Introduction to
FORENSIC PSYCHOLOGY

Research and Application

CURT R. BARTOL ■ ANNE M. BARTOL

EDITION

3

Los Angeles | London | New Delhi
Singapore | Washington DC

Los Angeles | London | New Delhi
Singapore | Washington DC

FOR INFORMATION:

SAGE Publications, Inc.
2455 Teller Road
Thousand Oaks, California 91320
E-mail: order@sagepub.com

SAGE Publications Ltd.
1 Oliver's Yard
55 City Road
London EC1Y 1SP
United Kingdom

SAGE Publications India Pvt. Ltd.
B 1/I 1 Mohan Cooperative Industrial Area
Mathura Road, New Delhi 110 044
India

SAGE Publications Asia-Pacific Pte. Ltd.
33 Pekin Street #02-01
Far East Square
Singapore 048763

Acquisitions Editor: Jerry Westby
Editorial Assistant: Erim Sarbuland
Production Editor: Karen Wiley
Copy Editor: Teresa Herlinger
Typesetter: C&M Digitals (P) Ltd.
Permissions Editor: Karen Ehrmann
Proofreader: Laura Webb
Indexer: Sheila Bodell
Cover Designer: Janet Kiesel
Marketing Manager: Erica DeLuca

Printed in the United States of America.

Library of Congress Cataloging-in-Publication Data

Bartol, Curt R., 1940-

Introduction to forensic psychology: research and application / Curt R. Bartol, Anne M. Bartol.—3rd ed.

p. cm.

Includes bibliographical references and index.

ISBN 978-1-4129-9175-9 (pbk. : acid-free paper)

1. Forensic psychology. I. Bartol, Anne M. II. Title.

RA1148.B37 2012 614'.15—dc22 2011000513

This book is printed on acid-free paper.

11 12 13 14 15 10 9 8 7 6 5 4 3 2

Contents

List of Boxes, Tables, and Figures

Tables

Figures

Preface

This book is intended to be a core text in undergraduate courses in forensic psychology, including those enrolling criminal justice majors and social work majors. However, the book is also addressed to general readers and mental health professionals seeking a basic overview of the field. Although many people associate forensic psychology with criminal profiling, crime scene investigations, and serial murder, the field is much broader in scope. In fact, forensic psychology is an engaging yet difficult field to survey because of its topical diversity, wide range of application, and very rapid growth.

For some time now, there has been a spirited debate about how forensic psychology should be defined and who should be called a forensic psychologist. We discuss this in Chapter 1 and refer to it periodically in the book. For our purposes, forensic psychology will refer *broadly* to the production and application of psychological knowledge and research findings to the civil and criminal justice systems. Forensic psychologists may be involved in clinical practice, in consulting and research activities, and as academicians, and they work in many contexts.

The book is organized around five major subareas of the field: (1) police psychology, (2) psychology and law or legal psychology, (3) the psychology of crime and delinquency, (4) victimology and victim services, and (5) correctional psychology (including institutional and community corrections for both adults and juveniles). Victimology and victim services represent the newest areas in which forensic psychologists are beginning to participate in increasing numbers.

The text concentrates on the *application* side of the field, focusing on research-based forensic practice. Throughout the book, we emphasize the professional application of psychological knowledge, concepts, and principles to both the civil and criminal justice systems. The topics included in the text are largely dictated by what forensic psychologists and psychologists practicing in forensic settings do on a day-to-day basis. Consequently, we cover such subjects as threat assessment for schools, child custody evaluations, competency and sanity evaluations of criminal defendants, counseling services to victims of crime, death notification procedures, screening and selection of law enforcement applicants, the assessment of posttraumatic stress disorder (PTSD), and the delivery and evaluation of intervention and treatment programs for juvenile and adult offenders. The practice of forensic psychology involves—among other things—assessments, research, consultation, the design and implementation of treatment programs, and expert courtroom testimony.

One of the major goals of the text is to expose readers to the many careers related to forensic psychology. During our years of teaching, it became apparent that an overriding concern of many students was to discover what kinds of employment opportunities are available in their chosen major or favorite subject area. In an effort to answer some of these questions, we provide examples of forensic practice. And, new to this edition, we include the personal narratives of 16 professionals in the field. These "Personal Perspectives" should provide readers with information about career choices as well as helpful advice about pursuing their goals.

Because students are often drawn to the word *forensic* without realizing the many branches of practice contained within the label, the book begins by covering the forensic sciences *in general*. It then moves on to the various levels of graduate training, internships, and fellowships relevant to forensic *psychology*. It will become very clear to aspiring forensic psychologists at the outset that they will have to pursue several years of graduate education (perhaps even postdoctoral training) and, in many cases, certification and licensure to practice. However, we also wish to emphasize that work in forensic areas can be enormously rewarding and filled with the personal satisfaction of knowing that one can make a difference in the lives of others. These common themes are evident in the Personal Perspectives narratives in the text.

Another major goal of the text is to emphasize the multicultural perspective that is an integral part of the day-to-day work of all practicing and research psychologists. Well-trained forensic psychologists recognize that ethnic and racial sensitivity is critical to successful practice, and they know they must be constantly vigilant to the injustices that can result from a monocultural perspective. Researchers in the field must pay attention to this as well.

Some features of the text should make it relatively accessible, even to readers without extensive background in psychology. Key terms appear in boldface in the text narrative (their definitions can be found in the glossary), and lists of key concepts and review questions appear at the end of each chapter. Every chapter begins with a list of objectives to help students obtain a sense of what is ahead. The text also includes an extensive list of references that will aid readers to find more material on the subject areas covered. Material in boxes (Perspectives and Focus) not only provides more information about career options, but also should prompt discussion on contemporary issues relevant to the practice of forensic psychology. For example, there are Focus boxes relating to drug courts, hate crimes, school shootings, wrongful convictions, and cognitive-behavioral treatment. Some boxes highlight decisions of the U.S. Supreme Court that are relevant to the practice of forensic psychology, such as decisions on the insanity defense or the sentencing of juvenile offenders.

The third edition includes a number of changes, many of which were made at the recommendation of peer reviewers. We will not repeat here the substantial changes that were made from the first edition to the second, where the order of chapters was changed. This edition retains the chapters as ordered in the second edition. However, in this third edition we have done the following:

- Provided updated material on defining forensic psychology and new material on the status of the field
- Used Aumiller and Corey's overview of police psychology as a basic framework for restructuring Chapter 2
- Discussed in some detail Laurence Steinberg's developmental dual systems model of adolescent risk taking
- Added other new topics, including but not limited to online sexual predators, autoerotic asphyxia, mental health needs of children exposed to intimate partner violence, and complicated bereavement of homicide covictims
- Substantially reorganized the material on profiling
- Covered recent findings on the mental health needs of delinquent youth
- Added new boxes, including those on drug courts, doctoral programs in forensic psychology, the "choking game," the Innocence Project, and bias crime

In addition, we have expanded on topics covered in previous editions, including—but again not limited to—PTSD, female sex offender typologies, the assessment of sex offenders, assessments of juveniles, police interrogation procedures, research on eyewitness identification, the psychological adjustment of victims of sexual assault, family preservation models of treatment for juveniles, and the long-term effects of child abuse, among others.

We have continued to emphasize important topics of great interest to our readers, such as serial and other murders, acquaintance rape, the relationship between mental disorders and crime and violence, sexual deviance, death penalty mitigation, restorative justice initiatives, arson and typologies of juvenile firesetters, sexual harassment, and criminal sentencing.

Numerous topics in this book deserve far more attention than we have been able to give them here; other topics relevant to forensic practice, particularly in the civil context, are left uncovered. We have not reviewed the empirical research or covered the legal and clinical ground that would be expected in a more advanced text. Nevertheless, we hope that this introductory material will prompt readers to explore topics of interest in more depth. The text should serve as an overview of the field of forensic psychology and an invitation to learn more about this very attractive and exciting career option.

Acknowledgments

We thank the academic and professional colleagues who reviewed the second edition of the book and offered detailed, chapter-by-chapter commentary and suggestions for revision. The reviewers were as follows: Lori Wallendael, University of North Carolina Charlotte; Ronald S. Truelove, Ball State University; David Campbell, Humboldt State University; Fadia Narchet, University of New Haven; Mandi Burnette, University of Rochester; Byron Greenberg, Virginia State University; Jackie Helfgott, Seattle University; and Cindy Moore, University of South Florida/Hillsborough Community College.

We are also extremely grateful to the 16 scholars and practitioners who wrote about their backgrounds and experiences and, in many cases, gave advice to students thinking of career opportunities in this field. It has been a pleasure to work with them, and we know that readers will appreciate hearing from so many smiling, happy professors and psychologists.

Once again, Jerry Westby, SAGE publisher, kept us on task with his gentle reminders that still another edition of the book was needed and his support throughout the revision process. We appreciate also the work of Jerry's editorial assistants, first Nichole O'Grady and then Erim Sarbuland, who among many of their tasks helped gather and coordinate photographs that are new to this edition. Our own editorial assistant Gina Cook helped with many of the details, such as locating valuable resources and preparing boxes, tables, and figures, and SAGE production editor Karen Wiley worked quietly and efficiently to orchestrate the many details about which we remain blissfully unaware. We were fortunate again to have the assistance of a most perceptive and thoughtful copyeditor, Teresa Herlinger, who surely ranks among the best. We are grateful as well to the many behind-the-scenes folks at SAGE who are instrumental in producing the book.

Finally, and as always, our family—immediate and extended—kept us grounded, reminding us that deadlines, though important, can be flexible and that life is enhanced immeasurably when there are kids to romp with, beaches to stroll on, and little and big victories and milestones to celebrate.

Part I

Introduction

1

Forensic Psychology

When the space shuttle *Columbia* disintegrated upon reentry into the Earth's atmosphere on February 1, 2003, "forensic investigators" from various federal agencies were immediately sent to the crash sites in an effort to identify the causes of the accident. They were forensic scientists trained to uncover evidence that may or may not eventually end up in a court of law. Likewise, when a bomb nearly detonated in New York's Times Square in 2010, this near catastrophe was investigated by scientists representing various federal and state agencies. Also in 2010, both independent and government-employed scientists began to study the cause and effects of the explosion aboard the Deepwater Horizon oil rig in the Gulf of Mexico that resulted in the deaths of 11 workers and the subsequent spillage—over 86 days—of an estimated 75,000 barrels of oil a day into the Gulf. As these examples indicate, the term *forensic* refers to anything pertaining or potentially pertaining to law, both civil and criminal.

Investigations of this sort almost invariably occur whenever there are unexpected and unexplained events that are not obvious natural disasters. In these contexts, scientists can perform numerous functions. They may be able to determine whether human factors—for example, terrorism, sabotage, or negligence—caused the tragedies. The information they provide can help in identifying those responsible. In the case of the oil spill, scientists tried to determine not only how the explosion occurred, but also how to stop the leakage and the extent of damage to wildlife and the environment.

Forensic science has become an all-encompassing professional activity and a popular career choice among students. Nearly every conceivable profession, including psychology, has a forensic specialization. Many people are confused about the various "forensic" areas and assume that professionals within these fields do largely the same thing. It will become clear, however, that they do not. Although **forensic psychology** is the subject of this text, it is helpful to begin with illustrations of other forensic sciences for comparison purposes. In other words, it is important for readers to know at the outset what forensic psychology is *not.*

The Forensic Sciences

Examples of the forensic professions, in addition to forensic psychology, include forensic engineering, forensic linguistics, forensic oceanography, forensic medicine, forensic computer investigation, forensic social work, forensic pathology, forensic anthropology, forensic archaeology, and forensic accounting. The focus of each discipline is evident from the terms. Forensic linguistics, for example, is concerned with the in-depth evaluation of language-related characteristics of text, such as grammar, syntax, spelling, vocabulary, and phraseology, either to profile an offender or to determine whether specific writing samples are from the same author (H. C. Black, 1990). Forensic anthropology refers to the identification of skeletal, badly decomposed, or otherwise unidentified human remains. Forensic pathology is that branch of medicine concerned with diseases and disorders of the body that relate to questions that might come before the court. The forensic pathologist—popularized in television shows such as *CSI, Bones,* and *NCIS,* and in the novels of Patricia Cornwell—examines the bodies of crime victims for clues about the victim's demise. Forensic anthropologists and forensic pathologists often work in conjunction with homicide investigators to identify a decedent; discover evidence of foul play; and help establish the age, sex, height, ancestry, and other unique features of a decedent from skeletal remains.

Forensic laboratories are usually maintained or sponsored by governmental agencies specifically to examine physical evidence in criminal and civil matters. The scientists working in these laboratories are expected to prepare reports and provide courtroom testimony on the physical evidence if needed. Alternately, private laboratories provide services to governmental agencies on a contractual basis or employ scientists who conduct independent research.

Scientists from both public and private laboratories may be asked to examine and testify about latent fingerprints, hair fibers, firearms and ballistics, explosives and fire debris, toxic material, and other pertinent evidence found at or near a crime scene or tragic accident. Some forensic labs are better at investigating certain types of evidence than others. For example, a lab maintained by the Food and Drug Administration (FDA) was instrumental in investigating a major product-tampering case that occurred in the United States in 1982. Seven persons in the Chicago area collapsed and died soon after taking Tylenol capsules. The capsules had been purchased in six different stores, and victims included a 12-year-old girl, a woman who had just returned from the hospital after giving birth, and three members of one family. Chemical investigation revealed that the capsules had been laced with cyanide. FDA chemists developed fingerprinting-like techniques that allowed authorities to trace the cyanide back to the specific manufacturer and distributor (Stehlin, 1995). The cyanide compound was identified as potassium cyanide with a purity of 90%. The compound is usually used in industries involved in metal electroplating, metal extraction, and both photographic and cinematographic film processing. Unfortunately, despite the fact that the poison was identified and the source was traced, the perpetrator was never found. The FDA lab continues to apply the "fingerprinting" techniques to identify cyanide origins, and since 1980, FDA chemists have developed techniques to screen for more than 250 of the most toxic poisons commonly available to the public (Stehlin, 1995).

With increased threats of mass violence and events such as the anthrax scare that followed the September 11, 2001, terrorist attacks in New York and Washington, D.C., quick forensic chemical-detection methods such as those described above have become especially crucial. In addition to terrorism-related concerns, also critical are forensic techniques that can address more common crimes, such as drug trafficking, computer crimes, and a wide variety of white-collar offenses that involve fraudulent documents. We highlight a few of these techniques below.

Example of Forensic Science: Forensic Entomology

Forensic laboratories often employ scientists who specialize in **forensic entomology,** which is the study of insects (and their arthropod relatives) as it relates to legal issues. This specialty is becoming increasingly important in criminal and civil investigations. For example, entomological investigations of termite infestation may be used to support civil litigation dealing with real estate, pest control, or landlord–tenant disputes. In another context, forensic entomology may be useful in investigations of food contamination. Scientists try to determine where an infestation occurred (e.g., which plant or store), when it occurred, and whether it was accidental or the possible result of human tampering. (Whether there actually was negligence or criminal intent, though, is left to the courts to decide.)

In criminal investigations, forensic entomology is used to determine the time since death (postmortem interval), the location of the death, placement or movement of the body, and manner of death. For example, because insects will feed first on soft-tissue areas of the head, such as the eyes and nasal passages, and any open wounds, they often will neglect undamaged flesh that will be left intact to harden. Consequently, the feeding patterns of insects often provide invaluable clues about the nature of a death.

Forensic entomology can also be applied to investigations of drug trafficking. Insects are sometimes found in drugs, and the identity of these insects can help in pinpointing where the drugs were produced or packed. In some cases, forensic entomologists can establish from the DNA of body or head lice whether two individuals had contact with each other (Mumcuoglu, Gallili, Reshef, Brauner, & Grant, 2004). Forensic entomology can also help in determining whether parents or caregivers have abused their children by intentionally using wasps or bees to sting them as a form of punishment. Fortunately, these instances are rare.

Another Example: Questioned Documents

Still another science represented in forensic laboratories is forensic document examination. This science analyzes handwriting, print fonts, the authenticity of signatures, alterations in documents, charred or water-damaged paper, the significance of inks and papers, photocopying processes, writing instruments, sequence of writing, and other elements of a document to establish authorship and authenticity. The process is often called **questioned document examination or analysis.** The questioned document may be a check, a threatening letter, a hold-up note, a credit application or receipt, a will, an investment record, a tax form, or a medical record (R. Morris, 2000). Questioned document analysis can be applied to many types of investigations, including fraud, homicide, suicide, sexual offenses, blackmail, bombings, and arson. Questioned handwriting analysis, for example, may include the forensic examination of a signature, handwritten letter, entries on a form, or even graffiti on a wall (R. Morris, 2000). A forensic document examiner (FDE) may be asked to examine and render opinions on the authorship of writing on building walls; recover engraved or obliterated writing on different types of surfaces; or determine the brand or model of typewriters or keyboards, printers, embossers, inks, and printing processes (R. Morris, 2000).

Closely related to forensic document analysis is forensic ink analysis, a little-known crime-fighting tool that is sometimes used to show that certain documents have been backdated or altered. Most of the ink analysis today is done by the U.S. Secret Service's Forensic Services Division, "which maintains the world's largest library of ink samples with more than 7,000 entries" (Maremont, 2003, p. A4). There is also a small group of private forensic experts who do ink analysis, primarily for medical malpractice suits, patent battles, or cases involving disputed wills. The ink analysis is especially effective in examining the ink of ballpoint pens, which contains a variety of different dyes and drying properties. Ink analysis played a role in the 1973 conviction of mass murderer Juan Corona, who hacked to death 25 migrant workers near Yuba City, California (Maremont, 2003). Usually, however, ink analysis is used in investigations of business fraud or, in rare cases, by the Internal Revenue Service for income tax cases.

Computer Evidence Recovery

Anyone who has experienced hard drive failure can recall the momentary panic it engenders. Surprisingly, most "lost" data can actually be recovered. Furthermore, as embarrassed politicians, their staffs, and high-profile professionals and public figures have learned, e-mail messages do not inevitably disappear in cyberspace, even with the press of the delete key.

Computer evidence recovery, also called forensic data recovery, involves e-mail and Internet analysis, along with sophisticated hard drive, diskette, and memory stick recovery techniques of orphaned, fragmented, and erased data. A computer evidence recovery specialist has the training to search, seize, and analyze magnetic media originating from a variety of operating systems pursuant to the execution of a search warrant or subpoena. Without specialized training, though, a law enforcement officer armed with a search warrant would not be advised to open computer files from the office of a person suspected of Internet fraud or one suspected of distributing child pornography. The major goal of the specialist or investigator is to recover the data without modifying the original media or the image of the media. These skills are used in a wide variety of investigations, such as financial fraud, embezzlement, sexual harassment, child pornography, program vandalism, identity theft, document forgery, software piracy, narcotics trafficking, and money laundering. Computer evidence recovery was a key law enforcement technique in bringing to justice Robert Hansen who, while he was an FBI agent, engaged in spying for the Soviet Union and Russia for over 15 years.

The data evidence recovery process involves an analysis of the computer make and capacity, the computer's time and date settings, hard drive partitions, data and operating system integrity, computer virus evaluation, files, and software. The analysis will also usually involve careful evaluation of *shadow data,* which is the information that remains on a disk, hard drive, or memory stick even after the data are ostensibly erased, damaged, or lost. Many people engaging in various forms of illegal activity think they are safe by making deletions or using software designed to cover their tracks, not realizing that a well-trained computer data recovery expert can access almost any information sent or received. As an example, Wardwell and Smith (2008) describe a method that was used in a child exploitation case to recover data from CD-RW discs that the suspect had erased.

Forensic data recovery also may be a powerful tool to clear a person of wrongdoing. For example, Clark (2002) describes a case of a successful businessman living in an upscale neighborhood, happily married with two children, who was accused of accessing and distributing child pornography. One evening, police appeared at his door to execute a search warrant. They seized his computer, took him into custody, and charged him with distribution of child pornography, though he strongly denied the allegations. His attorney contacted a computer evidence recovery service, which was able to demonstrate that the pornography was stored in his computer on dates the man wasn't even in town. Apparently, he had unknowingly downloaded a "Trojan Horse," enabling the computer cracker to have access to his computer. (Distinctions sometimes are made between a computer *cracker,* who maliciously breaks into computers for the purpose of damaging data or sending out viruses, and a *hacker,* who tries to get through holes in computer codes to prove a point or play a joke.)

The computer specialist in the above case was able to prove that someone else had been storing the pornography on the individual's computer without his knowledge.

As is apparent from the previous illustrations, forensic investigations usually require expertise in chemistry, biology, physics, or other sciences, including the science of computer technology. Although television, movies, and popular novels provide numerous graphic examples of forensic examinations of evidence, the extensive scientific preparation required to work in forensic laboratories is usually not emphasized. The scientists depicted typically have access to state-of-the-art equipment, and they are often glamorous and/or have complex emotional lives. Many students express a keen interest in the forensic sciences and seriously consider pursuing a career in the field without fully understanding what it is or what is required to reach their goal. The field of forensic psychology involves a very different type of preparation and is significantly different in content, but it too requires considerable preparation. Nonetheless, there are many different avenues to entering this field, as will become apparent in this text.

Forensic Psychology: An Overview

Forensic psychology—like many specialties in psychology—is difficult to define precisely. As John Brigham (1999) writes, if you ask a group of psychologists who interact with the legal system in some capacity, "Are you a forensic psychologist?" many will say yes, some will say no, and a majority will probably admit they really do not know. Referring to his own testimony in court, Brigham notes that, when asked the question, his most accurate current response would be, "Well, it depends." As Brigham points out, the professional literature on the subject adopts one of two prominent definitions. Some of the literature refers to forensic psychology *broadly* as the *research* and *application* of psychological knowledge to the legal system, whereas some of it prefers a more narrow approach, limiting forensic psychology to the *application* and *practice* of psychology as it pertains to the legal system. We (Bartol & Bartol, 1987) have offered the following definition: "We view forensic psychology broadly, as both (1) the research endeavor that examines aspects of human behavior directly related to the legal process . . . and (2) the professional practice of psychology within, or in consultation with, a legal system that embraces both civil and criminal law" (p. 3). Ronald Roesch (cited in Brigham, 1999) suggests a narrow definition: "Most psychologists define the area more narrowly to refer to clinical psychologists who are engaged in clinical practice within the legal system" (p. 279). This definition may be too restrictive because it seems to imply a specialty called "forensic *clinical* psychology." Furthermore, it excludes—among others—clinicians who offer counseling services to inmates and perform other corrections-related tasks. The broad definition, on the other hand, includes not only clinicians (also called practitioners) but also social, developmental, counseling, cognitive, experimental, industrial-organizational, and school psychologists—some but not all of whom are clinicians. The common link is their contribution to the legal system. We recognize, however, that only a small proportion of their work may be performed in this context.

DeMatteo, Marczyk, Krauss, and Burl (2009) note that the lack of consensus for defining forensic psychology as well as the activities it comprises has continued. "[T]here is considerable disagreement over the scope of forensic psychology and what activities (i.e., research, assessment, and treatment) and roles should appropriately be considered the exclusive province of forensic psychology" (p. 185). They point out that increasing dissatisfaction with narrow conceptualizations recently led the American Psychology-Law Society to endorse a broad definition (see Committee on the Revision of the Specialty Guidelines for Forensic Psychology, 2006; hereinafter "Committee"), one that would embrace the contributions of researchers as well as clinicians. Nevertheless, in its most recent draft of the guidelines (Committee, 2010), the group still favors an approach narrower than that taken in the present text.

In this text, we will continue to adopt a *broad* definition of forensic psychology but will focus primarily on forensic practice and what psychologists working in the field actually do. That is, we emphasize the professional *application* of psychological knowledge, concepts, and principles to civil and criminal justice systems. It should be understood, however, that this application must be based on solid research; thus, the research prong of our original definition (Bartol & Bartol, 1987) has not disappeared. The practice of forensic psychology, as it will be treated here, includes investigations, studies, evaluations, advice to attorneys, advisory opinions, and depositions or testimony to assist in the resolution of disputes relating to life or property in cases before the courts or other law tribunals. It can—and does—encompass situations before they reach the court as well as those situations following the court decision. It includes activities as varied as the following: courtroom testimony, child custody evaluations, screening and selection of law enforcement candidates, and clinical services to offenders and staff in correctional facilities. It also includes research and theory building in criminology; the design and implementation of intervention, prevention, and treatment for youth offenders; and counseling of victims of crime. Almost a decade ago, Tucillo, DeFilippis, Denny, and Dsurney (2002) observed,

> A growing number of clinicians provide expert witness testimony addressing a variety of issues, such as competency to stand trial, criminal responsibility, child custody, personal injury or handicap, and suitability to work in law enforcement. In addition to this major trend in clinical psychology and neuropsychology, developmental and experimental psychologists have come into demand for their expert opinions on such matters as the reliability of eyewitness testimony and lie detection. (p. 377)

This growth has continued, and it is reflected in the development of professional organizations devoted to research and practice in the field, significant increases in the number of books and periodicals focusing on the topic, the development of undergraduate and graduate training programs, and the establishment of standards for practitioners working in the discipline (DeMatteo, Marczyk, et al., 2009; Heilbrun & Brooks, 2010; Otto & Heilbrun, 2002). (See Focus 1.1 for important historical benchmarks in forensic psychology.)

For our purposes, forensic psychology will be divided into five subspecialties: (1) police psychology, (2) psychology of crime and delinquency, (3) victimology and victim services, (4) legal psychology, and (5) correctional psychology. Police psychology, correctional psychology, and legal psychology tend to be the more *applied* branches of forensic psychology, whereas the psychology of crime and delinquency and of victimology tend to be more *research* focused. It should be noted, though, that each branch has both research and applied aspects. Furthermore, psychologists conducting research in one area of forensic psychology may consult with or train practitioners in other areas. Likewise, the clinical experience of applied psychologists helps to inform theory development and suggest hypotheses to research psychologists. Finally, many practitioners do engage in research, although a very common complaint among them is the lack of time and resources for doing that.

FOCUS 1.1. HISTORICAL BENCHMARKS IN FORENSIC PSYCHOLOGY

1893—First psychological experiment on the psychology of testimony is conducted by J. McKeen Cattell of Columbia University.

1903—Louis William Stern of Germany establishes a periodical dealing with the psychology of testimony (*Beiträge zur Psychologie der Aussage [Contributions to the Psychology of Testimony]*).

(Continued)

(Continued)

1908—Publication of Hugo Münsterberg's *On the Witness Stand,* arguably one of the first professional books on forensic psychology. The book launched Münsterberg's career in forensic psychology, and some scholars consider Münsterberg, a Harvard professor of psychology, the father of forensic psychology.

1911—J. Varendonck was one of the earliest psychologists to testify in a criminal trial, which was held in Belgium.

1913—First time that psychological services are offered within a U.S. correctional facility (a women's reformatory in New York State).

1917—William Marston develops the first modern polygraph.

1917—Louis Terman becomes the first American psychologist to use psychological tests in the screening of law enforcement personnel.

1918—First inmate classification system developed by psychologists, established by the New Jersey Department of Corrections. New Jersey also becomes the first state to hire full-time correctional psychologists on a regular basis.

1921—First time an American psychologist testifies in a courtroom as an expert witness (*State v. Driver,* 1921).

1922—Karl Marbe, a psychology professor at the University of Würzburg, Germany, becomes the first psychologist to testify at a civil trial.

1922—Psychologist-lawyer William Marston becomes the first to receive a faculty appointment in forensic psychology, as "professor of legal psychology" at American University. Marston also conducted the first empirical research on the jury system.

1931—Howard Burtt's *Legal Psychology* is published—the first *textbook* in the forensic area written by a psychologist.

1961—Hans Toch edits one of the first texts on the psychology of crime, *Legal and Criminal Psychology.*

1964—Hans J. Eysenck formulates the first comprehensive and testable theory on criminal behavior advanced by a psychologist and publishes it in the book *Crime and Personality.*

1968—Martin Reiser becomes the first full-time police psychologist in the United States. He is hired by the Los Angeles Police Department and became instrumental in establishing police psychology as a profession.

1972—Under the guidance and leadership of the American Association for Correctional Psychology (AACP), Stanley Brodsky, Robert Lewinson, and Asher Pacht, correctional psychology becomes recognized as a professional career.

1974—The first successful interdisciplinary psychology and law program is developed at the University of Nebraska–Lincoln.

1978–The American Board of Forensic Psychology begins professional certification of diplomates in forensic psychology.

1978–The American Psychological Association approves a clinical internship in corrections at the Wisconsin Department of Corrections.

1991–The American Academy of Forensic Psychology and American Psychology-Law Society publishes *Specialty Guidelines for Forensic Psychologists*.

2001–The American Psychological Association recognizes forensic psychology as a specialty.

2006–The Committee on the Revision of the Specialty Guidelines for Forensic Psychology recommends a broader definition that encompasses research as well as clinical practice.

Here are examples of things that forensic psychologists (depending on their specialty) may be asked to do:

Police Psychology

- Assist police departments in determining optimal shift schedules for their employees.
- Assist police in developing psychological profiles of serial offenders.
- Establish reliable and valid screening procedures for law enforcement officer positions at various police and sheriff departments.
- Train police officers on how to deal with mentally ill citizens.
- Provide counseling services to officers after a shooting incident.
- Provide support services to the families of law enforcement officers.

Psychology of Crime and Delinquency

- Evaluate the effectiveness of preschool intervention strategies designed to prevent violent behavior during adolescence.
- Conduct research on the development of psychopathy.
- Consult with legislators and governmental agencies as a research policy advisor on the prevention of stalking.
- Consult with school personnel on identifying troubled youth who are potentially dangerous.
- Develop a psychological test for assessing risk among the mentally ill.

Victimology and Victim Services

- Evaluate and treat persons who are the victims of crime or witnesses of crime.
- Conduct psychological assessments for personal injury matters having to do with such things as auto accidents, product liability, sexual harassment and discrimination, and medical negligence or worker's compensation.
- Educate and train victim service providers on psychological reactions to criminal victimization, such as post-traumatic stress disorder.
- Assess, support, and counsel those who provide death notification services.
- Educate service providers on the impact of multiculturalism when victims seek mental health and support services.

Legal Psychology

- Conduct child custody evaluations, visitation risk assessments, and child abuse evaluations.
- Assist attorneys in jury selection through community surveys and other research methods.

- Perform evaluations of a defendant's competency to stand trial.
- Consult with attorneys and the courts concerning custody decisions, conflict resolution, and the validity of assessment procedures used in the evaluation of various psychological conditions.
- Conduct competency evaluations for the civil court.

Correctional Psychology

- Establish reliable and valid screening procedures for correctional officer positions at correctional facilities.
- Assess inmates entering prison for both mental health needs and suitability for prison programs.
- Provide individual and group treatment for inmates.
- Evaluate the effectiveness of programs for juvenile and adult offenders, such as victim–offender reconciliation programs, sex offender treatment, or health education programs.
- Develop a stress management program for correctional personnel.

It should be mentioned that the above list would be shortened considerably if we were to adopt a narrower definition of forensic psychology. Forensic psychologists also teach in colleges and universities and conduct research that is relevant to the legal system, such as research on eyewitness testimony, the comprehension of *Miranda* rights, and jury decision making. Throughout the book, text boxes in most of the chapters will introduce you to professionals who are engaged in these activities.

The work settings in which forensic psychologists are found include, but are not limited to, the following:

- Private practice
- Family courts, drug courts, and mental health courts
- Child protection agencies
- Victim services
- Domestic violence courts and programs
- Forensic mental health units (governmental or private)
- Sex offender treatment programs
- Correctional institutions (including research programs)
- Law enforcement agencies (federal, state, or local)
- Research organizations (governmental or private)
- Colleges and universities (teaching or research)
- Juvenile delinquency treatment programs
- Legal advocacy centers (e.g., for the mentally ill or developmentally disabled)

In today's economic climate, many students are worried that they will not secure employment upon graduation from college or upon earning an advanced degree. A *New Yorker* magazine cover (May 24, 2010), titled "Boomerang Generation," says it all. A young man is seen posting his just-minted PhD degree on the bedroom wall of his childhood home, among the academic and sports trophies of his youth, as his discouraged parents look on.

It is a reality that government grants and positions are being cut, and these affect scientists at all levels. Forensic psychology has thus far not been extensively damaged, however, and the outlook for career opportunities in its many facets is bright (Clay, 2009). Keep in mind, though, that with greater competition for available dollars comes greater accountability in the provision of services. For example, in the treatment arena, treatment providers are asked to document that their services are effective, in other words, that they are based on research evidence. As we will see later in the book, "evidence-based treatment" has become an important term in the correctional lexicon as well as in other areas of human service. Therefore, the need for psychologists capable of conducting evaluation research is great.

Forensic Psychology Compared to Forensic Psychiatry

Psychologists, especially clinical, counseling, and forensic psychologists, are often confused with psychiatrists by the public and the media. Today, the lines of separation between the two professions are becoming increasingly blurred. Clinical, counseling, and some forensic psychologists, along with psychiatrists, are trained to provide direct treatment services to persons with emotional, cognitive, or behavioral problems.

Psychiatrists are medical doctors (MDs) (or, in some cases, doctors of osteopathy [DOs]), who specialize in the prevention, diagnosis, and treatment of mental, addictive, and emotional disorders. Psychologists do not hold a medical degree, although some may have earned related degrees, such as a Master of Public Health (MPH). Another major distinction between the two has been the license to prescribe drugs, including psychoactive drugs. Traditionally, psychologists have not been permitted by law to prescribe any medication. Now, even that distinction is beginning to disappear. On March 6, 2002, New Mexico became the first state in the United States to allow properly trained psychologists to prescribe psychoactive drugs, or drugs intended to treat mental disorders. On May 6, 2004, Louisiana became the second state in the country to pass a law authorizing properly trained psychologists to prescribe certain medications for the treatment of mental health disorders. In that state, these psychologists are called "medical psychologists." Psychologists in the military also have prescription privileges. To date, though, psychologists in no other states have gained prescription privileges, although legislation has been introduced in numerous states. In April 2010, Oregon became the most recent state to deny these privileges. Medical associations typically have resisted extending prescription privileges, maintaining that this will lead to abuses and decrease the quality of patient care. Nevertheless, even among clinical psychologists there is not universal support for prescription privileges or authority, although most surveys find at least a majority in favor (e.g., Baird, 2007; Sammons, Gorny, Zinner, & Allen, 2000).

Many psychiatrists, like psychologists, work in a variety of forensic settings, including the court, correctional facilities, and law enforcement. Psychiatrists who are closely associated with the law are often referred to as **forensic psychiatrists.** In some areas, such as issues relating to insanity determination by the courts, psychiatrists are more visible—and sometimes more preferred—than psychologists. As we will discuss in a later chapter, this reflects a greater comfort on the part of some judges with the medical model approach to mental disorder (Melton, Petrila, Poythress, & Slobogin, 1997). Psychologists and psychiatrists seem to be equally involved in pretrial assessments of juveniles and custody evaluations, while psychologists are more likely than psychiatrists to consult with law enforcement and offer treatment in the correctional system. Law-related research tends to be the bailiwick of psychologists, although some psychiatrists are engaged in conducting and publishing such research also.

Finally, clinical social workers are often found working in forensic arenas. Social workers may counsel victims of crimes or families of victims and offenders, and provide substance abuse and sex offender treatment to offenders, among other functions. In many correctional facilities, social workers are part of the treatment team, typically under the supervision of psychologists. In corrections, as in other areas, collaboration among professionals is crucial. Therefore, although our text focuses on the work of psychologists, it is important to stress that contributions from other disciplines cannot be overlooked.

Ethical Issues

With the increasing opportunities available to forensic psychologists, numerous pragmatic and ethical issues also have been raised. Prescription authority, mentioned briefly above, is one example. Other ethical issues have been raised regarding dual relationships between the psychologist and the client, conflicts of interest, issues of confidentiality, and the tension between punishment and rehabilitation (A. Day & Casey, 2009; Ward & Birgden, 2009). In recent years, contentious issues have revolved around psychologists participating in military interrogations, treating death row inmates to render them competent to be executed, making recommendations in child custody cases, labeling juveniles as psychopathic, and establishing proper boundaries between assessment and treatment. For example, with respect to establishing boundaries, Greenberg and Shuman (1997, 2007) have argued forcefully that a psychologist should not both conduct a forensic examination and treat the same individual, even though the psychologist might be very competent in both roles. In fact, Greenberg and Shuman consider the forensic and therapeutic role irreconcilable if exercised with the same individual. Some practitioners have objected strongly to this view, suggesting that if adopted it would deprive therapists of the opportunity to testify objectively about their clients (Heltzel, 2007). This and other controversial topics will be covered in the chapters ahead.

Careers in Psychology

Since the 1970s, there has been an enormous expansion of the profession of psychology in general (Reed, Levant, Stout, Murphy, & Phelps, 2001). Psychology encompasses a wide spectrum of topics, ranging from engineering designs (human factors) to animal behavior, and has a place in every imaginable setting. Psychologists can be found in "personnel selection and training, developing user-friendly computer software, the delivery of psychological services to victims of natural and man-made disasters, the profiling of serial killers, the creation of effective commercials that increase the sale of a product, and so on" (Ballie, 2001, p. 25). Currently, there are over 152,000 members and affiliates of the **American Psychological Association (APA) (www.apa.org).** The APA, based in Washington, D.C., is the largest association of psychologists worldwide. Another 18,000 psychologists from the United States and abroad, whose specialties span the entire spectrum of scientific, applied, and teaching areas, are members of the **Association for Psychological Science (APS) (www.psychologicalscience.org)**, the second-largest psychological organization in the United States. The APS, also based in Washington, D.C., is a nonprofit organization dedicated to the advancement of scientific psychology. In addition to the APA and APS, psychologists belong to many other professional organizations at the national, state, and local levels. It is estimated that there are at least 300,000 practicing psychologists worldwide who provide a wide range of services (Donn, Routh, & Lunt, 2000; Lunt & Poortinga, 1996).

Education and Training

About 75,000 undergraduate psychology majors graduate each year from the nation's colleges and universities (APA, 2003a; B. Murray, 2002b). Starting salaries for graduates with a bachelor's degree range from $18,000 to $45,000, depending on the job type and location, with an average of approximately $29,000. Psychology majors most often find employment in the areas of management, teaching, counseling, social work, and sales. As most psychology graduates become quickly aware, the bachelor's degree does provide a basic foundation in the field of psychology, but it does not adequately prepare a person to be a professional psychologist. The minimum educational requirement for psychologists is the master's degree. In addition, specialization in psychology usually begins at the graduate level, although many undergraduate programs offer concentrations in certain areas, such as social psychology, education psychology, or human development. Graduate programs in psychology most often offer graduate degrees in experimental, biopsychology, developmental, cognitive, clinical, counseling, school, and industrial/organizational psychology. The last four represent the more applied or practitioner's side of psychology. Most recently, as we will see shortly, forensic psychology has become a fifth applied branch in the field, although the other four applied sectors have historically made significant contributions to various forensic topics and settings.

Graduate Training: Master's Level

At the master's level, clinical, counseling, and school psychology attract the most students (B. Murray, 2002b). In some states, graduates of master's degree programs in psychology—with the appropriate clinical training—may be eligible for licensure as psychological associates (LPAs) or psychologist-master's level (MacKain, Tedeschi, Durham, & Goldman, 2002). In other states, graduates with master's degrees in psychology are not allowed to practice *psychology* (at least they aren't allowed to use the label) and are instead licensed with *nonpsychology* titles, such as licensed mental health counselor, marriage and family therapist, or psychotherapist (MacKain et al., 2002).

In a survey conducted in North Carolina, Sally Joy MacKain and her associates (2002) asked state and private employers if they employed LPAs. Through this method, they were able to identify 345 master's-level psychologists working within the state. The researchers discovered that 158 were employed at mental health centers, 108 were with the state department of corrections, 54 were working at residential centers that serve the developmentally disabled, and 25 were employed at state psychiatric hospitals. Employers indicated that LPAs were as marketable as other master's-trained clinicians, such as social workers and counselors. Eighteen percent of the employers stated they were more likely to hire psychologists than other master's-trained clinicians, and 49% said they were "just as likely to hire them." In fact, some employers reported difficulty in finding enough LPAs for their positions. Salaries for LPAs ranged from $27,000 to $45,000 with a median of $30,500, a range similar to that of other master's-level clinicians.

In addition to employers, MacKain et al. (2002) also surveyed 60 LPAs. More than half the graduates interviewed (54%) stated they were definitely planning or were considering entering a doctoral program within the next 5 years, suggesting that the opportunities presented by the LPA alone may be limited. Of the LPAs, 36% were employed in community mental health centers, 24% were working in state corrections or the courts, 16% were involved in private inpatient or outpatient facilities, 10% were in university or college settings, and 8% were in nonprivate agencies. Currently, there is no accreditation of master's programs in psychology through the APA. However, since 1995, applied master's programs have been able to seek accreditation from the Master's in Psychology Accreditation Council (MPAC) (Hays-Thomas, 2000). Approximately 14,500 master's degrees in psychology are awarded each year (APA, 2003a).

Graduate Training: Doctoral Level

At the doctoral level, clinical psychology attracts the largest number of students of all the applied specialties and is considered the entry-level credential for the independent practice of psychology (APA, 1978; Hayes-Thomas, 2000). Every year, approximately 1,200 students earn PhDs and another 700 students earn PsyDs in clinical psychology (B. Murray, 2002a, p. 33). The *PhD* degree (Doctor of Philosophy) requires a dissertation and is well accepted in the academic world as appropriate preparation for scientists and scholars in many fields across the globe (Donn et al., 2000). It is regarded primarily as a research-based degree. A *dissertation* refers to a substantial paper based on the PhD candidate's original research, which should make a significant contribution to the research literature. The *PsyD* (Doctor of Psychology) is a graduate degree designed primarily for students who wish to become practitioners rather than researchers. The first PsyD program was established in 1968 by Donald R. Peterson at the University of Illinois (Peterson, 1968). Although many PhD psychologists have questioned the soundness of the PsyD since its early beginnings, especially in view of its limited research focus, the degree has received increasing professional recognition in recent years and has attracted the interest of many students. More than 50 institutions have awarded 9,000 PsyDs during the past 30 years. Overall, approximately 4,300 doctoral degrees in psychology are awarded each year (APA, 2003a, n.p.).

Usually, salaries for those with the doctorate are highest in the private sector and lowest for those in academe (college or university teaching and research). The overall median 9- to 10-month faculty salary was $76,090 in 2009, whereas the overall 11- to 12-month median salary for doctoral-level psychologists in the applied field was $120,000 (Finno, Michalski, Hart, Wicherski, & Kohout, 2010). The salary for a beginning assistant professor might be in the $40,000 to $60,000 range. Those working for the government fall somewhere in between an academic salary and a salary in the applied field, with a 2009 median salary of $86,293. Interestingly, one private practitioner quoted in Clay (2009) estimated that forensic psychologists in clinical practice typically earn $200,000 to $400,000 a year.

Licensure

According to Tucillo et al. (2002), by 1977 every U.S. state had laws relating to the licensure of psychologists, and in 1990 all Canadian provinces regulated the practice of psychology. In 1987, in an effort to encourage standardized licensing requirements, the APA developed the Model Act for State Licensure of Psychologists (see APA, 1987) to serve as a prototype for drafting state legislation (Tucillo et al., 2002). One of the chief criteria to qualify for licensing is possession of the doctoral degree. Professional psychologists are also ethically obligated to comply with the standards pertaining to their practice, as outlined by the **Ethical Principles of Psychologists and Code of Conduct** (American Psychological Association, 2002, 2003b, 2010). Guidelines are also offered in a number of areas associated with research and clinical practice. A good example is the **Specialty Guidelines for Forensic Psychologists** (Committee on Ethical Guidelines for Forensic Psychologists, 1991), which are presently under revision. Among other things, the "Specialty Guidelines" assert that "forensic psychologists are responsible for a fundamental and reasonable level of knowledge and understanding of the legal and professional standards that govern their participation as experts in legal proceedings" (1991, p. 658). An important distinction between standards and guidelines should be noted. Psychologists are expected to comply with *standards,* and there is an enforcement mechanism in place in case they do not. For example, a violation in the Code of Ethics could result in a complaint to the APA's Professional Conduct Board and, ultimately, loss of one's license to practice psychology (although such drastic consequences are rare). By contrast, the *guidelines* are aspirational; psychologists are strongly encouraged—but not required—to abide by them.

Employment

A survey on where psychologists with new doctorates find employment indicated that about three-fourths are employed in higher education or human service settings (such as schools or hospitals) (D. Smith, 2002c). The rest were working in business, government, or private practice. About 25% of new doctorates find employment in academic positions at 4-year colleges and universities. Most of the graduates have a strong foundation in research methodology and analysis that allows them to work in a variety of occupations. "Rather than being stereotyped as a professor or therapist, more and more psychologists are being seen as applied scientists" (Ballie, 2001, p. 25).

The Applied Specialties

At present, there are five subspecialties of applied psychology: clinical, counseling, school, industrial/organizational, and forensic psychology. Although these subspecialties may have distinct features, journals, associations, and interests, they also have many things in common. The similarities between counseling psychology and clinical psychology, in particular, are far greater than the differences. The clinical psychologist typically experiences 9 or 12 months of supervised internship in a clinical setting, where the theories and methods acquired in graduate training can be applied to human behavior problems. The counseling psychologist will have received much the same training as the clinical psychologist, including the internship. In the past, the major distinction between the two was their focus. The **counseling psychologist** was trained to evaluate and treat (counsel) persons with adjustment problems, such as those relating to education, job, and personal and marital relationships. The **clinical psychologist** was trained to evaluate and treat persons suffering more serious behavior and mental problems found in mental hospitals or psychiatric clinics. This distinction is rapidly becoming blurred, however.

Both counseling and clinical psychologists are employed in a wide assortment of settings, including college and university counseling centers, university research and teaching positions, independent practice, health care settings, hospitals, and the legal-forensic system. About 40% of the doctoral-level practitioners are in private or independent practice (Reed et al., 2001). Both counseling and clinical psychologists (at the doctorate level) are licensed in all 50 states, usually under the same designation of "licensed practicing psychologist."

In clinical and counseling practice throughout the United States, psychologists are finding that their clients are often from cultural backgrounds different from their own. "The majority of service providers are European Americans with middle-class values and orientation; a sizeable portion of the diverse client populations are African-Americans and underserved with mixed values and orientations" (E. F. Morris, 2001, p. 563). A growing Black middle and upper class contribute to the diversity. In addition, psychologists are encountering in their practices more persons of Latino, Asian, Native American, and Middle Eastern heritage. It is extremely crucial for practicing psychologists to be knowledgeable about and sensitive to the cultural values and norms held by persons to whom they are providing service. This may be especially important for forensic psychologists. Members of racial and ethnic minorities are often overrepresented in the populations these psychologists serve (Carter & Forsyth, 2007). Furthermore, the psychologists are often not chosen by those they evaluate or treat, but they nevertheless are called on to assist in making decisions that may drastically affect the lives of these individuals.

Clinical and counseling psychologists who are service providers to diverse populations should at a minimum be aware of their own assumptions and biases regarding cultures that are different from their own, understand their clients' worldviews, and use only culturally appropriate interventions and techniques (C. D. Erickson & Al-Timini, 2001; Sue, Arredondo, & McDavis, 1992). It is interesting to note that only half of the doctoral-level clinicians in one survey felt competent to provide services to African Americans despite their training exposure and diverse clientele (Allison, Crawford, Echemendia, Robinson, & Kemp, 1994; E. F. Morris, 2001).

The APA (1993) has begun to take notice of this important issue by publishing its "Guidelines for Providers of Psychological Services to Ethnic, Linguistic, and Culturally Diverse Populations." The guidelines emphasize, for example, that psychologists "consider the validity of a given instrument or procedure and interpret resulting data, keeping in mind the cultural and linguistic characteristics of the person being assessed" (p. 46). The guidelines further recommend that "psychologists who do not possess knowledge or training about an ethnic group seek consultation with, and/or make referrals to, appropriate experts as necessary" (p. 46). The APA (2005) also has published "Guidelines for the Accreditation of Programs in Professional Psychology," which includes sections on cultural differences.

It should also be recognized by forensic psychologists that the legal system they are working with might be unprepared to deal with many complex issues not only of culture, ethnicity, and race, but also of sexual orientation. Same-sex marriages or unions, adoptions by gay and lesbian couples, custody evaluations when one party seeking custody is gay or lesbian, and same-sex domestic violence are examples.

School psychology is a specialty involved in the evaluation, diagnosis, and reduction of social, emotional, and cognitive problems of school-age children. In many ways, the tasks of **school psychologists** are very similar to those of child clinical psychologists, but school psychologists tend to be more focused on the school environment and its influences on the child. They work not only with children with problems but also with parents, teachers, and school administrators. Many school psychologists do not have a PhD or other doctoral degree, but many states provide certification and licensing for school psychologists who have the requisite master's degree and an internship within a school setting. Qualified school psychologists are always in demand, and some years have seen major shortages (Dittmann, 2002). Compounding the shortages is the fact that approximately 45% of the students in public schools are from racial or ethnic minorities, often with very different linguistic experiences (Sue, Bingham, Porché-Burke, & Vasquez, 1999). As we will see shortly, school psychologists are increasingly becoming involved in forensic settings.

Industrial/organizational (I/O) psychologists help develop strategies that build better organizations and improve the well-being of employees. They work in a variety of areas within the organization, including selection and placement, training and development, organizational development and change, performance measurement and evaluation, quality of work life, consumer psychology, and human factors. The I/O psychologist may assist in fashioning accommodations for the disabled, offer employee workshops on sexual harassment, or counsel employees who have experienced workplace victimization. The training for this specialty usually involves a heavy emphasis on research design, statistics, knowledge of the research literature as it relates to organizations, and a 1-year internship within a relevant organization.

Forensic Psychology as a Specialty

In August 2001, the Council of Representatives of the American Psychological Association voted to recognize forensic psychology as another specialty. Although this is an important step forward, recall that other specialties also provide services in forensic settings. At the time, the council adopted a narrow rather than broad definition of forensic psychology: "It was ultimately decided that the petition for specialization should define forensic psychology narrowly, to include the primary clinical aspects of forensic assessment, treatment, and consultation" (Otto & Heilbrun, 2002, p. 8). As DeMatteo, Marczyk, et al. (2009) posit, this definition

> only encompasses clinically based areas of psychology and therefore excludes practitioners without clinical degrees. Under this narrow and restrictive definition, research psychologists in the fields of social, experimental, and cognitive psychology would not be considered forensic psychologists, despite the obvious contribution that these researchers can make in certain legal contexts (e.g., reliability of eyewitness testimony, perceptions of jurors). (p. 185)

As noted above, several years later, the Committee on the Revision of the Specialty Guidelines for Forensic Psychology (2006) recommended a broader definition that would encompass both clinical practice and research. The latest—fifth—draft of these yet-to-be-adopted new guidelines (Committee, 2010) continues to include the research prong.

Educational and Training Requirements in Forensic Psychology

The growth in the field is demonstrated by the continuing development of graduate programs in forensic psychology throughout the world, particularly in Canada, the United States, the United Kingdom, and Australia. In August 2010, the website GradSchools.com was listing 101 forensic psychology graduate programs, at both the MA and PhD or PsyD levels. Some were campus based and others were online programs. In the United States alone, it is estimated that nearly 50 programs offer graduate training in forensic psychology. Approximately 12 offer a master's degree specifically in the area, while most doctoral programs are in broader areas but allow students to obtain a formal concentration in forensic psychology, legal psychology, or psychology and law (DeMatteo, Marczyk, et al., 2009). A small minority of programs offer a PhD specifically in forensic psychology. (See Focus 1.2 for a list of representative programs.)

FOCUS 1.2. REPRESENTATIVE DOCTORAL PROGRAMS IN FORENSIC PSYCHOLOGY

Alliant International University	PhD or PsyD in Forensic Psychology
Arizona State University	Law and Psychology JD/PhD
California State Univ., Fresno	Joint PhD in Forensic and Behavioral Sciences
Carlos Alibizu Univ., Miami	PhD Clinical Psych with forensic concentration
Dalhousie University	PhD with forensic specialization
Drexel University	JD/PhD or PhD with forensic concentration
Edith Cowan University	PhD in Forensic Psychology
Florida International University	PhD with emphasis in Legal Psychology
Fordham University	Clinical PhD with forensic concentration
Illinois School of Professional Psych	Clinical PhD with forensic concentration
John Jay College of Criminal Justice	PhD in Forensic Psychology
Massachusetts School of Prof. Psych	Clinical PhD with forensic concentration
Nova Southeastern University	PsyD with clinical forensic concentration
Pacific University	PsyD with emphasis in Forensic Psychology
Sam Houston University	PhD in Clinical Psych with emphasis in Forensics
Simon Fraser University	PhD in Clinical-Forensic Psychology and PhD in Law and Forensic Psychology
University of Alabama	PhD with Psychology-Law concentration
University of Florida	JD/PsyD joint degree
University of Illinois at Chicago	PhD with Psychology and Law concentration
University of Nebraska	JD/PsyD joint degree
University of Nevada–Reno	PhD in Social Psych with Psych & Law concentration
Widener University	JD/PsyD joint degree

Thus, it is a mistake to believe you need a degree specifically in forensic psychology to work in the field. Many graduate programs in clinical psychology, counseling psychology, and criminal justice, among others, have forensic concentrations that provide students with academic and *training* opportunities in forensic psychology, whether through specific course work or internships. Furthermore, many psychologists recommend a broad background in psychology, such as would be obtained by a clinical or counseling degree, rather than a degree in forensic psychology. In reality, there are different avenues through which to work in forensic psychology, as you will see when you read the personal perspectives provided throughout this text.

Most of the graduate programs in the United States concentrate on either clinical or counseling psychology as it relates to corrections or on social psychology as it relates to legal psychology or psychology and law. Some universities offer a combined JD (law degree) and PhD as part of the academic package. Formal programs offering specific degrees in police psychology are virtually nonexistent in the United States and Canada, although there are several programs called "investigative psychology" in the United Kingdom. Academic and research institutions in Canada have long supported research in correctional psychology, and the curricula in Canadian forensic programs reflect this strong research or empirical emphasis. It is important to mention, also, that students with psychology backgrounds often enroll in doctoral programs that confer degrees in criminal justice, such as the distinguished programs at the State University of New York at Albany, the University of Cincinnati, and the University of Maryland. Although they are not psychologists, professors and researchers with doctoral degrees in criminal justice make significant contributions to research, teaching, and practice in this area. (Dr. Emily Salisbury, profiled in Personal Perspective 1.1, is an example.)

PERSONAL PERSPECTIVE 1.1

Pathways to a PhD

Emily J. Salisbury, PhD

OK, I admit it—I had to dig through my notes from graduate school and look up the precise definition of "forensic psychology." Despite efforts to have me diligently memorize this definition during my Master of Forensic Psychology program, the exact words had escaped me: "The research and application of psychological knowledge to the legal system." No doubt, this definition is outlined somewhere in the early pages of this textbook. If you're reading this text, you probably are taking a course in forensic psychology or a related subject area. Some of you may even hope to be a "forensic psychologist." However, it's important to understand that this label is somewhat misleading—that is,

you don't have to be a forensic psychologist to work in the world of forensic psychology.

Students immediately perk up when I tell them I have a degree in forensic psychology (perhaps because of the mass influx of television shows focusing on anything "forensic" or crime-related). But I am not a psychologist, and I don't even teach in a psychology department at my university. I teach and conduct research within a Criminology and Criminal Justice (CCJ) department, and my PhD is in criminal justice (and I'm not the only faculty member in my CCJ department with a background in psychology). As students who may be interested in this field for a profession, you may find it useful to learn how my academic path led me to where I am now, since I work in the realm of forensic psychology without actually being a clinical or forensic psychologist.

While grinding through my MA (yes, I used the word "grind" because it truly was an enormous leap from undergraduate to graduate-level study), many topics interested me, but I kept coming back to the ideas of risk assessment and the principles of effective correctional intervention. In other words, I was intrigued with the method of identifying offenders likely to recommit crimes, and the types of programs that can improve the lives of these offenders and increase the likelihood that they stop committing criminal acts. Not surprisingly, basic principles of psychology have a lot to say about changing offender behavior!

By the time I was approaching graduation, I knew I had learned a tremendous amount, but had no idea what I wanted to do with this prestigious advanced degree in forensic psychology. For a time, I was convinced that all I wanted were my nights and weekends back from studying—I swore I could not endure one more exam, let alone another 5 years of school, even with a PhD on the horizon. Several women in my small cohort (we were all women that year—not an uncommon scenario these days in graduate school) graduated and went on to work in the "field" as research analysts specializing in legal research for government or private firms; one was even hired as an investigator for the NCIS (Naval Criminal Investigative Service). We were all jealous of her.

But a couple of other women were convinced they wanted to pursue a PhD, including my best friend in the program. Jen was recruited to attend the University of Cincinnati, and upon her return from visiting the school, she encouraged me to seriously reconsider this option. But 5 more years!?! Could I do it? The thought of having to do this massive thing called a dissertation felt overwhelming. Yet, in the end, after much reflection and consultation with mentors like Curt Bartol, I knew that (a) I wanted to push myself; (b) if I waited, life would become more complicated, making the goal more challenging to achieve; (c) there would be many "baby steps" along the way to prepare me for the dissertation; and (d) if I could attend with my best friend, it wouldn't be so bad.

My psychology background during the early years of my criminal justice PhD program was extremely beneficial, especially at a program such as Cincinnati's. The faculty appreciated and emphasized psychological perspectives, and they were experts in the specializations I was interested in—risk assessment and correctional rehabilitation. Furthermore, I learned that although the field of criminology and criminal justice originally developed within sociology, it has become its own distinct area of study and increasingly multidisciplinary. It integrates not only sociology, but also psychology, biology, genetics, gender and ethnic studies, public administration, public health, and many other fields. My psychology background fit very well with criminology and the study of individual, micro-level causes of criminal behavior. Indeed, if you want to know something about how to effectively change offending behavior at a basic, individual level, you need to know something about how and why people behave the way they do and what is likely to assist them in making that change (i.e., psychology!).

(Continued)

(Continued)

Yet, in other ways, I had quite a bit of catching up to do during my doctoral career. I had taken only one survey criminal justice course and had never taken a sociology course. I was barely aware of the most basic criminological theories that you learn in Crim 101. Fortunately, I felt prepared enough overall, especially in the most difficult areas of statistics and research methodology (which tend to be relatively rigorous in psychology programs), and never worried that I couldn't "hang" with the rest of my cohorts. It was tough, especially with a full year of statistics during the first year, but Jen and I helped each other make it through.

Within the first few weeks of my second year at Cincinnati, I felt anxious and concerned that I had not yet connected with a faculty member to advance my research skills (an important aspect to a PhD student's academic development). Literally a day later, I received an e-mail from Dr. Pat Van Voorhis asking me if I was interested in joining her federal research grant developing a gender-responsive risk and needs assessment specifically for women offenders. I felt very relieved and fortunate to have the opportunity. My experience as a research assistant allowed me to develop my applied research skills, such as learning how to code and enter data into databases like SPSS, developing relationships with criminal justice agencies, understanding the importance of institutional review board (IRB) processes, and preparing and delivering research presentations to stakeholders.

Looking back on it now, I am very grateful that I had the opportunity to pursue graduate work in the fields of forensic psychology and criminology because I love continuing to learn about these subjects, sharing my knowledge with students, and conducting research in these areas. Although the demands of academic work are high, a professor's lifestyle can be very flexible and rewarding. Part of the work required of academic scholars is to simply *think* and immerse oneself deeply into the inquiry. This essentially means that professors don't ever really leave work behind at the office—in fact, they often have two offices, one at school and one at home. As you can imagine, then, I never truly got my "nights and weekends back" as I had once hoped. But I've learned to manage the intensity. I also understand that not many people get paid to think about social problems and how to more effectively understand and begin to solve them.

With that said, I don't wish to over-romanticize the profession. There are certainly days that the job is very difficult and taxing (i.e., when you know students aren't reading material; when a coauthor refuses to meet writing deadlines; and, of course, when you have to deal with the overall stress surrounding the goal of tenure and the publication requirements to achieve it). However, the rewards far outweigh the challenges. I enjoy learning and teaching students how to learn—I get to do both of these constantly as part of my job and share it with others.

For those of you thinking of pursuing graduate work, regardless of whether you seek a career in academe, I encourage you to speak to mentors, professors, and current graduate students to see what life will really be like as a graduate student, and to choose a program wisely, based on your needs and interests. It is especially important to research the faculty with whom you will be working. If your interests don't match well, the program will likely not be a good fit for you. Lastly, but perhaps most importantly, it's critical to find out what funding opportunities are available, since the time commitment of graduate school is similar to that of a full-time job.

For those of you thinking, "I never want to give up my nights and weekends—I'm so done studying after undergrad!" you'd be surprised at how quickly the years go by when you are studying issues that interest you.

Dr. Salisbury is an Assistant Professor in the Division of Criminology and Criminal Justice at Portland State University. She earned an MA in forensic psychology from Castleton State College, and a PhD in criminal justice from the University of Cincinnati. She loves playing soccer and tennis, backpacking, and exploring Oregon's cities and landscapes.

In addition to obtaining a doctorate, some clinicians become certified or become diplomates in forensic psychology. A **diplomate** is a professional designation signifying that a person has been certified as having advanced knowledge, skills, and competence in a particular specialty. Diplomate certification in forensic psychology attests to the fact that an established organization of peers has examined and accepted the psychologist as being at the highest level of excellence in his or her field of forensic practice. The psychologist must be licensed to qualify for diplomate status. Some of the psychologists profiled in boxes throughout this book are diplomates in forensic psychology.

In approximately 17 states, forensic psychologists must obtain licenses or state-issued certificates in order to engage in forensic practice, such as conducting competency evaluations or providing treatment services in a psychiatric facility. Virtually all of the laws relating to this certification were passed after the year 2000, which is testament to the growth in this field. Heilbrun and Brooks (2010) have published a helpful table summarizing these statutes.

Another level of certification is "board certification," which can add stature to an individual's credentials if he or she is called to testify in court. On a national level, the predominant organization that provides board certification in forensic psychology (as well as 12 other specialty areas) is the American Board of Professional Psychology (ABPP). In addition, the American Board of Forensic Psychology (ABFP) has provided board certification since 1978 and is now affiliated with the ABPP (Heilbrun & Brooks, 2010). Another certifying body is the American Board of Psychological Specialties (ABPS), which is affiliated with the American College and Board of Forensic Examiners. Criteria used by the various boards and organizations to grant credentials or titles vary widely (Otto & Heilbrun, 2002). According to Heilbrun and Brooks, with regard to board certification, the ABFP "appears to be the most rigorous, requiring a credentials review, a work sample review, and the passing of both a written and an oral examination for all candidates" (p. 229).

As referred to earlier, the American Academy of Forensic Psychology and the American Psychology-Law Society published the *Specialty Guidelines for Forensic Psychologists* (SGFP) (Committee on Ethical Guidelines for Forensic Psychologists, 1991), which is now under revision. According to Otto and Heilbrun (2002), "The primary goal of the SGFP is to improve the quality of forensic psychological services by providing guidance to psychologists delivering services to courts, members of the bar, litigants, and persons housed in forensic, delinquency, or correctional facilities" (p. 7).

We now turn to a discussion of the five major areas in the research and practice of forensic psychology to be covered throughout the text.

Police Psychology

Police psychology is the research and application of psychological principles and clinical skills to law enforcement and public safety (Bartol, 1996). Police psychologists are often not included in the umbrella category of forensic psychologist, and—like correctional psychologists—some do not consider themselves such. The term *police psychology* is somewhat imprecise because it appears to exclude other law enforcement agents, such as deputy sheriffs, fish and wildlife agents, airport security, marshals, constables, and many types of other state and federal agents. The term *law enforcement* is more encompassing. However, critics of that term note that enforcement of the law is only one of many tasks performed by police and that law is often enforced selectively. The real work of police is maintaining order, providing service, keeping the peace, and being coproducers—with citizens—of public safety. Rather than adopt one or the other viewpoint—each has its merits—we will use *police* and *law enforcement officers* interchangeably and broadly to include the wide variety of agents listed above.

The relationship between psychology and law enforcement has waxed and waned over the years, with considerable forensic psychology involvement followed by a period of quiescence. Overall, though, as law enforcement agencies have become more professional, law enforcement supervisors and directors better educated, and the public more critical and concerned, there has been a substantial increase in the need for services provided by police psychologists. They perform preemployment psychological assessments, fitness-for-duty evaluations (FFDEs), special unit evaluations, hostage team negotiations, and deadly force incident evaluations. Special unit evaluations include the selection and training of special weapons and tactics teams (SWATs), tactical response teams (TRTs), and hostage negotiation teams (HNTs). Forensic psychologists are also increasingly asked to do investigative-type activities, such as criminal profiling, psychological autopsies, handwriting analysis, and eyewitness (or earwitness) hypnosis. Larger police departments usually hire full-time, in-house police psychologists, whereas the smaller departments usually use psychological consultants.

In a survey of 152 police psychologists (Bartol, 1996), 89% of the respondents said they had PhD degrees, followed by EdD degrees (4.5%), master's degrees (3.6%), and PsyD degrees (2.7%). Most of the PhDs had obtained their degrees in clinical psychology (60.7%), counseling (17%), or industrial/ organizational psychology (8%). Twenty-five percent of the respondents were women. Participants in the nationwide survey were also asked to indicate the type of services they provided to police during a typical month, as well as the amount of time they usually spent at each activity. Respondents said that preemployment screening and assessment consumed the largest percentage (34.3%) of their time. A significant amount of time was also spent in providing services to officers and their families (28.7%), followed by fitness-for-duty evaluations (6.8%), training of personnel (6.9%), and administrative work (3.9%).

Currently, there are no formal graduate programs in the United States specifically focused on police psychology. It is best for students entering the field to earn a doctorate in psychology (especially clinical, counseling, or industrial/organizational) and, while in the graduate program, work with a faculty member who is involved in police psychology and preferably has worked with the law enforcement community. It is also advisable to complete a doctoral or postdoctoral internship in an agency or organization that deals directly with police organizations. A few police departments (e.g., the Los Angeles Police Department, the Los Angeles Sheriff's Department, the Metro-Dade Police Department in Florida, and the New York Police Department) do offer pre- or post-training in police psychology. More common internships are those that involve a formal schedule of supervision and training, as well as an opportunity for some degree of police training, ranging from ride-alongs to attendance at a police academy. Regardless of the career path taken, it is critical that a person interested in police psychology become highly familiar with the nature of police work, its policies and procedures, and gain an understanding of the police culture. (Dr. Robert Woody discusses this in Personal Perspective 1.2. as does Dr. Ellen Kirschman in Chapter 2 [Personal Perspective 2.2].) Some practitioners estimate that for police psychologists to be highly effective, socialization into the police culture may take up to 3 years beyond the usual academic and clinical training (Finn & Tomz, 1997). An aspiring police psychologist should also plan on being available 24 hours a day for the agency and be willing to work in different locations (e.g., on the street, at the academy, or in an officer's home).

PERSONAL PERSPECTIVE 1.2

The Reality of a Career in Law Enforcement

Robert Henley Woody, PhD, ScD, JD

Throughout my career as a psychologist and attorney, I have had many contacts with law enforcement personnel. I have also been a sworn law enforcement officer (LEO) (emphasizing training). I have been affiliated with a county sheriff's department, a city police unit, and a statewide coordinating agency.

In teaching undergraduate students in forensic psychology (primarily from the Departments of Psychology, Sociology, and Criminal Justice), I have been somewhat surprised at the great amount of interest in becoming a law enforcement officer, but there is often a lack of awareness of the reality of a law enforcement career. It seems that TV and film portrayals foster misconceptions—no, every LEO is not physically attractive; excitement and astute intellectual analyses are not part of the daily routine; a crime is not solved in an hour; and career outcomes are not always positive.

To enter law enforcement, a person must graduate from an accredited academy and usually must pass a written test (e.g., a state examination). There are variations among law enforcement training academies, but generally the curriculum is tightly structured by the state-level coordinating agency, and the substance is geared to high school graduates. Reportedly, there is, because of cost, resistance politically and from within agencies to *requiring* any college-level training for certification or employment, and it is believed that the large majority of recruits completing the academy will not have a lasting career in law enforcement. Consequently, law enforcement is usually thought of as an occupation, not a profession per se.

At present, there is an inclination to admit recruits who represent diversity (e.g., in terms of race, gender), which may jeopardize reliable and valid selection criteria. In other words, the tests and selection criteria that have been used for years and may be valid for White males may not be valid for other individuals who are still qualified. Also, there is preference for youth; as one state-level authority said, "We don't want to invest resources in anyone who will not be able to give us at least 25 years of service."

(Continued)

(Continued)

Although objective "cognitive" examinations (e.g., multiple-choice questions) are used, dexterity and performance in the "high liability" areas are strict requirements, namely in defensive tactics, firearms, vehicular maneuvers, and first responder skills. Police agencies do not want to be sued if LEOs demonstrate a lack of these abilities. Physical fitness, good health, and a blemish-free personal history are essential.

Being hired does not assure continued employment, though. The first year of employment almost always represents additional "on-the-job training," and failure to satisfy the training officer assigned to oversee the "new hire" can lead to termination. In some agencies, an attrition rate of 50% for first-year hires is not unusual. A high attrition rate is costly and seems to be attributable to faulty selection procedures by both trainers and employing agencies.

Certainly agencies differ and personnel have unique assignments, presumably based on competencies. However, there is reason to believe that—as a general principle—the threshold requirement for continued employment is compliance with the chain of command. High intelligence and advanced education are not of particular value, as opposed to understanding the functions and having the personal and practical skills to fulfill expectations. In many departments, if an LEO has more intelligence or education than someone within the chain-of-command, it is likely to be viewed negatively.

Constant evaluation by the chain of command is a frequent source of stress, and one not often noted in the law enforcement research literature. Day-to-day duties tend to be routine and uncreative (some LEOs might say monotonous). It takes years of high performance ratings and gradual skill-oriented training to advance in rank. Often, promotion is dependent on "following directions" and being a "team player."

Many LEOs report dissatisfaction and stress from the possibility of danger as well as from boredom, administrative policies, lack of career advancement, poor financial rewards, public disdain, and political interference. Also, there is always the looming possibility of illness or injury, which could restrict or end an LEO's career. In reality, however, the percentages of LEOs sidelined *significantly* by illness or injury is relatively small.

Despite the negatives, LEOs seem to like the field of law enforcement and recognize its contribution to bettering society. However, many LEOs are also prone to be disappointed in the lack of intellectual stimulation, job security, and chances for advancement.

Because of job dissatisfaction and stress, it is not surprising that, in their personal lives, some LEOs experience depression, marital conflicts and divorce, domestic violence, abuse of alcohol and other substances, and a range of unhealthy conduct. There is debate as to whether the incidence of these negative conditions is greater for LEOs than for the general population.

The foregoing comments do not constitute a condemnation of law enforcement. To the contrary, law enforcement is essential to society, and LEOs deserve admiration, praise, and rewards. Perhaps as importantly, they deserve support services to help them deal with the stressors of law enforcement work. The basic message is that a career in law enforcement has rewards, but also uncertainties and adverse employment-related conditions. Rather than a long-time career, it is not unusual for an LEO who wishes to maximize personal opportunities to view an entry into law enforcement as but a stepping-stone on the career trail.

Dr. Woody is a Professor of Psychology and former Dean for Graduate Studies and Research at the University of Nebraska at Omaha. He is a psychologist, attorney, and musician, and a former sworn law enforcement officer. He is a Diplomate in Clinical and Forensic Psychology, ABPP; member of the Florida, Michigan, and Nebraska bar associations; and a licensed psychologist in Florida and Michigan. He has authored 33 books and over 200 articles for professional sources.

Psychology of Crime and Delinquency

The psychology of crime and delinquency is the *science* of the behavioral and mental processes of the adult and juvenile offender (Bartol, 2002). It is primarily concerned with how criminal behavior is acquired, evoked, maintained, and modified. Recent psychological research has focused on the offender's cognitive versions of the world, especially his or her thoughts, beliefs, and values and how those that are inconsistent with leading a lawful life can be modified. It assumes that various criminal behaviors are acquired by daily living experiences, in accordance with the principles of learning, and are perceived, coded, processed, and stored in memory in a unique fashion for each individual.

Criminal psychology examines and evaluates prevention, intervention, and treatment strategies directed at reducing criminal behavior. Research in crime and delinquency has discovered, for example, that chronic violence usually develops when children do poorly in school, do not get along with peers, have abusive parents, and attend schools that do not control disruptive and violent behavior (Crawford, 2002). Research has also found that social rejection by peers and others can lead to serious, violent offending: "A great deal of psychological functioning is predicated on belonging to the group and enjoying the benefits, both direct and indirect, of that belongingness" (Benson, 2002, p. 25). When this sense of belongingness is removed or restricted, a feeling of isolation and social exclusion occurs that tends to produce significant changes in behavior, such as an increase in aggression, violence, and other maladaptive behaviors. Under these conditions, human behavior may become impulsive, chaotic, selfish, disorganized, and even destructive. School shooters, for example, frequently express a sense of social isolation and rejection.

Researchers have also found, however, that well-designed and carefully executed prevention programs can prevent violence and a lifelong career path of crime. For example, the Fast Track Prevention Program, developed by researchers at Duke University, Pennsylvania State University, Vanderbilt University, and the University of Washington, has shown highly promising results in reducing juvenile crime. We will discuss more such programs in the chapters on crime and delinquency. Of late, applied psychologists working in school settings have found an increased need for their services, as we noted above. This has led to a keen interest in a new subdivision of school psychology.

Forensic School Psychology

Educational programs are required for young people in correctional and psychiatric facilities throughout the country, and some states have established special school districts within these facilities (Crespi, 1990). The challenges for forensic school psychologists within these contexts are considerable. Although the primary focus of public and private schools in the community is obviously education, such education in most correctional or psychiatric settings may be secondary to the reasons for confinement.

Rehabilitation of the juveniles—which includes but is not limited to education—is crucial. Consequently, assessment and counseling services are critical roles for the school psychologist within these settings. Although many forensic school psychologists primarily work with mentally disordered offenders and youth in correctional facilities, they also work with public and private schools on issues that potentially relate to the legal system. For example, a psychologist in a public school setting might be asked to assess a student's potential for being violent after being suspended from school temporarily as a result of sending threatening letters to his teacher.

Forensic school psychologists may not call themselves such—they may think of themselves simply as psychologists or school psychologists. However, if they routinely interact with a multitude of legal issues, we would consider them deserving of that special title. Forensic school psychologists may work with local schools concerning school suspensions and expulsions, as well as possible placement of a youth into a residential school program and its concomitant implications for the youngster's home school district. They face issues relating to the limitations of client privilege; tactics during contested special education cases; and expectations of judges, attorneys, and facility staff pertaining to mental status and the client's potential placement in institutional settings (Crespi, 1990).

The need for additional consultation with school psychologists within the public and private schools systems across the United States took on chilling urgency in the late 1990s when a rash of school shootings made headlines. Communities across the nation that had previously had a low profile—West Paducah, Kentucky; Jonesboro, Arkansas; Pearl, Mississippi; Springfield, Oregon—suddenly became well known because of the violence that erupted within their schools. Since then, sporadic episodes of a student taking a gun to school or a student killing a school principal have been publicized. The most striking case of mass murder was the killing of 12 students and one teacher at Columbine High School in Littleton, Colorado, in April 1999. Twenty other students were injured, some seriously, during that incident. The two teenage boys who were responsible for the shootings apparently committed suicide in the school library during the tragedy. To the public and news media, the shooters appeared to be two ordinary boys from normal middle-class families living in a suburb of Denver. As more information became public, the shooters were described as isolated teenagers fascinated by weapons and often ridiculed by other students. Although there had been a number of school shootings prior to Columbine (at least 10 school shootings between 1996 and 1999), the Columbine shootings prompted a great deal of alarm and concern from parents across the United States. In addition, the media and some experts were quick to generalize about the "skyrocketing school violence problem" and demanded some kind of threat or risk assessment to identify those youth who might have similar intentions. Therefore, risk assessments became more common. Such an assessment would occur, for example, when a student makes a spoken or written threat to harm classmates or teachers. Once a youth has been assessed, he or she may then be counseled in the school setting or in the community or may even be expelled from school. As noted above, that assessment task often falls to the school psychologist.

Despite the media attention directed to Columbine and the other school tragedies, it is important to keep school violence in perspective. The school shootings described occurred during a time when juvenile violent crime was decreasing nationwide. Whenever the news media highlight certain events and dramatize their significance, the events seem to be more widespread and frequent to people than they really are. This phenomenon is called the **availability heuristic.** In reality, although the shootings were terrible and tragic, they were not representative of the juvenile crime picture as a whole. Furthermore, although the media understandably report incidents of children having guns on school premises and we periodically learn of still another instance, there is no documentation that this is a widespread problem. It is of course important to be alert for possible dangers facing school-age children and the adults who work with them in the schools, but the reality is that the risk of victimization in the school environment is smaller than in private homes or the community at large (O'Tool, 2000). Any risk, of course, is still unacceptable.

Victimology and Victim Services

Victimology refers to the study of persons who have experienced either actual or threatened physical, psychological, social, or financial harm as the result of the commission or attempted commission of crime against them. The harm may be direct or primary (experienced firsthand) or indirect or secondary (experienced by family members, relatives, survivors, or friends because of their closeness to the victim) (Karmen, 2001).

Violent victimization of children, such as terrifying abductions, school shootings, and sexual attacks, can disrupt the course of child development in very fundamental ways and can be associated with emotional and cognitive problems over the course of the life span (Boney-McCoy & Finkelhor, 1995). In adults, there is strong evidence that the effects of criminal victimization—such as assault, robbery, and burglary—are both pervasive and persistent (Norris & Kaniasty, 1994). Until recently, psychological services were received by a very small fraction of crime victims (2%–7%) (Norris, Kaniasty, & Scheer, 1990). In fact, it has only been within the past 30 years that criminal victimology has become recognized as a scientific and professional field of study (Karmen, 2001). Increasingly, forensic psychologists are beginning to play major roles in the research, evaluation, and treatment of crime victims from diverse cultural contexts and age groups. These activities will be covered in greater depth in Chapters 10, 11, and 12.

Students wishing to pursue a research career in victimology probably should obtain a research doctorate in psychology, criminal justice, social work, or sociology. Those desiring careers as practitioners in the field would be advised to obtain a doctorate in clinical or counseling psychology or an MSW (Master of Social Work). However, there are other training opportunities and career paths as well.

Over the past 25 years, for example, the field of victim services has become a rapidly growing profession, and not all of these services relate to crime victims. Today, there is greater understanding of victims' issues due to legislation enacted to support victims' rights, increased funding for victim services, efforts by victim advocates, and active research in victimology. Victim services concentrating on victims of sexual assault; domestic violence; and partner, child, and elder abuse have especially grown in recent years, and legislation has broadened the scope of understanding and services for victims. Colleges and universities now routinely offer courses, majors, and concentrations in victimology.

The National Victim Assistance Academy (NVAA), funded and sponsored by the U.S. Department of Justice's Office of Victims of Crime (OVC), has led the way in developing curriculum standards to be used at the national and state levels. The NVAA currently offers two distinct levels of training and education: (1) the Foundation-Level Academy and (2) the Advanced Topic Series. The Foundation-Level Academy, which began in 1995, is a comprehensive, 40-hour, academic-based course of study in victimology, victims' rights, and victim services for victim services professionals and allied professionals. The Advanced Topic Series involves workshops consisting of 20 to 24 hours of academic-based training in selected concentrations, such as program management, specific training/education, skills, and techniques.

Legal Psychology

Legal psychology is an umbrella term for the scientific study of a wide assortment of topics reflecting the close relationship between psychology and the courts. These topics include competencies and criminal responsibility (insanity defense), civil commitment, the psychology of the jury, the psychology of evidence, child custody determinations, family law issues, eyewitness identification, and the effects of pretrial publicity on jury decision making. As treated here, legal psychology includes both research and application of behavioral and social science to criminal and civil courts. Once they have earned their PhD degrees, people with a background in legal psychology often obtain post-doctoral positions in various agencies and research facilities like the Federal Judicial Center, the National Center for State Courts, the FBI, or the National Institute of Mental Health.

A caveat is in order, however. It is not unusual to see the terms *legal psychology, psychology and law,* and *forensic psychology* used interchangeably in academic and professional literature. Although we use *legal psychology* here as a subarea of forensic psychology, we recognize that this is not a universal approach. We also recognize the considerable overlap between legal psychology and the other subareas we have carved out. The psychology of evidence, for example, is of intense interest to police psychologists, who might be advising the law enforcement community on facial composites or the reliability of eyewitness testimony. In fact, we discuss these topics in the police chapters. The legal psychologist is far more likely than the police psychologist to be conducting research in these areas, however. Likewise, legal psychology and victimology intersect when psychologists perform risk assessments and some custody evaluations. The point here is that the various subareas of forensic psychology are not mutually exclusive. (See Focus 1.3 for an example of a specialization that may be valuable in several subareas of forensic psychology.)

FOCUS 1.3. FORENSIC NEUROPSYCHOLOGY

The term **forensic neuropsychology** refers to the application of knowledge from the neuropsychological profession to legal matters. Neuropsychology is the study of the psychological effects of brain and neurological damage and dysfunction on human behavior. Clinical neuropsychology is the applied branch of the field that focuses on the assessment and diagnosis of neurological damage. Forensic neuropsychologists provide information in legal cases on such things as dementia, brain damage, and intellectual functioning. The neuropsychologist may be asked to testify as to the extent of a person's impairment and be expected to answer questions relating to employment fitness, the need for a guardian or health care provider, chances of full recovery, or the extent of rehabilitation.

Interestingly, tragedies associated with wars bring this topic into focus. Many veterans of conflicts in Iraq and Afghanistan have suffered traumatic brain injuries (TBIs) as a result of encountering improvised explosive devices (IEDs) in the course of their military duty. Likewise, children who were victims of child abuse or adult victims of domestic violence may also suffer TBI. With increasing awareness of the extent of these injuries, military veterans and victims of crime are in need of assessments from neuropsychologists. Neuropsychological assessment procedures and tests include measures that evaluate general intelligence, language, memory, attention, thought processes, perceptual-motor functioning, and emotional status.

Forensic neuropsychology is a profession that is developing very rapidly and has a very bright and promising future. The best career route for a student interested in this field is to pursue a PhD in clinical psychology with a heavy emphasis on biopsychology and an internship focusing on clinical neuropsychology. Many neuropsychologists are certified by the American Board of Clinical Neuropsychology.

One of the numerous topics holding considerable interest for legal psychologists is the psychology of false confessions, a topic we discuss again in Chapter 2. Most people are aware that suspects—for a wide variety of reasons—sometimes confess to crimes they did not commit. A suspect may be afraid, may want the notoriety attached to confessing, may desire to protect the real perpetrator, or simply may think that no one will believe in his or her innocence. What surprises many people, however, is this: Some suspects who are truly innocent come to believe they are truly guilty. Current research strongly suggests that skillful manipulation by law enforcement officers can lead to this form of false confession (Kassin, 1997; Kassin, Goldstein, & Savitsky, 2003; Kassin & Kiechel, 1996; Loftus, 2004). Loftus observes that "we have every reason to believe that some people who are presented with false evidence that they committed a crime might actually come to believe that they did" (p. i). Legal psychologists have been at the forefront of studying this bizarre phenomenon.

Another topic of interest to legal psychologists is the creation of facial composites from the memory of eyewitnesses. Composites are considered indispensable aids to criminal investigation by most police agencies. Composites are reconstructions of faces through memory, and they are built either with the help of an artist's sketching skills or by using the various commercial kits available to law enforcement. In recent years, kits have been replaced by computer-based systems where features are stored on disks and the face is put together on a video display unit. Interestingly, research by forensic psychologists has revealed that computer systems are no more effective in developing accurate facial composites than kits or artists (Koehn & Fisher, 1997; Kovera, Penrod, Pappas, & Thill, 1997). In addition, this research has consistently found that facial composites developed from the memory of eyewitnesses are poor models of the "real" face of the offender. However, facial composites may be helpful in narrowing the field of suspects and providing leads for law enforcement investigators. For example, a sketch of a bank robber, disseminated by the media, may sufficiently represent the true perpetrator that it leads to an acquaintance alerting police. Such sketches almost invariably produce many false leads, however. In one noteworthy rape case that will be mentioned again in Chapter 3, police circulated a composite based on the victim's description of her assailant; a restaurant owner believed the composite resembled one of his busboys, and the busboy was arrested. The victim identified him in a lineup, and the individual was eventually convicted, despite his protestation of innocence. Years later, DNA evidence cleared him.

Family Forensic Psychology

Many legal psychologists are becoming increasingly involved in family law, so much so that specializing in **family forensic psychology** is a good career option. For example, the 2000 census indicated a baby boom in gay and lesbian families as well as a major increase of cohabitating, single-parent, and grandparent-led families (Grossman & Okun, 2003); the census of 2010 is not likely to see a decline. In 2007, the Centers for Disease Control (CDC) reported that 39.7% of all births in the United States were to unmarried women. These changes affect the formation of families as well as family maintenance and dissolution, and they also present a challenge to our traditional ideas of what a family is and how families function.

> Family courts are struggling with unprecedented issues over visitation and custody with lesbian, gay, and cohabitating parents who split up; whether surrogate mothers or donors of eggs or sperm have any parental rights; and the implications of children who are doing well living with a grandparent when a parent is released from jail and wants to reclaim these children. (Grossman & Okun, 2003, p. 163)

In recent years, issues relating to immigration status have led to questions about the legal rights of children whose parents entered the United States illegally or who entered legally but their visas expired and were not renewed. In addition, many legal immigrants must cope with the myriad challenges they face adjusting to schools, places of work, and housing situations. Practicing psychologists often consult with public and nonprofit agencies that provide these families with counseling and other services.

Family forensic psychologists are concerned with abuse; adoption; alternative families; child support; divorce, including custody, relocation, and conflict resolution; elder law, including estate planning; family business; guardianship; juvenile justice; paternity; reproductive and genetic technologies; and other areas such as termination of parental rights. Family forensic psychology is involved in civil and criminal cases when the understanding of family dynamics and family systems is essential, for example, in cases involving visitation to prisons, release programs, and the impact of sentencing on family members (Grossman & Okun, 2003). The best-known areas of family forensic psychology involve child custody, family violence, and the assessment and treatment of juveniles, all topics that will be covered in some detail later in the book. We will describe the other newer topics as we encounter them throughout various sections of the text.

Correctional Psychology

Correctional psychology is arguably the fastest growing branch of forensic psychology, though we acknowledge that many psychologists working in corrections prefer to call themselves "correctional psychologists" rather than "forensic psychologists." The number of persons incarcerated in the United States is now over 2.3 million and growing daily (Sabol, Hinton, & Harrison, 2007). Although only a portion (7–10%) of these individuals qualify as "chronic offenders," it is estimated that each chronic offender costs society about $1.3 million over the course of the offender's lifetime (Crawford, 2002). Of particular significance to psychologists is the large number of mentally disordered persons in the nation's jails and prisons, a topic we will cover in detail later in the book. In addition to those incarcerated, more than 4 million persons are under correctional supervision in the community, such as on probation or parole. Clearly, there is a great need for the services of correctional psychologists.

Fortunately, correctional psychology has changed dramatically since the 1970s, when the prominent psychologist Ned Megargee (1974) remarked, "By and large, psychology as a scientific discipline has not made a substantial contribution to the applied area of corrections" (p. 44). Even so, Megargee himself had developed one of the first classification systems for use with inmates, which remains in use in many prisons today. Since that time, correctional and research psychologists have made substantial contributions to corrections, particularly pertaining to inmate classification systems, psychological assessments, program/treatment evaluation, crisis intervention strategies, and sex offender and substance abuse treatment.

As the number of opportunities for psychologists in corrections has proliferated, psychologists have increasingly discovered that correctional psychology is an exciting, rewarding, and challenging field (L. Richardson, 2003). The **correctional psychologist**'s major goal is to help in inmate rehabilitation, treatment, and reintegration into the community. Correctional psychologists also work with offenders who are serving their sentences, or part of their sentences, in the community, such as those on probation or parole. The services they provide may include crisis intervention, long-term and short-term therapy, group therapy, and substance abuse treatment. Psychologists in these settings administer a wide variety of psychological assessment techniques (intellectual, personality, aptitude, vocational, and educational), interpret results, and prepare comprehensive reports. Their recommendations are considered in decisions to release prisoners, change their security levels, or assign them to a variety of programs. Likewise, some of the same tasks are performed in juvenile correctional settings, which we will cover in the last chapter.

Correctional psychologists also offer consultative services relating to corrections staff, which may include screening and selection, employee assistance counseling, and mental health consultation with hostage negotiation or crisis support teams. Research opportunities are often available, particularly—although not exclusively—in the larger prison systems, including the Federal Bureau of Prisons.

Research psychologists often study the psychological effects of correctional systems on prisoner behavior. Topics include the general effect of imprisonment on special populations of offenders, such as the mentally disordered or the elderly; the effects of crowding; the effects of isolation; and the outcome of various rehabilitative programs. Interestingly, psychologists who practice in correctional settings are sometimes criticized for aligning themselves with prison administrators, and they may be confronted with ethical quandaries, such as when asked to perform custody-related functions like supervising or restraining inmates. Nevertheless, many correctional psychologists find great personal and professional satisfaction working in these settings. In addition, as we will note in Chapter 12, there is ample evidence to support the positive impact of psychology on the correctional system.

Psychologists working in and as consultants to correctional facilities often join associations representing their common interests. Examples are the American Correctional Association (ACA) and the **International Association for Correctional and Forensic Psychologists (IACFP)**. The latter is guided by a series of recently updated standards (Althouse, 2010) that provide the minimum acceptable levels for psychological services offered to offenders, whether they are adults or juveniles held in local, state, or federal facilities, as well as in the community. The standards cover a wide range of principles as well as services, including staffing requirements, confidentiality issues, mental health screening, professional development, informed consent, segregation, and a host of other topics relating to this work.

Defining Forensic Psychology—A Recap

The foregoing sections indicate that the field of forensic psychology, as we define it broadly, provides ample opportunities for psychologists interested in interacting with some aspect of the law. We have devoted separate sections of this book to each of the five subareas defined above.

A decade ago, Otto and Heilbrun (2002) posited that if forensic psychology (particularly legal psychology) was to continue to grow and develop as a viable discipline, it had to become more mainstream. At the time, a relatively small group of forensic specialists devoted themselves full-time to this field, whereas a much larger group of psychologists provided occasional forensic services or provided such services only within a circumscribed area, such as child custody evaluations. They argued that forensic psychology, as a field, must acknowledge the fact that forensic practice was occurring at a variety of levels and for different reasons. The field must develop a plan to ensure that forensic practice overall was well-informed and competent. This plan was especially needed in the area of forensic testing and assessment.

More recently, Heilbrun and Brooks (2010) commented on the remarkable expansion of the field over the past decade, noting there has been substantial progress. "The field has matured: the recognition of the importance of the foundational science is stronger, and we are closer to identifying best practices across a range of legal contexts that are addressed by forensic psychology research and practice" (p. 227). In proposing an agenda for the next decade, they emphasize the need for interdisciplinary and intercultural collaboration; continuing improvement in the quality of forensic mental health assessments; a better integration of science and practice; and better outreach to a variety of settings, many of which are covered in this text. It appears that the field is gaining increasingly more adherents to the broad rather than narrow conceptualization of forensic psychology, although there is still debate about who should be considered a "forensic psychologist" (Committee, 2010).

SUMMARY AND CONCLUSIONS

As recently as 30 years ago, the term *forensic psychology* had barely been introduced into psychological or legal literature. Today, as we have seen, it is a commonly encountered term, but it still defies definition. Although some favor a narrow definition limiting it to clinical practice, the contributions of research psychologists may be undermined by such an approach. The Committee on the Revision of the Specialty Guidelines for Forensic Psychology (2006, 2010), as well as the writings of prominent forensic psychologists (e.g., DeMatteo, Marczyk, et al., 2009; Heilbrun & Brooks, 2010), recognize the importance of contributions from researchers. In addition, though, it is important to consider the context in which psychology is practiced. Limiting forensic psychology to work with civil and criminal courts does not recognize well enough the law-related functions performed by psychologists working with law enforcement, corrections, or victims. Finally, the many contributions of psychologists who study the psychology of crime and delinquency deserve to be included in this field. The legal system surely can benefit, for example, from research on the developmental paths to delinquency or research on the prevention and control of sex offending.

We have persisted, then, in advocating for a broad definition of forensic psychology, one that could divide it into the five subareas covered in this chapter. In each of the areas discussed, numerous career opportunities exist. Both undergraduate and graduate programs have rapidly seen the need for preparation for careers in forensic psychology, whether by offering degree programs in the field or by offering concentrations within a broader program, such as a doctorate in clinical, counseling, or developmental psychology. Furthermore, professionals themselves are regularly offered opportunities for licensing, certification, and continuing education.

KEY CONCEPTS

American Psychological Association (APA)

Association for Psychological Science (APS)

Availability heuristic

Clinical psychologist

Computer evidence recovery

Correctional psychologist

Counseling psychologist

Diplomate

Ethical Principles of Psychologists and Code of Conduct

Family forensic psychology

Forensic entomology

Forensic neuropsychology

Forensic psychiatry

Forensic psychology

Forensic school psychology

Industrial/organization (I/O) psychology

International Association for Correctional and Forensic Psychology (IACFP)

Legal psychology

Police psychology

Questioned document examination or analysis

School psychologist

Specialty Guidelines for Forensic Psychologists

QUESTIONS FOR REVIEW

1. Contrast the narrow and broad definitions of forensic psychology.

2. Contrast forensic psychology and other forensic sciences.

3. Identify the five subspecialties of forensic psychology covered in this text and provide illustrations of the contributions of forensic psychologists in each one.

4. Explain the difference between the PhD and the PsyD.

5. What are the five applied branches or specializations in psychology, as recognized by the APA?

6. How has the American Psychological Association responded to the need to provide services to a diverse client population?

7. What is meant by the term "prescription privileges" when applied to psychologists? Briefly discuss the progress psychologists have made in obtaining these privileges and discuss possible objections that would be raised.

Part II

Police and Investigative Psychology

2

Police Psychology

CHAPTER OBJECTIVES

- Explore the specialization of police psychology and its many tasks.
- Emphasize the importance of police culture and stress that it is not necessarily homogeneous.
- Discuss job analysis and the assessment of candidates for law enforcement positions.
- Describe the roles of psychologists and mental health professionals in working with officer post-shooting traumatic reactions, psychological problems, and fitness-for-duty evaluations.
- Review special unit evaluations and the police psychologist's responsibilities in hostage-taking incidents.
- Examine the psychological aspects of police interrogation methods and the risk of false confessions.

Approximately 18,000 agencies qualify as law enforcement agencies in the United States, operating at four levels of government: federal, state, county, and local or municipal. In addition, there is a wide range of private and public safety agencies. Some are private security agencies, and others are supported by public funding, such as campus police departments on public university and college campuses. Virtually every university or college campus, public or private, has a public safety department, whose officers may or may not be armed and may or may not be invested with police powers.

As we mentioned in Chapter 1, the relationship between psychology and law enforcement has waxed and waned over the years. More recently, as law enforcement departments have become more professional and the public has demanded more accountability, the role of psychological services in law enforcement has become more critical and prevalent.

Police psychology is the research and application of psychological knowledge and clinical skills to law enforcement and public safety. Precisely when a partnership between law enforcement and psychology first began is unclear, though. To a certain extent, community psychologists offered some type of consulting service to police, usually on an "as needed" basis, throughout the 20th century. Viteles (1929) discovered that police departments in Germany were using psychologists in a variety of ways at least as early as 1919. Chandler (1990) noted that in 1966, the Munich police were employing a full-time in-house psychologist to train officers to deal with patrol problems, such as crowd control.

In the United States, police psychology probably began as a viable profession in 1968 when Martin Reiser, EdD, was hired as a full-time in-house psychologist by the Los Angeles Police Department (LAPD). An in-house psychologist is one who is retained as a regular employee of the agency, in contrast to a psychological consultant, who is independent of the agency but contracted to provide special services. Today, the great majority of police psychologists are consultants. Their practice may be devoted exclusively to law enforcement, or they may be community psychologists who work with police as needed. This latter group may not even call themselves police psychologists; rather, they may think of themselves as clinical, professional, counseling, or practicing psychologists who offer services to the law enforcement community. Many are affiliated with specialized professional groups like the APA Division 18 (Psychologists in Public Service, Police and Public Safety Section) or the Society for Police and Criminal Psychology.

In 1969, Martin Reiser presented a paper at the Western Psychological Association Convention in Vancouver, British Columbia, titled "The Police Department Psychologist." The paper was later published, in 1972. Chandler (1990) suggests that the presentation of the paper probably marked the official beginning of American police psychology.

There is little doubt that Reiser was the most prolific writer on police psychology in the United States throughout the 1970s. He also established the first graduate student internship in police psychology at the LAPD, in conjunction with the California School of Professional Psychology. However, it remains debatable whether Reiser was the first full-time psychologist employed by a police department in the United States. It is likely that some psychologists were employed by American police agencies prior to 1969—and as we noted, many others were consultants—but their work may have become lost in history. Reiser (1982) himself, in a collection of published papers, asserted that he was not at all sure he was the first full-time police psychologist in the United States. For now, though, we will refer to the year 1968—the year he was officially hired—as the "beginning" of police psychology in the United States.

As also mentioned in Chapter 1, a police psychologist does not have to be a present or former police officer to be an effective service provider to law enforcement agencies. However, the police psychologist must be highly familiar with and knowledgeable about what policing involves, as well as the police culture, which, as we will note below, is far less homogeneous than previously assumed (Paoline, 2003). Woody (2005; see also Personal Perspective 1.2) notes that one of the clear requirements to be a successful police psychologist is to recognize and understand this culture, and he adds that the psychologist should reasonably accommodate it as long as it does not endanger the public safety; police ethics; or the mental, physical, or behavioral health of the officer. Police psychologist Ellen Kirschman, who is profiled in Personal Perspective 2.2, also mentions the importance of appreciating the police culture.

Nearly all occupations have a "culture." Manning (1995) describes occupational cultures as having "accepted practices, rules, and principles of conduct that are situationally applied, and generalized rationales and beliefs" (p. 472). The occupation of law enforcement is unique in that the working environment is not only potentially very hostile or dangerous, but officers have also been granted the legitimate power to create, display, and maintain their authority over the public (Paoline, 2003). Consequently, police officers work together to develop and maintain a unique occupational culture that values control, authority, solidarity, and isolation (L. B. Johnson, Todd, & Subramanian, 2005).

The coping mechanisms prescribed by the police culture are often essential in handling the many stressors that this unique work environment entails (Paoline, 2003). Officers, perhaps more than people in other occupations, depend on one another for the protection and social and emotional support they need to do their jobs. Paoline has perceptively observed, though, that researchers, scholars, and practitioners (including psychologists) often make the mistake of assuming that there is a single, homogenous police culture. He emphasizes that police cultures may vary in terms of the style, values, purpose, and mission of the organization itself, starting from the top down. The culture of a federal agency, for instance, is likely to be different from a county sheriff's department's culture. The culture may also vary according to rank. The street cop culture is apt to be quite different from the cultures in administration and supervision. In addition, there may be "subcultures" within the ranks, with some officers adopting a different style of policing from that of others. Some may play by the book, whereas others may go beyond departmental procedures and policies. Finally, the changing face of law enforcement as a result of recruitment of women and ethnic and racial minorities has certainly affected the concept of police culture. Paoline notes, "As police forces have become more heterogeneous, one would expect a single cohesive police culture to give way to a more fragmented occupational group. The modal officer of the past . . . is continually changing as the selection and recruitment of officers has diversified" (p. 208).

In short, claiming to be an expert without understanding and earning the acceptance and respect of a police agency, and without acknowledging the many facets of police culture, will likely lead to limited success for a new or inexperienced psychologist. Entry into the field of police psychology for most psychologists usually begins with providing limited consulting services to police agencies, such as screening and selection, or psychotherapy or counseling of police officers and their families. If the psychologist proves effective, trustworthy, and credible, the department may begin to request a variety of other services such as help with management problems, shift work assignments, fitness-for-duty evaluations, or evaluation of officers who have applied for promotion.

Ride-along programs, in which the psychologist accompanies police officers in patrol cars, are usually helpful in educating psychologists about the realities of the police experience (Hatcher, Mohandie, Turner, & Gelles, 1998). As experience accumulates and the agency becomes more familiar with the psychologist and his or her work, the psychologist may be asked to do many other things, such as evaluate an alleged use of excessive force incident, or become a member of the hostage/crisis negotiation team. "The invitation to the psychologist to participate in the hostage/crisis negotiation team appears to depend upon three factors: (1) mutual acceptance, (2) professional credibility (timely provision of critical information and behavioral analysis), and (3) an ability to function in the field setting" (Hatcher et al., 1998, p. 462). We will discuss the role of the police psychologist as an integral member of the hostage/crisis negotiation team later in the chapter.

In sum, psychologists specializing in providing psychological services to law enforcement participate in a wide variety of tasks, including helping in the screening and selection of candidates for entry positions as well as promotion, conducting **fitness-for-duty evaluations (FFDE),** assessing deadly force incidents, counseling after critical incidents, and doing special unit evaluations. Special unit evaluations include the selection and training of special weapons and tactical teams (SWATs), tactical response teams (TRTs), and hostage negotiation teams (HNTs). Psychologists also provide counseling or psychotherapy services, such as may be required after a shooting incident when an officer uses deadly force or witnesses a police colleague killed in the line of duty.

Some psychologists also engage in helping law enforcement officials solve crimes, such as by examining the scene, consulting on possible motives, and even "profiling" possible perpetrators. This type of work is more likely to be called investigative psychology, and it will be the focus of Chapter 3.

Finally, psychologists also develop and implement training programs and mental health programs for public safety personnel, including critical incident stress debriefings (commonly abbreviated CISDs), crisis intervention techniques, and stress management. *Critical incidents* refers to tragedies, death, serious injuries, hostage situations, and other threatening situations that the police frequently encounter. CISDs are commonly implemented in public safety departments (including those with emergency service personnel) across the United States, Canada, the United Kingdom, and other parts of the world (L. Miller, 1995).

To help organize the material in this chapter, we adopt the approach of Aumiller and Corey (2007), who divide police psychology into four general and overlapping domains of practice: (1) assessment, (2) intervention, (3) operational support, and (4) organizational/management consultation. (Table 2.1 shows some of the more common activities associated with each domain.) Aumiller and Corey were able to identify over 50 activities or services that police psychologists may be expected to provide. We will describe in more detail some of these activities as we go through this chapter and Chapter 3.

Table 2.1 Some of the More Common Activities and Tasks of a Police Psychologist

Assessment	Intervention	Operational	Consulting & Research
Job analysis	Individual therapy & counseling	Crisis & hostage negotiations	Research activities pertaining to law enforcement issues
Psychological evaluations of police applicants	Group, couple, & family therapy and counseling	Police academy education & training	Management and organizational consultation
Fitness-for-duty evaluations	Critical incident early intervention and debriefing	Threat assessments	Supervisory consultation
Psychological evaluations of specialty police units	Critical incident stress management and therapy	Criminal activity assessment and offender profiling	Development of performance standards for agency personnel
Emergency consultations concerning the seriously mentally disordered	Substance abuse and alcohol treatment	Operational-related consultation and research	Mediation

Assessment Tasks

Job Analysis

In order to evaluate whether someone is a good candidate for law enforcement, one must first understand what the job involves. This means understanding the true nature of the daily tasks expected, not as reflected in popular culture. Job analysis is the process of identifying and analyzing how, where, and why a particular job is done. For our purpose here, job analysis refers to a systematic procedure for identifying the skills, abilities, knowledge, and psychological characteristics that are needed to do public safety work successfully. The first step is to understand what officers do on a day-to-day basis. In the past, many law enforcement screening procedures have been based on intuition and "gut feelings" rather than a comprehensive analysis of job requirements. However, without a job analysis to justify the choice of psychological measures, it is extremely difficult for the psychologist doing the screening to know what he or she is looking for—let alone measure it. (See Personal Perspective 2.1, in which Dr. Cary Rostow describes his work in this regard.)

Job analyses have revealed characteristics that are desirable, and sometimes necessary, for all successful police officers. For example, successful candidates need to have good judgment and common sense, appropriate decision-making skills, interpersonal skills, a solid memory, good observation talents, and communication skills (both oral and written) (Spielberger, 1979). Integrity and trustworthiness are certainly other important traits. Although the emphasis that each agency places on the above characteristics may differ slightly, they tend to be universal psychological requirements for law enforcement. Thus, police psychologists often recommend a screening out of applicants who demonstrate a lack of these attributes. Mental disorders and serious behavioral problems, of course, are clear reasons for refusal to hire.

Police psychologists who do assessments for police screening, selection, and promotions should be familiar not only with the literature on job analysis, but also with how to conduct their own analysis. An agency may require psychological strengths that are beyond the general requirements listed above, such as the ability to work in special units with victims of sexual abuse, searching for missing children, or hostage negotiation. In addition, a job analysis must be carefully done. Data are often subjected to legal scrutiny concerning gender, racial, salary, promotional, selection, and—more generally—psychological testing issues. For example, a police applicant who feels he has been unfairly evaluated may challenge the agency's selection appraisal system on the grounds that it is not job-related or is discriminatory.

There are various procedures for doing a comprehensive job analysis, but most are done through interviews and questionnaires. In some cases, observations of job behavior may be necessary. In police work, for example, officers and supervisors are asked what is done on a daily basis; what skills and training they believe are necessary; and what temperament, personality, and intellectual capacities best fit particular tasks or responsibilities. The information gathered from a well-done job analysis is summarized as a job description that details what is done, how it is done, and why it is done (McCormick, 1979; Siegel & Lane, 1987).

PERSONAL PERSPECTIVE 2.1

Police Psychology: A Game for "Professional Guessers" or a Science?

Cary Rostow, PhD

Among the most interesting aspects of having a long-term general, community-based practice of clinical psychology is that, given sufficient time and opportunity, the practitioner will be approached by various agencies to perform specialized psychological work. When this happened to me about 15 years ago, my career was set on a very different path.

I was approached by a self-insuring, local governmental risk pool, which is a sort of insurance company owned by members of a public organization and which financially covers legal claims made against member agencies for such issues as police misconduct. When a serving officer or firefighter is accused of violating the civil rights of any person, that person may make a claim for civil damages under federal or state law. The executives associated with this agency told me that defending claims of this sort and settling with the plaintiffs placed a great strain on their finances. They noted that only a few officers were responsible for the lion's share of the costs and settlements they were compelled to cover. Since we had a good reputation as a respected practice that had provided forensic services in the past, the executives asked us to find a way to identify problem officer candidates at the "application for work" stage and screen them out before they became a departmental liability.

For those of you who have not read the work of the late Paul Meehl (1920–2003), I suggest that Dr. Meehl (1989) offered more useful advice than almost any other psychologist regarding the sort of problem that we were forced to consider. So, approaching the problem as Dr. Meehl suggested, we explored the police selection literature in the area of officer screening. We were disheartened by our review of the literature that had been generated over the previous 30 or so years. *What we found can best be described as an unproven collection of standard or common mental health procedures and techniques applied to nonclinical vocational screening in an inadequate and unconvincing manner.* For example, experimental samples tended to be very small in size, many studies used single instruments that generated small statistical significance regarding the outcome measure, and researchers tended to use analogue samples (such as college students instead of real officer candidates), thereby limiting the *generalizability of findings.* To make matters worse, many studies tended to have limited and questionably relevant measures of outcome (e.g., still employed vs. not employed 6 months

after data collection) that offered little actual guidance for the future user in making liability forecasts. The time interval between testing and post-measure was often calculated in weeks or months at most, often concluding at a time when actual officers are still under supervision and have limited occasion for misconduct. The impression that we received was that selection screening of officer candidates was little more than the use of concepts and constructs familiar to those in clinical work but without any confirmation of the validity of the measure for purposes of identifying officers who would show misconduct. Paul Meehl and his students have warned against this approach.

My professional colleague Dr. Bob Davis and I formed a company called Matrix, Inc., and we began a 4-year research project. At first, we interviewed law enforcement executives and documented the kinds of problems that they wished to avoid in the future (usually those that cost them money or embarrassed them). We also began to search court records and legal reports that specified ways in which police officers incurred actual liability for their departments. This was an eye-opener, as we encountered behaviors ranging from sexual inappropriateness and excessive force to behavior unbecoming an officer and insubordination. We used available test instruments in order to obtain psychometric samples of potentially useful data for analysis regarding probable later misconduct.

The next step was to compose psychometric tools and a research questionnaire based upon police executive reports and case law. Once this was accomplished, we began the practice of screening officer candidates by using the types of technologies that were typically used for the diagnosis of persons with mental problems

(Continued)

(Continued)

(e.g., the Minnesota Multiphasic Personality Inventory–Revised [MMPI-2]). This was followed up with detailed, objective feedback for the departments regarding the conduct of the officers. We then began a refinement program to measure how our actuarial decision making was holding up. Pathological items, items that did not predict misconduct, and redundant items were eliminated, and those remaining guided the development of new methods for liability screening.

Using a set of powerful statistical analytic tools, Matrix, Inc. created a police officer database and a backward-stepping regression equation that yielded about 95% accuracy in forecasting general officer misconduct. We developed subscale predictions of misconduct in specific areas of liability (such as excessive force and sexual inappropriateness) so as to be able to suggest remediation for acceptable officer candidates with some identifiable weaknesses. In other words, if a candidate was strong in other areas but showed some potential for misconduct somewhere down the line, we suggested ways in which the department could help the officer, once hired, overcome the weak area.

We followed the costs to departments over time (lawsuit expenses, settlement costs, etc.) and demonstrated significant taxpayer savings with the use of our new methodology. Thus, it may be safely assumed that such findings implied an indirect measure of improved officer conduct. We named this procedure the *M-PULSE*© *Methodology* or *Matrix-Psychological Uniform Law Enforcement Selection Evaluation*.

The defensibility and utility of our approach drew us into similar work for firefighters (where we developed the *M-FLAME*© or *Matrix*

Firefighter Liability Assessment and Management Evaluation), probation and parole officers, corrections officers, wildlife agents, and nuclear plant workers, all an outgrowth of similar technology that had succeeded with the M-PULSE©. Intimate contact with hundreds of municipal and state agencies eventually created a demand for us to work in the area of fitness-for-duty evaluations (FFDEs), a somewhat different task in which we evaluate officers who may be unable to meet the safety and "business necessity" aspects of public security or protection work because of some crisis in their personal or work lives.

In 2004, we published *A Handbook for Psychological Fitness-for-Duty Evaluations in Law Enforcement* (Rostow & Davis, 2004), which has come to be widely employed in the fitness-for-duty process. We approached the FFDE problem from the perspective that mental health or clinical methodology alone is insufficient or inappropriate for the vocational or occupational issues raised in such evaluations, and we developed a set of FFDE guidelines and procedures for practical use. For example, we have worked out methods that involve the sort of information that can and cannot be addressed in an FFDE for regulatory and forensic reasons. As a result, I am in contact with attorneys, municipal executives, and police psychologists around the country who employ some version of our system, and with whom I regularly consult.

Matrix, Inc., has grown so that we now contract to support several hundred police departments and many firefighting departments, corrections departments, probation offices, and nuclear plants. We are in constant contact with our associates around the country and are expanding service to new areas on a regular basis. We now spend a good part of our professional day performing some aspect of professional police psychology, consulting, evaluating, screening, and researching our procedures and products.

Paul Meehl was right all along: The world is open to those who wish to enlarge the boundaries of science in its application to psychological problems and not so much to those who want to cling to the methods of the past.

Dr. Rostow is the president of Matrix, Inc., a professional police psychology corporation, and received his PhD in clinical psychology at Northern Illinois University in DeKalb. He is licensed as a clinical psychologist, clinical neuropsychologist, and medical psychologist (prescribing psychologist) in the State of Louisiana. He holds a postdoctoral master's degree in psychopharmacology and is a Diplomate in Police Psychology from the Society for Police and Criminal Psychology.

Preemployment and Post-Offer Psychological Evaluations

As stated by Aumiller and Corey (2007), nearly all law enforcement agencies are subject to law, regulations, or accreditation standards that require psychological evaluations of public safety candidates. These psychological evaluations—usually in the form of personality measures—help to ensure that the candidates are free of mental or emotional impairments that would interfere with effective, responsible, and ethical job performance as a police officer. A candidate who is severely depressed, or one who has strong paranoid tendencies or is prone to aggressive behavior with minimal provocation, is unlikely to perform well as a law enforcement officer.

In the mid-20th century, psychologists often gave intelligence tests to law enforcement candidates, and agencies used scores on these tests to help in their hiring decisions. However, over the years it became clear that intelligence tests per se were not effective measures of how an officer is likely to perform on the street. Although some psychologists continue to use these tests as a standard practice in other contexts (e.g., school assessments and prisoner intake), they are not as commonly used in psychological screening of law enforcement applicants. However, it should be emphasized that a majority of police agencies and police academies still require a written or aptitude test for entrance to the academy. Interestingly, it has been documented that neither high intelligence nor a college education necessarily means that an individual will be a good police officer (Henderson, 1979; Spielberger, Ward, & Spaulding, 1979). Nevertheless, college-educated officers have been shown to have better communication skills, and they have earned promotions at a higher rate than non–college-educated officers (Cole & Smith, 2001). And, as noted above, officers with a college education also have an effect on changes in the police culture (Paoline, 2003).

In most cases, only licensed or certified psychologists or psychiatrists who are trained and experienced in psychological assessment instruments and their interpretation should conduct candidate evaluations. It is also important that the examiners be knowledgeable about what law enforcement demands as well as the research literature on public safety. Finally, the examiner must be aware of developments in the law relating to the hiring of candidates. For example, one of the most far-reaching federal laws in this regard is the Americans with Disabilities Act, which we discuss below.

Americans with Disabilities Act of 1990

The **Americans with Disabilities Act (ADA)** is a far-reaching civil rights law that prohibits discrimination and mandates equal treatment of all individuals regardless of physical or mental disabilities. Its sections on employment prohibit public employers and private employers with 15 or more employees from discriminating against any qualified person with a disability who can perform the essential (as opposed to marginal or incidental) functions of the job he or she holds or seeks. A qualified individual with a disability is an employee or job applicant who meets the legitimate skill, experience, education, or other requirements of a job. As such, the law has a significant effect on day-to-day police practices and—for our purposes here—on screening procedures used in law enforcement. The police psychologist who designs employment screening, selection, and promotional procedures for police agencies must be familiar with all the nuances of the act.

In balancing an individual's rights under the ADA and an organization's right to know of an applicant's physical and mental fitness, the Equal Employment Opportunity Commission (EEOC) has divided disability inquiries into two stages: (1) pre-offer of employment and (2) post-offer/pre-hire. At the pre-offer stage, a police agency, for example, must not ask applicants any health or fitness questions that elicit information about disabilities. The agency *may* ask general "job performance" questions, such as presenting a scenario and asking the candidate how he or she would handle it. At the post-offer/pre-hire stage, a police department may make direct inquiries about disabilities and may require applicants to undergo medical and psychological examinations. Such post-offer inquiries are allowed because the employer, by making a conditional offer of employment, can rescind that offer only if it can be shown that the person is unable to perform the essential functions of the job even with reasonable accommodation.

The ADA affects law enforcement agencies beyond accommodating and providing for equal opportunity for employment within the agency. The ADA affects nearly everything that police officers do, including receiving citizen complaints; interviewing witnesses; arresting, booking, and holding suspects; operating telephone ("911") emergency centers; providing emergency medical services; and enforcing the laws. In all these activities, the agency must try to make reasonable accommodations in its services to people who are disabled. In one noteworthy case, police were sued after they arrested a wheelchair-bound suspect and transported him to the police station without his wheelchair. They apparently thought the chair was a prop, but it was not.

Screening Out and Screening In

One of the more challenging tasks for the police psychologist is the process of screening-out compared to screening-in police officer candidates, usually through the use of personality measures. Screening-out procedures try to eliminate those applicants who demonstrate significant signs of psychopathology or emotional instability or who lack the *basic* ability or mental acuity to perform the job in a safe and responsible manner. Screening-out procedures are those most commonly used by police psychologists when screening police candidates (Varela, Boccaccini, Scogin, Stump, & Caputo, 2004). Screening-in procedures, on the other hand, are intended to identify those attributes that distinguish one job applicant as being potentially a more effective officer than another. Implicit in this approach is the ability to rank-order applicants, allowing agencies to select the top candidates from a pool that passed the initial screening procedures. This approach assumes that there are traits, habits, reactions, and attitudes that distinguish an outstanding officer from a satisfactory one. To date, there is virtually no evidence that psychologists have reached this laudable goal in any satisfactory, valid manner, although some psychological measures seem to be performing better than others.

Before discussing some of the instruments commonly used in police screening, it is helpful to review the importance of validity in psychological testing. Validity addresses the question, Does a test or inventory measure what it is designed to measure? Although psychologists discuss many types of validity, three are of particular relevance here: concurrent validity, predictive validity, and face or content validity.

Concurrent validity is the degree to which a test (or inventory) identifies a person's *current* performance on the dimensions and tasks the test is supposed to measure. Many personality measures are called inventories rather than tests. An *inventory* is usually a list of items, often in question form, used in describing or investigating behavior, interests, and attitudes. A *test* is a standardized set of questions or other items designed to evaluate knowledge or skills.

To develop a concurrently valid inventory (or to consider using an established inventory), the psychologist should assess the personality, interests, or attitudinal characteristics of already-employed police officers to establish predictors of good performance. Typically, the inventory is administered to officers representing varying degrees of success in law enforcement work, with "success" determined by supervisor evaluations, peer ratings, or both. For example, if a high percentage of officers evaluated by supervisors as "successful" respond differently to certain questions on a scale from a group of "unsuccessful" officers, the scale is considered a good evaluator of *current* on-the-job performance. Applicants who subsequently take the exam should obtain scores that are similar to those of the successful officers in order to be assessed as good candidates for employment.

Research that examines the current performance of individuals already on the force has a critical limitation, however, because it ignores the important psychological characteristics of those officers who were hired but dropped out because of various problems during the course of their career path. Thus, significant segments of the population are missed. One of the primary reasons for using any screening instrument is to discover the potential dropouts or failures as soon as possible in their careers, which could save both time and money for the department.

Predictive validity is the degree to which an inventory *predicts* a person's subsequent performance on the dimensions or attributes the inventory (or test) is designed to measure. In other words, an instrument has predictive validity if it is able to identify which candidates will and will not succeed at law enforcement work. As a research procedure, predictive validation is more useful and rigorous than concurrent validation, but it is rarely implemented because it requires a longitudinal design in which officers must be evaluated over an extended period of time, usually several years. Candidates are tested during a preemployment stage and then followed over their careers to see how the initial testing results could have predicted eventual problems and successes. If a test or inventory is able to distinguish those who eventually perform well from those who do not, it has high predictive validity and it is a powerful device for the screening and selection of candidates prior to entry into law enforcement.

A test or inventory has face validity if its questions appear relevant to the tasks needed in law enforcement—in other words, someone looking at the inventory will attest that it seems relevant, regardless of whether it really is. **Face validity** refers not to what the test actually measures but to what it superficially *appears* to measure (VandenBos, 2007). In reality, there may be no empirical support for these assumptions. However, face validity has value because examinees believe the exam is at least pertinent to the job for which they are applying. In addition, Otto et al. (1998) emphasize the importance of face validity for application in the legal context because any measuring instrument should look pertinent and relevant to the legal questions at hand. Judges, lawyers, and jurors may have more faith in a test or inventory with face validity. Psychologists know, though, that unless other types of validity are also ensured, a test with high face validity has little overall worth with regard to measuring what it is supposed to measure.

In summary, of the above three forms of validity, predictive validity is the most desirable to achieve but also the most challenging to establish. Face validity is probably the easiest to establish and is also desirable, particularly if we must persuade non-psychologists of the value of an inventory. However, face validity alone is not sufficient if an inventory or test has no other type of validity.

Commonly Used Inventories in Police Screening

There is a lack of consensus concerning which personality inventory or measure is most useful in the screening and selection process. Research on law enforcement screening (e.g., Cochrane, Tett, & Vandecreek, 2003) indicates that the following six personality measures are currently the most commonly used:

- The Minnesota Multiphasic Personality Inventory—Revised (MMPI-2)
- The Inwald Personality Inventory (IPI)
- The California Psychological Inventory (CPI)
- The Personality Assessment Inventory (PAI)
- The NEO Personality Inventory—Revised (NEO PI-R)
- The Sixteen Personality Factor Questionnaire—Fifth edition (16-PF)

To say they are commonly used is not to say they are the best measures, however. As we note below in discussing each, the jury is still out as to which is most deserving of continued use. Furthermore, many agencies make use of alternative approaches (e.g., see Dr. Rostow's comments in Personal Perspective 2.1). However, it is critically important for alternative psychological measures to be validated.

The most commonly used psychological instrument in public safety screening is the MMPI-2. Police officer candidates often know it by its length ("that endless test"—it has 557 questions). The MMPI-2 is primarily a measure of abnormal behavior, however, so it is usually considered a better "screening out" than "screening in" test. In other words, as traditionally used it can detect pathology, but it is less efficient at detecting positive qualities that might be helpful for law enforcement. Nevertheless, recent research has indicated that the MMPI-2 has shown good results in predicting police officer performance (Caillouet, Boccaccini, Varela, Davis, & Rostow, 2010; Detrick, Chibnall, & Rosso, 2001; Sellbom, Fischler & Ben-Porath, 2007), although there are indications that other personality inventories may be slightly better at this task (Varela et al., 2004). In a meta-analysis of personality testing in law enforcement, Varela et al. found results that suggest psychological inventories that measure normal personality traits may be slightly superior to those that measure abnormal personality, which is traditionally a focus of the MMPI-2. Most of the research on the MMPI as it relates to law enforcement has been of the concurrent validation variety.

Some research focusing on predictive validity of the MMPI and MMPI-2 has been conducted and shown some promise, provided the intent was to identify psychopathology or behavioral problems (Bartol, 1991). Far too much of the research on the MMPI-2 has incorrectly assumed that the inventory has the capacity to appraise both emotional status and *normal* personality traits, however. The MMPI and MMPI-2 were both originally designed to identify possible psychopathology and behavioral deviations and *not* normal personality traits. To force the instrument into doing something it is not equipped to do is unlikely to produce encouraging results. In summary, then, the MMPI-2 has better use as a screening-out measure to identify candidates least suited for law enforcement work, rather than as a screening-in measure to confirm the existence of positive attributes.

The *Inwald Personality Inventory* (IPI) is a 310-item, true–false questionnaire that has 26 scales. The IPI was specifically designed to measure the suitability of law enforcement and public safety candidates based on a variety of personality traits and behavioral patterns (Inwald, 1982; 1992). It was developed to measure both normal personality traits and deviant behavioral patterns, such as job difficulties, substance abuse, driving violations, absence abuse (missing excessive days of work), and antisocial attitudes. The IPI also contains a 19-item validity scale called "Guardedness," which is intended to identify those individuals resistant to revealing negative information about themselves (the MMPI-2 has a similar "Lie" scale). As Inwald (1992) states, "When a candidate denies such items, a strong need to appear unusually virtuous is indicated" (p. 4). If this score is low, the other scale scores may be affected due to socially desirable responses from the respondent.

Robin Inwald (who developed the IPI) and her associates continue to do research in an effort to improve the reliability and validity of the IPI. So far, the research suggests that the IPI, in *some* situations, does slightly better than the MMPI-2 in predicting the performance of public safety personnel and probably is a useful instrument when used in combination with other screening instruments. One strength of the IPI is that it has good face validity. The IPI is used in the preemployment screening process by about 12% of all municipal police departments across the country (Cochrane et al., 2003). The IPI has remained at roughly that percentage of use in preemployment screening over the past decade.

The *California Psychological Inventory* (CPI) (Gough, 1987) contains 462 true-or-false questions designed to measure various features of the normal personality. An earlier version, called Version I, has 480 questions. The inventory is to be used with both adolescents and adults to predict how individuals will behave and react in a variety of interpersonal situations (Murphy & Davidshofer, 1998). The items are grouped into 20 scales developed to measure attributes of personality involved in interpersonal behavior and social interaction (K. R. Murphy & Davidshofer, 1998). Norms of law enforcement applicants are available from the publisher (Consulting Psychologists Press, Inc.). The nationwide survey conducted by Cochrane et al. (2003) revealed that approximately 25% of the departments responding indicated that they used the CPI in their screening procedure.

Some success has been reported for the ability of the CPI to predict performance, both during training and in the field. Topp and Kardash (1986) compared the CPI scores of police recruits who passed academy training with the scores of those who failed or resigned from the academy prior to graduation. Based on CPI score patterns, the researchers described those who graduated as more outgoing, stable, venturesome, confident, controlled, and relaxed. In a recent comprehensive meta-analysis assessing the overall validity of personality measures as predictors of the job performance of law enforcement officers, Varela et al. (2004) discovered that prediction was strongest for the CPI compared to the MMPI or IPI. Varela and his coauthors reasoned that one possible explanation for the superior performance of the CPI is that the CPI is designed to measure *normal* personality traits, in contrast to the MMPI-2, which—as we mentioned previously—is designed to measure psychopathology. They write,

> personality measures that are designed to assess normal personality traits, such as the CPI, may be more useful in this context because they provide information that is not obtained during the initial screening process. For instance, the CPI was designed to provide information about consistent styles of interpersonal behavior. Because being a successful police officer requires effective interpersonal skills . . . the CPI may be a useful measure for predicting this important aspect of officer performance. (p. 666)

The *Personality Assessment Inventory* (PAI) (Morey, 1991) is a self-administered, objective inventory of adult personality that provides information on "critical clinical variables." The PAI contains 344 statements. Respondents are asked to rate the degree each statement is true of themselves on a 4-point scale (1 = *very true,* 2 = *mainly true,* 3 = *slightly true,* 4 = *false*). Responses to statements determine scores on 4 validity scales, 11 clinical scales, 5 treatment scales, and 2 interpersonal scales. Research suggests that the PAI may be a decent predictor of violence, suicide, aggression, and substance abuse and may be a reasonable instrument to use in the selection of police officers. However, considerably more research needs to be done before any firm conclusions can be made about its suitability in this last context.

The *NEO Personality Inventory—Revised* (NEO PI-R) (Costa & McCrae, 1992) is specifically designed to measure the five major domains of personality, called the "Big Five" and often remembered with the acronym OCEAN. They are (1) openness to experience, (2) conscientiousness, (3) extraversion, (4) agreeableness, and (5) emotional stability (which taps neuroticism). The NEO PI-R contains six trait or facet measures that define each of the five personality domains. Taken together, the 5 domain scales and 30 facet scales of the NEO PI-R facilitate a comprehensive and detailed assessment of normal adult personality.

At first, the five-factor model of personality as measured by the NEO was thought to be the answer to the ongoing search for a comprehensive and valid measure of personality and was met with enthusiasm by those involved in personnel selection. So far, though, the NEO has had mixed success. In a meta-analytic study, Barrick and Mount (1991) found that, except for openness to experience, the other four Big Five domains correlated significantly but only moderately with police performance. J. Black (2000) investigated the predictive validity of the NEO PI-R in police officers in New Zealand. He administered the NEO PI-R to recruits at the beginning of training and then analyzed how well the scales predicted outcomes at the end of training. He found significant relationships between the conscientiousness, extraversion, and neuroticism domains and several performance measures conducted during the training. Similarly, Detrick, Chibnall, and Luebbert (2004) examined the predictive validity of the NEO PI-R in relation to police academy performance in a large metropolitan area of the midwestern United States. They found that high scores on three facets of the neuroticism domain, and lower scores on one facet scale of the conscientiousness domain, were related to performance during academy training. Disciplinary and absenteeism factors were predicted by multiple facets. The vulnerability facet scale also emerged as a significant predictor of nongraduation. Overall, the authors concluded that the study provided support for the validity of the NEO PI-R as a predictor of police academy performance.

In a more recent study, Detrick and Chibnall (2006) found that the NEO PI-R may also be a powerful tool for predicting officer performance in the field. Based on NEO PI-R test data, the best entry-level police officers were described as "emotionally controlled, slow to anger, and steady under stress; socially assertive with high need for stimulation; guarded regarding others' motives and strategic in social exchange; and highly conscientious, goal-oriented, and disciplined" (p. 282). According to Detrick and Chibnall, these characteristics represent a very useful benchmark for psychologists to consider in evaluating law enforcement applicants.

The Sixteen Personality Factor Questionnaire (16-PF) is another instrument designed to measure normal adult personality traits. The questionnaire contains 185 items that require a person to answer along a 3-point Likert-type scale. A Likert scale usually requires respondents to indicate their reactions to various statements on a response scale ranging from "strongly agree" to "strongly disagree." The items on the 16-PF are grouped into 16 primary factor scales representing the dimensions of personality initially identified by Raymond Catell (cited in K. R. Murphy & Davidshofer, 1998). The questionnaire was based on a series of factor-analytic studies of items that contained personality dimensions that differentiate normal individuals. The 16-PF has been heavily researched and consistently demonstrates solid reliability and validity. The Cochrane et al. (2003) survey reported that the 16-PF was used by about 19% of the police departments in their preemployment screening procedures. Only a very limited amount of research has been done on its ability as a valid predictor of law enforcement performance, however.

Fitness-for-Duty Evaluations

Police officers, emergency personnel, crisis team members, and firefighters who witness an especially disturbing event—such as the deaths of young children, the terrorist attacks on the World Trade Center on September 11, 2001, plane crashes, the devastation that accompanied Hurricane Katrina, or catastrophes involving fellow colleagues—may exhibit intense emotional or psychological reactions. In some cases, evaluations are needed to determine whether the officer has the mental and psychological stability to continue as an effective officer on the street, at least for the foreseeable future. Therefore, a **fitness-for-duty evaluation (FFDE)** is conducted. This requires a much more extensive assessment than the psychological screening evaluation for initial employment positions.

It is important to mention that forensic psychologists are often asked to perform FFDEs for organizations in addition to law enforcement agencies. Large private corporations, federal agencies, universities, hospitals and other health care agencies, and licensure bureaus often ask them to do FFDEs (Bresler, 2010). The basic goal of any FFDE is "to ascertain to what extent an employee is, or is not, able to meet job expectations" (p. 1). However, our focus here is on FFDEs designed to serve law enforcement agencies.

The order or request for the FFDE for law enforcement comes from the department supervisor or head and is normally conducted by a police psychologist or qualified licensed psychologist who is highly familiar with police psychology issues and research. It is ordered or requested when an officer displays behavior that raises serious questions as to whether he or she is fit to carry out public safety duties. Behavior that may prompt concerns includes such things as one or more complaints of unnecessary or excessive force or any conduct indicating the officer has difficulty controlling his or her behavior. Other behaviors may include irrational verbal statements; evidence of hallucinations or delusions; suicidal statements or behaviors; inappropriate or excessive use of alcohol; use of illegal drugs; or behavioral signs of mental instability, serious depression, or emotional overreactions. A. V. Stone (1995) estimates that excessive force questions accounted for 19% of FFDE referrals. If the officer's behavior immediately or directly threatens safety, a supervisor or chief may instantly relieve the officer of duty or reassign him or her until an FFDE is completed. However, any long-term decision to reduce an officer's rank or duties or terminate that individual may be subject to a legal challenge.

It should be noted that some agencies require these evaluations as standard procedure after a critical incident (such as a fatal shooting). Therefore, it should not be assumed that a request for an FFDE occurs only when there are signs that an officer is facing problems on the job. In addition to carrying out the evaluation, the examining psychologist should recommend intervention methods or reasonable accommodations that would help improve the officer's effectiveness. These may involve counseling, retraining, or treatment.

Psychologists conducting the FFDE are advised to employ a variety of methods in their assessments, including psychological tests and a standard clinical interview that assesses mental status. They should obtain background information from files, the officers themselves, and other significant parties if possible. The evaluations must be done with the informed consent of the officer, but the examiner is under no obligation to explain the results to the officer. The "owner" of the FFDE is essentially the agency requesting the evaluation. On the other hand, the agency is not entitled to any more psychological information regarding an employee than is necessary to document the presence or absence of job-related personality traits, characteristics, disorders, propensities, or conditions that would interfere with the performance of essential job functions (International Association of Chiefs of Police [IACP], 2002).

The FFDE report usually includes the psychological measures used, a conclusion regarding the determination of fitness for duty, and a description of the functional limitations of the officer. In most instances, the FFDE report is provided to the department as a confidential personnel record. Periodic evaluations of the officer may also be necessary. The IACP (2002) recommends that the psychologist conducting the FFDE include performance evaluations, commendations, testimonials, internal affairs investigation, preemployment psychological screening, formal citizen/public complaints, use-of-force incidents, officer-involved shootings, civil claims, disciplinary actions, incident reports of any triggering events, medical/psychological treatment records, or other supporting or relevant documentation related to the officer's psychological fitness for duty. The IACP further recommends that personality, psychopathology, cognitive, and specialized tests that have been validated be used in the assessment process.

The FFDE is not limited to law enforcement but can be used by any occupational group. In addition, in law enforcement agencies, unsworn employees such as dispatchers, administrative assistants, and community service officers may be referred for evaluation if there is reason to believe that the employee cannot perform his or her job in a safe or effective manner due to a mental health problem (Fischler, 2001). In addition, as indicated above, fitness-for-duty evaluations are particularly useful in assessments of firefighters, emergency crisis teams, emergency medical technicians (EMTs), and paramedics.

Special Unit Evaluations

Psychological assessments are also done as standard procedure for members of special teams, such as special weapons and tactics teams (SWATs) and tactical response teams (TRTs); undercover agents; and narcotics, internal affairs, and crisis/hostage negotiation teams, to determine if they are psychologically fit to undergo the pressures and possess the judgment requirements of high-stress positions. Special units usually deal with the execution of high-risk search warrants or high-risk arrest warrants, barricaded persons, hostage situations, heavily armed offenders, terrorist acts, and suicidal persons. Normally, team members are evaluated on a yearly basis to identify problems before they develop into more serious behavioral patterns that would interfere with effective job performance.

Successful members of SWAT teams, for example, tend to be "self-disciplined, conscientious, adherent to rules, comfortable accepting rules, conforming, and helpful" (Super, 1999, p. 422). However, very little research has focused on the validity of assessment procedures used to identify special team selection. As concluded by Super, "There is a serious need for rigorous research regarding psychological assessment and special unit appointments" (p. 422).

Conclusions on Personality Testing for Law Enforcement Personnel

Although many different assessment techniques and personality inventories are currently used in the screening, selection, and promotion of law enforcement officers, it is usually not known whether many of these testing procedures are valid predictors of effective on-the-job law enforcement performance. This is a sobering fact because any selection procedure should ultimately be validated. If a psychological test is designed to predict how well applicants will perform in law enforcement, we must have solid, empirical evidence that it in fact does predict performance on the job. If not, the test is essentially useless as a predictor of future performance. Empirical investigations evaluating relationships between initial selection standards (predictors) and the actual job performance of law enforcement officers should be undertaken, and police psychologists should lead the way in this endeavor.

There are many different kinds of validity, but one of the more important types is predictive validity. To repeat what was said earlier in this section, **predictive validity** is the degree to which a test predicts a person's subsequent performance on the dimensions and tasks the test is supposed to measure. If a test claims to be able to predict which candidates develop into good or outstanding police officers, its predictive validity should be high, discriminating those who eventually perform well from those who do not. If there is empirical evidence that the instrument does have predictive validity, a test is a powerful device for the screening and selection of candidates prior to entry into law enforcement. Obviously, a device that could do this would save both the candidate and the agency valuable time as well as potential difficulty and embarrassment.

Suppose we have a very high incidence of citizen complaints within a particular department. The complaints not only affect public confidence in the department but also result in a high turnover rate. In an effort to identify both the individuals most prone to citizen complaints and the situations engendering them, the police psychologist administers a battery of psychological tests or inventories before the officers are hired and follows them over a number of years, collecting supervisory reports, police affidavits, and any documents pertaining to complaints. The psychologist then correlates the preemployment measures with these documents, paying particular attention to those officers who leave or against whom complaints are filed. If all goes well, the psychologist should be able to identify those tests or inventories that predict poor police–citizen relationships and use those specific measures in future screening of police officers for those departments.

We should be careful to add a note of caution with respect to the above illustration, however. The best way to deal with citizen complaints may not be to screen out ahead of time those who are most susceptible to them. Rather, the best way may be to improve training, communication with the public, and working conditions, thus minimizing the opportunity for stress to appear. An important thing to remember about predictive validity, therefore, is that it predicts adaptability to the status quo or to the situation as it exists. When the situation changes, the predictive validity of an instrument also changes.

As suggested by the above example, single psychological tests as predictors of effective law enforcement performance take considerable and carefully designed research. This is partly due to the diversity and complexity of behaviors required of law enforcement officers, but it is also due to varying work situations across departments. Police duties range from preventing and detecting crime to investigating accidents, intervening in disputes, handling domestic disturbances, and responding to a wide range of requests from the public. Police today also encounter more individuals who are mentally ill, homeless, and in need of support services (see Photo 2.1 of homeless people being evicted). The smaller the department, the more varied are the responsibilities of individual officers. It is not unusual to find a local, small-town law enforcement officer offering first-aid tips to an elementary school class and, on the same day, dealing with a violent domestic altercation. Because specialization is a luxury very small departments cannot afford, it is very difficult to establish objective performance criteria

Photo 2.1 Police officers talk with a homeless man as they serve eviction notices in Sacramento's tent city, April 2009. The homeless, including men, women, and children, were advised to relocate to a shelter in the city. Critics of the evictions maintain that the shelters were less safe than the makeshift shanties that had been erected.

on which to base predictions. Some officers may perform very competently on certain tasks while failing at others. The officer who relates exceptionally well to fun-loving teenagers may perform poorly in crisis situations involving depressed adults.

To tap the heterogeneity of law enforcement activities, screening devices should contain a number of predictors based on a multitude of behaviors, and few psychological measures are able to do this. In addition, because law enforcement work differs substantially from one jurisdiction to another, a test may be adequate for a given department but may not suffice elsewhere. Rural or small-town law enforcement may require different behaviors and talents from metropolitan or urban law enforcement work. Also, many states have sheriff's departments that frequently offer very different services from those of municipal or state law enforcement agencies.

The broad scope of law enforcement, together with the urgent need for more vigorous and sophisticated methods of study, warn us that we should expect few solid conclusions in the research literature as to what are adequate predictors of success or failure in law enforcement work. As expected, the literature is littered with inconclusive or mixed results. This does not mean that reliable and valid psychological assessment is beyond reach. It may mean, though, that a successful testing program may have to be tailor-made to the needs of a particular agency. In addition, it is certainly acceptable to "screen out" those candidates who exhibit gross indicators of problems, such as mental disorder, highly aggressive or antisocial behaviors, or poor judgment.

Intervention Responsibilities

Stress Management

The term *stress* became the overriding theme from the mid-1970s to the early 1980s. More than ever before, police psychologists were called on to identify and dissipate stress, which, if left unmanaged or untreated, could result in an array of psychological and physical health problems for the officer and potentially put the public at risk due to faulty judgment and decision making. *Stressors, burnout, post-traumatic stress disorder (PTSD)*, and *critical incident trauma* became standard terms in the police psychologist's vocabulary. The focus on stress was significant because it moved police psychologists away from their traditional testing functions and into a much larger realm of opportunity and services. Consequently, psychologists began to offer not only stress management but also crisis intervention training, hostage negotiation training, domestic violence workshops, and substance abuse and alcohol treatment.

Occupational Stressors in Law Enforcement

Many researchers, as well as the officers and their families, consider law enforcement to be one of the most stressful of all occupations, with correspondingly reported high rates of divorce, alcoholism, suicide, and other emotional and health problems (Finn & Tomz, 1997). "Police officers regularly deal with the most violent, impulsive, and predatory members of society, put their lives on the line, and confront miseries and horrors that the rest of us view from the sanitized distance of our newspapers and TV screens" (L. Miller, 1995, p. 592). However, persons in many occupations may argue that they face more physical danger than law enforcement officers. Construction workers, miners, stunt pilots, firefighters, and demolition workers are all exposed to potential death and physical injury. Paramedics and other medical personnel, though less likely to be exposed to physical harm, contend that theirs is as stressful as any occupation. However, perhaps few occupations encounter the wide variety of stressors, ranging from organizational demands (e.g., shift work) to the nature of police work itself (e.g., exposure to violence, suffering, and tragedy at all levels), as consistently as law enforcement.

A common strategy employed in the police stress literature is to divide the occupational stressors identified by police officers into four major categories: (1) organizational, (2) external, (3) task related, and (4) personal.

Organizational stress refers to the emotional and stressful effects that the policies and practices of the police department have on the individual officer. They include poor pay, excessive paperwork, insufficient training, inadequate equipment, weekend duty, shift work, inconsistent discipline or rigid enforcement of rules and policies, limited promotional opportunities, poor supervision and administrative support, and poor relationships with supervisors or colleagues. Organizational stressors in major departments may also include antagonistic subcultures within the department, such as intense competition between specialized units, precincts, or even shifts. Being investigated by the internal affairs division is another troubling stressor.

One study from the early 2000s reveals that excessive shift work contributes to more errors in judgment and greater increases in stress than perhaps any other factor in the police environment (Vila & Kenney, 2002). Some officers work more than 14 hours a day on a regular basis, and some "moonlight" for extra income. Excessive hours on the job not only interfere with sleep and eating habits but also raise havoc with family life and responsibilities. Furthermore, irregular hours often interfere with social get-togethers and family activities, isolating the officer even more from social support systems. Also, the organizational structure of large police departments often promotes office politics, lack of effective consultation, nonparticipation in decision making, and restrictions on behavior. Currently, organizational stressors are considered to be the most prevalent and frustrating source of stress for most law enforcement personnel (Bakker & Heuven, 2006; Finn & Tomz, 1997).

Task-related stress is generated by the nature of police work itself, such as inactivity and boredom; situations requiring the use of force; responsibility of protecting others; the use of discretion; the fear that accompanies danger to oneself and colleagues; dealing with violent or disrespectful, uncivil individuals; making critical decisions; frequent exposure to death; continual exposure to people in pain or distress; and the constant need to keep one's emotions under close control.

Law enforcement is frequently confronted with interpersonal violence, confrontational interactions with individuals, and emotionally charged encounters with victims of crimes and accidents (Bakker & Heuven, 2006). Police are expected to keep their emotions under control, a process that has been referred to as "emotional labor" (G. A. Adams & Buck, 2010; Grandey, 2000). Furthermore, they must regulate their emotional *expressions* to conform to societal norms and expectations. Although this is expected to some degree in many other occupations (e.g., lawyers, physicians, health care workers), this is especially expected of police officers on a day-to-day basis. Police officers are expected to regulate their emotions to display a facial and physical expression that is neutral, solid, and controlled. Moreover, police officers are expected to master the art of constantly switching between the human and controlled emotional expression (Bakker & Heuven, 2006), because sometimes a more "human" response is desired, as when an officer must inform people of the death of a loved one. Grandey calls this emotional regulation "surface acting," which is accomplished by suppressing the emotion that is actually felt (e.g., anger or sadness) and faking the appropriate emotion that the situation (or job) demands. Some researchers refer to this response as emotional dissonance (Adams & Buck, 2010). In essence, "emotional dissonance is the discrepancy between authentic and displayed emotions as part of the job" (Bakker & Heuven, 2006, p. 426). Increasing evidence supports the view that emotional dissonance has detrimental effects on health and well-being (Heuven & Bakker, 2003).

Task-related stress also occurs when officers experience role conflict, such as being at once an enforcer of the law, a social worker, a counselor, and a public servant (Finn & Tomz, 1997). Over the past 30 years, there has been increasing police interaction with mentally ill individuals, for example, which requires special skills on the part of the officer (see Focus 2.1). Community-oriented policing (COP), an approach whereby police and citizens work more closely together in positive endeavors, has added new pressures. It requires that officers "give up" a certain amount of control by "walking the beat," meeting with citizens, and adopting a service orientation more than a crime-fighting orientation. COP does not ignore crime or public safety, but it encourages police to form partnerships with citizens to prevent crime and improve safety for the public. Although its benefits are apparent, some officers find it difficult to adapt to its accompanying changes in strategies and policies.

FOCUS 2.1. POLICE AND THE MENTALLY DISORDERED

A woman entered a bodega in Brooklyn and openly began to remove small items from the shelves and place them in a shopping bag. Noticing her disheveled appearance and obvious mental disorder, the bodega owner asked her to replace the items and leave; when she continued to take items and became verbally abusive, he called the police. Officers who arrived on the scene persuaded the woman to accompany them to a local mental health clinic.

In a more serious incident, a mentally disordered individual entered a church on a Sunday morning where the congregation was assembled. He made threatening statements and brandished a knife. Police arrived on the scene and tried to talk him into putting down the knife. They eventually shot the person to death, with members of the congregation watching in horror. The shooting split the congregation as well as the town in which this occurred; many people believed police should have been able to handle this differently, while others supported the officers' actions.

Law enforcement officers are routinely the first line of response for situations dealing with mentally disordered citizens in crisis (Borum, Deane, Steadman, & Morrissey, 1998). Many people with severe mental impairments—either mental illness or mental disability—will experience at least one arrest, and many will be arrested more than once (McFarland, Faulkner, Bloom, Hallaux, & Bray, 1989). Cuellar, Snowden, and Ewing (2007) found that one-fourth of 6,624 individuals with a serious mental illness had at least one arrest, mostly for nonviolent crimes like trespassing or shoplifting or public order offenses like disturbing the peace.

It is estimated that about 10% of police contacts involve people who are mentally disordered (Borum et al., 1998). According to one of the leading experts in the area, psychologist Linda Teplin (2000), officers who encounter a mentally disordered person creating a disturbance generally have three basic choices: (1) Transport the person to a psychiatric facility; (2) arrest the person; or (3) resolve the matter on the spot, such as by moving the person on or contacting the family or a mental health provider. The research on this issue finds that police try to resolve the problem on the spot 72% of the time, make an arrest 16% of the time, and initiate emergency hospitalization 12% of the time (Teplin, 1986, 2000).

In practice, these three choices have some positives and some negatives. Transporting an irrational person is fraught with bureaucratic obstacles and the legal challenges of obtaining emergency commitment. An arrest is often the only option available to the officer when individuals do not appear to be disturbed enough to be accepted by a psychiatric facility but the deviance is sufficient enough not to be ignored. Arrest also may be preferred when the person is unknown by the police, in contrast to the "neighborhood characters" whose strange but harmless behaviors are well-known by the police who patrol the area. The third choice, to resolve the situation "on the spot," requires finesse and understanding on the part of the officer and is not appropriate in all cases. If a serious crime is involved, for example, the officer has little choice but to arrest.

Research has shown that police officers very much want training in dealing with seriously mentally disordered individuals, and are convinced such training is critical in their work (Demir, Broussard, Goulding, & Compton, 2009; Vermette, Pinals, & Applebaum, 2005). Although some have advocated, and some departments have adopted, special teams to handle the mentally disordered, the teams cannot be everywhere. Thus, it makes more sense for police or consulting psychologists to provide training workshops to help *all* officers develop strategies for dealing with those who are mentally disordered, even though special teams may still be warranted.

Demir et al. (2009) described a program called crisis intervention team (CIT) training that has shown significant success in helping police officers make better decisions when dealing with seriously mentally disordered citizens. Psychologists can also help by developing referral sources for mentally disordered individuals who may need to be protected from themselves. Finally, mental health courts (to be discussed in the next chapter), are one option for diverting individuals with mental health needs from criminal justice processing and providing them with needed services.

Stressful assignments, such as undercover duty or drug raids, also play a role in the stress equation. Police officers also fear air- or blood-borne diseases, either intentional (e.g., terrorists) or accidental, and exposure to toxic or hazardous materials (Dowling, Moynihan, Genet, & Lewis, 2006). More recently, budget cutbacks and fiscal uncertainty due to the economy have resulted in concerns about job security and opportunity for advancement. Many departments in recent years downsized or experienced hiring and promotional freezes because of across-the-board budget cuts (Finn & Tomz, 1997). Deployment of National Guard troops to the Middle East also taxed the ranks of police departments, particularly in small departments.

Critical Incidents: A Special Case

Perhaps the most troubling task-related stress in police work is dealing with **critical incidents.** These are emergencies and disasters that are nonroutine and unanticipated, such as a shooter on the loose on a college campus or a family hostage-taking situation involving young children. These events tend to be very stressful primarily because they threaten the perceived control of the police officers (Paton, 2006), and they can produce a number of psychological, neurological, and physical symptoms, including confusion, disorientation, chest pain, sweating, rapid heart rate, and loss of memory. These symptoms may occur during or shortly after the critical incident. However, delayed post-incident stress symptoms may occur weeks or months after the incident. They include restlessness, chronic fatigue, sleep disturbances, nightmares, irritability, depression, problems in concentration, and substance and alcohol abuse.

Considerable research strongly supports the effectiveness of immediate intervention after traumatic events (A. T. Young, Fuller, & Riley, 2008). Moreover, it appears that this intervention is especially effective if it occurs quickly, at or near the location of the crisis (Everly, Flannery, Eyler, & Mitchell, 2001; A. T. Young et al., 2008). Some psychologists work as members, advisors, or consultants on critical incident stress management (CISM) teams or critical incident stress debriefing (CISD) teams. They are sometimes called crisis intervention teams (CITs). The primary focus of these teams is to minimize the harmful effects of job stress as a result of very unusual crisis or emergency situations.

Many departments do not wait for an officer to be confronted with a critical incident. Rather, as part of candidate training they are provided with pre-incident education, which helps prepare officers by psychologically immunizing them to anticipate and understand how traumatic events may affect them. Furthermore, with experience on the job, police officers usually go through a desensitization process whereby they become accustomed to many taxing events that can be expected to occur within the normal routine of policing. However, some traumatic events may be considered extraordinary and beyond preparation. Critical incidents most likely to cause high levels of stress include the following: the suicide or fatal shooting of a colleague; the accidental killing or wounding of a citizen; death or serious injury to a child; events that draw high media coverage; and events involving a number of deaths, such as large fires, terrorist bombings, or large natural disasters such as hurricanes, earthquakes, or tornadoes.

External stress refers to an officer's ongoing frustration with the courts, the prosecutor's office, the criminal justice process, the correctional system, the media, and public attitudes. Available data suggest that for every 100 felony arrests, 43 are typically dismissed or not prosecuted (Finn & Tomz, 1997). Although this is not necessarily a bad thing, police often find it troubling. Moreover, many law enforcement officers feel court appearances are excessively time consuming, and they are often frustrated over what they perceive as inefficiency and "unjust" court decisions.

Personal stress refers to stressors involving marital relationships, health problems, addictions, peer group pressures, feelings of helplessness and depression, discrimination, sexual harassment, and lack of accomplishment. Some officers worry about their competency to do the job well or worry about doing something against regulations. Many police officers feel that the nature of their work has an adverse effect on their home life and social life. Older officers, because of their long stressful careers, are especially vulnerable to serious physical, mental, and health problems (Gershon, Lin, & Li, 2002). In addition, female officers appear to be more prone to depressive symptoms and suicide due to stress factors than male officers (Violanti et al., 2009). This finding is not surprising and does not imply a weakness on the part of the officer; rather, it is more likely a symptom of the traditionally male environment in which the female officer works. We will discuss this in more detail shortly.

Although criminal justice literature frequently mentions exceedingly high divorce rates and general marital unhappiness among law enforcement officers, documentation is very difficult to obtain. Borum and Philpot (1993), in their study, found that divorce rates among police families were no higher than those found in the general population. Similar results are reported by Aamodt (2008). Yet, there is little doubt that the whole family suffers the stressors inherent in law enforcement. In one study of 479 spouses of police officers, 77% reported experiencing unusually high amounts of stress from the officers' job (Finn & Tomz, 1997). According to Finn and Tomz, the most common sources of spousal stress include the following:

- Shift work and overtime
- An officer's cynicism, need to feel in control at home, or inability or unwillingness to express feelings
- The fear that the officer will be hurt or killed
- The officer's and other people's excessively high expectations of their children
- Avoidance, teasing, or harassment of children because of their parent's job
- The presence of a gun in the home

PERSONAL PERSPECTIVE 2.2

My Career Path as a Police Psychologist

Ellen Kirschman, PhD

My career has been shaped by intuition, opportunity, chance, and personal preference. I have no formula, other than to say that you should follow what interests you deeply and supports your strengths and preferences in life. It takes time, experience, and a lot of trial and error to know what these are.

I like variety and stimulation. I hate being confined to an office. I'm active, directive, and want to feel part of a team. I have opinions that I'm not shy about expressing. I like to laugh. I love stories. I'm curious. It was never in the cards for me to sit in an office every day of the week, counseling people or doing psychological assessments.

How I got started

Decades ago, I was a newly minted psychiatric social worker, earning my stripes in an outpatient psychiatric clinic attached to a large hospital. Several of my clients were married to cops. Stories about their marriages ranged from the usual marital complaints about lack of communication to more frightening events involving guns. As I had been taught in grad school, I called the husbands (there weren't that many women cops back then) and asked them to join us in counseling only to be told, in so many words, that coming within 25 feet of a psychiatric clinic was an intolerable humiliation. Better to sacrifice the marriage than lose their jobs. More often than not, the wives dropped out of therapy soon after.

Around that time, I saw a television documentary about family life in America, one segment of which featured a police officer and his wife. They quarreled often when he came home from work. He wanted peace and quiet and she wanted to talk. When the cameras followed the officer at work, it was clear why he needed quiet at home. He spent his entire shift in the chaos of his inner-city beat. People were either yelling at him or at each other. His hours were spent solving problems. When his wife saw the film footage of his work, she was amazed. She had no idea how loud and chaotic his day was. How had it happened, I wondered, that two well-meaning,

articulate people hadn't talked about this before? I decided, with the naïveté and enthusiasm of an early career therapist, that if I could explain the realities of police work to officers' families, I could cure their marriage problems. I put together a class titled "I Love a Cop" and took it to my local community college. When the college catalogue came out, the class filled to quota immediately and there were 40 women on the waiting list. I had struck a need I hardly knew existed. This was 1977. Very few departments recognized how much police work affected officers' families.

Shortly after that, I enrolled in a doctoral program and completed my PhD. Many years later, with a lot more experience under my belt, I wrote the book *I Love a Cop: What Police Families Need to Know* (2007, Revised Edition).

My first real police job

My first real police job after my doctorate was a half-time position consulting for a local police agency. There were no benefits and no pension, but it was a front-row seat to police culture. My office was located between the locker room and the briefing room, and I spent most of my time counseling, training, and doing management consultation. When I wasn't on-site, I saw clients in my private office and provided debriefings, crisis intervention, peer support training, and family orientations for other departments on an as-needed basis. Through the years, I have worked for dozens of law enforcement and public safety agencies, local to federal, from California to Asia. Every week has been different. I have had a great deal of control over my time, sometimes working 60 hours a week, sometimes 10. This has allowed me to write two books and travel when I wanted. I haven't made a lot of money. Police psychologists can earn substantial

(Continued)

(Continued)

incomes, but that was never one of my objectives. My goal was to make a difference in the lives of the people who do one of society's most difficult jobs, and in the lives of their families.

What you will need

In my experience, police psychology is a multidisciplinary field—a quilting of anthropology; group relations theory; systems theory; forensics; family therapy; and organizational, clinical, social, educational, and criminal psychology. Most of these can be studied in graduate school. But there are some things graduate school won't teach you, or won't emphasize enough.

1. The need for a support system: Depending upon the path you take, some fields of study will be more important to you than others. Assessment, for example, has been a minor part of *my* work, but I have colleagues who do nothing *but* assessment and I can call on them for help. Networking with colleagues is my #1 tool. Through my membership in various police psychology organizations, I have almost instant access to expertise and support from people with different skills from mine. I recommend joining a professional organization. Many have opportunities for students, including mentoring programs and the opportunity to present papers and be published.

Police psychology can occasionally be lonely, and sometimes the responsibility is terrifying. I have felt terrified after an officer was killed by friendly fire and the suffering of the other officers was almost unbearable to watch. I have lost sleep knowing that a working officer is deeply depressed or possibly suicidal, or when an officer's future career was hinging on my opinion about whether or not she was fit for duty. Police psychology, like police work, has consequences. Often there are multiple clients to consider: the officer, his or her agency, and the community.

Boundaries are clearer in theory than reality. Ethical dilemmas abound. No one should do this work without the support of a knowledgeable community of colleagues and mentors.

2. The need to understand police culture: Without specific understanding of the culture in which law enforcement officers work and the jobs they are mandated to do, it is easy to make clinical errors based on stereotypes, personal bias, or—even worse—television cop shows. The importance of becoming culturally competent cannot be overestimated. Cops are not eager clients. It takes a lot for them to seek help and very little to lead them to decide they no longer need it. Psychologists who make mistakes don't get second chances.

The issue of guns is one example where understanding the culture is critical. Years ago, as a neophyte psychologist participating in a role-playing exercise, I made the mistake of asking the actor-officers to leave their weapons in their cars rather than bring them into my office. "Would I ask you to take off your eyeglasses before doing therapy?" someone asked. "Guns are part of our uniforms. If you're afraid of guns, you shouldn't be working with cops."

Over the years I have learned that, while there are rare times when it is appropriate or even necessary to take an officer's weapon—during a depressive episode, for instance—for the most part, cops and guns go together. To separate them is to remove an essential part of the officer's identity. Many officers also carry weapons off-duty, which can be a problem for their families. Some officers are required to do this by their department; others choose to do so voluntarily. While there are risks involved in carrying a weapon off-duty, I have come to understand that officers are like doctors who keep medical bags in their cars in case they come upon an accident where people are in need of emergency medical attention. To be unable to act in a crisis runs counter to cops' dedication, their identities, and the social mandate to protect and serve.

How to get started

Stay out of trouble. A bad police record can stop you before you start. Police departments won't want to consult a police psychologist with a criminal history about operational issues or ongoing investigations. Stay in school. In the United States, the terminal degree for police psychology is a PhD. People with a master's get counseling jobs in law enforcement, but they often don't get the same respect and they don't have the same earning potential as those with doctorates. If you're going for your master's, you might as well stick it out for another few years. It will be worth it. Joining a professional organization and finding a mentor who can guide you and introduce you to other police psychologists are other good ideas.

Ask if you can shadow these professionals at work. Get as much experience as you can. This will broaden your perspective and add to your credibility. Go to your local police department and ask to go on a ride-along. Don't presume to know what officers need; spend some time observing them at work and then ask. Don't fake it. Cops can spot a phony a mile away. And don't forget to make whatever you do fun. Humor is what saves the day for police officers. Finally, examine your own attitudes toward police officers. Be aware of any stereotypes or judgments you hold, positive or negative. The more knowledge and experience you have, the more you'll be able to consider every action and every officer with objectivity and compassion for the difficulty of the job they're asked to do.

In addition to *I Love a Cop*, Dr. Kirschman is the author of *I Love a Fire Fighter: What the Family Needs to Know* and an as-yet-unpublished mystery about a fictional police psychologist. She spends much of her time training, writing, and volunteering at the West Coast Post-Trauma Retreat—a 6-day retreat for first responders with post-traumatic stress disorder (PTSD). Dr. Kirschman received the 2010 award for outstanding contribution to the practice of police and public safety psychology from Division 18 of the American Psychological Association, police and public safety section.

In light of the above data, it is not surprising that police departments are increasingly hiring either full-time police psychologists or psychological, counseling, or mental health consultants who are available to consult on cases as well as offer their services to individual officers and their families. (Personal Perspective 2.2 introduces you to Dr. Ellen Kirschman, a police psychologist who works closely with families of law enforcement officers.) Delprino and Bahn (1988) reported that 53% of police agencies in their sample used counseling services for job-related stress. Since that survey, police psychologists have moved from providing counseling services for stress to a broad range of law enforcement–related activities (Dietz, 2000). About one-third of these agencies also hired psychologists to provide relevant workshops and seminars. In addition, many family support groups are appearing throughout the United States, frequently at the instigation of police spouses who band together to discuss and solve common problems.

Peer counseling programs are available in a number of departments, but many police officers prefer to work with mental health professionals who are knowledgeable about police work but who are *not* police officers themselves. Officers are often resistant to discussing with other police officers problems that are generally unacceptable within the police culture, such as sexual dysfunction, fear of getting hurt, or inability to use force when necessary in the line of duty. This varies, though, because other officers distrust clinicians whom they may perceive as working for the police administration. In any case, it seems that psychologists must be careful *not* to try to act and talk like police officers as a means of gaining acceptance, or they may be labeled as "cop wannabes."

It is probably fair to speculate that most law enforcement officers have experienced one or more highly stressful situations, though they have not necessarily sought professional help in dealing with them. It is the atypical officer, for example, who has *never* been worried about getting hurt, *never* experienced marital problems, *never* seen a dead child, and *never* had sleep problems. At least one of these must have been experienced. In the following sections, we will cover two situations that are less common and thus perhaps far more problematic to the individual officer who experiences them.

Post-Shooting Traumatic Reactions

A **post-shooting traumatic reaction (PSTR)** represents a collection of emotions and psychological response patterns that may occur after a law enforcement officer shoots a person in the line of duty—which in itself is usually considered a critical incident. The traumatic reaction is especially likely when the victim dies. Fortunately, in contrast to what is depicted in so many media portrayals of police work, most law enforcement officers complete their career without ever firing a weapon in the line of duty. About 350 to 400 individuals are shot and killed by law enforcement officers each year, and another 200 are wounded (Federal Bureau of Investigation [FBI], 2008). Laurence Miller (1995) estimates that in the United States, two-thirds of the officers involved in shootings demonstrate moderate to severe psychological problems after the shooting, and about 70% leave the force within 7 years after the incident. Unfortunately, PSTR has not been subjected to well-executed empirical research, and most of the information on the topic comes from anecdotal or self-report surveys. As Zeling (1986) wrote, "The study of post shooting trauma is illustrative of a concept in police psychology that is widely accepted yet has little empirical support" (p. 410). Nevertheless, some studies do indicate that some degree of trauma is experienced by officers after a shooting. However, crucial variables are likely to be the age of the shooting victim (e.g., a 16-year-old youth versus a 34-year-old multiple offender); the officer's personal characteristics; and, of course, the circumstances surrounding the shooting.

Solomon and Horn (1986) surveyed 86 law enforcement officers who had been involved in a critical incident involving a shooting. The researchers found that one of the most prominent psychological effects that occurred during the incident was perceptual distortions involving time, sight, and sound. Eighty-three percent of the officers reported that they experienced a distortion of time during the shooting. Most of them said that time seemed to slow down to a point where everything appeared to be happening in slow motion. One officer remembered thinking, "How come I'm moving so slowly?" On the other hand, some officers thought everything sped up during the event. Other officers reported visual distortions (56%), and many experienced auditory (sound) distortions (63%). The most frequent visual distortion was "tunnel vision," in which the officer became so focused on one object that everything else at the scene went unnoticed. This phenomenon is frequently experienced by victims of a terrifying event as well. Some officers reported seeing everything more vividly and in greater detail than normal. Auditory distortions centered on not hearing sounds (such as the shots fired, shouts, commands given) or hearing them less or more intensely.

Following the incident, officers experienced a number of psychological reactions. The five most common were a heightened sense of danger, anger, sleep difficulties, isolation/withdrawal, and flashbacks. Specifically, officers involved in shooting incidents often lost their sense of invincibility and began to perceive their job as more dangerous than they originally thought. They were often angry at the victim of the shooting, at the department, at colleagues, or at society in general for putting them in the position of having to shoot someone. They had difficulty both falling asleep and staying asleep because of thoughts of the episode. Many needed to withdraw for a while, including taking a leave of absence, to get their thoughts together and to work through what happened. Finally, reoccurring thoughts of the scene intruded into their daily lives.

Solomon and Horn (1986) found that these common reactions varied widely in intensity. About 37% of the officers described their reactions as mild, 35% as moderate, and 28% as severe. The intensity of these reactions is similar to that reported by Stratton, Parker, and Snabbe (1984). The above researchers also agree that the intensity of the reaction depends partly on the perceived "fairness" of the shooting incident. According to Solomon and Horn,

> Being outnumbered, having a limited field of fire due to bystanders, going against a shotgun when armed with a revolver, and having to shoot someone who points an unloaded weapon (unknown to the officers), are examples of factors affecting the "fairness" of the situation. (p. 390)

The standard operating procedure in large agencies after a critical incident—such as a shooting—is to immediately contact the on-duty post-shooting peer support team members and the police psychologist. The psychologist will consult with supervisors to determine whether he or she should arrange to meet with the involved officers at that time or see the officer at a later time. Police psychologists generally realize that police officers have a reputation for shunning mental health services under a wide range of circumstances. Laurence Miller (1995) writes that some officers have a notion of the psychotherapy experience as akin to brainwashing, a humiliating, infantilizing experience in which they lie on a couch and sob about their toilet training. More commonly, the idea of needing "mental help" implies weakness, cowardice, and lack of ability to do the job.

Despite these apprehensions, many agencies require that the involved officer or officers receive immediate attention from both the peer support group and the police psychologist, regardless of the circumstances. Popular entertainment media often portray these psychology professionals as semi-caricatures, and the police actors often resist going to see them. In some TV portrayals, they are resented almost as much as the dreaded internal affairs divisions. Nevertheless, in reality some officers prefer to go to a respected mental health professional than to a peer support group. Both options should be available. It is also standard procedure at most agencies for the involved officer to immediately be placed on administrative leave for 3 days or longer. During that leave, it is usually common practice to recommend that the officer see the police psychologist for critical incident stress debriefings (CISDs). Usually, the CISD takes place within 24 to 72 hours after the critical incident and normally consists of a single group meeting that lasts approximately 2 to 3 hours (L. Miller, 1995). Thereafter, affected personnel may be seen individually or in groups.

Police Suicide

Data on the prevalence or frequency of police suicide are extremely difficult to obtain. The common assumption is that suicide among police officers is one of the highest of any occupational group in the United States (Violanti, 1996). It is estimated that twice as many officers (about 300 annually) die by their own hand as are killed in the line of duty (Violanti et al., 2009). Moreover, most victims are young patrol officers with no record of misconduct, and most shoot themselves while off-duty (L. Miller, 1995). A study of police suicide conducted by Aamodt and Stalnaker (2001), however, suggests that the suicide rate among police officers may be significantly lower than commonly believed. The authors point out that the incident reports usually compare the rates of police suicide to the rates found in the general population. According to Aamodt and Stalnaker, if researchers would compare the police suicide rate to the rates found in that sector of the population that is comparable to police officer age, gender, ethnic/minority, and racial group, they would discover that the police suicide incidence is significantly lower than often reported. Similar results have also been reported by Stack and Kelley (1999); Hem, Berg, and Ekeberg (2001); and Loo (2003). However, even if suicide rates among police officers are not higher than found in the general population, suicide is still a serious problem.

Police suicide may result from a number of factors, including psychological reactions to critical incidents, relationship difficulties, internal investigations, financial difficulties, frustration and discouragement, and easy access to weapons (Herndon, 2001). The overwhelming reason for police suicide, however, appears to be difficulties in marital or intimate partner relationships, followed by legal problems and internal investigations (Aamodt & Stalnaker, 2001).

If suicide rates for law enforcement personnel are lower than previously assumed, this might be explained by several factors. These include the sophisticated screening procedures and rigorous evaluations at the time of hiring, increased use of stress awareness training, better police training, increased counseling opportunities, and the many services provided by police psychologists and other psychologists working closely with police agencies.

Operational Responsibilities

The biggest shift in the role of police psychology in recent years has been in the area of operational support (Dietz, 2000). As police departments have become more specialized, psychological input has become important in crisis negotiations, hostage-taking incidents, criminal behavior assessments, and threat assessments.

Hostage-Taking Incidents

An area where police psychologists often serve as consultants involves hostage-taking incidents. A *hostage situation* is characterized by a person (or persons) holding victims against their will who are used to obtain material gain, deliver a sociopolitical message, or achieve personal advantage. Typically, the hostage taker threatens to take the lives of victims if certain demands are not met within a specified time period. A *barricade situation* is one in which an individual has fortified or barricaded himself or herself in a residence or public building or structure and threatens violence either to himself or herself or to others (see Photo 2.2). Included in the broad hostage-taking category are abductions and kidnappings, vehicle abductions (including aircraft or other forms of public transportation), and some acts of terrorism. Nearly 80% of all hostage situations are "relationship-driven" in that perceived relationship difficulties and resentment appear to be the precipitating factor (Van Hasselt, Flood, Romano, Vecchi, de Fabrique, & Dalfonzo, 2005).

Photo 2.2   A law enforcement officer wearing a protective suit investigates the lobby of the Discovery Communications building in Maryland following a hostage situation that had occurred earlier in the day, September 1, 2010. The gunman, who had held three persons hostage, was shot and killed by police.

Most police experts classify hostage takers into four very broad categories: (1) political activists or terrorists, (2) prisoners, (3) individuals who have committed a crime, and (4) individuals with mental disorders (Fuselier, 1988; Fuselier & Noesner, 1990). Political terrorists, who take hostages primarily to gain publicity for their cause, are considered the most difficult to deal with. Their demands often go beyond the authority of the local police departments and usually require the involvement of federal officials. According to Fuselier (1988), political terrorists take hostages for four basic reasons:

> (a) to show the public that the government cannot protect is own citizens; (b) to virtually guarantee immediate coverage and publicity for their cause; (c) to support their hope that after repeated incidents the government will overreact and place excessive restrictions on its citizens; and (d) often to demand the release of members of their group who have been incarcerated. (p. 176)

The hostage taker who committed a crime is usually trapped while committing the crime, such as robbery or domestic violence, and is trying to negotiate some form of escape. Prisoners, on the other hand, usually take hostages (usually correctional personnel) to protest conditions within the correctional facility. Persons with mental disorders take hostages for a variety of reasons but primarily to establish their sense of control over their life situations. Research *suggests* that more than 50% of all hostage-taking incidents are perpetrated by individuals with mental disorders (Borum & Strentz, 1993; Grubb, 2010). Consequently, the need for well-trained psychologists as part of the crisis negotiation team is becoming increasingly apparent to many police agencies.

In the early 1970s, the FBI and police departments began to set up specialized hostage negotiation teams that included a designated negotiator, tactical assault team (TAC), command structure, and support personnel (Butler, Leitenberg, & Fuselier, 1993; Fuselier, 1981). Psychologists were usually part of the support team. Today, the "third generation" of crisis/hostage negotiation teams usually has five designated primary members: (1) the primary negotiator (the primary talker), (2) the secondary negotiator (monitors negotiations and offers suggestions), (3) the intelligence officer (seeks and organizes incoming information), (4) the psychologist (whose functions will be described shortly), and (5) the tactical liaison (maintains communications with SWAT and command) (Hatcher et al., 1998). Psychologists rarely are the primary negotiators (less than 7%), usually because of their limited training and experience in hostage negotiations. Even if the psychologist has advanced training and experience in such matters, it is recommended that he or she be used as a negotiation consultant to maintain a more objective role in assessing the situation and to provide advice on how to deal with individuals with various mental disorders.

Individuals aspiring to be on the crisis/negotiation teams as psychologists, however, should realize that multiyear training—as expected of all crisis/negotiation team members—is necessary to become an effective member of the team. Part of that training may require some "street experience" such as ride-alongs with experienced officers and as informed observers in hostage/barricade situations. "The chaos of the field or street situation, the military-like police command structure, and presence of real personal risk can come as quite a shock, no matter how professionally well trained one is" (Hatcher et al., 1998, p. 463).

An estimated 30 to 58% of law enforcement agencies with a crisis/hostage negotiation team use a mental health professional in some capacity, of which 88% are psychologists as opposed to psychiatrists, social workers, and other professionals (Butler et al., 1993; Hatcher et al., 1998). However, the use of psychologists on crisis/hostage negotiation teams appears to be on the increase (Call, 2008; Van Hasselt et al., 2005). According to Hatcher et al. (1998), in hostage and barricade situations, four types of roles for non–law enforcement personnel have developed: (1) the consultant/advisor, (2) the integrated team member, (3) the primary negotiator, and (4) the primary controller. The psychologist is most likely to be in the consultant/advisor role with a variety of tasks. "Pre-incident, psychologists provide selection, training, police input, and conceptual development services to law enforcement" (p. 464). During the selection process, the psychologist would assist in identifying personnel who are likely to be effective and skillful negotiation team members. To date, however, studies have not been done to determine what selection procedures and psychological tests are best at determining the effectiveness of negotiation team members.

Approximately 40% of law enforcement agencies use psychologists for advice at the scene of hostage-taking or barricade incidents (Hatcher et al., 1998). The on-scene psychologists might be expected to profile and assess the suspect, possibly trying to determine his or her motivation, vulnerabilities, and danger-ousness. In addition, the psychologists might be expected to suggest some dialogue strategies or psychologi-cal tactics that are likely to defuse the situation. The on-scene psychologists also might be asked to assess the hostages with the goal to determine which hostages may engage in behaviors that may enhance or diminish their chances of survival. In some situations, the hostage taker may expect the hostages to do the talking dur-ing the incident. According to Hatcher et al., "The successful resolution of most hostage incidents requires that the crisis/hostage negotiation team devote almost equal interest to managing the hostages as to managing the hostage taker" (p. 465).

The psychologist, as an advisor/consultant, may assist in witness interviews and the review of other col-lateral information on the incident (Hatcher et al., 1998). Family members, friends, neighbors, coworkers, employers, and hostages who escaped or were released during the situation may provide important pieces of information that will lead to an understanding of the hostage taker and help in the eventual resolution of the incident. Those psychologists who are well trained and experienced in hostage negotiations can also offer use-ful analysis of the decision-making strategy to the team.

Research by Butler et al. (1993) discovered that police agencies that used a psychologist to assess suspects reported significantly fewer incidents in which the hostage taker killed or seriously injured a hostage. More specifically, police agencies that used a psychologist reported more hostage incidents ending by negotiated sur-render and fewer incidents resulting in the serious injury or death of a hostage. The data confirmed the obser-vation that psychologists can make valuable contributions in resolving hostage incidents with a lessened chance of injury or death.

In more recent years, there has been a discernible shift in the cultural diversity of hostage takers and kidnappers (Giebels & Noelanders, 2004). This trend demands that psychologists increase their efforts to study and identify cultural differences in approaches to social interaction and understand how violent indi-viduals from various cultures are likely to react to efforts to dissuade them from causing harm to their victims (Giebels & Taylor, 2009). According to Giebels and Taylor, "a more sophisticated understanding of cross-cultural communication will help police formulate culturally sensitive negotiation strategies and enhance their appreciation of why perpetrators react the way they do" (p. 5). In addition, forensic psycholo-gists and other mental health personnel can play a critical role in the training of negotiators and police offi-cers by providing workshops and training sessions in cultural differences in persuasive arguments during crisis negotiations.

Criminal Activity Assessment

In many large departments, police psychologists are involved in criminal activity assessment (Dietz, 2000). According to Dietz, "This role allows the psychologist to work with criminal investigator units to identify, understand and help explain crime patterns" (p. 3). Some of this work involves offender profiling, to be dis-cussed in the next chapter. Terrorism, however, is a topic of enormous importance in today's society. The nature of terrorism is fundamentally psychological. Its primary aim is to generate fear and psychological debilitation in a civilian population. Given the nature of terrorism, it is clear that psychology has a critical role to play in understanding it, counteracting it, and treating its traumatizing effects (Levant, Barbanel, & DeLeon, 2004).

Psychologists who participate in evaluating terrorist activity and patterns usually serve as consultants to specialized police units by primarily focusing on the motives, decision making, and behavioral patterns of terrorists (Aumiller & Corey, 2007). They also help maintain optimal performance levels of these units, whose members face extreme stress levels during terrorist attacks.

Threat Assessment

Threat assessment is a process to determine the credibility and seriousness of a threat and the likelihood that it will be carried out. It is accomplished through a variety of strategies, analyses, and techniques. In the past, a majority of law enforcement investigations of violent crime were conducted *after* the offense was committed (Borum, Fein, Vossekuil, & Berglund, 1999). Today, with new stalking laws, restraining orders, hate crime laws, and increased concerns about violence in the schools and the workplace, law enforcement and mental health professionals have been asked to provide assessments of potential violence against targeted individuals or groups. Consequently, professionals are not being asked simply to assess risk for general violent behavior but to assess risk for specific types of violence. "The task . . . is to determine the nature and degree of risk a given individual may pose to an identified or identifiable target(s)" (Borum et al., 1999, p. 324). A good threat assessment provides authorities with a suspect individual's risk for both potential violence and disruptive behavior (Axelrod, 2009). The assessment report should also give recommendations and directions for intervention and target hardening, which refers to making it more difficult for an assailant to reach the desired target. Security locks, martial arts training, bodyguards, German shepherds, and so forth, are all examples of target hardening.

Borum and his colleagues also point out that advances in threat assessments have moved from dangerousness being viewed as a personality trait that is not subject to change, toward more sophisticated models where dangerousness is viewed as highly dependent on situations and circumstances, is constantly subject to change, and varies along a continuum of probability. For example, in cases of potential parental abduction of children, numerous factors must be evaluated. Among the factors are distrust and lack of respect for legal authority, unsubstantiated allegations of child sexual abuse, and suspected exposure of young children to neglect or criminal activities (Johnston, Girdner, & Sagatun-Edwards, 1999). Cyberstalking and bullying provide additional examples where forensic psychologists are asked to conduct threat assessments.

In most cases, threat assessments are done through teams consisting of law enforcement and psychologists or other mental health professionals. When businesses are targeted, security management personnel may also be involved in the process.

Consulting and Research Activities

In describing the roles of the consulting police psychologist, Aumiller and Corey (2007) mention the development of performance appraisal systems, which "involves the design and development of organizational policies, processes and instruments for measurement and feedback of individual job performance" (p. 75). These activities are intended to increase performance improvement and help in the career development of the individual officer. In some cases, they may be used in promotional considerations. Consulting psychologists may also be expected to participate in the resolution of interpersonal conflict among individuals within the organization or between the department and the community.

Consulting psychologists often do some training and education to assist agency personnel in optimizing their leader, management, and supervisory effectiveness (Aumiller & Corey, 2007). In general, consulting and in-house psychologists are frequently shifting their roles to meet the crisis or problems that must be dealt with on an ongoing basis. In this section, we discuss a few of the concerns police administrators might have, including creating opportunities for women and ethnic minorities on the force and confronting problems involving excessive force and corruption.

Gender and Ethnic Minority Issues in Policing

As noted by Cole and Smith (2001), before the 1970s, many police departments did not hire non-Caucasians. However, the makeup of departments changed beginning in the late 1970s. A survey of the nation's 50 largest cities discovered that, between 1983 and 1992, 29% of the departments reported an increase of 50% or more in the number of African American officers, and 20% reported a similar increase in the number of Latino officers (Cole & Smith, 2001). In 1993, police officers representing racial and ethnic minorities made up approximately 20% of all local police departments across the country (Bureau of Justice Statistics, 1993).

Progressive police departments today continue to seek candidates who can demonstrate intercultural sensitivity and interpersonal skills for dealing with a wide spectrum of minority groups. This positive reaching out to previously underrepresented groups—which is the essence of affirmative action programs—does *not* mean that departments adopt quotas in which they deliberately hire to achieve a given percentage of women or a specific racial or ethnic group, nor does it mean that they hire unqualified candidates. Failure to recognize this, however, has led to court challenges to these recruitment strategies. To date, departments seeking to bring qualified women and minorities on board have had to overcome these challenges.

Nevertheless, there remain concerns that selection procedures may be screening out women as well as racial and ethnic minority groups. At the turn of the 21st century, women still remained a small minority in law enforcement nationwide, comprising only 11.2% of the sworn police officers, a figure that is less than 3 percentage points higher than in 1990. In large departments, women accounted for 12.7% of the sworn officers. In small and rural departments (fewer than 100 police officers), women comprise an even smaller number—8.1% of the officers. The most recent official report on women in law enforcement (Langton, 2010) indicates that their percentages increased, but only slightly, during the 2000s. In 2008, the last year in which data were reported, women comprised just over 15% of federal law enforcement officers; in local police departments and sheriff's agencies, their percentages were slightly lower (12%–15%) if the departments were greater than 100 officers. In medium size departments they ranged between 6% and 9%, and in small departments between 3% and just over 5%.

The major impediment to women gaining a greater proportion of representation in some of the law enforcement agencies across the country is the common perception that policing is a male-oriented profession, requiring physical strength and a display of physical prowess for many of the tasks. This perception seems to hold even though there is considerable evidence that women are as capable at police work as men. Consequently, many women are reluctant to apply, especially when a department has the reputation of being hostile toward women or has a high female officer turnover rate.

Researchers also have found that women are making some slow progress in acquiring promotions and administrative positions, although they still encounter continuing resistance from police managers, supervisors, and administrators (Martin, 1989, 1992). Less than 4% of supervisory positions are held by female officers, though the percentages are higher in larger departments (National Center for Women & Policing, 2002). The National Center for Women & Policing's website indicated in 2010 that there were now 232 female chiefs of police across the United States.

Worden (1993) found very few differences between male and female officers in their *attitudes* toward policing. She writes, "Overall, female as well as male police officers were predictably ambivalent about restrictions on their autonomy and the definition of their role, only mildly positive about their public clientele, complimentary of their colleagues, and unenthusiastic about working conditions and supervisors" (p. 229). She attributes (cautiously) much of this gender similarity in policing to "occupational socialization," a process that seems to wash out many of the major differences in gender roles. Occupational socialization refers to the learning of attitudes, values, and beliefs of a particular occupational group (Van Maanen, 1975). In general, women have the ability to become socialized into the police culture as successfully as men.

A. Morris (1996) reports that among New York Police Department (NYPD) officers, women as well as ethnic minorities received substantial social and psychological support from their police colleagues, and the women officers described mostly positive professional and social interactions while on the job. The one major gender difference identified by Morris was that women officers, compared to their male colleagues, were less likely to socialize off the job with other police officers. Their closest personal friends also tended to be outside the police community. This observation is not surprising if we consider that women police officers are likely to have families, including dependent children, to whom they prefer to give their off-duty attention. Women officers may feel more isolated in the male-dominated police work environment and consequently family life becomes a stronger source of social support (Violanti et al., 2009).

Accumulating research, both in the United States and internationally, indicates that the style of law enforcement used by women as a group may be more effective than the policing styles employed by men as a group (Bureau of Justice Assistance, 2001). For example, many law enforcement administrators, peer officers, and many members of the public are convinced that female officers are more skillful at defusing potentially dangerous or violent situations (Balkin, 1988; Seklecki & Paynich, 2007; Weisheit & Mahan, 1988). L. B. Johnson (1991) reports evidence that women officers seem to have a "gentling effect" when dealing with the public. Moreover, Worden (1993) found that women police officers seem to be guided more by altruistic and social motives than men, who tended to be more motivated toward the financial rewards of the occupation.

The research to date demonstrates that, overall, women officers are better at defusing and de-escalating potentially violent confrontations with citizens and less likely to become involved in incidents of excessive force (Bureau of Justice Assistance, 2001). Moreover, women officers as a group generally possess better communication and social skills than their male colleagues and are better able to facilitate the cooperation and trust required to implement a community policing model (Bureau of Justice Assistance, 2001). It is also likely that many women officers respond more effectively in dealing with situations involving violence against women (such as domestic abuse or sexual assault), although more research is needed in the area. Some research (e.g., Rabe-Hemp & Schuck, 2007) suggests that women officers may be at greater risk of being assaulted in domestic violence situations, especially when the assailant is drug or alcohol impaired. Nevertheless, hiring more women is likely to be an effective way of addressing the problems of excessive force and citizen complaints and also of improving community policing in general. It should also reduce the problem of sex discrimination and sexual harassment by changing the climate of the agency.

Excessive Force

Up to this point, we have given very little attention to the problem of "bad apples" in law enforcement, or the negative side. Both the entertainment and the news media show no such restraint. Bad cops are often portrayed in these venues, and some critics believe that by its very nature, law enforcement attracts or promotes the badness: "You go in as an idealistic kid and exit corrupt and with a guilty conscience, or none."

The repeated showings of the videotape documenting the L.A. police beating of Rodney King in the early morning hours of March 3, 1991, created nationwide concern about excessive force by law enforcement. Primarily as a result of the King incident, the U.S. Department of Justice called for research that would identify the nature, extent, and strategies for controlling the use of force by the nation's law enforcement personnel (Scrivner, 1994). Over the past two decades, many jurisdictions have installed video surveillance systems in "high-activity areas" that police often patrol. In Denver, for example, two police officers in 2009 were filmed beating two men outside a nightclub with a leather-encased metal club. Although an investigation did not conclude that the force used by the officers was excessive, a civil suit brought by the two men was settled out of court, and the officers were suspended without pay for a short period of time.

When the level of force exceeds what is considered justifiable under the circumstances, it is called **excessive force.** Excessive force is unacceptable behavior demonstrated by an individual officer, or it might be a pattern and practice of an entire law enforcement agency. In many instances, excessive force probably reflects some combination of both.

Prior to the 1970s, the police had wide discretion in the use of force, including deadly force (Blumberg, 1997). Police agencies often had poorly defined or nonexistent policies regarding the use of force generally. Mark Blumberg writes that, prior to 1970,

> Investigations into police shootings were sometimes conducted in a half-hearted manner, and police agencies often did not keep records of all firearm discharges by officers. In addition, social science research on this topic was practically nonexistent and no meaningful attempt to measure the incidence of police killings on a national basis had been undertaken. (p. 507)

How common is the use of force by police officers today? And under what circumstances or in what contexts does it occur? After all, police officers are in one of the very few occupations that is permitted and sometimes encouraged to use force (Brooks, 1997). The National Institute of Justice (NIJ) (K. Adams et al., 1999) released a report summarizing what is known about police use of force. The report found the following:

- Police use force infrequently.
- Police use of force typically occurs at the lower end of the force spectrum, involving grabbing, pushing, or shoving.
- Use of force typically occurs when police are trying to make an arrest and the suspect is resisting.

Another source of information about police use of force comes from surveys conducted in the general population concerning their contacts with law enforcement. In 1996, the U.S. Census Bureau interviewed a national randomly selected sample of 6,421 persons age 12 or older (Greenfeld, Langan, & Smith, 1997). Interviewers determined that 1,308 persons out of the total had face-to-face contact with the police during that year. Of those 1,308 persons, only 14 (less than 1%) said they were hit, pushed, choked, threatened with a flashlight, restrained by a police dog, threatened with or actually sprayed with chemical or pepper spray, threatened with a gun, or experienced some other form of force. Unfortunately, the small number of persons who were the subject of police force prevents a reliable comparison of police use of force experienced by Black, Latino, or other minority or ethnic respondents. These data suggest, however, that the use of police force is a relatively rare phenomenon.

Additional data from citizen complaints, use-of-force reports, and observational methods consistently indicate that only a small percentage of police–public interactions involve the use of force (K. Adams et al., 1999). As mentioned above, available data also indicate that most uses of force are at the lower end of the force spectrum, mostly grabbing or holding. This finding is not a surprise, considering that police officers are trained to use force progressively along a continuum, and the usual departmental policy requires that officers use the least amount of force necessary to accomplish their goals.

Police psychologist Ellen Scrivner (1994), in a report sponsored by NIJ, investigated some of the psychological attributes characteristic of officers who engage in excessive force. (As an aside, Dr. Scrivner is now Deputy Director of the NIJ, appointed under the Obama administration.) Police psychologists assigned to conduct fitness-for-duty evaluations should be knowledgeable about the behaviors outlined in the report. Scrivner identified five different officer profiles that are prone to excessive force complaints or charges:

1. Officers with personality patterns that reflect a lack of empathy for others and antisocial, narcissistic, and abusive tendencies

2. Officers with previous job-related experiences such as involvement in justifiable police shootings

3. Officers who experienced early career–stage problems having to do with their impressionability, impulsiveness, low tolerance for frustration, and general need for strong supervision

4. Officers who had a dominant, heavy-handed patrol style that is particularly sensitive to challenge and provocation

5. Officers who had personal problems such as separation, divorce, or perceived loss of status that caused extreme anxiety and destabilized job functioning

The Scrivner (1994) study focused primarily on the psychological profiles of individual police officers. It was not intended to give attention to the properties of entire police organizations that may implicitly (or explicitly) promote or condone excessive force within their ranks. For example, an agency may have an aggressive policing policy that encourages confrontational tactics that increase the probability of violence on the part of officers as well as members of the public. As K. Adams et al. (1999) state, "A major gap in our knowledge about excessive force by police concerns characteristics of police agencies that facilitate or impede this conduct" (p. 11). Adams and his colleagues further assert that

> many formal aspects of the organization—such as hiring criteria, recruit training, in-service programs, supervision of field officers, disciplinary mechanisms, operations of internal affairs, specialized units dealing with ethics and integrity, labor unions, and civilian oversight mechanisms—plausibly are related to the levels of officer misconduct. (p. 11)

As suggested above, knowledgeable police psychologists should also realize that, in some cases, the law enforcement agency itself might be a major factor in implicitly (or explicitly) encouraging the use of excessive force by its officers. Possibly, agencies may be placed on a continuum signifying the degree of aggressive policing they advocate in the community, especially in areas that have high crime rates. At one pole, the agency advocates that minimum force be applied when dealing with suspects, but at the other pole, the agency encourages force—and, if necessary, excessive force—in dealing with the suspects.

In summary, research data consistently show that only a small minority of police officers engage in excessive force in dealing with the public. Fortunately, an "early warning system," used by an increasing number of departments, can help supervisors identify problem officers early and intervene through counseling or training to correct problem behaviors (S. Walker, Alpert, & Kenney, 2001). **Early warning systems** are data-based management tools, usually consisting of three basic phases: (1) selection, (2) intervention, and (3) post-intervention monitoring (Bartol & Bartol, 2004). The criteria by which officers are selected vary from agency to agency but usually include some threshold combination of citizen complaints, civil litigation, firearms discharge or use-of-force reports, high-speed pursuits, and resisting-arrest incidents (Walker et al., 2001). Some early research on the effectiveness of early warning systems suggests that they are effective, especially if used in combination with departmentwide attempts to raise standards of performance and improve the quality of police services.

Assessing the Potential for Police Corruption

The term *police corruption* covers a wide range of illegal behaviors that represent a violation of the public trust. Accepting bribes, confiscating drugs or drug money, planting evidence, and soliciting sexual activity in exchange for giving a suspect a "break" are all illustrations. Can police psychologists assist departments in selecting out candidates who are likely to be engaged in corrupt activities?

The Defense Personnel Security Research Center (PERSEREC) conducted one of the most extensive studies on the ability of personality measures to identify eventual police corruption and misconduct. The PERSEREC began the Police Integrity Study in 1992, using four commonly used personality inventories in law enforcement: the MMPI-2, IPI, 16-PF, and CPI. Sixty-nine departments met all the prerequisites for participation and supplied personality test data on 878 officers, of whom 439 demonstrated misconduct and 439 did not. The preemployment personality inventories most frequently administered to those officers when they originally applied to their respective departments was the MMPI-2 (92.7%), followed by the CPI (41.0%), 16-PF (11.2%), and IPI (11.0%).

Overall, the study concluded that only modest improvements in combating corruption could be made by using the personality data collected. The personality inventories that had any success tended to indicate that those officers who engaged in misconduct or corruption during their careers had more of the following characteristics:

- Difficulty getting along with others
- Delinquent histories
- Indications of maladjustment, immaturity, irresponsibility, or unreliability

Basically, however, the study found that the *single* best predictor of corruption was not a personality measure administered prior to hire, but rather misconduct on the job after employment had begun and usually relatively early in the officer's career.

In other words, none of the preemployment psychological tests currently being used by law enforcement departments appears to offer a general scale or dimension that can reliably and validly differentiate officers at the beginning of their career who are likely to violate the public trust later in their career (Boes, Chandler, & Timm, 2001). Rather, the *strongest* predictor was post-hire misconduct. Officers who got into trouble for misconduct early in their careers were most likely to be punished for later acts of corruption.

Furthermore, the study found that the decision of whether or not to engage in acts of corruption is largely shaped by environmental factors, such as opportunity combined with the values particular police subcultures allowed or that were condoned by certain departments. However, as will be discussed in the section on criminal profiling in Chapter 3, the tendency toward misconduct, including misconduct and corruption by police officers, is more likely to be some combination of personality interacting with the situation, rather than personality or situation alone.

One final but very important topic in which psychologists could provide enormous assistance relates to police interrogations and the many dangers of psychologically coercing a suspect to confess to something he or she did not do. The police psychologist could be especially helpful in providing balanced training to interrogators and educating them about the extant research in the area.

Police Interrogation and False Confessions

The primary aim of police interrogation is to obtain a confession from a suspect or to gain information that may lead to a conviction. Experienced police interrogators use a wide variety of methods and techniques that are tailored to their personality and style. Skillful and legally useful interrogation involves the application of psychological principles and concepts. Although we cover this topic in this chapter, it should be emphasized that police psychologists are less likely to be conducting research on interrogation-related issues than are psychologists associated with academic institutions who are conducting research in legal psychology (e.g., Kassin et al., 2007; Rogers et al., 2009; Rogers et al., 2010). Nevertheless, police psychologists may serve as consultants, training officers in methods of interview and interrogation. In addition, they should be very aware of the pitfalls and myths surrounding the process.

Numerous researchers have criticized the Reid model of interrogation (Inbau & Reid, 1967; Inbau, Reid, Buckley, & Jayne, 2004), which is the predominant method used across the United States today (Kassin et al., 2010; L. King & Snook, 2009). The model is a confrontational one, pitting police interrogators against the suspect, under understandably stressful conditions, and its overall purpose is to obtain a confession. Western European countries and some parts of Canada, by contrast, focus on gathering information, or investigative interviewing (Beune, Giebels, & Taylor, 2010; Bull & Milne, 2004). This technique emphasizes rational arguments and being kind as methods of persuading the interviewee to provide information. The Reid method has some aspects of this—for example, it begins with an "interview" and moves on to the "interrogation" stage if enough information has been derived from the person to consider him or her a suspect, at which point it becomes accusatory. Despite criticisms, the Reid model is so firmly established in police procedure that it is unlikely to disappear or even be modified substantially. Many police are far more resistant to giving up this cherished approach than to changing lineup procedures, which will be discussed in the next chapter. Furthermore, the U.S. courts by and large have been supportive of police interrogation methods, unless they involve the most flagrant violations.

The U.S. Supreme Court, for example, has granted law enforcement wide latitude in trying to obtain confessions from suspects (see, generally, Leo, 1996). Despite the landmark ruling in *Miranda v. Arizona* (1966) establishing the basic rule that suspects in custody must be informed of their right to remain silent and their right to an attorney prior to being questioned, courts have allowed police to lie or trick suspects, such as by pretending they have eyewitness testimony or evidence that does not exist. Virtually every year since the *Miranda* decision was announced, the U.S. Supreme Court has decided at least one case relative to Miranda warnings. Many of these have been decided in favor of law enforcement, leading some commentators to observe that Miranda has been substantially watered down over the years or is even on life support. One 2010 case, *Berghius v. Thompkins,* is illustrative. Thompkins was informed of his rights to remain silent, and he refused to sign a waiver of those rights when it was placed before him. However, he did not specifically ask for an attorney or say he did not want to speak to police; had he done that, police would have been obliged to stop questioning him. Since he did not explicitly refuse to speak, they began to question him. During almost 3 hours of questioning, however, he remained silent. Then he was asked, "Do you pray to God to forgive you for shooting that boy down?" and he answered yes. The confession was used as evidence against him, and Thompkins was convicted.

The four dissenting Justices, in an opinion written by the then-newest Justice, Sonia Sotomayor, wrote that because Thompkins had remained silent during almost 3 hours and did not explicitly waive his right against self-incrimination, his subsequent "confession" should not have been used against him. However, the majority decision, which is now the law of the land, stated that suspects must *actively assert their wish to remain silent;* simply remaining silent—even for nearly 3 hours—is not enough. The Justices in the majority noted that Thompkins at any time during the questioning could have told officers he did not wish to speak to them—and he did not do so.

A confession must be freely and voluntarily given if it is to be used as evidence; it cannot be coerced. A waiver of one's rights must be voluntary, knowledgeable, and intelligent—and some jurisdictions, to avoid a situation such as what occurred in the *Thompkins* case, require a signed waiver before allowing the interrogation of a suspect in custody without a lawyer's presence. Even so, many legal psychologists over the years have explored whether suspects truly understand the significance of their Miranda rights. A long line of research in developmental and legal psychology (e.g., V. G. Cooper & Zapf, 2008; Grisso, 1981, 1998; Rogers, Harrison, Shuman, Sewell, & Hazelwood; Rogers et al., 2009, 2010) indicates that many individuals, including but not limited to juveniles and persons with mental disorders or deficiencies, have difficulty understanding the significance of a Miranda warning. Even words that are typically used in these warnings—words like "consult," "entitled," "interrogation"—are unfamiliar to many suspects. Richard Rogers and his colleagues (e.g., Rogers et al., 2007,

2009, 2010) have developed and validated a Miranda Vocabulary Scale (MVS) as well as a Miranda Quiz that can be used to test an individual's understanding of the rights guaranteed in the Supreme Court's landmark *Miranda* ruling. (Dr. Rogers' work is highlighted in Personal Perspective 6.2 in Chapter 6.)

False Confessions

Another issue relating to interrogation is the troubling matter of false confessions. As a result of recent DNA exonerations, it has become increasingly clear that a disturbing number of convictions were the result of false confessions gained through questionable procedures or illegal tactics (Kassin et al., 2007). A false confession "is an admission to a criminal act—usually accompanied by a narrative of how and why the crime occurred—that the confessor did not commit" (Kassin et al., 2010, p. 5). These DNA exonerations and other high-profile cases leading to the convictions of innocent people have prompted increased scrutiny of police interviewing and interrogation methods and strategies. We must emphasize that only a percentage of DNA exonerations involved false confessions, however. Numerous individuals cleared by DNA evidence never confessed to their crimes; on the contrary, they maintained their innocence from the moment of their arrest. (Focus 2.2 highlights the work of the Innocence Project, a research and advocacy group for prisoners believed to have been wrongfully convicted.)

However, as the DNA exonerations came rolling in, many stories did involve false confessions and how they were obtained. "Many of these stories recount horrific tales of psychologically—and, in some cases, physically—abusive interrogations of children and adults, including many who were cognitively impaired" (Kassin et al., 2007, p. 382). These stories and the other high-profile cases have underscored the enormous role that psychologists can play in the research, investigation, and prevention of wrongful convictions (Kassin et al., 2010). It should be emphasized that some of these wrongful convictions are the result of eyewitness misidentification, a topic to be discussed in the next chapter. Police psychologists should be aware of this and provide guidelines and procedures to law enforcement on how to minimize eyewitness identification errors (see Technical Working Group for Eyewitness Evidence, 1999). Our focus in this section, however, is on interrogation and false confessions.

Kassin (2008) contends that throughout the criminal justice system, confessions are met with naïve and uncritical acceptance. He finds that this naïveté is strongly buttressed by five myths: (1) Innocent people cannot be induced to confess through the use of legal and noncoercive interrogation tactics; (2) police investigators are often convinced they can identify truth tellers from liars during interviews, and consequently feel they are able to determine who should be interrogated; (3) relying on some combination of intuition and corroboration, many police officers and other criminal justice personnel believe they can distinguish between true and false confessions; (4) people facing interrogation are protected by their constitutional rights to silence and to counsel; and (5) if the confession was coerced and is erroneously admitted at trial, appellate courts can reasonably determine whether the error was harmless. We reiterate that Kassin stresses that the above are myths, not facts.

At this point, no one can accurately estimate the rate of police-induced **false confessions** across the United States or the number of wrongful convictions caused by false confessions (Kassin et al., 2010; Leo & Ofshe, 1998), but the research clearly indicates that people can be induced to confess. It should be understood at the outset, though, that most convictions are the result of the evidence acquired at the crime scene or through witness reports rather than through interrogations and a confession from the suspect.

Nevertheless, when a suspect does confess, the confession is universally treated as damning and compelling evidence of guilt; it is likely to dominate all other case evidence and lead to a defendant's conviction (Leo & Ofshe, 1998). As a society, then, we should be particularly wary of the false confession, as well as the confession that is coerced. According to Leo and Ofshe, American police are poorly trained about the dangers of interrogation and false confession. "Rarely are police officers instructed in how to avoid eliciting confessions, how to understand what causes false confessions, or how to recognize the forms false confessions take or their distinguishing characteristics" (p. 437). This is one important training service that police psychologists should be able to provide.

Most American police are exposed to only a cursory review of interviews and interrogation at the police academy and receive more extensive training when they become detectives or interrogation specialists at the police agency. However, police investigators are often convinced in their ability to tell who is lying and who is not during interviews and interrogations. This confidence stems from some combination of on-the-job experience and police training programs that promise increased accuracy in deception detection (Kassin et al., 2007). Some programs claim an 85% accuracy rate after the training. Unfortunately, research continually reveals that training does not produce reliable improvement. In a majority of research findings, police investigators and other professionals perform only slightly better than chance after the training (Kassin et al., 2010).

Interrogation of suspects usually is undertaken after the police investigator(s), on the basis of an interview or investigation, determine or "feel" that the suspect is culpable. Consequently, in many instances, the interrogation process begins with an assumption of guilt, and the tactics employed in the interrogation are intended to break down the anticipated resistance of the suspect. As stated by Kassin et al. (2010), "the modern American police interrogation is, by definition, a guilt-presumptive and confrontational process—aspects of which put innocent people at risk" (p. 27).

We must emphasize that estimates of *false* confessions are not high; the great majority of individuals who confess to crimes probably committed them. In Europe, 12% of prisoners report that they have confessed to crimes they did not commit (Gudjonsson, 2003). In North America, police investigators estimate that about 5% of innocent people confess to crimes during interrogation (Kassin, 2008). But why does even this relatively small number confess? People confess to crimes they did not commit because they are promised lighter sentences, to protect others, because they are mentally ill, because they want to become "celebrities," because they are exhausted after an extensive interrogation process, because they have little faith that they will be believed, as well as other reasons. In addition, some innocent people confess to a crime they did not commit because they come to believe (usually through persuasion) that they actually did do it.

In 1989, a 28-year-old investment banker was jogging in New York's Central Park when she was attacked, beaten, raped, and left for dead. Her skull had multiple fractures, her eye socket was crushed, and she could not remember the incident. She was subsequently hospitalized for 6 weeks. A number of robberies and other assaults also occurred during that night, which police described as a night of "wilding"—a term used for youth on a rampage. Within 48 hours after the attack, five Black and Latino suspects, ages 14 to 16, were arrested and charged with the rape. Police detectives aggressively interrogated the young suspects, *and all confessed.* Four of the confessions were videotaped, which—when showed during the trial—were convincing, "with each and every one of the defendants describing in vivid—though, in many ways, erroneous—detail how the jogger was attacked, when, where, and by whom, and the role that he played" (Kassin & Gudjonsson, 2004, p. 34). All were convicted and sent to prison.

Thirteen years later, Matias Reyes, serving a prison sentence for three rapes and a murder, confessed to the attack of the Central Park jogger. He said he acted alone. Reyes' unique knowledge of the crime and the DNA match on the samples recovered from the victim convinced the prosecutor's office that the five convictions should be vacated. Kassin and Gudjonsson (2004) assert that "The case of the Central Park jogger revealed five false confessions resulting from a single investigation." Furthermore, "During extensive interrogations, the men were pressured, ill-treated, and confronted with scientific evidence supposedly indicating that two of them had traces of explosives on them" (p. 34). One of the defendants served 11 years, and the other four served 7 years for the attack. The case is often used as a prime illustration of coercive police interrogation tactics that have the strong potential of resulting in false confessions. Police, however, have consistently denied that the confessions were coerced. The case regained public attention in 2009, when the five individuals brought a civil suit against the city.

The Innocence Project (2010), mentioned above and highlighted in Focus 2.2, tries to keep a running tally of false confessions across the United States. Included in the list is the story of Eddie Joe Lloyd, a mentally ill individual who was persuaded to confess to the murder of a 16-year-old girl. Lloyd had written to police offering suggestions for solving recent crimes; when he was questioned, police told him that by confessing he would help them "smoke out" the real killer. Lloyd spent nearly 20 years in prison before being exonerated by DNA evidence in 2002.

FOCUS 2.2. THE INNOCENCE PROJECT

It is now clear that some people who are serving time in prisons have been wrongfully convicted. The Innocence Project is an independent nonprofit organization whose mission is to free these individuals and to reform the system that is responsible for their imprisonment. In some cases, the convictions are partly attributable to "false confessions" or to other incriminating statements made to police, but in the majority of cases the individuals have consistently maintained their innocence.

The Project was founded in 1992 by Barry Scheck and Peter Neufeld at the Benjamin N. Cardozo School of Law at Yeshiva University. DNA testing is the primary means the Project has employed, and as of 2010, a total of 258 people in the United States have been exonerated. Seventeen of these individuals had been sentenced to death.

According to the project's website (www.innocenceproject.org), eyewitness misidentification played a role in over 75% of convictions that were ultimately overturned. Judges and juries had weighed this eyewitness testimony heavily at their trials. Ronald Cotton, whose case was alluded to in Chapter 1, was convicted after his accuser identified him as the man who had raped her. Another prisoner, Calvin Willis, was released after serving almost 22 years in prison for raping a 10-year-old girl. The girl was one of three sleeping in a house, but she denied identifying Willis even though police said she had.

Unvalidated or improper forensic science, false confessions, and the testimony of informants also play a role in DNA cases that are ultimately overturned. Daniel Gristwood, the father of five children, was submitted to 15 hours of interrogation, and had no sleep for 34 hours before he provided false statements to police that resulted in his conviction for killing his wife. He spent 10 years in prison before being exonerated (Norris & Redlich, 2010). The true perpetrator ultimately confessed. In another example, as mentioned in the text, Eddie Joe Lloyd was led to believe he was helping police "smoke out" the real killer of a 16-year-old girl by confessing falsely that he had killed her. Lloyd was mentally ill.

What happens to individuals who are exonerated? The answer is not clear, and there is likely wide variation in their success at rebuilding their lives. Furthermore, all states do not provide financial compensation for the years they have been imprisoned. According to Norris and Redlich (2010), only 27 states, the District of Columbia, and the federal government do provide for such post-exoneration reparation, and only 60% of 250 exonerated individuals have been compensated.

In a summary of the research literature, Kassin and Wrightsman (1985) identified three types of false confessions: (1) voluntary, (2) coerced-compliant, and (3) coerced-internalized. The first type, **voluntary confessions,** refers to a self-incriminating statement made without any external pressure from law enforcement. A well-known example of this type of voluntary false confession, Kassin (1997) notes, is when more than 200 people came forward and confessed to kidnapping the Charles Lindbergh baby, the most famous kidnapping case in U.S. history. Charles Lindbergh was an American hero who was the first man to fly solo over the Atlantic Ocean. On March 1, 1932, the first-born child of Lindbergh and his wife, Anne, was kidnapped for ransom and later found dead. The child was 20 months old. Although Bruno Richard Hauptmann was convicted and executed for the crime, doubts about his guilt have persisted around the case for years. As Kassin notes above, a large number of other individuals confessed to the crime, ostensibly in an effort to receive recognition or fame.

The coerced-compliant and the coerced-internalized false confessions, as their names imply, involve pressure from police officers. Research has indicated that skillful manipulation, deception, or suggestive tactics under stressful conditions may lead to false confessions (Gudjonsson, 1992; Kassin, 1997). The case of Eddie Lloyd, mentioned above, is a good example. Under these circumstances, even an innocent person may come to believe that he or she is guilty of the crime. Kassin attributes much of the coerced false confession phenomenon to such psychological concepts as compliance and internalization, processes first identified by Kelman (1958). *Compliance* is a form of conformity in which we change our public behavior—but not our private beliefs or attitudes—to appease other people or reduce social pressure or threats from others. *Internalization,* on the other hand, refers to changes in our private thoughts or beliefs that occur because we sincerely believe in the issue or perspective.

Coerced-compliant false confessions, Kassin (1997) concludes, are most likely to occur after prolonged and intense interrogation experiences, especially in situations when sleep deprivation is a feature. The suspect, desperate to avoid further discomfort, admits to the crime even though this person knows he or she is innocent. In the interesting case of Eddie Lloyd noted above, Lloyd apparently thought he was helping police by admitting to a crime that he knew he did not commit. These are examples of compliance without internalization.

In June 2001, *The Washington Post* examined the tactics of Prince George County's homicide detectives, who were able to coerce four men to confess to crimes they did not commit (Witt, 2001). The detectives used a variety of highly coercive methods and threats, including extremely long hours of interrogation combined with sleep deprivation, and ignored or refused the suspects' request for a lawyer. In one case, the suspect was slammed against the wall, threatened with execution, and deprived of sleep until he confessed. All four suspects were later exonerated by DNA evidence. In addition to these cases, the *Post* found in its review of hundreds of police and court documents that the detectives had habitually used coercive methods and violated the rights of suspects during interrogation over a period of years. Some of the interrogations lasted 32, 35, 51, and even 80 hours (Witt, 2001).

Coerced-internalized false confessions, on the other hand, occur when innocent persons—who are tired, confused, and highly psychologically vulnerable—come to believe that they actually committed the crime (Kassin, 1997; Kassin & Kiechel, 1996). This is an example of compliance eventually developing into an internalization of the belief. In addition, the pressures to confess may not necessarily originate from police officers but may come from family members, friends, religious figures, and colleagues who communicate to the suspect that he or she will feel better by doing the right thing and admitting to the offense (or atoning for his or her sins) (J. T. McCann, 1998).

Perhaps the most famous case of what *may* be a coerced-internalized confession is that of Paul Ingram, a deputy sheriff from Olympia, Washington. In 1988, his two daughters accused him and a number of others (actually, 30 members of the sheriff's department were accused) of satanic ritual abuse and sexual abuse.

The charges grew out of events sponsored by Ingram's church, the Church of Living Water. As a suspect, Ingram was subjected to 23 interrogations by detectives over a 5-month period, hypnotized, provided with graphic details of the crime, pressured by his church minister—who believed he was "80% evil"—to confess, put through exorcism by this same minister to purge the demons from him, and told by a court-appointed therapist that sex offenders often repress memories of their crimes (Fizel, 1997; Kassin, 1997). Ingram, saying he did not want his daughters to suffer through a trial, confessed, pleaded guilty, and was convicted of six counts of third-degree child rape. He received a 20-year sentence. It should be noted that Ingram was the first person who ever actually pleaded guilty to satanic ritual abuse. Ingram was released on April 8, 2003, after serving 14 years of his 20-year sentence. Upon release, he was required to register as a sex offender in the state of Washington and was rated as a Level-3 sex offender, the highest risk to reoffend. Many people believe that Ingram was rightly convicted, even if the details surrounding his crimes were exaggerated. However, others note that there has never been any forensic or physical evidence to establish that any of the ritual abuse or sexual abuse ever took place.

Summary

The spate of prisoners who have been cleared in recent years as a result of DNA evidence suggests that something went wrong as they were processed through the criminal justice system. Although many things could have gone wrong (e.g., inadequate assistance of counsel, misidentification by eyewitnesses), we have focused in this chapter on the interrogation process, which may have resulted in a false confession. However, even a "true" confession can be overturned by the courts if it is illegally obtained, in violation of the suspect's constitutional rights. Law enforcement agents, therefore, must learn to "do it right."

Meissner, Hartwig, and Russano (2010) recommend that, given the number of training manuals and training programs that promote flawed interrogation methods, the ability to offer more effective and sound alternatives is of critical importance. These researchers call for a systematic research-based approach that identifies promising interrogation techniques in which "truth" can be established (Meissner, Russano, & Narchet, 2010). Their proposal urges police psychologists and other researchers to seek opportunities to partner with police investigators in developing interrogation techniques. This integrative approach has proved very successful in the United Kingdom (see Bull & Soukara, 2010).

Messiner and Lassiter (2010) propose five recommendations for reforming police interrogations:

1. Record all interrogations from beginning to end.

2. Prohibit the use of psychologically manipulative interrogation tactics that have been shown to produce false confessions.

3. Protect vulnerable persons (e.g., juveniles, developmentally disabled persons) in the interrogation room.

4. Ensure the appropriate administration (knowing and intelligent waiver) of Miranda rights prior to interviewing a suspect.

5. Train law enforcement investigators regarding factors that contribute to false confessions.

Taking such preventive measures would not only increase public confidence in police but would also make it far less likely that evidence, including confessions, obtained during the interrogation or interview process will be disallowed from the final trial proceeding.

SUMMARY AND CONCLUSIONS

Individual psychologists have likely consulted with various law enforcement agencies in the United States throughout the 20th century, but police psychology as a subfield of applied psychology was not officially recognized until the late 1960s. Since then, it has expanded rapidly. Police psychologists today participate in the screening and selection of law enforcement candidates, conduct promotional exams and fitness-for-duty evaluations, provide counseling services to officers as well as their families, offer workshops in stress management, and assist in hostage negotiation training. In addition, there is a rich store of psychological research on topics relating to law enforcement work, most of which is conducted by academic or legal psychologists. Examples of such research include police handling of those with mental disorders, excessive force, adaptations to stress, gender differences in policing, police response to crisis situations, police interrogations, and reliability and validity of various instruments for use in screening.

Police work attracts a wide variety of people, and for many different reasons. Psychologists often participate in the screening and selection of candidates for law enforcement positions, typically by administering and evaluating psychological tests designed to identify desirable characteristics or detect problem behaviors. Before engaging in these consulting activities, it is recommended that psychologists conduct a job analysis to know specifically which tasks candidates will be expected to perform. We reviewed the most common tests used in the screening and selection of law enforcement but emphasized that other measures are available as well. It is important, though, that the approach taken be empirically validated.

Police psychologists in recent years have been giving more attention to legal issues relating to procedures used in hiring and promotional exams. Screening and selection procedures must be scrutinized carefully to ensure that women and ethnic and racial minorities are not unfairly dropped from the applicant and promotional pools. In addition, the Americans with Disabilities Act prohibits employers from discriminating against disabled persons who can perform essential functions of the job. The ADA has already led to changed testing procedures in many departments; numerous departments give the MMPI-2 only after a conditional offer of employment, for example, but others have deleted items that inquire about health-related issues. Other departments have preferred to adopt tests, such as the CPI, that have no apparent intrusive questions.

Psychologists have a good deal to offer law enforcement in the way of stress management and other clinical services. Police work ranks high among stressful occupations. We discussed a number of occupational stressors that officers encounter, including those that are organizational, external, task-related, and personal.

The chapter ended with coverage of special topics that have captured the attention of legal psychologists over the past 20 years, comprehension of Miranda rights and the matter of false confessions. It is apparent that many individuals, particularly but not limited to juveniles and people with mental disabilities, do not understand the significance of their constitutional rights. Some law enforcement officers may not believe it is their job to assure that people understand their rights, but many citizens will disagree. Nevertheless, it should be the role of the consulting psychologist to do whatever he or she can to promote sensitivity on the part of the law enforcement community in this regard. The psychology of false confessions has attracted considerable research interest in recent years, with the realization that a surprising number of suspects confess to crimes they did not commit. Forensic psychologists consulting with law enforcement may be able to offer interrogation strategies that will minimize the likelihood that a false confession will occur.

KEY CONCEPTS

Americans with Disabilities Act (ADA)

Coerced-compliant false confessions

Coerced-internalized false confessions

Concurrent validity

Critical incidents

Early warning systems

Excessive force

External stress

Face validity

False confessions

Fitness-for-duty evaluation (FFDE)

Job analysis

Organizational stress

Personal stressors

Personality assessment

Post-shooting traumatic reaction (PSTR)

Predictive validity

Screening-in procedures

Screening-out procedures

Situational testing

Task-related stress

Voluntary confessions

QUESTIONS FOR REVIEW

1. What has job analysis revealed about police work?

2. List and describe briefly the six personality measures currently most used in police screening.

3. Give examples of each of the four types of stressors that are common in law enforcement.

4. Provide examples of five gender issues relating to law enforcement.

5. Other than candidate screening, describe any three special evaluations that might be conducted by a police psychologist.

6. Discuss the common psychological reactions police may have to a shooting incident.

7. In the Scrivner study, what five different officer profiles were prone to excessive force complaints?

8. Name and describe the forms of false confessions identified by Kassin.

3

Investigative Psychology

CHAPTER OBJECTIVES

- Explore the many ways psychology contributes to investigations of criminal behavior.
- Define profiling and distinguish among five categories.
- Examine the history, methods, limitations, and problems of profiling.
- Evaluate the strengths and weaknesses of predicting human behavior.
- Describe the psychological autopsy.
- Introduce geographical profiling.
- Review the history, research, and application of the polygraph.
- Assess the usefulness of forensic hypnosis.
- Investigate the psychology of pretrial identification methods, such as lineups, photo spreads, and face recognition procedures.

In 1985, psychologist David Canter (1995) was called to Scotland Yard to explore the possibilities of integrating existing investigation procedures and techniques with psychological principles. As a consultant to British police, Canter began calling this enterprise "investigative psychology," the application of psychological research and principles to the investigation of criminal behavior. Eventually he developed a graduate program in investigative psychology at the University of Surrey in England and, 10 years later, moved to the University of Liverpool to direct a graduate program in investigative psychology there. He remains director of the Centre for Investigative Psychology and is a professor at the University of Liverpool and the University of Huddersfield. The International Research Centre for Investigative Psychology, in conjunction with the University of Huddersfield, offers MSc (Master of Science) and PhD degrees in investigative psychology under the leadership of Professor Canter and Professor Donna Youngs. To our knowledge, there is no comparable program in the United States or Canada, although graduate programs like those in Focus 1.2 offer education in topics covered in this chapter.

From a psychological perspective, three fundamental questions characterize all criminal investigations (Canter & Alison, 2000): (1) What are the important behavioral features associated with the crime that may help identify and successfully prosecute the perpetrator? (2) What inferences can be made about the characteristics of the offender that may help identify him or her? (3) Are there any other crimes that are likely to have been committed by the same person? These questions are central to the entire process of investigative psychology. This may or may not involve the task of "profiling," which is so fascinating to the public, the media, and many students of forensic psychology. And, when forensic psychologists attend career forums, give lectures, or even interact with other parents at their children's sports events, they are often asked about profiling!

Profiling in its various forms also has gained popularity in law enforcement circles since first used by the Federal Bureau of Investigation in 1971 (Pinizzotto & Finkel, 1990). It has intrigued the public through such films as *Silence of the Lambs, Kiss the Girls, Hannibal,* and *Red Dragon,* and TV series such as *CSI* and its various spin-offs in the United States as well as *Cracker* in the United Kingdom. Despite the media attention and popular TV and movie depictions of highly successful and probing profilers employing sophisticated techniques to identify the offender, reality is far from that picture. If the number of actual success stories in profiling were compared to the total number of misses or failures, the ratio of hits to misses might be close to chance. Furthermore, it should be emphasized that there are very few full-time employment opportunities for professional criminal profilers, even highly experienced ones, though some forensic psychologists do include profiling in their lists of professional activities. Although profiling is fascinating, students aspiring to become forensic psychologists should keep their career options open to the many other forensic areas that are growing and emerging each year and not narrow their career interests to such limited topics as profiling.

Nevertheless, because of this fascination, we begin the chapter by focusing on profiling and summarize the research on its validity. Is profiling useful? Successful? How exactly is it done? Are some profiling techniques more acceptable than others, and how does one distinguish a "good profiler" from one who might be seeking media attention? Later in the chapter, we discuss topics that are also relevant to investigative psychology, namely the polygraph, forensic hypnosis, and facial composites based on information provided by eyewitnesses. These activities apply psychological concepts and research to principles of criminal investigation. As you will see, when properly applied, they can help police solve crimes.

Profiling: The Psychological Sketch

Criminal profiling—perhaps the predominant task associated with investigative psychology in the public mind—requires sketching the significant behavioral, cognitive, emotional, and demographic features of a person believed to be responsible for a crime. Is the person likely to be a young, male, unmarried, unemployed blue-collar worker with highly aggressive tendencies who makes frequent appearances on the bar scene, or is the person likely to be a female, semiskilled substance abuser? Perhaps the perpetrator is even more likely to be a middle-aged loner with a steady income who seldom draws attention to himself. Note the importance of the word "likely" in each of these speculative comments.

Over the years, interest in profiling has waxed and waned, and it is often fueled by sensational media events. After a series of school shootings in the 1990s, considerable attention was directed at developing profiles of the type of high school student who would be likely to open fire on classmates or school officials. In the fall of 2002, when the Washington, D.C., area was terrorized by sniper shootings, sniper profiles were the rage.

Interestingly, many profilers were off base in their predictions. Today, nearly a decade after the September 11 terrorist attacks, law enforcement officials continue to seek profiles of persons who might be engaged in terrorist activity. Nevertheless, despite its enormous public and media interest—including depictions of profilers in the entertainment media—profiling is not a *frequent* investigative activity of police officials or psychologists. In fact, many police psychologists question the technique. In a nationwide survey of police psychologists, for example, 70% said they did not feel comfortable profiling and seriously questioned its validity and usefulness (Bartol, 1996). Ten years later, Torres, Boccaccini, and Miller (2006) reported a similar finding.

Interestingly, though, there may be a tendency to embrace profiling under a different name, namely criminal investigative analysis (often used as a more technical name for profiling). The Torres et al., 2006, survey discovered that forensic professionals who were asked to evaluate the term *criminal investigative analysis* found it significantly more reliable and valid than those asked to rate the term *profiling*. The Torres et al. findings support the position that when we attach a more scientific-sounding name to this practice, profiling is viewed more favorably. A similar view appears to be held by the courts (Cooley, 2008; Risinger & Loop, 2002). According to Torres et al., "Many professionals who engage in profiling work believe that profiling testimony is more likely to be admitted into court when it is called something other than profiling" (p. 53).

Moreover, it appears that a majority of *police investigators* believe that criminal profiling is useful (Snook, Cullen, Bennell, Taylor, & Gendreau, 2008). For example, as mentioned in Snook et al., J. L. Jackson, van Koppen, and Herbrink (1993) reported that 5 out of 6 police officers surveyed in the Netherlands thought that criminal profiling had some usefulness. In the United Kingdom, Copson (1995) found that about 83% of police officers believed that criminal profiling was operationally useful, and 92% claimed they would seek criminal profiling advice again. Many years ago, Pinizzotto (1984) discovered that 17% of police officers thought profiles were useful. However, to our knowledge, no recent survey on the value of profiles has been conducted on police officers in the United States.

There continues to be extensive debate on the effectiveness of the profiling endeavor, whether or not it is cloaked in scientific terminology. Therefore, an area desperately in need of attention from forensic psychologists is profiling *research*. In other words, it is critical that we learn how reliable or valid the various profiling procedures and methods currently used are and how (or if) they can be improved to allow meaningful application to law enforcement and other forensic realms. We will address this debate later in the chapter. For the moment, it is important to acknowledge that profiling is *pervasive*, even though it is not a *frequent* activity in which forensic and specifically police psychologists engage.

It is also important to understand the categories or forms of profiling, depending on the purpose and methods used. Profiling can be divided into the following five, sometimes overlapping categories: (1) crime scene profiling, (2) suspect-based profiling, (3) the psychological autopsy, (4) geographical profiling, and (5) psychological profiling. The first, second, and fourth forms represent profiling of *unknown* individuals. The third and fifth forms represent profiling of *known* individuals. Partly because of the overlapping nature of these categories, the terms are sometimes used interchangeably, and—as we will describe below—other terms also are used. Students asked to write a research paper on profiling have undoubtedly encountered a rather confusing array of labels for what may appear to be the same enterprise.

Crime Scene Profiling

Crime scene profiling is a method developed by the FBI's **Behavioral Science Unit** (BSU; see Focus 3.1) to provide investigative assistance to law enforcement in cases of serial homicide or serial rape (Homant & Kennedy, 1998). (Personal Perspective 3.1 introduces you to Dr. Anthony Pinizzotto, former senior forensic psychologist with the BSU, who continues to give lectures on applied investigative psychology.) Crime scene profiling is the process of identifying cognitive tendencies, behavioral patterns, emotional dispositions, and demographic variables of an unknown offender based on characteristics of the crime scene. This process also may be called *criminal profiling, criminal investigative analysis,* or *crime scene investigation* by some professionals. Based on crime scene information and the predicted characteristics and habits of the offender, the profiler tries to describe who the offender or offenders might be and predict where and how the next crime may occur. To a very large extent, the profiling process is dictated by the quality of the data collected on previous offenders who have committed similar offenses. For example, if the profiler believes, on the basis of research, that most burglars are male, are under 30, and commit their burglaries within a 20-mile radius of where they live, these are helpful clues in searching for suspects. On the other hand, profiling can go horribly wrong if the string of burglaries being investigated by police is committed by a small group of 40-year-olds from two states away.

PERSONAL PERSPECTIVE 3.1

Priest, Law Enforcement Officer, Forensic Psychologist

Anthony J. Pinizzotto, OSFS, PhD

Over 40 years ago, I joined the Oblates of Saint Francis de Sales (OSFS), a religious congregation, to study for the Catholic priesthood. In 1978, I was ordained a priest. Ten years later, I joined the FBI. In 2008, after 20 years of service with the FBI, I retired as the senior scientist and forensic psychologist from the Behavioral Science Unit in Quantico, Virginia, but I have never retired from the priesthood. It's a strange combination: Roman Catholic priest, clinical forensic psychologist, and law enforcement. It occurred by coincidence, thoughtful and deliberate choices . . . and, I think, some providence.

Before ordination to the priesthood, I worked as an intern corrections counselor and investigator, and while pursuing graduate degrees, joined

the Metropolitan Police Department in Washington, D.C., as a uniformed reserve officer. It was in D.C. that I realized how interesting and exciting a career in law enforcement can be. But I never lost my interest in psychology, so I decided to bring the two fields of law and psychology together by studying forensic psychology at John Jay College of Criminal Justice in New York. Then it was on to Georgetown University for a PhD in psychology. My dissertation examined the area of psychological "profiling" of crime scenes.

While teaching at Georgetown, I was recruited by the FBI to conduct research on felonious law enforcement assaults and deaths. At that time, I teamed up with Mr. Edward F. Davis, a retired lieutenant from the D.C. Police Department with whom I had worked back in 1975. He was now working for the FBI. For the next 20 years, Ed and I interviewed over 150 individuals who either feloniously assaulted or killed law enforcement officers. We also interviewed many of the officers who were feloniously assaulted in the line of duty. We learned a great deal from those officers' experiences. The results and analyses of those interviews can be found in three Department of Justice publications: *Killed in the Line of Duty* (1992), *In the Line of Fire* (1997), and *Violent Encounters* (2006).

In 1990, the U.S. Congress passed the **Hate Crime Statistics Act**. This act required the collection of reported instances to law enforcement of crimes committed against an individual that were wholly or in part based on the victim's race, religion, ethnicity, or sexual orientation. The Attorney General of the United States mandated the FBI to collect these data as part of the Uniform Crime Reports (UCR). One of the most interesting and rewarding assignments I was given was to develop a program for law enforcement to define, identify, investigate, and report these data to the FBI. I worked with men and women from federal, state, county, and municipal law enforcement agencies who had dedicated much of their careers to the investigation of these crimes. Together with these officers, and with members of various human interest groups, we developed a very comprehensive program, which is used to this day by law enforcement agencies across the country to identify, collect, and report hate-related crimes to the UCR Program of the FBI.

Since my retirement in 2008 from the FBI, I continue to work within the criminal justice field as a consultant to law enforcement officers and agencies in areas of crime scene evaluation and analysis; use of force; stress; perception, memory, and recall; and psychology and the martial arts. As a priest, I live and work at a parish church in northern Virginia. This gives me the opportunity to minister to the spiritual and psychological needs of law enforcement officers, firefighters, and military personnel as well as many other parishioners.

Students continue to ask, "What can I do to become a good forensic psychologist and work in law enforcement?" The answer is pretty simple: Get an excellent educational foundation in the behavioral sciences. Become very knowledgeable about research methodology and statistical analysis. It's important that you are able to read *critically* the research that is out there. In order to ask the right questions about the research you read, you must understand methodology. . . . Don't ever accept research results simply because they're published in some journal. Read, understand, question. Finally, in whatever area within the criminal justice system you hope to work . . . get practical, hands-on experience. It's very difficult to really understand the criminal justice system from the outside!

It's strange how life turns out when you just happen to be at the right spot at the right time . . . [thanks to] coincidence; thoughtful and deliberate choices; and, of course, providence.

Dr. Pinizzotto received his PhD in psychology from Georgetown University 8 years after his ordination. He now lives and works in a parish in northern Virginia and remains active as a consultant to law enforcement. He continues to present lectures in applied investigative psychology throughout the United States and Europe and has rekindled his interest in sports psychology. In his spare time, he has returned to some of the activities that kept him energized in the past: classical music, hiking, camping, archery, hunting . . . all with his faithful companion, Champ, his 14-year-old beagle.

It should be emphasized, at the outset, that crime scene profiling—even in its most sophisticated form—rarely can point directly to *the* person who committed the crime. Instead, the process helps develop a manageable set of hypotheses for identifying who *may* have been responsible for the crime. If done competently, a profile will provide some statistical probabilities regarding the demographic, geographic patterns, and psychological features of the offender. More important, it should eliminate very large segments of the population from further investigation.

Contrary to popular belief, this profiling is not and should not be restricted to serial murder or serial sexual assaults. It has considerable *potential* value when applied successfully to crimes such as arson, terrorist acts, burglary, shoplifting and robbery, Internet crimes, and white-collar crimes such as bank fraud or embezzlement.

FOCUS 3.1. THE FBI ACADEMY BEHAVIORAL SCIENCE UNIT

The FBI Behavioral Science Unit (BSU) is one of the instructional components of the FBI's Training Division in Quantico, Virginia. Its mission is to develop and provide training, research, and consultation programs in the behavioral and social sciences for the FBI and law enforcement community that will improve or enhance the administration, operational effectiveness, and understanding of crime. This work includes conducting high-impact research and presenting a variety of cutting-edge courses on topics such as applied criminal psychology, clinical forensic psychology, crime analysis, and death investigation.

The BSU focuses on developing new and innovative investigative approaches and techniques for solving crimes by studying offenders and their behaviors and motivations. Some of this research is conducted in partnership with outside researchers and through interagency agreements with the Department of Justice and Office of Justice Programs. The Unit staff consists of supervisory special agents and veteran police officers with advanced degrees in the behavioral sciences such as psychology, criminology, sociology, and conflict resolution.

The BSU also coordinates with and supports other FBI units, such as the National Center for the Analysis of Violent Crime (NCAVC) and the Critical Incident Response Group (CIRG), which provides operational assistance to the FBI field offices and law enforcement agencies. In 2008, the BSU, under the leadership of Dr. Gregory M. Vecchi, unit chief of the BSU, started the suprisingly named Evil Minds Research Museum. The museum collects serial killer items such as paintings, artwork, and correspondences. It is believed that the materials may provide unique insights into the killers' motivations, personalities, and thought processes. The BSU started the Evil Minds Research Museum Visiting Scholar Program for the purpose of analyzing and researching the artifacts in the museum.

Source: Behavioral Science Unit, FBI Academy (http://www.fbi.gov).

Dynamic and Static Risk Factors in Prediction

An important issue in the prediction and profiling of human behavior is the distinction between **dynamic risk factors** and **static risk factors** (Andrews & Bonta, 1998; Andrews, Bonta, & Hoge, 1990). They are referred to as "risk factors" because they are associated with or predictive of antisocial behavior. **Dynamic risk factors** are those that change over time and situation. For example, substance abuse and negative attitudes toward women have potential for change, in contrast to **static risk factors** like parental criminality or someone's own early onset of antisocial behavior. In short, dynamic factors can change, whereas static factors cannot.

Dynamic factors can be subdivided into stable and acute dynamic factors (Hanson & Harris, 2000). **Stable dynamic factors,** although they are changeable, usually change slowly and may take months or even years, if they change at all. Consider, for example, one's attitudes about violent pornography or one's long-time association with deviant peers. **Acute dynamic factors,** on the other hand, change rapidly (within days, hours, or even minutes), sometimes dependent upon mood swings, emotional arousal, and alcohol or other drug-induced effects. Hanson and Harris found that acute dynamic factors, such as anger and subjective distress, were better predictors of the tendency of sex offenders to reoffend than were the more stable dynamic factors, such as the sex offender's attitudes about women. Nonetheless, both are risk factors to be addressed not only in prediction, but also in the treatment of sex offenders.

It is important for a profiler to be aware of the role of risk factors, both static and dynamic, as well as the difference between the stable and acute dynamic factors, particularly in the case of serial offenders. These offenders, whether rapists, burglars, arsonists, killers, or pedophiles, often change their **modus operandi (MO)** as they become more proficient at their crime. Or, as Turvey (2002) points out, the MO may change due to an offender's deteriorating mental state, the increased use of drugs or alcohol, or changes in lifestyle and habits.

The MO refers to the actions and procedures an offender uses to commit a crime successfully. It is a behavioral pattern that the offender learns as he or she gains experience in committing the offense. However, it is subject to change. For example, burglars are continually changing their procedures and techniques to better accomplish their goals, and serial killers often become more daring and risky in their selection of victims. Because the offender generally changes the MO until he or she learns which method is most effective, investigators may make a serious error if they place too much significance on the MO when linking crimes.

Investigators may make another serious error if they believe offenders lack intellectual skills. Turvey (2002) suggests that some offenders improve their MO through educational and technical materials: "Professional journals, college courses, textbooks, and other educationally oriented media available at a public library, or now via the Internet, can provide offenders with knowledge that is useful toward refining their particular MO". (p. 232). Turvey further writes, "arsonists may read *Kirk's Fire Investigation . . .* rapists may read *Practical Aspects of Rape Investigation . . .* murderers may read *Practical Homicide Investigation . . .* and bank robbers may subscribe to security magazines" (p. 232). In addition, many offenders read newspaper, magazine, and television accounts of their crimes, which sometimes provide clues that the police have identified concerning the MO. Such accounts may prompt the offender to alter his or her methods of operation. In some instances, the offender may perfect the MO by engaging in a career or profession that enhances the methods used, such as an arsonist joining a volunteer fire department or even becoming a fire investigator.

Crime Scene Concepts and Terminology

The profiling literature sometimes makes distinctions among crime scenes that are organized, disorganized, or mixed. These classifications emerged as a result of interviews with incarcerated sexual murderers in the 1980s by representatives of the BSU. The interviews were conducted in an effort to identify some common behavioral characteristics and motives of serial killers (Ressler, Burgess, & Douglas, 1988; Ressler, Burgess, Hartman, Douglas, & McCormick, 1986). In the late 1980s, further study focused on the behavioral and motivational features of serial rapists (Hazelwood & Burgess, 1987, 1995).

An **organized crime scene** suggests planning and premeditation on the part of the offender. The crime reveals signs that the offender maintained control of himself or herself and the victim(s) and took considerable cautions to elude apprehension. In addition, it is also apparent that the victim or victims were selected rather than being randomly attacked. A **disorganized crime scene,** on the other hand, suggests that the offender committed the crime without planning. Essentially, the crime scene looks chaotic, indicating the offender acted on impulse, rage, or some other intense emotional state. High emotions tend to "disorganize" a person's thought processes and behavior. Think of what happens when a person becomes uncontrollably angry. Often, the disorganized offender obtains his or her victim or victims by chance. The victim is simply at the wrong place at the wrong time. The **mixed crime scene** has both organized and disorganized aspects. For example, a crime may have begun as a carefully planned one but quickly deteriorated into a disorganized crime when things failed to go as originally planned and unanticipated strong emotions set in.

Crime scenes are rarely as neat as portrayed here, however, and some research (e.g., Kocsis, Cooksey, & Irwin, 2002) suggests that the organized–disorganized classification scheme may have very limited usefulness. It is probably more realistic to assume that crime scenes exist somewhere along a continuum, with the organized label at one pole of the continuum and the disorganized label at the other. Even calling a crime scene "mixed" does not tell whether it has more features of the organized or disorganized crime. So, by using one of these three terms we try to fit crime scene analysis into an unrealistic classification system, or **typology.** In contemporary psychology, the term *typology* refers to a particular system for classifying personality or other behavioral patterns. Usually, the typology is used to classify a wide assortment of behaviors into a more manageable set of brief descriptions, which can be useful but should be employed guardedly. When we place people (in this case, people responsible for a crime scene) into behavioral categories, we assume that behavior is consistent across time and place. Crime scene typologies are constructed on the premise that human behavior (e.g., of the offender) is largely the same from situation to situation—and this is not necessarily the case. The concept of typologies will be discussed again in Chapters 8 and 9, when criminal violence and sexual assaults are covered.

Another concept sometimes encountered in crime scene profiling or analysis is **undoing.** Undoing is a behavioral pattern evident at the scene in which the offender tried to psychologically "undo" the crime. For example, a distraught or emotionally upset offender who has killed the victim may try to undo his or her actions by placing the body in bed, perhaps even resting the head on a pillow, and covering the body with blankets. The perpetrator also may place the victim upright in a chair, trying desperately to return the victim to a natural-looking state.

Trophy taking is another behavioral pattern sometimes encountered in crime scene analysis. Although it is more common in violent crime, it may occur in burglary as well. A crime scene **trophy** is a meaningful souvenir taken by the offender to remember the incident, to psychologically control the victim, or both. It could be anything: a piece of clothing, a photograph, a piece of jewelry, or even—in the case of a murdered victim—a body part. One of the more infamous trophy takers in the United States was the serial killer Jeffrey Dahmer, who collected body parts in glass jars filled with formaldehyde as well as photographs depicting victims at various stages of their deaths.

Trophy taking also may be a part of a signature of the offender. The **signature** is a symbolic communication by the offender that goes beyond what is necessary to commit the crime. The **signature** is thought to be related to the unique cognitive processes of the offender and, because it is relatively consistent in its characteristics, it may be more useful in the profiling process than the MO. In other words, the signature probably has greater stability than the MO. For example, some burglars tailor their styles (or their signature) to convey messages to victims and investigators, hoping to induce some strong emotional reactions from the victims, such as fear or anger. The burglar may leave a frightening or threatening note or "violate" some personal item, such as intimate clothing, a photograph, or a diary. Consequently, the emotional reactions of burglarized victims often run the gamut from anger and depression to fear and anxiety (B. B. Brown & Harris, 1989).

Related to the signature is the issue of psychopathology. Experienced profilers have argued for many years that profiling serial violent offenders is most successful when the offender exhibits some form of psychopathology at the scene of the crime, such as sadistic torture, evisceration, postmortem slashings and cuttings, and other mutilations (Pinizzotto, 1984). The reasoning behind this assertion is that when a person is mentally disordered, he or she demonstrates greater consistency in behavior from situation to situation. The assumption here is that anyone who commits these outrageous offenses must be mentally disordered, an assumption we will discuss again in Chapter 4. However—even if we concede the mental disorder—it is open to debate whether persons with mental disorders are more consistent in their behavioral patterns than stable individuals. Systematic empirical research on the topic is lacking.

Staging is another behavioral pattern sometimes found at a crime scene, a suspected suicide, or an accidental death. Staging is the intentional alteration of the scene prior to the arrival of the police. It is usually done for one of two reasons: either to redirect the investigation away from the most logical suspect or to protect the victim or the victim's family from public embarrassment (Douglas & Munn, 1992). Thus, staging may be done by the perpetrator or by someone who discovers the victim or evidence of a crime. In the case of a death, staging is frequently done by someone who has a close association or relationship with the victim. For example, the victim may have become an accidental death victim by practicing autoerotic asphyxia.

Autoerotic asphyxia refers to obtaining sexual excitement from *hypoxia* (lack of oxygen), usually accomplished through near strangulation or suffocation while masturbating. The euphoria produced by the hypoxia is believed to enhance masturbatory sensations and orgasm intensity. Participants use a variety of methods to deprive themselves of oxygen (also called *hypoxyphilia* by mental health professionals), including ligature hanging, near suffocation or smothering by plastic bags or duct tape, inhalation of noxious chemicals (such as butane or nitrous oxide), or submersion underwater. Unfortunately, most of what is known about this practice comes from studies of fatalities (Hucker, 2008). *Autoerotic death* refers to an unanticipated death that results while the participant is engaged in solo or accompanied sexual activity "and the arousal-enhancing device designed to rescue the participant fails" (Schields, Hunsaker, & Hunsaker, 2005, p. 45).

Death due to suspected autoerotic asphyxiation (AEA) is divided into two broad categories, typical and atypical. *Typical* autoerotic death denotes ligature asphyxiation due to some binding around the neck, such as a dog collar, belt, or bungee cord. It is believed to be the most common autoerotic method practiced. Unfortunately, it also has a high potential to be fatal when things go wrong. When practiced as solo sexual activity, the presence of a distinct release mechanism may confirm to forensic investigators that the fatality was accidental (Schields et al., 2005). A *release mechanism* refers to an escape strategy the victim has devised for releasing the neck ligature or bindings before losing consciousness, such as quick-release devices, slipknots, or readily available physical supports (feet touching the floor). Sometimes, however, lack of oxygen to the brain results in unintended loss of consciousness, causing accidental death. In many cases, practitioners employ protective padding about the neck to prevent telltale ligature marks. It should be mentioned, however, that in rare cases, suicidal intentions by the practitioner were intended from the outset (Hucker & Blanchard, 1992). Such cases may require a psychological autopsy to determine the motivations of the deceased individual.

Unlike typical cases, *atypical* autoerotic asphyxiation does not involve ligature binding around the neck. In other words, practitioners deprive themselves of oxygen but do not use ligatures. Instead, they achieve sexual gratification by other means, such as plastic bags covering the head or the entire body (Behrendt, Buhl, & Seidl, 2002; Schields et al., 2005), face masks (Janssen, Koops, Anders, Kuhn, & Püschel, 2005), experimentation with electricity (Klintschar, Grabuschnigg, & Beham, 1998; Schott, Davis, & Hunsaker, 2003), or compression of the chest or abdomen (Schields et al., 2005).

It is estimated that there may be as many as 250 to 1,200 AEA deaths in North America each year (Cowell, 2009). Estimates are almost certainly inaccurate, however, since there are no centralized data sources and most AEA deaths probably go unreported. Distressed family members who discover the victim in a "compromised" condition may feel compelled to alter the situation (e.g., by dressing the victim or hiding paraphernalia), perhaps to make it appear as either a homicide or a suicide. Distinguishing AEA cases from suicide is difficult in some instances, as will be noted shortly in the section on the psychological autopsy.

A 7-year retrospective study by Sauvageau (2008) suggests a lower incidence of autoerotic deaths and a higher percentage of female and atypical autoerotic fatalities than previously reported in U.S. studies. In North America and Germany, the primary victims of known autoerotic deaths are white, young, middle-class, unmarried males. Approximately 30% of the male victims are found nude, and approximately 25% are found wearing women's clothing (Breitmeier et al., 2003; Douglas & Munn, 1992). Often, pornographic materials and sexual aids are present. Females also engage in AEA but apparently in much smaller numbers than males (Behrendt et al., 2002; Gosink & Jumbelic, 2000). One of the most disturbing phenomena in recent years is the apparent increase in deaths of children playing "the choking game," although this is not necessarily autoerotic in nature (see Focus 3.2).

In a comprehensive review of the research on autoerotic deaths between 1954 and 2004, Sauvageau and Racette (2006) found a 21:7 male-to-female ratio overall. A majority of known females victims were found naked, and most died from a single ligature around the neck. Although the evidence of sexual props is rarely found in female AES deaths, there are exceptions. Behrendt et al. (2002) studied the accidental autoerotic deaths of four women. All women were found immobilized by self-tied ropes, string, or handcuffs. Overall, the four cases closely mirrored findings from scenes of males with various paraphernalia and props.

FOCUS 3.2. THE CHOKING GAME

A troubling aspect in asphyxiation practices over the past few years has been the increasing involvement of school-age children in so-called "choking games" (Cowell, 2009). Children call these games various names, including black hole, suffocation roulette, space cowboy, blackout, rising sun, flatlining, funky chicken, space monkey, and several other names. Choking games probably have been practiced in small groups for generations but they appear to have increased in frequency in recent years. According to a 2008 report from the Centers for Disease Control and Prevention, at least 82 choking game deaths among youths aged 6–19 years occurred during 1995–2007 in the United States. The typical age range is between 9 and 15 years with a male:female ratio of about 2 to 1 (Andrew & Fallon, 2007). Some children may be as young as 7 years old. Le and Macnab (2001) investigated four deaths and one near death due to strangulation by hanging from cloth towels in dispensers located in Canadian schools. The victims, all males ages 7 to 12, were playing the choking game by pulling down a loop of the cloth towel, wrapping the towel around their necks, and hanging from it until they lost consciousness. It appears that many young children who engage in the choking game are motivated more by the thrill than by seeking an intense erotic high, and they certainly do not intend to die.

In a follow-up study, Macnab, Deevska, Gagnon, Cannon, and Andrew (2009) surveyed 2,504 students in Texas and Canadian schools (Grades 4 to 12). The survey revealed that 68% of the children had heard about the choking game, 45% knew someone who had played it, and 6.6% reported having tried it. Of the number who tried the practice, 55% were male. More revealing was the finding that 40% of the youths did not believe there was any risk (of death or brain damage) in participating in the game. Another recent survey (McClave, Russell, Lyren, O'Riordan, & Bass, 2010) revealed that one-third of the surveyed pediatricians and family practitioners were completely unaware of the choking game.

Interestingly, children who practice the choking game are often average to above-average students who normally shun alcohol and drugs (Andrew & Fallon, 2007). As further noted by Andrew and Fallon, "The magnitude of risk is clearly lost on the child lulled into a false sense of security inherent in the belief that this activity is a drug-free, and therefore perfectly safe, high" (p. 305). Investigators and researchers believe that a majority of adult AEA practitioners began their ritual during childhood or adolescence (Andrew & Fallon, 2007; Friedrich & Gerber, 1994).

Suspect-Based Profiling

Whereas crime scene profiling examines features of the crime, suspect-based profiling is derived from the systematic collection of behavioral, personality, cognitive, and demographic data on previous offenders. In most instances, the suspect-based profile summarizes the psychological features of persons who *may* commit a crime, such as drug trafficking, detonating a bomb, or hijacking a plane. The end product of suspect-based profiling should describe people from various groups. "For example, someone driving at a certain speed, at a certain time of day, in a certain type of car, and of a certain general appearance may fit the profile of a drug courier and be stopped for a search" (Homant & Kennedy, 1998, p. 325). "General appearance," as used in the above quote, may refer to suspicious behavior, age, or manner of dress, but it also unfortunately has referred to race or ethnicity.

Probably the best known and most controversial type of suspect-based profiling is racial profiling, which refers to "police-initiated action that relies on the race, ethnicity, or national origin rather than the behavior of an individual or information that leads the police to a particular individual who has been identified as being, or having been, engaged in criminal activity" (Ramirez, McDevitt, & Farrell, 2000, p. 53). Thus, while other types of suspect-based profiling may be acceptable, racial or ethnic profiling is not.

In recent years, racial profiling became so well known to ethnic minorities or people of color during traffic stops that they began to label the phenomenon "driving while Black" or "driving while Brown" (abbreviated as DWB), as a play on the legally accepted term DWI (driving while intoxicated). Racial profiling is based on the assumption by some law enforcement officials that ethnic or racial minorities are most often used as couriers of illegal drugs or other contraband. This unwarranted assumption has led to a disproportionate number of "pretext" stops of people of color. A *pretext stop* is one in which a driver is pulled over for a mild traffic infraction, such as crossing the center line or driving a vehicle with a defective taillight. The stop allows the officer to conduct a visual search of the vehicle and, under some conditions, order drivers and even passengers out of the car.

In 2010, immigration emerged as a hot-button political issue, particularly but not exclusively in states bordering Mexico. The combination of high unemployment rates and concerns about drug trafficking led to a desire among some for a "crackdown" on individuals entering the United States illegally or remaining here after temporary visas have expired. Note that two separate problems are identified here: (1) cross-border transportation of illegal drugs and (2) immigration status that is not documented. Note also that this issue comes to the fore particularly at a time when the economy is only slowly recovering and many individuals remain without jobs. Undocumented immigrants are believed to be ready to take low-paying jobs and "not make waves" lest their status be discovered.

However, numerous undocumented immigrants seek asylum because of abuses suffered in their homeland. They work hard and raise their families, and the children of these families attend colleges and universities. Many want their status legalized but have waited years for this to occur, often due to language barriers or bureaucratic inefficiency. In 2010, an Arizona law went into effect requiring police in that state to question the immigration status of individuals they stopped legally, even if the stop was only for a traffic violation. Opponents argued that the law targeted persons of Hispanic descent, and the press reported numerous anecdotal instances of national groups and prominent individuals boycotting the state's tourist industry as a result. A federal judge subsequently struck down portions of the law on the basis that immigration was a federal and not a state matter. As this book is going to press, the legal complexities of this case continue, with Arizona officials attempting to craft a law that will be acceptable to the courts, and opponents continuing to argue that this approach sends the wrong message.

Ethnic or racial profiling has been used beyond the detection of drug couriers or undocumented immigrants. It has also been used in traveler or passenger profiling, although this is of relatively recent origin. Airline-related crimes (e.g., skyjacking, passenger assault, terrorist activities) have made many of us uneasy since September 11, 2001. Interestingly, airline-related crimes have a history dating back to the mid-20th century when skyjacking was often considered more "daring" than "frightening" (see Focus 3.3). Since 9/11, ethnic or racial minorities who fit the "profile" of terrorists (such as persons of Middle Eastern descent or origin) have been subjected to more extensive security screenings in airports or at immigration checkpoints. Moreover, the discovery of explosive devices in shoes, underwear, and cargo led the Transportation Security Administration (TSA) to initiate full-body scans or "patdowns" of all air travelers in many airports across the United States in 2010. Some critics of these measures believe that, even if all passengers are subjected to full-body scans, persons of Middle Eastern descent are more likely to be taken aside for more invasive patdowns. Air passenger profiling is a highly controversial topic, but is used in varying forms at airports around the world. A number of experts strongly believe that some sort of passenger profiling that includes race and nationality should be implemented as part of aviation security (Aviation Daily, 2002). Other experts disagree. Human rights groups have criticized techniques or procedures that single out people on the basis of gender, race, ethnicity, age, appearance, religion, or country of origin. Katie Corrigan, legal counsel for the American Civil Liberties Union, believes passenger profiling of any kind sets a dangerous precedent and is an ineffective security measure (Aviation Daily, 2002; Steinbock, 2003), because professional terrorists can employ ways to defeat whatever profile strategy is in use. For example, as mentioned above, passenger profiling has focused on those persons who have the physical appearance that suggests they are of Middle Eastern descent. Yet some convicted individuals—including the shoe-bomber Richard Reeve—did not conform to the profile, while other individuals did but were not singled out or detained.

And at this writing, the U.S. Department of Justice has indicted Colleen R. LaRose, an American woman from Pennsylvania (also known as "Jihad Jane") for using the Internet to recruit jihadist fighters (mostly women) and help terrorists across the globe. U.S. Attorney Michael L. Levy at a news conference said that the blonde, blue-eyed American woman's alleged acts shatter any lingering thought that we can spot a terrorist based on appearance (J. Adams, 2010).

Rather than focusing on race, religion, or nationality, it appears that passenger profiling that focuses on behavioral patterns and characteristics might be more effective. This type of suspect-based profiling is less objectionable. In the United States, major airlines have used a suspect-based profiling system known as the Computer Assisted Passenger Prescreening System (CAPPS) (Armstrong & Pereira, 2001). CAPPS, a more limited version of the passenger prescreening systems used in Europe and Israel, was created after the midair explosion of TWA flight 800 over Long Island Sound in 1996, which resulted in the deaths of 230 people. At first, it was thought that the explosion was the result of a terrorist attack, but further investigation revealed the cause to be frayed electrical wiring in or near the fuel tanks located in the midsection of the aircraft.

CAPPS uses basic data disclosed by passengers when they reserve and buy tickets—such as their names, addresses, and how they paid for tickets—to look for patterns that identify potential terrorists. For example, passengers who purchase one-way tickets, pay in cash, travel alone, buy tickets for passengers with different last names on the same credit card, or buy tickets with the same credit card shortly after another transaction are targeted for further investigation or closer surveillance (Armstrong & Pereira, 2001). At the present, though, it appears that these behavioral profiles are used in conjunction with the body scans and searches of all passengers.

Do these suspect-based techniques actually work? CAPPS did flag two of the four hijackers aboard American Airlines Flight 77 (which crashed into the Pentagon) as suspicious when they checked in at Dulles Airport on the morning of September 11, 2001. Unfortunately, neither man was questioned or searched at the airport, although their bags were carefully scanned before being loaded onto the plane. Following the attacks on September 11, passengers as well as baggage were searched before flights, a practice that continues today, as all air travelers are well aware.

In reference to the drug courier profiles, critics have argued that although they help discover evidence of drug trafficking, they are also so broad in their description that they can apply to a great number of passengers and result in the temporary detention and questioning of numerous innocent individuals. The same concerns are raised about the Arizona law mentioned above that targets many law-abiding individuals.

After the terrorist attacks of September 11 and with the heightened threat of more terrorism, psychologists and behavioral scientists were asked to further develop profiles that would help security personnel identify potential terrorists from passenger lists. These suspect-based profiles usually take into consideration the clothes the passenger is wearing, the person's nationality, travel history, behavioral patterns while at the airport, and even the book that he or she may have just purchased at the airport bookshop. That is, to improve their ability to identify potential terrorists, profile researchers would examine the buying habits, dress patterns, and cultural and social backgrounds of previous airline terrorists.

In recent years, the TSA has trained more than 2,000 airport security personnel in various methods to identify suspicious behavior and facial expressions that suggest terrorist or destructive intentions (Bradshaw, 2008). The training in passenger profiling is partly based on the research of psychologist Paul Ekman (2009), and the success of a 2002 pilot program at Boston's Logan International Airport (Bradshaw, 2008). However, the technique developed by Ekman is far from foolproof. Ekman admits that 9 out of every 10 persons detected have perfectly innocent reasons for their suspicious behavior. This hit-to-miss ratio concerns the American Civil Liberties Union (ACLU). "Many travelers may be subjected to undue attention simply because they have a fear of flying, feel intimidated by being scrutinized by uniformed screeners or are carrying items that cause them shame, such as legal but erotic literature" (Bradshaw, 2008, p. 10).

FOCUS 3.3. A BRIEF HISTORY OF AIRLINE HIJACKING

Profiling of potential hijackers and terrorists is not new. The word *hijack* originated in the Midwest around 1912 to 1920 and is a shortened form of a command meaning, "Hold your hands up high, Jack" (Dailey & Pickrel, 1975b). Apparently, it was first used by bands of individuals who habitually robbed farmers, and it eventually came to mean the use of force or trickery to compel individuals to do things they did not want to do. In 1961, *Time* magazine coined the term *skyjacking* to refer to the seizure of aircraft.

After the first official hijacking of an American aircraft occurred in 1961, a trickle of these events continued until the epidemic years between 1968 and 1978. In 1968, there were 36 skyjackings, 20 of them involving American aircraft, with most diverted to Cuba (Arey, 1972). This "contagion effect" became even more apparent in 1969 when there were 71 skyjackings, 58 of which were diverted to Cuba from the United States and other parts of the world. Some skyjackers were homesick Cubans, some claimed to be political activists, but most apparently wanted to become significant and newsworthy.

(Continued)

(Continued)

Sixty-nine skyjackings occurred in 1970, and similar instances continued until the United States began to clamp down on airport security. One of the skyjacking incidents that attracted extensive media attention was the case of D. B. Cooper, who hijacked an aircraft, demanded and received money and a parachute, and then jumped from the plane. The FBI does not believe he survived the jump, but there is little evidence to support this claim. The Cooper story became well-known, with much speculation about whether he lived or died from his jump. Books, posters, T-shirts, rock songs, and a movie—*The Pursuit of D. B. Cooper,* starring Robert Duvall and Treat Williams—document the considerable ongoing interest in the heist. A restaurant in Salt Lake City was even named after him. His daring feat also illustrates a good example of the **contagion** or **copycat effect**. Cooper himself may have been reacting to the early rash of skyjackings mentioned above. However, his demand for money and a parachute prompted others to do the same.

Of the 19 foiled hijacking attempts in 1972, a total of 15 included the demand for both money and parachutes. During the same year, three hijackers demonstrated that it was possible to survive a jump from a 727 by parachuting out the back (all were later captured or shot). The Federal Aviation Administration (FAA) soon required all 727s to be fitted with a device that automatically locks the rear door while in flight. The idea of demanding a ransom and parachutes may not have originated with Cooper, however. A hijacker, with a gun, tried to take over an Air Canada plane just 12 days prior to the Cooper hijacking. The hijacker demanded money and parachutes but was subdued by the flight crew when he tried to put on the parachute. Cooper, though, decided to use a bomb in a briefcase instead of a gun, a plot that he may have copied from the 1970 movie *Airport.*

Not long after the Cooper skyjacking, in August 1972, the FAA issued a directive that all U.S. carriers had to either search or deny boarding to those who fit a certain profile (Daile & Pickrel, 1975a). The profile had been developed by FAA psychologists in response to the rash of skyjackings in the late 1960s and early 1970s.

They had concluded that, in general, skyjackers were different from the usual air traveler of that time in such aspects as socioeconomic class and mannerisms in the airport terminal (Daile & Pickrel, 1975a). The "typical" skyjacker was generally an "unsuccessful" member of society, was inadequate socially and occupationally, was lacking in resourcefulness, appeared to have substantial feelings of helplessness or hopelessness, and perhaps was suicidal. Apparently, the skyjacking was a way of improving his or her situation and gaining some control and significance in the world. However, although the skyjacker profile was helpful at first, it eventually proved inadequate and incomplete because cultural, social, political, and security forces are always in a state of flux. Consequently, the most useful profiles must be continually evaluated and updated with new information.

The pre-boarding procedure mandated by the FAA seemed to work. During the years 1973 and 1974, only four American aircraft were involved in skyjackings, none of which turned out to be successful in terms of getting the skyjacker flown to the desired destination (Civil Aeronautics Board, 1975).

The Psychological Autopsy

A third category of profiling is the **psychological autopsy,** which refers to a procedure that is done following a person's death in order to determine his or her mental state prior to the death. For instance, determining whether a death is due to the choking game (see Focus 3.2) or autoerotic participation or suicide is extremely important, especially for parents and other family members and friends. Some parents of young victims are often relieved to learn that their child's death was accidental rather than a suicide. In other cases, what appears to be a suicide might actually be a homicide.

The psychological autopsy was originally devised to assist certifying officials in clarifying deaths that were initially ambiguous, uncertain, or equivocal as to the *manner* of death (Shneidman, 1994a). The method was first used in 1958, when the Los Angeles medical examiner/coroner Theodore J. Murphy consulted Edwin S. Shneidman, Director of the L.A. Suicide Prevention Center, for assistance in determining the cause of an unusually high number of equivocal, or unexplained, deaths. Shneidman is generally credited with coining the term "psychological autopsy."

The postmortem psychological analysis is also called the **reconstructive psychological evaluation (RPE),** or **equivocal death analysis (EDA)** (Poythress, Otto, Darnes, & Starr, 1993), but the more common term is **psychological autopsy** (Brent, 1989; Ebert, 1987; Selkin, 1987). The EDA, or the equivocal death psychological autopsy (EDPA), is usually reserved for those investigations conducted by law enforcement officials, especially the FBI, who primarily examine the crime scene material and other information directly available to the police (Canter, 1999; Poythress et al., 1993). Psychological autopsies may also be important in determining insurance payments and national security issues (Ebert, 1987). Psychological autopsies differ from other forms of profiling in two important ways: (1) The profile is constructed on a dead person, and (2) the identity of the person is already known.

An *equivocal death* is one where the manner of death is unknown or undetermined, and it is believed that about 5 to 20% of all deaths are equivocal (Shneidman, 1981; T. J. Young, 1992). The term *manner* has special significance in any death investigation. Basically, "the manner of death refers to specific circumstances by which a death results" (La Fon, 2008, p. 420). There are five generally accepted manners of death: natural, accident, suicide, homicide, and undetermined (La Fon, 2008).

Today, the psychological autopsy is primarily undertaken in an effort to make a reasonable determination of what may have been in the mind of the deceased person leading up to and at the time of death—particularly if the death appears to be a suicide (see Focus 3.4). La Fon (2008) identifies two basic types of psychological autopsy: suicide psychological autopsy (SPA) and equivocal death psychological autopsy (EDPA). The goal of the SPA is to identify and understand the psychosocial factors that contributed to the suicide. The goal of the EDPA, on the other hand, is to clarify the mode of death and to determine the reasons for the death. Although the cause of death is generally clear, the manner (or mode) is often unclear (T. J. Young, 1992). For example, T. J. Young gives the example of a parachutist who falls to the ground from an altitude of 5,000 feet and dies as the result of multiple injuries. In this case, an investigator cannot immediately ascertain whether the parachute malfunctioned (accident), or whether the parachutist intentionally jumped with a bad parachute (suicide). Alternately, the parachute may have been tampered with by someone else (homicide), or the parachutist may have suffered a heart attack during the jump (natural).

In most instances, the psychological autopsy is done for insurance purposes. Although some insurance policies do compensate the family if the cause of death is determined to be suicide, many policies do not. Consequently, if the manner of death is equivocal, it is in the best financial interest of the insurance company to hire a forensic psychologist to do a complete psychological autopsy to determine whether the death was more likely the result of suicide or some other cause. The forensic psychologist would do this

> by looking at lifestyle, behavioral history, as well as the characterological elements that contribute to that history: the degree of ambivalence, the clarity of cognitive functioning, the amount of organization or obsession, the state of turmoil or agitation, and the amount of psychic pain. (Shneidman, 1994a, p. 76)

A vast majority of the psychological assessments to uncover a person's thoughts and feelings prior to their death have been done in the United States, usually in civil or criminal litigation (Canter, 1999). The procedure consists largely of conducting interviews with family members and people who knew the decedent; the examination of personal documents (suicide notes, diaries, and letters); and other materials, such as the autopsy by the medical examiner, other medical reports, and police reports. Forensic psychologists who develop psychological autopsies do their own interviews, conduct background investigations, and examine other pertinent information that they believe will contribute to a meaningful forensic report. It is crucial to realize, though, that psychological autopsies are subject to the same judicial scrutiny as other scientific methods. To be accepted as evidence in courts, these autopsies must pass the tests for reliability and validity, as will be discussed in some detail in Chapter 4. For that reason, many proponents of these autopsies emphasize the importance of standardizing the procedure (see Focus 3.4).

FOCUS 3.4. HOW A PSYCHOLOGICAL AUTOPSY IS PERFORMED

The psychological autopsy is a process constructed to identify and evaluate the behavior, thoughts, moods, and events that led up to and may have contributed to a person's death. The investigation usually requires interviews with family members, relatives, friends, acquaintances, supervisors, teachers, physicians, and coworkers. The investigator (usually a forensic psychologist or mental health professional) writes a comprehensive report detailing the relevant factors and significant events prior to the death. The report most often includes an opinion as to the mode or manner of death.

In gathering material for the report, the investigator researches the history of any known alcohol or substance abuse, mood or emotional changes, and potential psychological stressors. Medical, psychological/psychiatric, educational, military, and employment histories are scrutinized. If available, the coroner's report, the police report, and laboratory results (e.g., toxicological profile) are also utilized. Pre-death behaviors are also noted, such as paying up insurance policies, giving away important possessions, and arrangements for family and pets. E-mails, written notes, and recent books read all are typically examined. The quality and nature of relationships are probably most important to the assessment process, especially relationships with spouse, children, and other intimates in the person's life. This can be difficult to obtain, because those close to the deceased may be reluctant to provide information that would place the deceased or themselves in a negative light. Also, a careful attempt at reconstructing the events that occurred on the day before the death adds a critical piece of information.

There is, however, no *standard* for conducting such a procedure, so it is not unusual for the results of these autopsies to be disallowed in court proceedings. An impressive effort to propose a standard protocol, particularly in the case of suspected suicides, was made by Snider, Hane, and Berman (2006). Their protocol includes recommended documentation, site of death, demographics, recent symptoms and behaviors, precipitants to the death, psychiatric history, physical health, substance abuse, family history, firearm history, attachments and social supports, emotional reactivity, lifestyle and character, access to care, and other areas of inquiry.

According to La Fon (2008), the U.S. military is one of the major consumers of psychological autopsies: "Each branch of the Armed Forces, including the Navy, Army, and Air Force, have the task of conducting an EDPA for every equivocal death that occurs either on base property or to military personnel" (p. 422). Both civilian and military forensic psychologists conduct these autopsies, and they are conducted both in cases of equivocal death and suspected suicide. In most cases, the beneficiaries of the deceased military personnel receive remuneration regardless of the cause of death. Interestingly, there is indication that the suicide rate among military personnel during the wars in Iraq and Afghanistan has been higher than during any other war or occupation. Nevertheless, for some families, the cause of death is never firmly established, even when an official finding has been released. For example, in 2010, the family of an officer was told that her 2009 death on base was the result of a self-inflicted gunshot wound to her temple, a determination the family strongly challenged. They continued to pursue the case, insisting on a more extensive investigation by the military, which was done and which arrived at the same conclusion. Presumably, the military's investigation involved a psychological autopsy.

In legal contexts, the psychological autopsy is frequently conducted to reconstruct the possible reasons for a suicide and ultimately to establish legal culpability on the part of other persons or organizations. For example, if a police officer shoots himself on the steps of the state capitol building, the message he was trying to send to all those concerned may be unclear. Family members of the deceased, convinced the department had poor stress management techniques or nonexistent early detection procedures for identifying emotional problems in their officers, may sue the department for emotional and financial damages. Under these conditions, a mental health professional may be retained to do a reconstruction of the victim's mental state during and before the incident. Psychological autopsies have also been part of civil proceedings in the private sector, where it was necessary to ascertain whether certain events on the job affected the persons—such as various kinds of harassment by fellow workers or supervisors—or whether certain job-related accidents prompted the eventual suicide. Failure of the company or organization to have adequate policies and procedures in place for handling problems of this sort may be sufficient reason to find the company liable. As noted above, however, results of psychological autopsies are not always accepted as evidence in courts under the *Daubert* standard, which will be described in more detail in Chapter 4 (*Daubert v. Merrill Dow Pharmaceuticals, Inc.*, 1993).

Another purpose of psychological autopsy is to use it as a research tool to collect data that are likely to be useful in the prediction and prevention of suicide (T. J. Young, 1992). For example, research indicates that a majority of suicide victims communicate their intentions to at least one person before killing themselves. Many victims also leave suicide notes. Research also indicates that psychological autopsies can be of therapeutic value to survivors (Ebert, 1987; Henry & Greenfield, 2009).

_rogress has been made on determining the reliability and validity of the psychological still needs to be done, and even psychologists who conduct such autopsies are concerned their reliability and validity (Snider et al., 2006). Recent research indicates that the psycho- _ows considerable promise for determining suicide intentions of the deceased (Portzky, Aude- eringen, 2009). Of course, the quality of the psychological autopsy will depend significantly on _nowledge, experience, and clinical acumen of the investigator (J. L. Knoll, 2008). Poythress et al. er warn that

> persons who conduct reconstructive psychological evaluations should not assert categorical conclusions about the precise mental state or actions suspected of the actor at the time of his or her demise. The conclusions and inferences drawn in psychological reconstructions are, at best, informed speculations or theoretical formulations and should be labeled as such. (p. 12)

Ault, Hazelwood, and Reboussin (1994) posit that a psychological autopsy is an investigative technique that is ultimately "a professional opinion based on years of law enforcement experience with indirect assessment and violent death" (p. 73). Selkin (1994) argues that clear, definitive procedures for carrying out psychological autopsies have yet to be developed, and investigators have a long way to go before standardized methods for conducting the psychological autopsy are established. Others agree with the statement that no definitive standards have been developed but do feel that progress is being made toward a standardized procedure (J. L. Knoll, 2008, 2009; Snider et al., 2006; see Focus 3.4).

Poythress et al. (1993) make three recommendations for forensic psychologists to follow when doing psychological autopsies or equivocal death analyses. First, the use of these procedures and techniques should not be extended to non-death situations (such as burglary or kidnapping), at least until the reliability and validity of the methods are clearly established. Second, in legal and quasi-legal contexts, psychologists who conduct reconstructive psychological evaluations should not make conclusions about the *precise* mental state or actions suspected of the actor at the time of his or her demise. Third, psychologists, mental health professionals, and social scientists should be careful not to mislead consumers about the accuracy of conclusions drawn from these psychological reconstructions, unless the research data support such conclusions. Currently, the research data are inconclusive about the accuracy of such methods, and clearly more well-executed research needs to be undertaken before firm conclusions about the validity of psychological autopsies can be made. It should be emphasized, however, that efforts toward establishing an accepted standardized procedure for conducting the autopsy, as well as improving its reliability and validity, are presently being undertaken (J. L. Knoll, 2008, 2009; Snider et al., 2006).

Geographical Profiling and Mapping

Offending patterns often occur or cluster within certain geographical areas, such as a specific area of a city. There are two major ways these crime patterns may be analyzed: geographical profiling and geographical mapping. **Geographical profiling** refers to the analysis of geographical locations associated with the spatial movements of a *single* serial offender, whereas **geographical mapping** is concerned with analyzing the spatial patterns of crimes committed by numerous offenders over a period of time. We should emphasize, though, that both procedures may be used in tandem or together. In a sense, geographical mapping focuses on identifying the "hot spots" of certain types of crime. The procedure has been used in Europe since the first half of the 19th century and began to be used in the United States during the early 1900s. It continues today in more sophisticated fashion and is often demonstrated in popular law enforcement TV shows like *CSI*. It is not unusual for urban police departments to train some officers as geographical mappers or to hire someone who specializes in that task, either full-time or as a consultant. One version of such mapping is CompStat, a system of tracking crime and managing resources, that was pioneered in New York and is used in other major cities as well. Although some departments have credited this system with effecting a decrease in violent crime, it is not without controversy. A program that aired on National Public Radio's *This American Life* in late summer of 2010 highlighted abuses of that system by commanders in one precinct who ordered illegal arrests of citizens and downgraded the seriousness of some criminal offenses, making it appear that serious crime had decreased.

Geographical profiling—as opposed to mapping—focuses on the offender rather than the spatial patterns. In 1995, D. Kim Rossmo wrote a doctoral dissertation at Simon Frasier University's School of Criminology (Vancouver, British Columbia) on this method, which has become a promising tool for serial offender identification (cited in Bartol & Bartol, 2004). Rossmo, who became the detective inspector in charge of the Vancouver Police Department's Geographic Profiling Section, developed a computer program called *Criminal Geographic Targeting* (CGT). It is designed to analyze the geographical or spatial characteristics of a specific offender's crimes. Basically, the program creates a topographical map that assigns different statistical probabilities to various areas that seem to fall into the offender's "territory." The primary goal of the technique is to pinpoint the location of the offender's residence or base of operations. CGT takes into account known movement patterns, possible comfort zones, and hypothesized "hunting patterns" for victims of a specific offender.

Rossmo (1997) classifies the "hunting patterns" of the offenders into four groups: (1) hunter, (2) poacher, (3) troller, and (4) trapper. Some serial offenders tend to commit their crimes within a certain region and are therefore geographically stable. Others are more transient, moving from place to place. According to Rossmo, "Hunters are those criminals who specifically set out from their residence to look for victims, searching through the areas in their awareness spaces that they believe contain suitable targets" (p. 167). The crimes of the hunter tend to be geographically stable and often occur near the offender's place of residence or neighborhood. Poachers tend to be more transient, usually traveling some distance from their residence or neighborhood in search of their victims. Those in the third group, the trollers, are not specifically searching for victims but rather randomly encounter them during the course of some other activity. Offenders in the fourth group, the trappers, create situations to draw victims to themselves. "Trapping" may be accomplished through entertaining potential victims, placing want ads, taking in boarders, or assuming positions or occupations where potential victims come to them.

Rossmo (1997) recommends that geographical profiling be combined with criminal profiling for maximum effectiveness in developing probabilities for offender identification. In addition, he admonishes that geographical profiling is essentially an investigative tool that does not necessarily solve crimes but should help in the surveillance or monitoring of specific locations.

Psychological Profiling

As we noted earlier in the chapter, terms associated with profiling are often used interchangeably, and there is also plenty of overlap between different categories. It comes as no surprise, then, that psychological profiling is often called criminal profiling, crime scene profiling, or suspect-based profiling. As we use the term here, however, psychological profiling refers to gathering data on a *known individual* or individuals, such as by tests and interviews with that person or those who know him or her. For example, results of an MMPI-2 test or other screening measures may be part of that person's psychological profile. Likewise, a psychologist might obtain a psychological profile of a famous actor, political figure, or mass murderer based on data acquired in interviews or from case records and other documents. David Canter—whom we credited with coining the term *investigative psychology*—and his colleague Laurence Alison (2000) point out that psychological profiling is basically an offshoot of psychological testing and assessment procedures.

Psychological profiling was used by the U.S. Office of Strategic Services (OSS) during World War II in an effort to identify the tendencies and thought processes of Adolf Hitler (Ault & Reese, 1980). It is very likely, though, that the technique predated the OSS by several hundred years in earlier efforts to understand the thinking of kings and military leaders. Although psychological profiling is still used by military and intelligence organizations, today it is often used for identifying and predicting dangerous individuals in society, a procedure known as risk or threat assessment.

As defined in Chapter 2, *threat assessment* is a process to determine the credibility and seriousness of a threat and the likelihood that it will be carried out. Risk assessment is often used in evaluating "individuals who have violated social norms or displayed bizarre behavior, particularly when they appear menacing or unpredictable" (Hanson, 2009, p. 172). Both of these highly similar assessments are accomplished through various kinds of evaluation measures, observations, and interviews. In most instances, the agency or parties requesting the threat or risk assessment report want more than a statistical statement about the chances of a damaging or violent act occurring. They usually want an estimate of the potential consequences, and what can be done to reduce those chances (Hanson, 2009).

Risk and threat assessments involve predicting the likelihood that a specific individual will be dangerous or violent to others *at some point in time.* These assessments examine psychological risk factors that reveal a propensity for violence in threatening or potentially dangerous individuals. The assessment also tries to determine what specific situations or circumstances might have or will set the person off. For example, threat assessments are often used in predicting whether a student (or students) is dangerous to members within a school. Investigators of juvenile school shooters, for instance, have repeatedly found that two of the major precipitating events of the violence are peer rejection and being bullied. Similarly, workplace violence often occurs in reaction to a perceived injustice toward the offender.

Risk assessments are usually conducted on a regular basis in correctional institutions, a process that may focus on whether the individual is dangerous to him- or herself or others at the facility, or may be after he or she gets out into the community. Many instruments are used for this purpose. Among the most empirically valid are the Violence Risk Appraisal Guide (VRAG), Historical Clinical Risk-20 (HCR-20), the Level of Service Inventory—Revised (LSI-R), the Static-99, and the Sex Offender Risk Appraisal Guide (SORAG). Risk assessment methods to assess domestic violence have become increasingly valuable in recent years. Two of the more popular and well-researched instruments for this purpose are the Ontario Domestic Assault Risk Assessment (ODARA) and the Domestic Violence Risk Appraisal Guide (DVRAG) (see Hilton, Harris, & Rice, 2010).

As characteristic of all forms of profiling, risk and threat assessments involve judgments about uncertainty. While risk or threat assessments provide some statistical probability of occurrence, they are never certain. In addition, research has consistently demonstrated that common sense is not a reliable guide to what matters in these assessments (Hanson, 2009). For over 50 years, statistical models that rely on measurable, valid risk factors have been, in a majority of cases, superior to clinical judgment or professional opinion (Hanson, 2005, 2009; Meehl, 1954). Nevertheless, many clinicians today argue very persuasively that these instruments must be balanced with sound, clinical judgment developed through years of experience and training.

We will return to psychological profiling—particularly risk assessment—in the chapter on psychology and the courts (Chapter 4). Having reviewed various forms of profiling, it is important that we turn our attention briefly to psychological concepts relative to the prediction of human behavior. The ultimate goal of profiling is prediction. Psychologists have long been involved in the enterprise of behavioral prediction, with the assumption that if we can predict with reasonable accuracy, we can prevent and treat those behaviors that are most dangerous to society and to the individual. If we can predict that an individual will be violent, for example, we can take steps to prevent the violence, including offering treatment addressing the violent tendencies.

Unfortunately, as we saw in the earlier discussions of static and dynamic factors, predicting behavior is not easy or simple—and many psychologists today prefer to forego that enterprise entirely. Crime scene profiles, psychological autopsies, suspect-based profiling, geographical profiling, and psychological profiling all assume to a large extent that psychologists can predict (or postdict [after the fact]) human behavior. However, in past years, forensic evaluators were wrong twice as often as they were right in predicting crime and violence (Hanson, 2009). It may be that crime scene and geographical profilers are no more accurate, but there is no way to know for sure since currently the field lacks testable theory and empirical support (Lilienfeld & Landfield, 2008; Snook et al., 2008).

Problems With Profiling

Contemporary researchers on profiling (Alison, Bennell, Ormerod, & Mokros, 2002; Alison & Canter, 1999) identify two main flaws with the current state of profiling, particularly crime scene and geographical profiling. One is the assumption that human behavior is consistent across a variety of situations; the other is the assumption that offense style or crime scene evidence is related to specific psychological characteristics. The second point refers to the tendency of profilers to believe that specific clues gathered at the crime scene (such as signatures) reveal certain generalizable psychological characteristics and thought patterns of certain types of offenders.

Alison et al. (2002) further assert that

(a) most current profiling methods rely on a naïve and outdated understanding of personality and the trait approach; (b) global traits, or broad personality types, are unlikely to be useful in predicting criminal behavior; (c) it is unlikely that the classification of offenders into broad personality types would enable the profiler to relate clusters of sociodemographic characteristics to different types; (d) a theoretical framework that emphasizes the importance of Person × Situation interactions in generating behavior may lead to a more productive research endeavor; (e) profiling should be used with extreme caution in criminal investigations, and not at all as evidence in court, until research demonstrates its predictive validity. (p. 116)

The above points underscore the observation that many professional profilers, especially those who rely on crime scene information, tend to rely on unsubstantiated assumptions about personality theory, the power of that personality or disposition to virtually override the influence of all situations, and the validity and accuracy of the profiling process itself. They rely too heavily on "gut feelings," believing they have special knowledge to put the pieces of the puzzle together, and too little on science.

The tendency to rely heavily or exclusively on gut feelings, intuition, hunches, subjective experiences, or whatever nonscientific approaches a profiler may take in forming his or her opinion puts offender profiling in serious jeopardy in the eyes of the court. Courts in the United States, Canada, Australia, and the United Kingdom are requiring criminal profiling to meet a rigorous standard in order to be admitted as valid scientific evidence in the courtroom (see, generally, Bosco, Zappalà, & Santtila, 2010, for a review of this important issue). For example, profiling has never been admissible in the British legal system as expert evidence because of its lack of established reliability and validity (Gregory, 2005). The standards that the courts in the U.S. are following are the *Daubert* standard and the Federal Rules of Evidence (FRE), to be discussed in more detail in Chapter 4.

A common error by profilers is the failure to consider the power of the situation to influence behavior. And remember, part of the situation is the victim and all the characteristics brought to the incident by that individual or individuals. As noted by Jenkins (1993), "The failure to consider victim-oriented factors often leads researchers to misunderstand the nature of such activity" (p. 462). The lack of a victimology perspective generates confusion and often leads to further flaws in the development of offender profiles. Jenkins strongly asserts that an overlooked tool available to profilers is examining characteristics of the victim because "offenders and victim comprise a common and interdependent ecology" (p. 463). Cromwell, Olson, and Avary (1991) also discuss the importance of the victim perspective in their study of burglary. Cromwell and his colleagues contend that the activities of the victim play a critical role in how burglars pick a home to burglarize, how they enter, and how long they remain. Cromwell et al. believe that "most burglaries in the jurisdictions studied appeared to result from a propitious juxtaposition of target, offender, and situations" (p. 47).

Profiling is ultimately based on the assumption that human behavior is consistent across time **(trans-temporal consistency)** and place **(trans-situational consistency)**. The profile process, by its very nature, presupposes that crime scene clues provide the skillful investigator with clues of the perpetrator's personality traits, habits, and even thought processes. Furthermore, there is an assumption that key factors of the personality identified at the crime scene should generalize to other situations, including future crimes.

The ability to predict the behavior and tendencies of individuals across different situations (trans-situational consistency) is very much open to debate. For example, some researchers (e.g., Mischel, 1968; Mischel & Peake, 1982) argue that human behavior across different situations is inconsistent and that notions of stable behavioral dispositions or personality traits are largely unsupported. Research by Merry and Harsent (2000) cogently illustrates that most criminal behavior, such as burglary, changes as the dynamics of the situation change. Consequently, crime scene activity is likely to be different from crime to crime. Although trans-situational consistency remains highly questionable, consistency across time, or temporal consistency, is acknowledged. As long as situations are similar, people will likely respond the same way over their life spans. But when situations change, behavior is apt to change. Therefore, criminal behavior that has been reinforced in a particular context is more apt to recur in a similar context than across a wide variety of different settings. A person who had engaged in a lifetime of burglary, for instance, is more likely to burglarize again if surrounded by similar psychosocial situations that have a perceived reward value. Therefore, there is trans-temporal consistency in behavior if the perceived situation is the same. On the other hand, if his or her environment has changed substantially (e.g., long-time partner in crime has died, or the person has aged to the point where physical agility has substantially deteriorated), the burglarizing is less likely to continue.

Mischel and Peake (1982) conclude, on the basis of their research findings, that behavior is highly dependent on the nature of the situation and that humans discriminate between situations and respond accordingly. Can we expect a shy child to be socially withdrawn on *all* occasions—even with family? He or she may be shy when meeting strangers (trans-situational consistency) but not shy in familiar, family gatherings. Consider the typical skyjacker profile, identified by Dailey and Pickrel (1975a) and discussed in Focus 3.3. Lacking resourcefulness and having feelings of helplessness are examples of mood states and behavioral patterns that may well *not* have trans-situational consistency. In fact, Hanson and Harris (2000) would call these acute dynamic risk factors, which are highly changeable. Although research by Bem and Allen (1974) and Kenrick and Springfield (1980) does suggest that *some* behaviors are consistent across both time and place, it is clear that *most* are not.

Trans-situational consistency is a critical issue in the formulation of any classification system or profile system, but we have seen that it is risky to assume it exists. Yet belief in "personality profiles" persists, not only with respect to criminal behavior but also in areas involving employment screening. Thus, a company may want to know what type of person makes the best salesperson, or a law enforcement agency may want to know who from a pool of applicants will make the best officer.

The intricate interaction of personality and situation creates problems for profilers. Personality research and theory building, 20 or 30 years ago, emphasized the person to the exclusion of the situation. It was assumed that personality structures and traits were the center and driving force of all human behavior. Once these attributes were delineated, accurate prediction was almost guaranteed. In this sense, to say an individual had an aggressive personality was to infer a corresponding list of behaviors, most of them negative. As we have noted, however, the situation and the meaning of that situation for the person are crucial variables. Rather than relying on a global conclusion that an officer has an "aggressive personality," an agency would do well to try to determine how the officer handles himself or herself in various situations. When someone is described as aggressive, it does not mean he or she is aggressive all the time and across all situations. "It means [he or she is] more likely than other people to be aggressive in certain circumstances" (Hanson, 2009, p. 177).

The above discussion emphasizes that accurate assessment and prediction require not only an evaluation of the person, but also an evaluation of the psychosocial environment within which the behaviors we are trying to predict occur. Failure to consider the context of the behavior is destined to produce disappointing results.

Suspect-Based Profiling Limitations

In addition to the limitations mentioned above on crime scene and geographical profiling, suspect-based profiling is (or should be) a nomothetic enterprise in that it tries to make *general* predictions about offenders based on clusters of data gathered from previous offenders. A **nomothetic approach** refers to the search for general principles, relationships, and patterns by examining and combining data from *many* individuals. Research psychology is largely nomothetic as opposed to idiographic in scope. The **idiographic approach** emphasizes the intensive study of *one* individual, usually called the case study. A case study of the coping behaviors of an individual or the biography of a famous person is an example of the idiographic approach.

Unfortunately, some profilers take the idiographic approach rather than the nomothetic and consequently are in danger of missing the mark; this is especially so if taking the nomothetic approach would emphasize situational variables. For example, data gathered on many offenders might reveal that the late-afternoon hours are a prime time for burglaries in a particular geographical area, yet a certain clinician might have had four burglars on her caseload over several years of personal experience in dealing with offenders, each of whom committed the crime in the early morning hours. She might then infer that early morning hours are the time most burglaries will likely occur. Too many profilers and clinicians prefer exclusive use of the idiographic approach, even though research has continually revealed that predictions based on statistical probability, calculated from research on clusters of offenders under various conditions, are far more accurate. Predictions based on statistical probability and data are called **actuarial predictions,** as opposed to **clinical predictions** which are based on subjective experience.

On the other hand, there are serious problems with singling out individuals from group data, so actuarial predictions have their own shortcomings. For example, if data have revealed that an ethnic, religious, or minority group is overrepresented in the commission of a specific type of crime, then there will be a strong tendency for investigators to focus on members of that group when a crime of that type is committed or is threatened to be committed.

Psychological Autopsy Limitations

As described earlier, the conclusions and inferences drawn from psychological autopsies are far too often informed speculations that lack standardized protocol backed by systematic research. In addition, considerable systematic research needs to be conducted for establishing the reliability and validity of psychological autopsies. However, as mentioned, strides are being made in that direction as researchers are suggesting standard protocols.

Psychological Profiling Limitations

Psychological profiling has many of the same limitations as the other forms of profiling, but considerable progress has been made in this area during the past 25 years (Hanson, 2005, 2009). Research on the predictive accuracy of current risk and threat assessment instruments is extremely robust. Most of these instruments demonstrate levels of predictive accuracy superior to that of professional opinion (Hanson, 2009). This is because the instruments are largely based on actuarial prediction rather than strictly on clinical prediction. Nonetheless, actuarial prediction combined with structured clinical judgment is a worthy approach.

Overall Limitations

There are other general problems with profiling, in addition to those mentioned above. Some recent studies indicate that a large proportion of the conclusions and predictions contained within profile reports are both ambiguous and unverifiable (Alison, Smith, Eastman, & Rainbow, 2003; Alison, Smith, & Morgan, 2003). That is to say, statements are so vague that they are open to a wide range of interpretations. For example, what does it mean that someone is "a loner" or "goes to church regularly"?

Moreover, there seems to be a tendency for some police investigators to "creatively interpret" the ambiguous information contained within profiles to fit their own biases about the case or the suspect. They select those aspects of the profile that they perceive as fitting the suspect while ignoring the many conclusions and predictions that do not seem to fit.

> If a suspect does arise during the investigation, officers may wish to actively ignore the information that does not fit the suspect, or perhaps unwittingly exaggerate the merits of the information that might fit and not appreciate the extent to which the information could fit a wide range of individuals (Alison, Smith, et al., 2003, p. 193).

The strong preference to have one's views confirmed is known as **confirmation bias.** "When it operates, it places us in a kind of closed cognitive system in which only evidence that confirms our existing views and beliefs gets inside; other information is sometimes noticed but is quickly rejected as false" (Baron & Byrne, 2000, p. 8). In short, confirmation bias is the tendency to notice and remember information that lends support to our views on something, such as a suspect. It is a tendency that might be prevalent not only in the subjective interpretations of a profile but also in its creation.

Although there are many flaws in current profiling methods, if conducted appropriately, profiling could have a promising and extremely useful future. Despite the concerns of many critics, some psychologists who engage in this practice defend it vigorously (see, e.g., Dern, Dern, Horn, & Horn, 2009). If profilers take into account the interaction between the person and the situations (and the influence of the victim), the science of profiling can lead to more accurate and helpful sketches of the offender. In addition, profilers should be cautious about relying exclusively on trait theory and rely more on contemporary psychological theory and research on human behavior. They should look for the conditional probability of certain behaviors occurring under certain situations instead of assuming that behavior remains consistent across all situations. All of this will require greater reliance on and involvement in well-executed scientific research.

The Polygraph

The main character in the television show *Lie to Me* is depicted as a psychologist who is invariably able to detect lying in suspects and other individuals, primarily through their nonverbal behaviors. Once again, the media portrayal does not mesh with reality. Most forensic psychologists would be far more modest about these abilities; although some behaviors suggest that an individual is not telling the truth, there is no sure way to ascertain this. Licking one's lips may indicate nothing more than the fact that one is nervous or thirsty; and it is not unusual to be nervous if one is being interviewed or questioned by law enforcement officials.

A more scientific method of attempting to detect truthfulness is the polygraph, commonly called the "lie detector." It is important to stress, though, that the polygraph does not really detect lies or deception, but only the neurophysiological responses that accompany emotional reactions to guilt, shame, and anxiety. The instrument usually records heart rate, blood pressure, breathing rate, and skin conductance. *Skin conductance* refers to how well the skin conducts a small, imperceptible electrical current that is affected by slight changes in perspiration. Presumably, when one tries to deceive, there are telltale bodily or physiological reactions that can be measured with sophisticated equipment and detected by a trained examiner called a polygrapher. In addition to observing the physiological measures, the skillful polygrapher makes behavioral observations and notations to infer truth or deception in the subject being examined (see Photo 3.1 depicting a polygrapher administering a polygraph test). There is little doubt that the polygraph can accurately measure and record the physiological responses of the peripheral nervous system. Whether it can detect actual lying and deception is another matter. As William Iacono (2008), one of the foremost researchers in this area, notes, "It is generally recognized that there is no physiological response that is uniquely associated with lying" (p. 1295).

A Brief History of the Polygraph

The modern polygraph has been used in some form for nearly a century, and much cruder versions of its components existed as far back as 300 B.C. (Trovillo, 1939). The Bedouins of Arabia, for example, required those making conflicting statements to lick a hot iron. The one whose tongue was not burned was considered truthful (B. M. Smith, 1967). The ancient Chinese required suspects to

Photo 3.1   A polygrapher administers a polygraph test to a subject.

put rice powder in their mouths and then spit it out (B. M. Smith, 1967). If the powder was dry, the individual was lying. The common principle underlying these and other similar methods used throughout history is that the tense, nervous person (the one who is lying) has less saliva (dry mouth and tongue) and thus is more likely to have his or her tongue burned, spit drier rice powder, or even be less able to swallow the "trial slice" of bread, as practiced centuries ago in England.

The idea of lie detection caught on rapidly in the United States during the 1920s and 1930s after John Larson was asked by the chief of police in Berkeley, California, to develop a "lie detector" to solve a case under investigation (Barland & Raskin, 1973). This instrument, according to Barland (1988), became "the first true polygraph used for lie-detection purposes" (p. 75). A number of well-publicized successes by Larson and one of his students, Leonarde Keeler, catapulted the polygraph into the limelight. Eventually, Keeler began to teach a 2-week course for police and military examiners, which soon developed into a 6-week course (Barland, 1988; Keeler, 1984). The increasing demand for polygraph examiners resulted in the formation of at least 30 polygraph schools across the United States (Barland, 1988).

Current Usage of the Polygraph

During its early beginnings in the United States, the polygraph was used almost exclusively in criminal investigations. However, as criminal suspects became more aware of their right not to incriminate themselves, and as civil libertarians challenged the instrument's validity, the use of the polygraph has become less common. Furthermore, the U.S. Congress severely limited the extent to which *private* employers can use the polygraph with the passage of the **Employee Polygraph Protection Act,** enacted in 1988. This law has, in effect, ended preemployment polygraphic screening by *private* employers as well as the periodic testing of employees to verify their good behavior (Iacono & Patrick, 1999). We still see examples of suspects volunteering to take a polygraph to clear their names or the polygraph used in counterintelligence investigations. Polygraph evidence can be admitted in a criminal hearing or trial, but only if the defense introduces it; the defendant cannot be forced to take a polygraph (*U.S. v. Piccinonna,* 1989). For the most part, however, its major uses are in personnel selection or screening by *government* agencies and certain strategic industries, such as nuclear energy.

U.S. governmental counterintelligence polygraph tests far outnumber the tests given at other organizations or all other agencies (Krapohl, 2002). Meesig and Horvath (1995) report that approximately 99% of the large police agencies and 95% of the small police departments in the United States require the polygraph as an integral and indispensable part of their preemployment screening procedures. Furthermore, polygraph screening of police, law enforcement, or governmental security applicants has either remained the same or increased in recent years.

Currently, a variety of private and government-sponsored polygraphy schools are in operation, almost all of which are accredited by the American Polygraphy Association. The American Association of Police Polygraphists also provides a list of 22 recognized schools on their website (policepolygraph.org/polyschools.htm). For many years, the most prestigious and intensive school has been the one operated by the Department of Defense (the Department of Defense Polygraph Institute, or DoDPI). The Department of Defense has traditionally been responsible for the training of all polygraphers employed by federal agencies, with the exception of the CIA, as well as polygraphers employed by many local and state agencies.

On January 25, 2007, the Department of Defense issued a new directive governing polygraphy policy, which changed the name DoDPI to the Defense Academy for Credibility Assessment (DACA). The DACA is currently under the operational control of the U.S. Defense Intelligence Agency. This change in name reflects a shift from exclusive use of the usual polygraph to including non-polygraph techniques for detecting deception, such as thermal imagery, to be discussed below. The directive also established the Psychophysiological Detection of Deception (PDD) Program, which is a 520-hour curriculum of courses designed to prepare an individual for a polygraph career in law enforcement or counterintelligence.

The typical polygraph examiner in the United States today does not have graduate psychological or research training, nor are all polygraph examiners licensed or graduates of accredited schools. In addition, the profession has "almost no input or oversight from psychology" (Iacono & Patrick, 1999, p. 467). On the other hand, many individual psychologists obtain polygraph training and become accredited polygraphers.

Many polygraph examiners also have shifted to computerization—called computerized polygraph systems (CPS)—to replace the conventional chart or graph method. Physiological data are stored digitally and are plotted with a printer. Software enables the computer to provide a probability statement as to the likelihood that a person was truthful when responding (Iacono & Patrick, 1999).

Traditional Procedures Used by Polygraphers

Polygraphers use several polygraph techniques or approaches to determine deception or truthfulness during the examination. The basic approach is to compare physiological reactions to different types of questions. The most commonly used procedure for lie detection in criminal investigations and forensic settings is the **control question technique (CQT),** developed by John Reid (Bashore & Rapp, 1993; R. E. Reid & Inbau, 1977). The CQT was renamed the **comparison question technique** in 1999 (Iacono, 2008). The most commonly used procedure for detection in *preemployment* screening is the **relevant/irrelevant question technique,** developed by

J. A. Larson (1932). The other two less popular techniques are the **directed lie test** and the **guilty knowledge test (GKT)**. The CQT is, by far, the procedure most preferred by professional polygraphers in forensic situations in the United States and Canada (Ben-Shakhar, 2002). However, its use has been seriously questioned (Iacono & Patrick, 2006) even though it has been used and researched for more than 60 years. According to Iacono and Patrick, "the CQT has little more than chance accuracy with innocent people and can be easily defeated by guilty people by deliberately augmenting responses to control questions." (p. 584). Because of its extensive use, we will briefly review how the typical CQT is administered.

Although there are many variants of the CQT approach, it is fundamentally based on three types of questions: (1) irrelevant or neutral questions, (2) relevant questions, and (3) control or comparison questions. Irrelevant questions are those posed about neutral topics and information, such as date of birth, name, age, birthplace, mother's maiden name, or education. They usually are asked at the beginning and end of the examination, but they also may be interspersed between other questions to bring the individual down to a normal physiological baseline following questions that elicit emotional reactions.

The relevant question probes whether the subject committed the offense that is under investigation—for example, "On December 20th, did you enter the home of Simpson O'Brien?" It is recommended that emotionally laden words not be employed, since the subject may react more to the words than the question itself.

The control or comparison question is based on a known or assumed lie. In forensic cases, this question probes the integrity of a subject by asking about possible past misbehaviors—for example, "Have you ever lied to a person of authority?" or "Have you ever committed a sexual act you were ashamed of?" Consequently, the CQT is sometimes called the "probable lie test" because it assumes the questions are likely to elicit lies (Iacono, 2008).

The assumption is that innocent people will respond more strongly to the comparison or control question than the relevant question. By contrast, guilty people are expected to respond more strongly to relevant questions directly related to details about the crime. Most examinations result in conclusions of either deception or non-deception (Iacono, 2008). Again we must emphasize that criminal suspects cannot be forced to take a polygraph; however, some may be encouraged to take one voluntarily to clear their names—and may then find that their results are used against them: "You flunked the polygraph. Now let's make a deal." On the other hand, some jurisdictions require convicted offenders on probation or parole to take polygraphs as a condition of their continued freedom in the community. We will discuss this further below.

Critics of traditional polygraph procedures have argued that the fundamental assumptions on which they are based are flawed and that there is essentially no sound scientific support for their validity (Bashore & Rapp, 1993). These critics believe that these frequently used procedures have not been subjected to rigorous scientific investigation and that the claims of their validity by their proponents are largely based on subjective evaluations. Today, the polygraph continues to be a highly controversial topic on philosophical, legal, theoretical, scientific, and ethical grounds. In a survey of scientists knowledgeable about the polygraph, Iacono and Lykken (1997) found that a majority of the respondents

> believed that polygraphic lie detection is not theoretically sound, claims of high validity for these procedures cannot be sustained, the lie test can be beaten by easily learned countermeasures, and polygraph test results should not be admitted into evidence in courts of law. (p. 462)

Despite the controversy—and as mentioned above—polygraphs continue to be used in a wide variety of governmental contexts, including criminal investigations, counterintelligence and national security screening, and civil litigation and post-conviction assessments. The last category includes situations in which the polygraph is used with sex offenders to detect deception in an effort to control recidivism. For example, one survey revealed that 35 states were using polygraph testing for monitoring convicted sex offenders (Consigli, 2002).

Countermeasures

Countermeasures are anything that an examinee might do to "fool" the polygraph and the examiner (Bartol & Bartol, 2004). Many types of countermeasures are possible, but most fall into the categories of physical, mental, drugs, hypnosis, or biofeedback, which allows the individual who has learned it to control his or her autonomic body functions, such as heart rate or skin conductance. The most common physical countermeasures are either pain or muscle tension. For example, in an effort to deceive the polygrapher, biting one's lip or tongue or subtly jabbing oneself with a pin may induce enough pain to promote a physiological response that masks the subject's response to questions from the polygrapher.

Available research suggests that mental countermeasures may be as effective in deceiving the polygraph as physical ones (Ben-Shakhar & Dolev, 1996; Honts, Devitt, Winbush, & Kircher, 1996). Mental countermeasures include any deliberate attempt by an examinee to alter his or her thought patterns during the polygraph test to deceive the polygrapher. Examples would include counting backwards from 100, thinking of a sexually arousing scene, imagining walking one's dog on a beautiful spring morning, or thinking of a very peaceful scene (such as canoeing on a moonlit lake on a summer evening). Any thought that either minimizes the emotional impact of relevant questions or increases physiological arousal across all questions qualifies as a mental countermeasure. Although physical countermeasures are often detectable by experienced polygraphers, mental countermeasures are far more difficult to detect (Ben-Shakhar, 2002).

It should be emphasized, however, that research indicates that spontaneous countermeasures in which the examinee tries to influence the outcome of the polygraph without forethought, planning, or training are largely ineffective (Honts & Amato, 2002). Untrained respondents who use physical, behavioral, and cognitive measures to deceive the polygrapher are rarely successful, although as mentioned above, Iacono and Patrick (2006) note that the CQT can be defeated by those who are guilty. In addition, there is very little evidence that drugs—sometimes referred to as "general state countermeasures" because they influence the entire neurophysiological system—can be used as an effective countermeasure to polygraph testing (Honts, 1987; Honts & Amato, 2002), and this includes alcohol (Honts & Perry, 1992). Hypnosis has also been tried as a countermeasure. The primary strategy in the use of hypnosis as a countermeasure is to induce a form of amnesia for the behavior in question. However, there is no evidence to date that hypnosis is an effective countermeasure in untrained respondents either (Gudjonsson, 1988).

An important issue concerning the use of the polygraph in criminal investigations is its accuracy with psychopaths, who are portrayed as skilled liars and manipulators with a limited capacity for anxiety or guilt (Patrick & Iacono, 1989). The possibility that psychopaths might be able to beat the polygraph is a concern because most of the research reveals that psychopaths—who will be discussed in detail in Chapter 7—constitute a sizable proportion of violent and repetitive offenders. Although the evidence on the issue remains unclear, some preliminary data from Patrick and Iacono suggest that under certain conditions, guilty psychopaths can be detected at about the same rate as guilty non-psychopaths.

Although individuals are not likely to beat the polygraph on their own, training in physical and mental countermeasures *may* be effective (Ben-Shakhar, 2002; Krapohl, 2002). Charles Honts and his research group (Honts, Hodes, & Raskin, 1985; Honts, Raskin, & Kircher, 1987) report that a significant proportion of highly motivated respondents can be trained to beat polygraph tests. The possibility of effective countermeasures is especially pertinent when the polygraph is used for espionage purposes. Spies and intelligence agents are probably well trained and largely effective in the use of countermeasures for defeating polygraph results.

Honts and Amato (2002) report that scientific studies examining the effects of countermeasure training on the polygraphic results will be very limited in the foreseeable future, however. This is partly due to the fact that research on countermeasures is difficult to conduct unless one has access to considerable resources and governmental financial support. Since the beginning of the 1990s, polygraphic research in the United States has been centered at the DACA (Honts & Amato, 2002). Currently, the DACA has a policy that all countermeasures research on the polygraph will be classified and not open to the scientific community or the general public. Apparently, the federal government is concerned that current employees or future applicants to governmental jobs might learn how to effectively control the results of the polygraph.

Research on the Polygraph

Many researchers continue to be very wary of the polygraph and its overall accuracy. Historically, professional field polygraphers have claimed extraordinary accuracy rates, ranging from 92 to 100% (Bartol & Bartol, 2004). Most biopsychologists and research psychologists find these statistics to be highly questionable. In addition to occasional arithmetic errors, none of the published reports gave any details of the methods and procedures used or of the criteria used to decide accuracy rates. Currently, the research conducted under laboratory or controlled conditions indicates that the correct classification of truthful and deceptive examinees ranges between 70 and 80% (Krapohl, 2002). However, the accuracy can be increased slightly through careful and intensive training of the examiner. Furthermore, in lab studies, computerized polygraph systems, in contrast to human evaluations, are slightly more accurate for detecting both innocent and deceptive respondents (Kircher & Raskin, 2002). Although there have been numerous polygraphic research studies conducted under realistic or field conditions, they are subject to debate, largely because their quality is low (National Research Council, 2003).

The accuracy of the polygraph in detecting who is telling the truth and who is being deceptive is a highly complicated issue.

> A number of factors—such as the specific technique used, the nature of the population tested, the issues to be resolved, the context of the examination, whether one is trying to detect truth or deception, the training of the examiner, what cues the examiner considers besides the polygraphic data, or even whether one is examining the victim or the suspect—all must be carefully considered before any tentative conclusions can be advanced. (Bartol & Bartol, 2004, p. 285)

Many professional polygraphers believe that the polygraph may be more accurate with criminal suspects than with victims (Barland, 1988). Many of these polygraphers also believe that people who have committed property crimes (theft, burglary) are more difficult to detect than those who have committed violent crimes, such as physical or sexual assault, robbery, or murder, primarily because the amount of emotional baggage is usually higher for the latter than for the former (F. S. Horvath, 1977). The polygraph is also believed to be more accurate when a suspect denies having physically committed a specific, illegal act and less accurate when the suspect admits the act but denies criminal intent (Barland, 1988). In other words, it is more difficult to determine what a person was thinking than what a person actually did.

In recent years, there has been growing interest in the use of the polygraph in the supervision and treatment of sex offenders (Grubin, 2002, 2008; Iacono & Patrick, 2006). It is believed that the polygraph—compared with case records or offender self-reports—provides more complete and accurate information about an offender's history, sexual interests, and offense behavior, thereby enabling more effective and targeted treatment strategies (Grubin, 2008). Some mental health and criminal justice professionals also think the polygraph is helpful in monitoring behavior and achieving adherence to prevention goals. One survey estimated that in the United States, polygraph examinations were used with 70% of community sex offenders in 2002 (McGrath, Cumming, & Burchard, 2003). In England, legislation was passed in 2007 that mandated polygraphic testing of sex offenders by the probation service on a trial basis (Ben-Shakhar, 2008; Grubin, 2008).

The use of polygraph testing for offenders has been criticized, however. As pointed out by Grubin (2008)—as well as the British Psychological Society (2004)—the criticism has centered on three main issues: (1) concerns regarding how the polygraphic examinations are conducted, (2) the lack of scientific validity of the procedure, and (3) ethical concerns. Ben-Shakhar (2008) asserts that there are many major flaws in the reliability as well as other scientific shortcomings in polygraph examinations of sex offenders. Some forensic clinicians, however, continue to argue that the polygraph is highly useful in the management and treatment of convicted sex offenders.

Thermal Imaging

Another promising area in lie detection is thermal imaging, a procedure that "focuses on the use of a mid-level infrared thermal camera which looks at the spectrum of body heat based on changes in facial blood flow" (Capps & Ryan, 2005, p. 9). Current research is seeking to determine if discernible changes in facial blood flow may be a reliable indicator of deception. The research focuses on peripheral nervous system functioning.

More recent research on lie detection focuses on neural activation in areas of the brain that process personally relevant, emotionally arousing information (B. G. Bell & Grubin, 2010). One way to measure this activation is by doing an MRI scan of the brain. The procedure is called functional magnetic resonance imaging (fMRI). The reliability, safety, and availability of fMRI have prompted attempts to use it for lie detection (Langleben, 2008). Increased activation in certain areas of the brain during lies has been observed in most fMRI studies of deception (Kozel et al., 2005; Langleben, 2008; Lee et al., 2002). However, the accuracy of fMRI-based lie detection appears to vary with the type of questions asked, countermeasures, and other unexplored variables (Langleben, 2008).

Functional brain imaging is a new development and awaits much more research before any conclusions can be advanced concerning its usefulness in the detection of deception. The brain processes underlying deception are not well understood (Iacono, 2007). Consequently, this emerging new area will unlikely become available as a reliable and valid tool in determining deception anytime soon (Iacono, 2008).

Forensic Hypnosis

Compared with efforts to detect deception, efforts to obtain information by means of hypnosis are quite rare. Nevertheless, they do occur, but typically more with victims of crimes than with suspects. For example, a victim of an aggravated assault who seems to have "blocked out" the appearance of his or her assailant might be hypnotized in an effort to help the victim recall features that would help in identifying the perpetrator. However, this is a procedure that should be used only by highly trained and properly credentialed professionals.

In hypnosis, a mental health, general health, or forensic professional suggests to a person that he or she try to experience particular changes in sensations, perceptions, thoughts, and behavior. Hypnosis is usually established by what is commonly referred to as an *induction procedure*. Although there are many different induction procedures, most center on suggestions for relaxation, calmness, and well-being. Induction instructions usually include asking the participant to imagine or think about pleasant experiences or things. During the induction, the participant may be sitting comfortably or lying down while concentrating on a "target" (such as a lit candle) while listening to the hypnotist's voice. The participant is usually encouraged to drift into a sleep-like state while always hearing the hypnotist's voice. Overall, most people find the experience very pleasant and relaxing.

People differ widely in their responses and susceptibility to hypnosis. "Some people respond to almost all suggestions, some respond to a few or none, and most respond to some suggestions but not others" (Braffman & Kirsch, 1999, p. 578). The ability to be hypnotized is believed to be an enduring and stable attribute, which peaks during the life cycle in late childhood and declines gradually thereafter (Spiegel & Spiegel, 1987). Among the factors that are important in inducing hypnosis are the following: (1) the level of trust the participant has in the hypnotist, (2) the participant's motivation and desire to cooperate, (3) preconceived notions the participant has about hypnosis, and (4) the context and reasons for the hypnosis (e.g., entertainment or critical information gathering). Trust, motivation, a strong belief in hypnotism's powers, and a serious context (such as a criminal investigation) inspire most people to become hypnotized, but this does not mean that they will accurately recall events. Apparently, what distinguishes truly being hypnotized from simple behavioral compliance is the person's ability to experience suggested alterations in perception, memory, and mood (Orne, Whitehouse, Dinges, & Orne, 1988).

A person's ability to experience hypnotic suggestions is most often inhibited by fears and concerns arising from some common misconceptions. Contrary to some depictions of hypnosis in books, movies, or on television, people who have been hypnotized do not lose control over their behavior. Furthermore, "(t)he general opinion among researchers is that participants are capable of lying when hypnotized" (Wagstaff, 2008, p. 1284). Hypnotized individuals remain aware of who and where they are, and unless some form of temporary forgetfulness is specifically suggested, they usually remember what transpired during the hypnosis. It has long been known that all the experiences and responses that are elicited during hypnosis can also be produced in a normal state without hypnotic induction (Braffman & Kirsch, 1999). Hypnosis does, however, increase suggestibility. As noted by Braffman and Kirsch, "The only thing which characterizes hypnosis as such and which gives any justification for calling it a 'state' is its generalized hypersuggestibility" (p. 578). The hypersuggestibility aspect, however, is the one feature that is most troubling to forensic investigators and researchers concerned with recollections of witnesses or victims of crime incidents. In fact, "[t]he subject's willingness to accept fantasy as reality during the hypnotic experience, together with the often dramatic vividness of recollections in hypnosis, may inspire great confidence that the recalled material is true to fact" (Orne et al., 1988, p. 25). This *induced* confidence, for example, may soundly convince the witness that his or her ambiguous view of the offender was much clearer than it really was.

Hypnosis has long been used in a variety of ways: as a form of entertainment (getting some people in an audience to do humorous things, presumably without their awareness), as a method to encourage people to give up smoking or lose weight, as a procedure in several branches of medicine for pain reduction, and as a means of enhancing the memory of eyewitnesses and victims in the criminal justice system. A common belief among some practitioners is that hypnosis can exhume long-forgotten or buried memories, such as repressed memories of sexual abuse. This belief has frequently been bolstered by anecdotal or clinical claims describing cases in which previously inaccessible memories have been brought to light by the mysterious hypnotic trance. Enhancement or revival of memory through hypnosis is known as **hypnotic hypermnesia.** Enhancement or recovery of memory through *nonhypnotic* methods, such as free association, fantasy, or recall technique, is called **nonhypnotic hypermnesia.**

Despite its long and varied history, precisely how hypnosis works remains a mystery, nor do we understand why some persons are readily susceptible to its influence but others are impervious. We do know that hypnosis seems to have little significant biological changes on bodily functioning other than those that occur in normal relaxation. We know also that hypnosis is not the same as sleep or a form of sleepwalking. But we know little more than this.

Currently, two major theoretical perspectives have been proposed for explaining the mechanisms behind its effects. One perspective, known as the **hypnotic trance theory,** assumes that hypnosis represents a *special state of consciousness* that promotes a high level of suggestibility and changes in bodily experiences. Under this special state of consciousness, the theory maintains, the hypnotized person may be able to do things that he or she could not do under a normal state of consciousness. For example, the person might regress to childhood and vividly remember or act out events that have been repressed or put out of consciousness for an extended period of time. While in the trance, participants may be instructed to feel little or no pain or to perform acts that they are unable to do when not hypnotized. The hypnotic trance theory holds that individuals can be instructed or trained to sense, feel, smell, see, or hear things that are not possible during normal consciousness.

For some individuals, hypnosis can substantially improve their ability to remember things. Generally, trance theory contends that the deeper the "hypnotic trance," the more intense, detailed, and vivid a scene becomes to the participant. Historically, the most influential perspective on hypnotic trance theory was from Ernest Hilgard (1986). The research evidence supporting this position, however, is very slim and overall not very convincing.

The second major theory is referred to as the **cognitive-behavioral viewpoint,** which contends that respondents are not in a special state of consciousness when they *appear* hypnotized. Rather, hypnosis is a product of certain attitudes, motivations, and expectancies toward the "hypnotic state"—not a "true" alteration of consciousness. According to the cognitive-behavioral viewpoint, people who have a positive attitude toward hypnosis and are highly motivated to be hypnotized actually role-play the "trance" by closely following many of the suggestions provided by the hypnotist. For example, when the hypnotist suggests to them that they feel relaxed, they will try and probably will feel relaxed. Or when the hypnotist suggests their eyes will tear up from staring so long at the target, their eyes will begin to tear.

Theodore X. Barber, one of the chief spokespersons for the cognitive-behavioral perspective (Barber, Spanos, & Chaves, 1974), hypothesized that the good hypnotic respondent is one who not only has the proper mixture of attitude, motivation, and expectancy, but also has the ability to think and imagine with the hypnotist. According to Barber, the good hypnotic respondent is similar to a person watching a captivating video or movie. This person experiences—sometimes intensely—the emotions and actions portrayed by the actors on the screen. In this sense, the "hypnotized" person is mesmerized by the imagery created in his or her mind.

Martin Orne (1970; Orne, Dinges, & Orne, 1984), who was one of the 20th century's foremost authorities on hypnosis, hypothesized a similar viewpoint to the cognitive-behavioral theory, arguing that role-playing accounts for much of the so-called hypnotic phenomenon. That is, participants act the way they *think* a truly hypnotized individual would act. Orne believed that "a prerequisite for hypnosis is the willingness to adopt the role of the 'hypnotic subject,' with its implicit social contract for uncritical acceptance of appropriate suggestions administered by the hypnotist" (Orne et al., 1988, p. 23). The "hypnotic subject" is willing to relinquish his or her sense of reality temporarily, hold any critical thinking in abeyance, and concentrate on what the hypnotist says. He called this state "trance logic" to describe the behavior of hypnotized participants who appeared to display a "peaceful coexistence between illusion and reality" (Orne, quoted in Kihlstrom, 2001, p. 754). Orne has found in his research that the material described under so-called hypnotic trances is often inaccurate and embellished with many intervening events that occur between the initial incident and the hypnotic session. It appears that some hypnotic participants are highly susceptible to distortions, suggestions, and leading questions posed by the hypnotist. Particularly if the interrogator is a police officer convinced of the powers of hypnosis, he or she is apt to inadvertently suggest events, details, or behaviors that were not present during the crime. The hypnotized witness or victim, eager to please the interrogator, can easily imagine a scene decorated with subjective fantasies and thoughts in line with the suggestions of the questioner. Under these suggestible conditions, the hypnotized participant may begin to be convinced of the accuracy and power of hypnosis to the same degree as the hypnotist. Furthermore, the participant also may become increasingly convinced of the accuracy of his or her revised account of the imagined scene, in contrast to the original (prehypnotic) account.

Orne became well-known as a result of his skillful evaluation of Kenneth Bianchi, the accused "Hillside Strangler" who terrified women and young girls in the Greater Los Angeles area in the late 1970s (see Focus 3.5). Bianchi maintained under hypnosis that his alter personality, "Steve Walker," had committed the murders. Bianchi's lawyer then argued that because Bianchi was suffering from a multiple personality disorder, he should not be held responsible for the serial murders. Ultimately, he was hoping for a successful insanity defense. Orne, however, was able to convince the court that Bianchi was merely playacting the different personalities while pretending to be hypnotized. Bianchi, because of Orne's testimony, dropped the multiple personality act and agreed to testify against his co-murderer, Angelo Buono, and to accept a life sentence without the possibility of parole. Orne's critical perspective on forensic hypnosis influenced more than 30 state Supreme Court decisions as well as the U.S. Supreme Court. He also developed guidelines for forensic hypnosis that were adopted by the Federal Bureau of Investigation (Kihlstrom, 2001).

FOCUS 3.5. THE CASE OF THE HILLSIDE STRANGLER

At least 12 women and girls, ranging in ages from 12 to 27, were victims of the Hillside Strangler, who terrorized the Los Angeles area in 1977 and 1978. The name "Hillside Strangler" was assigned to this serial killer because the nude bodies of many of the young women were conspicuously displayed on the hillsides in the Los Angeles area.

Kenneth Bianchi, who eventually pled guilty to the Hillside killings, had a very checkered career, holding at least 12 different jobs during a 9-month period following graduation from high school. During that time, he engaged in a wide variety of illegal activities, ranging from the use of stolen credit cards to the pimping of juvenile prostitutes. Although his life's ambition was to become a police officer, Bianchi also claimed to be a psychologist by falsifying his degrees and credentials. At age 26, he began to live with a woman in a common-law relationship, and the woman bore him a son. Soon after the birth of his son, Bianchi's common-law wife moved to Bellingham, Washington, where Bianchi soon joined her. However, not long after his arrival, the police in Bellingham had compelling evidence that Bianchi may have murdered two university students in that small city. Bianchi was arrested on January 11, 1979, and charged with their murders. An investigation also revealed that the killings in Washington followed a pattern very similar to those of the Hillside Strangler in California.

Bianchi had seen a film shortly before his arrest called *Sybil*, in which Sally Field played a schizophrenic suffering from multiple personalities set in motion by childhood abuse. In the film, one of the personalities Sybil displayed was a spiteful, vicious, manipulating alter ego who chronically tormented the normally pleasant and sedate Sybil. Apparently, Bianchi got his inspiration from the film to play a person haunted by a lustful, murderous alter ego who was out of his control. Bianchi thought his uncontrollable "other person" would provide the key ingredient for a successful insanity defense and absolve him of the crimes.

Under hypnosis during a forensic examination, Bianchi revealed his alter ego as Steve Walker, who admitted killing the two Bellingham women. But evildoer Steve Walker didn't stop there; he went on to confess to the Hillside Strangler murders while implicating Bianchi's cousin, Angelo Buono, as playing a major role in the killings. After two other forensic experts examined Bianchi and found his "performance" convincing, the police brought in one of the world's best-known experts on hypnosis, psychiatrist Martin T. Orne. During a forensic interview, Orne, doubtful about the veracity of the surfacing of multiple personalities through hypnosis, set a trap for the unsuspecting Bianchi. Orne told Bianchi in passing that multiple personality disorders almost always contain at least three different persons. Bianchi took the bait, and during the next hypnotic session, he introduced three more characters, including a prominent one called "Billy."

(Continued)

(Continued)

Orne's testimony, combined with the testimony of another expert, completely undermined the validity of Bianchi's multiple personality claim, and he was offered a plea bargain: If he were to come clean and to testify against his cousin, he would in return receive a life sentence without the possibility of parole. Bianchi, realizing his act was up, accepted the plea bargain to avoid the death penalty. Because of Bianchi's testimony, his cousin, Buono, was convicted of nine murders but was spared the death penalty by the jury. He died in prison on September 21, 2002, at age 67 after apparently suffering a heart attack in his cell. Bianchi, as part of the plea bargain, pled guilty to five murders and is currently serving a 118-year sentence at the Walla Walla State Penitentiary in the state of Washington.

When forensic hypnosis is used as a method to recall events that may be anywhere from several hours to several years old, the fundamental assumption is that human memory functions like a videotape: All the events and details are stored completely and accurately and, with the proper procedure, can be recalled or brought to consciousness intact. This assumption, however, is without much research support (Bartol & Bartol, 2004). Human perception and memory are flawed and permeated with inaccuracies and distortions. The frailties of perception and memory, combined with the highly suggestive medium under which hypnosis is conducted, provide a situation in which critical inaccuracies have a high probability of occurring. Memory recall under hypnosis is extremely malleable and manipulable, especially in highly suggestible respondents (Haber & Haber, 2000). Therefore, leading or suggestive questions may have a substantial effect on the respondents' recall of events after they are hypnotized (Kebbell & Wagstaff, 1998; Wagstaff, 2008). The danger is particularly high when the forensic examiner is untrained or uninformed about the power of questioning suggestible respondents. In addition, the tendency to make up things to fill the gaps in memory appears to be greater under hypnosis (Orne et al., 1988).

It is important, therefore, that the forensic psychologist be aware of the research and the many dangers of poorly conducted interviews when hypnosis is used, whether used with crime victims, witnesses to a crime, or criminal defendants. As noted by Scheflin, Spiegel, and Spiegel (1999), "When hypnosis is used for forensic purposes, strict guidelines must be scrupulously followed" (p. 491). Hypnosis can be a useful tool if used properly and with the understanding that it is no shortcut or replacement for standard investigative procedures (Scheflin et al., 1999). After extensively reviewing the literature on the topic, Wagstaff (2008) concluded that, despite many misconceptions about hypnosis, it should not be outrightly banned as an *investigative* technique. Indeed, some of the procedures associated with hypnosis, like meditation, relaxation, and eye closure, can yield useful information. Hypnosis can help, for instance, when trauma has occurred and it is difficult for the person to mentally or physically revisit the scene without the relaxation and concentration states that can be accomplished through this procedure.

Identifying the Offender: Other Procedures

Police officers routinely interview witnesses to a criminal incident. Typically, this task requires attempts at some form of identification of the offender, especially the facial features. The identification of suspects by witnesses begins as soon after the offense as possible. Police investigators usually obtain verbal descriptions of the perpetrators from witnesses or show them photographs to obtain a preliminary identification. In some instances, the police will have witnesses look over photos of individuals with previous records, either to identify the specific offender or to obtain an approximation of the offender's appearance. Some police agencies routinely ask witnesses to examine a group of photographs (photo boards, photo spreads, or mug shots) that are fairly well matched to the physical characteristics described by the witnesses, including the person the police suspect to be the guilty party. This section will examine the many pitfalls of other procedures designed to gather identification clues about the offender.

Identifying the Face

Courts, particularly criminal courts, rely heavily on eyewitness recognition as critical evidence either for or against the defendant. An accumulation of scientific studies, however, demonstrates that the accurate recognition of a relatively unfamiliar face is an extremely complex and error-ridden task (Bartol & Bartol, 2004); as we saw in the previous chapter (Focus 2.2), witness misidentification is the main culprit in many wrongful convictions. Research also reveals that the accuracy of facial recognition depends greatly on the type of face being recalled. For reasons unknown, some faces are easier to identify than others. Highly unique faces, for example, are better recognized than plain or average faces (M. E. Cohen & Carr, 1975; Going & Read, 1974), and distinct faces are easier to recognize than are typical faces (Chiroro & Valentine, 1995; MacLin & Malpass, 2001). Faces high and low in attractiveness also are easier to recognize than faces judged to be of medium attractiveness (Shepherd & Ellis, 1973). Not surprisingly, the longer a person views a face, the better the recognition of the face at a later time (MacLin, MacLin, & Malpass, 2001).

Unconscious Transference

On occasion, witnesses identify persons they have seen at some other time and place as the perpetrators of a more recent crime. This phenomenon, called **unconscious transference,** occurs when a person seen in one situation is confused with or recalled as a person seen in another situation. It is called "unconscious" because people do not realize they are doing it. A witness may have had limited exposure to a face (e.g., in a grocery store) and, on seeing the face at a later time, may conclude that it is the offender's. Loftus (1979) believes that unconscious transference is another feature of the fallible and malleable nature of human memory, where earlier input becomes "tangled up" with later input. As we noted above, research has continually shown that human memory is not like a videotape or DVD that stores things exactly as seen. Rather, memory is continually changing or being revised in line with our cognitive beliefs and versions of the world. Most psychologists would agree that "memory is a risky route to figuring out the past" (Turtle & Want, 2008, p. 1245).

The phenomenon of unconscious transference illustrates that it is highly possible that a fast-food worker, who is witness to a robbery of the restaurant, might incorrectly identify as the perpetrator an occasional customer who may have some of the features of the actual culprit. However, for unconscious transference to occur, the previous encounters with the innocent face must have been relatively brief. *Frequent* encounters with customers by the witness are unlikely to trigger unconscious transference involving those particular customers.

Own-Race Bias (ORB)

There is now considerable evidence that people are much better at discriminating between faces of their own race or ethnic group than faces of other races or ethnic groups (Bartol & Bartol, 2004). Researchers call this phenomenon **own-race bias (ORB),** or it is sometimes referred to as "own-race effect" or "cross-race effect." Scientific research across a wide band of cultures and countries has documented ORB, and it exists across diverse ethnic groups (Meissner & Brigham, 2001; Sporer, 2001). Unfortunately, ORB accounts for a fair amount of identification errors, or false alarms. *False alarms* refer to those situations when a witness identifies the wrong person as the offender. Although the frequency of false alarms seems to be increasing in our society, racial attitudes or prejudice do not seem to account for this phenomenon in a majority of cases (Meissner & Brigham, 2001).

Although there are several possible explanations for ORB, the most popular is called the **differential experience hypothesis.** The hypothesis states that individuals will have greater familiarity or experience with members of their own race and will thus be better able to discern differences among its members. Furthermore, it is the frequency of meaningful and positive contacts with other races that develops the skill to differentiate between racial or ethnic faces (MacLin & Malpass, 2001; Yarmey, 1979). For example, having close friends of other races or ethnicities is more likely to promote better facial recognition than having frequent but casual exposure. This other-race effect is obviously a critical aspect in the identification of suspects by eyewitnesses.

Pretrial Identification Methods

Lineups and Photo Spreads

In the spring of 2009, the television show *60 Minutes* aired a sobering segment about an individual—Ronald Cotton—who had been convicted of rape and sent to prison, largely based on the victim's identification of him as her assailant. Unfortunately, the victim—though certain at the time that she was identifying the right man—had been mistaken. Eleven years later, DNA evidence exonerated him, and Cotton was released from prison. Interestingly, he refused to blame the victim for the mistake, and the two have since remained in contact, even collaborating on a book about the incident. Both appeared on the *60 Minutes* segment.

Pretrial identification methods are especially vulnerable to biases and error, and many forensic researchers would say that the above victim's mistake was an honest one. She truly believed that the individual in the lineup had raped her. Sometimes, mistakes can occur because of the actions of the investigating officers, ranging from very blatant practices to more subtle innuendo. Consider, for example, a police investigator suggesting to an undecided witness that she should look more closely at "the second one from the right." Because of a number of problems associated with lineups, researchers suggest that victims be shown suspects sequentially rather than as a group, as we will note below.

It is interesting to note, though, that even lineups that are "suggestive" can pass muster in some jurisdictions. In the key case of *Manson v. Braithwaite* (1977), the U.S. Supreme Court ruled that a lineup can be suggestive, but if the identification is reliable it may still be used in court. To establish "reliability," courts should decide whether the witness had the opportunity to view the crime; gave attention; and provided a good, consistent description. Furthermore, not too much time should have elapsed between the crime and the identification, and the victim must be certain. Note that all of the above criteria would have been met in the case against Cotton, mentioned above.

Photo identification methods (photo spreads or photo boards) are commonly used, particularly if no "live" suspect is in custody. They may include file photographs of suspects or convicted offenders, sometimes interspersed with photos of police officers in plain clothes.

Whether in a lineup or viewed sequentially, live suspects in particular should fit the description the witness gave police. In other words, they should have similar characteristics—such as age, physical stature, race, hairstyle, and facial hair—that were included in the original witness description. It is also well-known that, before appearing in lineups, many suspects will try to change their appearance to mislead eyewitnesses, a tactic that is often successful (Cutler, Penrod, & Martens, 1987). If the witness remembered the offender as a 6-foot, 6-inch individual with black, curly hair and a beard, the lineup is obviously biased if only one person in six fits that description.

For a lineup to be considered fair, its functional size should approximate the nominal size—these are two terms critical for psychologists consulting with police to understand. The **functional size** of the lineup refers to the number of participants who resemble the suspect. No matter how many others are standing in the line, the test is effectively limited to that number. **Nominal size** of the lineup refers to the actual number of members within the lineup. In a simple lineup of six persons, the functional size will decrease as the physically dissimilar members of a lineup increase. If all the members of a six-member lineup have an equal probability of being selected on the basis of crucial characteristics, the functional size is six. If only three resemble the suspect, the functional size is three and the nominal size is six (see Photo 3.2 depicting a police lineup).

Another area of pretrial identification that must be closely monitored is that of **commitment bias.** When a witness has initially identified a face, even an incorrect one, he or she will be more likely to choose that face again. In the example used at the beginning of this section, the victim on more than one

Photo 3.2   Three individuals of similar height, age, and ethnicity in a police lineup. On the basis of research on this topic, what questions would you raise about this particular lineup?

occasion confirmed to police that Cotton was her assailant. Commitment bias is most likely to occur when witnesses are eager to please police investigators and further assume that the police have good evidence against someone in the pretrial identification process. Because of commitment bias, a witness who initially identifies a suspect, but with some doubt, is more likely to identify the suspect in subsequent exposures with greater conviction. In other words, each time the witness identifies the suspect as the perpetrator of the crime, the witness becomes more convinced that this was indeed the person who committed the crime.

One controversial identification procedure is called the **show-up.** "This is an identification procedure in which police present a single suspect to the eyewitness(es) to see if the eyewitness(es) will identify that person as the perpetrator" (Wells, 2001, p. 795). Unlike the lineup, there are no distractors, also called foils, in a show-up procedure. A *distractor* or *foil* is anyone in the line-up who is not the suspect. A show-up is legal in the United States as long as it occurs soon after the offense (within hours) or under circumstances that would make a lineup impracticable or impossible. For example, if a crime victim is hospitalized and not likely to live, police may bring in a suspect for identification (*Stovall v. Denno,* 1967). A more common type of show-up occurs when police drive a witness by someone on the street and ask whether that is the perpetrator. Research shows that show-ups are far more likely to lead to mistaken identification than lineups, however (Wells, 2001). This is because in a lineup, the error of mistakenly identifying a suspect is spread out among the foils and distractors. Even in a sequential lineup, the witness is aware that other possibilities will be presented. In the show-up situation, on the other hand, there is only one choice, right or wrong.

In 2001, the American Psychology-Law Society (AP-LS), in an effort to make certain that forensic psychologists and other personnel in the criminal justice system were aware of ways to improve lineup procedures, published a comprehensive document known as the "*Police Lineups*" white paper (Wells, 2001). The document made four recommendations for implementing valid procedures in conducting lineups or photo spreads (see Wells et al., 1998). First, the panel recommended that the person *putting together* the lineup or photo spread know which member of the lineup or photo spread is the suspect; however, the person *administering or conducting* the lineup should *not* know. In addition, the eyewitness should be informed that the person administering the lineup does not know which person is the suspect in the case. This recommendation is designed to prevent the witness from looking for subtle clues or identifying information from the officer administering the lineup. This has come to be called the **double-blind lineup** indicating that neither the witness nor the officer administering it is aware of the true suspect. Second, eyewitnesses should be clearly told that the suspect might *not* be in the lineup or photo spread. Under these conditions, the witness will not feel compelled to make an identification if he or she does not believe the suspect is in the lineup. Third, the suspect should not stand out in the lineup or photo spread as being clearly different from the distractors, based on the eyewitness's (or eyewitnesses') previous description. Fourth, a clear statement should be taken from the eyewitness at the time of identification, prior to any feedback from the police that would inform the witness whether he or she had chosen the "right" suspect. This last recommendation is based on the observation that witnesses are often susceptible to inadvertent or intentional communication about the suspect during the lineup or immediately after it occurs. Findings from research reported in the white paper were incorporated into a 44-page government guide for law enforcement officers working with eyewitness identification (Reno, 1999).

Since these recommendations were made, numerous legal psychologists and prisoner advocacy groups (e.g., The Innocence Project, highlighted in Focus 2.2) have advocated for changes in the procedures used in police lineups. They also assert that the sequential, double-blind procedure has the greatest likelihood of avoiding misidentification. At least two states (New Jersey and North Carolina) and several jurisdictions (e.g., Madison, Wisconsin; Boston, Massachusetts; Virginia Beach, Virginia) have implemented the sequential double-blind as standard procedure in lineups (Innocence Project, 2010).

SUMMARY AND CONCLUSIONS

Investigative psychology is perhaps the newest area of specialization for forensic psychologists, having begun in 1985 with the work of David Canter in England. It focuses on identifying features of a crime and likely characteristics of its perpetrator. The generic term *profiling,* as used in this chapter, is subsumed under investigative psychology. We discussed five overlapping forms: crime scene profiling (often called criminal profiling), suspect-based profiling, psychological autopsies, geographical profiling, and psychological profiling. It is important to realize, though, that these terms are very often used interchangeably in the literature.

Investigative psychology also includes research and practice in broader areas, such as polygraphy, forensic hypnosis, facial recognition, and other pretrial identification methods, all covered in this chapter. Essentially, we have included a variety of areas in which psychologists provide consulting services to law enforcement agencies in their investigations of crimes.

Profiling, though not a dominant activity performed by most forensic psychologists, has gained considerable media attention. If done correctly, profiling can provide statistical probabilities of features of an individual, including an offender, but it is far from a foolproof procedure. Perpetrators may change their methods and techniques as they become more skilled and more daring.

Psychological autopsies—more formally called reconstructive psychological evaluation—are performed after a person has died and the cause of the death is uncertain or equivocal. The psychologist conducting the autopsy tries to reconstruct the victim's behavior and thought processes leading up to the death. This procedure is often used in cases of apparent but questionable suicide. Psychological autopsies are also used—though less frequently—in civil cases in an effort to determine whether a third party may have contributed to the death. For example, an employer may have failed to respond appropriately to signals of extreme emotional distress or threats of suicide on the part of an employee. As yet, there is no established, standard method for conducting a psychological autopsy, and its validity has yet to be demonstrated.

Geographical profiling analyzes spatial characteristics to yield probabilities of a perpetrator residing or offending in a particular location. We described four "hunting patterns" that are examined. Geographical profiling is used primarily to solve serial crimes, in which a pattern of offending occurs over time. It is more likely to yield positive results when combined with criminal profiling, although we must caution that the scientific status of the latter remains in question.

We discussed some of the reasons profiling is difficult. Chief among these is the fact that much of human behavior is not consistent across different situations. Dynamic risk factors of an individual, particularly those that are acute—such as mood swings and drug-induced effects—contribute to this lack of consistency. In addition, crime scene evidence does not necessarily relate to specific psychological characteristics of the perpetrator. Although some professional profilers are cautious about the power of their predictions, others are too ready to rely on unsubstantiated assumptions, some of which are based on outdated interpretations of personality theory. In sum, profiling—though fascinating to the public—is an enterprise that must be approached with extreme caution, at least until research demonstrates that it has greater predictive validity.

The polygraph is not strictly an investigative technique in the narrow sense because it is used in a wide variety of criminal and civil contexts. In law enforcement, it is used primarily in the selection of candidates for law enforcement positions and much less in criminal investigation. The dominant method is apparently the CQT, though questions are raised about its validity. Results from polygraph tests are not admitted into courts against the wishes of criminal defendants, but they have been allowed in some courts to support a defendant's contention that he or she did *not* commit the crime. It appears that the polygraph is also being used more extensively in counterintelligence and by federal agencies than it has been in the past. Polygraphs are also used to monitor offenders in the community who are on probation or parole; this is particularly the case for sex offenders. Like the other techniques discussed in this chapter, the polygraph has not garnered impressive research results with respect to reliability and validity. Nevertheless, some researchers do support its use in limited situations and when administered by highly trained polygraphers.

We ended the chapter with a discussion of forensic hypnosis and the construction of police lineups. Hypnosis is a controversial topic, particularly when used to elicit repressed memories of traumatic events in victims of crime. It may also be used to enhance recall of nonvictim eyewitnesses to a crime. Although the weight of the scientific evidence is still very much against its use, research over the past decade has begun to challenge early assumptions. The lineup is a pretrial identification method that is very subject to error on the part of the eyewitness. This is especially so when the officer administering the lineup is aware of the identity of the suspect, because the officer may consciously or unconsciously communicate the "correct" choice to the witness. In recent years, psychologists have made significant research contributions relating to the construction and administration of police lineups. Some of their recommendations, including a preference for sequential, double-blind identification procedures, have been incorporated into government guidelines used by law enforcement officers nationwide.

KEY CONCEPTS

Acute dynamic factors	Commitment bias
Autoerotic asphyxia	Comparison question technique (CQT)
Behavioral Science Unit (BSU)	Confirmation bias
Clinical predictions	Contagion or copycat effect
Cognitive-behavioral viewpoint	Countermeasures

Crime scene analysis

Criminal profiling

Differential experience hypothesis

Directed lie test

Disorganized crime scene

Double-blind lineup

Dynamic risk factors

Employee Polygraph Protection Act

Equivalent death analysis

Functional size (of a lineup)

Geographical mapping

Geographical profiling

Guilty knowledge test (GKT)

Hypnotic hypermnesia

Hypnotic trance theory

Idiographic approach

Mixed crime scene

Modus operandi (MO)

Nominal size (of a lineup)

Nomothetic approach

Nonhypnotic hypermnesia

Organized crime scene

Own-race bias (ORB)

Psychological autopsy

Reconstructive psychological evaluation

Relevant/irrelevant question technique

Show-up

Signature

Stable dynamic factors

Staging

Static risk factors

Trans-situational consistency

Trans-temporal consistency

Trophy

Typology

Unconscious transference

Undoing

QUESTIONS FOR REVIEW

1. What three questions are central to the process of investigative psychology?

2. Distinguish between criminal profiling, crime scene analysis, and racial profiling.

3. How does the psychological autopsy differ from criminal profiling? What are the two basic types of psychological autopsy?

4. Distinguish between geographical profiling and geographical mapping.

5. According to Rossmo, what are the four "hunting patterns" of serial offenders?

6. Give at least three reasons why psychological profiling is so often inaccurate.

7. List any five findings from the research on the polygraph.

8. What are the advantages and disadvantages of using forensic hypnosis?

9. What were the four recommendations made by researchers regarding lineups and photo spreads in the "Police Lineups" white paper?

Part III

Legal Psychology

4

Consulting
and Testifying

CHAPTER OBJECTIVES

- Describe the relationship between psychology and the law.
- Introduce the reader to the court system.
- Describe the judicial process.
- Define and describe what is meant by expert testimony.
- Discuss the legal standards for the admission of scientific evidence in the courtroom.
- Describe professional responsibilities of psychologists who work in forensic settings.
- Provide an overview of forensic risk assessment.

The psychologist is a common sight in the courtroom today, both on the witness stand and, less frequently, sitting at the defense or prosecution table as a jury or trial consultant. Even when psychologists are not actually in the courtroom, their presence may be felt in the reports they have prepared or sworn statements they have made that are entered into the court record. Very early in the case, when attorneys are gathering information and preparing their trial strategy, a psychologist may be called to testify during a deposition. **Deposition** refers to proceedings during which potential witnesses are questioned by attorneys for the opposing side, under oath and in the presence of a court recorder, although typically away from the courtroom. For instance, lawyers for a plaintiff in an employment discrimination suit may depose the psychologist who administered and evaluated promotional exams. As another example, in a criminal case, the judge at a sentencing hearing may have access to a report detailing an offender's mental status based on a psychological assessment.

Psychology's entry into the courtroom did not come easily. Until the 1960s, psychiatrists were the only mental health experts recognized in many courts. Those courts that *did* welcome psychologists tended to limit their tasks to very specific areas, such as reporting on the results of intelligence tests or personality inventories. Criminal courts were particularly reluctant to accept expert testimony from a nonmedical professional when a defendant's criminal responsibility or sanity was in question. Because mental disorder was considered a disease, the professional with a medical degree—the psychiatrist—was believed to be the appropriate expert. Although there were exceptions, for the most part, the courtroom was the province of the psychiatrist, not the psychologist.

In 1962, however, a federal appeals court in *Jenkins v. U.S.* ruled that the lack of a medical degree did not automatically disqualify psychologists from providing expert testimony on the issue of mental disorder. Jenkins had pleaded not guilty by reason of insanity to sexual assault charges. Interestingly, the judge at his trial had allowed psychologists to testify that he did not have the required mental state to be found responsible, but the judge then told the jury to disregard the psychologists' testimony. "A psychologist is not competent to give a medical opinion as to a mental disease or defect," the judge said. Jenkins was convicted, but he appealed his conviction claiming that the judge's jury instruction violated his right to due process. The American Psychological Association and the American Psychiatric Association both filed briefs with the federal court on behalf of their respective professions. Psychologists, of course, hoped that the court would support their entry as experts; psychiatrists hoped to preserve their near-exclusive reign.

The federal appeals court supported psychologists, ruling that a psychologist with proper credentials could indeed provide competent testimony on the issue of mental disorder. Gradually, after the *Jenkins* case, psychologists began to provide testimony not only on issues relating to mental disorder, but also on a wide range of issues about which they were conducting research. For example, they provided data on subjects as diverse as the influence of pretrial publicity on juries, the effects of pornography on adolescents, and the influence of advertisements on consumers (Bartol & Bartol, 1999).

This chapter will offer many additional examples of psychologists working directly in courtroom settings, as well as behind the scenes at tasks relevant to the judicial process. Although most of us are familiar with the appearance of a courtroom either from personal experience or from media portrayals, knowledge of how courts are set up and how a case proceeds through various stages is less widespread. Therefore, the chapter begins with an overview of the structure and process in both criminal and civil courts.

Court Structure and Jurisdiction

In the United States, federal and state courts exist side by side, independent of one another, sometimes in the same geographical location. In most sizable cities, one can find municipal or county courts in one building and the federal court building not too far away. This **dual-court system** exists to recognize the unity of the nation as a whole, on one hand, and the sovereignty of the 50 individual states on the other. Among their many functions, federal courts interpret and apply the U.S. Constitution and acts of Congress; settle disputes between states or citizens of different states; and deal with such specialized matters as bankruptcies, copyrights, and patents. Persons accused of violating federal criminal laws are also processed in federal courts. State courts interpret and apply state constitutions and laws passed by state legislatures. They also settle disputes between citizens or between the government and citizens within the state. A group of taxpayers, for example, may challenge a state education funding plan that increases the taxes of property owners living in certain communities. In recent years, much has been made of the overwhelming workload of federal courts. To ease this burden, state courts will sometimes settle disputes between citizens of different states, as long as the parties agree to have their case heard in a state rather than a federal court (Abraham, 1998).

All courts, federal and state, are either established under the U.S. Constitution or the constitutions of the various states, or are created as needed by Congress or state legislatures. The constitution or the legislative enactment also specifies the court's **jurisdiction**, or authority. All courts have **subject matter jurisdiction** and

geographical jurisdiction as outlined in the law. For example, a family court may have authority over divorce, custody, adoption, and delinquency matters (subject matter jurisdiction) in a given county within the state (geographical jurisdiction). Many courts have only **limited jurisdiction,** or limited authority, meaning that they can only settle small disputes or deal with preliminary issues in a major case. By contrast, courts of **general jurisdiction** have broad authority over a vast array of both simple and complex cases, both civil and criminal. **Appellate jurisdiction** refers to a court's authority to hear appeals regarding decisions of lower courts.

Courts present an often confusing array of physical structures, terminology, and individuals with an equally confusing array of titles and roles. Some court proceedings are conducted at a table in the basement of a town hall at 10 PM, whereas others are conducted in dignified, velvet-curtained surroundings. Increasingly today, more court proceedings—particularly at the early stages of a case—are conducted via closed-circuit television. A **defendant** being detained in jail, for example, may "appear" before a judge for a bail reduction hearing. However, the defendant is in the jail and the judge is in his or her courtroom 5 miles away. Via closed-circuit television, the judge may reduce the bail and communicate to the defendant the conditions under which he or she is being released.

The structure of the federal court system is actually quite simple. The federal courts may be divided into four basic levels, two trial court levels and two appeals or appellate levels (see Table 4.1). At the trial court levels are courts of limited jurisdiction (e.g., magistrate judge's courts, bankruptcy courts) and general jurisdiction (U.S. district courts). At the appellate level are the intermediate courts of appeal for the various circuits and the court of last resort, the U.S. Supreme Court.

Table 4.1	Federal Courts

Highest Appellate Court

    U.S. Supreme Court

Intermediate Appellate Courts

    U.S. Courts of Appeals

- 12 Regional Circuit Courts of Appeals
- 1 U.S. Court of Appeals for the Federal Circuit

Trial Courts

    U.S. District Courts

- 94 judicial courts
- U.S. Bankruptcy Court

    U.S. Court of International Trade

    U.S. Court of Federal Claims

Federal Courts and Other Entities Outside the Judicial Branch

    Military Courts (trial and appellate)

    Court of Veterans Appeals

    U.S. Tax Court

    Federal Administrative Court

By contrast, state court structures can be quite complicated. No two state court systems are identical, leading to the often-made comment that we have 51 very different court systems in the United States: the federal system and the systems of each of the 50 states. Nonetheless, common features exist. Like the federal system, all states have trial and appellate courts, with the trial courts being divided into those of limited and general jurisdiction. At the very lowest level are courts overseen by a justice of the peace or a magistrate who presides over minor civil and criminal matters. This level also may include municipal courts—sometimes called traffic courts, night courts, or city courts. These lower courts are courts of limited jurisdiction and typically cannot conduct major civil trials or felony trials. At the next level are county courts, which have been called the "workhorse of the average judiciary" (Abraham, 1998, p. 155). County courts are courts of general jurisdiction, handling a wide range of both civil and criminal cases. Every state also has a court of last resort, which is the highest appellate court in that state, but not all have *intermediate* appeals courts. In addition, states often have a variety of **specialized courts,** which deal only with particular matters. Family courts, drug courts, mental health courts, and domestic violence courts are all examples of specialized courts. These courts are often of particular interest to psychologists because of the subject matter with which they deal. (See Personal Perspective 4.1 for a profile of Dr. Allison Redlich, a professor and researcher with an interest in mental health courts.)

PERSONAL PERSPECTIVE 4.1

Why Mentoring Matters

Allison Redlich, PhD

The first step toward my eventual career probably was taken in high school, when I volunteered at a state mental hospital in my home state of Pennsylvania. At that time, the residents there were inaptly referred to as "chronics" because of their severe mental illness. I'll never forget "George," who emerged naked from the locker room into the pool area! This was a sight for my 17-year-old eyes. Today, the state hospital has closed its doors, as have so many similar institutions in the United States. As a high school student, I did not

know that I would become a research psychologist and that some of my research would be applicable to people like George.

Today, I am an assistant professor in the School of Criminal Justice at the University at Albany, State University of New York. A large portion of my research is on mental health courts and the police interrogation of vulnerable suspects, including persons with mental illness and juveniles. Some scholars have said that the closing of state mental institutions and the concomitant lack of

(Continued)

(Continued)

community services and assistance led to the criminalization and reinstitutionalization (into jails) of persons with mental illness. My research concerns offenders with mental illness (and other vulnerabilities) in the criminal justice system.

After majoring in psychology in college, I applied to grad school, but did not get into any of the 15 clinical psychology programs, despite above-average grades and recommendations. (I learned later that I did a few things right and many things wrong when applying, so be sure to talk to as many people as you can about the process.) These denials turned out to be a fortunate occurrence, however, as I learned my passion was for applied research, not clinical psychology. Instead of going to grad school immediately, I was fortunate to obtain a research assistantship at the National Institute of Child Health and Human Development (NICHD), working with Michael Lamb and his colleagues. During the 2 years I spent there, I assisted on projects relating to children's disclosures of sexual abuse, which piqued my interest in psychology and the law and vulnerable persons' interactions with the legal system.

From NICHD, I left for the University of California, Davis, to obtain my doctoral degree, studying with Gail S. Goodman, the "founding mother" of child witness research. I learned a great deal about the capabilities, limitations, and perceptions of child-victim witnesses during forensic interviews and was able to apply this knowledge to children who were being questioned. This is where my interest in interrogations and false confessions grew, one that has developed into an active program of research. The 5 years I spent with Gail as a teacher and mentor were extremely fruitful. In addition to gaining an education in psychology and the law, I learned how to be a research psychologist. Being a researcher is not simply about "knowing your stuff" (which of course you need to succeed as well); it also entails all of the unspoken rules and offerings of precious advice on how to achieve success.

After UC Davis, I completed a postdoctoral fellowship at Stanford University in the Department of Psychiatry and Behavioral Sciences, working with Hans Steiner. I continued my education by collaborating on research with juvenile offenders housed at the California Youth Authority, a facility akin to prison for both male and female juveniles. We interviewed and assessed the juveniles for mental and substance use disorders, and I was able to observe firsthand how crimes do not define the person, particularly when said person is a youth.

From there, it was an easy transition into my next position, which was senior research associate at Policy Research Associates (PRA) in upstate New York. I spent 6 years at PRA, working with Henry (Hank) Steadman. There, I also had the opportunity to interact with other high-profile scholars in the field of mental health law, including John Monahan, John Petrila, and Paul Appelbaum. At PRA, I focused much of my effort on mental health courts and other forms of mandated treatment. Although this was a different topic area from my previous experiences, I immersed myself in it and in the end, believe I greatly expanded my knowledge as well as my network of colleagues. At PRA, I also learned a great deal about conducting large-scale field studies, which has been a tremendous asset. Finally, I retained my interest in police interrogation and initiated a program of research on the interrogation of persons with mental illness.

The next step in my journey was a return to academe. Some have told me that I did the impossible by returning after 6 years. Although

I was achieving success at PRA, I began to feel the itch to apply for faculty positions. I also knew that soon I would age myself out (in terms of time since I obtained my PhD) of assistant professor positions and lacked the teaching experience to be viable for associate professor positions. I decided to take it one step at a time and applied for only one position. Luckily for me, this position also happened to be in one of the leading departments of criminal justice, *and* it did not require me and my family to uproot and relocate.

About 2 years ago, when I joined the faculty at University at Albany, admittedly, I was unsure of what to expect. But the truth is that being a professor suits me to a tee. A typical day involves working at my desk with my door open. Much of my time is spent writing—papers, lectures, chapters, presentations, grants, reviews, letters of recommendation, and so forth. Sometimes my work involves testifying in court, attending conferences, and traveling within the United States and abroad.

Another portion of my time is spent meeting with students as a teacher and mentor. If I have been successful at what I do, I attribute it in large part to the mentors I have had over the years, including the luminaries in the field mentioned above. Not surprisingly, I place a high premium on mentoring. To those of you who are thinking about graduate school and careers in forensic psychology, I encourage you to seek out as many mentors as you can. Most people are nice, even the ones that you may find intimidating before you get to know them. And, the field of forensic psychology is small enough that mentors are never too far way. Having a helpful, hardworking, and caring mentor—especially in graduate school—can make all the difference.

If asked as a graduate student whether I would flip-flop from academe, to a private research firm, and back to academe, I probably would have said that that course was unlikely. My journey has been a nontraditional one. However, I'd like to think that along the way I kept my options open by being prolific and productive; this gave me the flexibility to choose what was right for me at certain points on my career path. The key for me was a focus on my next goals and the discipline to accomplish what I needed to, when I needed to. This preparation and work ethic have allowed me to take advantage of the opportunities that have come my way.

To end on a personal note, I am a proud wife and mother of two young children. Balancing work and home life does not have to be an issue. There is plenty of time to enjoy both.

Dr. Redlich earned her BA in psychology from The Pennsylvania State University and, as noted above, her MA and PhD in developmental psychology from the University of California, Davis. She enjoys spending time with her family, playing with her dog and two cats, and doing crossword puzzles.

The federal and state systems intersect when a case moves—or attempts to move—from the state court to the federal courts. Although there are a variety of ways in which this can happen, perhaps the most common is when an individual has lost his or her case after having exhausted all appeals in state courts. If a substantial federal question has been raised, the case may be heard in the federal courts. For example, when a state law is said to violate the U.S. Constitution, federal courts may ultimately decide whether it truly does. In 2003, in *Lawrence and Garner v. Texas*, the U.S. Supreme Court examined a state law that made it a crime for two individuals of the same sex to engage in certain intimate sexual conduct. The majority opinion held that this law violated the liberty interests guaranteed by the Constitution. In deciding *Lawrence and Garner v. Texas*, the Court overruled an earlier case, *Bowers v. Hardwick* (1986), in which it had ruled that a similar Georgia statute was *not* unconstitutional. As this book is going to press, the California "Proposition 8" case is making its way through the courts. After the California Supreme Court ruled that gay marriage was legal in California, voters passed a state constitutional amendment outlawing it. Supporters of gay marriage took the issue back to the courts, arguing—among other things—that Proposition 8 itself violated the equal protection clause of the 14th Amendment of the U.S. Constitution. At this writing, a federal court of appeals (9th circuit) is considering the case. Observers on both sides of this issue agree that the case will eventually be heard by the U.S. Supreme Court, which is the final arbiter of federal constitutional issues.

It should be noted, though, that the Supreme Court has virtually unlimited discretion as to whether it will accept a case for review. On average, it agrees to hear only about 10 to 15% of the cases that come to its attention (Abraham, 1998).

Mental Health Courts

Mental health courts are a possible solution to the vexing problem of crime—typically minor crimes—committed by individuals with mental disorders. Although they operate in different ways, most of these courts involve an immediate screening by a mental health clinician or team, which then makes a treatment recommendation to the presiding judge. Although defendants or their guardians may have to consent to go to this specialized court, avoiding placement in a traditional jail setting is a strong incentive for doing so. Some mental health courts accept defendants only after they have pleaded guilty to a criminal offense. In that case, the judge orders mental health treatment as a condition of probation and carefully supervises the progress of this treatment. Psychologists or other mental health professionals associated with the court work cooperatively with the judge to follow the individual through his or her course of treatment.

Observers have expressed a range of concerns about mental health courts, with the subjective decision-making power of the judge being a major theme. In most mental health courts, clinicians screen clients and make recommendations, but it is the judge who decides whether the individual is making sufficient progress. Many mental health professionals believe this should be a clinical decision (Hasselbrack, 2001). Other observers have expressed concerns that judges want early intervention and efficient processing, but the mental health professional needs time to conduct an assessment that is accurate and complete (Goldkamp & Irons-Guynn, 2000). Still others are concerned that adequate resources are not made available to provide recommended treatment (Steadman, Davidson, & Brown, 2001).

Mental health courts and other problem-solving courts (e.g., drug courts, domestic violence courts) face numerous challenges and require continuing research attention. However, drug courts in particular have been subjected to many evaluation studies and meta-analyses and have received positive reviews, including for reductions in recidivism of at least 1 to 3 years (see Hiller et al., 2010, and references therein; see also Focus 4.1). Problem-solving courts emphasize dispositions such as mental health treatment, various other kinds of treatment, the provision of social services, and ongoing judicial monitoring (DeMatteo, 2006; for a review of these courts, see also Huddleston, Marlowe, & Casebolt, 2008; Petrila, 2005).

FOCUS 4.1. DRUG COURTS: FEATURES AND OUTCOMES

Drug courts are increasingly becoming an integral component of the criminal justice system. By the end of 2007, a total of 2,147 such courts had been implemented in the United States (Huddleston et al., 2008).

The drug court addresses substance abuse as a health problem rather than a crime problem, and the professionals (judges, lawyers, treatment providers) act as a team to achieve treatment goals.

Initially, defendants who appeared before them were charged with nonviolent and/or misdemeanor offenses relating to their substance abuse, but felony defendants are increasingly treated in drug courts as well (Huddleston et al., 2008). Substance abuse treatment is provided, and defendants are monitored for compliance. However, noncompliance does not necessarily result in immediate punishment, such as imprisonment, because substance abuse treatment providers are aware that relapse is common. Therefore, graduated sanctions may be employed depending upon the severity of the noncompliance.

The following is a summary of the key components of drug courts (Huddleston et al., 2008):

- Alcohol and other drug treatment services are integrated with justice system processing.
- Both prosecution and defense lawyers work cooperatively, using a non-adversarial approach, to promote public safety while protecting the rehabilitation needs of participants.
- Participants are identified early and placed in a drug court program.
- A continuum of treatment and rehabilitation services is offered.
- Participants are expected to abstain from alcohol and other drugs and are monitored frequently by testing.
- A coordinated strategy governs drug court responses to participants' compliance.
- Judges interact on an ongoing basis with each participant.
- Program goals and effectiveness are monitored.
- Interdisciplinary education of those involved in implementing and maintaining the courts promotes an effective operation.
- Drug courts, public agencies, and community organizations form partnerships to generate local support and enhance the court's effectiveness.

Research indicates that 50 to 75% of drug court participants "graduate" from the program (Belenko, DeMatteo, & Patapis, 2007). Interestingly, though, research also suggests that not all participants had serious drug problems in the first place, raising questions about use of resources for this purpose (DeMatteo, Marlowe, Festinger, & Arabia, 2009). In their study of 284 participants, DeMatteo et al. found that about one-third probably did not have serious drug problems when they entered the program. The participants were not necessarily mismatched to the programs, but they may have been managed in a less intensive manner, the researchers noted.

Civil and Criminal Courts

The distinction between criminal and civil courts essentially refers to the type of case that is being heard. In large courthouses, certain rooms are set aside for civil cases and others for criminal cases. In small communities, however, the same courtroom may be used for criminal proceedings one day and a civil trial the next. Furthermore, the same judge may be presiding over all proceedings. The distinction between civil and criminal cases rests primarily on who brings the action and, to a lesser extent, the disputative versus punitive nature of a case. In a **civil case,** two or more parties (litigants) approach the legal system, often seeking resolution of a dispute. In the most common of civil actions, the **plaintiff** seeks relief or a remedy from the defendant, maintaining that he or she has been personally harmed. This relief or remedy could come in the form of a court injunction (an order to stop some practice), a protective order (such as an order to remain beyond a certain distance from an individual), or damages (a money award) for losses suffered. Although civil cases are normally between private individuals or organizations, governments also may be involved. For example, a state may file a civil action against an employer for allegedly discriminatory hiring practices, in violation of the state's antidiscrimination laws. A **criminal case**, on the other hand, involves an alleged violation of rules deemed so important that the breaking of them incurs society's formal punishment, which must be imposed by the criminal courts. In a criminal case, the government, represented by the prosecutor, brings the action against the individual.

Sometimes, the lines between civil and criminal cases are blurred. In most states, for example, if a juvenile is accused of committing a crime, he or she will most likely be brought to a juvenile or family court, which is considered a civil rather than a criminal setting. Juvenile courts are more informal and are typically closed to the public. However, they have aspects of criminal proceedings, such as the defendant's right to a lawyer and the opportunity to confront and cross-examine one's accuser and other witnesses. Disputes between private persons or organizations, such as breaches of contract, libel suits, or divorce actions, are clearly civil cases. Certain actions, however, can incur both civil and criminal penalties. This often happens in cases involving corporate malfeasance. The massive cases of Enron Corporation, Anderson Accounting Firm, and WorldCom in 2002 included alleged violations of both criminal and civil laws. In 2010, a mining disaster in which 29 coal miners lost their lives in West Virginia represented the worst mine disaster in 25 years in the United States. Also in 2010, an offshore oil spill in the Gulf of Mexico cost the lives of 11 oil workers and is now recognized as the worst environmental disaster in U.S. history. At present these cases, which possibly involved violations of both civil and criminal laws, are still under investigation.

Despite media coverage suggesting the opposite, most cases reaching the courts are civil rather than criminal, and civil cases are often more complex. The backlog of civil disputes is very high, and the process of achieving settlement can be tedious. In addition, civil courts deal with extremely emotionally wrenching issues, including the personal disputes that occur among family members and intensely personal matters such as those requiring end-of-life and other medical decisions.

The Judicial Process

The judicial process consists of a series of steps or stages through which litigants proceed. In high-profile or complex cases, the process can be very lengthy, sometimes taking years to complete, especially in civil cases. In the 1990s, tobacco and asbestos litigation cases threatened to immobilize the courts. Even relatively simple cases can get bogged down in the courts, however. These delays can be problematic in both criminal and civil cases, for all parties involved and for many different reasons. For example, in criminal cases, evidence deteriorates, and crime victims, as well as defendants, are held in abeyance. The defendant also may be confined in jail, unable to post bail. In civil cases, both plaintiffs and defendants have their lives on hold until the court proceedings have been terminated. On the other hand, delays also can be functional, such as when they encourage a settlement, allow more extensive investigation, or uncover new witnesses who may come forward and help absolve an innocent defendant.

It is helpful to divide the judicial or court process in both criminal and civil cases into four broad stages: (1) pretrial, (2) trial, (3) disposition, and (4) appeals. Various court appearances and hearings can occur at each of these stages, and there are many illustrations of what practicing psychologists can contribute. In the following discussion, we will emphasize those proceedings at each stage that are most likely to involve the assistance of the forensic psychologist. Unless otherwise specified, the discussion relates to both civil and criminal cases.

In addition, although we describe a process that is typical in courts across the United States, the proceedings and what they are called may vary across jurisdictions.

The Pretrial Stage

The courts can become involved in a *criminal* case very early, when police contact a judge or a magistrate to obtain a warrant to search or to arrest a suspect. Most arrests and most searches do not require warrants, however, so a court's first contact with a criminal case is typically either at the initial appearance or at the arraignment. However, in the federal system and some states, the prosecutor must obtain an indictment from a grand jury very early in the process. The **grand jury** is a body of citizens that reviews the evidence provided by the prosecutor and decides whether there is sufficient evidence to indict (formally accuse) the individual.

The **initial appearance** occurs if an arrested individual is being held in jail rather than released or cited to appear in court at a later date. Detained individuals must appear before a judge or magistrate, usually within 24 hours, to ensure that there are legal grounds to hold them.

Because jail detention can be an extremely stressful occurrence, detainees are screened for evidence of mental disorder or psychological crisis. Although jail officers or social caseworkers often perform this initial screening, which does not invariably occur, a consulting psychologist or psychiatrist may be called in if a detainee appears to be in major psychological crisis. Some large jails have psychologists, psychiatrists, or other mental health professionals on staff, but the typical jail setting employs them on a contract or as-needed basis. As indicated above, communities across the United States are experimenting with mental health courts to divert some defendants away from traditional criminal courts. Similarly, suspects with substance abuse problems or even those arrested in some domestic violence incidents may be diverted to drug or domestic violence courts. (See Focus 4.1 for a summary of common features of drug courts.)

The next pretrial step relevant to psychological practice is the **arraignment,** an open proceeding at which formal charges are read. At the arraignment, the presiding judge asks defendants if they understand the charges, informs them of their right to counsel, and asks them to enter pleas.

At this point, it is not unusual for persons charged with minor offenses and even many felonies to plead guilty and receive an immediate fine or sentence. Others plead *nolo contendere,* indicating that they will not contest the charges but are not admitting their guilt. For purposes of the criminal law, a *nolo contendere* plea has the same effect as a guilty plea; that is, a conviction is entered on the record.

Since the 1990s, forensic psychologists and psychiatrists have given considerable attention to the issue of a person's competency to plead guilty. This is an important matter because approximately 90% of criminal defendants plead guilty at arraignment or change their not-guilty plea to guilty before a trial date (Neubauer, 2002). Another possible plea—one highly relevant to forensic psychology—is not guilty by reason of insanity (NGRI), which is actually a not-guilty plea accompanied by notice that insanity will be used as a *defense.* When an NGRI plea is being considered, the forensic psychologist or psychiatrist is typically asked to examine the defendant and determine whether an insanity defense could be supported. This evaluation—called a criminal responsibility (CR) or mental state at the time of the offense (MSO) evaluation—is usually requested or arranged by the defense lawyer. A separate inquiry, whether the defendant is competent to stand trial, may be conducted at the request of the defense lawyer, the prosecutor, or the presiding judge. Criminal responsibility and competency examinations will be covered in detail in Chapter 5.

The not-guilty plea sets the trial process in motion. The next step is one or more pretrial hearings, during which witnesses, arresting officers, and other parties may present evidence. Numerous decisions may be made during these pretrial hearings. They include whether evidence is admissible, whether a trial should be moved because of extensive pretrial publicity, whether a youth should be transferred to juvenile court, whether a defendant is competent to stand trial, and whether bail should be denied because of the alleged dangerousness of a defendant.

Forensic psychologists are involved extensively during the pretrial stage in both juvenile and adult criminal cases. In cases where a judge must decide whether a juvenile's case should be heard in criminal court or in juvenile court, psychologists frequently assess the juvenile and file a report (or testify) as to the juvenile's level of development and ability to be rehabilitated. As noted above, when the mental health of a defendant is in question, the psychologist is again called on to perform an assessment. If a defendant is subsequently determined not competent to stand trial, psychologists may be involved in treating the defendant to restore competency. Defendants also may be evaluated with reference to their potential dangerousness or risk to the community if allowed free on bail pending their next court appearance.

The pretrial process in *civil* cases has parallels to the above but many differences as well. Those filing suits are called plaintiffs, and those being sued are defendants. The plaintiff's lawyer files a complaint outlining the alleged wrong and the desired remedy. The defendant is served with the complaint and is given a time limit in which to respond. As in criminal cases, there may be extensive negotiation between parties. In addition, there are pretrial conferences with the judge in an attempt to facilitate a settlement. In civil cases, forensic psychologists are more likely to be involved behind the scenes, consulting with one or the other attorney in the preparation of a case. A neuropsychologist, for example, may be asked to conduct a variety of tests on a plaintiff who is suing his employer for hazardous work conditions that resulted in a near-fatal accident and substantial injury to the brain.

The **discovery process** is an important component of the pretrial process in both criminal and civil cases. This requires each side to make available information at its disposal to the other side in the preparation of its case. The exact type of information to be made known is regulated by statute. For example, in virtually all states and the federal government, the prosecutor is expected to inform the defense lawyer about information that might exculpate (or help clear) the defendant. The defense lawyer, however, is not bound to inform the prosecutor of evidence that might inculpate (or work to the detriment of) his or her client. However, if the defendant plans to raise a defense based on mental state (e.g., insanity or duress), the defense lawyer is expected to share the contents of a court-ordered psychological evaluation with the prosecutor. It should be noted, though, that there is wide variation in state laws relating to the amount of information that the defendant is entitled to from the prosecutor.

As part of the discovery process, **depositions** (defined earlier in chapter) may be required. The deposition is part of the court record, and information obtained therein may well reappear at the trial. Recall that potential witnesses are questioned under oath and in the presence of a court reporter. Forensic psychologists are advised to review the transcription of a deposition very carefully, in the event that clerical errors might have been made (A. K. Hess, 1999).

The Trial Stage

In both criminal and civil cases, trials follow a similar pattern of stages. If it is to be a trial by jury (as opposed to a trial before only a judge, called a **bench trial or court trial**), the first step is to select jurors from a jury pool that is representative of the community. The process of selecting jurors from a pool for a particular trial is relevant to those forensic psychologists who serve as trial consultants to lawyers. In all jury trials, potential jurors are questioned by lawyers and sometimes by the presiding judge. This process, formally called the *voir dire*, is done to uncover bias and to attempt to produce an objective jury. In addition, the *voir dire* allows lawyers to select individuals whom they believe will be sympathetic to their case. When jury consultants are involved, they have often gathered information about potential jurors from public records or even from interviews with their acquaintances. The lawyer can then use this information in forming questions to ask of a potential juror. The consultant also may sit at the defense or prosecution table and make inferences based on a potential juror's nonverbal behavior or reaction to questions. These inferences are then communicated to the lawyer who has hired the consultant, and the lawyer must decide whether to "strike" the individual from the jury. We will discuss this aspect of jury consultation in more detail later in the chapter.

Lawyers have two avenues by which to strike or remove a potential juror. One, the **peremptory challenge,** allows the lawyer to reject a potential juror without stating a reason. Based on a "gut feeling" or on the recommendations of a consultant, a lawyer may decide that a given individual would not be receptive to the lawyer's side. The U.S. Supreme Court has placed some limitation on these challenges, ruling that they may not be exercised on the basis of race or gender (*Batson v. Kentucky,* 1986; *J.E.B. v. Alabama,* 1994). For example, a lawyer cannot remove all women from a jury because the lawyer believes women would not be sympathetic to his client. If the presiding judge suspects that this is being done, the judge must inquire into the lawyer's reasons to ensure that the peremptory challenge is not being used in a discriminatory fashion. There is, however, no constitutional right to peremptory challenges. In fact, in the latest case involving peremptories, *Rivera v. Illinois* (2009), the Court unanimously ruled that, if a judge made a good faith error in denying a peremptory challenge, this did not require an automatic reversal of a conviction provided all seated jurors were qualified and unbiased.

The second avenue for striking a potential juror is the **challenge for cause.** Here, a specific reason for removing the individual is offered. For example, the potential juror may have had a past relationship with one of the parties or may even be an outspoken advocate on a matter that is crucial to the case at hand. A potential juror who has already formed a strong opinion of the case is also apt to be removed "for cause."

During the presentation of evidence and cross-examination of witnesses, forensic psychologists who serve as trial consultants may continue to sit at the defense or prosecution table, conducting tasks similar to those performed during jury selection. Alternately, they may be working behind the scenes helping an attorney in ongoing case preparation, including the preparation of witnesses. The most visible role for psychologists during the trial is that of expert witness. These topics will be covered in some detail in the pages ahead.

The Disposition Stage

In a criminal case, when a judge or jury renders a verdict of not guilty, the case is over and the defendant is free to go. If the defendant is convicted, however, a decision must be made whether to incarcerate the individual and for how long and, in death penalty cases, whether to impose the ultimate penalty or an alternative life sentence. Often judges will order convicted offenders to undergo treatment, such as substance abuse or psychological treatment for sex offenders. (See Photo 4.1, depicting the sentencing hearing of a public figure who was ordered to participate in substance abuse treatment.) The role of the forensic psychologist at sentencing can be a critical one. In civil cases, when

Photo 4.1 Lindsay Lohan and her attorney awaiting her sentencing after violating probation in two drunk driving cases. Lohan was sentenced to 90 days in jail and ordered to participate in an inpatient substance abuse program.

a verdict favors the plaintiff, a **judgment** is handed down, specifying the remedy to be borne by the defendant. In deciding on a remedy, judges and juries often consider testimony relating to the psychological harm a plaintiff may have suffered. It should be noted that the juvenile process—which is civil—also might involve a "sentence," which is called a **disposition** in juvenile courts. Here, psychologists may be asked to offer opinions on the type of rehabilitative strategies that could be used for a particular juvenile.

In many felony cases, sentencing judges have obtained a **presentence investigation** (PSI) report. This is a document that has been prepared by an agent of the criminal justice system (typically a probation officer) or by a private firm. The PSI is a social history that includes information about the offender's family background, employment history, level of education, substance abuse, criminal history, medical needs, and mental health history, among other factors. PSI reports often include a *victim impact statement,* which is a summary of what the victim suffered—both physically and emotionally—as a result of the crime. Psychologists who have examined the offender or the victim may submit a report that is appended to the document. Alternately, information obtained by psychologists may be included within the PSI itself.

The Appellate Stage

Neither civil nor criminal cases necessarily end with the trial and disposition stages. Defendants who are losing parties have a variety of options for appealing their convictions, their sentences, or the judgments against them. A person convicted of a crime may appeal his or her conviction on a number of grounds, including errors made during the pretrial or trial stages or inadequate assistance of counsel. Likewise, sentences may be appealed for being disproportionate to the crime committed or on the basis of errors made during the sentencing hearing. The vast majority of criminal appeals are unsuccessful; roughly 1 out of 8 criminal appellants wins on appeal (Neubauer, 2002). A "win" does not mean that the convicted person will be free, however. When appeals courts rule in favor of convicted offenders, they almost always order new trials, a resentencing, or a lower court review of the case consistent with the appellate court's decision. It should be noted that a prosecutor cannot appeal a not-guilty verdict (this would violate the Constitution's prohibition against double jeopardy), but he or she can appeal a sentence that is considered too lenient. This is very rarely done, however.

Appeals of civil cases often revolve around a defendant's appeal of a judgment or a jury award. In recent years, for example, defendants have been appealing large damage awards given to plaintiffs by civil juries, and some judges have reduced these awards. Judgments in civil cases also are notoriously difficult to enforce, and when defendants do not comply, plaintiffs must initiate further legal action. "The arduous process of litigation may prove to be only a preliminary step to the equally protracted travail of collecting the award" (Neubauer, 1997, p. 331).

The individual forensic psychologist has little to do with the appellate stage, although he or she may have considerable stake in the outcome. In some cases, the psychologist's role during the earlier stages of the case may itself be in question. During the 1980s, for example, many individuals convicted of child sexual abuse appealed their convictions on the basis that psychologists who had interviewed alleged victims unduly influenced their testimony. In 2003, a federal appellate court ruled that a new trial might be required in a double-murder case because a psychologist who testified at the original trial had misrepresented his credentials (Ewing, 2003). Interestingly, the appeals court indicated that the false credentials themselves were not the critical factor that would determine the need for a new trial; rather, the critical factor was whether the prosecutor knew or should have known that the testimony was perjured (Ewing, 2003). And, in 2009, a federal appeals court ruled that "profiling" testimony provided by an expert witness nearly 30 years ago was "quackery," and that the witness had inflated his credentials with the knowledge of the county district attorney. The defendant in the case, who was ultimately convicted and imprisoned and challenged his imprisonment from his prison cell, was granted a new trial.

Another way in which forensic psychologists are connected with the appellate stage is through the filing of ***amicus curiae*** (friend of the court) **briefs.** An amicus brief is a document filed by interested parties who did not participate directly in the trial but either have a stake in the outcome or have research knowledge to offer the appellate court (Saks, 1993). Amicus briefs are typically filed by organizations on behalf of their members. The American Psychological Association, for example, has filed numerous briefs with state and federal appellate courts on topics such as involuntary civil commitment, sexual orientation, professional licensing, child testimony in sexual assault cases, the forced medication of inmates, and the effects of employment discrimination. (Focus 4.2 includes excerpts from the *amicus curiae* brief filed in a recent case involving juvenile crime. That case will be discussed again in Chapter 6.)

Appellate courts, of course, do not necessarily rule in accordance with the weight of the social science evidence. The U.S. Supreme Court case *Boy Scouts of America v. Dale* (2000) is illustrative. In that case, the APA submitted a brief that outlined a long line of psychological and social science research supporting equal treatment for gays and lesbians. For example, the brief cited the overwhelming research that gays and lesbians are no more likely to abuse children than are heterosexuals and are equally likely to form loving, long-term relationships with other adults. Nevertheless, the Court ruled that the Boy Scouts—as a private organization—had a First Amendment right to exclude homosexuals from serving as scoutmasters. Although the *Dale* case appears to conflict with the Court's later decision in *Lawrence and Garner v. Texas* (2003), there was a significant difference in that in the Texas case, the state was punishing people for what the Court determined to be private consensual behavior within their home.

Other cases have been decided more in accordance with social science evidence. *Atkins v. Virginia* (2002) involved the execution of individuals who are developmentally disabled. The brief writers argued that, considering the decision-making abilities of persons whose mental development is below the normal range, it violated common standards of decency to put these individuals to death. In a 6–3 decision, the Supreme Court agreed, ruling that persons with an IQ below 70 who were so developmentally disabled that they could not perform for themselves the daily tasks of living could not be put to death. Likewise, the Court has outlawed the death penalty for juveniles 17 and under (*Roper v. Simmons*, 2005) as well as life without parole sentences for juveniles not convicted of murder (see Focus 4.2).

Some time ago, Grisso and Saks (1991) urged psychologists not to be discouraged when appellate courts did not rule in line with social science evidence. The U.S. Supreme Court's expertise in constitutional analysis, as well as the numerous other sources of information available to the Justices, must be considered. Grisso and Saks maintained that the Court does not directly *reject* social science evidence but rather has often based its decisions on other grounds. *Boy Scouts v. Dale* is a case in point. The Court did not disagree with the points made by the APA and other groups that filed similar briefs. Rather, they found that, as a private organization, the Boy Scouts had a First Amendment freedom of association and thus could (but did not have to) reject individuals for leadership positions based on their sexual orientation. Nevertheless, it can be very frustrating for forensic psychologists and researchers in other social sciences when appellate courts seem to ignore the social science evidence offered to them.

In this and the following two chapters, we will turn our attention to a discussion of specific tasks assumed by psychologists in their interaction with the civil and criminal courts. In this chapter, we discuss their work as trial consultants, both in preparation for the trial and during the trial itself, and their participation as expert witnesses.

FOCUS 4.2. AMICUS CURIAE BRIEF: *GRAHAM v. FLORIDA*

Terrance Jamar Graham's family background is littered with unfortunate circumstances, including parents addicted to crack cocaine and a diagnosis of ADHD (attention deficit/hyperactivity disorder). He was 16 years old when he was arrested and charged with armed burglary and attempted robbery of a restaurant. Graham's case was heard in criminal court, and he was convicted and placed on probation. While on probation, he was allegedly involved in a home invasion, although he denied this charge. He did admit to associating with the young adults who perpetrated the offense and fleeing from the scene. Because he violated the conditions of his probation, he was returned to court and then sentenced to life without parole for a combination of offenses including the original armed burglary, attempted robbery, and probation violations.

The U.S. Supreme Court ruled in *Graham v. Florida* (2010)—along with a similar companion case—that a sentence of life without the possibility of parole for juvenile offenders who did not commit murder was cruel and unusual punishment in violation of the 8th Amendment of the Constitution.

Along with other professional organizations (The American Psychiatric Association, the National Association of Social Workers, and Mental Health America), the American Psychological Association had filed an amicus curiae brief arguing against the life sentence.

Citing extensive research in developmental psychology and neuroscience, the brief stated, among other things, that

- Juveniles have a lesser capacity for mature judgment.
- Juveniles are more vulnerable to negative external influences.
- Their unformed identify makes it less likely that their offenses evince a fixed bad character and more likely that they will reform.
- Their psychosocial immaturity is consistent with emerging research on brain development.
- It is disproportionate punishment to sentence them to die in prison with no opportunity to demonstrate reform.

The research findings summarized above will be discussed again in Chapter 6, where we focus on issues relating to juveniles in the justice system.

Source: American Psychological Association (2010).

Trial and Litigation Consultation

Psychologists often consult with key players in the judicial process, particularly lawyers. There appears to be no shortage of tasks to perform, both before the trial and during the trial itself, and the work can be quite lucrative. Although members of other professions can and do serve as trial consultants (e.g., sociologists, economists, political scientists), the majority of trial consultants are psychologists (Strier, 1999). They do not necessarily consider themselves "forensic psychologists," however, despite the fact that they work in the forensic arena.

Furthermore, trial consultants are often associated with major, nationwide consulting firms based in metropolitan areas. Examples are DecisionQuest and The Advocates.

In recent years, some of the literature in this area (e.g., Davidson, 2004; Finkelman, 2010) has distinguished between trial or jury consultants and litigation consultants, conceptualizing "trial or jury consultation" as a more narrow term that focuses primarily on traditional activities like aiding in the selection of jurors or helping in the preparation of witnesses. By contrast, "litigation consultation" is conceptualized as a more expanded version of these traditional roles, which can embrace such broader activities as assessing trial strategy or assessing the economic or emotional impact of going to trial (Finkelman, 2010). As R. Newman (2010) states,

> Although jury consulting is often viewed as attempting to ensure a fair trial, litigation consulting is seen as helping to gain a competitive advantage; the former activity is intended to achieve the court's objective whereas the latter is intended to achieve the objective of the attorney who hired the consultant. (p. 76)

While we appreciate the effort to make this distinction, we see considerable overlap in these terms—and to date most of the research literature uses "trial or jury consultation," even when describing the broader activities mentioned above. Furthermore, it is a challenge to argue that the attorney who hires a jury consultant is not intending to achieve his or her objective. In the future, distinctions between these terms may become the norm; for the present, we will continue to use the more common terms "trial or jury consultation."

Trial or jury consultants often have backgrounds in industrial psychology or social psychology, but this is not a requirement. The two main areas in which they work are in jury selection and in assisting the lawyer during the trial process, although in recent years work with jury selection has lessened. Increasingly, consultants help attorneys at a variety of trial preparation tasks, such as preparing witnesses and making decisions about particular trial strategies (Boccaccini, 2002; B. Myers & Arena, 2001). As an example, a lawyer might wonder what type of mental health professional to contact for the purpose of testifying about the effects of posttraumatic stress disorder. In his or her role as trial consultant, the psychologist would offer suggestions. The psychologist also might help to prepare these experts for the trial or help the attorney interpret clinical reports provided by mental health practitioners. In addition, once a jury has been seated, the consultant may inform the lawyer about existing jury research. One noted trial consultant firm advertises its success at helping lawyers get into the minds of jurors (Duboff & Neufer, 2010).

Again, though, the case that actually goes to trial is the exception. The great majority of both civil and criminal cases (often as much as 90%) are resolved through negotiation or mediation. Both parties want to avoid the time, expense, and unpredictability of a protracted trial, and—in criminal cases—a defendant may decide to plead guilty to protect another person or in exchange for a lighter sentence. As mentioned in Chapter 2, even persons who are not guilty sometime plead guilty, a reality that members of the public often have difficulty comprehending.

The cases that do go to trial are often high-profile cases in which the defendants (both criminal and civil) have a good deal to lose if the verdict does not come out in their favor. In the criminal context, they may be cases in which the defendant is truly innocent, despite the fact that probable cause to believe he or she committed the crime has been established. They may be death penalty cases or cases that would incur a long prison sentence. In the civil context, cases that go to trial may involve highly emotional situations in which one or both sides do not wish to compromise, such as litigation over custody of dependent children or the contesting of a will. They also may be those in which a corporate defendant stands to lose millions of dollars or even faces corporate dissolution if found to be at fault. The highly litigated case against A. H. Robins Company in the late 1970s and 1980s is a case in point (see Finley, 1996). Robins manufactured the Dalkon Shield, a birth control device that was subsequently found to produce numerous negative consequences (e.g., extreme bleeding, maiming, cramping, nausea, infections) for the women who used it. Women all across the United States sued Robins, and one jury, in Kansas, returned a $7.5 million punitive damages verdict against the company. Robins eventually filed for bankruptcy. Thus, when stakes are high, defendants (and occasionally prosecutors) with the financial means to do so are willing to assume considerable expense to hire experts to assist them in their jury selection and other trial preparation work.

Scientific Jury Selection

Scientific jury selection is the application of social science techniques in an effort to find a jury that will be favorably disposed toward one's case. This process may include attitude surveys within the community in an attempt to determine representative views on matters dealing with the upcoming case. Defense lawyers representing a corporate client being sued for illegally dumping hazardous wastes might want to know how members of the community in general view corporate crime. More important, what are the demographic profiles of persons who are friendly toward corporations? And what of the anti-corporation individual: What type of individual is most likely to be favorably disposed toward someone suing a large corporation? In the 1970s and 1980s, scientific jury selection was the rage, but it appears to have diminished in recent years, probably because of the extensive research required. Trial consultants who engage in scientific jury selection must conduct surveys, set up focus groups, interview community members, and employ other research strategies to try to help predict who will likely be a good juror for their client.

At the pretrial stage, lawyers are also concerned about the effect of publicity that could be prejudicial to their client's case. Thus, trial consultants may be asked to conduct surveys of the community and collect evidence of negative publicity, which would support a motion for a change of venue (change in the location of the trial). Once the trial is over, consultants also may be asked to conduct posttrial interviews with members of the jury who agree to be interviewed. This allows insight not only into the decision making of the jurors, but also into the effectiveness of the strategies engaged in by attorneys during the trial itself.

Witness Preparation

Trial consultants also help attorneys prepare witnesses and determine effective strategies for presenting evidence and persuading jurors (B. Myers & Arena, 2001). In preparing for the trial date, attorneys on each side of the conflict often meet with the witnesses they will be calling to the stand. This is done "to review, discuss, and sometimes modify the substance and delivery of their anticipated testimony" (Boccaccini, 2002, p. 161). In the case of lay witnesses who are not accustomed to a courtroom appearance, this prior meeting with lawyers (or sometimes with trial consultants) is considered an important step to avoid "surprises" in the testimony and to lessen the courtroom-related stress that witnesses may experience. Although attorneys are obviously concerned about the substance of a witness's testimony, they also are concerned about the presentation. The task of preparing witnesses may be shared with a trial consultant, part of whose task is to coach an individual in how to be a persuasive, confident witness. Finkelman (2010) emphasizes that "ethics require that preparation is limited to presentation techniques, rather than attempting to alter factual circumstances" (p. 14). Even psychologists serving as expert witnesses may benefit from coaching, as Dr. Stanley Brodsky indicates in Personal Perspective 4.2.

On the basis of his review of the available literature on this topic, Boccaccini (2002) notes that **witness preparation** involves three broad components: witness education, attorney education, and modification of testimony delivery. *Witness education* orients the witness to the courtroom process and reviews with the witness his or her previous statements (e.g., to police or during pretrial depositions) to ensure that there will be no contradictions. *Attorney education* allows the lawyer to be totally familiar with the information held by the witness. The *modification of testimony delivery* involves coaching the witness in such behaviors as speaking, dressing, and responding to the judge or the cross-examining attorney. (See Photo 4.2, illustrating a witness who was likely coached in how to describe the incident she observed.) Very little is known about the extent to which these strategies are used or whether such preparation affects the final outcome of the case.

Certain aspects of witness preparation are controversial because they may reinforce in the witness a memory that is actually quite weak. Recall the discussion about commitment bias in Chapter 2. An initially uncertain witness can be led to be very certain by police statements that imply approval of his or her lineup identification.

Photo 4.2 An eyewitness demonstrates in court the beating she saw from her apartment window after the Super Bowl in January 2000.

In a similar fashion, rehearsal of one's testimony during witness preparation is likely to increase one's confidence in that testimony. Research on eyewitness testimony indicates that jurors are more likely to believe or find credible a witness who speaks clearly and appears highly confident (Penrod & Cutler, 1995).

This may also be true of criminal defendants who take the stand in their own defense, although there is little research available on this matter. We are aware of a case in which a defendant was acquitted of rape, characterizing the incident as a consensual encounter of the "one-night stand" variety. In interviews with jurors after the not-guilty verdict, one juror told a reporter that the defendant was the only one among all of the witnesses to maintain eye contact with both attorneys while he was on the witness stand.

Suggestive questioning by attorneys or trial consultants also might lead witnesses to recall details that they did not initially remember. "Objectively false but subjectively true testimony can be created when a witness's memory of an event is distorted during the course of witness preparation, leading them to give unknowingly false or misleading testimony" (Boccaccini, 2002, p. 166). In fact, as mentioned in earlier chapters, eyewitness memory itself, even without the benefit of witness preparation, is extremely fallible. Such information has been a principal source of evidence in both criminal and civil cases. The expanding psychological research in the area, however, indicates that the judicial system should carefully examine some of its assumptions about eyewitness testimony. Psychological research has strongly suggested that evidence gained through eyewitness questioning and testimony is often teeming with inaccuracies and misconceptions, regardless of how certain the eyewitness claims to be. In fact, the "commonsense" view that the more confident a witness is about what he or she saw, the more accurate the witness tends to be is simply not supported by research data. The research consensus concludes that human perception and memory are unreliable sources of information where the original input is altered; partially lost; or transformed into a view that fits our experiences, expectations, and needs. In some cases, eyewitness testimony barely resembles the incident as it "actually" occurred.

The *Voir Dire*

During the trial itself, trial consultants perform a different group of tasks. The first stage of the trial is the jury selection process, technically called the *voir dire*. This involves the questioning of potential jurors to best ensure a nonbiased jury. Here, the pretrial research done by the trial consultant—if it was done—is put to practical use, as lawyers attempt to remove from the jury persons who will not likely be sympathetic to their side and select those who would be. The consultant may suggest *voir dire* questions to lawyers and make inferences about prospective jurors based on their responses or even on their nonverbal behavior (Strier, 1999).

Also during the trial, a "shadow jury" may have been set up. These are individuals similar in demographics to persons who are serving on the actual jury. If possible, members of the shadow jury should be in the courtroom on a daily basis to hear the testimony. The trial consultant keeps in close touch with them, noting, for example, their reactions to the evidence as it is being presented as well as to the tactics and strategies of the respective lawyers. Information from the shadow jury can then be transmitted to the trial consultant's client. During the trial, the trial consultant also may suggest questions or strategies to the lawyer.

The efficacy of these approaches has yet to be demonstrated scientifically, although there are anecdotal accounts of success in major trials. Defense lawyers in a number of politically related trials in the 1960s and 1970s, for example, credited jury consultants with helping them to select jurors when their clients were acquitted. Since that time, defense teams in a number of other high-profile cases that ended in acquittals (e.g., the O. J. Simpson case) have hired consultants. Although their help in selecting jurors may have contributed to the overall success of the defense in these cases, numerous other factors are relevant. Defendants able to afford trial consultants, for example, are also able to afford lawyers who can devote their full attention to the case, in contrast to less economically advantaged defendants. This raises concerns about the fairness of using consultants. In politically charged trials, when the individual defendants themselves do not have the financial resources to hire consultants, supportive interest groups may provide funds for the consultants. However, the average criminal defendant or the average litigant in a civil suit is usually unable to afford such services.

Trial Consultation: The Main Concerns

Research psychologists tend to be very skeptical of trial consulting, particularly the aspect of attempting to select jurors sympathetic to one's case. As mentioned earlier, some aspects of witness preparation also raise concern. With respect to scientific jury selection, comments by Ellsworth and Reifman (2000) are representative: "Jury researchers have searched in vain for individual differences—race, gender, class, attitudes, or personality—that reliably predict a person's verdict and have almost always come up empty handed" (p. 795). In a similar vein, law professor John Conley (2000) expressed wonderment "at the vast sums of money that lawyers and clients expend on jury-selection 'experts' who purport to produce psychological profiles of 'ideal' jurors for particular cases" (p. 823).

The lack of oversight of trial consulting has also been noted. As Strier (1999) observed, both for-profit and nonprofit trial consulting can now be found online, but whether online or not, it is largely unregulated:

"There are no state licensing requirements, nor is there any binding or meaningful code of professional ethics" (p. 96). Others have observed that there are no qualifications or education requirements, so trial consultants work with few restrictions (Griffith, Hart, Kessler, & Goodling, 2007). B. Myers and Arena (2001), acknowledging the legitimacy of such concerns, nevertheless are supportive of trial consultation. Psychologists, they believe, can help to restore the balance in the presently unbalanced scales of justice. They agree, though, that better standards in training and methodology are needed if the field is to advance.

There is indication, too, that jurors might be leery of trial consultation, although the research on this issue is very sparse. Griffith et al. (2007) surveyed jury-eligible individuals in two states on their perceptions of trial consultants. Although there were wide individual differences influenced by income, ethnicity, age, gender, and belief in the fairness of the system, overall 18% of those surveyed said they would be biased *against* the side using a trial consultant, while less than 0.25% said they would be biased *in favor* of the side that used a trial consultant. The researchers remarked that the side using a trial consultant might want to downplay this use, such as by limiting "face time" with the jury, while the side not using a consultant might want to be sure that the jury is aware of this use. According to Griffith et al. the public might have a more favorable view of trial consultants if they could be persuaded that they did not compromise the fairness of the system. This might be done by having trial consultants provide more pro bono work and by educating the public better about the services they provide.

Expert Testimony

In addition to working behind the scenes or sitting in the courtroom as trial consultants, psychologists also may be found on the witness stand, testifying as expert witnesses in a wide range of cases. This very visible role has produced extensive research and commentary. Expert testimony has been the subject of three significant Supreme Court decisions over the past decade. Together, the three decisions (*Daubert v. Merrill Dow Pharmaceuticals, Inc.*, 1993; *General Electric Co. v. Joiner*, 1997; *Kumho Tire Co. v. Carmichael*, 1999), collectively referred to as *Daubert* or the *Daubert* trilogy, articulate the standard to be applied by federal courts in deciding whether expert testimony—including that of psychologists—should be admitted if it is challenged by the opposing lawyer. By the end of the 20th century, 30 states also had adopted a standard identical to or closely related to *Daubert* (Parry & Drogan, 2000). We will discuss this in more detail shortly.

Expert testimony may occur in a variety of pretrial hearings, during both civil and criminal trials or delinquency proceedings, or during sentencing or disposition hearings. In each of these contexts, the role of the expert witness is to help the judge or the jury in making decisions about matters that are beyond the knowledge of the typical layperson. Most jurors and judges, for example, are not versed in neurology and the fine workings of the brain. Thus, a neuropsychologist may be called to testify about the effects of physical trauma—such as a severe head injury—on brain functioning. Likewise, most jurors and judges are unfamiliar with the psychological effects of ongoing physical abuse or experiencing a highly traumatic event such as a rape or a kidnapping; in such cases, experts on child abuse or on posttraumatic stress disorder (PTSD) might be called to the stand. Psychologists also have valuable information to convey to courts relative to eyewitness identification, pretrial publicity, human perception and memory, the credibility of child witnesses, or the effect of divorce on children.

Clinical psychologists are also frequently called to testify about the results of evaluations they have conducted. In the criminal context, for example, psychologists often conduct court-ordered evaluations of a defendant's competency to stand trial or of his or her mental state at the time of the crime. In these situations, the psychologist will submit a written report to the judge and the attorneys. If the parties do not agree with the psychologist's conclusions, or if the judge wishes additional information or clarification, the psychologist may then be called to testify. In highly litigated cases—such as in a serious violent crime or a custody dispute—another clinician may be called to testify as well. This resulting "battle of the experts" is often disparaged: "If you look hard enough, you'll find a 'so-called expert' willing to testify to anything."

In light of the above, it is no wonder that testifying as an expert is not for everyone. (This point is made quite clearly by Dr. Stanley Brodsky, a prominent psychologist with many years of courtroom, research, and teaching experience, in Personal Perspective 4.2.) Experts are often subjected to withering cross-examination, and they understandably may arrive at different opinions on issues. The case of Elizabeth Smart, who was kidnapped from her bedroom at 14 and found alive and living with her captors 9 months later, is illustrative. In 2009, Brian David Mitchell—one of her accused captors—was found competent to stand trial after a 10-day competency hearing during which opposing psychologists provided their assessments, one giving the opinion that he was competent and the other giving the opinion that he was delusional and was not competent. Mitchell's trial began in November 2010 but was interrupted early on when he suffered a seizure in the courtroom and was hospitalized. According to media reports, the trial was disrupted daily by the defendant's hymn singing. Mitchell's attorneys argued that their client was mentally disordered and therefore not responsible for his actions, but the defense was unsuccessful. Mitchell was convicted December 10, 2010.

PERSONAL PERSPECTIVE 4.2

On the Witness Stand

Stanley Brodsky, PhD

The cross-examining attorney had just asked the psychologist on the witness stand how much she was getting paid. After she answered, the attorney moved a little closer to the witness stand, just barely visibly wet his lips with his tongue, and then, in a booming voice, demanded,

"That's a great deal of money, isn't it, doctor?"

The psychologist paused before answering. Then she leaned forward a little, and in a quiet, assured voice, answered,

"Not at all. It is exactly the right amount of money, given how much time I have worked on this evaluation and given my training."

The unstated implication in the attorney's question was that the psychologist was a bought witness, a hired gun whose opinion could be purchased. The perception of witnesses as "bought" has been studied (Cooper & Neuhaus, 2000), with the conclusion that high fees and out-of-town witnesses are more likely to lead to this perception. In our sample cross-examination, the attorney next asks,

"You think you're pretty smart, don't you?"

This question has the potential of putting the psychologist in a difficult position. If she answers, "Yes, I do," she may come across as arrogant or egotistical. If she says, "No," then she may be acknowledging that she is not smart. Part of my interest is in how psychologists and other expert witnesses manage such challenging questions. No single perfect answer exists, but one possible answer to the "You're so smart" question, could be,

"It is considered unprofessional and unbecoming for psychologists to engage in anything that hints of bragging."

This give and take between cross-examining attorneys and testifying experts has been the subject of my research and writing. I find the exchanges to be an intriguing psychological process, in which attorneys seek to diminish the believability of the expert, while the experts seek to maintain their composure and credibility.

I am involved in these issues of expert testimony in three ways. First, I conduct evaluations myself. At different times, I assess defendants and occasionally plaintiffs for issues related to the law. When the cases come to trial (and more often than not, they are settled or plea-bargained), I testify about my findings. Second, I teach mental health professionals about how to testify as an expert witness. Even experienced PhDs and MDs find themselves anxious about testifying in court, and sometimes competent and knowledgeable professionals can become flustered and ineffective when they testify. I lead workshops in which I pose the challenging questions and situations to participants, and teach them how to understand and master these situations. Finally, I lead a witness research lab in the Department of Psychology at The University of Alabama, in which we study what aspects of testimony are convincing to jurors and what components are detrimental. Some of the issues we study in the research lab (with findings in parentheses) are the following:

How does race affect credibility of expert witnesses? (With impressive credentials, African American experts are seen as more credible; with modest credentials, less credible.)

How does confidence of the testifying expert influence credential judgments by jurors? (The most credibility is seen in moderately confident experts.)

Is there a difference between jurors' judgments about very brief, thin slices of testimony compared to longer periods of testimony? (No)

How does head nodding by jurors relate to what they think of testifying experts? (When mock jurors are instructed to nod their heads during testimony, they rate the testifying expert much more positively.)

How much do jurors respond to remorse behaviors and observations of defendant remorse by experts? (Jurors are suspicious of remorse shown by defendants, because they think the defendants are just trying to get lighter sentences.)

How should women experts handle personal and gender-intrusive cross-examination questions like, "Have *you* ever been physically or sexually abused?" (Assertive rebukes to the questioners work best.)

When I testify, I find the experience always intellectually challenging. Expert witnesses never know exactly what they will be asked. Sometimes attorneys ask whether we have had sufficient training or relevant clinical experience. Sometimes they hand experts a photocopy of an article and ask the experts to read aloud a passage that contradicts their testimony. Now and then I am given a copy of an article I have written that appears in part to refute a piece of my testimony. This is a mistake on the part of the attorney. After all, those of us who write journal articles are experts on our own body of knowledge.

(Continued)

(Continued)

Even if the quoted passage seems to undermine my testimony, I will observe that the passage was taken out of a broader context or that I have learned a great deal since I wrote the article.

For students who may be considering whether they want to go into this field, ask yourselves if you enjoy vigorous verbal exchanges with other people. Reflect on whether you are okay with subjecting yourself to careful scrutiny. Think over whether you are able to think and speak well, spontaneously but with preparation. Remember that most psychologists do not begin as poised and composed on the witness stand. Instead, new experts often seek consultation from colleagues, attend workshops on how to be effective in court, and read over the books on the subject. My own books in this area are titled *Testifying in Court*, *The Expert Expert Witness*, and *Coping With Cross-Examination*, and are all published by the American Psychological Association. They are full of examples of the common ways in which attorneys try to control the content and emotions of testifying experts, and the ways in which experts can respond comfortably and masterfully.

Dr. Brodsky is a professor of psychology at The University of Alabama where he coordinates the Psychology-Law PhD concentration. His PhD was in clinical psychology from the University of Florida. He spends much of his leisure time traveling and exploring cultures new to him. His hobby is photography, and his office is decorated with photos from Cuba, India, Greece, New Zealand, and Puerto Rico.

Research with mock juries suggests that the response to expert testimony is lukewarm or guarded, rather than wholeheartedly supportive (Nietzel, McCarthy, & Kerr, 1999), and that clinical testimony is favored more than the research-based testimony provided by academicians (Krauss & Sales, 2001). In a survey of 488 adult residents in one state, Boccaccini and Brodsky (2002) found that the public was far more likely to believe expert witnesses who worked with patients rather than those who engaged in academic activities. (For more findings from the research on jurors and experts, see Dr. Brodsky's comments in Personal Perspective 4.2.) Respondents also were more likely to believe experts who received no payment for testifying, and there was some preference for those who came from the community. Expert testimony will be covered again in the next two chapters. For the present, it is important to look at issues that are common to all such testimony.

Expert Certification

To qualify as an expert witness, a psychologist must first establish his or her credentials, including the requisite advanced degree, licensing or certification if relevant, and research or practical experience in areas about which he or she is testifying. As mentioned at the beginning of this chapter, until the mid-20th century, courts were divided over whether psychologists were competent to testify on mental health issues, so the typical expert on issues such as insanity, competency to stand trial, dangerousness, or amenability to treatment was a psychiatrist. In *Jenkins v. United States* (1962), however—as noted earlier in the chapter—an influential federal appellate court acknowledged that psychologists as well as psychiatrists could qualify as expert witnesses. In each case, it is left to the discretion of the trial judge to accept or reject an individual's qualifications as an expert, subject to review by appellate courts. However, as mentioned in Chapter 1, laws in some states require specific credentials or licensing to perform some of the evaluations and subsequently testify in court proceedings (Heilbrun & Brooks, 2010).

The expert's credentials may be critical to the final outcome of the case. Recall the two cases mentioned earlier in the chapter, one of which occurred nearly 30 years ago and the person ultimately convicted was granted a new trial. In that case, the federal court indicated that the then-prosecutor knew that the expert witness was inflating his credentials. In the other case, a double-murder, a psychologist who testified for the prosecution falsified his credentials and testified about a supposed "syndrome" that no one else had ever heard of (Ewing, 2003). According to Ewing, cases like this illustrate a new concern among forensic psychologists:

> This has recently become an issue within the field of forensic psychology—to what extent are some psychologists presenting credentials in court purchased from vanity or mail order boards (credentials sold with little or no scrutiny of credentials or competence) to pad their credentials? (p. 84)

Ewing cautions lawyers who call on expert witnesses to carefully vet their résumés before putting them on the stand. Unfortunately, incidents such as those described above damage the reputation of psychology as a whole and erode public confidence in both law and mental health professionals.

Legal Standards for the Admission of Scientific Evidence

Even though an expert has the professional background to qualify for certification as an expert witness, it is possible that the presiding judge will not allow the evidence the expert has to offer. Under federal law and the law of the states that have adopted similar standards, if the opposing lawyer challenges the introduction of the evidence, the judge must decide whether the evidence is reliable, legally sufficient, and relevant to the case at hand. This was the standard for federal courts announced by the U.S. Supreme Court in its 1993 decision, *Daubert v. Merrill Dow Pharmaceuticals, Inc.* (see Focus 4.3). The *Daubert* rule replaced an earlier standard (announced in *Frye v. U.S.*, 1923), which was loosely known as the "general acceptance" rule. According to that earlier standard, the expert's evidence must have been gathered using scientific techniques that had reached a general acceptance in the science field. Once that standard had been met, all relevant testimony would be admissible.

Over the years, the *Frye* standard lost favor because—among other things—it was considered to be too stringent, presenting an obstacle to the introduction of evidence that had not yet reached "general acceptance." For example, evidence of "battered woman syndrome" or evidence obtained through hypnosis might be too controversial to be considered widely accepted by mental health practitioners. In the Federal Rules of Evidence, adopted in 1975, Congress provided a different standard. The pertinent rule, Rule 702, did not require general acceptance, but it did require that evidence be relevant and reliable. Even relevant information could be excluded, however, if it would serve to prejudice the jury. In *Daubert,* the Supreme Court supported the standard set by the Rules of Evidence. It did not completely denigrate the "general acceptance" criterion, however. Rather, it announced that general acceptance by the scientific community could be taken into consideration in deciding whether evidence was reliable. General acceptance should not, however, be a *necessary* condition. Although this may appear to be a more liberal standard, some research indicates it has had the opposite effect, as we will see next.

FOCUS 4.3. THE *DAUBERT* TRILOGY

The *Daubert* standard makes the judge a gatekeeper who must evaluate evidence—including the testimony of a mental health practitioner—and decide whether it should be admitted. To provide some guidance to judges, the Court listed five factors for them to take into consideration:

(1) Whether theories and techniques used by the witness have been tested;

(2) Whether they have been subjected to peer review and publication;

(Continued)

(Continued)

(3) Whether there is a known error rate;

(4) Whether the techniques are subject to standards governing their application;

(5) Whether the theories and techniques used are widely accepted by others in the profession.

So, in deciding whether any scientific evidence—such as DNA testing, polygraph results, psychological test results, neurological exams, profiling data—should be admitted into a court proceeding, for example, a judge would be expected to apply the above criteria to that evidence.

In a later case, *General Electric Co. v. Joiner* (1997), the Supreme Court said it would not second-guess judges unless they clearly abused their discretion in allowing or not allowing testimony. According to the Court, the trial court judge in the *Joiner* case had conducted a careful review of the scientific information that would have been offered by four different experts before concluding that it should not be admitted. Following that case, some commentators have suggested that the psychologist or other expert must take care to explain carefully to judges how and why his or her information is reliable and relevant. In other words, the testimony evaluated by the judge in the *Joiner* case may have been based on good science, but the experts may not have explained their work adequately.

In *Kumho Tire Co. Ltd. v. Carmichael* (1999), the Supreme Court ruled that *all* expert testimony—whether it is based on scientific, clinical, or technical knowledge—is subject to the same *Daubert* standard of relevance and reliability. Thus, clinical psychologists are clearly held to the same standard, something that was not clear until the Court's ruling in the *Kumho* case. As Otto and Heilbrun (2002) have stated, the mantle of science has been placed over the shoulders of practitioners as well as researchers.

State courts are free to adopt their own rules of evidence, but in practice many use federal rules as a model. Approximately 30 states use *Daubert*-like criteria for the admission of scientific evidence. Some courts already have seen the *Daubert* trilogy as an invitation to give very careful scrutiny to a variety of psychological tests used by clinicians in their assessment practices. In addition, the professional literature has hosted spirited debates over the relevance and reliability of these measures. For example, psychologists do not always agree on the relevance and reliability of the Rorschach Comprehensive System (RCS), which is a method of scoring Rorschach "inkblot" tests (e.g., Grove, Barden, Garb, & Lilienfeld, 2002). Similar disagreements occur over practices and assessments in other contexts, such as child custody evaluations, repressed memory, hypnosis, and use of the polygraph (Otto & Heilbrun, 2002).

In spite of the above discussion, it is important to emphasize that a judge will not conduct a review of the relevance and reliability of the expert's testimony in all cases. Judges apply the *Daubert* standard only when an attorney challenges the *introduction* of the evidence. Shuman and Sales (2001) write that,

> like most other rules of evidence, *Daubert* relies on trial lawyers to identify issues of admissibility (e.g., the reliability of the expert testimony) and choose whether to raise them before the trial judge, to present on issues of credibility to the jury, or to ignore these issues. (p. 71)

Shuman and Sales (2001) add that a lawyer may not recognize that certain expert testimony is based on unreliable methods; alternately, the methods used by the lawyer's own expert may be just as faulty. In neither case would the lawyer be likely to challenge the opposing expert. In still another scenario, the lawyer may wait until the opposing expert is on the witness stand and within view of the jury before questioning the credibility of the information. Finally, pretrial *Daubert* motions cost money, take up court time, and require judges and lawyers to master science as well as the law. For all of the above reasons, they are not likely to become enthusiastically embraced in the nation's courtrooms (Shuman & Sales, 2001).

However, a review of civil cases in federal district courts indicates that judges do appear to be excluding more scientific evidence than ever before in the wake of *Daubert.* Dixon and Gill (2002) reviewed a sample of federal civil cases between 1980 and 1999 in which expert testimony was offered. The experts represented a variety of fields, including health care and medicine; engineering and technology; the physical sciences; the social and behavioral sciences; and business, law, and public administration. The researchers found significant changes after the Court announced its decision. For example, specifically referring to the social and behavioral sciences, judges rejected expert testimony as unreliable in 43% of the cases over a 10-year period prior to *Daubert.* After the *Daubert* decision, they rejected testimony in 61% of the cases between 1995 and 1997. Interestingly, in the 2-year period from 1997 to 1999, the rejection rate went down to 47%, suggesting the possibility that experts might have been better prepared to address the reliability of their finding.

The study also revealed that general acceptance of the evidence by others in the profession was no longer sufficient for the admission of expert evidence. However, *lack* of general acceptance was a barrier to admission. In other words, it had not become easier for novel or unusual evidence to be accepted. Dixon and Gill (2002) concluded that, since *Daubert,* federal judges—at least in civil trials—have heeded the instructions of the Supreme Court and have increasingly acted as gatekeepers for reliability and relevance:

> The evidence suggests that since *Daubert,* judges have examined the reliability of expert evidence more closely and have found more evidence unreliable as a result. Our analysis, however, does not allow us to conclude whether this increased scrutiny resulted in better outcomes. (p. 269)

In other words, from the results of their study, Dixon and Gill could not say that the excluded evidence should have been admitted (or that admitted evidence should have been excluded). They did suggest, though, that judges might not be knowledgeable enough about scientific methodology to make informed and accurate determinations. One way to evaluate this, they added, would be to assemble an independent panel of experts to review evidence offered in court cases and compare the panel's assessment of that evidence to the judge's decisions.

Since the *Daubert* decision, considerable research and commentary has addressed the Court's assumption that judges, who rarely have a scientific background, would be able to evaluate scientific evidence. Kovera, Russano, and McAuliff (2002) maintain that most judges and most jurors are similar in their ability to identify flawed expert evidence because neither has received formal training in the scientific method. They further maintain that such individuals cannot differentiate between valid and flawed research. Jurors, as the research has consistently indicated, are highly unlikely to be able to distinguish the flawed research, even when an opposing expert highlights these flaws (Cutler & Penrod, 1995; Cutler, Penrod, & Dexter, 1989). Neither jurors, nor judges, nor lawyers typically can understand the importance of control groups or appreciate the relative merits of small and large sample sizes (Kovera et al., 2002).

Kovera and her colleagues (Kovera & McAuliff, 2000; Kovera et al., 2002) asked judges and attorneys to evaluate studies that represented four methodological variations: a valid study, a study that was missing a control group, a study that contained a confound, and a study that used a non-blind confederate. Judges were asked whether they would admit the evidence; lawyers were asked whether they would file a motion to exclude it. Judges admitted flawed research at the same rates as they admitted valid testimony. When attorneys wanted evidence excluded (which was almost invariably), it had no relationship to their perceptions of the scientific reliability of the evidence. Kovera and her colleagues conclude that it remains likely that some "junk science" will make its way into the courtroom and that some valid evidence will be excluded.

Although the fallout from the *Daubert* decision continues to be investigated, expert witnesses continue to face other challenges in the courtroom. As many commentators have remarked, testifying in court is not an exercise for the faint of heart. Expert witnesses—just like lay witnesses— face the possibility of being subjected to grueling cross-examination. Even very low-profile trials or pretrial proceedings can produce anxiety for the expert being subjected to sharp cross-examination. Some experts also struggle with their concerns about confidentiality, "ultimate opinion" testimony, and the prediction of dangerousness or assessment of risk. We will discuss each of these hurdles below, beginning with the problem of confidentiality.

The Confidentiality Issue

The obligation to maintain confidentiality in the patient–therapist relationship is fundamental. In the courtroom setting, though, confidentiality is not absolute. When clinicians have been asked by the court to evaluate a defendant, the results of that evaluation are shared among the judge and the lawyers. In these situations, the clinician's client is the court, not the individual being examined. The evaluation also may be discussed in the open courtroom if the clinician is called to the stand. In such cases, persons who have been evaluated have been warned of the limits of confidentiality at the outset of the evaluation. Even the confidentiality of test data is not guaranteed if the client signs a release or if the court orders it released.

Under the "Specialty Guidelines for Forensic Psychologists" (Committee on Ethical Guidelines for Forensic Psychologists, 1991), clinicians are advised to inform the individual of the nature and purpose of an evaluation, as well as who will be receiving a report. They also should ensure that the individual is informed of his or her legal rights.

> If the person [being assessed] is not the client, the psychologist owes no duty of confidentiality to that person, but, because of the requirement of informed consent, must make the fact known to the person being assessed that the information to be obtained is not confidential. (Ogloff, 1999, p. 411)

Nonetheless, even if notified of the limits of confidentiality, the individual in reality has little choice in submitting to the evaluation if he or she has not requested it. In addition, the individual may suffer harm as a result of the psychologist's participation in the evaluation process (Perlin, 1991).

When it is not evaluation but rather psychotherapy or treatment that is at issue, all courts recognize the patient–therapist privilege, although it is not absolute. The U.S. Supreme Court, for example, has firmly endorsed confidentiality in federal courts (*Jaffe v. Redmond,* 1996). Redmond was a police officer who shot and killed an allegedly armed suspect who she believed was about to kill another individual. The suspect's family sued, maintaining that he was not armed and that Officer Redmond had used excessive force, a civil rights violation. When the plaintiffs learned that Redmond had attended counseling sessions with a psychiatric social worker after the shooting, they subpoenaed the social worker, who confirmed that the officer had been a patient. However, the social worker refused to answer specific questions about treatment. The judge in the case refused to recognize a therapist–patient privilege and informed the jury that they were entitled to presume that the testimony would have been damaging to Redmond's case. The jury found for the plaintiffs, but the Seventh Circuit Court of Appeals threw out the verdict.

In its 7–3 decision, the U.S. Supreme Court affirmed the appeals court's decision. The Justices not only recognized the importance of the psychotherapist–patient privileged communication but also placed licensed social workers under this protective cloak. The Court did not consider the privilege absolute—or totally protected under all conditions—but did not specify when it would *not* apply. It is likely, however, that restrictions of the psychotherapist–patient privilege in federal courts would be similar to those in the states. For example, the privilege generally does not apply when patients voluntarily introduce their mental health into evidence. Confidentiality also is not protected when a patient sues the therapist, because the therapist is entitled to use otherwise privileged information to defend himself or herself (Ogloff, 1999).

The law places other limits on confidentiality that do not directly affect courtroom testimony. For example, in many states, clinicians have a **duty to warn or protect** third parties who may be in danger from a patient who has threatened their lives. The duty to warn or protect is referred to as the *Tarasoff* requirement, named after a court ruling (see Focus 4.4). The specific requirements vary by state, which is why it is alternatively called a duty to warn and a duty to protect. In some states, for example, therapists are expected to notify the threatened individual directly (warn), whereas in other states, therapists can meet the requirement by contacting law enforcement authorities or by taking active steps to have their patient institutionalized (protect). In those states with duty to warn or duty to protect legislation, psychologists who fail in this duty are subject to being sued in civil court by victims who suffer harm at the hands of their clients. In all states, practitioners also are required by law to report evidence of child abuse (and, in some cases, elder or other abuse) encountered in their practice to appropriate parties, which may include law enforcement or social service agencies. Although many clinicians say they can live within the spirit of *Tarasoff* and other reporting requirements, others have been critical of the violation of trust that these requirements engender.

FOCUS 4.4. *TARASOFF'S* DUTY TO PROTECT

In some jurisdictions, mental health professionals can be held liable for not warning potential victims of violence or physical harm at the hands of their patients. In late 1969, a young California woman was murdered by a man who two months earlier had confided to his psychologist his intention to kill her. Although the psychologist, who was employed by the University of California, had notified campus police of the death threat, he informed no one else except his supervisor. After the murder, the woman's parents sued the university, the psychologist, and the police for failing to warn the family and take action against the offender. This case established the well-known *Tarasoff v. Regents of the University of California* (1974, 1976) ruling.

In *Tarasoff*, the California Supreme Court first held that, in certain circumstances, when a mental health professional determines that a patient or client is a serious danger to another, the professional has a **duty to warn** the intended victim that he or she may be in danger. Two years later, the court redefined the clinician's responsiblity as a **duty to protect**. This difference is an important one, because protection need not require notification to the intended victim, but it does require *active* steps on the part of the mental health professional. The court believed that the need to protect persons from serious harm takes precedence over the confidentiality of the therapist–patient relationship.

(Continued)

(Continued)

The duty to protect doctrine has since been adopted via statute or common law by a majority of states (DeMatteo, 2005a; Reisner, Slobogin, & Rai, 2004). Some states, such as Virginia and Washington, have explicitly rejected the doctrine (DeMatteo, 2005). Many states have also made modifications to the doctrine since the California cases. For example, on July 16, 2004, in *Ewing v. Goldstein*, the California Court of Appeals expanded Tarasoff by asserting that a communication from a patient's *family member* is the same as the patient's own communication, which may require a therapist's duty to protect. For example, if an individual tells a therapist that his brother—the therapist's patient—has threatened to harm their mother, the therapist may have a duty to protect her.

Ultimate Issue or Ultimate Opinion Testimony

The testimony provided by expert witnesses is different from that provided by lay witnesses. Recall that a main role of the expert is to assist triers of fact (judges and juries) in matters about which they would not otherwise be knowledgeable. In most jurisdictions, *lay* witnesses can testify only to events that they have actually seen or heard firsthand. Their opinions and inferences are generally not admissible. *Expert* witnesses, on the other hand, testify to facts they have observed directly, to tests they may have conducted, and to the research evidence in their field. Moreover, the opinions and inferences of experts not only are admissible but are also often sought by the courts.

However, there is considerable debate among mental health professionals about the wisdom of offering an opinion on the "**ultimate issue.**" The **ultimate issue** is the final question that must be decided by the court. For example, should the expert provide an opinion about whether the defendant was indeed insane (and therefore not responsible) at the time of his crime? Should the expert recommend which parent should be awarded custody? Should the expert declare that a defendant is competent to be executed? Should the expert recommend that a juvenile's case be transferred to criminal court? It is quite clear that courts frequently request and hope for such opinions (Melton, Petrila, Poythress, & Slobogin, 1997, 2007; Redding, Floyd, & Hawk, 2001; Slobogin, 1999). Recall that during the Mitchell competency hearing mentioned above, relative to the Elizabeth Smart kidnapping, the expert witnesses were asked whether, in their opinion, Mitchell was competent to stand trial. In one study, even despite a statutory prohibition on ultimate opinion testimony in insanity cases, judges and prosecutors said they had a strong desire for clinical opinion (Redding et al., 2001). Defense attorneys were less likely to support this.

Those who oppose ultimate issue testimony (e.g., Melton et al., 1997, 2007) believe—among other things—that it is highly subject to error. The expert may misunderstand the law, may apply hidden value judgments, or may believe a particular outcome is best for an individual, even if legal criteria are not met. A clinical psychologist, for example, may truly believe that an individual needs to be placed in a secure mental health facility and treated for a serious mental disorder, even if the person does not technically meet the criteria for institutionalization. Thus, the psychologist might offer the opinion that the individual is not competent to stand trial, knowing that if the individual is ruled incompetent, he or she will most likely be sent to a mental hospital and will receive some treatment. This is not to say that the psychologist is trying to evade the law; he or she may truly believe the person is incompetent in a clinical sense, without fully understanding the legal criteria for incompetency.

Opponents of ultimate issue testimony also fear the undue influence of the expert on the fact finder. They stress that decisions such as whether an individual was insane at the time of the crime or whether a father or a mother should be awarded custody of a minor child are legal decisions. Asking the expert to express his or her opinion suggests that great weight will be placed on that opinion, when in fact the decision must be made by a judge or a jury and must be based on legal factors.

There is partial research support for the assumption of undue influence. Research suggests that the expert's opinion heavily influences judges in *pretrial* situations but not judges or juries at the *trial* stage. On issues such as competency to stand trial or the dangerousness of a defendant (warranting a denial of bail), the influence of the expert is substantial (Melton et al., 1997, 2007). This may be one reason why opposing experts are important, to offset an advantage gained by one side; in many pretrial situations, however, only one expert is called upon, typically at the request of the court. In other words, in pretrial situations attorneys may agree to have a court-appointed clinician examine the defendant. Trial jurors, however, do not seem to be unduly swayed by the opinions of experts (Nietzel et al., 1999). This may be because opposing experts and aggressive cross-examination are more likely in a trial situation than in a pretrial. Furthermore, jurors perceive experts as "hired guns" who would not be placed on the stand if their opinions did not support the side that called them. Jurors do listen to expert testimony, but "the effect is modest and leaves opportunity for both foes and fans of ultimate opinion testimony to find support for their positions" (Nietzel et al., 1999, p. 41).

Those who favor testimony on the ultimate issue (e.g., Rogers & Ewing, 1989) argue that judges often depend on it and that such testimony can be carefully controlled, particularly by means of effective cross-examination. They note also that judges and lawyers are becoming increasingly sophisticated about possible sources of error in an expert's opinion; to believe otherwise is to insult their intelligence. Furthermore, in pretrial situations in both criminal and civil cases, judges typically ask an opinion of the clinician who has been appointed by the court and who is acceptable to both parties. These court officers have come to value and trust the professional's opinion as a result of having him or her involved in past cases. Finally, forensic psychology has developed rapidly, and many graduate and postgraduate programs now offer internships, specialized training, and other opportunities for psychologists and other clinicians to learn the laws. As a result, the quality of evaluations has improved significantly over the past decade.

Nevertheless, reflecting the lack of consensus on the matter of ultimate issue testimony, the American Psychological Association has not taken a stand on whether it should be provided, even when courts request it. The 1994 "Guidelines for Child Custody Evaluations in Divorce Proceedings" (APA, 1994), for example, specifically refer to the lack of consensus. Guideline 14 notes that psychologists "are obligated to be aware of the arguments on both sides of this issue and to be able to explain the logic of their own practice." The guideline further states that, if they choose to make a custody recommendation, it should be derived from sound psychological data and based on the best interests of the child. In addition, they should guard against "relying on their own biases or unsupported beliefs in rendering opinions in particular cases." Likewise, the "Specialty Guidelines for Forensic Psychologists" (Committee on Ethical Guidelines for Forensic Psychologists, 1991) neither encourage nor discourage ultimate issue testimony. The Guidelines note only that "professional observations, inferences, and conclusions must be distinguished from legal facts, opinions, and conclusions" (p. 663).

Surviving the Witness Stand

Courtroom testimony can be a stressful experience, even for those who appear in court on a regular basis. Cross-examination by an opposing attorney is particularly discomfiting. Forensic psychologists, like other expert witnesses, may enter the courtroom totally confident in their professional knowledge and the evidence they are about to present. However, faced with the grueling questions of a legal adversary and frustrated with legal rules of evidence that limit their testimony, they may wish for a very quick end to a painful experience.

Forensic psychologist Mark Cunningham—who is featured in Personal Perspective 5.2 in Chapter 5—says that it helps for the expert to be aware of the techniques used by the cross-examining attorney. First, the cross-examining attorney tries to attack the data, methodology, or science. If these are sound, the expert's qualifications are questioned. If these are impeccable, the attorney may assert bias or lack of integrity on the part of the expert witness. If all else fails, the attorney may emphasize the money being paid the expert to testify. See also Personal Perspective 4.2 for wisdom offered by Dr. Brodsky on this matter. As he points out, the expert can calmly acknowledge the money while indicating that she deserves it based on her training and expertise.

Despite the pitfalls, numerous forensic psychologists have learned to negotiate the landscape of the court-room and have developed the skills needed both to provide the court with specialized knowledge and to respond to cross-examination in a calm, professional matter. This is crucial, because it is not unusual for cross-examining attorneys to berate or insult experts, their field of study, or methods used in their research. The professional literature contains ample advice for psychologists preparing to testify as expert witnesses (e.g., Brodsky, 1999, 2004; Poythress, 1979). Today, most graduate programs with specializations in forensic psychology offer courses or workshops on testifying in court.

Other scholars have offered advice not only for the witness stand but also for a wide range of meetings and proceedings that are part of the trial preparation process (e.g., Heilbrun, 2001; Heilbrun, Marczyk, & DeMatteo, 2002; A. K. Hess, 2006). Expert witnesses are urged to establish a communicative relationship with the attorney who has called them early in the legal process so that each side will know what can realistically be expected from the other.

> Some attorneys stereotypically view psychologists as soft thinkers, lacking in discipline, while psychologists often regard attorneys as narrowly focused, rigid, and inflexible. These stereotypes result from a failure to understand the other's professional needs at the outset of the consultation. (Singer & Nievod, 1987, p. 530)

Pretrial *preparation* is essential, and psychologists should not allow themselves to be persuaded to enter the courtroom without advance notice and sufficient preparation time (Singer & Nievod, 1987). They are advised to gather information carefully; pay attention to details of the case and the legal issues involved; remain impartial; and keep clear, organized notes (Chappelle & Rosengren, 2001). Many expert witnesses today maintain that well-prepared PowerPoint exhibits are helpful if not essential. It should never be assumed that notes, correspondence, and tape recordings would not need to be made available to attorneys for both sides under the rules of discovery. At some point in the proceedings, considering *Daubert* and other relevant cases, either the judge or the opposing attorney is likely to inquire whether the techniques or theories on which the expert is relying have been scientifically evaluated. The error rate is also important. Thus, in the process of preparing his or her testimony, the expert witness must take care to address these questions.

Expert witnesses are also advised to pay particular attention to their nonverbal behavior in the courtroom. Any behaviors that suggest arrogance, confusion, hostility, or anxiety are to be avoided. Chappelle and Rosengren (2001), reviewing the literature on expert testimony, remarked that the need to maintain composure is a theme in this literature. The knowledge offered by the expert is more likely to be accepted by judge and jury if the expert projects a professional, confident, and respectful persona.

Psychologists are often advised to read Ziskin and Faust's (1994) *Coping With Psychiatric and Psychological Testimony*, in order to get a sense of what the opposition might be thinking. Ziskin and Faust are critical of psychological and psychiatric testing, research, and diagnosis, and their book is on many an attorney's reading list. "Their express purpose is to embarrass mental health professionals out of the courtroom" (A. K. Hess, 1999, p. 551).

The Assessment of Risk

Forensic psychologists are very often asked to predict the likelihood that a particular individual will be "dangerous" to him- or herself or to society. This question becomes relevant when courts decide whether to release a person on bail, whether to place a mentally disordered individual in a psychiatric treatment facility against his or her will, or whether to hold a juvenile in a secure setting. Although *dangerousness* typically refers to violent or aggressive behavior, a wide range of behavior is included under that rubric. For example, threatening to harm someone, setting an empty barn on fire, and assaulting one's neighbor could all be considered violent behaviors, even though only one results in actual injury to another individual. Can psychologists or any other clinicians predict such behavior with any degree of confidence?

Some clinicians—those called to testify in criminal and juvenile courts during the last quarter of the 20th century—were quick to say that they could make such predictions. "On a scale of 1 to 10, with 10 being the most dangerous, this person is an 11," one psychiatrist was fond of saying. Others made statements such as, "For his own good, this juvenile must be locked up; he will definitely commit more crime if not institutionalized." These types of predictions were cited in court cases (e.g., *Barefoot v. Estelle,* 1983) in which individuals challenged their bail denials, their sentences, or their confinements. For the most part, courts have allowed clinicians to make predictions but have also acknowledged their fallibility. In a juvenile case, *Schall v. Martin* (1984), for example, the U.S. Supreme Court recognized that predictions of behavior were imperfect and fraught with error but ruled nevertheless that they had a place in the law. The case involved juveniles who were held in secure detention prior to their delinquency hearings, partly because there was a serious risk that they would commit more illegal activity if allowed to remain free.

Today, many forensic psychologists are careful to point out the fallibility of behavioral prediction. Although they acknowledge that prediction is an important aspect of the services they provide to courts and other institutions, they are carefully guarded in their conclusions. When it comes to predicting violence, many now prefer the term *risk assessment* to *prediction of dangerousness.* The word *risk* communicates the important point that in their evaluation, psychologists are providing courts or other agencies with a probability statement that a given individual will behave in an inappropriate manner. The probability assessment may be based on clinical judgment or on certain "predictor variables" that are in the individual's background. For example, past violent behavior, age, lack of an adequate system of social supports, alcohol or other substance abuse, and a history of serious mental disorder together are good indicators that a person is likely to be violent once again (J. Monahan, 1996).

Remarkable strides have been made over the past decade in identifying factors that increase the probability that someone will commit a violent act. As presented in Chapter 3, *static risk factors* are those in a person's life that are not subject to change, such as one's age when the first violent offense was committed or a history of parental criminality. *Dynamic risk factors* are those that can be changed, such as substance abuse or unemployment. Incorporating those factors, psychologists have developed and tested numerous instruments that can be used to evaluate the *likelihood* that an individual will commit serious antisocial behavior.

In communicating the likelihood of violence, however, psychologists should avoid dogmatic and definitive statements and should specify the conditions under which the behavior is likely to occur. The consistency of human behavior varies across situations; a person may display highly aggressive behavior in one context but be very docile in others. Most domestic abusers, for example, do not display in their workplaces or in their social situations the violent behavior they display in the home. Finally, when possible, psychologists should offer proscriptive measures that might be taken to avert the violence. This may include strategies to help the individual avoid situations that have led to problem behavior, such as staying away from bars or stores selling pornographic materials. In addition, as Heilbrun et al. (2002) state, "Monitoring has been empirically demonstrated to lower an individual's risk for engaging in violent or antisocial behavior" (p. 462). The forensic psychologist offering a risk assessment may recommend that the individual be kept under close supervision in the community.

Risk Assessment Instruments

A variety of instruments are available to psychologists engaged in the risk assessment enterprise (see Focus 5.5 in the following chapter), and the research literature now contains numerous studies evaluating these instruments (Quinsey, Harris, Rice, & Cormier, 2006). Of particular interest are instruments designed to assess the risk of sexual or other violent offending. The tests often are based on actuarial or statistical data, rather than clinical impressions, although some instruments make use of both actuarial data and structured clinical judgment (e.g., the Structured Assessment of Violence Risk for Youth (SAVRY); Borum, Bartel, & Forth, 2005; Borum, Lodewijks, Bartel, & Forth, 2010). The instruments are typically designed by gathering information on a large group of individuals within a target population (e.g., paroled offenders, youths in detention, or patients in a mental institution). On the basis of data from that group, the researcher identifies key variables (predictor variables) that are associated with the behavior of concern (e.g., violence). People are then rated on the number of these variables they have in their present lives or backgrounds, with some factors being weighted more heavily than others. An individual with a score below the cutoff for a particular risk assessment instrument would be judged as being at a high risk of offending. Although the empirical literature has consistently supported the superiority of **actuarial data** over clinical data in predictions of human behavior, some forensic psychologists are not comfortable with the use of risk assessments to the exclusion of clinical factors, which led to the development of instruments that included some clinical judgment. Heilbrun et al. (2002, p. 478) summarize their concerns as follows. Actuarial instruments, they say,

- Focus on a small number of factors and may ignore important factors that are idiosyncratic to the case at hand (e.g., recent legal or medical problems);
- Are passive predictors, focusing primarily on relatively static variables, such as demographics and criminal history;
- May include risk factors that are unacceptable on legal grounds, such as race or sex, and may ignore risk factors that have unknown validity but are logical to consider (such as threats of violence);
- Have been developed to predict a specific outcome over a specific period of time in a specific population, and they may not generalize to other contexts;
- Have a restricted definition of violence risk and cannot address the nature of the violence, its duration, its severity or frequency, or how soon it may occur.

Heilbrun et al. (2002) add that clinicians themselves—unless they are sufficiently schooled in psychometric theory—may tend to overuse or underuse the actuarial instruments. Although acknowledging the value of risk assessment instruments, they also caution forensic psychologists not to undermine the role of clinical judgment in their assessments of risk. Nevertheless, "the problem with the judgment-based approaches is that they are inherently speculative" (p. 478).

Others have noted (e.g., Doren, 2002) that clinical examiners often adjust the scores on risk assessment instruments upward or downward to incorporate data that might not be covered by the instrument. As an example, a psychologist might increase the risk level if the individual has experienced a recent, highly stressful event that the psychologist believes might affect his or her judgment and lead this person to be aggressive or violent. T. W. Campbell (2003) observes—based on the research in this area—that upward or downward adjustments do not improve the quality of the prediction. We will discuss risk assessment again in Chapter 5. For the time being, it is important to be aware that neither risk assessment instruments nor clinical judgment is a perfect predictor of human behavior.

The clinical–actuarial debate also extends to the issue of which type of testimony is preferred by judges and juries. It is often reported in the literature that courts are more favorably disposed to information that comes from clinical data than from actuarial or statistical data (e.g., Krauss & Sales, 2001; Melton et al., 1997). Studies with mock jurors—a common approach in jury research—also indicate that jurors underuse or misunderstand statistical data (Cunningham & Reidy, 1999; B. C. Smith, Penrod, Otto, & Park, 1996). However, the *actual effect* of expert testimony (regardless of the form) on jury verdicts is assumed rather than documented, and as we noted earlier in the chapter, some research suggests it may not be that significant (Nietzel et al., 1999). In addition, a study involving risk assessment with sexually violent predators indicated that jurors did not value one form of testimony (clinical or actuarial) over the other (Guy & Edens, 2003). This may not be the last word on jurors and actuarial versus clinical testimony.

SUMMARY AND CONCLUSIONS

The main purpose of this chapter has been to introduce the structure and process in criminal and civil courts along with some of the specific tasks performed by forensic psychologists in those settings. After reviewing court structure and discussing basic concepts relating to criminal and civil cases, we provided illustrations of the work psychologists do at each of the major stages of the court process. In the next two chapters, these court-related tasks will be described in greater detail.

A major undertaking for forensic psychologists is to serve as expert witnesses in both criminal and civil courts, not necessarily at trial but, even more commonly, at a variety of pretrial and posttrial proceedings (e.g., a bail hearing, a sanity hearing, a sentencing hearing). It is now clear that all experts—from the physical, behavioral, and social sciences, as well as those representing medicine, law, and business—fall under the mantle of science identified in the *Daubert* case, at least in federal courts. Courts in most states also have adopted *Daubert* or highly similar standards as well. We discussed the reliability and relevance requirements associated with that case and some of the research on its effect. It appears that, since *Daubert,* many judges are scrutinizing and rejecting expert testimony more than before.

Although there are concerns that *Daubert* will allow more "junk science" to be admitted into courts, the evidence thus far does not indicate that this is happening. It is also not clear how much "good science" is rejected because judges are unable to evaluate it properly. More research addressing how well judges are performing their gatekeeper function is needed before conclusions can be reached on this issue.

The present chapter also covers issues that cause some psychologists to pause before agreeing to participate in court proceedings. Some psychologists are not comfortable divulging information that in other contexts would be confidential, even though they are allowed (and sometimes required) to do so by the law. When psychologists are asked to conduct an evaluation, the client is often not the individual being evaluated but the court. In that case, copies of the psychologist's report are sent to court as well as to attorneys on both sides of the case.

The patient–therapist relationship is different from the relationship between the examiner and the person being evaluated. Courts have respected patient–therapist confidentiality, but even that may give way in certain situations when balanced against other interests. In many jurisdictions, for example, therapists have a duty to warn or to protect when their clients have made serious physical threats against an identified third party. The patient–therapist privilege also gives way when a patient sues a therapist.

Some forensic psychologists also resist being pressed for an opinion on legal matters or being subjected to grueling cross-examination by an opposing lawyer. Yet each of these is a routine occurrence in courtroom appearances. Judges often want to know the psychologist's conclusion as to whether an individual is competent to stand trial, whether someone is insane, or who would be the better of two parents in a custody battle. Technically, these are legal issues—the "ultimate" issues to be decided by the court, not the psychologist. Although some forensic psychologists are willing to express these opinions, others find them out of their purview.

The communication of risk is another area that presents ethical concerns to many psychologists. Today, psychologists often prefer to engage in the enterprise of "risk assessment" rather than the "prediction of dangerousness." Given the fallibility of predictions of dangerous behavior, it is important that the legal system refrain from pressing psychologists for definitive answers as to whether a given individual "will" be violent, although we are optimistic that the great majority of psychologists would resist such pressure. In assessing risk, many psychologists provide the courts with probabilities that a given individual will engage in antisocial behavior, or indicate the level of risk, and they are careful to note the limitations of their data. In addition, research indicates that mental health practitioners also try to offer strategies for managing the risk whenever possible. The communication of risk also may be based on clinical findings, such as deductions made from information obtained in a clinical interview or on the basis of performance on personality inventories or projective tests. Many forensic psychologists today incorporate both clinical and actuarial data in their reports and in their testimony. The themes introduced in this chapter will be developed in the following two, where we describe in greater detail the contributions made to both criminal and civil courts.

KEY CONCEPTS

Actuarial data

Amicus curiae

Appellate jurisdiction

Arraignment

Bench trial (court trial)

Challenge for cause

Civil case

Criminal case

Defendant

Deposition

Discovery process

Disposition

Dual-court system

Duty to warn or protect

General jurisdiction

Geographical jurisdiction

Grand jury

Initial appearance

Judgment

Jurisdiction

Limited jurisdiction

Peremptory challenge

Plaintiff

Presentence investigation

Scientific jury selection

Specialized courts

Subject matter jurisdiction

Tarasoff requirement

Ultimate issue

Voir dire

Witness preparation

QUESTIONS FOR REVIEW

1. What is the significance of *Jenkins v. U.S.* to forensic psychology?

2. Review the main steps or stages of the judicial process and provide illustrations of tasks forensic psychologists might perform at each one.

3. Describe and discuss key features of mental health courts and drug courts.

4. Name any two cases in which an organization of national psychologists filed *amicus curiae* briefs with the U.S. Supreme Court. Briefly summarize the question before the Court and the organization's stand on the issue raised.

5. Scientific jury selection is less prevalent today than in the past. Give at least three reasons why this might be so.

6. Discuss the tasks psychologists perform in witness preparation. What are the pros and cons of psychologists participating in these tasks, particularly as they relate to lay witnesses?

7. List three findings from research on the influence of expert testimony on jurors.

8. Identify the cases in the *Daubert* trilogy and state the key holding or rule in each one.

9. Summarize each side of the argument as to whether an expert should provide an opinion on the "ultimate issue."

10. What are the pros and cons of using actuarial instruments in forensic assessment?

5

Consulting
With Criminal
Courts

CHAPTER OBJECTIVES

- Describe typical roles of psychologists consulting with the criminal courts.
- Describe the legal standards for competency and criminal responsibility.
- Provide an overview of psychological inventories and testing instruments used in evaluating criminal competency.
- Provide an overview of assessment procedures in evaluating criminal responsibility.
- Provide an overview of psychological evaluations for offender sentencing.
- Outline the roles and dilemmas for psychologists in capital sentencing.

Zacarias Moussaoui, the man known as "the 20th 9/11 hijacker," was indicted on six charges related to the 9/11 conspiracy in December 2001. He was sentenced to life in prison on May 3, 2006. In the 4-1/2 intervening years, Moussaoui refused to enter a plea, fired his court-appointed attorney, was ordered to submit to a mental evaluation, and received permission to represent himself (a decision the judge in the case later reversed, citing inflammatory and unprofessional briefs he submitted). Moussaoui then pled guilty after being psychologically evaluated and determined competent to plead. At his sentencing hearing, against the advice of his attorney, he gave damaging testimony against his own interests.

On November 10, 2009, former astronaut Lisa Nowak pleaded guilty to charges of felony burglary of a car and misdemeanor battery. Military charges are still under consideration. Prior to her guilty plea, Nowak's attorney had indicated that she would plead not guilty by reason of insanity, but possibly after evaluations performed by forensic psychologists, the strategy changed. Nowak had been charged in 2007 with the attempted kidnapping of another astronaut who was in a relationship with her former lover, a man who was also an astronaut. In an incident widely covered and derided in the media, Nowak had driven virtually non-stop some 900 miles over a short period of time, after packing items including a black wig, latex gloves, pepper spray, a drill, and a folding knife.

Albert Crowel was convicted of his third driving-while-intoxicated offense. At the time of the incident, he was driving with a suspended license. He had a 6-year history of substance abuse but had never received treatment for this problem. He also had been convicted of domestic assault, for which he had served a 2-year prison term. In prison, he had participated in a program for violent offenders and had been a model prisoner. At his sentencing hearing, the defense lawyer called to the stand a forensic psychologist who had examined Crowel and concluded that he would be a good candidate for a substance abuse program that was available in the community, on an outpatient basis. The psychologist also reported that he was a very low risk for further violence.

The above three scenarios, reporting on actual court cases, illustrate some of the most common roles performed by psychologists and psychiatrists consulting with criminal courts: competency evaluations, assessment of mental state at the time of the offense (sanity evaluations), and presentencing evaluations. In these roles, the clinicians conduct **forensic mental health assessments (FMHAs).** By far, the most frequent is the assessment of competency to stand trial, also called adjudicative competence. At the end of the 20th century, it was estimated that some 60,000 criminal defendants were evaluated for this purpose every year (Bonnie & Grisso, 2000); since then, the number has increased steadily given a steady increase in arrest rates (Zapf & Roesch, 2006). Zapf and Roesch also estimate that the cost of both competency evaluations and the treatment to restore individuals to competency probably reaches $1 billion annually. It is important to emphasize, as well, that the term *adjudicative competence* covers not only competency to stand trial, but also competency to waive one's rights, competency to serve as one's own lawyer, and competency to plea bargain, among other "competencies."

Sanity evaluations—also called criminal responsibility (CR) or mental state at the time of the offense (MSO) evaluations—are believed to be less frequent than competency evaluations. However, many defendants—like Lisa Nowak—indicate they will use the insanity defense and ultimately do not, presumably after evaluations do not support it. CR evaluations also are often combined with evaluations of competency to stand trial. That is, some jurisdictions allow the examiner to evaluate both competency and sanity, although in other jurisdictions this is frowned upon or even forbidden. At sentencing, psychological and psychiatric input is the exception rather than the rule, but it is becoming more common, particularly if the sentencing judge is interested in knowing an offender's amenability to respond well to substance abuse treatment or sex offender treatment. Clinical input is also sought in death penalty cases, particularly when the court wishes to appraise the "dangerousness" of the offender being sentenced.

This chapter will be devoted primarily to these three areas: competency, insanity, and sentencing. Throughout the chapter, we will be referring to the forensic psychologist, but it is important to remind readers that forensic examiners are often psychiatrists or psychiatric social workers. In addition, we will cover the controversy surrounding the civil commitment of sexual predators after they have served their criminal sentences, a topic that reminds us of the interrelationship between criminal and civil courts. It should be noted that an important service provided by forensic psychologists—the assessment of victims of crime—will be covered in Chapters 10 and 11. Before beginning with the main material, though, we will discuss a less traveled area, the bail denial process.

Preventive Detention

Because criminal defendants are considered to be innocent until proven guilty in a court of law, there is a presumption that they will be free pending their trial or the final resolution of their case. At their initial appearance or their arraignment, the law allows judges and magistrates to set bail to ensure that the defendant will return to court for the next scheduled hearing in the case. Research has consistently shown that the great majority of defendants who are released on bail do return to court (Neubauer, 2002).

The U.S. Constitution does not guarantee a right to bail; it only specifies that the bail must not be excessive (*U.S. v. Salerno*, 1987). Thus, some defendants are denied bail on the basis of their dangerousness. In most jurisdictions, if an individual is charged with a capital crime (one that carries a possible life sentence or a sentence of death), dangerousness is presumed and bail is usually (but not invariably) denied. However, for a number of violent crimes that are not capital crimes, prosecutors may ask the judge to deny bail. A request like this is not unusual in domestic violence situations, such as when a woman expresses intense fear that the person who allegedly assaulted her will be released prior to trial and may harm her again. In these cases, defendants are entitled to a hearing on the issue of their dangerousness before the presiding judge can deny bail. At the hearing, the prosecutor presents evidence of the defendant's dangerousness, and the defense lawyer refutes that evidence by cross-examining the prosecution's witnesses and presenting evidence and witnesses in the defendant's favor.

Forensic psychologists, then, may be asked to "predict the dangerousness" of the defendant charged with the violent crime. As we discussed in the previous chapter, the preferred term in the psychological literature is *risk assessment*. In addition to conducting such an assessment and filing a written report, the psychologist may be called to testify during the bail hearing. Risk assessments conducted for bail decision-making purposes are very similar to risk assessments conducted for other release decisions in the criminal justice process. For example, at sentencing, judges often must decide whether to place an offender on probation or send him or her to prison. A risk assessment may also occur when an imprisoned offender has become eligible for parole or early release. Because sentencing will be discussed later in the chapter, we will defer the discussion of risk assessment until that point.

Criminal Competencies

Photo 5.1   A courtroom drawing of Zacarias Moussaoui, an avowed al-Qaeda agent, testifying in federal court at his sentencing hearing in 2006. Moussaoui pled guilty to conspiracy charges in the September 11, 2001, terrorist attacks and was sentenced to life in prison.

We began this chapter with an illustration of competency to stand trial. In that case, the case of the "20th hijacker," the defendant was found competent and was ultimately sentenced to life in prison (see Photo 5.1). Approximately 20% of individuals whose competency is questioned are found not competent to stand trial. It should be noted, however, that although courts and statutes continue to use the term *competency to stand trial*, the psychological research literature is increasingly replacing the term with *adjudicative competence* (e.g., Mumley, Tillbrook, & Grisso, 2003; Nicholson & Norwood, 2000). This is in response to the theory proposed by Richard Bonnie (1992), who suggests that competency to stand trial must involve both "competency to proceed" and "decisional competency." As Bonnie has stated, courts thus far have focused almost exclusively on the competence to proceed without thoroughly taking into account the complex decisional abilities that are required of defendants in a wide variety of contexts—for example, competency to plead guilty, to represent themselves, and to engage in plea bargaining. Bonnie and others (e.g., Mumley et al.) urge psychologists evaluating defendants to consider these abilities very carefully. Thus, the term **adjudicative competence** is increasingly being used in the literature to recognize Bonnie's important contribution (Mumley et al., 2003).

Adjudicative competence also is broad enough to subsume a wide range of abilities defendants are expected to possess. For example, if defendants waive their rights to lawyers, the law says they must be competent to do so. If they plead guilty to a crime—and thereby waive their right to a jury trial with all of the due process protections that a trial entails—they must be competent to do so. It is estimated that 90% of criminal defendants plead guilty rather than going to trial.

Criminal defendants have much to lose in the face of criminal prosecution (e.g., their freedom and sometimes their lives). Therefore, the law guarantees them a number of due process protections, including the right to a lawyer during custodial interrogation, the right to a lawyer at every critical stage of the criminal proceedings, and the right to a jury trial in most felony and some misdemeanor cases. Again, if they waive these rights, they are supposed to be competent to do so. The U.S. Supreme Court has often reiterated that a waiver of constitutional rights must be knowing, intelligent, and valid (e.g., *Fare v. Michael C.,* 1979).

Legal Standard for Competency

Due process also requires that defendants not be tried if they do not have a sufficient present ability to help their attorneys and a rational and functional understanding of the proceedings against them. This is the standard for competency to stand trial that was announced by the U.S. Supreme Court in the 1960 case *Dusky v. U.S.* and has been adopted in most states. The Supreme Court ruled in *Dusky* that defendants are competent to stand trial if they have "sufficient present ability to consult with [their] lawyer with reasonable degrees of rational understanding . . . and a rational as well as a factual understanding of the proceedings" (p. 402). Competency requires not only that defendants understand what is happening, but also that they be able to assist their attorneys in the preparation of their defense. This has become known as the ***Dusky* standard**. The two requirements created a "two-pronged" standard. However, many clinicians have pointed out that the law does not give enough attention to the *level* of competency required in a particular case (e.g., Brakel, 2003; Roesch, Zapf, Golding, & Skeem, 1999). For instance, a defendant might meet the standard for competency if charged with retail theft in a straightforward case. The same defendant, charged with manslaughter and facing what is expected to be a protracted trial, might not meet the standard.

The Supreme Court has ruled (*Godinez v. Moran,* 1993) that the *Dusky* standards apply to guilty pleas as well; that is, defendants pleading guilty must have a rational understanding of the court process. Again, some mental health professionals believe that this "one size fits all" approach leaves much to be desired. Guilty pleas, they argue, should be scrutinized very carefully because of their implications. The waiver of a number of constitutional rights that a guilty plea entails requires decisional competence that many defendants simply do not have.

It is not altogether clear whether the unitary standard announced in the *Moran* case applies to proceedings before arraignment or after the verdict (Perlin, 2003). Waivers—and the question of competency—can occur during the police interrogation stage, while police are conducting searches, during lineups, at a sentencing hearing, at a hearing on the revocation of probation or parole, or during the appeals process, for example. The Supreme Court's opinion did not touch on these, although the concurring opinion of Justice Kennedy suggested that the *Godinez* rule might possibly not apply in these pretrial and after-verdict situations (Perlin, 2003).

In some criminal cases, defendants choose to waive the right to an attorney and to represent themselves, a right guaranteed under the U.S. Constitution (*Faretta v. California*, 1975) but which is exercised by very few criminal defendants. Alternatively, some defendants choose to ignore the advice of their attorneys and proceed with a defense that the attorney believes is not in their best interest. Two high-profile criminal cases in the 1990s led many scholars to question the wisdom of allowing criminal defendants who are presumably mentally disordered to take such an approach (e.g., Litwack, 2003; Slobogin & Mashburn, 2000). Theodore Kaczynski (the Unabomber) was an apparently delusional defendant who rejected the advice of his attorney to plead not guilty by reason of insanity. He subsequently pleaded guilty and avoided a death sentence, but had he taken his attorney's advice, he *might* not have been convicted. Colin Ferguson, who opened fire on a Long Island commuter train, killing six people and injuring many others, was allowed to waive his right to a lawyer and represent himself during his trial.

Many scholars and observers believe that the trial of Colin Ferguson was an embarrassment to our system of justice (Perlin, 1996). Some argue that he was not competent to stand trial; others argue that he was competent to stand trial but not competent to defend himself. Ferguson was evaluated by two psychologists who found him educated and articulate but suffering from paranoid personality disorder (Slobogin & Mashburn, 2000). Nevertheless, they believed he was competent to stand trial under the *Dusky* standard, and the judge agreed. Ferguson rejected the advice of his attorney that he plead not guilty by reason of insanity, insisted on defending himself, and was allowed to do so. "Ferguson proceeded to represent himself in a fashion that observers unanimously considered bizarre" (Slobogin & Mashburn, 2000, p. 1608). During the trial, he made rambling statements, proposed conspiracy theories, and tried to call President Clinton as a witness. Critics of that trial process (e.g., Perlin, 1996; Slobogin & Mashburn, 2000) believe he was not competent to reject an insanity defense and should not have been allowed to represent himself, although others disagree (e.g., Litwack, 2003). Ferguson is presently incarcerated in the New York prison system, serving life sentences. Over 10 years after the Ferguson case, the Supreme Court ruled that a defendant who was competent to stand trial was not necessarily competent to serve as his own lawyer (See Focus 5.1, *Indiana v. Edwards*).

FOCUS 5.1. *INDIANA v. EDWARDS*

Ahmad Edwards, an individual with schizophrenia, had a lengthy psychiatric history. In relation to the present case, Edwards had tried to steal a pair of shoes from a department store. In the process, he fired at a security officer and wounded a bystander. He was charged with attempted murder, battery with a deadly weapon, criminal recklessness, and theft.

Edwards's case illustrates the circuitous route criminal cases can take on the road to the actual trial. The defendant had three different competency hearings; he was found incompetent in the first and was hospitalized for competency restoration. In a second hearing he was found competent, but his lawyer soon asked for another competency evaluation; in a third hearing he was found incompetent, was rehospitalized, and subsequently found competent to stand trial. He then asked to represent himself but was denied the request, was appointed a lawyer, and was ultimately convicted. Edwards appealed to the Indiana Court of Appeals, arguing that his right to represent himself was violated. The court agreed with Edwards and ordered a new trial. The state then appealed to the Indiana Supreme Court, and that court also agreed with Edwards. As a last resort, the state of Indiana asked the U.S. Supreme Court to review the decision, which it agreed to do.

When the case reached the U.S. Supreme Court (*Indiana v. Edwards, 2008*), the Court ruled that a judge could *insist* that a seriously mentally ill defendant be represented by a lawyer, even if he was found competent to stand trial; in other words, just because a defendant was competent to stand trial, this did not mean he was competent to represent himself. It is interesting to note, though, that Indiana also asked the Court to allow a unitary standard that would deny criminal defendants the right to represent themselves at trial if they could not communicate coherently with the court or a jury. The Supreme Court rejected that unitary standard, preferring to have judges make the determination on a case-by-case basis, and based on their information and observations of the defendant.

Like most cases that reach the level of the U.S. Supreme Court, the *Edwards* case is obviously more complex than what we can present here. However, it is now clear that, although defendants still have a constitutional right to self-representation, states can allow judges to deny that right to seriously mentally ill defendants. Had that ruling been in effect at the time of the Ferguson case, described above, one wonders whether the Long Island Railroad trial might have proceeded differently.

The Byron Keith Cooper case provides another sobering illustration of the problems that can occur when the mentally ill are charged with crimes (*Cooper v. Oklahoma,* 1996). Cooper, charged with the murder of an elderly man, was originally ruled incompetent to stand trial (IST), was treated in a mental institution for 3 months, and then was found competent, although his lawyer had argued that he was not. His behavior during the competency hearing and the trial was bizarre at best. He refused to wear civilian clothes during his trial, claiming that these clothes were burning him, so he wore prison overalls. He crouched in a fetal position and talked to himself during much of the trial. However, the state of Oklahoma required that defendants persuade the court of their incompetence by **clear and convincing evidence,** and the judge in the case concluded that Cooper had not met that burden (see Focus 5.2 for a review of burdens of proof). The U.S. Supreme Court emphasized that states could require defendants to establish their incompetence by a **preponderance of the evidence** but no more than that. Cooper's behavior may not have demonstrated his incompetence according to the clear and convincing standard, but it would be difficult to argue that it was not demonstrated by a preponderance of the evidence. In other words, is it more likely than not (the preponderance standard) that Cooper was incompetent to stand trial?

There are several reasons why competency evaluations are so common—recall that approximately 60,000 defendants are evaluated for competency every year. First, questions about a defendant's adjudicative competence can arise at many different stages of the criminal process. In Byron Cooper's case, questions about competence were raised five different times, the last time at his sentencing hearing. The defendant in the *Edwards* case had had three competency hearings and two hearings on whether he could represent himself at trial. Second, an unknown number of criminal defendants are reevaluated over a period of years because they are charged with additional crimes. In virtually every state, certain defendants charged with misdemeanors or lesser felonies are well-known to both the judicial system and the mental health system. They continually appear before the court, are sent for competency evaluation, are found incompetent (or competent), are hospitalized (or not), have charges dropped (or plead guilty), spend time on probation (or in jail), and go forth into the community until their next criminal charge. The mental health courts mentioned in Chapter 4 are intended to prevent the perpetuation of this revolving door process by diverting nonviolent, mentally disordered individuals from the criminal process and providing community supervision and meaningful treatment. Finally, developments in forensic psychology itself may explain the frequency of competency evaluations. As we will discuss later in the chapter, the evaluation process has been made considerably simpler with the development of competency assessment instruments and the training of graduate and postgraduate students in making these assessments.

FOCUS 5.2. BURDENS OF PROOF

In adversary proceedings, the final legal decision requires that proof be established at a specified level.

Beyond a Reasonable Doubt

This is the standard of proof required in all criminal proceedings as well as delinquency proceedings when a juvenile is charged with a crime. It is proof that is just short of absolute certainty. "In evidence [it] means fully satisfied, entirely convinced, satisfied to a moral certainty" (H. C. Black, 1990).

Clear and Convincing Proof

This is the standard required in some civil proceedings, such as when the state wishes to commit an individual to a mental hospital against his or her will. It is an intermediate standard, resulting in "reasonable certainty of the truth of the ultimate fact in controversy. Clear and convincing proof will be shown where the truth of the facts asserted is highly probable" (H. C. Black, 1990).

Preponderance of the Evidence

This is proof that one side has more evidence in its favor than the other. It is "evidence which is of greater weight or more convincing than the evidence which is offered in opposition to it; that is, evidence which as a whole shows that the fact sought to be proved is more probable than not" (H. C. Black, 1990). It is the standard required in most civil suits and may be relevant to criminal proceedings as well. For example, when states require criminal defendants to prove they are incompetent to stand trial, they cannot require this by a standard more demanding than the preponderance of the evidence.

Evaluating Adjudicative Competence

Forensic psychologists evaluate defendants for adjudicative competence in a number of different settings. For example, a brief competency screening may be carried out very early in criminal processing while the defendant is being held in jail. Defendants also may be evaluated in the community, on an outpatient basis, while on pretrial release. (See Personal Perspective 5.1, in which forensic psychologist Kirk Heilbrun mentions a clinic in which graduate students are trained for these and other purposes.) Although such outpatient evaluations are on the increase (Roesch et al., 1999), many defendants are evaluated while hospitalized in a public mental facility. In fact, most states either permit or require hospitalization for both the evaluation of competence and the treatment to restore competence (R. D. Miller, 2003). Outpatient *evaluation* is far more common than outpatient *treatment,* however. In other words, the estimated 20% of defendants who are found incompetent to stand trial are usually hospitalized for treatment, whether or not they were evaluated in the community.

PERSONAL PERSPECTIVE 5.1

My Life as a Forensic Psychologist

Kirk Heilbrun, PhD

I have always enjoyed the chance to work on diverse tasks. The Boulder model, emphasizing the importance of the clinical psychologist as a scientist-practitioner, offers an ideal framework for this kind of professional diversity. I have been employed in settings that are mostly applied, such as a forensic hospital, a federal prison, and a specialized treatment unit for juveniles. When I worked in those settings, I always tried to be involved in research and writing on the individuals who were assessed and treated, and ideas that occurred to us as we were providing professional services.

For the last 15 years, I have worked in an academic setting—at MCP Hahnemann University, then Drexel University—in Philadelphia. This job has offered me the chance to work in four domains: *teaching and training* (undergraduates as well as graduate students), *research and scholarship*, *administrative leadership*, and *forensic practice*. These areas often overlap. For example, training graduate students requires teaching courses and seminars, but it also requires research mentorship and clinical supervision.

I constantly look for ways to be as efficient as possible across areas. One of the first goals I set when I arrived at the university in 1995 was to establish a departmentally based forensic assessment clinic that would provide high-quality psychological evaluations to courts and attorneys at reasonable rates, while involving graduate students on a practicum basis in this clinic. This has been accepted well by judges and attorneys in the Philadelphia area, so we have had enough referrals to stay busy without becoming overwhelmed. Doctoral students who take this practicum must also have taken the two-quarter forensic assessment series I teach. This means I have the chance to work with them in the classroom, earlier in their training, and then in the clinic when they have become more advanced. Some students have developed research ideas from their classroom or clinic experience; they may write theses or dissertations using principles of forensic assessment that are taught in the classroom or using archival data collected through the clinic. Graduate students who plan to make forensic assessment a part of their professional lives enjoy the chance to participate in this practicum.

I have also had the opportunity to chair the psychology department for about a decade. This is a challenging and important job that involves the day-to-day tasks needed to run a department, the occasional intensive attention to a crisis, and the predictable yearly tasks such as faculty evaluations and budget planning. It requires

(Continued)

(Continued)

a broad perspective within psychology, though. Faculty members and students within the department are often quite specialized, and the department chair must know enough about their areas to be able to describe them to a dean or provost. Promoting the department for purposes of university planning or fund-raising means communicating the department's strengths and needs in language that non-psychologists can understand—and appreciate.

There is some predictability within my professional life, but it is never boring. I have research meetings scheduled weekly on several topics with my graduate student teams and faculty colleagues. I work on clinic cases and supervision two mornings a week. I am in the classroom weekly or twice weekly. I must build in time to run research projects, write papers and chapters, review submissions to journals, and edit drafts of forensic reports. But sometimes the unexpected intrudes. A crisis in the department, a reporter asking for a comment, a colleague requesting a consultation—each can demand thoughtful attention. Being productive means staying busy doing everything you have committed to do, and much of what you are asked to do beyond that, to contribute to your department, university, and profession—and staying interested yourself!

Dr. Heilbrun is Professor and Head, Department of Psychology, Drexel University, and coordinator of the forensic concentration within the doctoral program in clinical psychology. His research and practice interests include forensic mental health assessment, violence risk assessment and management, and diversion of mentally disordered offenders. He enjoys travel, reading, and racket sports.

It should be noted that the persons referred for competency evaluations tend to be those with a past history of mental disorder or those presenting signs of current mental disorders. The typical evaluation is conducted when defendants are deemed mentally disordered, such as suffering from schizophrenia or psychosis (Mumley et al., 2003). Therefore, competency evaluations often are prompted by a defendant's past history of psychiatric care, institutionalization, bizarre behavior at arrest, or attempt to commit suicide while held in detention. On the other hand, developmental disability, emotional distress, or even advancing age might lead to questions about a defendant's competence. For example, a defendant charged with vehicular homicide might be so distraught over the incident that she is unable to meet the standard for adjudicative competence. In such situations, the individual is less likely to require hospitalization during the evaluation process.

The request for an evaluation may come directly from the defense attorney or from the court. It is important for psychologists to note the difference. When the defense requests and pays for the evaluation, the client is the person being examined and the report goes to his or her representative, the defense attorney. Depending on the evaluation's results, the attorney may or may not share the report with the prosecutor. When the evaluation is court ordered, even if ordered at the request of the defense attorney, the client is the court. Motions for court-ordered examinations may be made by the defense attorney (whose client is unable to pay for a private evaluation), the prosecutor, or the judge. The examiner should expect that the report of a court-ordered evaluation will be shared among all parties.

Research indicates that most competency evaluations are court ordered and that no more than one evaluation is performed (Melton et al., 1997, 2007), although some jurisdictions do require at least two evaluations. And, in high-profile cases, such as the kidnapping of Elizabeth Smart mentioned in Chapter 4, or in cases that might involve a life sentence or the death penalty, competing evaluations are more likely. When there are no opposing experts, though, judges almost always accept the recommendation of clinicians conducting the evaluation (Cruise & Rogers, 1998; Melton et al., 1997). Some researchers report agreement rates well over 90% (Cruise & Rogers, 1998; Zapf, Hubbard, Galloway, Cox, & Ronan, 2002). In at least this pretrial context, therefore, clinicians seem to have considerable influence on the courts. However, competency evaluations, like many other forensic mental health assessments, raise the "ultimate issue" question discussed in Chapter 4. Competency is a legal issue, not a clinical issue, and there continues to be debate over whether a psychologist should express an opinion as to whether the defendant is competent to stand trial.

As in all forensic mental health evaluations, the assessment of adjudicative competence should begin with a notice to the person being evaluated of the limits of confidentiality and the purpose of the evaluation (see Focus 5.3 for a list of factors common to all evaluations; see also Heilbrun, Grisso, & Goldstein, 2009). As noted above, unless the psychologist is hired directly by the defense attorney for an appraisal of his or her client's competency and general mental status, the competency report will be shared among the attorneys and the presiding judge. For this reason, examiners are often reminded to carefully limit the report to the defendant's present status and not to include information that might provide details about the crime itself (Grisso, 1988; Roesch et al., 1999).

Examiners are also warned about avoiding the **dual relationship** of evaluator and treatment provider. If a psychologist has been seeing the defendant in a therapist–patient relationship or has any other prior relationship with the defendant, the psychologist should not examine the defendant for adjudicative competence. Recall from Chapter 1 that dual relationship still remains a contentious issue among some forensic psychologists, however.

The examination process itself varies widely according to the examiner's training and theoretical orientation. As Cruise and Rogers (1998) stated, "There is no clear consensus on a standard of practice for competency evaluations" (p. 44). Some examiners conduct only a clinical interview, whereas others conduct an interview and administer a variety of projective or objective tests. Other examiners file a generic report that includes behavioral observations of the defendant and extensive background information. Traditionally, competency evaluations tended to include a good deal of information that was irrelevant to the issue of whether the defendant was competent to stand trial (Grisso, 1988). In recent years, with more guidance provided to clinicians, misconceptions about competency evaluations have lessened, and reports have improved in quality (Roesch et al., 1999).

FOCUS 5.3. FACTORS COMMON TO FMHAs

Although forensic mental health assessments (FMHAs) are conducted for a wide variety of reasons, they have at least the following features in common:

Before meeting with the person being assessed, the examiner should

- Understand the purpose of the referral;
- Decline to conduct the evaluation if there is a conflict of interest or if the examiner has ethical or moral objections to participating;
- Gather background information and records when available;
- Be knowledgeable about the law relative to the assessment;
- Clarify and agree on the time and method of payment;
- Clarify when a report is needed and to whom it should be submitted.

(Continued)

(Continued)

Before conducting the evaluation, the examiner should

- Explain its purpose to the person being evaluated;
- Stress that this is not a treatment relationship;
- Explain the limits to confidentiality;
- Warn the examinee of the possible uses of the examination;
- Tell the examinee who will be getting copies of the report;
- Obtain the examinee's written consent, if consent is needed.

The examiner's written report should

- Be clearly written and free of slang or excessive "jargon";
- Be submitted within a reasonable time after the evaluation has been completed;
- State the purpose of the report, identify the legal issues, and note who requested the report;
- Specify documents reviewed and any tests/inventories that were administered;
- State clearly the basis for any conclusions reached;
- Be submitted with an awareness that a variety of individuals will see the report.

Competency Assessment Instruments

Over the past 20 years, researchers have developed and attempted to validate a variety of instruments for the assessment of competency to stand trial. Some are screening instruments generally taking under 30 minutes to administer, whereas others are more elaborate instruments based on both interviewing and test administration. Screening instruments serve as quick appraisals to determine if someone is potentially incompetent; if so, they are then referred for a more extensive examination. Also available is a computer-assisted tool—the CAD-COMP (Computer-Assisted Competence Determination of Competency to Proceed)—which is heavily based on the defendant's self-reports of his or her background, legal knowledge, and behaviors (Barnard et al., 1991). Zapf and Viljoen (2003) and Zapf and Roesch (2006) have provided recent reviews of these assessment instruments. Although we do not provide a comprehensive review here, we will discuss a few of the instruments for illustrative purposes.

The **Competency Screening Test** is a sentence-completion test that is intended to provide a quick assessment of a defendant's competency to stand trial. The test taps the defendant's knowledge about the role of the lawyer and the rudiments of the court process. For example, defendants are asked to complete the following: "When a jury hears my case, they will . . . ." If defendants score below a certain level, they are evaluated more completely. The test's main advantage is the ability to screen out quickly the obviously competent defendants. According to Roesch et al. (1999), the test has a high false-positive rate (53.3%), identifying many competent defendants as incompetent. Because persons so identified in a screening test are likely to be hospitalized for further evaluation, this presents a significant deprivation of liberty for the defendant who would otherwise be free on bail. On the other hand, some defendants unable to post bail might prefer the security of a hospital to the chaos and crowded conditions of some jails. Nevertheless, hospitalization is no bargain.

The **Georgia Court Competency Test (GCCT)** and its Minnesota State Hospital revisions (GCCT-MSH) have received mixed reviews. These are short tests—17 and 21 items, respectively—that some examiners prefer to use primarily as a screening mechanism. The GCCT apparently has good internal consistency and interrater reliability, and it has a promising screen for malingering or feigning incompetence (Gothard, Rogers, & Sewell, 1995). **Internal consistency** refers to the degree to which all items on a particular test measure the same thing. **Interrater reliability** refers to the extent to which different examiner or test administers agree with the ratings in judging a person's abilities or characteristics. However, the test has been criticized for its lack of addressing decisional competency (Zapf & Viljoen, 2003)—in other words, how well a person can make important decisions.

The MacArthur Foundation Research Network on Mental Health and the Law initially developed the MacArthur Structured Assessment of the Competencies of Criminal Defendants (MacSAC-CD) (Hoge et al., 1997). This was a rather cumbersome research tool that led to a shorter instrument, the **MacArthur Competence Assessment Tool—Criminal Adjudication (MacCAT-CA),** containing 22 items. Defendants are provided with a vignette describing a situation in which a person is charged with a crime and are asked questions about it. They are also asked questions about their own situation. Shortly after its introduction, the MacCAT-CA began to receive good reviews as being superior to other assessment instruments (Cruise & Rogers, 1998; Nicholson, 1999; Zapf & Viljoen, 2003).

Despite the continuing development of forensic assessment instruments, they do not appear to be widely used in forensic practice, particularly by practitioners who serve as occasional experts (Skeem, Golding, Berge, & Cohn, 1998). A study by Borum and Grisso (1995) indicated that 36% of psychologists in their sample never use such forensic assessment instruments, whereas 40% use them almost always or frequently, a finding that—according to Zapf and Roesch (2006)—indicated a slow increase. The research literature tends to support the use of these instruments, both for their efficiency and for the fact that trained examiners, using the instruments, achieve a high level of interexaminer reliability (Zapf & Roesch, 2006).

Assessment of Malingering

Virtually every type of forensic mental health assessment requires some appraisal of possible **malingering** (or faking) on the part of the person being evaluated. For a variety of reasons, criminal defendants may pretend they have symptoms of a serious disorder when they actually do not. Rogers (1997) has described malingering as a response style in which the individual consciously fabricates or grossly exaggerates his or her symptoms. He observes that this is understandable in the light of the individual's situation. The obvious example is the offender who pretends to be mentally ill, believing that the judge is less likely to sentence him to prison. In the competency context, a defendant may pretend to have symptoms of a mental disorder to postpone the trial or avoid going to trial altogether. Although we discuss malingering in this chapter, it should not be assumed that this problem is limited to the criminal context. As we will note in Chapter 6, individuals being assessed in civil cases may be equally motivated to feign symptoms.

Forensic psychologists have at their disposal a variety of validated tests for detecting malingering. The Structured Interview of Reported Symptoms (Rogers, 1992) is a well-regarded instrument for detecting the malingering of psychotic symptoms. Another example is the Test of Memory Malingering (Tombaugh, 1997). In addition, some commonly used psychological tests, such as the Minnesota Multiphasic Personality Inventory (MMPI-2) and the Millon Clinical Multiaxial Inventory—III (Millon, 1994), as well as some forensic assessment instruments (e.g., the **Rogers Criminal Responsibility Assessment Scales [R-CRAS]**), also have power to detect malingering. There is, though, no foolproof way to detect malingering (Butcher & Miller, 1999). As Heilbrun et al. (2002) assert, it is important for the clinician to use multiple measures rather than one or two tests to assess this.

Restoration to Competency

Research indicates that approximately 15 to 20% of defendants referred for competency evaluations are ultimately found incompetent. Persons found incompetent tend to be those with a history of institutional treatment or diagnosis of a serious mental disorder. Research also suggests that a clinical diagnosis, when included in a competency evaluation report, is a strong predictor of a finding of incompetence (Cochrane, Grisso, & Frederick, 2001). Interestingly, forensic examiners are often advised not to include diagnoses in their reports (Golding & Roesch, 1987; Grisso, 1986). The diagnosis may not be accurate, and even if it is, it is subject to misinterpretation on the part of persons not trained as mental health practitioners.

The majority of persons found incompetent to stand trial are those suffering from schizophrenia and psychotic symptoms (Morse, 2003). Although mental disorder seems to be a requirement for most incompetency determinations, mental disorder itself—even serious mental disorder—is not *sufficient*. Andrea Yates, a woman who drowned five of her children in a bathtub in 2001 and whose case was publicized widely, had a long history of mental disorder. Yet she was found competent to stand trial and was convicted in a first trial. (The conviction was later overturned, and she then was found not guilty by reason of insanity. She remains institutionalized in a psychiatric facility.) Once an individual has been found incompetent to stand trial (IST), efforts are made to restore the person to competence to bring him or her to trial. Clinicians typically are asked to make some assessment of the likelihood that an individual will be restored to competency. If restoration is highly unlikely, the state must decide whether to drop the criminal charges and, if necessary, initiate **involuntary civil commitment** proceedings.

Every state has its examples of defendants who were found incompetent to stand trial and who are held in institutions for seemingly very lengthy periods. In the federal system, we have the example of Russell Weston, charged in the deaths of two Capitol police officers in July of 1998. As of this writing, 13 years after the fact, Weston remains hospitalized and has not been brought to trial. The U.S. Supreme Court did place a limit on this practice, ruling in *Jackson v. Indiana* (1972) that incompetent defendants could not be held indefinitely if there was no likelihood that they would be restored. However, they can be subjected to civil commitment, as mentioned above. In most states, periodic hearings are held to assess an incompetent defendant's status; defendants are kept institutionalized as long as some progress is being made. Some states do not allow incompetent defendants to be held for longer than the maximum sentence they would have served had they been convicted. Research suggests that the average period for inpatient treatment is 6 months, but many defendants are held for much longer periods (R. D. Miller, 2003).

Restoration of competence need not be done in an institution. Like competency evaluations, treatment for incompetent defendants can be provided in community settings. In fact, many legal commentators as well as clinical practitioners believe that outpatient treatment rather than institutionalization should be made available to more defendants found IST (R. D. Miller, 2003; Roesch et al., 1999). R. D. Miller surveyed mental health program directors across the United States and found that, though outpatient *evaluation* was on the increase, outpatient *treatment* to restore competence was rare: "Despite the availability of outpatient treatment, few states utilize it very often" (p. 384). Miller found that 18 states *required* the hospitalization of incompetent defendants and 21 *permitted* it, but without specific criteria for doing so. In five states, incompetent defendants had to meet civil commitment criteria before they could be hospitalized. In 21 states, there were no effective time limits on hospitalization, whereas in 11 states, the limit was between 1 and 5 years.

R. D. Miller (2003) notes that the length of stay for forensic patients—such as those found incompetent to stand trial or not guilty by reason of insanity—is measured in months or years, but the length of stay for non-forensic civil patients is measured in days or weeks. Thus, although most states have made significant progress in "deinstitutionalizing" those with mental disorders, the liberty interests of forensic populations remain unacknowledged. Although conceding that some defendants clearly need hospitalization for both evaluation and—if found incompetent—for treatment, Miller notes that hospitalization is overused: "For defendants who have demonstrated their ability to remain safely in the community before determination of their competence, there is little justification for hospitalization" (p. 386).

According to Roesch et al. (1999), "The disposition of incompetent defendants is perhaps the most problematic area of the competency procedures" (p. 333). Many researchers have observed that, although **restoration to competency** is the intent, IST defendants are rarely treated differently from other hospitalized populations (Siegel & Elwork, 1990). For the IST defendant, however, restoration should focus not only on his or her decisional capacities, but also on his or her understanding of the criminal process. In other words, depending on the defendant's individual situation, restoration may require education about the legal system. To illustrate, we will use the example of a defendant who is intellectually disabled and has been found incompetent to stand trial.

In recent years, much attention has been given to the plight of individuals with developmental or intellectual disabilities, still termed "mental retardation" (MR) in much of the literature, who are arrested and processed by the criminal justice system. Intellectual disability does not guarantee that an individual will not be held responsible for a crime; indeed, prisons and jails in the United States are believed to hold a substantial number of convicted offenders who are intellectually disabled. Furthermore, as Zapf and Roesch (2006) have noted, persons with mild disability may try to "hide" it, even from their lawyers. Thus, the issue is not raised either in pretrial evaluations or in mitigation for the offense, if they are convicted.

However, when individuals with developmental disabilities are found incompetent to stand trial, restoration is unlikely to occur because of the chronicity of their condition. S. D. Anderson and Hewitt (2002) reported on an education program in Missouri that specifically addressed the restoration needs of these defendants. The program consisted of a series of classes in which defendants learned about the legal system and participated in role-playing activities. The competency training had very little success, with only one-third of all defendants restored to competency. The defendant's IQ contributed to the outcome, but the IQ score was just short of reaching statistical significance. According to the researchers, "Persons with certain levels of MR may inherently lack the skills needed to actively participate in trial proceedings. Abilities such as abstract reasoning, decision-making, and so forth are not only difficult to teach but are extremely difficult to learn" (p. 349). Once again, this speaks to the importance of mental health courts and their ability to divert some individuals from the criminal process.

Although states vary in their approaches to restoring competency, the most common means of doing this appears to be through medication (Roesch et al., 1999). Psychoactive drugs are widely administered in the efforts to restore competency. In fact, in the study mentioned above, S. D. Anderson and Hewitt (2002) noted that—before a special program was initiated—defendants with intellectual disability had been treated with **psychoactive medication** just like other IST defendants. In recent years, the involuntary administration of these drugs has received considerable national attention. Both a high-profile case involving the alleged shooter of Capitol police officers (the Weston case) and the U.S. Supreme Court case *Sell v. United States* (2003) revolved around this issue.

Drugs and the Incompetent Defendant

Antipsychotic or psychoactive drugs have improved significantly in effectiveness, but they still may produce unwanted side effects, including nausea, headaches, loss of creativity, inability to express emotions, and lethargy in some individuals. In one key case that reached the U.S. Supreme Court (*Sell v. United States*), a defendant found incompetent to stand trial refused to take antipsychotic medication that was intended to restore him to competency. Charles Thomas Sell was a former dentist charged with fraud, and he had a history of mental disorder and bizarre behavior, including once calling police to report that a leopard was boarding a bus. During an earlier period of hospitalization he had taken antipsychotic medication. Sell's case proceeded through a number of administrative and court hearings. Staff at the federal medical facility, as well as a federal magistrate, determined that he was dangerous to others and therefore required involuntary medication. He had apparently become infatuated with a nurse and had inappropriately accosted her, though he had not physically harmed her. A district court judge and the 8th Circuit Court of Appeals both ordered the medication on different grounds. These courts did not consider him dangerous, but they did approve the forced medication to render him competent to stand trial.

In 2003, the U.S. Supreme Court sent the case back for further inquiry (*Sell v. United States,* 2003). According to the Justices, Sell's dangerousness had not been established, a fact that had been noted by the federal district court and the court of appeals. However, those lower courts had not sufficiently reviewed the possible trial-related risks and side effects of the medication. "Whether a particular drug will tend to sedate a defendant, interfere with communication with counsel, prevent rapid reaction to trial developments, or diminish the ability to express emotions are matters important in determining the permissibility of medication to restore competence," the Court said.

Sell's alleged crimes (Medicaid fraud, mail fraud, and money laundering) were not violent. However, the crimes allegedly committed by Eugene Russell Weston, the shooting death of two Capitol police officers and the wounding of two others in the summer of 1998, were. Like Sell, Weston had a history of mental disorder that included serious delusional symptoms. Like Sell, he was found incompetent to stand trial and, like Sell, he resisted taking the medication that was intended to restore him to competence. He languished in federal detention for 3 years, unmedicated, while his lawyers argued before various courts that he should not be forced to take medication against his will. In July 2001, a federal court of appeals ruled that the government's strong interest in bringing this defendant to trial overrode his right to remain free of psychoactive drugs and therefore allowed the medication. The Supreme Court refused to hear the case, leaving the decision of the lower court standing.

Although some might wonder if the Court would rule differently today, in light of its decision in the *Sell* case, there are distinguishing features. Weston's alleged crime, the nature of his illness, and his past violent behavior all suggest that he is a probable threat to others. Furthermore, the crime of which he is charged—murder—is a capital offense, one that the government has a strong interest in prosecuting. More important, though, the court in Weston's case carefully considered the side effects of the medication and was careful to note that heightened scrutiny was required before forcing medication on incompetent defendants. Significantly, 13 years after the offense, Weston remains hospitalized and medicated and has yet to be tried. In another high-profile case, the kidnapping of Elizabeth Smart discussed in Chapter 4, codefendant Wanda Barzee was initially found incompetent to stand trial. A judge ordered her to be forcefully medicated, and she subsequently chose to plead guilty rather than go to trial. She is now serving 15 years in prison.

The medication controversy extends to the trial process itself. Although defendants often respond well enough to medication to render them competent to stand trial, continual medication during the trial itself is often, if not invariably, warranted. In other words, to remain competent, the defendant must continue to be medicated. Yet the medication itself may affect the defendant's ability to participate in the proceedings, as the Supreme Court observed in the *Sell* case. Medication also creates an interesting conundrum for defendants who have raised an insanity defense. We will return to this issue later, after introducing the concept of insanity and its assessment.

Insanity

A person cannot be held responsible for a crime if he or she did not possess the "guilty mind" that is required at the time the criminal act was committed. The law recognizes a number of situations under which the guilty mind is absent. For example, if a person acts in self-defense, believing he or she is in imminent danger of grave bodily harm, that person will not be held responsible provided a judge or a jury agrees with his or her perceptions. Likewise, if a defendant charged with sexual assault can convince a judge or jury that the alleged victim consented to the sexual activity, he or she will not be held responsible. When it is mental disorder that robs the individual of a guilty mind, the law refers to this as **insanity.**

The distinction between insanity and competency to stand trial is crucial. Competency refers to one's mental state *at the time of the criminal justice proceedings* (e.g., when waiving the right to a lawyer, pleading guilty, standing trial). Sanity (or criminal responsibility) refers to mental state *at the time of the crime.* It is possible for a person to be insane yet competent to stand trial or sane but incompetent. Obviously, it is also possible for people to be both insane and incompetent or sane and competent. Furthermore, in contrast to competency to stand trial, where the *Dusky* standard is universal, there is no uniform standard for determining insanity. Federal courts and state courts use a variety of "tests" for this purpose, a common one being knowledge of the difference between right and wrong. In some states, even if a person knows the difference between right and wrong, the evidence of an inability to conform his or her conduct to the requirements of the law will suffice. For example, in these states a person who—as the result of a mental disorder—is compelled by "voices" to kill his victim could be excused. The U.S. Supreme Court has given wide latitude to states to decide their own insanity standards (see Focus 5.4).

Over the past 20 years, changes in the federal law as well as the law in numerous states have made it more difficult for defendants pleading not guilty by reason of insanity to win acquittal. The following are examples of why this defense has become more difficult:

- The federal government and some states now no longer allow defendants to claim they could not control their behavior; if they knew the difference between right and wrong, they can still be held responsible.
- The federal government and most states now require defendants to prove their insanity by a preponderance of the evidence.
- A minority of states abolished the insanity defense.
- In federal courts and in some states, forensic examiners are not allowed to express an ultimate opinion on whether the defendant was insane.

Interestingly, research indicates that juries sitting on cases involving the insanity defense very rarely apply the tests for insanity, so changes in the tests may not be that significant. Rather, insanity cases appear to be decided more on moral grounds or on what jurors believe is the "right" decision rather than on correct legal grounds. In her first trial, Andrea Yates was found guilty of killing her children despite evidence of a long history of psychiatric disorder. There are clearly exceptions, though. John Hinckley was tried in the attempted assassination of President Ronald Reagan and the shooting of his press secretary, James Brady, in 1980. The federal jury carefully applied the federal standard that was in effect at that point in time, and it found Hinckley not guilty by reason of insanity.

It should be noted that cases in which defendants actually plead not guilty by reason of insanity are rare, comprising a mere 1 to 3% of all criminal cases (Golding, Skeem, Roesch, & Zapf, 1999). Furthermore, despite media publicity surrounding the insanity defense—one commentator (Perlin, 2003) has referred to it as the "media darling"—the defense is usually not successful. Most defendants who argue that they were not criminally responsible are found guilty, which may be one reason why individuals who initially indicate they will use the defense change their mind.

The rates of acquittal vary widely by jurisdiction, though. Some multistate surveys have found acquittal rates of 20 to 25% (Cirincione, Steadman, & McGreevy, 1995). Although a "success" rate of 1 in 4 may surprise some observers, acquittal does not bring freedom to NGRI defendants. The defense may be used in both misdemeanor and felony cases, and it is sometimes used to obtain treatment for an individual who might not otherwise qualify for civil commitment. Consider the following example.

A person who is mentally disordered breaks into a home to obtain shelter for the night (breaking and entering). Because he is not a danger to himself or others, nor is he gravely disabled, he would not be eligible for involuntary hospitalization. Charged with a crime, though, he may be referred for a competency evaluation. The evaluation allows his hospitalization for at least a temporary period, which may be sufficient to stabilize his mental disorder. Returned to court, he is found competent, but his attorney wonders whether a defense of not guilty by reason of insanity could be supported. The defendant is returned to the hospital for another evaluation, which concludes that such a defense could indeed be supported. The prosecutor and defense attorney stipulate to the report (accept its findings), and the judge enters a not-guilty verdict. The acquitted individual then may be returned to the hospital for more treatment. Such "backdoor" commitments are believed to be common in many communities where community mental health services and resources for the mentally disordered are not available.

In approximately 13 states, an alternative verdict of **guilty but mentally ill** can be returned. This interesting but troubling verdict form allows judges and jurors a middle ground, supposedly reconciling their belief that the defendant "did it" with their belief that he or she "needs help." It makes little difference in the life of the person who obtains this verdict, however. Defendants found guilty but mentally ill are still sent to prison and are no more likely to receive specialized treatment for their disorder than other imprisoned offenders (Borum & Fulero, 1999; Bumby, 1993; Zapf, Golding, & Roesch, 2006).

Assessment of Criminal Responsibility

The evaluation of a defendant's criminal responsibility at the time of the crime is widely recognized by clinicians as an extremely complex one. Note that it is, by definition, retrospective. The clinician must look back and attempt to gain some understanding of the defendant's state of mind at the crucial point in the past when the crime was committed. This may be weeks or even months after the event itself. According to Golding et al. (1999), the clinician must determine whether and what sort of disturbances existed at the behavioral, volitional, and cognitive levels and clarify how those disturbances relate to the criminal act. Melton et al. (1997) have likened the clinician's role to that of an investigative reporter, who gathers information and documents from a wide variety of sources. Likewise, D. L. Shapiro (1999) notes that in addition to a clinical interview, the evaluator should obtain copies of police reports, hospital records, statements of witnesses, any past psychological tests, and employment records, if possible.

All of the cautions mentioned in our discussion of competency evaluations (and the principles in Focus 5.3) apply here as well. One point on which clinicians seem to lack consensus, though, is the appropriateness of conducting **dual-purpose evaluations.** It is not unusual for clinicians to conduct evaluations of a defendant's competency to stand trial and criminal responsibility at the same time. In fact, statutes in many states encourage this practice. Judges will frequently order both a competency evaluation and a **criminal responsibility evaluation** "to see whether an insanity defense could be supported." In one study (Warren, Fitch, Dietz, & Rosenfeld, 1991), 47% of competency evaluations also addressed questions of sanity. Although this seems like an efficient and cost-saving practice, it poses problems, and some scholars have been extremely critical of the process (e.g., Roesch et al., 1999). They emphasize that competency and criminal responsibility are very separate issues requiring separate determinations. According to Roesch et al., it is "cognitively almost impossible" for a judge to keep them distinct when the reports are combined. In addition, an evaluation of criminal responsibility is likely to include a good amount of background information that should be irrelevant to the limited question of whether the defendant is competent to stand trial.

Clinicians have access to forensic assessment instruments similar to those discussed in the competency evaluation process to help in their CR evaluations. By far, the most dominant are the Rogers Criminal Responsibility Assessment Scales (R-CRAS), developed by Richard Rogers (1984). (Dr. Rogers is featured in Personal Perspective 6.2.) Defendants are rated on a number of characteristics, including psychopathology, reliability of their report of the crime, organicity, cognitive control, and behavioral control. Rogers has used a quantitative approach and notes that the R-CRAS has been validated through a series of empirical studies (Rogers & Sewell, 1999; Rogers & Shuman, 1999).

A second instrument, the Mental State at the Time of the Offense Screening Evaluation (MSE; Slobogin, Melton, & Showalter, 1984), is, as its name implies, a way of both screening out the clearly not insane as well as screening in the "obviously insane" (Zapf et al., 2006). Compared with the R-CRAS, the MSE has received less research attention. Zapf et al. report that there have not been any published studies of its reliability, although its validity was established by Slobogin et al.

The use of instruments for assessment of criminal responsibility may be on less solid ground than the use of instruments to assess competency (Grisso, 1996; Nicholson, 1999). Far more research has been conducted on competency assessment, and the *Dusky* standard has remained relatively stable through the years. As we noted earlier, the MacCAT-CA in particular shows promise as an instrument that will take competency assessment to a higher level. In light of their complexity and the wide range of information that must be obtained in sanity assessments, however, the greatest use of assessment instruments may be as screening measures (e.g., the MSE) or as supplementary information to a more comprehensive examination procedure.

Insanity Trials

Once a defense attorney has received a clinician's report suggesting that an insanity defense could be supported, the attorney hopes for a verdict that his or her client is not guilty by reason of insanity. As in the competency context, this is a legal decision, not a clinical decision, and it is one that must be rendered by a judge or a jury. Research indicates that judges are far more sympathetic to the insanity defense than are juries, so a bench trial is more likely to result in a not-guilty verdict than a jury trial (Callahan, Steadman, McGreevy, & Robbins, 1991). Juries also have been found to have many negative attitudes toward, as well as misconceptions about, the insanity defense (Bailis, Darley, Waxman, & Robinson, 1995; Golding et al., 1999; Perlin, 1994). They often do not realize, for example, that defendants found NGRI do not often "go free," but are subject to civil commitment and hospitalization.

The most difficult insanity cases are those in which defendants are charged with serious crimes and go to trial. A critical issue that has emerged in recent years pertains to the case of the medicated defendant. As we noted earlier, defendants found incompetent to stand trial are typically given psychoactive medications to restore them to competency. However, to maintain trial competency, defendants may need continued medication. Thus, during their trials, juries see them in a calm, often emotionless state that is far different from the mental state they claim they were in at the time of the crime. Recall that the Supreme Court expressed some concern about this in the *Sell* case. In an earlier case, the Court had ruled that defendants claiming an insanity defense have a right to be seen by a judge or jury in their natural, unmedicated state (*Riggins v. Nevada*, 1992).

FOCUS 5.4. *CLARK v. ARIZONA* (2006): RECENT DECISION ON INSANITY DEFENSE

On June 21, 2000, Officer Jeffrey Moritz of the Flagstaff, Arizona, Police Department responded to citizen complaints that a pickup truck with loud music blaring was circling a residential block. When he located the truck, Moritz pulled over Eric Clark (age 17). Within a minute of the traffic stop, Clark shot the officer, who died soon after calling for police backup. Clark ran off on foot but was arrested later that day and was charged with first-degree murder for intentionally and knowingly killing a police officer in the line of duty. Clark was first found incompetent to stand trial and committed to a mental hospital. Two years later, the trial court found his competence restored and ordered him to be tried.

Clark, who had been diagnosed with paranoid schizophrenia, argued that he was mentally ill at the time of the crime and believed that Flagstaff had been taken over by hostile aliens. Arizona had adopted a variant of the *M'Naghten standard* for determining insanity. Although the state had originally used the two-pronged M'Naghten standard, it had recently dropped the first component, which stipulates that a person must be able to understand what he is doing—or appreciate the nature and quality of his actions. This "cognitive capacity" element is no longer part of Arizona law. Under current law, an individual was insane only if he was unable to understand that his actions were wrong, a so-called "moral incapacity" standard. A jury apparently believed that Clark understood that his actions were wrong and convicted him of first-degree murder. He was sentenced to 25 years to life in prison.

In appealing his conviction, Clark argued that Arizona's elimination of the first part of the traditional M'Naghten test violated his due process rights. On June 29, 2006, the U.S. Supreme Court ruled in favor of Arizona by a 5-to-4 vote. The Court held that the abbreviated version of the M'Naghten standard was within the state's right, as no universal standard of what constitutes insanity has been established. In other words, there is considerable disagreement on the insanity defense. In essence, the Court affirmed that insanity standards are substantially open to state choice (DeMatteo, 2007b). The American Psychological Association, however, felt that the Court missed the opportunity to establish a Constitutional rule that precludes punishing an offender who, because of mental illness, lacked rational appreciation of his criminal conduct (DeMatteo, 2007b).

The case highlights the need for forensic psychologists and psychiatrists to be highly familiar with the standards for insanity in the states in which they practice. Fine distinctions such as the one illustrated in *Clark v. Arizona* may be relevant in choosing assessment measures as well as questions to be addressed to the defendant who is being examined.

Treatment of Defendants Found Not Guilty by Reason of Insanity

When a defendant is found not guilty by reason of insanity, he or she will rarely be free to go. All states and the federal government allow a period of civil commitment in a mental institution or, less frequently, on an outpatient basis. In practice, hospitalization is the most common outcome of a finding of not guilty by reason of insanity, and also in practice, numerous individuals found NGRI are hospitalized for longer than the time they would have served had they been convicted (Golding et al., 1999). John Hinckley, found NGRI after shooting President Ronald Reagan and seriously wounding Press Secretary James Brady, has remained hospitalized for about 30 years, although he has been allowed visits to his parents' home in nearby Virginia (see Photo 5.2).

Civil commitment cannot be automatic, however. A hearing must be held to document that the individual continues to be mentally disordered, in need of treatment, and a danger to the self or others. Commitment also cannot be indeterminate, without periodic reviews of the need for commitment. Most states require NGRI patients to prove they are no longer mentally ill and dangerous in order to be released. However, an individual cannot be held solely based on dangerousness if there is no longer evidence of mental illness (*Foucha v. Louisiana*, 1992). The exception may be the case of sexually violent predators, who we will discuss later in the chapter.

Recall that persons found incompetent to stand trial are hospitalized with the goal of being restored to competency, so that the legal process may continue. Especially in serious cases, the state has a

Photo 5.2   St. Elizabeth's Hospital in Washington, D.C., where John Hinckley has been held since 1981, when he shot President Ronald Reagan and seriously wounded Press Secretary James Brady, leaving him brain damaged. Hinckley was found not guilty by reason of insanity. In 2003, he was granted unsupervised visits to the home of his parents in neighboring Virginia. He has progressed from short day visits to overnight visits. Although his mental illness has been in remission and clinicians say he is not a danger, his periodic requests for permanent release from the hospital have been denied.

strong interest in bringing them to trial. In the case of persons found NGRI, the state cannot retry them—this would be an example of double jeopardy, which is in violation of the Constitution. Thus, if they are institutionalized, they receive treatment that is usually indistinguishable from the treatment received by other hospitalized patients. In recent years, some states have crafted programs that are particularly directed at persons found NGRI, both in forensic hospitals and in community settings. Furthermore, aware that many insanity acquittees have "significant lifelong psychopathological difficulties" (Golding et al., 1999, p. 397), some states discharge individuals on a conditional basis and provide follow-up and monitoring services in the community. We will discuss outpatient commitment for a variety of individuals in more detail in the following chapter.

Sentencing Evaluations

Criminal sentencing in the United States went through a period of "reform" during the last quarter of the 20th century. Until that time, sentencing was primarily indeterminate, with offenders being sent to prison for a range of years (e.g., 5 to 10). Indeterminate sentencing was based on a rehabilitative model of corrections; it was assumed that prisoners would be provided with rehabilitative services while in prison and that they would be released when they had made sufficient progress. Alternatively, offenders could be placed on probation to serve their sentences in the community, but again with the assumption that rehabilitation would be offered.

The psychologist or psychiatrist might be asked to evaluate the offender and offer a recommendation for treatment, which would then be forwarded to correctional officials.

Although rehabilitation remains an important consideration, it is no longer the dominant consideration in the sentencing schemes of the federal government or approximately 15 states today. These jurisdictions have adopted determinate sentencing, which attempts to make the punishment fit the crime and have an offender serve the sentence he or she supposedly deserves, regardless of individual characteristics and the extent to which rehabilitation is accomplished. The sentencing discretion provided to the judge in these states is usually quite limited; judges are usually provided with guidelines that take into consideration the seriousness of the crime and the individual's prior record in determining the appropriate sentence. Additional factors—such as the offender's age or the extent to which he or she might be a good candidate for a particular program—are not taken into account at sentencing. For this reason, the psychologist's role in recommending rehabilitation strategies has been diminished in these states.

In determinate sentencing states, though, courts may consider evidence of diminished mental capacity or extreme emotional distress and may reduce the sentence that would otherwise be imposed. In addition, psychologists may be called on to assess risk or to testify as to whether the individual might benefit from specific types of treatment, such as substance abuse, anger management, or sex offender treatment. In short, sentencing evaluations may focus on treatment needs, the offender's culpability, or future dangerousness (Melton et al., 1997).

Regardless of whether the jurisdiction has determinate or indeterminate sentencing, however, the forensic psychologist might be called in to assess an offender's *competency* to be sentenced. There is very little literature on this as a separate competency assessment, and we have virtually no information on how often it occurs.

In those states where indeterminate sentencing is still in effect, the psychologist may still play a crucial role. The defense attorney is the legal practitioner who is most likely to contact the clinician. The attorney is attempting, in this context, to craft the best sentencing package for his or her client. Thus, a lawyer trying to keep his or her client in the community rather than imprisoned might offer to the court a report from a forensic psychologist suggesting that the client would likely benefit from substance abuse treatment, which is only intermittently available in the state prison system.

Risk Assessment

Clinicians are now being called in frequently to assess the offender's dangerousness to society. As we noted at the beginning of the chapter, such risk assessments may occur very early in the criminal justice process, when a decision is being made whether to deny bail to a defendant who has been charged with a violent crime and would allegedly be dangerous if released. Furthermore, as discussed in Chapter 4, many clinicians today see their task as one of assessing risk rather than predicting dangerousness. This is to emphasize that human behavior, including that which is violent, cannot be comfortably predicted. Rather, the best a clinician can do is assess probabilities based on a variety of factors in the individual's unique situation. Risk assessments are useful to the courts in deciding whether an individual should remain in the community.

Heilbrun et al. (2002) emphasize the importance of clarifying the purpose of the risk assessment, as in all forensic mental health assessments. They note that the clinician must ascertain "whether the purpose . . . is to predict future behavior (e.g., provide a classification of risk or a probability of the likelihood of future violence), to identify risk factors and include recommendations for reducing risk, or both" (p. 461). They add that if the purpose is one but not the other, it may not be appropriate to address the other. We might illustrate this with the following example: A lawyer requesting a risk assessment prior to representing his or her client at a sentencing hearing may be interested only in an identification of risk factors and strategies for reducing risk in the hope that the judge will agree to place the convicted individual on probation. To include a statement that the individual has an extremely high probability of reoffending would be problematic for the client.

Instruments for assessing risk are more widely available and empirically supported than are instruments for assessing the reduction of risk, or the second question referred to above (Heilbrun et al., 2002). Yet, even though researchers have developed empirically sound instruments for assessing risk, even the most well-known (e.g., the Violence Risk Appraisal Guide [VRAG], the Historical/Clinical/Risk Management Scale [HCR-20], and the Iterative Classification Tree [ICT]) have their limitations. (These and other instruments are listed in Focus 5.5.). "If they were developed on different populations, or predict outcomes that are different from what is being assessed in the immediate case, or use an outcome period that is not applicable, then they might not be particularly useful in that case" (Heilbrun et al., 2002, p. 461).

Readers should also recall the limitations of actuarial risk assessment, as discussed in Chapter 4. On the whole, however, actuarial assessment has fared better than clinical prediction in terms of success at accurately foretelling whether an individual will engage in violent behavior. Nevertheless, the combination of actuarial assessment and structured or guided clinical judgment may be the most worthwhile approach.

For purposes of assessing change in risk *level,* Heilbrun et al. (2002) recommend a number of strategies, even if instruments are not widely available. They suggest, for example, assessing the dynamic risk factors that were in operation at the time of the individual's violent act and determining whether they still exist. Recall that dynamic risk factors are those that can change. For example, at the time of the alleged assault, the individual had just lost his job; he has since gained new employment. "Protective factors" that may have inhibited violence in the past should also be assessed to see if they are still in place. An example of a protective factor would be a stable marital relationship or a child who looks up to the individual and for whom he is responsible. Heilbrun et al. also recommend close observation of an individual's behavior, modification of the environment that may be conducive to violent behavior, and an assessment of the impact on monitoring, "which has been empirically demonstrated to lower an individual's risk for engaging in violent behavior" (p. 462).

FOCUS 5.5. RISK ASSESSMENT INSTRUMENTS

The risk assessment enterprise includes a variety of instruments that researchers have designed specifically to assess risk of violence among certain populations. As noted in the chapter, there is no perfect test for predicting that a person will or will not engage in violent or other antisocial behavior. Nevertheless, some of the more promising instruments and guidelines are the following:

HCR-20 (Webster, Harris, Rice, Cormier, & Quinsey, 1994). The Historical/Clinical/Risk Management Scale is a 20-item instrument that includes items based on a person's background (historical), attitudes or mental disorders (clinical), and external risk factors (R) such as housing or family support. It assesses violence risk among persons with serious psychiatric or personality disorders.

Iterative Classification Tree (Monahan, Bonnie, et al., 2001). Developed on psychiatric patients, the Iterative Classification Tree (ICT) is a yes/no flowchart that takes into consideration both clinical observations and variables traditionally associated with a prediction of violence. It is particularly effective at identifying those individuals at high risk and low risk of offending.

(Continued)

(Continued)

SARA (Kropp & Hart, 2000). The Spousal Assault Risk Assessment (SARA) guide assesses an individual's risk of committing violence against a spouse or intimate partner. It may be used in situations when a release decision is being considered (such as bail or parole). It assesses risk factors relating to psychosocial adjustment (such as employment or relationship problems) as well as the seriousness of criminal offenses.

VRAG (Harris, Rice, & Quinsey, 1993). The Violence Risk Appraisal Guide (VRAG) is based on 12 variables, including such background variables as alcohol abuse and elementary school malad-justment, as well as present mental status, such as schizophrenia and symptoms of psychopathy. It assesses the risk of violence in the community over a relatively long period (e.g., average is 7 years).

LSI-R (Andrews & Bonta, 1995). The Level of Service Inventory–Revised assesses dynamic and static risk factors to determine offender needs for services as well as risk of reconviction, includ-ing for violent offenses. It is used in many correctional facilities and has attracted a long line of research.

SAVRY (Borum, Bartel, & Forth, 2005). The Structured Assessment of Violence Risk for Youth is, as its name implies, designed for use with adolescents aged 12 to 18 years. It takes into consid-eration both static and dynamic risk factors as well as protective factors, and research suggests it can predict nonviolent as well as violent offending (Vincent, Chapman, & Cook, 2010).

Researchers have also developed instruments designed to assess risk among sex offenders, includ-ing juvenile sex offenders. These instruments are less widely accepted, primarily because they have not yet been subjected to extensive empirical research, although this situation is changing rapidly (e.g., Viljoen, Elkovitch, Scalora, & Ullman, 2009, pertaining to juvenile measures). Examples are the Min-nesota Sex Offender Screening Tool–Revised (Mn-SOST-R) (Epperson, Kaul, & Hesselton, 1998); the Static-99 (Hanson & Thornton, 2000); the Estimate of Risk of Adolescent Sexual Offense Recidivism (ERASOR); and the Registrant Risk Assessment Scale (Ferguson, Eidelson, & Witt, 1998), which was developed in New Jersey to evaluate and place sex offenders into risk tiers for sex offender registration purposes. Juvenile assessment instruments will be discussed again in later chapters.

Capital Sentencing

Risk assessments are useful to courts in the 38 death penalty states, as well as the federal government and the military, where the decision between life and death may revolve around the extent to which the individual is a danger to society. As noted by Melton et al. (2007), "the modern death penalty process has been shaped by a long series of United States Supreme Court decisions" (p. 265). In cases in which offenders face a potential death sentence, forensic psychologists and other forensic professionals sometimes work with the defense team to present arguments for mitigation, a process known as **death penalty mitigation.** *Mitigation* in this sense means to reduce the sentence by avoiding the death penalty. In a recent Supreme Court case (*Cone v. Bell*, 2009), a Vietnam-era veteran went on a crime spree during which he killed an elderly couple; he was ultimately convicted and sentenced to death. The Supreme Court vacated the death sentence, stating that the veteran's drug addiction and his diagnosed posttraumatic stress disorder (PTSD) should have been considered as mitigating circumstances by the sentencing jury.

Death penalty mitigation investigations are comprehensive psychobiological evaluations of potential neuropsychological deficits, mental disabilities, mental disorders, and conditions that may have affected a defendant's criminal actions. The psychologist also may be asked to provide a more general evaluation of the offender's psychological functioning to learn whether there is anything that might lessen the offender's culpability for the crime. (See Personal Perspective 5.2, which introduces you to Dr. Mark Cunningham, who does extensive research and consulting work relating to the death penalty.)

Some clinicians, however, also work with the prosecutor who seeks evidence *against* mitigation or evidence of **aggravating factors** associated with the crime. Thus, if a psychologist or psychiatrist gives the opinion that the individual is not developmentally disabled or is likely to engage in serious violent behavior, this would bolster the prosecutor's argument against mitigation. This aspect of capital sentencing is particularly controversial, and it may create ethical problems for some psychologists, as Dr. Cunningham notes in Personal Perspective 5.2. Some researchers have suggested that the psychopath designation should not be used at this phase of the criminal process. Psychopaths are widely believed to be cold, unfeeling, nonresponsive to treatment, and—of course—dangerous.

PERSONAL PERSPECTIVE 5.2

Capital Defendants, Capital Sentencing, and Capital Inmates

Mark D. Cunningham, PhD, ABPP

Where some people's recreational passion is golf or tennis, mine is scholarly writing. I am a clinical psychologist by graduate training, a forensic psychologist by career evolution, and a researcher and scholar by avocation. I am in independent practice. Capital sentencing (i.e., death penalty jeopardy) determinations are my subspecialty. I was in mid-career before I figured out that when you have a good mind, nothing is quite as enjoyable as challenging those faculties with scientific investigations and their real-world applications. Research and writing are not only enormously stimulating in their own right, but also have the collateral returns of camaraderie with coauthors, the realization of an identity as a scientist, and the satisfaction of illuminating an issue that has been incompletely or even erroneously understood. My research efforts have been recognized with the *2006 American Psychological Association Award for Distinguished Contributions to Research in Public Policy* and the *2005 Texas Psychological Association Award for Outstanding Contribution to Science*. These awards are a demonstration that psychologists in independent practice, as well as academicians, can make meaningful scientific contributions. Please allow me to describe some of this research.

(Continued)

(Continued)

Representation of Mississippi death row inmates: As of 1998, indigent death row inmates in Mississippi had not been provided with state-funded attorneys at an important stage of their appeals known as postconviction proceedings.

By comprehensively assessing the intellectual capabilities, literacy level, psychological status, specific knowledge of post-conviction law, and legal aptitude of inmates on Mississippi's death row, Dr. Mark Vigen and I established that these prisoners were wholly deficient to represent themselves. Soon after being informed of the findings of this study through a highly detailed affidavit I authored, the Mississippi Supreme Court (*Jackson v. State* 1998) reversed its prior rulings and found that death row inmates did not have the capability to represent themselves in state post-conviction efforts, and thus their meaningful access to the courts *did* entail a right to appointed and state-funded representation in post-conviction proceedings. This was the first such ruling by a high court in the United States. Our research findings were credited for this extraordinary change in public policy.

Violence risk assessment in capital prosecutions: Expert testimony by mental health professionals regarding the likelihood of future acts of violence by capital defendants has been notoriously unreliable and ethically controversial. This was largely due to the absence of either a reliable methodology or relevant group statistical data (i.e., base rate data) to anchor these predictions. These same deficiencies also drive public policy decisions regarding capital prosecutions, legislative and clemency considerations, and conditions of death row confinement. In providing expert testimony in capital cases as well as in my scholarship and research, I have articulated a scientifically sound capital risk assessment methodology based on rates and correlates of violence in prison and on capital parole. Subsequent scholarship has refined the applications and implications of this methodology and data. My colleagues and I have further explored these considerations through a series of studies, some quite large in scale (i.e., $N = 2{,}000$–$50{,}000$), on rates and correlates of prison violence, and the institutional conduct of capital offenders and other inmate groups.

We have also tested the capability of capital jurors to predict the future violence of a capital offender and to utilize this as a consideration in death penalty sentencing, finding that the predictions of these jurors were no better than random guesses. This has enormous public policy implications. Jury appraisal of the "dangerousness" of capital offenders has been a factor in many of the death sentences handed down in the past 35 years.

Relationship of offense of conviction and life-without-parole sentencing to prison misconduct: In a number of studies, my colleagues and I established that convicted murderers and capital murderers are not a disproportionate source of prison violence. Contrary to popular "nothing to lose" expectations, we also found that life-without-parole inmates were often better adjusted than short-term inmates. I testified regarding these research data before the Criminal Justice Committee of the Texas Senate in 2005 as this legislative body considered legislation to provide a life-without-parole sentencing option at capital sentencing. The bill was signed into law, and our research findings were identified as critical to its passage.

Conditions of confinement for death-sentenced inmates: My colleagues and I examined the 11-year policy of the Missouri Department of Corrections of "mainstreaming" death-sentenced inmates in the general prison population of a maximum security prison rather than segregating them on a death row. The mainstreamed death-sentenced inmates we studied had frequency rates and prevalence of institutional violence that were quite similar to life-without-parole inmates, and well below fellow inmates that were sentenced to parole-eligible terms. The findings of this study also have significant public policy implications, as they cast serious doubt on the security-driven assumptions that have resulted in the segregation of death-sentenced inmates elsewhere in the nation. This finding has important constitutional implications as well. If death-sentenced prisoners are not a disproportionate risk of serious violence in prison, then their confinement under draconian super-maximum conditions does not serve a legitimate penological interest and arguably represents a violation of the Eighth Amendment bar against cruel and unusual punishment.

From clinician to forensics to research: Though trained in a "scientist-practitioner" model in my doctorate program at Oklahoma State University, I had anticipated a career as a practitioner more than a researcher. True to this expectation, I established an independent practice that gradually evolved from clinical to forensic in focus. In early 1995, I became board-certified (American Board of Professional Psychology, ABPP) in forensic psychology. The several-year process of intensive study of research and case law in preparing for this board-certification examination reawakened the scientist in me and stimulated 15 years of research and scholarship. Forty-six publications and a remarkable career niche have followed.

Dr. Cunningham received his PhD in clinical psychology from Oklahoma State University and completed a 2-year postdoctoral training program at the Yale University School of Medicine. He was an assistant professor of psychology at Hardin-Simmons University in Texas for 2 years and has since been in independent practice. He is board-certified (ABPP) in clinical and forensic psychology. His practice is national in scope.

After the reinstitution of the death penalty in the United States in 1976, the first case to consider mitigating evidence in capital cases was *Lockett v. Ohio* (1978) (R. King & Norgard, 1999). Sandra Lockett was convicted of felony murder as an accomplice in the robbery of a pawnshop during which the owner was killed (She encouraged the robbery and drove the getaway car.). In 1978, Ohio passed a statute that *required* individuals convicted of aggravated murder to be given a death sentence. The defense argued that the Ohio statute was unconstitutional because it does not allow the sentencing judge to consider mitigating factors in capital cases, which is required by the Eighth and Fourteenth Amendments. At sentencing, Lockett offered evidence from a psychologist who reported that she had a favorable prognosis for rehabilitation. Among other things, she was only 21 years old at the time of the offense and had committed no other major offenses. The U.S. Supreme Court agreed and stated,

We conclude that the Eight and Fourteenth Amendments require that the sentencer, in all but the rarest kind of capital case, not be precluded from considering, as a mitigating factor, any aspect of a defendant's character or record and any of the circumstances of the offense that the defendant proffers as a basis for sentence less than death. (pp. 604–605)

The Court overturned the Lockett sentence and asserted that a law which prohibits one from considering mitigating circumstances is unreasonable and unconstitutional. Although mitigating factors vary among jurisdictions, most mitigators are phrased in legislation in terms that invite the participation of forensic practitioners (Melton et al., 1997). For example, many jurisdictions allow mitigation circumstances to include intellectual disability, mental or emotional distress, or the inability to appreciate the criminality of one's actions. Age, a childhood marred by extensive abuse, neuropsychological deficits, and—as noted above—PTSD are other examples.

The U.S. Supreme Court abolished capital punishment for offenders under the age of 16 in *Thompson v. Oklahoma* (1988) and in 2005, in *Roper v. Simmons,* it struck down the death penalty for all juveniles up to age 18. Thus, if a 16- or 17-year-old commits a capital murder, he is not eligible for the death penalty, regardless of his age at the time of the trial. In recent years, the Court also has ruled that neither intellectually disabled offenders (*Atkins v. Virginia,* 2002) nor offenders who are so mentally ill that they cannot understand what is happening to them (*Ford v. Wainwright,* 1986) are eligible for the death penalty. Furthermore, someone who is mentally ill at the time of execution cannot be executed. Finally, persons who commit rape (*Coker v. Georgia,* 1977), including rape of a child (*Kennedy v. Louisiana,* 2008), cannot be executed if their victims did not die. Regardless of the heinous nature of these offenses, the death penalty is to be limited to situations resulting in murder. Despite these limitations, over 3,000 individuals were on death row in the United States at the end of 2010 (www.deathpenaltyinfo.org). (See Photo 5.3, depicting a death chamber in Texas.)

Photo 5.3 Image of the death chamber in Huntsville, Texas, where prisoners are put to death by lethal injection.

According to Heilbrun et al. (2002), "Capital sentencing evaluations are among the most detailed and demanding forensic assessments that are performed" (p. 116). The clinician is called in to provide a broad-based report that will presumably assist in determining whether a person convicted of a capital crime should be sentenced to death. Some psychologists have strong moral objections to participating in any phase of a death penalty case, with particular antipathy toward assessing risk at the sentencing stage. Many also do not choose to participate in assessments of competency for execution, which occur later in the criminal process, as the execution date is approaching. Evaluations of competency to be executed will be discussed in Chapter 12.

In light of a long line of research documenting the deficiencies of clinical predictions of dangerousness, many forensic examiners are reluctant to rely on clinical impressions alone (Heilbrun et al., 2002). Nevertheless, as we noted in this and earlier chapters, actuarial or statistical data are not foolproof, either. In the death penalty context, actuarial data may be especially suspect. Cunningham and Reidy (1998, 1999) have brought attention to a problem dealing with the base rate, which is the fundamental group statistic in risk assessment. The base rate of murderers, they say, does not justify a prediction of dangerousness in death penalty cases. As a group, convicted murderers are neither violent in prison nor violent if released on parole (Bohm, 1999; Cunningham, Sorensen, Vigen, & Woods, in press).

In sum, the role of the forensic psychologist at capital sentencing is both crucial for obtaining possible evidence in mitigation and controversial for its contribution to the jury's prediction of dangerousness. Cases in which the death penalty is a possible outcome are unique. As the U.S. Supreme Court has so frequently observed in its death penalty opinions, death is different, and there is a bright line separating capital from noncapital cases. In *Furman v. Georgia* (1972), where the death-is-different principle was first expressed, the Court noted that death is "an unusually severe punishment, unusual in its pain, in its finality, and in its enormity." The bright line that separates death penalty cases from those in which death is not a possible outcome is one that many psychologists prefer not to cross. Yet, others believe that they are in a unique position to document the existence of mitigating factors that may spare a convicted offender the death sentence.

Sex Offender Sentencing

Psychologists have conducted extensive research on the nature, causes, and treatment of sexual offending. Because of their expertise, psychologists are often asked to provide assessments of convicted sex offenders to help courts decide on a just punishment. In many jurisdictions, these evaluations are known as "psychosexual assessments." They are typically very broad based, with the psychologist providing a wealth of background information, test results, observations, and—in some cases—risk assessments. Psychosexual assessments also typically include recommendations for treatment and for managing any risk believed to be posed by the offender. For example, if an offender will almost assuredly be sent to prison, the evaluator may indicate that he is a good candidate for a sex offender treatment program known to be available in the prison system. For an offender who may be placed on probation, the evaluator might suggest that the supervising probation officer pay close attention to his employment status because he was particularly vulnerable to committing offenses during periods in which he was laid off from work.

Heilbrun et al. (2002) warn clinicians to be very careful in using some of the typologies to classify sex offenders in their reports to the courts. Although the typologies may be useful in clinical practice and may be intuitively appealing, few have received empirical support. Typologies also offer convenient and catchy "labels" that may follow an offender throughout his prison career, again with little validity. An offender tagged by professionals as a "sadistic rapist" or a "fixated child molester" may encounter adjustment problems in prison over and above the problems faced by inmates with more innocuous or "normal" labels—burglar, killer, or even rapist. In addition, the typologies may unjustly confine an offender to a higher security level than is warranted or limit his opportunity for participation in work programs or for early release.

According to Heilbrun et al. (2002), more promising than typologies are the risk assessment scales that have been developed specifically for sex offenders (see Focus 5.5). As with other risk assessment instruments, though, care must be taken to choose the appropriate instrument and to be sure it is used in combination with other methods of assessment.

It should be emphasized that both the ethical code of the American Psychological Association (1992, 2002b) and the "Specialty Guidelines for Forensic Psychologists" (Committee on Ethical Guidelines for Forensic Psychologists, 1991) make it clear that psychologists should use validated instruments. Furthermore, they should acknowledge the limitations of the instruments they do use and should communicate their findings in a manner that will promote understanding and avoid deception.

Civil Commitment of Sexually Violent Predators

In the 1980s and 1990s, Congress as well as many state legislatures passed laws and funded programs that were designed to address the many problems associated with sex offending. Most of us are familiar with variants of these laws or programs that are named after the victims of heinous offenses (e.g., Sex Offender Registration and Notification Act [SORNA], Megan's Law, the Adam Walsh Child Protection and Safety Act, the Amber Alert). As a group, these legislative enactments provide resources for police in the prevention of sex offending as well as services for victims and their relatives. Many of the laws also provide for registration of sex offenders after they have been released from prison and, in some instances, community notification. Today, names of registered sex offenders are widely dispersed on the Internet.

In the early part of the 21st century, the U.S. government increasingly placed mandates on states to revise their systems pertaining to the classification of sex offenders, thereby presumably making registration and notification laws more consistent across the country (A. J. Harris, Lobanov-Rostovsky, & Levenson, 2010). Researchers are just beginning to assess the effects of these mandates (e.g., Freeman & Sandler, 2009; A. J. Harris, Lobanov-Rostovsky, et al., 2010), and some question the efficiency of these procedures as well as the effect on those sex offenders who, based on sex offender research (e.g., Hanson & Morton-Bourgon, 2005), are unlikely to recidivate. (See A. J. Harris & Lurigio, 2010, for a comprehensive review.) In addition, the monitoring of sex offenders living in the community—such as community notification and residency restrictions—are believed to conflict with or interfere with treatment goals, particularly for those who are mentally ill (A. J. Harris, Fisher, Veysey, Ragusa, & Lurigio, 2010).

The policy issues relating to sex offenders and former sex offenders living in the community are important. Less widely publicized is the commitment of violent sex offenders to mental institutions for indeterminate periods, against their will, after they have completed their prison sentences. In some states, the law also allows persons charged with violent sex offenses to be detained in mental institutions rather than in jails. Approximately 16 states and the federal government have such provisions, cumulatively known as sexually violent predator (SVP) statutes. Estimates of the number of individuals detained or committed under these laws range from 1,300 to 2,209 (La Fond, 2003). Janus and Walbek (2000) report that these commitment schemes are exceedingly expensive, with the annual cost per patient ranging from $60,000 to $180,000. This does not include the cost of commitment proceedings or capital costs for constructing needed facilities.

Numerous legal, ethical, and practical issues have been raised about this practice. However, the U.S. Supreme Court has allowed it, provided the offender has a history of sexually violent conduct, a current mental disorder or abnormality, a risk of future sexually violent conduct, and a mental disorder or abnormality that is connected to the conduct (*Kansas v. Hendricks*, 1997). In *Kansas v. Hendricks*, the Court held that dangerous sexual predators may be civilly committed against their will upon expiration of their prison sentences. In *Kansas v. Crane* (2002), the Court added that the state also has to prove that the individual has *some inability* to control his behavior. (The Kansas Supreme Court had ruled that the individual had to be found *unable to control* his dangerous behavior; the federal Court ruled that this was too heavy a burden for the state to bear.) In its most recent ruling on this issue (*U.S. v. Comstock*, 2010), the Court allowed the *federal* government also to hold violent sexual offenders beyond their prison sentence if they were mentally ill. The government could either keep them in federal facilities or transfer them to state mental institutions, with a state's permission. They are, however, entitled to periodic reviews of their mental status. The forensic psychologist or psychiatrist may be called in to assess this status. As a result of these and other developments, training sessions, workshops, and publications are now available to offer guidance to psychologists conducting evaluations of individuals designated as sexually violent predators (e.g., Heilbrun, Grisso, & Goldstein, 2008; Melton et al., 2007).

Although the involuntary civil commitment of SVPs technically comes under the purview of civil law, it is so closely related to the criminal justice process and to the risk assessment instruments discussed above that we cover the topic here. In the following chapter, civil commitment of other individuals will be discussed.

Forensic psychologists may face a number of dilemmas relative to the assessment of sexually violent predators. The usual concerns about the assessment of risk, including the use of specialized instruments for use with sexual offenders, must be considered. Although progress has been made on risk assessment in a number of contexts, the enterprise is by no means on solid empirical ground. This is an important point to make in all legal contexts, but when it comes to sexually violent predators, there are additional ethical considerations. Because of the nature of this type of crime, courts are highly likely to err on the side of caution and to accept any documentation provided by the clinician; the high numbers of offenders who have been committed under these statutes suggest that commitment is not difficult to achieve.

It is also important to note that commitment does not require evidence of a recognized mental disorder; mental "abnormality" is sufficient. Researchers have found that many sex offenders do not suffer from mental disorder or mental illness. Nevertheless, the statutes often allow them to be civilly committed. In an analysis of sex offender commitment in Minnesota, Janus and Walbek (2000) learned that more than half of the 99 men in the study for whom diagnostic information was available had not been diagnosed with a sexual deviation disorder. Although other diagnoses were present (e.g., dementia, 2%; antisocial personality disorder, 26%; substance abuse or dependency, 52%), 10% had no diagnosis other than substance abuse or dependency. It should be noted that the civil commitment of persons other than SVPs requires a diagnosis of mental disorder or illness; a substance abuse or dependency diagnosis would not qualify. Under *U.S. v. Comstock* (2010), civil commitment in the federal system also requires the finding of a mental disorder.

An additional concern expressed in the literature is the possible lack of treatment that accompanies SVP commitment (Janus, 2000; Wood, Grossman, & Fichtner, 2000). Although the statutes typically include a provision that treatment will be offered if available, most statutes do not guarantee that this will occur. "Nevertheless, many states claim that sex offender commitments are aimed at treatment, and that they are providing effective—or at least state of the art—treatment" (Janus & Walbek, 2000, p. 347).

Critics of these commitment statutes maintain that they are really being used to extend punishment rather than provide treatment (La Fond, 2000). In other words, treatment is a secondary purpose. It should be noted also that not all sex offenders are mentally disordered to begin with, as Janus and Walbek's (2000) Minnesota study confirms. In fact, some researchers maintain that most are not: "The absence of a major mental disorder unique to offenders who commit sex crimes suggests that mental health treatment for most sex offenders needs to be questioned" (L. M. J. Simon, 2000, p. 295).

Still another concern is that sex offender commitment seems to result in very lengthy confinement. Recall from earlier in the chapter that the confinement of persons to civil mental institutions for non-forensic purposes is more likely to be measured in terms of days or weeks, whereas forensic populations are measured in terms of months or even years. Janus and Walbek (2000) observed that committed sex offenders almost never get released. They note that, "[a]s a practical matter, the burden of proof to support discharge is a heavy one" (p. 346). This is illustrative of an observation that has frequently been made about sex offenders: "Historically, sex offenders have been singled out for differential treatment by the legal and mental health systems" (L. M. J. Simon, 2000, p. 275).

In light of some of the above concerns, La Fond (2003) has advanced an interesting but undoubtedly controversial argument for outpatient commitment for violent sexual predators. Some SVPs, he believes, could benefit from initial outpatient treatment, whereas others could benefit from outpatient commitment as a transitional measure after institutionalization. La Fond refers to the consensus among treatment providers that persons who are enrolled in sex offender treatment programs within a secure facility should be followed up in the community to achieve maximum treatment outcomes. Thus, for those SVPs who get treated within the prison or the mental institution, outpatient commitment would provide continuing supervision and treatment upon release. Yet, **sexually violent predator statutes** in most of the states that have them do not provide for such outpatient commitment. When they do, there is very little evidence that it is used (La Fond, 2003).

The above are only some of the many issues that have been raised about the wisdom and ethics of involuntary civil commitment for sexually violent predators. Psychologists are likely to be involved in both the assessment and the treatment (if provided) of sexual offenders. Some evaluators may assume, when conducting risk assessments, that treatment will be provided once the individual is civilly committed. As we have seen, this is not necessarily the case. In addition, as we will discuss again in Chapter 12, the *effectiveness* of sex offender treatment programs is still very much in question, even though there is positive movement in this area. Although the forensic psychologist does not set social policy, he or she should be aware of the research and the growing controversy in this matter.

SUMMARY AND CONCLUSIONS

This chapter has reviewed a wide variety of tasks performed by forensic psychologists in their interaction with criminal courts. The available research suggests that the dominant tasks revolve around the various competencies that criminal defendants must possess to participate in criminal proceedings. Competency to stand trial, competency to waive the right to a lawyer, competency to plead guilty, and competency to be sentenced are examples. The psychological literature uses the term *adjudicative competence* to embrace all of these separate competencies. Adjudicative competence—as conceived by Richard Bonnie—also includes the important aspects of being able to communicate effectively with one's attorney and making decisions across a wide range of contexts.

There appears to be no consensus about how competency evaluations should be conducted, although most guidelines and publications indicate that the traditional clinical interview by itself does not suffice. Although some psychologists administer traditional psychological tests, instruments specifically designed to measure competency are now widely available. Among the most promising is the MacCAT-CA, developed by researchers from the MacArthur Foundation. The results of the competency evaluation appear to have a significant effect on a judge's decision, with judges almost always agreeing with recommendations offered by the examiner.

Psychologists also conduct sanity evaluations, more formally known as assessments of criminal responsibility or mental state at the time of the offense. These evaluations are far more complex than most evaluations of adjudicative competence—but there are exceptions. The assessment of criminal responsibility requires the collection of a large amount of background data, interviews with the defendant, and contacts with other individuals who may be able to provide insight into the defendant's state of mind when the crime was committed. The Rogers Criminal Responsibility Assessment Scales (R-CRAS) and the Mental State at the Time of the Offense (MSO) screening evaluation are the dominant instruments available for this purpose, though research suggests they are less likely to be used than are competency assessment instruments.

A controversial topic relating to both competency and insanity is the administration of psychoactive medication against an individual's will. Medication is the dominant way of treating incompetent defendants to render them competent to stand trial. However, medicated defendants may suffer a variety of side effects, some of which may interfere with their capacity to participate in the trial process. The U.S. Supreme Court has indicated that extreme care must be taken before medicating defendants against their will to restore them to competency. In the case of a non-dangerous defendant charged with a nonviolent offense, the Court disallowed the forced medication because the lower courts had not sufficiently considered its side effects. However, the Court refused to hear another case—and thus allowed the involuntary medication of an incompetent defendant who was charged with a serious violent crime and was deemed to be dangerous. The Court has ruled, though, that defendants have a right not to be medicated during their trials if they are pleading not guilty by reason of insanity and want jurors to see them in their natural, non-medicated state.

Psychologists also consult with criminal courts as judges are preparing to sentence an offender. These sentencing evaluations are conducted primarily to determine whether the offender would be a good candidate for a particular rehabilitative approach, such as substance abuse treatment or a violent offender program. Sentencing evaluations also may involve assessments of risk, however, because courts are often interested in an appraisal of the convicted offender's dangerousness. Risk assessment remains an imperfect enterprise, but a variety of valid instruments are available for this purpose. In this chapter, we reviewed some of the major concerns surrounding risk assessment of special populations, such as sex offenders and defendants convicted of a capital crime and facing a possible death sentence.

The chapter ended with a discussion of sexually violent predators and their indeterminate commitment to civil mental institutions. Approximately 15 states now allow such a commitment, provided that the offender is dangerous and has a mental disorder or some mental abnormality—a very broad term that has been criticized by many scholars. Although statutes often indicate that treatment will be provided, it is widely suspected that the primary intention of these statutes is to keep sexual predators incapacitated.

KEY CONCEPTS

Adjudicative competence

Aggravating factors

Capital sentencing

Clear and convincing proof

Competency Screening Test

Criminal responsibility evaluation

Death-is-different principle

Death penalty mitigation

Dual-purpose evaluations

Dual relationship

Dusky standard

Forensic mental health assessments (FMHAs)

Georgia Court Competency Test (GCCT)

Guilty but mentally ill

HCR-20

Insanity

Involuntary civil commitment

Iterative Classification Tree

MacArthur Competence Assessment Tool—Criminal Adjudication (MacCAT-CA)

Malingering

Mitigating factors

Preponderance of evidence

Psychoactive medication

Restoration to competency

Rogers Criminal Responsibility Assessment Scales (R-CRAS)

SARA

Sexually violent predator statutes

QUESTIONS FOR REVIEW

1. List at least five competencies in criminal suspects and defendants that might have to be assessed by forensic psychologists.

2. State and explain the differences between the three burdens of proof discussed in this chapter.

3. List at least five aspects that are common to all FMHAs.

4. Why are dual and multiple relationships problematic?

5. Why are the following cases significant to forensic psychology: *Riggins v. Nevada*, *Jackson v. Indiana*, and *Foucha v. Louisiana*?

6. Compare and contrast the cases of Charles Sell and Russell Weston.

7. Provide illustrations of how changes in federal and state statutes have made it more difficult for defendants pleading not guilty by reason of insanity.

8. Compare the assessment of competence to stand trial and that of sanity/criminal responsibility.

9. List the instruments commonly used in the assessment of risk.

10. What is the role of the forensic psychologist in (a) capital sentencing and (b) sexually violent predator proceedings?

6

Consulting
With Juvenile
and Civil Courts

CHAPTER OBJECTIVES

- Describe the roles and responsibilities of psychologists consulting with noncriminal courts.
- Introduce the juvenile court system and its history.
- Review landmark U.S. Supreme Court cases pertaining to the rights and protection of juveniles.
- Introduce the methods and procedures used in psychological assessments of juveniles.
- Discuss juvenile comprehension of constitutional rights.
- Review social science research on false confessions of juveniles.
- Examine the roles of psychologists and other mental health professionals in family and probate courts, including child custody evaluations and arrangements.
- Introduce issues involving competence to consent to treatment.
- Examine the many questions and problems concerning involuntary civil commitment.
- Explore the challenges of psychologists and other mental health professionals in evaluating the effects of sexual harassment.

The criminal courts discussed in Chapter 5 tend to get the most public and media attention, but the courts that are the subject of this chapter are noteworthy for different reasons. The average citizen is far more likely to come into contact with a civil court than a criminal court. Claims of breach of contract, sexual harassment, libel, invasions of privacy, age discrimination, and medical malpractice are all brought before the civil courts. These courts settle property disputes and adjudicate contested wills. Judges and juries decide such highly emotional issues as who will obtain custody of minor children, whether an individual is competent to make decisions about medical treatment, and the extent to which a victim of discrimination suffered emotional distress. They declare juveniles delinquent and allow persons to be committed to mental institutions against their will. In some of the most highly litigated cases in recent years, civil courts have dealt with numerous suits against corporations, such as tobacco, asbestos, insider trading, and fraud cases.

Not surprisingly, forensic psychologists have been extensively involved in this arena and in virtually every form of litigation mentioned above. Because of the wide array of issues that reach the civil courts, it is impossible to present a comprehensive review of the work of forensic psychologists in one chapter. Instead, we will represent their work by focusing on select activities. First, we discuss consultation with juvenile courts, which are sometimes referred to as "quasi-civil" because they have many features of criminal courts. Then we will cover family and probate courts, where issues involving divorce, child custody, child neglect, civil commitments, and competency to make medical decisions may be decided. Finally, we review disputes in civil courts involving personal injury (mental and physical) and discrimination. Please remember that each state—as well as the federal government—has its unique way of organizing and naming its courts and determining their jurisdiction. In many states today, for example, juvenile delinquency proceedings take place within the family court, not in a separate juvenile court. Likewise, custody may be litigated in probate, family, or courts labeled "superior courts" in some states. Civil commitment proceedings may occur in mental health courts, probate courts, family courts, or in the nonspecialized district or county courts. Therefore, although we divide the material to follow into sections, students should be aware that considerable overlapping does occur.

Juvenile Courts

The juvenile justice system provides numerous opportunities for the forensic psychologist. Various statistics indicate that juveniles today are more likely to come into contact with police, courts, and correctional facilities than at any other time in history. Arrest data reveal that police take into custody some 2.5 million juveniles every year. While most juveniles reach juvenile court as a result of an arrest, about 15 to 19% are referred by parents, school personnel, social agencies, or probation departments (C. Knoll & Sickmund, 2010; Puzzanchera, Adams, & Sickmund, 2010; Sickmund, 2004). In 2002, 1.6 million delinquency petitions were filed with juvenile courts (Stahl, 2006). A **petition** is a written document filed in juvenile court alleging that the juvenile is a delinquent or in need of protection and requesting that the court assume jurisdiction over the juvenile. In 1998, a total of 327,700 juveniles were being held in juvenile detention facilities prior to adjudication (Puzzanchera, Stahl, Finnegan, Tierney, & Snyder, 2003) and 102,388 were held in residential treatment facilities (Sickmund, 2006), though this number had declined to 81,000 in 2008 (Sickmund, 2010).

An unknown number of juveniles, chiefly between the ages of 14 and 18 (but sometimes younger), are tried in criminal rather than juvenile courts. (See Redding, 2010, for a comprehensive review of this issue.) Nevertheless, the juvenile crime rate—which began to rise quite dramatically in the 1980s—has been stabilizing, suggesting that juveniles today are not significantly more likely than in the past to commit crimes, particularly serious crimes. In the late 1990s, for example, the arrest rate for violent juvenile crime dropped 9%; the juvenile homicide rate dropped 31% (Howell, 1998). However, public officials, clinicians, and legal and social service professionals alike are concerned about the still-disturbing patterns of juvenile crime, particularly substance abuse, violence, and sex offending, as we will see in the next chapter.

Juvenile courts may exist as separate entities or may be part of a broader "family court" or "domestic court" system. In general, they operate more informally than criminal courts and employ a different lexicon or terminology (see Focus 6.1). Regardless of how these courts are structured, judges, lawyers, and social service representatives consult with psychologists and other clinicians for a wide variety of reasons. A defense lawyer may require an assessment of her client's overall intellectual functioning. When juveniles waive their constitutional rights, such as the right to remain silent or the right to a lawyer during police interrogation, judges (and defense lawyers) often want to know whether the juveniles possessed the necessary cognitive skills to make such a waiver. Psychological assessments may be sought to determine whether a youth is a threat to society or is amenable to rehabilitation. In addition to this, juvenile court judges as well as lawyers often want to know whether treatment is available to meet the needs of a given young offender, along with the cost of such treatment and the probability that it will be effective. (See Personal Perspective 6.1, in which Dr. Michele Peterson-Badali discusses her interests in the law, teaching, and research that benefits young people.)

In addition to the above assessment tasks, psychologists are called on to offer treatment to juveniles, both within juvenile facilities and in community settings. In this chapter, we will discuss psychological involvement at the early stages of the juvenile process, up to and including the adjudication of delinquency. A separate chapter—Chapter 13—is devoted to juvenile corrections. In that chapter, we will cover a variety of rehabilitation programs and treatment strategies for dealing with delinquent youth.

FOCUS 6.1. COMMON TERMS IN JUVENILE COURTS

Intake

The intake is the juvenile's first contact with the juvenile justice system following police custody. Here a decision is made whether to dismiss the case, handle it informally, or refer it formally to juvenile court. About half of all cases are handled informally. This may include referral to a social service agency, informal probation, or even the payment of some fines or voluntary restitution.

Intake workers also decide whether a juvenile should be detained, though a judge must review the detention, typically within 48 hours. Intake officers may be probation officers, social workers, or representatives from the prosecutor's office.

Diversion

This is the process of steering youth away from court and referring them to a structured program. The decision to refer a youth to diversion is usually made by intake workers or by prosecutors. Diversion programs vary widely, usually requiring youth to admit their actions, sign contracts, and agree to certain conditions (e.g., perform community service). Some diversion programs include teen courts, where juveniles are "judged" and "sentenced" by peers.

Delinquency Petition

This is the formal document prepared by the prosecutor that states the allegations against the juvenile and asks the juvenile court to adjudicate the juvenile a delinquent.

Preventive Detention

Juveniles may be detained securely to prevent them from committing additional offenses. Although an intake worker may make the initial detention decision, a judge or magistrate must review the need for continued detention. Juvenile courts often use detention as an opportunity to order psychological evaluations and other tests.

(Continued)

(Continued)

Waiver Petition

This is the prosecutor's request that the juvenile's case be transferred to criminal court.

Delinquency Hearing (or Adjudicatory Hearing)

This is the equivalent of a trial in criminal court. Like adults, the juvenile has a right to have a lawyer, to confront and cross-examine witnesses, and to remain silent. The prosecutor must prove all elements of the offense beyond a reasonable doubt. However, the juvenile does not have a constitutional right to a trial by jury.

Blended Sentencing

In approximately half the states, both juvenile and criminal courts are allowed to impose juvenile or adult sanctions on certain juveniles (usually dependent on ages of juveniles and crime charged).

Aftercare

Aftercare is the equivalent of adult parole. This involves supervision of the juvenile after release from some form of residential treatment.

PERSONAL PERSPECTIVE 6.1

Meshing a Love of Law With Interest in Youth

Michele Peterson-Badali, PhD, CPsych

While I feel as if I've been in psychology forever—having earned a PhD in applied psychology at the University of Toronto in 1990 and having been a university professor for many years—it wasn't the career that I initially envisioned for myself. In fact, from the time I can first remember thinking about my career, and for many years after that, I was certain I wanted to be a lawyer. My dad practiced law for over four decades and when I was little, every night over dinner I'd ask, "Did you close any deals?" (He did a lot of real estate law.) "Did you solve any problems?" And every night when he said goodnight he'd teach me a new legal term; I was probably the only 7-year-old on my block who knew what "hearsay" and "non sequitur" meant!

When I finished high school early, I decided to work for my dad for a year before heading off to university. I loved that year—and I worked for him every summer after that until I graduated—but I also discovered that a career in law was not for me. I honestly can't place what it was that changed my mind, but after my first year of university and "Psych 101," I became fascinated with psychology. During my undergraduate years, my interests in cognitive and developmental psychology were born and grew, but once I hit graduate school—initially studying infant memory—I realized two things. One, I wanted to do work that had a direct application to the lives of young people. Two, I still loved law. I was fortunate to be able to combine my passions when I conducted the research for my master's thesis, which examined children's understanding of some of the basic tenets of Canadian youth justice law, such as the right to legal representation. From that point, I began a research program that focused on the application of psychological theories and methods to real-world issues in youth justice law, policy, and practice. And for me, that meant a career as a university professor: conducting research, teaching, and training a new generation of psychology researchers and practitioners.

I've since worked on a number of issues that are tied together by a common theme: a concern for the rights of children and youth. I have been involved in projects examining adolescents' legal competencies, young people's understanding of critical due process rights (like the rights to silence and to legal counsel), peer violence in youth custody facilities, young people's adjustment to incarceration, the role of parents in youths' justice system experiences, and effective rehabilitation practices for young people. Every day, lawmakers, administrators, and practitioners make decisions affecting the lives of youths.

My goal in all of my research projects has been to contribute to a base of evidence that will inform these decisions. This means that I and my fellow researchers must identify questions and issues that are relevant to current policy and practice, design studies that are methodologically sound, and communicate the results clearly—and to multiple audiences—in a way that will have maximum impact. Achieving this goal also means reaching out to the people making the laws as well as to those working with youth on a daily basis, both as partners in the research process and when it comes to disseminating the research findings and their implications. This helps us ensure that we are doing meaningful research that is communicated back to the people who can use it.

I have also discovered that partnering with *young people* is just as important, and finding out how youth themselves understand and experience the justice system has been a key focus of my research for many years. For example, laws are passed and policies implemented with the goal of preventing or reducing offending, but what are the assumptions about human behavior that underlie these laws? And do they accurately reflect how young people think and act? There is plenty of research evidence to suggest that common—and popular—approaches such as boot camps and prison sentences are *not* effective in reducing youth crime, though they may make politicians and members of the public feel good. Hearing directly from young people can add to our understanding of why such approaches have not achieved their stated goals, as well as what the critical elements of *successful* policies and programs might be.

Results of studies that I've been involved with informed the Canadian government's decision not to lower the minimum age of criminal responsibility from 12 to 10 years of age. They were used in

(Continued)

(Continued)

an inquest into the death of a teenager in custody, contributing to the jury's recommendations to prevent and address peer violence in youth jails. They have also been used in court proceedings. In one case, for example, a lawyer familiar with our research was able to demonstrate that his clients did not adequately comprehend their rights prior to giving statements to the police. The statements were ruled inadmissible. However, while it is gratifying to see research have a direct impact on the lives of young people, it is important not to overstate the strength or generalizability of findings; in other words, research must be used in a way that is valid and meaningful.

Perhaps the most important lesson that I have taken away from my career as a psychologist is to remember that whoever we work with, whether in the context of assessment, intervention, or research—and whether the individuals are offenders, victims, witnesses, family members, or students—each person has his or her own unique set of circumstances, strengths, and needs. Always striving to maintain our awareness of that humanity helps remind us of the need to treat individuals with respect and dignity, rather than simply as a means to *our* goals.

Whether this is the one and only forensic psychology course you take or the first step in a career in the field, enjoy your studies and good luck!

Dr. Peterson-Badali worked as a clinical psychologist before joining the faculty at the University of Toronto, where she is an associate professor in the Department of Human Development and Applied Psychology. Her primary teaching areas are psychological assessment; ethics; and children, psychology, and law. She is also the busy mom of three teenagers, work that doesn't seem to decrease as they get older, she says. For balance, she also finds time for fun: cooking, travel, getting away to her summer cottage, and just hanging out with family and friends.

Historical Background

It is important for forensic psychologists working with the juvenile justice system to be aware of its history. Many concerned advocates for juveniles today fear that problems very similar to those of old have reoccurred or, in some cases, never really disappeared. Furthermore, the history of the juvenile court is also very much the history of family courts because separate courts with exclusive jurisdiction over family matters did not emerge in most states until the last quarter of the 20th century.

The first juvenile court was established in the United States in 1899, in the state of Illinois. A broad group of social activists had influenced the Illinois legislature to establish a judicial system for children that was to be separate from that faced by adults. Children were presumed to be in need of protection, less accountable for their offenses than adults, and more amenable to rehabilitation once they had strayed. Furthermore, many children were neglected by their parents or guardians and required the intervention of the state for their own best interest. Thus, the first juvenile court was intended to serve the needs of *all* children who needed supervision, including those who violated the law. Other states followed Illinois' lead, and by 1925, all but two states (Maine and Wyoming) had established similar courts with exclusive jurisdiction over minors, usually defined as children younger than age 18 (Bartol & Bartol, 1998; Tappan, 1949).

The courts were strongly based on a *parens patriae* rationale. The doctrine of ***parens patriae*** (literally, "parent of the country"), first applied to children in a Pennsylvania case (*ex parte Crouse,* 1838), gives the state the power to intervene in a child's life, even over the objections of the parents, because such intervention is presumed to be in the best interest of the child. The doctrine has survived and remains a strong component of much juvenile law today, although the law is also very oriented toward recognizing the legal rights of juveniles, at least in principle.

Prior to the establishment of the juvenile courts, children who allegedly broke the law were handled through the social service system or were taken before criminal courts. In the mid-19th century, the nation's largest cities had **Houses of Refuge,** which were institutional settings presumably intended to protect, nurture, and educate neglected or wayward children. Children who were sent to Houses of Refuge were poor or homeless, were considered incorrigible, or had committed usually minor law violations—or some combination of the above. Houses of Refuge in the 19th century—with some exceptions—very rapidly earned the reputation of being emotionally cold facilities that often exploited their young charges by contracting their domestic and manual labor to households in the community (Bernard, 1992).

Young offenders who were processed in criminal courts were allowed to remain in the community if they stayed out of trouble. This is similar to the probation of today, but there were few probation officers available to monitor behavior and offer support and guidance as needed. The early probation officers were volunteers or police officers assigned to this special duty (Cromwell, Killinger, Kerper, & Walker, 1985). It was not until the end of the 19th century that states began to authorize probation and provide funds for probation officers on a systematic basis. Before that time, probationary status was available only in areas where volunteers or police were available. Many young offenders, then, were sentenced by criminal courts to serve time in prisons or reformatories. The latter were intended primarily for first-time offenders. Their purpose was to give these offenders a second chance, offering them education and discipline in preparation for a law-abiding life. Like the Houses of Refuge, many of those reformatories were criticized for abusing young offenders, ruling by fear, and not delivering on their promise to provide education and rehabilitation (Bernard, 1992; R. Johnson, 1996).

When we consider the above problems, the motives of those who fought for the establishment of a separate court for juveniles appear noble. Few will disagree that children need more protection than do adults and that children, on the whole, are less cognitively and emotionally mature than most adults. Once they reach adolescence, their abilities to make decisions and their emotional maturity vary widely. Indeed, the competence of adolescents to make decisions in their own interests is a hot topic in child development research today (see, generally, Grisso & Schwartz, 2000; Steinberg, 2010). Children and adolescents are also vulnerable to exploitation. Institutional settings that degrade, humiliate, fail to educate, and fail to nurture the young cannot protect or rehabilitate them.

In addition, few will disagree that some children are neglected and physically abused in their own homes and require the intervention of a protective state. At the end of the 19th century, then, a separate court with the mandate of focusing exclusively on the needs of children seemed to be a major improvement over what had been occurring.

However, some scholars have strongly questioned the actions of those who worked to establish these juvenile courts, suggesting that they were primarily motivated by their desire to control the children of the poor, who were considered all too visible reminders of growing inequality in society (A. Platt, 1969). Poor children were considered offensive ruffians, spending too much time on the streets and threatening the comfortable lifestyles of those who were more privileged. Thomas Bernard (1992) suggests that social reformers were first and foremost interested in bringing about social change. However, they gave up their efforts to improve social conditions that produce crime and reverted instead to trying to "fix" children and their families:

> Eventually, social workers stopped trying to change the rich and powerful and started trying to change the poor and powerless. The seeds of both casework and social reform had been present at the beginning of the juvenile court, but only the seeds of casework sprouted and grew. The seeds of social reform withered and died. (p. 102)

The juvenile courts clearly were trying to change children and their families, but it is highly questionable whether they were effective. Until the 1960s, they operated very informally, and judges and other court officers had very broad discretion over the lives of juveniles. The courts were supposedly intended to help juveniles, preferably within the community and within their own homes. Sometimes, parents themselves took their children to these courts if they considered them "incorrigible." (See Photo 6.1 depicting a young boy with his parents in court.) Proceedings were informal and closed to the public, and all aspects of the juvenile's life were subjected to inquiry by the court. Psychiatrists and psychologists working in child guidance clinics provided judges with cognitive and personality test results and offered recommendations based on their interviews with the child and family members (Rothman, 1980).

Photo 6.1   A boy accompanied by his parents appearing before a juvenile court judge in the 1920s.

Gradually, despite the allegedly good intentions of the founders of the juvenile court movement, the courts gained the reputation of being authoritarian, imposing unreasonable expectations on juveniles and their families, particularly the economically disadvantaged. When these expectations were not met, juvenile judges were not averse to sending juveniles to secure training schools, where they encountered punitive treatment rather than effective rehabilitation. These decisions to institutionalize were routinely made with little attention to due process of the law; juveniles in most courts did not have the assistance of lawyers, nor did they have reasonable opportunity to confront the witnesses against them or to challenge the actions of court officials. Juvenile courts also routinely urged—and in some cases required—juveniles to confess their offenses. When juvenile court judges believed that the juveniles were not appropriate for juvenile court, they would transfer them to criminal court, where they would presumably be treated the same as adults.

Supreme Court Decisions

Two U.S. Supreme Court cases in the 1960s signaled a need to change procedures in juvenile court. One—*Kent v. U.S.* (1966)—required that a judge hold a hearing before transferring a juvenile to adult court (see Focus 6.2). At that hearing, the juvenile had a constitutional right to have the assistance of an attorney and to challenge the transfer. The Court also suggested factors that judges could consider in deciding whether the transfer was appropriate. These included the child's age, the seriousness of the crime, prior record with the juvenile court, the prospect of rehabilitation if kept in the juvenile system, the likelihood of being rehabilitated if transferred to criminal court, and the threat to the security of the community if not transferred. The Supreme Court opinion in *Kent* also presents a scathing indictment of the juvenile court system as it operated at that time, serving as a precursor of the landmark case that would follow, *In re Gault* (1967).

FOCUS 6.2. *KENT v. UNITED STATES*

Although the U.S. Supreme Court had heard other juvenile cases, the first far-reaching Court decision dealing directly with a juvenile offender was *Kent v. U.S.* (1966). Morris Kent Jr., was no angel. The 16-year-old was charged with housebreaking, robbery, and rape while on probation under the jurisdiction of the District of Columbia Juvenile Court. When arrested, Kent admitted committing the offenses and was confined in a receiving home for children. The juvenile court, however, soon transferred his case to adult criminal court over the very strong objections of his attorney who argued that Kent could be rehabilitated if maintained in a juvenile setting. In criminal court, Kent was found not guilty by reason of insanity regarding the rape charge but was found guilty of housebreaking and robbery. He was sentenced to 30 to 90 years and transferred to a mental institution in accordance with the insanity finding. Kent appealed the original decision of the juvenile court to transfer his case to criminal court.

In reviewing Kent's appeal, the U.S. Supreme Court recognized that there was no constitutional requirement for a separate juvenile court system. In their unanimous decision, the Justices strongly criticized the procedures of the juvenile court and the unchecked discretionary power it had over the lives of juveniles. In essence, the Supreme Court signaled that it would begin to change substantially the procedures through which juveniles could be processed, and it gave guidelines for judges to use in deciding whether to transfer a juvenile case.

The transfer decision remains one of the most significant phases of the juvenile court process, with increasingly more juvenile cases being transferred to adult criminal courts. Consequently, forensic psychologists and other mental health professionals are frequently called upon to advise judges about the wisdom of transferring juveniles to criminal courts in this manner.

The following year, in a landmark juvenile case (*In re Gault*, 1967), the Supreme Court dramatically altered procedures associated with delinquency hearings. Gerald Gault had been taken into custody by police, taken to the police station, and subjected to two hearings before a judge who ultimately adjudicated him delinquent and sent him to a juvenile training school, where he could have been kept until his 21st birthday. Gerald was 15 years old at the time of his offense. His crime? He had placed an obscene phone call to his next-door neighbor. Although his parents were present at the delinquency hearing, Gerald was not represented by counsel, and his alleged victim did not appear in court to testify against him.

In a lengthy opinion that traced the history of the juvenile court in the United States, the Supreme Court noted that Gerald Gault, like Morris Kent before him, had been subjected to proceedings that could only be characterized as "a Kangaroo court." The Court therefore ruled that juveniles facing delinquency proceedings and possible institutionalization had, at a minimum, the following constitutional rights:

- The right to written notice of the charges against them
- The right to confront and cross-examine witnesses against them
- The right against self-incrimination (often referred to as a privilege, but actually a right)
- The right to the assistance of a lawyer in their defense

Although *In re Gault* (1967) was a decision widely hailed by children's rights advocates, it should not be assumed that it cured all of the ills of juvenile courts. Just over 20 years after the *Gault* case, Barry Feld (1988) reported research that fewer than half of all juveniles were represented by lawyers in delinquency proceedings. Other research across 15 states suggests higher rates of representation, 65 to 97% depending on the jurisdiction. Nevertheless, even with a lawyer, there is some question as to whether juveniles can participate *effectively* in their defense.

When juveniles are *not* represented by lawyers, it is likely that they waived that constitutional right. In some cases, this was done on the advice of parents or other authority figures. Juveniles also have a constitutional right to a lawyer during custodial interrogation, but most juveniles speak to police without a lawyer present (Grisso, 1998). Thus, the validity of waivers—that is, whether the juveniles understood the consequences of giving up this right—is another topic of great interest to researchers.

Against this historical backdrop, we now turn to the specific tasks that are performed by forensic psychologists in consultation with the juvenile courts.

Juvenile Assessment: An Overview

As we noted in Chapters 4 and 5, assessment is an essential component of the daily professional life of the forensic psychologist. Also called psychological evaluation, assessment refers to all the techniques used to measure and evaluate an individual's past, present, or future psychological status. It may be considered "the act of determining the nature and causes of a client's problem" (Lewis, Dana, & Blevins, 1994, p. 71). Thus, interviews, observations, and reviews of records and other documents are all part of the assessment process. Typically, the psychologist also administers a variety of tests and inventories to measure the juvenile's cognitive abilities and personality attributes.

The assessment often includes phone or in-person interviews with relevant adults, including family members, and peers. Some forensic psychologists recommend observing the juvenile in a natural setting (e.g., in school, with parents and siblings at home) if possible. Although some forensic psychologists urge very wide-ranging assessment, others believe assessments should be limited in scope and should address only the referral question (e.g., did this juvenile possess the necessary cognitive ability to waive his or her right to a lawyer?). Until recently, in most jurisdictions there were no clinical requirements and few legal restrictions associated with these assessments; the specific approach taken was left to the individual clinician. Now, increasingly more states are endorsing specific guidelines or certification procedures for clinicians who will be submitting evaluation results to the courts (Heilbrun & Brooks, 2010). In addition, there is a wealth of information in the form of handbooks, guidelines, and research studies that offer suggestions to clinicians (e.g., APA, 1996; Grisso, 1998; Kruh & Grisso, 2009; Melton et al., 1997, 2007; Weiner & Hess, 2006).

The clinical literature advises forensic psychologists to be extremely cautious in assessing juveniles if their practice has been limited primarily to adults. "It is possible to conduct a seemingly competent evaluation but fail to obtain the data necessary to construct a complete picture of the developmental and familial context for the youth's clinical presentation and delinquent behavior" (Heilbrun et al., 2002, p. 187). Heilbrun et al. add that normal adolescent defensiveness and mistrust may make youths appear cold and remorseless. For instance, children of ethnic and racial groups that have experienced discrimination in society may be distrustful of authority figures, including the mental health professionals evaluating them. Adolescents as a group also may be reluctant to disclose embarrassing information that may actually help in their defense. For example, a juvenile may be charged with assaulting an individual who sexually abused him in the past, and the juvenile may be reluctant to disclose that abuse. Examiners also must be alert to the possibility of serious psychopathology, which can be overlooked in adolescents by clinicians accustomed to the symptomatology and clinical presentations of adults (Heilbrun et al., 2002).

Although assessment is an essential component of treatment, treatment does not necessarily accompany assessment. In fact, as we mentioned in earlier chapters, psychologists are warned to avoid—or at least be cautious of—dual roles of evaluator and treatment provider. Because of this distinction between assessment and treatment, we discuss them as separate tasks and in separate chapters. (Treatment of juveniles is covered in Chapter 13.) Nevertheless, clinicians are often advised to include recommendations for treatment in assessment reports, if such treatment is known to be available (Grisso, 1998).

Assessment of Competence to Waive Miranda Rights

There is good evidence that many juveniles cannot understand their constitutional rights (Grisso & Schwartz, 2000; Rogers et al., 2010). Psychologists who evaluate them must be knowledgeable not only about the law, but also about adolescent development and decision making (Grisso, 1998; Heilbrun et al., 2002). Like adults, juveniles have a constitutional right not to incriminate themselves during their dealings with the criminal justice system. Juveniles do not have to answer questions posed by police while in custody (*Fare v. Michael C.,* 1979; *Miranda v. Arizona,* 1966). (See Photo 6.2 of juvenile taken into custody.) In addition, they do not have to take the stand during a delinquency proceeding (*In re Gault,* 1967). Closely associated with this right against self-incrimination is the right to an attorney. The above cases also established that juveniles have a right to have an attorney present during custodial interrogation and have a right to the assistance of counsel in delinquency proceedings.

Photo 6.2 A juvenile is led to a police car by a law enforcement officer after being taken into custody.

In reality, many if not most juveniles waive these constitutional rights, as do many adults. The police questioning of juveniles who have been taken into custody is far more likely to occur solely in the presence of a parent or legal guardian than in the presence of an attorney. Research suggests strongly that these adults often encourage the juveniles to cooperate with police, answer their questions, and confess to their offenses. "At the time of their children's arrests, many parents themselves are anxious, fearful, or confused during the police encounter. Others are angry at the youth and contribute to the coercive pressure of the interrogation" (Grisso, 1998, p. 44).

Recall that under the law, a waiver is a valid one if it is made willingly, knowingly, and intelligently. At what age can the average juvenile meet this standard? Moreover, even if the average juvenile can meet the standard, what about *this* juvenile who is being confronted by police under stressful conditions? In *Fare v. Michael C.* (1979), the Supreme Court noted that a juvenile's waiver of the right to a lawyer before being questioned by police while in their custody (custodial interrogation) should be given very careful scrutiny if it comes to court attention (see Focus 6.3). Thus, when defense attorneys challenge these waivers or when judges themselves decide there is reason to question their validity, forensic psychologists may be called in to evaluate the juveniles' cognitive development and the extent to which they understood what they were doing.

FOCUS 6.3. *FARE v. MICHAEL C.*

The U.S. Supreme Court case *Fare v. Michael C.* (1979) involved a juvenile's waiver of his right to an attorney during police interrogation. Michael C. was a 16-year-old charged with rape and robbery. After arrest and at the police station, he was told he had a right to see an attorney, but he apparently interpreted this *Miranda* warning as a police trick. Described as immature, distraught, and poorly educated, Michael C. repeatedly asked to see his probation officer instead of a lawyer. He was told his probation officer would be contacted after he answered some police questions. Asked again if he wished to see an attorney, he said he did not.

The Court expressed concern as to whether juveniles have the capacity to fully understand the warning giving to them, the nature of their constitutional rights, or the consequences of waiving them. The Court, therefore, warned judges to consider the social circumstances of the interrogation as well as the age, education, background, and intelligence of the juvenile.

Nevertheless, in this case the Court did not determine that Michael C.'s rights were violated. Although the Justices who dissented believed that the request to see the probation officer was the equivalent of a request to seen an attorney in this situation, the majority did not agree.

Psychologist Thomas Grisso is a leading expert in adolescent development, the legal rights of juveniles, and a variety of forensic assessments. Early research by Grisso (1981) found that most juveniles age 14 and younger did not understand the meaning of the *Miranda* warning, nor the implications if they chose to waive their rights. Juveniles who were slightly older—15 and 16—had similar difficulty if they were of below-average intelligence. Most recently, Redlich, Silverman, and Steiner (2003) found that age and suggestibility were strong predictors of *Miranda* competence. Interestingly, juveniles who had frequent contacts with police, though not significantly less likely to comprehend their **Miranda rights** than those without frequent contact, had much more trouble understanding the vocabulary used in *Miranda* warnings (e.g., "consult" or "interrogation"). As researchers like Rogers et al. (2010) have demonstrated, this lack of understanding is not restricted to juveniles.

Grisso (1998) recommends three standardized instruments that may be helpful to the clinician in performing this assessment. The first is the Comprehension of Miranda Rights (CMR) and its offshoots (e.g., the Comprehension of Miranda Rights—Recognition [CMR-R], the Comprehension of Miranda Vocabulary [CMV], and Function of Rights in Interrogation [FRI]). The second type of standardized instrument is any standardized test of cognitive ability. The third is personality inventories. Grisso also recommends a review of school, mental health, and juvenile court records, when available, as well as interviews with parents or caretakers along with the youth himself or herself. In other words, Grisso recommends conducting a very extensive assessment in an effort to determine whether the youth provided a valid waiver of the right to an attorney during custodial interrogation.

Psychologist Richard Rogers and his colleagues (e.g., Rogers et al., 2009, 2010) also have conducted extensive research on juvenile comprehension of *Miranda* rights, and they have developed and validated a Miranda

Vocabulary Scale (MVS) to assess an individual's understanding of very basic terms used by police. (Dr. Rogers discusses this research in Personal Perspective 6.2.) Helms (2003) also found wide geographical differences in the understanding of *Miranda*, suggesting that psychologists should be aware of research findings relating to their own practice areas as well as the broad research findings.

PERSONAL PERSPECTIVE 6.2

Graduate Research and Forensic Psychology

Richard Rogers, PhD, ABPP

I spend about 20 hours each week working with master's and doctoral students in forensic psychology on their graduate research. Graduate faculty members provide considerable diversity in how they approach graduate student training and mentorship, ranging from highly individualized relationships to very structured research teams that can range from 8 to 12 students. I like working with a research team where everyone has an opportunity to contribute. Although there are typically two coordinators for the larger team projects, we try to avoid a strictly hierarchical structure that might disadvantage new team members. Seniority on my team is much less valued than self-initiative, originality, and writing skills.

Importantly, I see the research team as a collaborative effort with each member making important contributions. Team members look after each other and are invaluable to me. Besides their own individual research (theses and dissertations), all of my students become involved in larger team projects. Currently, two major projects involve (1) assessment of malingering (e.g., feigning a mental disorder), and (2) *Miranda* comprehension and reasoning (e.g., understanding the right to counsel).

For those students considering a career in forensic psychology, the most common path is a doctoral degree in clinical psychology followed by further specialization in forensic psychology. I think that the success of your graduate training and subsequent career is strongly influenced by your choice of a major professor and subsequently developing a working relationship with this faculty member and her or his students.

I wrote this introduction to give you some initial ideas about what is involved in graduate research. You need to consider the structure of the team, your comfort level with the major professor, and the success of past graduate students when judging your fit with a particular program. In subsequent paragraphs, I address my own views and values on several important considerations for graduate research in forensic psychology.

(Continued)

(Continued)

Herd Instinct

Certain topics capture the interests and imagination of undergraduate students. Forensic researchers are not immune to these influences and, consequently, often become self-limiting in their topics of research. In the 1980s, eyewitness research became very popular, with 180 peer-reviewed articles listed in a PsychINFO search; this interest has only continued to grow with a present total of 972 refereed articles.[1] For a more clinical topic, psychopathy is now in vogue with 1,876 referred articles of which the majority (1,181) was published since 2000. Although these are important topics, when do we reach a point of diminishing returns?

I counsel my graduate students to avoid the herd instinct and find relevant topics that interest them and have not been over-researched. For example, thousands of juvenile offenders waive their *Miranda* rights without a clear understanding of the concept of self-incrimination. How many peer-reviewed studies have investigated this? I found only 11 empirical studies. I think it is self-evident that original contributions to forensic psychology are likely to be achieved with important yet emerging topics rather than simply following the herd. That said, I do have two students conducting thesis research on psychopathy. In both cases, however, they are considering competing hypotheses. For example, is psychopathy better than antisocial personality disorder at predicting violence? Alternatively, does general impulsivity override both psychopathy and antisocial personality disorder? These students' originality and initiative convinced me that they were not following the herd, but instead making important contributions to the field.

Research in the Trenches

I strongly believe that an integral part of research training in forensic studies is in the trenches. By the *trenches*, I mean personally conducted with relevant clinical and forensic populations. I fully realize that this is not possible for every study. For example, our research team is investigating the effects of situational stressors (e.g., being caught "red-handed" in a mock crime) on *Miranda* comprehension; it would be impractical and likely unethical to conduct this research with detained custodial suspects. Nonetheless, graduate training in forensic research should include direct participation in one or more studies of forensically relevant topics with the *appropriate samples*. To underscore this key point, what else can be learned about psychopathy of forensic relevance from studying apparently successful, law-abiding college students?

Graduate students are commonly tempted to use existing data sets for their thesis and dissertation. I receive frequent e-mails from inquiring students wanting to mine preexisting data. For certain areas of psychology, such as health practices, such secondary analyses may be unavoidable. For clinical-forensic research, my own personal view is that graduate training must give students a real-world perspective on relevant measures and populations, and the sometimes grim realities of conducting this challenging research. For example, research on juvenile

---

[1]The numbers of referred articles in this section are only approximate based on PsychINFO abstract searches of key terms on June 26, 2010. Of course, cumulative numbers will continue to increase.

offenders often copes with disaffected youth in frequently chaotic institutional settings.

Also on a personal note, I think secondhand data often results in second-rate research. Why rely upon someone else's originality and the constraints of their research design rather than conduct your own original research? At least for me, I try to wring every bit of original analyses

and articles out of my data. I do not think that forensic research will appreciably advance by further examining the remnants of originality left in mine or others' data sets. I recognize there are occasional exceptions, but I still think I would be remiss in my mentoring role if I did not encourage my graduate students to find their own way rather than walk in someone else's shadow.

Dr. Rogers is a Regents Professor of Psychology at the University of North Texas, where he focuses primarily on research and graduate training. His pioneering research includes the development of standardized assessments for malingering, insanity, competency to stand trial, and Miranda-related abilities. His accomplishments have been recognized by national awards from the American Psychological Association, the American Psychiatric Association, the American Academy of Forensic Psychology, and the American Academy of Psychiatry and the Law.

False Confessions

In addition to evidence that juveniles have trouble understanding their constitutional rights, there is evidence that they sometimes confess to crimes they did not commit. As we discussed in Chapter 2, a false confession may occur for a wide range of reasons, some of which relate to psychological tactics used by police (e.g., Kassin, 1997; Kassin & Kiechel, 1996; G. Richardson, Gudjonsson, & Kelly, 1995). For example, police may deceive a suspect into thinking they have evidence that they do not actually have, or they may befriend the suspect into thinking they are his or her only link to freedom. A juvenile eager to go home, or a juvenile who wants to protect a family member or friend, may decide to tell police what they want to hear. An evaluating clinician clearly should be alert to this possibility.

Although false confessions are of concern regardless of the age of the suspect, it should come as no surprise that juveniles may be particularly susceptible to making them. Redlich and Goodman (2003) examined the suggestibility of three different age groups (12- and 13-year-olds, 15- and 16-year-olds, and 18- to 26-year-olds) in an experimental situation similar to many used in the false confession research (e.g., Kassin, 1997). (Recall that Dr. Redlich was highlighted in Personal Perspective 4.1.) Participants were given a computer task and told to not press a particular key. They were then told that they had pressed it when they really had not. In some experimental situations, the experimenter provides participants with "false evidence," in this case that they pressed the key. Researchers then tabulate the number of "false confessions" and try to determine what, in addition to age, distinguishes participants who "admit" to something they did not actually do from those who do not.

Redlich and Goodman (2003) examined whether (a) scores on the Gudjonsson Suggestibility Scale (GSS) and (b) the presentation of false evidence would predict and facilitate a false confession. The GSS is an instrument designed to measure the extent to which individuals are susceptible to being influenced by others. Results indicated that 69% of all participants falsely confessed or complied, 39% internalized (believed they had pressed the forbidden key), and 4% confabulated (made up details about their behavior during the study). However, significant age differences emerged. For the mid-level age group (15- and 16-year-olds), false confessions occurred particularly when false evidence was presented. The youngest age group falsely confessed both when false evidence was presented and when it was not. In general, the two youngest age groups were more likely to say they had done something wrong than were the young adults. With respect to individual differences, scores on the GSS predicted compliance (admitting to the "offense") but not internalization or confabulation.

Research on the psychology of false confessions is still in its infancy (or perhaps its early childhood), and its ecological validity is questionable. **Ecological validity** refers to whether results obtained in a laboratory setting can be applied to the natural environment as well as whether events in the natural environment can be adequately represented in the laboratory. "It is ethically problematic to accuse someone of an actual crime in the laboratory" (Redlich & Goodman, 2003, p. 154). Nevertheless, there is reason to be concerned about what are widely accepted police interrogation processes, particularly when the suspects are juveniles or other vulnerable individuals, as discussed in Chapter 2. Police interrogation involves intimidating authority figures and a high level of stress, both of which have been demonstrated in other social psychology experiments to elicit compliance (e.g., Milgram, 1974). The present study suggests that juveniles are significantly more susceptible to this influence than are young adults, although all age groups are affected.

Evaluating Adjudicative Competence

Juveniles whose cases are heard in criminal courts must, like adults, be competent to stand trial. Otherwise, the trial of an incompetent defendant violates due process of the law (*Drope v. Missouri*, 1975; *Dusky v. U.S.*, 1960). When a juvenile's case is heard in criminal court, competency to stand trial—if it is raised—is measured in accordance with the *Dusky* standard discussed in Chapter 5. Recall from that chapter that the standard for competency to stand trial is a sufficient present ability to consult with one's lawyer and a rational and factual understanding of the proceedings. Although most courts have not set a separate standard for juveniles, the *Dusky* standard is altered in some jurisdictions to inquire more carefully into the juvenile's decision-making abilities (Oberlander, Goldstein, & Ho, 2001).

This is a good move because many developmental psychologists and legal advocates for children believe that adjudicative competence in juveniles and adults is not identical. Even if a juvenile is knowledgeable about the role of the attorney and able to understand the charges, he or she may not be an *effective* participant in these proceedings. According to Richard Bonnie (1992), effective participation requires an ability to make decisions, weigh alternatives, and understand consequences—abilities he referred to as "decisional competency."

Juveniles may be particularly at a disadvantage when it comes to **decisional competency.** Although adults also may have deficits related to effective participation, juveniles—given their stage of development—are more likely to have these deficits and are thus at greater jeopardy. In addition, those juveniles who come before the juvenile courts are even more likely than other juveniles to be intellectually disabled, mentally disordered, or emotionally or socially immature. The problem does not disappear if the juveniles are transferred to criminal court. In fact, it might be even greater, because criminal court judges are not attuned to the needs of juveniles, having dealt with the legal question of competency primarily with adult defendants.

Competency to stand trial—or adjudicative competence—in the *juvenile* court has emerged as an issue only since the early 1990s. At this point, statutes or case law in about half the states *require* an inquiry into adjudicative competency in juvenile courts. In the remaining states, the competency inquiry is raised on a case-by-case basis.

MacArthur Juvenile Competence Study

In an effort to shed some light on the juvenile competency question, the MacArthur Research Network began gathering data in 1999 for a multisite study of adjudicative competence in juveniles. Major questions addressed by the research were the following (see the **MacArthur Juvenile Competence Study** home page at www.mac-adoldev-juvjustice.org):

- Compared to adults in the criminal justice system, do youth in the juvenile justice system more often manifest deficits in abilities related to adjudicative competence?
- If so, on what abilities are these differences most apparent, and how are those abilities related to development?
- What types of youth are at greatest risk of adjudicative incompetence due to developmental immaturity? Might developmental immaturity interact with mental disorders to create increased risks of deficits in abilities related to adjudicative incompetence? Is there an age below which incompetence to stand trial should be presumed?
- What methods could clinicians and courts use to identify youth who are seriously deficient in abilities related to adjudicative competence?

In the first phase of the above study, Grisso et al. (2003) compared abilities of 927 adolescents in juvenile detention facilities and community settings and 466 young adults (ages 18–24) in jails and community settings in Philadelphia, Los Angeles, northern and eastern Virginia, and northern Florida. In addition to a standard battery of tests and record reviews, the groups were asked to respond to vignettes and were administered the MacArthur Competence Assessment Tool—Criminal Adjudication (MacCAT-CA) and a newly developed MacArthur Judgment Evaluation. The two youngest adolescent groups (ages 11–13 and 14–15) were 3 times and 2 times (respectively) as likely as the young adults to be seriously impaired in competence-relevant abilities. The 16- and 17-year-old juveniles did not differ from the young adults.

In addition to age, intelligence was also a predictor of poor performance. Gender, ethnicity, socioeconomic background, prior experience with the legal system, and symptoms of mental health problems were not predictors (although few individuals with serious mental health problems were included in the sample). The adolescents also tended to make choices that reflected compliance with authority and psychosocial immaturity. Grisso and his colleagues (2003) recommend that legal standards recognize immaturity as a possible indicator of incompetence to stand trial. In other words, children who are immature are unlikely to meet the standard for competency in criminal court. They recommend also that states rethink transferring juveniles age 13 and younger to criminal courts, given the high proportion of youth in that age group who were considered significantly impaired (about 30% total, but more than half of those with below-average intelligence).

The Lawyer–Client Relationship

In a separately published study, Schmidt, Reppucci, and Woolard (2003) reported on 203 juveniles and 110 adults who were given vignettes relating to attorney–client issues. In the vignette, an individual was charged with a robbery, and the respondents were asked a variety of questions as to what the defendant should do. Age had a significant effect on responses to the vignettes. Juveniles were more likely to say the defendant should deny guilt to his lawyer, less likely to recommend that he should communicate honestly, and more likely to be influenced by short-term consequences as opposed to long-term consequences. Juveniles who had previously been detained within the juvenile justice system were even more distrustful of defense attorneys than juveniles who had had less or no experience with the system. However, juveniles previously charged with property offenses (and presumably aware that lawyers had been helpful) were trustful. Black, Latino, and Asian juveniles were more distrustful than White juveniles.

Schmidt et al. (2003) believe that the results of their study highlight the importance of taking developmental differences into consideration when looking at the attorney–client relationship. Together with other researchers (e.g., Buss, 2000; Tobey, Grisso, & Schwartz, 2000), they recommend that lawyers receive training in developmental issues relating to children and adolescents, and guidance in how to effectively represent young clients, based on knowledge from developmental psychology. In a similar vein, clinicians conducting evaluations of adjudicative competency in juveniles are advised to gather information about the attorney–client relationship, including, if possible, an interview with the juvenile's attorney (e.g., Barnum, 2000). As Grisso (1999) has observed, a juvenile may be highly capable cognitively but may still be reluctant to accept that an adult such as a public defender is working for him or her and in this juvenile's best interest.

Another study exploring the relationship between juveniles and their lawyers provides a somewhat different—but certainly not optimistic—view. Pierce and Brodsky (2002) recruited 163 male juveniles and young adults with experience in the juvenile or criminal justice system. Participants were in residential facilities, a group home, or a day diversion program. On measures of *trust* (in lawyers, in others, or in authority), there were no significant age differences. However, there was pervasive distrust in lawyers within the group. Significant differences in *understanding the role of counsel* emerged as a function of age, with juveniles ages 12 to 14 years (the youngest group in the study) demonstrating the least understanding. In addition, those youth who were least trustful of attorneys, regardless of age level, were also the ones who demonstrated the least understanding of attorney roles. Cognitive abilities were also negatively correlated with both trust and understanding. In other words, the less cognitively developed the youth, the more distrustful of lawyers and the more lacking in understanding of their function. Black participants were less trusting and understanding than White participants, even when intellectual functioning was controlled. However, Blacks with higher intellectual functioning were less trustful than Whites with higher intellectual functioning, a finding that Pierce and Brodsky interpreted as "justified cynicism regarding the treatment of Black individuals in this society" (p. 104). Once again, psychologists evaluating the competency of juveniles to participate in court proceedings should take into account not only developmental and cognitive differences but also cultural differences.

All of the above material on cognitive development seems especially crucial today, with increasing research evidence that adolescents, as a group, are lacking in decision-making skills that would serve their own best interests. Recall the APA brief in the case of *Graham v. Florida*, discussed in Chapter 4. In that case—to be discussed again briefly below—the Supreme Court cited a long line of research in developmental psychology indicating very clearly that the adolescent brain has not reached its full maturity, a fact that often affects the decisions that they make. Very few adults today would want to be held fully accountable for some of their actions as teenagers.

Complicating the matter of juveniles effectively helping their lawyers is the reality that some lawyers in juvenile court do not provide the zealous advocacy that they provide for adults in criminal courts. Barry Feld (2000) points out that many well-meaning attorneys truly believe it is in their client's best interest to be adjudicated delinquent and receive treatment. As Feld notes—and as we will discuss in Chapter 13—the efficacy of many treatment programs is questionable. On the other hand, successful programs do exist. Forensic psychologists consulting with defense attorneys should be aware of the evaluation literature and should advise lawyers to advocate for a disposition "package" for their clients that would be the most likely to achieve rehabilitation.

If the lawyer is inclined to recommend a plea bargain, psychologist Richard Barnum (2000) recommends that examining clinicians determine the extent to which the juvenile is willing to undergo the treatment that will likely accompany it. Plea negotiation is increasingly common in the juvenile system, just as it is in criminal courts. Yet, developmentally, youth are far less likely than adults to understand the stakes and ramifications of admitting guilt. There are both risks and benefits. For example, although juvenile probation will allow the youth to remain in the community, it may require a lengthy period of supervision and frequent, unannounced home visits. "Whether the juvenile actually understands what may be involved in elaborate probation agreements and treatment contracts, may be critical issues in determining his competence to take part in a negotiated solution" (Barnum, 2000, p. 196). Barnum also notes that, even though the juvenile court may be rehabilitative, the loss of liberty involved may be far greater than the juvenile would receive for the same offense in criminal court. Recall the *Gault* case, in which the juvenile faced a 6-year confinement for making an obscene phone call.

Finally, in evaluating adjudicative competency, clinicians are advised to evaluate the juvenile–parent relationship and assess how well the parent or guardian understands the juvenile's capacities and needs. Barnum (2000) notes that this can be a cumbersome process but adds, "When there is doubt about the juvenile defendant's autonomous competence, it is appropriate to examine the parent's ability to provide appropriate support and advice to make up for the youth's deficits" (p. 213).

There is less agreement in the literature on whether specific treatment recommendations should be made or on whether clinicians should express an ultimate issue opinion: Is this juvenile competent to stand trial (or to participate in juvenile proceedings)? Barnum (2000) considers it unethical for clinicians to express an ultimate legal opinion, even though courts may press for it. He does not, however, believe it problematic for the clinician to provide treatment recommendations, but they should be phrased in a conditional way—for example, "If the defendant is found incompetent . . ." or "If the defendant is found competent and adjudicated delinquent . . . ." Barnum warns, "Having carefully avoided offering an opinion as to the ultimate opinion of competence, the consultant may introduce new confusion if she offers a clinical recommendation that is available only to an adjudicated delinquent" (p. 220). Barnum believes that if treatment recommendations are made, the clinicians must be careful to distinguish between those recommendations aimed at establishing competence and those aimed at overall clinical care.

Amenability to Rehabilitation

The decision as to whether a juvenile is likely to benefit from rehabilitative services and what types of services are most promising may be made at several points during juvenile justice processing. In addition, **amenability to rehabilitation** commonly takes into consideration a juvenile's present treatment needs. Two contexts in which courts request these evaluations are the judicial waiver decision and the disposition decision.

Waiver Decisions

Judges in both criminal and juvenile courts are often faced with the decision whether to transfer jurisdiction of juveniles, or "waive" a juvenile to the other court. Most **judicial waivers** are made at the request of prosecutors who want to prosecute juveniles in adult courts. In making the transfer decision, judges consider factors such as those recommended by the U.S. Supreme Court in *Kent v. U.S.* (1966), discussed earlier in the chapter.

The transfer by judges is only one of several possible forms of waiver. A great number of juveniles are tried in criminal courts as a result of **legislative waiver,** also called **statutory exclusion** or **waiver by statute.** These are waivers whereby the legislative branch has ordained that juveniles of specified ages will have their cases heard in criminal courts when charged with specific crimes. For example, in the vast majority of states, a 15-year-old charged with murder will automatically be tried in criminal court. (A criminal court judge may transfer his or her case to juvenile court, but this very rarely occurs.) Still another form of waiver, **prosecutorial waiver,** gives prosecutors the authority to decide whether the case will be taken to juvenile court or criminal court. Most state statutes allow some combination of these waivers, depending on the age of the juvenile and the seriousness of the offense. Opponents of waivers argue that they are overused and unjustifiably consign too many adolescents to the adult system, where the emphasis is on punishment more than on rehabilitation (Bishop, 2000). In addition, current research indicates that transferring juveniles to adult criminal courts increases their recidivism and promotes life-course criminality. Furthermore, the potential of having their cases heard in criminal court apparently does not deter juveniles from committing crime (Redding, 2010).

Even when juveniles have been transferred to criminal courts, however, an amenability for rehabilitation evaluation may be requested. A defense attorney, for example, may desire such an assessment for help during the plea negotiation process or during the sentencing phase, if his or her client is convicted.

The most recent juvenile justice decision delivered by the U.S. Supreme Court, *Graham v. Florida* (2010), highlights the importance of amenability for rehabilitation. As you may recall, Graham, who was on probation, took part in a home invasion during which an elderly couple was harmed. He was tried in criminal court and was given a sentence of life without parole (LWOP). At the beginning of the 21st century, some 2,500 prisoners who were juveniles at the time of their crimes were serving LWOP sentences. The U.S. Supreme Court has now established that a LWOP sentence is cruel and unusual punishment for juveniles, at least in cases that did not involve murder. At sentencing, Graham had not been given the opportunity to argue that society should not give up on him, that as a juvenile he was able to be rehabilitated. It is hard to conceive of a mental health practitioner who would be willing to consign Graham to a life sentence without the possibility of parole for crimes he had committed when he was 17 years old and in which no victim died.

There is considerable debate about even trying juveniles in criminal courts, a phenomenon that has increased steadily in recent years. All but one state (Nebraska), along with the District of Columbia, enacted or expanded transfer provisions between 1992 and 1999 (Sickmund, 2003). Juveniles being considered for transfer to criminal court have a good deal to lose. Prosecution in criminal court involves public proceedings, a criminal record if found guilty, and possible incarceration in an adult prison. A juvenile who is considered an unlikely candidate for rehabilitation in the juvenile system is not likely to get rehabilitative services once transferred to adult settings. Research has also documented that juveniles charged with serious crimes in criminal courts and juveniles facing property offenses in juvenile courts both get harsh dispositions (Podkopacz & Feld, 1996). However, juveniles sentenced in criminal courts typically get longer sentences than those in juvenile court for similar crimes (Redding, 2010).

Disposition

Disposition is the equivalent of sentencing in the adult context. Once a juvenile has been adjudicated a delinquent in a delinquency hearing, the judge chooses from a variety of disposition alternatives, ranging from community-based services to confinement in a secure facility. In most jurisdictions, juvenile judges themselves do not choose among a variety of community alternatives, however. The judges place juveniles in the custody of juvenile justice officials (e.g., a juvenile correctional agency or a department of human services), who determine the best program approach for each juvenile. Placement in a secure facility, however, must be made by a juvenile court. In either case—community setting or institution—psychological assessment may occur later in the process rather than in consultation with the juvenile court. Juvenile correctional officials may want help deciding on a programmatic approach for a particular juvenile. A juvenile probation officer, for example, may wonder whether a boy on her caseload is a good candidate for a substance abuse program in the community. We will discuss these assessments again in Chapter 13.

The extent to which psychologists actually do consult with the juvenile courts for amenability to rehabilitation evaluations varies by jurisdiction. It appears that they are used more prior to judicial waivers than prior to disposition, though after *Graham v. Florida*, we may see them occurring more in criminal courts. Podkopacz and Feld (1996) found that court psychologists had examined and filed reports on 46% of juveniles facing transfer proceedings in their Minnesota sample, with percentages increasing in later years (63% in 1991 and 57% in 1992). By comparison, Hecker and Steinberg (2002) found that only 2 to 3% of juvenile cases in the jurisdiction they studied were referred for psychological assessment *prior to disposition.* A slightly higher percentage (10–15%) was referred for screening, as opposed to full assessment. (It is possible, though, that the records of juveniles not referred contained psychological reports of evaluations that had been conducted earlier in the juvenile process.) It should be noted that in both of the above studies, the recommendations of the clinicians carried heavy weight with judges.

Conducting the Evaluation

A number of manuals and suggestions are available for psychologists conducting psychological evaluations relating to transfer and disposition decisions (e.g., Grisso, 1998; Melton et al., 1997, 2007). As Hecker and Steinberg (2002) observed, though, "an empirically validated 'gold standard' for the predisposition evaluation of juvenile offenders remains elusive" (p. 300). Psychologists are typically advised to review the juvenile's files, including school, social service, and juvenile court records. In addition, they are advised to obtain information about family history and substance use and abuse, as well as assess intellectual, academic, personality, and vocational functioning, using a range of possible measures. Furthermore, although most juvenile offenders are not *seriously* emotionally disturbed, mental health needs are common, and—according to recent research—very prevalent (e.g., Grisso, 2008). Juveniles in correctional facilities, for example, are believed to have mental health issues ranging from conduct disorders to severe depression and suicidal tendencies (LeCroy, Stevenson, & MacNeil, 2001). Developmental disabilities and cognitive impairment also plague both institutionalized juveniles and those under community supervision (Day & Berney, 2001). Many juvenile offenders also are substance abusers, often with significant chemical dependency problems, and many others are sex offenders. Developing and validating instruments for the evaluation of juvenile sex and violent offenders (e.g., J-SOAP, ERASOR, Static-99, Static-2002; see Focus 5.5) have become robust activities in recent years. The psychologist assessing juveniles, therefore, should be aware of both assessment techniques and the range of treatment and rehabilitation services available, in the community as well as within institutional settings.

Many psychologists are concerned about the possible negative effects of labeling juveniles. Of particular concern are those labels that suggest the prospects for change are not good. In recent years, for example, juvenile psychopathy has received considerable research attention. It has prompted the development of a special version of Hare's Psychopathy Checklist, the Psychopathy Checklist: Youth Version (PCL:YV) (Forth, Kosson, & Hare, 1997). Some researchers have argued, though, that it is premature to place this pessimistic label on juveniles who may possess psychopathic characteristics that they may well outgrow (Edens, Skeem, Cruise, & Cauffman, 2001; Edens & Vincent, 2008; Seagrave & Grisso, 2002). Edens, Skeem, et al. (2001) also suggest that labeling adolescents this way may violate the two ethical principles of social responsibility and do no harm. There is also concern that labeling a juvenile as a psychopath will be harmful in various legal proceedings (Viljoen, MacDougall, Gagnon, & Douglas, 2010); in an amenability for rehabilitation evaluation, for example, this would almost assuredly guarantee that he or she will be transferred to criminal court. Somewhat in response to the above controversy, many researchers now prefer to refer to "juveniles with psychopathic characteristics" (e.g., callousness) rather than "juvenile psychopaths." In addition, research on both identification and treatment of such juveniles is expanding rapidly (Salekin, Leistico, Trobst, Schrum, & Lochman, 2005) as is research on protective factors that might reduce the likelihood that psychopathy would develop (Salekin & Lochman, 2008).

Another pessimistic label that might be problematic is *life-course persistent offender* (LCP), in accordance with Moffitt's (1993a) adolescent limited (AL)-LCP dichotomy, which will be discussed again in Chapter 7. Some diagnostic categories in the *Diagnostic and Statistical Manual of Mental Disorders,* 4th edition, text revision, or *DSM-IV-TR* (American Psychiatric Association, 2000) (e.g., ADHD, conduct disorder), are problematic if the individuals working with the juvenile after the assessment do not understand their limitations as well as their significance. Labels that make their way into files of juveniles in correctional facilities or community programs may be as damaging as labels that make their way into school files of non-delinquent children.

Hecker and Steinberg (2002) appraised the quality of psychological evaluations submitted to juvenile courts prior to disposition as well as the effect of the reports on judges' decision making. They reviewed 172 predisposition reports submitted to juvenile courts in Philadelphia between 1992 and 1996 by four independent practitioners who were licensed psychologists in Pennsylvania.

Findings included the following:

- A vast majority of the assessments included a standardized measure of intellectual functioning, but few included a standardized personality measure; instead, projective tests were typically administered for measuring personality.
- There were no statistically significant individual differences in either judges' acceptance/rejection of recommendations or among clinicians in whether their recommendations were accepted or rejected.
- A high percentage of recommendations were accepted; in fact, recommendations were fully rejected in only 8 of the 172 cases.
- Many reports lacked information about the juvenile's mental health, criminal, or substance abuse history, all of which the researchers considered crucial information because of their links to recidivism.
- Judges were most likely to accept recommendations if the reports included information about mental health, regardless of the quality of this information. This was troubling to the researchers, who believed that reports did not include sufficient detail in this area, as noted above.

Hecker and Steinberg (2002) emphasized that their study may not be representative of other jurisdictions, considering the small number of judges and clinicians as well as the small number of cases in their sample. Nevertheless, they described a useful coding scheme by which researchers might evaluate predisposition reports, along with their impact on judicial decisions in other jurisdictions.

In sum, research on amenability to rehabilitation evaluations suggests that they vary widely in quality, despite the fact that there is some consensus on what should be included in the evaluation reports. Most sources recommend comprehensive evaluations that will assess the juvenile's family background; determine developmental, cognitive, and emotional functioning; and identify promising treatment options. Evaluators are advised to avoid labels that might be pessimistic and suggest that there is little hope for the juvenile. As Grisso (1998) has noted, a pessimistic report may become a self-fulfilling prophecy if the rehabilitation staff becomes discouraged. "Reservations about the prospect for change . . . should always be coupled with suggestions to staff that might increase the prospects" (p. 192).

Family and Probate Courts

As mentioned in Chapter 4, states are increasingly establishing specialized courts to deal with a very wide range of civil and criminal matters, such as mental health, drug, and family-related issues. Family courts are a good example of this trend, having jurisdiction over virtually all matters pertaining to the family, including delinquency matters. Thus, in many states, the juvenile courts discussed in the previous section are actually a subset of family courts. Probate courts, though also specialized, have a longer history. These are the courts that have general powers over wills and administration of estates. In some states, they can appoint guardians and approve the adoption of minors (H. C. Black, 1990).

Both family and probate courts deal with some of the most emotionally charged and contentious issues in society. In most states, family courts—sometimes called domestic courts—are the venue for litigating divorce proceedings and making custody decisions, although these proceedings also may occur in courts of general jurisdiction (e.g., superior courts or district courts, depending on the state). Family courts also have the power to remove neglected and abused children from their homes and place them into temporary custody of the state, as well as the power to revoke parental rights permanently. In states where minors must notify a parent and obtain parental consent before obtaining an abortion, family courts can override that requirement in the best interest of the girl seeking the abortion. In domestic violence situations, family court may be the place where a victim seeks a temporary or permanent restraining order against an abuser. Adoptions are finalized in family or probate courts. Similarly, contested wills, decisions about competency to make medical decisions, and involuntary commitments to mental institutions come under the jurisdiction of some—but not all—family or probate courts. In light of the powers listed above, it is not surprising that psychologists and other mental health professionals play a role in the day-to-day operation of these courts and that family forensic psychology is a rapidly developing specialization (see Focus 6.4).

FOCUS 6.4. FAMILY FORENSIC PSYCHOLOGY

In June 2003, the *Journal of Family Psychology* published a special issue devoted to the intersection of family psychology and family law. According to the editors of this special issue, its primary goal was "to introduce readers to new and emerging opportunities for research and practice in the areas where family psychology and family law overlap" (Grossman & Okun, 2003, p. 163).

Family psychologists—whether clinicians or researchers—have extensive knowledge about human development and systems theories. Forensic psychologists have knowledge and expertise in assessment and consultation with courts and legal professionals. They also know legal theories and procedures that relate to clinical practice and have experience at providing expert testimony. Family forensic psychologists, then, represent a combination of the knowledge and skills of forensic psychologists and family psychologists.

Grossman and Okun (2003) define family forensic psychology as

the study of families, members of family units, organizations, and larger systems from a family systems perspective in assessment and intervention regarding interaction with the legal system. Among the areas that assessment and intervention include are prevention, education, evaluation, various forms of conflict resolution, treatment, and outcome assessment. Family forensic psychologists provide expertise to the legal system. (p. 166)

Family forensic psychology can make contributions in all of the following areas: adoption; divorce, child custody, and visitation; conflict resolution and mediation; juvenile justice; assessment of parental fitness (e.g., when parents have a psychiatric diagnosis); termination of parental rights; elder law and estate planning; child–parent relationships when parents are imprisoned; guardianship; reproductive rights and technologies; and family violence. Because all of these issues are increasingly being adjudicated in family courts and other specialized courts, family forensic psychologists should continue to be in high demand.

Child Custody Evaluations

Among the most contentious areas faced by family courts are those involving divorce and child custody, most particularly when custody is contested. Although it is estimated that children are involved in about 40% of divorces (L. S. Horvath, Logan, & Walker, 2002), the majority of these do not require a custody decision by the court. Instead, custody is not contested because parents, alone or with the help of a mediator, have agreed on a mutually satisfactory custody arrangement. Studies suggest that courts make decisions in 6 to 20% of all divorce cases (Melton et al., 1997). When courts do make decisions, however, they turn to mental health professionals. Research suggests that psychologists are the most frequent examiners (Mason & Quirk, 1997), but they are also apparently highly paid compared with other examiners, such as social workers. Bow and Quinnell (2001) reported that the average charge for a custody evaluation performed by a licensed psychologist in private practice was $3,335. Thus, many courts use mental health practitioners who are associated with public court service agencies, such as master's-level psychologists or clinical social workers (L. S. Horvath et al., 2002).

At the outset, we must acknowledge that individuals other than the child's biological or adoptive parents may seek custody of minor children. In fact, over the past decade, family courts have seen an unprecedented explosion in both custody and visitation requests from stepparents, grandparents, other relatives, gay and lesbian partners of deceased biological or adoptive parents, cohabiting but nonmarried parents who have split up, family friends, and surrogate mothers (Grossman & Okun, 2003). Although legal parents clearly have both constitutional and civil rights to be involved in their children's lives, the rights of other individuals, including grandparents, are not universally well-defined. The U.S. Supreme Court has denied grandparents a *constitutional* right to see their grandchild over the objection of the child's competent mother (*Troxel v. Granville,* 2000), but statutes in many states have recognized that grandparents should not completely be barred from their grandchildren, except under rare circumstances (e.g., grandparent has abused the grandchild). Moreover, in the Granville case, the mother had not totally deprived the grandparents of visitation privileges but had refused to allow more than one visit every month. Thus, although the decision did not represent a victory for grandparents, it is unclear what would have been decided had the mother refused to allow *any* visits.

Child Custody Standards

Historically, courts have relied on a number of different standards for determining child custody. The primary standard was the **tender years doctrine,** in which it was presumed that the children, particularly girls and very young children, were best left in the care of the mother. An early appellate case (*People v. Hickey,* 1889) suggested that even if the father was without blame, he had an "inability to bestow on [the child] that tender care which nature requires, and which it is the peculiar province of the mother to supply" (Einhorn, 1986, p. 128). Today, the tender years doctrine has given way in most states to a standard that does not presume that either parent is naturally better than the other, but rather looks at what is in the best interest of the child, known as the **best interest of the child standard (BICS).**

Krauss and Sales (2000) maintain that the dominant "best interest of the child" standard should be replaced by a **least detrimental alternative standard.** They argue that psychological knowledge, in its present state, cannot determine which custody arrangement is truly in the child's best interest. At best, psychological knowledge can help in identifying which arrangement would do the least harm. Psychological assessment instruments, according to Krauss and Sales, tend to be pathology focused, identifying deficits more than strengths. In that sense, a custody evaluation would be more efficient at "screening out" the custody arrangement that would create problems for the child rather than making a determination that one parent would be better than the other. Interestingly, representatives of **family forensic psychology** suggest that the legal principle should be the best interests of the child *in relation to the family* (Grossman & Okun, 2003).

Deciding what is in the best interest of the child sounds sensible, but the process of arriving at that determination remains highly subjective and controversial. A number of researchers have noted that custody evaluations—compared with other psychological services—are disproportionately associated with ethical problems and complaints to state licensing boards (Bow & Quinnell, 2001; Kirkland & Kirkland, 2001). The APA (1994) has published a list of 16 guidelines for child custody evaluation, which focus on the purpose of the evaluation, the competence needed by the psychologist, and specific recommended procedures such as using multiple methods of data gathering and clarifying financial arrangements. The guidelines are recommendations and suggestions that are *aspirational* rather than mandatory. By comparison, APA *standards* are mandatory and may be accompanied by an enforcement mechanism (APA, 1993). The Ethical Principles and Code of Conduct of the APA (2002b) is an illustration of standards as opposed to guidelines.

Like competency to stand trial and criminal responsibility evaluations, custody evaluations also raise the "ultimate issue" question that was introduced in Chapter 4. Should examiners make a recommendation as to which parent should be given custody of the child? The APA guidelines do not take a position on this beyond advising psychologists to be aware of both sides of the ultimate issue controversy and to be aware of their own biases in making custody recommendations. This caveat is particularly relevant when we consider the changing definitions of family that go beyond the traditional definition of individuals related by blood or marriage.

Methods of Evaluation in Child Custody Cases

Several studies have examined the methods used by psychologists in conducting custody evaluations (e.g., Ackerman & Ackerman, 1997; Bow & Quinnell, 2001; Keilin & Bloom, 1986; LaFortune & Carpenter, 1998). These studies suggest that evaluators progressed from relying almost exclusively on interview data (Keilin & Bloom, 1986) to using a wide range of assessment measures, including tests developed specifically for custody evaluations (Bow & Quinnell, 2001). However, these tests themselves have been criticized by some psychologists for not being grounded in sufficient research before being used in practice (Krauss & Sales, 2000; Otto & Heilbrun, 2002).

In their survey of 198 psychologists in 38 states, Bow and Quinnell (2001) found that psychologists were testing parents more and children less. In other words, they made greater use of parent rating scales and parenting inventories and less use of cognitive and personality tests for children. According to their own reports, psychologists were following the APA (1993) guidelines by using multiple methods of data collection and attending seminars and workshops to gain more expertise at this task. Although Bow and Quinnell identified problem areas relating to ethical issues, they concluded that psychologists seemed to be doing a better job of conducting custody evaluations than early studies indicated. Interestingly, almost all respondents (94%) provided a recommendation to the court as to which parent should gain custody.

L. S. Horvath et al. (2002) used a different methodology to research custody evaluation procedures—a method that, it is hoped, will be adopted by other researchers in different jurisdictions. Rather than asking psychologists to report their own practices, Horvath et al. performed a content analysis of evaluations in 60% of custody cases decided in one court over a 2-year period. (**Content analysis** is a technique in which the researcher carefully examines the content of documents to discover common elements.) A total of 102 evaluation reports were examined. The evaluators represented a variety of professionals, including social workers; child protective service investigators; and clinical, counseling, and educational psychologists. Both private and court-appointed evaluators were represented in the sample. Horvath et al. found that there was considerable variability in the contents of the reports and in methods of the evaluations, leading them to the conclusion that there was no standardized approach for conducting custody evaluations. More disturbingly, though, the researchers found that parent interviews often failed to address variables that would seem critical to custody determination.

> In particular, evaluators frequently neglected assessment of domestic violence and child abuse, adequate assessment of parenting skills, assessment of health status, and formal psychological testing. . . . It is also noteworthy that approximately 40% of the evaluations relied on only two methods of assessment to determine a custody arrangement. (p. 7)

L. S. Horvath et al. (2002) found that some differences emerged across professionals and between private and public evaluators. For example, private evaluators were more likely to include formal psychological testing of both parents and children. MSWs (those with a master's in social work) were more likely to include home visits. None of the educational psychologists included parent–child observations in their reports, whereas 62.5% of the MSWs and 76.2% of the clinical and counseling psychologists included these observations.

The content analysis confirmed information derived from self-report studies (e.g., Bow & Quinnell, 2001; LaFortune & Carpenter, 1998) that examiners almost always offer custody and visitation recommendations (only 8 of the 102 evaluations did not include these). L. S. Horvath et al. (2002) were able to compare the recommendations to the final decision. The final determination was exactly as evaluators recommended in 27.3% of the cases and similar to the recommendations but with a few modifications in 63.6% of the cases. It appears, therefore, that the examiner's opinion carries considerable weight in crafting the final custody and visitation arrangements. Considering the problems identified by these researchers in the reports they examined, this is a sobering fact. Horvath et al. recommend that continuing efforts should be made to develop a standard of practice so that, at the least, custody evaluations will contain information that is essential to deciding what is in the best interest of the child.

Visitation Risk Assessments

Closely related to the custody issue is the issue of visitation, and visitation recommendations are almost invariably included in custody assessments. Ideally, children should have access to both parents, and each parent also has the right to be involved in his or her child's lives. However, it is not uncommon for a custodial parent to challenge or request a change in the visitation rights of the non-custodial parent. This usually occurs under the premise that the non-custodial parent is emotionally or physically damaging the child—or presents a strong risk of inflicting such harm. In some high-profile media cases, the custodial or non-custodial parent has absconded with the child or children, claiming that this was done to protect the child from abuse by the other parent.

Consequently—in addition to custody evaluations—psychologists and other mental health practitioners are sometimes asked to conduct "visitation risk assessments" to help courts decide whether visitation rights should be limited or abrogated completely. For example, on the basis of such an assessment, the family court judge may decide to require that all visits be supervised by the child's social service caseworker or by a court-appointed guardian.

The psychologist conducting the visitation risk assessment ideally interviews both parents and, depending on the circumstances, may also interview the child. The psychologist's role is to determine whether there is evidence of a psychological problem or behavior pattern that would likely lead to inappropriate and potentially harmful interactions between parent and child. Like the custody evaluations discussed above, there is no "standard of practice" for visitation risk assessments. However, there is more research available on custody evaluations than on visitation risk assessments.

Research on Custody Arrangements

Custody arrangements tend to fall into one of four patterns, each of which can encompass physical or legal custody (K. D. Hess, 2006). The patterns are (1) sole custody, the most common; (2) divided (or alternating) custody, which typically gives one parent custody for segments of the year; (3) split custody, in which one or more children go with one parent and other children go to the second parent; and (4) joint custody, where the parents share legal or physical custody "so as to assure the access of the child to both parents in a frequent and continuing manner" (K. D. Hess, 2006, p. 106).

Psychologists and other mental health practitioners conducting custody evaluations should be aware of the vast store of research on the effects of divorce and custody arrangements (e.g., Bricklin & Elliott, 1995; Johnston, 1995; Maccoby, Buchanan, Mnookin, & Dornsbusch, 1993; Wallerstein, 1989). However, sifting through this research can become an exercise in frustration because—as Krauss and Sales (2000) have observed, methodologically sound studies have reached different conclusions. Particularly equivocal has been research comparing joint custody to sole custody arrangements (e.g., Bauserman, 2002; Gunnoe & Braver, 2001), leading to conclusions that no one arrangement is clearly superior to the other. It has been observed, though, that when custody is contested, psychologists and other practitioners are likely to encourage placement with the parent who is most likely to foster contact between the child and the non-custodial parent (K. D. Hess, 2006).

Numerous factors have been found to play a part in a child's adjustment to divorce (see K. D. Hess, 2006, for a review) and custody arrangements, including—but not limited to—the child's age and gender, hostility between parents, parenting skills, the quality of the parent–child relationship, and emotional and physical health of the parents. These factors should be taken into consideration when performing custody evaluations, but examiners should be careful not to generalize from the group data reported to what is in the best interest of the particular child or children involved in the presenting case.

Decisional Competency

Psychologists, as well as other clinicians, may be asked to evaluate whether an individual was or is capable of making a critical decision in his or her best interest. Persons who have reached adulthood are presumed to be capable of making these decisions. Likewise, they are expected to take responsibility for decisions that resulted in disastrous consequences. This decisional autonomy extends to such areas as consenting to medical treatment, joining a cult, engaging in a business contract, enlisting in the military, drafting a will, refusing medication or life-prolonging treatment, or consenting to participate in psychological or medical research. The presumption that one is capable of making decisions can be overcome if it can be demonstrated to the satisfaction of a court that the person was not mentally or physically competent at the time the decision was made (or is being considered). In most jurisdictions, the burden of proof in these situations is a preponderance of the evidence, but some jurisdictions require clear and convincing evidence, which is a higher standard (see Focus 5.2 in the previous chapter for a review of the burdens of proof). When a court determines that an individual is or was not competent, it invalidates a decision that was made (e.g., the terms of a will or a decision to forgo medical treatment). If the person is still alive, the court will usually appoint a guardian to decide what is in the person's best interest.

Testamentary Capacity

One decision that is frequently challenged—though not often successfully—is the competence to make a will, called **testamentary capacity.** In most states, this would come under the purview of a probate court.

As Slovenko (1999) has noted, making a will actually requires only minimal competency and is an easy task. The law requires only that one be "of sound mind" when making a will. Specific requirements are that individuals (1) know they are making a will, (2) know the nature and extent of their property, (3) know the objects of their bounty, and (4) know how their property is being divided (Melton et al., 2007). As Melton et al. point out, it is possible for someone to be forgetful, addicted to narcotics or alcohol, mentally disordered, or have a low threshold of cognitive functioning, yet still be capable of making a will. The evaluation of testamentary capacity is usually retrospective, such that it requires the evaluator to interview those who knew the individual, review any available records, and draw inferences about the individual's mental state at the time the will was formulated. In many respects, it is similar to the psychological autopsy (discussed in Chapter 3), although far less detailed. However, in some situations, lawyers advise their clients to be evaluated for testamentary capacity at the time they execute their wills. Psychological assessment would especially be warranted if the individual exhibits signs of dementia, has a mental disorder that includes periods of cognitive incapacity, or has some intellectual disability.

Competence to Consent to Treatment

Perhaps even more frequent than evaluations of testamentary capacity are evaluations of a person's competence to make decisions regarding medical and psychological treatment. These decisions require informed consent, which generally requires that the individuals must be told of the possible consequences of the treatment; must be mentally capable of understanding what they are consenting to; and must be doing so of their own free will, without coercion. Each of these three elements is scrutinized separately by courts when questions of informed consent come before them. Interestingly, research suggests that being told of the consequences—referred to as disclosure—is particularly problematic. "The most general thing that can be said about disclosure in health and mental health settings is that there is rarely adherence to the spirit of informed consent" (Melton et al., 1997, p. 352). Melton et al. note that consent forms are lengthy and beyond comprehension, patients often lack information about alternative treatments, and negative information (e.g., about side effects) is often omitted. A variety of explanations are offered for this failure to adhere to the spirit of disclosure requirements. For example, treatment providers may wish to protect their patients from excessive worry, or they may fear that they themselves will appear professionally weak by not knowing precisely how the patient will react to the treatment. Obviously, the quality of disclosure is an important component in a subsequent evaluation of consent to treatment. That is, if the individual did not receive sufficient information about treatment alternatives or about the risks associated with the treatment, the consent was not informed.

Measure of Competence to Consent to Treatment

The competence of mentally disturbed individuals to consent to treatment has been studied extensively by researchers associated with the MacArthur Foundation (e.g., Appelbaum & Grisso, 1995; Grisso, Appelbaum, Mulvey, & Fletcher, 1995). Their research has, in turn, been the subject of considerable scholarly comment (see, generally, Winick, 1996). The MacArthur Competence Study (Appelbaum & Grisso, 1995) assessed and compared decision-making competence in three groups: persons hospitalized with serious mental illness, persons hospitalized with medical illness, and community volunteers who were not patients. Despite some decision-making deficits, those hospitalized with mental illness were still capable of making decisions, as reflected on measures of decision-making ability. The exceptions were patients with schizophrenia who had severe psychiatric symptoms; nevertheless, the majority of patients with schizophrenia still performed adequately. Hospitalized patients with depression demonstrated intermediate levels of decision making. The MacArthur researchers developed a tool—the **MacArthur Competence Assessment Tool—Treatment (MacCAT-T)**—for use by clinicians who evaluate treatment competence. The interview format allows clinicians to test decision-making competence in four areas: (1) ability to state a choice, (2) ability to understand relevant information, (3) ability to appreciate the nature of one's own situation, and (4) ability to reason with the information provided.

Although the MacCAT-T has received favorable reviews (e.g., Winick, 1996), some researchers and scholars have issued cautionary notes. Kirk and Bersoff (1996) suggest that the instrument sets too low a standard for decision-making competence, focusing as it does on competencies rather than disabilities. In other words, under the instrument, too many individuals would be found to make competent decisions in their best interest, and their decisional disabilities would be overlooked. In addition, Stefan (1996) made a compelling argument that the MacCAT-T is not sufficiently sensitive to race, class, and gender differences in the determination of incompetence.

Kapp and Mossman (1996) believe there are inherent problems in any attempt to construct a universal test of decisional capacity to make medical choices. Although the MacArthur group clearly warned that their measures were still in the experimental stage, Kapp and Mossman expressed concern that clinicians will rush too quickly to adopt the competency assessment tool and that courts will accept it too readily. They note also that numerous other instruments are currently available to assess competency, many of which are accompanied by research testing their validity (e.g., the Mini-Mental State Examination [MMSE], the Geriatric Depression Scale, the Alzheimer's Disease Assessment Scale). Kapp and Mossman believe it is far more useful to develop a *process* than a universal test (or *capacimeter*) for evaluating competency to consent to treatment: "What is needed . . . is a credible process for collecting, critically examining, and drawing up usable guidelines from our extensive research and practice experience" (p. 95). Critiques such as these highlight the need for forensic psychologists evaluating competency matters to exercise judgment in their approach and in communicating their findings to legal decision makers.

Incapacitation: Special Condition

Another decisional competency area that has been controversial involves persons who are comatose or cognitively incapacitated and in a permanent vegetative state. Obviously, they cannot make decisions in their best interest. However, if their wishes are known, they will generally (although not invariably) be honored. The tragic cases of two young women, Karen Ann Quinlan and Nancy Cruzan, brought this issue directly to the courts. Quinlan ingested alcohol and other drugs at a party and subsequently collapsed. She remained comatose and on life support systems with physicians giving no hope to her parents that she would ever be revived. The parents went to court to secure permission to remove their daughter from life support. The state Supreme Court in that case (*In re Quinlan,* 1976) ruled that the wishes of a comatose person should be honored if she had made it clear what she would want in the event that she should become incompetent; the parents then had to persuade the courts that this was what she would have wanted.

Nancy Cruzan was a young woman severely injured in an automobile accident that left her in a permanent vegetative state. In that case, the U.S. Supreme Court supported Missouri's law requiring clear and convincing evidence that Cruzan would want life-sustaining procedures to be terminated (*Cruzan v. Director, Missouri Department of Health,* 1990). Together, these two cases prompted many people to prepare **advance directives** in the event they became physically incapacitated. In some instances, family members or other interested parties challenge these advance directives, maintaining that the incapacitated person was not mentally competent at the time he or she formulated them. In these situations, the forensic clinician is asked to make an assessment similar to that involved in testamentary capacity. In recent years, advance directives for mental health care have also been promoted, in case a person should become psychologically incapacitated (Monahan, Bonnie, et al., 2001; Stavis, 1999). In other words, individuals with mental disorders are urged—in their stable and lucid periods—to make it clear that they would (or would not) accept certain interventions, such as psychoactive medication, if they became too mentally disordered to make autonomous decisions at some point in time.

Although the Supreme Court has made it clear that competent individuals have a constitutional right to refuse life-prolonging treatment, it has not thus far supported the idea of aggressively hastening one's death. To date, it has been left to states to craft their own legal rules in this matter. Only one state, Oregon, allows terminally ill individuals to request, and physicians to prescribe, medication that will help them die. This law, Oregon's Death with Dignity Act, is itself presently being challenged in the courts. However, the law has spurred the need for a new form of psychological assessment, the evaluation of competency to make decisions that will hasten one's death.

Hastened death evaluations are discussed in the forensic psychology literature, along with proposed guidelines for conducting them (e.g., Allen & Shuster, 2002; Werth, Benjamin, & Farrenkopf, 2000). Although opponents of laws such as the one that passed in Oregon say they undermine the value of life, supporters say they recognize the dignity and privacy of the individual who does not wish to postpone the inevitable death he or she faces in the near future. Interestingly, even if the Oregon law were to be overturned, some individuals would still choose to hasten their death with the assistance of a compassionate physician, and no psychological or psychiatric evaluation would be required. It is highly unlikely, then, that hastened death evaluations will be in significantly increased demand.

Involuntary Civil Commitment

Closely related to competency to consent to treatment is the issue of hospitalizing individuals for psychological/psychiatric treatment against their will. Every state allows such commitment, both on emergency and extended bases. The typical statute allows an emergency commitment of 3 to 10 days and an extended commitment for a 3- to 6-month period subject to recommitment proceedings. Although standards vary somewhat depending on the state, the party seeking the commitment always has to prove by at least clear and convincing evidence that the individual is mentally ill and in need of treatment (*Addington v. Texas,* 1979). Interestingly, in the case of mental *retardation*, now more aptly called intellectual disability, commitment can be achieved by a less rigid standard, preponderance of the evidence (*Heller v. Doe,* 1993). Whether mentally disordered or developmentally disabled, the individual must be deemed a danger to self or others *or* so gravely disabled that this person is unable to meet his or her basic needs. It should be noted that, although individuals have a right to legal representation at commitment hearings, there is evidence that lawyers often function paternalistically instead of advocating for the legal rights of their clients (Perlin & Dorfman, 1996). This is not unlike the situation of lawyers representing juveniles in delinquency proceedings, when they believe it is in the juvenile's interest to obtain treatment rather than aggressively forcing the state to prove the juvenile's guilt beyond a reasonable doubt.

An extremely controversial area in involuntary commitment is the civil commitment of sexual predators. Less controversial, but still of concern, is the civil commitment of persons found not guilty by reason of insanity. Both of these topics were addressed in the previous chapter and will not be revisited here.

The Supreme Court has ruled that persons who are seriously mentally disordered are unable to consent "voluntarily" to being institutionalized (*Zinermon v. Burch,* 1990). Burch, a mentally disordered individual who was found wandering along a highway in a highly disoriented condition, had signed forms voluntarily admitting himself into a mental institution. He later attempted to rescind his agreement. The Supreme Court declared his original admission invalid because, in his severely mentally disordered state, he could not have validly consented. Accordingly, persons who are unable to make competent decisions must be admitted to mental institutions via the involuntary commitment route described above (Slovenko, 1999).

Outpatient Civil Commitment

Civil commitment also can be achieved on an outpatient basis—in fact, statutes often require this least restrictive alternative if it can reasonably be provided. Courts are empowered to issue "**outpatient treatment orders**" or "orders of nonhospitalization." These orders typically require that the individual live in his or her own home or alternative group or foster home and comply with a medication regimen. Outpatient civil commitment has been a hot topic in the research literature, probably surpassing interest in institutional confinement (see, generally, Winick & Kress, 2003b).

Until recently, most states required that an outpatient order be based on showing that the individual was both mentally disordered and dangerous to self or others. Some states are now beginning to allow outpatient orders without the dangerousness component. Called **preventive outpatient treatment,** this approach allows the state to intervene before the individual's condition becomes worse. "The new broadened criteria still require mental illness, but instead of the dangerousness standard, they require a need for treatment to prevent further deterioration that would predictably lead to dangerousness based on the individual's illness history" (Hiday, 2003, p. 11). Hiday adds that the person must be judged unable to seek or comply with treatment voluntarily. In addition, like the outpatient orders based on a dangerousness standard, it must be determined that the individual can survive safely in the community with available supervision.

Schopp (2003) has provided an additional description of outpatient civil commitment that helps clarify the situations under which it occurs. He notes that outpatient commitment can take three forms. First, persons who were institutionalized under civil commitment statutes requiring mental disorder and the dangerousness standard are conditionally released to the community; if they fail to meet the conditions of their release, they are subject to being returned to the institution. Second, persons who are eligible for institutional confinement under the civil commitment statutes are placed on an alternative mandatory treatment status in the community. Third, persons who would not qualify under the dangerousness standard but who are considered to need treatment to prevent further deterioration are assigned to preventive commitment.

Researchers are continuing to explore the effectiveness of involuntary outpatient treatment, which is increasingly being used in all three forms described by Schopp (2003). The main questions revolve around whether individuals can be "coerced" to get better; in other words, does treatment "work" if a person is forced to get it? In reviewing this literature, Hiday (2003) notes that early studies almost invariably found positive outcomes on a number of factors. For example, patients ordered to outpatient treatment had lower rehospitalization rates; better compliance with medication and other treatment; and generally better adjustment in the community than comparison groups of patients, such as those who were discharged without outpatient orders. Hiday also reports on a second generation of research, conducted in North Carolina (Swartz, Swanson, & Hiday, 2001) and New York City (Steadman, Gounis, & Dennis, 2001), that is more empirically based, including random assignment to outpatient commitment and non-outpatient commitment groups. Both groups received mental health and social services in the community. The North Carolina study again found that patients under outpatient orders had significantly more positive outcomes than those not under these orders. The New York study, though, found no significant differences, a finding that Hiday (2003) attributes to technical problems in the research. She notes that, despite the study's conclusions, New York State's Department of Mental Health remains supportive of outpatient commitment and reports positive outcomes for patients under those orders—including declines in harmful behavior and homelessness and an increase in medication compliance.

Not everyone is supportive of outpatient commitment, however, particularly when it is not based on dangerousness criteria. Civil libertarians have argued that such preventive commitment raises many legal questions without ensuring that effective treatment will be provided (e.g., Winick, 2003). Persons who would otherwise not qualify for civil commitment are forced to take medications and comply with other treatment regimens against their will. This, they say, is a dangerous expansion of the already overwhelming power of the state. The New York study (Steadman, Gounis, & Dennis, 2001), which reported no differences between those subjected to mandatory treatment and those who were not, provides additional support for this perspective—if forced treatment is no better than voluntary treatment, why force treatment? Such debates among reasonable people have a long history in the literature on civil commitment and will not likely be resolved in the near future.

It is also important to note that the research supportive of any form of outpatient commitment generally indicates that such treatment is effective only if it continues for a period of at least 6 months and is accompanied by the provision of intensive services (Winick & Kress, 2003a). Thus, forensic psychologists who are providing treatment to patients under such orders should be aware of the need to sustain these services.

Role of Forensic Psychologists

Regardless of the nature of the involuntary commitment (inpatient or outpatient and its variations), the assessment skills of forensic psychologists are required to help determine whether the individual meets the standards for commitment. If a showing of dangerousness is required, the psychologist again engages in the risk assessment enterprise we have discussed in earlier chapters. Melton et al. (1997, 2007) warn that this is an area where clinicians must exercise extreme caution, considering the inadequate legal representation provided to so many individuals and the potential loss of freedom they are encountering. Demonstrating the presence of mental illness and determining treatment needs of the individual are probably the easier of the clinician's tasks. The accompanying assessment of dangerousness (or risk) is more formidable. All of the cautions about risk assessment referred to in earlier chapters should be recalled here as well.

The individual's potential for dangerousness to self involves an assessment of suicide risk. Clinicians should be informed about general research on demographics of suicide (e.g., males at higher risk, married persons at lower risk) as well as the individual's own clinical history. Interviews with the individual also may uncover *suicide ideation,* or fantasies of killing oneself. Both the frequency and intensity of such ideations should be considered. However, as Melton et al. (1997, 2007) note, the track record of mental health professionals at predicting suicide is very poor. They urge clinicians to refer to the person's risk compared with others in the population rather than simply state that he or she is a danger to himself or herself.

Other Civil Disputes

It has become commonplace to state that we are a litigious society, seeking redress through the courts for a wide range of alleged wrongs done to us by others. There are a variety of ways in which we may approach the civil courts, including—but not limited to—a civil rights claim, a claim of a breach of contract, intellectual property claim (e.g., a patent case), a prisoner case, or a labor case (e.g., unfair labor practices). The most common civil suit is the **tort,** which is the legal term for a civil wrong in which a plaintiff alleges some negligence on the part of the defendant. Courts consider torts on such matters as defamation, invasion of privacy, toxic harm, and personal injury, to name but a few. The redress sought is typically some form of financial compensation. To be awarded damages, though, the plaintiff must be able to demonstrate some physical harm or mental injury as a result of the actions of the defendant. Mental injury may also be referred to as emotional distress, emotional harm, or psychic trauma. Although courts were initially reluctant to accept these claims of mental injury, they have become far more commonplace, "at least in part because of an increased willingness by courts to accept diagnosis and prognosis as legitimate skills" (Melton et al., 1997, p. 374). A plaintiff alleging emotional distress is subject to being evaluated not only by a clinician contacted by his or her lawyer, but also by a clinician hired by the defendant. In the usual case, the plaintiff hires the psychologist.

Psychologists also may be called as expert witnesses in these civil suits to testify more generally on the effects of the alleged wrong, without examining the plaintiff. For example, in a civil suit alleging discrimination on the basis of gender—a civil rights violation—a psychologist with research expertise on gender stereotyping may be called as an expert witness. As we noted in Chapter 4, researchers continue to examine the effects of the *Daubert* standard. Thus far, it appears that judges—particularly federal judges—are scrutinizing expert testimony more carefully and are rejecting more such testimony than they were in the years before the *Daubert* decision (see, generally, Studebaker & Goodman-Delahunty, 2002). How well judges are performing this gate-keeping function has yet to be determined, however (Dixon & Gill, 2002). It is interesting to note, though, that psychologists appear to be expert witnesses in a relatively small number of civil trials compared with other medical and mental health professionals. For example, Krafka, Dunn, Johnson, Cecil, and Miletich (2002) obtained information on 297 federal civil trials in 1998, involving 1,281 expert witnesses. Clinical psychologists comprised 3.4% of the total medical/mental health experts, and other medical/mental health experts (including research psychologists) comprised 14.8% of the total.

In the following section, we will discuss two additional areas in which forensic psychologists consult with civil courts. In both cases, psychologists are asked to evaluate claims of mental harm, often as the result of another individual's behavior.

Sexual Harassment

Sexual harassment may be broadly defined as unwelcome sexual advances, requests for sexual favors, and other verbal or physical conduct of a sexual nature (Hellkamp & Lewis, 1995; Till, 1980). Civil claims of sexual harassment arise most frequently in employment and educational contexts, where harassment qualifies as discrimination in violation of Title VII of the Civil Rights Acts of 1971.

Many people work in environments where "dirty jokes," innuendoes, sexual banter, or comments on a coworker's clothes are a regular occurrence, and some do not mind this. Others do mind but try to ignore them, or they put the offending individual in his or her place. One need only watch a few episodes of the popular show *Mad Men* for examples of each of these approaches—though the show is set in the early 1960s, before the era of social consciousness on this issue. Still other individuals find that a pattern of such conduct is so uncomfortable, interferes so much with work productivity, and produces so much emotional distress that they file complaints or leave the workplace. When inappropriate and harassing behaviors reach extremes, this is when the legal system is most likely to be brought into the picture.

For many years, the Supreme Court recognized two primary forms of sexual harassment: *quid pro quo* and hostile environment (*Meritor Savings Bank v. Vinson,* 1986), a distinction which is now disappearing despite its logic. In *quid pro quo* harassment, the offender uses his or her position of power to obtain sexual favors in exchange for something of presumed value to the victim. For example, a supervisor promises a promotion if the victim sleeps with him, or punishes the victim who refuses his advances by recommending a demotion. In hostile-environment harassment, the offender's actions have created an unacceptably negative environment that has made it difficult for normal work or social interaction to occur. In this second category, the offender may be a coworker or a supervisor.

To qualify as illegal, the behavior must be more than irritating or mildly offensive. It must be severe and pervasive, so much so that it alters conditions of the victim's employment (*Harris v. Forklift Systems, Inc.,* 1993). The conduct also must be objectively offensive—or offensive to a reasonable person—not just subjectively offensive to the plaintiff (*Harris v. Forklift Systems, Inc.,* 1993). Examples of such conduct from actual court cases include the following: a fellow worker posting pictures of erect penises on women's lockers; a supervisor ordering a clerk to reach into his pocket for change; constant repetition of extremely vulgar jokes, even after a request that these cease; consistent, noticeable ogling of a person's body, particularly focusing on women's breasts or the genital area; exposure or threatened exposure of one's genitals; licking the neck and arm of a fellow worker, while panting; and sending images of violent pornography and degradation of women via office computers.

Some courts prefer a "reasonable woman" standard on the premise that men might not understand the effects of sexual harassment on women. However, because men as well as women may be victims of sexual harassment, other courts use a "reasonable victim" standard. In a review of the legal standards applied in sexual harassment cases, Goodman-Delahunty (1999a) maintains that the reasonable victim standard avoids gender bias and is most reflective of the spirit of sexual harassment law. Finally, although plaintiffs typically seek compensation for mental anguish and pain and suffering (e.g., anger, anxiety, loss of self-esteem, fear, or feelings of humiliation), extensive psychological harm need not be demonstrated for a plaintiff to prevail (*Harris v. Forklift Systems, Inc.,* 1993). In other words, the Supreme Court has recognized that some victims of sexual harassment may experience its negative effects without also experiencing debilitating psychological deterioration.

Psychologists have a variety of tasks to perform relating to sexual harassment. They may consult with employers in setting up educational programs on the topic, including providing information on the effects on victims. They may also offer counseling services to victims of harassment. In the present chapter, we discuss their role in civil suits. Either side—plaintiff or defendant—might hire a psychologist to evaluate the claims of emotional distress made by the plaintiff. The psychologist is also asked to address the question of whether the particular behavior of the defendant, if it did occur, could reasonably lead to the mental injury experienced by the plaintiff. In these examinations, the evaluator is asked not only to document the disorder, but also to eliminate other possible sources that are unrelated to the alleged harassment. Both clinical and research psychologists also might be called as expert witnesses to testify on gender stereotyping or on the general psychological effects of sexual harassment. In the sexual harassment context as well as other contexts (e.g., custody evaluations), psychologists are warned to avoid dual relationships in which they both serve as evaluators or expert witnesses *and* offer treatment (Heilbrun et al., 2002; Hellkamp & Lewis, 1995).

In sexual harassment suits, the alleged victim may be compelled to undergo a psychological or psychiatric evaluation at the request of the defendant. Compelled examinations occur when the plaintiff claims any more than ordinary distress as a result of the harassment. For example, she may claim that the actions of the defendant not only were irritating or embarrassing but also caused a mental disorder, such as a major depressive disorder (Kovera & Cass, 2002) or PTSD. In compelled evaluations, the defendant asks the court to order an evaluation by a clinician contacted by his or her attorney. The defendant must show good cause for why the plaintiff should undergo it. Kovera and Cass note that courts tend to deny motions for a compelled examination if the disorder occurred in the past rather than being current. Furthermore, "simply claiming emotional damages does not put one's mental health into controversy and thus does not warrant a compelled mental health examination" (p. 99). Rather, motions are more likely to be granted if the plaintiff meets a number of criteria, such as claiming *severe* disorder and signifying intent to put forth her or his own expert to substantiate any claims. A compelled evaluation is likely to open the way for a psychologist to gain information about sexual history, including sexual abuse, and this information is then made available to the opposing party. Shortly, we will explain why this is so controversial. As in all evaluations, then, it is critical that the examining clinician inform the person being evaluated of the potential use of the report.

Psychological Measures of Sexual Harassment

The dominant instrument for assessing sexual harassment from the perspective of the alleged victim is the **Sexual Experiences Questionnaire (SEQ)** (Fitzgerald & Shullman, 1985), which has developed with updated versions (e.g., Fizgerald, Magley, Drasgow, & Waldo, 1999). The SEQ has been referred to as "the most theoretically and psychometrically sophisticated instrument available for assessing incidence and prevalence of sexual harassment" (Cortina, 2001, p. 165). Despite this comment, it is important to emphasize that, for legal purposes, the mental health practitioner does not decide whether sexual harassment occurred in a particular case. Furthermore, some researchers are more guarded in their appraisal of the SEQ: "As a measure of the psychological definition of sexual harassment, the SEQ has been shown to be a reliable and valid assessment of unwanted social-sexual workplace treatment, which generally (but not legally) conforms to the construct of sexual harassment" (Stockdale, Logan, & Weston, 2009).

The SEQ lists 29 specific behaviors and asks respondents whether they have ever experienced them on a scale of *never* to *often*. Five types of harassment are measured: gender harassment, seductive behavior, sexual bribery, sexual coercion, and sexual imposition.

As with the great majority of instruments described in this text, the SEQ was developed from research focusing almost exclusively on White participants. Although acknowledging the usefulness of the SEQ, several researchers have noted that research on sexual harassment does not sufficiently take into consideration differences in ethnic and cultural norms that might affect non-White victims. J. H. Adams (1997) argued persuasively that sexual harassment of Blacks is reflective of both sex and race discrimination and that it perpetuates both gender and racial stereotypes. Cortina (2001) notes that Latinas might be more likely than non-Latinas to take offense at unwanted sex-related behavior in the workplace because of cultural norms emphasizing respect, dignity, and harmony in in-group relations. On the other hand, those Latinas who emigrated from countries where sexual harassment is more accepted might interpret fewer of the behaviors on the SEQ as harassing behaviors. After conducting focus group interviews with Latina working women, Cortina added new items to the SEQ (SEQ-L) to assess behaviors that were particularly relevant to Latina experiences. For example, focus group interviews suggested that the Latina women were offended by being addressed informally in Spanish when a more formal mode of address was expected and by being called Spanish pet names. They were also offended when someone stood too close or expected them to behave in certain ways *because of their ethnicity* (e.g., as a Latina, she was expected to wear sexy clothes). None of these behaviors were included in the original SEQ.

We have only touched the surface of the rapidly developing research on ethnic and race differences in attitudes and responses to sexual harassment. Clearly, though, it is incumbent on forensic psychologists working with culturally diverse groups to be aware of these findings and to be sensitive to between-group differences.

Private Life Issues in Sexual Harassment Cases

One controversial aspect of sexual harassment suits involves the private life of the victim, particularly her sexual history. Some defendants have argued that a plaintiff who has an active sex life with multiple partners is unlikely to be offended by their behavior, despite the fact that research does not support this assumption (Kovera & Cass, 2002). Although many states have passed "rape shield laws" to protect victims of rape from having their sexual history exposed in court, such protections are rarely available to plaintiffs in sexual harassment suits if their history is part of the psychological record (Kovera & Cass, 2002). Thus, when psychologists evaluate plaintiffs in sexual harassment suits, particularly when the examination is a compelled one, they should be aware that information about the plaintiff's sexual past could be appropriated by the defense and used to its advantage. This is not to suggest that defendants in sexual harassment suits should not have resources to defend themselves against false claims; rather, it is to emphasize that anyone, regardless of sexual history, can be subjected to hostile environments and unwelcome sexual advances.

Defendants also have argued that victims who were prior victims of sexual assault or domestic violence might be hypersensitive to social situations involving sexual overtones. This hypersensitivity, they say, results in an aversion to even the most benign interactions. Some psychologists agree, maintaining that prior abuse alters the perceptions of victims and leaves them susceptible to revictimization as adults. In arguing against this perspective, other researchers point out that there is no empirical evidence that many victims of sexual harassment were victims of past abuse (Fitzgerald, Buchanan, Collinsworth, Magley, & Ramos, 1999). Furthermore, even if they were victims of such abuse, reviews of the literature (e.g., Stockdale, O'Connor, Gutek, & Geer, 2002) indicate that there is no strong and consistent relationship between past victimization and attitudes and perceptions about sexual harassment, although some studies do show a relationship. Stockdale et al. (2002) conducted a series of studies in which participants were provided with written scenarios or videos of a sexual harassment case. Those who reported prior abuse did not differ significantly from those who did not in their perceptions of the validity of the claim. Stockdale et al. concluded that, on the basis of the available research, it is unwarranted to make assumptions about plaintiffs or jurors in sexual harassment cases who may have experienced prior sexual abuse. This research is obviously of import to forensic psychologists, particularly those who interview plaintiffs or help attorneys select jurors in sexual harassment cases.

Another area of intense interest is the presence of PTSD in victims of sexual harassment. It is not unusual for someone seeking damages for sexual harassment to put forth that diagnosis—or at least symptoms of PTSD—in support of her or his claims. Reviewing the literature, Stockdale et al. (2009) note that many studies document symptoms of PTSD in victims of sexual harassment. However, they also note that some researchers have contended that PTSD or its symptoms could be a result of prior experiences, such as child sexual abuse or intimate partner violence. In an effort to shed light on this issue, Stockdale et al. studied 445 women who were part of a larger study on abuse and whose responses on a variety of measures indicated that they had experienced behaviors that would qualify as workplace harassment. The women had sought orders of protection from abuse but were not involved in sexual harassment litigation. They were interviewed and administered surveys, but questions about experiences with harassment were not salient, suggesting that they had little to gain by exaggerating symptoms. Controlling for prior trauma, prior abuse, prior psychological functioning, and prior PTSD, Stockdale et al. found that symptoms of PTSD were evident in women who had been subjected to serious harassment and were severe enough for a diagnosis of PTSD. They concluded,

> for those women (or men) who are litigating their claims of sexual harassment, this study sheds doubt on the assumption that claims of PTSD should be dismissed if evidence of prior trauma or prior psychological dysfunction is produced. Indeed our findings lend credibility to their claims of emotional and psychological damages due to sexual harassment. (p. 415)

Employment Compensation and Personal Injury Claims

Employment compensation laws were passed to avoid extensive tort actions on the part of employees who were injured in the course of their work. In passing these laws, Congress and state legislatures also recognized the formidable task faced by the injured worker pitted against his or her powerful employer. Under tort law, the employee would have to prove some fault on the part of the employer. This was a long, involved process that rarely resulted in a successful claim and often left the worker and his or her family in poverty (Melton et al., 1997). Under the employment compensation system, employers agree to insure their workers, and workers agree not to seek the greater compensation that they might possibly achieve if they filed a civil suit and succeeded in proving some negligence on the part of the employer.

Although **employment compensation claims** involve physical injuries, psychic injury or emotional distress is also typically asserted. To use a hypothetical example, Jason is employed by a roofing company that often repairs roofs that were damaged by severe weather conditions. While replacing shingles on a roof that is three stories high, Jason is caught by a wind gust and swept off the roof, suffering extensive back injuries. In addition to this physical injury, Jason claims extreme emotional distress that includes fear of heights manifested in an inability to climb ladders, take escalators, or accompany his 10-year-old son on a skiing chairlift. Note that Jason is not claiming that his employer was at fault for dispatching him to repair the roof on a high-wind day. He is merely stating that he should be compensated for his lost wages, the physical and neurological effects of the fall (e.g., debilitating back pain, recurring headaches), and the life changes necessitated by his fear of heights.

Evaluations of mental injury—both psychological and neurological harm—also occur in a wide variety of personal injury litigation that is not necessarily employment related. For example, mental health is included in "pain and suffering" and "emotional distress" claims by individuals who were injured in car accidents, in a fall in a neighbor's yard, or by a cup of excessively hot coffee served by a fast-food chain. Plaintiffs also claim psychological and neurological harm from exposure to environmental contaminants or from defective products.

Melton et al. (1997) state that evaluations of mental injury have many similarities to the inquiry into the mental state at the time of the offense (MSO), which we covered in Chapter 5. Like MSO evaluations, they are retrospective and complex. However, mental injury evaluations are also *prospective,* in the sense that they must make some judgment about the plaintiff's future functioning: Will the plaintiff be able to function as he or she functioned prior to the claim? In the case of employment compensation claims, what is the extent of the loss in earning capacity suffered by the plaintiff?

As in other mental injury claims, the psychologist is advised to gather an extensive store of information in an attempt to compare the past and present functioning of the individual as well as project into the future. If the injury is work related, all information pertinent to the workplace is relevant to the inquiry. Melton et al. (1997) point out that personality inventories are helpful, particularly if they can be compared with inventories taken before the injury occurred. In addition, they remind the psychologist to investigate the extent of physical injury, using neurological tests if needed, in addition to mental injury. Furthermore, the evaluator should be attuned to the possibility of posttraumatic stress disorder.

In a summary article on personality assessment in personal injury litigation, Butcher and Miller (1999) suggest that the Minnesota Multiphasic Personality Inventory (MMPI-2) is superior to any other specific inventories because it can be interpreted objectively and can differentiate between persons with mental health problems and those who are not psychologically disturbed. They caution, however, that a psychological test cannot determine whether a person's physical injuries are based on organic conditions or derive from personality factors. And, of course, without the results of a test administered prior to the injury, the forensic psychologist cannot assess how the individual's pre-injury personality might influence his or her current functioning. The psychologist can, though, "provide indication of the severity and long-term stability of the individual's problems" (Butcher & Miller, 1999, p. 110).

As we noted in Chapter 5, malingering and the exaggeration of symptoms have received considerable attention in the research literature (e.g., Gothard et al., 1995; Mossman, 2003; Rogers, 1997). In all mental injury evaluations, psychologists and other clinicians must be concerned about the possibility that the individual being evaluated is "faking" the symptoms he or she is claiming, or presenting them as being much worse than they are. Butcher and Miller (1999) emphasize that there is no foolproof way to assess malingering, although the MMPI-2 appears to have valid indicators. Continued research is needed, however, before firm conclusions can be drawn.

Butcher and Miller (1999) also advise the evaluator to be extremely conscious of the role of the individual's lawyer: "One of the most problematic factors encountered in forensic assessment is the tendency of many attorneys to guide their clients through a desired strategy for responding to psychological test items" (p. 110). They advise clinicians to try to determine whether the individual has been "coached" by the lawyer and the extent and nature of the coaching. Basically, the individual should be asked what he or she has been told. The final report should reflect how this coaching might have affected the results of the examination.

After a comprehensive discussion of mental injury evaluations, Melton et al. (1997) conclude with three general points about communicating with the courts relevant to these assessments. First, they urge clinicians to not rely overly on diagnoses because these will not explain why a particular individual reacted in a particular way to the particular events. Second, they emphasize that a longitudinal history of the impairment, its treatments, and efforts at rehabilitation is necessary. Third, they maintain that conclusory information should be avoided. Clinicians should provide descriptive reports of their findings but allow the legal decision makers to decide the critical legal question of whether the plaintiff should be compensated.

SUMMARY AND CONCLUSIONS

As we have stated throughout these early chapters, there is no shortage of tasks for forensic psychologists to perform in a given context. Consultation with the civil courts is no exception. In this chapter, we have attempted to provide a representative sampling, but several areas were left untouched or only lightly addressed. For example, forensic psychologists participate in a wide variety of personal injury litigation and disability evaluations other than the employment compensation claims that were highlighted here. Likewise, they participate in discrimination suits other than sexual harassment, such as race, age, disability, and gender discrimination in both employment and non-employment situations. They perform assessments of families and of children at risk in child protection proceedings. They evaluate children who have allegedly been sexually abused and whose parents wish to file civil charges against the alleged perpetrators. These and numerous other areas have contributed to making forensic psychology the exciting and growing field that it is.

Consultation with the juvenile courts is an area that has been heavily researched; consequently, we covered this in some detail. Traditionally rehabilitation oriented, the juvenile courts today resemble criminal courts in many ways, although rehabilitation is still a primary focus. Psychologists have a major role to play in assessing the extent to which juveniles are amenable to rehabilitation—but just as important, it is incumbent on them to avoid pessimism, to be aware of available programs, and to suggest alternative approaches. Negative—and possibly invalid—labels should be avoided. These labels may prompt prosecutors or judges to transfer juveniles to criminal courts or encourage staff of juvenile facilities to expend less energy on juveniles who may be perceived as hopeless.

Psychologists also have an important role to play in assessing whether juveniles understood the consequences of waiving their constitutional rights. The adjudicative competence of juveniles is heavily researched, with recent studies suggesting that juveniles as a group have considerable deficiency in both understanding their rights and being able to fully participate in juvenile proceedings. With this knowledge, it is critical for forensic psychologists to pay attention to the lawyer–juvenile relationship, as well as the parent–child relationship, in juvenile cases.

Child custody evaluations are among the most controversial for forensic psychologists. They are emotionally laden, have engendered ethics complaints, and raise numerous questions as to what is the proper standard for making custody decisions. A major concern in this area is the instruments that are sometimes used to assess parental abilities because few have been submitted to empirical validation. Furthermore, because there is no one clearly identified preferred custody arrangement, psychologists must be cautious about research that suggests one form of custody is superior to the other.

The chapter included discussion of involuntary civil commitment, most particularly commitment to outpatient treatment. This form of commitment is increasing in virtually every state, but it raises important questions about the civil liberties of individuals who would otherwise not be eligible for institutional confinement. Many forensic psychologists are supportive of this form of commitment, primarily because it allows individuals to receive needed treatment in a community setting. Thus far, research on treatment effectiveness has demonstrated positive results, particularly if the treatment continues beyond a 6-month period and is accompanied by intensive services.

We covered a variety of contexts in which decisional competencies might be assessed. Chief among these is the competency to make medical and legal decisions. Of particular concern, however, is the problem encountered when individuals are incapacitated and unable to make decisions in their own interest. A different problem relates to an individual's decision to hasten his or her death. Oregon has pioneered legislation allowing individuals to request the assistance of physicians in this matter, an approach that has prompted the need for psychological evaluations of whether the individual is mentally competent to request such assistance.

We ended the chapter with discussion of research and issues relating to sexual harassment and mental injury claims. Evaluations of persons who bring sexual harassment claims—particularly compelled evaluations—should be done with extreme caution. Although a number of inventories, including the SEQ, are available, they are just beginning to address the perceptions and experiences of different cultural groups. Furthermore, a controversial aspect of sexual harassment evaluations is the relevance of information about the private life of the person who has allegedly been harassed. Relatedly, when PTSD is said to occur as a result of the harassment, defense attorneys may argue that the trauma was more the result of early abuse than the more recent harassment. Psychological research indicates, though, that PTSD is not an unlikely consequence of sexual harassment, even when no prior abuse has occurred.

KEY CONCEPTS

Advance directives

Amenability to rehabilitation

Best interest of child standard (BICS)

Content analysis

Decisional competency

Disposition

Ecological validity

Employment compensation claims

Family forensic psychology

Houses of Refuge

Involuntary civil commitment

Judicial waivers

Least detrimental alternative standard

Legislative waiver/statutory exclusion or waiver by statute

MacArthur Competence Assessment Tool—Treatment (MacCAT-T)

MacArthur Juvenile Competence Study

Miranda rights

Outpatient treatment orders

Parens patriae

Petitions

Preventive outpatient treatment

Prosecutorial waiver

Sexual Experiences Questionnaire (SEQ)

Sexual harassment

Tender years doctrine

Testamentary capacity

Tort

QUESTIONS FOR REVIEW

1. Summarize the positive and negative features of juvenile courts from the turn of the 20th century to the 1960s.

2. State the significance of *U.S. v. Kent* and *In re Gault* for juveniles charged with crime.

3. What type of information is commonly gathered in a juvenile assessment?

4. What has research uncovered about the ability of juveniles to understand *Miranda* rights?

5. List at least five findings from the MacArthur Juvenile Competence Study.

6. Compare and contrast the various forms of "waiving" juveniles to criminal courts.

7. Provide three findings from the research literature on custody evaluations and the effects of custody arrangements on children.

8. Provide illustrations of when a forensic psychologist might be asked to assess competence to consent to treatment.

9. What are three different forms of outpatient civil commitment?

10. What is the role of the forensic psychologist in evaluating mental injury and sexual harassment cases?

Part IV

Criminal Psychology

7

The
Development
of Delinquent
and Criminal
Behavior

CHAPTER OBJECTIVES

- Define criminal behavior and juvenile delinquency.
- Define antisocial behavior, conduct disorder, and antisocial personality disorder.
- Review the offenses for which juveniles are most frequently charged.
- Review the developmental approach to criminal behavior.
- Summarize theories of Terrie Moffett, Gerald Patterson, and Laurence Steinberg.
- Identify developmental factors most relevant to criminal behavior.
- Identify psychological factors associated with school violence.
- Specify the relationship between ADHD and delinquency.
- Identify those fire-setting behaviors that are precursors to offending.
- Review research on adult psychopathy and juveniles with psychopathic characteristics.

Crime can be defined as "an intentional act in violation of the criminal law committed without defense or excuse, and penalized by the state as a felony or misdemeanor" (Tappan, 1947, p. 100). In other words, criminal behavior is intentional behavior that violates a criminal code—it did not occur accidentally, and the person's action cannot be justified (e.g., self-defense) or excused (e.g., insanity). To be held criminally responsible, a person must have known what he or she was doing during the criminal act and know that it was wrong under the law. To convict someone of a criminal offense, the prosecution (the government) generally must prove that the defendant committed a *voluntary act* (*actus reus*) intentionally, or with a *guilty* state of mind (*mens rea*). The statute defining the offense will specify what actions and what mental states (together called "elements") constitute a particular crime (La Fond, 2002). If a case goes to trial, the judge or jury can convict the defendant only if the prosecutor proves all elements beyond a reasonable doubt (The burdens of proof were outlined in Focus 5.2 in Chapter 5.). However, if a defendant pleads guilty, the prosecutor is spared the burden of doing so, and a conviction is still entered on the record.

The spectrum of criminal behavior is extremely wide, ranging from minor offenses like criminal trespass to murder. In recent years, the public has become much more aware of corporate and political crimes, categories of offenses that have long captured the interests of criminologists who believe that extensive harm can be perpetrated by those holding extreme wealth or political power. Major corporations, such as Enron (a dominant energy leader), WorldCom (a telecommunications giant), Global Crossing (worldwide computer networking services), and others were involved in serious accounting improprieties that misled and betrayed investors. In the case of Enron, the wrongdoing affected the retirement, security, and jobs of its employees. Fraud in the banking industry, insider trading, violations of human rights, and corruption among public officials are examples of other criminal offenses that began to receive more public attention at the turn of the 21st century.

Although many people from all socioeconomic groups break laws, only a small percentage become persistent offenders who commit numerous serious crimes, including crimes of a violent nature. An even smaller group commits the unusual, high-profile crimes that gain media attention, such as the individual who opens fire on his fellow workers. Because psychologists have been particularly interested in studying these two groups, we focus on them in the text. In the present chapter, we discuss people who demonstrate a habitual, persistent offending history of committing serious crimes. We will especially concentrate on those offenders who often lead a *lifelong* criminal career of engaging in a wide variety of criminal offenses. Good examples of repetitive, chronic offenders are the life course–persistent offender discussed in the following section on juvenile delinquency and the psychopath, discussed later in the chapter. In Chapters 8 and 9, we will narrow our focus to crimes involving sexual assault, intimidation, and violence, such as murder, stalking, hate crime, and arson—again, crimes that lend themselves particularly well to psychological research and theory.

The purpose of the present chapter is to provide an overview of criminal behavior, with a focus on the developmental factors that are involved in the formation of serious or repetitive criminal behavior. Empirical research indicates that persistent antisocial behavior does not *usually* begin in adulthood but rather quite early in life, with signs sometimes appearing even during the preschool years (Moffitt, 1993a, 1993b). Consequently, the best place to start is by examining the developmental trajectory of the emerging juvenile offender.

It is important to avoid the temptation to seize on one cause or single explanation of crime, though. Although "the crime problem" *as a whole* can be attributed to any number of broad societal factors—racism, poverty, glorification of violence, sexism, and the availability of handguns are examples—the cause of a *given individual's* criminal behavior is unlikely to be unidimensional. The causes of crime and delinquency are multiple, complex, and probably result mostly from some complicated interaction of several influences.

The Juvenile Offender

Definition of Juvenile Delinquency

Juvenile delinquency is an imprecise, social, clinical, and legal label for a broad spectrum of law- and norm-violating behavior. At first glance, a simple legal definition appears to be adequate: *Delinquency is behavior against the criminal code committed by an individual who has not reached adulthood.* But the term *delinquency* has numerous definitions and meanings beyond this one-sentence definition. In some states, the legal definition also includes status offending, which is not behavior against the "adult" criminal code but is behavior prohibited *only* for juveniles. For example, running away, violating curfew laws, and truancy all qualify as **status offenses.**

In addition, social, legal, and psychological definitions of delinquency overlap considerably. Social definitions of delinquency encompass a broad gamut of youthful behaviors considered inappropriate, and not all are technically crimes. These youthful behaviors include aggressive actions, truancy, petty theft, vandalism, drug abuse, sexual promiscuity, and even incorrigibility. The behavior may or may not have come to the attention of the police and, in fact, often does not. If the behavior is known to the police, it is not unusual for "social delinquents" to be referred to community social service agencies or to juvenile courts, but these youth do not qualify for the legal definition of delinquent unless they are found at a court hearing to have committed the crime for which they are charged. Therefore, *legally speaking,* a **juvenile delinquent** is one who commits an act against the criminal code *and who is adjudicated delinquent by an appropriate court.* The legal definition is usually restricted to persons younger than age 18, but states vary in their age distinctions. A handful of states give criminal courts, rather than juvenile courts, automatic jurisdiction over juveniles at age 16. Furthermore, all states allow juveniles to be tried as adults in criminal courts under certain conditions and for certain offenses.

Psychological or *psychiatric* definitions of delinquency include the symptom-based labels of "conduct disorder" or "antisocial behavior." **Conduct disorder** (often abbreviated CD) is a diagnostic designation used to represent a group of behaviors characterized by *habitual* misbehavior, such as stealing, setting fires, running away from home, skipping school, destroying property, fighting, being cruel to animals and people, and frequently telling lies. Under this definition—like the social definition discussed above—the "delinquent" may or may not have been arrested for these behaviors, and some are not even against the criminal law. CD is described more fully in the fourth edition of the American Psychiatric Association's (1994) *Diagnostic and Statistical Manual of Mental Disorders,* commonly referred to as the *DSM-IV,* and the more recent, slightly modified version of the manual, referred to as the *DSM-IV-TR* (American Psychiatric Association, 2000). The *TR* stands for "text revision." A fifth revision of the *DSM* (*DSM-V*) is scheduled for release in May 2013. The *DSM* is regarded as a decision-making tool for clinicians and as a guidepost for researchers (Moffitt et al., 2008).

The more psychological term *antisocial behavior* is usually reserved for more serious habitual misbehavior, which involves actions that are directly harmful to the well-being of others. It is to be distinguished, however, from **antisocial personality disorder (ASP, or APD),** a psychiatric diagnostic label reserved primarily for *adults* at least 18 years of age who displayed conduct disorders as children or adolescents and who continue serious offending well into adulthood.

Although psychologists use the terms conduct disorder and antisocial behavior, a growing number of them describe and try to understand crime and delinquency through developmental, cognitive, and even biopsychological processes. For example, Terrie Moffitt's (1993a) theory explains crime from a developmental perspective, and Robert Hare's (1996) concept of criminal psychopathy offers an intriguing delineation of the emotional, cognitive, and biopsychological factors involved in repetitive, serious offending over a lifetime. As we discuss later in the chapter, Hare and his followers believe that there are fundamental differences in brain functioning between the true psychopath and the "normal" population. More recently, Laurence Steinberg and his colleagues (Steinberg, 2007; Steinberg, Cauffman, Woolard, Graham, & Banich, 2009; Steinberg & Monahan, 2007) have gathered revealing scientific evidence on adolescent cognitive and psychosocial development and how these relate to decision making, peer influence, and impulsivity. We will review each of these perspectives shortly.

The Nature and Extent of Juvenile Offending

The amount of delinquent behavior—both what is reported and what is unreported to law enforcement agencies—is essentially an unknown area. We simply do not have complete data on the incidence of juvenile delinquency, broadly defined. However, although incomplete, we do have some statistics collected by law enforcement agencies, the courts, and juvenile correctional facilities.

Unlawful acts committed by juveniles can be divided into five major categories:

1. Unlawful acts against persons

2. Unlawful acts against property

3. Drug offenses

4. Offenses against the public order

5. Status offenses

Juvenile courts in the United States handled an estimated 1.66 million delinquency cases in 2007, which averages 4,600 cases per day (Puzzanchera, Adams, & Sickmund, 2010). In addition, approximately 31 million youths are under some form of juvenile court jurisdiction in any given year, with 79% of them being between the ages of 10 and 15 (Puzzanchera et al., 2010). In 2008, approximately 81,000 juveniles were in residential placement in publicly or privately operated juvenile facilities (Sickmund, 2010). Recent data indicate that 23% of the cases handled by juvenile courts concerned person offenses (violent offenses), 39% of the cases were property offenses, 12% dealt with drug law violations, and 26% were public order offenses (Puzzanchera, Stahl, Finnegan, Tierney, & Snyder, 2004). Public order offenses include obstruction of justice, disorderly conduct, weapons offenses, liquor law offenses, and nonviolent sex offenses such as lewd behavior. Many of the crimes committed by adolescents are done in groups or youth gangs.

The first four categories listed above are comparable in definition to crimes committed by adults. **Status offenses,** on the other hand, are acts that only juveniles can commit and that can be adjudicated only by a juvenile court. As discussed earlier, typical status offenses range from misbehavior, such as violations of curfew, underage drinking, running away from home, and truancy, to offenses that are interpreted very subjectively, such as unruliness and ungovernability (beyond the control of parents or guardians). The most common status offenses referred by law enforcement agencies are underage drinking (92%), running away from home (40%), ungovernability (11%), and truancy (10%) (Sickmund, 2003).

The juvenile justice system historically has supported differential treatment of male and female status offenders. Adolescent girls, for example, have often been detained for incorrigibility or running away from home, while the same behavior in adolescent boys was ignored or tolerated. In recent years, as a result of suits brought on behalf of juveniles, many courts have put authorities on notice that this discriminatory approach is unwarranted. For example, the arrest rate for status offenses of runaways is now about equal for girls and boys (Puzzanchera, 2009; Snyder, 2008). The reasons they run away, though, are often different.

Youth crime data are collected from a mixture of sources: (1) official records of police arrests, such as the FBI's Uniform Crime Reports (UCR); (2) reports from victims, such as the National Crime Victimization Survey (NCVS); (3) self-reports of delinquent involvement, in which national samples of youth are asked to complete questionnaires about their own behavior, such as in the National Youth Survey (Elliott, Ageton, & Huizinga, 1980) and Monitoring the Future (MTF); (4) juvenile court processing, as reported by the National Center for Juvenile Justice (NCJJ); (5) juvenile corrections, as reported in the monograph *Children in Custody (CIC)*; and

(6) probation and parole statistics, as reported in various governmental publications. The last three sources of information have the major disadvantage of greatly underestimating the number of actual offenses because, even more than in the criminal system, a very high proportion—perhaps a majority—of cases are either undetected or dismissed before reaching the courts. In other words, because of parental involvement, negotiations, and community programs, many offenders are diverted before they go to juvenile court. To add to the problem of obtaining statistics on juvenile offenders, juvenile court dockets do not always reflect serious offending. Referrals by parents, schools, probation officers, and other courts, either for status offenses or for supervision, make up much of a court's delinquency workload. Because of this confusion, perhaps the most complete official nationwide compilation of juvenile offenses today remains the FBI's UCR. Consequently, we will touch briefly on the juvenile offending data as presented in this document. Knowledge about the UCR will be useful in discussing adult crime as well.

The Uniform Crime Reports

The FBI's UCR, first compiled in 1930, is the most frequently cited source of U.S. crime statistics. The UCR is an annual document containing accounts of crime *known to law enforcement* agencies across the country, as well as *arrests*. The UCR does not include conviction data; it is strictly law enforcement information and does not tell us anything about whether individuals arrested were found guilty. The UCR is available on the FBI website at www.fbi.gov.

The UCR divides crimes in several ways, including by age, gender, and race of persons arrested, as well as by city and region of the country. The two major divisions of serious crimes are classified as violent crimes and property crimes. The four offenses that qualify as violent are (1) murder and nonnegligent manslaughter, (2) forcible rape, (3) robbery, and (4) aggravated assault. The four offenses that qualify as property are (1) burglary, (2) larceny-theft, (3) motor vehicle theft, and (4) arson. Table 7.1 illustrates the distribution of juvenile arrests for these offenses for 2008.

Table 7.1   Juvenile Arrests for Violent and Property Crimes, 2008

Offense Charged	Total Arrests, All Ages	Under Age 18	Under Age 10
Total	1,762,590	413,960	2,814
Violent crimes	457,455	73,970	469
Murder	9,888	974	1
Forcible rape	16,916	2,505	8
Robbery	100,738	27,522	61
Aggravated assault	329,913	42,969	399
Property crimes	1,305,135	339,990	2,345
Burglary	236,219	64,418	554
Larceny-theft	982,997	251,483	1,480
Motor vehicle theft	75,135	19,068	20
Arson	10,784	5,021	291

Source: Federal Bureau of Investigation (2009).

The UCR is not the sole method of recording police data on reported crimes and arrests. Since 1989, the FBI has collected data through the National Incident-Based Reporting System (NIBRS). The NIBRS collects data on crime incidents and arrests within 22 categories. For each offense known to law enforcement within these categories, incident, victim, property, offender, and arrestee information are gathered when available. The goal of the NIBRS is to modernize crime information and address many of the shortcomings that had been identified in the UCR.

Nationally, juveniles made up about 15% of the persons arrested in the United States during 2008. They were arrested for 16% of the violent crime and 26% of the property crime (FBI, 2009). It should also be emphasized that crime and arrest rates move in cycles, often due to the social, economic, and political climates that occur within a society at any given time. Therefore, although rates have decreased in recent years, they may—for a variety of reasons—also suddenly increase in future years.

One point needs to be made clear at the outset: A small percentage of offenders are responsible for a large proportion of the total crimes committed (M. R. Chaiken, 2000; Coid, 2003). In any given population, the most persistent 5 or 6% of offenders are responsible for at least 50 to 60% of known crimes (Farrington, Ohlin, & Wilson, 1986; Lynam, 1997). On the other hand, it is also important to note that many reported serious offenses never result in a police contact (Bartol, 2002). Self-report surveys—those in which people report their own offending—suggest that serious, repetitive juvenile offenders escape detection about 86% of the time (Elliott, Dunford, & Huizinga, 1987). These figures clearly indicate that measures of juvenile offending substantially underestimate the overall juvenile crime rate, although the adult crime rate is underestimated as well, because many crimes committed by adults are not reported to police. Finally, frequent offenders usually do not specialize in any one particular kind of offending, such as theft, larceny, or drug trafficking. Instead, they tend to be involved in a wide variety of offenses, ranging from minor property crimes to highly violent acts.

The Developmental Perspective

Over the past three decades, the contemporary study of crime and delinquency has adopted a developmental perspective. If we follow groups of individuals from birth to adulthood, we learn a great deal about how antisocial behavior develops (Hartup, 2005). There is solid research evidence, for example, that serious, persistent delinquency patterns and adult criminality begin in early childhood, and some signs even can be seen during the preschool years. Researchers have discovered discernible differences between young children who ultimately became serious delinquents and those who did not. For example, there are differences in childhood experiences, biological and genetic predispositions, social skills, and expressions of feelings for others. The emerging developmental approach emphasizes the neurological, biological, mental, emotional, and social influences on children and how these in turn may affect the emergence of delinquency and adult criminal behavior.

Perhaps the most fruitful approach is to conceptualize development as following a path or trajectory. Research has strongly supported the hypothesis that people follow different developmental pathways in their offending or non-offending histories. Some youth, for example, engage in defiant and disobedient behavior at very young ages, and this sometimes progresses into more severe forms of violence and criminal behavior during adolescence and young adulthood (Dahlberg & Potter, 2001). Other youth display early signs of cruelty to animals, bullying, firesetting, and substance abuse, and these behavioral patterns continue well into adulthood. Many young people display very few signs of antisocial behavior during their childhood, but participate in some vandalism, theft, alcohol consumption, and drug experimentation during adolescence. Developmental theory has clearly been the most instrumental in identifying and documenting the various developmental pathways related to antisocial behavior.

The Moffitt Theory

Seminal research conducted by Terrie Moffitt (1993a, 1993b) indicated that delinquency could be best under-stood if we view it as progressing along at least two developmental paths. Because the Moffitt theory is one of the dominant theories in the psychology of crime and delinquency today, it is important that we cover it in some detail. We must emphasize at the outset that, although most of Moffitt's research identifies the *two* paths that will be covered below, more recent research by Moffitt and many other scholars strongly suggests that a two-path theory is not sufficient. However, it is a good place to begin.

On one path, we see a child developing a lifelong trajectory of delinquency and crime beginning at a very early age, probably around 3 or even younger. Moffitt (1993a) reports that

> across the life course, these individuals exhibit changing manifestations of antisocial behavior: biting and hitting at age four, shoplifting and truancy at age ten, selling drugs and stealing cars at age sixteen, robbery and rape at age 22, and fraud and child abuse at age 30. (p. 679)

These individuals, whom Moffitt calls **life course–persistent offenders** (**LCPs**), continue their antisocial ways across all kinds of conditions and situations. The occasional hitting by a 4-year-old is not cause for concern; if it persists, though, it may be. Moffitt (1993a, 1993b) finds that many LCPs exhibit neurological problems during their childhoods, such as difficult temperaments as infants, attention deficit disorders *or* hyperactivity in elementary school, and additional learning problems during their later school years. Some of these neurological problems are present before or soon after birth. These same children may develop judgment and problem-solving deficiencies that become apparent when they reach adulthood.

LCPs generally commit a wide assortment of aggressive and violent crimes over their lifetimes. Moreover, LCPs as children miss opportunities to acquire and practice prosocial and interpersonal skills at each stage of development. This is partly because they are rejected and avoided by their childhood peers and partly because their parents and other caretakers become frustrated and give up on them (Coie, Belding, & Underwood, 1988; Coie, Dodge, & Kupersmith, 1990; Moffitt, 1993a). Furthermore, disadvantaged living conditions, inadequate schools, and violent neighborhoods are factors that are very likely to exacerbate the ongoing and developing antisocial behavioral pattern. Based on available data, the number of LCPs in the male juvenile offender popu-lation is estimated to be somewhere between 5 and 10% (Moffitt, Caspi, Dickson, Silva, & Stanton, 1996). "Less than 10% of males should show extreme antisocial behavior that begins during early childhood and is thereaf-ter sustained at a high level across time and across circumstances, throughout childhood and adolescence" (Moffitt, 1993a, p. 694). Less than 2% of females can be classified as early starters in a persistent career of crime (Coid, 2003).

The great majority of "delinquents" are those individuals who take a second path: They *begin* offending during their adolescent years and *stop* offending somewhere around their 18th birthday. In essence, these ado-lescent delinquent behaviors arise from peer and social environmental factors, and the offending tends to be temporary. Moffitt labels these individuals **adolescent-limited offenders** (**ALs**). Moffitt (1993a) estimates that a majority of adolescents are involved in some form of antisocial behavior during their teens, but then the antisocial behavior stops as they approach the responsibilities of young adulthood.

The developmental histories of the ALs do not demonstrate the early and persistent antisocial problems that members of the LCP group manifest. Interestingly, the frequency—and, in some cases, the violence level—of the offending *during the teen years* may be as high as that of the LCP youth, however. In effect, the teenage offending patterns of ALs and LCPs may be highly similar during the teenage years (Moffitt et al., 1996):

> The two types cannot be discriminated on most indicators of antisocial and problem behavior in adolescence; boys on the LCP and AL paths are similar on parent-, self-, and official records of offending, peer delinquency, substance abuse, unsafe sex, and dangerous driving. (p. 400)

That is, a professional could not easily identify the group classification (AL or LCP) simply by examining juvenile arrest records, self-reports, or the information provided by parents *during the teen years*.

The AL delinquent is most likely to be involved in offenses that symbolize adult privilege and demonstrate autonomy from parental control (Bartol, 2002), such as vandalism (usually school property), theft, drug and alcohol offenses, and other status offenses like running away or truancy. In addition, AL delinquents may engage in crimes that are profitable or rewarding, but they also have the ability to abandon these actions when more socially approved behavioral patterns become more rewarding and acceptable to significant others. For example, the onset of young adulthood brings new opportunities, such as leaving high school for college, obtaining a full-time job, and entering a relationship with a prosocial person. AL delinquents are quick to learn that they have something to lose if they continue offending into adulthood. During childhood, in contrast to LCP children, AL youngsters have learned to get along with others. Research has consistently shown that social rejection by peers in the elementary school grades is a potent risk factor for the development of antisocial behavior problems in adolescence and adulthood (Dodge & Pettit, 2003; Laird, Jordan, Dodge, Pettit, & Bates, 2001). Therefore, by adolescence, AL youth normally have a satisfactory repertoire of academic, social, and interpersonal skills that enable them to "get ahead" and develop lasting relationships. Their developmental histories and personal dispositions allow them the option of exploring new life pathways, an opportunity not usually afforded the LCP youth.

A growing body of research is finding, though, that a simple dual developmental path may not adequately capture all the variations in criminal careers (Donnellan, Ge, & Wenk, 2000). Using data from three studies of crime and delinquency conducted in London, Philadelphia, and Racine, Wisconsin, some researchers (D'Unger, Land, McCall, & Nagin, 1998; Nagin, Farrington, & Moffitt, 1995; Nagin & Land, 1993) have identified four developmental paths that perhaps more comprehensively reflect the reality of offending patterns. The four paths are (1) the adolescent-limited offenders, (2) the life course–persistent offenders (also called "high-level chronic offenders"), (3) the low-level chronic offenders (LLCs), and (4) those with a non-offending pattern (NCs). The ALs followed Moffitt's (1993a, 1993b) hypothesized offending pattern, beginning in their early teens, peaking at around age 16, and then showing a steady decline during their late teens and early adulthood (Nagin et al., 1995). The LLCs, on the other hand, exhibited a rise in offending through early adolescence, reached a plateau by mid-teens, and remained at the same offending level well past age 18. The LCPs demonstrated their usual pattern of beginning antisocial behavior early and remaining at a high level throughout their lifetimes. Interestingly, research by H. R. White, Bates, and Buyske (2001) suggests that it might be meaningful to introduce a fifth category, characterized by youth who engage in relatively little delinquency in early adolescence but for whom delinquency increases from late adolescence into adulthood.

Other researchers are interested in exploring gender differences in pathways, which is referred to as the "gendered pathway" approach. Though Moffitt (Moffitt & Caspi, 2001) found evidence that her theory fit both males and females, other researchers (e.g., Fontaine, Carbonneau, Vitaro, Barker, & Tremblay, 2009) have found significantly lower percentages of girls falling squarely into the theory, particularly on the LCP path. In addition, scholars focusing on gendered pathways refer to differences in risk factors between girls and boys that can lead to a later onset of antisocial behavior in girls (Salisbury & Van Voorhis, 2009; recall that Dr. Salisbury was introduced in Personal Perspective 1.1). In sum, the topic of gendered pathways represents one that should be of continuing interest to scholars.

Coercion Developmental Model

Like Moffitt and others, Gerald Patterson and his colleagues also believe that **early starters** in antisocial behaviors are at greater risk for more serious criminal offending as they grow older. However, the Patterson group focuses far more on the role of parenting than on specific characteristics of the child. The Patterson model argues that poor parental monitoring of child activities, disruptive family transitions (e.g., divorce), and inconsistent parental discipline are major psychosocial contributors to early-onset delinquency (Brennan, Hall, Bor, Najman, & Williams, 2003; Patterson, 1982). More specifically, the model posits that the key predictor of early-onset offending is the family environment in which the child learns to utilize **coercive behaviors** (e.g., temper tantrums, whining) to escape aversive parental discipline and authority.

Coercion theory sees an interaction between the behaviors of the child and the parent. Certain children—especially those with irritable temperaments and dispositions—are more likely to elicit inept parenting strategies. Essentially, the parent and the child each behave in a way that is aversive to the other in an attempt to control the other's behavior. As the child's aversive and coercive behaviors increase in intensity and frequency, the parent eventually acquiesces, unwittingly reinforcing the child's behavior. As the child becomes increasingly irritating, the parent further escalates power-assertion techniques and tries to apply coercive or forced compliance methods on the child. In simple terms, coercive theory explains how parents and children mutually "train" each other to behave in ways that increase the children's aggressive behavior and decrease the parents' control over these aversive and aggressive behaviors (Granic & Patterson, 2006).

Coercive exchanges between parents and children may emerge as early as when the child is 18 months of age (Granic & Patterson, 2006). At approximately 18 to 24 months, a normal behavioral pattern for many children is to become oppositional to authority, saying "no" to just about anything, and throwing occasional attention-getting tantrums. For most children, these behaviors peak at the end of the second year. However, for some, the beginnings of coercive exchanges may be triggered by the reinforcing nature of parental responses to these oppositional patterns and outbursts. In other words, by throwing a tantrum the child gets the attention she wants and, possibly, the outcome she was seeking, such as being allowed to watch one more video. Under these conditions, coercion eventually becomes the child's primary interpersonal strategy and thus generalizes to environments outside the home. According to the theory, antisocial behaviors progress from coercive parent–toddler interactions to similar interactions with teachers, peers, and others in the social environment. The socially inept child who uses coercive methods in dealing with others, however, soon finds she is rejected by peers.

The theory identifies two developmental trajectories of antisocial behavior. "One trajectory leads to early arrest (prior to age 14) and adult crime and the other to late-onset arrests and desistence from adult crime" (Patterson & Yoerger, 2002, p. 147). Overall, though, the model takes the position that both the early- and late-start trajectories represent variations of the *same basic processes*. Specifically, social-environmental influences—such as divorce, poverty, or parental depression—work in combination with inept parenting and deviant peer socialization to engender different levels of delinquent and antisocial behavior.

Hartup (2005) considers coercive developmental theory to be one of the most brilliant achievements of the 20th century for explaining the links between parent–child relationships and the development of antisocial behavior. Zoccolillo et al. (2005) call the theory one of the most comprehensive models in the field of child aggression. In general, the theory has been well-supported in the research literature.

A Development Dual Systems Model of Adolescent Risk Taking

Laurence Steinberg and his associates have formulated a theoretical model that offers an intriguing *neurological* explanation for Moffitt's adolescence-limited offenders. The model is based on a collection of empirical studies from developmental psychology and neuroscience. Steinberg (2008, 2010) hypothesizes that reward seeking and impulsivity develop along different timetables and have different neurological influences during adolescent and young adult development. Moreover, the differences in the timetables help account for the well-known high levels of risk taking during adolescence. As a general rule, and as most parents and caretakers have learned, adolescent behavior is characterized by impulsiveness, sensation seeking, a lack of future orientation, and strong susceptibility to peer pressure and influence. Risk taking during this period includes reckless driving, binge drinking, smoking cigarettes, and engaging in spontaneous unprotected sex. Teenagers "know" they should not drag race at 88 miles an hour, they "know" the harm in smoking tobacco, they "know" the dangers of sexually transmitted diseases, but nevertheless many still engage in risky behaviors. What is more, there are no gender differences in these behavioral patterns.

Impulsivity and rapid mood swings, so characteristic of many teens, is likely associated with immature self-control mechanisms, which take time to develop during the adolescent and young adult years. Sensation seeking "refers to the tendency to seek out novel, varied, and highly stimulating experiences, and the willingness to take risks in order to attain them" (Steinberg et al., 2008, p. 1765). Developmental psychologists have long observed that teens lack a "future orientation." Compared with adults, they are more likely to focus on the here and now and less likely to think about the long-term consequences of their decisions or actions. When they do think about the long-term consequences, they are inclined to give less weight to future consequences than to immediate risks and benefits (Scott & Steinberg, 2008). Moreover, as highlighted by Moffitt's theory, risk taking during the teen years may also involve committing a variety of criminal acts. Self-report studies have revealed that nearly 90% of adolescent boys admit to committing offenses for which they could be incarcerated (Scott & Steinberg, 2008).

Considerable research evidence supports the conventional wisdom that adolescents are more oriented toward peers and more responsive to peer influence than to the influence of adults (Scott & Steinberg, 2008). The increased importance of peers leads teens to modify their behavior in order to fit in and receive peer approval. Furthermore, numerous studies have consistently shown that susceptibility to peer influence plays a significant role in instigating adolescents to engage in antisocial behavior (K. Erickson, Crosnoe, & Dornbusch, 2000; Scott, Reppucci, & Woolard, 1995). Risky behaviors and most crimes committed by adolescents are usually committed in groups and are seldom premeditated (K. C. Monahan, Steinberg, & Cauffman, 2009; Warr, 2002; Zimring, 1998). In fact, Moffitt (1993a) contends that the desire for adolescents to impress peers is the core reason for most delinquency. The greater prevalence of group risk-taking behaviors and criminal offending is probably due to the fact that adolescents spend more time with their peer groups than adults do (Steinberg, 2008).

On the other hand, it appears that the very way the human brain develops may explain some of the behavior of youth during the adolescent years. Over the past 15 years, researchers have had a strong and sustained interest in patterns of brain development during adolescence and young adulthood (Steinberg, 2008).

> Enabled by the growing accessibility and declining cost of structural and functional Magnetic Resonance Imaging (MRI) and other imaging techniques, such as Diffusion Tensor Imaging (DTI), an expanding network of scientists have begun to map out the course of changes in brain activity during this period of development, and, to a more modest degree, link findings on the changing morphology and functioning of the brain to age differences in behavior. (Steinberg, 2008, p. 81)

Recall that Steinberg's research was cited in the U.S. Supreme Court case *Graham v. Florida* (2010). In that case, the Court ruled that a sentence of life without parole was cruel and unusual punishment for individuals who committed their crimes during adolescence, at least when the crime was not murder. The Court had already determined that the death penalty is cruel and unusual punishment for anyone who was 17 or under when they had committed their crime, including murder (*Roper v. Simmons*, 2005). In both cases, research on cognitive abilities of juveniles helped inform the decisions of the majority of the Supreme Court Justices.

Steinberg (2008) asks two fundamental questions about the high risk-taking propensity of teens: Why does risk-taking behavior increase between childhood and adolescence? And, why does risk-taking decline between adolescence and adulthood? He theorizes that risk taking increases between childhood and adolescence because of developmental changes in the regions of the brain he calls the *socio-emotional system.* The specific regions of the brain believed to be involved include a complex neurological network consisting of the amygdala, nucleus accumbens, orbitofrontal cortex, medial prefrontal cortex, and superior temporal sulcus. These neurological changes lead to significant increases in reward-seeking and stimulation-seeking activity during adolescence.

On the other hand, risk-taking behavior *declines* between adolescence and adulthood because of developmental changes in the regions of the brain he labels the *cognitive control system,* which is primarily located in the front areas of the brain. These growth changes, he contends, improve the person's capacity for self-regulation and regulate the socio-emotional system. The increase in reward-seeking needs occurs early and is relatively abrupt, whereas the increase in self-regulatory competence occurs gradually and is not usually complete until an individual has reached the mid-20s. These two systems constitute the basic components for Steinberg's **dual systems model.** Steinberg argues that risk taking and criminal behavior during adolescence can be best understood and explained by the interaction between the socio-emotional and cognitive control systems.

From Steinberg's (2008) perspective, the observed high and abrupt risk-taking behavioral patterns of adolescence are primarily due to increases in sensation seeking that are linked to increases in neurotransmitter activity within the socio-emotional system areas of the brain. The neurotransmitter dopamine and an increase in dopamine receptors are largely responsible for these changes. On the other hand, the emergence of the cognitive control system lags behind the socio-emotional system. The gradual development of cognitive control or self-regulation systems during adolescence and early adulthood are linked to neurological and network maturation in the frontal cortex, especially the prefrontal regions. Research confirms the hypothesis that adolescents tend to recruit the cognitive control network less selectively and efficiently than do adults (Steinberg, 2008).

Steinberg believes resistance to peer influence is achieved by cognitive control of the impulsive reward-seeking behavior (the socio-emotional system). Steinberg and Monahan (2007) found that gains in self-reported resistance to peer influence continue to age 18 and beyond. Furthermore, the impact of peers on risky behavior continues to be very evident even among college undergraduates averaging 20 years of age (M. Gardner & Steinberg, 2005). (During political campaigns, it is sometimes remarked that—with the exception of a serious violent offense—no candidate for office should be judged on anything that occurred when he or she was in high school or college.) As the cognitive control system matures, however, conditions of heightened arousal in the socio-emotional system that in earlier years led to risk taking are increasingly controlled. As mentioned previously, this maturity is largely completed by the mid-20s in most individuals. "Some things just take time to develop, and mature judgment is probably one of them" (Steinberg, 2008, p. 100).

Steinberg emphasizes that not all teens exhibit dangerous, harmful, or reckless behaviors. As we have noted throughout the chapter, individuals follow different developmental trajectories and reach different levels of maturity at different ages (Steinberg, Graham, et al., 2009). In addition, a wide assortment of factors influence sensation-seeking and risky behavior, including opportunities to engage in antisocial risk taking, parental and adult supervision levels, individual temperamental differences, and availability of alcohol and drugs. These same factors also play an important role in the early formation of persistent or life-course antisocial behavior.

Interestingly, there is growing scientific evidence that intellectual maturity is reached several years before psychosocial maturity (Steinberg, Graham, et al., 2009). Adolescents age 16 or older have basically the same logical reasoning abilities and verbal skills as adults. In addition, "adolescents are no worse than adults at perceiving risk or estimating their vulnerability to it" (Steinberg, 2008, p. 80). In other words, as mentioned above, they "know" that drag racing at high speeds on a country road is dangerous. However, even though teens can articulate the risks involved in some of their behavior, the socio-emotional system takes over in certain situations, especially in the presence of peers. These situations are most likely to occur when adolescents are emotionally aroused, absent adult supervision, and facing choices with apparent immediate rewards and few obvious or immediate costs—the very conditions that are likely to undermine adolescents' decision-making competence (Steinberg, 2007).

In sum, Steinberg's dual systems theory provides an excellent conceptual platform for understanding the adolescent-limited offenders and why teenagers often engage in risky, dangerous behavior, even when they know better. Fortunately, risky behavior in most cases fades as the individual gets older. For the serious, persistent offender, however, violent antisocial behavior persists well into adulthood. Studies consistently underscore the fact that specific early behavior problems frequently precede the development of serious antisocial behavior. In the next sections, specific developmental factors that are believed to be most closely linked to these antisocial patterns well into adulthood will be presented.

Developmental Factors in the Formation of Persistent Criminal Behavior

Daniel Waschbusch (2002) reports that "disruptive behavior problems in childhood typically include hyperactivity, impulsivity, inattention, oppositional behaviors, defiance, aggression, and disregarding the rights of others" (p. 118). According to Waschbusch, these disruptive behavior problems affect 5 to 10% of children and adolescents and account for more than 50% of referrals to mental health clinics. When left untreated, disruptive children are likely to experience peer rejection, have problems in school, demonstrate difficulties getting along with others, and exhibit persistent delinquent behaviors. In many instances, the persistent delinquency behaviors develop into long-term chronic, adult, violent and antisocial behavioral patterns. Similarly, four of the most prominent features of Moffitt's LCPs or serious, persistent offenders that are continually reported in the research literature are (1) hyperactive-impulsive attention problems, (2) conduct problems, (3) deficient cognitive ability, and (4) poor interpersonal or social skills (often resulting in peer rejection). It is important, therefore, that in order to understand more fully the formation of life-course antisocial behavior, we cover each in some detail.

Attention Deficit/Hyperactivity Disorder (ADHD) and Delinquency

The term **attention deficit/hyperactivity disorder** (ADHD) encompasses a wide variety of terms frequently used in mental and educational contexts, such as minimal brain dysfunction (MBD), attention deficit disorder (ADD), and hyperactive-impulsive attention (ADHD-HI) problems or simply "hyperactivity." We will use the term most commonly used today, *ADHD*. All the terms, however, refer basically to three central behaviors: (1) excessive motor activity (cannot sit still, fidgets, runs about, is talkative and noisy), (2) impulsivity (acts before thinking, shifts quickly from one activity to another, interrupts others, does not consider consequences of behavior), and (3) inattention (does not seem to listen, is easily distracted, loses things necessary for tasks or activities). Together, the three behaviors result in the child's inability to regulate and organize his or her behavior in different situations.

Another symptom cluster that should not be confused with ADHD is **oppositional defiant disorder (ODD),** which has often been linked to crime. ODD symptoms include arguing with adults, refusing adults' requests, deliberately trying to annoy others, blaming others for mistakes, and being spiteful or vindictive (Kosson, Cyterski, Steuerwald, Neuman, & Walker-Matthes, 2002).

Although ADHD is the leading psychological diagnosis for children living in the United States (Flory, Milich, Lynam, Leukefeld, & Clayton, 2003; Nigg, John, et al., 2002), estimates of the incidence of ADHD in school-age children range widely from 1 to 20% (American Psychiatric Association, 2000; Developmental Disabilities Branch, 2000), and 3 to 9% in the normal adult population (Sevecke, Kosson, & Krischer, 2009). To date, however, no systematic nationwide research has been conducted to identify the extent, seriousness, or nature of ADHD. The research has consistently revealed that boys outnumber girls, but the ratios reported have ranged from 2:1 to 9:1 (R. W. Root & Resnick, 2003). According to Root and Resnick, Black children appear to receive the diagnosis more often than other racial or ethnic minority children, although the reasons for this finding are debatable. In addition, ADHD symptoms manifest themselves early in development, usually during the preschool years (Deault, 2010). It is important to realize that all children (and adults) have certain levels of inattention, overactivity, and impulsivity in situations, but for the diagnostic label of ADHD to be assigned, the symptoms must be unusually persistent and pronounced (Root & Resnick, 2003). Although most studies have been carried out in the United States and Europe, research has also supported the validity of ADHD in developing countries (Rohde et al., 2001) and across different cultures (Barkley, 1998).

Furthermore, a significant percentage of ADHD children show the same persistent symptoms into adulthood (Lara et al., 2009; Nigg, Butler, Huang-Pollock, & Henderson, 2002; Mannuzza, Klein, Bessler, Malloy, & LaPadula, 1998). In a comprehensive study of 10 countries, Lara et al. (2009) report that roughly 50% of childhood cases of ADHD continue to meet the full criteria for the disorder as adults. In other words, many people do not "outgrow" ADHD. The observation that ADHD is prevalent among adults is a recent conclusion, however.

Educators find that ADHD children have difficulty staying on task, remaining cognitively organized, sustaining academic achievement in the school setting, and maintaining control over their behavior. ADHD is puzzling, and its cause is largely unknown. Some scientists contend that ADHD children are born with a biological predisposition toward inattention and excessive movement; others maintain that some children are exposed to environmental factors that damage the nervous system. Loeber (1990) reveals how exposure to toxic substances during the preschool years can interfere with a child's neurological development, often resulting in symptoms of ADHD. For example, children exposed to low levels of lead toxicity (from paint or airborne contaminants) are more hyperactive and impulsive and are easily distracted and frustrated. They also show notable problems in following simple instructions. Some researchers observe that ADHD children do not possess effective strategies and cognitive organization with which to deal with the daily demands of traditional school. These children often have particular difficulty in understanding and using abstract concepts. ADHD children also seem to lack cognitive organizational skills for dealing with new knowledge and information. Nonetheless, it is believed that numerous gifted, brilliant individuals were or could have been diagnosed with ADHD when they were children, so it is a mistake to focus on the problematic aspects of this diagnosis. In addition, it is believed that numerous children are misdiagnosed.

Some research suggests that one of the primary causal factors appears to be inhibitory problems due to neuropsychological deficits (Barkley, 1997, 1998; Nigg, Butler, et al., 2002). The inhibitory problems may be primarily due to motor (behavioral) control (Nigg, 2000). Overall, the extant research underscores the possibility that the causes of ADHD are probably multiple and extremely difficult to tease out of the many ongoing interactions occurring between the nervous system and the environment.

Although many behaviors have been identified as accompanying ADHD, the major theme is that ADHD children are perceived as annoying and aversive to those around them, and therein may lie the problematic aspects. ADHD children often continually seek and prolong interpersonal contacts and eventually irritate and frustrate those people with whom they interact. Because of these annoying and socially inappropriate behaviors, they are often rejected by peers, especially if they are perceived as aggressive (Henker & Whalen, 1989).

This pattern of peer rejection appears to continue throughout the developmental years (Dodge & Pettit, 2003; J. B. Reid, 1993). In many ways, then, ADHD appears to be more a disorder of interpersonal relationships than simply a disorder of hyperactivity. Some researchers find that ADHD children generally lack friendship and intimacy (Henker & Whalen, 1989). Moffitt (1990) reports that children between the ages of 5 and 7 who demonstrate the characteristics of both ADHD and antisocial behavior not only have special difficulty with social relationships but also have a high probability of demonstrating these problems into adolescence and beyond.

Experts argue that the most common problem associated with ADHD is delinquency and substance abuse (Beauchaine, Katkin, Strassberg, & Snarr, 2001). The data strongly suggest that youth with symptoms of both ADHD and delinquent behavior are at very high risk for developing lengthy and serious criminal careers (Mannuzza et al., 1998; Moffitt, 1990; Pfiffner et al., 1999; Satterfield, Swanson, Schell, & Lee, 1994). Other studies indicate that prevalence estimates for adjudicated adolescents range from 14 to 19% and from 20 to 72% for incarcerated adolescents (Vermeiren, 2003). One study of antisocial youth in a secure facility found that nearly half of the adolescents demonstrated symptoms of ADHD (S. Young et al., 2010). David Farrington (1991), in his well-regarded research, also found that violent offenders often have a history of hyperactivity, impulsivity, and attention deficit problems. The relationship between ADHD and delinquency and adult crime is an area demanding much more research by forensic psychologists interested in studying crime and delinquency. It must be stressed, however, that the child with ADHD should not be labeled as the delinquent or the criminal of tomorrow.

The most common method of treatment for ADHD is medication (especially methylphenidate, more commonly known as Ritalin, and the central nervous system stimulant Adderall and its derivatives). However, although medication apparently helps many children, many others exhibit numerous side effects, some of them severe. Counseling and psychotherapy are often used, often in conjunction with medication, but with limited success with this puzzling phenomenon, particularly over the long term. As many practitioners realize, ADHD children generally demonstrate multiple problems that can be best managed through treatment strategies that take into account all the factors impinging on the child at any given time (see Root & Resnick, 2003, for an excellent review). These treatment approaches are called "multisystemic" and will be dealt with more fully in Chapter 13.

Conduct Disorders

ADHD frequently co-occurs with a diagnostic category called "conduct disorders" (Coid, 2003; Connor, Steeber, & McBurnett, 2010; Offord, Boyle, & Racine, 1991; J. B. Reid, 1993). Waschbusch (2002) reports, for instance, that about 50% of disruptive children exhibit the basic symptoms of both ADHD and conduct disorders (CD). If disruptive children have the symptoms of one, about half of them also have symptoms of the other. Not only does the presence of CD increase the symptoms of ADHD, but the combination of the two is an especially powerful predictor of a lifelong course of violence, persistent criminal behavior, and drug abuse (Flory et al., 2003; Molina, Bukstein, & Lynch, 2002; Pfiffner et al., 1999). As mentioned previously, conduct disorder consists of a cluster of maladaptive behaviors characterized by a variety of antisocial behaviors. Examples of this misbehavior include stealing, fire setting, running away from home, skipping school, destroying property, fighting, telling lies on a frequent basis, and being cruel to animals and people. CD is generally considered to be a serious childhood disorder because it appears to be a precursor to chronic criminal behavior during adulthood (Lahey et al., 1995). According to the *DSM-IV* (American Psychiatric Association, 1994), the central feature of conduct disorder is the *repetitive* and *persistent* pattern of behavior that violates the basic rights of others.

The *DSM-IV* recognizes two types of conduct disorder: childhood onset and adolescent onset. Childhood-onset CD occurs when the pattern begins before the age of 10. This pattern often worsens as the child gets older and is more likely to lead to serious and persistent criminal behavior into adulthood (Frick et al., 2003).

According to Frick and colleagues, "In addition, children in the childhood-onset group are characterized by more aggression, more cognitive and neuropsychological disturbances, greater impulsivity, greater social alienation, and more dysfunctional backgrounds than are children in the adolescent-onset group" (p. 246).

On the other hand, adolescent-onset CD is characterized by the absence of any maladaptive behavior before the age of 10. After age 10, those with adolescent-onset CDs tend to exhibit fewer problems in interpersonal and social skills but do reject traditional rules and formal procedures. They often associate with deviant peers in forbidden activities to show their independence and self-perceived maturity (Frick et al., 2003). In many respects, the two types of CD follow the developmental paths of Moffitt's (1993a, 1993b) LCPs (childhood onset) and ALs (adolescent onset).

Behavioral indicators of childhood-onset CDs can be observed in children's interactions with parents or caretakers well before school entry (J. B. Reid, 1993). For example, children who are aggressive, difficult to manage, and noncompliant in the home at age 3 often continue to have similar problems when entering school. Furthermore, as we noted, these behaviors show remarkable continuity through adolescence and into adulthood. CD children frequently have significant problems with school assignments, a behavioral pattern that often results in their being mislabeled with a "learning disability." It is important to note that students with genuine learning disabilities are not necessarily conduct disordered. In other words, the two designations may overlap, but each is also a distinct categorization. Similar to ADHD children, aggressive CDs are at high risk for strong rejection by their peers. This rejection generally lasts throughout the school years and is very difficult to change (J. B. Reid, 1993). As described above, children who are consistently socially rejected by peers miss critical opportunities to develop normal interpersonal and social skills. Lacking effective interpersonal skills, these youth *may* meet their needs through more aggressive means, including threats and intimidation.

An estimated 6 to 16% of boys are believed to have behavioral features of CD (American Psychiatric Association, 2000). The prevalence in girls ranges from 4 to 9.2% (Cohen, Cohen, & Brook, 1993; Zoccolillo, 1993). Overall, the sex ratio for CD appears to be 2.5 males for each female (Moffitt et al., 2008). It should be mentioned, however, that the *DSM-IV* does not include sex-specific criteria for CD, and many clinicians and researchers are advocating for sex-specific criteria to be used in the *DSM-V*. Some feel that the current diagnostic category in the *DSM-IV* fails to accurately detect CD among girls (see Moffitt et al., 2008 for a comprehensive review).

An interesting study by Anna Bardone and her colleagues (Bardone, Moffitt, & Caspi, 1996) found that CD patterns in girls are a strong predictor of a lifetime of problems, including poor interpersonal relations with partners/spouses and peers, criminal activity, early pregnancy without supportive partners, and frequent job loss and firings. Similar to CD boys, CD girls—without intervention—often lead a life full of interpersonal conflict.

We must remind ourselves that there are multiple factors associated with delinquency, including serious and chronic offending. This part of the chapter has focused on various deficiencies within the individual—hyperactivity, conduct disorder, and impulsivity, to name a few. Children live within a social system, however. The behavior and reactions of adults such as parents, caretakers, and teachers significantly affect the child's behavior. In some cases, the "deficiencies" described here are due to abuse, maltreatment, neglect, or simply ignorance about effective child-rearing techniques. In these, as well as in other cases, intervention by competent and caring adults can avert a lifetime of continual offending.

Cognitive Ability and Crime

In addition to the emphasis on developmental pathways, ADHD, and conduct disorders, recent research on crime and delinquency has identified the importance of cognition and mental processes in the development of antisocial behavior and violence. These include language acquisition, self-regulation, and executive functions.

(We covered self-regulation to some extent in the section on Steinberg's dual systems model.) Developmental research also has been instrumental in identifying the enormous influence of multiple contexts (e.g., school, peers, and families) in the learning and continuation of delinquency and criminal behavior. This emphasis has highlighted the importance of considering the many complex interactions among genes and the environment, family members, peers and friends, and cultural and ethnic background in all discussions of antisocial behavior.

Intelligence

A number of developmental theories posit a role for intelligence in the development of delinquency. For example, Moffitt (1993a) hypothesizes that the more serious, persistent offenders should demonstrate lower intelligence or cognitive ability than non-offenders. She writes, "The verbal deficits of antisocial children are pervasive, affecting receptive listening and reading, problem solving, expressive speech and writing, and memory" (p. 680). It is clear that a person's intellectual performance will vary on different occasions, in different domains—as judged by different criteria—and across the life span. In the past two decades, there has been a concentrated effort to develop the idea of broader, multiple intelligences, rather than just one single type of intelligence, and to have an appreciation of abilities that previously either were ignored or were considered not very important in understanding human behavior. Every student reading this book knows that some people are "book smart but not street smart." Some people find it difficult to express themselves orally or in writing but are able to create works of art or build a sturdy house. Who would argue that the street smart person or the creator of art or builder of houses is not intelligent?

Although intelligence is a controversial topic—particularly due to skepticism about the validity of "IQ" testing—it has become apparent today that intelligence exists in multiple forms and relates to a wide assortment of abilities. Howard Gardner (2000), for example, describes nine different types of intelligences or cognitive styles (see Table 7.2). There are probably more types, such as wisdom, spirituality, synthesizing ability, intuition, metaphoric capacities, humor, and good judgment (H. Gardner, 1983, 1998, 2000), many of which have been used to describe resilient persons. Gardner considered two of the primary nine—insight into oneself

Table 7.2 Howard Gardner's Different Intelligences Model	
Intelligence	**Definition**
(1) Linguistic	Possessing a good vocabulary and reading comprehension skills
(2) Visual/spatial	Ability to visualize objects, find one's orientation in space, and navigate from one location to another
(3) Logical-mathematical	Ability to think logically, reason deductively, detect patterns, and carry out mathematical operations
(4) Interpersonal	Ability to understand and interact with others effectively
(5) Intrapersonal	Ability to understand and know oneself
(6) Existential	Tendency to ponder the meaning of life, death, and the nature of reality
(7) Kinesthetic	Ability to dance well, handle objects skillfully, and be a competent athlete
(8) Musical	Ability to hear, recognize, and manipulate patterns in music
(9) Naturalistic	Ability to see patterns in nature and discriminate among living things (plants and animals)

Source: Gardner (1983, 1998, 2000).

and the understanding of others—features of **emotional intelligence.** Emotional intelligence is the ability to know how people and oneself are feeling and the capacity to use that information to guide thoughts and actions. A deficiency in this form of intelligence may play a prominent role in human violence.

Standard intelligence tests (IQ tests) measure only the first three forms of the Gardner multiple intelligences model. Even if we presume that standard tests are valid (and caution is urged here), the delinquents who scored low on the standard tests may well be higher in other types of intelligence.

Individuals who chronically engage in violence may lack significant insight into their own behavior and possess little sensitivity toward others. They tend to misread emotional cues from others and become confused and angry in ambiguous social situations. For example, highly aggressive children often have a **hostile attribution bias.** That is, they are more likely than less aggressive children to interpret ambiguous actions of others as hostile and threatening. Research consistently indicates that highly aggressive and violent adolescents "typically define social problems in hostile ways, adopt hostile goals, seek few additional facts, generate few alternative solutions, anticipate few consequences for aggression, and give higher priority to their aggressive solutions" (Eron & Slaby, 1994, p. 10). These hostile cognitive styles, combined with deficient interpersonal skills, are more likely to result in aggression and violence in certain social situations.

Highly aggressive and antisocial children appear to be less equipped cognitively for dealing with ambiguous or conflictual situations. Research strongly supports the idea that highly aggressive individuals possess biases and cognitive deficits for dealing with and solving problematic social encounters with others. Children and adolescents who engage in severe peer aggression show more distorted thought patterns that support aggressive behavior. According to Pornari and Wood (2010), "They make more justifications and rationalizations in order to make a harmful act seem less harmful and to eliminate self-censure" (pp. 88–89). Research also indicates that serious delinquent offenders are deficient in being able to cognitively put themselves in the place of others or to empathize (Pepler, Byrd, & King, 1991). As a result, these youth are less concerned about the negative consequences of violence, such as the suffering of the victim or the social rejection they receive from their peers.

Ironically, although the early research on IQ and delinquency can be criticized for its lack of attention to social factors, it is likely that intelligence, in a broader sense, *does* play a role. Most particularly, Gardner's (1983) concept of *emotional intelligence* may be a key factor in the development of habitual and long-term offending. Put another way, the chronic offender may or may not be "intelligent" in the traditional sense; however, he or she is unlikely to be high in emotional intelligence.

More importantly, however, early school failure seems to play a more critical role in the development of delinquency and crime than the traditional measures of intelligence predict (Dodge & Pettit, 2003). In addition, research indicates that retention in kindergarten and in the early grades—being "held back"—has significant detrimental effects on healthy development (Dodge & Pettit, 2003).

Related to verbal intelligence and thinking is language development. There have been a number of studies indicating that low language proficiency is associated with antisocial behavior, as will be discussed in the next section.

Language Development

Verbal deficits and impaired language development are closely associated with serious delinquency (Leech, Day, Richardson, & Goldschmidt, 2003; Muñoz, Frick, Kimonis, & Aucoin, 2008; Vermeiren, De Clippele, Schwab-Stone, Ruchkin, & Deboutte, 2002). Antisocial behavior and aggression have been linked to low language proficiency as early as the second year of life and throughout the life span (Dionne, 2005). According to Keenan and Shaw (2003), language is the "primary means by which children learn to solve problems nonaggressively and effectively decrease negative emotions such as anger, fear, and sadness" (p. 163). By the end of the preschool period, the average child has internalized—primarily through the use of language—rules that are associated with the ability to inhibit behavior, follow rules, and manage negative emotions (Keenan & Shaw, 2003; Kochanska, Murray, & Coy, 1997). In addition, according to Keenan and Shaw, the child demonstrates more empathy and prosocial behavior toward others as a result of language development. As noted by Dionne, "language becomes for most children a social tool for increased prosocial interactions" (p. 335).

Delayed language development appears to increase stress and frustration for many children and impede normal socialization (Keenan & Shaw, 2003). Toddler language development at ages 6 months, 18 months, and 24 months predicts later delinquency and antisocial behavior for boys, even when other influences are accounted for (Nigg & Huang-Pollock, 2003; Stattin & Klackenberg-Larsson, 1993). A higher incidence of language delay also has been observed among male children who display disruptive behaviors during the preschool years and antisocial behaviors during the school years (Dionne, Tremblay, Boivin, Laplante, & Pérusse, 2003; Stowe, Arnold, & Ortiz, 2000). The evidence for a similar pattern for girls remains sparse and inconclusive.

How might the above relationships be explained? Early language delay and limited communication skills may predispose a child to use more physically aggressive tactics for dealing with others, especially peers. Frustrated about not getting his needs met through normal communication and social strategies, the child is drawn to more physically aggressive behaviors to get his way. This aggressive behavioral pattern, however, is likely to produce a circular effect, since aggressive and disruptive behaviors interfere with creating a positive social environment for language development and normal peer interactions. Therefore, aggressive or antisocial behaviors may, in turn, curtail language development. In contrast to children with language deficits, verbally advantaged children may benefit from their verbal skills by developing prosocial behaviors and may thus steer away from the antisocial trajectories (Dionne, 2005; Dionne et al. 2003).

N. J. Cohen (2001) asserts that language provides an important cognitive tool for controlling one's own behavior, impulses, and emotions. According to Dionne (2005), "Emotion regulation and self-regulation are generally viewed as requiring complex linguistic tools such as the ability to analyze social situations, organize thoughts about one's own emotions, and plan behavior according to social roles" (p. 346).

Self-Regulation Skills

As emphasized by Steinberg and his associates, whose research was discussed above, self-regulation is one of the most important skills in the prevention of antisocial behavior. **Self-regulation** is defined as the capacity to control and alter one's behavior *and* emotions. It also includes the ability to shift focus and attention and to activate and change behavior (Eisenberg et al., 2004). The reader will recognize that self-regulation includes *both* behavioral and emotional regulation. Being able to control and shift emotions, especially anger, is a pivotal skill important for maintaining prosocial behavior and avoiding aggressive or violent behavior. Research documents that not only is poor behavioral and emotional self-regulation related to aggression and violent delinquency, but it is also related to the early onset of substance use and the escalation of use during adolescence (Wills & Stoolmiller, 2002; Wills, Walker, Mendoza, & Ainette, 2006).

In their relationships with adults, children begin to acquire strategies that enable them to control their behavior and emotions in numerous ways. Although self-regulation skills may reflect some temperamental qualities whose origins may have some genetic component, it is clear that such skills are malleable and can be taught or improved upon by parents, caregivers, or others in the social environment (Buckner, Mezzacappa, & Beardslee, 2003). Sensitive and consistent caregiving and warm but firm parenting styles have been associated with the development of self-control and compliance with social rules. As we learned from Steinberg's dual systems research, self-regulation abilities take time to mature fully. Still, young children can learn to control many of their basic impulses and behaviors at a fairly early age.

Features of self-control begin to emerge in the second year, as does the concern for others. During the third year of life, children are expected to become reasonably compliant with parental requests and to internalize the family standards and values for behavior. By 17 months of age, however, approximately 80% of children show some form of physically aggressive behavior (Tremblay et al., 1996). Moreover, this physical aggression is not usually learned but appears to be a "natural" development of childhood. In addition, while most demonstrate physical aggression at 17 months, not all do so at the same frequency and with the same vigor (Tremblay & Nagin, 2005). As self-regulation develops, physically aggressive behavior usually decreases substantially from the third year onward. During mid-adolescence, however, many exhibit another peak in physical aggression but show a decrease during early adulthood (Dionne, 2005). However, there is a significant increase in verbal and indirect aggressions with age (Vaillancourt, 2005), suggesting that physical aggression may still exist but that children learn how to be aggressive in different ways (Tremblay & Nagin, 2005). A large factor in this learning or socialization is the development of self-regulation and enhanced executive functions.

Executive Functions

Closely related to self-regulation is the concept of **executive functions**, which refers to deliberate problem solving and the regulation of one's thoughts, actions, and emotions (Tremblay, 2003; Zelazo, Carter, Reznick, & Frye, 1997). Not only do executive functions recognize and inhibit inappropriate behavior, but they also direct focus and attention to external events and organize information for higher-order reasoning. They also prioritize the steps necessary for solving problems. In sum, executive functions are involved in the planning, regulation, and control of purposive behavior. As further described by Marie Banich (2009), "[executive function] involves an *individual* guiding his or her behavior, especially in novel, unstructured, and nonroutine situations that require some degree of judgment" (p. 89, italics original).

Current research and theory supposes that executive functioning resides predominantly in the prefrontal lobe of the cortex (or front part of the brain). There may be other cortical areas that contribute, but to date they have not been convincingly identified. Not surprisingly, studies have also repeatedly reported strong links between those individuals with symptoms of ADHD and poor executive functioning (Brocki, Eninger, Thorell, & Bohlin, 2010; Miller & Hinshaw, 2010).

Several studies of children and adolescents have documented a relationship between different aspects of executive functions and antisocial behavior (A. B. Morgan & Lilienfeld, 2000; Nigg, Quamma, Greenberg, & Kusche, 1999; Séguin & Zelazo, 2005; Tremblay, 2003). Children and adults with good executive functions are well-organized, diligent, focused on completing tasks, and skillful in their approach to resolving problems (Buckner et al., 2003). They are adept at focusing attention, able to concentrate well, and flexible in their thinking. All these features are the opposite characteristics of those persons who manifest persistent and violent offending histories.

Deficient Interpersonal Skills and Peer Rejection

Research examining social influences has discovered that peer rejection is one of the strongest predictors of later involvement in persistent, serious offending, especially violence (Cowan & Cowan, 2004; Dodge, 2003). This rejection starts early. Even around age 5, aggressive, belligerent children are unpopular and are excluded from peer groups (Dodge & Pettit, 2003; Patterson, 1982).

Children may be rejected by peers for a variety of reasons, but aggressive behavior appears to be a prominent one. Kids reject those peers who rely on various forms of physical and verbal aggression as a method for getting what they want. Peer-rejected children are not only aggressive, but they also tend to be argumentative, inattentive, and disruptive. Furthermore, boys who are both peer rejected and aggressive have a variety of behavioral, social, and cognitive deficits and display low levels of prosocial behavior in general (Coie & Miller-Johnson, 2001). This cluster of deficits frequently results in poor school and academic performance (Buh & Ladd, 2001; Dodge & Pettit, 2003). Peer acceptance is crucial during early development, and those who receive it turn out far differently from their rejected peers. Children who are liked and accepted by their peer group in the early school years are far less likely to become antisocial in their later years (Laird et al., 2001; Rubin, Bukowski, & Parker, 1998). It should be emphasized, however, that almost all the research on the effects of peer rejection, aggression, and delinquent behavior has focused on boys.

As pointed out previously, recent research on the development of delinquent and criminal behavior has identified ADHD features, which appear to have a strong biological component. There are many other potential biopsychological factors that may contribute to the development of antisocial behavior. In the next section, we will consider some of them.

Biological Factors

Children are born with a range of genetic makeups, neurological predispositions, and temperaments. During the past two decades, researchers have made significant advances in discovering the many biological and neurological factors that may play important roles in the development of antisocial and violent behavior (see Raine, 2002, and Tremblay, Hartup, & Archer, 2005, for comprehensive reviews). According to Tremblay and Côté (2005), the increasing number of biopsychosocial studies appears to be largely due to the development of sophisticated biological measures that are relatively easy to use with humans. They use molecular genetics, brain scans, and radio immunoassays of saliva as examples of the improved measuring techniques. For example, the latest neurodevelopmental imaging studies indicate that the brain is still growing and maturing well beyond adolescence (DeMatteo, 2005c). A recent National Institute of Mental Health (NIMH) investigation suggests that brain maturation may not peak until age 25 (Beckman, 2004), a finding which supports Steinberg's dual systems theory concerning maturation of the self-control system.

One important point must be made, however. Researchers have continually emphasized that biological or neurological factors do not act in isolation. Neurobiological development is continually influenced by the psychosocial and physical environment across the life span. For example, it is becoming increasingly apparent to behavioral scientists that a lack of physical contact, verbal stimulation, and social responsiveness from parents and caregivers can substantially alter the rate of intellectual, emotional, and social development in children (Dahlberg & Potter, 2001).

Temperament

Developmental scientists have continually documented the strong association between a child's difficult **temperament** and the development of persistent antisocial behavior (e.g., Bates, Pettit, Dodge, & Ridge, 1998; Rubin, Burgess, Dwyer, & Hastings, 2003; Shaw, Owens, Giovannelli, & Winslow, 2001). The mere mention of a child's "difficult temperament" may alienate some readers; after all, children—especially babies—should be loved, cuddled, and nurtured. If they are "difficult," it is seen as the fault of the caretaker.

According to the research literature, though, temperament (1) has a constitutional or biological basis, (2) exists at birth and continues across the life span, and (3) can be influenced by the psychosocial environment (Else-Quest, Hyde, Goldsmith, & Van Hulle, 2006; Lahey & Waldman, 2003). Temperament is generally viewed as individual differences in emotional expression, motor activity, and sensitivity to simulation.

Without doubt, adults should be able to adapt to temperamental differences in children. We cannot fault the infant or the young child for the hand he or she has been dealt. Nevertheless, an understanding of temperament is important, because heritable or biological predispositions may be a critical factor in the early formation of delinquency and crime. "Ill-tempered" children may be at higher risk to engage in antisocial behavior than "easy" children. Specifically, a smiling, relaxed, socially interactive child (easy) is apt to generate a different social response from caregivers than a fussy, tense, and withdrawn one (ill-tempered). A chronically ill-tempered child may become so frustrating and discouraging to his parents or caregivers that they feel over-whelmed and helpless in their ability to deal effectively with the child. The caregiver's resulting frustration may feed into the behavior of the child in a reciprocal fashion, engendering a disruption in the caregiver–child relationship. This frustration may progress into physical or emotional abuse or neglect by the caregivers, which in turn may progress into future behavioral problems.

Genetic Influences

Over the past 30 years, more than 100 twin and adoption studies have examined the relationship between genes and aggression or violence (Pérusse & Gendreau, 2005). Not surprisingly, most scientists have concluded that both genetic and environmental factors are important in the development of antisocial behavior. Some scholars (e.g., Rhee & Waldman, 2002) have estimated that environment plays a significantly more important role in the development of antisocial behavior than does genetics. Moreover, some researchers have further suggested that genetics may play a more prominent role in the development of those who commit property crimes, and plays a less important role in the development of those who commit violent crimes (Pérusse & Gendreau, 2005). However, despite a fairly large quantity of research on the relationship between genetics and antisocial behavior, the evidence remains largely inconclusive.

Brain Chemistry

Earlier, we discussed self-regulation and executive functions and their involvement in antisocial behavior. As we also pointed out, scientists have discovered that, to a large extent, these functions are found in front parts of the brain, known as the frontal cortex. According to Pihl and Benkelfat (2005), "the frontal lobes are seen as responsible for planning, controlling, and verifying behavior in the presence of goals, working within a context and providing control over the more automatic subcortical systems" (p. 273). As previously noted, the frontal cortex is one of the last parts of the brain to mature, probably as late as age 25 (Gogtay et al., 2004).

A biochemical that is found in heavy concentrations in this region of the brain is dopamine. Dopamine is actually one of the neurotransmitters, which are biochemicals involved in the transmission of neural impulses within the nervous system. Without neurotransmitters, communication within the mammalian nervous system would be impossible. The assumption by the scientific community is that low concentrations of dopamine in the frontal cortex may be linked to poor self-regulation and faulty executive functions.

Another neurotransmitter that has been linked to poor impulse control and violent behavior is serotonin. Basically, many individuals who act aggressively or violently toward others may have abnormally low levels of serotonin (Coscina, 1997; Lesch & Merschdorf, 2000; Loeber & Stouthamer-Loeber, 1998). There is also some evidence that levels of serotonin may partially explain the differences in physical aggression between men and women (Verona, Jointer, Johnson, & Bender, 2006). Low levels of serotonin are also linked to depression and suicide (Pihl & Benkelfat, 2005).

Other neurotransmitters are believed to be associated with violence and antisocial behavior, such as nor-epinephrine and GABA. There will probably be many more as the research continues, but it is unlikely that research will discover that neurotransmitters are the sole causes of violent or aggressive behavior.

Hormones and Aggression

The two hormones that have been implicated in influencing physical aggression and antisocial behavior are the androgen testosterone and the stress hormone cortisol (Van Goozen, 2005). Several studies have found that antisocial children and adults often have low levels of cortisol. The evidence to date suggests that the more aggressive the behavior, or the more serious the antisocial behavior, the lower the level of cortisol (see Van Goozen, 2005, for a review). Similar to neurotransmitters, it is highly likely that many additional hormones will be linked to aggressive or antisocial behavior.

Other Social Developmental Influences

Many other developmental factors have been identified as contributing to a child's trajectory toward a life of committing serious crime and violence. The experience of physical abuse in early life significantly increases the risk of future antisocial conduct (Dodge & Pettit, 2003; Mayfield & Widom, 1996). On the other hand, warmth and appropriate behavioral management by parents have been found to have very positive outcomes on the developmental trajectories of their children (Dishion & Bullock, 2002; Dodge & Pettit, 2003). The amount of exposure that the child has to aggressive peers in day care or preschool also appears to have significant effects on the child's later aggressive behavior. In addition, children who spend large amounts of time in unsupervised after-school self-care in the early elementary grades are also at high risk of participating in antisocial behavior (Sinclair, Pettit, Harrist, & Bates et al., 1994).

Poverty is also a powerful risk factor. Although many children growing up poor do not engage in serious antisocial behavior or delinquency, poverty does create multiple barriers to healthy development. Communities under financial strain are often plagued by inadequate educational and health systems and often have a large number of families experiencing disruption brought about by limited occupational resources and family breakdown. In these areas, schools tend to be inadequate and day care services limited. Unsafe levels of lead and other toxic materials have been found in significantly higher amounts in economically deprived areas than in middle- or upper-income communities (Narag, Pizarro, & Gibbs, 2009).

School Violence

As noted in Chapter 1, in the 1990s, a rash of school shootings across the United States made headlines and brought the topic of school violence into sharp focus. Communities that had previously had a low profile—West Paducah, Kentucky; Jonesboro, Arkansas; Pearl, Mississippi; Springfield, Oregon— suddenly became notorious. The most infamous case was the mass murder of 12 students and 1 teacher at Columbine High School in Littleton, Colorado, in April 1999. The two teenage boys who did the shooting apparently committed suicide during the incident (see Photos 7.1 and 7.2). An additional 20 students were injured. To the public and news media, the shooters appeared to be two ordinary boys from normal, middle-class families living in an affluent suburb of Denver. Although there had been a number of school shootings prior to Columbine (there had been at least 10 school shootings between 1996 and 1999), the Columbine shooting prompted a great deal

Photo 7.1 Eric Harris, left, and Dylan Klebold on a surveillance tape in the cafeteria at Columbine High School on April 20, 1998. The two shooters also made videos of themselves target practicing shortly before the incident.

Photo 7.2 Covered by police, students run from Columbine High School on April 20, 1998.

of alarm and concern nationwide. In addition, the media and some experts were quick to make gross generalizations about the school violence problem. O'Tool (2000) lists the usual wrong or unverified impressions of school shooters often promoted by the news media (see Focus 7.1).

Despite the media attention given to Columbine and other schools where violent incidents had occurred, it is important to keep school crime, including violence, in perspective. Note that the school shootings described here occurred during a time when juvenile violent crime on the whole was going down; thus, although the shootings were terrifying, they were not representative of the juvenile crime picture. Furthermore, although the media understandably report incidents of children having guns on school premises, there is no documentation that this is a widespread problem. Although it is important to be alert to possible dangers facing school-age children and the adults who work with them in the schools, the reality is that the risk of victimization is smaller in that environment than in private homes or the community at large. Still, each school-based attack has had a stressful and lasting effect on the school in which it occurred, the surrounding community, and the nation as a whole. Consequently, although many parents, teachers, and school officials across the nation are pleased that the *nationwide* statistics of school crime and violence are decreasing, they—understandably—want their children and the children in their local district to have a safe school environment. One way to improve the safety of youth in our nation's schools is through threat assessment, a strategy in which many mental health professionals and forensic psychologists are becoming increasingly involved. Although threat assessment was briefly described in Chapter 2 as it pertained to the duties and responsibilities of psychologists working for law enforcement agencies, this section will focus on the target itself, which in this case is the school. Mass murders outside the school context, such as workplace killings and sniper attacks, are discussed in Chapter 8.

FOCUS 7.1. PUBLIC MYTHS ABOUT SCHOOL SHOOTERS

News coverage magnifies a number of widespread incorrect or unverified impressions of school shooters. Among them are the following:

- All school shooters are alike.
- The school shooter is always a loner.
- School shootings are exclusively revenge motivated.
- Easy access to weapons is the most significant risk factor.
- Unusual or bizarre behaviors, interests, and hobbies are the hallmarks of the student destined to become violent.

Source: O'Tool (2000, p. 4).

Threat Assessment

Threat assessment is a set of investigative and operational activities designed to identify, assess, and manage individuals who may *pose* a threat of violence to *identifiable targets,* such as the school environment (Borum et al., 1999). "A threat is an expression of intent to do harm or act out violently against someone or something. A threat can be spoken, written, or symbolic—for example, motioning with one's hands as though shooting at another person" (O'Tool, 2000, p. 6).

Threat assessment is innovative in two ways: (1) It does *not* rely on descriptive, demographic, or psychological profiles, and (2) it does *not* rely directly on verbal or written threats as a threshold for risk (Borum et al., 1999). More specifically, threat assessment is different from "profiling" in that it looks at the pathways of ideas, thinking patterns, and behavior that may lead to violent action. Profiling is designed to reduce the number of possible suspects within any given population by sketching the "type" of person who may have committed a certain category of crime (see Chapter 3). Threat assessment, on the other hand, concentrates on determining the *seriousness* of a threat that has already been made and—if the assessment suggests it is serious—setting up procedures and strategies to protect the intended target. "Instead of looking at demographic and psychological characteristics, the threat assessment approach focuses on a subject's thinking and behaviors as a means to assess his/her progress on a pathway to violent actions" (Borum et al., 1999, p. 328).

Therefore, the crucial step in threat assessment is to determine whether the threatener is *making* a threat or *posing* a threat. Thousands of threats are made on public officials (and schools) every year, but a vast majority of them are not based on real intentions to carry them out. On the other hand, those who *pose* a threat are regarded as serious and may not even communicate their intentions to the threatened target directly. Interestingly, none of the 43 people who attacked a public figure (such as the U.S. president) over a 50-year period in the United States communicated a threat directly to the intended target (Borum et al., 1999; Fein & Vossekuil, 1999). However, in several of the school shooting cases, the shooters had communicated their intentions to other students who did not take them seriously; did not tell adults; or, in one case, even turned out to watch. It should be emphasized that all threats should be taken seriously and evaluated. The competent threat assessment tries to distinguish who is serious and who is not.

Because of their expertise in working with threats against public figures and other members of the public, several federal agencies, including the FBI and the Secret Service, have put together threat assessment guidelines to help school personnel, students, and parents identify warning signs of potential violence directed at the school environment. In response to the demand for such, the U.S. Secret Service has been especially involved, establishing the Secret Service National Threat Assessment Center (NTAC) (see Focus 8.2). In June 1999, following the attack at Columbine High School, the U.S. Secret Service and the Department of Education launched a collaborative effort called the Safe School Initiative (SSI) (Borum et al., 1999). This included an intensive study of 37 U.S. school shootings involving 41 perpetrators that have occurred over the past 25 years (see Focus 7.2). The goal of the project was to examine thoroughly the thinking, planning, and behaviors engaged in by students who carried out school attacks. In addition, the perceived rash of school violence has thrust mental health professionals and school psychologists into the role of assisting school districts and the local communities in the development of prevention and treatment programs directed at juvenile violence (Evans & Rey, 2001). It also has initiated considerable applied research by forensic psychologists across the country.

According to the FBI (O'Tool, 2000), threats may be divided into four types: (1) direct, (2) indirect, (3) veiled, and (4) conditional. A *direct* threat specifies a target and is delivered in a straightforward, clear, and explicit manner. For example, a caller might say, "I placed a bomb in the school cafeteria and it will go off at noon today." An *indirect* threat is more vague and ambiguous. The specific motivation, the intention, and the target are unclear and open to speculation: "If I wanted to, I could kill many at the school at any time." This is the type of threat that had most frequently been made, according to the SSI.

A *veiled* threat strongly implies but does not explicitly threaten violence. For example, a student might receive an anonymous note in his locker that reads, "We would be better off without you around anymore." The message clearly hints at a potential violent act but leaves the seriousness and meaning of the note for the threatened victim to interpret. A *conditional* threat is most often seen in extortion cases. It often warns that a violent act will occur unless certain demands or terms are met, such as occurred during the Washington, D.C., sniper killings in the fall of 2002. The message was this: "If you don't pay us 10 million dollars, none of your children will be safe." Without the condition attached, this would have been a veiled threat.

Researchers from the SSI have concluded that those involved in school shootings did not "just snap"; they planned their attacks ahead of time (Vossekuil, Fein, Reddy, Borum, & Mozeleski, 2002). In many cases, the incident was planned at least 2 weeks beforehand. Interestingly, the researchers found that when juveniles plan targeted violence, they often tell at least one person about their plans, give out specifics before the event takes place, and usually obtain the weapons they need from their own home or a relative's home. Unfortunately, the person or persons who were told about the impending incident were peers and friends, and rarely did these informed youth bring the information to an adult's attention.

Another observation from the SSI report was that, in many school shootings, friends and fellow students influenced or encouraged the attacker to act. For example, Evan Ramsey, age 16, who killed his principal and a student and wounded two others in Bethel, Alaska, in 1997, explained, "I told everyone what I was going to do." In fact, so many students had heard about his planned attack that 24 students crowded the lobby mezzanine to watch. One student even brought a camera to record the event.

According to the SSI report, for more than half of the school shooters, the motive was revenge. In many cases, long-standing bullying or harassment played a key role in the decision to attack. However, there are many other motives or reasons for school violence. O'Tool (2000) suggests a list:

> Threats are made for a variety of reasons. A threat may be a warning signal, a reaction to fear of punishment or some other anxiety, or a demand for attention. It may be intended to taunt; to intimidate; to assert power or control; to punish; to manipulate or coerce; to frighten; to terrorize; to compel someone to do something; to strike back for an injury, injustice or slight; to disrupt someone's or some institution's life; to test authority, to protect oneself. The emotions that underlie a threat can be love; hate; fear; rage; or desire for attention, revenge, excitement, or recognition. (p. 6)

In summary, it should be emphasized that there is no accurate or useful profile of "the school shooter" or threatener. According to the SSI report, the personalities and social characteristics of the shooters varied considerably. They came from a variety of social backgrounds and varied in age from 11 to 21 years. Family situations ranged from intact families to foster homes. Academic performance ranged from excellent to failing. Most were not diagnosed with any mental disorder, and a majority had no history of drug or alcohol abuse. However, more than three-fourths of school shooters did threaten to kill themselves, make suicidal gestures, or try to kill themselves before their attacks. Nevertheless, serious, long-standing, major depression did not appear to be a prominent feature in their backgrounds.

Most school shooters did have easy access to guns. As noted in Focus 7.2, in nearly two-thirds of the incidents, school shooters obtained guns from their own home or from that of a relative. The SSI report suggests, therefore, that although guns may be easy to obtain for many youth, when the notion of an attack exists, any effort to acquire, prepare, or use a weapon may signal an attacker's progression from a thought to an action.

FOCUS 7.2. SECRET SERVICE SAFE SCHOOL INITIATIVE REPORT

What we know about school shooters:

- Attackers talk about their plans to others. Prior to most incidents, the attacker told someone about his idea or plan. In more than three-fourths of incidents, the attacker told a friend, schoolmate, or sibling about his idea for a possible attack before taking action.
- Attackers make plans. Incidents of targeted violence at school are rarely impulsive. In almost all incidents, the attacker developed the idea to harm the target before the attack.
- There is no stereotype or profile. There is no accurate or useful profile of the "school shooter." The personality and social characteristics of the shooters vary substantially.
- Attackers had easy access to guns. Most attackers had used guns previously and had access to guns. In nearly two-thirds of incidents, the attackers obtained guns used in the attack from their own home or that of a relative.
- School staff are often first responders. Most shooting incidents were not resolved by law enforcement intervention. More than half of the attacks ended before law enforcement responded to the scene. In these cases, faculty or fellow students stopped the attacker.
- Attackers are encouraged by others. In many cases, other students were involved in some capacity. In almost half of the cases, friends or fellow students influenced or encouraged the attacker to act.
- Bullying can be a factor. In a number of cases, bullying played a key role in the decision to attack. A number of attackers had experienced bullying and harassment that were long-standing and severe.
- Warning signs are common. Most attackers engaged in some behavior prior to the incident that caused concern or indicated a need for help.

Source: U.S. Secret Service (2000).

Juvenile Firesetting

A particularly important offense category that most often involves juveniles is arson, or **firesetting.** We include it in this chapter because firesetting is usually a symptom of serious antisocial behavior that can be the precursor of many years of chronic offending.

According to the U.S. Fire Administration (2009), there were an estimated 32,500 intentionally set structural fires in 2008. During the same year, 10,784 individuals were arrested for intentionally set fires in the United States. Nearly 50% of these arrests were juveniles (FBI, 2009). Besides school violence, firesetting is the only violent crime where juveniles represent nearly a majority of the arrests. Of those juveniles arrested, nearly 60% were under the age of 15. The majority (75%) of arson fires involved community or public buildings such as churches, jails, or schools. In a typical year in the United States, fires set by children and youth claim the lives of approximately 300 individuals and destroy more than $300 million worth of property (Putnam & Kirkpatrick, 2005). Children are also often the victim of firesetting and arson fires, accounting for 85% of the lives lost in intentionally set fires in the United States (U. S. Fire Administration, 2004). Next to deaths caused by motor vehicle accidents, fires are the leading cause of death among young children (Stickle & Blechman, 2002).

The term *firesetting* refers to "intentional acts planned to produce a disturbance or to bring about damage or harm" (Chen, Arria, & Anthony, 2003, p. 45). Most firesetters are young males. Some studies have found that between 75 and 85% of all firesetting is done by males, with increasing percentages of females in the 13- to 17-year-old group (FBI, 2003; Stadolnik, 2000). In a comprehensive study of 1,016 juveniles and adults arrested for arson and fire-related crimes, Icove and Estepp (1987) discovered that vandalism—prompted by a wish to get back at authority—was the most frequently identified motive, accounting for 49% of the arsons in the sample. This finding has been consistently supported in other research (e.g., E. Robbins & Robbins, 1964), which reveals that most fires set by juveniles are motivated by the wish to get back at authority or gain status or are prompted by a dare or a need for excitement. Feelings of anger, being ignored, or depression are commonly reported before acts of firesetting (Chen et al., 2003).

Many arson fires set by youth go undetected, unreported, or unsolved (Zipper & Wilcox, 2005). It is estimated, for example, that less than 10% of the fires set by juveniles are reported (Adler, Nunn, Northam, Lebnan, & Ross, 1994). Zipper and Wilcox report that, of the 1,241 Massachusetts juveniles referred for counseling services because of firesetting, only 11% of the blazes these youths started were reported. No one reported these incidents because witnesses or caretakers did not consider the behavior dangerous; no loss of life or significant destruction of property occurred. In these situations, many people worry that charging juveniles with arson will give them a criminal record that will hamper their future careers.

Developmental Stages of Firesetting

Child firesetters have attracted considerable interest among developmental psychologists. The general consensus is that childhood firesetting goes through discernible stages. For example, Gaynor (1996) identifies three developmental phases: (1) fire interest, (2) fireplay, and (3) firesetting. Fascination and experimentation with fire appear to be common features of normal child development. Kafrey (1980) discovered that fascination with fire appears to be nearly universal in children between 5 and 7 years old. This fascination with fire begins early, with 1 in 5 children setting fires before the age of 3. As the child gets older, fireplay (experimentation) normally takes place between the ages of 5 and 9. In this stage, the child experiments with how a fire starts and how it burns. Unfortunately, children during this phase are especially vulnerable to the hazards of fire because of their lack of experience with it and ways to extinguish it if it flares out of control (Lambie, McCardle, & Coleman, 2002). By age 10, most children have learned the dangers of fire. However, if they continue to set fires at this point—especially damaging ones—they probably have graduated into the firesetting stage. These youths most often intend to use fires to destroy, as a form of excitement, or as a communicative device to draw attention to themselves and their perceived problems.

Experts find that children who *continue* to set fires after age 10 frequently demonstrate poor social skills, inadequate social competence, and poor impulse control compared to their peers (Kolko, 2002; Kolko & Kazdin, 1989). Some experts have found that persistent firesetters, compared to non-firesetters, are more likely to have attention deficit/hyperactivity disorders (Forehand, Wierson, Frame, Kempton, & Armistead, 1991), and many are rejected by their peers. Some studies report that approximately 74% of youth firesetters have been diagnosed with conduct disorders (Chen et al., 2003). In addition, a majority of children who set fires beyond the normal fascination and experimental stages tend to have poor relationships with their parents and also appear to be victims of physical abuse (H. F. Jackson, Glass, & Hope, 1987). One recent investigation found that maltreated and abused children, compared to their non-maltreated peers, set significantly more fires, demonstrated more versatility in their ignition sources, had more variety in the items or targets they burned, and were more likely to set fires out of anger due to family stressors (C. Root, MacKay, Henderson, Del Bove, & Warling, 2008).

Lambie et al. (2002) report that firesetting is often only one segment of a cluster of antisocial behaviors, the motives for which occur for a variety of reasons and typically include impulse control problems and misdirected anger and boredom. Other researchers have commented on the wide range of criminal offending engaged in by firesetters, beyond firesetting (Gannon & Pina, 2010). For instance, there is some evidence that children who are consistently cruel to animals and other children also tend to engage in consistent firesetting behavior (Slavkin, 2001). Furthermore, a very large majority of firesetters known to the juvenile justice system have committed many other serious juvenile acts besides arson (Ritvo, Shanok, & Lewis, 1983; Stickle & Blechman, 2002). Interestingly, Stickle and Blechman found that "firesetting juvenile offenders exhibit a pattern of developmentally advanced, serious antisocial behavior consistent with an early starter or life-course–persistent trajectory" (p. 190). As might be expected, research has revealed that a greater portion of the persistent firesetters are boys than girls, at a ratio of about 9 to 1 (Zipper & Wilcox, 2005).

Firesetting Typologies

Based on clinical assessments of known firesetters, Kolko (2002) developed a typology that identifies four types of firesetters: (1) curious, (2) pathological, (3) expressive, and (4) delinquent. The typology is built on the assumption of differences in motivation, although it does take into consideration individual and environmental influences. In brief, the curious firesetter uses fire for fascination purposes, the pathological is driven by psychological or emotional problems, the expressive sets fires as a cry for help, and the delinquent uses fire as a means to antisocial or destructive ends (Putnam & Kirkpatrick, 2005). The types are not mutually exclusive, in that a juvenile could use fire as a cry for help for his or her psychological distress.

The Criminal Psychopath

"Is Joran Van der Sloot a psychopath?" In 2010, this headline screamed at us from the Internet, followed by numerous comments and blog entries on the subject. Van der Sloot, often described as "the Dutch playboy," was charged in the killing of a Peruvian woman, Stephany Flores Ramirez, and was a suspect in the disappearance of Alabama teenager Natalee Holloway. Van der Sloot had a history of reckless, impulsive, attention-getting behaviors and was frequently described as unremorseful or callous. But is he a psychopath?

Probably no topic has caught the attention of forensic psychologists interested in the development of habitual criminal behavior more in recent years than the topic of psychopathy. (See Personal Perspective 7.1, in which Dr. Adelle Forth discusses her research interests in this area.) The term **psychopath** is currently used to describe a person who demonstrates a discernible cluster of psychological, interpersonal, and neuropsychological features that distinguish him or her from the general population. In addition, the psychopath, according to this definition, may or may not engage in habitual criminal behavior. This is a main reason why a psychopath should be distinguished from a *sociopath,* the common term for someone who commits repeated crime. As we will see shortly, career criminals are not necessarily psychopaths.

PERSONAL PERSPECTIVE 7.1

Teaching Forensic Psychology and Studying Psychopaths

Adelle Forth, PhD

I am an associate professor of forensic psychology at Carleton University in Ottawa, Ontario. Although I enjoy teaching all levels of undergraduate and graduate courses, my two favorite classes are the second-year Introduction to Forensic Psychology and the third-year Forensic Psychology Honours Seminar.

In the second-year course, I have the chance to introduce the students to the field of forensic psychology. As you glance over the chapters in this textbook, it becomes clear that forensic psychology is a diverse discipline with a host of intriguing topics. In the third-year course, students read journal articles in order to provide them with an understanding of how knowledge accumulates and the methodologies used in forensic psychology. Students select readings from key forensic journals like *Law and Human Behavior, Criminal Justice and Behavior,* and *Behavioral Sciences and the Law* and are asked to identify the main components of an empirical article and develop an idea for future research. They also develop the necessary skills to do their honours thesis in forensic psychology. I always incorporate real-world activities in this class. For example, students participate in a mock dangerous offender trial. The case is modeled after one that I testified in as an expert witness, one in which a man had repeatedly violently assaulted his common-law wife. The students take on the roles of the expert

witnesses and lawyers from the prosecution and defense sides. I get to play the role of the judge! In the actual case, the judge decided the accused was not a dangerous offender and gave him a sentence of 8 years and ordered that he be supervised for a minimum of 10 years after release.

Each year, when I tell students my area of research is psychopathy, the first question is always, "What made you interested in psychopaths?" Students also ask, "Did you date a psychopath?" "Is your brother a psychopath?" "Is your twin sister a psychopath?" To these questions I answer, "None of the above." I tell them that in the third year of my undergraduate psychology degree at the University of British Columbia, I took a forensic psychology course taught by Professor Robert Hare. We spent a huge chunk of that course reading and learning about psychopaths, and I was fascinated. I volunteered to work in his lab, then completed my BA, MA, and PhD working under his mentorship, and I continue to collaborate with him today.

What keeps me interested in studying psychopaths is that there are still so many questions yet to be answered. Although research in psychopathy has increased dramatically over the past few decades, we are still looking for answers to questions like, What are the underlying cognitive and social factors associated with psychopathy? What is the interaction between genetic predispositions and environmental factors? What works best for preventing psychopathy? Why do some psychopathic individuals respond to intervention whereas others do not? How do psychopathic traits manifest across different cultures and countries?

During my academic career, I have developed two assessment measures, both focused on adolescents. My colleagues and I have developed the *Hare Psychopathy Checklist: Youth Version (PCL-YV)* in order to provide researchers and clinicians with a method to identify psychopathic features in adolescents. I have also coauthored the *Structured Assessment of Violence Risk in Youth (SAVRY)*, a structured professional judgment measure designed to assess static and dynamic risk for future violence.

There is one area of psychopathy that has been neglected by researchers: victims of psychopaths.

I have recently begun a program of research to rectify this omission. My students and I have recently completed a large survey of men and women who have been victims of psychopaths. The survivors described an enormous amount of emotional, physical, and financial harm perpetrated by psychopaths, harm that has had long-term consequences for them. As one survivor stated, "Humanity needs to know what psychopathy is, how it behaves and the harm it can do if left uncensored and undetected" (Survey participant, December 30, 2008). We are currently identifying potential "red flags" for psychopathic behavior and the forms of deception and manipulation used by psychopaths. In the future, we will be doing in-depth interviews with survivors to better understand what can be done to help them.

Dr. Forth earned her PhD in forensic psychology at the University of British Columbia and has taught at Carleton University since 1991. To balance her academic life, she spends time looking after her four "rescue" ferrets, two German Shepherds, and one long-suffering cat. She also tries to find forever homes for abused and abandoned ferrets. Finally, she volunteers as a dog trainer, teaching humans how to better communicate with their four-legged friends, as well as competing in obedience trials with her own two dogs. In her spare time, she enjoys reading UK crime writers like P. D. James, Minette Walters, and Ian Rankin.

Many psychopaths have no history of serious antisocial behavior, and the converse may also be true. That is, many persistent, serious offenders are not psychopaths. For our purposes here, the term *criminal psychopath* will be reserved for those psychopaths who demonstrate a wide range of persistent antisocial behavior. As a group, they tend to be "dominant, manipulative individuals characterized by an impulsive, risk-taking and antisocial lifestyle, who obtain their greatest thrill from diverse sexual gratification and target diverse victims over time" (Porter et al., 2000, p. 220). As further noted by Stephen Porter and his colleagues, "Given its relation to crime and violence, psychopathy is arguably one of the most important psychological constructs in the criminal justice system" (p. 227). Nevertheless, some scholars believe the emphasis on psychopathy is unjustified, particularly as it relates to juveniles, as we will discuss shortly.

General Behavioral Characteristics of Psychopaths

Hervey Cleckley (1941) was one of the first to outline the behavioral characteristics of psychopaths. He was a professor of psychiatry and neurology at the Medical College of Georgia during the 1930s and remained there until the 1950s. Cleckley is credited with completing one of the most comprehensive works on the psychopath, titled *The Mask of Sanity*. The book went through five editions, and his clear writing style, in combination with the subject area, captivated public and scholarly interests for many years.

Cleckley (1941) identified what he thought were 10 cardinal behavioral features characteristic of the true psychopath: (1) selfishness (also called egocentricity), (2) an inability to love or give genuine affection to others, (3) frequent deceitfulness or lying, (4) lack of guilt or remorsefulness (no matter how cruel the behavior), (5) callousness or a lack of empathy, (6) low anxiety proneness, (7) poor judgment and failure to learn from experience, (8) superficial charm, (9) failure to follow any life plan, and (10) cycles of unreliability. By no means do all researchers in the field of psychopathy agree with this list, but the behavioral features outlined serve as a starting point for further discussion in this section.

An important distinction underlying much of the behavioral descriptions is what Quay (1965) refers to as the psychopath's profound and pathological stimulation seeking. According to Quay, the actions of the psychopath are motivated by an excessive *neuropsychological* need for thrills and excitement. It is not unusual to see psychopaths drawn to such interests as race-car driving, skydiving, and motorcycle stunts.

Antisocial Personality Disorder and Psychopathy

Psychiatrists, clinical psychologists, and mental health workers often use the term *antisocial personality disorder (ASP/APD)* to summarize many of the same features found in the criminal psychopath. Antisocial personality disorder refers specifically to an individual who exhibits "a pervasive pattern of disregard for, and violation of, the rights of others that begins in childhood or early adolescence and continues into adulthood" (American Psychiatric Association, 1994, p. 645). In other words, the antisocial personality disorder appears closely aligned with the persistent offender, such as the LCP offender.

It should be emphasized that, although there are many behavioral similarities, the terms *antisocial personality disorder* and *psychopathy* are not synonymous. Antisocial personality disorder refers to broad behavioral patterns based on clinical observations, whereas psychopathy refers not only to specific behavioral patterns but also to measurable cognitive, emotional, and neuropsychological differences. In addition, ASP is so broad in its scope that between 50 and 80% of male inmates qualify as meeting its criteria (Correctional Services of Canada, 1990; Hare, 1998; Hare, Forth, & Strachan, 1992). In contrast, only 11 to 25% of male inmates meet the criteria for psychopathy (Hare, 1996). These data suggest that the construct of psychopathy may be a more precise indicator—and a better predictor of violence—than the more global construct of ASP.

Prevalence of Criminal Psychopathy

Overall, Hare (1998) estimates that the prevalence of psychopaths in the general population is about 1%, whereas in the adult prison population, estimates range from 15 to 25%. Some researchers (e.g., Simourd & Hoge, 2000) wonder, however, whether these estimates are not somewhat inflated. Simourd and Hoge report that only 11% of the inmate population they studied could be identified as criminal psychopaths. The inmates used in the Simourd and Hoge study were not simply inmates in a medium-security correctional facility. All 321 were serving a current sentence for violent offending, more than half of them had been convicted of a previous violent offense, and almost all of them had extensive criminal careers. Therefore, percentage estimates of criminal psychopathy within any given population should be tempered by the type of facility, as well as the cultural, ethnic, and age mix of the targeted population.

Offending Patterns of Criminal Psychopaths

Although some psychopaths have little contact with the criminal justice system, many have continual contact with the system because of persistent, serious offending. For example, Gretton, McBride, Hare, O'Shaughnessy, and Kumka (2001) point out that criminal psychopaths generally "lack a normal sense of ethics and morality, live by their own rules, are prone to use cold-blooded, instrumental intimidation and violence to satisfy their wants and needs, and generally are contemptuous of social norms and the rights of others" (p. 428). Criminal psychopaths manifest violent and aggressive behaviors—including verbal abuse, threats, and intimidation—at a much higher rate than is found in other populations (Hare, Hart, & Harpur, 1991). In some cases, this persistent offending is extremely violent in nature.

Criminal psychopaths are "responsible for a markedly disproportionate amount of the serious crime, violence, and social distress in every society" (Hare, 1996, p. 26). Hare posits, "The ease with which psychopaths engage in . . . dispassionate violence has very real significance for society in general and for law enforcement personnel in particular" (p. 38). Hare refers to a 1992 report by the FBI that found that nearly half of the law enforcement officers who died in the line of duty were killed by individuals who closely matched the personality profile of the psychopath. In addition, the crimes of psychopathic sex offenders are likely to be more violent, brutal, unemotional, and sadistic than those of other sex offenders (Hare, Clark, Grann, & Thornton, 2000). Some serial murders described as unusually sadistic and brutal also tend to have many psychopathic features (Hare et al., 2000; M. H. Stone, 1998). It should be emphasized, though, that very few psychopaths are serial killers.

The relationship between psychopathy and sexual offending appears to be a complex one. For example, the prevalence of psychopaths among child molesters is estimated to be from 10 to 15%; among rapists, it is between 40 and 50% (Gretton et al., 2001; Porter et al., 2000). Research also indicates that rapists who have psychopathic characteristics are more likely to have "nonsexual" motivations for their crimes, such as anger, vindictiveness, sadism, and opportunism (Hart & Dempster, 1997).

Many of the murders and serious assaults committed by non-psychopaths occurred during domestic disputes or extreme emotional arousal. On the other hand, this pattern of violence is rarely observed for criminal psychopaths (Hare et al., 1991; Williamson, Hare, & Wong, 1987). Criminal psychopaths frequently engage in violence as a form of revenge or retribution or during a bout of drinking. Many of the attacks of non-psychopaths are against women they know well, whereas many of the attacks of criminal psychopaths are directed toward women who are strangers. Hare et al. (1991) observe that the violence committed by criminal psychopaths was callous and cold-blooded, "without the affective coloring that accompanied the violence of nonpsychopaths" (p. 395).

According to Porter et al. (2000), research suggests that psychopaths reoffend faster, violate parole sooner, and perhaps commit more institutional violence than non-psychopaths. In one study (Serin, Peters, & Barbaree, 1990), the number of failures—or violations of the conditions of their release—of male offenders released on an unescorted temporary absence program was examined. The failure rate for psychopaths was 37.5%, whereas none of the non-psychopaths failed. The failure rate during parole was also examined. Although 7% of non-psychopaths violated parole requirements, 33% of the psychopaths violated their requirements. In another study (Serin & Amos, 1995), 299 male offenders were followed for up to 8 years after their release from a federal prison. Sixty-five percent of the psychopaths were convicted of another crime within 3 years, compared to a reconviction rate of 25% for non-psychopaths. Quinsey, Rice, and Harris (1995) found that within 6 years of release from prison, more than 80% of the psychopaths convicted as sex offenders had violently recidivated, compared to a 20% recidivism rate for non-psychopathic sex offenders.

High recidivism rates are also characteristic of adolescent offenders with psychopathic characteristics. According to Gretton et al. (2001), these offenders are more likely than other adolescent offenders to escape from custody, violate the conditions of probation, and commit nonviolent and violent offenses over a 5-year follow-up period. The high recidivism rates among adult and juvenile psychopathic offenders have prompted some researchers to conclude that there is "nothing the behavioral sciences can offer for treating those with psychopathy" (Gacono, Nieberding, Owen, Rubel, & Bodholdt, 1997, p. 119). This may be because psychopaths tend to "be unmotivated to accept their problematic behavior and often lack insight into the nature and extent of their psychopathology" (Skeem, Edens, & Colwell, 2003, p. 26). Other researchers take a decidedly different perspective and believe that untreatability statements concerning the psychopath are unwarranted (Salekin, 2002; Skeem, Monahan, & Mulvey, 2002; Skeem, Poythress, Edens, Lilienfeld, & Cale, in press; Wong, 2000). There is *some* evidence that psychopaths who receive larger "doses" of treatment are less likely to demonstrate subsequent violent behavior than those who receive less treatment (Skeem et al., 2003).

Psychological Measures of Psychopathy

Currently, the most popular instrument for measuring criminal psychopathy is the 22-item **Psychopathy Checklist (PCL)** (Hare, 1980) and its 20-item revision **(PCL-R)** (Hare, 1991). More recently, the PCL-R has been published in a second edition, which includes new information on its applicability in forensic and research settings. It has been expanded for use with offenders in other countries and includes updated normative and validation data on male and female offenders.

A 12-item short-form version has also been developed, called the **Psychopathy Checklist: Screening Version (PCL:SV)** (Hart, Cox, & Hare, 1995; Hart, Hare, & Forth, 1993), as well as the **Psychopathy Checklist: Youth Version (PCL:YV)** and the **P-Scan: Research Version.** The P-Scan is a screening instrument that serves as a *rough* screen for psychopathic features and as a source of working hypotheses to deal with managing suspects, offenders, or clients. It is designed for use in law enforcement, probation, corrections, civil and forensic facilities, and other areas in which it would be useful to have some information about the possible presence of psychopathic features in a particular person. Of course, the P-Scan needs much more research before it can be used as a valid instrument in practice. All five checklists are conceptually and—with the exception of the P-Scan—empirically similar.

The instruments are largely based on Cleckley's (1941) conception of psychopathy but are specifically designed to identify psychopaths in male prison, forensic, or psychiatric populations. Because the PCL-R is currently the most frequently used as both a research and clinical instrument, it will be the center of attention for the remainder of this section. The PCL:YV is beginning to be researched more extensively and will be covered in more detail in the section on juveniles with psychopathic features.

The PCL-R assesses the affective (emotional), interpersonal, behavioral, and social deviance facets of criminal psychopathy from various sources, including self-reports; behavioral observations; and collateral sources, such as parents, family members, friends, and arrest and court records, which can help to establish the credibility of self-reports (Hare, 1996; Hare et al., 1991). In addition, item ratings from the PCL-R, for instance, require some integration of information across multiple domains, including behavior at work or school; behavior toward family, friends, and sexual partners; and criminal behavior (Kosson, Cyterski, Steuerwald, Neuman, & Walker-Matthes, 2002). Typically, highly trained examiners use all this information to score each item on a point scale of 0 to 2, which measures the extent to which an individual has the disposition described by each item on the checklist (0 = *consistently absent*, 1 = *inconsistent*, 2 = *consistently present*). Scoring is, however, quite complex and requires substantial time, extensive training, and access to a considerable amount of background information on the individual. A score of 30 or above usually qualifies a person as a primary psychopath (Hare, 1996). In some research and clinical settings, cutoff scores ranging from 25 to 33 are often used (Simourd & Hoge, 2000). Hare (1991) recommends that persons with scores between 21 and 29 be classified as "middle" subjects who show many of the features of psychopathy but do not fit all the criteria. Scores below 21 are considered "non-psychopaths."

So far, the research has strongly supported the reliability and validity of the PCL-R for distinguishing criminal psychopaths from criminal non-psychopaths and for helping correctional psychologists in risk assessments of inmates (Hare, 1996; Hare et al., 1992). In addition, the instrument provides researchers and mental health professionals with a universal measurement for the assessment of psychopathy that facilitates international and cross-cultural communication concerning theory, research, and eventual clinical practice (Hare et al., 2000). Currently, the PCL-R is increasingly being used as a clinical instrument for the diagnosis of psychopathy across the globe, although it appears to be most powerful in identifying psychopathy among North American White males (Hare et al., 2000).

Core Factors of Psychopathy

One finding that has clearly emerged from the research on the PCL-R is that psychopathy is multidimensional in nature. **Factor analysis** is one statistical procedure designed to find different dimensions or factors in test data. When expert ratings of psychopathy on the PCL-R were submitted to a factor analysis, at least two behavioral dimensions or factors came to light (Hare, 1991; Harpur, Hakstian, & Hare, 1988; Hart et al., 1993). Factor 1 reflects the interpersonal and emotional components of the disorder and consists of items measuring remorselessness, callousness, and selfish use and manipulation of others. The typical psychopath feels no compunction about using others strictly to meet his or her own needs. Factor 2 is most closely associated with a socially deviant lifestyle, as characterized by poor planning, impulsiveness, an excessive need for stimulation, proneness to boredom, and a lack of realistic goals. In criminal psychopaths, some researchers have found that Factor 1 appears to be associated with planned predatory violence, whereas Factor 2 appears to be related to spontaneous and disinhibited violence (Hart & Dempster, 1997). Factor 1 is also linked to resistance to and inability to profit from psychotherapy and treatment programs (Seto & Barbaree, 1999). Factor 2 appears related to socioeconomic status, educational attainment, and cultural/ethnic background, whereas Factor 1 may be more connected with biopsychological influences (Cooke & Michie, 1997). Research also suggests that Factor 1 may be a more powerful indicator of psychopathy than Factor 2 (Cooke, Michie, Hart, & Hare, 1999).

More recent research with both children and adults, however, reveals that there may be *three* behavioral dimensions at the core of psychopathy rather than just the original two (Cooke & Michie, 2001; Frick, Bodin, & Barry, 2000; Kosson et al., 2002). Cooke and Michie, for example, found from their factor analysis of PCL-R data that psychopathy probably consists of three core factors: (1) arrogant and deceitful interpersonal style, (2) impulsive and irresponsible behavioral style (highly similar to the original Factor 2), and (3) deficient affective experience. Factors 1 and 3 are actually subdivisions of the original Factor 1 reported in earlier studies. The term *deficient affective experience* refers to the lack of sincere positive emotions toward others and the demonstration of callousness and lack of empathy. The terms *arrogant* and *deceitful interpersonal style,* on the other hand, refer to the glibness, superficial charm, and grandiose sense of self-worth that are so characteristic of the psychopath.

Research has shown that adult psychopaths usually exhibit significant antisocial behavior in their childhoods (Seagrave & Grisso, 2002). It is reasonable, therefore, to expect researchers to begin searching the developmental trajectory of psychopathy to identify tomorrow's psychopaths. The next section examines what we currently know about the childhood of the psychopath.

Juvenile Psychopathy

One of the serious shortcomings of the extensive research conducted on psychopathy is that it has focused almost exclusively on White adult males (Frick et al., 2000). Consequently, research on juvenile (adolescent and child) psychopathy is limited, but it is rapidly growing. However, as we mentioned in Chapter 6, attempts to apply the label *psychopathy* to juvenile populations are strongly resisted, and they "raise several conceptual, methodological, and practical concerns related to clinical/forensic practice and juvenile/criminal justice policy" (Edens, Skeem et al., 2001, p. 54). Over the past decade, scholars have engaged in spirited debates on this issue (Edens & Vincent, 2008; Salekin, Rosenbaum, & Lee, 2008; Viljoen et al., 2010). Some debate has focused on whether psychopathy can or should be applied to juveniles at all. Can features of adult psychopathy be found in children and adolescents in the first place? Second, even if psychopathy can be identified in adolescents, the label may have too many negative connotations. More specifically, the label implies that the prognosis for treatment is poor, a high rate of offending and recidivism can be expected, and the intrinsic and biological basis of the disorder means little can be done outside of biological interventions. A third debate contends that psychopathy assessments of youth must achieve a high level of confidence before they can be employed in the criminal justice system (Seagrave & Grisso, 2002).

Several instruments for measuring pre-adult psychopathy have been developed in recent years, including the Psychopathy Screening Device (PSD) (Frick, O'Brien, Wootton, & McBurnett, 1994), the Childhood Psychopathy Scale (CPS) (Lynam, 1997), and the PCL:YV (Forth et al., 1997). All three instruments began primarily as research measures rather than as clinical-diagnostic measures but are now likely to be seen in clinical practice. This is particularly true of the PCL:YV.

The PCL:YV, designed for assessing psychopathy in adolescents age 13 or older, is a modified version of the PCL-R. Basically, the instrument attempts to assess psychopathy across the youth's life span, with an emphasis on school adjustment and peer and family relations. Similar to the adult PCL-R, the PCL:YV requires a lengthy standardized, semistructured clinical interview and a review of documents by a well-trained psychologist. Scores of 0 (*consistently absent*), 1 (*inconsistent*), or 2 (*consistently present*) for each of the 20 behavioral dimensions of psychopathy represent the scoring system. The instrument—like the PCL-R—generates a total score and two factor scores. Factor 1 reflects an interpersonal/affective dimension and includes items that measure glibness/superficial charm, grandiosity, manipulativeness, dishonesty, and callousness. Factor 2 reflects behavioral or lifestyles features such as impulsiveness, irresponsibility, early behavioral problems, and lack of goals.

The PSD is a behavior rating scale in which some of the items on the PCL-R were rewritten for use with children (Frick et al., 2000). Currently, the PSD comes in three versions: (1) a teacher version, (2) a parent version, and (3) a self-report version. Using the teacher and parent versions of the PSD, Frick et al. (1994) found (through a factor analysis) that juvenile psychopathy may be made be up of two major dimensions. One dimension was labeled callous-unemotional and the other impulsivity-conduct problems. Later, however, Frick et al. (2000) found evidence (again through a factor analysis) to support a *three*-dimensional core for childhood psychopathy. Two of the factors (callous-unemotional and impulsivity) were similar to the core dimensions found for adults in Frick et al.'s earlier study. However, the construct of impulsivity seems to be much more complex in children than in adults, and the researchers discovered that the construct may be subdivided into impulsivity and narcissism (grandiose sense of self-worth).

One of the major problems of identifying juvenile psychopaths is that psychopathy may be very difficult to measure reliably because of the transient and constantly changing developmental patterns across the life span, especially during the early years. For example, psychopathic symptoms in childhood may look very different from those exhibited in adulthood (Hart, Watt, & Vincent, 2002). That is, some of the behavioral patterns of children and adolescents may be similar to psychopaths for a variety of reasons but may not really be signs of psychopathy.

Children in an abusive home often demonstrate an abnormally restricted range of emotions that are similar to the emotional characteristics of psychopathy. Actually, they may be the child's way of coping in a very stressful home environment (Seagrave & Grisso, 2002). Furthermore, Seagrave and Grisso assert that

"Some adolescent behavior may . . . appear psychopathic by way of poor anger control, lack of goals, and poor judgment, but is actually influenced by parallel developmental tasks encountered by most adolescents" (p. 229). Going against the rules is part of many adolescents' attempts to gain autonomy from adult dominance, such as what is found in adolescent-limited offending. In addition, adult criminal psychopaths often have been psychologically scarred by years of drug and alcohol abuse, physical fighting, lost opportunities, and multiple incarcerations (Lynam, 1997). Consequently, adult psychopaths may present a very different population pool compared to the juvenile psychopath.

Edens, Skeem, et al. (2001) also point out that some of the items on the various psychological measures of psychopathy (especially the PCL-R and the PCL:YV) are inappropriate for use with adolescents, or for use with certain populations, such as female adolescents (Edens, Campbell, & Weir, 2007) or various ethnic groups (Leistico, Salekin, DeCoster, & Rogers, 2008). Some items focus on such things as the lack of goals and irresponsibility. If these features are not present, then the adolescent might receive scores in the psychopathy direction. However, adolescents generally have not crystallized their life goals and responsibilities to any great extent, and consequently such items "seem less applicable as definitive markers of psychopathy for adolescents than for adults" (Edens et al., 2007, p. 58). We must be careful, then, not to generalize what we know about the adult psychopath to a juvenile who has been given the same label.

Nevertheless, many researchers are persisting in their attempts to identify juvenile psychopaths and measure psychopathic tendencies. In a study examining the prevalence rate of psychopathy among children, Skilling, Quinsey, and Craig (2001) found in a sample of more than 1,000 boys in Grades 4 to 8 that 4.3% of the sample could be classified as psychopathic on every measure employed in the study. These data suggest that the percentages reported in the prison population may not be as inflated as some researchers suppose.

Lynam (1997) designed a research project that compared juvenile and adult psychopaths. Using the CPS, Lynam reported results that suggested psychopathy begins in childhood and can be measured reliably in children ages 12 and 13. Lynam found that psychopathic children, like their adult counterparts, were the most aggressive, severe, frequent, and impulsive offenders, a characteristic that was stable across time. Moreover, he discovered that the CPS was a better predictor of serious delinquency than socioeconomic status, previous delinquency, IQ, or impulsivity.

Research so far does indicate that there is some validity in measures of juvenile psychopathy (Kosson et al., 2002; Murrie & Cornell, 2002). Recent research also indicates that juvenile psychopathy may have a genetic basis and may run in families (Forsman, Lichtenstein, Andershed, & Larsson, 2010; Viding & Larsson, 2010). In addition, functional magnetic resonance imaging studies show potential areas of the brain are active in juvenile psychopaths when performing certain tasks (Salekin, Lee, Schrum Dillard, & Kubak, 2010). Other studies suggest that psychopathic youth may have specific physical brain abnormalities (J. P. Newman, Curtin, Bertsch, & Baskin-Sommers, 2010; Shirtcliff, Vitacco, Gostisha, Merz, & Zahn-Waxler, 2009). However, many scholars remain concerned about the implications of bringing evidence of psychopathy or psychopathic features to the attention of the courts.

In a recent study, Viljoen et al. (2010) reviewed 111 American and Canadian cases involving adolescent offenders and found that psychopathy evidence is becoming increasingly common and appears to be influential in the decision making of judges, although it was not necessarily a key factor. Evidence of psychopathy or psychopathic features was found in about half the cases. Juveniles whose cases did not indicate psychopathy or psychopathic features received more lenient sentences than those whose cases did. In addition, "psychopathy evidence appeared very influential in some cases, including those in which decisions were made to transfer a youth to adult court or place the youth in an adult jail" (p. 271). According to Viljoen et al., "psychopathy evidence was commonly used to infer that a youth would be very difficult or impossible to treat" (p. 271).

The Female Psychopath

Similar to the research on juvenile psychopathy, very little research has been conducted on the extent to which psychopathy exists in females. There are few statistics on the ratio of male to female psychopaths, but it has been generally assumed that males far outnumber their female counterparts. Based on PCL-R data, Salekin, Rogers, and Sewell (1997) reported that the prevalence rate of psychopathy for female offenders in a jail setting was 15.5%, compared to a 25 to 30% prevalence rate estimated for men.

In another study, Salekin, Rogers, Ustad, and Sewell (1998) found, using a PCL-R cutoff score of 29, that 12.9% of their sample of 78 female inmates qualified as psychopaths. In another investigation involving 528 women incarcerated in Wisconsin, Vitale, Smith, Brinkley, and Newman (2002) reported that 9% of their participants could be classified as psychopaths, using the recommended cutoff score of 30 on the PCL-R. Because the known psychopathic population is dominated by men, little research has been directed at women, although both Hare and Cleckley included female psychopaths in some of their work. Nevertheless, Hare's PCL and PCL-R (Hare, 1980, 1991, respectively) have been developed almost exclusively for use on male criminal psychopaths. Some preliminary studies using the PCL-R suggest that female criminal psychopaths may demonstrate different behavioral patterns from those of male criminal psychopaths (Hare, 1991; Vitale et al., 2002).

There is some preliminary evidence that female psychopaths may be less aggressive and violent than male psychopaths (Mulder, Wells, Joyce, & Bushnell, 1994). Female psychopaths may also recidivate less often than male psychopaths. In fact, the evidence suggests that psychopathic female inmates may have recidivism rates that are no different from the recidivism rates reported for non-psychopathic female inmates (Salekin et al., 1998).

Recent research using the PCL-R shows considerable promise in identifying gender differences in psychopathy. Salekin et al. (1997) have found evidence of at least two broad categories of female psychopaths. One category appears to be characterized by interpersonal deception, sensation seeking, proneness to boredom, and a lack of empathy or guilt. The other group appears to be characterized by early behavioral problems, promiscuous sexual behavior, and adult antisocial (not violent) behavior. In recent years, we have seen a renewed interest in studying the female psychopath.

Racial/Ethnic Differences

Kosson, Smith, and Newman (1990) noticed that most measures of psychopathy have been developed using White inmates as subjects. In their research, they found that psychopathy, as measured by Hare's PCL, does exist in African American male inmates in a pattern that resembles that of White male inmates. However, Kosson et al. found one important difference: African American criminal psychopaths tended to be less impulsive than White criminal psychopaths.

On one hand, this finding raises some questions as to whether the PCL is entirely appropriate to use with African American inmates. On the other hand, Vitale et al. (2002) found no significant racial differences in the scores and distributions of female psychopaths. More specifically, Vitale et al. reported that 10% of the 248 incarcerated White women who participated in their study reached the cutoff scores of 30 or higher on the PCL-R compared to 9% of the 280 incarcerated African American women who had similar scores. A meta-analysis by Skeem, Edens, and Colwell (2003) supports the conclusion that the differences between Blacks and Whites are minimal. Questions remain, however, as to the potential differences among other minority or disadvantaged groups.

Some researchers have raised the intriguing and serious issue of whether the stigmatizing diagnosis of psychopathy is likely to be used in a biased manner among minority or disadvantaged groups (Edens, Petrila, & Buffington-Vollum, 2001; Skeem, Edens, & Colwell, 2003; Skeem, Edens, Sanford, & Colwell, 2003). In essence, the consequence of being diagnosed a psychopath is becoming more serious (Skeem, Edens, Sanford, et al., 2003). As pointed out by Skeem, Edens, and Colwell, Canada and the United Kingdom use the diagnosis of psychopathy to support indeterminate detention for certain classes of offenders, and that furthermore,

> There is evidence that psychopathy increasingly is being used as an aggravating factor in the sentencing phase of U.S. death penalty cases, where it has been argued that the presence of these personality traits renders a defendant a "continuing threat to society." (p. 17)

In addition, as we learned earlier, there is concern that a diagnosis of psychopathy may be used to justify decisions to transfer juvenile offenders to the adult criminal justice system, typically based on the assumption that psychopathy is untreatable. Therefore, any differences in psychopathy scores related to race, ethnicity, or age would raise significant criminal justice and public policy issues (Skeem, Edens, & Colwell, 2003). Edens, Petrila et al. (2001) suggest that perhaps the PCL-R should be excluded from capital sentencing until more solid research on its ability to predict future dangerousness in minority and disadvantaged individuals is established. It would be wise, therefore, for forensic psychologists to refrain from using diagnostic indicators of psychopathy at the sentencing phase until considerably more research is undertaken.

SUMMARY AND CONCLUSIONS

Criminal behavior involves an extremely wide range of human conduct and is committed by individuals of all ages and across all social classes. In this chapter, we have been concerned with that subset of criminal behavior that includes persistent, serious offending over time. Consequently, we have examined early origins of such offending by focusing on developmental factors associated with the antisocial acts of chronic juvenile offenders. In addition, we have examined offending patterns over the life span by focusing on the criminal psychopath.

As a group, juvenile offenders tend to grow out of crime—which is to say, they do not grow up to become chronic adult offenders. From the statistics on juvenile arrests, it is impossible to tell how many different juveniles are involved (as some are arrested more than once) as well as which of these particular juveniles will become long-term offenders. We know from the research that a small percentage (5–6%) of offenders is responsible for a large proportion of juvenile crime. We know also that chronic offenders do not specialize but rather are involved in a wide variety of offenses. Forensic psychologists attempt to identify those juveniles who are at risk of serious, chronic offending. Psychologists are also involved in providing treatment for these juveniles, a topic we will return to in Chapter 13.

In their attempts to identify juveniles at risk, many psychologists today have adopted developmental or cognitive approaches. Developmental studies—such as those conducted by Terrie Moffitt and her colleagues—suggest that differences in impulsivity, aggressiveness, social skills, and empathy for others can distinguish persistent from non-persistent offenders. Moffitt's (1993a) dual-pathway hypothesis (LCP vs. AL offenders) has contributed significantly to theory development in this area. Most recently, though, Moffitt as well as other researchers have suggested that more than two developmental pathways are needed.

The most recent developmental studies have identified such factors as early exposure to aggressive peers and rejection by peers as contributing to later antisocial conduct. Developmental theory also suggests that conduct disorders, differences in cognitive abilities, and ADHD all play a significant role in facilitating chronic antisocial behavior in children and adolescents. However, they certainly do not "cause" it. Although each of these correlates with delinquency, a cautionary note is necessary. "Deficiencies" in children may well be due to abuse, neglect, or lack of resources or understanding on the part of the adults in their lives. Focusing on behavioral problems in children without attending to their broader social systems is unwise.

The topic of school violence became salient after highly publicized school shootings in the 1990s. Although victimization in school is a problem, it must be kept in perspective. Studies show that serious school crime is declining and that children are safer in school than in many communities and, unfortunately, many homes. Nevertheless, forensic psychologists have been increasingly asked to conduct threat assessments when school officials are concerned that a particular student or students may pose a threat to others in the school.

Recent data suggest that juvenile firesetting is a considerable social problem, with juveniles responsible for almost half of all arsons. As a group, children are fascinated with fire, and some experimental play with matches or other incendiary devices is not unusual. Persistent firesetting, as well as that which continues past age 10, are signs of serious developmental problems, however. Researchers have concluded that firesetting is usually only one in a cluster of antisocial behaviors and have begun to develop and test typologies of juvenile firesetters.

We discussed in some detail the criminal psychopath, a designation that has been given to a significant minority of adults. Although it is estimated that only 1% of the total adult population would qualify as psychopathic, estimates of the number of imprisoned psychopaths have reached 15% (although some believe these estimates are inflated). Psychopaths are problematic, not only because of their offending patterns but also because of their resistance to change. For this reason, a diagnosis of psychopathy may be the "kiss of death" at capital sentencing. A variety of instruments are offered to measure psychopathy, the most widely known being Robert Hare's (1991) PCL-R. We noted that gender, race, and ethnicity differences in psychopathy are beginning to merit research attention.

Although there is debate over whether the concept of psychopathy can be applied to juveniles, efforts to develop instruments for measuring this construct are robust and ongoing and the instruments are increasingly being used in clinical practice. However, the concept of juvenile psychopathy—*if such a construct exists*—may have important implications for the prevention of serious delinquency if clinicians can intervene and provide effective treatment. Nevertheless, as in the adult population, psychopathy is likely to be limited to a very small subset of juvenile offenders. Even so, the concerns expressed by many researchers should be very carefully considered. A psychopathic label placed on a juvenile may virtually guarantee his or her transfer to a criminal court.

KEY CONCEPTS

Adolescent-limited offenders (ALs)	Executive functions
Antisocial personality disorder	Factor analysis
Attention deficit/hyperactivity disorder (ADHD)	Firesetting
Coercive behaviors	Hostile attribution bias
Conduct disorder	Juvenile delinquent
Crime (definition of)	Life course–persistent offenders (LCPs)
Early starters	National Incident-Based Reporting System (NIBRS)
Emotional intelligence	Oppositional defiant disorder (ODD)

Psychopath

Psychopathy Checklist (PCL)

Self-regulation

Status offenses

Temperament

Threat assessment

QUESTIONS FOR REVIEW

1. Discuss the differences between legal and psychological definitions of delinquency.

2. What are the main sources of youth crime data?

3. Explain how Moffitt's original dichotomy of juvenile offending has been modified in recent years.

4. What are at least three explanations of ADHD?

5. What are three alternative explanations for the IQ–delinquency connection?

6. What is intelligence? How has Howard Gardner contributed to psychology's understanding of this concept?

7. What are five commonly held myths about school shooters?

8. How does threat assessment differ from criminal profiling?

9. List Cleckley's behavioral features of the psychopath.

10. State the controversy over labeling juveniles as psychopaths.

8

Psychology of Violence and Intimidation

CHAPTER OBJECTIVES

- Introduce the reader to the statistical and research data on violent crime.
- Assess the psychological effects of violent media and violent video games on aggressive behavior.
- Examine the research and clinical data on criminal homicide, including multiple murder and serial killers.
- Review the psychological factors involved in workplace violence.
- Review the demographic and psychological aspects involved in hate and bias crimes.
- Review the psychological trauma and potential violence of being stalked.

Violence both terrifies and fascinates us. Although we are concerned about perceived increases in violent crime rates and fearful of becoming victims of violence, we also support images and depictions of violent activity in the entertainment media and often demand such details in the news media. Interestingly, violence is somewhat difficult to define precisely because it has so many meanings and conjures up such a broad spectrum of images (G. Newman, 1979). Moreover, it occurs in many situations and under a wide variety of conditions, and there are numerous explanations for why it occurs.

Violence is commonly defined as *physical* force exerted for the purpose of inflicting injury, pain, discomfort, or abuse on a person or persons or for the purpose of damaging or destroying property. Such physical force, however, may be condoned by society. We allow police to use reasonable force against an individual resisting arrest, a football player to tackle his opponent, a soldier to kill his or her enemy, and crime victims to protect themselves from serious bodily harm. It is the violence committed without justification that we are concerned with in this chapter, specifically criminal violence.

It should be noted that *violence* and *aggression* are not interchangeable terms. Whereas violence involves physical force, **aggression** may or may not involve such force. Aggression can be defined as behavior perpetrated or attempted with the intention of harming another individual (or group of individuals) physically or psychologically (Bartol & Bartol, 2011). A protester who blocks someone's entry into a business that allegedly discriminates against a racial or ethnic group is performing an aggressive act, not a violent act. Even though we may agree with the protester's action as a matter of principle, it is still aggressive. Likewise, refusing to speak to someone who has insulted you in the past is an aggressive act, not a violent act, one which psychologists would call "passive aggressive." Thus, all violent behavior is aggressive behavior, but not all aggressive behavior is violent behavior. Although the concept of aggression has been studied extensively by psychologists, we are concerned primarily in this chapter with the subset that is violent behavior. Nevertheless, nonviolent aggression will also have its place, particularly when we discuss crimes of intimidation.

Two increasingly interconnected streams of research on violence have emerged in recent years. One research stream has examined the many characteristics and demographics of the individual violent offender; the other has examined the immediate contexts and environments in which violence most often occurs (Hawkins, 2003). Studies focusing on the former have examined the social, psychological, and biological factors in interpersonal offending. Studies on the latter tradition have examined family, peer, local community, and neighborhood effects on varying levels of violence. In recent years, each area of research has recognized the importance of the other. That is, researchers acknowledge that both individual factors and environmental influences must be taken into account in their efforts to understand violence. Research has shown, for example, that the relationships among racial/ethnic composition; feelings of anger, resentment, and frustration; and homicide rates are contingent—at least in part—on the level of economic deprivation, joblessness, drug use, and number of gangs within a given community (C. C. Johnson & Chanhatasilpa, 2003).

Forensic psychologists frequently encounter violence—as well as aggression in general—sometimes even on a daily basis. Their clients may threaten to harm others. They may be asked to assess the risk of violence in a given individual. They may themselves be placed at risk of violence. They may be offering psychological services to victims of violence. In a court setting, they may be asked to testify about the effects of violence on a victim of a crime or a plaintiff in a civil suit. Therefore, an understanding of the prevalence, the causes, and the effects of violence is critical for forensic psychologists.

We will begin this chapter with data on violent crime, including information on gender and race/ethnic differences. This will be followed by a discussion of theoretical perspectives on violence offered by research psychologists. We will then focus on the specific violent crimes of homicide and workplace violence. The chapter ends with a discussion of crimes of intimidation, which represent a form of aggression that may or may not result in violence but produce fear in the victims. The chapter that follows this one is devoted to another very disturbing violent crime, sexual assault.

UCR Data on Violent Crime

In the Uniform Crime Reports (UCR), as discussed in the previous chapter, the four violent crimes are murder and nonnegligent manslaughter, forcible rape, robbery, and aggravated assault. Together, reports of these crimes comprise the violent crime rate provided annually to the public (see Figure 8.1 for trends in violent crime). In addition, arrest data on the above crimes as well as simple assault are also provided. According to the UCR (FBI, 2009), aggravated assault accounts for the largest share of violent crimes known to police

| Figure 8.1 | Five-Year Trend in Violent Crime |

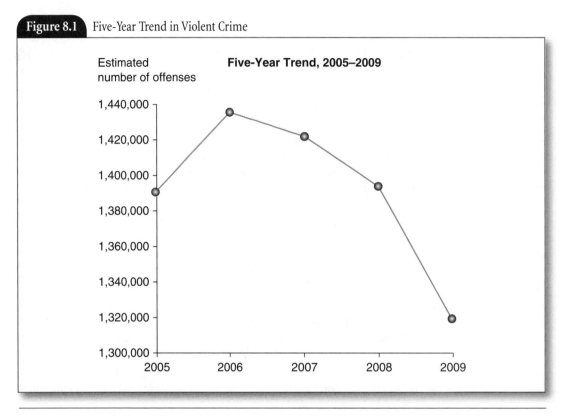

Source: Federal Bureau of Investigation, 2010.

(approximately 60%), and murder accounts for the smallest share (approximately 1%) (see Figure 8.2). Personal weapons, such as hands, fists, and feet, were used in 6.1% of the homicides committed in 2008; firearms in 66.9%; and knives or cutting instruments in 13.4% of the incidents. Other dangerous weapons were used in the remaining 13.7% of the offenses.

In 2008, an estimated 45% of the violent crimes and 17.4% of property crimes were cleared by arrest or some other means. During that same year, the clearance (or solved) rate for murder was 63%. The **clearance rates** for aggravated assault, forcible rape, and robbery were 55%, 40%, and 27%, respectively.

The geography of violence is largely distributed across two primary locations—the home and the street. Additional locations—e.g., schools, bars, places of work—comprise smaller percentages of violence. Until recently, much of the emphasis on stopping violent crimes has been directed at the more visible street crimes and less at violence within the homes. Street crimes are far more likely to come to the attention of police and thus more likely to be represented in official statistics. However, women and children are more likely to be harmed by violence in their homes and by people they know than by strangers on the street. Thus, both researchers and law enforcement officials have given increasing attention to studying, preventing, and responding to this category of violent crime. Workplace and school violence also are drawing more attention. We will address these issues more completely in Chapters 10 and 11, in which we discuss the effects of violent crime on its victims.

| Figure 8.2 | Violent Crime Distribution in the United States, 2009 |

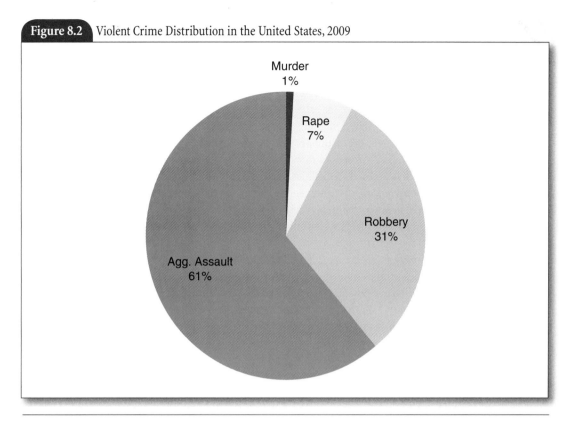

Source: Federal Bureau of Investigation, 2010.

Gender, Race, and Ethnic Differences in Criminal Violence

UCR data consistently indicate that males account for 87 to 90% of total arrests for violent crimes in any given year. Males account for about 90% of the annual arrests for murder, and females the remaining 10% (FBI, 2002b, 2009). This ratio is characteristic of other countries as well (Bartol, 2002). Arrest rates for aggravated assault are slightly different, showing a ratio of 80% male to 20% female. Although women's violent crime rate increased faster than the men's rate for a brief period in the mid-1990s, women continue to be far underrepresented in the violent crime statistics. The two dominant explanations for the gender discrepancies in violent offending are (1) socialization factors (women are less likely than men to be encouraged to be violent) and (2) biological factors (e.g., some researchers have linked the male hormone testosterone to aggression).

Women also are said to have less opportunity to commit the violent street crimes that come to the attention of police. Thus, some theorists have suggested that violence perpetrated by women may go undetected and unreported because it is more likely to occur in the privacy of the home. Even if this were so, it would be unlikely to narrow the gender gap in violent offending because much male violence in the home also goes undetected and unreported.

Although gender differences in violent offending have garnered some interest, it is racial and ethnic differences that have produced the most commentary. Race differences in crime and violence remain emotionally and politically charged, divisive topics in the United States and in many other societies around the world (Hawkins, 2003). National surveys conducted in the United States, for example, suggest that a majority of White respondents believe Blacks and Latinos are more prone (innately and culturally) to violence than Whites or Asians (Bobo & Kluegel, 1997). These beliefs demonstrate the continual existence of racial stereotypes as misguided explanations of criminal violence in this country.

Official crime data can be partly blamed for perpetuating these stereotypes. According to these data, African Americans in the United States are involved in criminal homicide and other forms of violence at a rate that far exceeds their numbers in the general population. For example, although African Americans make up about 13.5% of the U.S. population, they accounted for more than 39% of all arrests for violent crimes in 2008 (FBI, 2009). These figures probably reflect social inequalities, such as lack of employment and educational opportunities, racial oppression in its many forms, discriminatory treatment at the hands of the criminal justice system, and law enforcement practices in inner-city areas where many African Americans reside. It is extremely important to emphasize that race or ethnic differences in violent crime are *not* due to genetic or biological factors, such as racial differences in innate aggressive traits. As we shall see shortly, researchers have explored and sometimes uncovered links between biology and aggression, but these links are not racially or ethnically related.

Latinos are now the largest ethnic minority group in the United States. The Latino population in the United States more than doubled between 1980 and 2000 and is likely to continue increasing. U.S. Census 2010 estimates projected 9 births for every 1 death among Latinos, whereas for Whites, the ratio was 1:1 (Cruz, 2010). The estimated Latino population, representing 15.5% of the U.S. population, currently exceeds the African American population. A large proportion of this Latino population growth is due to a rise in the number of recent immigrants. Empirical research on Latino crime is surprisingly scarce (Martinez, 2003).

Preliminary data suggest that the Latino violence rate falls significantly *below* the rates found for economically deprived African Americans and Caucasians (Martinez, 2002; Reidel, 2003). Martinez attributes these findings partly to the fact that Latinos generally have high rates of labor force participation—despite being traditionally characterized as the working poor—and have close and highly supportive ties to the local community and family. Although there are many influences that play a role, this labor-relationship pattern probably reduces violent crime involvement and criminal activity in general. Shihadeh and Barranco (2010) assert that it is a mistake to characterize Latino communities as one undifferentiated group, as previous research has done. They point out that some Latino communities have changed in recent years and consequently are more likely to show higher rates of violent crime. For example, years ago Latino migrants were more likely to settle in large Latino communities where they were protected by a shell of common culture and language. Today, Latino migrants are more likely to venture into new, less established communities that are more isolated from their culture and language. This recent shift in migration patterns may lead to higher rates of crime and violence among some sectors of the Latino population. Still, much more research needs to be undertaken before meaningful conclusions about the relationship between violence and Latino ethnicity can be advanced.

Interestingly, research findings from industrialized nations across the globe do not lend themselves to simple explanations for the different rates of violence among groups, cultures, or subcultures. "Group differences in rates of crime and violence observed in those areas of the world do not appear to be easily explained by traditional notions of minority versus majority, white versus nonwhite, and possibly economically disadvantaged versus advantaged" (Hawkins, 2003, p. xxiii). After years of research into the many causes of crime, Farrington, Loeber, and Stouthamer-Loeber (2003) stated the following in reference to the overrepresentation of violent crime by Blacks:

> We are left with [the] conundrum of why African-American boys are more violent. . . . The challenge for future researchers is twofold: to explain the remainder of the racial difference in behavior, and to explain the even greater disproportionateness in official violence. (p. 237)

We must be careful not to focus exclusively on any one racial or ethnic group, however, to the exclusi of others. Although great attention has been paid to the street crimes of African American males, the researc microscope has ignored other groups. There is an indication, for example, that intimate partner and family violence may be far more prevalent among Asian Americans than among other ethnic groups. In the National Violence Against Women Survey, 25% of Asian women indicated they had been physically or sexually assaulted by family members or intimates (M. Lee, 2002). Overall, many puzzles remain in any attempts to explain the ethnic and racial distribution of violence and its changes over time (Hawkins, 2003).

Much more research needs to be conducted on ethnic minorities and crime across a variety of settings and environments. Using simple categories such as Black, Latino/Hispanic, Asian, Native American, Middle Eastern, and White does not truly capture the multiethnic mixture characteristics of communities across the nation. Cultures and subcultures are complex and psychologically rich, and meaningful research investigations on ethnic/minority differences in violence require a deep appreciation of this complexity.

Practicing forensic psychologists must become highly knowledgeable about the beliefs, attitudes, values, traditions, and expected behaviors of each ethnic or racial group or subculture with which they interact if they are to be effective and helpful to offenders and their victims. *Ethnocentrism,* or viewing others strictly through one's own cultural perspectives, often encourages people—including mental health professionals—to form stereotypes and biases that limit their ability to assess and treat those from diverse backgrounds (Feindler, Rathus, & Silver, 2003). An understanding of violence involves an examination of the demands and expectations that cultures place on people, especially the poor, the oppressed, and the disenfranchised.

Theoretical Perspectives on Violence

Criminal violence can be classified along several continuums. For example, one continuum can represent the amount of planning involved in the act. At one pole, the act is highly calculated and planned (cold-blooded), but at the other pole, the act can be characterized as highly impulsive and emotionally driven behavior with virtually no planning (e.g., crimes of passion). In psychological literature, violence may represent different forms of aggression, ranging from instrumental aggression to reactive aggression, with equal elements of both occurring at the middle sections of the continuum. **Instrumental violence** "occurs when the injury of an individual is secondary to the acquisition of some other external goal" (Woodworth & Porter, 2002, p. 437). The external goal may be money, status, security, or material goods. **Reactive violence**—also called expressive violence—refers to physical violence precipitated by a hostile and angry reaction to a perceived threat or dangerous situation. Reactive violence, therefore, "is often the impulsive and unthoughtful response to a provocation, real or imagined" (APA, 1996, p. 8). An angry person who "flies off the handle" and shoots a friend over a petty argument represents an obvious example. More often than not, the aggressor—once the emotions calm down—cannot believe what he or she did or understand how he or she could lose control to that level. In many cases, though, it is difficult to clearly differentiate whether the violence is instrumental or reactive—it often appears to include some mixture of both instrumental and reactive factors. Consequently, violent actions often fall in the middle ranges of the instrumental–reactive continuum, similar to what is found in the normal curve (see Figure 8.3).

An interesting question emerges when we examine these two polar opposites on the violence continuum in reference to the criminal psychopaths discussed in Chapter 7. Are they more likely to commit instrumental or reactive forms of violence? Recall that psychopaths demonstrate a lack of empathy or remorse and have shallow emotions in general. However, they are also impulsive and highly reactive to provocative situations. Woodworth and Porter (2002) have initiated some research into this area by studying both psychopathic and non-psychopathic offenders who committed homicide. According to these researchers, psychopaths tend to engage in the more instrumental, goal-driven (e.g., to obtain money or drugs) homicides, whereas

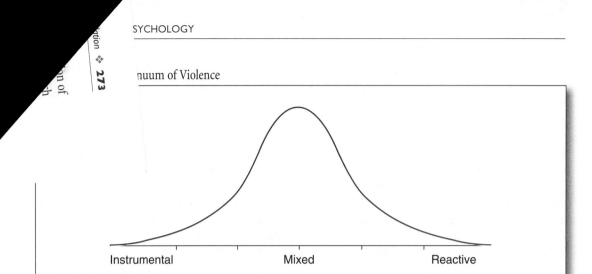

nuum of Violence

Instrumental — Mixed — Reactive

non-psychopathic offenders engage in predominately reactive, spontaneous violence (e.g., in the context of a heated argument). Psychopaths who murdered were primarily motivated to advance their own cause and exhibited little empathy or concern for their victims. Woodworth and Porter were surprised, though, at the overall level of instrumental violence characterizing *all* homicides, whether committed by psychopaths or non-psychopaths. The majority of the offenders did not simply "snap" and kill their victims in an uncontrollable emotional rage. The researchers suggest that future study should examine whether the results might generalize to other types of criminal violence, offenders, and subcultures.

The Causes of Violence

The causes of violence are multiple. The psychological literature usually divides these causes into four highly overlapping categories: (1) biological, (2) socialization, (3) cognitive, and (4) situational factors.

The *biological factors* refer to the wide array of neurological, physiological, or chemical influences on aggression and violence. Recent advances in the neurosciences have revealed that biological factors, interacting with the social environment, may have some significant influences on child development. The exact nature of these influences remains largely unknown. Child development researchers have found links between aggression and brain damage resulting from a variety of environmental factors. These include toxic materials found in the environment (e.g., lead paint), traumatic head injury (e.g., as the result of child abuse or accident), dietary deficiencies (especially prenatal), alcohol and drug ingestion by the mother during critical fetal developmental stages, and birth trauma. The best approach, of course, is to prevent these from occurring in the first place. Once the deficits do occur, attempts to remove or remedy the biological cause may include active biological treatment in the form of medication. However, and equally important, a supportive and competent social environment has been found to neutralize or reduce the effects that these biological factors exert on any propensity toward violence.

Socialization factors refer to those processes through which a person learns patterns of thinking, behavior, and feeling from his or her early life experiences (APA, 1996). More specifically, according to the APA, "Scientists use the term socialization to describe the process by which a child learns the 'scripts' for specific social behavior, along with the rules, attitudes, values, and norms that guide interactions with others" (p. 3). Furthermore, children can learn as much from observing significant or admired others in their environment as from their own experiences. Considerable research indicates that aggressive, antisocial, and violent behaviors are often learned from significant others (including TV, movie, or fictional characters) and are held in reserve for response to specific social situations. This is a good argument for limiting young children's exposure ⌐ violent media images, a topic that will be addressed shortly.

Cognitive factors refer to the ideas, beliefs, and patterns of thinking that emerge as a result of interactions with the world during a person's lifetime. Research has revealed that violent individuals have different ways of processing and interpreting that information. "They tend to perceive hostility in others when there is no hostility" (APA, 1996, p. 5). As the reader may recall from Chapter 7, this notable tendency is referred to as *hostile attribution bias.* Violent people are also less efficient at thinking of nonviolent ways to solve social conflicts and disagreements. They also tend to be more accepting of violence in general. Some young males—especially members of violent groups or gangs—have adopted the belief that it is acceptable to react to every perceived or imagined sign of disrespect with aggression. Aggressive children and adolescents have more antisocial, violent beliefs than their nonaggressive peers (Shahinfar, Kupersmidt, & Matza, 2001).

Situational factors refer to the characteristics of the environment, such as stress or aggression in others, that encourage or engender violent behavior. As pointed out by many researchers, "Often we seek the causes of violence in the person and ignore the contributing effects of the situation" (APA, 1996, p. 6). Almost any aversive situation—such as excessive heat, continuous loud noise, or crowded living conditions—can provoke aggression and violence in those persons submitted to such conditions. Neighborhoods, schools, family, and peers can all be conducive to the development of violent behavior. The presence of weapons increases the chances that the conflict will occur in the first place and that it will have lethal consequences once it does occur.

It is also clear that children who grow up in deprived environments where poverty, frustration, and hopelessness are prevalent are at much greater risk for later involvement in violence than other children. Childhood aggression can predict adult violence in some individuals. Research has discovered that approximately 10% of highly aggressive children grow up to account for 50 to 60% of the majority of violent crimes (Bartol & Bartol, 2011). During their childhood, these individuals exhibit aggression, disobedience, and disruptions at home and in school; are disliked and avoided by peers; are neglected by parents and teachers; and are likely to fail in school, eventually dropping out. Unsupervised and susceptible to the pernicious influence of other delinquent youth, they grow up to be antisocial, aggressive, and violent young adults. They are likely to become involved in abusive spousal relationships, and they often abuse their own children. But not every child growing up under these conditions follows this destructive path, and the example of such children has provided valuable insights into how to design prevention programs.

Despite the complexity and multitude of causes, human violence is ultimately a learned behavior. And because it is learned, it can be unlearned or altered, or conditions can be changed so that it is not learned in the first place. Furthermore, violence is a behavior that is acquired early in life—in many cases, *very* early in life, as we saw in Chapter 7. Consequently, prevention of violence should likewise begin very early in life.

The Effects of Violent Media

Over the past 40 years, a significant amount of research literature has strongly supported the observation that media violence viewing is one factor contributing to the development of aggression and violence (Huesmann, Moise-Titus, Podolski, & Eron, 2003). The majority of the research has focused on the effects of watching dramatic violence on TV and film. A wide variety of research projects have continually arrived at the same fundamental conclusion: Exposure to dramatic violence on TV and in the movies is related to violent behavior. In addition to the hundreds of research findings, three major national studies have concluded that *heavy* exposure to televised violence is one of the most significant causes of violence in society (APA, 2003c). They are the Surgeon General's Commission Report (Surgeon General's Scientific Advisory Committee on Television and Social Behavior, 1972), the National Institute of Mental Health's Ten-Year Follow-Up (1982), and the American

ociation's Task Force on Television in Society (1992). According to the APA (2003c), these
iat viewing a steady diet of violence on the screen has the following negative effects:

he viewer's fear of becoming a victim, with a corresponding increase in self-protective behaviors and
trust of others.
...sensitizes the viewer to violence. That is, viewers often become less sensitive to the pain and suffering of others.
- It encourages some individuals to become more involved in violent actions.
- It demonstrates how desired goods and services can be obtained through the use of aggression and violence.
- Sexual violence in X- and R-rated videotapes has been shown to increase sexual aggression in some males.

It is important to distinguish between short-term and long-term effects of media on aggressive behavior
and violence. Long-term effects occur as a result of learning and storing violent and aggressive material into
the cognitive system that eventually "crystallizes" and is difficult to change as the child gets older. Young children are especially open to new learning, and these experiences often have a greater impact during the early
developmental years than learning events that occur during adulthood. Moreover,

In recent theorizing, long-term relations have been ascribed mainly to acquisition through observational learning of
three social-cognitive structures: schemas about a hostile world, scripts for social problem solving that focus on
aggression, and normative beliefs that aggression is acceptable. (Huesmann et al., 2003, p. 201)

Observational learning refers to the very strong tendency of human beings to imitate any significant or
admired person or model they observe. Children are especially prone to doing this. Consequently, observation
of specific aggressive behaviors around them increases children's likelihood of behaving exactly that way. Over
time and with frequent exposure to aggressive behavior, children develop beliefs (schemas) that the world is
basically a hostile place, that aggression is an acceptable social behavior, and that the best way to solve conflicts
and to get things is to be aggressive.

Huesmann and his colleagues (2003) found strong long-term effects of media violence observed in early
childhood that carried over into adulthood:

Overall, these results suggest that both males and females from all social strata and all levels of initial aggressiveness
are placed at increased risk for the development of adult aggressive and violent behavior when they view a high and
steady diet of violent TV shows in early childhood. (p. 218)

Media violence encourages, stimulates, and reinforces aggressive behavior. Furthermore, aggressive
children tend to enjoy aggressive media. Huesmann et al. (2003) suggest that "aggressive children feel happier and more justified if they believe they are not alone in their aggression, and view media violence to
make them feel happier because it convinces them that they are not alone" (p. 202). Huesmann et al. also
posit that media violence appears to have *short-term* effects on adults, but the real *long-term* effects seem to
occur only with children. The effects are not only found in children who are already violence-prone but also
in almost all children.

In addition, the Huesmann et al. (2003) study found that violent films and TV programs that have the most
deleterious effects on children are not always the ones that adults and critics perceive as most violent. What type
of scene is the most deleterious to children? "It is one in which the child identifies with the perpetrator of
the violence, the child perceives the scene as telling about life like it is, and the perpetrator is rewarded for the
violence"(p. 218). In other words, violent media that portray an admired perpetrator as successful through the
use of violence appear to have a greater impact on the child's observational learning of aggression and violence

over the long haul. The researchers suggest that the easiest way to reduce the effects of media violence on children is to restrict children's exposure to such violence. The persons in the best position to do this, particularly with young children, are parents or caretakers.

Violent Video Games

Virtually everyone reading this textbook has likely played video games, some perhaps for hours at a time. (See Photo 8.1 for illustration of two children captivated by a video game.) Many of you have played *violent* video games. Has that made you more violent? Has it desensitized you to the effects of violence? Has it caused you serious psychological harm? In the spring of 2011, the U.S. Supreme Court is expected to address this last question, when it announces its decision in *Schwarzenegger v. Entertainment Merchants Association*. The case involves a California law passed in 2005 banning the sale of violent video games to children under 18 and imposing a $1,000 fine on any retailer caught doing so. The games in question were those that depicted killing, maiming, dismembering, or sexually assaulting the image of a human. However, the California Supreme Court struck down the law in 2009, stating there was no conclusive evidence that these games seriously harmed children. The state of California appealed that decision to the U.S. Supreme Court, and oral arguments were heard in November 2010. Interestingly, the American Psychological Association decided not to file an *amicus curiae* brief, presumably because the research remained equivocal as to the evidence of harm (Azar, 2010).

The effect of violent video games on violence became a serious topic for study after the series of school shootings that occurred during the late 1990s.

Photo 8.1 Girl and boy captivated by a video game. Research on the effect of *violent* video games on children is equivocal, but it does appear that they have a negative effect on children who have already displayed violent tendencies or have witnessed violence in their families.

The shooters in these cases were often students who habitually played violent video games. For example, Eric Harris and Dylan Klebold, the Columbine (Colorado) High School students who murdered 13 persons and wounded 23 before killing themselves, were fascinated with the bloody video game *Doom,* one of the earliest and most successful of all violent video games. "Harris created a customized version of *Doom* with two shooters, extra weapons, unlimited ammunition, and victims could not fight back—features that are eerily similar to aspects of the actual shootings" (C. A. Anderson & Bushman, 2001, p. 353).

Research also suggests that violent video games increase or encourage aggressive behavior not only in children but also in young adults, both males and females (C. A. Anderson & Bushman, 2001). A recent meta-analysis by Anderson et al. (2010) provides the strongest evidence to date of harmful effects. Nevertheless, this research is not unequivocal; that is, some studies challenge these conclusions. Some recent researchers criticize earlier research relating to violence in the media—including video games—on methodological grounds and say its results are inconclusive (e.g., Ferguson et al., 2008; Savage & Yancey, 2008).

According to Anderson and colleagues (2001, 2010), though, exposure to violent video games increases aggression-related thoughts and feelings and decreases prosocial behavior. Even so, the *long-term effect* of heavy exposure to violent video games over the course of a person's life remains unknown at this time, which could partly explain the APA's decision not to file a brief in the California case. The overwhelming majority of people who play video games today, including violent games, do not commit acts of violence. Nevertheless, the games could have a desensitizing effect on some individuals. In addition, they may have a particularly negative effect on individuals who are already violence-prone.

Criminal Homicide

Homicide is the killing of one person by another. **Criminal homicide** is the causing of the death of another person without legal justification or excuse. The criminal law recognizes two major levels of criminal homicide, murder and manslaughter. **Murder** is the term reserved for the "unlawful killing of one human by another with malice aforethought, either expressed or implied" (H. C. Black, 1990, p. 1019). **Manslaughter** refers to an *unintended* killing that results from *unjustifiable* conduct that places others at risk (Morawetz, 2002). The individual who aimlessly fires a loaded weapon, even if he or she does not "intend" to kill anyone, is still responsible for that person's death if the victim happens to be in his or her path. According to Morawetz, manslaughter also includes an *intended* killing "for which there is mitigation, acts that are provoked by the victim, or that result from temporary and understandable circumstances that compromise the actor's normal responsibility" (p. 398). For example, a father who comes upon a car accident, discovers that his daughter has been killed, and chokes to death the inebriated driver of the car that hit her would likely be charged with nonnegligent manslaughter, not murder. Most states have additional gradations in their homicide statutes, depending on the level of seriousness.

First-degree murder, for instance, is usually considered a capital offense, punishable by death or life in prison. The UCR includes both murder and "nonnegligent" manslaughter under the term *criminal homicide* for reporting purposes.

According to the UCR, approximately 16,272 persons were murder victims in 2008 (FBI, 2009). The murder rate in the United States during that year was 5.4 murders for every 100,000 inhabitants. The murder rate as reported in the UCR is based solely on police investigations as opposed to the determination of a court, medical examiner, coroner, jury, or other investigative or judicial body. In other words, the UCR provides data on the homicides known to police and—if solved—on the persons arrested. Recall also that the UCR does not tell us whether the 9,859 persons arrested and charged in 2008 were convicted. Also, not included in the UCR murder statistics are deaths police believe were caused by negligence, suicide, accidents, or justifiable homicide.

During 2008, UCR contributing agencies submitted supplemental information concerning homicides. The Supplementary Homicide Report (SHR) collects data on the age, sex, and race of both the victim and the offender; the type of weapon used; the relationship of the victim to the offender; and circumstances surrounding the incident. The circumstances are listed in Table 11.1 in Chapter 11. The relationship of the victim to the offender will also be reported in Chapter 11, which deals with violent victimology.

Criminal homicide, like sexual assault, is a heterogeneous phenomenon, associated with different contexts, motivations, and types of offenders (Woodworth & Porter, 2002). Consequently, any attempt to make broad generalizations about people who commit criminal homicide—particularly murder—is risky. Nevertheless, researchers have drawn tentative conclusions about the types of individuals who commit this ultimate violent act. For example, most murders are single-incident offenses involving only one victim—and murderers generally do not commit another murder, even after release from prison. The "typical murder" is committed either during the course of committing another offense—most often a robbery—or is perpetrated against an intimate or an acquaintance. The typical murder also is committed during early adulthood, between the ages of 18 and 25 (see Table 8.1).

Table 8.1	Age Distribution of Murder Offenders, 2008		
Age	**Total**	**Male**	**Female**
Total (all ages)	16,277*	10,568	1,176
Under 18	951	870	80
Under 22	3,527	3,229	289
9 to 12	9	8	1
13 to 16	496	447	48
17 to 19	1,772	1,632	138
20 to 24	2,713	2,450	252
25 to 29	1,893	1,696	193
30 to 34	1,049	922	125

Source: Federal Bureau of Investigation (2009).

*4,533 cases were listed as unknown regarding gender.

An unknown number of murderers kill themselves after they have committed their crimes—typically very shortly thereafter and in the same location. The clinical characteristics of homicide-suicide are similar across the globe. Perpetrators of homicide-suicide are mostly men (95% in the United States), and the homicide victims are usually women (85% in the United States) (Hillbrand, 2001). In a majority of cases, the offender and victim(s) are relatives. Most cases involve one killer and one victim (90%) (Hillbrand, 2001). Despair, hopelessness, and depression are common among perpetrators of murder-suicides. In fact, the clinical or psychological characteristics are more typical of suicide than homicide. For example, there is not a lifelong pattern of impulsivity or violence.

A distinct form of homicide-suicide involves politically motivated terrorists who commit acts such as suicide bombings. In such incidents, a single terrorist may strap himself or herself with explosives that are later detonated at targeted locations. As in the September 11, 2001, attacks on the World Trade Center and the Pentagon, these may be perpetrated by individuals acting in small groups. Individuals who commit homicide-suicide, whether politically motivated or not, seldom utter threats or give warnings of the impending killings.

Forensic psychologists are most likely to be called on to consult regarding the atypical murder. A psychologist may be asked, for example, for a profile of a serial killer or asked to assess the risk that he will strike again within a given locality. Consequently, in the following sections, we devote more coverage to these atypical crimes. The topic of single or typical murders reoccurs in Chapters 10 and 11, when we discuss the effects of violent crime on victims. Persons whose loved ones have been murdered or who themselves have survived an attempt to kill them often seek the help of psychologists and other clinicians in coping with their traumatic experiences.

Multiple Murder

Multiple murder (also called multicide) is usually divided into three somewhat overlapping major-offender patterns based on the timing of the act. **Serial murder** usually refers to incidents in which an individual (or individuals) separately kills a number of individuals (usually a minimum of three) over time. The time interval—sometimes referred to as the "cooling-off" period—may be days or weeks but more likely months or years. **Spree murder** normally refers to the killing of three or more individuals without a cooling-off period, usually at two or three different locations.

A convenience store robber who kills some individuals at the store and kills a number of others during a countywide chase would be an example of a spree murderer. A classic example is illustrated by Charles Starkweather. In 1958, the 19-year-old Starkweather went on an 8-day killing spree in Nebraska during which he and his 14-year-old girlfriend, Caril Ann Fugate, murdered 10 persons, including her parents. Starkweather was executed by electricity on June 25, 1959, and Fugate was sentenced to life in prison. She was paroled in 1977. The Starkweather episode formed the basis for several movies, including Oliver Stone's 1994 film, *Natural Born Killers*. Compared with serial and mass murderers, spree murderers have received very little research attention and will not be discussed in detail below.

Mass murder involves the killing of three or more persons at a single location with *no* cooling-off period between the killings. The FBI identifies two types: classic and family. An example of a classic mass murder is when an individual barricades himself inside a public building, such as a fast-food restaurant, randomly killing the patrons and any other persons he has contact with. This very scenario occurred in 1991, when George Hennard smashed his pickup truck through a restaurant window in Killeen, Texas, and fired on a lunchtime crowd with two semiautomatic handguns. He killed 22 people, was wounded by a policeman, and then killed himself. Another example is the January 2011 incident in Tucson, Arizona, when six persons (including a 9-year-old girl and a federal judge) were killed and 13 persons (including a member of the U.S. House of Representatives) were wounded.

In a family mass murder—by far the more common of the two—at least three family members are killed by another immediate family member or relative. Very often, the perpetrator kills himself or herself. Thus, family mass murders are also often examples of homicide-suicides.

What the public knows about multiple murder is largely based on misinformation and myth. The more sensational aspects of serial murder, for example, associate it with sexual sadists who prey on strangers to satisfy sexual fantasies. Researchers and scholars do not seem immune to the alluring features of multiple murder either. Fox and Levin (1998) have observed that the scholarly accounts are too often based on media sources or unstructured interviews with convicted offenders: "Indeed, the ratio of scholarly books to research articles is unusually high, reflecting an abundance of speculation and a paucity of hard data" (pp. 409–410). It is with this caveat in mind that we review the following information.

What little empirical research on multiple murder has been conducted has occurred within the past 20 years, largely in response to high-profile, multiple homicide incidents, such as the serial offenders David Berkowitz ("Son of Sam"), Theodore Bundy, Robert Yates, John Wayne Gacy, Donald Harvey, Jeffrey Dahmer, and Gary Ridgway. (See Photo 8.2 of Theodore Bundy.) Ridgway, known as the "Green River Killer," pleaded guilty in November 2003 to the murders of 48 women, more than any other serial killer in U.S. history to date. In the past, researchers and criminologists have assumed that multiple murderers were basically similar to single-victim offenders and therefore did not require special study. Recent research, however, has revealed that multiple murder does involve different motivations, victims, demographics, and psychological features that differentiate much of it from the more ordinary single-victim homicide.

The considerable variation in the behavioral, emotional, and cognitive features of multiple murderers has prompted some researchers (R. M. Holmes & DeBurger, 1988; R. M. Holmes & Holmes, 1998; Ressler et al., 1988) to develop typologies, or classification systems, that allow some appreciation of the complexity of the crime. We will cover one of these typologies later in the chapter.

Although multiple murders receive considerable media attention because of their drama and sensational qualities, they are statistically rare occurrences. The frequent onslaught of violence and multiple murder in the entertainment media eventually develops the impression that these incidents are much more frequent than they actually are. When multiple murders do occur, news media depict repetitive, graphic, and dramatic accounts of the violence. The normal cognitive reaction of people watching is to store the vivid details and then have these details ready at the "top of their mind" for future reference. The result of this process is the public's tendency to conclude that violence and multiple murders are dramatically increasing when they really are not. This phenomenon, defined in Chapter 1, is called the **availability heuristic** and is based on the observation that humans prefer cognitive simplicity and are often strongly influenced by what they see and hear most often and most recently (Tversky & Kahneman, 1973). Mass and serial murders *seem* to be on the increase in the United States because accounts in the media are readily available. However, a careful review of the data simply does not lend support to this perspective. Even if statistics sometimes indicate that serial murders have increased, this apparent increase may be due to better communication and computer systems between state and federal law enforcement agencies over the past 20 years. For example, the **Violent Criminal Apprehension Program (ViCAP)** (see Focus 8.1) is designed to communicate with and help the nation's law enforcement agencies to investigate, identify, track, apprehend, and prosecute violent serial offenders.

Photo 8.2 Serial killer Ted Bundy in a sheriff's office shortly after his arrest in 1978, at age 32. Bundy eventually confessed to over 30 murders and was executed in 1989.

FOCUS 8.1. ViCAP: SHARING DATA TO SOLVE VIOLENT CRIME

ViCAP—the Violent Criminal Apprehension Program—is an FBI-sponsored data information center for crimes of violence, particularly murder. Law enforcement officials across the United States are able to enter information on solved cases into the database, as well as request the FBI's assistance in solving particularly difficult cases. The cases examined by ViCAP include the following:

- Solved or unsolved homicides or attempts, especially those that (1) involve an abduction; (2) are apparently random, motiveless, or sexually oriented; or (3) are known or suspected to be part of a series;

(Continued)

(Continued)

- Missing persons, in which the circumstances indicate a strong possibility of foul play and the victim is still missing; and
- Unidentified dead bodies, in which the manner of death is known or is suspected to be homicide.

As cases are entered into the database, they are compared continually against all other cases to detect signature aspects of homicide—such as a note left at the scene—and similar patterns (e.g., victim's age, season of the year). If ViCAP analysts detect similar patterns, as they would in the case of serial murder, the law enforcement agencies involved are notified. ViCAP can then assist agencies in coordinating an investigation, such as obtaining search warrants and conducting laboratory tests.

The FBI refers to ViCAP as a "timeless tool" because it carries information from many years back. For example, in 1989, Pennsylvania law enforcement officers entered a case that had been solved in 1951 in which a man had murdered a young girl. Shortly after that, Illinois law enforcement officers entered an unsolved murder case from 1957, also involving the death of a young girl. ViCAP analysts noticed similarities in the two cases, allowing Illinois investigators to solve the murder in their state after nearly 40 years.

Source: Federal Bureau of Investigation (2000).

Serial Killers

Despite the extensive commentary and media interest, there has been surprisingly little empirical research on serial murder. Most of the scientific research is limited to archival research or case studies. "The literature on serial murder is largely the product of broad-based descriptive study of large numbers of cases of serial killers or the result of individual case studies" (Skrapec, 2001, p. 46). Consequently, most of the following information will be descriptive in nature, and the identification of motives will be largely based on the self-reports provided by the killers themselves. Self-reports, although informative, are not the most objective measures available. They only provide information pertaining to what offenders want to reveal. Before we discuss serial killers, though, it is important to keep in mind a very useful statement noted by Candice Skrapec (p. 52) from the work of Kluckhohn and Murray (1953). To paraphrase, every human is, in certain respects, (a) like all other humans, (b) like some other humans, and (c) like no other human. That is, there are many characteristics of serial killers that are common to everyone, there are *some* identifiable commonalities among serial killers, and then there are a few significant differences.

What does a serial killer look like? Physically, serial killers can be placed on a continuum, with Theodore Bundy, the handsome, charming, intelligent law student who brutally killed dozens of women in the Pacific Northwest, at one pole, and Arthur Shawcross, the dour, rumpled, aging serial killer of primarily prostitutes in the Rochester, New York, area at the other pole. There is no one identifiable serial killer type based on physical appearance, social class, or personality attributes. Research suggests that most serial killers are males, but there are exceptions, such as Aileen Wuornos, convicted of killing six men, who was executed by lethal injection in 2002.

Serial killers have many of the same personality traits or behavioral features as the general public. However, the one trait that appears to separate them from the norm is their exceptional interpersonal skill in their presentation of self (Fox & Levin, 2003). Their ability to charm and "fool" others often elevates them beyond suspicion and makes them difficult to apprehend. This may explain why victims allow serial killers into their homes or go willingly with them on dates or other engagements. In reference to this issue, Joseph Fisher (1997) describes a serial killer who held two communities in constant fear for several months. He writes,

> Perhaps most unsettling for the community was the behavior of the victims; some of whom were reported to have gone willingly with their killer even though they may have known what lay ahead. This blind trust and the killer's exploitation of that trust seemed to have an eerie, supernatural quality. (pp. xiii–xiv)

It is a mistake to assume that serial murderers are seriously mentally disordered in the clinical sense of that term. Some are, but most are not. Although their thought patterns may be considered to be extremely aberrant when it comes to sensitivity and concern for other human beings, a vast majority of serial killers fail to qualify as psychotic or "crazy" in the traditional diagnostic categories of mental disorders. Serial killers have developed versions of the world characterized by values, beliefs, perceptions, and general cognitive processes that facilitate repetitive murder, often in a brutal, demeaning, and cold-blooded manner. They are drawn to committing murders that draw interest and send spine-chilling fear into the community, and their motives appear incomprehensible to the general public. The motives of many serial killers seem to be based on psychological rewards of control, domination, media attention, and excitement rather than material gain. But the labels "sick," "crazy," or "psychotic" explain little and offer little hope in the quest for understanding the processes in the development of this behavior.

Unlike the typical single-victim murderer who commits the homicide in early adulthood, serial murderers generally begin their careers of repetitive homicide at a relatively late age, usually in their late 20s or early 30s. Jenkins (1988) concludes that most begin their killings between the ages of 24 and 40, and R. M. Holmes and Holmes (1998) report that most known serial killers are between the ages of 25 and 35. The National Center for the Analysis of Violent Crime (NCAVC) reports that the average age of serial killers at the time of their first murder is 27.51 years and at their last murder is 32.11 years. The age of their victims, on the other hand, varies widely, ranging from infants to the very old. Arthur Shawcross, for example, murdered at least 11 adults, but his first two victims were children.

Although some serial killers have extensive police records, the records mainly reflect a series of petty thefts, embezzlements, and forgeries rather than a history of violence (Jenkins, 1988). Single-victim homicides often involve family, intimates, or acquaintances, whereas serial murder most often involves strangers, especially if the offender is male. Female serial murderers present a different story, however, because they most often murder those with whom they share a relationship such as husbands, intimates, and acquaintances, including individuals who are in their care.

An examination of the victim selection of known male serial murderers will reveal that they prefer victims offering easy access and transience. Often the victim's disappearance is not reported to police. For example, victims are often prostitutes, runaways, young male drifters, and itinerant farm workers whose family and friends may not immediately realize that they are missing. With experience, improving skills, and a need for greater challenge, serial killers often move to more difficult victims, such as university or college students, children, the elderly, or the solitary poor. Very rarely do serial murderers break in and terrorize, torture, and kill middle-class strangers in their homes.

The geographic location preferred by serial killers most often tends to be a specific location. For some unknown reason, serial murderers seldom kill victims in the communities where they (the murderers) were born. They do, however, often select victims near their *current* residence or place of work. Hickey (1997) estimates, for example, that 14% of serial killers use their homes or workplaces as the preferred location, whereas another 52% commit their murder in the same general location or area, such as the same neighborhood or city. This tendency suggests that geographical profiling may be an invaluable aid in the identification of serial murderers. However, this still leaves more than 30% of offenders who apparently commit crime across a much wider geographical area.

As noted above, serial killers are primarily males, and they often have a preference for one gender over the other. Jeffrey Dahmer, for instance, murdered at least 17 young males in Wisconsin and Ohio during the early 1990s. Dahmer drugged, strangled, dismembered, and—in some cases—consumed the flesh of his victims. John Wayne Gacy sexually assaulted and killed at least 33 boys in Illinois during the 1970s. He buried most of his victims in the dirt basement of his house. Robert Yates, on the other hand, murdered at least 17 prostitutes and homeless women in the state of Washington during the 1990s. Gary Ridgway targeted girls and women in the Seattle area during the 1980s and 1990s, mainly runaways and prostitutes.

A serial murderer may choose his victims because they hold profound meaning for him in terms of his life experiences (Skrapec, 2001). Interviews and descriptions of serial killers suggest that one of the dominant motives for their behavior is the power and control over another person's life that the crime offers them. "For these killers, murder is a form of expressive, rather than instrumental, violence" (Fox & Levin, 1998, p. 415). In keeping with the control theme, serial killers, unlike typical murderers, usually do not use a firearm to murder their victims. Although they may use a firearm to intimidate and control their victims, serial killers prefer a method of killing that provides the maximum amount of control and dominance over the victims. Choking, stabbing, and other methods of delayed death are ways the killer can maintain the life-or-death mastery over the helpless victims.

Serial killers also tend to be inspired by detailed and elaborate fantasies rich with themes of dominance (Fox & Levin, 2003; Skrapec, 1996). Prentky et al. (1989), for instance, found that 86% of the 25 serial killers they studied had violent fantasies on a regular basis, compared with only 23% of the 17 single-victim murderers. However, it should be mentioned that a majority (58%) of the serial killers in their sample had above-average intelligence compared to only 29% of the single-victim murderers. Therefore, the two groups were not completely matched in all important factors. In reference to this difference, Prentky et al. state, "While intelligence seems to have little bearing on the quality or content of the fantasy, it does influence how well fantasy is translated into behavior (i.e., how organized the crime is) and how successfully the offender eludes apprehension" (p. 888). The researchers further state that "fantasy, as it is defined in this study, is an elaborated set of cognitions (or thoughts) characterized by preoccupation (or rehearsal), anchored in emotion, and originating in daydreams" (p. 889). Furthermore, the more the fantasy is rehearsed in the mind of the potential killer, the stronger the association between the fantasy content and the actual behavior becomes, eventually lowering the restraints that normally would inhibit acting out the fantasy itself. Eventually, the individual will actually act on the fantasy. At this point, Prentky et al. suggest, the serial killer engages in a series of progressively more accurate "trial runs" in an attempt to enact the fantasy as it is imagined. In other words, the killer will continue to try to improve on his cognitive script through trial and error. Because the trial runs can never quite match the fantasy entirely, the need to restage the fantasy with a new victim is always there. As Fox and Levin (1998) note, "The killer's crime can increase in severity as he constantly updates his fantasy in a never-ending spiral of image and action" (p. 417).

Many serial killers augment their fantasies with hard-core pornography, which often contains themes of violence, dominance, and bondage (Fox & Levin, 1998, 2003). Police investigators often uncover extensive libraries of films and tapes that portray acts of rape and murder. It is not clear, however, whether the violent pornography engenders thoughts of violence or whether violence-prone individuals prefer violent pornography. The answer may lie in some combination of both.

Many serial killers also collect memorabilia or souvenirs of their victims, such as items of clothing, audiotapes or photographs of the murder, and—in rare cases—body parts. Called trophies (as noted in Chapter 3), these "souvenirs" vividly remind the killer of the incident, enhancing his fantasies even further.

Serial Killer Typologies

In contemporary psychology, the term *typology* refers to a particular system for classifying personality or behavior patterns. Usually, the typology is used to classify a wide assortment of behaviors into a more manageable set of brief descriptions. There are many problems with typologies, however, such as considerable overlap between categories. Rarely is one classification independent and separate from the others. In addition, some individuals can qualify for two or more classifications at once. For example, if the typology is based primarily on motive, the offender may demonstrate a combination of motives for the crime. Moreover, placing individuals into various categories is based on the questionable assumption that behavior is consistent across both time and place. Still, typologies are useful in highlighting the complexity of human behavior and the variety of motives and scripts.

Several typologies of serial killers have been proposed in recent years, but we will concentrate only on the R. M. Holmes and DeBurger (1985, 1988) and R. M. Holmes and Holmes (1998) scheme for illustrative purposes. Holmes and DeBurger classify serial killers into a typology based on motive. The typology outlines four types: (1) visionary, (2) mission-oriented, (3) hedonistic, and (4) power/control.

The **visionary type** is driven by delusions or hallucinations that compel him (or her) to kill a particular group of individuals. According to R. M. Holmes and DeBurger (1988), this type of serial killer is psychotic—which is atypical because serial killers are not usually mentally disordered—and suffers from a severe break with reality. He or she is probably the most difficult to understand for investigators and the public alike. The crime scene is chaotic and has an abundance of physical evidence, often including fingerprints and even the murder weapon (R. M. Holmes & Holmes, 1998).

When the visionary type does kill, it will usually be well within his comfort zone (near his residence, place of recreation, or workplace). Therefore, geographical profiling would seem to be a very useful tool in the detection of this offender. Unlike most serial killers, however, the visionary murderer has no ideal victim type (IVT). That is, there are rarely any common physical (hair color, sex, age, or race), occupational, or personality traits that connect the victims. In addition, the murder is usually spontaneous and characterized by very little planning, and the victim is simply in the wrong place at the wrong time.

The **mission-oriented type** believes that there is a particular group of people who are considered undesirable and who must be destroyed or eliminated. The undesirables may be prostitutes; homosexuals; "street people"; or members of a particular religious, racial, or minority group. Unlike the visionary type, this serial killer is not psychotic or otherwise mentally disordered.

The **hedonistic type** strives for pleasure and thrills, and, in the killer's mind, people are simply objects to use for one's own enjoyment. According to R. M. Holmes and Holmes (1998), hedonistic killers may be divided into three subtypes based on the primary motive for the murder: lust, thrill, and comfort. The *lust* serial killer's primary motive is exclusively sex, even if the victim is already dead (an activity called necrophilia): "He kills for sex; it is a propelling element in the motivation to kill and in the enjoyment he receives from his activities" (p. 93). Furthermore, "The killer kills in ways that reflect both the fantasy and the manner in which the fantasy is to be satisfied" (p. 93). The lust killer, according to Holmes and Holmes, is always seeking the IVT that is sexually appealing to him. Ted Bundy, for example, reported that the way a woman walked and talked was an important factor in his victim selection.

The ***thrill* killer** is primarily motivated to induce pain or a terrified reaction from the victim. The pain and terror engendered, in combination with the process of the murder itself, are highly stimulating and exciting for the killer. Usually, the killer has no relationship with his victim, although he may have followed her for some time. Similar to the lust killer, the thrill murderer selects victims based on certain physical characteristics that feed into his fantasies.

The motive for the *creature-comfort* **killer** is to acquire activities (business interests) or objects (money) that provide a comfortable and luxurious lifestyle. The killer's victims presumably stand in the way of achieving this. "The comfort killer's main objective is to enjoy life and to be sufficiently in control of immediate circumstances so that 'the good life' can be attained" (R. M. Holmes & Holmes, 1998, p. 119). Moreover, "overt, blatant displays of fatal aggression are not characteristics of this type; most comfort-oriented murderers tend to kill quietly if the situation permits" (p. 119). For the comfort killer, the act of murder is incidental to the pursuit of material gain and a comfortable lifestyle. Presumably, comfort killers dispose of their victims when they have identified a potential *new* "mark." In many ways, comfort killers resemble the behavioral characteristics of a criminal psychopath. Some writers (S. T. Holmes, Hickey, & Holmes, 1991) have pointed out that female serial killers often fall into this category.

The **power-control killer** obtains satisfaction from the absolute life-or-death control he has over the victim. Sexual components may or may not be present, but the primary motive is the extreme power and dominance over the helpless victim. These killers also tend to seek specific victims who appear especially vulnerable and easy to victimize.

Mass Murder

Compared to serial murder, relatively little research has been done on mass murderers. Perhaps this is because mass murder, although horrible and troubling, is not as intriguing, mysterious, or frightening as serial murder. Furthermore, mass murder usually happens suddenly and unpredictably—rarely is there any sequel. A long-term search for the perpetrator is not necessary. It is often clear who the offender is, although the motives are sometimes unclear. Some earlier FBI investigators (Douglas, Ressler, Burgess, & Hartman, 1986) have found it useful to divide mass murder into two major types mentioned previously: *classic* and *family*. Due to the many global examples of mass murder publicized in recent years, a third category—terrorist mass murder—should probably be added. Although the United States encountered these primarily in the 1995 bombing of the Federal Building in Oklahoma City in which 168 people were killed, as well as in the terrorist attacks on September 11, 2001, in which 3,047 people were killed, other countries such as Ireland, Iraq, and Afghanistan have encountered terrorist mass murder on a regular basis.

As mentioned earlier, an example of a classic mass murder is when the person barricades himself inside a public building—such as a restaurant or school—and randomly kills persons with whom he has contact. A family mass murder is when at least three family members are killed (usually by another family member). Most often, the incident occurs within the family residence. In one rural town, a woman was dropped off at her home after spending an evening working with friends on crafts for a church fair. She walked into the house and was confronted by her 17-year-old son, who had shot to death his father and younger brother and sister. He killed his mother, wrote a note revealing his actions, and then killed himself. The boy had sexually assaulted his sister, who threatened to reveal her victimization to her parents.

It is commonly assumed that suicide is a primary motive of many mass murderers. In other words, the individual planned to die at the crime scene after killing as many as possible, either at his own hand or by police gunfire. However, Grant Duwe (2000), on the basis of his examination of 495 mass killings over a 21-year time period, concluded that only 21% of mass murderers committed suicide, another 2% attempted suicide, and 3% were fatally shot by the police. It appears that family mass murders are the type that are most likely to result in the perpetrator's taking his or her own life.

The motives of mass murderers are highly variable. "The motivations for mass murder can range from revenge to hatred, from loyalty to greed; and the victims can be selected individually, as members of a particular category or group, or on a random basis" (Fox & Levin, 1998, p. 430). However, according to Fox and Levin, a majority of mass murderers are driven by revenge, and their victims are apparently chosen because of what they have done or what they represent. Mass murderers are frequently described as frustrated, angry people who feel helpless about their lives. They are usually between the ages of 25 and 45 (average age at time of murder is approximately 30), and they are generally convinced there is little chance that things will get better for them. Their personal lives have been failures by their standards, and they have often suffered some tragic or serious loss, such as losing a job or being abandoned by a spouse or partner. George Hennard, the 35-year-old described earlier who drove his pickup truck into the plate glass window of a restaurant in Texas, killing 22 patrons and wounding 27, had lost his cherished job as a merchant marine. He also apparently had an intense hatred of women and minorities. The 17-year-old described above who killed his family and himself does not fit the above profile, however. His crime appears to be one motivated by guilt for past actions and fear of what would occur if these actions were revealed.

Mass murderers are often socially isolated and withdrawn people who lack a strong social network of friends or supporters. Compared with serial murderers, they are more likely to be mentally disordered in the clinical sense. Their isolation is probably due to some combination of an active dislike of people and their own inadequate social and interpersonal skills. Attacking several or many others at one time provides these lonely, angry people a chance to get even, to dominate others, to take control, and to gain recognition.

An example of a classical mass murder is the Virginia Tech massacre. On April 16, 2007, Seung-Hui Cho shot and killed 32 people and wounded 25 others on the campus of Virginia Poly-technical University in Blacksburg. (See Photo 8.3, a photo of Cho released to the media.) He killed two students in a dormitory, and over 2 hours later killed 30 people in a classroom building. Cho, a 23-year-old senior majoring in English, was described by those who knew him as a lonely, troubled, isolated, bullied, and peer-rejected indi-vidual who was extremely angry at the world for the way he was treated during most of his lifetime.

Photo 8.3 Seung-Hui Cho, the Virginia Tech shooter, sent this photo of himself to the media shortly before perpetrating his crimes.

Some of his English professors found his papers unusually violent and frightening. On the Virginia Tech cam-pus, Cho was seen by students as quiet, strange, and basically noncommunicative.

Cho had come into contact with law enforcement on several occasions for allegedly stalking female stu-dents at Virginia Tech. Two of the incidents resulted in verbal warnings from campus police. Because of deep depression, he was also detained temporarily at a behavioral health center because he was considered an immi-nent danger to himself and others.

The Virginia Tech massacre is the most violent in American college history. The second most violent inci-dent occurred at the University of Texas on August 1, 1966, when Charles Whitman opened fire from the 28th floor of the Texas Tower, killing 16 and wounding 31 students below.

In the wake of the Virginia Tech and Columbine killings, many schools and universities across the nation have set up established "threat assessment" centers in an attempt to gauge the likelihood that a given individual is likely to harm others. Forensic psychologists are often consulted to carry out these assessments. (See Personal Perspective 8.1 for an introduction to Dr. Kris Mohandie, a psychologist who includes threat assessment among his many professional activities.) (See also Focus 8.2 on the National Threat Assessment Center.)

FOCUS 8.2. NATIONAL THREAT ASSESSMENT CENTER

The National Threat Assessment Center (NTAC), run by the U.S. Secret Service, was created to provide leadership and guidance to the emerging field of threat assessment. Specifically, the NTAC offers timely, realistic, useful, and effective advice to law enforcement and other professionals and organizations with responsibilities to investigate or prevent targeted violence.

Building on recent studies of U.S. assassins, attackers, and near-lethal approachers of public officials, the NTAC will develop and provide threat assessment training and conduct operational research relevant to public official, workplace, stalking/domestic, and school-based violence. In addition, the NTAC will offer its assistance to organizations interested in developing threat assessment programs.

Source: U.S. Secret Service (2003). Also available online at http://www.secretservice.gov.

Mass murderers often take a very active interest in guns. Unlike serial murder, about two-thirds of the mass killings (both classic and family) involved the use of guns, usually semiautomatic firearms with high magazine capacities (Duwe, 2000). In other words, they prefer weapons that make it easier to kill many people quickly.

The data reported by Duwe (2000) do not bear out reports claiming that most mass murders take place at the workplace. In fact, workplace massacres are quite rare, accounting for only 4% of the total incidents, whereas 27% of the incidents involved offenders who killed their victims in a public place, such as a park, restaurant, or college campus. The January 2011 shooting in Tucson occurred in front of a supermarket where a Congresswoman was meeting on a Saturday morning with her constituents. In Duwe's study, though, almost two-thirds of mass murders took place within a residential setting, often involving family members or acquaintances. Thus, a majority of mass murders can be classified as family mass murders.

Workplace Violence

Workplace violence is a complex phenomenon, encompassing a wide assortment of threatening and injurious behaviors that occur within one's place of employment. Workplace violence is somewhat of a misnomer because it refers not only to the more physically violent incidents but also to the subtle behavior that *threatens* violence, such as coercion, intimidation, outright threats, and harassment. In fact, although the media report the more serious violence, the incidents that actually occur most frequently in the workplace are *threats* of violence (J. W. Budd, Arvey, & Lawless, 1996). It is estimated that approximately 7% of those in the workforce are threatened every year, amounting to more than 6 million workers in the United States (Barling, Rogers, & Kelloway, 2000). Persons who report being *physically* assaulted in the workplace average around 2.5% of the U.S. workforce or approximately 2 million workers per year (Gregorie & Wallace, 2002).

PERSONAL PERSPECTIVE 8.1

From LAPD to the Private Sector: An Unusual and Exciting Career Path

Kris Mohandie, PhD

I have always had an interest in criminality and abnormal psychology—I recall while growing up listening with interest to media reports of events like the Manson murders, the Patty Hearst kidnapping and Symbionese Liberation Army shootout, and terrorist events (primarily aircraft hijackings) that punctuated the late 1960s and 1970s.

I obtained my bachelor's degree in behavioral science from Cal Poly Pomona in 1984, having rapidly gravitated toward psychology during my first year of undergraduate education, then enrolled in the PhD program at the California School of Professional Psychology in Los Angeles (CSPP-LA). There I had the opportunity to do several internships; my first one was doing juvenile diversion counseling at the Anaheim Police Department. I spent my time at this practicum working on the same floor as the juvenile detectives and obtained my first exposure to the law enforcement milieu and culture. Next, I completed an internship at Pomona Valley Mental Health, a community mental health center that served a very diverse population. There I was able to do rotations with the psychiatric emergency team, day treatment, as well as outpatient mental health services. The exposure to seriously mentally ill and sometimes violent people, both in ongoing treatment as well as in the crisis evaluation context, would prove invaluable to my later career.

After obtaining my doctorate, I was hired by Dr. Martin Reiser, the first police psychologist, as a postdoctoral fellow with the Los Angeles Police Department (LAPD). Shortly thereafter, I became a full-time member of LAPD's growing police psychology staff, where I remained until 2003. In addition to providing the usual clinical services to a law enforcement population, I received training and experience in "operational" psychological roles, including consultation to the crisis/hostage negotiation and SWAT team, homicide and sex crime units, and the Threat Management Unit, which managed stalking and threat cases. My consultation experience with the crisis negotiation and SWAT team was one of the most rewarding, stimulating, and challenging aspects of the work. In real time, I would be on scene, assessing and profiling barricaded suspects, jumpers, hostage takers, as well as hostages, offering psychological profiles, assessing threat risk, and suggesting dialogue strategies. There are very few contexts of which I am aware, where dynamics of unfolding violence can be observed and experienced in the moment. It was essential to be able to think on one's feet, with lives in the balance, under less-than-ideal circumstances.

I recall, in about 1990, arriving solo to my first hostage incident involving a parolee armed with an AK-47 who had a child hostage—an older victim had managed to jump from the second story.

(Continued)

(Continued)

Shots had been fired by the subject. I arrived to find a tense negotiation unfolding, with the first responding sergeant in "dialogue" that initially consisted of yelling. In short order, we were able to get the situation calmed down somewhat and the sergeant presented a quieter delivery. However, the sound of metal clacking against teeth as the subject placed the gun in his mouth quickly raised the stakes again, and he had to be talked through this crucial point in the crisis situation. Later, through listening, empathy, the passage of time, and crisis reduction, including the delivery of some requested cigarettes, we not only got the subject to release the child, but eventually surrender himself without further incident. Other cases included numerous attempted jumpers, a patient who shot several doctors at County USC hospital and took hostages, interrupted attempted murder-suicides, the North Hollywood robbery shoot-out, and the O. J. Simpson barricade.

There were many other tense and memorable events, including the Spielberg stalking case, in which a delusional offender's belief that he needed to abduct the famous movie director propelled him to show up at Mr. Spielberg's residence on multiple occasions with duct tape, box cutters, and handcuffs. Other interesting crimes included false victimization cases, in which individuals staged and falsely claimed to be victims of stalking, rape, and other related offenses.

Throughout my career, I have met some great professional police officers. Together with SWAT Lieutenant Mike Albanese, I have traveled to prisons and interviewed a number of violent offenders. We also interviewed hostages who had survived these events. We traveled around the country providing training to other departments and hostage negotiator associations, which enabled us to meet some amazing people doing this incredible

work, and to learn from their experiences and case debriefs. I met people from the FBI, was invited to attend their hostage negotiation training in 1994, and later had the opportunity to consult for this agency on an ongoing basis.

In about 1992, I became involved with private practice consultation in the area of threat assessment after meeting experienced police and forensic psychologist Dr. Chris Hatcher. He assembled a network of police psychologists from throughout the country who would assist private and public companies in the area of workplace violence prevention. We would assess and interview individuals who were identified as potential threats, including disgruntled employees, unstable outsiders, and stalkers who were raising concerns. I learned techniques for safely conducting evaluations, how to consult with attorneys and private security professionals, as well as methods of investigative interviewing. It brought me fast-forward from my first "accidental" workplace violence case in 1988 involving an individual who had purchased a black market Uzi and told me he was going to kill multiple people at his workplace, related to a worker's compensation dispute and pride issue. We were fortunate to avert catastrophe in that early case, but my work in subsequent years with Dr. Hatcher and others provided strategies that were purposeful and effective at defusing these ticking time bombs. This work, as well as my experience consulting with the Threat Management Unit at the LAPD, inspired me to seek out and interview other types of violent offenders in prison, including a number of notorious mass murderers and stalkers. Lessons learned from these offenders were insightful and enhanced our ability to keep people safe and interrupt individuals who were careening out of control on their violent pathway.

During my years at LAPD, I began to participate in a variety of scientific and scholarly writing projects for peer-reviewed journals. Many of these writings were collaborations with established forensic psychologists, particularly with the much accomplished Dr. J. Reid Meloy. To date, I have authored and coauthored a number of publications on subjects such as hostage negotiation, adult and adolescent mass murder, human captivity and victimology, police shootings and suicide by cop, and stalking.

I left the LAPD in 2003 to pursue full-time private consultation. My specialties and interests are extreme violence, violent offending, victimology, suicide by cop, stalking, and threat assessment. For many years now, I have regularly worked in the area of forensic psychology. I am often consulted by criminal prosecutors, defense attorneys, and civil attorneys in all of these areas, and have testified in numerous civil and criminal court cases, including multiple capital murder cases. I continue to work with various local, state, and federal agen-

cies, and regularly consult with the private sector on matters of risk and threat management.

My days are interesting and varied with a fair amount of focused travel. I am never bored by my career and have been grateful to get paid to do what I enjoy doing. I do make time for leisure and other activities, which is important for maintaining balance.

I have some recommendations for those interested in pursuing a career in police or forensic psychology. Attend an accredited graduate school (with a PhD or PsyD program) in clinical psychology; obtain a breadth of experience that gives you a solid general background in clinical psychology; ground yourself in ethical practice; and develop mentors that can guide you to helpful experiences, resources, and sound decisions. There are now numerous scientific and scholarly publications in a multitude of relevant areas—read all you can. Think about making your own contributions. Recognize the opportunities in many experiences to serve your future career aspirations.

As indicated above, Dr. Mohandie has had a long and varied career as a police psychologist, consultant, expert witness, and researcher. His company—Operational Consulting International—is based in Southern California. He gives lectures, workshops, and training sessions across the United States and Canada. He also consults with media and makes frequent media appearances on topics relating to violence, stalking, and hostage negotiation.

Nevertheless, approximately 1,000 employees are murdered in the workplace each year (Gregorie & Wallace, 2002), and an additional 1.5 million workers are victims of non-homicidal violence, not including threats. Homicide is the third leading cause of death in American workplaces and the second leading cause of fatal occupational injury for women (Iowa Injury Prevention Research Center, 2002). Firearms are used in about 80% of the workplace homicides. Retail sales workers (especially fast-food and convenience store employees) tend to be the most frequent victims, largely because robbery is the primary motive of job-related homicides (Occupational Safety and Health Administration [OSHA], 2001).

Neither schools nor colleges and universities are immune from workplace violence. In February 2010, Amy Bishop, a 42-year-old college professor at the University of Alabama in Huntsville, opened fire on colleagues during a biology department meeting, killing three and wounding three. Interestingly, and apparently unbeknownst to those who knew her in Alabama, Bishop had violent incidents in her past. In 1986, she shot to death her brother, an 18-year-old freshman at Northeastern University, in a case that was then ruled accidental. After the Alabama shooting, the Massachusetts case was reopened, and in June 2010, Bishop was charged with the murder of her brother. According to news reports, Amy Bishop also was the prime suspect in a 1993 mail bombing attempt on a professor from Harvard Medical School. (Bishop had obtained her PhD in genetics from Harvard.) She also had once punched a stranger in a restaurant in an argument over a child seat. Bishop and her husband have four young children.

Other examples of workplace violence in academe have included graduate students who shot professors on their dissertation committees and teachers killed by former boyfriends in the parking lot of the school. In 2009, a laboratory technician at Yale University—24-year-old Raymond Clark III—was charged with the on-campus murder of graduate student Annie M. Le shortly before her scheduled wedding day. Note that we are making a distinction between these work-related incidents and the school violence that is directed specifically at students and that was discussed previously.

One-third of victims of workplace violence between 1993 and 1999 reported that they believed that the perpetrator was under the influence of alcohol or drugs at the time of the crime. In approximately 8 out of 10 workplace homicides, the perpetrators and victims were strangers. Coworkers and former coworkers were responsible for 7% of the workplace homicides, and husbands and boyfriends were responsible for 3% (Bureau of Justice Statistics, 2001b). Although retail workers tend to be the most frequent victims of *homicide,* other occupational groups are at greater risk of *violence* in general because of the nature of their job. Police officers are victims of the highest rate of workplace violence, followed by correctional officers, taxi drivers, private security guards, and bartenders. In the 1980s, the phrase *"going postal"* became part of the national lexicon after a series of workplace shootings by distressed postal workers. In actuality, postal workers were no more likely to commit workplace violence than other occupational groups, but the convergence of several crimes among this group led to the misconception. Occupational risks for workplace violence per 1,000 workers are listed in Focus 8.3.

Physical workplace violence has been classified into four major types on the basis of the assailant's relationship to the workplace (California Occupational Safety and Health Administration, 1995; Gregorie, 2000; LeBlanc & Kelloway, 2002). In the first type, the assailant does not have a legitimate relationship to the workplace or to the victim. He or she usually enters the workplace to commit a criminal action, such as a robbery or theft. Robbery is the principal motive for most workplace homicide, accounting for 85% of workplace deaths (Gregorie & Wallace, 2000). The second type of assailant is the recipient of some service provided by the workplace or victim and may be either a current or a former client, patient, or customer. Most often, this individual is unhappy with the product or service he or she received from the agency or company. In August 2010, an individual entered the headquarters of the Discovery Channel in Maryland and took several people hostage. Although this could have ended in violence toward the hostages, the man—who had previously expressed dissatisfaction with the media outlet—was himself shot by police (see Photo 2.2). The third type of assailant has an employment-related involvement with the workplace, as a current or former employee, supervisor, or manager. This assailant is often referred to as a "disgruntled employee" who enters the workplace to punish or get back at some individual or the agency or company in general. Amy Bishop was allegedly irate because her colleagues did not support her bid for tenure. According to Gregorie and Wallace, disgruntled employees account for approximately 10% of workplace homicides. The fourth type has an indirect involvement with the workplace because of a relationship with an employee, such as a current or former spouse or partner. Often, this situation concerns domestic violence or spousal/partner abuse.

Few systematic studies have examined the predictors or causes of workplace violence. Most of the work to date has focused on either (a) describing the assailant or (b) identifying the job characteristics that increase the risk for violence (LeBlanc & Kelloway, 2002). Considerably more research is needed to identify the causes and implement preventive measures in the workplace. Nevertheless, many places of employment have been sensitized to this issue and have increased their levels of security in response to fear and uneasiness among employees.

This may be due, at least partly, to the dramatic increase in workplace violence litigation (Kaufer & Mattman, 2002). The legal action and civil lawsuits at this point in time concentrate on four major areas: (1) negligent hiring (failure to screen employees properly), (2) negligent retention (failure to terminate unsuitable and threatening employees), (3) negligent supervision (failure to monitor performance), and (4) inadequate security (Kaufer & Mattman, 2002).

Consequently, legal and regulatory obligations for employers to provide safe and secure work environments are bound to increase, and mandatory prevention and training programs are likely to be commonplace across all private and public organizations in the near future. As should be apparent, forensic psychologists increasingly are called on to conduct threat assessments, or to assess the risk of violence in an individual about whom fellow workers or supervisors are concerned. Perhaps more important, however, psychologists working within workplace settings should be attuned to the culture of the workplace and play a critical role in facilitating a working environment that promotes cooperation and mutual respect among and between employees and supervisory personnel.

We have thus far discussed only violence and threats of violence in the workplace, but we must emphasize that other workplace issues also merit careful attention. Discrimination—be it on the basis of race, gender, ethnicity, age, sexual orientation, or religion—remains of major concern. One particular form of discrimination—sexual harassment, covered in Chapter 6—is also noteworthy. In fiscal year 2008, the U.S. Equal Employment Opportunity Commission (EEOC) received 13,869 charges of sexual harassment (U.S. EEOC, 2009). Sixteen percent of those charges were filed by men. Moreover, even though there has been a leveling off of filings with the EEOC over the past 10 years, the data underscore the fact that sexual harassment is still quite common in the workplace. One recent study (Fineran & Gruber, 2009) found that more than half of teenage girls experience some form of sexual harassment at their place of work. It is a distressing behavior that explicitly or implicitly affects an individual's employment; unreasonably interferes with an individual's work performance; and creates an intimidating, hostile, or offensive work environment. In addition, a number of investigations have substantiated a link between posttraumatic stress disorder, depression, and sexual harassment (Fineran & Gruber, 2009). More pertinent to our discussion here, harassing behavior may lead to stalking, which may in turn lead to violence.

Likewise, racial and ethnic discrimination in the workplace also may lead to violence. In addition, discrimination in all of its contexts has similarities to bias crimes and to crimes of intimidation, to which we now turn our attention.

FOCUS 8.3. OCCUPATIONAL RISKS FOR WORKPLACE VIOLENCE

Highest rates of workplace violence per 1,000 workers:

Police officers: 306.0

Correctional officers: 217.9

Taxi drivers: 183.8

Private security guards: 117.3

Bartenders: 91.3

(Continued)

(Continued)

Mental health professionals: 79.5

Gas station attendants: 79.1

Convenience and liquor store clerks: 68.4

Mental health custodial workers: 63.3

Junior high/middle school teachers: 57.4

Bus drivers: 45.0

Special education teachers: 40.7

High school teachers: 28.9

Nurses: 24.8

Source: Bureau of Labor Statistics (1999).

Hate or Bias Crimes

Hate crimes—also called **bias crimes**—are criminal offenses motivated by an offender's bias against a group to which the victim either belongs or is believed to belong. Note that neither hatred nor prejudice alone is sufficient to constitute a hate crime. There must be an underlying criminal offense—for example, an assault, vandalism, arson, or murder—that is *motivated* by the hatred or prejudice. It is not a crime to hate; however, demonstrated hatred against the victim of a crime based on prejudice can enhance the sentence given the perpetrator if he or she is convicted.

The groupings—or protected categories—most commonly identified in bias crime laws are race, religion, gender, disability, sexual orientation, and ethnicity. (See Focus 8.4 for illustrations of recent incidents that qualify as hate crimes.) It is important to note that these are inclusive categories; that is, bias crime statutes protect all members of all races (not just Blacks or Whites) and persons of all sexual orientations (not just gays and lesbians). In addition, statutes in some states also provide penalties for bias crimes against certain age groups (e.g., the elderly) or members of the military. The **Hate Crime Statistics Act** of 1990 requires the FBI to collect data and provide information on the nature and prevalence of violent attacks, intimidation, arson, or property damage directed at persons or groups because of bias against their race, religion, sexual orientation, or ethnicity. In September 1994, the Violent Crime Control and Law Enforcement Act amended the Hate Crime Statistics Act to include physical and mental disabilities in the data collection. Note that gender—commonly covered in hate crime statutes—is not one of the specified categories. Also in 1994, Congress passed the Hate Crime Sentencing Enhancement Act, which provides for longer sentences for such crimes. In 1996, due to dramatic increases in the burning of places of worship (especially African American churches located in the southeastern sections of the United States), the Church Arson Prevention Act was signed into law. More recently, the Hate Crime Prevention Act of 1999 prohibits persons from interfering with an individual's civil or constitutional rights, such as voting or employment, by violence or threat of violence due to his or her race, color, religion, or national origin.

FOCUS 8.4. HATE CRIME EXAMPLES

The following are only a few illustrations of bias-related incidents, all reported in the media during the summer of 2010. Although criminal activity is indicated in each, they may or may not all be charged as bias crimes.

- A young man, Kevin Shea, was sentenced to 8 years for his role in the stabbing death of an Ecuadorean immigrant, Marcelo Lucero, as he walked near a train station. In all, seven teens were implicated in the attack, most charged with gang assault, conspiracy, and related charges. Jeffrey Conroy, who actually stabbed Lucero, received a 25-year sentence for manslaughter as a hate crime. Prosecutors said the group of teens went to the area "in search of Hispanics."
- A cabdriver in New York City was stabbed and robbed after being asked whether he was Muslim. The day after the incident, the driver commented, "Until yesterday I felt safe here."
- Vandals spray-painted anti-Muslim and racial epithets on the wall of a mosque, shortly before Eid, the celebratory time marking the end of Ramadan, the time of prayer and fasting. Three men in their early 20s were arrested. Residents of the small community in which this occurred were outraged, saying that the diverse community has lived peacefully without such expressions of hatred.
- A gay pastor and his partner were attacked and robbed at gunpoint in a park by six male teens. The teens first asked them if they were gay.
- A 17-year-old Mexican immigrant on his way home from work as a busboy was beaten and robbed by three young men who shouted anti-Mexican epithets. This happened despite a heavy police presence in the area and was apparently the eleventh time in a 3-month period that a hate crime task force had investigated such incidents.

Based on national statistics, hate crimes appear to account for a relatively small percentage of all criminal violence. However, documenting hate or bias crimes is difficult because the intentions of the offender are not always obvious or clear-cut. Consequently, law enforcement agencies record hate crimes only when the investigation reveals facts sufficient to conclude that the offender's actions were bias motivated. Evidence most often used to support the existence of bias includes oral comments, written statements, or gestures made by the offender at the time of the incident, or drawings or graffiti left at the crime scene (Strom, 2001). In addition, there is tremendous state-to-state variation in the degree to which law enforcement officers are trained and encouraged to recognize and record hate crimes. In 2008, there were 7,783 reported incidents of hate crimes nationwide, and in 2009 this decreased only slightly to 6,604 (FBI, 2010).

Available data indicate that a majority of hate crimes are motivated by racial bias (51.3%), followed by religious bias (19.5%), sexual orientation bias (16.7%), ethnic/national origin bias (11.5%), and disability bias (1.0%) (FBI, 2009). Since the events of September 11, suspected incidents of bias crimes against Muslims are believed to have increased, but documentation is difficult to obtain; moreover, Muslims—like members of many other groups—may be reluctant to report their victimization to police. We discuss this again in the next chapter. Examples of a disability bias include biases against a person with a physical disease, a mental disorder, or intellectual disability. Hate crimes on college campuses demonstrate a broad spectrum of criminal conduct, ranging from threats to sexual assaults to bombings. They occur at virtually every type of college or university and in every part of the country and are a significant problem on many campuses (Wessler & Moss, 2001). Offenders may include students, former students, or nonstudents.

Approximately two-thirds of hate crimes are directed at individuals, whereas the remaining targets are businesses, religious institutions, or other institutions and organizations. More than 4 out of 5 violent hate crimes reported in the FBI's National Incident-Based Reporting System (NIBRS) involve the victimization of a single individual within a single incidence (Strom, 2001). The majority of persons (three-fourths) suspected of committing hate crimes are White males. NIBRS data indicate that more than a third of persons arrested for hate crimes are younger than 18, and more than half are younger than age 25 at the time of arrest. Younger persons (younger than age 18) are more likely to be arrested for property-related offenses, such as vandalism, whereas older persons are more likely to be arrested for violent hate crime.

Hate crime violence appears to have its roots in an individual's learned prejudice against particular social groups. This learned prejudice, combined with fear, can escalate into violence when a member of the prejudicial group believes his or her lifestyle is under attack. Interestingly, two-thirds of those arrested for hate crimes reside in the locality in which the crime occurred (Strom, 2001).

Stalking: The Crime of Intimidation

Stalking is defined as "a course of conduct directed at a specific person that involves repeated physical or visual proximity, nonconsensual communication, or verbal, written, or implied threats sufficient to cause fear in a reasonable person" (Tjaden, 1997, p. 2). The term refers to

> repeated and often escalating unwanted intrusions and communications, including loitering nearby, following or surveying a person's home, making multiple telephone calls or other forms of unwanted direct and indirect communications, spreading gossip, destroying personal property, harassing acquaintances or family members, sending threatening or sexually suggestive "gifts" or letters, and aggressive and violent acts. (Abrams & Robinson, 2002, p. 468)

Stalking is as old as the history of human relationships, and yet it has only been within the past two decades that the behavior has been recognized as unlawful (Beatty, Hickey, & Sigmon, 2002). The release of films such as *Fatal Attraction* (Paramount Pictures, released 1987), *Sleeping With the Enemy* (20th Century-Fox, released 1991), and *Cape Fear* (Universal Studios, released 1991) contributed to increasing salience about this problem in the minds of the public. Increased coverage by the news media of the stalking of celebrities (e.g., David Letterman, Rebecca Schaeffer) also led to stalking becoming a household term. (See also Personal Perspective 8.1, where Dr. Mohandie mentions famous cases of celebrity stalking.) Some commentators refer to stalking as the "crime of the nineties" (L. Sheridan & Davies, 2001).

Stalking is an extremely frightening, emotionally distressful, and depressing crime of intimidation. Not surprisingly, clinicians have discovered that the longer the duration of the stalking—regardless of whether the behaviors are intrusive, violent, or some combination of both—the greater the potential damage to the victim (McEwan, Mullen, & Purcell, 2007). Anti-stalking laws exist in all 50 states, the District of Columbia, and Canada. Although most states define stalking in their statutes as the willful, malicious, and repeated following and harassing of another person, some include such activities as lying-in-wait, surveillance, nonconsensual communication, telephone harassment, and vandalism (Tjaden & Thoennes, 1998a). Some states require that at least two stalking incidents occur before the conduct is considered criminal.

One of the most comprehensive studies on stalking was conducted by the Center for Policy Research and published in a monograph titled *Stalking in America: Findings From the National Violence Against Women Survey*

(Tjaden & Thoennes, 1998b). The project, cosponsored by the National Institute of Justice and Centers for Disease Control and Prevention, was a nationally representative phone survey of 8,000 women and 8,000 men, 18 years or older. The survey was conducted between November 1995 and May 1996 and provides empirical data on the prevalence, characteristics, and consequences of stalking.

The survey found that 8% of women and 2% of men reported that they had been stalked at some point in their lives (Tjaden, 1997). In most instances, the stalking lasted less than 1 year, but some individuals were stalked for more than 5 years. According to the research reported by Mullen, Pathé, and Purcell (2001), however, repeated unwanted communications and imposed contacts that go on for more than 2 weeks are highly likely to last for months or even years. In one recent, extensive survey (National Crime Victimization Survey), 11% of the victims of stalking said they had been stalked for 5 year or more (Baum, Catalano, Rand, & Rose, 2009).

Researchers believe that the motives of most stalkers are to control, intimidate, or frighten their victims. The fears and emotional distress generated by stalking behavior are many and varied. About 1 in 5 victims feared bodily harm to themselves and 1 in 6 feared for the safety of a child or other family member. About 1 in 20 feared being killed by the stalker (Baum et al., 2009).

In the study referenced above, the stalker was male 87% of the time, and the victim was female 80% of the time. Eighty percent of the stalkers are believed to be White, at least 50% are between the ages of 18 and 35, and many earn above-average incomes. In most stalking incidents, the victims (particularly women) knew their stalker. Approximately half of the female victims were stalked by current or former marital or cohabiting partners, and a majority of these women (80%) had been physically assaulted by that partner either during the relationship, during the stalking episode, or during both. In about a third of the cases, the stalkers vandalized the victim's property, and about 10% of the time, the stalker killed or threatened to kill the victim's pet. Only 7% of the victims thought their stalkers were mentally disordered, psychotic, crazy, or abusers of alcohol or drugs.

Another comprehensive study of stalking was cosponsored by the National Institute of Justice and the Bureau of Justice Statistics (B. S. Fisher, Cullen, & Turner, 2000). The project involved a phone survey of 4,446 female students at 223 colleges and universities, conducted from February to May 1997. The primary screening question used to measure stalking was the following: "Since school began in fall 1996, has anyone—from a stranger to an ex-boyfriend—repeatedly followed you, watched you, phoned, written, e-mailed, or communicated with you in other ways that seemed obsessive and made you afraid or concerned for your safety?"

The key findings of the study were the following:

- Thirteen percent of the college women had been stalked since the school year began.
- Of the victims, 80.3% knew or had seen their stalker before.
- Stalking incidents lasted on average about 2 months.
- Thirty percent of the women reported being injured emotionally and psychologically from being stalked.
- In 10.3% of incidents, the victim reported that the stalker forced or attempted sexual contact.
- Overall, 83.1% of stalking incidents were not reported to police or campus law enforcement.

It should also be noted that some mental health professionals who deal regularly with persons having mental or emotional difficulties have become the victims of stalking by their clients (Gentile, Asamen, Harmell, & Weathers, 2002). According to Gentile et al., the stalkers of mental health professionals may be either single or divorced at the time of the stalking. The majority of these clients (62%) were diagnosed as having a mood disorder. In another survey, about 2 out of 3 university counselors had experienced some type of harassing behavior or stalking behavior from a current or former client (Romans, Hays, & White, 1996).

In an effort to better understand stalkers, some researchers have proposed typologies, or classification systems. One of the first systematic studies on stalkers was done by Zona, Sharma, and Lane (1993) in their work with the Los Angeles Police Department's Threat Management Unit (also mentioned in Focus 8.1). These researchers developed a classification system that focused on individuals who stalked entertainment celebrities and divided stalkers into three behavioral clusters: (1) erotomanic, (2) love obsessional, and (3) simple obsessional (categories that will be defined shortly). A few years later, researchers shifted their focus from "star stalkers" to men who stalked their ex-partners (Emerson, Ferris, & Gardner, 1998; Kurt, 1995). Star stalkers were assumed to be predominately mentally disordered persons who were driven by delusions in their pursuit of their favorite celebrity, whereas ex-partner stalkers were seen as asserting their power over women through violence and intimidation (Mullen et al., 2001).

More recently, Mohandie, Meloy, Green-McGowan & Williams (2006) studied a large sample of 1,005 male and female stalkers. They concluded that they could be grouped into four categories based on their relationship to the victim: (1) the Intimate stalker, who pursues a current or former sexual intimate; (2) the Acquaintance stalker, who pursues someone he or she knows but with whom he or she has not ever been sexually intimate; (3) the Public Figure stalker, who pursues a public figure with whom he or she has never had a relationship; and (4) the Private Stranger stalker, who pursues someone he or she has never met but is aware of because the victim is in the stalker's environment (such as a neighbor or fellow college student). Mohandie et al. found that these groups had different violence rates, with the Intimate stalker being the most likely (74%) to use violence against his or her victim and the Public Figure stalker being the least likely (2%). Using the same data set, M. Meloy, Mohandie, and Green (2008) and M. Meloy and Mohandie (2008) have published studies focusing only on female stalkers.

Another often-cited stalking typology, one that focuses more on the motives for stalking than on the relationship between the stalker and his or her victim, was outlined by Beatty et al. (2002). It consists of four broad categories, the first three of which are similar to those proposed by Zona et al. (1993): (1) simple *obsession* stalking, (2) love obsession stalking, (3) erotomania stalking, and (4) vengeance stalking. The term *obsession* refers to recurrent ideas, thoughts, impulses, or images that a person tries to control or satisfy through various actions. It should be emphasized that this typology has not been validated by empirical research but should serve as a springboard for future research and hypothesis development. The following descriptions of the four stalker categories follow Beatty et al.'s definitions.

Simple obsession stalkers are the most common, accounting for 60% of the stalkers, and represent behavior that is a continuation of a previous pattern of domestic violence and psychological abuse in an intimate relationship. Consequently, the targeted victim is often a former spouse, and the majority of offenders are males. These stalkers appear to be more intelligent and better educated than most other stalkers (J. R. Meloy & Gothard, 1995). The stalking is hypothesized to be prompted by the offender's feelings of low self-esteem and helplessness. Apparently, the offender increases his own self-esteem by demeaning and demoralizing his former spouse and may take drastic steps if he perceives the victim is trying to remove herself from the controlling situation. Simple obsession is the category of stalking that is most likely to result in murder. It is very similar to the Intimate stalker described by Mohandie et al. (2006).

Love obsession stalkers and their victims tend to be casual acquaintances, such as neighbors or coworkers, but such stalking may also involve complete strangers, such as a celebrity. The primary motivation of these stalkers is to establish a personal relationship with the targeted victim. Like simple obsession stalkers, these individuals may have very low self-esteem and may be haunted by feelings of helplessness and depression. Presumably, these stalkers believe that by associating with persons who display exceptional qualities and high status, they can correspondingly raise their own levels of self-esteem and worthiness. Often, the love obsession stalker is so desperate to develop a relationship with the victim that he or she is willing to accept a negative or destructive relationship, sometimes resorting to violence in an effort to win the attention of the unwilling victim. A classic example of this type of stalker is John Hinckley, who was convinced he could win the love of actor Jodie Foster by shooting President Ronald Reagan.

Erotomania stalking is considered highly delusional, and the offender is often plagued by serious mental disorders, most often schizophrenia. Erotomania stalkers believe that the relationship with their victim already exists, in contrast to the simple and love obsession stalkers. Erotomania stalkers are usually less dangerous to the victims, but their irrationality is troubling and unpredictable to the victims. Margaret Ray, the woman who stalked talk show host David Letterman for nearly 10 years, illustrates this type of stalker. She apparently believed throughout that time that she was Letterman's wife and the mother of his child. She was discovered on his New Canaan, Connecticut, property on many occasions; was arrested driving his car; and sent him flowers and candy. Eventually, the troubled woman committed suicide by kneeling in front of a speeding train in Colorado.

Vengeance stalkers are quite different from the other three types because they do not seek a personal relationship with their targeted victims. Instead, these stalkers try to elicit a particular response—such as fear, or change of behavior such as moving to another area—from their victims. Vengeance is their prime motivation. An illustration of this kind of stalker is when an employee who is fired from his job begins to stalk and harass the supervisor who he believes is responsible for the firing, in hopes of ruining the supervisor's life.

When Does Stalking Usually Stop?

What terminates stalking? Some stalkers stop pursuing their current victim when they find a new "love" interest. About 18% of the victims in the Center for Policy Research Survey (Tjaden & Thoennes, 1998b) indicated that the stalking stopped when stalkers entered into a relationship with a new person. Law enforcement interventions also seem to help. Fifteen percent of victims said the stalking ceased when their stalkers received a warning from the police. Interestingly, more formal interventions such as arrest, conviction, or restraining orders do not appear to be very effective—perhaps serving to antagonize the stalker. When it comes to persistent, frightening stalking that creates risks to personal safety, the survey suggests that the most effective method may be for the victim to relocate as far away from the offender as possible, providing no information of the person's whereabouts to the stalker or to individuals who might communicate that information. Victims of stalking should not be expected to bear the burden of such an impractical approach, however.

Predictions of Violence in Stalking Cases

Many stalking victims want to know the likelihood that they will become the victim of a violent act (Rosenfeld & Harmon, 2002). According to Rosenfeld and Harmon, "Determining which stalkers represent a significant risk of violence, and differentiating those individuals from the remaining offenders who may pose less risk of physical harm, has clear and significant implications for victims, clinicians, and the legal system" (p. 685). Recall that Mohandie et al. (2006) found that Intimate stalkers had the highest rate of violence in their four groups.

In an effort to identify features that may differentiate violent stalkers from nonviolent stalkers, Rosenfeld and Harmon (2002) analyzed 204 stalking and harassment cases referred for court-ordered mental health evaluations in New York City. Results supported the findings of previous researchers (e.g., Palerea, Zona, Lane, & Langhinrichsen-Rohling, 1999) who found that former spouses or intimates of stalkers were most at risk.

> Specifically, intimate stalkers threatened persons and property (including physical violence toward the victim), were more likely to "make good" on their threats by following them with some form of violent behavior, and used more physical approach behaviors in contacting their victims than non-intimate stalkers. These results illustrate the importance of accounting for the presence of an intimate relationship when assessing for violence risk in stalking cases. (Palerea et al., 1999, p. 278)

Violent *threats* and drug abuse also appear to be significant predictors of stalking violence. Rosenfeld and Harmon (2002) also found that variables such as the stalker's prior criminal history and previous violent *behavior* did *not* emerge as good predictors of violence. This was surprising because Palerea et al. (1999) reported that a history of violence was the strongest predictor in their data. McEwan, Mullen, Mackenzie, and Ogloff (2009) also found that stalkers who are rejected by ex-intimates, who have a history of violent behavior, and who have made threats, present the greatest risk of violence. The differences between the studies, however, may be due to the fact that Rosenfeld and Harmon had access to much more information—official records of arrest and convictions as well as stalker self-reports and victim reports—than the Palerea group did. Palerea et al. used data obtained from 223 police files maintained by the Los Angeles Police Department. Consequently, the difference between the two studies might be a function of the quality and quantity of the data collected. Research so far has not indicated that psychiatric history is associated with violence against persons or property. Quite possibly, though, if the stalkers were divided into an empirically-based typology, more significant results in this regard might be forthcoming.

Juvenile stalkers appear to be more dangerous and violent than adults. In an investigation of 299 juvenile stalkers, Purcell, Moller, Flower, and Mullen (2009) found that juveniles participated in higher levels of threats and violence than typically found in adult stalking. Over half of the victims (54%) of juvenile stalkers were physically attacked, some sustaining significant injuries, and another 2% were sexually assaulted resulting in serious injury. These data also indicate that juvenile stalkers prefer a more direct means of contact with their victims, mostly via unwanted approaches or unsolicited phone calls, e-mails, or text messages. According to Baum et al. (2009), about 1 in 4 adult victims reported having experienced some form of cyberstalking, such as e-mail (83%) or instant messaging (35%).

Cyberstalking is analogous to traditional forms of stalking in that it incorporates persistent behaviors that engender apprehension and fear. However, with the advent of new technologies, traditional stalking has taken on entirely new forms through mediums like e-mail, text messaging, and social networking sites. It is possible that such incidents may be more common than traditional forms of stalking. This is because the basic apparatus of the Internet facilitates not only anonymity but also contact with an immense field of potential victims. Cell phones and the Internet have provided far-reaching and unregulated opportunities for cyberstalkers to harass unsuspecting victims. In addition, there is a considerable amount of personal information available through the Internet, and cyberstalkers can easily and quickly locate private information about a target.

Unsolicited e-mail is one of the most common forms of harassment, including hate, obscene, or threatening mail. Other forms of harassment include sending the victim viruses or high volumes of electronic junk mail (spamming). E-mail stalking can result from an attempt to initiate a relationship, repair a relationship, or threaten and traumatize a person. It is often accompanied by traditional stalking such as threatening phone calls, vandalism of property, threatening mail, and physical attacks (Gregorie, 2000).

SUMMARY AND CONCLUSIONS

Violence, the definition of which indicates that it requires some display of physical force, is essentially atypical human behavior when we compare it with the vast amount of human behavior that is nonviolent. Nonetheless, it remains a fascinating area of study as well as a pervasive aspect of popular culture. In fact, as we saw in this chapter, the increasingly violent images in the media have prompted research studies that in turn have led to calls for limiting the exposure of children—particularly young children—to these images.

In Spring 2011, the U.S. Supreme Court is expected to rule on whether states can ban the sale of certain violent videos to children. We also saw in this chapter that aggression, a construct frequently studied by psychologists, does not necessarily result in the physical force that we defined as violence. In addition, society actually condones some forms of violence, which further complicates any attempts to prevent it, predict it, or treat those who display violence or who are its victims.

The chapter focused primarily on criminal violence as it is defined in the law and in crime statistics. The four Part I (formerly known as "index") violent crimes—murder and nonnegligent manslaughter, forcible rape, aggravated assault, and robbery—together comprise about one-third of all Part I crimes. Persons arrested for these crimes are predominantly male (87–90%), although the violent crime rate for females began to increase faster than the male rate in the 1990s. Women continue to appear in arrest statistics far less often than men, however, a phenomenon for which a variety of explanations has been proposed. The most common explanations relate to either socialization or biological differences.

Race and ethnic differences in violent crime have received greater attention, and these differences are among the most troubling to researchers and policy makers alike. African Americans, particularly African American males, continue to make up a disproportionate part of official statistics on violent crime. The chapter emphasized that numerous social factors can explain these differentials and guarded against attributing any biological factors to the differences. In addition, we warned against focusing on one racial group to the exclusion of others, noting that researchers are beginning to explore differences among ethnic groups.

Psychologists and criminologists as a group often discuss violence as being instrumental, or reactive/expressive, or some combination of both. Studies suggest that the great majority of criminal violence—including homicide—is instrumental. Offenders commit the crime to achieve a particular goal, be it material goods, recognition, or political change. Psychologists and criminologists also have explored biological, social, cognitive, and situational factors as explanations for violent behavior. At present, it appears that a combination of all four categories of factors is the best way to approach the study of violence. However, we emphasize that, although some researchers have found biological links to aggression, any biological predisposition can be attenuated (or lessened) with careful attention to social, cognitive, and situational factors. To use one example, the social environment of a child who is highly aggressive as the result of some brain damage can be modified to make it less likely that that child will display violent behavior.

The chapter gave considerable attention to criminal homicide, the violent crime that is the least frequent but has received considerable research attention. The separate violent crime of sexual assault will be discussed in detail in the following chapter. The typical homicide is the single killing committed either in the course of another felony—most often a robbery—or committed against a relative or acquaintance. Young adult males are the most likely perpetrators of these single murders. Atypical murders—particularly those that qualify as multiple murders (serial, spree, and mass murders)—have most fascinated and frightened the public. We discussed in detail both serial and mass murderers because they have been the subject of considerable scholarly commentary and research attention.

Serial murderers—so called because of the time interval between their killings—generally begin their murderous behavior at a later age than single murderers. Most are male, but their victims may be male or female—they generally show a preference for one or the other. Although there is no "serial murderer personality" or profile, serial murderers as a group appear to be persuasive and to delude their victims into thinking that they pose no danger to them. Serial murderers *as a group* are not mentally disordered in the traditional sense; that is, they do not fit traditional diagnostic categories of mental illness, although some qualify as criminal psychopaths. In some typologies of serial murderers, however, one type does display psychotic behavior.

The best-known typology (R. M. Holmes & Holmes, 1998) divides serial murderers into visionary, mission-oriented, hedonistic, and power-control types, with the visionary murderer being the most likely to engender a clinical diagnosis. Mass murderers—who kill three or more individuals during one incident—are generally divided into classic and family types, but a terrorist mass murder type should also be added. Although there are highly publicized illustrations of mass murders in public places, most mass murders seem to be family murders. When the perpetrator is a member of the family, he or she is also likely to commit suicide in conjunction with the incident. Compared with serial murderers, mass murderers are more likely to be isolated, disenchanted, and ineffective individuals whose crime is precipitated by what they perceive as a tragic loss, such as abandonment by a significant other or loss of employment.

Workplace violence includes homicides, but the vast majority of workplace violence incidents do not end in death. In fact, most of these incidents are not actually violence but rather *threats* of violence. Study of this phenomenon has increased in recent years, as has litigation on the part of employees who believe their employers did not adequately protect them from threats or from actual violent incidents. Forensic psychologists have critical roles, not only in alerting employers to potentially violent individuals in the workplace but also in facilitating a working environment that fosters acceptance and cooperation among all employees. However, a substantial portion of workplace violence is committed by outsiders or by former workers or supervisors.

The chapter ended with a discussion of bias crimes and stalking. Of the two, bias crimes qualify more directly as criminal violence, if the underlying offense is a violent crime—and data indicate that in the majority of cases, it is. Although the federal government and all states provide penalties for bias crimes, the FBI only gathers data on those associated with race/ethnicity, religion, sexual orientation, or mental or physical disability. We cautioned that many bias crimes likely go unreported to police. In addition, police agencies vary greatly in the extent to which they enforce bias crime statutes or record bias crimes.

Stalking is sometimes referred to as the crime of the 1990s. The most recent research efforts give some attention to cyberstalking as well as the more traditional approaches such as following, sending mail, or telephoning victims. Researchers have proposed typologies of stalkers that are similar to the typologies proposed for serial killers and mass murderers. Although not violent in itself, stalking engenders fear—sometimes debilitating fear—in its victims. An undetermined percentage of stalkers do ultimately exhibit violent behavior. We discussed recent efforts to distinguish between those stalkers who are likely to be violent and those who will cease their stalking behavior without harming their victims. At present, it appears that victims who are former intimate partners of the stalker are most at risk of being physically harmed. Past violent behavior does not appear to be a strong predictor of violence *in stalkers*, but the research is somewhat inconsistent on this point and needs further attention.

KEY CONCEPTS

Aggression	Cognitive factors
Availability heuristic	Creature-comfort killer
Bias crimes	Criminal homicide
Biological factors	Cyberstalking
Clearance rate	Erotomania stalking

Hate Crime Statistics Act

Hedonistic type

Instrumental violence

Love obsession stalkers

Manslaughter

Mass murder

Mission-oriented type

Murder

Observational learning

Power-control killer

Reactive violence

Serial murder

Simple obsession stalkers

Situational factors

Socialization factors

Spree murder

Thrill killer

Vengeance stalkers

Violence

Violent Criminal Apprehension Program (ViCAP)

Visionary type

Workplace violence

QUESTIONS FOR REVIEW

1. Identify and provide examples of the two tracks of psychological research on violence.

2. Provide illustrations of gender, race, and ethnic differences in violence.

3. What are the four categories of causes of violence?

4. Summarize the negative effects of constant viewing of violence in the media.

5. Distinguish among single murder, serial murder, mass murder, and spree murder.

6. List and define the typologies of serial killers.

7. What are the two major types of mass murder?

8. Why is the term *workplace violence* somewhat of a misnomer?

9. Describe the four major categories of workplace violence.

10. List any five findings from the research on stalking.

Psychology of Sexual Assault

CHAPTER OBJECTIVES

- Define sexual assault and rape, and identify the incidence of each.
- Examine the characteristics of men who rape and sexually assault.
- Acquaint the reader with the Massachusetts Treatment Center and Groth typologies for rapists and child molesters.
- Define and review the research and clinical data on pedophilia.
- Review research on juvenile sex offenders, both male and female.
- Describe the procedures for the psychological assessment of sex offenders.

Sexual assaulters attack others for a wide variety of reasons. After three decades of research, it is clear that sexual assault is a multidetermined behavior committed by a heterogeneous group of offenders. Sexual gratification is often not the primary reason, whereas desire for power, control, and dominance frequently is. Addressing the heterogeneity of sexual offenders and their motives is critical if we are to identify effective strategies for offender management and treatment (S. L. Brown & Forth, 1997).

In this chapter, we provide a comprehensive summary of the incidence and complexity of sexual assault, the known characteristics and developmental histories of the various sex offenders, and the methods commonly used to assess and evaluate sex offenders. The effect of sexual assault on victims will be covered in Chapter 11, and the treatment of convicted sex offenders will be described in Chapter 12. This chapter will also cover typologies of sexual offenders that are often used by both law enforcement officials and mental health professionals. Typologies, which place people into categories or groupings, are an important first step in the understanding and management of sexual assault. A typology is useful in classifying a wide assortment of behaviors, attitudes, motives, and beliefs into a manageable set of meaningful descriptions. It helps put order into an otherwise chaotic mass of observations, a process that enables research, assessment, prevention, treatment, and policy planning to take place. Offender typologies also highlight the enormous complexity of sexual offending and emphasize that there is no one single type of sex offender. Nevertheless, as we saw in Chapter 8 with the discussion of typologies of stalkers, typologies are not perfect tools and must continually be revised and validated.

Definitions of Sexual Assault and Rape

Legal definitions of what constitutes a sexual offense vary widely from state to state. In a majority of states, the broad term *sexual assault* has replaced the term *rape* in the criminal statutes. **Rape** is a narrower term, referring to forced penetration in vaginal, anal, or oral regions. Sexual assault recognizes that victims may be violated in other ways as well. In addition, in an effort to include males as victims, the statutes are becoming increasingly gender neutral.

The definitions used in federal criminal law parallel the changes in definitions in many states. To begin with, the Federal Criminal Code (Title 18, Chapter 109A, Sections 2241–2243) definition of sexual assault does not even use the term *rape* and does not require the victim to label the act as rape to meet the criteria (legally called the elements) for the crime (Kilpatrick, Whalley, & Edmunds, 2002). Second, the federal code distinguishes between two types of sexual abuse on the basis of the degree of force or threat of force used: (1) aggravated sexual abuse and (2) sexual abuse.

Aggravated sexual abuse by force or threat of force, according to the federal code, is when a person "knowingly causes another person to engage in a sexual act or . . . attempts to do so by using force against the person, or by threatening or placing that person in fear that the person will be subjected to death, serious bodily injury, or kidnapping." The federal code also tries to take into consideration recent increases in the use of "date rape drugs" or "acquaintance rape drugs" by defining *aggravated sexual abuse by other means*. This occurs when a person knowingly renders another person unconscious and thereby engages in a sexual act with that other person. Aggravated sexual abuse by other means also occurs when a person administers to another person by force or threat of force, or without the knowledge or permission of that person, a drug, intoxicant, or similar substance and thereby (1) substantially impairs the ability of that person to appraise or control conduct and (2) engages in a sexual act with that person.

The Federal Criminal Code defines sexual abuse—as opposed to aggravated sexual abuse—in two ways, in terms of whether it involves the following:

1. Causing another person to engage in a sexual activity by threatening or placing that person in fear; or

2. Engaging in a sexual act with someone when that person is incapable of declining participation in or communicating unwillingness to engage in that sexual act.

Governmental Definitions

As we discussed in Chapter 7, the U.S. government has three major crime measures, each published in a separate document: the Uniform Crime Reports (UCR), the National Incident-Based Reporting System (NIBRS), and the National Crime Victimization Survey (NCVS). All three measures define sexual assault slightly differently. The UCR divides sexual offending into two categories: (1) forcible rape and (2) sexual offenses. The first is considered one of the eight crimes for which both crime rates and arrest data are gathered. According to the UCR, forcible rape is "the carnal knowledge of a female forcibly and against her will. Assaults or attempts to commit rape by force or threat of force are also included; however statutory rape (without force) and other sex offenses are excluded" (FBI, 2002b, p. 29). The rape of female victims where no force is used and the victim is under the age of consent are categorized under other sex offenses.

Statutory rapes are part of a list of less serious offenses for which only arrest data are collected. It is estimated, however, that approximately 25% of the sex crimes committed against minors and reported to the police involve statutory rape (Troup-Leasure & Snyder, 2005). The UCR program counts each offense in which a female of any age is forcibly raped or on whom an assault to rape or attempt to rape is made. Of the total rapes reported for 2001, about 90% were classified as rapes, and the remainder were categorized as attempts.

The UCR program does *not* recognize rape when males are the victims. These sexual assaults on males are classified as simple or aggravated assaults or sex offenses, depending on the nature of the crime and the extent of the injury. The UCR also does not tabulate cases in which the offender uses threats of *nonphysical* force to obtain sex, such as threatening a person with a loss of job or other punishment if this person does not comply. However, some state legislatures have broadened the definition of force and have criminalized sex obtained by certain nonphysical forms of coercion (Kinports, 2002).

The relatively new NIBRS, also discussed in Chapters 7 and 11, has the potential to yield fairly detailed descriptions of sexual assaults reported by participating law enforcement agencies. The NIBRS divides crimes into two major categories: Group A and Group B. Group A contains the 46 most serious crimes, including sexual offenses, and Group B contains 11 of the less serious offenses, such as passing bad checks. The sex offenses in Group A are divided into two subcategories, forcible and non-forcible. The forcible offenses include forcible rape, forcible sodomy, sexual assault with an object, and forcible fondling. For these offenses, the NIBRS provides, among other things, data that include the following:

- Demographic information on all victims
- Levels of victim injury
- Victim's perceptions of offender's age, gender, race, and ethnicity
- Victim–offender relationship

The NIBRS also collects information on the weapons used, location of the incident, and the demographics of the offender (if arrested). Like the UCR, the NIBRS is based on law enforcement data and does not include information on convictions.

The National Crime Victimization Survey is a government-sponsored survey of victims of crime. In the NCVS, rape is defined as forced sexual intercourse in which the victim may be either male or female. Sexual assault—on the other hand—includes a wide range of victimizations involving attacks in which unwanted sexual contact occurs between the victim and the offender(s). Threats and attempts to commit such offenses are included in the victimization data reported by the NCVS.

Many existing laws require that both force and lack of consent be proven before an individual can be convicted of rape or sexual assault. Traditionally, for example, a lack of resistance by the victim was interpreted as evidence of consent. Ironically, at the same time, victims were often advised not to resist because that would only anger the rapist even more. Although no jurisdiction still adheres to the requirement that the victim must have resisted "to the utmost," some state courts continue to require some reasonable resistance unless the force exercised by the offender prevented the victim from resisting (Kinports, 2002). The issue of consent is a critical component in many cases involving rape or sexual assault because persons accused of these crimes who choose to go to trial often use consent as their defense when their alleged victim was an adult.

Statutory rape is the unlawful sexual intercourse with a female younger than the age of consent, which may be anywhere between 12 and 18, depending on the jurisdiction and state statute. Most states, however, use a cutoff point of age 16 or 18. The age of consent is an arbitrary legal cutoff considered to be the age at which the person has the cognitive and emotional maturity to give meaningful consent and understand the consequences. If the female was below the age of consent, the state is not required to prove that the intercourse was without her consent, as she is presumed incapable of consenting because of her young age. Moreover, a mistake made by the offender as to the victim's age is usually not a valid defense. Kinports (2002) writes, "Although this crime was traditionally justified as a means of preserving an unmarried girl's economic value to her father, today it is seen as a way of protecting vulnerable children" (p. 737). Increasingly, many contemporary state statutes are becoming gender neutral, encompassing both boys and girls. Therefore, the female teacher who has "consensual" sex with her 15-year-old male student can be charged with statutory rape. Furthermore, most states exempt peer relationships from statutory rape laws by requiring a minimum age for the offender or an age differential (typically 2 years) for the youths.

Rape by fraud refers to the act of having sexual relations with a consenting adult female under fraudulent conditions. A frequently cited example is when a professional psychotherapist has sexual intercourse with a patient under the guise of "effective treatment."

Despite these broad and much-needed shifts in definition, *rape* and *sexual assault* are still used interchangeably in both law and research to describe crimes that involve unwanted and illegal sexual acts. This is especially true with official government documents, such as those published by the U.S. Department of Justice. Even there, use of the term *rape* is increasingly reserved for sexual acts that involve actual or threatened sexual penetration, whereas *sexual assault* refers to a wide range of sexual attacks, including rape. Put another way, rape is always sexual assault, but sexual assault is not always rape.

Mindful of the distinctions and changes in definitions and requirements, we will continue to use the term *rape* when it is clear that penetration is an issue. Otherwise, *sexual assault* will be used. In addition, our discussion of research studies and typologies will employ the terminology favored by the researchers who conducted and developed them.

Prevalence and Incidence of Rape and Other Sexual Assaults

National victimization surveys indicate that the vast majority of sexual assaults are never reported to law enforcement (Kilpatrick et al., 2002). Both the NCVS and data from nongovernmental sources support this observation. Nongovernmental surveys include the National Women's Study (NWS) (Kilpatrick, Edmunds, & Seymour, 1992), the National Violence Against Women Survey (NVAW) (Tjaden & Thoennes, 1998a), and the National Survey of Adolescents (NSA) (Kilpatrick & Saunders, 1997). According to the NCVS, only about one-third of sexual assaults are reported to authorities. The NWS found that only 16% of rapes were reported to the police or other authorities, and the NSA discovered that only about 14% were reported. In addition, national studies also indicate that victims are reluctant to label the experience as a sexual assault if the attacker is a spouse, boyfriend, or acquaintance (Acierno, Resnick, & Kilpatrick, 1997). Victims with disabilities are even less likely to report sexual assaults because of their social isolation and fear (Kilpatrick et al., 2002). Many of the assailants are family members or caretakers, and the victims fear loss of support or services if they report.

According to the UCR, 90,491 forcible rapes of females (females of any age are counted) were recorded during 2001 (FBI, 2002b). Based on that volume, 62.2 of every 100,000 females were victims during the year. The rate of forcible rapes during the past 10 years has shown a discernible downward trend, but as always we should be cautious in interpreting these statistics.

For UCR purposes, an offense is "cleared" when at least one person is arrested and charged or when circumstances beyond the control of law enforcement preclude an arrest for a crime that has been solved. The latter would occur when a victim decides not to cooperate with police or a suspect dies before an arrest can be made. Nationally, 41.2% of rapes reported to police were cleared during 2009 (FBI, 2010). However, it is important to emphasize that most rapes are not reported to police.

The NVAW survey reports that about 15% of the adult women in the United States have been raped sometime during their lives, and another 2.8% have been victims of attempted rape (Kilpatrick et al., 2002; Tjaden & Thoennes, 1998a). For adult men, lifetime prevalence estimates for being victims of sexual assault and attempted sexual assault were 2.1% and 0.9%, respectively. Survey research in the United States and Canada suggests that more than 50% of college women have been victims of some form of sexual assault (Morry &

Winkler, 2001). The NWS found that about 13% of adult women had been victims of completed rape, and about 14% had been victims of other types of sexual assault. The NSA reports that an estimated 13% of female adolescents and 3.4% of male adolescents had been victims of sexual assault at some point.

Date or Acquaintance Rape

Date rape (also called **acquaintance rape**) refers to a sexual assault that occurs within the context of a dating relationship. In a national study of nearly 4,500 college women, Bonnie Fisher et al. (2000) found that 10% reported having been raped in their lifetimes and another 11% reported having experienced an attempted rape involving threatened or actual physical force. Another 35% said they had experienced some form of nonconsensual sexual contact. A very large portion of the rapes occurred during a dating situation. The Fisher et al. study estimates that 9 out of 10 of the college women knew the man who raped them while in college. In another survey, over one-fourth of the college women had experienced unwanted sexual contact ranging from kissing and petting to oral, anal, or vaginal intercourse since enrolling in college (Gross, Winslett, Roberts, & Gohm, 2006). The survey discovered that 41% of the offenders were boyfriends, followed by friends (29%), and acquaintances (21%).

The connection between alcohol use and date or acquaintance rape is strong. In more than half of sexual assaults involving dating partners, alcohol had been consumed by either one or both partners (Gross, Bennett, Sloan, Marx, & Jurgens, 2001; Ullman, Karabatsos, & Koss, 1999). Women who consume alcohol may be perceived by many young males as sexually available (Abbey, Zawacki, & McAuslan, 2000), and thus are more likely to be the targets of sexual predators (Abbey, Zawacki, Buck, Clinton, & McAuslan, 2004). However, as Sarah Ullman (2007) warns, "women's drinking in and of itself should not be assumed to increase their risk of sexual victimization" (p. 419). She notes that research has found that rapes where only offenders were drinking were related to greater rape completion and victim injury, "suggesting a greater role of offender, not victim, drinking in assault outcomes" (p. 419). Clearly, the role of drinking with respect to injury received is a complicated one and is in need of further study.

In many date rapes, the male believes he is entitled to "payback" because he probably initiated the date, paid most of the expenses, and drove his vehicle. A decade ago, M. S. Hill and Fischer (2001) found in their study of male college students that "feelings of entitlement" appear to be a central feature in date rape behaviors and attitudes. Changing concepts of "dating," such as the couple agreeing to share the cost or the woman initiating the date, will likely begin to diminish this payback attitude. However, feelings of entitlement may well be a key feature in other forms of sexual assault, including marital rape and incest. An understanding of the "feelings of entitlement" issue may significantly help in the development of rape prevention, education, and intervention programs. (See Photo 9.1, depicting students participating in a rape awareness workshop.)

Photo 9.1   A student leads a workshop on acquaintance rape prevention for male students on a college campus.

Under date rape conditions, it should be mentioned that the victim often blames herself for the attack and is often blamed by others for presumably arousing her date (see B. L. Shapiro

& Schwarz, 1997). Moreover, in some cases a sexual assault by a date or acquaintance may be more traumatizing than an assault by a stranger because of the implicit trust involved and the violation of that trust.

Demographics of Men Who Rape

One of the most consistent demographic findings about rapists is that, as a group, they tend to be young. According to data reported in the UCR, for instance, nearly half of those arrested for forcible rape are younger than age 25, and more than 16% of those arrested are younger than age 18 (FBI, 2001). Another consistent finding is that many men convicted of rape manifest a wide spectrum of antisocial behavior across their early life span. Warren, Hazelwood, and Reboussin (1991) report that in their sample of serial rapists, 71% were involved with shoplifting, 55% were assaultive to adults, 24% set fires, and 19% were violently cruel to animals during childhood and adolescence. Nearly 28% of convicted rapists released from prison are rearrested for a new violent crime within 3 years after release. In addition, about 8% of these released rapists are arrested again for another charge of rape within that time frame. In fact, released rapists are more than 10 times as likely as non-rapists to be rearrested for rape, and those offenders who have served time for sexual assault are nearly 8 times as likely as those convicted of other crimes to be rearrested for a new sexual assault (Greenfeld, 1997).

In about 12% of the reported rapes, the offender used a firearm, 7% used a knife, and 80% involved the use of physical force only (Greenfeld, 1997). Murders that involve rape and other sex offenses are referred to as sexual assault murders. Sexual assault murders account for less than 1% of all homicides with known circumstances in the United States. Surprisingly, though, according to Greenfeld, offenders younger than age 18 have accounted for more than 10% of the sexual assault murders that have taken place since 1976. A vast majority of the victims killed in sexual assaults are young White females killed by young White males. Twenty-five percent of the victims are younger than age 18, and 2% are younger than age 12. More than 80% of sexual assault murders are *intra*racial (victim and offender are of the same race or ethnic origin). In addition, sexual assault murders are far more likely to involve strangers than rape alone or nonlethal sexual assault.

As a group, sex offenders appear to be deficient in social skills and intimacy and are often described as lonely. Furthermore, child molesters, on average, appear to be more deficient in intimacy and are lonelier than rapists, who, in turn, appear to be lonelier and more lacking in intimacy than non–sex offenders (W. B. Marshall, 1996). Despite these generalizations, researchers know that sex offenders are not a homogeneous group. Several attempts have been made to capture their heterogeneity into categories or types. In the following sections, we will discuss the best known of these attempts to classify offenders.

Typologies of Men Who Rape

As mentioned earlier, classification systems, based on either personality traits or behavioral patterns of individuals, are called typologies, and they have been moderately successful in their ability to add to our understanding of criminal behavior. Chief among the criminal typologies are those pertinent to men who rape. It is important to realize, however, that individuals do not always fit neatly into a particular type; they only approximate it. There are very few "textbook examples." Underscoring this point, Don Gibbons (1988) wrote that classification systems or typologies generally consist of

> criminological foundations that assume that real life persons can be found in significant numbers who resemble the descriptions of offenders in the various typologies that have been put forth. . . . [R]esearchers have often failed to uncover many point-for-point real life cases of these hypothesized types of offenders. (p. 9)

Another problem with typologies is that very few of them have been subjected to empirical verification or validation studies, and they sometimes encourage stereotypes of offenders (B. K. Schwartz, 1995). That is, typologies can promote a tendency for the public and professionals to jam people into their favorite categories without empirical support or thoughtful consideration of individual differences between offenders.

However, typologies can be very useful in organizing a vast array of behavioral patterns that would otherwise be a confusing muddle. They are also useful in correctional facilities for risk management, such as deciding where to place an inmate, or in treatment programming, such as deciding what particular treatment technique or strategy might be most beneficial for an inmate or offender. The "acid test" of the usefulness of a typology, however, is its ability to estimate the risk of particular offenders to reoffend (Quinsey, 1986).

Many rape typologies have been suggested, including that used by the FBI (Hazelwood & Burgess, 1987), the Selkin typology (Selkin, 1975), the Nagayama-Hall typology (Nagayama-Hall, 1992), and the Nicholas Groth typology (Groth, 1979). The most empirically based typology, however, is the Massachusetts Treatment Center's typology, which has drawn and continues to draw considerable research attention.

The Massachusetts Treatment Center Rapist Typology

A group of researchers at the Massachusetts Treatment Center (MTC) (M. Cohen, Garafalo, Boucher, & Seghorn, 1971; M. Cohen, Seghorn, & Calmas, 1969; R. A. Knight & Prentky, 1987; Prentky & Knight, 1986) has developed an empirically based and useful typology based on the behavioral patterns of convicted rapists, including the appearance of aggressive and sexual patterns in the sexual assaults. It also provides an excellent framework for describing the psychological characteristics of rapists in general.

The MTC researchers believe that rape is a multidetermined behavior that can best be explained by models incorporating a multitude of dimensions. An empirically-based typology that takes into account all possible categories of rape behavior is such a model. Originally, the researchers identified four categories of rapists: displaced aggressive, compensatory, sexual aggressive, and impulsive. These have been replaced with a new typology. The MTC classification system now identifies *four* major types based on the rapist's primary motivation (opportunistic, pervasively angry, sexual, vindictive) and *nine* subtypes (R. A. Knight, Warren, Reboussin, & Soley, 1998; see Figure 9.1). The new system is called the **MTC:R3** and has been subjected to extensive research by the MTC group as well as other researchers (Barbaree & Serin, 1993; Barbaree, Seto, Serin, Amos, & Preston, 1994; G. T. Harris, Rice,& Quinsey, 1994).

The nine discrete rape subtypes are differentiated on the basis of six variables that have been consistently found by clinicians and researchers to play an important role in the behavioral, emotional, and thought patterns of a wide array of rapists (and child molesters). Before covering the typologies themselves, we will discuss the six variables, which are as follows:

- Aggression
- Impulsivity
- Social competence
- Sexual fantasies
- Sadism
- Naïve cognitions or beliefs

In a sense, these six variables form the "building blocks" for the development and ongoing revision of the MTC rape typology, and each should be described separately to get a deeper understanding of typology subtypes. It should be understood at the outset that certain variables appear to be more prominent in some rapists than in others.

Aggression

For our purposes here, aggression may be divided into two broad categories: (1) instrumental or strategic violence, and (2) expressive aggression or nonstrategic violence (Prentky & Knight, 1991). The former represents the type of aggression used by rapists to gain victim compliance. There is usually no anger present in instrumental aggression, except in reaction to a victim's lack of cooperation or compliance. Expressive aggression, on the other hand, is used by rapists to hurt, humiliate, abuse, or degrade the victim in some way. This form of aggression goes way beyond simply obtaining victim compliance and is often extremely violent. Sexual desire may not even be the primary motivation for the attack. This instrumental–aggressive dichotomy model does have its limitations, however, as some rapists demonstrate a mixture of both. As Prentky and Knight (1991) point out, "Those rapists who intend only to force victim compliance are likely to vary widely in the amount of aggression evident in their offenses" (p. 647). It may depend on the extent of victim resistance, the level of alcohol or drugs ingested by the offender, the presence of other aggressors or victims, and the context in which the attack occurs. Furthermore, sometimes the expressive aggression is "sexualized," and sometimes it is not. However, the instrumental–expressive dichotomy does serve as a useful springboard for discussing most of the MTC subtypes.

Impulsivity

There is considerable research and clinical evidence that impulsivity is a significant factor in many sexual assaults and criminal behavior in general. Lifestyle impulsivity has been found to be a powerful predictor of recidivism and frequency of offending (Prentky & Knight, 1986, 1991). Some impulsive people seem to have an overpowering deficiency in self-control and continually revert to old behavioral patterns, regardless of the costs. Research has consistently found that lifestyle impulsivity emerges as one of the strongest and most meaningful ways to differentiate repetitive rapists and other repetitive sex offenders such as child molesters. It is also the major focus of many treatment programs designed to change the antisocial behavior of sex offenders. As noted by Prentky and Knight (1991), "Clinicians have long recognized the importance of impulsivity for relapse and have introduced self-control and impulsivity management modules into treatment" (p. 656).

Social Competence

Sexual offenders have often been described as having poor social and interpersonal skills, especially when dealing with the opposite sex (Prentky & Knight, 1991). The MTC researchers refer to this characteristic as *social competence*, a concept that plays an important role in developing the various subtypes of the MTC typology. This feature is especially prominent in the behavioral patterns of child molesters. There are also consistent research findings that rapists as a group are not assertive in their everyday relationships with others. It should be realized that social competence represents a wide range of different abilities, such as social assertiveness, communication skills, social problem solving, social comfort, and political savvy, and consequently should be understood as a complex skill that is developed within a variety of contexts.

Sexual Fantasies

Sexual fantasy refers to any mental imagery that is sexually arousing or erotic to the individual (Leitenberg & Henning, 1995). Many clinicians believe that sexual fantasy is a necessary precursor to deviant sexual behavior. As stated by Leitenberg and Henning, "There seems to be little question that many men who commit sexual offenses frequently have sexually arousing fantasies about these acts and masturbate to these fantasies regularly and presumably more often than nonoffenders" (p. 487). In one clinical study of men who had been convicted of sexual homicide, approximately 80% had sexual fantasies related to sexually assaultive behavior (Burgess, Hartman, & Ressler, 1986), and the percentage appears to be even higher for serial sexual murders (Prentky et al., 1989). In fact, most treatment programs for sex offenders include a component designed to directly change sexual fantasies (Leitenberg & Henning, 1995). Some research has discovered that the content, frequency, and intensity of deviant sexual fantasies often differentiate between single and serial sexual murderers (Prentky & Knight, 1991).

It should be noted that it is not unusual for people to have sexual fantasies that would be inappropriate, or even criminal, for them to act on. Briere and Runtz (1989) found that 21% of male college students in an anonymous survey admitted that children sometimes attracted them sexually, and 9% of the sample said they have sexual fantasies about children (Leitenberg & Henning, 1995). In a survey conducted by Malamuth (1981), 35% of male college students felt there was some likelihood that they would sexually assault if they could be sure of getting away with it. In another study, 60% of a group of 352 male undergraduates indicated that they might rape or force a female to perform sexual acts against her will if given the opportunity (Briere, Malamuth, & Ceniti, 1981). Nevertheless, research (e.g., Dean & Malamuth, 1997) suggests that although aggressive or violent sexual fantasies are common in some college males, the degree to which these fantasies translate into an actual sexual assault depends on the individual's empathy for others. More specifically, those men who are highly self-centered are more likely to be sexually aggressive and act out their sexual fantasies. "There is no evidence that sexual fantasies, by themselves, are either a sufficient or a necessary condition for committing a sexual offense" (Leitenberg & Henning, 1995, p. 488).

Sadism

"Typically, central to the definition of sadism is a pattern of extreme violence in the offense that has often focused on erogenous areas of the body and that may be considered bizarre or appear ritualized" (Prentky & Knight, 1991, p. 652). Sadism is illustrated by cruel and malicious acts that are enjoyed by and often sexually arousing to the offender. Sadistic rapists, compared to other types of rapists, tend to offend more frequently against victims who are close friends, intimates, or family (Prentky, Burgess, & Carter, 1986).

Naïve Cognitions or Beliefs

Research indicates that offense-justifying attitudes are prevalent among males prone to rape and, to some extent, among the general male population as well. Similar to sexual fantasies, irrational attitudes and cognitive distortions usually are a major focus of most treatment programs for sex offenders.

Sexual socialization and social learning play very critical roles in the development of those who choose to sexually assault. Sexual behavior and attitudes toward women are acquired through the day-to-day contacts with family members, peers, entertainment models, and the media in general. Koss and Dinero (1988) found that sexually aggressive men expressed greater hostility toward women, frequently used alcohol, frequently viewed violent and degrading pornography, and were closely connected to peer groups that reinforced highly sexualized and dominating views toward women. These same men were more likely to believe that force and coercion are legitimate ways to gain compliance in sexual relationships. Koss and Dinero conclude, "In short, the results provided support for the developmental sequence for sexual aggression in which early experiences and psychological characteristics establish conditions for sexual violence" (p. 144).

Research reveals that a majority of sexually aggressive men subscribe to attitudes and ideology that encourage men to be dominant, controlling, and powerful, whereas women are expected to be submissive, permissive, and compliant. Such an orientation seems to have a particularly strong disinhibitory effect on sexually aggressive men, encouraging them to interpret ambiguous behaviors of women as come-ons, to believe that women are not really offended by coercive sexual behaviors, and to perceive rape victims as desiring and deriving gratification from being sexually assaulted (Lipton, McDonel, & McFall, 1987).

Rape myths and misogynistic attitudes appear to play a major role in sexual assault. Rape myths are "attitudes and beliefs that are generally false but widely and persistently held, and that serve to deny and justify male sexual aggression against women" (Lonsway & Fitzgerald, 1994, p. 134). Not all rapists tend to have these attitudes, but men who do subscribe to them hold more rape-supportive points of view (Chapleau & Oswald, 2010; Good, Heppner, Hillenbrand-Gunn, & Wang, 1995) and date rape–supportive points of view (M. S. Hill & Fischer, 2001; Truman, Tokar, & Fischer, 1996). Recent research on rape in prisons—a topic that is gaining more attention from the research community—suggests that inmates who sexually assault others and prison officials who ignore or deny the seriousness of this behavior tend to subscribe to rape myths (Neal & Clements, 2010).

According to findings reported by Chapleau and Oswald (2010), the stronger the cognitive association between power and sex, the more likely it is that men endorse rape myths and report a higher likelihood that they would rape. Furthermore, the more strongly men accept rape myths, the stronger the tendency that they will misperceive women's attire and behavior as "asking for it" or misperceiving their own sexual interest as "uncontrollable." Similarly, an important European study by Bohner, Jarvis, Eyssel, Siebler (2005) provides further evidence that rape myths serve to justify sexual aggression, "not only after it has occurred but also by increasing the likelihood of future violence" (p. 827).

Researchers have also explored the "macho personality constellation," which is characterized by having callous sexual attitudes, believing that violence is manly, and getting excitement from taking high risks (M. S. Hill & Fischer, 2001; Mosher & Anderson, 1986). Some sexually aggressive men also believe that women must be kept in their place—even if it means humiliating them—and the best way to achieve this world order is to assault them physically and sexually. The underlying cognitive framework that most sexually aggressive men seem to have is hostility toward women (Lonsway & Fitzgerald, 1995).

In his ongoing research on sexual aggression, Neil Malamuth and his colleagues (Malamuth, Linz, Heavey, Barnes, & Acker, 1995) have identified several characteristics that distinguish sexually aggressive males from their less aggressive counterparts. The more important characteristics include (1) an insecure, defensive, hypersensitive, and hostile-distrustful orientation toward women; (2) gratification from being able to control and dominate women; and (3) a strong tendency to misread cues from women.

Malamuth and his associates (Malamuth, Heavey, & Linz, 1993; Malamuth, Sockloskie, Koss, & Tanaka, 1991) argue that sexually aggressive men have beliefs (or schema) that predispose them to regard women as untrustworthy. These men do not believe what women say or do, especially when it pertains to romantic or sexual interests. In short, these men are highly suspicious of women and perceive communication from women as having the opposite meaning of what was intended. Malamuth et al. (1991) note that societies and subcultures that regard power, toughness, dominance, aggressiveness, and competitive selfishness as masculine qualities tend to produce men who are hostile to women and to the qualities associated with femininity, such as gentleness, empathy, and sensitivity. "The display of these traditionally feminine characteristics may signify to some men a loss of appropriate identity, whereas engaging in dominance and aggression, including in the sexual arena, may reinforce the idea that they are 'real men'" (Malamuth et al., 1995, p. 354). For such men, sexual aggression may be a way to reaffirm their sense of masculinity, as advocated by that particular society or subculture.

Malamuth also has found that sexually aggressive men have information-processing deficits in their ability to separate seductive from friendly behavior or hostile from assertive behavior (Malamuth & Brown, 1994; W. D. Murphy, Coleman, & Haynes, 1986). For example, rapists are less accurate than non-rapists in reading women's cues in first-date interactions (Lipton et al., 1987). This deficit is especially apparent when the woman's communication is direct, clear, and strong. If she protests too much, it means—to the sexually aggressive male—that she really means the opposite. To the sexually aggressive male, she is game-playing and attempting to be seductive by using assertiveness or aggression.

The misinterpretation of communication (both verbal and nonverbal) is not limited to the sexual assault context. It is often a key element found in highly aggressive and violent persons, including children. Kenneth Dodge and his associates, for example, discovered that highly aggressive children often have what he calls a **hostile attribution bias,** as described in Chapters 7 and 8. That is, children prone to high levels of aggression are more likely to interpret ambiguous actions of others as hostile and threatening than their less aggressive peers (Dodge, 1993). They are apt to perceive aggression and attack where none was intended. Research has consistently shown that violent youth "typically define social problems in hostile ways, adopt hostile goals, and seek few additional facts, generate few alternative solutions, anticipate few consequences for aggression, and give higher priority to their aggressive solutions" (Eron & Slaby, 1994, p. 10). This information-processing deficiency may be the result of the lack of opportunity during early childhood to develop social and interpersonal skills for detecting correct cues from others.

On the other hand, there is some empirical evidence that women who have severe victimization histories are less adept at identifying the cues that signal risky situations. Yeater, Treat, Viken, and McFall (2010) conducted a study using 194 undergraduate women who were between the ages of 18 and 24 years of age and from diverse ethnic and cultural backgrounds. As part of the study, the students read vignettes describing social situations that varied on dimensions of sexual victimization risk and potential impact on women's popularity. Near the end of the study, the participants were administered the Sexual Experiences Survey (SES) and the Rape Myths Acceptance Scale. The SES responses were used to quantify the severity of victimization experiences. The researchers found that those women who had severe victimization histories had difficulty identifying those situations that suggested high risks of being sexually assaulted. In addition, the researchers found that fear of losing the relationship with a man or losing popularity in general obscured their ability to identify high-risk situations. Lastly, those participants who demonstrated a higher acceptance of rape myths were less skillful at identifying high-risk situations. According to Yeater and her colleagues, "endorsement of rape-supportive attitudes appears to interfere with both women's and men's use of information that may help guide effective decision making in heterosexual interactions" (p. 383).

We should be careful not to imply that these women would be at fault if they were raped, simply because they misread high-risk situations. The tendency to blame victims for their victimization is one that often occurs in society, particularly but not exclusively in cases of sexual assault: "If you had locked your door, you wouldn't have been burglarized." "How could you fall for that scam? If it sounds too good to be true, it isn't." "If you hadn't gone to that bar, you wouldn't have been raped." However, women as well as men can benefit from information that disproves rape myths and from learning effective strategies to help avoid victimization (Ullman, 2007).

MTC:R3

As described previously, the MTC:R3 rape typology consists of nine discrete rapist types who are differentiated on the basis of the six variables already discussed. This section describes these nine types in more detail, and the typology is illustrated in Figure 9.1. Thus far, the research has focused almost exclusively on male rapists. Although a small percentage of reported rapes involve women as offenders, these women are almost invariably operating in partnership with a male offender. In recent years, though, some researchers are suggesting that the prevalence of independent female sexual offending has been underestimated, chiefly due to society's reluctance to accept that women sexually offend or that their offending is harmful to their victims (Becker, Hall, & Stinson, 2001).

Figure 9.1 Breakdown of Four Categorizations of Rapist Type Into Nine Rapist Subtypes (MTC:R3)

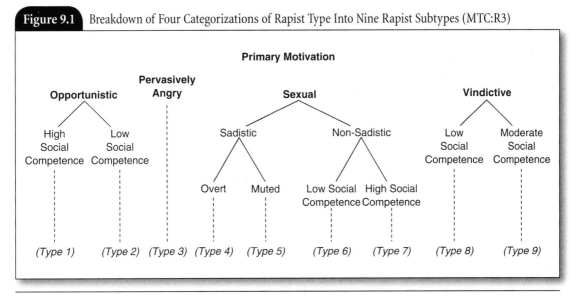

Source: Knight, R. A., Warren, J. I., Reboussin, R., & Soley, B. J. (1998). Reprinted with permission from Sage, on behalf of the International Association for Correctional and Forensic Psychologists.

Thus, whereas our discussion of the MTC:R3 typology focuses on the male as perpetrator, we recognize that there are many unanswered questions about female offenders.

The Opportunistic Rapist (Types 1 and 2)

The impulsive or **opportunistic rapist** engages in sexual assault simply because the opportunity to rape presents itself. Thus, this offender type is motivated more by contextual factors and opportunity than by any internally driven sexual fantasy (Prentky & Knight, 1991). The rape may occur within the context of some other antisocial act, such as a robbery or burglary. Alternatively, the victim could be a woman encountered at a bar or party. The most prominent characteristic of these offenders is their impulsivity and lack of self-control, resembling those qualities of an immature child. More important, this poor impulsive control leads to a pervasive and enduring lifestyle of impulsive and irresponsible behavior, frequently leading to an extensive criminal career. Thus, rape becomes only one of many antisocial behaviors in this person's repertoire.

The opportunistic rapist is not perceived to be "person oriented" and sees the victim only as a sexual object. He seems to have little concern for the victim's fear or discomfort. Opportunistic offenders consistently engage in troublesome acting-out behavior throughout their childhood, adolescence, and into adulthood. To be classified as an opportunistic rapist according to the MTC:R3, the offender must show the following:

- Callous indifference to the welfare and comfort of the victim
- Presence of no more force than is necessary to force the compliance of the victim (instrumental aggression). Any excessive force or aggression rules out this type.
- Evidence of adult impulsive behavior, such as frequent fighting, vandalism, and other impulse-driven antisocial behaviors

The MTC researchers have discovered that opportunistic rapists can be subdivided on the basis of their social competence and the developmental stage at which their high impulsivity is first noticed. The opportunistic offender who is high in social competence—a Type 1 rapist—manifests impulsivity in *adulthood*. The Type 2 rapist, on the other hand, is low in social competence and demonstrates impulsivity during *adolescence*.

The Pervasively Angry Rapist (Type 3)

The **pervasively angry rapist** demonstrates a predominance of global and undifferentiated anger that pervades all areas of the offender's life. These rapists are angry at the world in general, and their anger is directed at both men and women. The acts reflect capricious and random violence directed at whoever gets in the way at the wrong time and wrong place (Prentky & Knight, 1991). When these men attack women, their violent and aggressive behaviors exhibit a minimum or total absence of sexual arousal. Their attacks are characterized by high levels of aggression, and they inflict considerable injury on their victims. S. L. Brown and Forth (1997) report that psychopaths who sexually assault fall most often into the opportunistic or the pervasively angry categories.

The occupational history of the pervasively angry rapist is usually stable and often reveals some level of success. He perceives himself as athletic, strong, and masculine. More often than not, his occupation is a "masculine" one, such as truck driver, carpenter, mechanic, electrician, or plumber. His friends typically describe him as having a quick, violent temper (S. T. Holmes & Holmes, 2002). These offenders experienced chaotic and unstable childhoods and family life. Many of them were adopted or foster children who were often neglected or abused.

According to R. A. Knight and Prentky (1987), an offender must demonstrate the following characteristics to be classified as the pervasively angry type:

- Presence of a high degree of nonsexualized aggression or rage expressed through verbal or physical assault that clearly exceeds what is necessary to gain compliance of the victim (expressive aggression)
- Evidence of adolescent *and* adult unsocialized, antisocial behavior
- Carries out attacks that are usually unplanned and unpremeditated

So far, no particular subtypes have been identified for the pervasively angry rapist. Therefore, this type of rapist is referred to simply as Type 3.

Sexually Motivated, Sadistic Rapists (Types 4 and 5)

The motivation for the next four types is "sexual" in that their attacks are characterized by the presence of protracted sexual or sadistic fantasies that strongly influence the assaults. A discernible pattern of sexual preoccupation and fantasy is what all four have in common. The **sexually motivated rapist** is subdivided into sadistic or nonsadistic, and each is further subdivided (see Figure 9.2). Sadistic sexual offenders are either "overt" (Type 4) or "muted" (Type 5), depending on whether their sexual-aggressive acts are directly expressed in violent attacks (overt) or are only fantasized (muted). The muted offender's motive is the victim's fear or some violent fantasy that aids in his sexual arousal. That is, the victim's fear excites him, or he relies on some rehearsed sexual fantasy during the act to excite him. The overt sadistic rapist demonstrates *both* sexual and aggressive elements in his assault. In essence, the victim's actual (not fantasized) pain and discomfort are prerequisites for his sexual excitement. He believes his victims fundamentally "enjoy" being abused, forcefully raped, aggressively dominated, and controlled. Therefore, this type of rapist interprets the victim's resistance and struggle as a game, and the more the victim resists, the more excited and aggressive he becomes. At first, the attack may begin as attempts at seduction, but with increasing resistance from the victim, aggressive behaviors become increasingly prominent. On the other hand, rage or high levels of violence are precipitated in the offender when the victim, out of abject fear or helplessness, becomes passive and submissive, so it seems to be a no-win situation for the victim. In this context, in the offender's eyes, the victim is no longer playing the "game" properly.

Overt sadistic rapists are frequently married, but they show little commitment to the marriage. Their backgrounds often are replete with antisocial behavior, beginning during adolescence or before and ranging from truancy to rape-murder. They have often had severe behavior problems in school, and throughout their lifetimes they have displayed poor behavior control and a low frustration tolerance. They manifest consistently more paraphilias than the other types of rapists. **Paraphilia** is the term for a class of sexual disorders and deviations in which sexual arousal occurs almost exclusively in the context of inappropriate objects or individuals (Durand & Barlow, 2000). The essential features of paraphilias "are recurrent, intense sexually arousing fantasies, sexual urges, or behaviors generally involving 1) nonhuman objects; 2) the suffering or humiliation of oneself or one's partner; or 3) children or other nonconsenting persons that occur over a period of at least 6 months" (American Psychiatric Association, 1994, p. 522).

Some examples of paraphilias include the following:

- **Frotteurism**—sexual arousal from touching or rubbing against a nonconsenting person, usually in a crowded public place
- **Voyeurism**—sexual arousal from observing an unsuspecting person who is undressing, naked, or engaged in sexual activity
- **Sexual masochism**—sexual arousal in response to being humiliated, beaten, whipped, bound, or otherwise made to suffer
- **Sexual sadism**—sexual arousal gained from inflicting real or simulated physical pain or psychological suffering on another person
- **Fetishism**—achieving sexual arousal by using, fondling, or smelling inanimate objects, such as shoes, undergarments, leather, stockings, or purses
- **Partialism**—achieving sexual arousal by touching or fondling body parts not normally associated with sexual activity, such as feet or ears.

On occasion, the Type 4 rapist engages in sexual sadism that is so extreme that the victim may be murdered. To qualify as an overt, sadistic rapist, the offender must demonstrate the following:

- A level of aggression or violence that clearly exceeds what is necessary to force compliance of the victim
- Explicit, unambiguous evidence that aggression is sexually exciting and arousing to him. This can be illustrated either by descriptions indicating that the offender derives sexual pleasure from injurious acts to the victim, or the injurious acts are focused on parts of the body that have sexual significance.

To qualify as a sadistic, muted rapist, on the other hand, the offender must demonstrate the following:

- Instrumental aggression or enough force to gain compliance
- Evidence that sexual fantasies of violence or the victim's fear excite him

Sexually Motivated, Nonsadistic Offenders (Types 6 and 7)

The **nonsadistic rapist** engages in a sexual attack because of an intense sexual arousal prompted by specific stimuli identified in the intended victim. Although rape is, by definition, clearly a violent act, aggression is not the significant feature in the attack of the sexually motivated, nonsadistic rapist. Rather, the fundamental motivation is the desire to prove sexual prowess and adequacy to the victim. This type is also known as the "power reassurance rapist" (S. T. Holmes & Holmes, 2002). These men live in a world of fantasy, oriented around themes of how victims will yield eagerly under attack, submit to pleasurable intercourse, and find their skill and performance so outstanding that the victims will plead for a return engagement. These rapists fantasize that they will at last be able to prove their masculinity and sexual competence to themselves and the victims. In their sexual assaults, these rapists are described as being highly sexually aroused and showing obvious disturbances involving lack of control and cognitive-perceptual distortions of reality.

The victim of such a rapist is most often a stranger, but the rapist has probably watched and followed the victim for some time. Certain stimuli have drawn his attention and excited him. For instance, he may be attracted to college or professional women who normally would not be attracted to him. S. T. Holmes and R. M. Holmes (2002) report that nonsadistic, sexually motivated rapists prefer women who are approximately their own age and race, especially those residing in the same neighborhood or close to their place of employment. The attacks are often done at night, with a time interval between attacks of 7 to 15 days. If the victim physically resists his attack, the nonsadistic rapist is likely to flee from the scene. During the entire incident, there will be very low levels of aggressive behavior on his part. Sometimes, if he is successful, he may contact the victim at a later time to inquire about her well-being or even to ask for a date. Generally, this type of rapist confines his illegal activity to sexual assault and is not involved in other forms of antisocial behavior.

Assignment to the nonsadistic categories requires the following behavioral indicators:

- Presence of verbalizations aimed at self-reassurance and self-affirmation
- Behaviors that reflect, albeit in a distorted fashion, an attempt at establishing an amorous relationship with the victim
- Concerns for the victim's welfare, comfort, and enjoyment of the sexual experience

Research (e.g., R. A. Knight & Prentky, 1987; R. A. Knight et al., 1998) has shown that there may be at least two subtypes of nonsadistic, sexually motivated rapists, similar to the two subdivisions of the opportunistic rapist. One group may be described as quiet, shy, submissive, and socially inadequate. Although they are dependable workers, their poor social skills and resulting low self-esteem prevent them from succeeding at occupational advancement. This type of person is usually classified as low socially competent, or Type 6. The second subtype may be more socially adaptable and competent and achieve more occupational advancement and professional development. This rapist is classified as highly socially competent (Type 7) (see Figure 9.2).

Vindictive Rapists (Types 8 and 9)

In an effort to express his anger toward women, the **vindictive rapist** uses the act of rape to harm, humiliate, and degrade women. A violent sexual assault is, in this rapist's eyes, the most humiliating and dominating act possible. The victims are brutally assaulted and subjected to sadistic acts such as biting, cutting, or tearing of parts of the body. In most instances, the victims are complete strangers, although the victim may possess certain characteristics that attract the assailant's attention. Often, in addition to using physical abuse, this attacker will use a great deal of profanity and emotional abuse through threats. Resisting this particular rapist may engender more violence from him.

Although many of these rapists are married, their relationships with women are characterized by periodic irritation and violence, and they probably engage in domestic violence and wife abuse. These men generally perceive women as demanding, hostile, and unfaithful individuals who need to be dominated and controlled. They sometimes select their victim because they perceive something in her behavior or appearance that communicates assertiveness, independence, and professional activity. The assault usually follows some precipitating events involving a wife, girlfriend, or mother that he generalizes to all women. Upon arrest, the offender often attributes his offense to an "uncontrollable impulse." Like the opportunistic and nonsadistic rapists, vindictive rapists can be subdivided into their degree of social competence types, although here they are divided into low and moderate rather than low and high.

To qualify as a vindictive rapist, the following behaviors must be evident:

- Clear evidence, in verbalization or behavior, of the intent to demean, degrade, or humiliate the victim
- No evidence that the aggressive behavior is eroticized or that sexual pleasure is derived from the injurious acts
- The injurious acts are not focused on parts of the body that have sexual significance

Summary

Although human beings rarely fit neatly into typologies, the MTC rape typology is useful in understanding rape and helps in treatment and in the prediction of recidivism. It takes into consideration behavioral patterns, rather than simply personality traits, as well as the context within which the behavior patterns occur. However, the MTC typology needs refinement and reconstruction, a process the group has been pursuing for a number of years. R. A. Knight and Prentky (1990) conclude that "the MTC:R3 is a typological system that was developed to increase understanding of the etiology of sexual offending and to help predict recidivism. It might be that an alternative typology or a variant of MTC:R3 can be developed to maximize detection" (p. 78).

However, rape typologies in general also may be of little use to the *victim* of sexual assault, and may even be a liability. Some typologies, for example, suggest that resisting some rapist types will only make them angrier and will also make it more likely that the victim will be severely physically harmed or even killed. Ullman (2007) remarks that the woman in the process of being assaulted is unlikely to make a determination about which category the rapist falls into. More importantly, however, contemporary research indicates that women who scream loudly or fight back are more likely to avoid a completed rape; on the other hand begging, pleading, and trying to reason with the rapist are less likely to be effective (Ullman, 2007).

The Groth Rapist Typology

Nicholas Groth (1979; Groth, Burgess, & Holmstrom, 1977) has proposed typologies for both rapists and child molesters that are somewhat similar to the MTC systems. We will cover the **Groth rape typology** in this section and the **Groth child molester typology** in the next section. Although the MTC:R3 was largely built on research and statistical analyses, the Groth typology has been largely clinically developed and has not been adequately tested for reliability and validity. Mental health workers, though, tend to like the Groth classification system because it is simple and straightforward to use. In addition, many police investigators continue to use the system in the development of psychological profiles of sex offenders.

The Groth system is based on the *presumed* motivations and aims that underlie almost all rapes. According to Groth (1979), rape is a "pseudosexual act" in which sex serves merely as a vehicle for the primary motivations of power and aggression. He asserts that "rape is never the result simply of sexual arousal that has no other opportunity for gratification. . . . Rape is always a symptom of some psychological dysfunction, either temporary and transient or chronic and repetitive" (p. 5). Rape, he says, "is always and foremost an aggressive act" (p. 12). On this basis, Groth divides rape behavior into three major categories: (1) anger rape, (2) power rape, and (3) sadistic rape.

In **anger rape,** the offender uses more physical force than necessary to gain compliance and engages in a variety of sexual acts that are degrading or humiliating to the woman. He also expresses his contempt for the victim through abusive and profane language. Rape, for the anger rapist, is a violent act of conscious anger and rage toward women. According to Groth (1979), sex is actually "dirty," offensive, and disgusting to the anger rapist, and this is the reason why he uses the sexual act to defile and degrade the victim. To illustrate, Groth quotes one rapist: "I wanted to knock the woman off her pedestal, and I felt rape was the worst thing I could do to her" (p. 14). Very often, his attacks are prompted by a previous conflict with or humiliation by some significant woman in his life, such as a wife, supervisor, or mother. However, some anger rapists are also reacting to a recent upset that does not necessarily involve a woman, such as being rejected from military service, being fired, being burdened by financial debts, or being harassed by others. Considerable physical injury to the victim is common in such rapes.

The offender in **power rape** seeks to establish power and control over his victim. Consequently, the amount of physical force and threat used will depend on the degree of submission shown by the victim: "I told her to undress and when she refused I struck her across the face to show her I meant business" (Groth, 1979, p. 26). The goal of the power rapist is sexual conquest, and he will try everything in his power to overcome any resistance. Sexual intercourse is his way of establishing his masculine identity, authority, potency, mastery, and domination as well as providing sexual gratification. According to Groth, the victim is sometimes kidnapped or held captive in some fashion, and she may be subjected to repeated sexual assaults over an extended period of time. However, the offender is often disappointed that the assault did not live up to his expectations and fantasies: "Everything was pleasurable in the fantasy, and there was acceptance, whereas in reality of the situation, it wasn't pleasurable, and the girl was scared, not turned on to me" (a rapist quoted in Groth, 1979, p. 27).

The third pattern of rape proposed by Groth is the **sadistic rape,** which includes both sexual and aggressive aspects. The sadistic rapist experiences sexual arousal and excitement at the victim's maltreatment, helplessness, and suffering. The assault may involve bondage and torture, and he often administers physical abuse to various parts of the victim's body. Prostitutes, women he considers promiscuous, or women representing symbols of something he wants to punish or destroy often incur the wrath of the sadistic rapist. The victim may be stalked, abducted, abused, and sometimes murdered.

Groth (1979) estimated that more than half of the offenders evaluated or treated by his agency (Connecticut Sex Offender Program) were power rapists, 40% were anger rapists, and only 5% were sadistic rapists. Interestingly, Groth asked convicted sex offenders to rate the sexual pleasure they had received from the rape on a scale from 1 (*little or none*) to 10 (*extremely satisfying*). Most of the offenders gave ratings of 3 or less, indicating low sexual pleasure from the act. In fact, Groth found that many men failed to have orgasms during the rape. Most reactions from the sex offenders in the sample to the sexual aspects of the attack ranged from disappointment to disgust. Moreover, none of the offenders thought rape was more rewarding or gratifying sexually than consensual sex. Similar results have been reported by Warren, Reboussin, Hazelwood, and Wright (1989).

One of the major contributions of the Groth typology is that it questions the notion that rapists are motivated largely by sexual desire or that rapists are all the same. However, although the descriptions of the offenders are intuitively appealing, empirical evidence in support of the reliability and validity of the typology is lacking. Very few research studies have examined the typology in recent years. Of the two major typologies, the MTC version is by far the more heavily researched and validated.

Pedophilia

If you are reading this text, you probably consider sexual crimes against children among the most heinous in our society. However, if the statistics are accurate, it is also likely that you or some of your classmates have been victimized by such crimes. As we discuss next, the incidence of childhood sexual victimization is highly disturbing; moreover, like other crimes against children, it is often not reported to police or social service agencies. (Personal Perspective 9.1 introduces you to Dr. Michael Bourke, a psychologist whose professional work with the U.S. Marshals Service focuses on preventing such crimes.)

PERSONAL PERSPECTIVE 9.1

From the Federal Bureau of Prisons to the U. S. Marshals Service

Michael L. Bourke, PhD

I currently serve as the Chief Psychologist of the United States Marshals Service (USMS), the nation's oldest law enforcement agency. Since George Washington appointed the first 13 U.S. Marshals in 1789, the Marshals Service has been unique in its mission and scope of authority. The men and women who wear the badge referred to as "America's Star" are extremely adept at hunting fugitives, protecting the federal judiciary and federal witnesses, accounting for noncompliant sex offenders, and accomplishing the myriad tasks put before them. The work is as challenging and exciting today as it was in the days of the legendary Old West, and there is nothing quite like watching a team of Deputy United States Marshals as they track, locate, and apprehend men and women wanted by the law.

Within the USMS, I head the Behavioral Analysis Unit (BAU), a component of the National Sex Offender Targeting Center (NSOTC). The NSOTC is an intelligence and investigative "hub" for sex offender investigations of all types, and the BAU is tasked with four primary missions: (1) to provide operational support, including behavioral profiling, to USMS investigators in the field; (2) to provide case consultation to federal, state, local, and tribal law enforcement

officers; (3) to conduct research relevant to the identification, apprehension, and prosecution of sex offenders; and (4) to "safeguard," a term used to describe the psychological monitoring of individuals at risk for exposure to traumatic material (e.g., child pornography and other disturbing media).

It may be of interest that I am both an operational psychologist (a subset of police and military psychologists) and a sworn law enforcement officer. I am not a criminal investigator, but as a result of my deputation and law enforcement status I am able to participate in operational matters, including fugitive "sweeps" of individuals wanted for sexual offenses. This allows me to maintain a perspective I otherwise would not have about the difficulties USMS deputies face on a daily basis.

My Career "Path"

When I was asked to contribute to this textbook, a colleague suggested that students might be interested in my "career path." This idea made perfect sense at the time, but as I sat down to write, I found to my dismay that there was no discernable path I could describe. I came to my current position much as a child moves a toy

(Continued)

(Continued)

soldier up the side of a dirt hill: a great deal of haphazard marching, an occasional push through or around obstacles, and sudden leaps of flight when I took a risk without knowing precisely where I would land. Thankfully, I nearly always found myself farther up the hill than the place from which I had leapt!

Similarly, during my academic training and professional preparation, I rarely encountered any paths that were likely to lead to a specific career in the landscape of clinical or forensic psychology. As a result, my graduate school classmates and I chose to journey "cross country" by scrambling for forensic training experiences wherever and whenever we could find them. We volunteered in jails, sought practica within the court system, and rode along with and helped train law enforcement officers in surrounding communities, to name but a few relevant experiences. Considering where I am today, I am convinced that this circuitous path was the best one for me.

My Early Career: Correctional Psychology

Prior to accepting my current position with the USMS, I spent nearly two decades working part-time or full-time within correctional settings. While work with incarcerated individuals can be rewarding, it is not for everyone. I can assure you there is no sound quite like the slamming of the gates of a prison sallyport. They simultaneously shudder and crash with a finality that leaves no question you have surrendered control over your own egress and that you are *locked in* a world like no other. Much forensic work occurs inside secure facilities of one type or another. If this environment instills fear or creates feelings of pronounced anxiety, it is fairly obvious that

correctional psychology may be the wrong field for you. But you should also consider another line of work if you feel *nothing* when you enter; that is, if the sound of the gates fails to jolt you into switching from your normal self to the guarded persona you assume inside the walls. Working safely and effectively inside correctional environments requires a certain type of vigilance, an ability to keep your instincts and senses on alert. It is important to notice when something is "just wrong"—atypical movement in one part of the prison yard; the absence of normal sounds from the wing of a housing unit; or just a different, inexplicable feel to the cafeteria.

I first heard the slam of a prison gate at the age of 19 when I reported to a large, maximum-security prison to begin my undergraduate internship. (As an assignment in one of my law enforcement administration classes, I shadowed a correctional psychologist for a semester.) The following year, I worked briefly in a secure psychiatric facility, which was my first introduction to the challenges that come with working with the chronically mentally ill. After graduation, I worked for 2 years as a truant officer and then began my graduate studies in clinical psychology. Throughout graduate school, I worked in a variety of correctional settings—a juvenile detention center, where I evaluated youth for the courts; several county jails, where I ran programs with drug offenders; and a state prison, where I worked with maximum-security female inmates.

When it came time to apply for a predoctoral internship, I found that despite my primary interest in policing, there were no training opportunities offered within police environments. The only forensic training sites were located in secure facilities (prisons and forensic hospitals). I decided to complete my internship at a federal prison in Fort Worth, Texas. At FMC Fort Worth, I was fortunate to receive outstanding supervision from very skilled clinical psychologists; they provided training on various types of forensic evaluations, including dangerousness assessments and those relating to competency and sanity. It was interesting and challenging work, and I had the opportunity to work with patients who presented with a fascinating array of clinical diagnoses, including some that are only rarely, if ever, encountered by private practitioners. For those who are interested in conducting forensic evaluations (e.g., competency, sanity, dangerousness), there may not be a better training ground than a federal prison. The cases are fascinating, the ethical standards are high, and some of your colleagues are among the best in the field.

Upon completion of my internship, I relocated to North Carolina to begin working in the Federal Bureau of Prisons' Sex Offender Treatment Program. I attended the Federal Law Enforcement Training Center (FLETC) in Glynco, Georgia, to become a federal law enforcement officer. Then, for the next 8 years, I evaluated and treated inmates in three sex offender treatment programs housed at this institution. From 2006 to 2008, the last 2 years of my correctional career, I had the unique opportunity to work with offenders who had been civilly detained as Sexually Dangerous Persons.

In the spring of 2001, I was asked if I was interested in becoming a forensic polygraph examiner. I quickly agreed to attend the Department of Defense's Polygraph Institute (DoDPI [later renamed the Defense Academy for Credibility Assessment, or DACA]), the polygraph school for federal law enforcement officers and members

of the U.S. intelligence community. Upon graduation, I began to polygraph the sex offenders in our treatment program to ascertain if they had honestly disclosed their entire sexual offense history. Not surprisingly, many had not, and the polygraph became an effective therapeutic tool for breaking through denial and learning about undisclosed and undetected sexual offenses. In 2008, I left the Federal Bureau of Prisons to join the United States Marshals Service.

Rewards and Challenges of a Typical Day

Put simply, I absolutely love my job. It is an honor and a privilege to work for an agency with a long and distinguished history, and the colleagues with whom I work are simply outstanding. From a mission standpoint, there are few, if any, more challenging and more rewarding areas of law enforcement than the fight against sexual assault and exploitation. It's a job where, each day, I have the opportunity to make a difference—to bring closure to the family members of victims, to prevent further violence against children and other vulnerable populations, and to bring dangerous men and women to justice.

There is no typical day in the BAU. I regularly train law enforcement officers, members of the judiciary, and others who work in the field of child exploitation, so I often fly to various cities to speak at conferences or annual meetings. I have accompanied the USMS Director to "the Hill" for congressional or White House briefings. I occasionally conduct interviews for television and other media outlets. I have participated in the extradition of prisoners from foreign countries. I periodically go to the firearms range for weapons qualification. I design and carry out research,

(Continued)

(Continued)

and I supervise the research efforts of BAU analysts. I assist with training our investigative staff, including our elite team of Sex Offender Investigative Coordinators. I may provide on-site support at the scene of a criminal investigation. And I create behavioral profiles and provide consultation to investigators around the world as they attempt to identify, locate, and apprehend fugitive sex offenders.

As far as challenges, working for any government agency can have its share of frustrations. Funding for projects and programs waxes and wanes, administrations change, and one can always find examples of bureaucratic red tape that seems to bog down the process. Fortunately, as a smaller federal law enforcement agency, the USMS enjoys far less bureaucracy than other law enforcement agencies, and for this reason I think we are able to accomplish things faster and more efficiently than might otherwise be the case.

As a final comment, I will make the assumption, since you are reading this textbook, that you and I are at least somewhat alike. On an emotional level, you are excited by the disciplines of psychology and criminal justice, and you are particularly intrigued by at least one of the unique and fascinating careers that emerge when the two fields are combined. On an intellectual level, you likely think the study of human behavior—particularly aberrant behavior—is a fascinating and complex area of inquiry. If so, and if on a deeper level you are committed to making a difference in the lives of others, I urge you to identify the core values that inspire you.

I suspect that things have not changed much in the decade since I earned my doctoral degree. Based on the calls and e-mails I receive, many students have an unrealistic or inaccurate understanding of what types of positions exist in the world of forensic psychology, and which credentials would improve their chances of securing a certain position. Even if you do not secure a highly sought-after position, a fascinating array of other jobs await in the forensic arena, including interesting work in local, state, or federal law enforcement; within the military and the intelligence communities; and within correctional and forensic mental health facilities. I encourage you to be open to opportunities that arise as you journey forward, and to take risks and avail yourself of them whenever possible.

I am not suggesting you embark on your professional journey without a specific career goal in mind, though, and there is no substitute for directed, intentional effort. I wholeheartedly believe you should select and follow a road you find fascinating and think will be fulfilling. To choose wisely, I recommend you identify that which inspires you to enter and work in the field. Are you committed to making a difference in the lives of neglected children? Are you especially passionate about reducing crimes against elderly adults? Does the thought of practicing law in mental health court excite you? *Next, set goals based on your value system rather than because you think it will lead to a particular job 10 years down the road.* Finally, no matter what road you may choose or opt to create, I wish you much fulfillment in your life's work.

Dr. Bourke obtained his undergraduate degree from the University of Oklahoma and his PhD in clinical psychology from Nova Southeastern University. He currently resides with his family in the Washington, D.C., area, though he remains a Sooner at heart.

Definitions of Pedophilia

Pedophilia *is commonly* known as "child molestation" or child sexual abuse, but pedophilia—as defined in the *DSM-IV*—is not necessarily a crime. It is a psychological condition, defined as a condition in which, "over a period of at least 6 months, recurrent, intense sexually arousing fantasies, sexual urges, or *behaviors* involving sexual activity with a prepubescent child or children (generally age 13 years or younger)" occur (American Psychiatric Association, 1994, p. 528, italics added). We added the italics to emphasize that the fantasies or urges themselves are not criminal; they become so only if and when the individual acts upon them. The *DSM-IV* further specifies that some pedophiles are sexually attracted only to children (the exclusive type), whereas others are attracted sexually to both children and adults (nonexclusive type). The psychologist, then, wants to prevent the urges from translating into criminal activity or, if the activity has already occurred, treat the person so that it does not happen again. This is not a simple thing to do.

For the purposes of this text, we are focusing on the pedophile who has taken the step into criminal activity. If the child victim is the offender's relative—sometimes referred to as *intrafamilial* child molestation—the pedophilia is called **incest.** By far the largest group in this category is fathers who molest their sexually immature daughters or stepdaughters (Rice & Harris, 2002). *Extrafamilial* child molestation, on the other hand, refers to sexual abuse from a person *outside* the family. However, the two categories probably overlap, perhaps to a large extent. Rice and Harris, for example, report that a significant number of intrafamilial molesters have also offended outside the family.

Some Demographics of Child Molesters

Although there is considerable age variability, pedophiles tend to be older than those who rape other adults, ranging between the ages of 36 and 40. Prentky, Knight, and Lee (1997) assert that the more an offender's sexual preference is limited to children, the less socially competent he is likely to be. In this context, social competence refers to the offender's strength and range of social and sexual relationships with adults. Many studies (e.g., W. L. Marshall, Barbaree, & Fernandez, 1995; W. L. Marshall & Mazzucco, 1995; Prentky et al., 1997) have continually documented the observation that pedophiles are inadequate socially, lack interpersonal skills, are under-assertive, and have poor self-esteem.

Perhaps because of the extremely negative attitudes the public has toward child sexual abuse, pedophiles rarely take full responsibility for their actions. Many claim that they went blank, were too intoxicated to know what they were doing, could not help themselves, or did not know what came over them. Overall, they demonstrate a strong preference for attributing their behavior to external forces or motivating factors largely outside their personal control.

Few crimes are considered as despicable as the sexual abuse of children, and yet so little is understood about its causes, incidence, and reoffense risk (Prentky et al., 1997). Data on pedophilia are difficult to obtain because there are no central or national objective recording systems for tabulating sexual offenses against children. The available evidence suggests, though, that pedophilia is grossly underreported, both to police and in official statistics. This is due partly to children's fears of retaliation from the family member who is the perpetrator. However, in some cases it is also because another adult is aware of the offending but persuades the child not to reveal it. With regard to official statistics, offenders may be arrested and prosecuted under a variety of statutes and for a variety of offenses, including child rape, aggravated assault, sodomy, incest, indecent exposure, and lewd and lascivious behavior. Although the UCR program lists arrests for sex offenses, it does not differentiate pedophilia from the mixture of other possible sexual offenses. In addition, arrests are reported for crimes against children, but not all crimes against children are sex offenses. Self-report surveys are somewhat more instructive. These surveys indicate that from a quarter to a third of all females and a tenth or more of all males in the United States have been sexually molested during childhood (Finkelhor & Lewis, 1988; Peters, Wyatt, & Finkelhor, 1986).

The classification, diagnosis, and assessment of child molesters—like those of rapists—are complicated by a high degree of variability among individuals in relation to personal characteristics, life experiences, criminal histories, and motives for offending. "There is no single 'profile' that accurately describes or accounts for all child molesters" (Prentky et al., 1997, p. v). Perhaps the best way to provide a solid framework for any presentation on the complex nature of pedophilia and the offenders involved is through a discussion of two well-known typologies. Again they are the research-based typology of the Massachusetts Treatment Center (MTC:CM3) and the more clinically based Groth typology. Like the rapist typologies discussed earlier, these typologies have been formulated primarily with reference to male offenders, but this situation has changed in recent years, as we will discuss shortly.

The MTC:CM3

Similar to their development of the MTC:R3 for rape typing, the Massachusetts Treatment Center researchers (Cohen et al., 1969; R. A. Knight, 1989; R. A. Knight & Prentky, 1990; R. A. Knight, Rosenberg, & Schneider, 1985) have also developed one of the most useful typologies or empirically-based classification systems for pedophiles yet constructed. Called the **MTC:CM3** (Child Molesters, Revision 3), the system underscores the importance of viewing pedophilia as characterized by multiple behavioral patterns and intentions. The MTC:CM3 classifies child molesters according to variables on two basic dimensions, or axes (see Figure 9.3). The first dimension focuses on the degree of fixation the offender has on children and the level of social competence demonstrated by the offender. The second dimension focuses on the amount of contact with children, the level of injury to the victim, and the amount of sadism manifested in the attack.

The First Dimension

The MTC researchers have distinguished four types of child molesters based on this dimension:

- High fixation, low social competence (Type 0)
- High fixation, high social competence (Type 1)
- Low fixation, low social competence (Type 2)
- Low fixation, high social competence (Type 3)

The term *fixation* refers to the intensity of pedophilic interest or the degree to which the offender is focused on children as sexual objects. High fixation means that the offender demonstrates an exclusive and long-standing preference for children as sexual objects, whereas a low fixation connotes that children *and* adults can or have served as sexual objects for the offender. Social competence refers to the level of social and interpersonal skills, assertiveness, and self-esteem possessed by the offender. Low social competence signifies that the offender has inadequate social skills, is unassertive in dealing with adults, and demonstrates poor self-esteem. High social competence means the opposite.

The **Type 0** child molester displays a long-standing preference for children as both sexual and social companions. He has never been able to form a mature relationship with adult peers, male or female, and he is described by people who know him as socially immature, passive, timid, and dependent. He feels most comfortable with children. The Type 0 pedophile is rarely married and has a history of steady employment, although the type of

Figure 9.2 A Flow Chart of the Decision Process for Classifying Child Molesters

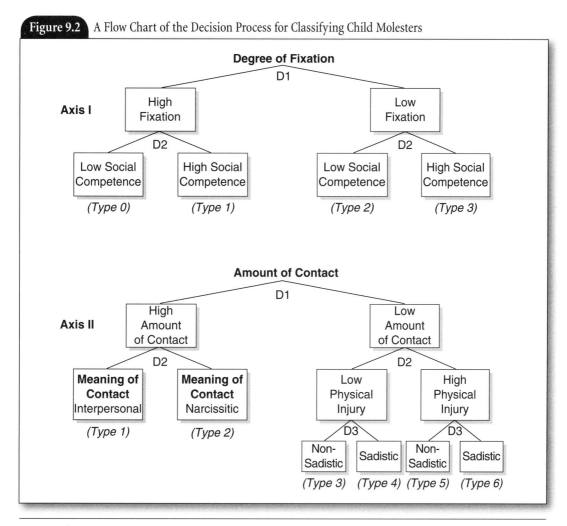

Source: Knight, R. A., Warren, J. I., Reboussin, R., & Soley, B. J. (1998). Reprinted with permission from Sage, on behalf of the International Association for Correctional and Forensic Psychologists.

work is often below his ability and intellectual capacity. Sexual contact with the child occurs after the two become fully acquainted through a number of social encounters. He rarely is aggressive or uses physical force and rarely engages in genital intercourse. The behavior is generally restricted to touching, fondling, or caressing the child. However, this pedophile is the most difficult to treat and is most likely to recidivate because he is not disturbed or troubled about his exclusive preference for children.

Type 1 is similar to Type 0 in his child molestation strategies but tends to be more socially competent in dealing with the world, has higher self-esteem, and usually has a good work history in line with his competence.

Type 2 child molesters have low fixation. They have had a fairly normal adolescence and good peer relationships and sexual experiences, but they later developed feelings of sexual inadequacy and self-doubt. These feelings of inadequacy were further exacerbated by failures in their occupational, social, or sexual lives. The Type 2 offender's background almost always includes alcohol abuse, divorce, and a poor employment history. Each pedophilial act is usually precipitated by a significant disappointment related to the offender's sexual and social inadequacy in interaction with either female or male peers. Unlike Types 0 and 1, the low fixated/low socially competent offender prefers victims who are strangers and who live outside his neighborhood or area. The victims are nearly always female, and he seeks genital sex with the victim. Unlike Type 0 and 1 child molesters, this offender often feels remorseful for his actions and is willing to change.

The Second Dimension

MTC researchers have also discovered that child molesters can be distinguished on the basis of how much daily contact they seek with children (see Figure 9.2).

The "amount of contact" dimension identifies six types of child molesters:

High contact, interpersonal interests (Type 1)

High contact, sexual interests (Type 2)

Low contact, low physical injury, exploitative (Type 3)

Low contact, low physical injury, psychologically sadistic (Type 4)

Low contact, high physical injury, aggressive (Type 5)

Low contact, high physical injury, victim pain (Type 6)

A high-contact offender has regular contact with children within both sexual and nonsexual contexts (R. A. Knight et al., 1989). These high-contact offenders often engage in occupations or recreational activities that bring them into frequent contact with children, such as bus driver, schoolteacher, Little League coach, or Boy Scout leader. The MTC research team identified two kinds of offenders who intentionally seek more extensive contact with children: (1) the *interpersonal* offender (Type 1), who seeks the frequent company of children for both social and sexual needs, and (2) the *narcissistic* offender (Type 2), who seeks the company of children primarily for sexual needs. The narcissistic offenders molest children they do not know, and their sexual acts with children are typically genitally oriented (R. A. Knight, 1989).

Another group of pedophiles includes low-contact seekers. In general, low-contact child molesters come into contact with children only when they decide to sexually assault a child. Low-contact child molesters are subdivided into those who administer very little physical injury to their victims and those who administer high physical injury. Low physical injury is indicated by the absence of physical injury to the victim and the presence of such acts as pushing, shoving, slapping, holding, verbal threats, or other intimidation tactics. Low physical injury offenders are further classified into two types: (1) exploitative, nonsadistic offenders (called Type 3), and (2) muted or symbolic, sadistic offenders (Type 4). The Type 3 offender uses no more aggression or violence than is necessary to obtain victim compliance. Type 4, on the other hand, engages in a variety of frightening, painful, or threatening acts, none of which causes significant physical injury to the child.

Finally, the MTC:CM3 classifies two types of child molesters who administer a high amount of physical injury to their victims: (1) the aggressive offender (Type 5) and (2) the sadistic offender (Type 6). High injury is characterized by hitting; punching; choking; sodomizing; or forcing the child to ingest disgusting things, such as urine or feces. The Type 5 offender is drawn to children for both aggressive and sexual reasons, but sadism is not the primary need. He is extremely angry about all things in his life and is generally violent toward people, including children. The sadistic or Type 6 offender obtains sexual pleasure from the pain, fear, and physical harm he inflicts on the child. He exploits the child's vulnerability any way he can and attempts various strategies and ploys to get the child to comply. This pedophile does not care about the emotional or physical well-being of the victim and sees the child strictly as a sexual object. This offender usually has a long history of criminal and antisocial behavior. His relationships with peers are unpredictable, difficult, and stormy. He is unpleasant to be around, uncomfortable to work with, and generally moody and irritable. His very poor and abrasive interpersonal skills may be the principal reason he selects children as victims (R. A. Knight et al., 1985). This individual is very difficult to treat.

The aggressive-sadistic or Type 6 child molester is apt to have a long history of antisocial behavior and poor adjustment to his environments. Type 6 pedophiles most often prefer male children. Because the primary motive is to obtain sexual gratification without consideration for the victim, these offenders often assault the child viciously and sadistically. The more harm and pain inflicted, the more this individual becomes excited. Type 6 pedophiles are most often responsible for child abductions and murders by strangers. They are very difficult to treat, but, fortunately, they are also very rare. A well-known example of this offender would be John Wayne Gacy, Jr., who raped and sadistically murdered 33 teenage boys and young men and buried their bodies in the cellar of his suburban Chicago home.

The Groth Typology

Another often-cited typology that classifies child molesters is the one proposed by Nicholas Groth (1979; Groth & Burgess, 1977). Groth classifies child molesters on the basis of the longevity of the behavioral patterns and the offender's psychological aims. If the sexual preference for children has existed persistently since adolescence, he is classified as an *immature* or *fixated* child molester. Like the MTC system's high-fixation type, the fixated child molester has been sexually attracted to children throughout his life. Groth argues that this fixation is due to a lack of psychological development. On the other hand, if the child molester has managed to develop some normal aspects to his relationships with adults but turns to children for sexual comfort when stressed or when he experiences a blow to his self-esteem, he is called a *regressed* child offender.

As mentioned above, Groth further subdivides child molesters on the basis of their intentions or psychological goals. He identifies two basic types: (1) sex-pressure offenders and (2) sex-force offenders. The sex-pressure offender tries to entice the child into sexual acts through persuasion or cajolement or to entrap the child by placing him or her in a situation in which he or she feels indebted or obligated. Attractive gifts or "thoughtful" favors are the most common strategies. The sex-force offender, on the other hand, uses threat of harm or brute physical force. The offender either intimidates the child by exploiting the child's helplessness, naïveté, or trust, or simply physically overpowers the child.

Groth believes the sex-force type can be subdivided into the *exploitative* type, who use the threat of force to overcome victim resistance, and the *sadistic* type, who derive great pleasure in harming the child. The exploitative offender employs verbal threats, restraint, manipulation, intimidation, and physical strength to overcome the child's resistance. His intent is not to physically harm the child but to obtain the child's compliance. According to Groth, the sadistic type eroticizes the pain he administers to the child. He uses more force than necessary to gain compliance and may even commit what some police investigators call a "lust murder." The physical and psychological abuse is necessary for him to experience sexual excitement and gratification. Often, the child is beaten, choked, tortured, and violently sexually abused. Fortunately, this type of offender is very rare.

The Groth system has traditionally been the one most often used by police and federal law enforcement investigators, largely because it is intuitively appealing. In many ways, the Groth typology is similar to the MTC child molester classification system, although it has not been developed much beyond Groth's original formulation. Furthermore, and as pointed out by Heilbrun, Marczyk, and DeMatteo (2002), the Groth child molester typology remains speculative and continues to have very little empirical research to support it.

Female Sex Offender Typologies

Traditionally, female sex offenders have received very little research attention, and consequently have been poorly understood, but this research neglect has been changing in recent years. Donna Vandiver and Glen Kercher (2004), for example, developed a clinically useful and research-derived typology of female sex offenders. They based their typology on 471 registered adult female sexual offenders in Texas and were able to identify six types. They are the following:

1. Heterosexual nurturers

2. Noncriminal homosexual offenders

3. Female sexual predators

4. Young adult child exploiters

5. Homosexual criminals

6. Aggressive homosexual offenders

Heterosexual nurturers represented the largest group. The women in this group victimized only males with an average age of 12. The offenders were generally in mentorship, care-taking, or teachers roles, such as the teacher-lover category in which a teacher engages in a "romantic" relationship with one of her students or a counselor with one of her clients. A large segment of the women in this group did not believe the relationship was abusive or psychologically damaging to their child victim. These offenders appeared to be motivated by a desire for intimacy to compensate for unmet emotional and social needs and did not recognize the inappropriateness of the relationship. Vandiver and Kercher (2004) found that this group had a low recidivism rate.

Noncriminal homosexual offenders made up the second-largest group. This group preferred early adolescent females as victims with an average age of 13. These female offenders appeared to have similar characteristics as heterosexual nurturers except that their victim preferences were females. Similar to heterosexual nurturers, these offenders were unlikely to have a criminal record or to recidivate.

Female predators sexually abused both male (60%) and female children (40%) who averaged 11 years of age. Members of this group were largely repeat offenders who engaged in a wide variety of crimes.

Females who fell into the young adult child exploiters group were those who sexually assaulted young victims (average age of 7) of both genders. These offenders themselves were the youngest of the six offender groups, with an average age of 28. About half of the victims were related to the offender and were sometimes the offender's own child. Their crimes appeared to be associated with domestically violent relationships with other women.

In a study of 390 female sex offenders in New York State, Sandler and Freeman (2007) also were able to identify six categories. In addition, their sample was highly similar to Vandiver and Kercher's (2004) sample on demographic variables, such as offender age and race. However, Sandler and Freeman's research did not completely support some of the offender characteristics reported by Vandiver and Kerscher. This is to be expected as the development of female sex offender typologies is in its earliest stages.

Sandler and Freeman (2007) did find support for the heterosexual nurturer and young adult child exploiter categories identified by Vandiver and Kercher (2004), but some descriptors of the four other categories were different. One major difference was the gender of the victims. Sandler and Freeman discovered that many of the female offenders did not *consistently* victimize one gender more than the other.

Overall, the samples between the two studies were different. For one thing, the two states had different codes or registry requirements for sex offenders, so that an offender registered at a certain level in one may not have been registered at the same level in the other state. Furthermore, Vandiver and Kercher's (2004) sample included females who may or may not have served time in prison, although their offenses were considered serious enough to warrant arrest and prosecution (Gannon & Rose, 2008).

Although the two studies advance our knowledge concerning female offenders, neither project was able to obtain additional data relating to co-offenders (Gannon & Rose, 2008). That is, did the females offend alone or with a co-offender, such as a male partner? In addition, Gannon and Rose assert there is very little research on the sexual interests, empathy, intimacy deficits, and self-regulation of female sex offenders. This information is a necessary goal if forensic psychologists and other mental health professionals are to develop risk assessments and provide treatment.

Online Sexual Predators

The explosive growth of Internet use among youth has both positive and negative effects on the health and development of children and adolescents (Ybarra & Mitchell, 2007). Because of the Internet's anonymity, one negative impact is the opportunity for child molesters to engage in sexual solicitation of young adolescents. According to the Growing Up With Media Survey involving 1,588 youth, 15% of the participants reported an unwanted sexual solicitation online in 2006 (Ybarra & Mitchell, 2008). Other surveys support these data (Mitchell, Wolak, & Finkelhor, 2005). Surveys also indicate that most of the sexual solicitations occurred via instant messaging or public chat rooms.

According to Janis Wolak and her colleagues (Wolak, Finkelhor, Mitchell, & Ybarra, 2008), most Internet-initiated sex crimes involve adult men who use the Internet to meet and seduce underage youth into sexual encounters. They utilize various online communications in these endeavors, including instant messages, social networking avenues (blogs, Facebook, Myspace), e-mail, gaming sites, and chat rooms. One study (Malesky, 2007) found that three-quarters of online offenders said they monitor chat room dialogues in an attempt to identify potential victims. As a result of these and other activities, many states now have passed "luring" statutes, making it a crime to deceive children or adolescents through the electronic media for purposes of engaging them in sexual activity.

Surprisingly, current research indicates that the typical Internet child molester does not use trickery to assault children (Wolak, Finkelhor, & Mitchell, 2004). In a great majority of cases, the victims are fully aware they are communicating with adults; only 5% of the offenders pretended to be adolescents. In addition, offenders rarely deceive victims about their sexual interests. "Sex is usually broached online, and most victims who meet offenders face to face go to such meetings expecting to engage in sexual activity" (Wolak et al., 2008, p. 113). Perhaps more surprisingly, the National Juvenile Online Victimization (N-JOV) study reports that three-quarters of victims who had face-to-face sexual encounters with offenders did so more than once (Wolak, Mitchell, & Finkelhor, 2003). Ninety-nine percent of the victims of Internet-initiated sex crimes were 13 to 17 years old, and none were younger than 12. Available data suggest that online molesters do not usually seek unsuspecting victims as much as they seek those youths who are susceptible to seduction (Wolak et al., 2008). Nevertheless, it is a crime for an adult to engage in sexual activity with an underaged person, even if that person is "willing" to do so. As a result, most online offenders—because they engaged in non-forced sexual activity with victims too young to consent to sex with an adult—are charged with statutory rape and/or other offenses associated with luring statutes.

Wolak and her colleagues (2008) assert that many youths are vulnerable to online child molesters because they lack the mature judgment and emotional self-regulation necessary for healthy relationships that involve sexual intimacy (recall the Steinberg research discussed in Chapter 7). Engaging in early sexual behavior, especially with an unknown adult, presupposes risk taking, a common behavioral pattern of adolescence, as we learned in Chapter 7. Adolescents who have histories of sexual or physical abuse appear to be especially vulnerable (Mitchell, Finkelhor, & Wolak, 2007).

Online child molesters are usually not violent or sadistic offenders, nor do they lack interpersonal skills to gain the confidence and acquiescence of victims. That said, the word "usually" should be emphasized. About 5% of the offenders in the N-JOV survey used threats or violence or attempted sexual assault. Abduction, however, is rare. For example, none of victims in the N-JOV study (Wolak et al., 2004) were forced to accompany offenders. Still, about one-quarter of the cases began with missing persons reports, because the victim either ran away to be with the offender or lied to parents about his or her whereabouts.

Juvenile Sex Offenders

According to FBI statistics (FBI, 2002b), about 16% of those arrested for forcible rape and 19% of those arrested for all other sex offenses (except prostitution) are younger than age 18. The NIBRS reports that 23% of sexual assault offenders are younger than age 18 (Snyder, 2000). The extent of the offending may be underestimated because, for a variety of reasons, many (perhaps a majority) of juvenile sex offenders are unknown to the criminal justice system. Several studies do suggest, however, that at least 20 to 30% of rapes and 30 to 50% of child molestations may be committed by adolescents (Cellini, 1995). Most of the research on juvenile sex offenders has concentrated on adolescent males while neglecting preadolescent males and females and adolescent female sex offenders. Nevertheless, there are exceptions, as we will see shortly.

Juvenile male sex offenders represent a heterogeneous population and defy any unitary profile or simple description. They come from all ethnic, racial, and socioeconomic groups. "However, what is known is that about 70% of adolescent sexual offenders come from two-parent homes, most attend school and achieve average grades, and less than 4% suffer from major mental illness" (Becker & Johnson, 2001, p. 274). Further research indicates that the median age of juvenile sex offenders is between 14 and 15, more than 90% know their victims, and more than one-third of the offenses involved the use of force (National Council of Juvenile and Family Court Judges [NCJFCJ], 1993). The victims are often substantially younger than the juvenile offender, are most often female (75%), and are usually relatives or acquaintances (Righthand & Welch, 2001). The median age of victims is 7 years old (NCJFCJ, 1993). Babysitting or some form of child care frequently provides the opportunity to offend, especially for female sex offenders.

Juvenile sex offenders frequently engage in a wide range of nonsexual criminal and antisocial behavior. They tend to shoplift, steal, set fires, bully, assault others (including adults), and are often cruel to animals. One study, for example, reported that more than half of all juvenile sex offenders were abnormally cruel to animals, including their own pets (Tingle, Barnard, Robbins, Newman, & Hutchinson, 1986).

Although most juvenile sex offenders attend school and achieve average grades, a significant number are truant, demonstrate behavioral problems, and have learning disabilities. Moreover, although juvenile sex offenders are described as ranging from social outcasts to popular athletes and from academically gifted students to tough delinquents (Cellini, 1995), research continually reveals that most juveniles with sexual behavioral problems have significant deficits in social competence and getting along with others (Becker, 1990; R. A. Knight & Prentky, 1993). As we found in Chapter 7 for life course–persistent (LCP) delinquents in general, inadequate interpersonal skills, poor peer relationships, and social isolation are among the social difficulties identified in these juveniles (Righthand & Welch, 2001).

The types of sexual offenses committed by juveniles vary widely, ranging from noncontact offenses (such as exhibitionism and voyeurism) to sexual penetration. About half of the contact offenses involve oral–genital contact or attempted or actual vaginal or anal penetration (Righthand & Welch, 2001). Juvenile sex offenders usually use more force when assaulting peers or adults than they do with younger children.

Many adult sex offenders began their sexual abusive behavior in their youth. Research studies report that 47 to 58% of adult sex offenders committed their first offense during adolescence or younger (Cellini, 1995; Cellini, Schwartz, & Readio, 1993).

Many experts and mental health professionals have made the point that a juvenile's own sexual victimization in childhood is a primary cause of later sex offending. Yet, such abusive experiences have not consistently been found to differ significantly from those of other juvenile offenders (R. A. Knight & Prentky, 1993; Spaccarelli, Bowden, Coatsworth, & Kim, 1997). We also must be careful not to assume that someone who was sexually abused as a child will then go on to abuse others. In a recent British study, the researchers found that only 12% of the 224 boys who had been sexually abused as children later became sexually abusive themselves (Salter et al., 2003). Although the figure may reflect only the abuse that came to official attention, it does underscore the point that most children who are sexually abused do not become victimizers themselves.

The role of child maltreatment in the etiology of sex offending appears unclear and much more complicated than previously supposed (R. A. Prentky, Harris, Frizzell, & Righthand, 2000). There is some evidence, though, that abused children exhibit less empathy toward others than their non-abused peers, have trouble recognizing appropriate emotions in others, and have difficulty taking another person's perspective (R. A. Knight & Prentky, 1993).

Female Juvenile Sex Offenders

According to the latest FBI statistics, juvenile females accounted for 10% of all juveniles arrested for sex offenses (excluding forcible rape and prostitution) (FBI, 2010). Nevertheless, like adult female sexual offending, the prevalence of juvenile female sexual offending may be underestimated. Research on girls who have committed sex offenses has been relatively rare, and existing studies have been limited by small sample sizes and other methodological restrictions and problems (Becker et al., 2001; Righthand & Welch, 2001). Most of the available research has focused on adult female sexual offenders (Bumby & Bumby, 1997) and—as discussed above—that research itself is very limited. As Becker et al. observe, "Society in the past has been disbelieving in regards to the presence or potential threat of female sexual perpetrators" (p. 30). They add that the mental health professionals in routine clinical interviews rarely or never ask females about possible sexual aggression or paraphilias.

Fehrenbach and Monastersky (1988) report that most adolescent girls who sexually victimized young children did so while taking care of children or babysitting. The victims of the 28 female sex offenders they studied were 12 years old or younger, and they were mostly acquaintances (57%), followed by siblings (29%) and other relatives (14%). Mathews, Hunter, and Vuz (1997) provided data on 67 female adolescent offenders who ranged in age from 11 to 18. More than 90% of their victims were acquaintances or relatives. Both of the above studies also found that a high percentage of the abusers (50% and 77.65%, respectively) themselves had a history of being sexually abused. Bumby and Bumby (1997) found that adolescent female sex offenders tended to be depressed, have a poor self-concept, have a suicide ideation, and have been victims of sexual abuse during childhood.

Future Directions

Becker and Johnson (2001) recommend that future clinical research on juvenile sex offending concentrate on the following four areas: (1) theory development that addresses the etiology of the behavior, (2) the development of classifications systems or typologies that encompass all juvenile ages and both genders, (3) further development of treatment interventions for different classifications of juvenile sexual offenders, and (4) treatment outcomes studies with long-term follow-ups.

Recidivism Rates of Sex Offenders

Recidivism refers to the repetition of criminal behavior. Usually, it is measured in four ways: (1) rearrest, (2) reconviction, (3) resentence to prison, and (4) return to prison with or without a new sentence (Langan & Levin, 2002). The observed rate of new sexual offenses among known sexual offenders is 10 to 15% after 4 or 5 years (Hanson, 2001; Hanson & Bussière, 1998). However, not all offenders reoffend at the same rate. As a group, child molesters commit a new but similar sexual offense at a higher rate than rapists. On the other hand, research suggests that rapists generally do not confine their repeat crimes to sexual offenses but engage in a wide variety of violent crimes, including violent sexual ones (Quinsey, Harris, Rice, & Cormier, 1998). Child molesters, however, tend to repeat their offenses of child sexual abuse and usually do not engage in other types of violent crimes.

Age Factors

A study by R. Karl Hanson (2001) confirms prior research that, on average, the rate of recidivism for rapists decreases with age. Hanson analyzed data from 10 follow-up studies of sex offenders released from prisons. He found important differences in recidivism risk according to both age and offense type. The highest-risk age period for adult rapists was between 18 and 25 years, with a gradual decline in recidivism risk as the offender got older. Extrafamilial child molesters were far more likely to recidivate than either intrafamilial child molesters or rapists. The highest-risk period for extrafamilial child molesters was between the ages of 25 and 35; moreover, there were only modest declines in their recidivism risk until after the age of 50. Intrafamilial child molesters, on the other hand, were at highest risk between the ages of 18 and 25, and they were the least likely of the three groups to recidivate, particularly after age 25.

Hanson (2001) notes that the age differential in recidivism between rapists and child molesters as a group might be attributable to a greater delay in the detection and prosecution of offenses against children than for offenses against adults. Another factor that may enter into the reported differences in age is that child molesters may be more skillful at avoiding detection.

Recidivism of Juvenile Sex Offenders

In general, research has found that the juvenile offender recidivism rate for sex offenses ranges between 2% and 14% (Reitzel, 2003; Rubinstein, Yeager, Goodstein, & Lewis, 1993; Sipe, Jensen, & Everett, 1998). M. A. Alexander (1999) reports an overall sexual recidivism rate (based on rearrest) of 7%, with juvenile rapists having the highest sexual reoffending rate of all juvenile sex offenders. More important, however, is the finding by some researchers (Alexander, 1999; Hunter & Becker, 1999) that juvenile sex offenders are less likely to reoffend than adult offenders.

Assessment of Sex Offenders

Assessment of sex offenders is an extremely challenging undertaking because of the heterogeneous and multidimensional nature of the persons who commit such crimes. Comprehensive assessment strategies include evaluations of the offender's needs (psychological, social, cognitive, and medical), family relationships, risk factors, past criminal history, and risk management considerations (Righthand & Welch, 2001). Forensic psychologists assess sex offenders not only to decide on a treatment plan but also to gauge their likelihood of further offending. These **psychosexual evaluations** often are conducted at the request of judges, lawyers, parole officers, or other agents of the criminal justice system.

Unstructured clinical interviews have traditionally been the most commonly used assessment procedure for evaluating sex offenders (Dougher, 1995). An unstructured interview is one that imposes minimal structure on the interviewee by asking open-ended questions rather than preset questions that are designed to control the discussion. The interviewee is allowed to answer the questions with wide freedom and minimal direction. The assessment interview with sex offenders is usually problematic, though, because the sex offender has a strong tendency to deny or conceal his "true" thoughts, feelings, or deviant behaviors (Abel, Lawry, Karlstrom, Osborn, & Gillespie, 1994). Consequently, the information gathered is often unreliable and distorted and must be viewed with skepticism. It is important, therefore, that the clinician obtain as much collateral or outside information as possible during the assessment process to corroborate or supplement the interview material. Collateral information includes psychological and medical reports, previous statements made by the offender, police reports, arrest reports, and other information from those persons who know the offender (Dougher, 1995). Even when all these informational sources are taken into account, forensic psychologists and other practitioners who rely on unstructured assessment methods and clinical judgment are often inaccurate in their predictions of sexual offending. "It is widely accepted that evaluations based on unstructured professional judgment are less accurate than structured risk assessments" (Hanson & Morton-Bourgon, 2009, p. 1). As mentioned in Chapter 3, this observation was also made over 50 years ago by Paul Meehl (1954). In recent years, however, even researchers strongly devoted to actuarial risk assessment have been receptive to including *structured* clinical judgment in these methods. This allows clinicians to add their unique observations to the data gathered from the actuarial instruments.

The use of various psychological tests for the assessment of sex offenders also has a long history. These tests are primarily focused on identifying personality characteristics or developing a psychological profile of the already-known offender. Usually, the tests are of the paper-and-pencil variety, where respondents answer "true" or "false" to items that ask about their thoughts, attitudes, and behaviors. Assessments based on psychological tests and inventories have largely focused on **risk assessment measures,** specifically the likelihood of recidivism or reoffense. These instruments are used in various jurisdictions to place sex offenders in risk tiers, which are then used in accord with community sexual offender notification regulations and civil commitment statutes (Heilbrun et al., 2002). For example, sex offender notification statutes typically require that low-risk offenders only register with police. In the case of high-risk offenders, it is expected both that they register and that police notify the community where they take up residence.

However, the success of psychological inventories in identifying those sex offenders who will reoffend is, at best, very marginal. The development of actuarial risk assessment measures over the past 15 years has been a major improvement in prediction of sexual offending. Actuarial prediction is based on quantified experience and data rather than on the more subjective information, such as clinical judgment. The Static-99 is currently the most widely used sex offender risk assessment tool in the world. It is a 10-item actuarial instrument created by R. Karl Hanson and David Thornton (2000). The 10 items cover static, historical factors, such as the number of prior offenses, victim characteristics, and the offender's age. The items were selected strictly on the basis of empirical relationships with recidivism and ease of administration (Hanson & Morton-Bourgon, 2009). The popularity of Static-99 is probably due to its cost-effectiveness and its applicability to a wide range of sexual offenders (Hanson, Helmus, and Thornton, 2010). However, its accuracy in predicting sexual and violent recidivism could be improved. In an effort to improve predictive accuracy, Hanson and Thornton (2003) developed the Static-2002. Preliminary study has, indeed, indicated that the Static-2002 is more accurate for the prediction of sexual, violent, and general recidivism, but more research is needed on the power of subscales to identify psychologically meaningful attributes (Hanson et al., 2010).

According to a survey of forensic psychologists conducted by Archer, Buffington-Vollum, Stredny, and Handel (2006), the second most commonly used risk assessment instrument for adult sex offenders is the Sexual Violence Risk-20 (SVR-20), developed by Boer, Hart, Knopp, and Webster (1997). The SVR-20 covers aspects of the offender's criminal history and psychological characteristics. The items are designed to evaluate the risk for sexual recidivism and to help in case management.

It should be emphasized that fully effective risk assessment for sex offender recidivism will require more than a single risk assessment instrument. The forensic psychologist should be prepared to examine a wide range of complex factors in the assessment process. The best methods of combining risk factors into an overall evaluation remain an active topic of scientific debate in forensic psychology. For example, Hanson and Morton-Bourgon (2009) argue that the ideal risk assessment procedure should not only provide accurate prediction of criminal sexual behavior, but it should also provide information useful for case management. This approach involves the utilization of dynamic risk factors, discussed in Chapter 3. As you may recall, dynamic risk factors are those characteristics of a person that can be changed. Case management that focuses on changeable risk factors should also be able to reduce recidivism. Hanson and Morton-Bourgon (2005) were able to identify several dynamic factors characteristic of persistent sexual offenders that have the potential of being useful case management and treatment targets, including sexual preoccupation, deviant attitudes, intimacy deficits, and self-regulation problems.

The instruments described above are largely intended for adult sex offenders. There have also been several risk assessment methods devised for evaluating juvenile sex offenders. Examples include the Juvenile Sex Offender Assessment Protocol—II (J-Soap-II; Prentky et al., 2000; Prentky & Righthand, 2003); the Estimate of Risk of Adolescent Sexual Offender Recidivism (ERASOR; Worling & Curwen, 2001); the Juvenile Sexual Offense Recidivism Risk Assessment Tool—II (JSORRAT-II; Epperson, Ralston, Fowers, & DeWitt, 2006); and the Multiplex Empirically Guided Inventory of Ecological Aggregates for Assessing Sexually Abusive Adolescents and Children (MEGA; Miccio-Fonseca, 2006). Some of these procedures are based on static risk factors (those that are historical or unchangeable), while others utilize dynamic factors (Griffin, Beech, Print, Bradshaw, & Quayle, 2008).

Importantly, juvenile risk assessment procedures pay attention not only to dynamic risk factors but also to strength and resilience factors (also called protective factors) in the life of the youthful offender and his or her family. Examples of protective factors are the consistent presence of a stable adult in the youth's life—such as a grandparent or respected teacher—and having someone in whom the youth can confide. One relatively new and promising assessment instrument, the AIM2 (Griffin et al., 2008), incorporates static and dynamic strengths along with concerns (risk factors). The instrument is intended for young men between 12 and 18 years of age who are known to have sexually abused or assaulted others. The AIM2 consists of 75 items, designed to measure static concerns, dynamic concerns, static strengths, and dynamic strengths. Although there is much research needed, the assessment approach represented by the AIM2 seems warranted for both juvenile and adult sex offenders.

SUMMARY AND CONCLUSIONS

Sex offending is of grave concern in contemporary society. Statistics indicate that sexual victimization is a reality for many individuals, and it is well acknowledged that most such victimization does not come to official attention. Forensic psychologists are highly likely to come into contact with both offenders and victims. In this chapter, we covered the assessment tasks of psychologists in relation to sexual offending; sex offender treatment and work with victims will be covered in later chapters.

The terms *rape* and *sexual assault* are often used interchangeably, but we have made some distinction between them. *Sexual assault* is a broader term that covers a wide range of offenses, including rape. *Rape* is typically used to refer to sexual crimes in which vaginal, anal, and sometimes oral penetration of the victim occurred. Increasingly, more state statutes are forgoing the term *rape,* however, to define instead forms and degrees of sexual assault (e.g., aggravated; sexual assault of a child; forcible sodomy). Research literature continues to report studies using the term *rape,* and offenders are routinely called rapists as opposed to sexual assaulters.

Statistics reporting on the incidence and prevalence of sexual offending often are not comparable, partly because of the differences in terminology. Nevertheless, it is possible to discern a variety of patterns. It appears, for example, that probably no more than one-third of all sexual assaults are reported to authorities. Victims themselves may not label the attacks as rapes or as sexual assaults; when they do, they are often fearful of the consequences of revealing their victimization. Although the official rate of forcible rape has shown a downward trend, statistics and surveys about date rape, child sexual abuse, and juvenile sex offending indicate continuing cause for concern. Also of increasing interest is the topic of sexual offending by both adult and adolescent females. Although some studies in this area are available, they are often limited by their small sample sizes. By far, the greatest amount of research has focused on male offenders.

Research has indicated that men who rape often manifest a wide range of antisocial behavior in addition to their sexual offenses. Sex offenders as a group appear to be deficient in social skills and in their ability to maintain positive intimate relationships with others. A number of variables have also been found to play a key role in the behaviors, emotions, and thoughts of sex offenders. These include aggression, impulsivity, social competence, sexual fantasies, sadism, and naïve beliefs, such as those demonstrated in a rapist's acceptance of society's "rape myths."

Nevertheless, sex offenders are not a homogeneous group. That very clear conclusion, based on numerous research studies, has led to the development of typologies or methods of classifying sex offenders for the purpose of both predicting deviant sexual behavior and providing treatment to offenders.

We reviewed two prominent typologies for both rapists and child molesters: the research-based typologies developed by the Massachusetts Treatment Center and the more clinically-based typologies offered by Nicholas Groth. Mental health professionals as well as law enforcement and correctional officials are probably more familiar with the Groth typologies, but they are the least validated. The MTC rapist typology divides rapists according to one of four primary motivations: opportunistic, pervasively angry, sexual, and vindictive. Three of the four are further subdivided, resulting in nine rapist subtypes. The Groth typology identifies three forms of rape: anger, power, and sadistic rape.

Pedophilia—the clinical term for a condition in which sexually arousing fantasies, urges, or behaviors involving sexual activity with children repeatedly occur—is both underreported and often difficult to treat. It is a challenge to obtain data on the prevalence of sexual abuse of children, and available evidence suggests that these behaviors are widely underreported. Both the MTC researchers and Groth have developed classification systems for child molesters, as they have for rapists. The MTC system classifies child molesters on two separate axes, one focusing on the offender's degree of fixation and the other on the amount of contact, level of injury, and extent of sadism demonstrated in the attack. Several radically different types of child molesters are especially difficult to treat. The first is the Type 0 offender, who has a long-standing and highly fixated preference for children as both sexual and social companions. Types 5 and 6, aggressive and sadistic offenders, inflict pain and physical harm on their victims, including harm that may result in death. Because of the nature of their crimes, they are unlikely to be included in treatment programs. Forensic psychologists who treat child molesters often do work with Type 0 offenders, however.

Groth's typology classifies offenders first on the basis of the longevity of their behavior patterns: They are either immature (or fixated) or regressed. Groth also considers their psychological aims: They pressure or they force. Finally, offenders who force are subdivided into exploitative and sadistic types.

Although most research has been carried out with male sex offenders, female offenders are receiving increasingly more attention. It is highly unlikely that female offenders can be conceptualized or treated in the same way as male offenders. In the chapter, we reviewed proposed typologies as well as some of the characteristics that distinguish them from male offenders. Although some female sex offenders engage in highly predatory behavior with strangers, the great majority appear to offend against those who are in their care.

The chapter also covered the topic of luring children and adolescents into sexual activity via the Internet, an activity believed to be on the increase. However, it is important to acknowledge that most of the victims lured in this way are adolescents who are aware that their predators are adults and also are aware that sexual activity is desired. Such luring is still criminal and to be condemned, but if sexual activity occurs, it is most likely to be considered statutory rape.

In recent years, researchers have been paying increasing attention to the problem of juvenile sex offenders. Statistics suggest that between 25 and 50% of sexual assaults may be perpetrated by adolescents. Although we must be guarded in accepting these figures, it is clear that juvenile sexual offending is of concern. As with adult offending, most of the research to date has been directed at males as perpetrators. Juvenile sex offenders are a heterogeneous group, and they frequently engage in a wide variety of nonsexual offending and exhibit behavioral problems. The typical juvenile sex offender has significant deficits in social competence, but again there are exceptions. It is important to point out that children who are sexually victimized do not necessarily become sex offenders. However, it is likely that significant numbers of juvenile sex offenders—both male and female—were themselves victimized. Even so, the relationship between prior sexual victimization and juvenile sex offending is not clear and merits additional research before firm conclusions can be offered. The recommendations made by Becker and Johnson (2001) bear repeating. Theory development, typologies, additional treatment interventions for different classifications of juveniles, and evaluation research are all sorely needed.

Sex offender recidivism rates reflect the importance of preventing and treating the behaviors discussed in this chapter. Adult offenders as a group show higher recidivism rates than juveniles, although the sex offending of adults decreases with advancing age. These rates vary among offender types, though. Furthermore, not all reoffend at the same rate. Child molesters, for example, commit new offenses more often than rapists. Rapists, however, have been found to engage in other violent crimes in addition to rape.

The psychological assessment of sex offenders is a crucial task for forensic psychologists. Offenders are assessed not only for their amenability to treatment but also for their level of risk—or dangerousness—to society. An assessment may be performed, for example, to help a judge decide whether to incarcerate an offender or place him on probation. The Massachusetts Treatment Center has developed an assessment instrument to be used in tandem with its classification system, and over the past decade many other instruments have been developed by other researchers. However, as Becker and Johnson (2001) stress, no one test can determine that an individual has committed an offense or predict recidivism.

KEY CONCEPTS

Acquaintance rape	Pervasively angry rapist
Anger rape	Power rape
Date rape	Psychosexual evaluations
Groth child molester typology	Rape
Groth rape typology	Rape by fraud
Hostile attribution bias	Rape myths
Incest	Recidivism
MTC:CM3	Risk assessment measures
MTC:R3	Sadistic rape
Nonsadistic rapist	Sexually motivated rapist
Opportunistic rapist	Statutory rape
Paraphilias	Typology
Pedophilia	Vindictive rapist

QUESTIONS FOR REVIEW

1. Define rape and explain how and why the term is being replaced in many criminal statutes.

2. What are the demographic features of men who rape?

3. Briefly summarize the MTC classification system, along with what it is based on.

4. What six variables have consistently been found to play an important role in the behavior, emotional, and thought patterns of rapists?

5. Contrast the MTC and the Groth rapist typologies on both their (a) classification system and (b) research support.

6. What are the two basic dimensions on which child molesters are classified according to the MTC:CM?

7. Contrast the MTC and Groth child molester typologies on both their (a) classification system and (b) research support.

8. Discuss juvenile sex offenders according to their antisocial conduct, the victims they choose, and their own history of victimization.

9. Are female juvenile sex offenders different from male juvenile sex offenders? Explain your answer.

10. List any five psychological measures designed to assess recidivism among adult or juvenile sex offenders.

Part V

Victimology and Victim Services

10

Forensic
Psychology
and the Victims
of Crime and
Other Wrongs

CHAPTER OBJECTIVES

- Describe the psychological effects of being victimized and introduce the reader to the role played by mental health professionals in working with victims.
- Emphasize the multicultural aspects of working with victims.
- Describe the legal rights of victims.
- Survey official victimization data.
- Review hate and bias crime victimization.

We are all victims of crime. Whether or not we have been robbed, assaulted, deprived of our life savings or pension funds, or burglarized, we have all experienced the social and financial costs of crime. Even so-called **victimless crimes**—e.g., illegal drug use, prostitution, and illegal gambling—can be said to be harmful to society and leave victims in their wake. Many of us have experienced the fear of crime as well. It is not unusual to hear of women applying for permits to carry guns or signing up for self-defense classes following a string of sexual assaults in a small town or city, for example. In addition, many citizens are victimized by crime without being aware of it. Medical insurance fraud is a good example of this. How many beneficiaries of

Medicare or Medicaid are able to review and monitor the statements submitted by medical practitioners on their behalf? It is estimated that health insurance fraud costs taxpayers millions of dollars annually.

When we speak of crime victims, however, we are most likely referring to individuals who have been physically or emotionally harmed by known crimes against themselves or their property. The U.S. government, which has been collecting victimization data since the early 1970s, focuses its efforts on the types of crimes that are highlighted in the media—assaults, burglaries, robberies, larcenies—and rarely on white-collar offenses or political crimes. Likewise, forensic psychologists and other mental health providers are far more likely to assess and treat victims of rape, child abuse, attempted murder, or robbery than victims of insider trading or illegal government surveillance. Moreover, when members of the public are asked about their fear of crime, they are more worried about child abduction than they are about credit card fraud, despite the relative rarity of the former and frequency of the latter. Child abduction is, of course, a serious, emotionally wrenching crime compared with fraud. Yet the person who is the victim of credit card fraud suffers both financial and emotional harm. The point made here is that victimization comes in many forms and touches people in numerous ways. Although we may focus in this chapter on the forms of victimization most likely to be encountered by mental health providers, the backdrop is victimization in its broadest sense.

Psychologists will be increasingly employed as consultants, instructors, expert witnesses, evaluators, therapists, and service providers to victim service organizations in the coming years. Their help will be needed in many areas, including those involving victims of domestic violence, child abuse, elderly abuse, violent crime, and hate/bias crimes. One skill area that will be especially in demand is the assessment of a victim's crime-related experiences and responses. For example, such assessments are desirable when someone sues for damages or seeks disability or other compensation relating to a crime (Carlson & Dutton, 2003). Another important forensic task is the assessment of a child to determine if a crime occurred or the extent to which it had negative psychological effects.

The chapter begins with an overview of the issues that forensic psychologists must deal with concerning victimization of people of diverse cultures and backgrounds, sexual orientation, disability, and religious preferences. We will then discuss victim rights and their ramifications.

Though we are focusing on criminal victimization, it is important to emphasize that much victimization occurs in the civil context; that is, people are victims of civil wrongs, such as discrimination, sexual harassment (which is a form of discrimination), unsafe working conditions, and negligence on the part of others in numerous other settings. Sometimes the wrongs done by others result in physical losses, such as brain damage or the loss of a limb; at other times, wrongs can result in severe psychological symptoms, such as depression or post-traumatic stress disorder. Thus, while the greater part of the chapter will focus on what is known about victims of *crime*, the psychological impact of being victimized and the various roles played by forensic psychologists in victim services are similar in civil contexts.

Multiculturalism and Victimization

"**Multiculturalism,** in its broadest terms, not only is defined by race and ethnicity but also involves topics of gender, sexual orientation, and disability" (Bingham, Porché-Burke, James, Sue, & Vasquez, 2002, p. 75, emphasis added). Recognizing and respecting individual differences in culture, religious preference, sexual orientation, disabilities, and gender are important to sensitive and effective work with victims. Each person has his or her unique way of viewing the world through the lens of cultural and linguistic experiences. Currently, the racial/ethnic composition of the United States is approximately 79% White; 13% Black; 5% Asian; and 16% Hispanic, Latino or Spanish origin (U.S. Census Bureau, 2009). One in 50 Americans now identifies as "multiracial." By the year 2030, it is estimated that the composition will be 60% White, 19% Latino, 13% Black, and 7% Asian (Ogawa & Belle, 2002). Native Americans are now recognized by the Bureau of the Census as represented by more than 500 separate nations and tribes with 187 different languages (Ogawa & Belle, 2002).

In addition, there are an estimated 3.5 million Arab Americans living in the United States (U.S. Census Bureau, 2009), who represent perhaps one of the most misunderstood ethnic groups in recent years (C. D. Erickson & Al-Timini, 2001). They are also one of the most diverse ethnic groups in the United States in terms of their cultural and linguistic backgrounds, political and religious beliefs, family structures and values, and acculturation to Western society. Arab Americans represent 22 countries as diverse as Egypt, Lebanon, Morocco, Tunisia, Syria, Palestine, and Yemen. The exact number of Arab Americans is unknown because they are often reluctant to identify themselves for fear of possible negative social reactions, particularly in the wake of the terrorist attacks of September 11, 2001. In fact, the FBI reported a 1,600% increase in hate crimes against this population in the year after the events of September 11th (Padela & Heisler, 2010). A survey conducted by Padela and Heisler, two years after September 11th, found evidence that many Arab Americans continue to experience negative emotional states that have led to a variety of mental health problems, such as depression and stress disorders.

By the year 2050, it is projected that 50% of the U.S. population will consist of "ethnic minorities" (Bernal & Sharrón-Del-Río, 2001; C. I. Hall, 1997). The shift in racial/ethnic composition is projected to be more dramatic in some states, such as California and Texas, and will present enormous challenges and opportunities to victim services providers, as well as to providers of other social services. Members of immigrant families are often afraid to ask for help due to language barriers, fear of deportation, and poor understanding of their rights in the community (Ogawa & Belle, 2002). If they are here temporarily or are undocumented, the challenges are multiplied, because there may be abrupt interruptions of services and difficulties in long-range planning.

> Once in the United States, undocumented aliens become easy prey for employment exploitation, consumer fraud, housing discrimination, and criminal victimization because assistance from government authorities is attached to the fear of deportation. There is an epidemic of sexual assaults, for example, committed upon undocumented Latinas. (Ogawa & Belle, 2002, p. 6)

As we commented in Chapter 1, these concerns have intensified in recent years, with irrational fears of "other" groups and the unsettled state of the economy contributing to the mix. Immigration status should not dictate whether individuals get an education, get protection from a society, or receive victim services. A decade ago, it was observed that "almost 20 million international refugees throughout the world have been forced by extreme abuse of human rights to flee their home countries" (Gorman, 2001, p. 443), many fleeing to the United States. At that time, the U.S. Immigration and Naturalization Service had authorized about 200,000 asylum cases, and another 90,000 undocumented immigrants received amnesty permitting them to stay in the country (Gorman, 2001). Many of them had been abused and tortured in their home countries, and they were vulnerable to becoming victims of crime here. In working with refugees, promoting a sense of safety is an important task that requires a high degree of cross-cultural sensitivity. Today, refugees from many Middle Eastern nations ravaged by wars have sought to build new lives in the United States and other Western nations. In addition, an unknown number of immigrants—chiefly women and both male and female adolescents—are lured to this country for work purposes, only to be victimized by those who engage in sex trafficking.

Well-trained forensic psychologists and other clinicians must recognize that the traditional psychological concepts and theories used in assessment and treatment approaches were developed from predominately Euro-American contexts and may be limited in their application to racial and culturally diverse populations

(Sue, Bingham, Porché-Burke, & Vasquez, 1999). Christine Iijima Hall (1997) has admonished that Euro-American psychology may become culturally obsolete if it is not adapted to reflect a multicultural perspective. According to Hall, this will require psychology to make "substantive revisions in its curriculum, training, research, and practice" (p. 642). Heeding these words as well as those from many other scholars, the professional associations such as the APA have published guidelines for working with diverse populations, as mentioned in Chapter 1. Most recently, the APA has published the *APA Handbook of Intercultural Communication,* edited by David Matsumoto (2010), which should be of great help to practicing psychologists.

Forensic psychologists should be especially attuned to the potential injustices and oppression that may result from *monocultural* psychology. C. I. Hall (1997) writes that "people of color and women have been misdiagnosed or mistreated by psychology for many decades" (p. 643). Even psychologists of color or those who are gay/lesbian/bisexual or from diverse backgrounds are not always knowledgeable about the psychological issues of other cultural groups or of their own groups. As Hall notes, "Color, gender, and sexual orientation do not make people diversity experts" (p. 644). Although these challenges are crucial to all forensic settings, they may be particularly important for those who provide victim services. Without appreciation of their cultural backgrounds, some individuals become not only victims of crime but also victims of the criminal justice system and victims of the mental health professions that do not truly recognize their needs.

Victims With Disabilities

A neglected area in victimization research and practice is consideration of persons with disabilities. Victims in this instance extend not only to criminal victimization but also to discrimination and harassment in the workplace, as well as abuse and neglect in the home that fall short of criminal offending. Laws banning discrimination against persons with disabilities in work settings and public services open up new areas of opportunity for forensic psychologists. It should be noted that individuals with drug addictions are often covered by these laws.

> Psychologists may find opportunities to consult in the determination of reasonable workplace accommodation for persons with psychiatric, learning, and intellectual disabilities and to provide expert testimony in employment discrimination cases. Psychologists also have an essential role in evaluating neurological, learning, and psychological impairment and function as part of the process of determining reasonable accommodation for both students and employees with disabilities. (C. J. Gill, Kewman, & Brannon, 2003, p. 308)

Much of the recent activity in working with the disabled has been prompted by the Americans with Disabilities Act, implemented July 26, 1992. The act applies to public employers and private employers with 15 or more employees. It prohibits discrimination (a) in the hiring process; (b) regarding terms, conditions, and benefits of employment; and (c) in access to work-related amenities, facilities, and functions (Goodman-Delahunty, 2000). Employees who become victims of crime may suffer substantial, long-term psychological problems that may interfere with or hamper their employment opportunities, advancement, and quality of life. The interested reader is encouraged to consult an article by Jane Goodman-Delahunty (2000), who identifies some common legal pitfalls for practitioners and forensic psychologists and provides suggestions for how to avoid these pitfalls when providing services to employers or to employees with psychological impairments.

Approximately 15 to 20% of the U.S. population has some type of disability (C. J. Gill et al., 2003; Olkin & Pledger, 2003), broadly defined as a physical or mental condition that substantially limits one or more of the individual's major life activities. In addition, the prevalence of severe disability is different among racial and ethnic groups. For example, according to one report, in the population ages 16 to 64, a total of 7.4% of Whites had severe disabilities compared to 12.7% of Blacks, 11.7% of American Indians, 9.1% of Hispanic/Latino origin, and 4.5% of Asians (Tyiska, 1998). The explanations for these differences are likely to be wide-ranging, and likely include access to health care, economic circumstances, victimization, and many other possible factors.

Criminal victimization data indicate that victimization rates for children and adults with disabilities far exceed those of individuals who do not have disabilities (Office for Victims of Crime, 2009). Youth (ages 12 to 19) with a disability experience violence at twice the rate as those without a disability (Rand & Harrell, 2009). In addition, persons with disabilities are often victims of harassment, discrimination, and emotional abuse. Many people with disabling conditions are especially vulnerable to victimization because of their real or perceived inability to resist or flee or to notify others. About 68 to 83% of women with developmental disabilities will be sexually assaulted in their lifetime, which represents a 50% higher rate than in the rest of the population (Tyiska, 1998). In addition, people with developmental disabilities are more likely to be revictimized by the same person, and more than half of those victimized never seek assistance from legal or treatment services (Pease & Frantz, 1994).

It should be noted that disability is listed along with race, gender, age, sexual orientation, and other dimensions of human diversity in the Ethical Principles of Psychologists and Code of Conduct (APA, 2002b, 2010). Psychologists working in forensic settings, therefore, may require specialized training and experience to be competent professionals in working with the disabled.

Well-executed research on the victimization of people with disabilities and the impact it has on their lives is desperately needed. Not everyone agrees, for example, that the victimization rates are substantially higher among people with disabilities. According to Okin and Pledger (2003), "Although the assertion that rates of all types of abuse are higher for children and adults with disabilities is legion in the literature, there is little to support this assertion, and rates found vary unbelievably from study to study" (p. 302). However, the first national study on crime against persons with disabilities was released in October of 2009 by the U.S. Justice Department's Bureau of Justice Statistics (BJS). The study was based on data from the National Crime Victimization Survey (NCVS) and does indicate that crime is experienced by adults (ages 35 to 49) and youth (ages 12 to 19) with disabilities at a much higher rate than reported for persons of similar ages and without disabilities. However, the survey also found that the rate of violence did not differ by disability status for persons age 50 or older. Perhaps the discrepancies in the research reviewed by Okin and Pledger are due, in part, to failure to compare age groups.

Legal Rights of Victims

Although it can be said that victims of crime—particularly violent crime—will always be affected by what happened to them, society has taken some steps to try to "make up for" their victimization. Crime victims' bills of rights have been enacted in all states, half of which provide for mandatory restitution unless compelling reasons to the contrary are stated on the record. In addition, at least 31 states have passed victims' rights constitutional amendments, and at least 10 of these provide for mandatory restitution (M. Murray & O'Ran, 2002). **Restitution** is a remedy for the recovery of some measure of economic and psychological wholeness. It is an attempt to restore a victim's original financial, physical, or psychological position that existed prior to the loss or injury. Undoubtedly, this is a laudable if somewhat high-sounding goal. However, crime victims have consistently reported their frustrations in obtaining adequate and timely restitution both from offenders and from public funds allocated for this purpose (Karmen, 2009).

Victims of crime can use two legal venues. Criminal courts deal with that aspect of the justice system that determines guilt or innocence with reference to crime and metes out criminal sanctions. Although criminal courts do not provide direct compensation to victims, they do allow them to speak out at sentencing or have their statements read to the court. In some states, victims are also notified prior to all court appearances, and—if the defendant is eventually convicted and imprisoned—they are notified of parole hearings. They also may be given the opportunity to speak out at these hearings. The civil courts allow crime victims to seek civil remedies for the physical, financial, and psychological injuries they have suffered as a result of criminal acts, permitting vindication of their rights and recovery of financial reparations from the offenders (Gaboury & Edmunds, 2002). As illustrated in the high-profile O. J. Simpson case of the early 1990s, a defendant may be acquitted in criminal court but found responsible for a death in a civil court, but these instances are rare. Simpson was found not guilty of killing Nicole Brown Simpson and Ronald Goldman in criminal court; later, a civil jury held him responsible for those deaths and awarded the family $3.5 million. Students should review Focus 5.2 (Burdens of Proof) for one possible explanation.

Civil litigation can be a complex, difficult, and expensive process, however. Lawyers may ask forensic psychologists, such as those specializing in neuropsychology, to help determine the extent of injuries. For example, psychologists may assess a victim of crime or a civil wrong for the presence of PTSD or other psychological after-effects of victimization. This is done to determine a value that can be placed on the victim's injuries, which in turn helps a jury award damages. Compensation for the cost of psychotherapy can be included in the damages awarded.

Cases involving personal injuries or civil wrong that are not crime related include sexual harassment, wrongful termination due to gender discrimination, unnecessary medical procedures, and injuries suffered from using faulty products, to name but a few. Sexual harassment suits are a particularly controversial area, especially when the victim of harassment has symptoms of PTSD.

Although both the civil and the criminal process can be stressful for the victim, the criminal justice process is especially intimidating and frustrating. From the moment some victims call police, they may find themselves faced with a spiral of events that is seemingly out of their control. They may perceive that police do not respond quickly enough, for example, and when police do arrive, victims may believe that police are not sensitive enough to the experience they suffered. Victims often find it difficult to understand why their property cannot be recovered or, if recovered, why it cannot be immediately returned. Victims of violent crime are fearful that their aggressor will be released on bail; if convicted and imprisoned, they are fearful that he or she will be released on parole.

It is a reality in law that the Constitution of the United States protects the rights of suspects and defendants but not the rights of victims. Criminal suspects do not have to speak with police, for example, and if they choose to do so, they are guaranteed the right to an attorney during police questioning. Defendants have the right to an attorney during every critical stage of the court proceedings, including arraignments, pretrial hearings, trials, and sentencing. In contrast, victims are not represented by lawyers unless they choose to hire a lawyer during a civil proceeding. Although it can be argued that the prosecutor is essentially the lawyer for the victim, the prosecutor is technically the lawyer for the government and may pay very little attention to the physical, financial, or emotional needs of victims. Victims often have to take time off from work or other obligations to appear in court, and when cases go to trial, they are subjected to the scrutiny of the media and grueling cross-examination in a courtroom in which they must be confronted by the defendant. As a result, victims have often complained that they are the forgotten component of the criminal justice process or are twice victimized—once when the crime first occurs and again when they encounter the criminal justice process.

Although the above reality strikes many citizens as unfair, it occurs because suspects and defendants have so much to lose from the criminal justice process, in which the awesome power of the state is brought to bear against the individual. A person accused of crime stands to lose his or her freedom, sometimes for life. Under the law, if we are ready to take away a person's freedom—in some cases even his or her life—we must "do it right" by providing the protections in accordance with the Constitution. The law does not plan to take away the freedom of the victim, and hence the victim's rights are not guaranteed in the Constitution.

This logic often does not convince victims or their advocates, however. In the 1970s, the nation saw a major trend in the direction of ensuring that victims, too, would have certain rights under the law. Thus, beginning in 1980, when Wisconsin passed the first "victims' bill of rights," states began to pass laws providing victims with certain statutory, if not constitutional, guarantees and protections. Congress, in the Victim and Witness Protection Act of 1982, enacted similar provisions into federal law. The Office for Victims of Crime (OVC) was created the following year. Throughout the 1980s, Congress passed a number of similar laws and funded programs designed to help victims. In addition, virtually every state fiscal budget now provides funding for victim advocates or victim assistants. These are professionals who serve as liaisons between the victim and the criminal court process. They perform a wide range of services aimed at informing victims of what they will encounter and offering support during this trying period. Unfortunately, these positions and services are often faced with threatened or actual budget cuts.

Notification

Most states now have laws requiring **notification** of victims at various stages during the criminal justice process. For example, if a person charged with a violent crime against the victim is about to be released on bail, the victim is notified; if a convicted offender is about to be released from jail or prison, the victim is notified. Even if an offender will be out of prison for a limited time period, as in a work release program, the victim may be notified. Some states also require notification when a plea negotiation has been reached. Not surprisingly, all states require that victims be notified if an offender has escaped from prison.

Allocution

There are several decision-making points at which a victim's input may be accepted. The right of **allocution** is the right to speak out during these proceedings. Chief among them are the bail hearing, the sentencing hearing, and the parole board hearing. At bail setting, victims are sometimes allowed to argue for a higher bail or, more commonly, to ask that the defendant be forbidden from contacting them. All states allow victims to speak out at sentencing hearings, either in person or in prepared written statements.

Presentence reports—which are documents prepared by probation officers or other professionals to help judges reach sentencing decisions—typically include a *victim impact statement.* The person preparing the report interviews the victim and obtains information about the extent of his or her suffering. A victim of an aggravated assault, for example, might describe being unable to sleep peacefully, recurring nightmares, expensive meetings with a psychiatrist, and his continuing fear of walking alone. When there is no presentence report, victims are allowed to present statements to the presiding judge or to appear in court and testify directly about what they have experienced. In death penalty cases, survivors of the victim are allowed to have the sentencing jury hear details about the suffering they have experienced (*Payne v. Tennessee,* 1991). A minority of states also allow victims to appear at parole board hearings to protest an offender's release.

Compensation

Although the physical and psychological impact of crime may be considered the most obvious aspect, the financial impact can also be devastating. "The financial losses incurred as a result of crime (unforeseen medical expenses, psychological counseling costs, and the need to replace stolen property) can be as debilitating as any other type of injury suffered by crime victims" (Gaboury & Edmunds, 2002, p. 2).

All 50 states, plus the District of Columbia, Puerto Rico, and the Virgin Islands, have compensation programs that can pay for medical and counseling expenses, lost wages and support, funeral bills, and variety of other costs (Eddy & Edmunds, 2002). In some cases, the money is derived from state taxes or grant sources; in others, it comes from offenders themselves. An inmate may be earning money in a prison work program, for example, and a percentage of that income is allocated to the victim of the crime. It is also common for states to deny convicted offenders the right to profit from books they may write about their crimes. Called "Son of Sam" laws, after the infamous serial murderer David Berkowitz, who claimed he was controlled by the devil through a dog called "Sam," these laws sometimes redirect the income to the victim or to a victim's fund.

Despite the enactment of these laws, they do not seem to be working to the advantage of the great majority of victims. Research has indicated that only a small percentage of victims are even aware of their existence (Karmen, 2009; National Center for Victims of Crime [NCVC], 1999). As noted earlier, victims also report that **compensation** takes time and is rarely provided in total.

Notification, which places an added burden on agents of the criminal justice system, seems particularly problematic. It is often not clear who has the responsibility to keep the victim informed, and consequently, no one takes on this task. In communities with well-funded victims' advocates or victims' assistance programs, notification is more likely to occur, but as indicated above, victims' assistance programs may be the first to go when budgets are tight.

Likewise, most victims do not exercise their right of allocation at bail, sentencing, or parole hearings. When they do, the research is mixed with respect to their effectiveness, although results are slightly weighed in favor of their having influenced parole decision makers. For example, several studies document that victims appearing before parole boards have been successful at delaying the offender's release (Karmen, 2009).

Victims are not typically successful at having sentences *increased*, however. After reviewing studies on the effect of victims' rights legislation, Karmen (2001) notes, "Even with all the new options, does institutionalized indifference toward the victims' plight still pervade the justice system? The answer seems to be a qualified 'yes,' according to some preliminary findings gathered from evaluation studies" (p. 317).

Restorative Justice

One philosophical approach that directly provides services to victims is **restorative justice.** Restorative justice is not easy to define because it encompasses a vast array of practices in different areas of the criminal justice system (Daly, 2002). According to Daly, "Restorative justice is used not only in adult and juvenile criminal matters, but also in a range of civil matters, including family welfare and child protection, and disputes in schools and workplace settings" (p. 57). Rather than focusing exclusively on punishing the individual offender, the primary goal of restorative justice is to involve a larger segment of the community in deciding what should be done about criminal offending and the harm perpetrated on its victims. Basically, the mission of restorative justice is to "make whole" the victims and the community that have suffered from the offender's crime, while also reintegrating the offender into the community when appropriate (Karmen, 2001). "It is guided by values that emphasize healing and social well-being of those affected by crime" (Presser & Van Voorhis, 2002, p. 162). Typically, a community reparative board functions as mediators to help resolve conflict and restore or repair both the victim and the offender. The victim plays a major role in the process and may receive some form of restitution. In instances where no crime has been committed (e.g., a school dispute or a serious disagreement between neighbors), the goal is to settle the dispute in an informal manner and achieve a satisfactory outcome for all involved.

Restorative or reparative justice is closely associated with a "mediation" philosophy, or an approach that attempts to solve problems by compromising and finding common ground rather than by using conflict tactics.

School children today are often exposed to mediation strategies to avoid playground fights or resolve a variety of peer conflicts, and mediation may be used in workplaces to resolve disputes between front-line workers and supervisors or administrators. Likewise, attempts at peaceful resolution may be recommended in divorce situations, including custody disputes. It may be surprising that mediation approaches are used in the criminal context as well.

Programs based on the restorative justice philosophy do not focus only on mediation; they try to hold offenders accountable for their actions and make them responsible for repairing harm to victims and the community (Lemley, 2001). This is done through the process of negotiation, mediation, victim empowerment, and reparation (Rodriguez, 2007). Restorative justice can be applied when the offender has already been sentenced and is in jail, in prison, or on probation. However, it can also be used as an alternative to prosecution for less serious crimes. Meetings among victims, their offenders, and community members represent common procedures, and decision making is carried out by both lay and legal participants.

Crime Victimization Data

Information about victimization in our society is best obtained from victims themselves. Persons who have been assaulted or burglarized can tell us when and where the crime occurred, whether they reported it to police, and the degree of physical and emotional harm they experienced, among many other things. These victimization statistics also help us understand the distribution of crime, including its geographical and temporal characteristics. Are certain regions of the country more "crime-prone" than others, for example, or are certain months of the year more likely to see a reduction in crime? When victims know something about the person or persons who victimized them, victimization data also can provide information about those who commit crime.

The preeminent victimization survey in the United States is the **National Crime Victimization Survey (NCVS),** sponsored by the Bureau of Justice Statistics (BJS) and conducted by the Census Bureau. The NCVS reports the results of contacts with a large national sample of households (approximately 76,000) representing 135,300 persons older than age 12. On an annual basis, a member of the household is first asked whether anyone experienced crime during the previous 6 months. If the answer is yes, the victim is interviewed more extensively on the frequency, characteristics, and consequences of the criminal victimization. The same households are re-contacted every 6 months for a period of 3 years. The NCVS is currently designed to measure the extent to which households and individuals are victims of rape and other types of sexual assault, robbery, assault, burglary, motor vehicle theft, and larceny. The survey includes both crimes reported and those not reported to the police. Consequently, there are differences between NCVS data and the FBI's Uniform Crime Report data.

The NCVS was introduced in 1973 and was then known as the National Crime Survey (NCS). Until that time, the government's main measure of crime in the United States was the FBI's UCR, which reflected crimes that were known to police along with arrest data. Many people—for a variety of reasons—do not report their victimizations to police, however. The NCS was developed to try to tap the "dark figure" of crime, or the crime that did not come to the attention of police. A victimization rate, expressed by the number of victimizations per 1,000 potential victims, is reported to the public. Developers of the NCS reasoned that some crime victims might be more willing to report their victimization to interviewers than to police. Furthermore, interviewers could probe and learn more about the effects of victimization. Over the years, these predictions have been borne out because victimization data continually indicate that, overall, at least half of all crimes are not reported to police. Not surprisingly, this figure varies according to specific crimes; reporting rates of auto theft, for example, are dramatically higher than reporting rates of sexual assault.

The NCS was revised in the 1980s and substantially redesigned in 1992, when its name was changed to the National Crime Victimization Survey. Among the changes were the addition of questions asking victims how law enforcement officials responded when they reported their victimizations. Victims also were asked more details about the crime, including whether the perpetrator appeared to be under the influence of alcohol or illegal substances and what they were doing at the time of the crime (e.g., going to work, shopping). The redesign also included a more sensitive and comprehensive approach to asking victims about sexual assault (Karmen, 2001). In addition to reports of household victimization, the BJS also sponsors supplementary reports, such as surveys of school and workplace victimization and victimization of commercial establishments.

Ethnic/Minority Differences in Victimization

Recent NCVS data, tabulated by the BJS (Rand, 2009), provide information on the criminal victimization of five ethnic/minority or racial groups: White, Black, American Indian, Hispanic, and Asian. The American Indian classification is based on those NCVS respondents who identified themselves as persons of Indian, Eskimo, or Aleut descent. Asians were defined in this context as Japanese, Chinese, Korean, Asian Indian, Vietnamese, and Pacific Islander. Pacific Islander includes those persons who identified themselves as Filipino, Hawaiian, Guamian, Samoan, and other Asian. Respondents who identified themselves as Mexican American, Chicano, Mexican, Puerto Rican, Cuban, Central or South American, or other Spanish origins were classified as Hispanic. All the groups are extremely diverse, but the rapidly growing Hispanic/Latino group reflects perhaps the greatest diversity. Because of this diversity, the BJS considered the "Hispanic" category as consisting of persons of any race in this tabulation. In other words, some Hispanics also report that they consider themselves White, Black, American Indian, or Asian, a point that needs to be considered when examining the statistical data on crime rates.

The most recent NCVS data (Rand, 2009) show that Blacks experience higher rates of violence than persons of all other races. In addition, individuals of more than one race experience violent crime at rates that are 2 to 3 times higher than Whites, Blacks, or persons of other racial groups. For decades, Blacks have consistently been disproportionately represented among homicide victims, especially Black males. Blacks are usually 6 times more likely than Whites and 8 times more likely than persons of other races to be murdered (Rennison, 2001). (See Table 10.1 for data on race and victimization.)

Studies have shown that approximately 70% of inner-city youth have been victimized by violent acts, including being threatened, chased, hit, beaten up, sexually assaulted, or attacked with a knife or gun, and 85% of these youth report having witnessed violent acts (Kliewer, Lepore, Oskin, & Johnson, 1998). A survey of U.S. adults revealed that 43% had witnessed interpersonal violence, and 5% had a friend or relative die from homicide or suicide (D. M. Elliott, 1997; Hillbrand, 2001). Many children and youth (from ages 6 to 18) who are continually exposed to violence develop difficulty concentrating and learning, as well as anxiety, fear, depression, and **posttraumatic stress disorder (PTSD).**

Various kinds of violence have different types of impact on those individuals who experience and witness it. In other words, all violence is not the same. Violence between parents (interparental violence) may be more damaging to the psychological health of a young child than being beaten and chased at school. Furthermore, interparental violence in which weapons are used, such as guns or knives, may be more upsetting to children than those incidents not involving weapons (Jouriles et al., 1998).

Approximately 25% of the victims of violent crime are injured, many of them severely (T. Simon, Mercy, & Perkins, 2001). Moreover, several studies have shown that the psychological impact of being a victim of violence differs from that of being a witness to violence (Shahinfar et al., 2001). Research also has found that adolescents who had been physically abused were at a higher risk to commit violent behavior themselves than those who had simply witnessed abuse (Shahinfar et al., 2001).

Table 10.1	Rate of Violent Victimization by Type of Crime and Race, 2008			
	Rate of Victimizations			
Per 1,000	**White**	**Black**	**Other race**	**Two or more races**
Total violent crime	18.1	25.9	15.2	51.6
Rape/sexual assault	0.6	1.9	0.9	1.9
Robbery	1.6	5.5	3.0	6.8
Aggravated assault	3.0	5.3	2.8	6.8
Simple assault	12.8	13.3	6.8	36.1

Source: Rand (2009).

Psychological Effects of Criminal Victimization

Psychological Impact of Violence

A summary statement by the APA's "Human Capital Initiative Report" (1996) begins this section well:

> Violence harms its victims both physically and psychologically. It traumatizes victims, bystanders, and family members alike. It can trigger paralyzing anxiety and fear, long-lasting depression, or deep anger. Although a substantial amount of effort has been devoted to finding the best ways to treat violent offenders, little research has been conducted on the best ways to treat the victims of violence to minimize their psychological problems. Standard treatments for depression and anxiety may be inappropriate in these cases. Programs to treat victims have been shown to be most effective when they are delivered in natural locations, such as schools, community groups, health care environments, and when they are culturally relevant and age- and sex-specific. Therapies that are more specific to different types of victimization have yet to be developed. (p. 9)

The impact of criminal violence extends even beyond the direct victims and their families and friends. For several decades, it has been widely recognized that Americans have a substantial fear of becoming victims of crime, and that this fear is especially strong among women and the elderly (Dansie & Fargo, 2009; Schafer, Huebner, & Bynum, 2006). Daily reports of crime victimization in the media exacerbate the fear but other things do too. Perceptions of neighborhood safety, ability to defend oneself, and other factors also contribute.

The psychological impact of criminal violence on its direct victims is substantial and far-reaching. In fact, in many cases, the psychological trauma experienced by victims of crime may be more troubling to the victim than the physical injury or the loss of property. Psychological reactions to criminal victimization can range from mild to severe. Mild reactions to stress are characterized by a variety of symptoms, including minor sleep disturbances, irritability, worry, interpersonal strain, attention lapses, and the exacerbation of prior health problems (Markesteyn, 1992). Severe reactions, on the other hand, may include serious depression, anxiety disorders, alcohol and drug abuse problems, and thoughts about or attempts at suicide (S. D. Walker & Kilpatrick, 2002). One of the most devastating and common reactions to criminal victimization is *posttraumatic stress disorder*. Posttraumatic stress disorder, abbreviated PTSD, is so important in the understanding and treatment of criminal victimization that it will be worthwhile to discuss the symptoms and what is known about it in some detail.

Posttraumatic Stress Disorder (PTSD)

PTSD is a common psychological reaction to a highly disturbing, traumatic event, and it is usually characterized by recurrent, intrusive memories of the event. The memories tend to be vividly sensory, are experienced as relatively uncontrollable, and evoke extreme distress (Halligan, Michael, Clark, & Ehlers, 2003). As we will note below, it is now documented that many veterans of wars in Vietnam, the Persian Gulf, Iraq, and Afghanistan have suffered or still suffer from PTSD, and it is likely that veterans of earlier wars did as well, although the condition was not recognized. According to the *DSM-IV* (American Psychiatric Association, 1994), PTSD is

> the development of characteristic symptoms following exposure to extreme traumatic stress or involving direct personal experience of an event that involves actual or threatened death or serious injury, or other threat to one's physical integrity; or witnessing an event that involves death, injury, or threat to the physical integrity of another person; or learning about unexpected or violent death, serious harm, or threat of death or injury experienced by a family member or other close associate. (p. 424)

The precipitating event would be substantially distressing to almost anyone and is "usually experienced with intense fear, terror, and helplessness" (American Psychiatric Association, 1994, p. 424).

PTSD is diagnosed by a mental health professional when the biological, psychological, and social effects of trauma are severe enough to have impaired a victim's social and occupational functioning. PTSD may be either acute (when duration of symptoms is less than 3 months) or chronic (when symptoms last longer than 3 months), or the victim may show a delayed onset (when at least 6 months have passed between the traumatic event and the onset of symptoms). The usual course is for symptoms to be strongest soon after the event and then diminish over time. Symptoms may be more severe and longer lasting if the trauma is perceived by the victim as intentionally human made rather than an accident or a natural catastrophe. In other words, victims of violence such as rape, war, or a terrorist attack would be more likely to have long-lasting and more severe symptoms than those persons who experience a hurricane, earthquake, tornado, or an *accidental* plane crash.

PTSD symptoms include intense fear, helplessness, or horror. In addition, the victims continually re-experience the traumatic event in their thoughts and reactions, persistently avoid things that remind them of the incident, and have persistent symptoms of high levels of anxiety and stress that were not present before the trauma. The symptoms usually wax and wane, coming back and then going into remission for a time.

Surveys estimate that lifetime prevalence (meaning sometime in their lifetime) of PTSD among American adults ranges between 7 and 12% (Breslau, 2002; Kessler et al. 2005; Ozer, Best, Lipsey, & Weiss, 2003). Many Americans across the nation experienced considerable trauma after terrorists flew two airliners into the World Trade Center and another into the Pentagon, killing more than 3,000 persons. Still more were killed when passengers deflected a fourth plane that crashed into the ground in Pennsylvania. However, research done prior to the attacks on September 11th indicated that of the 50 to 60% of the U.S. population who are exposed to traumatic stress, only 5 to 10% develop PTSD (Ozer et al., 2003). These data suggest that people's reactions to stress are unique and different for each individual. Nevertheless, for many years PTSD was under-recognized in routine clinical practice when PTSD symptoms were not the presenting complaint (Franklin, Sheeran, & Zimmerman, 2002), but with more knowledge about its existence this could be changing.

The lifetime prevalence of PTSD for women is twice that for men (10.4% vs. 5.0%), according to a nationally representative sample of 5,877 people ages 15 to 45 years (Kessler, Sonnega, Bromet, Hughes, & Nelson, 1995). The prevalence of PTSD is high among immigrants and refugees in the United States, particularly those who immigrated because of war or political persecution and torture (Gorman, 2001; Ozer et al., 2003). In a national survey of male and female Vietnam War veterans (Weiss et al., 1992), it was estimated that 30.9% of men and 26.0% of

Photo 10.1 An Iraq War veteran suffering from PTSD speaks with a physical therapist before attending a treatment session. In recent years, the documented instances of veterans experiencing symptoms of PTSD have increased.

women met the diagnostic criteria for PTSD at some point since their service in Vietnam (Ozer et al., 2003). Fifty percent of the veterans of the wars in Iraq and Afghanistan seeking treatment screen positive for PTSD, although much fewer receive an "official" diagnosis of the disorder (Ramchand et al., 2010). Among those previously deployed military personnel not seeking treatment, the prevalence estimates range from 5 to 20% (see Photo 10.1).

About 25 years ago, Kilpatrick et al. (1985) conducted a random community survey of more than 2,000 adult women who had personally experienced such trauma as rape, sexual molestation, robbery, and aggravated assault. The women were asked—among other things—whether they had thoughts of suicide after the incident, had attempted suicide, or had had a "nervous breakdown." The results clearly indicated that rape caused the most psychological trauma, with 19% of the rape victims having attempted suicide, 44% reporting suicide ideation at some point after the rape, and 16% saying that they had had a nervous breakdown. A comparison sample of women who had *not* been victims of any traumatic incidents reported the following: 2.2% had made suicide attempts, 6.8% had suicide ideation, and 3.3% said they had had nervous breakdowns in their lifetimes. H. S. Resnick, Kilpatrick, Dansky, Saunders, and Best (1993) found that 32% of rape victims met the criteria of PTSD at some point in their lives following the incident. Similarly, a study titled *Rape in America: A Report to the Nation* found that 31% of the women who had been raped developed symptoms that fully meet the criteria of PTSD (Kilpatrick, Edmunds, & Seymour, 1992). The same report indicated that rape victims are 3 times more likely than nonvictims to suffer major depression and 4 times more likely to show PTSD symptoms.

The psychological aftermath of exposure to traumatic life experiences is highly variable, with some persons adjusting well and others showing significant adverse emotional and psychological consequences of considerable duration (G. N. Marshall & Schell, 2002). Many researchers continue to search for an array of personal, social, and environmental factors that may contribute to PTSD. However, research on who is most susceptible to PTSD is unclear. It is apparent, though, that social support is both a prevention factor before the person experiences trauma and a factor that helps the person recover faster after the trauma has occurred (Ozer et al., 2003).

The research literature suggests that psychological harm is not qualitatively dissimilar for victims of different criminal offenses but rather is a matter of degree. That is, although the psychological reactions displayed by victims of sexual assault, robbery, burglary, and kidnapping vary in intensity, the nature of their distress is similar (Markesteyn, 1992). Therefore Markesteyn proposes that, in general, a victim's reactions and recovery may be mediated by three classes of variables: (1) victims' pre-victimization characteristics, (2) victims' post-victimization abilities to cope, and (3) factors related to the criminal event. Pre-victimization variables refer to such things as ethnic/minority background, religious or spiritual beliefs, socioeconomic status, gender, and age. Perhaps, as we noted above, one of the most important pre-victimization variables is the quality and availability of supportive relationships. Factors related to the criminal event include the degree of violence involved and the location of the crime (e.g., at home or outside the home). Victims who are attacked in an environment they perceive as being "safe" have been shown to experience more negative reactions than those attacked in "unsafe" locations (Markesteyn, 1992). Post-victimization factors include the various coping mechanisms available to crime victims, such as ability to place the blame appropriately, perceived control over their lives, and social and professional support. Fear of being re-victimized is especially powerful as a post-victimization reaction. For example, mugging victims report an increased sense of vulnerability and an extreme awareness of themselves as potential targets of another mugging. Robbery victims refrain from going out at night, change their place of employment, move to a new house, or acquire weapons for self-defense (Cohn, 1974). On the basis of an extensive research literature review, Markesteyn concluded that, "almost without exception, the research has demonstrated a correlation between the positive support people receive and their ability to adapt to and successfully overcome stressful life events" (p. 25). Victim services intervention appears to be especially critical.

Short-term psychological reactions to nondomestic assaults (robbery, aggravated and simple assaults) experienced by 40% of victims include anger, difficulty sleeping, uneasiness, confusion, bewilderment, denial, and fear (Markesteyn, 1992). The most serious reactions of depression, helplessness, loss of appetite, nausea, and malaise are reported by 20 to 40% of the victims. Most of these effects persist for up to 3 weeks; 3 to 6 weeks later, approximately 15% of victims feel "very much" affected, and about 5% have lifelong reactions. Victims who do not receive support from others, especially professional intervention and treatment, are particularly at risk for developing subsequent psychological problems.

Homicide Victimization

On average, approximately 16,000 to 17,000 people are murdered each year in the United States (FBI, 2009). Homicide victims represent the smallest proportion (.002%) of violent crime victims, but the psychological devastation experienced by the families of victims is enormous. Approximately 1 in every 10,000 Americans will become a victim of homicide during his or her lifetime, a rate that has doubled since World War II (APA, 1996). The nation's youth are especially vulnerable, with nearly 3 of every 10,000 young males likely to be victims of homicide prior to their 18th birthday (APA, 1996). Murder rates of young minority males living in impoverished areas of large cities are much higher, with 1 in every 333 becoming a victim of a homicide before reaching the age of 25. The homicide rate of juveniles in the United States is very high compared to other developed, industrialized nations.

Homicides of young children are committed primarily by family members (71%), usually by "personal weapons" (such as hands and feet) used to batter, strangle, or suffocate victims (Finkelhor & Ormrod, 2001b). According to Finkelhor and Ormrod, although victims include approximately equal numbers of boys and girls, offenders include a disproportionate number of women. Children at the highest risk for homicide are those younger than age 1. Usually, children in this age group are killed by relatives who do not want the child or believe they are ill-equipped to provide for the child. When young children (younger than 5 years of age) are killed by parents, it is usually as a result of the demands and the constant attention they require. Two of the most common triggers of young-child homicide are crying that will not stop and toileting accidents (U.S. Advisory Board on Child Abuse and Neglect, 1995). These fatalities appear to be more common in conditions of poverty and in families marked by divorce or absence of the father.

Middle childhood (ages 6–11) is a time when homicide risk is relatively low, whereas the risk of homicide for teenagers (ages 12–17) is high, remaining constant at 10% higher than the average homicide rate for all persons (Fox & Zawitz, 2001). Unlike homicides of children younger than age 12, relatively few homicides of teenagers (9%) are committed by family members.

As pointed out by Finkelhor and Ormrod (2001b), the actual homicide rate for young children may be higher than the statistics suggest. Homicides of young children are difficult to document because they can resemble deaths resulting from accidents and other causes. A child who dies from sudden infant death syndrome (SIDS) may be difficult to distinguish from one who has been smothered, or a child who has been intentionally dropped may have injuries similar to those who died from an accidental fall (Finkelhor & Ormrod, 2001b).

Relationship of the Offender to the Victim

Figure 10.1 shows the relationship of the victim to the offender, based on 2001 data reported by the FBI. As illustrated, about 13% of the homicides were a result of one family member killing another family member. Figure 10.1 also shows the number of victims killed within the family and other known relationships, with wife and acquaintance victims being the most common.

Figure 10.1 Relationship of Homicide Victims to Offenders

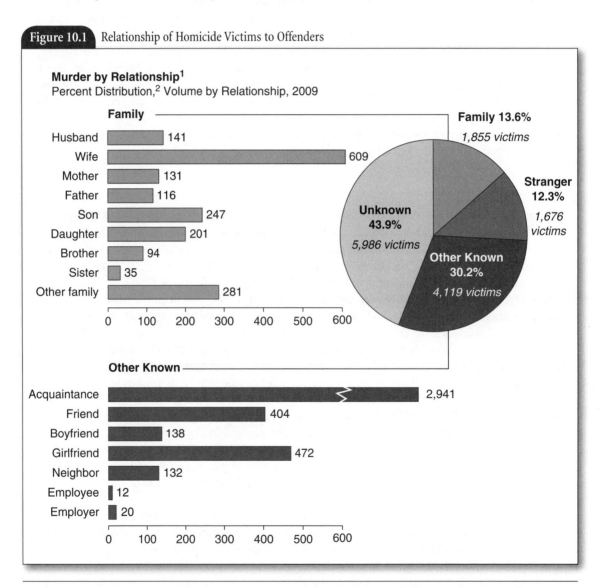

Note: Figures are based on 13,636 murder victims for whom supplemental homicide data were received, and includes the 5,986 victims for which the relationship was unknown.

[1]Relationship is that of victim to offender.

[2]Due to rounding, the percentages may not add up to 100.0.

Death Notification

Notification of family members of a death that resulted from violent crime is among the most challenging for professionals whose responsibility it is to deliver the message (C. A. Ellis & Lord, 2002). The best available data indicate that nearly 2% of the adults in the U.S. population have lost an immediate family member due to criminal homicide (Amick-McMullan, Kilpatrick, & Resnick, 1991; S. D. Walker & Kilpatrick, 2002). It is also very often the most traumatic event in the lives of family members and loved ones. Not only is **death notification** highly stressful and intense, but the survivors have also had no time to prepare psychologically.

An inappropriate or poorly done notification can prolong survivors' grieving process and delay their recovery from the trauma for years. In the victimology literature, survivors are often referred to as "covictims," a term that will be defined and discussed below. During notification and thereafter, the covictim's needs may include (1) an opportunity for ventilation of emotion; (2) calm, reassuring authority; (3) restoration of control; and (4) preparation for what they need to do next (C. A. Ellis & Lord, 2002).

Forensic psychologists would most likely be involved in death notification by training and providing supportive counseling to police officers, mental health professionals, and death notification teams who are expected to provide the services to families and covictims of violent crime on a regular basis. There are several models for training death notifiers, but the best-known and probably the most heavily relied on model was developed by Mothers Against Drunk Driving (MADD) (C. A. Ellis & Lord, 2002). Even with the availability of the training protocol offered by MADD, however, many death notifiers lack formal training (Stewart, Lord, & Mercer, 2001). Several other handbooks or manuals with training suggestions for death notification are also available. The U.S. Office for Victims of Crime (OVC), in cooperation with the National Sheriffs' Association, has prepared a handbook titled *First Response to Victims of Crime 2001* (Gillis, 2001), and the National Organization for Victim Assistance (1998) has published the second edition of the *Community Crisis Response Team Training Manual.* Chapter 6 of the manual is directly related to procedures and suggestions for death notification. Janice Lord (1997, 2001) has also been a leading expert in developing practices for death notification and has written several manuals or brochures for the OVC. In 1995, the OVC supported the MADD protocol in revising their death notification curriculum and tested it in seven sites (C. A. Ellis & Lord, 2002). Experienced death notifiers reported that their greatest unmet educational needs were the following:

- Specific details on how to deliver a notification
- How to manage immediate reactions of the family
- How to manage their own reactions
- General aspects of death notification

According to C. A. Ellis and Lord (2002), death notifiers should be sensitive, mature, positive, and calm persons who sincerely wish to become notifiers. Stressed, anxious individuals who lack confidence in delivering the message properly probably should not be selected as notifiers. Because death notification is a stressful event for all participants, burnout is a prominent danger for those professionals who are intimately involved on a regular basis. An important role for the psychologists in these situations is to provide support and counseling to the victim service providers and be watchful for burnout symptoms.

Reactions of Homicide Covictims

My brother was killed by another kid 16 years ago, when he was 15. My family's never been the same. People who talk about "closure" or "moving on" just don't get it. There's never "closure."

My father's in jail because he killed my mother. He can rot there forever. I don't care.

These statements, made some years ago by students in our classes, highlight the terrible suffering and grief faced by what are called **covictims** of violent crime. Both direct victims and those who are close to them are likely to feel the effects of what occurred for many years to come. This is particularly so with violent crimes.

The term covictim is often used to emphasize the depth of the homicide's emotional impact.

In the aftermath of the murder it is the covictim who deals with the medical examiner, the criminal and juvenile system, and the media. The term covictim may be expanded to any group or community that is touched by the murder: a classroom, a dormitory, a school, an office, or a neighborhood. Most of the individuals who make up these communities are wounded emotionally, spiritually, and psychologically by a murder, some more deeply than others. (C. A. Ellis & Lord, 2002, p. 2)

To be effective, victim service providers must be knowledgeable and carefully trained to deal with the wide range of reactions and needs of victims and covictims as well as the investigative and judicial processes involved in homicide cases. Competent, well-trained service providers are responsible and ethical professionals who recognize cultural diversity, understand the role that culture and ethnicity play with regard to individuals and groups, and understand the socioeconomic and political factors that affect these groups (C. I. Hall, 1997). Covictims may respond to the notification of the death of their loved ones in a way that is compatible with their cultural/ethnic ways of dealing with death, in combination with their psychological, emotional, and spiritual strengths and weaknesses.

Family members exhibit a wide range of emotions when a loved one is murdered. The available research suggests that the reactions of survivors of homicidal death differ significantly from those of people who grieve the loss of a loved one who died nonviolently (Sprang, McNeil, & Wright, 1989). The process of mourning for families of murder victims lasts longer, is more intense, and is more complex (Markesteyn, 1992). The grief reactions of homicide survivors appear to be deeper, display rage and vengefulness more often, and result in longer-lasting anxiety and phobic reactions (Amick-McMullen, Kilpatrick, Veronen, & Smith, 1989; Markesteyn, 1992). As pointed out by L. Miller (2008), "the cruel and purposeful nature of murder compounds the rage, grief, and despair of the survivors" (p. 368). The greater the perceived intentionality and malevolence of the murder, the higher is the covictims' distress. Covictims often suffer from intrusive and repetitive images of the violence; nightmares; and episodic, turbulent emotions of anger and grief. Excessive yearning or searching for the deceased, feelings of loneliness or emptiness, a sense of purposelessness or futility, and emotional numbness or detachment are also frequent symptoms of grief brought on by a violent death of a loved one (Carlson & Dutton, 2003). In addition to these symptoms, homicidal death bereavement responses include rage, desire for revenge directed toward the killer, and frustrations with the criminal justice system (S. A. Murphy et al., 1999).

Covictim reactions may be especially intense if the deceased was subjected to torture, sexual assault, or other intrusive or heinous acts (C. A. Ellis & Lord, 2002). Covictims often need to be reassured that the death was quick and painless and that suffering was minimal. "If the death was one of torture or of long duration, they may become emotionally fixated on what the victim must have felt and the terror experienced" (C. A. Ellis & Lord, 2002, Chap. 12, p. 8). If the offender was of another racial/ethnic or other minority group, the covictim may develop a biased view of that particular group, which may have to be dealt with during counseling.

Complicated Bereavement

A particular challenge for counselors and psychologists is when the survivors cannot find any kind of meaning in the death, a situation that is quite common for parents who lose a child through a violent death, such as murder or suicide (L. Miller, 2008). In his review of the grief literature, Neimeyer (2000) writes,

Taken together, these studies document that the 'search for meaning' plays a compelling role in the grief of the great majority (70–85%) of persons experiencing sudden, potentially traumatizing bereavement, although a significant minority apparently copes straightforwardly with their loss, without engaging in deep-going reflection about its significance. (p. 549)

According to Neimeyer, the quest for meaning in a violent death is an individual odyssey but appears to center around finding benefit in the experience. Grief counselors find that it is helpful to survivors to shift from an early emphasis on finding an answer to the question of "why" the death occurred, to a later focus on the positive benefits of the loss. For example, an individual may find new meaning in his or her life and set forth on a path to a new, positive life direction. More specifically, a person may decide to live more fully in the present, and develop a more compassionate and expressive approach to others.

Some experts indicate that survivors who cannot "find meaning" are far more likely to experience a syndrome called *complicated bereavement* (Neimeyer, Prigerson, & Davies, 2002). Complicated bereavement as discussed by Neimeyer et al. involves symptoms that are not considered psychologically healthy. They can include prolonged and obsessive searching for the loved one, preoccupation with thoughts of the death, excessive irritability and bitterness, disbelief, and lack of acceptance of the death. There often are serious suicide thoughts in a desire to rejoin the loved one. While some of these symptoms are characteristic of the grieving process, it is their length and intensity that distinguish complicated bereavement from "normal" bereavement.

The grief literature indicates that most survivors of *nonviolently* bereaved family members eventually make a reasonable recovery and move on as best they can. By contrast, survivors of those who die violent deaths take longer to recover. S. A. Murphy et al. (1999) reported that one-third of the parents of children who died violent deaths continued to show their trauma responses and psychological distress at least 2 years after the child's death. In a later study (S. A. Murphy, Johnson, & Lohan, 2002), two-thirds of the parents (both mothers and fathers) met the diagnostic criteria for mental distress (depression, anxiety, cognitive disorganization, detachment from their world) 5 years after the violent death of their child. Clinicians and researchers interested in bereavement believe that the grief process that follows the violent death of a loved one represents a distinctive type of grief response that requires special training and skills to treat effectively (Carlson & Dutton, 2003).

Sexual Assault Victimization

Characteristics of the Victims

Age

Rape and sexual assault are primarily crimes against youth, at least according to available statistics. These statistics must be viewed guardedly, however, in light of the low reporting rates of sexual assault in general. Older women, married women, and men, for example, may be less likely to report this type of victimization. The National Women's Study (Tjaden & Thoennes, 1998a) reported the following data concerning the age of victims:

- 32% of sexual assaults occurred when the victim was between the ages of 11 and 17.
- 29% of all forcible rapes occurred when the victim was younger than age 11.
- 22% occurred between the ages 18 and 24.
- 7% occurred between ages 25 and 29.
- 6% occurred when the victim was older than 29 years old.

Again, these data must be viewed cautiously, because sexual assault of older individuals—including the elderly—within their residences are likely to go unreported, as are incidents of marital and acquaintance rape.

For example, Rennison (2002b) reports that 63% of completed rapes, 65% of attempted rapes, and 74% of completed and attempted sexual assaults are not reported in the United States.

Additional data collected from the National Incident-Based Reporting System add a more comprehensive picture, but the age distribution differs. NIBRS indicates that more than two-thirds of all victims of sexual assault reported to law enforcement agencies were juveniles (younger than age 18) (Snyder, 2000). More than half of all juvenile victims were younger than age 12. More specifically, 33% of all victims of sexual assault reported to law enforcement were ages 12 through 17, and 34% were younger than age 12. Fourteen percent of victims were younger than age 5 (see Figure 10.2). In fact, for victims younger than age 12, the 4-year-olds were at greatest risk of being sexually assaulted.

NIBRS data indicate juveniles were the largest majority of the victims of forcible fondling (84%), forcible sodomy (79%), and sexual assault with an object (75%), but they were the victims in less than half (46%) of forcible rapes (Snyder, 2000).

Although babysitters are responsible for a relatively small portion of the crimes against young children (4.2%), children at risk of physical assaults by babysitters are younger (ages 1–3) than those at risk of sex crimes (ages 3–5) (Finkelhor & Ormrod, 2001a). Males constitute the majority of sex-offending babysitters reported to the police (77%), whereas females make up the majority of physical assaulters (64%).

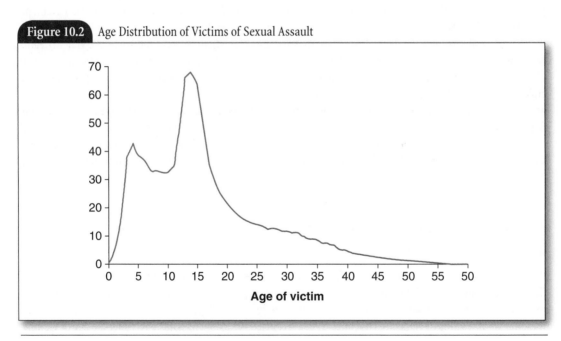

Figure 10.2 Age Distribution of Victims of Sexual Assault

Age of victim

Source: Snyder (2000).

Gender

Overall, an estimated 91% of the victims of rape and sexual assault are female (Greenfeld, 1997). The NIBRS data on juvenile victims show that females were more than 6 times as likely as males to be victims of sexual assault (Snyder, 2000). Moreover, 89% of the victims younger than age 6 were female. The majority of juvenile victims of forcible sodomy (54%) were males, whereas young females were the large majority of victims in incidents of sexual assault with an object (87%) and forcible fondling (82%).

The child molester, or pedophile, is almost always male, but the victim may be of either gender. As mentioned in Chapter 9, however, researchers are beginning to question the assumption that females rarely commit sexual assaults against children (Becker et al., 2001; Sandler & Freeman, 2007). Heterosexual pedophilia—male adult with female child—appears to be the more common type, with available data suggesting that three-quarters of male pedophiles choose female victims exclusively (Langevin, 1983; Lanyon, 1986). Homosexual pedophilia—adult male with male child—appears to be substantially less frequent, occurring in about 20 to 23% of the reported cases. A small minority of pedophiles prefer children of either gender.

Extent of Injury to Victims

Data on physical injury from sexual assault reveals that

- 70% of rape victims reported no physical injuries;
- 4% sustained serious physical injuries;
- 24% received minor physical injuries.

These data suggest that most victims will not exhibit overt physical evidence that most people believe is characteristic of violent sexual attacks. Unfortunately, many people who see no clear evidence of physical injury will conclude that the victim must have consented. In addition, even though some attacks do not result in physical injury or death, sexual assaults inflict enormous psychological harm on victims, especially children.

Relationship of the Victim to the Offender

Rape

The legal scope of forcible rape has traditionally been confined to imposed sexual contact or assault of adolescent and adult females who are not related to the offender. In view of the fact that rape most often occurs between acquaintances, relatives, and spouses, this traditional definition is drastically outdated. Kilpatrick et al. (2002), for example, report compelling evidence that most rapes are of intimate partners and not strangers. Their data indicate that

- 24.4% of rapists were strangers;
- 21.9% were husbands or ex-husbands;
- 19.5% were boyfriends or ex-boyfriends;
- 9.8% were relatives;
- 14.6% were other nonrelatives, such as friends or neighbors.

Still, many people (including the victims themselves) do not define sexual attacks as rape unless the assailant is a stranger. Thus, if the victim is sexually assaulted by a husband, boyfriend, or a "date," she is unlikely to report the incident. Criminal justice officials and the general public frequently feel that marital or date rape is unimportant because they believe that it is less psychologically traumatic to the victim and more difficult to prove. Prosecutors, for example, admit they are reluctant to prosecute marital or date rape cases because of concerns that it is difficult to convince juries that husbands or boyfriends could be sexual assailants. However, available data suggest that more than 40% of the total rapes that occur may be

Photo 10.2   At a Denim Day speak-out and rally in Los Angeles, high school students read T-shirts designed by survivors of sexual abuse. Clothesline projects like this one are a sobering reminder of the pain suffered by those who have experienced these crimes.

committed by husbands or male friends (Kilpatrick, Best, Saunders, & Veronen, 1988). (See Photo 10.2 depicting a clothesline project on behalf of survivors of sexual assault and domestic violence.)

Child Sexual Abuse

In most cases of child sexual abuse, the offender and the victim know one another, often very well, and the crime frequently involves relatives (incest). Many victims are simply looking for affection, wanting only to be hugged or cuddled or to have human contact. The offender frequently misinterprets this behavior as a form of "seduction" and misgauges the amount of power he has over the child. Very often, the child may participate in the molestation primarily because he or she is too frightened to protest. Research indicates that pedophiles, on average, tend to have positive feelings toward their victims, generally perceiving them as willing participants, and that they frequently victimize children living in their immediate households (Miner, Day, & Nafpaktitis, 1989). In many cases, the sexual behavior between the offender and the same child has gone on for a sustained period of time.

Additional Victim Data

Approximately 90% of the time, the rape or sexual attack involves a single offender. The most common reason given by adult victims of rape or sexual assault for reporting the crime to the police was to prevent further crimes by the offender against them. The most common reason given by the victim for *not* reporting the crime to the police was that it was considered a personal matter. Nationally, per capita rates of rape are found to be highest among residents ages 16 to 19, low-income residents, and urban residents (Greenfeld, 1997). There are no significant differences in the rate of rape or sexual assault among racial groups.

Juvenile victims were more likely to be victimized in a residence than adult victims (Snyder, 2000). The most common nonresident locations for sexual assaults of juveniles are roadways, fields/woods, schools, and hotels/motels. The weapons most commonly used in sexually assaulting juveniles were hands and fists.

Psychological Impact of Sexual Assault

Sexual assault produces a broad spectrum of psychological reactions in its victim. In some of the literature on sexual assaults, the woman "victim" is now often referred to as a "survivor," "a label that emphasizes her strength and avoids the connotation of passivity associated with the label of 'victim'" (Felson, 2002, p. 136). However, we will continue to use the more recognized term *victim* in this context to emphasize the point that we are talking about *victimization* of all kinds in this chapter and discussing the many *victim* services available. In a sense, all victims who do not die can be considered survivors.

Sexual victimization usually provokes some type of reaction and physical, social, psychological, and often economic or—in the case of students—academic loss. After a sexual assault, some student victims have difficulty concentrating, begin to miss classes, and fall behind in their school assignments. Some withdraw completely from high school or college. Furthermore, service providers and psychologists should be aware that many victims of sexual assault are often concerned about people finding out about the assault, including family members (Kilpatrick et al., 2002). As one student commented, "I never wanted to tell my mother; it would have broken her heart."

Among the more common psychological reactions to sexual assault are PTSD, shame, helplessness, anger, or depression. The quality of life usually suffers as victims experience sleeplessness, nightmares, social isolation, flashbacks, and intense feelings of insecurity. Some research has found that 94% of rape victims met symptomatic criteria for PTSD shortly after the assault, and 47% continued to show symptoms of PTSD 3 months after the assault (Foa, Rothbaum, Riggs, & Murdock, 1991). In another study, 16.5% of rape victims showed PTSD symptoms 17 years after the assault (Kilpatrick, Saunders, Veronen, Best, & Von, 1987). Some of the mental health problems become life threatening in nature. Rape victims are 4 times more likely than non–crime victims to have contemplated suicide. Moreover, "rape victims were also 13 times more likely than non–crime victims to have actually made a suicide attempt (13% vs. 1%)" (Kilpatrick et al., 2002, Chap. 10, p. 15).

Forensic psychologists and other psychologists working in forensic settings are often asked to do an assessment, provide treatment, or become an expert witness in sexual assault cases. The assessment may be done to evaluate the victim's claims, responses, and reactions, especially if they appear to be life threatening. The psychologist should be knowledgeable about the victim's cultural and ethnic background and how that culture perceives victims of sexual assault. A number of rating scales and psychological inventories are available to document the victim's level of trauma.

Expert testimony might occur in a criminal or a civil case. A civil case may involve a victim suing an alleged attacker to recover damages or suing a third party for failing to provide adequate protection. A psychologist might testify in support of the victim's claim of severe emotional injuries, such as PTSD, which has led to the devastation of the victim's social, occupational, and/or financial life.

Psychological Effects of Child Sexual Abuse

Child sexual abuse is the exploitation of a child or adolescent for another person's sexual and control gratification (Whitcomb, Hook, & Alexander, 2002). Research offers strong support for the assumption that sexual abuse in childhood (both violent and nonviolent) produces long-term psychological problems (Briere, 1988). Reports of severe depression, guilt, strong feelings of inferiority or inadequacy, substance abuse, suicidality, anxiety, sleep problems, and fears and phobias are common. Children may feel responsible for the abuse because no obvious force or threat was used by the adult, and only after the victims become adults do they realize that they were powerless to protect themselves.

The overwhelming evidence from both clinical and empirical studies is that most victims of sexual abuse are negatively affected by their experience (Haugaard & Reppucci, 1988). However, the long-term effects of child sexual abuse are unclear and appear to differ significantly from individual to individual. Although some victims apparently suffer no negative long-term consequences, studies with adults confirm the long-term effects of sexual abuse mentioned in the clinical literature for a majority of the victims (Browne & Finkelhor, 1986). For example, adults who were sexually victimized as children are more likely to manifest depression, self-destructive behavior, anxiety, feelings of isolation and stigma, poor self-esteem, and substance abuse. A history of childhood sexual abuse is also associated with greater risk for mental health and adjustment problems in adulthood.

Studies suggest that sexual abuse by fathers or stepfathers may have a more negative impact than abuse by perpetrators outside the home. Furthermore, the use of force or physical coercion in the assault usually results in more trauma for the child (Browne & Finkelhor, 1986). Experiences involving intercourse or attempted intercourse and genital contact by mouth also seem to be more troubling than acts involving touching of unclothed breasts or genitals. Penetration is especially traumatic for the young victim.

The child sexual abuse syndrome (CSAS), or **child sexual abuse accommodation syndrome (CSAAS)**, originally proposed by Summit (1983), is reserved for a cluster of behaviors that occur in children who have been victims of sexual abuse by a family member or by a trusted adult. According to Summit, children do not necessarily have an innate sense that sexual activity with an adult is wrong. However, if the sexual activity continues, the adults usually must pressure or threaten the child to prevent others from knowing about the activity. Often, the abuser presents these threats and pressures in such a way that the child is led to believe something terrible will happen (perhaps to a family member) if this "private" knowledge becomes known. Hence, the child is placed in the position of being responsible for the welfare of the family. The child also feels helpless to stop the activity. Thus, the child must "accommodate" these secrets and incorporate them into his or her daily living pattern.

However, there is still the question of whether the child sexual abuse syndrome actually exists. "At this point, professionals have not reached consensus on whether a syndrome exists that can detect child sexual abuse" (J. E. B. Myers, 1991, p. 82). Haugaard and Reppucci (1988) write, "The principal flaw with the notion of a specific syndrome is that no evidence indicates that it can discriminate between sexually abused children and those who have experienced other trauma" (pp. 177–178). Many of the behaviors listed by Summit (1983) may occur in any child who has experienced other types of trauma besides sexual abuse, although the behaviors usually do not demonstrate precocious sexual awareness. "As a result, one cannot reliably say that a child exhibiting a certain combination of behaviors has been sexually abused rather than, for instance, physically abused, neglected, or brought up by psychotic or antisocial parents" (Haugaard & Reppucci, 1988, p. 178).

Child sexual abuse accommodation syndrome has questionable validity as a meaningful diagnosis or indicator of sexual abuse. On the other hand, children are highly vulnerable to PTSD, a more useful concept in describing the psychological impact of child sexual abuse (Whitcomb et al., 2002).

In child sexual abuse cases, the forensic psychologist may be asked to evaluate the child to determine if the allegations have foundation and, if they do, what level of trauma has been experienced. The forensic psychologist may also be asked to assess the competency of the child to testify in the case and may also help in preparing the child to testify. Finally, the psychologist may act as an expert witness in the case, such as testifying about the validity of the child's memory or level of understanding.

Property Crime Victimization

Research on the effects of victimization in property crimes is very limited. Consequently, we will only touch briefly on this topic, focusing on the effects of burglary.

Psychological Impact of Burglary

According to the UCR, **burglary** is the unlawful entry into a structure, with or without force, with intent to commit a theft or other felony. According to the NCVS (BJS, 2002b), approximately 4 million residences are burglarized each year. Although there is a considerable amount of information on burglary and how to prevent it, very little information is available for how most people react or adjust to this frequent crime.

Burglary is officially classified as a property crime, but it is also in many ways an interpersonal crime (Merry & Harsent, 2000). Many victims of burglary feel psychologically traumatized beyond the simple material loss. The invasion of the safety, privacy, and sanctity of the home can be discomforting and stressful, and a victim may take a long time to recover from the invasion. According to Merry and Harsent, "[The home] is a special place that is central to our daily lives, a place that is at the beginning and end of most of our journeys; it is chosen and personalized" (p. 36). Some victims describe burglary as a rape of their home, especially in cases when the burglar disturbed or damaged personal photographs, letters, or diaries. The distress levels tend to be more pronounced when the invasion extends to personal sectors of the home, such as bedrooms, closets, chests of drawers, bathrooms, and desks. Some victims, after being burglarized, install security systems, increase and improve the locks, buy "guard" dogs, or even move to new homes.

Some burglars also try to upset the members of the residence by leaving messages or objects, vandalizing some personal items, or indicating they will be back. According to Merry and Harsent (2000), this aspect represents the "interpersonal dimension" of the crime. The emotional reactions of burglarized victims to these "signatures" often run the gamut from anger to fear and depression (B. B. Brown & Harris, 1989). It may well be that the victim's feelings of fear, vulnerability, or even anger are psychological reactions or "losses" that can be translated into psychological "gains" for the offender. Therefore, the burglar may gain psychologically as well as materially.

Most items stolen are never recovered, and if the property has unique or sentimental value for the victim, emotional reactions can be intense. It is not unusual for the victim or victims to become angry toward the police for their seeming lack of concern.

SUMMARY AND CONCLUSIONS

As we noted at the beginning of the chapter, forensic psychologists and other mental health practitioners will be increasingly employed as consultants, instructors, expert witnesses, evaluators, therapists, and service providers to victim service organizations in the coming years. In this chapter, we explored some of the many areas in which their services will be most needed in the very near future and emphasized the need for a deep appreciation for **multiculturalism** and diverse cultural norms and values. The knowledgeable forensic psychologist will also be capable of working with many victims with disabilities, a group that represents a very large, diverse, but underserved population in American society.

We reviewed some highlights of victim rights, with an emphasis on victims who must deal with the criminal justice system. Although victim rights and victim services may be provided for in both federal and state regulations, programs and providers often are not funded sufficiently.

Crime victimization data were covered briefly, focusing on some of the racial and ethnic-minority differences reported in the available victimization statistics. The psychological effects of criminal victimization, particularly violent victimization, were described in some detail. PTSD appears to be the most common psychological reaction to crime of all kinds, although the reactions are usually most intense and long lasting after a violent incident. The *covictims* of homicide incidents, especially when the dead victim is a family member, are usually devastated, and their suffering is often not recognized by others. Sexual assault also represents a highly traumatic event that is often followed by a wide range of psychological reactions and disorders, especially PTSD. Child sexual abuse, believed to be more prevalent than official statistics indicate, can have long-lasting psychological damage for some children that will remain with them for the rest of their lives. However, the chapter also emphasized that victims respond to trauma and disaster differently, with some coping extremely well while others struggle. In fact, many victims today prefer to refer to themselves as survivors rather than victims. Consequently, the existence of "textbook syndromes" as a direct result of victimization should be viewed cautiously and with the understanding that all victims do not exhibit a set pattern of symptoms.

Property crime victimization and its psychological consequences are unexplored areas. Thus, we could only briefly touch on the psychological effects of burglary victimization because it is one of the very few areas of property crime that has received any significant research. Research on the effects of white-collar crime victimization is needed as well. All crimes engender psychological effects and can leave emotional scars on their victims. Therefore, an area worth exploring for those forensic psychologists interested in doing research would be the psychological effects of these understudied but very common offenses.

KEY CONCEPTS

Allocution

Burglary

Child sexual abuse accommodation syndrome
  (CSAAS)

Compensation

Covictim

Death notification

Multiculturalism

National Crime Victimization Survey (NCVS)

Notification

Posttraumatic stress disorder (PTSD)

Restitution

Restorative justice

Victimless crimes

QUESTIONS FOR REVIEW

1. What is monocultural psychology, and what challenges does it present to forensic psychologists?

2. Are persons with disabilities more likely to be victims of crime? Explain your answer.

3. What are the two venues in which victims of crime may seek recourse?

4. List any five rights granted to victims as a result of the victims' rights movement.

5. What type of information about victimization is available from the NCVS?

6. List some of the common psychological effects of crime on its victims.

7. What role do forensic psychologists play in dealing with the covictims of criminal homicide?

8. What role do forensic psychologists play in dealing with adult victims of sexual assault?

9. What role do forensic psychologists play in dealing with victims of child sexual abuse?

10. Describe Summit's child sexual abuse accommodation syndrome and state the controversy associated with it.

11

Family Violence, Abuse, and Victimization ❖

CHAPTER OBJECTIVES

- Review the various issues in family violence and its psychological consequences.
- Describe intimate partner violence.
- Describe forensic assessment of domestic violence.
- Review research on child abuse and its psychological consequences.
- Emphasize the strengths and limitations of human memory in reporting victimization and crime.
- Examine child abduction and its psychological effects.
- Introduce elder abuse and neglect and review its devastating effects.

Forensic psychologists and other clinicians working within forensic settings frequently encounter both perpetrators and victims of violence among and within families and between intimate acquaintances. The tasks they perform include doing assessments, consulting with legal authorities and social service providers, testifying in courts, and providing psychotherapy for victims as well as offenders. As will be seen throughout this chapter, family violence in all of its manifestations is found at all socioeconomic levels and spares no age, race, religion, or ethnic group. However, with the economic downturn in recent years (2008–2010), the media are replete with stories about the link between families undergoing heavy financial strain and family violence. Yet despite the dramatic increase in stories about home foreclosures, job loss, and family violence, little contemporary empirical research has addressed the issue to date. Consequently, it is too soon to advance the argument that the current economic hardships for American families will lead to a significant increase in family violence.

The chapter begins with a discussion of the violence directed at spouses or other intimate partners, then moves to child abuse and the more serious or unusual physical forms of abuse, including infanticide, Munchausen syndrome by proxy, and shaken baby syndrome. Repressed and recovered memory is discussed in some detail because this topic has received considerable attention in recent years, especially in cases involving child sexual abuse. It is one of the most controversial topics in psychology today. Child and juvenile abduction is presented as a special area that has not received the professional attention it deserves. The chapter ends with another neglected topic, elder abuse. There is a rapidly growing demand for forensic gero-psychologists throughout the country, and we will describe some of the career opportunities in that expanding discipline.

Intimate Partner Violence

The broad term **family violence** (also known as domestic or intrafamilial violence) refers to any assault, including sexual assault, or other crime that results in the personal injury or death of one or more family or household member(s) by another who is or was residing in the same dwelling. It often occurs in intimate relationships, for instance, between current or former spouses, partners, or significant others. As such, it is more likely to be called *intimate partner violence (IPV),* a term that also encompasses violence in a relationship where the two individuals may not be living together (or have lived together). Approximately 13% of all homicides involve one family member killing another family member (FBI, 2002b). Nearly one third of the victims of family homicides were wives slain by a husband or ex-husband, usually during an argument (see Table 11.1) (FBI, 2009). Approximately 1 in 4 American, British, and Australian women report experiencing a physical assault by an intimate partner at some point in their lives (Bedi & Goddard, 2007).

Table 11.1 Murder Circumstances, by Relationship, 2008

Circumstances Total	Family Murder Victims	Husband*	Wife*
Total	1841	119	577
Romantic triangle	9	2	6
Argument over money	29	1	4
Other arguments	737	78	291
Arson	7	0	3
Robbery	4	1	1
Larceny-theft	5	0	1
Narcotic drug laws	9	0	1
Brawl due to alcohol	14	2	0
Other—not specified	707	20	172
Unknown	293	15	96

Source: Federal Bureau of Investigation (2009).

*The relationship categories of husband and wife include both common-law and ex-spouses.

Whether referred to as domestic, family, intrafamilial, or intimate partner violence, it is found across all ethnic and racial groups and all socioeconomic classes. It occurs against people of all ages, cultures, and living conditions. However, research indicates that violence directed at women is more likely to occur in homes characterized by poverty, communities with few resources, socially isolated immigrant families, and subcultures where there is greater acceptance of gender inequities (L. E. Walker, 1999).

It should be emphasized that both men and women perpetrate violence, and some studies suggest that there is little difference in aggression between the sexes in this regard (e.g., Archer, 2002; Straus & Gelles, 1990). As pointed out by Menard, Anderson, and Godboldt (2009), however, these studies often are based on large community samples that self-report aggression using such measures as the Conflict Tactics Scale (CTS), to be discussed below. Self-reported aggression in this context includes situations in which a couple may have a physical altercation that does not necessarily result in calling police and that does not represent a pattern of continuing or escalating violence (M. P. Johnson, 2006). By contrast, official data such as the NCVS, records from shelters, and studies by other researchers indicate that IPV *that is persistent and escalating* is perpetrated chiefly by men against women.

In addition, there appear to be different motivations for the violence used by men versus the motivations for women (Menard et al., 2009). The motivations for **intimate partner violence**—as they are for all forms of human violence—are highly variable, but the overriding motive of male offenders who abuse women is to establish or maintain power and control over them. When women use violence in domestic situations, it is most often for self-defense, in anticipation of violence, or in retaliation for violence perpetrated against them (Meuer, Seymour, & Wallace, 2002). Many male abusers are serial abusers. That is, if they leave or are left by one victim, they quickly become involved with another partner whom they soon abuse. Furthermore, this cycle of violence or pattern of abuse is not easily broken, as we shall see.

Typical Development of an Intimate Partner Violence Relationship

Meuer et al. (2002) outline the typical sequence that characterizes the pattern of such violence, which they refer to broadly as domestic violence. They identify nine stages. It should be noted that we use opposite-sex pronouns (he and she) in the illustrations below because heterosexual relationships are dominant in society. We also refer to the abuser as male because these are the most typical abusive relationships. However, IPV also occurs in same-sex relationships, a topic we will return to in the pages ahead.

Stage 1 of such relationships identified by Meuer et al. (2002) seems wonderful and intense, with the husband or partner taking an active interest in everything his spouse or partner does and everywhere she goes. He wants to be with her all the time, flatters her, confides in her, and proclaims he wants to spend the rest of his life with her. Meuer et al. observe that many victims mistake these obsessive and controlling behaviors as devotion, rather than recognizing them as red flags that may lead to an abusive relationship. *Stage 2* emerges when he begins to insist on knowing her whereabouts at all times, begins making decisions for her, and demands her loyalty to the relationship. He indicates he is in charge, will make the rules, and expects her to follow him and attend to his needs. During this stage, he also may begin to blame a former spouse or partner for the problems in a previous relationship, saying—for example—that that person had him arrested or unjustifiably obtained a restraining order against him. During *Stage 3,* the woman becomes adjusted to the attention, jealousies, and control he displays. She makes a commitment to him—usually under his pressure—and convinces herself that she is happy to be with someone who cares so much for her. *Stage 4* is characterized by the beginning of excessive control through psychological and emotional abuse. He begins to demand control over things dealing with all phases of her life, including clothing, hairstyles, and how she should act. He becomes angry if she deviates from his requests. His actions communicate that she is unattractive or that her appearance is somehow faulty.

Stage 5 is characterized by the first incident of physical abuse. The victim will probably view the response as an aberration that is unlikely to occur again. The abuser often says he is sorry and that it will never happen again. She accepts his apologies and explanation and may wonder what she did to prompt his behavior. In *Stage 6*, the psychological and physical abuse occurs again. The victim will ask why he is repeating such behavior, and he will, in turn, blame the victim for prompting his abusive behavior because she is not meeting his expectations. He makes it clear that she is responsible for setting him off and that it will not happen again if she changes her ways. The victim at this stage begins to internalize the blame more completely. *Stage 7* occurs roughly simultaneously with Stage 6. Meuer et al. (2002) refer to this stage as the beginning of the isolation process. The abuser wants to know who she spends time with and either asks her to not see them again or forbids her to see them again. He further makes it difficult for her to see anyone and gets excessively suspicious if she has a good time with anyone but him. Eventually, she stops seeing people of whom he disapproves, and she becomes increasingly isolated.

As the relationship continues, she experiences considerable emotional conflict and confusion. This phase represents *Stage 8*. The abuser blames the victim, and the victim is confused about what is wrong. In *Stage 9*, the abuser increases his use of psychological threats and physical force to gain and maintain control and dominance. If she confronts him or threatens to leave him, he escalates his use of threats and force. The victim may eventually conclude that it is safer to stay in the relationship than to leave. She may feel she cannot make it on her own for a variety of reasons.

During the later stages, the abusive behavior is usually followed by promises that he will never do it again. As noted by Meuer and her colleagues (2002), most IPV victims repeatedly attempt to leave the relationship but return when they believe they cannot overcome the obstacles of getting away from the abuser.

According to these researchers, leaving the relationship is not always the best approach and may increase the potential danger to the victim. Unfortunately, there has been evidence that victims who attempt to leave are often stalked, harassed, and threatened on an ongoing basis. The stalking may occur even when a divorce is filed or granted. It was originally believed that if a battered woman could be persuaded to leave the abusive relationship, the violence would stop, but "many batterers continue to harass, stalk, and harm the woman long after she has left him, sometimes resulting in someone's death" (L. E. Walker, 1999, p. 25). In many cases, most of the reported injuries from domestic violence occur *after* the separation of the couple. Some evidence also suggests that women who leave their batterers are at a 75% greater risk of being killed by their batterers than those who stay (M. Wilson & Daly, 1993).

The above perspective—that leaving may not be the best thing—is strongly resisted by advocates of victims of IPV, who maintain that getting out of the relationship is still precisely what victims must do. For the person being abused, it seems to be a no-win situation: "If I stay, this will get worse; if I leave, he will come after me." In addition, society itself places obstacles in the victim's path. For example, economic options are limited, and deeply entrenched cultural norms hold the victim responsible for dealing with the violence against herself (Dobash & Dobash, 2000). Also, community support is too often unavailable. If shelters, support groups, and a supportive law enforcement response were consistently present, the odds of successfully escaping an abusive situation would increase. In general, advocates maintain, the risk of staying is much greater than the risk of leaving. This is a complex issue and one not clearly resolved by the empirical data. However, it is probably fair to say that most practicing psychologists working with victims of abuse would be supportive of their efforts to leave but would also help them to identify the resources necessary to enable them to do that.

Psychological Characteristics of Batterers

Battering is a term often reserved for *physical violence* experienced in intimate relationships, in a dating relationship, marriage or partnership, or separation and divorce. Some researchers use the term *battering* to represent the more serious and frequent abuse, including the more severe *psychological abuse.* Men who batter often deny or minimize their use of violence, or blame it on others. In fact, the shoving, kicking, striking, hitting, or punching he does to the victim is often not seen by the batterer as abuse (Meuer et al., 2002). Rather, he justifies his behavior as being provoked by, triggered by, or in response to something done by the victim. In other words, he perceives his behavior as a natural and understandable reaction to frustration.

A strong predictor of whether a man will abuse his spouse or significant other appears to be whether he has experienced or witnessed violence in his own family while growing up (Meuer et al., 2002). Violence is learned behavior that is passed down from one generation to the next (Eron, Gentry, & Schlegel, 1994; L. E. Walker, 1999). Not all men from abusive or violent homes become abusers themselves. Those who do, compared to those who do not, are less capable of attachment to others; are more impulsive; are more lacking in social skills; and possess different attitudes toward women, the masculine role in the family, and violence. Some research has also indicated that many batterers have serious mental disorders in addition to their problems with power and control over women that encourage their use of violence (D. Dutton & Golant, 1995; L. E. Walker, 1999). It appears, therefore, that treatment programs that focus on both the batterer's emotional problems and his misguided beliefs and values may help in the amelioration of domestic violence for those abusers who show signs of psychopathology.

Similar to other offenders discussed in earlier chapters (e.g., rapists, stalkers), batterers also have been studied for purposes of suggesting typologies or batterer types. A well-validated typology of batterers would allow a systematic examination of how and why different men use violence against their wives and partners, as well as help in the design of effective prevention and treatment strategies for dealing with them. After a thorough review of the research literature on batterers in domestic situations, Holtzworth-Munroe and Stuart (1994) were able to identify three types of male batterers that emerge with consistency in a variety of studies: (1) family only, (2) dysphoric/borderline, and (3) generally violent/antisocial. The typology is based on the severity and frequency of the marital violence, the generality of the violence (only within the family or outside the family), and the amount of emotional or mental dysfunction exhibited by the batterer.

Family-only batterers are typically not violent outside the family and engage in the least amount of severity and frequency of violence. Their violence tends to be periodic, primarily when stress and frustration reach a peak, and they do not demonstrate discernible indications of severe mental disorders or psychopathology. In addition, they are least likely to have previous arrest records and alcohol problems and are most likely to apologize after the violence. Their major problems are being inappropriately assertive in their relationships and their tendency to misinterpret social cues. Consequently, they have resorted to violence rather than appropriate nonviolent means to resolve conflicts with their partners. This group is estimated to constitute about 50% of the known batterers (Holtzworth-Munroe & Stuart, 1994).

Dysphoric/borderline batterers exhibit mental disorders and are psychologically disturbed and emotionally volatile. These individuals often engage in moderate to severe spousal abuse, including psychological and sexual abuse. Although this group's violence is mainly confined to the family, they may also exhibit some extrafamilial violence. Their anger is generalized and explosive in nature and is apt to become displayed anytime they become frustrated. The disturbed batterer also tends to have serious alcohol and drug abuse problems. It is estimated that this group comprises about 25% of the known batterers.

Generally violent/antisocial batterers are more likely to use weapons and are more prone to inflict severe injury on wives, partners, and other family members, in addition to engaging in extrafamilial violence. They also are more likely to have an extensive history of contacts with police, including arrests and convictions. Generally violent batterers tend to be highly impulsive and explosive. Moreover, they exhibit serious problems with alcohol and drug abuse, and many show characteristics of psychopathy. Overall, they probably make up about 25% of the batterer group (Holtzworth-Munroe & Stuart, 1994).

Mental health professionals have made some progress in the treatment of batterers, both with programs in the community and in prison settings. However, researchers have not yet concluded that any specific approach to treating batterers is significantly more effective than others, assuming equivalent training of the providers and a comprehensive treatment strategy (APA, 2003b). Most treatment programs include some form of cognitive-behavioral psychotherapy, although the specifics vary with the types of abuse for which the offender is being treated. Waltz, Babcock, Jacobson, and Gottman (2000) suggest that generally violent batterers and disturbed batterers are unlikely to benefit from short-term treatments focusing on anger management. According to Waltz et al., these approaches often assume—incorrectly—that the acquisition of anger control and attitude change are sufficient. In addition, a variety of broader, more complex issues may interfere with short-term treatment approaches. Long-term treatment strategies that concentrate on cognitive-behavioral and psychopathological issues are more likely to be effective. How effective these strategies are for psychopaths who are batterers remains an unfinished story. We simply do not have enough empirical data to know what works with this troubling group.

For family-only batterers, treatments that focus on violence, abusive behavior, and relationship problems are likely to be successful for these men because they appear to be more sensitive and empathic to the needs of others. One thing is clear, however. The form of treatment used by mental health professionals must address the offender's use of dominance and control, as well as the attitudes and cognitions that underlie his acts of violence.

Dropping out of treatment programs is a common problem that many clinicians face with their clients. Research has found that batterers who complete their treatment programs are less likely to recidivate (Cattaneo & Goodman, 2005). Interestingly, the source of referral to treatment as well as supervision appear to have some effect on the completion of treatment; that is, batterers who are referred by courts—rather than enrolling in a program voluntarily—and who are supervised while attending the programs are more likely to complete their treatment (S. J. Barber & Wright, 2010). It seems clear, then, that efforts should be made on three fronts: mandate treatment, encourage retention in treatment, and supervise offenders to make it less likely that they will drop out of the program.

Battered Woman Syndrome

Battered woman syndrome (BWS) is a term first used by psychologist Lenore Walker (1979), who identified the syndrome based on a volunteer sample of abused middle-class women. In her clinical practice, Walker observed a cluster of behavioral, cognitive, and emotional features that she believes are frequently found in women who have been battered and psychologically abused *over a period of time* by their partners. She later documented BWS more fully on the basis of extended interviews with 435 battered women (L. E. Walker, 1984). The core features she identified include feelings of learned helplessness (Seligman, 1975), the development of survival rather than escape skills (e.g., appeasing the batterer rather than planning to leave), low self-esteem, and feelings of depression. Currently, Lenore Walker (2006, 2009) considers BWS to be a subcategory of post-traumatic stress disorder. In recent years, she has developed and modified the Battered Woman Syndrome Questionnaire (BWSQ) (see L. E. Walker, 2009).

Lenore Walker (1979, 1986) contends that battering relationships generally follow a three-stage cycle of violence: (1) the tension-building phase, (2) the acute battering incident phase, and (3) the honeymoon or contrition phase. The cycle has similarities to the nine-stage sequence later proposed by Meuer et al. (2002) and discussed earlier. During the tension-building phase, there may be minor physical, emotional, or verbal abuse. During this phase, the victim often tries to placate her abuser but with only limited success. This initial phase is followed by a second phase that is characterized by an escalation of serious physical violence and the inability of the woman to placate the batterer at all, no matter what she does. This acute battering phase is followed by the "honeymoon stage" (also referred to as the "loving contrition stage"), in which the batterer expresses his regret for the assaultive behavior and vows to change his ways. He may send her flowers, give her gifts, and pay a great deal of attention to her. At some point, however, he communicates to her that the incident was her fault. Soon, the violence cycle is repeated.

According to Lenore Walker (1979), a woman qualifies for BWS when she has experienced the complete cycle at least *twice.* Walker (1989) further suggested that the third stage of the cycle often disappears as the relationship continues to deteriorate over time and the violence increases. She argued that, over time, the tension-building phase becomes more common, whereas the contrition phase eventually drops out of the cycle completely. Unless some effective intervention takes place, when Stage 3 ends, many battered women are in grave danger of becoming homicide victims.

Although Lenore Walker (1986) admits that not all battered women report many of the features she described, other researchers continue to challenge her general propositions on BWS (Levesque, 2001) and its scientific validity (see McMahon, 1999). Roger Levesque argues that one of the real dangers of indiscriminately applying the BWS label to all battered women is that it may mistakenly lead the public, lawmakers, and the courts to perceive women's positions in violent relationships to be essentially identical. As Levesque points out, cross-cultural analysis indicates that the abusive relationship dynamics found in U.S. studies on mainstream culture may not apply to other societies, cultures, or even subcultures within the United States: "Thus, different groups may experience maltreatment events differently, which may exacerbate the difficulties others face in situations that happen to garner the same label" (p. 51).

The term *BWS* also portrays a stereotypical image of battered women as helpless, passive, or psychologically impaired, and the battering relationship is seen as matching a single, stereotypical pattern of all domestic violence cases (M. A. Dutton, 1996). In contrast to the expected stereotypical pattern of depression, helplessness, and passivity, many battered women demonstrate a wide range of behavioral patterns and emotions that often reflect survival skills and effective adaptations to a serious, life-threatening situation. Unfortunately, the BWS label undermines the enormous coping skills and psychological strength of many—if not most—battered women across a broad spectrum of cultural and social circumstances.

Evan Stark (2002) strongly recommends that psychologists and other mental health practitioners, when preparing forensic assessments and legal testimony for the courts, emphasize the *process* of unique coercive control used by some batterers, rather than focusing strictly on the generalized psychological trauma assumed to be experienced by all battered women. Stark argues that stressing the systematic use of the abuse, coercion, and control in a *particular* relationship and the harms associated with this complete domination is a more meaningful approach than simply trying to identify the psychological damage done to the victim. Many victims, he notes, do not exhibit clearly discernible clusters of psychological maladjustment, depression, and helplessness outlined in much of the literature, even though they may have been subjected to incredible amounts of coercion, domination, and abuse during a lengthy relationship. Furthermore, Stark concludes from the extant research that most battered women experience neither the cycle of violence nor learned helplessness. Some experience a range of psychological and behavior problems that fall outside the purview of BWS, whereas others demonstrate virtually no mental health problems at all. Stark also cautions about a common misconception that the severity of domestic violence can be measured by those physical injuries and emotional disturbances that come to the attention of the police and medical personnel. These groups do not learn about the tyrannical control and low-level violence that, when administered chronically and over an extended period of time, severely affect the victim's quality of life. Nevertheless, the behaviors may not follow an identifiable syndrome.

A minority of IPV victims kill their abusers; in fact, research consistently indicates that they are far more likely to be killed than to kill (Ogle, 2000). When they do kill, BWS has sometimes been used as a defense. Proponents of this approach argue that women suffering from BWS are in continuing fear of immediate and severe bodily harm (including death). Therefore, under the law of self-defense, they should be excused for killing an abusive partner. Although courts are more likely to allow than to exclude such expert testimony, and scholars agree that the victim's voice should be heard in this way (A. Hess, 2006; Slobogin, 1999), it does not guarantee that the defendant will be acquitted. Also, the term *battered woman syndrome* is used by most courts today to refer to the "generic issue of battering rather than to Walker's specific formulation" (Stark, 2002, p. 227). BWS has become a legal catchall phrase to refer to all victims of domestic abuse if it can be established that they display any symptoms of distress. However, "courts that rely exclusively on the Walker model have discounted the credibility of victims who appear strategic or aggressive rather than 'helpless' or dependent, particularly if they are from income or ethnic groups stereotypically portrayed as aggressive" (Stark, 2002, p. 227). Accordingly, a victim who exhibits emotional and cognitive strength is suspect because she does not demonstrate the classic characteristics, and many may conclude that she should have been able to do something about the situation earlier and more effectively.

Same-Sex Domestic Violence

Researchers in recent years have given considerable attention to the issue of IPV between members of the same sex. As a general proposition, virtually all of the literature reviewed above applies in this context as well. For example, Potoczniak, Mourot, Crosbie-Burnett, and Potoczniak (2003) find some striking similarities in the research literature in the violence cycle and stages of abuse between same-sex domestic violence (SSDV) and opposite-sex domestic violence (OSDV). Similar to OSDV perpetrators, SSDV perpetrators blame their partners, are extremely controlling, and are highly self-focused. SSDV victims also often follow many of the same characteristics described for OSDV victims. The major difference between OSDV and SSDV incidents appears to be how the community, police, medical personnel, and available help programs respond to the victims.

Turrell (2000) investigated same-sex domestic violence among lesbians, gay women, and gay men (female participants were allowed to choose between the labels *lesbian* and *gay woman*). Turrell discovered a sexual abuse prevalence rate of 13% for gay men, 11% for gay women, and 14% for lesbians in a past or present relationship. Of those who reported sexual abuse, other physical abuse was also common. Specifically, 44% of the gay men, 58% of the gay women, and 55% of the lesbians reported receiving physical abuse in a past or present relationship.

Potoczniak et al. (2003) point out, based on a study by J. Hill (2000), that gay, lesbian, and bisexual (GLB) persons involved in domestic violence are perceived by jurors as having a lower moral character than their heterosexual counterparts. In line with this type of reasoning, jurors feel also that rape committed against a GLB person by another GLB person of the same sex is not as serious as a heterosexual rape and consequently should receive a less severe penalty in a judicial setting (J. Hill, 2000).

Research also suggests that female victims of same-sex domestic violence find help at different places from those of the female victims of opposite-sex domestic violence. For example, OSDV victims find domestic violence shelters more helpful than many other resources, whereas female victims of SSDV reported these same shelters to be the *least* helpful (Potoczniak et al., 2003; Renzetti, 1992). Furthermore, SSDV female victims most often find friends to be the most helpful resources, followed by counselors and relatives. It is no surprise that SSDV female victims report that the police, attorneys, and medical professionals are generally *not* helpful. In addition, one of the very few studies that examined the help-seeking behaviors of gay male victims of SSDV (G. S. Merrill & Wolfe, 2000) found that many male victims not only sought help from friends and counselors but also found domestic violence programs for gay individuals very helpful (Potoczniak et al., 2003).

Mental Health Needs of Children Exposed to Intimate Partner Violence

Research on the effects of IPV on children began in the early 1980s and has followed a rapid growth since that time (Goddard & Bedi, 2010). Exposure to intimate partner violence occurs when children "see, hear, are directly involved in, or experience the aftermath of violence between their caretakers" (Olaya, Ezpeleta, de la Osa, Granero, & Doménech, 2010, p. 1004). According to this definition, approximately 15.5 million children living in the United States are exposed to IPV incidents every year (McDonald, Jouriles, Ramisetty-Mikler, Caetano, & Green, 2006). Some believe this estimate is too low (Knutson, Lawrence, Taber, Bank, & DeGarmo, 2009).

A large number of studies report that children exposed to IPV have different mental health needs than those children not exposed to IPV (Goddard & Bedi, 2010; Olaya et al., 2010). More specifically, these children are more likely to have symptoms of PTSD, mood problems, loneliness, lowered self-esteem, and a greater tendency toward self-harm. Other studies (Cummings, El-Sheikh, Kouros, & Buckhalt, 2009; Gelles & Cavanaugh, 2005; Goddard & Bedi, 2010) report that IPV exposure affects the child's ability to regulate his or her emotions and appears to be linked to a greater tendency toward violence during adolescence and into adulthood.

McGee (2000) describes some of the self-reports provided by IPV-exposed children and teens.

One [nightmare] was that when I was asleep he got a knife and stabbed me. (boy, age 5; p. 71)

I'd think about my mom being hit and then I just would walk out of school and come home. . . . I didn't like the thought of her being on her own with him, so I stayed home all the time. (girl, age 15; p. 81)

The relationship between child abuse and IPV exposure has been the subject of much controversy. Some researchers and practitioners argue that the two are different and therefore should remain distinct categories. On the other hand, evidence that IPV results in negative outcomes for the child has led some countries, such as Australia and the United States, to consider IPV as a form of psychological child abuse, a topic to be discussed in the next major section on child abuse (Bedi & Goddard, 2007; Goddard & Bedi, 2010).

The first step for clinicians working with troubled children is to identify the IPV home environment; that is, does IPV occur and if so, what is its severity and frequency? Most IPV-exposed children are reluctant to report or discuss the situation, and they may feel shame, guilt, or fear (Olaya et al., 2010). In addition, it is important for the psychologist to realize that there may be more than violence between adult partners happening. Research has demonstrated that co-occurring or different forms of child abuse are common in families identified for domestic violence (Margolin et al., 2009). The more frequent and severe the IPV, the more likely that various kinds of child abuse are also occurring. We will return to the topic of child abuse in more detail in the next major section of the chapter.

The Roles of the Forensic Psychologist in Domestic Violence Cases

Forensic psychologists are often asked to do risk assessments of batterers at all stages of the criminal justice process, from pretrial assessment to sentencing to correctional release. They may be asked to be an expert witness during a civil or criminal trial. If the batterer is a defendant in a criminal case, the psychologist may be asked to assess his level of danger if released on bail before the next court appearance. In a criminal trial in which a defendant assaulted or killed an abusive partner, the defense may request the forensic psychologist to identify whether the defendant qualified for BWS or PTSD. During the jury selection process in criminal cases, the forensic psychologist may also be asked to evaluate the extent of myths about family violence within the jury pool or community; once a jury has been chosen, a jury consultant might be asked to assess how these individuals are likely to respond to the testimony presented by both sides of the case. In civil matters, the psychologist may be asked to evaluate the family dynamics or parental suitability to help in custody decisions involving the children. Finally, in many instances, psychologists and other mental health professionals will provide crisis intervention or treatment consultation or provide the services themselves.

Forensic Assessment of Domestic Violence

Before engaging in any kind of assessment or treatment of domestic violence victims, the forensic psychologist must be keenly aware of the impact of cultural and lifestyle variables on the battered person's response to the abuse and her recovery (M. A. Dutton, 1992; T. L. Jackson, Petretic-Jackson, & Witte, 2002). For example, many cultural and social barriers impede help-seeking behavior for a wide spectrum of cultural groups. In some cultures, violence may even be condoned within the secrecy of the family, although there are currently world-wide attempts to change this tolerance (Kozu, 1999; McWhirter, 1999). For some minority women or immigrants, a language barrier makes it doubly hard to find help and support.

A multimodal approach is most often recommended for the assessment of battered victims and battering offenders. The term *multimodal* refers to the use of a combination of psychological instruments and information-gathering strategies, including open-ended interviews, structured interviews, questionnaires, and standard psychological measures. An open-ended interview allows people to respond "in their own words" or "tell their own story" with a minimum of redirection from the clinician. It allows considerable flexibility for the clinician to modify the goals, the questions, and the general flow of information from the person being interviewed. The structured interview involves a more standardized set of procedures and questions that lessen the clinician's freedom to redirect the information-gathering process. It normally asks specific, predetermined questions that restrict the evaluator's inquiries during the administration of the interview.

In the forensic setting, one of the most commonly used assessment instruments for determining the extent of intimate partner violence is the Conflict Tactics Scales (CTS), developed by Murray Straus (1979). The CTS measures the frequency and severity of behaviors that partners engage in during an argument (Levensky & Fruzzeti, 2004).

During the early stages of its development, CTS-generated data were surprising and controversial, indicating that 1 in 6 marriages had included an incident of physical violence, and that IPV appeared to be as high among women as it was among men (Langhinrichsen-Rohling, 2005). According to Langhinrichsen-Rohling, the CTS data gave us a look behind closed doors of intimate partner violence early on. Although widely used, researchers and practitioners have identified many limitations (see Levensky and Fruzzetti, 2004, for a comprehensive review of its limitations). As we observed above, some studies using the CTS led to the misleading conclusion that men and women were equally likely to engage in interpersonal violence, without taking into consideration the forms and motivation for the behavior. In an attempt to address the criticisms, a Revised Conflict Tactics Scale and child–parent CTS were later developed.

Assessment of Victim Reactions

Although the BWS is facing considerable opposition in the research community, there is support for the presence of PTSD symptoms in battered women, with rates ranging from 45% to 84% (T. L. Jackson et al., 2002). Several measures commonly used to assess the level of PTSD symptomatology are the PTSD Symptom Scale (Foa, Riggs, Dancu, & Rothbaum, 1993), the Posttraumatic Diagnostic Stress Scale (Foa, Cashman, Jaycox, & Perry, 1997), the Crime-Related Post-Traumatic Stress Disorder Scale (Saunders, Arata, & Kilpatrick, 1990), the Distressing Event Questionnaire (Kubany, Leisen, Kaplan, & Kelly, 2000), and the Traumatic Life Events Questionnaire (Kubany, Haynes, et al., 2000).

The forensic psychologist is likely to administer formal psychological tests and inventories or other appropriate psychological measures to determine whether any discernible changes in attitude, cognitive functioning, behavior, and emotions are a result of the abuse. In any forensic setting, documentation is critical at all phases of the assessment process. Documentation may include court records; police reports; mental health and medical records; investigative reports of friends, family, or neighbors or other witnesses; and related legal proceedings such as depositions, trial transcripts, and protection orders. The evaluator should be aware that "unconventional sources" might provide invaluable documentation. Unconventional sources include "date books, logbooks, telephone messages, diaries, letters (including threatening letters from partners), tapes, photographs, and other records" (Stark, 2002, p. 232).

The assessment of the family must also consider the age, social class, occupational status, level of acculturation, prior exposure to violence, normative approval of violence, family structure, and cultural coping strategies (T. L. Jackson et al., 2002; C. M. West, 1998). It is important for the clinician to also realize that the victim may have the distorted belief that she is the cause of the abuse and is at a loss about what to do about it. Unfortunately, very little empirical research on the effectiveness of therapeutic interventions with battered women has been conducted (Petretic-Jackson, Witte, & Jackson, 2002).

Risk Assessment: Is the Victim Safe?

Another important task for the forensic psychologist during assessment is to determine the level of danger the victim may be in as well as the likelihood that the victim may assault or kill the abuser, though this is rare compared with the violence perpetrated by the abuser. Practitioners who work with family violence agree that the ongoing safety of the victim must be considered first and foremost (Petretic-Jackson et al., 2002). Failure to put this factor into the equation may result in the death or serious injury of one or more family members. One instrument that may be useful for predicting risk in family situations is the **Spousal Assault Risk Assessment (SARA),** developed by Kropp, Hart, Webster, and Eaves (1998). The SARA is a 20-item checklist designed to screen for risk factors in individuals suspected of or being treated for spousal or family-related assault. It is used when a clinician wishes to determine the degree to which an individual poses a threat to his or her spouse, children, or other family members.

Another useful risk assessment measure is Danger Assessment (DA), developed by Jacquelyn Campbell (1995). The first part of the DA is designed to determine the severity and frequency of battering by presenting the victim with a calendar of the past year. He or she is then asked to mark the approximate dates when physically abusive events occurred and to rank the severity of the incident on a 1-to-5 scale (ranging from 1 = *low* to 5 = *use of weapon*). The second part of the DA is a 15-item questionnaire requiring a yes or no response to each item. The items are intended to provide an overview of the range of tactics used by the batterer.

Necessary Training for Domestic Violence Assessment

Forensic psychologists and other mental health workers who deal with domestic violence and its victims should have special training that emphasizes that assault by an intimate partner is a unique form of violence that differs in important ways from other forms. Whereas violence from strangers is often an isolated, one-time event, the type found in domestic violence is an ongoing situation characterized by repetitive abuse from a once-trusted person over a long period of time. In short, domestic violence is a process that has incalculable, cumulative effects over time. Moreover, the victim may feel trapped in the home or situation in which it occurs, often with no *perceived* hope for escape. "Because of marital commitments, financial ties, and child care, victims of intimate partner violence cannot as easily remove themselves from the situations as can victims of abuse by a nonintimate" (Petretic-Jackson et al., 2002, pp. 300–301). This perceived hopelessness may lead to depression and inhibiting feelings of helplessness for some victims, but—as noted above—many other victims handle the situation quite differently. Consequently, forensic psychologists and other clinicians must be prepared for the wide range of psychological symptoms and coping mechanisms that victims will display.

IPV, as well as domestic violence in general, is also apt to engender a variety of reactions from psychologists, especially if they or someone close to them have personally experienced such violence. Working with victims of domestic abuse (of both adults and children) is especially stressful, and when clinicians are exposed to trauma victims, it leads to a high incidence of professional burnout. The term **vicarious traumatization** has sometimes been used to describe the psychological distress that clinicians themselves experience as a result of working with traumatized victims (L. McCann & Pearlman, 1990; Petretic-Jackson et al., 2002).

Child Abuse

In 2008, an estimated 772,000 children were victims of maltreatment in the United States (U.S. Department of Health and Human Services [DHHS], 2010). These statistics indicate that about 12 out of every 1,000 children are victims of maltreatment each year, a rate that has been fairly consistent over the past decade. Children less than 1 year old had the highest rate of victimization at 21.7 per 1,000 children.

About 1,740 children died of maltreatment in 2008 in the United States, a rate of 2.33 per 1,000 children. Infant boys (younger than 1 year) had the highest rate of fatalities (19.21 per 100,000). About 50% of the children who die of maltreatment in the United States had already been referred to a child protection agency (National Resource Center on Child Sexual Abuse, 1996).

Types of Maltreatment

There are four major types of child maltreatment: (1) neglect, (2) physical abuse, (3) sexual abuse, and (4) emotional abuse. Neglect refers to failure to provide for a child's basic needs, such as lack of appropriate supervision or failure to provide necessary food, shelter, or medical care. Neglect may also include failure to educate a child or attend to special education or emotional needs. Physical abuse refers to anything that may cause physical injury such as punching, beating, kicking, biting, shaking, throwing, stabbing, choking, burning, or hitting. (See Photo 11.1 depicting a child's fear of physical abuse.) Sexual abuse includes activities by a parent or caretaker such as sexual fondling, incest, rape, sodomy, indecent exposure, and commercial exploitation through prostitution or the production of pornographic materials. Emotional abuse refers to behavior that impairs a child's emotional development or sense of self-esteem or worth and may include such things as constant criticism or rejection.

Photo 11.1   Boy on floor facing the wrath of an adult male.

According to the U.S. Department of Health and Human Services (2010), over two-thirds (70%)

of maltreatment victims experience neglect. About 15% are physically abused, and 9% are sexually abused. Only 7% reportedly are emotionally abused, a figure that probably is greatly underestimated. Boys and girls are about equally neglected or physically abused, but girls are 4 times more likely to experience sexual abuse. About one quarter of the victims experience more than one type of maltreatment. About 60% of children seen by a physician for an injury suggesting physical abuse will return with further inflicted injuries. Approximately 10% will eventually die from the continual abuse. About 10% of all children seen in emergency rooms have some form of non-accidental injury. Although abusive injuries are seen at all socioeconomic levels, fatal cases of abuse are most common in the poorer segments of the population. Children of all races and ethnicities experience child abuse.

Pet and Child Abuse

Research has discovered that pet abuse often accompanies child abuse (Arkow, 1998). That is, adults who abuse their children also tend to abuse the family pet, which is usually a treasured companion of abused children. Abusers often threaten to harm or kill a pet to frighten a child into secrecy about the abuse, particularly about sexual abuse. A strong relationship also exists between pet cruelty and spousal abuse. In one study, more than half of the victims at a women's shelter reported that their pets had been harmed or killed by their partner and that they delayed coming to the shelter for fear of harm to their pets left at home (Ascione, 1997). A growing body of research also suggests that violent people often commit considerable cruelty against animals in general, particularly against pets and stray animals (Merz-Perez, Heide, & Silverman, 2001).

Dynamics of Family Violence

Abusive families tend to be socially isolated and lack an extended social network of family and friends for social, financial, and emotional support. The family situation is usually unstable, punctuated by stormy relationships between adults, an unwanted child, financial constraints, heavy alcohol or drug abuse, or feelings of being trapped with little way out. The literature on abusers is consistent in outlining common characteristics of male and female abusers (e.g., Babcock, Waltz, Jacobson, & Gottman, 1993; Hornung, McCullough, & Sugimoto, 1981; Strauss & Gelles, 1990). For example, male abusers tend to be impulsive, immature, frustrated persons who believe it is their right as the "man of the household" to dominate the female. Males become especially abusive if they are forced into providing primary care while the woman works because they interpret this situation as a loss of self-esteem and their traditional masculine role. Female abusers tend to be overstressed, dominated, depressed, and frustrated. For both male and female abusers, the precipitating event for the abuse tends to be the infant's or child's crying, lack of toileting, or a soiled diaper. In recent years, a little girl was nearly blinded when her mother's boyfriend forced her to kneel in a corner and washed her eyes with bleach because she had urinated in her underwear.

In a long-ago case, a young divorced mother with three children under 3 (including 18-month-old twins), living in a small stark apartment far away from her parents and siblings, was receiving public assistance. Her check failed to arrive in time, and she was unable to heat her apartment or buy sufficient groceries; her telephone and electricity were shut off and the landlord threatened to evict her. When one of her twin boys cried consistently, she "lost it" and beat him, leaving severe bruises and nearly breaking his arm. We often wonder what happened to the above child, who was taken temporarily out of the home but eventually returned to his mother after several months during which social caseworkers tried to meet the family's needs. Stories like these abound in the files and in the minds of human service workers.

There are uncertainties concerning the relative contribution of child abuse to later psychopathology in the victim (Knapp & VandeCreek, 2000).

> Little is known about the impact of mitigating factors, such as having otherwise positive parental figures, receiving an early treatment after the abuse, or having a robust personality or a strong social network. Similarly, more needs to be known about the impact of exacerbating factors, such as having otherwise destructive parental figures, receiving blame or no treatment after the abuse, having a fragile personality, or lacking a strong social network. (Knapp & VandeCreek, 2000, p. 370)

Infanticide, Neonaticide, and Filicide

An estimated 1,200 to 1,500 young children are murdered each year by a parent or other person (Emery & Laumann-Billings, 1998). According to the FBI, two thirds of victims younger than 6 days old are murdered by their mothers, who are often young (younger than age 20) and unmarried (Finkelhor & Ormrod, 2001b).

Infanticide, although the term literally means the killing of an infant, has become the umbrella term for homicide of children up to 2 years of age, although a 1 year cutoff is sometimes used. Because there are significant differences between mothers who commit infanticide within the first 24 hours after birth and those who kill a slightly older child, two additional terms are often used in the research and clinical literature. Specifically, **neonaticide** refers to the killing of the newborn within the first 24 hours, whereas **filicide** refers to the killing of a child older than one year (P. J. Resnick, 1970). Mothers who commit neonaticide tend to be young, unmarried women who deny or conceal their pregnancy, fearing the disapproval or rejection from their family and society (Dobson & Sales, 2000). Mothers who commit filicide (where the child is over a year) tend to be older and married and often demonstrate symptoms of depression. Mothers in the second group are most often in situations they perceive as hopeless and dire. They believe that killing the child is the only way to prevent the child's suffering or potential suffering from living under adverse conditions.

Traditionally, women who kill their children have been viewed by the legal system (and the public) as very likely suffering from serious mental problems. Most often, the clinical diagnosis is "postpartum depression," a depressive episode believed to be brought on by childbirth. However, it is important to realize that three categories of mental reactions may be apparent after childbirth: postpartum blues, postpartum depression, or postpartum psychosis (Dobson & Sales, 2000). The most common is *postpartum blues,* characterized by crying, irritability, anxiety, confusion, and rapid mood changes. Approximately 50 to 80% of women show some minor features of postpartum blues between 1 and 5 days after delivery (Durand & Barlow, 2000). The symptoms may last for a few hours to a few days and are clearly linked to childbirth. Rarely do the symptoms last more than 12 days. The connection between postpartum blues and the killing of one's child has not been supported by the research literature.

The second category, *postpartum depression,* occurs during the weeks and months following childbirth. The symptoms include depression, loss of appetite, sleep disturbances, fatigue, suicidal thoughts, disinterest in the newborn child, and a general loss of interest in life's activities. The woman with postpartum depression often feels guilty for being depressed when she should be happy about a new baby. The incidence rate among childbearing women ranges from 7 to 17% in North America (Dobson & Sales, 2000). However, in contrast to postpartum blues, postpartum depression does not appear to be directly connected to childbirth but is more a clinical form of depression that is present before childbirth and may be a recurring disorder across the life cycle of the woman. Although women with postpartum depression may commit infanticide, research finds that this is not common after childbirth, and infanticide is not directly caused by it.

The third category of mental problems associated with the postpartum period is *postpartum psychosis,* a severe mental disorder that is rare, occurring in 1 out of every 1,000 women following delivery. Usually, the psychotic features are highly similar to the symptoms of serious bipolar depression and appear to be directly connected to childbirth. As noted by Dobson and Sales (2000), "A number of epidemiological studies have provided clear scientific evidence supporting the link between childbirth and postpartum psychosis" (p. 1106). Sometimes the psychosis is severe enough to lead to the mother's attempted suicide, together with an attempt to kill her baby (Kendall & Hammen, 1995). There is some documentation that many women (estimates range from 20 to 40%) who commit filicide are suffering from postpartum psychosis (Dobson & Sales, 2000).

Overall, few infanticides are committed by mothers who suffer depression, despair, or psychosis. Infant homicides can result from acts of omission, such as neglecting to watch the child in a hazardous environment, or acts of commission, such as delivering a swift blow to silence a crying infant. In many instances, however, it is difficult to determine whether the infant's death is due to an accident, biological deficiency of the infant (such as physical immaturity or genetic malformations), carelessness by the mother, or an intentional act to kill.

For example, sudden infant death syndrome (SIDS) is the number one cause of death in infants between the ages of 2 weeks and 1 year, although the risk is greatest between 2 and 4 months of age. It is estimated that 1 in every 350 live births will be a victim of SIDS. Unfortunately, the disorder is largely unpreventable and unpredictable, and currently there is no known cause or cure. The victims of SIDS are usually healthy, well-cared-for babies with no previous history of disease or illness. The parent or caretaker often finds the baby dead in its crib, usually in a normal sleeping position. In some cases, there may be some bloody fluid around the mouth and nose and some discoloration of the face and extremities, but these signs are not evidence of foul play or abuse. Consequently, an accurate appraisal of the cause of death often requires a careful autopsy by a skilled medical examiner, scene investigation, and careful review of the statements provided by parents or caretakers. We must emphasize that the vast majority of apparent SIDS deaths are not due to parental neglect or parental actions. However, in rare cases, infants as well as young children may be killed in such subtle ways that only a very careful forensic investigation can discover the cause and manner of the death.

Munchausen Syndrome by Proxy

Munchausen syndrome by proxy (MSBP) is a form of child abuse in which a parent (almost always the mother) *consistently* and *chronically* subjects a child to medical attention without any "true" medical condition or symptoms being present. MSBP was first applied to children by Money and Werleas (1976) and Meadow (1977). Prior to the mid-1970s, Munchausen syndrome was considered exclusively an adult disorder. "Adult Munchausen is characterized by an adult's chronic and relentless pursuit of medical treatment, involving some combination of consciously self-inflicted injury and falsely reported symptomatology" (Robins & Sesan, 1991, p. 285). The term *Munchausen syndrome* was apparently coined by the London physician Richard Asher (1951) to describe patients who consistently produced false stories about themselves to receive needless medical examinations, operations, and treatments. Asher named the syndrome after Baron von Munchausen, a distinguished German soldier and politician who was born in 1720 (Dowdell & Foster, 2000). Asher named the behavior after von Munchausen because of the many fabricated stories of incredible travels and brave military exploits he would tell to friends and acquaintances, including his physicians (Raspe, 1944).

In Munchausen syndrome by proxy, the child's presenting symptoms are either falsified or directly induced *by the parent*. In fact, the term *by proxy* refers to the parent's dominating influence in the presentation of symptoms to the medical staff. The most common cluster of symptoms reported by the parent concerning the child's condition involves seizures, failure to thrive, vomiting, diarrhea, asthma/allergies, and infections (see M. S. Sheridan, 2003, pp. 441–443, for complete list of symptoms). Symptom inducement by the parent may include adding fat to stools in order to produce a laboratory abnormality, initiating starvation in the child, placing blood into the child's urine sample before lab testing, or injecting contaminating or toxic material intravenously into the child's bloodstream (J. B. Murray, 1997; Pearl, 1995).

MSBP cases are found in homes of all socioeconomic levels, and the victims are most often young children ranging in ages from 6 months to 8 years. Both sexes appear to be equally susceptible to being victimized. The term *serial MSBP* is reserved for those cases involving more than one child in the same family (R. A. Alexander, Smith, & Stevenson, 1990).

The case histories of MSBP cases commonly illustrate an "over-involved" mother and an "emotionally distant" or physically absent father. MSBP mothers are often described as "emotionally empty" and lonely and often have experienced significant emotional, physical, and sexual abuse during their own childhood and young adulthood (Robins & Sesan, 1991). The mother often appears to others as the ideal parent and comes across as very concerned, devoted, attentive, and loving. However, she is also seen as overprotective and obsessed with the child's illness (M. L. Brown, 1997; Voltz, 1995).

The offending mother is often sophisticated about medical conditions, has some fascination with medical procedures and diagnosis, and may even be a health professional herself. Suspicions that MSBP may be present should be entertained when the parent is unusually attentive to the child and is very reluctant to leave the child's side during a medical examination or treatment. This, though, can be said of many if not most parents. A better sign is when a child has a series of recurring medical conditions that do not respond to treatment or follow an unanticipated course that is persistent, puzzling, and unexplained. Another indicator is when laboratory findings or symptomatology are highly abnormal and discrepant with existing medical knowledge. The extreme forms of this child abuse may lead to serious injury or death. Verification of MSBP can also be achieved when the symptoms disappear after the suspected perpetrator and victim are separated (M. S. Sheridan, 2003).

Although there have been many cases of MSBP reported in the literature, the prevalence or incidence of the problem is unknown, largely due to the difficulty of identifying actual illnesses as opposed to fabricated ones and the general lack of knowledge about this unusual form of child abuse. It should also be mentioned that there have been some reports that, in some cases, the "proxy" is a family pet (Tucker, 2002). In a survey sent to 1,000 veterinary surgeons asking them about non-accidental injuries in animals, a small number of the respondents believed that they had encountered MSBP perpetrated by some pet owners. In other words, some pet owners may deliberately hurt their pets to get sympathy and medical attention.

In most cases, child protection services are brought into play if MSBP is suspected, and rarely are criminal charges filed unless the behavior has resulted in serious injury or the child has died. The forensic psychologist may become involved at both the child protection and the prosecution stages of the case. If the parent is unwilling or unable to stop the behavior, the child may need to be removed from the home until effective intervention or some appropriate arrangement with the parent is accomplished. If the case is serious enough to warrant criminal charges, the forensic psychologist may become a "court appointed" evaluator, which means he or she is being asked directly by the court to provide pertinent information (Sanders & Bursch, 2002). Recall that, as mentioned in Chapter 1, many states now require special training and certification for those who provide these and similar services for courts (Heilbrun & Brooks, 2010).

In the case of MSBP, the psychologist must review all available medical records on both the child and the suspected parent and do a psychological assessment of both parent and child. According to Sanders and Bursch (2002), a significant number of women who engage in illness falsification on behalf of their children also complain of many unsubstantiated illnesses within themselves. Siblings should also be evaluated, as they too may have been subjected to MSBP. In most cases, the court will be interested in whether there is evidence that child abuse occurred, and how the child has been harmed as a result of the alleged abuse. The court may also be interested in treatment options for the perpetrator and what management or treatment programs are recommended. In keeping with forensic guidelines, though, psychologists should avoid serving as both the evaluator and the treatment provider if possible.

Shaken Baby Syndrome

Another form of child abuse is called **shaken baby syndrome (SBS),** in which a parent or caretaker shakes a baby so hard that serious brain damage occurs. The brain damage can result in intellectual disability, speech and learning disabilities, blindness, paralysis, seizures, hearing loss, or death. A baby's brain and blood vessels are very fragile and can be easily damaged by whiplash motions, such as shaking, jerking, and jolting. The neck muscles are not strong enough to control head movements, and rapid movement of the head can result in the brain being damaged from banging against the skull wall.

SBS is difficult to diagnosis, unless a witness accurately describes the incident. Medical personnel report that many babies symptomatic of SBS are brought in for medical attention for a fall, difficulty breathing, seizures, vomiting, altered consciousness, or choking. Sometimes the adults in these cases admit that they shook the baby, but it was done only in an effort to resuscitate the infant. To diagnose SBS, physicians look for bleeding in the retina or retinal detachment, blood in the brain, and increased head size indicating excessive accumulation of fluid in the tissues of the brain. Fixed pupils, inactivity, and breathing problems may also be evident. Spinal cord damage and broken ribs may also be present, depending on how the baby was held during the shaking.

Although there are not complete statistics on the frequency of SBS, there is consensus that brain trauma is the leading killer of abused children (more than 50%) and that shaking is involved in many of these cases (Duhaime, Christian, Rorke, & Zimmerman, 1998; Showers, 1999; Smithey, 1998). Russell (2010) writes that, of those children diagnosed with SBS, about 30% die as a result of their injuries, and only 15% survive with no lasting effects. C. A. Ellis and Lord (2002) estimate that 10 to 12% of all deaths related to abuse and neglect can be attributed to SBS. Furthermore, studies indicate that 70 to 80% of the perpetrators of SBS are male, and most often they are the parent of the child (Child Abuse Prevention Center, 1998; C. A. Ellis & Lord, 2002). The offender is usually in his early twenties (Showers, 1997). Both male and female babies are equally victimized, and SBS cuts across all socioeconomic levels. Frustration from a baby's incessant crying or from eating and toileting problems is usually reported as the precipitating event leading to the severe shaking. Ignorance of the dangers of shaking a baby is typical, and the overwhelming majority of offenders have poor child-rearing skills. In some hospitals today, parents are asked to watch educational videos on SBS and on infant care in general before leaving the hospital with their newborns.

Repressed and Recovered Memories

In the late 20th century, one of the most controversial topics in forensic psychology was the question of whether a "lost" memory of abuse or other crime can be recovered at a later time. The topic remains of great interest to some researchers today, although there is increasing skepticism that significant memories are buried and suddenly recovered (e.g., Alison, Kebbell, & Lewis, 2006). The topic is often referred to as **repressed memory;** recovered memory; or, less frequently, false memory (to imply questionable validity of the reported memory itself).

The notion of repressed memories has been around at least since the time of Sigmund Freud (1915/1957) and probably has been discussed in some capacity throughout the history of humankind. Freud, though, was certainly the most influential in bringing the concept into the limelight. Freud wrote that "the essence of repression lies simply in the function of rejecting and keeping something out of consciousness" (p. 105). To minimize anxiety and fear, we supposedly push out of our awareness painful or extremely troubling memories, and it is assumed we do this unconsciously. Current clinical thinking broadens the term *repression* to include a wide range of cognitive processes.

> Repression refers to the psychological process of keeping something out of awareness because of unpleasant affect connected with it. The "something" may be a memory (or part of a memory), a fantasy, a thought, an idea, a feeling, a wish, an impulse, a connection, and so forth. (Karon & Widener, 1999, p. 625)

Repression may include loss of memory of the trauma (amnesia) in some individuals and partial, fragmentary memory in still others.

According to Freud—and some contemporary clinicians—a repressed or submerged memory continues to linger in the unconscious until it is retrieved during psychotherapy or under certain other conditions, such as dream analysis, hypnosis, or some other "method of recovery." For many individuals, these repressed memories are never satisfactorily retrieved and may continue to raise havoc by causing psychological problems across their life spans—at least this is the position held by some clinicians. These clinicians are convinced that they encounter many forms of repression—particularly memories of early childhood abuse—during their routine practice. On the other side of the ledger are cognitive scientists who question the frequency of "true" repression and the clinical assumptions of how or why it occurs.

The courts have had to face the issue of repressed memories in numerous cases. Adults who were allegedly the victims of abuse, especially sexual abuse, claim in civil or criminal trials that they had initially forgotten these traumatic experiences but eventually remembered them, usually with the help or guidance of therapists and often under hypnosis or some other "discovery" process. The courts refer to repressed-then-recovered memory as "delayed discovery." The alleged abuser, often the father or another family member, having been named, disclaims abuse, countering that the victim's memories are false and that they have been implanted by the psychotherapist, investigator, or evaluator (Partlett & Nurcombe, 1998). The accuracy of these recollections has been the center of the contentious debate of experts spanning nearly 30 years, as well as among the experts providing testimony in the courtroom.

It should be noted that criminal prosecutions for child or adult sexual abuse cannot be brought after the statute of limitations has expired (*Stogner v. California*, 2003). The *statute of limitations* is the legal time limit placed on the filing of criminal charges or a civil complaint. In criminal cases, it is typically 1 year after the event, except for murder, for which the time period does not expire. In recent years, however, many states have begun to extend their statute of limitations in recognition that it may take years for victims of sexual abuse to come forward—even when repressed memories are not at issue. Many court cases in which sexual abuse is alleged are civil in nature. The widely publicized priest abuse cases are a case in point. Sexual abuse allegations also occur with some frequency in child custody and visitation cases.

In both civil and criminal sexual abuse cases, the defense tries to call an expert witness to challenge the testimony offered by the prosecution's or the plaintiff's witness. The focus is usually on questioning the circumstances under which the original report was elicited and the interviewing methods of investigators or other involved professionals (Berliner, 1998). Some victims, under the repeated urging of their psychotherapists and often combined with discovery methods such as hypnosis, come to remember (often suddenly) that they were sexually abused by parents, siblings, relatives, or strangers. Convinced that these abuses are the core ingredient of their maladjustment or current difficulties or that their abusers should be punished, a significant number of these victims seek redress through the courts, primarily civil courts. Although these recovered memories may have foundations in some (perhaps many) cases, these claims must be evaluated very carefully by the forensic psychologist before proceeding to the legal arena.

Lilienfeld and Loftus (1998) write, "The question of whether traumatic memories can be repressed for long periods of time (i.e., years or decades) and then suddenly recovered in intact form is perhaps the most controversial issue in clinical psychology today" (p. 471).

There are very few figures on how frequently repressed memory occurs in clinical practice. In one of the few studies conducted so far, Polusny and Follette (1996) reported that 72% of the psychologists whom they surveyed had *not* encountered a case of "repressed" memory in the past year, and 15% had seen only one repressed memory case during that time.

Special Expert Panels on Repressed Memory

According to McNally, Perlman, Ristuccia, and Clancey (2008), the controversy surrounding repressed and recovered memories of child sexual abuse has been among the most bitter in the history of psychology. In an effort to clear up some of the controversy and debate on repressed or recovered memories, the American Psychological Association appointed a "working group" of researchers and clinicians to study the issue and arrive at some consensus on what is known and how to proceed. Called the American Psychological Association (APA) Working Group on Investigation of Memories of Childhood Abuse ("Final Conclusions," 1998), the panel of clinicians and researchers was able to come to the following five conclusions:

1. Controversies regarding adult recollections should not be allowed to obscure the fact that child sexual abuse is a complex and pervasive problem in America that has historically gone unacknowledged.

2. Most people who were sexually abused as children remember all or part of what happened to them.

3. It is possible for memories of abuse that have been forgotten for a long time to be remembered.

4. It is also possible to construct convincing pseudo-memories for events that never occurred.

5. There are gaps in our knowledge about the processes that lead to accurate and inaccurate recollections of childhood abuse. (p. 933)

But there were far more important issues on which the APA Working Group could not agree, mostly concerning the nature of early memory of abuse and its recovery. Although the group clearly strove to find consensus, the debate between some clinicians and researchers apparently became heated and polarized, resulting in a special issue in the December 1998 edition of *Psychology, Public Policy, and Law* that presents both sides. In this section, we will focus on the dominant view generally accepted by the cognitive and developmental scientists, but we will also give some attention to other perspectives where appropriate.

Before we proceed, however, we should mention that a similar panel of experts on repressed or recovered memory met in the United Kingdom shortly before the APA group convened. The group, called the British Psychological Society's Working Party on Recovered Memories, was sponsored by the British Psychological Society (BPS) to publish a position statement on the phenomenon for the members of the BPS, the media, and the interested citizen. The final document, which took more than 10 months to be finalized, is commonly referred to as the BPS Report (see British Psychological Society, 1995). The conclusions of the BPS Report generally coincide closely with the conclusions of the APA Final Report described above. For example,

> Like the BPS Report, the APA Final Report concluded that it was possible for memories of abuse that had been forgotten for a long time to be remembered, but that it was possible to construct convincing pseudomemories for events that never occurred. (Davies, Morton, Mollon, & Robertson, 1998, p. 1080)

However, the authors of the BPS Report also concluded that the APA Working Group neglected some important research findings that should have been addressed. The British group, for instance, thought that the APA panel neglected to establish an agreed-on scientific framework on which to base their discussions. More specifically, "there appears to be little consensus over the relevant evidence and methods of proof. In the absence of such fundamentals, the temptation is to revert to a political framework, which is unproductive from the standpoint of advancing theory and practice" (Davies et al., 1998, p. 1080). But even more relevant to our discussion here is the observation by the British group that

> the Final [APA] Report contains little serious discussion as to how memory mechanisms might mediate such diverse effects: The cognitivists merely accuse the therapists of clinging to a scientifically unsupported view of repression, and the therapists look in turn to the recent work of Van der Kolk (e.g., Van der Kolk & Fisler, 1995) as providing a rationale for a special and different form of memory associated with trauma. (Davies et al., 1998, p. 1080)

Because the topic of repressed memory is so important in forensic psychological practice and because it sets the stage for understanding memory processes in witness and expert testimony in the courtroom, we will pay special attention to the issue in this section. We begin by briefly outlining some of what research has revealed about human memory in general.

Research Sketches of Human Memory and Its Limitations

In its simplest terms, memory involves acquisition, storage, and retrieval. *Acquisition,* also called the encoding or input stage, is the initial step in the memory process and overlaps considerably with the sensory perceptual process. *Sensory perception* is the process of organizing and making sense of the information received from the senses, such as sight, hearing, smell, taste, somatosensory receptors, and vestibular and kinesthetic senses. *Memory storage,* also called retention, is when information becomes "resident in memory" (Loftus, 1979). In the *retrieval* stage, the brain searches for the pertinent information and retrieves it, a process somewhat like searching for a document in a filing cabinet or on one's hard drive.

In any discussion of forensic matters and memory, it will be helpful to begin with four important points about memory made by three of the leading scientists in the area: Peter Ornstein, Stephen Ceci, and Elizabeth Loftus (1998a).

- Not everything gets into memory.
- What gets into memory may vary in strength.
- The status of information in memory changes in memory.
- Retrieval is not perfect (i.e., not all that is stored gets retrieved).

In reference to the first point, some experiences may not be recalled because they were not entered into memory in the first place. The human cognitive system is limited in its information-processing capacity and cannot simultaneously attend to everything going on in the environment. We have to be selective in what is noticed. Consequently, considerable information is never processed. Furthermore, information processing is influenced by prior knowledge and experience. In other words, to understand and interpret what is being experienced, the brain compares "new" material to "old" stored material. By analogy, the new material is fitted onto a "cognitive template" to see how it compares. How one "sees" the world is dictated to a large extent by cognitive templates that are already in place from previous experiences and knowledge.

Concerning the second point raised by Ornstein et al. (1998a), several factors may influence the strength and organization of the resulting memory "trace." In addition, strong memory traces may be readily retrieved, whereas weak traces may be more difficult to recover. The strength of the trace depends on such factors as the length of exposure to an event, the number of exposures, the age of the individual, and how significant or prominent the event is to the person. With increasing age (at least through young adulthood), there are corresponding changes in information-processing skills and the cognitive templates that have been developed from previous experiences.

The third point refers to what may happen once the information is stored and perhaps is one of the most important points concerning forensic issues. That is,

> the memory trace can be altered during the course of the interval between the actual experience and a report of it. The passage of time, as well as a variety of intervening experiences, can influence strongly the strength and organization of stored information. (Ornstein et al., 1998a, p. 1028)

Apparently, due to the experiences of current events, humans continually alter and reconstruct their memory of past experiences rather than simply store past events permanently and unchangingly. Memory is not like a video camera that accurately stores events on film to be played back when necessary. Moreover, this alteration or "reconstructive process" is often done without the person's complete awareness. The individual is aware of the content of memory but is not usually aware of the transformations that have occurred during encoding, retention, and retrieval. The perspective that memory is continually vulnerable to revision is known as the **reconstructive theory of memory.** Overall, though, this reconstructive process probably does not *substantially* alter the *major* theme of the original memory for most people, but it does introduce a number of errors in *specific* descriptions of the event. For example, witnesses to a car accident may all report that two cars collided (as opposed to three trucks), but the specific details of the incident may vary considerably.

Moreover, "without reinstating events or experiences (e.g., through rehearsal, prompts, or visualizations), the strength of a memory trace decreases over time, and this trace decay combines with interferences in the delay interval to make access to stored information and successful retrieval more difficult" (Ornstein et al., 1998a, p. 1028). In young children, memory traces are often not as strong because children generally lack the requisite knowledge and experience to fully appreciate the event. Thus, they may undergo more rapid decay than the memory traces of older children. A growing body of research also indicates that young children (such as preschoolers) are usually more susceptible to the influences of misleading information received after the event than are older children and adults (Ceci & Bruck, 1993; Ceci, Ross, & Toglia, 1987; Ornstein et al., 1998a).

The fourth point refers to the common observation that not everything in memory can be retrieved all the time. Social pressures, stress, anxiety, information overload, and the low strength of the information itself are some of the many factors that may interfere with quick and immediate retrieval under certain conditions. People's names are especially difficult to retrieve for many people.

Many clinicians believe that memory of traumatic events may be encoded differently from memory for unremarkable events (Alpert, Brown, & Courtois, 1998). More specifically, some suggest that the enormous differences between normal resting states and high levels of arousal might result in changing the entire process of how memories are stored and retrieved. In the APA Working Group Report, as mentioned previously, the clinical group placed considerable reliance on the work of Van der Kolk and Fisler (1994, 1995) as evidence for memory repression. As pointed out by Davies and his colleagues (1998), Van der Kolk and Fisler did emphasize the difference between memories of traumatic events and memories of events that are merely stressful. More specifically, Van der Kolk and Fisler (1994) stated that traumatic memories may somehow be "frozen" in their original form and unmodified by further experience. Consequently, reliving these traumatic experiences can be retraumatizing because retrieving them is actually like reexperiencing them. But note that this phenomenon refers to actively *avoiding* reliving the trauma, not *repressing* the event. If anything, Davies et al. note, Van der Kolk and

Fisler are referring to state-dependent memory rather than repressed memory. **State-dependent memory** refers to the research findings that the things we experience in one emotional or physiological state—such as happiness, fear, or even intoxication—are sometimes easier to recall when we are again in that same state. (See Focus 11.1 for more on this interesting phenomenon.) Although a person who does not like to revisit that same state of pain and trauma may avoid doing so as much as possible, it does *not* mean that person is *repressing* the memory, at least according to the typical clinical definition of repression.

FOCUS 11.1. STATE-DEPENDENT MEMORY

State dependence refers to the observation that a memory acquired in one state of consciousness cannot be recalled until the person returns to that same state of consciousness. Otherwise, the person will have great difficulty remembering the events if in a different psychological state. For example, if a person learns new material while under the influence of alcohol, he tends to recall it better if he is again under the influence of alcohol.

State-dependent learning was first described in 1784 but was not subjected to much scientific study until the 1960s (Eich, 1989; Schramke & Bauer, 1997). Early research concentrated on differences induced by drugs and alcohol, and then interest shifted to the effects of mood or emotional states on memory and learning. For example, research has discovered that negative events are recalled better when people are in a negative mood (Lewinsohn & Rosenbaum, 1987), and positive events are recalled better while in a positive mood (Ehrlichman & Halpern, 1988). Research now finds that state-dependent learning may be influenced by drugs, moods, levels of activation (e.g., anxiety levels), arousal (i.e., sleep and wakefulness), or environmental settings (i.e., where the memory was acquired) (Slot & Colpaert, 1999; Weingartner, Putnam, George, & Ragan, 1995). Pertaining to environmental settings, if you misplace your keys, trying to remember where you left them is often not as effective as physically retracing your steps in the actual environment. If a person hides money while intoxicated and forgets where the money was hidden, recall is likely to be enhanced by being similarly intoxicated and placed in the same environment.

The implications for forensic psychology are interesting. A person who witnessed a crime or traffic accident while under the influence may be better able to recall that incident if placed back into that same physiological or psychological state. In the case of environmental settings, it might be helpful if the witness also returns to the scene of the crime.

In addition, the scientific evidence clearly indicates that memories from early infancy are highly unreliable, incomplete, and full of error. The phenomenon of infantile or childhood "amnesia" has long been noted by developmental psychologists (Dudycha & Dudycha, 1941). *Infantile amnesia* refers to the common observation that adults are usually unable to recall events that occurred before the age of around 3 years. According to the BPS Report (BPS, 1995), for instance, "nothing can be recalled accurately from before the first birthday and little from before the second. Poor memory from before the fourth birthday is normal" (p. 29). Most of us have little trouble remembering certain things that occurred when we were 7 years of age, such as a birthday party or a special occasion, but prior to that, things often become quite hazy. Even some things about our seventh birthday or other ordinary memories of early childhood may be nothing more than reconstructions based on stories told to us by parents or relatives (Knapp & VandeCreek, 2000). However, scientists are not in complete agreement as to when this period of infantile amnesia ends for most children (Ornstein, Ceci, & Loftus, 1998b) or exactly why it occurs (Harley & Reese, 1999; see Focus 11.2). Interestingly, Roseanne Barr, the well-known television sitcom star of the 1990s, claimed after therapy that she remembered her mother sexually abusing her when she was 6 months old (Ornstein et al., 1998b, p. 1001).

FOCUS 11.2. INFANTILE AMNESIA

What is your earliest memory? It is widely believed by psychologists that a vast majority of humans cannot recall events that occurred prior to age 3, a phenomenon called infantile amnesia. For some unknown reason, adult memory of childhood events appears to begin sometime after the third or fourth birthday. Consequently, all those hours spent with a baby—rocking to sleep, playing, changing diapers, feeding, laughing, and cuddling—may be lost forever in the baby's mind. Childhood memories are fragile, but the common assumption is that *infant* memories are virtually nonexistent.

However, some recent research (Bauer, 1996) suggests that a baby may store those events but in a different kind of "preverbal" memory. It appears that even infants in the first year of life are able to retain bits of information about unique episodes over time (Mandler, 1988, 1990), but because they do not possess language skills, they cannot put these experiences into words at a later time. Very young children often rely on forms of memory (e.g., kinesthetic memory) that do not depend on verbal processing to be cognitively stored.

Other factors probably also contribute to the difficulty in recalling early childhood memories. Howe and Courage (1997) propose that childhood memories emerge as the cognitive self develops. The cognitive self is "a knowledge structure whose features serve to organize memories of experiences that happen to 'me'" (Howe & Crowe, 1997, p. 499). If the cognitive self is immature, the ability to recall remains disorganized and partly inaccessible. As children get older, the ability to maintain and organize information appears to increase. Other developmental aspects that probably affect childhood memory are the dramatic neurological and perceptual changes that occur during early childhood.

Whatever the mechanisms involved in early development, it appears that infants can "remember" or store events in memory in nonverbal ways. It is possible, therefore, that certain smells, tastes, and auditory and visual environmental cues may bring some undefined, distant memory to us, but we tend to be unable to articulate from where or when. Thus, well-articulated claims by victims of child abuse, based on their early infancy memories, probably should be held suspect until other corroborating evidence is gathered.

Claims and assertions of abuse during childhood are complicated by the fact that the very definition of abuse is culturally determined, and behaviors that would be taken by adults to be clear instances of abuse might not be viewed in a comparable fashion by children and vice versa (Ornstein et al., 1998b). For example, as Ornstein et al. point out, insertions of anal suppositories, urinary catheterization, and other invasive medical procedures during the first few years of life may be perceived by the young child as "abusive."

Many practitioners believe that traumatized children are more likely to reenact traumatic events than to describe them verbally (Alpert et al., 1998). Although many children are unable to give verbal descriptions of events that had taken place in their early years, they may show evidence of their memory in their behavior and play, where they reenact the abuse events (Alpert et al., 1998). It is clear that children interpret and respond to trauma according to their developmental level and maturity, but description of the behavioral pattern in children has been limited. Terr (1991, 1994) developed a model (derived from clinical observations of hundreds of traumatized children) of two types of childhood trauma, each with corresponding memory encoding and retrieval. By her description, Type I trauma consists of sudden, external, single events that result in stereotyped symptoms of childhood PTSD along with detailed memories, but also with misperceptions and mistimings regarding characteristics of the events. Type II traumas are those that involve "long-standing or repeated exposure to extreme external events" (Terr, 2003, p. 328). According to Terr, memory loss is most common in this kind of trauma. However, as pointed out by Ornstein et al. (1998b), scientists who study memory have found that repetition enhances memory rather than diminishing it: "Research on memory with children and adults suggests that people are more likely to forget an isolated event than a series of repeated events, even though the repeated events may become blended into a typical script" (p. 1000).

Perhaps more troubling for the courts and the psychological profession is that under certain circumstances, *false* memories of abuse can be created, often by psychotherapists or evaluators themselves. As reported by Roediger and Bergman (1998), "A substantial body of experimental evidence (buttressed by a long collection of anecdotal cases) shows that events that never happened can be vividly remembered, or that events can be remembered in ways quite different from the way they occurred" (p. 1102). Repeated suggestions, confrontations, or the use of highly suggestive "memory recovery" techniques may cause the creation of memories that are not true (Knapp & VandeCreek, 2000). A growing literature further suggests that it is relatively easy to create pseudo-memories in some individuals, but it may be more difficult in others. "The available evidence makes clear that individuals who have been exposed to repeated suggestive techniques over long periods of time sometimes provide highly detailed and coherent narratives that happen to be false"(Ornstein et al., 1998a, p. 1045). Hypnosis as a memory recovery technique especially runs the risk of creating, distorting, or magnifying memories. As discussed in Chapter 3, many forensic experts are very cautious about the use of hypnosis as a technique for obtaining information.

The tendency of clinicians to unintentionally engender symptoms or recollections in their patients is called the **iatrogenic effect** (*iatros* is the Greek word for *physician,* and *genic* refers to *cause*). In other words, clinicians who firmly believe in and are perceptually sensitive to certain symptoms as indicative of a specific disorder may, in effect, prompt the patient to think similarly. In this sense, certain therapists who are convinced that sexual abuse is the basic cause of many symptoms of maladjustment may have a strong propensity to look for and interpret a variety of behaviors as symptoms of sexual abuse. In effect, the clinician may encourage the reconstruction of memory in the patient to include accounts of sexual abuse that may have never occurred. In addition, the scientific research indicates that young children may be disproportionately vulnerable to suggestive influences, either during psychotherapy or more generally through daily living (Ceci & Bruck, 1993). However, Bruck and Ceci (2004) have also noted that susceptibility to suggestion is highly common in middle childhood as well.

In summary, repressed memory of childhood abuse and its recovery by psychotherapists or through suggestions via self-help books or workshops should raise some red flags for further inquiry and reasonable evaluation and assessment by the forensic psychologist. We do not mean to imply that it could not happen—only that the overwhelming bulk of the research evidence suggests that if it does, it is probably full of error and will need further corroboration from independent sources and careful assessment.

As asserted by two well-respected scientists, Roediger and Bergman (1998),

> Far more mysterious is how painful events, banished to an unconscious state for years though some mechanism of dissociation or repression, could be brought back to consciousness and recollected with great fidelity. . . . [N]o evidence from the voluminous literature on human memory makes us think this is possible. (p. 1095)

This is especially the case for adults who suddenly recollect from their "unconscious" traumatic events that happened 20 to 40 years previously.

By contrast, the research clearly indicates that memories of emotional events are reasonably good and accurate, and very rarely are they repressed or forgotten (Alison et al., 2006; Roediger & Bergman, 1998). Many people have reported their memories for high-impact events with considerable accuracy, a phenomenon referred to as **flashbulb memory** (R. Brown & Kulick, 1977). People in their 60s and older remember vividly what they were doing when they heard that President Kennedy was assassinated, and those older than 35 or 40 remember where they were when the space shuttle that contained teacher-astronaut Christa McAuliffe exploded in 1986. All but the youngest among us remember what we were doing when two hijacked airliners crashed into the World Trade Center on September 11, 2001. You likely recall some high-impact event that occurred during your childhood. People often feel that they remember with high accuracy even minor details of emotional events, such as earthquakes, tornadoes, and other natural disasters (Roediger & Bergman, 1998). Thus, many adults do vividly recall past abuse, including sexual abuse.

Roles of the Forensic Psychologist in Child Abuse Cases

In the past, clinicians rarely became involved in addressing forensic issues in child abuse before the cases were adjudicated (Melton et al., 1997). This has changed in recent years. Forensic psychologists are becoming involved much earlier in the process. Today, the forensic psychologist may assume a crucial role at the early stages of a case and then be asked to return to the role of a "neutral" expert in the adjudication and disposition. For example, the clinician may be asked by a court to determine whether child abuse or neglect occurred and, if it did occur, what should be done about it. The second question requires immediate (emergency), short-term, and/or long-term predictions and decisions and is essentially a risk assessment determination. According to Melton et al., the second question also focuses on the extent to which the child is in imminent danger. Early in the case, this might involve removing the child from the home for his or her protection.

It should be emphasized that many states are beginning to establish multidisciplinary teams for investigation, assessment, and intervention in child abuse or neglect cases. Consequently, the forensic psychologist rarely acts alone or without the expertise of other mental health professionals. Still, as pointed out by Melton et al. (1997, 2007), the forensic psychologist may be regarded as the team's sole expert in a variety of assessments and predictions.

The adjudication and disposition of the case refers primarily to the criminal proceedings against the alleged abuser. However, they may also occur in civil proceedings, such as custody hearings or hearings to decide whether visitation should be allowed. During adjudication, four issues that may involve the forensic psychologist are as follows:

1. What is the most appropriate procedure for taking a child's testimony?

2. Under what conditions is a child's out-of-court statement (hearsay) admissible?

3. Is the child competent enough to provide accurate testimony in abuse cases?

4. Did abuse or neglect occur, and if so, who is responsible?

The first issue—which first emerged in sexual abuse cases—concerns identifying what special procedures would allow a child to testify without being under enormous duress in the presence of the defendant. Moreover, "the child is notoriously vulnerable while giving evidence against abusers, especially parents, when proof of the charge will result in separation. Many children are highly suggestible and subject to recantation when faced with the reality of parental separation" (Partlett & Nurcombe, 1998, p. 1260). These problems of recantation and suggestibility are especially troubling when accusations of abuse made during custody proceedings give one parent an advantage over the other.

In criminal cases, recent legal rules in many states limit the defendant's confrontation with the child by allowing, under special circumstances, the child's testimony to be taken through closed-circuit TV, courtroom closure, or in some other way. Thus, the jury can observe and hear the testimony and the cross-examination while the child's distress and the defendant's possible attempt to intimidate are presumably minimized. If such a limitation on the defendant's right to confront witnesses against him is to occur, it first requires an assessment of the emotional consequences of the child's "interaction with a particular adult in a specific context" (Melton et al., 1997, p. 458). In 1987, the U.S. Supreme Court (e.g., *Maryland v. Craig,* 1987) "opened the door to testimony by mental health professionals in hearings to determine whether there is a necessity for special procedures to protect particular child witnesses" (Melton et al., 1997, p. 458).

Clinicians who evaluate abused children are required to be skillful and sensitive to a wide range of factors. K. S. Budd, Felix, Poindexter, Naik-Polan, and Sloss (2002) report that

> clinicians may be asked to assess the child's developmental or emotional functioning and needs, the effects of maltreatment on the child, the risk of harm should the child be united with his or her parents, the impact of separation from the biological family on the child's functioning, or the advantages and disadvantages of potential visitation or placement options. (p. 3)

In addition, the APA's Committee on Professional Practice and Standards (1998) recommends the use of a multimethod, multisource, multisession assessment approach in the evaluation of abused children. As pointed out by K. S. Budd et al. (2002), the standards also encourage that the forensic psychologist be highly sensitive to and knowledgeable about the cultural, socioeconomic, and diversity issues relevant to the child's situation. Furthermore, the standards highly recommend that the forensic psychologist interpret his or her findings conservatively. That is, the psychologist should acknowledge the limitations of the assessment findings and refrain from stating opinions or recommendations that are not adequately supported by the data. It is also emphasized that the evaluator should focus on the child's strengths rather than only on his or her deficits.

Assessment of child abuse or child protection cases is very common, yet few surveys describe in detail current practice or which evaluation procedures are most useful. In their survey of one urban juvenile court system, K. S. Budd et al. (2002) found that psychologists conducted 90% of the evaluations of children. Unfortunately, many of the evaluations were not based on multisource, multisession information but on much more limited data. However, many of the evaluations did emphasize the strengths of the child.

In a very helpful article, Bruck and Ceci (2004) review the many misconceptions that have emerged from the literature about children's ability to recall past events as well as the type of questions they should be asked. Among other things, Bruck and Ceci emphasize that children do disclose abuse if asked to do so, but that both preschoolers and slightly older (6- to 8-year-old) children can be very susceptible to suggestive, closed-ended questions.

In some cases, anatomically detailed dolls are used to help young children suspected of being sexually abused express themselves verbally on sexual topics. The practice of using them, however, has been questioned. Some experts (e.g., Bruck, Ceci, & Francoeur, 2000; Ceci & Bruck, 1993) contend that these dolls heighten the child's suggestibility and promote false stories. Others (e.g., Koocher et al., 1995) believe that, in the hands of well-trained professionals, they may be a useful communication tool, as long as they are used cautiously.

The expert testimony offered in child abuse cases is subject to the same legal rules as other forms of expert testimony (Berliner, 1998): "It must be relevant, not common knowledge; its value in helping prove the case cannot be outweighed by the potential for creating unfair prejudice; and it must be helpful to the trier of fact" (p. 11). Because forensic psychologists have been increasingly asked to serve as expert witnesses in child abuse cases in recent years, they would be wise to become familiar with the general nature of the disputes and the current status of relevant knowledge. The courts have scrutinized expert testimony in child abuse cases more carefully and more thoroughly as the amount of such testimony has correspondingly increased. Furthermore, as we discovered in Chapter 4, recent revisions in legal rules relating to the admission of expert testimony suggest that this scrutiny is apt to continue.

The psychologists may be asked in child abuse cases to provide expert testimony as *substantive evidence* or *rehabilitative evidence* (Berliner, 1998). An example of substantive evidence in this context would be professional opinions as to whether the child was abused or shares characteristics with abused children. An example of rehabilitative evidence would be testimony concerning the suitability of the child to tell his or her story. In other words, is the child credible, or is there an emotional or psychological problem that may hamper the veracity of the child's story or report?

> For example, if a child had exhibited reactions that were very unusual, such as severe dissociative symptoms, and these symptoms were used to discredit the child, the expert might properly explain the nature of dissociation and its possible association with a traumatic history. (Berliner, 1998, pp. 16–17)

In another situation, the psychologist may be asked to provide expert testimony for the defense, which seeks to discredit the child's testimony or to challenge it as being inconsistent with the reactions that would be expected if abuse actually had occurred. Patterns of behaviors or "syndromes" are not necessarily evidence of abuse, a fact that many courts and professionals have confused and misapplied. For example, the child sexual abuse accommodation syndrome (CSAAS) (Summit, 1983) does not necessarily verify that child sexual abuse occurred—nor did the originator of the term intend that the syndrome be applied that way (Berliner, 1998; Summit, 1992). In fact, because of the misapplication of the term, some courts have banned the term from being used at all (e.g., *Hellstrom v. Commonwealth,* 1992). Moreover, other scholars have questioned the assumptions or misconceptions that are associated with the CSAAS (Bruck & Ceci, 2004).

Child Abduction

A person is guilty of **child abduction** (kidnapping) if he or she unlawfully leads, takes, entices, or detains a child under a specified age with intent to keep or conceal the child from its parent, guardian, or other person having lawful custody. Child abduction is relatively rare among violent crimes against children and juveniles. It makes up less than 2% of all violent crimes against juveniles reported to law enforcement (Finkelhor & Ormrod, 2000). Kidnapping is most often divided into three classifications based on the identity of the perpetrator: (1) family kidnapping (representing 49% of reported kidnapping cases), (2) acquaintance kidnapping (27%), and (3) stranger kidnapping (24%). Most of the following data are drawn from the U.S. Department of Justice report, *Kidnapping of Juveniles,* prepared by Finkelhor and Ormrod. Their primary source for the data was the National Incidence-Based Reporting System (see Focus 11.3).

FOCUS 11.3. NATIONAL INCIDENT-BASED REPORTING SYSTEM

The U.S. Department of Justice is replacing its long-established Uniform Crime Reports (UCR) program with a more comprehensive National Incident-Based Reporting System (NIBRS). During the late 1970s, the law enforcement community called for the expanded use of the UCR and more detailed information on each criminal incident, in contrast to the straightforward statistics offered in the traditional UCR. In response to these concerns, the UCR reporting system was evaluated under federal contracts by Abt Associates of Cambridge, Massachusetts, which made a number of far-reaching recommendations for improvement. These recommendations formed the basis of the NIBRS under the support of the Uniform Federal Crime Reporting Act passed by the U.S. Congress in 1988. In this act, Congress required all federal law enforcement agencies, including those agencies within the Department of Defense, to collect and report more complete data to the FBI on two categories of offenses: Group A, which includes 46 serious offense categories, such as arson, assault, homicide, fraud, embezzlement, larceny-theft, and sex offenses, and Group B, which includes 11 less serious offenses, such as passing bad checks, driving under the influence of alcohol, engaging in disorderly conduct, drunkenness, nonviolent family offenses, and liquor law violations. The NIBRS is designed to collect a wide range of information on victims, offenders, and circumstances for a wide variety of offenses.

Under the NIBRS, local law enforcement agencies are asked to compile information on crimes coming to their attention, and this information is then added together at the state and national levels. For a crime to be counted, it simply needs to be reported and investigated. In addition, another major difference between the UCR and the NIBRS is that the NIBRS records *every* crime that occurs during one incident, in contrast to the UCR, which only records the most serious crime. Presumably, the added information from Group A data will become an indispensable tool for law enforcement agencies and researchers because it will provide detailed data about when and where specific types of crime take place, what forms they take, and the characteristics of their victims and perpetrators. Because reporting agencies are expected to submit a brief account of each incident, the NIBRS data include the number of offenders, the number of victims, and/or multiple attributes (e.g., weapons, property loss, drugs, alcohol) for each crime. The NIBRS has the promise of being the first explicitly computer-based and standardized reporting system in U.S. law enforcement, providing a rich source of data for researchers and policy makers.

Family kidnapping is committed mostly by parents (80%), a phenomenon so common in child abduction cases that it is labeled *parental abduction*. "Parental abduction encompasses a broad array of illegal behaviors that involve one parent taking, detaining, concealing, or enticing away his or her child from the parent having custodial access" (J. J. Wilson, 2001, p. 1). The U.S. Department of Justice (2010) estimates that there are 200,000 parental abductions annually in the United States. Parental abduction usually involves a child younger than age 6—most often around age 2. Both genders are equally victimized. The perpetrators are also evenly distributed (50% each) between men and women. The abduction generally originates in the home. Those children who become victims of family abduction are often thrust into a life of uncertainty and isolation, because the abductor is always fearful that he or she will be discovered and the child returned to the custodial parent.

Juveniles, similar to young children, are also more likely to be kidnapped by family members or acquaintances than by complete strangers. Acquaintances are people they know but who are not family members. Acquaintance kidnapping most often involves a teenage female victim (72%). The perpetrator is often a juvenile himself (30%) and is frequently a boyfriend or former boyfriend (18%). The most common motives are to seek revenge for being spurned, to force a reconciliation, to commit a sexual assault, or to evade parents who want to break up the relationship. In some instances, gang members kidnap other teenagers (whom they know) for intimidation, retaliation, or recruiting. A third type of acquaintance kidnapping involves family friends or employees (e.g., babysitters) who remove children from the family's home for the purpose of sexual assault or retaliation against the family. Acquaintance kidnapping victims suffer a higher rate of injury compared to victims of the other forms of abduction, possibly because the victim is usually older and therefore more likely to resist the abduction. Another reason may be that intimidation, which often is associated with more physical force, is the primary motive in many of these abductions.

Stranger kidnapping victimizes more females than males (64% compared to 36%). Most stranger kidnappings victimize teenage and elementary school–age victims (57% and 32%, respectively). Preschoolers are rarely targeted. The perpetrator is predominately male (95%). About 1 out of 5 stranger kidnappings is associated with another violent crime, such as sexual assault in the case of girl victims and robbery in the case of boy victims. This is the type of kidnapping most likely to involve the use of a firearm. The location of stranger kidnapping is associated primarily with the outdoors (58%), such as streets, highways, parks, waterways, and other public areas. Finkelhor and Ormrod (2000) point out that, based on NIBRS data, school is usually *not* the location for child abductions, including family abductions.

The National Incidence Study of Missing, Abducted, Runaway and Throwaway Children (NISMART) (Finkelhor, Hotaling, & Sedlack, 1990; Johnston & Girdner, 2001) is a report describing the results of a nationwide telephone survey conducted in 1988. The study determined estimates of the number of family abductions to both domestic and international destinations nationwide. More important to our discussion here, the NISMART survey reported some of the common behavioral and psychological characteristics of parental abductors. The following characteristics were outlined by Johnston and Girdner:

- Abducting parents are likely to deny and dismiss the other parent's value to the child. They believe that they, more than anyone else, know what is best for their child. In some cases, the motivation to abduct may also be an attempt to protect the child from a parent who is perceived to be likely to molest, abuse, or neglect the child, which in some instances may be a legitimate concern.
- Abducting parents usually take very young children (the mean age is 2–3). Such children are easier to transport and conceal, are unlikely to protest verbally, and may be unable to tell others their name or provide other identifying information.
- Most abducting parents are likely to have a supportive social network of family, friends, or social communities that provide assistance and emotional and moral support. This pattern is especially prevalent when the abductor has no financial or emotional ties to the geographical area from which the child was taken.
- Most custody violators do not consider their actions illegal or morally wrong, even after the involvement of the district attorney's office.
- Mothers and fathers are equally likely to abduct their children, although at different times. Fathers tend to abduct before there is a child custody order in place, whereas mothers tend to abduct after the court has issued a formal custody decree (p. 5).

Parental kidnappers who appear to be the most dangerous to the other parent or the child manifest paranoid, irrational beliefs and delusions that do not dovetail with reality (Johnston & Girdner, 2001). This risk is especially high in those abductors who have a history of domestic violence, hospitalization for mental disorders, or serious substance abuse. They may feel overwhelmed by their divorce and may be convinced that their former partner has betrayed and exploited them. Revenge may emerge as a dominant motive for the abduction. Fortunately, this type of parental abductor is relatively rare. Interestingly, one study found that approximately 75% of male abductors and 25% of female abductors had exhibited violent behavior in the past (Greif & Hegar, 1993).

Psychological Impact of Abduction

The experience of family abduction can be emotionally traumatic to both the child and the left-behind parent (Chiancone, 2001). The incident can be particularly damaging in cases in which force is used to carry out the abduction, the child is concealed, or the child is held for a long period of time. According to the NISMART survey, abductors use force in 14% of parental abductions and coercive threats in 17% (Chiancone, 2001; Finkelhor et al., 1990). The length of time separated from the left-behind parent is one of the major determinants of the emotional impact the incident has on the abducted child (Agopian, 1984). According to Chiancone, children held for short periods (less than a few weeks) usually do not give up hope of being reunited with the other parent and do not suffer significant emotional damage. However, the story is different for those children who experience long-term abductions. In reference to the Agopian study, Chiancone writes,

> They [the children] were often deceived by the abducting parent and frequently moved to avoid being located. This nomadic, unstable lifestyle made it difficult for children to make friends and settle into school, if they attended at all. Over time, younger children could not easily remember the left-behind parent, which had serious repercussions when they were reunited. Older children felt angry and confused by the behavior of both parents—the abductor for keeping them away from the other parent and the left-behind parent for failing to rescue them. (p. 5)

Chiancone (2001) also indicates that in long-term abductions, left-behind parents commonly experienced feelings of loss, rage, and impaired sleep, and more than half reported loneliness, fear, or severe depression. Social support and professional intervention are often important in helping them adjust to this traumatic experience.

One of the most dramatic cases of non-family child abductions took place in 1976 when a California school bus carrying 26 children, ages 5 to 14, was commandeered at gunpoint by three kidnappers. The kidnappers were attempting to arrange a $5 million ransom. The bus was later found empty, covered with bamboo and brush in a drainage ditch. The victims—19 girls and 7 boys—were driven for 11 hours in two darkened vans before being entombed in a moving van buried in a rock quarry. They remained buried for 16 hours in an 8-by-16-foot space until two of the oldest boys and the bus driver managed to dig the group out.

All three kidnappers were eventually captured. On December 15, 1977, a California superior court judge found the trio guilty of three counts of kidnapping with bodily harm, a conviction that in some jurisdictions carries a mandatory sentence of life in prison without the possibility of parole. The kidnapping was eventually dramatized in a made-for-TV move titled *They've Taken Our Children: The Chowchilla Kidnapping* (directed by Vern Gillum). Interestingly, the California Supreme Court refused to allow a suit by one of the kidnappers who claimed his role in the 1993 ABC docudrama had been distorted.

Psychiatrist Lenore Terr (1979, 1982, 1983) interviewed most of the victims and their parents 5 to 13 months after the kidnapping and again 4 years later. Virtually all the children suffered some short-term psychological effects, including sleep disorders, fear of being revictimized, and a variety of "unique" PTSD symptoms. Terr reported that the children, instead of demonstrating cognitive flashbacks, reexperienced the event through stereotyped, repetitive posttraumatic play (e.g., kidnapping games) that failed to diminish their anxiety about the abduction (McNally, 1991). One 5-year-old, for instance, began to bury her Barbie dolls, a process called behavioral reenactment. Some of the victims continued to have symptoms 4 or 5 years after the incident. The abduction underscores the short- and long-term psychological damage that often follows criminal victimization of children.

Elder Abuse and Neglect

Approximately 2.5 million older Americans are victims of various kinds of abuse each year (National Center on Elder Abuse [NCEA], 1999). **Elder abuse** is defined as the physical, financial, emotional, or psychological harm of an older adult, usually defined as age 65 or older (C. E. Marshall, Benton, & Brazier, 2000). Some researchers (Acierno, et al., 2010) use 60 as the minimum age when studying elder abuse. *Abandonment* is usually included in the definition of neglect and is characterized by such things as desertion of an elder at a hospital, a nursing facility, or other similar institution or public place such as a bus station. *Financial abuse* is also prevalent in cases of elder abuse. This refers to the illegal or improper use of an elder's funds, property, or assets. *Sexual abuse,* on the other hand, is relatively uncommon and refers to nonconsensual sexual contact of any kind with an elderly person. The laws that protect elders and the definitions of elder abuse vary from state to state, although all states have some form of legislation that addresses the problem (Berson, 2010).

The National Elder Mistreatment Study (Acierno et al., 2010) reports that a 1-year prevalence of elder abuse in the United States was 4.6% for emotional abuse, 1.6% for physical abuse, 0.6% for sexual abuse, 5.1% for neglect, and 5.2% for financial abuse by a family member. Overall, approximately 1 in 10 cognitively intact, elderly respondents reported experiencing some form of abuse during 2008. Relatively little of this mistreatment was reported to authorities.

Adult children are the most frequent abusers of the elderly (National Center on Elder Abuse, 1999). Other family members and spouses ranked as the next most likely abusers. Men tend to be the most likely perpetrators of elder mistreatment, although women are more likely to be involved in elder neglect (Administration on Aging, 1998). Most cases of elder abuse and neglect take place at home because most older Americans live at home rather than in nursing homes or institutions.

Because elder maltreatment is often subtle and provides few indications or clear or recognizable signs, it is extremely difficult to say exactly how many cases there are in the United States each year. It is estimated that only 1 out of 14 domestic elder abuse incidents comes to the attention of authorities (Pillemer & Finkelhor, 1988). The emotional or psychological abuse can range from name-calling or giving the "silent treatment" to intimidating and threatening the individual. It may also involve treating the older person like a child and isolating the person from family, friends, or regular activities. (See Focus 11.4 on the growing field of geropsychology.)

FOCUS 11.4. GEROPSYCHOLOGY: MEETING THE NEEDS OF OLDER ADULTS

The graying of the baby-boom generation and better quality health care have combined to make older adults the fastest growing age group. It is expected that persons older than age 65 will represent 20% of the population by 2030 (Qualls, Segal, Norman, Niederche, & Gallagher-Thompson, 2002).

Today, many people in their late 60s, 70s, and even 80s do not consider themselves old, and many also resist such euphemisms as "senior citizens." Although society recognizes the desire of older adults to maintain their independence, concerns are often raised about their capacity to live alone and to make decisions, including financial ones, in their own best interest. When they live in other settings—such as assisted living facilities or nursing homes—their well-being in such alternative living arrangements must be addressed.

Geropsychology is a specialty area devoted to the research, assessment, and treatment of older adults. Geropsychologists may be asked to evaluate an individual's competency or capacity to manage

(Continued)

(Continued)

funds, make informed decisions about medical treatment, or draft legal documents such as wills or real estate contracts. According to psychologists with expertise in this area, "A clinical assessment . . . in an older adult is an exacting task: It must be comprehensive, address a host of ethical and environmental issues, and address multiple co-morbidities" (Baker, Lichtenberg, & Moye, 1998, p. 151). Fortunately, the Department of Veterans Affairs (1996) has led the way in developing a helpful resource guide for geropsychologists for this purpose.

The treatment tasks of geropsychologists presume an understanding that older adults are different from young adults and have very unique mental health needs. In addition to diagnosable mental disorders such as depression or paranoia, they also may have cognitive impairments, including dementias that are associated with a variety of illnesses. On the other hand, most older adults are mentally healthy and have some of the same needs as their younger counterparts. For example, older adults benefit from cognitive stimulation and physical and emotional intimacy. Mentally healthy older adults often need emotional support when faced with crises such as the loss of a spouse or adult child, a debilitating physical illness, or a change in living situation.

The demand for both assessment and treatment of older adults is expected to increase well into the 21st century. According to Qualls (1998), three levels of specialization in geropsychology have been identified. **Generalists** will do limited work with older adults but have at least basic exposure to geropsychology. **Generalists with proficiency** will have achieved more in-depth study of aging and have a wider array of specialized skills. Qualls predicts that these practitioners will provide the majority of services to older adults. **Specialists** will operate at the expertise level. Having obtained advanced skills, they will conduct research and training, set standards and policies, and be responsible for generating new knowledge in the field.

Graduate training in psychology is rapidly recognizing the demand for geropsychological services, but not all programs even offer a course in aging. Readers interested in learning more about educational and career opportunities in this field are referred to APA Division 20 (Adult Development and Aging) and Division 12, Section II (Clinical Geropsychology).

Roles of the Forensic Psychologist in Elder Abuse Cases

Melton and his colleagues (1997) posit that, for the forensic psychologist, the issues of elder abuse and neglect are closely related to child abuse cases in many respects: "Evaluators should address many of the same domains in dispositional evaluation, and they should be alert to many of the same potential problems and role confusion" (p. 479). *Dispositional evaluation* refers to an assessment of the attitudes, desires, and motivations of an individual. There are, however, two major differences between forensic evaluations for child abuse and those for elder abuse.

> First, clinicians conducting dispositional evaluations in cases involving elders or other dependent adults need to be aware of the service alternatives for adults with disabilities, and they need to have a realistic view of the care needs that the victim presents. In that sense, the scope of an evaluation in an elder maltreatment case may have much in common with an evaluation for limited guardianship. (Melton et al., 1997, p. 479)

Guardianship refers to the appointment of authority over an individual's person or estate to another person when that individual is considered incapable of administering his or her own affairs. Guardianship can come in many forms, but the two that are most pertinent here are general and specific or special guardianship. As the name implies, a *general guardian* is one who has the responsibility for general care and control of the person and the estate, whereas the *specific guardian* is one who has special or limited powers and duties with respect to the person. For example, the specific guardian may have the legal authority to make only certain treatment decisions, whereas in other areas, the affected person is free to make other decisions. In other words, the guardian has limited authority.

The second major difference between child abuse and elder abuse evaluations is that the victim, unlike in child abuse or protection cases, is presumed to be competent until there is a legal determination otherwise. In addition, about one fourth of the complainants in the elder abuse cases are the victims themselves (Melton et al., 1997). Furthermore, there may be significant financial conflicts of interest, especially if the assigned caregivers are financially (and perhaps emotionally) dependent on the victim. Consequently, the clinician needs to be aware of and sensitive to the complicated relationships that may exist between the guardians and the victim.

SUMMARY AND CONCLUSIONS

Forensic psychologists are all too familiar with the results of violent victimization. When the perpetrator of the violence is a family member or an intimate partner, the effects are particularly devastating. Psychologists not only offer treatment to victims of violent crime but also evaluate them to assess the extent of their psychological injury. Results of those evaluations then may be used in civil or criminal proceedings. Psychologists also may evaluate or offer treatment to violent offenders, a topic that will be covered more fully in the remaining chapters. In this chapter, we have focused on the services provided to victims of violent crime, as well as the information that has been gathered on the characteristics and extent of the crime itself.

Family violence—as used in the title of this chapter—is a very broad term that encompasses each of the areas discussed. The term is not perfect. We have taken some liberty with it, as much of the violence described in this chapter is not technically between family members. Nevertheless, no other term adequately covers each area discussed herein. Many researchers use the term *domestic violence,* which includes spouse or partner violence, sibling violence, child abuse within the home, and elder abuse—but it does not technically cover intimate partner violence (IPV) if the partners do not reside in the same domicile.

Researchers have made considerable progress in their study of IPV. Whereas earlier studies focused primarily on female victims, often describing them as passive, depressed, and helpless, later research focused on descriptions of the abuse relationship and features of the male batterer. Likewise, researchers have explored IPV between same-sex couples and between couples in which the woman is the abuser. In the great majority of intimate partner abuse situations, however, the male is the abuser. We explored some of the issues faced by forensic psychologists who treat abusers and victims, as well as the challenges they face when giving expert testimony.

Child abuse is a continuing and disturbing problem. After reviewing statistics associated with this crime, we focused on the most severe forms, including infanticide, sexual abuse, and the little-researched Munchausen by proxy and shaken baby syndromes. Evaluations of children who have allegedly been sexually abused are among the most challenging for psychologists in forensic practice. A related area, alleged instances of child abuse in the distant past, has been extremely controversial for many psychologists. These cases often—but not inevitably—revolve around the issue of repressed or recovered memory. We presented the research associated with this topic as well as conclusions from both American and British working groups. Although the repressed memory issue is far from resolved—and it often pits research psychologists against clinicians—it is important to note that the empirical research to this point does not strongly support widespread forgotten memories. It is possible, though, that some victims of sexual assault do forget and do remember their victimization many years later.

The chapter ended with coverage of two areas that are under-researched by psychology, though not ignored by the law or by victim advocates. Child abduction and elder abuse have both received a good deal of public attention over the past two decades. Practicing psychologists are likely to encounter these issues primarily in the treatment context, such as when providing services to the elderly or to the parent or parents who are left behind in child abduction cases.

KEY CONCEPTS

Battered woman syndrome (BWS)

Battering

Child abduction

Dysphoric/borderline batterer

Elder abuse

Family-only batterer

Family violence

Filicide

Flashbulb memory

Generally violent/antisocial batterer

Geropsychology

Iatrogenic effect

Infanticide

Intimate partner violence (IPV)

Munchausen syndrome by proxy (MSBP)

Neonaticide

Reconstructive theory of memory

Repressed memory

Repression

Shaken baby syndrome (SBS)

Spousal Assault Risk Assessment (SARA)

State-dependent memory

Vicarious traumatization

QUESTIONS FOR REVIEW

1. Summarize Meuer, Seymour, and Wallace's stage theory of domestic violence.

2. What obstacles are placed in the path of victims of intimate partner violence who want to leave the relationship?

3. Why is the term *battered woman syndrome* controversial?

4. What progress has been achieved in the treatment of batterers?

5. What are the major differences between same-sex domestic violence (SSDV) and opposite-sex domestic violence (OSDV)?

6. List five measures used to assess symptoms of PTSD.

7. List and describe briefly the four major types of child maltreatment.

8. What are the key psychological features of Munchausen's syndrome by proxy?

9. What conclusions were reached by the APA Working Group on Investigation of Memories of Childhood Abuse?

10. What is the role of the forensic psychologist in child abuse cases? In parental abduction cases? In elder abuse cases?

Part VI

Correctional Psychology

12

Correctional Psychology in Adult Settings

CHAPTER OBJECTIVES

- Describe the tasks of psychologists and other mental health professionals in adult corrections.
- Sketch the correctional system and how it operates.
- Summarize the legal rights of inmates, including the right to treatment and the right to refuse treatment.
- Review the research on the psychological effects of imprisonment.
- Describe treatment approaches to dealing with specific groups of offenders.

Corrections today is a high-profile, complex operation that consumes very large portions of the operating budgets of the federal government and virtually all states. On December 31, 2008, about 1 in every 133 U.S. residents was in custody of state or federal prisons or local jails (Sabol, West, & Cooper, 2009). Overall, at the end of 2009, federal and state correctional authorities had jurisdiction over 1,613,656 prisoners (H. West, 2010). *Jurisdiction*, in this context, refers to the legal authority over a prisoner, regardless of where the person is held. The facilities include prisons, jails, privately operated correctional facilities, halfway houses, boot camps, farms, training or treatment centers, and hospitals. Eighty-seven percent of these prisoners were under the jurisdiction of state correctional authorities.

The majority of offenders (approximately two thirds) were under community supervision, which includes probation, parole, and their many variants. House arrest, electronic monitoring, halfway houses for newly released offenders, day reporting, and intensive supervision are examples of sanctions included under the term *community corrections. Probationers* represent the majority (84%) of offenders under community supervision (Glaze & Bonczar, 2009). *Probation* is a court-ordered period of correctional supervision in the community, usually as an alternative to incarceration. *Parole* is a period of conditional supervised release in the community following a prison term, and represents approximately 15% of offenders under community supervision. During the past 10 years, the number of offenders supervised in the community has increased dramatically (Glaze & Bonczar, 2009).

In recent years, there also has been a significant increase of detainees under the custody of U.S. Immigration and Customs Enforcement (ICE). Nationwide, the overall number of ICE detainees has doubled since 2000 (Sabol et al., 2009). Data from 2008 reveal that Mexican citizens represent over a third of the 34,000 detainees, followed by El Salvadorans, Guatemalans, and Hondurans.

In this chapter, we will focus on the services offered by forensic psychologists to the wide variety of individuals under correctional supervision, particularly in prisons and jails. In the United States, correctional psychology is a vibrant and growing field. (For illustrations, see the Personal Perspectives of Dr. Michael Bourke [9.1] and Dr. Philip Magaletta [12.2, this chapter].) In Canada, a long and rich tradition of correctional psychology has had an enormous impact on the field, particularly in the United States, Canada, and Europe (see Wormith & Luong, 2007, for a comprehensive review). Correctional treatment research by Canadian correctional psychologists (e.g., Andrews & Bonta, 1994; Hanson, Bourgon, Helmus, & Hodgson, 2009) has been instrumental in the development of correctional psychology as a viable profession (see also Personal Perspective 12.1, Dr. Marnie Rice, this chapter).

The chapter begins with this institutional focus, providing an overview of key concepts and the legal rights of inmates that are pertinent to psychological concepts. We then examine the assessment and treatment roles of correctional psychologists as well as aspects of the prison and jail environments that present obstacles to effective treatment. By far the greatest research attention is paid to the work of psychologists who consult with or work in institutional settings, yet forensic psychologists as a group are more likely to come into contact with persons under community supervision than inmates within correctional facilities. During the latter part of the chapter, therefore, we will focus on **community corrections** and the contributions of forensic psychologists in that realm.

PERSONAL PERSPECTIVE 12.1

Learning From Maximum-Security Psychiatric Patients

Marnie E. Rice, PhD

I am a registered (licensed) clinical psychologist in the province of Ontario and currently Research Director Emerita at the Mental Health Centre Penetanguishene, where I work part-time as a researcher. I am also Professor of Psychiatry and Behavioural Neurosciences (part-time) at McMaster University, Professor of Psychiatry (adjunct) at the University of Toronto, and Associate Professor of Psychology (adjunct) at Queen's University in Kingston, Ontario.

(Continued)

(Continued)

How did I get started? As I was about to finish my PhD in clinical psychology, I heard that a job was open as a psychologist to work on a behavioral program for male mentally disordered offenders in a maximum-security psychiatric hospital. My clinical experience as a student had primarily been in behavioral programs for autistic children, and I had never considered working with adult forensic patients, but my interest was piqued for several reasons. For one, the hospital was located in Ontario's "cottage country," just a couple of hours from the urban areas of southern Ontario where my family was located and where I grew up, and my husband and I were very interested in the active outdoor lifestyle we would be able to have there. Second, there was also a job there for my husband, who was just graduating from law school. Third, a friend told me that there was a psychologist there by the name of Vern Quinsey whom she highly recommended as a researcher from whom I could learn.

I'll never forget the first day I set foot in the Oak Ridge Division of the Mental Health Centre Penetanguishene in 1975. I was here to be interviewed for the position of psychologist on what was called the "Activity Treatment Unit," four wards of about 38 patients each, all run as a token economy. After my interview, I was taken to visit a ward. Perhaps in an attempt to dissuade me from any desire to work there (the attendants at the time were all male and they didn't particularly want a woman working there), I was taken to see "D ward," the ward that housed the most difficult patients. Many of them had developmental disabilities, had had lobotomies, or were severely psychotic. All were supposedly very aggressive, but the burly all-male ward attendants seemed at least equally intimidating. The place was dismal, and as the attendants

guided me down the corridor, we stopped at each patient's room so that the patient could perform for me. Each one had an act: Ricky walked on his hands, Fred danced, Clifford recited a poem, Art sang a song, and so on down the corridor. I felt that these patients were made to perform on cue for my benefit. I decided that day that the place was so bad that surely I could do some good. I'm still here over 35 years later.

From the beginning, it seemed like a natural fit to do research that could eventually help improve the assessment and treatment of the patients at our hospital. Vern Quinsey handed me an ongoing research project pretty much the day I started, and we have collaborated on most projects since then, with Grant Harris soon joining our research team. At the time I started working, the literature was clear that there was no such thing as "expertise" when it came to making predictions about future violence. It seemed this was one area where research could really make a contribution. Our first paper on this topic was published in 1993 (Harris, Rice, & Quinsey, 1993) and was titled, "Violent Recidivism of Mentally Disordered Offenders: Development of a Statistical Prediction Instrument." Interestingly, although this paper became (and still is) the most highly cited paper ever published in *Criminal Justice and Behavior*, it was first rejected by three other journals! After four books and numerous papers and book chapters on the topic of violence risk assessment, I believe our work has made a difference, and I'm still excited about continuing to make progress in this area.

One of my favorite publications by my colleagues and me is our evaluation of a maximum-security therapeutic community (Rice, Harris, & Cormier, 1992), titled "An Evaluation of a Maximum Security Therapeutic Community for

Psychopaths and Other Mentally Disordered Offenders." I like this study for several reasons: first, because the results surprised me—I had really expected to see that the therapeutic community program would be shown to reduce violent recidivism. (Remember, this was before the work of Andrews, Gendreau, Bonta et al. on risk, need, and responsivity). Second, the study pointed out to me that there was something fundamentally different about psychopaths inasmuch as the program seemed to make them worse. At the same time, it seemed to have the opposite effect for other patients. This was a very surprising finding and led us to our subsequent work on the nature of psychopathy. Finally, this work showed that if we knew just one thing about an offender—i.e., his score on the PCL—we could predict at much higher than chance levels whether or not he would commit another violent offense upon release. That finding helped lead to our future work on violence risk prediction.

Another favorite is a study we did to evaluate the effects of a staff training program we developed to reduce the amount and seriousness of violence in our hospital (Rice, Helzel, Varney, & Quinsey, 1985), on training for psychiatric hospital staff. I am proud of this work because it had a positive effect on violence within our hospital; the program is still used (with modifications) at both our own facility and others.

My interest in continuing my research is maintained by discovering new findings that allow us to refine the problem and ask new and more sophisticated questions. Sometimes our findings confirm what we thought, but other times they force us to rethink our hypotheses. It's still very exciting to me. The construct of psychopathy and whether it is best conceived as a set of enduring personality traits or as a set of behavioral tactics is a topic that I think still holds much promise for contributing to knowledge in the field of criminal justice.

To those considering entering the field, I will say that I'm still a big fan of the scientist-practitioner model, and would strongly advise pursuing a PhD rather than a PsyD. To me, the strong emphasis on research skills in a PhD program in psychology is what distinguishes us most from other clinical disciplines, and what has allowed psychologists to be major contributors to the clinical research literature in the criminal justice field.

Dr. Rice earned a BA in psychology from McMaster University, an MA in developmental psychology from the University of Toronto, and a PhD in clinical psychology from York University. She and her husband have two grown children who are "our proudest accomplishments." Her current part-time status allows her to pursue other interests, especially traveling with her camera to exotic locations. She says she always comes back with a new appreciation of her good fortune in having been born in Canada. When at home, she enjoys a variety of outdoor winter and summer sports.

Institutional Corrections

The United States has the highest **incarceration rate** of any industrialized country, with the numbers of inmates behind bars having increased steadily over the past quarter-century. Interestingly, Russia is a close second to the United States (Wilper et al., 2009). The greatest population increase in the United States has occurred in the federal prison system (BJS, 2002a) and is believed to be largely due to the nation's "war on drugs," whereby **mandatory sentences** have been in effect for individuals convicted of drug offenses.

However, rising incarceration rates also have been observed in virtually every state, even during periods of declining crime rates. Consequently, by the end of the 20th century, every state was facing overcrowding in at least one, and typically more, of its correctional facilities. In recent years, however, this overcrowding has eased somewhat as more states have taken steps to move offenders out of institutional settings or divert them to community programs.

The crimes for which offenders are incarcerated are not only those considered the most heinous. As of 2001, in state prisons, 51% of all offenders were serving time for violent offenses, 20% for drug offenses, 15% for public order offenses, and 14% for property offenses such as burglary or larceny (BJS, 2002a). In contrast to what we might expect from media coverage, robbery—not homicide—accounted for the great majority of the violent offenses. Although robbery is a serious crime and its effect on the victim should not be discounted, it does not necessarily include the *use* of force. The taking of property through *threat* of force—such as a weapon shown to the victim—is sufficient to classify a crime as a robbery. The point made here is that even the 51% of offenders serving time for violent offenses did not necessarily cause physical harm to their victims.

Women are less likely than men to be incarcerated for violent offenses. Yet, since 1990, the number of female prisoners has increased 108% (compared with a male increase of 77%) (BJS, 2001a), though to our knowledge no one is predicting that women will ever "catch up." By 2008, a total of 105,300 women were serving prison sentences of more than one year (Sabol et al., 2009). Presently, women make up 6.3% of all state and federal prison inmates and approximately 10% of all jail inmates and detainees in the United States. Women ages 35 to 39 make up the largest percentage of sentenced women prisoners under state or federal jurisdiction (Sabol et al., 2009).

Despite the rising incarceration rate, imprisonment does not seem to deter or rehabilitate a substantial number of offenders. Research on **recidivism**—typically measured by new arrests, new convictions, or sometimes by self-report data—is not encouraging. An oft-cited, but somewhat dated government survey of persons released from prison in 15 states found that, over a 3-year period, a very high number were rearrested, particularly those who had been imprisoned for property offenses (BJS, 2002c). For example, 78.8% of motor vehicle thieves, 77.4% of those who possessed or sold stolen property, 74.6% of larcenists, and 74% of burglars were rearrested within 3 years (BJS, 2002c). Although these data suggest that neither the imprisonment itself nor programs offered to inmates had a positive effect on those who reoffended, recidivism data must be interpreted very cautiously.

An arrest does not necessarily mean that an individual has indeed committed another offense. Even if he or she has, however, it does not mean that a former offender has not benefited in other ways from the rehabilitation programs offered in a correctional setting. Nevertheless, recidivism statistics such as those reported above lead some observers to question whether incarceration is the best route to take in dealing with the problem of crime, and others to question whether rehabilitation is a realistic goal. Furthermore, many legal scholars and researchers in the social sciences are concerned about the disproportionate confinement of the poor and racial or ethnic minorities. The conditions within many prisons, including overcrowding and violence within the facility, give further cause for concern. In recent years, for example, the disturbing topic of prison rape has received increasingly more research attention (Neal & Clements, 2010). Although few scholars advocate the total abolition of jails and prisons, there are increasing calls for alternatives to incarceration, especially for nonviolent offenders.

Forensic psychologists working in **institutional corrections,** then, must find ways to do their work within a system that is placed in the position of justifying its operations. The public wants its prisons but is resentful of the fiscal costs. Moreover, although public opinion surveys suggest continuing support for rehabilitation, individuals working in corrections have learned that rehabilitation-oriented programs are the first to go when budgets need to be cut. Even with scaled-down programming, it is not unusual for the corrections budget to consume a greater share of state coffers than the education budget. Indeed, college students are often appalled to learn that their own hefty yearly tuition fee may be smaller than the cost of maintaining an inmate in prison for a year.

The psychologist in a correctional setting also must work in an environment that often diminishes the likelihood of therapeutic success. Inmates get transferred to other prisons, correctional officers may not support the psychologist's role, administrators may cut their budgets, there is little time to conduct research, and the limitations on confidentiality suggest to inmates that psychologists are representatives of the prison administration, not advocates for their own interests. We will cover these and other issues later in the chapter.

For the time being, it is important to note that many professional groups have established a variety of guidelines and standards for providing services in correctional facilities. These include the *Standards for Health Services in Prisons,* published by the National Commission on Correctional Health Care (NCCHC, 2008), as well as the recently updated standards developed by the International Association for Correctional and Forensic Psychology (IACFP; Althouse, 2010), which was formerly the American Association of Correctional Psychology. These standards, to which we will refer later in the chapter, are intended to offer direction and support to practitioners. In addition, psychologists working in corrections are expected to conform to the ethical code of the American Psychological Association (APA), which was revised in 2003 and again in 2010 (APA, 2003a, 2010). Forensic psychologists are also provided with a set of specialty guidelines (Committee on Ethical Guidelines for Forensic Psychologists, 1991) that do not have the force of the ethics code but do offer suggestions for practice. Finally, psychologists must be aware of all relevant state and federal laws and regulations that are pertinent to the services they provide and the contexts in which they provide them.

Overview of Correctional Facilities

Persons detained, accused, or convicted, when not allowed to remain in their own homes, are housed in three types of facilities: jails, prisons, and community-based facilities. (Secure hospitals, such as psychiatric hospitals, are a fourth alternative.) **Jails** are operated by local governments to hold persons temporarily detained, held for lack of bail while awaiting trial or other court proceedings, or sentenced to confinement after having been convicted of a misdemeanor. **Prisons** are facilities operated by the federal government and all states for persons convicted of felonies and sentenced to terms of more than 1 year. **Community-based facilities** are less secure institutions, such as halfway houses or transition homes, typically intended as **intermediate sanctions** for offenders deemed to need less security than would be provided in jails or prisons but more than would be available in their own homes. Community-based facilities will be discussed later in the chapter.

On any given day, approximately half of the individuals held in jails are innocent; they are detainees, not convicted of the crime of which they are accused. Approximately another half are serving short-term sentences for misdemeanor offenses.

The proportion of detainees and sentenced misdemeanants varies widely by jurisdiction, however. In some facilities, up to 70% of the population comprises **pretrial detainees** who were unable to afford bail or who were denied bail because they were considered dangerous. Jails also may house a vast array of individuals awaiting transfer to prison, to a mental institution, to another state, to a juvenile facility, or to a military detention facility, though such individuals awaiting transfer usually make up a small portion (rarely more than 5%) of the jail population. In effect, though, jails hold a collection of persons at various stages of criminal, civil, or military justice processing. In some communities, jails also serve as temporary overnight shelters for individuals whom police arrest on minor charges, believing they need a safe haven.

In the federal system, pretrial detainees are held in **detention centers.** When space in federal detention centers is not available, persons accused of federal crimes or awaiting sentencing are detained in state or local jails. In fact, about two thirds of federal detainees are held in such facilities (Clear & Cole, 2000). Federal detention centers have been heavily publicized since the terrorist attacks of September 11, 2001, because the government held individuals for questioning about possible terrorist involvement. "Makeshift" detention centers were opened, and numerous individuals were turned over to Immigration and Naturalization Services (INS) and deported after secret deportation proceedings before immigration judges. When President Barack Obama took office in January 2009, one of his first actions was to announce his attention to close Camp Delta, the detention center in Guantanamo Bay. To date, this has not yet occurred, although the number of detainees has been reduced.

Prisons, operated by states or by the federal government, hold only persons convicted of felonies. They are classified by the level of security maintained over the inmates: minimum, medium, and maximum, with gradients sometimes in between these three main alternatives. Different custody levels are also found within as well as among prisons. Thus, an inmate may be kept in close custody in a medium-security prison for disciplinary reasons, and an inmate in a maximum-security prison may have attained "trustee" status, requiring minimal custody.

In the 1990s, **supermax prisons** were introduced in the federal government and approximately 41 states. These are extremely high-security facilities (or units within a maximum-security prison) supposedly intended to hold the most troublesome, violent inmates. As we will see later in the chapter, however, numerous concerns have been raised about these facilities. Prison systems also may include specialized facilities, such as work camps, classification centers, and units for inmates with mental disorders. Boot camps, prison farms, forestry centers, and ranches for young offenders who have committed primarily nonviolent crimes are other examples of specialized facilities.

In some states—e.g., Alaska, Connecticut, Delaware, Hawaii, Rhode Island, and Vermont—jails are under the control of the state rather than local government, and jail/prison functions are combined. Thus, detainees and sentenced offenders—both misdemeanants and felons—may be kept within the same facility, though they may be placed in separate housing units. A typical approach in these "mixed systems" is to have one or two facilities designated as maximum security, with the balance being medium- or minimum-security facilities capable of housing persons accused of crime as well as those who have been convicted and sentenced.

The federal prison system is highly organized and centralized under the **Federal Bureau of Prisons (BOP).** It consists of a network of facilities that are called penitentiaries, correctional institutions, prison camps, and halfway houses, as well as the detention centers referred to above. They are located on a continuum of five security levels: minimum, low, medium, high, and administrative. The nation's one federal supermax facility, located in Florence, Colorado, is classified at the administrative level. (See Focus 12.1 on career opportunities for psychologists in the BOP; see also Personal Perspectives 12.2, highlighting Dr. Philip Magaletta, who has had a lifelong career with the BOP.)

PERSONAL PERSPECTIVE 12.2

A Career in Corrections

Philip R. Magaletta, PhD*

When students ask about careers, I share that prisons chose me. When I signed the papers to work at a penitentiary, my first job after obtaining my doctorate, all I really knew was that I liked the Psychology Services staff I'd met and was impressed with the others involved in the daily operation of the facility. It came to pass that adding inmates to that mix was the reason I decided to stay.

Now let me back up a bit. I was fortunate to earn undergraduate and graduate degrees from Jesuit schools that train the whole person. Two core teachings from this experience stand out and are relevant to working in corrections. First, I should give serious consideration to living a life of service for others. Marriage, children, and friendships helped me realize this personally; clinical practice in corrections, as a true public service, helped me realize it professionally. Second, I should live effectively, which required that I develop as a contemplative in action. In other words, considering and reflecting on others and their point of view is equally important as engaging their world through action. As it turns out, the dual "custody and care" mission of the criminal justice setting and its implied integration of both public safety and public health principles requires that one be both reflective *and* actively involved.

Commencing my first postdoctoral job, I quickly learned that prisons are truly a series of nested systems. This reality required and allowed a psychologist to stretch and manifest all aspects of psychology as a public service: practice (including individual and group work, crisis intervention, psychopharmacological consultation, screening, and assessment), training, research, and administration. I continue to adhere to the belief that there is no greater, high-risk, high-need group than inmates and that psychology has barely begun to scratch the surface of the potential it holds for addressing their needs. The public health work we do with inmates and the public safety work we do for our communities is among the most challenging, rewarding, and hopeful areas of psychology that I know of.

That said, it is also quite true that criminal justice settings can be very demanding professionally and personally. For this reason, I advocate that students and early career professionals find strong mentors, sponsors, and supervisors when they embark upon this path. I consider myself quite lucky to have had the chance to work with some of the brightest students in psychology as well as the chance to receive mentoring from some outstanding professionals in our shared field of study. For that, I am both grateful and responsible for passing it on.

(Continued)

(Continued)

Clinical work in corrections is rarely the same from day to day. One reason for this is the heterogeneity of pathology across the population served. There is an extraordinary array of psychopathology present, much of which took years to develop. Not all of the services provided are related to psychopathology, though. Many of the services provided are mandated by policy and law. For example, due to the custodial nature of corrections, all inmates must be screened for mental health problems and program placement.

Although the daily work may appear different, it does typically require the same set of competencies. These typically include the functional competencies of screening/assessment and intervention. Each of these functional competencies is surrounded by and infused with one overarching foundational competency: interdisciplinary collaboration. What makes corrections work unique is that "interdisciplinary" is not limited to only "primary care model" interpretations. It means that daily, your work with screening, assessment, and interventions is achieved through collaboration with other corrections disciplines such as corrections officers, case managers, and the like. Best practices in mental health services delivery in correctional settings require clinicians that are able to understand, interact with, and respect these interdisciplinary partners.

My present responsibilities as an administrator allow me to continue the work of engineering pipelines back to graduate schools where psychologists are being trained. Building upon the work of others, we are involved in the daily task of attracting and retaining the brightest talent in graduate programs today. Over the past three decades, we have seen increasing numbers of students self-select into this line of work. They are increasingly aware (and thankfully, so are their graduate program faculty) of the distinctions and differences between the broad, generalist training required for effective clinical practice in corrections and the more specialized areas that are sometimes thought to be important by others concerned with graduate school enrollment.

In the future, criminal justice settings are likely to benefit from the work of clinical and counseling psychologists who have knowledge and skills in the area of psychopharmacology, geriatrics, and gangs, as well as continue to benefit from those trained to work with substance abusers, sexual offenders, and the seriously mentally ill. The risk-need frame for understanding the process of change will continue to yield evidence-based practice(s). In addition, both risk-need models and evidence-based practices will have a chance to flourish as the field begins questioning and then understanding the competencies required among staff who implement change programs. The prevailing thought is that all of these future emergent needs are best suited to an initial predoctoral level of study that is broad and general.

Dr. Magaletta is a licensed clinical psychologist presently serving as the Clinical Training Coordinator at the Washington office of the Federal Bureau of Prisons. He is also a faculty associate at The Johns Hopkins University. A graduate of University of Scranton, he earned his master's degree in 1992 from Loyola College in Maryland and his doctorate in clinical psychology in 1996 from St. Louis University. He is an active member of several professional associations and his work has been published in a number of books and journals. His areas of teaching and research include mental health services delivery to incarcerated populations, addictions counseling, spirituality, telehealth, and mental health workforce and education systems.

*The views and opinions presented are those of the author only and do not reflect the policy or opinion of the Bureau of Prisons or the Department of Justice.

In addition to the features summarized above, jails and prisons can be contrasted on an important point that affects the work of psychologists. Prisons are far more likely than jails to offer programs, including recreation, work programs, substance abuse treatment, and a variety of rehabilitative programs. This can be attributed to several factors. First, because a jail stay is relatively short, inmates are less likely to benefit from long-term programming. Second, most jails are operated by local governments and do not have funds available for much beyond their custodial function. Third, most jails are operated by law enforcement professionals, such as county sheriffs, rather than corrections professionals. The law enforcement community is not trained to provide services to offenders or alleged offenders; it is trained to enforce the law, protect the public, and provide service to the community. Programming for detainees and inmates is not considered a priority. Nevertheless, there are exceptions, and programming can be found in many jails nationwide. Short-term programs, such as those aimed at substance abuse, domestic violence, and prevention of disease, are examples. Furthermore, a professional organization—the American Jail Association—publishes standards for operating jails that include training staff and offering a variety of services to detainees and inmates.

Although psychologists are less likely to be involved in treatment programs in jails than in prisons, their *assessment* and *crisis intervention* services are often more in demand in these short-term settings. Some pretrial detainees, for example, need to be assessed for their competency to stand trial and the variety of other competencies that were discussed in Chapter 5. Whether or not competencies are in question, pretrial detainees are often confused; frightened; and worried about their social, legal, and financial status. In a confusing, noisy, often crowded environment, detainees may experience "entry shock" (Gibbs, 1992). This is particularly—but not exclusively—a problem for persons being held in jail for the first time. Suicide is the leading cause of death in jails (Clear & Cole, 2000). Research also documents that suicide rates are higher in jail than in prison; some estimates indicate they are at least 5 times higher (F. Cohen, 1998; Steadman, McCarty, & Morrissey, 1989). Although screening for suicide risk is typically done by non-psychological staff upon a detainee's or inmate's entry into the facility, mental health professionals are needed to do a more comprehensive assessment and to offer treatment to individuals who are at risk of taking their own lives. In spite of this, jails are much less likely than prisons to have well-developed mental health services available to inmates (Steadman & Veysey, 1997). It is for this reason that many communities have now begun to experiment with the mental health courts that were discussed in Chapter 4.

Correctional facilities—both jails and prisons—can be violent, noisy, disorganized, demeaning places that promote isolation, helplessness, and subservience through the use of overwhelming power, often by instilling fear. Although this is particularly true of large, urban jails and maximum-security prisons, there are clearly exceptions. On the other hand, correctional professionals maintain that both jails and prisons also can be operated in a humane fashion and can achieve society's dual hope of protecting the public from crime and rehabilitating offenders.

FOCUS 12.1. CAREER OPPORTUNITIES IN THE FEDERAL BUREAU OF PRISONS

Employment opportunities in the U.S. Federal Bureau of Prisons (BOP) are expected to increase in light of projected increases in the number of inmates. Psychologists in this setting have doctorate degrees, with about 60% of those employed having completed internships in federal prisons. BOP states that they have a continuous need for clinical psychologists around the country. Currently there are 400 doctoral-level psychologists working for BOP. The Bureau is a national leader in offering quality predoctoral internship training for students interested in becoming a professional psychologist.

(Continued)

(Continued)

Psychologists in the BOP are autonomous. They are the main providers of mental health services and—in contrast to psychologists in some state prison systems and mental hospitals—are not under the supervision of psychiatrists. Staff psychologists have the opportunity to be involved in the following:

- Forensic evaluations for the federal courts
- Psychological evaluations of candidates for the witness protection program
- Hostage negotiation training
- Drug abuse treatment programs
- Suicide prevention program
- Crisis intervention response team for trauma victims
- Predoctoral internship training program
- Employee assistant program
- Inpatient mental health program
- Staff training
- Research

Entry-level positions, for those who have just completed their doctorates, are at the GS-11 salary level but are automatically upgraded after successful completion of the first year. An annual continuing education stipend—currently $10,000—is guaranteed. Other benefits include the Federal Employee Retirement System, which, among other things, provides an attractive pension plan and allows retirement after 20 years provided an individual has reached age 50.

Source: U.S. Bureau of Prisons (http://www.bop.gov).

Legal Rights of Inmates

It is a well-established principle in law that inmates do not lose their constitutional rights at the prison gate. In a great number of U.S. Supreme Court decisions, especially during the 1960s and 1970s, the Court specified minimum rights that were guaranteed to inmates under the Constitution. The cases decided by the Court involved procedures, practices, and conditions of confinement in jails and prisons. In addition to federal constitutional protections, inmates also may have rights that are guaranteed under their state constitutions or under both federal and state statutes. In this section, we will summarize the key doctrines that are most relevant to psychologists consulting with correctional systems or offering direct services to inmates. This will, of necessity, omit legal protections that are important to inmates but are at most peripheral to the professional concerns of psychologists. For example, inmates have a constitutional right to receive mail (although it may be censored) and a constitutional right to observe religious practices (including dietary practices) unless those interfere with institutional security or create excessive economic burdens. Readers are referred to the excellent treatises by Fred Cohen (1998, 2000, 2003, 2008) and J. W. Palmer and S. E. Palmer (1999) for comprehensive coverage of correctional law that encompasses many areas not to be discussed here.

The principles to be discussed next clearly apply to cases involving prisoners, but they also apply to those serving jail sentences. For this reason, we are using the term *inmate* throughout this chapter as a more generic term to cover both groups. The rights of pretrial *detainees,* however, are somewhat different because these individuals have not been convicted of a crime. Nevertheless, in the name of institutional security, detainees can be subjected to many of the same conditions as sentenced misdemeanants, as will be noted shortly.

Right to Treatment

A right closely aligned with the interests of psychologists is the constitutional right of the inmate to receive adequate medical treatment. The case that established this right is *Estelle v. Gamble* (1976), in which an inmate argued that his Eighth Amendment right against cruel and unusual punishment, had been violated by the failure of prison officials to attend to his medical needs.

Gamble, a Texas inmate, was on a prison work assignment when a bale of cotton that he was loading on a truck fell on him. There followed 3 months of repetitive visits to prison medical staff, during which he was provided with muscle relaxants and other medications. By the end of this time period, he had received numerous different medications, blood tests, and blood pressure measurements, along with cell passes permitting him to stay in his cell. At one point, a prescription was not filled for 4 days because the staff had lost it. Eventually, he refused to work, saying that his pain was not dissipating, and he was brought before a prison disciplinary committee and then placed in solitary confinement as punishment. While in solitary, he asked to see a doctor for chest pains; a medical assistant saw him 12 hours later and hospitalized him.

Although *Estelle v. Gamble* involved treatment for a variety of physical ailments, it has widely been interpreted to include psychological or psychiatric assistance for serious mental disorders (F. Cohen, 2008). To deprive the inmate of adequate medical care violates the Eighth Amendment ban on cruel and unusual punishment. The question naturally arises, "What is 'adequate' medical treatment?" Inmates clearly do not have a right to "state-of-the art" treatment or therapy. In fact, in the *Gamble* case, even failure to obtain an X-ray of an inmate's lower back was not considered inadequate treatment. Although the Supreme Court in that case made it clear that inmates had a **right to treatment,** it did not second-guess the judgment of medical professionals who did not order the X-ray.

Estelle v. Gamble (1976) is also important because it set the standard for deciding in each case whether the Constitution had been violated. Inmates alleging such a violation would have to prove that prison officials were "deliberately indifferent" to their serious medical needs. Simple "negligence" would not be enough to amount to a constitutional violation (although negligence would be sufficient under some *state* laws). In a later case, *Farmer v. Brennan* (1994), the Court said that a prison official would not be liable unless that official both knew of and disregarded an excessive risk to an inmate's health and safety. The Court added that if an official *should have known* of a substantial risk but did not, the official's failure to alleviate the risk did *not* constitute cruel and unusual punishment.

Applied in the context of psychological treatment, it is clear that inmates should be offered treatment at least for their serious mental disorders, including psychoses, clinical depression, and schizophrenia. The IACFP (Althouse, 2010) standards do not distinguish between serious and milder disorders, suggesting that mental health treatment should be available for *all* mental disturbances. Moreover, the standards indicate that it is generally inappropriate for inmates needing acute, chronic, or convalescent mental health care to be treated in jails and prisons. Rather, they should be transferred to facilities that are set up specifically for these purposes.

In reality, both jails and prisons hold substantial numbers of individuals with severe disorders. The lack of adequate mental health care in jails and prisons across the United States is widely acknowledged by commentators and courts alike (F. Cohen, 2000; Heilbrun & Griffin, 1999; S. M. Morris, Steadman, & Veysey, 1997). Although specialized treatment exists for forensic populations, a great number of individuals with mental disorders continue to languish in jails and prisons without adequate psychological intervention. It has been estimated that at least 10 to 15% of men in jails and state prisons have severe mental disorders and are in need of treatment (Lamb, Weinberger, & Gross, 2004; Steadman, Osher, Robbins, Case, & Samuels, 2009). Preliminary data from the Mental Health Prevalence Project (MHPP; Magaletta, Dietz, & Diamond, 2005) suggest that the rates of psychiatric disorder among *federal inmates* may not be that different, and a later report confirms the preliminary findings:

> (O)ur overall estimates suggest that the populations may actually be more similar than previously thought. Although the two jurisdictions (i.e., federal and state) do house correctional populations that are dissimilar along certain demographic and criminological dimensions, mental health might not be one of them. (Magaletta, Diamond, Faust, Daggett, & Camp, 2009, p. 241)

In some jurisdictions, services are provided to fewer than 25% of the inmates requiring them (*Feliciano v. Gonzales,* 1998). Studies also indicate that the need among female inmates is even greater than among males (Clear & Cole, 2000), an estimate that is somewhat confounded by the fact that women, compared with men, may be more likely to self-disclose their need for mental health services. If not greater, however, the treatment needs are still different (Van Voorhis, Wright, Salisbury, & Bauman, 2010). The adequacy of medical services, including both physical and mental health, is a frequent point of litigation in class action suits brought by incarcerated individuals. (A *class action suit* is one brought on behalf of a group of people who have all allegedly been harmed by the actions of a defendant.) Interestingly, although there is a right to treatment for physical and mental disorders, there is no right to treatment for alcoholism or other substance abuse, as we will discuss shortly. These programs fall under the rubric of rehabilitation rather than medical treatment.

Right to Refuse Treatment

Although inmates have a right to treatment, they cannot be forced to participate in treatment programs. This applies to both physical and psychological treatment. However, if the state has a very strong interest in seeing the inmate's behavior changed, some leeway exists. In the Supreme Court case, *McKune v. Lile* (2002), the Court allowed prison officials to effectively punish an inmate for refusing to participate in a program, although the state argued—and the Court agreed—that it was not acting punitively. Lile was a convicted rapist within 2 years of completing his sentence and being released. The state had a strong interest in enrolling him in a sex offender treatment program that required him to disclose his history of offending, but it did not guarantee that the information would be confidential. Lile—apparently concerned that disclosing information could lead to future prosecution for crimes he had not previously been accused of—refused to participate. Prison officials told him that his refusal could lead to his being transferred to a more dangerous prison. In addition, they threatened to curtail a number of privileges, including canteen access and certain work activities. Lile then argued that he was essentially being forced to incriminate himself. In a close decision, a majority of five Justices did not agree. Thus, although inmates still may not be forced to participate in a treatment program, they can be persuaded to do so with threatened loss of privileges, provided that the state's interest in rehabilitation is high, as it was in this case.

In a similar fashion, inmates have a right to refuse medication, but this right can be overridden. Obviously, inmates cannot refuse treatment for a communicable disease, such as tuberculosis, that poses a risk to the prison population. Perhaps less obviously, the preservation of life may be given more weight than the inmate's own wishes. In a 1995 case, for example, an inmate with diabetes was forced to submit to monitoring of his blood sugar and to take insulin or other medications if ordered to by physicians (*North Dakota ex rel. Schuetzle v. Vogel,* 1995). On the other hand, a quadriplegic inmate who wished to die a dignified death was allowed by courts in California to reject force-feeding and other painful medical intervention (*Thor v. Superior Court,* 1993). One could argue cynically that, had the diabetic inmate been allowed to have his way, the prison system would have been faced with significant medical costs resulting from complications associated with his disease. The quadriplegic inmate presented no such economic threats. The cases were not decided on the economic issue, however, but rather on the right of competent individuals to self-determination of their medical needs balanced against the state's interest in preserving life.

The U.S. Supreme Court has issued one decision on the right of inmates to refuse treatment in the form of psychoactive drugs (*Washington v. Harper,* 1990). In Washington State, felons with severe mental disorders were housed in a special unit within the prison system. Antipsychotic drugs were frequently used to control disruptive behavior. If an inmate refused to be treated with these medications, he or she was allowed to challenge the treatment in an administrative hearing before a three-person panel comprising a psychologist, a psychiatrist, and a member of the prison administration. Harper and other inmates wanted a judicial review, before an independent court, rather than an administrative review. They also wished to be afforded a right to counsel, rather than the lay adviser allowed in the administrative hearing. The Supreme Court, in a 6–3 ruling, however, found no fault with the procedure in use. Essentially, prison officials can give an inmate psychoactive drugs against his or her will, but it must be determined in an administrative hearing that such medication is necessary to control the inmate's disruptive behavior. It is important to note, though, that state statutes may be even more restrictive than this, prohibiting medication that might be more for the convenience of the staff than truly medically necessary.

Courts have also begun to address the issue of forcing an inmate to take medication to render him or her competent to be executed. In 1986, in *Ford v. Wainwright,* the U.S. Supreme Court ruled that executing a death row inmate who was "insane"—or too mentally disordered to appreciate what was happening to him—violated the Constitution. (See also *Panetti v. Quarterman* [2007], in which a slim majority [5–4] of the court said that being *aware* that the state was putting the mentally disordered offender to death was not enough; the inmate must *appreciate the purpose* of this being done.) Since the *Wainwright* ruling, many forensic psychologists and forensic psychiatrists have been troubled. Some psychologists resist participating in evaluations of an inmate's **competency to be executed,** knowing that their recommendation could facilitate the inmate's death. Some psychiatrists—who have the authority to prescribe medication—have not wanted to prescribe psychoactive medication that would stabilize the inmate enough to allow him or her to be put to death. Furthermore, lawyers representing these death row inmates have argued that they should have a right to refuse the medication. Thus far, appeals courts have ruled that they do *not* have such a right.

Rehabilitation

People are often surprised to learn that, although there is a right to *treatment* for physical and mental disorders, an inmate has no constitutional right to **rehabilitation** in correctional settings. In this context, rehabilitation refers to a variety of programs that presumably should increase the likelihood that the inmate will not reoffend upon release from prison. In a wide range of cases, inmates have asked the courts to grant them constitutional rights to participate in substance abuse programs, job training programs, educational programs, and programs for violent offenders, among many others. They have consistently been rejected. This is not to say that such programs should not exist. In fact, "It is clear . . . that a penal system cannot be operated in such a manner that it impedes the ability of inmates to attempt their own rehabilitation, or simply to avoid physical, mental, or social deterioration" (J. W. Palmer & Palmer, 1999, p. 221). Thus, lack of *any* meaningful rehabilitative opportunities, particularly within a prison system, would be regarded with suspicion by the courts. The key principle is that individual prisoners do not have a constitutional right to participate in any particular program. Corrections officials are given the discretion to decide who will be assigned to these programs.

Prison Transfers

Inmates have no constitutional right to be held in a specific facility, including one in their home state or close to their family. In many prison systems, it is not unusual for prisoners to be moved from one facility to another, often with little or no notice. During the 1990s, some states experiencing prison overcrowding sent inmates to out-of-state facilities, both public and private, and courts generally upheld the policies. Transfers are typically made not only to manage space but also to break up gangs or to send a prisoner to a more or less restrictive setting. Likewise, corrections officials have broad leeway to assign inmates to various security levels within a facility or to assign them to special treatment programs. Generally, courts have upheld these classification decisions of prison officials unless they are demonstrated to be arbitrary, abusive, capricious, or discriminatory on racial or religious grounds. In addition, if inmates are assigned a special status that would limit substantially their eligibility for parole, work release, or furlough programs, some due process protections are afforded them under many state laws. For example, they may have a right to appear before a neutral decision maker (J. W. Palmer & Palmer, 1999). Neutral decision makers, though, are almost invariably within the institution, rather than being outside judicial or administrative forums.

The one type of **prison transfer** that has constitutional implications is the transfer to a civil mental institution. Inmates with mental disorders who are facing a transfer to a mental health facility outside of the prison system are entitled to a hearing before this occurs (*Vitek v. Jones,* 1980). Such a transfer, according to the Supreme Court, represents a significant deprivation of liberty, specifically because of the stigma of being in a mental institution and the lack of opportunity to earn *good time credits*—credits for good behavior that subtract from the offender's sentence—while institutionalized. Therefore, the Court required a variety of due process protections. They include (a) a written notice to the inmate, (b) a hearing at which clear and convincing evidence of the inmate's mental disorder and dangerousness is provided, (c) an independent decision maker, (d) testimony of witnesses on both sides, and (e) qualified assistance for the inmate (though not necessarily a lawyer). In reality, transfers to mental institutions are rarely challenged (F. Cohen, 2000, 2008). Furthermore, inmates with mental disorders, when transferred, are usually sent to a mental health unit or facility within the prison system. Because it is not clear whether such transfers require hearings such as those outlined in the *Vitek* case, prison systems sometimes provide them as a matter of policy if the inmate protests the transfer. In addition, the IACFP (Althouse, 2010) standards assume that hearings are required: "This requirement is not obviated by the receiving institution being in the same jurisdiction or the special management unit being within the same correctional facility" (Standard D-36, Discussion).

Inmates With Mental Disorders

A number of court cases, including U.S. Supreme Court cases, have addressed special situations encountered by mentally disordered inmates in the nation's prisons. Currently, the prevalence of mental disorders among inmates is high and exceeds the rate of mental disorders in the general population (Dressing & Salize, 2009). As mentioned earlier in the chapter, research indicates that at least 10 to 15% of men in jails and prisons have severe mental disorders (Lamb et al., 2004; Steadman et al., 2009). According to recent data reported by Steadman and associates, nearly one third of women held in jails have serious mental disorders. Not surprisingly, Fazel and Danesh (2002) estimate that 1 in 7 prisoners (both men and women) in western countries has serious mental disorders. Furthermore, Fazel and Danesh found that the need for psychological services for these inmates is substantial, in spite of the mandates for psychological services by the European Convention on Human Rights and other international charters.

The number of inmates with serious mental disorders is increasing significantly (Ashford, Sales, & Reid, 2001; Dressing & Salize, 2009). As described earlier, American inmates with serious mental disorders have a right to treatment under the disease model recognized in *Estelle v. Gamble* (1976). Although they may be able to refuse treatment, this refusal can be overridden if it is shown that the inmate is disordered and dangerous to the self or others (*Washington v. Harper,* 1990). In addition, as we saw above, courts are beginning to allow the forced medication of prisoners who, without the medication, would be incompetent to be executed. We will discuss the assessment of competency to be executed again later in the chapter.

The segregation of inmates with mental disorders raises many legal questions. Courts have allowed severely disturbed inmates to be placed in stripped-down observation cells—sometimes referred to as "safe cells"—for their own protection. They may be kept under extremely stark conditions while awaiting transfer to a treatment facility or until they can be stabilized with appropriate medication, but there are legal limitations on this type of confinement. A suit against the New York Department of Corrections (*Perri v. Coughlin,* 1999) is illustrative. Perri was an extremely disruptive, severely disordered inmate in the New York state prison system. He was held in an observation cell on three separate occasions, for a total of 108 days. The cell contained only a sink and toilet, and a brightly glaring light was on 24 hours a day. He had no clothes or blankets and had to sleep naked on the floor. The observation unit provided no opportunity for exercise, recreation, or group therapy. The lengthy confinement, coupled with failure to provide treatment, led to the court's decision to hold the New State Department of Corrections liable for damages (F. Cohen, 2000).

Privacy and Confidentiality

Inmates have very little right to privacy in prison or jail settings. Despite the fact that inmates often call their cells their "houses" or "homes," the law does not treat them this way. In the leading case on this issue, *Hudson v. Palmer* (1984), the Court gave corrections officials wide leeway in conducting unannounced cell searches without the presence of inmates. Prisoners had asked to be allowed to be present when the cell searches were conducted, arguing that their property—including objects having sentimental value—was sometimes destroyed or was missing after these searches. Although not condoning malicious destruction of property, the Court majority nevertheless left these searches to the discretion of prison officials, in the name of maintaining institutional security.

Some state and lower federal courts have given inmates a right to privacy with respect to supervision by correctional officers of the opposite sex. Female inmates have a right not to be observed by male correctional officers while showering or toileting and likewise male inmates have the same rights regarding female officers. Body cavity searches by opposite-sex correctional officers also have been prohibited. These searches, generally visual in nature, may be conducted after inmates have had visits with someone from the outside. They also may be conducted during routine searches for contraband.

Confidentiality of psychological records is a topic of more direct concern to the forensic psychologist. Psychologists have an ethical obligation to preserve inmate confidentiality to the maximum extent possible. The IACFP (Althouse, 2010) standards indicate that non-psychological staff should have access to confidential information only on a "need to know" basis and that psychological staff should supervise such releases and interpret information.

In the event that third parties within or outside the facility are provided with psychological information, "release of confidential information" forms should be completed by inmates and kept in the files. The standards also make it clear that inmates should be informed verbally and in writing of limits of confidentiality.

For example, they should be informed that if a psychologist is made aware of an escape plan or of a plan to harm another inmate, he or she is obliged to notify prison officials. In addition, psychologists should obtain completed informed consent forms from inmates before conducting an assessment or initiating treatment.

Interestingly, even more basic than confidentiality is the actual *adequacy* of the records. Despite the fact that lower courts have made it clear that adequate records are prerequisite to continuity of care (F. Cohen, 2008), there is widespread concern about poor record keeping in many correctional facilities. According to Fred Cohen, a lawyer and a scholar of correctional law,

> In my own work encompassing a large number of prisons, I would say that broadly deficient mental health records is the most consistently encountered problem I uncover. . . . What may be surprising is that even in relatively sophisticated systems, the mental health records are sometimes so deficient that there often is no treatment plan or only an old one that has not been changed or updated; what is there is illegible; there is no medical history or a clinically inadequate one; treatment recommendations are sparse or nonexistent; and there are no follow-up or progress notes. (Section 10.2)

He adds that "decent treatment" may in fact be occurring in some cases, but this would not be evident from the files. He includes in his book (2008) a helpful guide for ensuring a properly prepared mental health file.

The limits on confidentiality and requirements for informed consent are problematic for many psychologists who are considering work in correctional settings. According to the IACFP (Althouse, 2010),

> The correctional mental health services provider works *with* their clients, but *for* the department, facility, or agency, and must be able to differentiate and balance the ethical/legal obligations owed to the correctional organization or agency, community safety, and the offender, inmate, or resident client. (Standard C-6, Discussion, italics original)

This can be difficult for the psychologist who is accustomed to working both for and with the same client. Furthermore, some psychologists are concerned that a number of inmates who "consent" to assessment and treatment do so because they believe they have no choice.

Solitary Confinement

Inmates may be isolated from the general jail or prison population for a variety of reasons. We referred above to the isolation of those with mental disorders in observation cells. In addition, inmates may be placed in **disciplinary segregation,** as punishment for violation of rules, or in **protective custody,** to keep them away from other inmates who may prey on them. Supermax or ultramax facilities hold large numbers of allegedly violent and recalcitrant inmates in **administrative segregation** for years at a time. Courts have allowed corrections officials to segregate inmates but have placed some restrictions on the duration and the conditions of the confinement, particularly in the case of disciplinary segregation.

Conditions of segregation have been monitored more carefully than *duration* by the courts, though they are often considered in relation to the duration. Thus, placement in a stark cell with no opportunity to shower for 48 hours is not legally problematic; placement in the same cell and under the same conditions for 2 weeks would be. Hygiene, nutrition, the physical condition of the cell, and the physical condition of the inmate are all taken into consideration. "It is clear that there is not yet a minimum standard set on the number of days or other conditions that will constitute cruel and unusual punishment in punitive isolation in every situation" (J. W. Palmer & Palmer, 1999, p. 80). Thus, although psychologists may be concerned about the effects of isolation on the mental state of the inmate, and although inmates have argued unsuccessfully that isolation is per se cruel and unusual, the courts have placed limits on only the most egregious of situations.

Few limitations have been placed on the duration of protective custody or administration segregation, but again, conditions may be scrutinized. The Supreme Court has yet to hear a case involving conditions of confinement in supermax facilities, but lower courts have weighed in on this issue. Conditions vary in these facilities, depending upon the state—in some, for example, some inmates are provided with longer exercise periods and may have work assignments outside their cells. Interestingly, because these facilities are still quite new and "high tech," they often look modern and innocuous. (See Photo 12.1, depicting an inmate being led through a supermax facility shortly after its opening.) In a not-untypical facility, though, the inmates are held in cells for 24 hours a day, with the exception of a brief (up to 1 hour) exercise period, usually in a secluded space. They have no contact with other inmates. Food is brought to their cells by guards. The extraordinary high level of security needed to house inmates in supermax facilities results in extreme isolation and unprecedented restrictions on personal freedoms (DeMatteo, 2005c). Essentially, these institutions often function "very close to the edge of what the Constitution allows" (Collins, 2004, p. 2).

A lower federal court (*Madrid v. Gomez,* 1995) has made it clear that the above solitary conditions are particularly harmful to inmates who are at psychological risk or are presently mentally disordered. Reviewing conditions in the secure housing unit (SHU) at Pelican Bay State Prison in California, the

Photo 12.1 A prisoner being led through the new ultra-maximum-security facility in Florence, Colorado, 1995, built to house 484 offenders considered the most dangerous in the federal prison system.

court found that the following violated the Constitution's prohibition against cruel and unusual punishment: a pattern of excessive force by correctional officers within the facility, the lack of adequate provision of medical and mental health care, and the holding of inmates with mental illness in the SHU.

Nevertheless, the court did not find a constitutional violation in the SHU for *stable* inmates:

> Conditions in the SHU may well hover on the edge of what is humanly tolerable for those with normal resilience, particularly when endured for extended periods of time. They do not, however, violate exacting Eighth Amendment standards, except for the specific population subgroups [the mentally ill] identified in this opinion. (*Madrid v. Gomez,* 1995)

Pretrial Detainees

Under the law, persons accused of crime and held in jails or detention centers may not be punished. They are considered to be innocent unless and until they are proven guilty. Thus, a detainee cannot be placed in disciplinary segregation and lose good time credits, because he or she is not serving time. However, courts allow detainees to be placed in highly restrictive conditions and to suffer significant invasions of privacy in the name of institutional security. In addition, a detainee can be placed in isolation for violating the rules of the facility. In the landmark U.S. Supreme Court case on this issue, *Bell v. Wolfish* (1979), detainees in a federal facility challenged a number of actions taken by administrators in the name of institutional security. For example, they were placed in groups of three and more in what were intended to be two-person cells and sometimes in makeshift accommodations due to overcrowding. They were not allowed to stand and watch if their cells were searched. They were not allowed to receive packages containing food items or personal items from outside the institution. The facility had a "publishers only" rule, whereby books and magazines had to come directly from the publisher. Finally, they were submitted to visual body cavity searches after contact visits (visits from the outside). In a 6–3 decision, the U.S. Supreme Court ruled that these were not punitive conditions and were justified in the name of institutional security.

In addition to the constitutional protections discussed above, inmates may have certain rights under their state constitutions or laws passed by state legislatures. In some states, for example, inmates have a right to vote in national elections; there is no such constitutional right. Confidentiality of records, rights to participate in rehabilitation programs, and visitation rights are all areas that vary widely from state to state. The psychologist working in a correctional setting, then, must be aware not only of the federal constitutional principles, but also of the law specific to his or her own state.

Correctional Psychologists

Correctional psychologists are sometimes distinguished from psychologists working in correctional facilities. The correctional psychologist typically has "specific academic and/or program training in correctional philosophy, systems, offender management, forensic report writing, treatment aimed at reducing recidivism, and outcome research" (Althouse, 2000, p. 436). Many—if not most—psychologists working in corrections do not have this specific background. Furthermore, not all psychologists hold doctorates, whether PhDs or PsyDs. Although it is estimated that more than 90% of psychologists working in the Federal Bureau of Prisons hold doctorates, it appears that those working in state prisons and local jails are more likely to merely hold master's degrees or certificates of advanced study.

Nevertheless, psychologists at all levels clearly offer valuable services to corrections. For our purposes, therefore, we use the terms *correctional psychologist* and *psychologist working in corrections* interchangeably. This is consistent with the revised IACFP (Althouse, 2010) standards, which note that the same level of professional practice is needed irrespective of the training level or educational background of the service provider. The standards also recognize that these service providers often include other professional groups as well as psychologists. Finally, as mentioned in Chapter 1, correctional psychologists often do not consider themselves "forensic psychologists," though in the broad sense of this term we do so in the text.

Estimates of the number of psychologists working in correctional settings vary widely, partly because available surveys do not always include the many settings in which they can be found. According to Boothby and Clements (2000), more recent estimates indicate that more than 2,000 psychologists are now employed in correctional settings. In addition, some surveys count only those psychologists who work full-time within correctional systems. Other surveys maintain the distinction between *correctional psychologist* and *psychologist working in corrections* and count only the former. Memberships in professional organizations do not provide definitive answers because many psychologists who would be eligible for membership do not join these organizations.

Boothby and Clements (2000) conducted an extensive survey of 830 psychologists working in state and federal prisons across the United States. The great majority—88%—worked in the prisons full-time, whereas 12% provided services on a contractual basis. The survey did not include those working in jails or in juvenile facilities. Of their sample, 59% held doctorates and 37% were master's-level graduates. All psychologists working in federal prisons had doctorates, whereas state prisons employed master's- and doctoral-level psychologists about equally. An overwhelming majority of the psychologists (92%) identified themselves as Caucasian, and 62% were male and 38% female. The psychologists tended to work exclusively with one or the other gender. Thus, 82% worked only with male offenders, 8% only with female offenders, and 10% with both. The prison population itself comprises approximately 93% males and 7% females.

For some psychologists, a limitation of working in correctional settings is the amount of time they are able to allocate for research. Psychologists in the Boothby and Clements (2000) study reported that research endeavors occupied approximately 2% of their time. The IACFP (Althouse, 2010) standards recognize the difficulty of setting aside time for research due to the increasing demand for psychological services. Nevertheless, Standard F-1 encourages applied or basic research, and its discussion section recommends that qualified mental health staff be "afforded the opportunity for engaging in at least one evaluation or research project having practical relevance for correctional or forensic psychology" (Standard F-1, Discussion). Mental health staff also are encouraged to facilitate research projects from outside parties when possible.

In a follow-up study, Boothby and Clements (2002) reported on the job satisfaction of the psychologists in their survey. Satisfaction was measured on 18 job dimensions, including such items as opportunity for advancement, job security, salary, clear definition of roles, access to and influence on decision making, and safety. Overall, the psychologists were "moderately satisfied." They were most satisfied with safety, job security, and relationships with clients, and they were least satisfied with opportunities for advancement and professional atmosphere. The respondents were also asked to rate the importance of these 18 dimensions. All dimensions but one (job status or prestige) received average ratings of 3 or above on a 5-point scale, indicating that all of the 18 dimensions were important. However, the most important were autonomy, personally meaningful work, and achievement (although recognition of such achievement was not that important). Not surprisingly, salaries and the number of inmates in a facility were also correlated with job satisfaction, with high salaries and crowded conditions having opposite effects. Demographic variables such as age and gender were unrelated to job satisfaction. Correctional psychologists working in federal prisons were significantly more satisfied than those working in state systems on 8 of the 18 dimensions. These were opportunity for advancement, appropriate level of responsibility, job security, salary, achievement or success in job, status/prestige of job, professional atmosphere, and safety. Boothby and Clements concluded their report with a discussion of the implications for recruiting and retaining psychologists for work in correctional settings.

Since the Boothby-Clements research, a number of other studies have examined job satisfaction or burnout among staff in correctional facilities, although these studies are often not limited to psychology staff (e.g., Garland, MCarty, & Zhao, 2009). Two exceptions are the work of Mackain, Myers, Ostapiej, and Newman (2010) and Senter, Morgan, Serna-McDonald, and Bewley (2010). Mackain et al., using scales similar to those used by Boothby and Clements (2002), studied specific facets of satisfaction among prison psychologists in North Carolina and found that economic factors (health benefits, job security), work relationships, and perceived administrative support were related to job satisfaction. Senter et al. examined the effects of correctional work on psychologists' job and life satisfaction. The researchers also compared the level of occupational burnout of these correctional psychologists with that of psychologists working in other public service and non–public service settings. The results indicated that correctional psychologists experience greater degrees of burnout. In addition, they reported lower job satisfaction than non-correctional psychologists. Interestingly, correctional psychologists appear to be more satisfied with their personal lives than psychologists working in such settings as public psychiatric hospitals. These results suggest that psychologists employed in correctional facilities should be educated about the potential stressors of their work. Furthermore, students planning to become correctional psychologists should receive course work about the inherent stressors of correctional settings. Nonetheless, the stressors may not be as apparent as one would think; for example, in the Mackain et al. (2010) study, safety was not a major concern among the prison psychologists they studied.

We now turn our attention to the main tasks performed by correctional psychologists. For purposes of organization, these will be divided into two distinct but interrelated topic areas, assessment and treatment.

Psychological Assessment in Corrections

Psychological assessment refers to all of the techniques used to measure and evaluate an individual's past, present, or future psychological status. Assessment usually includes but is not limited to the use of psychological tests or measuring devices. The last two decades of the 20th century saw a large increase in the number of commercially available measures and tests specifically intended for use in forensic and other clinical settings. This includes a variety of inventories that are presently in use in prisons and jails across the United States. As an example, all inmates entering the Federal Bureau of Prisons are administered the Psychology Services Inmate Questionnaire (PSIQ), a fill-in-the-blank self-report form that assesses past mental health services and evidence of current psychological problems (Magaletta et al., 2009). In addition to tests and other measurement instruments, assessment involves interviews with the individuals being assessed, interviews with others, direct observations, and reviews of case records.

In corrections, assessment is warranted *at a minimum* at several points in an inmate's career: (1) at the entry level, when he or she enters the correctional system; (2) when decisions are to be made concerning the offender's reentry into the community; and (3) at times of psychological crisis. A more specialized type of assessment is also performed in death penalty cases, when questions are raised about an offender's competency to be executed. Beyond these very minimal requirements, however, reassessments should be done on an ongoing basis. "Behavioral changes in inmates, which occur as time is served, demand constant reassessment and reassignment" (J. W. Palmer & Palmer, 1999, p. 307).

For the correctional system intent on pursuing both security needs and rehabilitative goals, assessment also is a key component to providing treatment. James Bonta (1996) has identified three historical generations of assessment for the purpose of offering treatment. During the first generation, assessment was performed chiefly by individual clinicians who relied on their own professional experience and judgment. In the second generation, standardized assessment instruments were adopted, although these included primarily static risk factors (such as prior record or number of violent incidents within a facility) focused predominantly on making decisions about an offender's custody level. The third generation of assessment includes both risk and needs factors. Thus, a standardized risk/needs assessment instrument takes into consideration both prior violent incidents (a risk factor) and an offender's attitude toward authority (a needs factor). In recent years, a fourth generation has emerged combining actuarial approaches with structured clinical or professional judgment. We will discuss risk/needs assessments in more detail shortly.

Initial Inmate Screening and Classification

As a matter of institutional or systemwide policy, correctional facilities require entry-level assessments so that inmates can be "psychologically processed" and assigned to a particular facility or unit. Ideally, no individual should be placed in the general correctional population without having been screened for evidence of problem behaviors or mental states. Thus, screening should be done as soon as possible after entry into the facility.

In jails, especially for pretrial detainees, this screening process may be very cursory. It will focus on whether the inmate is a suicide risk, indications of substance abuse, history of hospitalizations and medications, and indicators of violence. Because few facilities have psychological staff available round the clock, initial screening may be done by corrections staff, such as caseworkers or corrections officers. The IACFP (Althouse, 2010) standards condone this practice as long as these individuals have been trained by psychological staff and this staff reviews all written reports. If there is evidence of mental disorder, suicide ideation, or depression or anxiety greater than would be normally expected, the individual should be referred for a more extensive evaluation. It appears that initial psychiatric evaluations of inmates occur in virtually all jails (Steadman et al., 1989).

In prisons, screening and classification become more complex. In many states, an offender is first sent to a classification or reception center, which may or may not be within the facility to which the offender is eventually sent. States with large prison systems (e.g., Texas, New York, California, and Florida) have centralized processing centers. The new prisoner may spend several days or even many weeks in this assessment center, separated from those already in the system, until assigned to an institution based on security needs as well as to specific programs. The classification committee may recommend, for example, that a prisoner be assigned to an aggression management program or an educational program to improve his reading level. The committee might recommend that another prisoner be offered substance abuse treatment and that contacts with her children be facilitated.

The reception unit in many prisons includes psychologists, psychiatrists, social workers, or other professionals who administer tests, interview the offender, review records, and offer programming and treatment recommendations. The IACFP (Althouse, 2010) standards recommend that all newly received inmates be briefly screened for mental illness and suicide risk "prior to being placed in a general population room or cell" and that those in need of a more comprehensive mental health evaluation be referred immediately to a qualified mental health provider (Standard D-17a). Detailed recommendations for the contents of these screenings are provided in standards D-17b through D-17g. "Initial assessment of the mental health status of the inmate at this crucial point can also prevent additional complications, including assault, suicide attempts, or rapid cognitive and emotional deterioration" (Standard D-17, Discussion).

Principles of Risk, Needs, Responsivity

In corrections, it is important to assess both needs and risks, particularly if a treatment regimen is to follow. In previous chapters, we have given some attention to risk factors, those that make it more likely that an individual will engage in antisocial behavior (e.g., parental criminality), as well as protective factors, those that cushion or protect the individual (e.g., a caring adult). Principles of risk/needs/responsivity (Andrews & Bonta, 1994) are now firmly established in the criminology literature.

Andrews and Bonta (1994) identified two main categories of needs: criminogenic and noncriminogenic. **Criminogenic needs** are dynamic factors (Gendreau, Cullen, & Bonta, 1994), subject to change. An offender's attitude toward employment or his or her degree of alcohol use are examples. "The importance of criminogenic needs is that they serve as treatment goals: when programs successfully diminish these needs we can reasonably expect reduction in recidivism" (Gendreau et al., 1994, p. 75). **Noncriminogenic needs** are those that may be subject to change but have been found to have little influence on an offender's criminal behavior. Psychological states such as depression, anxiety, or low self-esteem are examples. Although these states may lead to adjustment problems for the individual, they are not strongly correlated with criminal behavior in the great majority of offenders. However, these needs should still be addressed in treatment. The depressed or highly anxious offender still needs help.

One of the foremost risk/needs scales available in corrections is the **Level of Service Inventory—Revised (LSI-R)** (Andrews & Bonta, 1995), which is widely used in Canadian correctional facilities and used to a lesser extent in American corrections. The LSI-R—which is scored on the basis of records reviews and interviews with offenders—assesses offenders' criminogenic needs along 10 domains, including personality characteristics, pro-criminal attitudes, family/marital history, and substance abuse. The total score on the LSI-R can be used to assess the risk of future offending. The LSI-R has garnered considerable research (e.g., Gendreau, Little, & Goggin, 1996; Simourd & Malcolm, 1998). A number of recent studies have supported its use with male offenders (Hollin, Palmer, & Clark, 2003); female offenders (Folsom & Atkinson, 2007; E. J. Palmer & Hollin, 2007); and youthful offenders, both male and female (Catchpole & Gretton, 2003). Not all research supports its use with female offenders, however; as we will note below, a considerable amount of research suggests that needs of female offenders are different and are not tapped by many of the actuarial instruments in use (Van Voorhis et al., 2010). Although earlier surveys suggested that psychologists in the United States were less inclined to use actuarial instruments (Boothby & Clements, 2000; Gallagher, Somwaru, & Ben-Porath, 1999), this has changed, at least among clinicians engaged in the practice of forensic psychology (Heilbrun & Brooks, 2010). Part of this is due to the fact that, as Otto and Heilbrun (2002) predicted, instruments with good predictive ability are increasingly being sought as courts demand more scientific accountability.

More recently, researchers have developed assessment instruments that include a wider range of risk and needs factors and embrace a broad selection of criminological theories, in addition to the social learning theory that underlies the LSI-R. One such instrument is Correctional Offender Management Profiling for Alternative Sanctions (COMPAS; Northpointe Institute for Public Management, 1996), which is available as a software package. In addition to assessing risks and needs, COMPAS also assesses strength and protective factors. Preliminary research found good reliability and predictive validity and concluded that COMPAS was at least as effective as other major instruments (Brennan, Dieterich, & Ehret, 2009).

As prison inmates approach the end of their sentence, or as they approach a parole date, the psychologist may be called on to assess the inmates' risk of reoffending. Similar assessments also may be conducted when prison officials are considering a change in the offender's status, such as shifting him or her from a medium- to a minimum-security level. Because this is pertinent to the classification issues discussed above, it is important to keep in mind that the various assessment instruments to be covered below may be used for classification as well as release decision making.

Assessments for **release decisions** are usually prepared at the request of state parole boards (Brodsky, 1980), particularly in the case of inmates who have a history of mental disturbance or predatory behavior. The psychologist typically meets with the inmate, reviews his or her prison files, and administers psychological tests. As we have seen in previous chapters, psychology has made substantial progress in developing **risk assessment instruments** over the past 20 years (e.g., J. Monahan, Steadman, et al., 2001; Steadman et al., 1989). The Boothby and Clements (2000) survey, however, suggests that risk assessment *instruments* are not widely used. Nevertheless, instruments recommended for this purpose include the revised Psychopathy Checklist (PCL-R), discussed in Chapter 7, and the Violence Risk Appraisal Guide (VRAG) and the Historical/Clinical/Management Risk Scale (HCR-20), which were discussed in Chapter 5 (see Focus 5.6). Also mentioned in Chapter 5 were the instruments developed specifically to assess sex offender risk, a particularly intractable problem.

Use of Risk Assessment Instruments

Despite the proliferation of risk assessment instruments, it is uncertain whether they are being used extensively by many psychologists working in correctional settings. In fact, risk assessments themselves may not be performed that frequently. In the Boothby and Clements (2000) study, respondents reported that their most frequent assessments were of personality characteristics (42%), followed by intellectual assessment (19%). Only 13% of their assessments were risk assessments. The few psychologists who reported conducting risk assessments typically did not specify the instruments they used; when they did, the most commonly indicated was the PCL-R. However, by far the most common instrument used by the correctional psychologists in the study was the Minnesota Multiphasic Personality Inventory (MMPI), which was used in a variety of contexts by 87% of the respondents. "It seems that many correctional psychologists rely on instruments such as the MMPI, regardless of the referral question" (Boothby & Clements, 2000, p. 724). Put another way, regardless of the question the lawyer or court wanted answered (e.g., "Is this person likely to reoffend if granted parole?" or "Is this a good candidate for sex offender treatment?"), the correctional psychologist administered the MMPI. With many alternative measures being available today, however, it is likely that a similar study would produce different results.

Crisis Intervention

Inmates in both jails and prisons are susceptible to facing a wide variety of psychological crises that may require a forensic psychologist's assessment and treatment skills. Psychologist Hans Toch (e.g., Toch, 1992; Toch & Adams, 2002) has written extensively about the "mosaic of despair" that can overwhelm some inmates and even lead them to injure themselves or take their own lives. Crises of self-doubt, hopelessness, fear, or abandonment are not unusual in an incarcerated population. In addition, any inmate may be confronted with a situation that warrants a psychological consultation. Victimization by other inmates, news of the death of a loved one, and denial of parole are all examples of situations that can precipitate a psychological crisis in an otherwise stable inmate. When such a crisis occurs, prison officials are interested in obtaining from the psychologist both an immediate resolution of the crisis and long-range solutions that will help avoid a similar problem in the future.

In their research on psychological crises that result in self-directed violence (such as self-mutilation or suicide attempts), Toch and Adams (2002) found age, cultural, and gender differences. They state that young White and Latino inmates are the most likely groups to face acute psychological crises. Married inmates feel more vulnerable in jail, whereas single inmates suffer more in prisons. Women are most likely to have problems with loneliness, whereas Latino inmates are distressed if they face the abandonment of relatives. Toch and Adams emphasize, though, that response to the jail or prison environment is very individualistic, which suggests that correctional officials must be carefully attuned to the risks of suicide among particular inmates.

Assessment of Correctional Personnel

"For the most part, a psychologist's role in the employment selection process is not extensive" (Correia, 2001, p. 60). Although correctional officer candidates in prisons are likely to have taken entry-level examinations at correctional academies or at on-site facilities, these exams typically attempt to measure aptitude for the work and attempt to screen out major behavioral problems. Little research is available on the extent to which psychological tests are administered prior to employment. Those prison systems that administer psychological tests have predominantly used the MMPI and a test specifically designed for correctional officer use, the Inwald Personality Inventory (IPI) (Inwald, Knatz, & Shusman, 1982). Research on both suggests that they should be used with caution, however. The MMPI is intended primarily to identify gross mental disturbances; it is not helpful in "screening in" or identifying ideal characteristics in candidates for employment. The IPI, though validated for corrections officers, was found by its author to successfully predict the retention or termination of only 73% of the candidates in the research sample (Shusman, Inwald, & Landa, 1984). In the same study, MMPI profiles were found to predict 63%. No further published research on the IPI is apparently available, though Inwald (1992) has published a later study dealing with the IPI administered to law enforcement officers.

Psychological screening of correctional officer candidates has also been resisted by correctional officer unions and challenged in a number of court cases. Psychological screening of officers in jail settings is rare. Although professional jail organizations such as the American Jail Association (AJA) recommend the careful selection of correctional officers, candidates for these positions are typically screened primarily for prior criminal records and aptitude for the work.

The IACFP (Althouse, 2010) standards suggest that psychologists and other mental health practitioners may be involved in the psychological screening of security staff in specialized mental health units (Standard B-1b), but no details are offered. However, staff screening, staff training, and assignment of staff to various duties are all examples of the broad services that can be offered by psychologists to improve the jail or prison environment for the incarcerated offender. For example, psychologists can recommend—and sometimes even select—corrections officers for participation in a treatment program for certain offenders. Boothby and Clements (2000), in their review of the tasks performed by correctional psychologists, noted that less than 10% of the psychologists' time was spent at staff training. It is unclear whether screening and selection were included in this figure.

Competency to Be Executed

One very specialized area demanding the assessment skills of correctional psychologists revolves around the death penalty. The U.S. Constitution prohibits the execution of an offender who is so mentally disordered that he or she is unaware of the punishment that is about to be imposed and why he or she has to suffer it (*Ford v. Wainwright*, 1986). In *Atkins v. Virginia*, 2002, the Court also ruled that some intellectually disabled persons could not be executed. Specifically, if they had IQ scores below 70 and were unable to care for themselves independently, it was deemed cruel and unusual punishment to put them to death. In addition, the offender must appreciate the purpose of the execution (*Panetta v. Quarterman*, 2007). Thus, if an offender on death row challenges the execution on the basis of his or her mental disorder or intellectual disability, the forensic psychologist may be called in to perform an assessment of the offender's competency for execution. Together, these Supreme Court decisions reignited a long-standing philosophical debate on the critical role of mental health professionals with respect to offenders sentenced to die (e.g., Bonnie, 1990; Brodsky, 1980; Mossman, 1987; Radelet & Barnard, 1986). As we saw earlier in the chapter, federal court decisions allowing the forced medication of such inmates will certainly keep the controversy raging.

The great majority of psychologists working in correctional settings will never be asked to conduct an evaluation of a death row inmate's competency to be executed, for two main reasons. First, in states with the death penalty, the death row population is usually kept at one maximum-security facility, at least as these inmates approach their execution date. Only a small minority of psychologists work in or contract with these facilities. Second, prisoners under sentence of death are far more likely to appeal their death sentence on other grounds (e.g., inadequate assistance of counsel) than to raise the issue of incompetency. It is too early to tell whether the Court's recent case prohibiting execution of the intellectually disabled will significantly increase the numbers of offenders who challenge their execution on this basis.

Both the American Psychological Association and the American Psychiatric Association say that the ultimate decision as to whether the offender is competent to be executed should be made by the court and that adversarial expert witnesses are essential in this context. In other words, the psychologist or psychiatrist conducting the evaluation should neither be the sole examiner nor the decision maker.

A number of forensic psychologists have offered suggestions to their colleagues who may be conducting evaluations of competency to be executed (e.g., Heilbrun, 1987; Heilbrun et al., 2002; Small & Otto, 1991).

In a model report published by Heilbrun et al., psychologist Mark Cunningham used the following techniques in his competency assessment:

- Clinical and forensic interview of the prisoner;
- Psychological testing, including the MMPI-2 and the Personality Assessment inventory (PAI);
- Interview of a corrections officer on the death row unit;
- Cell observation;
- A second interview with the prisoner;
- Telephone interviews with friends, relatives, the prisoner's ex-wife, and his spiritual adviser, which ranged in length from 70 minutes to 12 minutes; and
- Reviews of numerous legal, health, military, and prison records, as well as journal entries and letters in support of clemency (p. 96).

Recall that both Dr. Heilbrun and Dr. Cunningham were highlighted in Personal Perspectives in Chapter 5.

Small and Otto (1991) note that it is important to inform the prisoner of the purpose of the evaluation, describe its procedure, and explain who will get the results as well as the implications of the findings. In addition, they recommend videotaping the assessment to document that the above steps have been taken, under the assumption that a court may scrutinize the evaluation process itself. Central to the evaluation, they say, is the clinical interview, in which the clinician should try to determine whether the prisoner understands that he or she was convicted and is about to be executed.

Treatment and Rehabilitation in Correctional Facilities

A dominant task of the psychologist in the correctional system is to provide *psychological treatment,* a term that encompasses a wide spectrum of strategies, techniques, and goals. Boothby and Clements (2000) reported that direct treatment took up approximately 26% of psychologists' time in correctional settings, second only to administrative tasks. In addition to those inmates who are mentally disordered, psychologists also provide services directly targeting substance abusers, sexual offenders, psychopaths, arsonists, and those prone to violence such as domestic abusers. In addition, virtually any inmate, regardless of his or her offense, may require treatment of symptoms such as depression, anxiety, and stress (including posttraumatic stress) that might not necessarily qualify as a full-fledged mental disorder.

Nonetheless, the mentally disordered are frequent recipients of services provided by psychologists and other mental health providers. As indicated at earlier points in the chapter, rates of mental disorder in jails and prisons are staggering. Escalating incarceration rates, the levels of violence in some prisons, and increasing use of solitary confinement have contributed to this problem (Kupers, 2009; Magaletta, Patry, Dietz, & Ax, 2007). Many inmates with mental disorders also have co-occurring substance abuse problems (M. D. White, Goldkamp, & Campbell, 2006). Inmates with mental disorders are more likely to be incarcerated for a violent offense than those without apparent mental disorders. In addition, an estimated 60% of the mentally disordered in state or federal prisons receive some form of mental health treatment during their period of incarceration, although a large segment of the treatment is in the form of medication.

The most common treatments used within correctional institutions are person-centered therapy, cognitive therapy, behavior therapy, group and milieu therapy, transactional analysis, reality therapy, and responsibility therapy (Kratcoski, 1994; Lester, Braswell, & Van Voorhis, 1992). Today, as mentioned above, psychological treatment often follows the risk/needs/responsivity principles of Andrews and Bonta, most specifically by reducing an offender's criminogenic needs (Andrews & Bonta, 2006).

It should be noted that psychologists are just one of several professional groups providing this therapy. Psychiatrists, social workers, and mental health counselors are also involved in most correctional facilities. This is an important point because the method of treatment used depends largely on the professional training and orientation of the clinician. Psychiatrists, for example, are more likely to favor psychoactive drugs as part of a treatment regimen, although recent studies suggest that this approach is increasingly being supplemented with individual therapy (Heilbrun & Griffin, 1999). Social workers are more likely to use group treatment approaches, in which inmates talk about their concerns, experiences, and anxieties while the clinician generally directs and controls the topic flow. As indicated by the Boothby and Clements (2000) study, group therapy does not seem to be the norm among psychologists in correctional facilities, but it is still widely used by other clinical professionals. Sixty percent of the treatment provided by the psychologists in that study was in an individual format. The researchers found this problematic, given the high need for mental health services in the nation's jails and prisons.

A different survey of 162 professionals representing a range of professional groups (R. D. Morgan, Winterowd, & Ferrell, 1999) indicated a far greater use of group therapy. In that study, 72% of the respondents offered group therapy to inmates, and their time was about equally divided between group and individual treatment. These practitioners also estimated that 20% of all inmates in their facilities received some group therapy. When delivered effectively, group therapy has several advantages over individual therapy in correctional settings. It is, of course, more practical, given the limited number of treatment staff and high prison population. In addition, group therapy provides inmates with opportunities for socializing, group decision making, developing altruism, and developing functional peer relationships that individual treatment typically does not provide (Morgan et al., 1999).

On a more negative note, few professionals in the above study (only 16%) reported that their departments were conducting research on the effectiveness of group or other therapy. Perhaps more sobering, 20% indicated that no supervision was offered to therapists who facilitated group therapy sessions.

Common Psychological Treatment in Corrections

A wide variety of treatment options are available to forensic psychologists offering therapy in correctional settings (Kratcoski, 1994). The treatment model—or treatment approach—adopted by a given professional may be influenced by a host of factors, including the psychologist's training; perceptions of "what works"; and, of course, the available resources within the facility. In the Boothby and Clements (2000) study, a large majority of respondents (88%) reported using a cognitive model, whereas 69% used a **behavioral model** and 40% a rational-emotive approach. As is obvious from these percentages, psychologists used various models, depending on the situation.

Behavioral Models

In the 1960s, psychologists consulting with correctional facilities made extensive use of behavior modification as a means of encouraging inmates to change (Bartol, 1980). Behavior modification included rewarding inmates for "good behavior" within the facility and removing privileges when behavior was unacceptable. For example, an inmate who had no disciplinary violations for a month might be given an increase in visits to the commissary, or prison store. Disruptive behavior might result in a loss of visiting privileges. By themselves, approaches that are based on such reinforcement strategies have shown little effectiveness. The main objection to such approaches is that change generated within the facility did not generalize to the real world, once inmates were released. Furthermore, in some facilities, legal advocates argued that the punishments imposed were sometimes arbitrary and in violation of inmate rights. Behavior modification as the sole approach to treatment eventually lost favor.

Cognitive-Behavioral Models

Cognitive models seek to change the very beliefs and assumptions that are at the core of an individual's behavior. Some researchers have argued (e.g., Mandracchia, Morgan, Gross, & Garland, 2007; Walters, 1996, 2006) that offenders as a group possess thinking styles or make thinking errors that encourage them to persist in antisocial behavior. Cognitive models, which are strongly based on social learning theory, encourage inmates to examine their beliefs and assumptions, recognize problems in judgment that have led them to criminal activity, develop self-awareness, and accept responsibility for their actions. Once this has been accomplished, inmates are taught decision-making strategies and social skills, as needed, for replacing behaviors that got them into trouble with prosocial behaviors. Because cognitive programs often have components that resemble aspects of behavioral programs, the term *cognitive-behavioral* is used. For example, many cognitive-behavioral programs make use of contracts and token economy systems, whereby individuals gain points when they demonstrate prosocial behaviors.

Cognitive-behavioral therapy also involves the reduction of criminogenic needs, in accordance with the theory of Andrews and Bonta (1994, 2006). The **cognitive-behavioral approach** appears to have the most promise in a variety of treatment contexts (Wormith et al., 2007). Pearson, Lipton, Cleland, and Yee (2002) performed a meta-analysis on the 69 primary research studies on the effectiveness of behavioral and cognitive-behavioral treatment and found the latter significantly associated with lower recidivism rates. The effect was mainly due to the cognitive components rather than the behavior modification interventions, however. That is, such aspects as problem solving, interpersonal skills training, role-playing, and negotiation skills training—all associated with a cognitive approach—were linked with effectiveness. Token economies, contingency management, and behavioral contracts—all associated with behavior modification—had little effect.

Wormith et al. (2007) also discuss a revived interest in positive psychology, which is closely related to principles of cognitive psychology. *Positive psychology* "promotes ideas and principles that facilitate optimal mental and physical health and militate against mental illness and dysfunctional thoughts, feelings, and behaviors" (p. 886). Clinicians who use this approach in correctional settings try to help inmates work toward desirable goals such as achieving meaning and happiness in their lives. Wormith et al. note that, while this does not seem consistent with a punitive-retributive model of criminal justice, it is worthwhile considering as an alternative to traditional forms of treatment.

Treatment of Special Populations

Like the general population, inmates vary widely in their background experiences and their needs. Although treatment should be individualized as much as possible to recognize these differences, programs are often established to address common needs of groups of offenders. For example, prisons—and to a lesser extent jails—may offer programs for inmates who are HIV positive, elderly inmates, female inmates who killed their abusers, sex offenders, psychopaths, inmates who are parents, substance abusers, inmates with developmental disabilities, and inmates under sentence of death. Although we will not cover all of these categories below, readers are advised that an extensive literature in correctional psychology is available (e.g., Ashford et al., 2001; Kratcoski, 1994).

Substance-Abusing Offenders

As noted above, substance abuse often co-occurs with mental disorders. Nevertheless, many individuals with substance abuse problems are not mentally disordered. With or without accompanying mental disorder, though, their numbers within correctional facilities are increasing. Statistics in recent years suggest that about one fifth of state prisoners and slightly over half of all federal prisoners are serving time for drug offenses. Even more revealing, however, is the fact that 53% of state and 45% of federal inmates in 2004 met the *DSM-IV* criteria for drug dependence or abuse (Welsh, 2007).

Although correctional facilities recognize the need for treatment of offenders with substance abuse problems, the availability of professional treatment is limited (Belenko & Peugh, 2005). Welsh (2007) reports that, although nearly half of drug-dependent inmates are in some type of substance abuse program, fewer than 15% receive treatment from a trained professional. Peer counseling, self-help groups, or drug education is more likely to be available. In addition to the need for more professional programs, there is great need for more research on identifying the specific needs of offenders and their performance in treatment programs (see, generally, Simpson & Knight, 2007).

One approach to the treatment of substance abusers that has received favorable research results is the therapeutic community (TC), discussed again later in this chapter. In this model, trained counselors interact with a small group of offenders, establishing therapeutic relationships and engaging them in a process of taking responsibility for and changing their substance-abusing behavior (De Leon, 1997, 2000). Prisons with TCs in place often contract out this program to private providers in the community, and it is typically offered to inmates who are preparing to leave the prison setting (Butzin, Martin, & Inciardi, 2005). At its best, a prison-based TC can be highly effective for offenders with substance problems. However, TCs also encounter obstacles to their smooth operation, including untrained staff, staff turnover, budget cuts, and changes in treatment providers (Farrabee et al., 1999; Saum et al., 2007). On the whole, however, "prison-based TCs coupled with aftercare treatment in the community can reduce both recidivism and relapse into drug use" (Wormith et al., 2007, p. 883).

Violent Offenders

Violent behavior has been defined as the intentional and malevolent physical injuring of another without adequate social justification (Blackburn, 1993). Psychological services to inmates who have committed violent crimes or who otherwise demonstrate propensities toward violent behavior are common in many correctional facilities. Corrections officials place a high priority on both controlling such behavior within prison and jail settings and reducing its likelihood once an inmate has been released. Therefore, programs that address this problem in the inmate population are appreciated, if not always well funded. As a group, however, violent offenders are extremely challenging. "When compared to other offenders, they tend to be less motivated for treatment, more resistant or noncompliant while in treatment, have higher attrition rates, demonstrate fewer positive behavioral changes while in treatment, and demonstrate higher recidivism rates posttreatment" (Serin & Preston, 2001, p. 254).

Serin and Preston (2001) note that a major impediment to treating violent offenders has been confusion over the definition of the population along with failure to recognize that violent individuals are not all alike. This lack of homogeneity, Serin and Preston emphasize, requires differential treatment, but differential treatment is rarely offered. For example, programs for violent offenders too often do not distinguish between offenders displaying instrumental aggression and offenders who have anger control problems. Instrumental aggression is coolly committed for the purposes of achieving a particular goal. Thus, it makes little sense to place an offender who commits his crimes using instrumental aggression into a program teaching him to control his anger. On the other hand, anger control is an important skill to develop in individuals who are impulsive; have substance abuse problems; or lack social, relationship, or parenting skills. Although differential treatment is an important goal, it is very difficult to achieve, particularly within an institutional setting. As Serin and Preston acknowledge, few settings have the resources—both financial and human—to provide multiple programs for different types of violent offenders. Even when more than one program is offered, the identification and matching of offenders with specific programs are challenging tasks. In addition, the population of violent offenders who qualify as psychopaths requires different strategies, as we will see shortly.

Programs vary widely in their approach. However, many programs have two common features: (1) teaching techniques for self-regulating aggression and (2) addressing cognitive deficits. In the first category, motivated offenders are taught relaxation skills or "stress inoculation" approaches to reduce the arousal that results in inappropriate aggression. In the second category, motivated offenders are challenged to confront the irrational beliefs or biases that lead to violence. Defining problems in hostile ways or failing to anticipate the consequences of aggressive behavior are examples. Programs that address cognitive deficits, therefore, strive to change the thinking patterns of offenders by persuading them that the approaches they have used to this point have not resulted in successful outcomes in their relationships with society or with others in their environment. A prerequisite to a successful program outcome, however, is the motivation of the offender.

Although a variety of violent offender programs have produced some positive treatment effects, "few provide the rigor (i.e., control groups) to conclude that intervention for violent adults reduces violent recidivism" (Serin & Preston, 2001, p. 260). Advocates of violent offender programs maintain that such programs at the least *reduce the risk* of future violence and should ideally be followed up with community supervision and treatment once inmates are released. Furthermore, even when studies do not demonstrate positive posttreatment effects, the design of the study itself—not the treatment offered—may be the problem. As always, more methodologically sound research is needed to continue the progress toward effective programming.

Interestingly, some research indicates that it is far more difficult to provide intensive treatment for high-risk offenders in the community than in a controlled prison environment. Despite the numerous challenges within an institutional setting that were discussed above, the clinician has more control within a residential program. In addition, *milieu* treatment—such as can be found in therapeutic communities within the facility—is a possibility. A major disadvantage of institutional treatment is the difficulty in generalizing it to noninstitutional settings (Quinsey et al., 1998).

It should be mentioned that pharmacological approaches are also used in the management of violent offenders, particularly those for whom violence can be attributed partially to biological factors. These would include some individuals with brain injuries, schizophrenia, dementia, and clinical depression, among other disorders. Antipsychotic medications are often used in prison settings to control acute violent behavior in a crisis situation, such as a psychotic episode. Nevertheless, the vast majority of violent offenders neither require nor would benefit from pharmacological treatment (Serin & Preston, 2001). When such treatment is indicated, it should also be accompanied by psychological interventions such as those mentioned above.

Criminal Psychopaths

As we discussed in Chapter 7, individuals who qualify as criminal psychopaths present special challenges to society as well as to prison administrators. It has been a long-standing conclusion that psychopaths are essentially untreatable and continually demonstrate low motivation in treatment or rehabilitation programs. Hare (1996) asserts,

> There is no known treatment for psychopathy. . . . This does not necessarily mean that the egocentric and callous attitudes and behaviors of psychopaths are immutable, only that there are no methodologically sound treatments or "resocialization" programs that have been shown to work with psychopaths. Unfortunately, both the criminal justice system and the public routinely are fooled into believing otherwise. (p. 41)

In fact, Hare suggests that group therapy and insight-oriented treatment programs may actually help the psychopath develop better ways of manipulating and deceiving others.

Psychopaths often volunteer for various prison treatment programs, show "remarkable improvement," and present themselves as model prisoners. They are skillful at convincing therapists, counselors, and parole boards that they have changed for the better. Upon release, however, there is a high probability that they will reoffend, and their recidivism rate is not usually reduced following treatment. "Treatment participated in by many psychopaths may be superficial, intended mainly for impression management" (Porter et al., 2000, p. 219).

Some evidence even suggests that psychopaths who participate in therapy are *more* likely to engage in violent crime following treatment than psychopaths who did not receive treatment. Rice, Harris, and Cormier (1992) investigated the effectiveness of an intensive therapeutic community program offered in a maximum-security psychiatric facility. (Dr. Rice mentions this study in Personal Perspective 12.1.) The study was retrospective, in that the researchers examined records and files 10 years after the program was completed. Results showed that psychopaths who participated in the therapeutic community exhibited higher rates of violent recidivism than psychopaths who did not. For non-psychopaths, the results were the reverse: Non-psychopaths were less likely to reoffend if they had participated in the program. Rice et al. note that the psychopaths in their study were an especially serious group of offenders, with 85% having a history of violent crimes. It is possible that a group of less serious offenders would show better results. Nevertheless, the researchers concluded, "The combined results suggest that a therapeutic community is not the treatment of choice for psychopaths, particularly those with extensive criminal histories" (p. 408).

Some recent preliminary data by Skeem et al. (2002) do suggest, though, that *under certain conditions,* some psychopaths do benefit from treatment. Specifically, both the level of violence and the frequency of offending can be reduced. The key appears to be the intensity of the treatment. Skeem et al. found that psychopathic psychiatric patients who received seven or more treatment sessions during a 10-week period were approximately 3 times less likely to be violent than psychopathic patients who received six or fewer sessions. These results support earlier findings reported by Salekin (2002), who also discovered that a range of treatment interventions appeared to be moderately successful for psychopaths, especially if the treatment was lengthy and intensive.

Likewise, Bonta (2002) has suggested that psychopathy should be considered a dynamic factor, not a static variable: "Antisocial personality . . . does not need to be viewed as such a stable, intractable aspect of the person" (p. 369). He argues that certain features of the antisocial personality—impulsiveness, risk taking, callous disregard for others, shallow affect, pathological lying—can be linked with realistic treatment goals. Note that although we have made a distinction between the psychopath and the individual with antisocial personality disorder (see Chapter 7), the behavioral characteristics of the antisocial personality as mentioned here are virtually indistinguishable from those of the psychopath. Obviously, much more research is needed before we can make any far-reaching conclusions about the effectiveness of treatment programs directed at criminal psychopaths.

Sex Offender Treatment

As we discussed in Chapter 9, sex offenders are an extremely heterogeneous group. Most of the research has focused on two predominant groups, rapists and child molesters. These are the two sex offender groups that are the most likely to be imprisoned and the most difficult to treat, although within each group, some types of offenders are more amenable to treatment. Recall that we gave considerable attention in Chapter 8 to the typologies developed in an attempt to understand these offenders. It should be noted that extreme care should be used in applying these typologies, very few of which have been submitted to empirical validation (Heilbrun et al., 2002). As we stated in Chapter 9 while discussing sex offender evaluations, a negative label (e.g., sadistic rapist) may have unfair consequences for the individual so labeled. In prison, it may hinder his adjustment to incarceration, may affect his security level, or may limit his chances for an early release. In addition, although many psychologists believe the risk assessment instruments specifically devised for sex offenders are useful, these instruments also have many limitations (T. W. Campbell, 2003).

The number of sex offenders under correctional supervision has reached alarming proportions. By the end of the 1990s, approximately 296,100 individuals convicted of rape or sexual assault—including assault of children—were in this category, with about 40% of them in jails or prisons (BJS, 2001a). Observers have noted, however, that these figures represent the offense for which an offender was convicted and sentenced; an undetermined number of additional inmates also have offended sexually in the past but are not incarcerated for sex offenses (Burdon & Gallagher, 2002). In addition, Burdon and Gallagher note that some prison inmates are clinical sex offenders but not legal sex offenders. That is, they have a clinically diagnosable paraphilic disorder that may or may not have resulted in a conviction.

Psychologists and other clinicians continue to search for effective strategies to prevent future crime by sex offenders who, *as a group*, are highly resistant to changing their deviant behavior patterns (Bartol, 2002). After an extensive review of the research and clinical literature on the subject, Furby, Weinroth, and Blackshaw (1989) were forced to conclude, "There is as yet no evidence that clinical treatment reduces rates of sex reoffenses in general and no appropriate data for assessing whether it may be differentially effective for different types of offenders" (p. 27). The Furby et al. review included all variants of therapeutic approaches.

Despite this pessimistic appraisal, other reviews have been more favorable. For example, meta-analyses of the sex offender treatment literature have indicated that, on the whole, sex offenders are better if they are treated than if they are untreated (e.g., Gallagher et al., 1999). A meta-analysis examining 69 studies (Schmucker & Losel, 2008) indicated that cognitive-behavioral programs had positive effects. The cognitive-behavioral approach has also received positive reviews from Laws (1995) and Hanson et al. (2009), who conducted a meta-analysis of 23 treatment programs offered in institutions and the community.

Cognitive-behavioral treatment contends that maladaptive sexual behaviors are learned according to the same principles as normal sexual behaviors and are largely the result of attitudes and beliefs. Cognitive-behavioral therapy, compared to traditional verbal, insight-oriented therapy, has demonstrated short-term effectiveness in eliminating exhibitionism and fetishism (Kilmann, Sabalis, Gearing, Bukstel, & Scovern, 1982), some forms of pedophilia (W. Marshall & Barbaree, 1990), and sexual violence and aggression (N. G. C. Hall, 1995; Polizzi, MacKenzie, & Hickman, 1999). Cognitive-behavioral treatment currently offers the most effective method for the temporary cessation of deviant sexual behavior in motivated individuals. (See Focus 12.2 for common features of cognitive-behavioral treatment programs.)

The key words relative to the success of cognitive-behavioral treatment are *temporary cessation* and *motivated individual.* There is now widespread agreement among researchers and clinicians that sex offenders cannot be "cured." The problem of cognitive-behavioral therapy—and all therapies for that matter—is not in getting the motivated offender to stop the deviant sexual patterns but in preventing relapse across time and situations. It is analogous to dieting. Although most dieting regimens are effective in getting the motivated individual to lose weight initially, the real problem is the eventual relapse into old eating patterns. Thus, a treatment approach demonstrating much promise in the treatment of sex offenders is called Relapse Prevention (RP). "RP is a self-control program designed to teach individuals who are trying to change their behavior how to anticipate and cope with the problem of relapse" (George & Marlatt, 1989, p. 2). The program emphasizes self-management; clients are considered responsible for the solution of the problem.

In accordance with the principles outlined by Andrews and Bonta, however, clinicians also need to work on reducing criminogenic needs in high-risk sexual offenders and in matching their treatment to the learning style of the client (Hanson et al., 2009). Negative peer associations, aimless use of time, an antisocial lifestyle, deviant sexual interests, and attitudes tolerant of sexual crime are examples of criminogenic needs. Interestingly, Bourke and Hernandez (2009) found that federal inmates convicted of offenses relating to Internet child pornography had a high incidence of self-reporting prior instances of hands-on child sex offenses. If this connection is documented in additional research, mental health clinicians treating sex offenders would regard child pornography as a criminogenic need that should be monitored and dealt with.

Sex offender treatment programs exist in virtually every state and in the federal prison system, and they represent a major endeavor engaged in by correctional psychologists, as well as community psychologists who have sex offenders among their patients. The programs vary widely in approach, in the extent to which they are evaluated, and in the degree of success when evaluation research is conducted. Recent meta-analyses (Hanson et al., 2009) are making progress in identifying the common features of those programs that are most likely to reduce recidivism. Treatment programs are less likely to be available to jail inmates because of the short-term nature of jail confinement. However, inmates who are subsequently released to the community may be referred to community treatment programs.

FOCUS 12.2. THE COGNITIVE-BEHAVIORAL APPROACH: KEY ELEMENTS

Of the many therapeutic interventions that have been tried in corrections, the cognitive-behavioral approach seems to hold the most promise. It consists of counseling (group and individual) and training whereby offenders develop cognitive skills that will presumably help them to adopt alternative, prosocial behaviors rather than the antisocial behaviors that resulted in their criminal convictions. There is no universally implemented cognitive-behavioral treatment program; rather, treatment providers decide on an approach consistent with their own training and the needs of the offenders under their care. Any or all of the following elements might be found in a cognitive-behavioral treatment program:

- Social skills development training (e.g., learning to communicate, be assertive rather than aggressive, and resolve conflicts appropriately)
- Decision making (e.g., learning to weigh alternatives, learning to delay gratification)
- Identifying and avoiding "thinking errors"—misguided assumptions that facilitated criminal offending (e.g., "women want to be shown who's boss")
- Training at solving problems (e.g., interpersonal problems with one's intimate partner)
- Self-control training and anger management (e.g., avoiding hostile attribution)
- Building self-esteem (e.g., recognizing good qualities and providing self-reinforcement)
- Cognitive skills training (e.g., learning to reason)
- Relapse prevention (learning to avoid situations that might lead to further offending)
- Practical skills training (e.g., applying for work)

As noted in the text, the cognitive-behavioral approach has shown success when programs are properly implemented and carried out and offenders are motivated to change. It is not perfect. However, although other therapeutic approaches (e.g., behavior modification, therapeutic communities) have not had promising results (with some exceptions), cognitive-behavioral therapy gives reason to hope.

Women Prisoners

In recent years, women's rates of incarceration have increased faster than men's rates, although, as noted earlier, very few scholars predict that they will ever "catch up." In 1970, there were only 5,600 women in prison; by 1980 there were 12,500; and by 1998 there were over 75,000 (Reichert, Adams, & Bostwick, 2010). As indicated at the beginning of the chapter, by 2008, a total of 105,300 women were serving prison sentences of more than 1 year (Sabol et al., 2009). Presently, women make up 6.3% of all state and federal prison inmates and approximately 10% of all jail inmates and detainees in the United States. (See Photo 12.2 depicting a female inmate in a cell.) Women ages 35 to 39 make up the largest percentage of sentenced women prisoners

Photo 12.2 A woman sits in a jail cell awaiting a court hearing. Although the number of women in jails and prisons is far less than the number of men, women's arrest rates have increased faster than those of men.

under state or federal jurisdiction (Sabol et al., 2009). Most women are in prison because of drug or property offending. Typical female offenders are mothers who are poor, undereducated, unskilled, and victims of physical and sexual abuse (Reichert et al., 2010). In addition, 20% of women entering U.S. prisons have abused alcohol, and 45% have abused drugs (Fazel, Parveen, & Doll, 2006).

Although increasing research attention is now being given to women inmates, they still remain forgotten offenders compared with males. Recent studies have focused on assessing needs and validating actuarial risk assessment instruments with female offenders (e.g., Folsom & Atkinson, 2007; E. J. Palmer & Hollin, 2007; Van Voorhis et al., 2010), but research on effective treatment approaches is not widely available. Yet mental health concerns are becoming increasing apparent. For example, in one recent study (Reichert et al., 2010), 60% of the incarcerated women in a state prison showed symptoms of PTSD or other mental disorders. Other studies have identified similar statistics (Owen, 2000). Since most female prisoners are likely to have prior abuse histories (between 60 and 85%), they are generally in need of trauma-based treatment (Messina, Grella, Burdon, & Prendergast, 2007). A vast majority of women offenders are also in need of substance abuse services.

As mentioned in the previous paragraph, many women serving time have had a history of victimization—often violent victimization and often at the hands of fathers, spouses, or intimate partners. As Owen (2000) observes, "Closely related to mental health problems is the need to recognize the impact of the physical, sexual, and emotional abuse experienced by women offenders" (p. 196). Treatment approaches that increase their self-confidence, recognize their victimization but enable them to take charge of their lives, and teach them life skills offer the best hope for women who are incarcerated.

Scholars agree that problems faced by female prisoners are similar to but also distinct from the problems faced by male prisoners. For example, due to the small numbers of women in prison, there are far fewer correctional facilities available, thus severely restricting opportunities for female inmates to be near their families or to have occupational, educational, or social activities while incarcerated. More important, their relationships with their children are often severely hampered, resulting in a more severe deprivation than is typically found for the male parent (MacKenzie, Robinson, & Campbell, 1989). This parent–child deprivation is especially severe for long-term women inmates, who may lose their major source of identity when they lose their parental role (Weisheit & Mahan, 1988). In essence, the available literature suggests that different treatment priorities may be warranted for women who are incarcerated (Van Voorhis et al., 2010).

Treatment in Jail Settings

Psychological treatment of inmates in jail settings is considerably different from treatment in prisons. The short-term nature of the jail stay—on average, 11 days—suggests that **crisis intervention** and limited treatment goals are typical. Moreover, treatment in jail settings is far more likely to consist of stabilizing medication rather than therapy. Nevertheless, the treatment models discussed above can still be implemented, even in short-term jail settings.

Steadman et al. (1989) have provided a helpful but now dated description of mental health services offered in 43 jails in 26 states. All jails in their study offered psychotropic medication, and almost all offered psychological evaluation and competency examinations (98% and 93%, respectively). Far fewer (60%) offered drug and alcohol treatment. Therapy or counseling was offered by 30%, whereas a mere 16% provided case management services for general mental health at release. Steadman et al. identified, described in detail, and provided illustrations of four basic types of service arrangements for mentally disordered inmates:

1. "Ad hoc," in which services were offered only on an emergency basis;

2. "Identification," in which correctional officers only identified disturbed inmates;

3. "Identification and treatment," in which disturbed inmates were both identified and were provided with treatment; and

4. "Comprehensive," in which identification, treatment, and referral services were all available (pp. 48–49).

The above taxonomy was not the researchers' main concern, however. Rather, they wished to examine the linkages between community resources and the delivery of mental health services to the jailed population.

> Instead of viewing the jail as a self-contained or closed system, an interorganizational approach to program development and evaluation looks beyond the jail to its linkages with a variety of other organizations in its environment, such as state mental hospital, psychiatric units in general hospitals, community mental health centers, and other health and human service agencies. (Steadman et al., 1989, p. 73)

Many of the existing programs offered services outside the jail, such as by transporting inmates to community clinics or offices. Internal programs, which were less in evidence, placed heavier demands on staffing, budgets, and institutional security.

A key finding of the research was that conflict between correctional staff and mental health staff was far less evident than the researchers had expected. Although some conflict existed, particularly when services were provided within the jail under the joint auspices of correctional and mental health personnel, the two professions shared the convergence of two goals: custody and therapy. Correctional staff indicated that therapists made their jobs easier, and therapists respected the needs of the custodial staff to keep the jail secure. Steadman and his colleagues (1989) attributed this to the short-term nature of a jail stay, essentially leaving no time for the huge ascendancy of one type of goal over the other, such as is more likely to occur in prison settings. They note that the jail is truly the client:

> If individual treatment were more ambitious, much more therapy in the form of individual counseling and group sessions would become more pervasive, and conflict, as well as service costs, would probably increase dramatically. However, given the nature of the jail, such treatment goals are unrealistic, while safety management needs are acute. (p. 103)

Providing treatment services to the non-sentenced jail population—the detainees—is especially challenging. First, it is impossible to predict how long the individual will remain in detention because pretrial release is a continuing possibility for the majority of detainees. Some detainees may have charges dismissed or they may plead guilty to their offenses, meaning that they will be placed on probation or transferred to prison. Second, even while in custody, numerous disruptions will occur in the individual's schedule. For example, court appearances, visits, meetings with attorneys, population head counts, and even recreational opportunities are unpredictable. Third, treatment services must be generic and not tied to criminal activity because the detainee is only charged with, not convicted of, crime. Thus, sex offender treatment or a program for domestic abusers is inappropriate when applied to detainees who are presumed innocent until proven guilty.

Even sentenced inmates serving time in jail provide challenges to the forensic psychologist, largely due to the short-term natures of their sentence. The therapist therefore must forgo long-term goals, even if he or she believes such goals are in the greater interest of the client. "Mental health professionals who are willing to work toward less traditional treatment goals can function within the jail with minimal goal conflict" (Steadman et al., 1989, p. 103). They are advised to develop release-planning goals that will link the individual to community-based mental health agencies. In addition, they are urged to keep in mind that the jail environment itself is crowded, noisy, and lacking in privacy, and that inmates have very little control over their lives. Such conditions can exacerbate mental disorder. Not surprisingly, therefore, "the primary treatment goals for jail inmates will usually be crisis stabilization and maintenance at an appropriate level of functioning while in custody" (Cox, Landsberg, & Paravati, 1989, p. 223).

As discussed at the beginning of this chapter, jails—sometimes even more than prisons—have a number of features that can impede efforts to offer treatment. Today, limited budgets and overcrowding are major concerns. Bowker and Schweid (1992) wrote about a program for intellectually disabled offenders in Cuyahoga County, Ohio. A special unit was opened in order to prevent the victimization of these offenders by other offenders. A counselor would meet with them weekly in group meetings to help them adjust to their environment and would consult with a team to address their needs. Eventually, overcrowding necessitated the closing of the special unit, and the developmentally disabled inmates then were shifted to a medical/psychological unit. Although the researchers noted there was hope that adding more space to the jail might revive the special unit, the problem that was faced is a common one in numerous jails that do not have the resources to separate inmates with special needs.

Treatment and Counseling of Correctional Officers

"Louis" prides himself on being a "take no prisoners" correctional officer. He is often assigned to accompany criminal justice students on their tours through the maximum-security facility where he works. Louis likes to roll up his pant leg to show students the scars he has received from inmate assaults. Research shows, however, that inmates rarely assault correctional officers.

"Sam" is a 35-year-old correctional officer in a maximum-security prison. His father, uncles, and several men in his hometown have been or are correctional officers. Sam is married and has two young children. He is having an affair with a female officer, and he has just learned that his wife wants a divorce. Sam has been involved in several altercations with inmates and is fearful of losing his job.

"Art" has been a correctional officer for 22 years and is respected if not liked by inmates. He treats them fairly but does not hesitate to give them tickets for rule violations. He cooperates with mental health providers, though he also thinks most of them are "conned" by the inmates. Art has felt safe in the prison environment and secure in his job, which brings a good salary and benefits. He has a stable family life and looks forward to retirement, when he will be able to travel, hunt, and fish. In the past few years, there has been talk about changing the focus of the prison to one that provides more mental health services, which would require transferring many inmates as well as correctional officers. Art is not happy about this possibility and is experiencing health problems as a result.

According to research and anecdotal reports, stress among correctional officers in both jails and prisons is widespread (Abt Associates, 2000; Huckabee, 1992; Lambert, Edwards, Camp, & Saylor, 2005). These officers face challenges ranging from threats of inmate violence to public derogation of their work, but in reality inmate violence against them is atypical. In the popular media, correctional officers are often depicted as callous, uneducated, and brutal. (Consider such films as *Shawshank Redemption, The Green Mile,* and *Monster's Ball.*) The professional, stable, intelligent officer—like Art—is portrayed as the exception rather than the rule. These media stereotypes are reflected in public attitudes toward correctional work; some officers comment that, when asked what they do for a living, they reply that they "work for the state" and hope to avoid further questions.

Within the prison or jails, correctional officers experience stress associated with understaffing and extensive overtime, low pay (particularly in jails), inmate violence, rotating shift work, and problems with coworkers (Abt Associates, 2000). Furthermore, overcrowding in many correctional facilities is accompanied by an increasing number of attacks against correctional staff. Nevertheless, most violence in prisons and in jails is believed to be inmate-on-inmate violence (Clear & Cole, 2000), and the research literature is consistent in reporting high rates of both violence and fear of violence among inmates (Listwan, Colvin, Hanley, & Flannery, 2010). However, even if they are not the direct recipients of assaults, correctional officers experience stress as a result.

For many reasons, psychological services to correctional officers are almost invariably delivered outside of the facility, on a contractual basis with the correctional system, and with guaranteed confidentiality. An exception might be on-site crisis counseling following a critical incident within the facility, such as a hostage-taking situation or the killing of a correctional officer. In such a situation, the facility's mental health professionals as well as professionals working in the community might conduct group debriefing sessions with affected correctional officers. For the most part, however, prison and jail systems contract with mental health professionals within the community. Alternatively, correctional officers are left to seek help on their own. Peer counseling programs, with or without guidance from psychologists and other mental health professionals, are also becoming increasingly available in correctional facilities. A report prepared for the Department of Justice (Abt Associates, 2000) describes approximately a dozen programs designed to address correctional officer stress in prisons, jails, and youth facilities. Although we emphasize in this chapter the assessment and treatment offered to inmates, it is obvious that psychologists and other mental health professionals must continue to make their services available to correctional staff as well.

Obstacles to the Treatment of Inmates and Staff

The correctional environment itself creates numerous challenges for the clinician offering services both to inmates and to staff. In this section, we discuss some of the main obstacles.

Confidentiality

As noted in earlier chapters, forensic psychologists often find that they cannot guarantee total confidentiality to the persons whom they assess or treat. This is especially true of psychologists working in correctional settings, particularly prisons and jails. For example, when the security of the institution is at stake, the inmate presents a threat of suicide, or a third party is in danger, confidentiality cannot be guaranteed. Limitations on confidentiality include "knowledge of escape plans, intentions to commit a crime in prison, introduction of illegal items (e.g., contraband) into prison, in addition to suicidal or homicidal ideation and intention, court subpoenas, and reports of child or elder abuse or neglect" (Morgan et al., 1999, p. 602). As we noted earlier in the chapter, psychologists and other treatment providers are advised to inform inmates of these limitations on confidentiality prior to the provision of assessment and treatment services. As a result of these limits, the inmate may perceive the treatment provider as a representative of the administration. When this happens, the work of psychologists in correctional facilities becomes especially challenging (Milan, Chin, & Nguyen, 1999).

Confidentiality is also a critical factor when psychologists are treating correctional officers. There are countless anecdotal reports of correctional officers (as well as law enforcement officers) who resist seeking help for psychological problems—from mild to very severe—because they fear that supervisors or coworkers will learn of this and lose confidence in their ability to do their job. For this reason, prison and jail systems sometimes go to great lengths to guarantee the anonymity of the officer being treated. In one program described in the Abt Associates (2000) report, for example, a chaplain assigns a number to an officer needing professional treatment. The officer then calls a psychologist, and all subsequent billing for services is done using only the number as identification. The chaplain serves as the intermediary, receiving bills and forwarding them to the appropriate fiscal office. In this way, correctional administrators presumably are never made aware of which officer has sought treatment.

Although patient–therapist confidentiality is sacrosanct, the fact that an individual has sought treatment may eventually be revealed. This is particularly the case when a civil suit is brought against the facility or agency and an individual officer is an essential part of the legal action. When a clinician is called to testify as a witness in a legal proceeding, confidentiality is not protected. An officer sued for excessive force, for example, cannot expect to keep confidential the fact that he or she has sought psychological treatment, either before or after the alleged incident. Even an officer using justifiable force may be subjected to some legal scrutiny. The *content* of the therapist–patient communication is privileged, but the *fact* that such communication took place is not (*Jaffe v. Redmond*, 1996).

Coercion

Another obstacle to successful treatment, particularly treatment of inmates, is its coercive aspect. Institutional treatment often—although not invariably—operates on the principle that psychological change can be coerced. Conversely, traditional forms of psychological treatment have been successful only when subjects were willing and motivated to participate. This basic principle applies regardless of whether the person is living in the community or within the walls of an institution that has overwhelming power over the lives of its inmates. Thus, although inmates have a **right to refuse treatment,** their refusal can create far more problems than their grudging acceptance. For example, refusal may mean transfer to another facility, delay in being released, or a restriction on privileges (*McKune v. Lile*, 2002).

In recent years, however, some researchers have begun to question the conventional wisdom that coercion and treatment cannot coexist (see generally, Farabee, 2002). An inmate may feel pressured to participate in a treatment program but may then come to accept its value. In addition, some studies indicate that even a recalcitrant inmate can eventually benefit from treatment programs (e.g., Burdon & Gallagher, 2002; Prendergast, Farabee, Cartier, & Henkin, 2002).

Environment

Another obstacle to effective treatment in prisons and jails is the unusual nature of the prison environment itself. The list of negative features ranges from overcrowding, violence, and victimization by both other prisoners and staff to isolation from families and feelings of a lack of control over one's life.

In the late 1950s and 1960s, a number of psychologists working in correctional settings helped establish therapeutic communities for inmates facing adjustment problems in prisons (Toch, 1980). As mentioned earlier in the chapter, these TCs were special living quarters where inmates would be housed separately from the rest of the prison population and would be involved in decision making, group therapy, and operating their own living quarters within the broad prison setting. Although these inmates did not have significantly better recidivism rates than other inmates (Gendreau & Ross, 1984), prison life was made more tolerable for them, and job satisfaction for the staff improved. Today, few prison programs offer therapeutic community settings, primarily because of budgetary constraints and space limitations. When available, they are more likely to be offered to inmates with substance abuse problems. Recall from our discussion of psychopaths that they do not appear to be good candidates for a therapeutic community approach. In general, research has documented the effectiveness of therapeutic communities when they are intensive, behavior based, and focused on targeting an offender's drug use (MacKenzie, 2000). Continuing research has shown positive results with the therapeutic community approach with respect to drug offenders (Saum et al., 2007).

Many observers note that prison environments are worse today than they were in the 1960s, when therapeutic communities were first proposed. Overcrowding, violence, and deteriorating physical conditions characterize a substantial number of the nation's prisons and jails. By the end of the 20th century, for example, state prisons as a group were operating between full capacity and 15% above capacity, and federal prisons were operating at 31% above capacity (BJS, 2001a). The overcrowding problem in jails was even more severe. Violence is also endemic in many prisons. It has been estimated that about 25,000 nonsexual assaults and close to 300,000 sexual assaults occur each year in the nation's jails and prisons (Clear & Cole, 2000). It is impossible to know the true number because many assaults may not be reported. In 2003, in an attempt to address this issue, Congress passed the Prison Rape Elimination Act (Office of Justice Programs, 2003), which, among other things, mandates prisons and jails to report incidences of rape of which they are aware. Most recently, psychologists themselves have written about the need to research the problem of prison rape and design programs for both prevention and treatment (Neal & Clements, 2010).

Living conditions for inmates who are kept in isolation for disciplinary reasons or presumably for their own protection (e.g., inmates with mental disorders) are particularly problematic from a psychological perspective, especially if the stays in isolation extend for months or even years at a time. As mentioned above, however, not everyone agrees that isolation is damaging, particularly because offenders are kept under varying conditions. Although it would be unfair to suggest that the typical jail or prison faces these seemingly intractable problems, correctional psychologists encounter them all too often, and they contribute significantly to the stress experienced by both inmates and staff.

Treatment is also made difficult by other aspects of even the most humane jail or prison environment. Jail sentences are typically short, so continuous treatment is highly unlikely to occur. In both jails and prisons, inmates "miss" appointments with clinicians for a wide variety of reasons. Even when inmates themselves want to attend, they may be prevented from doing so for security or disciplinary reasons. A cellblock may be locked down for a day, for example, while officials conduct cell searches, investigate a disturbance, or conduct medical tests. An inmate involved in an altercation may be placed in disciplinary segregation, making it unlikely that visits to a therapist will be allowed. For security reasons, prison inmates are transferred to other facilities with little warning. Finally, budgetary constraints in many facilities result in cutbacks to all but the most essential services.

Community-Based Corrections

As we noted at the beginning of the chapter, the great majority of adults under correctional supervision remain within the community, either in their own homes or in transitional or group homes, camps, ranches, or similar facilities. Community-based placements other than one's own home generally hold individuals for less than 24 hours a day, allowing them opportunity to work, attend school, participate in job training, or attend counseling or treatment sessions. Community-based facilities are operated by state or federal governments or by private organizations under government contract. In the criminal justice literature, such placements are referred to as "intermediate sanctions," representing points on a continuum between probation and jail or prison, as well as between prison and parole. They may also be referred to as "probation plus," or "parole plus." The offender who lives in a halfway house upon release from prison, for example, is on parole with the added restrictions imposed by the rules and supervision of the halfway house administration. Interestingly, in February 2003, the federal government announced that it was removing from federal judges the authority to send sentenced offenders to halfway houses rather than to federal prisons when the federal sentencing guidelines prescribed a prison sentence. Offenders who were most likely to benefit from judicial discretion were those convicted of white-collar offenses. The government indicated its goal was to end favorable treatment for these individuals.

Intermediate sanctions are also used with offenders who remain in their own homes, such as offenders assigned to house arrest or electronic monitoring. The forensic psychologist offering services to offenders under community correctional supervision, therefore, soon learns that they have a variety of living arrangements as well as conditions of release.

A common condition of release is the requirement that an offender attend counseling or therapy. Thus, many community psychologists have on their caseload individuals who have been ordered to seek treatment. We will not revisit here the issue discussed earlier in the chapter, revolving around whether change can be coerced. Although it is not irrelevant in this context, the coercion here is not as clear-cut as coercion within the institutional environment of the jail or prison, particularly the latter. Nevertheless, community psychologists are well aware that their clients might only be seeking help because of the fear that they could be incarcerated if they do not meet the conditions of release.

Like the psychologist working with detainees and inmates, the psychologist working in community settings performs both assessment and treatment tasks. Evaluations of an individual's competency to stand trial or competency to participate in a variety of judicial proceedings are often performed in the community, as we noted in Chapter 4. In addition, the community psychologist may assess an offender's appropriateness for a particular treatment program, such as a program for sex offenders. Risk assessments are increasingly being performed within the community, as well. For example, before downgrading a probationer from an **intensive supervision program** (defined further below) to "regular" probation, the court or the probation authority may ask the psychologist to assess the risk to the community if the probationer is no longer supervised as diligently. The principles associated with risk assessment, as well as with risk/needs assessment discussed earlier in this chapter and in Chapters 4 and 5, will not be repeated here. As we will see shortly, recent commentators are strongly advocating an assessment of an offender's criminogenic needs before undertaking community treatment.

The role of the psychologist in treating offenders in the community deserves our careful attention. In most ways, the principles applied and the standard of practice are no different from what the psychologist would adopt in the treatment of any other client. Nevertheless, a number of factors render the correctional client distinctive. The common thread among all of these factors is the importance of communication between the psychologist and the representatives of the criminal justice system. First, as noted above, the coercive nature of the treatment may create problems, although it is far less coercive than treatment in jails and prisons. Second, the psychologist may be placed in the untenable position of being an "enforcer," similar to the probation officer. Thus, if the client misses an appointment, the psychologist must decide whether to report this lapse to the probation officer, who may or may not see this as a serious problem. Third, in a somewhat related vein, the psychologist may be called on to make decisions involving privileges that he or she would rather not have to make. A parolee receiving treatment may wish to attend the out-of-state wedding of a sibling, for example, a decision that would typically be left to the supervising officer. Community psychologists are often called on to render opinions on such matters, which many believe are out of their purview. Fourth, the limits of confidentiality must be recognized and communicated to the individual. Typically, the client in these situations is not the offender but the supervising agency, which may be a court or a probation/parole department. In some jurisdictions, the court imposing the conditions of release may require periodic progress notes from the treating clinician. In addition, in the event that probation or parole is revoked, summary notes from the psychologist's records may be subjected to court scrutiny. Fifth and finally, the criminogenic needs of the offender require continual assessment and addressing.

The last decade of the 20th century saw some promising work describing and evaluating the work of psychologists vis-à-vis conditionally released offenders in community settings. Heilbrun and Griffin (1999), describing a number of well-regarded programs in the United States, Canada, and the Netherlands, concluded that there was no single "ideal" program; rather, it was important to use

> the full range of treatment modalities that have been developed during the past decade. . . . By employing treatments such as recently developed psychotropic medications, psychosocial rehabilitation, skill-based psychoeducational interventions designed to improve relevant areas of deficits, and relapse prevention, it is likely that treatment response in a forensic program will be enhanced. (p. 270)

Heilbrun and Griffin (1999) provide illustrations of community-based programs in eight states as well as Canada. Most of the programs described provided services to a hybrid population of individuals with mental disorders, including individuals found not guilty by reason of insanity (NGRI) as well as probationers and parolees assigned to treatment programs as a condition of their release or referred by probation/parole officers. Thus, most contacts were on an involuntary basis. Included were both outpatient and residential rehabilitation programs, with outpatient clinics offering both assessment and treatment. Some clinics offering substance abuse treatment also accepted voluntary clients.

In summarizing the programs they describe, Heilbrun and Griffin (1999) note that all emphasized the treatment of psychopathology and the management of aggressive behavior. "In order to meet both goals, programs may refuse to accept high-risk patients, who are generally regarded as more antisocial individuals" (p. 264). Interestingly, it is precisely high-risk offenders who have been found to benefit the most from intensive treatment programs.

This is a finding that has consistently emerged from research focusing on the variant of intermediate sanctions known as intensive supervision. **Intensive supervision programs (ISPs)** were intended for high-risk probationers and parolees who were nevertheless deemed not to require incarceration if a less costly alternative were available. (In reality, low-risk offenders were placed in these programs as well [Tonry, 1990].) Probation or parole officers supervising offenders on ISPs have smaller caseloads, provide round-the-clock team supervision, make frequent contacts, and presumably are less tolerant of any failure on the part of the offender to meet the conditions of release. Alcohol and illegal drug use are monitored closely and without notice. Despite these punitive conditions, evaluations of community ISPs have not been promising, and they have not proved cost-effective (Gendreau, Paparozzi, Little, & Goddard, 1993; Tonry, 1990).

Gendreau et al. (1994) have proposed **intensive rehabilitation supervision (IRS)** as a "second generation" approach to community supervision. "Based on the existing empirical evidence, a persuasive case can be made for abandoning intensive supervision programs that seek only to control and punish offenders in favor of programs that give equal primacy to changing offenders" (p. 74).

Because of their potential for frequent contact with high-risk offenders, IRS programs are likely to be able to match the risk level of offenders with their criminogenic and noncriminogenic needs. Recall that many criminogenic needs are dynamic risk factors, or factors that can change over time, such as an individual's attitude toward authority or employment. Recall also the following comment: "The importance of criminogenic needs is that they serve as treatment goals: when programs successfully diminish these needs, we can reasonably expect reduction in recidivism" (Gendreau et al., 1994, p. 75). Targeting noncriminogenic needs (e.g., anxiety, depression, and self-esteem) is less likely to produce significant reductions in recidivism (Andrews & Bonta, 1994).

Bonta, Wallace-Capretta, and Rooney (2000) conducted an experiment in which they assessed the effectiveness of an intensive rehabilitation approach operating in Newfoundland. The Learning Resources Program (LRP) provides such services to offenders as anger management, a cognitive-behavioral approach to substance abuse, individual counseling, and errors in thinking that might facilitate criminal activity. Bonta et al. compared three groups of offenders, two receiving treatment by the LRP and one receiving no treatment. The two groups receiving treatment were IRS participants and probationers who were chosen by probation officers as needing treatment. The third group consisted of incarcerated inmates who did not receive treatment but who would have been considered eligible for IRS had it been available. In other words, they qualified as high-risk inmates. Results at first showed no significant differences in recidivism between the two treated groups and the nontreated inmate group. However, when researchers divided the groups into high-risk and low-risk participants (using the LSI-R), a significant interaction effect was found: "The high-risk offenders who received relatively intensive levels of treatment showed lower recidivism rates than untreated high-risk offenders (31.6% vs. 51.1%)" (p. 325). In addition, low-risk offenders who received intensive treatment demonstrated higher recidivism than nontreated low-risk offenders (32.3% vs. 14.5%). This last finding did not surprise researchers because prior studies have indicated that low-risk offenders do not seem to benefit from intensive treatment and may, in fact, be hurt by it (Andrews & Bonta, 1998; Andrews et al., 1990).

Gendreau and his colleagues (1994) have identified a number of features associated with the effective rehabilitation of high-risk offenders, including those in the community. For example, the intensive rehabilitation services provided to the high-risk offender should occupy 40 to 70% of the offender's time for 3 to 9 months. The goal of treatment should be to reduce criminogenic needs—thus obviously necessitating an initial risk/needs assessment. Both the style and the mode of treatment should be matched to the offender's personality—thus, an anxious offender might work better with a relaxed, calm clinician. Gendreau et al. suggest also that the treating psychologist should advocate for the offender and link the offender with other community agencies, as long as these agencies offer appropriate services.

Thus, Gendreau and his colleagues (1994) have faith in community corrections treatment, particularly if it is targeted specifically at high-risk offenders and uses the intensive treatment approach. "The empirical evidence regarding ISP's is decisive: without a rehabilitation component, reductions in recidivism are as elusive as a desert mirage" (p. 77).

This is not to suggest that *non-intensive* treatment is not effective for low-risk offenders, however. As studies reviewed by Heilbrun and Griffin (1999) have demonstrated, substance abuse treatment and assistance in working toward independent living can be beneficial for motivated low-risk offenders. Programs with strong community ties; written contracts; group meetings; vocational resources; and assistance at tasks of daily living, such as managing money, have garnered positive research results.

SUMMARY AND CONCLUSIONS

This chapter has provided a description of the role of forensic psychologists working primarily with adult offenders (and sometimes with detainees) in both institutional and community settings. We began with an overview of jails and prisons, focusing on distinctions between the two that are most relevant to the psychologist. Because of their short-term nature, for example, jails offer fewer programs and are less likely to enable the psychologist to have long-range treatment goals. Jails also engender more crisis situations, such as suicide attempts by detainees. The chapter also included a brief review of those legal rights of inmates that are most likely to affect the work of psychologists. The right to treatment, the right to refuse treatment, and the right not to suffer cruel and unusual punishment are examples.

The work of psychologists in adult corrections can be divided into the two broad but overlapping areas of assessment and treatment. We reviewed the many situations under which psychologists are asked to assess various abilities of detainees and inmates, as well as their mental states. In recent years, psychology has seen the development of many assessment instruments for use in these forensic settings; studies indicate, however, that psychologists are not making extensive use of these instruments, preferring more traditional measures such as the clinical interview and the MMPI. At a minimum, assessment is needed when inmates enter the facility, before they are released, and when they are in crisis situations. Ideally, though, assessment should be a continuing enterprise and should occur as indicated throughout the inmate's stay.

The assessment of a death row inmate's competency to be executed is unlikely to involve the typical correctional psychologist. Nevertheless, this is an area of immense importance and one that has engendered considerable debate. Some psychologists, such as those who are philosophically opposed to the death penalty, believe they should not be involved in such assessments or in the subsequent treatment that may be needed. Others believe it is their professional duty to offer the services as they are required. Furthermore, because some courts have now given authorities the go-ahead to force medication on a death row inmate to render him or her stable enough to be executed, this issue will undoubtedly trouble some clinicians even more. We did not cover this debate in detail within the chapter, but we discussed suggestions given to those forensic psychologists who conduct "competency for execution" assessments. With the Supreme Court decisions in *Atkins v. Virginia* (2002) and *Panetti v. Quarterman* (2007), assessments of cognitive ability have become more frequent as well.

Psychologists are only one of several professional groups offering treatment services to inmates, both individually and in groups. The treatment model—or treatment approach—that tends to be the most favored is the cognitive-behavioral approach, although others are also in evidence. Cognitive-behavioral approaches—which have received the most positive evaluation results—are based on social learning theory. They assume that criminal behavior is learned much like other behavior and that the motivated inmates can "unlearn" the behavior. Consequently, these approaches encourage inmates to identify their thinking patterns, their assumptions, and their expectations, and to recognize the consequences of their behavior both for themselves and their victims. Research indicates that motivated inmates can benefit from these approaches, which are often used with a wide range of offenders, including violent offenders, sex offenders, and substance abusers. Among the least motivated inmates for such treatment are persistent violent offenders and psychopaths, although we hesitate to draw generalizations, particularly about the first group.

Features of the prison and jail settings can present numerous obstacles to effective treatment, so much so that some psychologists prefer not to approach this challenge. Limitations on confidentiality, budgetary restraints, violence and overcrowding within the facility, inmate schedules and inmate transfers, and sometimes lack of support from administrators and correctional officers are not unusual. Yet many psychologists find immense satisfaction performing this work. Professional organizations offer guidelines and provide support, and increasingly more research is published identifying effective strategies and approaches in a wide variety of situations.

The chapter ended with a review of community treatment programs with offenders who are on probation; on parole; or under intermediate sanctions, such as intensive supervision. In recent years, we have begun to see more descriptions and evaluations of community programs within the psychological literature. Although community programs provide their own special challenges (e.g., offenders not appearing for their treatment session or dropping out completely), they also have the advantage of being in a more realistic environment that does not present the numerous obstacles of institutional settings.

KEY CONCEPTS

Administrative segregation

Behavioral models

Cognitive-behavioral approach

Community-based facilities

Community corrections

Competency to be executed

Correctional psychologists

Criminogenic needs

Crisis intervention

Detention centers

Disciplinary segregation

Federal Bureau of Prisons (BOP)

Incarceration rate

Institutional corrections

Intensive rehabilitation supervision

Intensive supervision programs

Intermediate sanctions

Jails

Level of Service Inventory—Revised (LSI-R)

Mandatory sentences

Noncriminogenic needs

Pretrial detainees

Prisons

Prison transfer

Protective custody

Psychological assessment

Rehabilitation

Release decisions

Right to refuse treatment

Right to treatment

Supermax prisons

QUESTIONS FOR REVIEW

1. Explain the difference between institutional and community corrections.

2. What are the IACFP standards? List any five topics they cover.

3. List the main differences between prisons and jails.

4. Does the constitutional right to treatment include a right to psychiatric/psychological treatment? Explain your answer.

5. Which two categories of adult offenders have been found to be incompetent to be executed?

6. Why is it important for forensic psychologists working in correctional settings to be aware of both constitutional and state law relating to inmates?

7. Identify the tasks that might be assumed by psychologists in relation to both screening and classification of inmates.

8. Are forensic psychologists involved in the screening and treatment of correctional personnel? Explain your answer.

9. Provide an illustration of a treatment program for each of the following special populations: violent offenders, criminal psychopaths, women offenders, sex offenders, and inmates in jail.

10. What are three major obstacles to the treatment of prisoners and staff in prison settings?

13

Juvenile Corrections

In 2010, the U.S. Department of Justice released a report (Beck, Guerino, & Harrison, 2010) that gained considerable attention in the media. A survey of youth in 195 juvenile confinement facilities across the country indicated that about 12% had experienced one or more incidents of sexual victimization over the past year (or since their admission if they had not been confined that long). The time period covered was from June 2008 to April 2009, and the facilities included both state and large private residential centers. Incidents involving staff victimization were more prevalent than those involving other youth (10.3% of the youth reported staff victimization and 2.6% reported incidents involving other youths).

In a separate news item, a state director of an office of family and children's services stepped down from her position after it was learned that juvenile males in a state-run facility were rewarded for their good behavior by being allowed to have a party to which they could invite female friends and prostitutes from the outside. Drug use and sexual activity allegedly occurred at these parties.

And, in still other news flashes, juvenile detention or treatment centers have been closed after evidence of physical abuse and neglect of the mental health needs of the residents was obtained.

Stories like these come as no surprise to advocates for juveniles, many of whom argue forcefully that juveniles should be placed in secure confinement only as a last resort. We explore these arguments in this chapter, along with providing more positive information about the treatment of juveniles in both institutional and community settings.

Although much remedial work is needed in the care given to young offenders, conditions and programs vary both geographically and across facilities; clearly not all are represented by the negative examples.

Facilities that hold juvenile offenders vary widely in size, organizational complexity, and layout. Many of the facilities provide only one type of placement program, such as a boot camp or a detention center, while others are more complex. The complex facilities may consist of multiple buildings at a single location or have housing units at multiple locations. Facilities also differ in their security, the types of offenders they hold, and the average length of stay for the residents. Most youth (93%) are in facilities that provide a single primary program, whereas the remainder (7%) live in complex facilities (Sedlack & McPherson, 2010a).

Some facilities house youth who are in custody because the juvenile court wants to protect them. For example, they may have been abused or neglected, or they do not have a parent or guardian. In some instances, families may have voluntarily placed them in a private facility for mental health or substance abuse treatment. Consequently, about 12% of youth in residential placement live in facilities that house both offenders and non-offenders (Sedlak & McPherson, 2010a).

In 2007, the most recent year for which national juvenile court statistics are available, courts with juvenile jurisdiction handled an estimated 1,666,100 delinquency cases (Puzzanchera et al., 2010). Probation was the most severe sanction ordered in 58% of adjudicated delinquency cases. During that same year, courts ordered juveniles to out-of-home residential placements (such as training schools, treatment centers, boot or forestry camps, drug treatment, group homes, or private placements) in 9% of the cases. More significantly, the total number of cases in which youth were placed out of their homes (148,600) rose 42% between 1985 and 2007.

Particularly in the case of juveniles, institutionalization is—or theoretically should be—considered a last resort. Still, at the time of the report cited at the beginning of this chapter (June 2008 through April 2009), about 26,590 juveniles were in detention centers or public or private facilities across the United States (Sedlak & McPherson, 2010a). This figure represents 26% of the total youth in residential placement (See Table 13.1 for total numbers in residential placements). It should be mentioned that a community-based program may include a shelter, group home, or independent living subunit.

Juveniles, like adults, also may be provided with intermediate sanctions, which are less restrictive than residential placement but more restrictive than the standard probation under which the juvenile remains in his or her own home with conditions attached. Examples of intermediate sanctions are day reporting centers and intensive supervision programs.

A major difference between juvenile and adult corrections is the number of private facilities available. Although they do not hold as many juveniles (only 35% of the total youth offenders), they are more privately

Table 13.1 Youth in Residential Placement, by Type of Program

Program Type	Estimated Number of Youth	Percentage of Youth
Detention	26,590	26
Corrections	32,260	32
Camp	9,770	10
Community based	18,360	18
Residential treatment	14,070	14

Source: Sedlak & McPherson, 2010a.

operated than publicly operated facilities for juveniles (Bayer & Pozen, 2003; Snyder & Sickmund, 1995, 2006). Private facilities are operated by private nonprofit or for-profit corporations or organizations. Private facilities have the advantage of restricting their populations to those juveniles they believe they are best able to help, but they are not necessarily the best option for youth and may suffer from lack of oversight. Nevertheless, some innovative treatment programs have been tried and tested in private facilities.

As mentioned above, also included under the rubric of juvenile corrections is **juvenile detention,** which is defined as a *temporary* secure or nonsecure placement pending adjudication or during adjudication proceedings, up to a final disposition. In other words, some youth are held in detention following arrest; through their delinquency hearing; and up until the time the judge decides whether to place them on probation, order them to residential treatment, or neither one. Although the term *detention* is widely used to pertain to placement at any point in time, it should technically be used in the above limited sense.

Like adults, juveniles are presumed innocent until proven guilty. Adults, though, have a greater presumption of being released prior to their next court appearance. Adults may be denied bail and held in preventive detention if they are charged with a capital crime or demonstrated to be dangerous (*U.S. v. Salerno,* 1987). Juveniles, however, may be held in preventive detention for their own protection or if there is a serious risk that they will commit *any* crime before their next court appearance (*Schall v. Martin,* 1984). This gives juvenile judges a wide leeway to detain juveniles, although most juveniles are *not* detained. The number of delinquency cases involving detention increased 48% from 1985 to 2007. The largest increase (143%) was for crimes against persons, followed by drug offenses (100%). More male juveniles charged with an offense (24%) were held in secure facilities while awaiting court disposition than females (17%) (Puzzanchera et al., 2010).

Juveniles in detention have not been adjudicated and thus cannot technically be placed in rehabilitation programs. For example, a youth accused of sexual assault should not be placed in a treatment program for juvenile sex offenders because he has not been found guilty of that offense. Many public juvenile facilities have detention and treatment wings, with treatment reserved for those juveniles who have been adjudicated delinquent. On the other hand, juveniles in detention *can* be provided with substance abuse treatment, sex education, remedial education, and other such services during the time they are held.

Detention centers, compared with rehabilitation or treatment centers, also have come under scrutiny for their overcrowded conditions and disproportionate confinement of minority youth (though rehabilitation centers have not been totally absolved of problems in these regards). Because of these important differences, we will preserve the "pure" meaning of *detention.* Whenever the word is used, the reader should realize that it refers to *temporary* placement and that the youth under these conditions have not yet been adjudicated delinquent, with the exception of those who have been so adjudicated and are awaiting the judge's disposition (sentencing) decision.

In this chapter, we will provide a brief historical overview of juvenile corrections that supplements the historical background relating to juvenile courts provided in Chapter 5. The assessment tasks of forensic psychologists that were discussed in that chapter (e.g., evaluating comprehension of constitutional rights, adjudicative competence, and amenability to rehabilitation) will not be repeated here, but they remain relevant. For example, evaluation of a youth's adjudicative competence or amenability for rehabilitation is often conducted on youth who are held in secure detention.

In addition, adjudicated delinquents both in the community and in treatment facilities still have a constitutional right of access to lawyers and consequently might be evaluated for their ability to communicate with these lawyers, as well as to participate in post-conviction court proceedings (e.g., an appeal of the delinquency finding). Evaluations performed to determine whether the juvenile is a good candidate for a specific rehabilitation program are conducted for juvenile correctional officials as well as for the juvenile courts. Finally, the assessment enterprise is crucial to the treatment process. As McNeece, Springer, and Arnold (2001) have observed, assessment is the first active phase of treatment. It is also an ongoing activity that continues throughout treatment because the juvenile's needs as well as his or her situation may change.

The main focus of this chapter is the type of treatment options that are available to psychologists working as treatment providers in the juvenile system, in both community and residential settings. As an aside, we should note that—like the correctional psychologists discussed in the previous chapter—clinicians working with youth do not necessarily call themselves forensic psychologists. Relevant to the definitional dilemma we alluded to in Chapter 1, broad versus narrow definitions of the field continue to compete for favor. The fifth draft of the proposed Specialty Guidelines for Forensic Psychology (Committee, 2010) limits forensic treatment (of both adults and children) to those practitioners who "provide therapeutic services tailored to the issues and context of a legal proceeding" (Section 1.04). Elsewhere (Section 6.02.03), the draft committee noted, "Although some therapeutic services can be considered forensic in nature, the fact that therapeutic services are ordered by the court or are delivered to someone does not necessarily make them forensic." This terminology seems to exclude the treatment provider in a juvenile rehabilitation center as well as the correctional psychologist in an adult prison.

Some research indicates that nearly two-thirds of youth in juvenile detention centers and correctional facilities meet the criteria for one or more mental disorders (Grisso, 2008). It is also known that the symptoms of mental disorders in adolescence often lead to impulsive, aggressive, and violent behaviors, particularly when the adolescent has two or more mental disorders. In a recent, anonymous survey of youth in residential placements across the United States, 60% reported that they were easily upset, quick to lose their temper, and often angry (Sedlak & McPherson, 2010b). According to Grisso, various forms of clinical depression are found in about 10 to 25% of youth in juvenile justice settings. In the national survey by Sedlack and McPherson, about half of the youth offenders indicated they were depressed. Fazel, Doll, and Långström (2008) found similar results, although they also discovered that girls in detention or correctional facilities were 3 times more likely to be diagnosed with severe depression than boys. Available data (e.g., Sedlak & McPherson, 2010b) indicate that girls in custody have more mental health and substance use problems, and experience a more extensive history of abuse, than boys in custody (Blum, Ireland, & Blum, 2003; Hubbard & Pratt, 2002; Teplin, Abram, McLelland, Dulcan, & Mericle, 2002).

Grisso observes that depressed adolescents, male or female, are commonly very irritable, sullen, and hostile, unlike depressed adults who tend to be sad and withdrawn. The irritable moodiness of these youth increases the likelihood that they will provoke angry responses from their social environments, including peers. In far too many instances, these angry responses escalate to physical aggression and potential violence. This connection between anger and aggression may, in some cases, lead to self-injurious behavior like cutting or head banging.

In addition, Fazel and associates (2008) found that adolescents in detention and correctional facilities are about 10 times more likely to have psychosis (serious mental disorder) than the general adolescent population. These figures held for both boys and girls. Research also links psychiatric disorder in juveniles with suicidal behavior (Wasserman, McReynolds, Schwalbe, Keating, & Jones, 2010).

Developmental disabilities and cognitive impairments also plague both institutionalized juveniles and those under community supervision (Day & Berney, 2001). Many juvenile offenders also are substance abusers, often with significant chemical dependency problems. For instance, Loeber, Burke, and Lahey (2002) discovered that 40 to 50% of delinquent youth were found to have substance abuse disorders compared to only 15% of nondelinquent youth. Youth offenders with multiple limitations abound. It is not unusual, for example, for a juvenile rehabilitation facility to receive a depressed sex offender who abuses alcohol and has attempted suicide.

Grisso (2008) observes that some adolescents have a mental disorder for a significant period of time, while others show symptoms of a mental disorder for only a short time. On the other hand, some juvenile offenders do not have mental disorders, developmental disabilities, or substance abuse problems at all. Nevertheless, these adolescents would benefit from treatment programs addressing their violent behaviors or their chronic property offending. Furthermore, a substantial number of juvenile offenders have been victims of violence, including sexual assault, and many come from dysfunctional families. Over two-thirds of the youth responding to the Sedlak and McPherson (2010b) survey reported experiencing some form of trauma, including physical or sexual abuse. Consequently, programs that focus on treatment of juvenile offenders often address the effects of victimization. For example, they offer strategies for developing social skills and improving a self-concept that may have been shattered by years of abuse. A significant number of programs for juveniles incorporate family treatment along with individual and group treatment.

FOCUS 13.1. CRISIS IN DETENTION

The *proportion* of cases involving secure detention has remained stable or has dropped in recent years, but the *number* of cases has increased (Puzzanchera et al., 2003). This has placed a severe strain on detention facilities. In addition, as noted in the text, the disproportionate confinement of minority youth has been a major cause for concern. Fortunately, there is now a national movement—initiated in large part by the Annie E. Casey Foundation—to promote alternatives to detention for youth who do not truly need secure confinement. The Annie E. Casey Foundation is a private group dedicated to research and advocacy for the needs of children and adolescents.

In the mid-1990s, the foundation funded initiatives to reverse the trend of skyrocketing detention during the 1980s and early 1990s (Mendel, 2003). Various demonstration sites across the country obtained grants to perform better screening of youth at the intake stage, to determine whether secure detention was truly needed. For those youth not at risk of committing violent crime, alternatives such as the following have been adopted:

- Community custody, whereby youth are supervised by detention workers in their own homes or in unlocked group homes. Detention workers make frequent visits and link the youth with community services as needed.
- Youth reporting, whereby youth attend school during the day but check in with a reporting center after school or in the evenings. The reporting centers include activities and offer counseling and remedial skills as needed.
- Outpatient mental health clinics, where youth with emotional and behavioral problems are provided with counseling and/or medication as ordered by the juvenile courts.

Alternatives to the detention initiative have not reached all states, and many juvenile detention centers across the country remain overcrowded; understaffed; and lacking in sufficient services such as mental health screening, education, and recreational opportunities. Although the average length of stay in a detention facility is about 2 weeks, some youth remain in detention for months at a time. Because of the nature of detention, these juveniles are often emotionally upset, afraid, and resistant to staff, and violent behavior is not unusual. Although some juveniles clearly need secure confinement, it is also clear that many would benefit much more from the alternatives that are now being used.

Historical Overview

As we noted in Chapter 6, the history of juvenile justice in both the 19th and 20th centuries is rife with sobering accounts of juveniles confined to various institutions where they were subjected to punitive treatment rather than rehabilitation (Bernard, 1992; Rothman, 1980). The last half of the 20th century saw some improvement in this regard, with significant efforts made to end unjustified confinement. The U.S. Supreme Court's decisions in *Kent v. U.S.* (1966) and *In re Gault* (1967) questioned the predilections of the juvenile courts to be too quick to send delinquents to institutions where they were more likely to be exploited than rehabilitated.

Shortly after these Court rulings were announced, Congress also began to scrutinize the juvenile justice system. In 1974, Congress passed the landmark **Juvenile Justice and Delinquency Prevention Act (JJDPA),** a law that encouraged states to do better by the juveniles in their care. The act strongly advocated the diversion of juveniles from formal court processing whenever this could be accomplished.

In addition, Congress was particularly concerned about two groups of juveniles. These were the juveniles who were being detained in adult jails, sometimes within sight and hearing distance of adults, and the status offenders who had committed no "crimes" but were nevertheless being held in secure institutions, often with more serious delinquents. As described in Chapter 7, **status offenders** are juveniles whose offenses might include running away from home, "incorrigibility," or truancy (skipping school)—in other words, behaviors that only they can commit by virtue of their status as children or adolescents. The JJDPA mandated that states receiving funds for juvenile justice programs must remove all juveniles from adult jails and must also remove status offenders from secure institutions. The latter mandate is referred to as the **deinstitutionalization of status offenders (DSO)** requirement. Throughout the 1980s and 1990s, Congress passed numerous amendments to the JJDPA, some of which extended deadlines for states to meet the mandates of the law (I. M. Schwartz, 1989). Nevertheless, the JJDPA remains a strong piece of legislation supporting the rights of children in the juvenile justice system. A national office, the **Office of Juvenile Justice and Delinquency Prevention (OJJDP),** oversees the legislation, provides grants for research on juvenile issues, and helps set national juvenile justice policy.

By the end of the 20th century, both court decisions and legislation were in place to recognize the rights of juveniles while also providing them with protection and treatment. Despite this, numerous observers commented that the juvenile justice system was in disarray (e.g., Amnesty International, 1998; Feld, 1999). Of particular concern was increasing evidence that racial and ethnic minorities were disproportionately detained and incarcerated (Leiber, 2002; Snyder & Sickmund, 1995). This problem became known as **disproportionate minority confinement (DMC).** In a provocative article, Sampson and Laub (1993) demonstrated that communities characterized by racial inequality and containing a high concentration of the "underclass" (defined as families in poverty, female-headed households, minorities, and families receiving welfare benefits) were significantly more likely to confine children of these population groups.

It should be pointed out that government statistics show some decline in the overall use of *detention* for Black versus White youth. However, racial variation persists in drug cases, with detention used in 18% of drug cases involving White juveniles, 35% involving Blacks, and 20% involving other races. In addition, White youth were less likely than Black or other races to be ordered to *residential* placement (24% White, 30% Black, 25% other races) (Puzzanchera et al., 2003).

The treatment of girls and ethnic minorities also gained more attention as the 20th century came to a close. Researchers and scholars noted that, although girls had benefited from the movement to deinstitutionalize status offenders, the needs of girls in detention and treatment were not being met by the juvenile justice system (Chesney-Lind & Shelden, 1998; Federle & Chesney-Lind, 1992). Still others pointed to the need for culturally sensitive programs within the juvenile justice system to recognize the needs of Native American, Black, Latino, and Asian American youth (Eron et al., 1994). Those who support such ethnocentric programming do not say that it alone will make a difference if other principles for facilitating positive change are not applied. As W. R. King, Holmes, Henderson, and Latessa (2001) observed, these programs are syringes rather than cures: "Syringes do not heal people by themselves; however, syringes are indispensable tools for delivering medicine" (p. 501).

The overall conditions in juvenile detention and treatment facilities also received considerable attention nationwide (Amnesty International, 1998; Parent et al., 1994; Puritz & Scali, 1998). As suggested by the material in the opening of this chapter, not much seems to have changed. By statute and case law, juveniles held in institutions have a variety of legal rights, but they need advocates to see that these rights are acknowledged. They have a right to be in a sanitary environment and to be protected from other violent juveniles and abusive staff; as we see from the recent Department of Justice report (Beck et al., 2010), problems have been identified in a number of states. Juveniles also may not be held in excessive isolation or under unreasonable restraints, but most institutions permit the use of isolation and restraints when needed (Snyder & Sickmund, 1995). Juveniles must receive adequate medical care, mental health care, and education, and they must have access to legal counsel, family communication, recreation, exercise, and programming (del Carmen, Parker, & Reddington, 1998; Puritz & Scali, 1998). Despite these rights, a review of conditions of confinement in detention centers, training schools, camps, ranches, farms, and other facilities for juveniles nationwide indicated substantial and widespread problems in living space, health care, security, and control of suicidal behavior (Parent et al., 1994). (See Photo 13.1 of boys touring a detention facility.)

Photo 13.1   Sixth graders visit a juvenile detention facility as part of a program to warn them about the dangers of joining a gang. Although such programs may not do any harm, there is little evidence that they have a measurable effect on future delinquency.

Finally, by the end of the 20th century, numerous questions continued to be raised about the efficacy of treatment provided to juveniles, particularly in institutional settings. A noteworthy meta-analytic review of juvenile treatment programs (Whitehead & Lab, 1989) produced discouraging results. The authors analyzed evaluations of juvenile correctional treatment that had appeared in professional journals from 1975 to 1984 and found little positive impact on recidivism. In fact, many of the programs appeared to exacerbate recidivism. The authors also found no support for the superiority of behavioral interventions over other forms. Diversionary approaches, those intended to steer juveniles away from formal court processing, did show some favorable results, however.

Not all reviewers were as pessimistic as the Whitehead and Lab (1989) meta-analysis would suggest. As we noted in the chapter on adult corrections, many scholars and researchers have not given up on rehabilitation and are intent on documenting the effectiveness of some programs for some individuals. Psychologists have uncovered a number of principles associated with effective treatment. For example, cognitive-behavioral approaches and "multimodal approaches" that integrate group, individual, and family treatment to the extent possible have received good reviews. In a recent meta-analytic overview, Lipsey (2009) found three factors that were associated with program effectiveness: (1) a therapeutic intervention philosophy; (2) serving of high-risk offenders; and (3) quality of the program, meaning that the treatment providers were carefully trained and supervised and lapses in quality were quickly corrected. Interestingly, the Lipsey meta-analysis also found that the level of juvenile justice supervision (e.g., intensive supervision, probation, secure custody) did not show a relationship to the success of the intervention, suggesting that "effective treatment is not highly context dependent" (p. 143).

Despite these more optimistic appraisals, Grisso (2008) notes that the juvenile justice system is far from the most ideal place to treat delinquent youth, particularly those with mental disorders. Grisso points out that the role of the state in relation to the youth in custody is essentially adversarial. While some youth may benefit within the structure and guidance of a properly operated, secure program, effective treatment and rehabilitation for most youth is highly dependent on trust and sincere caring. "These conditions between youth and therapist often are difficult to maintain in secure juvenile facilities when the therapist is part of the system that restricts the youth's liberty" (p. 154). Consequently, placing greater emphasis on mental health treatment services in juvenile justice facilities may not be the best answer. Grisso argues that the more effective approach is providing treatment and rehabilitation services for troubled youth within the community at multiple levels of application. This approach would permit the juvenile justice system to engage in a more focused and limited rehabilitation role for those youths who are dangerous to others. We will discuss these in greater detail as we now turn to the treatment options available in juvenile correctional settings, both institutional and within the community.

Related to the above discussion are the observations by Sedlak and McPherson (2010a) concerning the mental health services provided in delinquent youth facilities. In their extensive survey, they discovered that mental health services in the form of evaluation, ongoing therapy, or counseling are nearly universal in the facilities studied. However, they also found that many mental health personnel were untrained or marginally capable of meeting the needs of the youth held in many of the facilities, a fact that suggests that the quality of the programs—seen as an essential factor by Lipsey (2009)—is lacking. For instance, only half of the youth surveyed were in facilities that provide mental health evaluations or appraisals. Moreover, despite the relatively high suicide risk in the juvenile population in residential placement, screening for suicide risk was not common. More than one fourth of youth were in facilities that did not screen for suicide risks at all, and another fourth are in facilities where the staff conducting suicide screenings are untrained. Sedlak and McPherson (2010b) conclude,

> Overall, current mental health services for youth in custody still fall short of key recommendations for practice, which suggest that all youth offenders receive suicide risk and other mental health screens and that all mental health screens and assessment be administered by property trained staff. (p. 3)

Approaches to Rehabilitation

Despite a trend toward punitiveness and a demand for greater accountability on the part of juveniles who commit crimes, the juvenile justice system in most states continues to be rehabilitative in orientation. Once processed through the juvenile courts—and often even before that point—juveniles are assigned to or placed in a wide variety of programs intended to prevent future offending as well as provide them with tools needed to move on to successful adult lives.

Group Home Models

For a wide variety of reasons, many juveniles cannot remain in their own homes, yet they do not need to be placed in a secure treatment facility. Group homes are a common alternative, allowing juveniles to remain in their community, attend school, and be provided with services in the community on an outpatient basis (e.g., counseling, therapy, substance abuse prevention program). It is an important principle of juvenile justice that the least restrictive placement should be used, a principle that critics charge is too often not honored in practice.

One of the most common models for the treatment of adolescents in a group home setting is the **teaching-family model,** initiated in 1967 with the opening of Achievement Place in Kansas. By the turn of the 21st century, there were approximately 134 such group homes in the United States for delinquents, abused and neglected children, and autistic and developmentally challenged children and young adults (Bernfeld, 2001). In the typical "teaching-family home," the teaching parents are a couple with specialized training and usually with master's degrees in human services. They live in a family-like situation with up to seven youths and have assistants available on a daily basis. Consultants serve in a supervisory capacity and integrate treatment, training, and specialized services as needed. "Almost without exception, consultants started out as practitioners and then obtained the extra training to become consultants" (Fixsen, Blasé, Timbers, & Wolf, 2001, p. 163).

Fixsen et al. (2001) have candidly reviewed the growing pains of the teaching-family model, noting how earlier attempts to replicate the apparent success of Achievement Place produced discouraging results. In 1978, the first meetings of the Teaching-Family Association were held, and the association continued to identify goals, produce ethical standards, and provide training and other services to individuals involved in this model (Teaching-Family Association, 1993, 1994).

Teaching-family homes originally operated primarily on a token-economy model—a behavior modification approach that was quite popular in psychology in the 1960s and 1970s for institutional settings. Residents would receive tokens or points for good behavior and could then exchange these points for privileges, such as longer recreation time or a more desirable work assignment. However, "bad" behavior resulted in loss of tokens and, consequently, the removal of privileges. Transferring the token economy to a natural setting, such as a group home, is more of a challenge (Reppucci & Saunders, 1974; Wolf, Kirigin, Fixsen, Blasé, & Braukmann, 1995). As a result, although reinforcement for good behavior and a system of points and privileges remain important aspects of the teaching-family home, additional treatment services are provided. The concept is usually not recommended, however, for adolescents with serious mental health problems or for those who have been charged with or found to have committed serious offenses.

The teaching-family home has many positive features that should be helpful to *nonserious* delinquents who are unable to remain in their own homes, at least temporarily. Warm and compassionate teaching parents, the maintenance of ties with natural family and with the community, and the opportunity to learn prosocial behaviors are among these features. Nevertheless, studies indicate that behavioral gains—including reductions in substance use and increases in prosocial behaviors—while adolescents are in the teaching-family home are typically not maintained when they have left (Mulvey, Arthur, & Reppucci, 1993).

In recent years, many have argued that group homes—like juvenile justice programs in general—should give more attention to cultural diversity and specific cultural needs of individual juveniles (e.g., Eron et al., 1994). Black, Latino, and Asian American youth, for example, can benefit from a group home placement that encourages them to acknowledge, learn about, and celebrate their cultural heritage. Evaluations of culturally sensitive programs indicate that they lower recidivism and increase self-efficacy (Eron et al., 1994; W. R. King et al., 2001). One such program, the House of Umoja in Philadelphia (also in Portland, OR), provides education, cultural treatment, counseling, and substance abuse treatment to Black male at-risk youth ages 15 to 18 (see Focus 13.2).

Likewise, gender-specific programming is critical. Girls, including delinquent girls, often have needs that are very different from those of boys. As mentioned earlier in the chapter, delinquent girls are more likely than boys to have been victims of child sexual abuse and intimate violence; in addition, they are more likely to be lacking in self-esteem (Budnick & Shields-Fletcher, 1998; Sedlak & McPherson, 2010b; Sorensen & Bowie, 1994). They are also less likely than boys to be charged with a violent offense (Snyder & Sickmund, 1999). Adolescent girls also are more likely than adolescent boys to suffer from mental disorders, particularly depression (Sedlack & McPherson, 2010b; Teplin et al., 2002). However, girls also may be more likely than boys to self-report symptoms of depression. Although group home options may appear to be warranted for girls, they often come to these homes with family backgrounds that may be even more complex than those of delinquent boys.

FOCUS 13.2. HOUSE OF UMOJA

In the early 1970s, David and Falaka Fattah established the first House of Umoja (Swahili for *unity*) in a Philadelphia neighborhood. Concerned about the rising numbers of African American youth who were joining gangs, the couple wanted to provide boys at risk with a sense of belonging, identity, and self-worth as an alternative to gang membership. The House of Umoja provided a safe haven, mediated gang conflicts, and offered counseling and positive adult role models. In addition, it promoted pride in the traditional cultural norms of the African American community, such as the importance of the extended family.

Today, the House of Umoja occupies a strip of 23 row houses in Philadelphia. It accepts boys between the ages of 15 and 18 who are referred by various social service agencies in the city, including juvenile courts. Individual and group counseling, parent education, educational support, cultural activities, and family planning information are all included in the program. Residents learn leadership and conflict resolution skills and are encouraged to provide service to others. When possible, staff members work with the families of the youth to involve them in treatment. Although some boys return to their homes, others move into independent living arrangements, linked with community services.

Like other private organizations providing services to juveniles, the House of Umoja receives funding from federal, state, and local governments as well as from private foundations. Although no published evaluation research is available, the House of Umoja has received positive reviews from such groups as the National Center for Neighborhood Enterprise (NCNE) and the Office of Juvenile Justice and Delinquency Prevention (OJJDP). According to the NCNE, the House of Umoja has "successfully transformed more than five hundred frightened, frustrated, and alienated young minority males into self-assured, competent, concerned, and productive citizens."

Family Preservation Models

Many advocates for children maintain that they should be kept in their own homes, with their own parents or close relatives, if at all possible (e.g., D. A. Gordon, 2002; Henggeler, 1996). They believe that providing a wide range of support services, even to highly dysfunctional families, is in the best interest of the children and adolescents who are part of these families. It must be acknowledged, however, that family preservation is not in the best interest of all children and adolescents. Despite the optimistic appraisals and documented success of family preservation that will be covered below, some juveniles may not be well served by intense efforts to make their family situation work for them. This is particularly true of children and adolescents who have been victimized in their own homes, by parents or caretakers or by siblings. As Chesney-Lind and Shelden (1998) indicate,

> Family counseling that is grounded in the notion that maintenance of the family unit is uppermost needs to be critically reviewed in light of the extreme physical and sexual violence that some girls in the juvenile justice system report. In some instances, the victimized girl or boy must be allowed to live away from the parents. (p. 219)

With this caveat, we turn now to a discussion of the positive aspects of family preservation.

Homebuilders

One highly regarded family preservation approach is the **homebuilders model,** an exemplary program for families in which one or more children are at risk of being removed from the home because of their antisocial behavior (Haapala & Kinney, 1988; Whittaker, Kinney, Tracy, & Booth, 1990). It is probably the oldest intensive family preservation services program in the United States. In the Homebuilders model, one or two caseworkers—typically social workers with master's degrees—work intensively with a family for a short period of time; they are available to the family around the clock and are highly proactive in obtaining needed services for the family. The goal is to prevent the out-of-home placement of children through intensive, on-site intervention, and to teach families new problem-solving skills. These services might be wide-ranging. For example, they might include a job for one of the family members, transportation, tutoring, family therapy, after-school programming, or a mentor for a young adolescent. An evaluation of the homebuilders program by Haapala and Kinney produced highly favorable results, with 87% of the children avoiding out-of-home placement within a year. The forensic psychologist is most likely to come into contact with Homebuilders as a consultant offering evaluation or treatment services in the community. The youth involved in the program are not those with serious delinquency problems, however.

Multisystemic Therapy

Another program that has received extensive research attention is the family preservation approach advocated by social psychologist Scott Henggeler, **multisystemic therapy (MST).** MST was specifically developed for application with serious juvenile offenders, including those responsible for violent crimes. MST is heavily based on the systems theory pioneered by psychologist Urie Bronfenbrenner (1979). According to this view, behavior is multidetermined and influenced heavily by interactions with one's social environment. Children and adolescents are embedded in various social systems (their families, their peer groups, their schools, and their neighborhoods). Effective intervention requires that the child or adolescent and all of his or her social systems be considered. Thus, MST attempts to promote behavior change within the youth's natural environment and uses the strengths within each of the various social systems to bring this about.

Henggeler (1996; Henggeler & Borduin, 1990) argues that secure institutions should be avoided if at all possible because antisocial behaviors are only reinforced when serious offenders live among other serious offenders. Thus, in addition to keeping juveniles in their own homes, another goal of MST is to help juveniles break bonds with antisocial peers and develop bonds with prosocial peers. Henggeler has acknowledged that this is one of the most difficult goals to achieve.

Like Homebuilders, MST makes a small team of treatment providers—in this case, therapists—available to families around the clock and helps facilitate a wide range of services. Most treatment providers are master's-level mental health professionals specially trained in the multisystemic approach. Clinical or forensic psychologists supervise the therapist and provide intensive treatment if needed. Therapists meet with youth in natural settings (e.g., the home or school or even in a local park). They identify both risk and resilience factors in a juvenile's life, across all of his or her social systems. For example, a risk factor at school may be an older boy who has goaded the juvenile into committing offenses in the past. A resilience factor at school may be an art class or a history class that the juvenile likes. Likewise, genuine affection among siblings is a resilience factor in the family; the impending loss of a father's employment is a risk factor. The treatment providers then provide strategies for addressing the risk factors and capitalizing on the resilience factors.

MST may involve intensive individual counseling, a factor that distinguishes it from Homebuilders and other **family preservation models** that target youth whose behavioral problems are usually less serious. MST therapists are generalists. "Because of the varying demands of each family, [they] must be capable of applying a range of empirically based therapeutic approaches . . . and tailoring interventions to the unique needs and strengths of each family" (T. L. Brown, Borduin, & Henggeler, 2001, p. 458). MST youth are often on probation after having been adjudicated delinquent, with offenses ranging from substance abuse to aggravated assault. However, MST also has been used for nonoffending child and adolescent populations and with youth from a variety of cultural and ethnic backgrounds (T. L. Brown et al., 2001; Edwards, Schoenwald, Henggeler, & Strother, 2001). Thus far, it has achieved favorable research reviews (e.g., Burns, Schoenwald, Burchard, Faw, & Santos, 2000; Henggeler, 2001; Schaeffer & Borduin, 2005).

To illustrate, Borduin, Schaeffer, and Heiblum (2009) conducted an evaluation of MST as compared to the usual community services (UCS) mandated by the juvenile court. All the youths and their families who participated in the study were referred by juvenile court personnel, and all had sex offending on their record. The arrest histories of the youth attest to their serious criminal involvement. The youths, whose mean age was 14, averaged 4.33 previous arrests for sexual and nonsexual felonies. Ninety-five percent of the youths were boys and most (73%) were White.

Families and youths received MST for 31 weeks on average; whereas the UCS group received cognitive-behavioral therapy for about the same length of time. The researchers measured the effectiveness of the treatment 9 years after initial contact. They selected a follow-up time period that was long enough to allow for adult arrest data on every youth.

Overall, MST had favorable results on family relations (increased cohesion and adaptability), peer relations (increased emotional bonding, social maturity, and decreased aggression), and improved academic performance. MST also created both short- and long-term changes in the youths' criminal behavior and incarceration. "Youths treated with MST reported decreases in person and property crimes at posttest and were less likely to be rearrested for sexual and nonsexual crimes with the 8.9-year follow-up period than were youths who received UCS" (Borduin et al., 2009, p. 35).

Similar positive results for MST have been reported recently by Curtis, Ronan, Heiblum, and Crellin (2009) in New Zealand, and by Glisson et al. (2010) in the Appalachian region of eastern Tennessee.

We should note, however, that a large portion of the research to date has been conducted by the individuals who developed the programs and deliver the services. Although this is not uncommon in evaluation research, the close oversight of the implementation and delivery of programs may affect the findings (MacKenzie, 2000). It is important that additional independent researchers in different settings also evaluate MST, along with other treatment programs for juveniles.

It is also crucial to highlight the fact that MST programs do not generally deal with youths who have serious mental disorders. Although there is considerable controversy in the juvenile justice literature about the prevalence of such serious disorder, no one can deny that it exists in at least some youth.

Functional Family Therapy

A program similar to MST is **functional family therapy (FFT)**, which was developed in the 1970s for behaviorally disturbed adolescents whose parents were unable to control their acting-out behaviors. According to Sexton and Turner (2010), "FFT has an established record of outcome studies that demonstrate its efficacy with a wide variety of adolescent-related problems, including youth violence, drug abuse, and other delinquency-related behavior" (p. 339). Furthermore, the positive outcomes of the therapy remain even after a 5-year follow-up, and it also appears to have a positive influence on the siblings of the targeted adolescent. It appears to be especially effective in reducing substance abuse (Waldron & Turner, 2008).

FFT combines social learning, cognitive-behavioral theory, interpersonal theory, and family systems theories (D. A. Gordon, 2002). It should be recalled from Chapter 12 that cognitive-behavioral approaches focus on a person's expectations and appraisals. The person is encouraged to examine how attitudes and beliefs may have contributed to his or her present situation. The individual works with the therapist to identify strategies for behavioral change. In functional family therapy, therapists work with the family as a unit and attempt to identify features of family dynamics that result in problematic interactions among members. Attention is focused away from the adolescent as the problem; rather, the family is viewed as a system, with members affecting one another's behaviors. Communication and problem-solving skills are taught, and participants are typically given homework assignments between sessions. Like MST, FFT is used in a wide variety of contexts, not just with youth who have come into conflict with the law. (See Photo 13.2 of family receiving therapy from a treatment provider.)

Photo 13.2   Family with therapist in a counseling session.

Although FFT has been used successfully with delinquents, including those referred by juvenile courts (D. A. Gordon, 2002), it seems less suited for serious delinquents remaining in the community than MST. The latter was specifically formulated to deal with serious delinquency, and it places considerable emphasis on intensive individual treatment as well as strengthening social systems both within and outside the family group. On the other hand, FFT may be better than MST at providing all members of the family group with skills and strategies to function effectively as a self-supporting group. Nonetheless, according to T. L. Brown et al. (2001), behavioral parent training approaches have not been demonstrably effective with serious juvenile offenders, primarily because of the multiple risk factors (e.g., marital distress, socioeconomic disadvantage, parental depression) that are relatively common in their families. Although FFT is not exclusively focused on parent training, it closely resembles such a model.

MST and FFT—to ensure program integrity—require extensive training on the part of those who will deliver the services, but neither one requires that treatment providers hold terminal degrees in the field. Those with master's degrees—and sometimes less—are able to offer treatment when they are well trained and supervised by clinical psychologists. Sexton and Turner (2010) also point out that FFT must be delivered in a clinically specific and precise manner to produce positive results. That is, the therapists must be well trained and supervised before the full desired effects can be achieved. Edwards et al. (2001) and D. A. Gordon (2002) have summarized the challenges faced in implementing each of these approaches in communities that have expressed interest in them. Supporters of both approaches have emphasized the need for continual communication between developers of these programs and the service providers, as well as the extensive training and initial supervision required to ensure that treatment will be delivered effectively.

Substance Abuse Models

Like adult offenders, juvenile offenders very often have substance abuse problems that accompanied past offenses and are predictive of future delinquent activity (Snyder & Sickmund, 1999; Weekes, Moser, & Langevin, 1999). In the case of juvenile offenders, however, the treatment must take into account their rapid physiological, psychological, and sociocultural development (McNeece et al., 2001). In other words, treatment providers must factor in the emotional turmoil and search for identity and acceptance that are often characteristic of adolescence. Like the other treatment programs discussed, programs that provide individual, group, and family therapy—a multimodal approach—seem to be the most effective for substance abusers.

We should note that many of the approaches discussed thus far in this chapter might include a substance abuse component. For example, both group home and family preservation models frequently implement substance abuse treatment. As stated above, for example, FFT seems to be particularly well-suited for treating adolescent substance abuse problems. Such treatment also is a component of virtually every publicly supported juvenile rehabilitation center. Private facilities, in which parents enroll their adolescents for inpatient substance abuse treatment, are also common. Interestingly, Ira Schwartz (1989), a one-time head of the OJJDP, argued forcefully that these private placements are overused and unwarranted for many youth, calling private treatment centers the new jail for middle-class kids. Moreover, there is very little evidence to support inpatient treatment over outpatient approaches for the vast majority of juvenile substance abusers (McNeece et al., 2001).

McNeece et al. (2001) reviewed the variety of programs available for both adult and juvenile substance abusers. These include individual, group, and family therapy; self-help programs; psychoeducational approaches; pharmacotherapy (e.g., Antabuse, methadone, and naltrexone); acupuncture; case management; and both inpatient and outpatient programs. They note that several states are developing specific assessment and receiving centers for juveniles with substance abuse problems. These centers may be attached to the juvenile court or a local drug court, or they may operate independently. Although such assessment and treatment centers may be a step in the right direction, follow-up services are desperately needed. In a study of six such assessment centers, McNeece and his colleagues (1997) learned that they provided short-term stabilization, but recommendations for extended treatment often were not followed due to lack of resources and shortage of staff. The crucial importance of follow-up services has been demonstrated in evaluation studies of many other juvenile programs as well.

The professional literature contains numerous descriptions and evaluations of substance abuse treatment programs for both adult and juvenile offenders (see, e.g., K. Knight & Simpson, 2007). For our purposes, we will discuss two illustrations, one representing inpatient and one representing outpatient treatment.

Inpatient Substance Abuse Treatment: An Example

Mears and Kelly (2002) reviewed programs for chemically dependent adjudicated juvenile offenders under the supervision of the Texas Youth Commission (TYC). The youth were located in one of five inpatient treatment sites. In accordance with key principles of effective intervention, treatment was cognitive-behavioral in approach and targeted dynamic, criminogenic needs (Cullen & Gendreau, 2000). Group counseling, peer accountability, and a low caseworker-to-youth ratio (1:8 to 1:10) were significant components of the program.

In addition, staff worked with the youth to develop individualized **relapse prevention** and community reintegration plans. Treatment was provided for at least 6 continuous months. The 332 juveniles (all but 5 were male) were compared with a control group of 220 youth who were eligible for the treatment but did not receive it because of limited bed space.

Mears and Kelly (2002) analyzed both a juvenile's performance in the program and subsequent recidivism (measured by arrest, whether or not the arrest was drug related). Although there were no significant differences in recidivism between control and treatment groups (a discouraging finding, at the least), researchers did find that youth who performed better in treatment were somewhat less likely to recidivate (but again, not significantly). More interestingly, researchers found differences among the treatment sites, with two of the sites demonstrating significantly greater success (with recidivism rates of 25% and 24%) and two significantly less (recidivism rates of 40% and 38%). The differences related to the quality of service delivery and the staff's commitment to carefully implementing the program. The two programs with the poorest results experienced staff turnover and seemed to suffer from "ongoing tension between emphasizing administrative and correctional versus rehabilitative concerns" (p. 110). In other words, those who ran the program and those who worked in it were not in agreement over its mission. Some believed it should be more punitive, whereas others were more dedicated to rehabilitation. The two best-performing sites had unified and consistent support for rehabilitation. One was a new program with better funding for staff and resources; the other had a "long-standing reputation as having a culture of rehabilitation, despite the fact that it generally handles the most serious and violent youth at TYC" (p. 110). Interestingly, psychologists were more involved at this site than at any of the others, suggesting that their presence may have made a difference. (The fifth site reported in the study had features of both the successful and less successful programs [e.g., commitment to rehabilitation but high staff turnover] and produced outcomes midway between the other two groups.) (See Photo 13.3 depicting juveniles in art class in a treatment facility.)

Photo 13.3 Juveniles in art class in a treatment facility. In addition to intensive treatment, a traditional education curriculum and classes such as art, health, and computer skills are important for youth in residential treatment facilities.

Mears and Kelly (2002) concluded from their findings that evaluations of treatment programs must take into account how well youth participate in the programs, as well as how carefully the programs are implemented and operated on a day-to-day basis. In addition, they note, those programs that are found effective may become even more so if they improve their service delivery and carefully monitor youth progress in the program.

Outpatient Substance Abuse Treatment: An Example

A recent evaluation of an outpatient substance abuse treatment program produced mixed results. O'Neill, Lidz, and Heilbrun (2003) evaluated the effects of an outpatient substance abuse treatment program on adolescents with psychopathic characteristics. The treatment program was developed for adolescent substance abusers as a group, not just those with psychopathic characteristics. The program involved twice-weekly, 1-hour sessions of individual therapy and daily group therapy sessions and was developed in accordance with a cognitive-behavioral model (J. J. Platt, Bux, Lamb, Lidz, & Husband, 1996). Among other things, the adolescents in the program would set goals for themselves; understand and modify their thoughts, feelings, and behaviors; and learn coping skills for maintaining appropriate behavior after discharge from the program. These are typical approaches taken by **cognitive-behavioral programs** and resemble the approach taken in the Texas sites discussed earlier. At this time, cognitive-behavioral principles are widely believed to be the most effective at facilitating positive change (Cullen & Gendreau, 2000).

We must repeat, as we stated in Chapters 4 and 7, that **juvenile psychopathy** is a controversial construct. Many clinicians and researchers are reluctant to label adolescents in this way. As Edens, Skeem, et al. (2001) have noted, some characteristics that are considered psychopathic in adults (e.g., impulsivity, poor behavioral controls, need for stimulation, callousness) may be normative in the adolescent developmental sequence. Furthermore, adolescents often appear callous and unfeeling to hide their fear and anxiety (Barnum, 2000). O'Neill et al. (2003) concede these points but consider the concept of juvenile psychopathy as one that merits more study, particularly if psychopathic characteristics are found to be related to treatment outcomes.

In the O'Neill et al. (2003) research, higher scores on the Psychopathy Checklist: Youth Version (PCL:YV) were positively associated with four behaviors: (1) rearrest risk, (2) high attrition from the program, (3) lower quality ratings of participation in the program, and (4) more frequent use of alcohol and drugs throughout the treatment program. "The majority of participants with a high level of psychopathic characteristics did not respond favorably to the treatment interventions provided in this program" (p. 309). Nevertheless, they cautioned that the concept of juvenile psychopathy should be limited to the research arena until research can better differentiate those adolescents with psychopathic characteristics who will maintain those characteristics into adulthood: "The premature application [of research results] for clinical and forensic purposes could inhibit the development of potentially promising interventions and could also significantly mislead legal decision-makers" (p. 309).

It is important to note that many of the participants, particularly those with low Psychopathy Checklist: Screening Version (PCL:SV) scores, did benefit from the program described in the O'Neill et al. (2003) research. Moreover, like the Mears and Kelly (2002) study discussed above, *quality of participation* in the program was a significant variable. Juveniles with high PCL:SV scores were rated lower on their level of cooperation while in treatment. The other variables found to be significant in the Mears and Kelly review—staff-related variables such as commitment to rehabilitation and turnover—were not assessed in the O'Neill et al. research. However, the program included daily "community" meetings during which participants and staff discussed rules, expectations, and problems, and recognized accomplishments. We might infer that these meetings would facilitate staff satisfaction, discourage turnover, and contribute to the program's positive effect on those youth who did not have psychopathic characteristics.

Boot Camps

Beginning in the early 1980s, boot camps gained popularity in adult corrections as a way of reducing overcrowding in adult prisons while providing nonviolent offenders with discipline and structure over an intense but short period of time (e.g., 30 to 120 days). In the late 1980s, they began to appear in juvenile corrections as well.

Boot camps are so called because they have many parallels with the military model. They are highly structured programs that, according to their supporters, instill discipline, respect for authority, and self-esteem in juveniles who generally have not been given the opportunity to learn these values. Boot camps are typically operated and staffed by correctional personnel who are not inclined to favor a therapeutic, rehabilitative approach with juvenile delinquents. There are exceptions, however. In some juvenile boot camps, for example, substance abuse treatment or violence prevention programs are provided.

The boot camp approach has lost support in recent years because of highly publicized abuses (see Focus 13.3) and because the evaluation research has not found them effective in reducing recidivism among adults or juveniles (Duwe & Kerschner, 2008; Kurlychek & Kempinen, 2006; Lipsey, 2009). A review of juvenile boot camp programs at three sites, sponsored by the Office of Juvenile Justice and Delinquency Prevention (1996), indicated that there was some hope for boot camps in which juveniles were offered substance abuse treatment and were provided with aftercare services for a 3-year period. Otherwise, the boot camp experience did not appear to significantly affect recidivism or self-efficacy. Negative effects of the boot camp experience were discovered at all three sites. The California Youth Authority (1997) published the results of its evaluation of its own boot camp program, with similarly discouraging results. Boot camps have also been criticized as being the wrong approach to take, particularly with juvenile girls (Chesney-Lind & Shelden, 1998). The boot camp experience includes heavy doses of demeaning comments and shouting on the part of staff. This "in-your-face" approach, critics say, is the last thing that girls need because too many girls have been subjected to this kind of treatment far too much in their own backgrounds.

On the whole, although boot camps remain appealing to some who believe that juveniles benefit from structure and discipline, they are not obtaining rave reviews. The research simply does not support their continued use as a rehabilitative strategy for juveniles. Of the more than three dozen studies conducted since the 1980s, only a very few have reported evidence that demonstrates a significant reduction in recidivism among boot camp participants (Duwe & Kerschner, 2008). In 2005, the Federal Bureau of Prisons decided to end its 14-year-old boot camps that operated in Pennsylvania, Texas, and California.

FOCUS 13.3. JUVENILE BOOT CAMPS: LESSONS LEARNED?

In the year 2000, the state of Maryland disbanded its juvenile boot camps and fired top juvenile justice officials after publicity surrounding allegations of physical and emotional abuse of juveniles. One news story recounted split lips and bloody noses inflicted by guards who slammed teens to the ground (Nelson, 2003). Maryland was only 1 of 27 states that operated juvenile boot camps in the 1990s, despite warnings from juvenile justice researchers that such punitive quick fixes do not reduce recidivism.

Even boot camps that include a rehabilitative aspect—such as educational programming and substance abuse treatment—have not produced highly favorable results. An evaluation of three sites sponsored by the Office of Juvenile Justice and Delinquency Prevention (OJJDP, 1996) indicated that some positive change occurred while the youth were in the 3-month camps. Once they graduated, however, positive change persisted only when they remained in aftercare for at least 5 months. Moreover, nearly one half of the juveniles who entered aftercare dropped out, were arrested for new offenses, or were terminated for not complying with aftercare rules. On balance, the very small positive change reflected in the research pales beside the evidence that—for the great majority of boot camp participants—the experience is negative.

The OJJDP was initially supportive of juvenile boot camps, even to the point of producing model guidelines to states interested in opening such camps. Even after the 1996 evaluation, the OJJDP indicated that the problems could be fixed by attention to the model guidelines and improved aftercare services. In 1997, though, the U.S. Department of Justice concluded that the efficacy of boot camps was questionable at best (Nelson, 2003).

Wilderness and Adventure Programs

Wilderness and adventure experiences are different from boot camps and seem to offer more hope as an effective strategy for *some* youth. A wide range of camps, ranches, and outdoor programs—most privately operated—are offered for juveniles. Among the most well-known are those offered by the Eckerd Foundation, a private organization based in Florida. Associated Marine Industries (AMI) is another such enterprise.

Like many other private programs, **wilderness and adventure programs** accept both juveniles who are at risk of committing delinquency and those who are already adjudicated. (At-risk juveniles are often the status offenders who are runaways or are considered incorrigible by their parents or guardians.) The offenses of adjudicated delinquents range from drug offenses to violent crime. Some but not all such programs accept juvenile sex offenders. Also like other private programs, and unlike public training schools or treatment centers, wilderness programs need accept only juveniles who meet their criteria—that is, those they believe would be helped by their program. Wilderness camps are often the "last chance" for juveniles before being sent to a secure training school. However, like boot camps, wilderness programs have received some negative publicity relating to their treatment of the youth in their care.

Wilderness and adventure programs, compared with boot camps, have received some favorable research reviews, but the studies are rarely empirically sound and almost never include a control group (T. L. Brown et al., 2001). In addition, as noted above, the programs are not limited to delinquents, making it impossible to gauge treatment efficacy for that group. T. L. Brown et al. report that only one study (Sale, 1992) included a delinquent sample of 30 adolescent offenders. Although the self-concept of the adolescents improved as a result of being in the program, there was no comparison group.

Published descriptions of these programs suggest that, although they do not subscribe to a common model, they have some things in common: They de-emphasize traditional classroom education and emphasize the progressive development of physical skills that are intended to improve self-efficacy. Self-efficacy is the belief that one is competent and can get things accomplished, and self-esteem is "one's attitude toward oneself along a positive–negative dimension" (Baron & Byrne, 2000, p. 169). Wilderness and adventure programs do, however, include some educational component, which correlates with an individualized education plan (IEP) formulated for each juvenile. They attempt to develop a positive peer culture, wherein youth support each other's prosocial behaviors and confront one another when antisocial behavior is displayed. They are far more likely than boot camps to include therapeutic components, such as drama therapy, development of communication and problem-solving skills, or individual counseling. Staff in these programs are typically young, idealistic, and supportive of the youth, yet they demand accountability and adherence to rules. However, it is unknown to what extent psychologists or other clinicians provide treatment services. One major criticism of wilderness programs is that the skills that might be obtained by youth in an outdoor environment do not necessarily translate to skills they will need to survive in an urban, suburban, or even rural environment. Also, like boot camp programs, wilderness programs rarely have intensive aftercare services.

From an evaluation viewpoint, it is extremely difficult to gauge the extent to which wilderness and adventure programs have a positive effect on recidivism or on the lives of juveniles who participate in them. There is a dearth of solid empirical research thus far available, even on individual programs. An early review (F. Kelly & Baer, 1978) compared boys in a traditional training school to boys in a wilderness-type program. A significant difference in recidivism over a 1-year period was found—with the wilderness boys doing significantly better—but the differences washed out over a 5-year period. Wilderness programs are very different from one another, defying an attempt at meaningful comparisons. However, evaluation research of individual programs is warranted and needed, particularly because this approach continues to have considerable appeal as a rehabilitative strategy for some juvenile offenders and at-risk youth.

Violence Prevention Programs

Violence is commonly defined as physical force exerted for the purpose of inflicting injury, pain, discomfort, or abuse on a person or persons. Some definitions include damage to or destruction of property. Thus, vandalism—an offense often seen in juvenile crime statistics—would be included. Programs for juveniles that are aimed at preventing and controlling violence focus primarily on physical harm done to other persons. In addition, although sexual assault is clearly a violent crime, it is typically approached in a separate (or additional) treatment program, as we will discuss shortly.

As we described in Chapter 7, violence may begin very early in a child's life and often occurs as a result of modeling from significant individuals in the child's social network—particularly parents, caretakers, peers, or media heroes. In recent years, as discussed in Chapter 8, increasing attention has been given to violent video games that are thought by many to desensitize children to brutality and encourage them to adopt violent strategies in their own lives. Also gaining attention is the **biological/neurological perspective,** with some researchers suggesting that biological, genetic, or neuropsychological factors make a significant contribution to aggression (e.g., Fishbein, 2000; Moffitt, 1993a; Raine, 1993). Although these researchers do not suggest that these factors "cause" violent crime or delinquency, they do indicate that some individuals may be predisposed to committing violent acts. Consequently, they urge early identification and intervention into the lives of individuals who may be at risk.

Violent behavior may suddenly appear in adolescence—for example, the 14-year-old who takes a gun to school and kills the principal or the 15-year-old who stabs his father to death. However, this one-time violence is highly atypical. Far more typical is the progression from early, aggressive behavior to more serious aggression as a child develops. Psychologist Arnold M. Goldstein (2002a) says, "Catch it low to prevent it high," indicating that low-level aggression could, if not nipped, turn into more serious behavior later on. He goes on to say,

> My central belief—a belief increasingly finding at least initial empirical support—is that we, as a society, have far too often ignored the very manifestations of low-level aggression which, when rewarded, grow (often rapidly) into those several forms of often intractable high-level aggression which are currently receiving a great deal of society's attention. (p. 169)

Arnold M. Goldstein (2002a) also believes that cursing, threats, insults, incivilities, vandalism, bullying, and harassment are all precursors to serious aggression. Thus, the 6- or 7-year-old who consistently bullies, bites, or hits his playmates will likely, if reinforced, move on to more serious assaultive behavior as an adolescent. Reinforcement may be in the form of internal or external rewards. Gaining status on the playground or having other children be afraid of him may be sufficient reinforcement, even if adult authority figures "punish" him for his misbehavior.

Most children who reach the juvenile courts on delinquency petitions are older than 10—most are between the ages of 12 and 17. Even so, approximately 9% of juvenile arrests involve children age 14 and younger. In addition, the most recent juvenile court statistics indicate that 24% of delinquency cases involving *crimes against persons* (e.g., assault, rape, robbery, violent sexual offenses) were committed by youths younger than age 14 (Knoll & Sickmund, 2010). By the teen years, the individual has already "learned" that his or her violent behavior brings some rewards. Therefore, the treatment of violent behavior usually involves "unlearning" strategies that have seemingly worked up to that point.

Most violence prevention programs geared at juveniles adopt a cognitive-behavioral or social learning perspective. "Cognitive interventions assume that an angry, aggressive state is mediated through a person's expectations and appraisals and that the likelihood of violence is increased or decreased as a result of this process" (Tate, Reppucci, & Mulvey, 1995, p. 778). Violent youth often see hostility where none is intended. Therefore, they are encouraged to reassess their assumptions that others are a threat to them. In some programs, these cognitive distortions are referred to as "thinking errors," a concept proposed by Yochelson and Samenow (1976). Youth—particularly those in residential treatment programs—may be asked to write down their thoughts and emotions as they occur. In group therapy sessions, they reveal what they have written, and the group and the treatment provider identify the thinking errors and suggest strategies for thinking differently.

A victim empathy component may be part of the treatment. For example, the juveniles are encouraged to put themselves in the place of the victim to appreciate what the victim suffered, sometimes through role-playing exercises. Violence prevention programs also typically provide juveniles with alternatives to violent behavior, teaching them decision-making skills to put to use when a potentially violent situation erupts. They are encouraged also to avoid placing themselves in volatile situations. Alcoholic substances, for example, are known to facilitate violent behavior, so substance abuse prevention is an important component of many violence prevention programs.

A. P. Goldstein and Glick (1987, 2001) describe **aggression replacement training (ART),** an approach taken with children and adolescents in a variety of settings, including community and residential treatment programs for delinquents. They note that adolescents who display highly aggressive behaviors are often also deficient or inadequate in socially desirable behaviors, such as identifying their own feelings or responding appropriately to slights or anger. The ART curriculum consists of (1) skillstreaming (teaching a broad range of prosocial behaviors), (2) anger control training, and (3) moral reasoning. In small groups, chronically aggressive adolescents are taught such skills as asking permission, having a conversation, giving a compliment, and dealing with embarrassment. They are also taught to identify triggers to their aggression and provided with techniques for reducing the level of their anger (e.g., counting backward, imagining a peaceful scene). The juveniles are also presented with moral dilemmas and encouraged to find a solution that is fair and just. The ART curriculum has been implemented in numerous residential and community facilities, as well as in a variety of school systems and gang prevention programs (see A. P. Goldstein & Glick, 2001, for a review). Although ART has produced cognitive-behavioral changes in violent adolescents, it has not yet been demonstrated to reduce violent behavior in juveniles after release from correctional facilities (Tate et al., 1995). A. P. Goldstein and Glick acknowledge that maintaining anger control beyond facility walls can be problematic. Nevertheless, they maintain that positive effects of the program persist, although not as strongly as in a controlled environment.

Guerra, Tolan, and Hammond (1994) observe that a common element related to treatment effectiveness for adolescent violence is the development of social interaction skills: "Improved social skills not only help individuals resolve conflict-producing situations with their peers, but enable them to get along in multiple social contexts" (p. 397).

In the juvenile justice system, programs for serious violent offenders generally operate within institutional settings, primarily in secure settings for youth. From a therapeutic perspective, institutionalization has the obvious advantages of intervening in a controlled setting, away from criminogenic influences in the youth's natural environment. It also allows intensive treatment, using both group and individual models. Unfortunately, evaluations of institutional treatment have produced mixed results, which is not surprising because the youth themselves are the most challenging to work with. Critics of institutionalization also point out, however, that a major disadvantage of secure treatment is the tendency of adolescents to align with one another and reinforce their own deviant behaviors (Henggeler, 1996). Interestingly, M. S. Jackson and Springer (1997) recommend taking advantage of this tendency to align; they suggest that those working with juveniles in incarcerated settings encourage the forming of "therapeutic gangs," which incorporate positive aspects of the juvenile gangs to which many incarcerated youth belonged. The "therapeutic gang" members work together to identify negative attitudes and values and look for positive alternatives.

Institutional programs also are unable to place much emphasis on working with the family, the environment to which the adolescent frequently returns. Supporters of multisystemic therapy, discussed earlier, make a good case for its use with violent youth who are allowed to remain in the community and within their own family environment.

Paint Creek

One institutional treatment program for serious (including violent) offenders that received avid research attention in the 1990s was Ohio's **Paint Creek** Youth Center, developed as an experimental program in 1984 (Greenwood & Turner, 1993). It continues today as a private facility for juveniles under different management. Our interest here is in its operation during the late 20th century along with the careful research that accompanied it.

Delinquent youth were randomly assigned to Paint Creek or to other, more traditional training schools in the state, allowing a control population for purposes of comparison. Such random assignment to treatment is rarely possible in juvenile justice research. Under the direction of a clinical psychologist, Paint Creek staff were trained to provide treatment that included well-defined behavioral goals and reinforcements for meeting them. Role-playing exercises to encourage **victim empathy,** reality therapy, development of a positive peer culture, and the identification of thinking errors were all critical components of the treatment.

The program served 30 to 35 boys at a time (compared with several hundred in the traditional programs). It involved daily group sessions, family group therapy twice a month, and intensive aftercare. In other words, the program seemed to have many features of a model approach to treating juveniles in an institutional setting. Unfortunately, the first published results of the Paint Creek program (Greenwood & Turner, 1993) were disconcerting. Although both youth and staff from Paint Creek were more favorable toward their program than were youth and staff from the traditional facilities, and although Paint Creek youth were held in confinement about 27% longer, there were no significant differences in either officially recorded or self-reported recidivism. Any reported gains (e.g., Paint Creek youth who completed the program reported less drug use) were modest at best. Greenwood and Turner suggested a number of possible interpretations for these findings. They reported, for example, that the youth in this study returned to disruptive environments; approximately one quarter experienced family deaths, deaths of friends, or being fired or laid off from their jobs within a 1-year period after leaving the program. It is possible that the chaotic environment of the more traditional training school did just as good a job preparing youth for the outside because it represented more accurately the life they would be leading. The researchers also suggested that more attention should be devoted to the aftercare component because the supervision and support provided by Paint Creek were not enough to make a significant difference.

The results of the Paint Creek experiment do not surprise those who are pessimistic about the prospects of rehabilitation, particularly within institutional settings. As we noted above, intensive treatment within the community is often preferred, even for serious offenders (Henggeler, 1996). Nevertheless, recall the findings from the Lipsey (2009) meta-analysis that context was not a crucial factor in program effectiveness. Again, therapeutic approach, high-risk offenders, and program quality were the critical issues. Moreover, many if not most juvenile justice professionals believe that treatment in a secure juvenile facility is warranted for *some* youth who commit serious crime—including violent crime—but should not be transferred to the adult criminal justice system.

Juvenile Sex Offender Treatment Programs

It is believed that a high percentage of all juvenile sex offenders were themselves sexually abused. Gray, Pithers, Busconi, and Houchens (1997) found that 86% of the children in their sample of serious juvenile offenders had been sexually abused themselves. As we discussed in Chapter 10, however, children who are sexually abused typically do not become abusers. Rather, the devastating effects of sexual abuse are more likely to be internalized and displayed in adjustment problems such as depression, self-destructive behavior, anxiety, and poor self-esteem in both children and adults (Browne & Finkelhor, 1986). Those victims who do become abusers suffer many of these adjustment problems as well. If we consider the well-documented effects of childhood sexual abuse, it is clear that juvenile sex offenders need a treatment program that not only works to prevent future offending, but also recognizes and addresses the emotional trauma they have experienced.

Adolescent sex offenders, left untreated, are highly likely to continue to offend into adulthood. It has been estimated that 47 to 58% of adult sex offenders committed their first offense during adolescence (Cellini et al., 1993). Becker and Johnson (2001) note that researchers and clinicians are becoming increasingly aware also that prepubescent children commit sexual offenses and that many of these offenses continue into adolescence. Recent juvenile court data show a slight decrease in the percentage of sex offenses (Puzzanchera et al., 2003), but over the 10-year period from 1989 to 1998, they increased quite dramatically (26% for forcible rape; 53% for other violent sex offenses). In addition, clinicians report increasing numbers of juvenile sex offenders in their own private practices (Cellini, 1995). Consequently, sex offender treatment, much like substance abuse treatment, is an essential component of many clinical practices. It is available in most public and many private juvenile rehabilitation facilities.

The assessment that precedes treatment for juvenile sex offenders often occurs before they have been adjudicated, however. Youth suspected of or charged with sexual offenses may be referred for evaluation, both by juvenile courts and by social service agencies. In these situations, "it is the job of the assessor to determine the probability that a deviant sexual act occurred, the reason for its occurrence, and whether or not there is need for intervention" (Becker & Johnson, 2001, p. 274).

Whether it occurs before or after a juvenile has been adjudicated delinquent, assessment of sex offenders is controversial. Because of the nature of sexual offending, courts and other juvenile justice officials are particularly interested in knowing not only whether the juvenile is likely to respond to treatment but also whether the juvenile is likely to reoffend. However, most assessment guidelines offered in the clinical literature have not been systematically evaluated. Cellini (1995) notes that, due to this absence of validated research instruments and assessment protocols, clinicians must be extremely cautious in making predictions or assessing risk: "There simply is no way to make clinical assumptions about the risk of re-offense or progression of adolescents' deviant sexual patterns" (Chapter 6, p. 4).

Practicing forensic psychologists and researchers recommend the gathering of extensive background and clinical information in any evaluations of juvenile sex offenders. According to Becker and Johnson (2001), the psychologist conducting the assessment should obtain the following:

- Family social, medical, and mental histories;
- Developmental history of the juvenile, including information about temperament as infant and toddler;
- School information;
- History of violent behavior;
- Alcohol and other substance abuse history;
- A detailed sexual history;
- Information about mental status.

Becker and Johnson made the additional comment, "One should assess the youth's general fund of knowledge and intelligence as well as insight and judgment" (p. 276).

A very wide range of treatment modalities is available for juvenile sex offenders, including individual and group treatment, family counseling, and psychoeducational classes. According to Cellini (1995), "Peer groups are the preferred method of treatment for 98% of the juvenile and adult programs currently being offered for sex offenders" (Chapter 6, p. 6). The typical peer group program takes a cognitive-behavioral approach, with sex offenders discussing their offenses and the effects on their victims, under the direction of a clinical moderator. Sex education is an important component; juvenile sex offenders are given factual information about human sexuality, and nondeviant sexual interests are promoted. They are encouraged to identify **thinking errors**—mistaken assumptions regarding their crimes or their victims—and to develop strategies to avoid future offending. Social skills and assertive skills training is an important component of many sex offender treatment programs as well. Although peer group treatment may be dominant, the literature also strongly advocates individual and family therapy when possible (Becker & Johnson, 2001). As is the case with programs for violent offenders, a multimodal approach, emphasizing group, individual, and family treatment, is most likely to be effective.

One controversial aspect of sexual offender treatment is the use of pharmacological agents to suppress libido and reduce sexual offending. These are not recommended for use with adolescents before the age of 16, who have not yet completed puberty (Becker & Johnson, 2001; Bradford, 1993). Becker and Johnson review the effects of other biological agents (e.g., antipsychotic medication, mood stabilizers, and various antidepressants) that may be indicated for some juveniles, though never in the absence of psychotherapeutic interventions.

It is widely believed that sex offenders are never completely "cured" but are always susceptible to reoffending (Cellini, 1995; Pithers et al., 1995). Thus, an important component of sex offender treatment programs is relapse prevention, whereby offenders are taught strategies for recognizing situations and avoiding stimuli that have led to their offenses in the past (e.g., visit with a particular acquaintance, playground, violent pornography).

As Becker and Johnson (2001) indicate, the literature on sex offender treatment is long on description and short on careful evaluation. Although many articles are published outlining the treatment methods used, there are very few controlled studies of effectiveness. In addition, the literature discusses primarily the sex offending of adolescent males, with very little written regarding female sex offenders or prepubescent children. This, too, is changing, though, as more researchers become aware that the sexual offending of women and girls is a topic worthy of attention (Becker et al., 2001).

SUMMARY AND CONCLUSIONS

In 1999, the U.S. juvenile justice system celebrated its 100th anniversary, if one marks its beginning with the establishment of the first juvenile court in 1899. As would be expected, the juvenile justice process of today hardly resembles the process of the first half of the 20th century. Or does it? Early juvenile courts were informal, paternalistic, often very judgmental, and children were rarely represented by lawyers. Clinicians—primarily psychiatrists and psychologists—consulted regularly with these courts, providing wide-ranging evaluations of a juvenile's emotional, cognitive, and mental status, as well as background information on the youth's social history. Although the courts were supposedly intended to "save" children from a life of poverty, they too often placed them in institutions that failed to provide the education, nurturing, and overall physical and emotional care that children need.

In the 1960s, a rights-oriented Supreme Court recognized these deficiencies in the juvenile justice system and attempted to correct them by providing juveniles with legal representation and other due process rights. In the 1970s, Congress passed the Juvenile Justice and Delinquency Prevention Act, landmark legislation that, among many other things, began to address conditions in juvenile facilities.

It is important for forensic psychologists working with the juvenile justice system to be aware of its history, which was reviewed in the present chapter as well as in Chapter 6. Many concerned advocates for juveniles today fear that problems similar to those of old have reoccurred or, in some cases, never really disappeared. In this chapter, we focused on issues that relate to juveniles while they are in detention or after they have been adjudicated delinquent. Conditions of confinement in many secure facilities are appalling, as the government report cited at the beginning of this chapter attests. There is documented overrepresentation of minority youth, particularly in secure confinement. The needs of juvenile girls have been overlooked, and the needs of juveniles from ethnic, racial, or sexual orientation minorities have been ignored. The effectiveness of many treatment programs has not been documented. These and many other problems have led to calls ranging from complete abolition of a separate system for juveniles to increasing its financial resources and making drastic changes in its procedures. Nevertheless, good juvenile facilities exist, and numerous professionals find juvenile work highly rewarding, believing they can help make significant changes in the lives of juveniles. Psychologists provide an extremely wide range of consulting services to juvenile justice. Although we reviewed their assessment tasks in Chapter 4, here we concentrated on the provision of treatment. It is important to emphasize once again, though, that treatment cannot be offered without both initial and ongoing assessment.

Programs abound, both in community and institutional settings, but the great majority of them have not been submitted to empirical investigation. When they are, the results are often disappointing, particularly for programs based in residential settings. However, the evaluation research of the past had many shortcomings, including failure in some cases to include control groups. Recent meta-analyses (e.g., Lipsey, 2009) have made impressive efforts at identifying effective treatment options. There is a great need for additional, well-designed evaluation research in juvenile as well as adult corrections.

Many researchers and clinicians today advocate community treatment if at all possible for a wide range of juvenile offenders, including substance abusers, sexual offenders, and some violent offenders. Family preservation models try intensely to keep juveniles within their own families. Critics of this approach maintain that it fails to recognize adequately that some children and adolescents are not well served by this emphasis.

Similar to what has been found with adult treatment programs, some common features of successful programs can be identified. Those based on cognitive-behavioral models, for example, have received very favorable reviews. Multimodal programs—those that attempt to incorporate group, individual, and family treatment—also produce good results. Programs that target offenders with high risks and high needs, work intensively with those offenders, and include a follow-up component are also well rated. The follow-up component is particularly important for juveniles because they so frequently return to an environment that facilitates their antisocial behavior. This may be why multisystemic therapy—the community-based approach that attempts to address strengths and weaknesses in the juvenile's various social systems (e.g., individual, family, school, community, employment setting)—is highly promising.

KEY CONCEPTS

Aggression replacement training (ART)	Deinstitutionalization of status offenders (DSO)
Biological/neurological perspective	Disproportionate minority confinement (DMC)
Boot camps	Family preservation models
Cognitive-behavioral programs	Functional family therapy (FFT)

Homebuilders model

Juvenile detention

Juvenile Justice and Delinquency Prevention Act
   (JJDPA)

Juvenile psychopathy

Multisystemic therapy (MST)

Office of Juvenile Justice and Delinquency
   Prevention (OJJDP)

Paint Creek

Relapse prevention

Status offenders

Teaching-family model

Thinking errors

Victim empathy

Wilderness and adventure programs

QUESTIONS FOR REVIEW

1. Define juvenile detention and summarize the major concerns relative to detention today.

2. Why is it important to distinguish between detention and treatment/rehabilitation?

3. What are the strengths and weaknesses of the teaching-family approach?

4. Compare and contrast Homebuilders, FFT, and MST on such factors as population served, treatment approaches, and evaluation research.

5. Provide illustrations of an inpatient and an outpatient substance abuse treatment program and summarize the advantages and disadvantages of each approach.

6. From a psychological perspective, what are the main problems with boot camps?

7. What is ART? Briefly summarize its curriculum.

8. Describe the Paint Creek treatment program.

9. Describe the Paint Creek evaluation study, focusing on the methodology and the results.

10. Based on the research literature, what conclusions can be drawn about juvenile sex offender (a) assessment and (b) treatment?

Glossary

Acquaintance rape See Date rape.

Actuarial data Statistical information compiled from databases and gathered by objective measures. Typically compared with clinical data, which are less structured, interview based, and more subjective in nature.

Actuarial predictions A prediction method that employs statistics to identify certain facts about a person's background and known behavior that can be related to the behavior being predicted, based on how groups of individuals with similar characteristics have acted in the past.

Acute dynamic factors Psychological characteristics that change rapidly (within days, hours, or even minutes) and include such things as mood swings, emotional arousal, and alcohol or other drug-induced effects.

Adjudicative competence The ability to participate in a variety of court proceedings. See also, Incompetence to stand trial.

Administrative segregation A form of custody exercised by prison administrators to isolate an inmate physically from the rest of the prison population for a variety of reasons, including but not limited to protection of the inmate.

Adolescent-limited offenders (ALs) Individuals who usually demonstrate delinquent or antisocial behavior only during their teen years and then stop offending during their young adult years.

Advance directive A document that allows persons to make advance decisions about life-sustaining procedures in the event of a terminal condition or persistent vegetative state, or any other later health care decision.

Aggravating factors Circumstances surrounding a crime that heighten its seriousness for purposes of sentencing. An example would be an excessively heinous or cruel method of carrying out a crime, such as a torture murder.

Aggression Behavior that is intended to cause harm or damage to another person.

Aggression replacement training (ART) Treatment program for aggressive children and adolescents consisting of skillstreaming (teaching a broad range of prosocial behaviors), anger control training, and moral reasoning.

Allocution The right to speak out during court proceedings, such as at the bail hearing, the sentencing hearing, or the parole board hearing. In all states, for example, victims are allowed to speak out at sentencing hearings.

Amenability to rehabilitation Refers to the types of treatment and rehabilitative services that are considered most promising for a juvenile offender during juvenile justice processing.

American Psychological Association (APA) The largest professional association for psychologists in the world, with 150,000 members as of 2010.

Americans with Disabilities Act (ADA) A federal law that guarantees equal opportunity for individuals with disabilities in state and local government services, public accommodations, employment, transportation, and telecommunications.

***Amicus curiae* brief** A document submitted to an appellate court by an outside party to call attention to some matter that might otherwise escape its attention.

Anger rape A rape situation, identified by Groth, in which an offender uses more force than necessary for compliance and engages in a variety of sexual acts that are particularly degrading or humiliating to the victim.

Antisocial personality disorder (ASP, also referred to as APD) A disorder characterized by a history of continuous behavior in which the rights of others are violated.

Appellate jurisdiction A court's authority to hear appeals from decisions of lower courts.

Arraignment The court proceeding during which defendants are formally charged with an offense, informed of their rights, and asked to enter a plea.

Association for Psychological Science (APS) A nonprofit organization of psychologists dedicated to the advancement of science in psychology. After the APA, it is the next-largest psychological association in the United States.

Attention deficit/hyperactivity disorder (ADHD) Traditionally considered a chronic neurological condition characterized by developmentally poor attention, impulsivity, and hyperactivity. More contemporary perspectives see the behavioral pattern as a deficiency in interpersonal skills.

Autoerotic asphyxia Refers to obtaining sexual excitement from hypoxia (lack of oxygen), usually through near strangulation, such as a near hanging.

Availability heuristic The cognitive shortcuts that people use to make inferences about their world. It is the information that is most readily available to use mentally, and is usually based extensively on the most recent material we gain from the news or entertainment media.

Battered woman syndrome (BWS) A cluster of behavioral and psychological characteristics believed common to women who have been abused in relationships.

Battering A term often reserved for *physical violence* experienced in intimate relationships such as a dating relationship, marriage or partnership, or separation and divorce.

Behavioral model Treatment approach based on the assumption that rewarding inmates for "good behavior" and removing privileges when behavior is unacceptable will produce positive changes in behavior.

Behavioral Science Unit (BSU) One of the instructional components of the FBI's Training Division at Quantico, Virginia. The BSU also coordinates with and supports other FBI units, such as the National Center for the Analysis of Violent Crime (NCAVC) and the Critical Incident Response Group (CIRG), which provides operational assistance to the FBI field offices and law enforcement agencies.

Bench trial Also called court trial. A civil or criminal trial in which the judge, rather than a jury, is the finder of fact, responsible for reviewing the evidence and rendering a verdict.

Best interest of child standard (BICS) The legal doctrine that the parents' legal rights should be secondary to what is best for the child.

Bias crimes Also called **hate crimes**. These are criminal offenses motivated by an offender's bias against a group to which the victim either belongs or is believed to belong.

Biological factors Any physical, chemical, genetic, or neurological condition associated with development of a specific behavior.

Biological/neurological perspective The research perspective that biological, genetic, or neuropsychological factors make a significant contribution to aggression. Although this perspective does not suggest that these factors "cause" violent crime or delinquency, it does indicate that some individuals may be biologically or neurologically predisposed to committing violent acts.

Boot camps Military-style, short-term facilities for juvenile delinquents. Most focus on instilling discipline rather than education or treatment.

Burglary The unlawful entry of a structure, with or without force, with intent to commit a felony or theft.

Capital sentencing Refers to a judicial process in which an offender faces a potential death sentence.

Challenge for cause Exercised by an attorney or judge whenever it can be demonstrated that a would-be juror does not satisfy the statutory requirements for jury duty.

Child abduction Unlawfully leading, taking, enticing, or detaining a child under a specified age with intent to keep or conceal the child from the parent, guardian, or other person having lawful custody.

Child sexual abuse accommodation syndrome (CSAAS) A term reserved for a cluster of behaviors that occur in children who have been victims of sexual abuse by a family member or an adult with whom the child has a trusting relationship.

Civil case An action at civil law, which is the part of the law concerned with noncriminal matters pertaining to the rights and duties of citizens.

Clear and convincing proof Legal standard achieved when the truth of the facts asserted is highly probable but does not reach the standard of proof beyond a reasonable doubt.

Clearance rate Law enforcement term for the proportion of reported crimes that have been solved through an arrest or exceptional means, such as a deathbed confession.

Clinical predictions Predictions based on subjective experience.

Clinical psychologist Doctoral-level psychologist who is trained in the research, assessment, diagnosis, evaluation, prevention, and treatment of mental or behavioral disorders.

Coerced-compliant false confessions Admissions of guilt most likely to occur after prolonged and intense interrogation experiences, especially in situations where sleep deprivation is a feature. The suspect, in desperation to avoid further discomfort, admits to the crime even knowing that he or she is innocent.

Coerced-internalized false confessions Occur when innocent persons—who are tired, confused, and highly psychologically vulnerable—come to believe that they actually committed the crime.

Coercive behaviors A key component of the Patterson coercive model, which asserts that a strong predictor of early-onset offending is the family environment in which the child learns to utilize coercive behaviors (e.g., temper tantrums, whining) to escape aversive parental discipline and authority.

Cognitive-behavioral approach An approach to therapy that focuses on changing beliefs, fantasies, attitudes, and rationalizations that justify and perpetuate antisocial or other problematic behavior. Commonly used in the treatment of many offenders, including those convicted of sex crimes.

Cognitive-behavioral programs Programs that examine beliefs and cognitions to produce changes in behavior; emphasizes the role of positive reinforcements. May include contracts and token economy systems, whereby individuals gain points when they demonstrate prosocial behaviors.

Cognitive-behavioral viewpoint In hypnosis research, the perspective that people holding positive attitudes to hypnosis role-play a trance situation and are not truly in an altered state of consciousness.

Cognitive factors The internal processes that enable humans to imagine, to gain knowledge, to reason, and to evaluate. Each person has his or her own cognitive version of the world.

Commitment bias The phenomenon that once a witness commits to a certain viewpoint, such as identification of a face, the witness is less likely to change his or her mind.

Community-based facilities Correctional facilities that are not institutions and allow supervision of juveniles or adults within their own homes or in special community facilities, such as halfway houses.

Community corrections The broad term for a wide variety of options that allow persons convicted of crime to be supervised in the community, such as being placed on probation; term also applies to parole, the supervision of former prisoners in the community.

Comparison question technique (CQT) Formerly control question technique. The most commonly used procedure by professional polygraphers, it is based on three types of questions: (1) irrelevant or neutral questions (2) relevant questions, and (3) control questions.

Competency Screening Test Sentence completion examination intended to provide a quick assessment of a defendant's competency to stand trial. The test taps the defendant's knowledge about the role of the lawyer and the rudiments of the court process.

Competency to be executed The legal requirement that a person convicted of a capital crime and sentenced to death must, at the time of execution, be emotionally stable enough to appreciate the reason he or she is being put to death.

Computer evidence recovery Also called forensic data recovery, involves e-mail and Internet analysis, along with sophisticated hard drive and diskette recovery techniques of orphaned, fragmented, and erased data.

Concurrent validity In psychological testing, validity measured by comparing one test with another, already established one.

Conduct disorder A diagnostic label used to identify children who demonstrate habitual misbehavior.

Confirmation bias The tendency to look for evidence that confirms preexisting expectations or beliefs.

Contagion/copycat effect A tendency for some people to model or copy a behavior or activity portrayed by the news or entertainment media.

Content analysis Technique in which the researcher carefully and systematically examines the content of documents to discover common elements.

Control question technique (CQT) See Comparison question technique.

Correctional psychologists Psychologists employed by prisons, jails, and other correctional facilities and programs, or who offer consulting services to these institutions and programs.

Counseling psychologist Similar to clinical psychologists, these individuals are traditionally trained to evaluate and treat (counsel) persons with adjustment problems, such as those relating to education, job, and personal and marital relationships.

Countermeasures Any effort or behavior by an individual undergoing a polygraph examination to avoid being evaluated as deceitful or dishonest.

Court trial Also called bench trial. Trial before a judge, with the judge—rather than a jury—serving as a trier of fact.

Covictims Individuals who are close to the victim of a serious crime, such as a murder, who must deal with the medical examiner, the criminal or juvenile justice system, and the media in the aftermath of a murder. Often used to emphasize the depth of homicide's emotional impact.

Creature-comfort killer Murderer whose primary motive is to acquire activities (business interests) or objects (money) that provide a comfortable and luxurious lifestyle.

Crime (definition of) Behavior in violation of the criminal code for which a range of penalties exist upon conviction.

Crime scene analysis The development of a rough behavioral or psychological sketch of an offender based on clues identified at the crime scene.

Criminal case An alleged violation of rules deemed so important that the breaking of these rules incurs society's formal punishment, which must be imposed by the criminal courts.

Criminal homicide The unlawful and intentional killing of a human being; the term encompasses both murder and nonnegligent homicide.

Criminal profiling The process of identifying personality traits, behavioral tendencies, and demographic variables of an offender based on characteristics of the crime.

Criminal responsibility evaluation Assessment usually designed to determine whether a defense of insanity can be supported. Also called "mental state at time of offense" evaluation.

Criminogenic needs Those dynamic risk factors that are empirically found to be related to criminal behavior.

Crisis intervention The intervention of mental health practitioners into emergency or crisis situations, such as suicide attempts, emotional agitation, or psychotic behavior displayed during confinement.

Critical incidents Tragedies, death, serious injuries, hostage situations, and other threatening situations that the police frequently encounter.

Cyberstalking Threatening behavior or unwanted advances directed at another using the Internet or other forms of online communication.

Date rape A sexual assault that occurs within the context of a dating relationship.

Daubert **standard** Guide to help determine whether expert scientific testimony meets criteria established by the Federal Rules of Evidence for reliability and relevance.

Death-is-different principle Cautionary warning that the death penalty is an unusually severe punishment, unusual in its pain, in its finality, and in its enormity. Consequently, all decisions in death penalty cases should be carefully weighed.

Death notification Procedure or process used for informing family members of a death resulting from violent crime, accident, or some other incident.

Death penalty mitigation In capital cases, attempts by the defense team to reduce or avoid the sentence of death for their client based on factors that lessen the offender's culpability. Examples of mitigating factors are age and a long history of violent victimization.

Decisional competency Ability to make decisions in one's own best interest. Juveniles—given their stage of development—are unlikely to have the cognitive sophistication and maturity to make such decisions when they come before the juvenile court.

Defendant Individual who is facing a legal action.

Deinstitutionalization of status offenders (DSO) Mandate from the JJDPA that states receiving funds for juvenile justice programs must remove all juveniles from adult jails and must also remove status offenders from secure institutions.

Deposition Proceedings during which potential witnesses are questioned by attorneys for the opposing side, under oath and in the presence of a court recorder, although typically away from the courtroom.

Detention centers Facilities where pretrial detainees are held.

Differential experience hypothesis States that individuals will have greater familiarity or experience with members of their own race and will thus be better able to discern differences among its members.

Diplomate Professional designation signifying that a person has been certified as having advanced knowledge, skills, and competence in a particular specialty.

Directed lie test A polygraph technique in which examinees are instructed to respond negatively and untruthfully to questions.

Disciplinary segregation Punishment (physical isolation) for violation of rules.

Discovery process The pretrial procedure by which one party in a civil or criminal case discloses to the other party information vital for his or her defense.

Disorganized crime scene Demonstrates that the offender committed the crime without premeditation or planning. In other words, the crime scene indicators suggest the individual acted on impulse or in a rage, or under extreme excitement.

Disposition The resolution of a legal matter. In criminal law, an example would be the sentence a defendant receives. In civil law, the disposition of a case may be a judgment in favor of the plaintiff.

Disproportionate minority confinement (DSM) The observation that racial and ethnic minorities are disproportionately detained and incarcerated.

Double-blind lineup A lineup during which the officer administering the lineup does not know the identity of the suspect, and the witness has been told that the officer does not know. This is done so that the officer cannot consciously or otherwise provide clues to the witness.

Dual-court system Refers to the fact that federal and state courts in the United States exist side by side, independent of one another, sometimes in the same geographical location.

Dual-purpose evaluations Assessment of both a defendant's competency to stand trial and criminal responsibility during the same evaluation.

Dual relationship Refers to psychologists offering treatment to a patient who also form other relationships with the patient or evaluate them for other purposes, e.g., competency to stand trial. Such dual relationships are in violation of ethical codes and are forbidden.

Dual systems model Developed by Laurence Steinberg. Steinberg contends that risk taking and criminal offending during adolescence are best explained by the dynamic interaction between the socio-emotional and cognitive-control systems.

***Dusky* standard** Relates to juvenile and adult competency to stand trial and decision-making abilities. The rule holds that defendants must be able to understand and appreciate the criminal proceedings against them and be able to assist their attorneys in their defense.

Duty to warn or protect Requirement from the *Tarasoff* case that clinicians must take steps to protect possible victims from serious bodily harm as a result of threats made by the clinicians' clients.

Dynamic risk factors Elements of a person's developmental history that change over time, such as attitudes, opinions, and knowledge and that are identified as predictors of offending.

Dysphoric/borderline batterers Batterers who exhibit mental disorders and are psychologically disturbed and emotionally volatile. These individuals often engage in moderate to severe spousal abuse, including psychological and sexual abuse.

Early starters Refers to those children who begin demonstrating antisocial behaviors early in their development. They are considered at greater risk for more serious criminal offending as they grow older.

Early warning systems Systems that help identify problem law enforcement officers early, before they become major problems.

Ecological validity The degree of practical or useful application of a theory or idea to the "real world."

Elder abuse Defined as the physical, financial, emotional, or psychological harm of an older adult, usually defined as age 65 or older.

Emotional intelligence Ability to know how people and oneself are feeling and the capacity to be able to use that information to guide thoughts and actions.

Empirically supported treatments Those psychotherapies or treatments that research has found effective in changing behavior and attitudes.

Employee Polygraph Protection Act A law passed by the U.S. Congress that severely limits the extent to which *private* employers can use the polygraph.

Employment compensation claims Claims involving physical injuries, psychological damage, or emotional distress sustained as a result of one's employment. Employers are required to insure their workers against injury while on the job.

Equivalent death analysis (EDA) Reconstruction of the personality profile and cognitive features (especially intentions) of deceased persons. Also called reconstructive psychological evaluation (RPE).

Erotomania stalking In this form of stalking, the stalker usually has serious mental disorders and is considered delusional. Public figures are typically the targets.

Ethical Principles of Psychologists and Code of Conduct Provides ethical guidelines for what is appropriate behavior in clinical and research practice for psychologists.

Excessive force Refers to situations where the level of force exceeds the level considered justifiable under the circumstances.

Executive functions Higher-order mental abilities involved in goal-directed behavior. They include organizing behavior, memory, inhibition processes, and planning strategies.

External stress Stress that is outside of one's daily tasks. In the law enforcement context, they include frustrations with the courts, the prosecutor's office, the criminal process, the correctional system, the media, and public attitudes toward policing.

Face validity Refers not to what the test actually measures but to what it superficially *appears* to measure.

Facial composites Graphic, artistic, or computer-driven drawings of suspect faces based on the memory of eyewitnesses.

Factor analysis A statistical procedure by which underlying patterns and personality characteristics are identified.

False confessions Admissions of guilt that are not valid and that may be induced by coercive interrogation procedures.

Family forensic psychology A specialty with extensive knowledge about human development, family dynamics, and the court system.

Family-only batterers Usually do not engage in violence outside the family. Their violence tends to be periodic, primarily when stress and frustration reach a peak.

Family preservation models Approaches that try to prevent youth with minor behavioral problems and their family from becoming dysfunctional. The major intention is to keep the family unit together.

Family violence Refers to any assault, including sexual assault, or other crime that results in the personal injury or death of one or more family or household member(s) by another who is or was residing in the same dwelling.

Federal Bureau of Prisons (BOP) The organizational structure for all facilities holding detainees and sentenced offenders in the federal system.

Fetishism Sexual attraction to inanimate objects.

Filicide Killing of one's child who is older than 1 year.

Firesetting An abnormal fascination with fire accompanied by successful or unsuccessful attempts to start harmful fires. Term used in child psychopathology literature.

Fitness-for-duty evaluation (FFDE) Conducted to determine the psychological ability of law enforcement officers to perform their essential job functions.

Flashbulb memory Refers to memory of high-impact events with considerable accuracy.

Forensic entomology Study of insects (and their arthropod relatives) as it relates to legal issues.

Forensic mental health assessments (FMHAs) Conducted by psychologists and psychiatrists consulting with criminal courts. Competency to stand trial assessments and criminal responsibility evaluations are prominent examples.

Forensic neuropsychology The application of knowledge from the neuropsychological profession to legal matters. Neuropsychology is the study of the psychological effects of brain and neurological damage and dysfunction on human behavior.

Forensic psychiatrists Medical doctors trained to provide direct treatment services to persons with emotional, cognitive, or behavioral problems relating to legal matters.

Forensic psychology The production of psychological knowledge and its application to the civil and criminal justice systems.

Forensic school psychology Branch of psychology dealing with legal matters within an educational context.

Functional family therapy (FFT) Developed in the 1970s for behaviorally disturbed adolescents whose parents were unable to control their acting-out behaviors, it combines social learning, cognitive-behavioral theory, interpersonal theory, and family systems theories.

Functional size (of a lineup) Number of participants in a lineup who resemble the suspect.

General jurisdiction Courts with broad authority over a vast array of both simple and complex cases, both civil and criminal.

Generally violent/antisocial batterers Batterers who are likely to use weapons and who are more prone to inflict severe injury on wives, partners, and other family members, in addition to engaging in extrafamilial violence.

Geographical jurisdiction Court authority over a specified geographical area of the country or state.

Geographical mapping Concerned with analyzing the spatial patterns of crimes committed by numerous offenders over a period of time.

Geographical profiling Focuses on the location of the crime and how it relates to the residence or base of operations of the offender. The fundamental assumption of geographical profiling is that serial offenders prefer to commit their crimes near their own residences.

Georgia Court Competency Test (GCCT) Short examination for initial screening for mental competency.

Geropsychology Branch of psychology concerned with older adults.

Grand jury A body of citizens (usually 23 in number) that is directed by the prosecutor to weigh evidence and decide whether there is enough to charge a person with a criminal offense.

Groth child molester typology Clinically developed classification system of pedophiles.

Groth rape typology Clinically developed classification system of rapists.

Guilty but mentally ill A verdict alternative in some states that allows defendants to be found guilty while seemingly affording them treatment for mental disorders.

Guilty knowledge test (GKT) A method of polygraphy in which the suspect is led to reveal facts about a crime or incident not known by the public.

Hate Crime Statistics Act A 1990 federal statute that directs the FBI to collect data on all crimes motivated by hatred of or bias against victims based on their race, ethnicity, religion, or sexual orientation. Physical or mental disability bias was added in 1997.

HCR-20 Historical/Clinical/Management Risk Scale for evaluating risk in offenders and inmates.

Hedonistic type Serial killer who strives for pleasure and thrills; in this killer's mind, people are simply objects to use for one's own enjoyment.

Homebuilders model Family preservation approach that tries to keep antisocial children in their homes and offers highly intensive services to the family for a short period of time.

Hostile attribution bias The tendency of some individuals to perceive hostile intent in others even when it is totally lacking.

Houses of Refuge Institutional settings intended to protect, nurture, and educate neglected or wayward children during the mid-19th century.

Hypnotic hyperamnesia The enhancement or revival of memory through hypnosis.

Hypnotic trance theory The perspective that hypnosis represents a special state of consciousness that promotes a high level of responsiveness to suggestion and changes in bodily feelings.

Iatrogenic effect A process whereby mental or physical disorders are unintentionally induced or developed in patients by physicians, clinicians, or psychotherapists.

Idiographic approach In a research context, the focus or study of one individual, such as by doing a case study. See also Nomothetic approach.

Incarceration rate Number of inmates per population.

Incest Sexual abuse of adolescents or children by immediate family or relatives.

Industrial/organizational (I/O) psychologists Those who work in the branch of psychology concerned with organizations, helping to develop strategies that build better organizations and improve the well-being of employees.

Infanticide Although this term literally means the killing of an infant, it has become synonymous with the killing of a child by a parent.

Initial appearance A court appearance by an arrested individual if he or she is being held in jail rather than released or cited to appear in court at a later date. Its purpose is to review the need for continuing detention. However, it also may apply to the first proceeding before a judge, whether or not the individual was detained.

Insanity In the legal context, this term describes a judicial determination that an individual's degree or quantity of mental disorder relieves him or her of criminal responsibility for illegal actions.

Institutional corrections Broad term for facilities that confine inmates as well as their rules, policies, and practices.

Instrumental violence Occurs when the injury of an individual is secondary to the acquisition of some other external goal of the offender.

Intensive rehabilitation supervision (IRS) Community supervision programs that match the risk level of offenders with their criminogenic and noncriminogenic needs.

Intensive supervision programs (ISPs) Correctional supervision of offenders who are on probation or parole but are assigned to heightened supervision or offered additional services.

Intermediate sanctions Supervision that is less restrictive than residential placement but more restrictive than the standard probation under which the juvenile or adult offender remains in his or her own home with conditions attached. Sometimes referred to as probation-plus or parole-plus. Examples of intermediate sanctions may include intensive supervision, day-reporting requirements, or electronic monitoring.

Internal consistency Refers to the degree to which all items on a particular test measure the same thing.

Interrater reliability Refers to the extent to which different examiner or test administrators agree with the ratings in judging a person's abilities or characteristics.

Intimate partner violence Crimes committed against persons by their current or former spouses, boyfriends, or girlfriends.

Involuntary civil commitment Procedure for committing a mentally disordered individual in need of treatment to a treatment facility.

Jails Facilities operated by a local government to hold persons temporarily detained, awaiting trial, or sentenced to confinement after having been convicted of a misdemeanor.

Job analysis Identification and analysis of the skills, abilities, knowledge, and psychological characteristics that are needed to do a job.

Judgment Judge specification concerning the remedy to be borne by the defendant.

Judicial waivers Involves waiving a juvenile to another court.

Juvenile delinquent Young person who commits an act against the criminal code and who is adjudicated delinquent by an appropriate court.

Juvenile detention *Temporary* secure or nonsecure placement pending adjudication or during adjudication proceedings, up to a final disposition.

Juvenile Justice and Delinquency Prevention Act (JJDPA) Landmark federal legislation passed in 1974 that attempted to address the needs of juveniles in the juvenile justice system as well as those considered at risk for delinquency.

Juvenile psychopathy Controversial topic that posits that certain juvenile offenders exhibit many of the psychopathic characteristics of adult psychopaths.

Least detrimental alternative standard Custody evaluation designed to "screen out" the custody arrangements that would create problems for the child.

Legal psychology Umbrella term for the scientific study of a wide assortment of topics reflecting the close relationship between psychology and the courts.

Legislative waiver/statutory exclusion or waiver by statute Waivers whereby the legislative branch has ordained that juveniles of specified ages will have their cases heard in criminal courts when charged with specific crimes.

Level of Service Inventory—Revised (LSI-R) Assesses dynamic and static risk factors to determine offender needs for services as well as risk of reoffending, including violent offenses.

Life course–persistent offenders (LCPs) A term by Terrie Moffitt to represent offenders who demonstrate a life-long pattern of antisocial behavior and who are resistant to treatment or rehabilitation.

Limited jurisdiction Court that settles small disputes or deals with preliminary issues in a major case.

Love obsession stalkers In this form of stalking, the stalker and victim are strangers or casual acquaintances. The stalker seeks a love relationship with the object of his or her obsession.

MacArthur Competence Assessment Tool—Criminal Adjudication (MacCAT-CA) Used by clinicians to evaluate competence to stand trial.

MacArthur Competence Assessment Tool—Treatment (MacCAT-T) Used by clinicians to evaluate ability to benefit from treatment.

MacArthur Juvenile Competence Study Multisite study of adjudicative competence in juveniles.

Malingering Response style in which the individual consciously fabricates or grossly exaggerates his or her symptoms.

Mandatory sentence Criminal sentence set by a legislature that establishes the minimum length of jail or prison time for specific crimes.

Manslaughter *Unintended* killing that results from *unjustifiable* conduct that places others at risk.

Mass murder Involves the killing of three or more persons at a single location with *no* cooling-off period between the killings.

Miranda **rights** Refers to requirement that suspects must be told they have the right to an attorney and the right to remain silent. They must also be informed that anything they say can be used as evidence against them in court.

Mission-oriented type Serial killer who believes that there is a particular group of people who are considered undesirable and who must be destroyed or eliminated.

Mitigating factors Conditions which, while not completely exonerating a defendant, might at least reduce the punishment if he or she is convicted. An example would be evidence of a childhood marred by extensive physical or sexual abuse.

Mixed crime scene Indicates that the nature of the crime demonstrates both organized and disorganized behavioral patterns.

Modus operandi (MO) Actions and procedures an offender uses to commit a crime successfully.

MTC:CM3 Empirically-based classification system for pedophiles that underscores the importance of viewing pedophilia as characterized by multiple behavioral patterns and intentions.

MTC:R3 Rape typology consisting of nine discrete rape types that are differentiated on the basis of six variables.

Multiculturalism Refers to sensibility to differences in race, ethnicity, gender, sexual orientation, and disability.

Multisystemic therapy (MST) A treatment approach for serious juvenile offenders that focuses on the family while being responsive to the many other contexts surrounding the family, such as the peer group, the neighborhood, and the school.

Munchausen syndrome by proxy (MSBP) An unusual form of child abuse in which the parent (usually the mother) or parents consistently bring a child for medical attention with symptoms falsified or directly induced by the parent or parents.

Murder The felonious killing of one human being by another with malice aforethought.

National Crime Victimization Survey (NCVS) Designed to measure the extent to which households and individuals are victims of rape and other types of sexual assault, robbery, assault, burglary, motor vehicle theft, and larceny in the United States.

National Incident-Based Reporting System (NIBRS) FBI's system of collecting *detailed* data from law enforcement agencies on known crimes and arrests.

Neonaticide The killing of a newborn, usually under 24 hours old.

Nominal size (of a lineup) Actual number of members within a police lineup who may or may not resemble the suspect.

Nomothetic approach Refers to the search for general principles, relationships, and patterns by examining and combining data from many individuals.

Noncriminogenic needs Needs that are subject to change but have been found to have little influence on an offender's criminal behavior. Psychological states such as depression, anxiety, or low self-esteem are examples.

Nonhypnotic hypermnesia Enhancement or recovery of memory through nonhypnotic methods, such as free association, fantasy, and recall techniques.

Nonsadistic rapist Rapist who engages in a sexual attack because of an intense sexual arousal prompted by specific stimuli identified in the intended victim. Aggression is not the significant feature in the attack.

Notification Requirement that victims be told about the status of an offender at various stages of the criminal justice process.

Office of Juvenile Justice and Delinquency Prevention (OJJDP) The federal agency charged with overseeing juvenile justice on the national level, providing grants for juvenile research and programs, and taking a leadership role in setting policies nationwide relative to juveniles.

Opportunistic rapist One who engages in sexual assault simply because the opportunity to rape presents itself.

Oppositional defiant disorder (ODD) Symptoms include arguing with adults, refusing adults' requests, deliberately trying to annoy others, blaming others for mistakes, and being spiteful or vindictive.

Organizational stress Refers to the emotional and stressful effects that the policies and practices of the police department have on the individual officer.

Organized crime scene Suggests planning and premeditation on the part of the offender.

Outpatient treatment orders Usually involve court orders that require an individual to live in his or her own home or alternative group or foster home and comply with a medication regimen.

Own-race bias (ORB) The finding that people are often better able to discriminate between faces of their own race than between those of other races or people of color.

Paint Creek A residential correctional program for delinquent youths where staff were trained to provide treatment that included well-defined behavioral goals and reinforcements for meeting them. The facility was the subject of a random experiment evaluating treatment effectiveness.

Paraphilia The clinical term for a condition exhibited in fantasies, urges, or behaviors involving nonhuman objects, suffering or humiliation of oneself or one's partner, or children or other nonconsenting persons.

Parens patriae The doctrine in law that establishes the right of the state to substitute its presumably benevolent decision making for that of individuals who are thought to be unable or unwilling to make their own decisions.

Partialism Refers to achieving sexual arousal by touching or fondling body parts not normally associated with sexual activity, such as feet, hair, or ears.

Pedophilia Clinical term for the sexual preference for children rather than adults.

Peremptory challenge A rule that allows a lawyer to request the removal of a prospective juror without giving reason.

Personal stress Stress that involves marital relationships, health problems, addictions, peer group pressures, feelings of helplessness and depression, and lack of achievement.

Personality assessment Historical trend in police psychology where the search for the police personality predominated.

Pervasively angry rapist Demonstrates a predominance of global and undifferentiated anger that pervades all areas of the offender's life.

Petition Written document filed in juvenile court alleging that the juvenile is a delinquent or in need of protection and requesting that the court assume jurisdiction over the juvenile.

Plaintiff Person or party who initially brings a legal suit.

Police culture The rules, attitudes, beliefs, and practices that are thought to be accepted among law enforcement officers as an occupational group.

Police psychology Branch of psychology focusing on law enforcement personnel.

Post-shooting traumatic reaction (PSTR) Represents a collection of emotions and psychological response patterns that may occur after a law enforcement officer shoots a person in the line of duty.

Posttraumatic stress disorder (PTSD) A cluster of behavioral patterns that result from a psychologically distressing event that is outside the usual range of human experience.

Power-control killer Type of serial murderer who obtains satisfaction from the absolute life-or-death control he has over the victim.

Power rape A rape situation, identified by Groth, in which the assailant seeks to establish power and control over his victim. Thus, the amount of force and threats used depend on the degree of submission shown by the victim.

Predictive validity Degree to which a test *predicts* a person's subsequent performance on the dimensions and tasks the test is designed to measure.

Preponderance of evidence Proof that one side in a legal dispute has more evidence in its favor than the other. It is the standard required in most civil suits and may be relevant to criminal proceedings as well.

Presentence investigation (PSI) Social history prepared by someone appointed by the court that includes information about the offender's family background, employment history, level of education, substance abuse, criminal history, medical needs, and mental health history.

Pretrial detainees Those persons held in jail before trial either because they are unable to afford bail or they were denied bail because they were considered dangerous.

Preventive outpatient treatment Treatment that may be court ordered to prevent a person from becoming dangerous.

Prisons Correctional facilities operated by state and federal governments to hold persons who are convicted of felonies and sentenced generally to terms of more than 1 year.

Prison transfer Process whereby prisoners are moved from one facility to another, sometimes without notice.

Prosecutorial waiver Provision that gives prosecutors the authority to decide whether the case will be taken to juvenile court or criminal court.

Protective custody A form of isolation in which the inmate is separated from others for his or her own safety.

Psychoactive medication Drugs that exert their primary effect on the brain, thus altering mood or behavior.

Psychological assessment Refers to all the techniques used to measure and evaluate an individual's past, present, or future psychological status. It usually includes interviews, observations, and various measuring procedures that may or may not include psychological tests.

Psychological autopsy Primarily undertaken in an effort to make a reasonable determination of what may have been in the mind of the deceased person leading up to and at the time of death—particularly if the death appears to be a suicide.

Psychopath An individual who demonstrates a distinct, physiologically based behavioral pattern that differs from the general population in its decidedly lower level of sensitivity, empathy, compassion, and guilt.

Psychopathy Checklist (PCL) Series developed by Robert Hare; currently the best-known instrument for the measurement of criminal psychopathy. Other versions include the PCL-R and the PCL-YV.

Psychosexual evaluations Assessment of sex offenders not only to decide on a treatment plan but also to gauge their likelihood of further offending.

Questioned document examination or analysis Examination of the validity of documents.

Rape Sexual assault by force or threat of force.

Rape by fraud The act of having sexual relations with a supposedly consenting adult female under fraudulent conditions, such as when a physician or psychotherapist has sexual intercourse with a patient under the guise of effective treatment.

Rape myths A variety of mistaken beliefs about the crime of rape and its victims held by many men and women.

Rape trauma syndrome (RTS) Consists of an "acute" state of extreme fear and other emotional, physical, and psychological symptoms experienced immediately after a rape.

Reactive violence Refers to physical violence precipitated by a hostile and angry reaction to a perceived threat or dangerous situation. Also called expressive violence.

Recidivism A return to criminal activity (usually measured by arrest) after being convicted of a criminal offense.

Reconstructive psychological evaluation (RPE) Reconstruction of the personality profile and cognitive features (especially intentions) after a person is deceased. Also called an equivocal death analysis.

Reconstructive theory of memory Perspective that memory is continually vulnerable to revision.

Rehabilitation Any attempt intended to bring about changes in behavioral or thought patterns.

Relapse prevention A method of treatment primarily designed to prevent a relapse of an undesired behavioral pattern.

Release decisions Judge's decisions concerning whether to confine an individual or place him or her on probation.

Relevant/irrelevant question technique A polygraph technique developed in 1917 by William Marston for criminal investigation. It is now the method of choice in employment or preemployment screening situations in which the polygraph is used.

Repressed memory State of being unaware a traumatic event occurred.

Repression Refers to the psychological process of keeping something out of awareness because of unpleasant effects connected with it.

Restitution Compensation provided to the victim of crime for the harm he or she suffered. May be obtained from public funds or from the offender.

Restoration to competency In criminal law, the process by which a person who was found incompetent to stand trial is rendered competent, such as by medication or psychological treatment.

Restorative justice Rehabilitative intentions designed to repair the damage done to the community and to victims by the offender's action. Sometimes referred to as the attempt to "make whole" victims and offenders.

Right to refuse treatment Right of persons to refuse treatment they perceive to be potentially hazardous, intrusive, or not in their best interest.

Right to treatment Statutory guarantee that stipulates that persons have a right to receive care and treatment suited to their needs.

Risk assessment The enterprise in which clinicians offer probabilities that a given individual will engage in violent or otherwise antisocial behavior based on known factors relating to the individual.

Risk assessment measures Instruments designed to estimate the level of dangerousness an individual might pose in a correctional facility or upon release.

Rogers Criminal Responsibility Assessment Scales (R-CRAS) Forensic examination designed to detect malingering (see Malingering).

Sadistic rape A rape situation, identified by Groth, in which the offender experiences sexual arousal and excitement as a result of the victim's torment, distress, helplessness, and suffering. The assault usually involves bondage and torture, and the rapist directs considerable abuse and injury to various areas of the victim's body.

Scientific jury selection The application of social and behavioral science techniques to assist attorneys in accepting jurors who will be favorably disposed toward their clients.

Screening-in procedures In the selection of law enforcement candidates, procedures intended to identify those personality and other attributes that distinguish one candidate over another as being potentially a more effective police officer.

Screening-out procedures Designed to eliminate those law enforcement applicants who demonstrate significant signs of psychopathology or emotional instability or who lack the *basic* ability or mental acuity to perform the job in a safe and responsible manner.

Self-regulation The ability to control one's behavior in accordance with internal cognitive standards.

Serial murder Incidents in which an individual (or individuals) kill a number of people (usually a minimum of three) over time.

Sexual Experiences Questionnaire (SEQ) Instrument available for assessing incidence and prevalence of sexual harassment.

Sexual harassment May be broadly defined as unwelcome sexual advances, requests for sexual favors, and other verbal or physical conduct of a sexual nature.

Sexual masochism Refers to sexual arousal in response to being humiliated, beaten, whipped, bound, or otherwise made to suffer.

Sexual sadism A deviation characterized by torture or killing and mutilation of other persons in order to achieve sexual gratification.

Sexually motivated rapist Characterized by the presence of protracted sexual or sadistic fantasies that strongly influence the assaults.

Sexually violent predator statutes Statutes addressing the fact that sex offender treatment programs within a secure facility should be followed up in the community to achieve maximum treatment outcomes.

Shaken baby syndrome (SBS) A form of child abuse in which an adult (usually male) shakes a baby so hard that it causes significant brain damage or death.

Show-up Identification procedure in which police present a single suspect to the eyewitness(es) to see if the eyewitness(es) will identify that person as the perpetrator.

Signature Any behavior that goes beyond what is necessary to commit the crime. Also called personation.

Simple obsession stalkers Stalkers who seek power and control after a failed relationship with the victim; often associated with past domestic violence.

Situational factors Characteristics of the psychosocial environment, such as stress or aggression in others, that encourage or engender violent behavior.

Socialization factors Those processes through which a person learns patterns of thinking, behavior, and feeling from his or her early life experiences.

Specialized courts Courts that deal only with particular matters. Family courts, drug courts, mental health courts, and domestic violence courts are all examples of specialized courts.

Specialty Guidelines for Forensic Psychologists Guidelines offered in a number of subject areas associated with research and clinical practice in forensic psychology.

Spousal Assault Risk Assessment (SARA) Evaluates an individual's risk of committing violence against a spouse or intimate partner.

Spree murder Refers to the killing of three or more individuals *without* a cooling-off period, usually at two or three different locations.

Stable dynamic factors Although they are changeable, these factors usually change slowly and may take months or even years to change.

Staging The intentional alteration of a crime scene prior to the arrival of the police.

State-dependent memory Refers to the research finding that the things we experience in one emotional or physiological state—such as happiness, fear, or even intoxication—are sometimes easier to recall when we are again in that same state.

Static risk factors Things about a person's developmental history that normally do not change, such as biological parents, gender, birth order, birth date, and ethnic background. Also called historical factors.

Status offenses A class of illegal behavior that only persons with certain characteristics or status can commit. Used almost exclusively to refer to the behavior of juveniles. Examples include running away from home, violating curfew, buying alcohol, or skipping school.

Statutory rape Rape in which the age of the victim is the crucial distinction, with the premise that a victim below a certain age (usually 16) cannot validly consent to sexual intercourse with an adult.

Subject matter jurisdiction Issues or legal matters over which a court has jurisdiction. For example, a family court may have authority over divorce, custody, adoption, and delinquency matters.

Supermax prisons High-security facilities (or units within a maximum-security prison) supposedly intended to hold the most troublesome, violent inmates.

***Tarasoff* requirement** Statutory stipulation that a therapist has the duty to warn and/or a duty to protect individuals threatened by his or her patient.

Task-related stress Stress related to the nature of the work itself. In a law enforcement context, for example, this includes the possibility of being killed in the line of duty.

Teaching-family model Group homes for delinquents, abused and neglected children, and autistic and developmentally challenged children and young adults.

Temperament Natural mood disposition determined largely by genetic and biological influences.

Tender years doctrine A legal assumption, derived from the traditional belief that the mother is the parent ideally and inherently best suited to care for children of a "tender age."

Testamentary capacity Competence to make a will.

Thinking errors Mistaken assumptions of juvenile sex offenders regarding their crimes or their victims.

Threat assessment Set of investigative and operational activities designed to identify, assess, and manage individuals who may *pose* a threat of violence to *identifiable targets,* such as the school environment.

Thrill killer Serial murderer whose primarily motivation is to induce pain or to terrify his or her victims.

Tort Legal term for a civil wrong in which a plaintiff alleges some negligence on the part of the defendant.

Trans-situational consistency Tendency of people to exhibit the same behavior and tendencies across different situations.

Trans-temporal consistency Tendency of people to exhibit the same behavior and tendencies across time.

Trophy Meaningful souvenir taken by the offender to remember the incident.

Typology Classification system.

Ultimate issue Final question that must be decided by the court, such as whether the defendant was indeed insane (and therefore not responsible) at the time of his crime.

Unconscious transference Occurs when a person seen in one situation is confused with a person seen in another situation.

Undoing A behavioral pattern found at the crime scene whereby the offender tries to psychologically "undo" the murder.

Vengeance stalkers These stalkers do not seek a relationship with their victims but rather are trying to elicit a response or change of behavior from the victim.

Vicarious traumatization Occurs when clinicians are exposed to a series of trauma victims, which often leads to a high incidence of professional burnout.

Victim empathy Psychologically, putting oneself in the place of a victim.

Victimless crimes Offenses that do not have a direct victim, such as illegal drug use, prostitution, and illegal gambling.

Vindictive rapist Offenders who use the act of rape to harm, humiliate, and degrade their victims.

Violence Use of physical force or destruction.

Violent Criminal Apprehension Program (ViCAP) Program designed to communicate with and help the nation's law enforcement agencies to investigate, identify, track, apprehend, and prosecute violent serial offenders.

Visionary type Serial killer driven by delusions or hallucinations that compel him (or her) to kill a particular group of individuals.

Voir dire A process that allows the judge and attorneys to question the prospective jurors and possibly disqualify them from jury duty.

Voluntary (false) confession A form of false confession in which the individual confesses to a crime without any pressure or coercion from the police or other individuals.

Wilderness and adventure programs Rehabilitative approaches for adjudicated delinquents (and preventive approaches for some youngsters at risk) that focus on skill building and the development of self-esteem.

Witness preparation Steps taken by lawyers to prepare victims and other witnesses for their testimony in court. This usually includes educating the witness about what to expect, fully informing the attorney about what the witness knows, and coaching the witness about courtroom behavior and how to respond to questions posed.

Workplace violence The aggressive actions, including homicides, that occur at the workplace, not necessarily caused by those who work within the organization.

Cases Cited

Addington v. Texas, 99 S. Ct. 1804 (1979).

Atkins v. Virginia, U.S. (2002).

Barefoot v. Estelle, 463 U.S. 880 (1983).

Batson v. Kentucky, 476 U.S. 79 (1986).

Bell v. Wolfish, 441 U.S. 520 (1979).

Berghuis v. Thompkins, 560 U.S., 130 S. Ct. 2250 (2010).

Bowers v. Hardwick, 478 U.S. 186 (1986).

Boy Scouts of America v. Dale, U.S. (2000).

Chevron v. Echazabal, U.S. (2002).

Claiborne v.United States (06–5618) (2007).

Clark v. Arizona, 126 S. Ct. 2709 (2006).

Coker v. Georgia, 433 U.S. 584 (1977).

Cone v. Bell, 556 U.S. , 129 S. Ct. 1769 (2009).

Cooper v. Oklahoma, 116 S. Ct. 1373 (1996).

Cruzan v. Director, Missouri Department of Health, 497 U.S. 261 (1990).

Daubert v. Merrill Dow Pharmaceuticals, Inc., 509 U.S. 579 (1993).

Drope v. Missouri, 420 U.S. 162 (1975).

Dusky v. U.S., 362 U.S. 402 (1960).

Estelle v. Gamble, 429 U.S. 97 (1976).

Ewing v. Goldstein, 15 Cal. Rptr. 3d 864 (Cal. Ct. App. 2004).

Ex parte Crouse, 4 Whart. 9 (Pa. Supreme Court, 1838).

Fare v. Michael C., 442 U.S. 707 (1979).

Faretta v. California, 422 U.S. 806 (1975).

Farmer v. Brennan, 511 U.S. 725 (1994).

Feliciano v. Gonzales, 13 F.Supp.2d 151 (D.P.R. 1998).

Ford v. Wainwright, 477 U.S. 399 (1986).

Foucha v. Louisiana, 504 U.S. 71 (1992).

Frye v. U.S., 54 app. D.C., 46, 47; 293 F 1013, 1014 (1923).

Furman v. Georgia, 408 U.S. 238 (1972).

Gall v. United States, 552 U.S. 38 (2007).

General Electric Co. v. Joiner, 522 U.S. 136 (1997).

Godinez v. Moran, 113 S.Ct. 2680 (1993).

Gonzales v. Oregon, 546 U.S. 243 (2006).

Graham v. Florida, 560 U.S., 130 S. Ct. 357 (2010).

Harris v. Forklift Systems, Inc., 510 U.S. 17 (1993).

Heller v. Doe, 509 U.S. 312 (1993).

Hellstrom v. Commonwealth, 825 S.W.2d 612 (Ky. 1992).

Hudson v. Palmer, 468 U.S. 517 (1984).

Indiana v. Edwards, 554 U.S. 164 (2008).

In re Gault, 387 U.S. 1 (1967).

In re Quinlan, 70 N.J. 10, 355 A.2d. 647, cert. denied sub nom. (1976).

Jackson v. Indiana, 406 U.S. 715 (1972).

Jackson v. State, No. 98-DP-00708-SCT, Miss. (August 13, 1998, withdrawn and reissued January 28, 1999).

Jaffe v. Redmond, 116 S. Ct. 1923 (1996).

J. E. B. v. Alabama ex rel T. B., 511 U.S. 127 (1994).

Jenkins v. U.S., 307 F.2d 637 (D.C. Cir. 1962 en banc).

Kansas v. Crane, 534 U.S. 407 (2002).

Kansas v. Hendricks, 521 U.S., 117 S. Ct. 2072 (1997).

Kennedy v. Louisana, 554 U.S., 128 S. Ct. 2641 (2008).

Kent v. U.S., 383 U.S. 541 (1966).

Kimbrough v. United States, 552 U.S. 85 (2007).

Kumho Tire Co. Ltd. v. Carmichael, 119 S. Ct. 1167 (1999).

Lawrence and Garner v. Texas, U.S. (2003).

Lockett v. Ohio, 438 U.S. 586 (1978).

Madrid v. Gomez, 889 F. Supp. 1149 (N.D. Cal. 1995).

Manson v. Braithwaite, 432 U.S. 98 (1977).

Maryland v. Craig, 497 U.S. 836 (1987).

McKune v. Lile, 536 U.S. 24 (2002).

Meritor Savings Bank v. Vinson, 477 U.S. 57 (1986).

Miranda v. Arizona, 384 U.S. 436 (1966).

North Dakota ex rel. Schuetzle v. Vogel, 537 N.W. 2d 358 (N.D. 1995).

Panetti v. Quarterman, 127 S. Ct. 852 (06–6407) (2007).

Payne v. Tennessee, 501 U.S. 808 (1991).

People v. Hickey, 86 Ill. App. 20 (1889).

Perri v. Coughlin, WL 395374 (N.D.N.Y. 1999).

Riggins v. Nevada, 504 U.S. (1992).

Rita v. United States, 551 U.S. 338 (2007).

Rivera v. Illinois, 556 U.S., 129 S. Ct. 1446 (2009).

Roper v. Simmons, 543 U.S. 551 (2005).

Schall v. Martin, 467 U.S. 253 (1984).

Schwarzenegger v. Entertainment Merchants Association, docket 08-1448; argued 11-2-2010.

Sell v. United States, 539 U.S. 166 (2003).

State v. Driver, 88 W.Va. 479, 107 S.E. 189 (1921).

Stogner v. California, U.S. (2003).

Stovall v. Denno, 388 U.S. 293 (1967).

Tarasoff v. Regents of the University of California, 17 Cal. 3d 425, 551 P.2d 334, 131 Cal. Rptr. 14 (Cal. 1976).

Thompson v. Oklahoma, 487 U.S. 815 (1988).

Thor v. Superior Court, 855 P.2d 375 (Cal. 1993).

Toyota v. Williams, 534 U.S. 184 (2002).

Troxel v. Granville, 530 U.S. 57 (2000).

U.S. v. Comstock, 560 U.S., 130 S. Ct. 1949 (2010).

U.S. v. Piccinonna, 885 F.2d 1529 (11th cir. 1989).

U.S. v. Salerno, 481 U.S. 739 (1987).

Vitek v. Jones, 445 U.S. 480 (1980).

Washington v. Harper, 494 U.S. 210 (1990).

Zinermon v. Burch, 110 S. Ct. 975 (1990).

References

Aamodt, M. G. (2008). Reducing misconceptions and false beliefs in police and criminal psychology. *Criminal Justice and Behavior, 35,* 1231–1240.

Aamodt, M. G., & Stalnaker, H. (2001). Police officer suicide: Frequency and officer profiles. In D. C. Sheehan & J. I. Warren (Eds.), *Suicide and law enforcement.* Washington, DC: FBI Academy.

Abbey, A., Zawacki, T., Buck, P. O., Clinton, A. M., & McAuslan, P. (2004). Sexual assault and alcohol consumption: What do we know about their relationship and what types of research are still needed? *Aggression and Violent Behavior, 9,* 271–305.

Abbey, A., Zawacki, T., & McAuslan, P. (2000). Alcohol's effects on sexual perception. *Journal of Studies on Alcohol, 61,* 688–697.

Abel, G. G., Lawry, S. S., Karlstrom, E., Osborn, C. A., & Gillespie, C. F. (1994). Screening tests for pedophilia. *Criminal Justice and Behavior, 21,* 115–131.

Abraham, H. J. (1998). The judicial process (7th ed.). New York: Oxford University Press.

Abrams, K. M., & Robinson, G. E. (2002). Occupational effects of stalking. *Canadian Journal of Psychiatry, 47,* 468–472.

Abt Associates, Inc. (2000). Addressing correctional officer stress: Programs and strategies. Washington, DC: U.S. Department of Justice, National Institute of Justice.

Acierno, R. H., Hernandez, M. A., Arnstadter, A. B., Resnick, H. S., Steve, K., Muzzy, W., et al. (2010). Prevalence and correlates of emotional, physical, sexual, and financial abuse and potential neglect in the United States: The National Elder Mistreatment Study. *American Journal of Public Health, 100,* 292–297.

Acierno, R. H., Resnick, H., & Kilpatrick, D. G. (1997, Summer). Health impact of interpersonal violence 1: Prevalence rates, case identification, and risk factors for sexual assault, physical assault, and domestic violence in men and women. *Behavioral Medicine, 23,* 53–67.

Ackerman, M. J., & Ackerman, M. C. (1997). Custody evaluations practices: A survey of experienced professionals (revisited). *Professional Psychology: Research and Practice, 28,* 137–145.

Adams, G. A., & Buck, J. (2010). Social stressors and strain among police officers: It's not just the bad guys. *Criminal Justice and Behavior, 37,* 1030–1040.

Adams, J. (2010, March 10). "Jihad Jane" and 7 others held in plot to kill Swedish cartoonist. *Christian Science Monitor,* pp. 1, 3.

Adams, J. H. (1997). Sexual harassment and Black women: A historical perspective. In W. O'Donahue (Ed.), *Sexual harassment: Theory, research, and treatment.* Boston: Allyn & Bacon.

Adams, K., Alpert, G. P., Dunham, R. G., Garner, J. H., Greenfield, L. A., Henriquez, M. A., et al. (1999, October). *Use of force by police: Overview of national and local data series: Research report.* Washington, DC: National Institute of Justice and Bureau of Justice Statistics.

Adler, R., Nunn, R., Northam, E., Lebnan, V., & Ross, R. (1994). Secondary prevention of childhood firesetting. *Journal of the American Academy of Child and Adolescent Psychiatry, 33,* 1194–1202.

Administration on Aging. (1998, September). *The National Elder Abuse Incidence Study: Final report.* Washington, DC: U.S. Department of Health and Human Services, Administration on Aging.

Agopian, M. W. (1984). The impact on children of abduction by parents. *Child Welfare, 63,* 511–519.

Alexander, M. A. (1999). Sexual offender treatment efficacy revisited. *Sexual Abuse: A Journal of Research and Treatment, 11,* 101–116.

Alexander, R. A., Smith, W., & Stevenson, R. (1990). Serial Munchausen syndrome by proxy. *Pediatrics, 8,* 581–585.

Alison, L. J., Bennell, C., Ormerod, D., & Mokros, A. (2002). The personality paradox in offender profiling: A theoretical review of the processes involved in deriving background characteristics from crime scene actions. *Psychology, Public Policy, and Law, 8,* 115–135.

Alison, L. J., & Canter, D. V. (1999). Professional, legal and ethical issues in offender profiling. In D. V. Canter & L. J. Alison (Eds.), *Profiling in policy and practice.* Aldershot, UK: Ashgate.

Alison, L. J., Kebbell, M., & Lewis, P. (2006). Considerations for experts in assessing the credibility of recovered memories of child sexual abuse: The importance of maintaining a case-specific focus. *Psychology, Public Policy, and Law, 4,* 419–441.

Alison, L. J., Smith, M. D., Eastman, O., & Rainbow, L. (2003). Toulmin's philosophy of argument and its relevance to offender profiling. *Psychology, Crime & Law, 9,* 173–183.

Alison, L. J., Smith, M. D., & Morgan, K. (2003). Interpreting the accuracy of offender profiles. *Psychology, Crime & Law, 9,* 185–195.

Allen, R. S., & Shuster, J. L. (2002). The role of proxies in treatment decisions: Evaluating functional capacity to consent to end-of-life treatments within a family context. *Behavioral Sciences and the Law, 20,* 235–252.

Allison, K. W., Crawford, I., Echemendia, R., Robinson, L., & Kemp, D. (1994). Human diversity and professional competence: Training in clinical and counseling psychology revisited. *American Psychologist, 49,* 792–796.

Alpert, J., Brown, L. S., & Courtois, C. A. (1998). Symptomatic clients and memories of childhood abuse: What the trauma and sexual abuse literature tells us. *Psychology, Public Policy, and Law, 4,* 941–945.

Althouse, R. (2000). AACP standards: A historical overview (1978–1980). *Criminal Justice and Behavior, 27*, 430–432.

Althouse, R. (Ed.). (2010). *Standards for psychology services in jails, prisons, correctional facilities, and agencies* (3rd ed.). International Association for Correctional and Forensic Psychology. Published in *Criminal Justice and Behavior, 37*, 749–808.

American Association for Correctional and Forensic Psychology. (2002). Standards for psychology services in jails, prisons, correctional facilities, and agencies. *Criminal Justice and Behavior, 27*, 433–493.

American Bar Association. (1979). *Juvenile justice standards project.* Chicago: Author.

American Psychiatric Association. (1994). *Diagnostic and statistical manual of mental disorders* (4th ed.). Washington, DC: Author.

American Psychiatric Association. (2000). *Diagnostic and statistical manual of mental disorders* (4th ed., text rev.). Washington, DC: Author.

American Psychological Association. (1992). Ethical principles of psychologists and code of conduct. *American Psychologist, 47,* 1597–1611.

American Psychological Association. (1993). Guidelines for providers of psychological services to ethnic, linguistic, and culturally diverse populations. *American Psychologist, 48,* 45–48.

American Psychological Association. (1994). Guidelines for child custody evaluations in divorce proceedings. *American Psychologist, 49,* 677–680.

American Psychological Association. (1996). *Reducing violence: A research agenda.* Washington, DC: Author.

American Psychological Association. (2002a, December). Amicus curiae brief in Sell v. U.S., no. 02–5664.

American Psychological Association. (2002b). Ethical principles of psychologists and code of conduct. *American Psychologist, 57,* 1060–1073.

American Psychological Association. (2003a). *Ethical principles of psychologists and code of conduct—2002.* Washington, DC: Author.

American Psychological Association. (2003b). Guidelines on multicultural education, training, research, practice, and organizational change for psychologists. *American Psychologist, 58,* 377–402.

American Psychological Association. (2003c). Is youth violence just another fact or life? In *APA Online: Public Interest Initiatives.* Washington, DC: Author. Retrieved December 15, 2010, from http://www.APA. org.

American Psychological Association. (2005). *Guidelines and principles for accreditation of programs in professional psychology.* Washington, DC: Author.

American Psychological Association (2009, July). Amicus curiae brief: Graham v. Florida and Sullivan v. Florida. *Supreme Court of the United States, Nos. 08-7412, 08-7621.*

American Psychological Association. (2010). *Ethical principles of psychologists and code of conduct—2010.* Washington, DC: Author.

American Psychological Association Committee on Professional Practice and Standards. (1998). *Guidelines for psychological evaluations in child protection matters.* Washington, DC: Author.

American Psychological Association's Task Force on Television in Society. (1992). *Big world, small screen: The role of television in American society.* Lincoln: University of Nebraska Press.

Amick-McMullen, A., Kilpatrick, D. G., & Resnick, H. S. (1991). Homicide as a risk factor for PTSD among surviving family members. *Behavioral Modification, 15,* 545–559.

Amick-McMullen, A., Kilpatrick, D. G., Veronen, L. J., & Smith, S. (1989). Family survivors of homicide victims: Theoretical perspectives and an exploratory study. *Journal of Traumatic Stress, 2,* 21–35.

Amnesty International. (1998). *Betraying the young* (Special report). New York: Author.

Anastasi, A. (1988). *Psychological testing* (4th ed.). New York: Macmillan.

Anderson, C. A., & Bushman, B. J. (2001). Effects of violent video games on aggressive behavior, aggressive cognition, aggressive affect, physiological arousal, and prosocial behavior: A meta-analytic review of the scientific literature. *Psychological Science, 12,* 353–359.

Anderson, C. A., Shibuya, A., Ihori, N., Swing, E. L., Bushman, B. J., Sakamoto, A., et al. (2010). Violent video game effects on aggression, empathy, and prosocial behavior in Eastern and Western countries: A meta-analytic review. *Psychological Bulletin, 136,* 151–173.

Anderson, S. D., & Hewitt, J. (2002). The effect of competency restoration training on defendants with mental retardation found not competent to proceed. *Law and Human Behavior, 26,* 343–351.

Andrew, T. A., & Fallon, K. K. (2007). Asphyxial games in children and adolescents. *American Journal of Forensic Medicine and Pathology, 28,* 303–307.

Andrews, D. A., & Bonta, J. (1994). *The psychology of criminal conduct.* Cincinnati, OH: Anderson.

Andrews, D. A., & Bonta, J. (1995). *The Level of Service Inventory—Revised.* Toronto, ON, Canada: Multi-Health Systems.

Andrews, D. A., & Bonta, J. (1998). *The psychology of criminal conduct* (2nd ed.). Cincinnati, OH: Anderson.

Andrews, D. A., Bonta, J., & Hoge, P. D. (1990). Classification for effective rehabilitation: Rediscovering psychology. *Criminal Justice and Behavior, 17,* 19–52.

Appelbaum, P. S., & Grisso, T. (1995). The MacArthur Treatment Competence Study I: Mental illness and competence to consent to treatment. *Law and Human Behavior, 19,* 105–126.

Archer, J. (2002). Sex differences in physically aggressive acts between heterosexual partners: A meta-analytic review. *Aggression and Violence, 7,* 313–351.

Archer, R. P., Buffington-Vollum, J. K., Stredny, R. V., & Handel, R. W. (2006). A survey of psychological test use among forensic psychologists. *Journal of Personality Assessment, 87,* 84–94.

Arey, J. A. (1972). *The sky pirates.* New York: Scribner's.

Arkow, P. (1998). The correlations between cruelty to animals and child abuse and the implications for veterinary medicine. In R. Lockwood & F. R. Ascione (Eds.), *Cruelty to animals and interpersonal violence: Readings in research and application.* West Lafayette, IN: Purdue University Press.

Armstrong, D., & Pereira, J. (2001, October 23). Nation's airlines adopt aggressive measures for passenger profiling. *Wall Street Journal,* p. A12.

Ascione, R. R. (1997). *Animal welfare and domestic violence.* Logan: Utah State University.

Asher, R. (1951). Munchausen's syndrome. *The Lancet, 1,* 339–341.

Ashford, J. B., Sales, B. D., & Reid, W. H. (Eds.). (2001). *Treating adult and juvenile offenders with special needs.* Washington, DC: American Psychological Association.

Ault, R., Hazelwood, R. R., & Reboussin, R. (1994). Epistemological status of equivocal death analysis. *American Psychologist, 49,* 72–73.

Ault, R., & Reese, J. T. (1980). A psychological assessment of criminal profiling. *FBI Law Enforcement Bulletin, 49,* 22–25.

Aumiller, G. S., & Corey, D. (2007). Defining the field of police psychology: Core domains & proficiences. *Journal of Police and Criminal Psychology, 22,* 65–76.

Aviation Daily. (2002, February 28). Passenger profiling important to aviation security, experts say. *Aviation Daily, 347*(40), 3.

Axelrod, E. M. (2009). Violence goes to the Internet: Avoiding the snare of the net. Springfield, IL: Charles C Thomas.

Azar, B. (2010). *Virtual violence: Researchers disagree about whether violent video games increase aggression.* Retrieved December 15, 2010, from http://www.apa.org/monitor/2010/12/virtual-violence.aspx.

Babcock, J. C., Waltz, J., Jacobson N. S., & Gottman, J. M. (1993). Power and violence: The relation between communication patterns, power discrepancies, and domestic violence. *Journal of Consulting and Clinical Psychology, 61,* 40–50.

Bachman, R. (1992). *Death and violence on the reservation.* New York: Auburn House.

Bailis, D., Darley, J., Waxman, T., & Robinson, P. (1995). Community standards of criminal liability and the insanity defense. *Law and Human Behavior, 19,* 425–446.

Baird, K. A. (2007). A survey of clinical psychologists in Illinois regarding prescription privileges. *Professional Psychology: Research and Practice, 38,* 196–202.

Baker, R. R., Lichtenberg, P. A., & Moye, J. (1998). A practice guideline for assessment of competency and capacity of the older adult. *Professional Psychology: Research and Practice, 29,* 149–154.

Bakker, A. B., & Heuven, E. (2006). Emotional dissonance, burnout, and in-role performance among nurses and police officers. *International Journal of Stress Management, 13,* 423–440.

Balkin, J. (1988). Why policemen don't like policewomen. *Journal of Police Science and Administration, 16,* 29–37.

Ballie, R. (2001, December). Where are the new psychologists going? *Monitor on Psychology, 32,* 24–25.

Banich, M. T. (2009). Executive function: The search for an integrated account. *Current Directions in Psychological Science, 18,* 89–94.

Barbaree, H. E., & Serin, R. C. (1993). Role of male sexual arousal during rape in various rapist subtypes. In G. C. Nagayama, G. C. N. Hall, R. Hirchman, J. R. Graham, & M. S. Zaragoza (Eds.), *Sexual aggression: Issues in etiology, assessment, and treatment.* Washington, DC: Taylor & Francis.

Barbaree, H. E., Seto, M. C., Serin, R. C., Amos, N. L., & Preston, D. L. (1994). Comparisons between sexual and nonsexual rapist subtypes: Sexual arousals to rape, offense precursors, and offense characteristics. *Criminal Justice and Behavior, 21,* 95–114.

Barber, S. J., & Wright, E. M. (2010). Predictors of completion in a batterer treatment program. *Criminal Justice and Behavior, 37,* 847–858.

Barber, T. X., Spanos, N. R., & Chaves, J. F. (1974). *Hypnosis, imagination, and human potentialities.* New York: Pergamon.

Bardone, A. M., Moffitt, T. E., & Caspi, A. (1996). Adult mental health and social outcomes of adolescent girls with depression and conduct disorder. *Development and Psychopathology, 8,* 811–829.

Barkley, R. (1997). Behavioral inhibition, sustained attention, and executive functions: Constructing a unifying theory of ADHD. *Psychological Bulletin, 121,* 65–94.

Barkley, R. (1998). *Attention deficit hyperactivity disorder* (2nd ed.). New York: Guilford Press.

Barland, G. H. (1988). The polygraph test in the USA and elsewhere. In A. Gale (Ed.), *The polygraph test: Lies, truth and science.* London: Sage.

Barland, G. H., & Raskin, D. C. (1973). Detection of deception. In W. F. Prokasy & D. C. Raskin (Eds.), *Electrodermal activity in psychosocial research.* New York: Academic Press.

Barling, J., Rogers, A. G., & Kelloway, E. (2000). Behind closed doors: In-home workers' experience of sexual harassment and workplace violence. *Journal of Occupational Health Psychology, 6,* 255–269.

Barnard, G. W., Thompson, J. W., Freeman, W. C., Robbins, L., Gies, D., & Hankins, G. (1991). Competency to stand trial: Description and initial evaluation of a new computer-assisted assessment tool (CADCOMP). *Bulletin of the American Academy of Psychiatry and the Law, 19,* 367–381.

Barnum, R. (2000). Clinical and forensic evaluation of competence to stand trial in juvenile defendants. In T. Grisso & R. G. Schwartz (Eds.), *Youth on trial: A developmental perspective on juvenile justice.* Chicago: University of Chicago Press.

Baron, R. A., & Byrne, D. (2000). *Social psychology* (9th ed.). Boston: Allyn & Bacon.

Barrick, M. R., & Mount, M. K. (1991). The Big Five personality dimensions and job performance: A meta analysis. *Personnel Psychology, 44,* 1–26.

Bartol, C. R. (1980). *Criminal behavior: A psychosocial approach.* Englewood Cliffs, NJ: Prentice Hall.

Bartol, C. R. (1991). Predictive validation of the MMPI for small-town police officers who fail. *Professional Psychology: Research and Practice, 22,* 127–132.

Bartol, C. R. (1996). Police psychology: Then, now, and beyond. *Criminal Justice and Behavior, 23,* 70–89.

Bartol, C. R. (2002). *Criminal behavior: A psychosocial approach* (6th ed.). Upper Saddle River, NJ: Prentice Hall.

Bartol, C. R., & Bartol, A. M. (1987). History of forensic psychology. In I. B. Weiner & A. K. Hess (Eds.), *Handbook of forensic psychology.* New York: Wiley.

Bartol, C. R., & Bartol, A. M. (1998). *Delinquency and justice: A psychosocial approach.* Upper Saddle River, NJ: Prentice Hall.

Bartol, C. R., & Bartol, A. M. (1999). History of forensic psychology. In A. K. Hess & I. B. Weiner (Eds.), *Handbook of forensic psychology* (2nd ed.). New York: Wiley.

Bartol, C. R., & Bartol, A. M. (2004). *Psychology and law: Theory, research, and application* (3rd ed.). Belmont, CA: Wadsworth/Thomson.

Bartol, C. R., & Bartol, A. M. (2011). *Criminal behavior: A psychological approach* (9th ed.). Upper Saddle River, NJ: Prentice Hall.

Bashore, T. R., & Rapp, P. E. (1993). Are there alternatives to traditional polygraph procedures? *Psychological Bulletin, 113,* 3–22.

Bates, J. E., Pettit, G. S., Dodge, K. A., & Ridge, B. (1998). Interaction of temperamental resistance to control and restrictive parenting in the development of externalizing behavior. *Developmental Psychology, 34,* 982–995.

Bauer, P. J. (1996). What do infants recall of their lives? Memories for specific events by one- to two-year-olds. *American Psychologist, 51,* 29–41.

Baum, K., Catalano, S., Rand, M., & Rose, K. (2009, January). *Stalking victimization in the United States.* Washington, DC: U.S. Department of Justice, Bureau of Justice Statistics.

Bauserman, R. (2002). Child adjustment in joint-custody versus sole-custody arrangements: A meta-analytic review. *Journal of Family Psychology, 16,* 38–53.

Bayer, P., & Pozen, D. E. (2003). *The effectiveness of juvenile correctional facilities: Public versus private management.* New Haven, CT: Economic Growth Center, Yale University.

Beatty, D., Hickey, E., & Sigmon, J. (2002). Stalking. In A. Seymour, M. Murray, J. Sigmon, M. Hook, C. Edwards, M. Gaboury, & et al. (Eds.), *National Victim Assistance Academy textbook.* Washington, DC: U.S. Department of Justice, Office of Victims of Crime.

Beauchaine, T. P., Katkin, E. S., Strassberg, Z., & Snarr, J. (2001). Disinhibitory psychopathology in male adolescents: Discriminating conduct disorder from attention-deficit/hyperactivity disorder through concurrent assessment of multiple autonomic states. *Journal of Abnormal Psychology, 110,* 610–624.

Beck, A. J., Guerino, P., & Harrison, P. M. (2010). *Sexual victimization in juvenile facilities reported by youth, 2008–09.* Washington, DC: U.S. Department of Justice, Bureau of Justice Statistics.

Becker, J. V. (1990). Treating adolescent sexual offenders. *Professional Psychology: Research and Practice, 21,* 362–365.

Becker, J. V., Hall, S. R., & Stinson, J. D. (2001). Female sexual offenders: Clinical, legal and policy issues. *Journal of Forensic Psychology Practice, 1,* 29–50.

Becker, J. V., & Johnson, B. R. (2001). Treating juvenile sex offenders. In J. B. Ashford, B. D. Sales, & W. H. Reid (Eds.), *Treating adult and juvenile offenders with special needs.* Washington, DC: American Psychological Association.

Beckman, M. (2004). Crime, culpability, and the adolescent brain. *Science, 305,* 596–599.

Bedi, G., & Goddard, C. (2007). Intimate partner violence: What are the impacts on children? *Australian Psychologist, 42,* 66–77.

Behrendt, N., Buhl, N., & Seidl, S. (2002). The lethal paraphiliac syndrome: Accidental autoerotic deaths in four women and a review of the literature. *International Journal of Legal Medicine, 116,* 148–152.

Belenko, S., DeMatteo, D., & Patapis, N. (2007). Drug courts. In D. W. Spring & A. R. Roberts (Eds.), *Handbook of forensic mental health with victims and offenders: Assessment, treatment, and research.* New York: Springer.

Belenko, S., & Peugh, J. (2005). Estimating drug treatment needs among prison inmates. *Drug and Alcohol Dependence, 77,* 269–281.

Bell, B. G., & Grubin, D. (2010). Functional magnetic reasonance imaging may promote theoretical understanding of the polygraph test. *Journal of Forensic Psychiatry & Psychology, 21,* 52–65.

Bell, D. J. (1982). Policewomen: Myths and reality. *Journal of Police Science and Administration, 10,* 112–120.

Bem, D. J., & Allen, A. (1974). On predicting some of the people some of the time: The search for cross-situational consistencies in behavior. *Psychological Review, 81,* 506–520.

Ben-Shakhar, G. (2002). A critical review of the Control Question Test (CQT). In M. Kleiner (Ed.), *Handbook of polygraph testing.* San Diego: Academic Press.

Ben-Shakhar, G. (2008). The case against the use of polygraph examinations to monitor post-conviction sex offenders. *Legal and Criminological Psychology, 13,* 191–207.

Ben-Shakhar, G., & Dolev, K. (1996). Psychophysiological detection through the guilty knowledge technique: The effects of mental countermeasures. *Journal of Applied Psychology, 81,* 273–281.

Benson, E. (2002, November). The perils of going solo. *Monitor on Psychology, 33,* 25.

Berliner, L. (1998). The use of expert testimony in child sexual abuse cases. In S. J. Ceci & H. Hembrooke (Eds.), *Expert witnesses in child abuse cases.* Washington, DC: American Psychological Association.

Bernal, G., & Sharrón-Del-Río, M. R. (2001). Are empirically supported treatments valid for ethnic minorities? Toward an alternative approach for treatment research. *Cultural Diversity and Ethnic Minority Psychology, 7,* 328–342.

Bernard, T. (1992). *The cycle of juvenile justice.* New York: Oxford University Press.

Bernat, J. A., Cahoun, K. S., Adams, H. E., & Zeichner, A. (2001). Homophobia and physical aggression toward homosexual and heterosexual individuals. *Journal of Abnormal Psychology, 110,* 179–187.

Bernfeld, G. A. (2001). The struggle for treatment integrity in a "dis-integrated" service delivery system. In G. A. Bernfeld, D. P. Farrington, & A. W. Leschied (Eds.), *Offender rehabilitation in practice.* Chichester, UK: Wiley.

Bersoff, D. N., Goodman-Delahunty, J., Grisso, J. T., Hans, V. P., Poythress, N. G., & Roesch, R. G. (1997). Training in law and psychology: Models from the Villanova Conference. *American Psychologist, 52,* 1301–1310.

Berson, S. B. (2010, June). Prosecuting elder abuse cases. *NIJ Journal, 265,* 8–9.

Beune, K., Giebels, E., & Taylor, P. J. (2010). Patterns of interaction in police interviews: The role of cultural dependency. *Criminal Justice and Behavior, 37,* 904–925.

Beutler, L. E. (1998). Identifying empirically supported treatments: What if we didn't? *Journal of Consulting and Clinical Psychology, 66,* 113–120.

Bingham, R. P., Porché-Burke, L., James, S., Sue, D. W., & Vasquez, M. J. T. (2002). Introduction: A report on the National Multicultural Conference and Summit II. *Cultural Diversity and Ethnic Minority Psychology, 8,* 75–87.

Bishop, D. M. (2000). Juvenile offenders in the adult criminal justice system. *Crime and Justice: A Review of Research, 27,* 81–167.

Black, H. C. (1990). *Black's law dictionary* (6th ed.). St. Paul, MN: West.

Black, J. (2000). Personality testing and police selection: Utility of the "Big Five." *New Zealand Journal of Psychology, 29,* 2–9.

Blackburn, R. (1993). *The psychology of criminal conduct.* Chichester, UK: Wiley.

Blanchard, R., Klassen, P., Dickey, R., Kuban, M. E., & Blak, T. (2001). Sensitivity and specificity of the phallometric test for pedophilia in nonadmitting sex offenders. *Psychological Assessment, 13,* 118–126.

Blum, J., Ireland, M., & Blum, R. W. (2003). Gender differences in juvenile violence: A report from Add Health. *Journal of Adolescent Health, 32,* 234–240.

Blumberg, M. (1997). Controlling police use of deadly force: Assessing two decades of progress. In R. G. Dunham & G. P. Alpert (Eds.), *Critical issues in policing: Contemporary readings* (3rd ed.). Prospect Heights, IL: Waveland.

Bobo, L. D., & Kluegel, J. (1997). The color line, the dilemma, and the dream: Racial attitudes and relations in American at the close of the twentieth century. In J. Higham (Ed.), *Civil rights and social wrongs: Black–White relations since World War II.* University Park: Pennsylvania State University Press.

Boccaccini, M. T. (2002). What do we really know about witness preparation? *Behavioral Sciences & the Law, 20,* 161–189.

Boccaccini, M. T., & Brodsky, S. L. (2002). Believability of expert and lay witnesses: Implications for trial consultation. *Professional Psychology: Research and Practice, 33,* 384–388.

Boer, D., Hart, S., Kropp, P., & Webster, C. (1997). *Manual for the Sexual Violence Risk-20 (SVR-20).* Vancouver, BC, Canada: Family Violence Institute.

Boes, J. O., Chandler, C. J., & Timm, H. W. (2001, December). *Police integrity: Use of personality measures to identify corruption-prone officers.* Monterey, CA: Defense Personnel Security Research Center.

Boeschen, L. E., Sales, B. D., & Koss, M. P. (1998). Rape trauma experts in the courtroom. *Psychology, Public Policy, and Law, 4,* 414–432.

Bohm, R. M. (1999). Deathquest: An introduction to the theory and practice of capital punishment in the United States. Cincinnati, OH: Anderson.

Bohner, G., Jarvis, C. I., Eyssel, F., & Siebler, F. (2005). The causal impact of rape myth acceptance on men's rape proclivity: Comparing sexually coercive and noncoercive men. *European Journal of Social Psychology, 35,* 819–828.

Boney-McCoy, S., & Finkelhor, D. (1995). Psychosocial sequelae of violent victimization in a national youth sample. *Journal of Consulting and Clinical Psychology, 63,* 726–736.

Bonnie, R. J. (1990). Dilemmas in administering the death penalty: Conscientious abstentions, professional ethics, and the needs of the legal system. *Law and Human Behavior, 14,* 67–90.

Bonnie, R. J. (1992). The competence of criminal defendants: A theoretical reformulation. *Behavioral Sciences & the Law, 10,* 291–316.

Bonnie, R. J., & Grisso, T. (2000). Adjudicative competence and youthful offenders. In T. Grisso & R. Schwartz (Eds.), *Youth on trial: A developmental perspective on juvenile justice.* Chicago: University of Chicago Press.

Bonta, J. (1996). Risk-needs assessment and treatment. In A. T. Harland (Ed.), *Choosing correctional options that work: Defining the demand and evaluating the supply.* Thousand Oaks, CA: Sage.

Bonta, J. (2002). Offender risk assessment: Guidelines for selection and use. *Criminal Justice and Behavior, 29,* 355–379.

Bonta, J., Wallace-Capretta, S., & Rooney, J. (2000). A quasi-experimental evaluation of an intensive rehabilitation supervision program. *Criminal Justice and Behavior, 27,* 312–329.

Boothby, J. L., & Clements, C. B. (2000). A national survey of correctional psychologists. *Criminal Justice and Behavior, 27,* 716–732.

Boothby, J. L., & Clements, C. B. (2002). Job satisfaction of correctional psychologists: Implications for recruitment and retention. *Professional Psychology: Research and Practice, 33,* 310–315.

Borduin, C. M., Schaeffer, C. M., & Heiblum, N. (2009). A randomized clinical trial of multisystemic therapy with juvenile sexual offenders: Effects on youth social ecology and criminal activity. *Journal of Consulting and Clinical Psychology, 77,* 26–37.

Borum, R. (1996). Improving the clinical practice of violence risk assessment: Technology, guidelines, and training. *American Psychologist, 51,* 945–956.

Borum R., Bartel, P. A., & Forth, A. E. (2005). Structured assessment of violence risk in youth. In T. Grisso, G. Vincent, & D. Seagrave (Eds.), *Mental health screening and assessment in juvenile justice.* New York: Guilford.

Borum, R., Deane, M. W., Steadman, H. J., & Morrissey, J. (1998). Police perspectives on responding to mentally ill people in crisis: Perceptions of program effectiveness. *Behavioral Sciences and the Law, 16,* 393–405.

Borum, R., Fein, R., Vossekuil, B., & Berglund, J. (1999). Threat assessment: Defining an approach for evaluating risk of targeted violence. *Behavioral Sciences and the Law, 17,* 323–337.

Borum, R., & Fulero, S. M. (1999). Empirical research on the insanity defense and attempted reforms: Evidence toward informed policy. *Law and Human Behavior, 23,* 375–394.

Borum, R., & Grisso, T. (1995). Psychological tests used in criminal forensic evaluations. *Professional Psychology: Research and Practice, 26,* 465–473.

Borum R., Lodewijks, H., Bartel, P. A., & Forth, A. E. (2010). Structured Assessment of Violence Risk in Youth (SAVRY). In R. L. Otto, & K. S. Douglas (Eds.), *Handbook of violence risk assessment: International perspectives on forensic mental health.* New York: Routledge/Taylor & Francis Group.

Borum, R., & Philpot, C. (1993). Therapy with law enforcement couples: Clinical management of the "high-risk lifestyle." *American Journal of Family Therapy, 21,* 122–135.

Borum, R., & Strentz, T. (1993, April). The borderline personality: Negotiation strategies. *FBI Law Enforcement Bulletin,* pp. 6–10.

Bosco, D., Zappalà, A., & Santtila, P. (2010). The admissibility of offender profiling in courtroom: A review of legal issues and court opinions. *International Journal of Law and Psychiatry, 33,* 184–191.

Bourke, M., & Hernandez, A. E. (2009). The "Butner Study" redux: A report of the incidence of hands-on child victimization by child pornography offenders. *Journal of Family Violence, 24,* 182–191.

Bow, J. N., & Quinnell, F. A. (2001). Psychologists' current practices and procedures in child custody evaluations five years after American Psychological Association guidelines. *Professional Psychology: Research and Practice, 32,* 261–268.

Bradford, J. M. W. (1993). The pharmacological treatment of the adolescent sex offender. New York: Guilford Press.

Bradshaw, J. (2008, July/August). Behavioral detectives patrol airports. *The National Psychologist,* p. 10.

Braffman, W., & Kirsch, I. (1999). Imaginative suggestibility and hypnotizability: An empirical analysis. *Journal of Personality and Social Psychology, 77,* 578–587.

Brakel, S. J. (2003). Competency to stand trial: Rationalism, "contextualism" and other modest theories. *Behavioral Sciences and the Law, 21,* 285–295.

Breitmeier, D., Mansouri, F., Albrecht, K., Böhm, U., Tröger, H. D., & Kleemann, W. J. (2003). Accidental autoerotic deaths between 1978 and 1997. Institute of Legal Medicine, Medical School Hannover. *Forensic Science International, 137,* 41–44.

Brennan, P. A., Hall, J., Bor, W., Najman, J. M., & Williams, G. (2003). Integrating biological and social processes in relation to early-onset persistent aggression in boys and girls. *Developmental Psychology, 39,* 309–323.

Brennan, T., Dieterich, W., & Ehret, B. (2009). Evaluating the predictive validity of the COMPAS risk and needs assessment system. *Criminal Justice and Behavior, 36,* 21–40.

Brent, D. A. (1989). The psychological autopsy: Methodological issues for the study of adolescent suicide. *Suicide and Life-Threatening Behavior, 19,* 43–57.

Breslau, N. (2002). Epidemiologic studies of trauma, posttraumatic stress disorder, and other psychiatric disorders. *Canadian Journal of Psychiatry, 47,* 923–929.

Bresler, S. A. (2010, Summer). The fitness for duty assessment: An evaluation well-suited for the forensic psychologist. *American Psychology-Law Society News.* Washington, DC: American Psychological Association.

Bricklin, B., & Elliot, G. (1995). Postdivorce issues and relevant research. In B. Bricklin (Ed.), *The child custody evaluation handbook: Research-based solutions and applications.* New York: Bruner/Mazel.

Briere, J. (1988). The long-term clinical correlates of childhood sexual victimization. *Annals of the New York Academy of Science, 528,* 327–334.

Briere, J., Malamuth, N., & Ceniti, J. (1981). Self-assessed rape proclivity: Attitudinal and sexual correlates. Paper presented at the American Psychological Association meeting, Los Angeles.

Briere, J., & Runtz, M. (1989). University males' sexual interest in children: Predicting potential indices of "pedophilia" in a non-forensic sample. *Child Abuse & Neglect, 13,* 65–75.

Brigham, J. C. (1999). What is forensic psychology, anyway? *Law and Human Behavior, 23,* 273–298.

Brink, J., Doherty, D., & Boer, A. (2001). Mental disorder in federal offenders: A Canadian prevalence study. *International Journal of Law and Psychiatry, 24,* 339–356.

British Psychological Society. (1995). *Recovered memories: The report of the working party of the British Psychological Society.* Leicester, UK: Author.

British Psychological Society. (2004, October 6). *A review of the current scientific status and fields of application of polygraph detection.* Leicester, UK: Author.

Brocki, K. C., Eninger, L., Thorell, L. B., & Bohlin, G. (2010). Interrelations between executive function and symptoms of hyperactivity/impulsivity and inattention in preschoolers: A two-year longitudinal study. *Journal of Abnormal Child Psychology, 38,* 163–171.

Brodsky, S. L. (1980). Ethical issues for psychologists in corrections. In J. Monahan (Ed.), *Who is the client? The ethics of psychological intervention in the criminal justice system.* Washington, DC: American Psychological Association.

Brodsky, S. L. (1991). *Testifying in court: Guidelines and maxims for the expert witness.* Washington, DC: American Psychological Association.

Brodsky, S. L. (1999). *The expert expert witness: More maxims for the expert witness.* Washington, DC: American Psychological Association.

Brodsky, S. L. (2004). *Coping with cross-examination and other pathways to effective testimony.* Washington, DC: American Psychological Association.

Bronfenbrenner, U. (1979). *The ecology of human development: Experiment by nature and design.* Cambridge, MA: Harvard University Press.

Brooks, L. W. (1997). Police discretionary behavior: A study of style. In R. G. Dunham & G. P. Alpert (Eds.), *Critical issues in policing: Contemporary readings* (3rd ed.). Prospect Heights, IL: Waveland.

Brown, B. B., & Harris, P. B. (1989). Residential burglary victimization: Reactions to the invasion of a primary territory. *Journal of Environmental Psychology, 9,* 119–132.

Brown, M. L. (1997). Dilemmas facing nurses who care for Munchausen syndrome by proxy. *Pediatric Nursing, 23,* 416–418.

Brown, R., & Kulik, J. (1977). Flashbulb memories. *Cognition, 5,* 73–99.

Brown, S. L., & Forth, A. E. (1997). Psychopathy and sexual assault: Static risk factors, emotional precursors, and rapists subtypes. *Journal of Consulting and Clinical Psychology, 65,* 848–857.

Brown, T. L., Borduin, C. M., & Henggeler, S. W. (2001). Treating juvenile offenders in community settings. In J. B. Ashford, B. D. Sales, & W. H. Reid (Eds.), *Treating adult and juvenile offenders with special needs.* Washington, DC: American Psychological Association.

Browne, A., & Finkelhor, D. (1986). Impact of child sexual abuse: A review of the research. *Psychological Bulletin, 99,* 66–77.

Bruck, M., & Ceci, S. J. (2004). Forensic developmental psychology: Unveiling four common misconceptions. *Current Directions in Psychological Science, 13,* 229–232.

Bruck, M., Ceci, S. J., & Francoeur, E. (2000). Children's use of anatomically detailed dolls to report genital touching in a medical examination. *Journal of Experimental Psychology: Applied, 6,* 74–83.

Buckner, J. C., Mezzacappa, E., & Beardslee, W. R. (2003). Characteristics of resilient youths living in poverty: The role of self-regulatory processes. *Development and Psychopathology, 15,* 139–162.

Budd, J. W., Arvey, R. D., & Lawless, P. (1996). Correlates and consequences of workplace violence. *Journal of Occupational Health Psychology, 1,* 197–210.

Budd, K. S., Felix, E. D., Poindexter, L. M., Naik-Polan, A. T., & Sloss, C. F. (2002). Clinical assessment of children in child protection cases: An empirical analysis. *Professional Psychology: Research and Practice, 33,* 3–12.

Budnick, K. J., & Shields-Fletcher, E. (1998). *What about girls?* Washington, DC: U.S. Department of Justice, Office of Juvenile Justice and Delinquency Prevention.

Buh, E. S., & Ladd, G. W. (2001). Peer rejection as an antecedent of young children's school adjustment: An examination of mediating processes. *Developmental Psychology, 37,* 550–560.

Bull, R., & Milne, R. (2004). Attempts to improve the police interviewing of suspects. In D. Lassiter (Ed.), *Interrogations, confessions, and entrapment.* New York: Kluwer Academic.

Bull, R., & Soukara, S. (2010). Four studies of what really happens in police interviews. In G. D. Lassiter & C. A. Meissner (Eds.), *Police interrogations and false confessions: Current research, practice, and policy recommendations.* Washington, DC: American Psychological Association.

Bumby, K. M. (1993). Reviewing the guilty but mentally ill alternative: A case of the blind "pleading" the blind. *Journal of Psychiatry and Law, 21,* 191–220.

Bumby, K. M., & Bumby, N. H. (1997). Adolescent female sexual offenders. In H. R. Cellini & B. Schwartz (Eds.), *The sex offender: New insights, treatment innovations and legal developments* (Vol. 2). Kingston, NJ: Civil Research Institute.

Burdon, W. M., & Gallagher, C. A. (2002). Coercion and sex offenders: Controlling sex-offending behavior through incapacitation and treatment. *Criminal Justice and Behavior, 29,* 87–109.

Bureau of Justice Assistance. (2001, June). *Recruiting & retaining women: A self-assessment guide for law enforcement.* Washington, DC: U.S. Department of Justice.

Bureau of Justice Statistics. (1993). *Law Enforcement Management and Administrative Statistics (LEMAS) survey.* Washington, DC: U.S. Department of Justice.

Bureau of Justice Statistics. (2001a). *Prisoners in 2000.* Washington, DC: U.S. Department of Justice.

Bureau of Justice Statistics. (2001b, December). *Violence in the workplace, 1993–1999.* Washington, DC: U.S. Department of Justice, Bureau of Justice Statistics.

Bureau of Justice Statistics. (2002a). *Corrections statistics.* Retrieved December 5, 2010, from http://www.ojp.usdoj.gov/bjs/correct.htm.

Bureau of Justice Statistics. (2002b). *National Crime Victimization Survey.* Washington, DC: U.S. Department of Justice.

Bureau of Justice Statistics. (2002c). *Recidivism of prisoners released in 1994.* Washington, DC: U.S. Department of Justice.

Bureau of Labor Statistics. (1999). *National census of fatal occupational injuries, 1998.* Washington, DC: U.S. Department of Labor.

Burgess, A. W., & Hazelwood, R. (Eds.). (1995). *Practical aspects of rape investigation: A multidisciplinary approach* (2nd ed.). New York: CRC Press.

Burgess, A. W., & Holmstrom, L. L. (1974). Rape trauma syndrome. *American Journal of Psychiatry, 131,* 981–986.

Burgess, A. W., Hartman, C. R., & Ressler, R. K. (1986). Sexual homicide: A motivational model. *Journal of Interpersonal Violence, 1,* 251–272.

Burns, B. J., Schoenwald, S. K., Burchard, J. D., Faw, L., & Santos, A. B. (2000). Comprehensive community-based interventions for youth with severe emotional disorders: Multisystemic therapy and the wraparound process. *Journal of Child and Family Studies, 9,* 283–314.

Buss, E. (2000). The role of lawyers in promoting juveniles' competence as defendants. In T. Grisso & R. G. Schwartz (Eds.), *Youth on trial: A developmental perspective on juvenile justice.* Chicago: University of Chicago Press.

Butcher, J. N., & Miller, K. B. (1999). Personality assessment in personal injury litigation. In A. K. Hess & I. B. Weiner (Eds.), The handbook of forensic psychology (2nd ed.). New York: Wiley.

Butler, W. M., Leitenberg, H., & Fuselier, G. D. (1993). The use of mental health professional consultants to police hostage negotiation teams. *Behavioral Sciences and the Law, 11,* 213–221.

Caillouet, B. A., Boccaccini, M., Varela, J. G., Davis, R. D., & Rostow, C. D. (2010). Predictive validity of the MMPI-2 Psy 5 scales and facets for law enforcement employment outcomes. *Criminal Justice and Behavior, 37,* 217–238.

California Occupational Safety and Health Administration. (1995). *Guidelines for workplace security.* Sacramento, CA: Author.

California Youth Authority. (1997). *LEAD: A boot camp and intensive parole program: Final impact evaluation.* Sacramento: Author.

Call, J. A. (2008). Psychological consultation in hostage/barricade crisis negotiation. In H. V. Hall (Ed.), *Forensic psychology and neuropsychology for criminal and civil cases.* Boca Raton, FL: CRC Press.

Callahan, L. A., Steadman, H. J., McGreevy, M. A., & Robbins, P. C. (1991). The volume and characteristics of insanity defense pleas: An eight-state study. *Bulletin of Psychiatry and the Law, 19,* 331–338.

Caillouet, B. A., Boccaccini, M., Varela, J. G., Davis, R. D., & Rostow, C. D. (2010). Predictive validity of the MMPI-2 Psy 5 scales and facets for law enforcement employment outcomes. *Criminal Justice and Behavior, 37,* 217–238.

Campbell, J. C. (1995). Prediction of homicide of and by battered women. In J. C. Campbell (Ed.), *Assessing dangerousness: Violence by sexual offenders, batterers, and child abusers.* Thousand Oaks, CA: Sage.

Campbell, T. W. (2003). Sex offenders and actuarial risk assessments: Ethical considerations. *Behavioral Sciences and the Law, 21,* 269–279.

Canter, D. (1995). Criminal shadows: Inside the mind of the serial killer. London: HarperCollins.

Canter, D. (1999). Equivocal death. In D. Canter & L. J. Alison (Eds.), *Profiling in policy and practice.* Burlington, VT: Ashgate.

Canter, D., & Alison, L. (2000). Profiling property crimes. In D. Canter & L. J. Alison (Eds.), *Profiling property crimes.* Burlington, VT: Ashgate.

Capps, J. G., & Ryan, A. (2005, Summer). It's not just polygraph anymore. *Psychological Science Agenda,* 9–10.

Carlson, E. H., & Dutton, M. A. (2003). Assessing experiences and responses of crime victims. *Journal of Traumatic Stress, 16,* 133–148.

Carter, R. T., & Forsyth, J. M. (2007). Examining race and culture in psychology journals: The case of forensic psychology. *Professional Psychology: Research and Practice, 38,* 133–142.

Castle, T., & Hensley, C. (2002). Serial killers with military experience: Applying learning theory to serial murder. *International Journal of Offender Therapy and Comparative Criminology, 46,* 453–465.

Cattaneo, L. B., & Goodman, L. A. (2005). Risk factors for reabuse in intimate partner violence: A cross-disciplinary critical review. *Trauma, Violence, and Abuse, 6,* 141–175.

Ceci, S. J., & Bruck, M. (1993). The suggestibility of the child witness: A historical review and synthesis. *Psychological Bulletin, 113,* 403–439.

Ceci, S. J., Ross, D. F., & Toglia, M. P. (1987). Suggestibility of children's memory: Psycholegal implications. *Journal of Experimental Psychology: General, 116,* 38–49.

Cellini, H. R. (1995). Assessment and treatment of the adolescent sexual offender. In B. Schwartz & H. R. Cellini (Eds.), *The sex offender: Corrections, treatment and legal practice* (Vol. 1). Kingston, NJ: Civil Research Institute.

Cellini, H. R., Schwartz, B., & Readio, S. (1993, December). *Child sexual abuse: An administrator's nightmare.* Washington, DC: National School Safety Center.

Centers for Disease Control and Prevention. (2008). Unintentional strangulation deaths from the "choking game" among youths aged 6–19 years—United States, 1995–2007. *Morbidity and Mortality Weekly Report, 57,* 141–144.

Chaiken, J. M. (Ed.) (1999, February). Foreword. *American Indians and crime* [Department of Justice publication]. Washington, DC: U.S. Department of Justice.

Chaiken, M. R. (2000, March). Violent neighborhoods, violent kids. *Juvenile Justice Bulletin,* 6–18. Washington, DC: U.S. Department of Justice.

Chandler, J. T. (1990). Modern police psychology: For law enforcement and human behavior professionals. Springfield, IL: Charles C Thomas.

Chapleau, K. M., & Oswald, D. L. (2010). Power, sex, and rape myth acceptance: Testing two models of rape proclivity. *Journal of Sex Research, 47,* 66–78.

Chappelle, W., & Rosengren, K. (2001). Maintaining composure and credibility as an expert witness during cross-examination. *Journal of Forensic Psychology Practice, 1,* 51–67.

Chen, Y-H., Arria, A., & Anthony, J. C. (2003). Firesetting in adolescents and being aggressive, shy, and rejected by peers: New epidemiologic evidence from a national sample survey. *Journal of the American Academy of Psychiatry and Law, 31,* 44–52.

Chenoweth, J. H. (1961). Situational tests: A new attempt at assessing police candidates. *Journal of Criminal Law, Criminology, and Police Science, 52,* 232–238.

Chesney-Lind, M., & Shelden, R. G. (1998). *Girls, delinquency, and juvenile justice* (2nd ed.). Belmont, CA: West/Wadsworth.

Chiancone, J. (2001, December). Parental abduction: Review of the literature. *Juvenile Justice Bulletin,* 14–18. Washington, DC: Office of Juvenile Justice and Delinquency Prevention.

Child Abuse Prevention Center. (1998). *Shaken baby syndrome fatalities in the United States.* Ogden, UT: Author.

Chiroro, P., & Valentine, T. (1995). An investigation of the contact hypothesis of the own-race bias in face recognition. *Quarterly Journal of Experimental Psychology, 48A,* 979–894.

Cirincione, C., Steadman, H., & McGreevy, M. (1995). Rates of insanity acquittals and the factors associated with successful insanity pleas. *Bulletin of the American Academy of Psychiatry and Law, 23,* 399–409.

Civil Aeronautics Board. (1975). *Supplement to the handbook of airline statistics.* Springfield, VA: National Information Service.

Clark, K. (2002, May/June). Data recovery: The forensics wave of the future. *The Forensic Examiner, 11,* 36–37.

Clay, R. A. (2009, November). Postgrad growth area: Forensic psychology. *GradPSYCH,* 35–36.

Clear, T. R., & Cole, G. F. (2000). *American corrections* (5th ed.). Belmont, CA: West/Wadsworth.

Cleckley, H. (1941). *The mask of sanity.* St. Louis, MO: C. V. Mosby.

Cochrane, R. E., Grisso, T., & Frederick, R. I. (2001). The relationship between criminal charges, diagnoses, and psycholegal opinions among federal defendants. *Behavioral Sciences & the Law, 19,* 565–582.

Cochrane, R. E., Tett, R. P., & Vandecreek, L. (2003). Psychological testing and the selection of police officers: A national survey. *Criminal Justice and Behavior, 30,* 511–527.

Cohen, F. (1998). *The mentally disordered inmate and the law.* Kingston, NJ: Civic Research Institute.

Cohen, F. (2000). The mentally disordered inmate and the law, 2000–2001 supplement. Kingston, NJ: Civic Research Institute.

Cohen, F. (2003). The mentally disordered inmate and the law, 2003 cumulative supplement. Kingston, NJ: Civic Research Institute.

Cohen, F. (2008). *The mentally disordered inmate and the law* (2nd ed.). Kingston, NJ: Civic Research Institute.

Cohen, M. E., & Carr, W. J. (1975). Facial recognition and the von Restorff effect. *Bulletin of the Psychonomic Society, 6,* 383–384.

Cohen, M. L., Garafalo, R., Boucher, R., & Seghorn, T. (1971). The psychology of rapists. *Seminars in Psychiatry, 3,* 307–327.

Cohen, M. L., Seghorn, T., & Calmas, W. (1969). Sociometric study of the sex offender. *Journal of Abnormal Psychology, 74,* 249–255.

Cohen, N. J. (2001). Language development and psychopathology in infants, children, and adolescents. Thousand Oaks, CA: Sage.

Cohen, P., Cohen, J., & Brook, J. (1993). An epidemiological study of disorders in late childhood and adolescence: II. Persistent disorders. *Journal of Child Psychology and Psychiatry, 34,* 869–877.

Cohn, Y. (1974). Crisis intervention and the victim of robbery. In I. Drapkin & E. Viano (Eds.), *Victimology: A new focus* Lexington, MA: Lexington Books.

Coid, J. W. (2003). Formulating strategies for the primary prevention of adult antisocial behaviour: "High risk" or "population" strategies. In D. F. Farrington & J. W. Coid (Eds.), *Early prevention of adult antisocial behaviour* Cambridge, UK: Cambridge University Press.

Coie, J. D., Belding, M., & Underwood, M. (1988). Aggression and peer rejection in childhood. In B. Lahey & A. Kazdin (Eds.), *Advances in clinical child psychology* (Vol. 2). New York: Plenum.

Coie, J. D., Dodge, K., & Kupersmith, J. (1990). Peer group behavior and social status. In S. R. Asher & J. D. Coie (Eds.), *Peer rejection in childhood* (). Cambridge, UK: Cambridge University Press.

Coie, J. D., & Miller-Johnson, S. (2001). Peer factors and interventions. In R. Loeber & D. P. Farrington (Eds.), *Child delinquents: Development, intervention, and service needs* (). Thousand Oaks, CA: Sage.

Cole, G. F., & Smith, C. E. (2001). *The American system of criminal justice* (9th ed.). Belmont, CA: Wadsworth/Thompson.

Collins, W. C. (2004). *Supermax prisons and the Constitution: Liability concerns in the extended control unit.* Washington, DC: National Institute of Corrections, U.S. Department of Justice.

Comer, R. J. (2004). *Abnormal psychology* (5th ed.). New York: Worth.

Committee on Ethical Guidelines for Forensic Psychologists. (1991). Specialty guidelines for forensic psychologists. *Law and Human Behavior, 15,* 655–665.

Committee on the Revision of the Specialty Guidelines for Forensic Psychology (2006). *Specialty guidelines for forensic psychologists* (second official draft). Retrieved December 13, 2006, from http://www.ap-ls.org/links/SGFP%20January%202006.pdf.

Committee on the Revision of the Specialty Guidelines for Forensic Psychology (2010). *Specialty guidelines for forensic psychology* (fifth draft 8/1/10). Retrieved November 20, 2010, from http://www.ap-ls.org/aboutpsychlaw/080110sgfpdraft.pdf.

Conley, J. M. (2000). Epilogue: A legal and cultural commentary on the psychology of jury instructions. *Psychology, Public Policy, and Law, 6,* 822–831.

Connor, D. F., Steeber, J., & McBurnett, K. (2010). A review of attention-deficit/hyperactivity disorder complicated by symptoms of oppositional defiant disorder or conduct disorder. *Journal of Developmental & Behavioral Pediatrics, 31,* 427–440.

Consigli, J. E. (2002). Post-conviction sex offender testing and the American Polygraph Association. In M. Kleiner (Ed.), *Handbook of polygraph testing.* San Diego, CA: Academic Press.

Cooke, D. J., & Michie, C. (1997). An item response theory analysis of the Hare Psychopathy Checklist—Revised. *Psychological Assessment, 9,* 3–14.

Cooke, D. J., & Michie, C. (2001). Refining the construct of psychopathy: Toward a hierarchical model. *Psychological Assessment, 13,* 171–188.

Cooke, D. J., Michie, C., Hart, S. D., & Hare, R. D. (1999). Evaluation of the screening version of the Hare Psychopathy Checklist—Revised (PCL-SV): An item response theory analysis. *Psychological Assessment, 11,* 3–13.

Cooley, C. M. (2008). Criminal profiling on trial: The admissibility of criminal profiling evidence. In B. E. Turvey (Ed.), *Criminal profiling: An introduction to behavioral evidence analysis.* Amsterdam: Elsevier/Academic Press.

Cooper, J., & Neuhaus, I. M. (2000). The "hired gun" affect: Assessing the effect of pay, frequency of testifying, and credentials on the perception of expert testimony. *Law and Human Behavior, 24,* 149–171.

Cooper, V. G., & Zapf, P. A. (2008). Psychiatric patients' comprehension of Miranda rights. *Law and Human Behavior, 32,* 390–405.

Copson, G. (1995). *Coals to Newcastle? Part I: A study of offender profiling.* London: Home Office, Police Research Group.

Cornwell, P. (2002). *Portrait of a killer: Jack the Ripper—case closed.* New York: Putnam.

Correctional Services of Canada. (1990). *Forum on corrections research, 2*(1) [Entire issue]. Ottawa, ON, Canada: Author.

Correia, K. M. (2001). *A handbook for correctional psychologists.* Springfield, IL: Charles C Thomas.

Cortina, L. M. (2001). Assessing sexual harassment among Latinas: Development of an instrument. *Cultural Diversity and Ethnic Minority Psychology, 7,* 164–181.

Coscina, D. V. (1997). The biopsychology of impulsivity: Focus on brain serotonin. In C. D. Webster & M. A. Jackson (Eds.), *Impulsivity: Theory, assessment, and treatment.* New York: Guilford Press.

Costa, P. T., & McCrae, R. R. (1992). NEO PI-R: The Revised NEO Personality Inventory. Odessa, FL: Psychological Assessment Resources.

Cowan, P. A., & Cowan, C. P. (2004). From family relationships to peer rejection to antisocial behavior in middle childhood. In J. B. Kupersmidt & K. A. Dodge (Eds.), *Children's peer relations: From development to intervention.* Washington, DC: American Psychological Association.

Cowell, D. D. (2009). Autoerotic asphyxiation: Secret pleasure lethal outcome? *Pediatrics, 124,* 1319–1324.

Cox, J. F., Landsberg, G., & Paravati, M. P. (1989). A practical guide for mental health providers in local jails. In H. J. Steadman, D. W. McCarty, & J. P. Morrissey (Eds.), *The mentally ill in jail: Planning for essential services.* New York: Guilford Press.

Crawford, N. (2002, November). Science-based program curbs violence in kids. *Monitor on Psychology, 33,* 38–39.

Crespi, T. D. (1990). School psychologists in forensic psychology: Converging and diverging issues. *Professional Psychology: Research and Practice, 21,* 83–87.

Cromwell, P. F., Killinger, G. C., Kerper, H. B., & Walker, C. (1985). *Probation and parole in the criminal justice system* (2nd ed.). St. Paul, MN: West.

Cromwell, P. F., Olson, J. F., & Avary, D. W. (1991). *Breaking and entering: An ethnographic analysis of burglary.* Newbury Park, CA: Sage.

Cruise, K., & Rogers, R. (1998). An analysis of competency to stand trial: An integration of case law and clinical knowledge. *Behavioral Sciences and the Law, 16,* 35–50.

Cruz, N. S. (2010, June 10). Minority population growing in the United States, Census estimates show. *Los Angeles Times,* p. A1.

Cuellar, A. E., Snowden, L. M., & Ewing, T. (2007). Criminal records of persons served in the public mental health system. *Psychiatric Services, 58,* 114–120.

Cullen, F. T., & Gendreau, P. (2000). Assessing correctional rehabilitation: Policy, practice, and prospects. In J. Horney (Ed.), *Criminal justice 2000: Vol. 3. Policies, processes, and decisions of the criminal justice system.* Washington, DC: National Institute of Justice.

Cullen, F. T., Wright, J. P., & Applegate, B. K. (1996). Control in the community: The limits of reform? In A. T. Harland (Ed.), *Choosing correctional options that work: Defining the demand and evaluating the supply.* Thousand Oaks, CA: Sage.

Cummings, E. M., El-Sheikh, M., Kouros, C. D., & Buckhalt, J. A. (2009). Children and violence: The role of children's regulation in the marital aggression–child adjustment link. *Clinical Child and Family Psychological Review, 12,* 3–15.

Cunningham, M. D., & Reidy, T. J. (1998). Integrating base rate data in violence risk assessments at capital sentencing. *Behavioral Sciences & the Law, 16,* 71–96.

Cunningham, M. D., & Reidy, T. J. (1999). Don't confuse me with the facts: Common errors in violence risk assessment at capital sentencing. *Criminal Justice and Behavior, 26,* 20–43.

Cunningham, M. D., Sorensen, J. R., Vigen, M. P., & Woods, S. O. (in press). *Criminal Justice and Behavior.*

Curtis, N. M., Ronan, K. R., Heiblum, N., & Crellin, K. (2009). Dissemination and effectiveness of multisystemic treatment in New Zealand: A benchmarking study. *Journal of Family Psychology, 23,* 119–129.

Cutler, B. L., & Penrod, S. D. (1995). *Mistaken identification: The eyewitness, psychology, and law.* New York: Cambridge University Press.

Cutler, B. L., Penrod, S. D., & Dexter, H. R. (1989). The eyewitness, the expert psychologist, and the jury. *Law and Human Behavior, 13,* 311–322.

Cutler, B. L., Penrod, S. D., & Martens, T. K. (1987). Improving the reliability of eyewitness identification: Putting content with context. *Journal of Applied Psychology, 72,* 629–637.

Dahlberg, L. L., & Potter, L. B. (2001). Youth violence: Developmental pathways and prevention challenges. *American Journal of Preventive Medicine, 20*(1s), 3–14.

Dailey, J. T., & Pickrel, E. W. (1975a, April). Federal Aviation Administration's behavioral research program for the defense against hijacking. *Aviation, Space and Environmental Medicine,* pp. 423–427.

Dailey, J. T., & Pickrel, E. W. (1975b). Some psychological contributions to defenses against hijackers. *American Psychologist, 30,* 161–165.

Daley, K. (2002). Restorative justice: The real story. *Punishment & Society, 4,* 55–79.

Dansie, E. J., & Fargo, J. D. (2009). Individual and community predictors of fear of criminal victimization: Results from a national sample of urban U.S. citizens. *Crime Prevention and Community Safety, 11,* 124–140.

Davidson, S. (2004, June/July). Litigation consultants: What happens when your client needs more than just an expert witness in a dispute resolution process. *CA Magazine,* pp. 42–44.

Davies, G., Morton, J., Mollon, P., & Robertson, N. (1998). Recovered memories in theory and practice. *Psychology, Public Policy, and Law, 4,* 1079–1090.

Day, A., & Casey, S. (2009). Values in forensic and correctional psychology. *Aggression and Violent Behavior, 14,* 232–238.

Day, K., & Berney, T. (2001). Treatment and care for offenders with mental retardation. In J. B. Ashford, B. D. Sales, & W. H. Reid (Eds.), *Treating adult and juvenile offenders with special needs.* Washington, DC: American Psychological Association.

Dean, K. E., & Malamuth, N. M. (1997). Characteristics of men who aggress sexually and of men who imagine aggressing: Risk and moderating variables. *Journal of Personality and Social Psychology, 72,* 449–455.

Deane, M. W., Steadman, H. J., Borum, R., Veysey, B. M., & Morrissey, J. P. (1999). Emerging partnerships between mental health and law enforcement. *Psychiatric Services, 50,* 99–101.

Deault, L. C. (2010). A systematic review of parenting in relation to the development of comorbidities and functional impairments in children with attention-deficit/hyperactivity disorder (ADHD). *Child Psychiatry and Human Development, 41,* 168–192.

DeHaan, J. (1997). *Kirk's fire investigation* (4th ed.). Upper Saddle River, NJ: Prentice Hall.

del Carmen, R. V., Parker, M., & Reddington, F. P. (1998). *Briefs of leading cases in juvenile justice.* Cincinnati, OH: Anderson.

Delprino, R. P., & Bahn, C. (1988). National survey of the extent and nature of psychological services in police departments. *Professional Psychology: Research and Practice, 19,* 421–425.

DeMatteo, D. (2005a, Winter). Legal update: An expansion of Tarasoff's duty to protect. *American Psychology-Law News, 25*(1), 2–3, 20.

DeMatteo, D. (2005b, Summer). Legal update: Juveniles and the death penalty. *American Psychology-Law News, 25*(2), 1, 6.

DeMatteo, D. (2005c, Fall). Legal update: "Supermax" prison: Constitutional challenges and mental health concerns. *American Psychology-Law News, 25*(3), 8–9.

DeMatteo, D. (2006, Winter). Legal Update: Problem-solving courts: Integrating treatment and criminal justice. *American Psychology-Law News, 26*(3), 10–11.

DeMatteo, D. (2007a, Summer). Competence to be executed: The Supreme Court stands poised to define the standard. *American Psychology-Law News, 27*(2), 1, 5.

DeMatteo, D. (2007b, Winter). The Supreme Court rules on the insanity defense and capital sentencing procedures. *American Psychology-Law News, 27*(1), 1, 5.

DeMatteo, D., Marczyk, G., Krauss, D. A., & Burl, J. (2009). Educational and training models in forensic psychology. *Training and Education in Professional Psychology, 3,* 184–191.

DeMatteo, D., Marlowe, D. B., Festinger, D. S., & Arabia, P. L. (2009). Outcome trajectories in drug courts: Do all participants have serious drug problems? *Criminal Justice and Behavior, 36,* 354–368.

Demir, B., Broussard, B., Goulding, S. M., & Compton, M. T. (2009). Beliefs about causes of schizophrenia among police officers before and after crisis intervention team training. *Community Mental Health, 45,* 385–392.

Department of Veterans Affairs. (1996). *Geropsychology assessment resource guide, 1996 revision.* Milwaukee, WI: National Center for Cost Containment.

Dern, H., Dern, C., Horn, A., & Horn, U. (2009). The fire behind the smoke: A reply to Snook and colleagues. *Criminal Justice and Behavior, 36,* 1085–1090.

Desmarais, S. L., & Reeves, K. A. (2007). Gray, black, and blue: The state of research and intervention for intimate partner abuse among elders. *Behavioral Sciences and the Law, 25,* 377–391.

Detrick, P., & Chibnall, J. T. (2006). NEO PI-R personality characteristics of high-performance entry-level police officers. *Psychological Services, 3,* 274–285.

Detrick, P., Chibnall, J. T., & Luebbert, M. C. (2004). The NEO PI-R as predictor of police academy performance. *Criminal Justice and Behavior, 31,* 676–694.

Detrick, P., Chibnall, J. T., & Rosso, M. (2001). Minnesota Multiphasic Personality Inventory—2 in police officer selection: Normative data and relation to the Inwald Personality Inventory. *Professional Psychology: Research and Practice, 32,* 481–490.

Developmental Disabilities Branch. (2000, December). *Attention-deficit/hyperactivity disorder.* Atlanta, GA: Centers for Disease Control and Prevention.

Dietz, A. S. (2000). Toward the development of a roles framework for police psychology. *Journal of Police and Criminal Psychology, 15,* 1–4.

Diliman, E. C. (1963). Role-playing as a technique in police selection. *Public Personnel Review, 24,* 116–118.

Dionne, G. (2005). Language development and aggressive behavior. In R. E. Tremblay, W. W. Hartup, & J. Archer (Eds.) (2005). *Developmental origins of aggression.* New York: Guilford Press.

Dionne, G., Tremblay, R., Boivin, M., Laplante, D., & Pérusse, D. (2003). Physical aggression and expressive vocabulary in 19-month-old twins. *Developmental Psychology, 39,* 261–273.

Dishion, T. J., & Bullock, B. M. (2002). Parenting and adolescent problem behavior: An ecological analysis of the nurturance hypothesis. In J. G. Borkowski, S. L. Ramey, & M. Bristol-Power (Eds.), *Parenting and the child's world: Influences on academic, intellectual, and social-emotional development.* Mahwah, NJ: Erlbaum.

Dittmann, M. (2002, December). Attracting more school psychology faculty. *Monitor on Psychology, 33,* 46–47.

Ditton, P. M. (1999). *Mental health and treatment of inmates and probationers.* Washington, DC: U.S. Department of Justice, Bureau of Justice Statistics.

Dixon, L., & Gill, B. (2002). Changes in the standards for admitting expert evidence in federal civil cases since the Daubert decision. Psychology, Public Policy, and Law, 8, 251–308.

Dobash, R. P., & Dobash, R. E. (2000). Feminist perspectives on victimization. In N. H. Rafter (Ed.), *Encyclopedia of women and crime.* Phoenix, AZ: Oryx.

Dobson, V., & Sales, B. (2000). The science of infanticide and mental illness. *Psychology, Public Policy, and Law, 4,* 1098–1112.

Dodge, K. A. (1993). Social-cognitive mechanisms in the development of conduct disorder and depression. *Annual Review of Psychology, 44,* 559–584.

Dodge, K. A. (2003). Do social information-processing patterns mediate aggressive behavior? In B. B. Lahey, T. E. Moffitt, & A. Caspi (Eds), *Causes of conduct disorder and juvenile delinquency.* New York: Guilford Press.

Dodge, K. A., & Pettit, G. S. (2003). A biopsychological model of the development of chronic conduct problems in adolescence. *Developmental Psychology, 39,* 349–371.

Donn, J. E., Routh, D. K., & Lunt, I. (2000). From Leipzig to Luxembourg (via Boulder and Vail): A history of clinical training in Europe and the United States. *Professional Psychology: Research and Practice, 31,* 423–428.

Donnellan, M. B., Ge, X., & Wenk, E. (2000). Cognitive abilities in adolescent-limited and life-course-persistent criminal offenders. *Journal of Abnormal Psychology, 109,* 396–402.

Doren, D. M. (2002). *Evaluating sex offenders.* Thousand Oaks, CA: Sage.

Dougher, M. J. (1995). Clinical assessment of sex offenders. In B. K. Schwartz & H. R. Cellini (Eds.), *The sex offender: Corrections, treatment and legal practice.* Kingston, NJ: Civic Research Institute.

Douglas, J. E., & Munn, C. (1992). The detection of staging and personation at the crime scene. In J. E. Douglas, A. W. Burgess, & R. K. Ressler (Eds.), *Crime classification manual.* New York: Lexington Books.

Douglas, J. E., Ressler, R. K., Burgess, A. W., & Hartman, C. R. (1986). Criminal profiling from crime scene analysis. *Behavioral Sciences and the Law, 4,* 401–421.

Dovidio, J., Gaertner, S., Kawakami, K., & Hodson, G. (2002). Why can't we just get along? Interpersonal biases and interracial distrust. *Cultural Diversity and Ethnic Minority Psychology, 8,* 88–102.

Dowdell, E. B., & Foster, K. L. (2000). Munchausen syndrome by proxy: Recognizing a form of child abuse. *Nursing Spectrum.*

Dowling, F. G., Moynihan, G., Genet, B., & Lewis, J. (2006). A peer-based assistance program for officers with the New York City Police Department: Report of the effects of Sept, 11, 2001. *American Journal of Psychiatry, 163,* 151–153.

Dressing, H., & Salize, H-J. (2009). Pathways to psychiatric care in European prison systems. *Behavioral Sciences and the Law, 27,* 801–810.

Duboff, R. D., & Neufer, N. L. (2010). Scoping the juror's head: What's going on in there? Retrieved December 15, 2010, from http://www.theadvocates.com/news/JurorPreconceptions-scopingthe juror.php.

Dudycha, G. J., & Dudycha, M. M. (1941). Childhood memories: A review of the literature. *Psychological Bulletin, 38,* 668–682.

Duhaime, A., Christian, C. W., Rorke, L. B., & Zimmerman, R. A. (1998). Nonaccidental head injury in infants: The "shaken-baby syndrome." *New England Journal of Medicine, 338,* 1822–1829.

D'Unger, A. V., Land, K. C., McCall, P. L., & Nagin, D. S. (1998). How many latent classes of delinquent/criminal careers? Results from mixed Poisson regression analysis. *American Journal of Sociology, 103,* 1593–1630.

Durand, V. M., & Barlow, D. H. (2000). *Abnormal psychology: An introduction.* Belmont, CA: Wadsworth.

Dutton, D., & Golant, S. K. (1995). *The batterer: A psychological profile.* New York: Basic Books.

Dutton, M. A. (1992). *Empowering and healing the battered woman.* New York: Springer.

Dutton, M. A. (1996, May). Validity and use of evidence concerning battering and its effects in criminal trials: NIJ Report to Congress. Washington, DC: U.S. Department of Justice, National Institute of Justice and U.S. Department of Health and Human Services, National Institute of Mental Health.

Duwe, G. (2000). Body-count journalism: The presentation of mass murder in the news media. *Homicide Studies, 4,* 364–399.

Duwe, G., & Kerschner, D. (2008). Removing a nail from the boot camp coffin: An outcome evaluation of Minnesota's Challenge Incarceration program. *Crime & Delinquency, 54,* 614–643.

Ebert, B. W. (1987). Guide to conducting a psychological autopsy. *Professional Psychology: Research and Practice, 18,* 52–56.

Eddy, D., & Edmunds, C. (2002). Compensation. In A. Seymour, M. Murray, J. Sigmon, M. Hook, C. Edmunds, M. Gaboury, et al. (Eds.), *National Victim Assistance Academy textbook.* Washington, DC: U.S. Department of Justice, Office of Victims of Crime.

Edens, J. F., Campbell, J., & Weir, J. (2007). Youth psychopathy and criminal recidivism: A meta-analysis of the psychopathy checklist measures. *Law and Human Behavior, 31,* 53–75.

Edens, J. F., Petrila, J., & Buffington-Vollum, J. K. (2001). Psychopathy and the death penalty: Can the Psychopathy Checklist—Revised identify offenders who represent "a continuing threat to society"? *Journal of Psychiatry and Law, 29,* 433–481.

Edens, J. F., Skeem, J. L., Cruise, K. R., & Cauffman, E. (2001). Assessment of "juvenile psychopathy" and its association with violence: A critical review. *Behavioral Sciences and the Law, 19,* 53–80.

Edens, J. F., & Vincent, G. M. (2008). Juvenile psychopathy: A clinical construct in need of restraint. *Journal of Forensic Psychology Practice, 8,* 186–197.

Edwards, D. L., Schoenwald, S. K., Henggeler, S. W., & Strother, K. B. (2001). A multi-level perspective on the implementation of multisystemic therapy (MST): Attempting dissemination with fidelity. In G. A. Bernfeld, D. P. Farrington, & A. W. Leschied (Eds.), *Offender rehabilitation in practice.* Chichester, UK: Wiley.

Ehrlichman, H., & Halpern, J. N. (1988). Affect and memory: Effects of pleasant and unpleasant odors on retrieval of happy and unhappy memories. *Journal of Personality and Social Psychology, 55,* 769–779.

Eich, E. (1989). Theoretical issues in state dependent memory. In H. L. Roediger & F. I. M. Craik (Eds.), *Varieties of memory and consciousness.* Hillsdale, NJ: Erlbaum.

Einhorn, J. (1986). Child custody in historical perspective: A study of changing social perceptions of divorce and child custody in Anglo-American law. *Behavioral Sciences & the Law, 4,* 119–135.

Eisenberg, N., Spinrad, T. L., Fabes, R. A., Reiser, M., Cumberland, A., Shepard, S. A., et al. (2004). The relations of effortful control and impulsivity to children's resiliency and adjustment. *Child Development, 75,* 25–46.

Ekman, P. (2009). Telling lies: Clues to deceit in the marketplace, politics, and marriage. New York: Norton.

Elliott, D. M. (1997). Traumatic events: Prevalence and delayed recall in the general population. *Journal of Consulting and Clinical Psychology, 65,* 811–820.

Elliott, D. S., Ageton, S. S., & Huizinga, D. (1980). *The National Youth Survey.* Boulder, CO: Behavioral Research Institute.

Elliott, D. S., Dunford, T. W., & Huizinga, D. (1987). The identification and prediction of career offenders utilizing self-reported and official data. In J. D. Burchard & S. N. Burchard (Eds.), *Prevention of delinquent behavior.* Newbury Park, CA: Sage.

Ellis, A. (1962). *Reason and emotion in psychotherapy.* Secaucus, NJ: Citadel.

Ellis, C. A., & Lord, J. (2002). Homicide. In A. Seymour, M. Murray, J. Sigmon, M. Hook, C. Edmunds, M. Gaboury, & et al. (Eds.), *National Victim Assistance Academy textbook.* Washington, DC: U.S. Department of Justice, Office of Victims of Crime.

Ellsworth, P. C., & Reifman, A. (2000). Juror comprehension and public policy: Perceived problems and proposed solutions. *Psychology, Public Policy, and Law, 6,* 788–821.

Else-Quest, N. M., Hyde, J. S., Goldsmith, H. H., & Van Hulle, C. A. (2006). Gender differences in temperament: A meta-analysis. *Psychological Bulletin, 132,* 33–72.

Emerson, R. M., Ferris, K. O., & Gardner, C. B. (1998). On being stalked. *Social Problems, 45,* 289–314.

Emery, R. E., & Laumann-Billings, L. (1998). An overview of the nature, causes, and consequences of abusive family relationships. *American Psychologist, 53,* 121–135.

Epperson, D. L., Kaul, J. D., & Hesselton, D. (1998, October). *Final report of the development of the Minnesotat Sex Offender Screening Tool—Revised (MnSOST-R).* Paper presented at the 17th Annual Research and Treatment Conference of the Association for the Treatment of Sexual Abusers, Vancouver, BC, Canada.

Epperson, D. Ralston, C., Fowers, D., Dewitt, J., & Gore, K. (2006). Juvenile Sexual Offense Recidivism Rate Assessment Tool-II (JSORRAT-II). In Prescott, D. (Ed.), *Risk assessment of youth who have sexually abused.* Oklahoma City, OK: Wood N' Barnes Publishing.

Equal Employment Opportunity Commission. (2009, March 11). *Sexual harassment.* Washington, DC: U.S. Equal Employment Commission.

Erickson, C. D., & Al-Timini, N. R. (2001). Providing mental health services to Arab Americans: Recommendations and considerations. *Cultural Diversity and Ethnic Minority Psychology, 7,* 308–327.

Erickson, K., Crosnoe, R., & Dornbusch, S. M. (2000). A social process model of adolescent deviance: Combining social control and differential association perspectives. *Journal of Youth and Adolescence, 29,* 395–425.

Eron, L., Gentry, J. H., & Schlegel, P. (Eds.). (1994). *Reason to hope: A psychosocial perspective on violence and youth.* Washington, DC: American Psychological Association.

Eron, L., & Slaby, R. G. (1994). Introduction. In L. D. Eron, J. H. Gentry, & P. Schlegel (Eds.), *Reason to hope: A psychosocial perspective on violence and youth.* Washington, DC: American Psychological Association.

Evans, G. D., & Rey, J. (2001). In the echoes of gunfire: Practicing psychologists' responses to school violence. *Professional Psychology: Research and Practice, 32,* 157–164.

Everington, C., & Luckasson, R. (1992). *The Competence Assessment for Standing Trial for Defendants with Mental Retardation (CAST-MR).* Worthington, OH: IDS.

Everington, C., Notario-Small, H., & Horton, M. L. (2007). Can defendants with mental retardation successfully fake their performance on a test of competence to stand trial? *Behavioral Sciences and the Law, 25,* 545–560.

Everly, G., Flannery, R., Eyler, V., & Mitchell, J. (2001). Sufficiency analysis of an integrated multicomponent approach to crisis intervention. *Advances in Mind-Body Medicine, 17,* 174.

Ewing, C. P. (2003). False credentials cause extensive fallout. *Monitor on Psychology, 34,* 84.

Farabee, D. (Ed.). (2002). Making people change [Special issue]. *Criminal Justice and Behavior, 29.*

Farberman, R. (2007). Council extends its stance on torture. *Monitor on Psychology, 38*(9), 14.

Farrington, D. P. (1979). Environmental cues, delinquent behavior, and conviction. In I. G. Sarason & C. D. Spielberger (Eds.), *Stress and anxiety* (Vol. 6). Washington, DC: Hemisphere.

Farrington, D. P. (1991). Childhood aggression and adult violence: Early precursors and later life outcomes. In D. J. Pepler & K. H. Rubin (Eds.), *The development and treatment of childhood aggression.* Hillsdale, NJ: Erlbaum.

Farrington, D. P., Loeber, R., & Stouthamer-Loeber, M. (2003). How can the relationship between race and violence be explained? In D. F. Hawkins (Ed.), *Violent crime: Assessing race and ethnic differences.* Cambridge, UK: Cambridge University Press.

Farrington, D. P., Ohlin, L. E., & Wilson, J. Q. (1986). *Understanding and controlling crime.* New York: Springer.

Faust, E., & Magaletta, P. R. (2010). Factors predicting levels of female inmates' use of psychological services. *Psychological Services, 7,* 1–10.

Fazel, S., & Danesh, J. (2002). Serious mental disorder in 23,000 prisoners: A systematic review of 62 surveyes. *The Lancet, 359,* 545–550.

Fazel, S., Doll, H., & Långström, N. (2008). Mental disorders among adolescents in juvenile detention and correctional facilities: A systematic review and metaregression analysis of 25 surveys. *Journal of American Academy of Child and Adolescent Psychiatry, 47,* 1010–1019.

Fazel, S., Parveen, B., & Doll, H. (2006). Substance abuse and dependence in prisons: A systematic review. *Addiction, 101,* 181–191.

Federal Bureau of Investigation. (2000). *Uniform Crime Reports—1999.* Washington, DC: U.S. Department of Justice.

Federal Bureau of Investigation. (2001). *Uniform Crime Reports—2000.* Washington, DC: U.S. Department of Justice.

Federal Bureau of Investigation. (2002a). *Hate crime statistics, 2001.* Washington, DC: U.S. Department of Justice.

Federal Bureau of Investigation. (2002b). *Uniform Crime Reports—2001.* Washington, DC: U.S. Department of Justice.

Federal Bureau of Investigation (2003). *Uniform Crime Reports—2002.* Washington, DC: U.S. Department of Justice.

Federal Bureau of Investigation. (2005). *Uniform Crime Reports—2004.* Washington, DC: U.S. Department of Justice.

Federal Bureau of Investigation. (2006). *Uniform Crime Reports—2005.* Washington, DC: U.S. Department of Justice.

Federal Bureau of Investigation. (2008). *Expanded homicide data—Crime in the United States, 2007.* Washington, DC: U.S. Department of Justice.

Federal Bureau of Investigation. (2009). *Crime in the United States—2008.* Washington, DC: U.S. Department of Justice.

Federal Bureau of Investigation. (2010). *Crime in the United States—2009.* Washington, DC: U.S. Department of Justice.

Federle, K. H., & Chesney-Lind, M. (1992). Special issues in juvenile justice: Gender, race and ethnicity. In I. M. Schwartz (Ed.), *Juvenile justice and public policy: Toward a national agenda.* New York: Maxwell-Macmillan.

Fehrenbach, P. A., & Monasterky, C. (1988). Characteristics of female sexual offenders. *American Journal of Orthopsychiatry, 58,* 148–151.

Fein, R. A., & Vossekuil, B. (1999). Assassination in the United States: An operational study of recent assassins, attackers, and near-lethal approaches. *Journal of Forensic Sciences, 50,* 321–333.

Feindler, E. L., Rathus, J. H., & Silver, L. B. (2003). *Assessment of family violence: A handbook for researchers and practitioners.* Washington, DC: American Psychological Association.

Feld, B. C. (Ed.). (1999). *Readings in juvenile justice administration.* New York: Oxford University Press.

Feld, B. C. (1988). In re Gault revisited: A cross-state comparison of the right to counsel in juvenile court. *Crime & Delinquency, 34,* 393–424.

Feld, B. C. (2000). Juveniles' waiver of legal rights: Confessions, Miranda, and the right to counsel. In T. Grisso & R. G. Schwartz (Eds.), *Youth on trial: A developmental perspective on juvenile justice.* Chicago: University of Chicago Press.

Felson, R. B. (2002). *Violence and gender reexamined.* Washington, DC: American Psychological Association.

Ferguson, C. J., Rueda, S. M., Cruz, A. M., Ferguson, D. E., Fritz, S., & Smith, S. M. (2008). Violent video games and aggression: Causal relationship or byproduct of family violence and intrinsic violence motivation? *Criminal Justice and Behavior, 35,* 311–332.

Ferguson, G. E., Eidelson, R. J., & Witt, P. H. (1998). New Jersey's sex offender risk assessment scale: Preliminary validity data. *Journal of Psychiatry and Law, 26,* 327–351.

Fernald, G. M., & Sullivan, E. B. (1924, October). Psychology and public safety. *California Monthly,* pp. 81–83.

Final conclusions of the American Psychological Association Working Group on Investigation of Memories of Childhood Abuse. (1998). Psychology, Public Policy, and Law, 4, 931–940.

Fineran, S., & Gruber, J. E. (2009). Youth at work: Adolescent employment and sexual harassment. *Child Abuse & Neglect, 33,* 550–559.

Finkelhor, D., Hotaling, G., & Sedlak, A. (1990). *Missing, abducted, runaway, and thrownaway children in America: First report.* Washington, DC: Juvenile Justice Clearinghouse.

Finkelhor, D., & Lewis, I. A. (1988). An epidemiologic approach to the study of child molestation. In R. A. Prentky & V. L. Quinsey (Eds.), *Human sexual aggression: Current perspectives.* New York: New York Academy of Sciences.

Finkelhor, D., & Ormrod, R. (2000, June). *Kidnapping of juveniles: Patterns from NIBRS.* Washington, DC: U.S. Department of Justice, Office of Juvenile Justice and Delinquency Prevention.

Finkelhor, D., & Ormrod, R. (2001a, September). *Crimes against children by babysitters.* Washington, DC: U.S. Department of Justice, Office of Juvenile Justice and Delinquency Prevention.

Finkelhor, D., & Ormrod, R. (2001b, October). *Homicides of children and youth.* Washington, DC: U.S. Department of Justice, Office of Juvenile Justice and Delinquency Prevention.

Finkelhor, D., Hotaling, G., & Sedlak, A. (1990). *Missing, abducted, runaway, and thrownaway children in America: First report.* Washington, DC: Juvenile Justice Clearinghouse.

Finkelman, J. M. (2010). Litigation consulting: Expanding beyond jury selection to trial strategy and tactics. *Consulting Psychology Journal: Practice and Research, 62,* 12–20.

Finley, L. M. (1996). The pharmaceutical industry and women's reproductive health. In E. Szockyj & J. G. Fox (Eds.), *Corporate victimization of women.* Boston: Northeastern University Press.

Finn, P., Talucci, V., & Wood, J. (2000, January). On-the-job stress in policing: Reducing it, preventing it. *National Institute of Justice Journal*, pp. 18–25.

Finn, P., & Tomz, J. E. (1997, March). *Developing a law enforcement stress program for officers and their families.* Washington, DC: U.S. Department of Justice.

Finno, A. A., Michalski, D., Hart, B., Wicherski, M., & Kohout, J. L. (2010, May). *Report of the 2009 APA salary survey.* Washington, DC: American Psychological Association.

Fischler, G. L. (2001). Psychological fitness-for-duty examinations: Practical considerations for public safety departments. *Illinois Law Enforcement Executive Forum, 1,* 77–92.

Fishbein, D. (2000). Neuropsychological function, drug abuse, and violence: A conceptual framework. *Criminal Justice and Behavior, 27,* 139–159.

Fisher, B. S., Cullen, F. T., & Turner, M. G. (2000). *Sexual victimization of college women.* Washington, DC: U.S. Department of Justice, National Institute of Justice.

Fisher, J. C. (1997). *Killer among us: Public reactions to serial murder.* Westport, CT: Praeger.

Fitzgerald, L. F., Buchanan, N. T., Collinsworth, L. L., Magley, V. J., & Ramos, A. M. (1999). Junk logic: The abuse defense in sexual harassment litigation. *Psychology, Public Policy, and Law, 5,* 730–759.

Fitzgerald, L. F., Magley, V. J., Drasgow, F., & Wado, C. R. (1999). Measuring sexual harassment in the military: The Sexual Experiences Questionnaire (SEQ-DoD). *Military Psychology, 11,* 243–263.

Fitzgerald, L. F., & Shullman, S. L. (1985). *Sexual Experiences Questionnaire.* Kent, OH: Kent State University.

Fixsen, D. L., Blasé, K. A., Timbers, G. D., & Wolf, M. M. (2001). In search of program implementation: 792 replications of the teaching-family model. In G. A. Bernfeld, D. P. Farrington, & A. W. Leschied (Eds.), *Offender rehabilitation in practice.* Chichester, UK: Wiley.

Fizel, D. (1997, February 26). The suspect confessed. Case closed? Not necessarily, researcher says [*APA News* Press Release]. Washington, DC: American Psychological Association.

Flory, K., Milich, R., Lynam, D. R., Leukefeld, C., & Clayton, R. (2003). Relation between childhood disruptive behavior disorders and substance use and dependence symptoms in young adulthood: Individuals with symptoms of attention-deficit/hyperactivity disorder and conduct disorder are uniquely at risk. *Psychology of Addictive Behaviors, 17,* 151–158.

Foa, E. B., Cashman, L., Jaycox, L., & Perry, K. (1997). The validation of a self-report measure of posttraumatic stress disorder: The Posttraumatic Diagnostic Scale. *Psychological Assessment, 9,* 445–451.

Foa, E. B., Riggs, D. S., Dancu, C. V., & Rothbaum, B. O. (1993). Reliability and validity of a brief instrument for assessing post-traumatic stress disorder. *Journal of Traumatic Stress, 6,* 459–474.

Foa, E. B., Rothbaum, B. O., Riggs, D. S., & Murdock, T. B. (1991). Treatment of posttraumatic stress disorder in rape victims: A comparison between cognitive-behavioral procedures and counseling. *Journal of Consulting and Clinical Psychology, 59,* 715–723.

Folsom, J., & Atkinson, J. L. (2007). The generalizability of the LSI-R and the CAT to the prediction of recidivism in women offenders. *Criminal Justice and Behaivor, 34,* 1044–1056.

Fontaine, N., Carbonneau, R., Vitaro, F., Barker, E. D., & Tremblay, R. E. (2009). Research review: A critical review of studies on the developmental trajectories of antisocial behavior in females. *Journal of Child Psychology and Psychiatry, 50,* 363–385.

Forehand, R., Wierson, M., Frame, C. L., Kempton, T., & Armistead, L. (1991). Juvenile firesetting: A unique syndrome or an advanced level of antisocial behavior? *Behavioral Research and Therapy, 29,* 125–128.

Forsman, M., Lichtenstein, P., Andershed, H., Larsson, H. (2010). A longitudinal twin study of the direction of effects between psychopathic personality and antisocial behavior. *Journal of Child Psychology and Psychiatry, 51,* 39–47.

Forth, A. E., Kosson, D. S., & Hare, R. D. (1997). *Hare Psychopathy Checklist: Youth Version.* Toronto, ON, Canada: Multi-Health Systems.

Fox, J. A., & Levin, J. (1998). Multiple homicide: Patterns of serial and mass murder. In M. Tonry (Ed.), *Crime and justice: A review of research* (Vol. 23). Chicago: University of Chicago Press.

Fox, J. A., & Levin, J. (2003). Mass murder: An analysis of extreme violence. *Journal of Applied Psychoanalytic Studies, 5,* 47–64.

Fox, J. A., & Zawitz, M. A. (2001). *Homicide trends in the United States.* Washington, DC: U.S. Department of Justice, Bureau of Justice Statistics.

Franklin, C. L., Sheeran, T., & Zimmerman, M. (2002). Screening for trauma histories, posttraumatic stress disorder (PTSD), and subthreshold PTSD in psychiatric outpatients. *Psychological Assessment, 14,* 467–471.

Freeman, N., & Sandler, J. (2009). Female sex offender recidivism: A large-scale empirical analysis. *Sexual Abuse: Journal of Research and Treatment, 21,* 455–473.

Freud, S. (1957). Repression. In J. Strachey (Ed. and Trans.), *The standard edition of the complete psychological works of Sigmund Freud* (Vol. 14). London: Hogarth. (Original work published 1915)

Freund, K. (1963). A laboratory method for diagnosing predominance of homo- and hetero-erotic interests in the male. *Behavior Research and Therapy, 1,* 85–93.

Frick, P. J., Bodin, S. D., & Barry, C. T. (2000). Psychopathic traits and conduct problems in community and clinic-referred samples of children: Further development of the psychopathy screening device. *Psychological Assessment, 12,* 382–393.

Frick, P. J., Cornell, A. H., Bodin, S. D., Dane, H. E., Barry, C. T., & Loney, B. R. (2003). Callous-unemotional traits and developmental pathways to severe conduct problems. *Developmental Psychology, 39,* 246–260.

Frick, P. J., O'Brien, B. S., Wootton, J., & McBurnett, K. (1994). Psychopathy and conduct problems in children. *Journal of Abnormal Psychology, 103,* 700–707.

Friedrich, W. N., & Gerber, P. N. (1994). Autoerotic asphyxia: The development of a paraphilia. *Journal of the American Academy of Child and Adolescent Psychiatry, 33,* 970–974.

Furby, L., Weinroth, M. R., & Blackshaw, L. (1989). Sex offender recidivism: A review. *Psychological Bulletin, 105,* 3–30.

Fuselier, G. D. (1981, June/July). A practical overview of hostage negotiations. *FBI Law Enforcement Bulletin,* pp. 1–11.

Fuselier, G. D. (1988). Hostage negotiation consultant: Emerging role for the clinical psychologist. *Professional Psychology: Research and Practice, 19,* 175–179.

Fuselier, G. D., & Noesner, G. W. (1990, July). Confronting the terrorist hostage taker. *FBI Law Enforcement Bulletin,* pp. 9–12.

Gaboury, M., & Edmunds, C. (2002). Civil remedies. In A. Seymour, M. Murray, J. Sigmon, M. Hook, C. Edwards, M. Gaboury, & et al. (Eds.), *National Victim Assistance Academy textbook.* Washington, DC: U.S. Department of Justice, Office of Victims of Crime.

Gacono, C. B., Nieberding, R. J., Owen, A., Rubel, J., & Bodholdt, R. (1997). Treating conduct disorder, antisocial, and psychopathic personalities. In J. B. Ashford, B. D. Sales, & W. H. Reid (Eds.), *Treating adult and juvenile offenders with special needs.* Washington, DC: American Psychological Association.

Gallagher, R. W., Somwaru, D. P., & Ben-Porath, Y. S. (1999). Current usage of psychological tests in state correctional settings. *Corrections Compendium, 24,* 1–3, 20.

Gannon, T. A., & Pina, A. (2010). Firesetting: Psychopathology, theory and treatment. *Aggression and Violent Behavior, 15,* 224–238.

Gannon, T. A., & Rose, M. R. (2008). Female child sexual offenders: Toward integrating theory and practice. *Aggression and Violent Behavior, 13,* 442–461.

Gardner, H. (1983). Frames of mind: The theory of multiple intelligences. New York: Basic Books.

Gardner, H. (1986). The waning of intelligence tests. In R. J. Sternberg & D. K. Detterman (Eds.), *What is intelligence?* Norwood, NJ: Ablex.

Gardner, H. (1993). Multiple intelligences. New York: Basic Books.

Gardner, H. (1998). Are there additional intelligences? The case for naturalist, spiritual, and existential intelligence. In K. Kane (Ed.), *Education, information, and transformation.* Englewood Cliffs, NJ: Prentice Hall.

Gardner, H. (2000). *Intelligence reframed: Multiple intelligences for the 21st century.* New York: Basic Books.

Gardner, M., & Steinberg, L. (2005). Peer influence on risk taking, risk preference, and risky decision making in adolescence and adulthood: An experimental study. *Developmental Psychology, 41,* 625–635.

Garland, B. E., McCarty, W. P., & Zhao, R. (2009). Job satisfaction and organizational commitment in prisons: An examination of psychological staff, teachers, and unit management staff. *Criminal Justice and Behavior, 36,* 163–183.

Gaynor, J. (1996). Firesetting. In M. Lewis (Ed.), *Child and adolescent psychiatry: A comprehensive textbook.* Baltimore: Williams & Wilkins.

Geberth, V. (1996). *Practical homicide investigation* (3rd ed.). New York: CRC Press.

Gelles, R. J., & Cavanaugh, M. M. (2005). Violence, abuse, and neglect in families and intimate relationships. In P. C. McHenry & S. J. Price (Eds.), *Families & change: Coping with stressful events and transitions* (3rd ed.). Thousand Oaks, CA: Sage.

Gendreau, P., Cullen, F. T., & Bonta, J. (1994). Intensive rehabilitation supervision: The next generation in community corrections? *Federal Probation, 58,* 72–78.

Gendreau, P., Little, T., & Goggin, C. (1996). A meta-analysis of the predictors of adult recidivism: What works! *Criminology, 34,* 401–433.

Gendreau, P., Paparozzi, M., Little, T., & Goddard, M. (1993). Punishing smarter: The effectiveness of the new generation of alternative sanctions. *Forum on Correctional Research, 5,* 31–34.

Gendreau, P., & Ross, R. R. (1984). Correctional treatment: Some recommendations for effective intervention. *Juvenile and Family Court Journal, 34,* 31–39.

Gentile, S. R., Asamen, J. K., Harmell, P. H., & Weathers, R. (2002). The stalking of psychologists by their clients. *Professional Psychology: Research and Practice, 33,* 490–494.

George, W. H., & Marlatt, G. A. (1989). Introduction. In D. R. Laws (Ed.), *Relapse prevention with sex offenders.* New York: Guilford Press.

Gershon, R. R. M., Lin, S., & Li, X. (2002). Work stress in aging police officers. *Journal of Occupational and Environmental Medicine, 44,* 160–167.

Gibbons, D. (1988). Some critical observations on criminal type and criminal careers. *Criminal Justice and Behavior, 15,* 8–23.

Gibbs, J. J. (1992). Jailing and stress. In H. Toch (Ed.), *Mosaic of despair: Human breakdown in prison.* Washington, DC: American Psychological Association.

Giebels, E., & Noelanders, S. (2004). *Crisis negotiations: A multiparty perspective.* Veenendall, The Netherlands: Universal Press.

Giebels, E., & Taylor, P. J. (2009). Interaction patterns in crisis negotiations: Persuasive arguments and cultural differences. *Journal of Applied Psychology, 94,* 5–19.

Gill, C. J., Kewman, D. G., & Brannon, R. W. (2003). Transforming psychological practice and society: Policies that reflect the new paradigm. *American Psychologist, 58,* 305–312.

Gill, R. E. (2007, September/October). Role of psychologists at detention centers approved. *The National Psychologist, 16*(5), 1–2.

Gillis, J. W. (2001). *First response to victims of crime 2001.* Washington, DC: U.S. Department of Justice, Office for Victims of Crime.

Glaze, L. E., & Bonczar, T. P. (2009, December). *Probation and parole in the United States, 2008.* Washington, DC: U.S. Department of Justice, Bureau of Justice Statistics.

Glisson, C., Schoenwald, S. K., Hemmelgarn, A., Green, P., Dukes, D., Armstrong, K. S., et al. (2010). Randomized trial of MST and ARC in a two-level evidence-based treatment implementation strategy. *Journal of Consulting and Clinical Psychology, 78,* 537–550.

Goddard, C., & Bedi, G. (2010). Intimate partner violence and child abuse: A child-centred perspective. *Child Abuse Review, 19,* 5–20.

Gogtay, N., Giedd, J. N., Lusk, L., Hayashi, K. M., Greenstein, D., Vaituzis, A. C., et al. (2004). Dynamic mapping of human cortical development during childhood through early adulthood. *Proceedings of the National Academy of Sciences, 101,* 8174–8179.

Going, M., & Read, J. D. (1974). Effects of uniqueness, sex of subject, and sex of photograph on facial recognition. *Perceptual and Motor Skills, 39,* 109–110.

Golding, S. L., & Roesch, R. (1987). The assessment of criminal responsibility: A historical approach to a current controversy. In I. B. Weiner & A. K. Hess (Eds.), *Handbook of forensic psychology.* New York: Wiley.

Golding, S. L., Skeem, J. L., Roesch, R., & Zapf, P. A. (1999). The assessment of criminal responsibility: Current controversies. In A. K. Hess & I. B. Weiner (Eds.), *The handbook of forensic psychology* (2nd ed.). New York: Wiley.

Goldkamp, J. S., & Irons-Guynn, C. (2000). *Emerging judicial strategies for the mentally ill in the criminal caseload: Mental health courts in Fort Lauderdale, Seattle, San Bernardino, and Anchorage.* Washington, DC: U.S. Department of Justice, Office of Justice Programs, Bureau of Justice Assistance.

Goldstein, A. M. (2002a). Low-level aggression: Definition, escalation, intervention. In J. McGuire (Ed.), *Offender rehabilitation and treatment.* Chichester, UK: Wiley.

Goldstein, A. M. (2002b). Teaching point: What kinds of cases do you avoid accepting because they would make it too difficult for you to remain impartial? In K. Heilbrun, G. R. Marczyk, & D. DeMatteo (Eds.), *Forensic mental health assessment.* New York: Oxford University Press.

Goldstein, A. P., & Glick, B. (1987). *Aggression replacement training.* Champaign, IL: Research Press.

Goldstein, A. P., & Glick, B. (2001). Aggression replacement training: Application and evaluation management. In G. A. Bernfeld, D. P. Farrington, & A. W. Leschied (Eds.), *Offender rehabilitation in practice.* Chichester, UK: Wiley.

Good, G. E., Heppner, P. P., Hillenbrand-Gunn, T. L., & Wang, L. (1995). Sexual and psychological violence: An exploratory study of predictors in college men. *Journal of Men's Studies, 4,* 59–71.

Goodman-Delahunty, J. (1999a). Civil law: Employment and discrimination. In R. Roesch, S. D. Hart, & J. R. P. Ogle (Eds.), *Psychology and law: The state of the discipline.* New York: Kluwer Academic/Plenum.

Goodman-Delahunty, J. (1999b). Pragmatic support for the reasonable victim standard in hostile workplace sexual harassment cases. *Psychology, Public Policy, and Law, 5,* 519–555.

Goodman-Delahunty, J. (2000). Psychological impairment under the Americans with Disabilities Act: Legal guidelines. *Professional Psychology: Research and Practice, 31,* 197–205.

Gordon, C. C. (1969). Perspectives on law enforcement: I. Characteristics of police applicants. Princeton, NJ: Educational Testing Service.

Gordon, D. A. (2002). Intervening with families of troubled youth: Functional family therapy and parenting wisely. In J. McGuire (Ed.), *Offender rehabilitation and treatment.* Chichester, UK: Wiley.

Gorman, W. (2001). Refugee survivors of torture: Trauma and treatment. *Professional Psychology: Research and Practice, 32,* 443–451.

Gosink, P., & Jumbelic, M. I. (2000). Autoerotic asphyxiation in a female. *American Journal of Forensic Medicine and Pathology, 21,* 114–118.

Gothard, S., Rogers, R., & Sewell, K. W. (1995). Feigning incompetency to stand trial: An investigation of the Georgia Court Competency Test. *Law and Human Behavior, 19,* 363–373.

Gough, H. G. (1987). *California Psychological Inventory administrator's guide.* Palo Alto, CA: Consulting Psychologists Press.

Grandey, A. A. (2000). Emotion regulation in the workplace: A new way to conceptualize emotional labor. *Journal of Occupational Health Psychology, 5,* 95–110.

Granic, I., & Patterson, G. R. (2006). Toward a comprehensive model of antisocial development: A dynamic systems approach. *Psychological Review, 113,* 101–131.

Gray, A. S., Pithers, W., Busconi, A. J., & Houchens, P. (1997). Children with sexual behavior problems: An empirically derived taxonomy. *Association for the Treatment of Sexual Abusers, 3,* 10–11.

Greenberg, S. A., & Shuman, D. W. (1997). Irreconcilable conflict between therapeutic and forensic roles. *Professional Psychology: Research and Practice, 28,* 50–57.

Greenberg, S. A., & Shuman, D. W. (2007). When worlds collide: Therapeutic and forensic roles. *Professional Psychology: Research and Practice, 38,* 129–132.

Greenfeld, L. A. (1997). *Sex offenses and offenders: An analysis of data on rape and sexual assault.* Washington, DC: U.S. Department of Justice, Bureau of Justice Statistics.

Greenfeld, L. A., Langan, P. A., & Smith, S. K. (1997, November). *Police use of force: Collection of national data.* Washington, DC: U.S. Department of Justice, Bureau of Justice Statistics.

Greenwood, P. W., & Turner, S. (1993). Evaluation of the Paint Creek Youth Center: A residential program for serious delinquents. *Criminology, 31,* 263–279.

Gregorie, T. (2000). *Cyberstalking: Dangers on the information highway.* Arlington, VA: National Center for Victims of Crime.

Gregorie, T., & Wallace, H. (2002). Workplace violence. In A. Seymour, M. Murray, J. Sigmon, M. Hook, C. Edmonds, M. Gaboury, & et al. (Eds.), *National Victim Assistance Academy textbook.* Washington, DC: U.S. Department of Justice, Office for Victims of Crime.

Gregory, N. (2005). Offender profiling: A review of the literature. *British Journal of Forensic Practice, 7,* 29–34.

Greif, G. L., & Hegar, R. L. (1993). *When parents kidnap: The families behind the headlines.* New York: Free Press.

Gretton, H. M., McBride, M., Hare, R. D., O'Shaughnessy, R., & Kumka, G. (2001). Psychopathy and recidivism in adolescent sex offenders. *Criminal Justice and Behavior, 28,* 427–449.

Griffin, H. L., Beech, A., Print, B., Bradshaw, H., & Quayle, J. (2008). The development and initial testing of the AIM2 framework to assess risk and strengths in young people who sexually offend. *Journal of Sexual Aggression, 14,* 211–225.

Griffith, J. D., Hart, C. L., Kessler, J., & Goodling, M. M. (2007). Trial consultants: Perceptions of eligible jurors. *Consulting Psychology Journal: Practice and Research, 59,* 148–153.

Grisso, T. (1981). *Juveniles' waiver of rights: Legal and psychological competence.* New York: Plenum.

Grisso, T. (1986). *Evaluating competencies: Forensic assessments and instruments.* New York: Plenum.

Grisso, T. (1988). *Competency to stand trial evaluations: A manual for practice.* Sarasota, FL: Professional Resource Exchange.

Grisso, T. (1996). Society's retributive response to juvenile violence: A developmental perspective. *Law and Human Behavior, 20,* 229–247.

Grisso, T. (1998). *Forensic evaluation of juveniles.* Sarasota, FL: Professional Resource Press.

Grisso, T. (1999). Dealing with juveniles' competence to stand trial: What we need to know. *Quinnipiac Law Review, 18,* 371–383.

Grisso, T. (2008). Adolescent offenders with mental disorders. *The Future of Children, 18,* 143–164.

Grisso, T., Appelbaum, P., Mulvey, E., & Fletcher, K. (1995). The MacArthur Treatment Competence Study: II. Measures of abilities related to competence to consent to treatment. *Law and Human Behavior, 19,* 127–148.

Grisso, T., & Saks, M. J. (1991). Psychology's influence on constitutional interpretation. *Law and Human Behavior, 15,* 205–211.

Grisso, T., & Schwartz, R. G. (Eds.). (2000). *Youth on trial: A developmental perspective on juvenile justice.* Chicago: University of Chicago Press.

Grisso, T., Steinberg, L., Woolard, J., Cauffman, E., Scott, E., Graham, S., et al. (2003). Juveniles' competence to stand trial: A comparison of adolescents' and adults' capacities as trial defendants. *Law and Human Behavior, 27,* 333–364.

Gross, A. M., Bennett, T., Sloan, L., Marx, B. P., & Jurgens, J. (2001). The impact of alcohol and alcohol expectancies on male perceptions of female sexual arousal in a date rape analog. *Experimental and Clinical Psychopharmacology, 9,* 380–388.

Gross, A. M., Winslett, A., Roberts, M., & Gohm, C. L. (2006). An examination of sexual violence against women. *Violence Against Women, 12,* 288–300.

Grossman, N. S., & Okun, B. F. (2003). Family psychology and family law: Introduction to the special issue. *Journal of Family Psychology, 17,* 163–168.

Groth, A. N. (1979). Men who rape: The psychology of the offender. New York: Plenum.

Groth, A. N., & Burgess, A. W. (1977). Motivational intent in the sexual assault of children. *Criminal Justice and Behavior, 4,* 253–271.

Groth, A. N., Burgess, A. W., & Holmstrom, L. (1977). Rape: Power, anger, and sexuality. *American Journal of Psychiatry, 134,* 1239–1243.

Grove, W. M., & Barden, R. C. (1999). Protecting the integrity of the legal system: The admissibility of testimony from mental health experts under Daubert/Kumho analyses. *Psychology, Public Policy, and Law, 5,* 224–242.

Grove, W. M., Barden, R. C., Garb, H. N., & Lilienfeld, S. O. (2002). Failure of Rorschach-Comprehensive-System-based testimony to be admissible under the Daubert-Joiner-Kumho standard. *Psychology, Public Policy, and Law, 8,* 216–234.

Grubb, A. (2010, June 18). Modern day hostage (crisis) negotiation: The evolution of an art form within the policing arena. *Aggression and Violent Behavior.*

Grubin, D. (2002). The potential use of polygraph in forensic psychiatry. *Criminal Behaviour and Mental Health, 12,* 45–55.

Grubin, D. (2008). The case for polygraph testing of sex offenders. *Legal and Criminological Psychology, 13,* 177–189.

Gudjonsson, G. H. (1988). A new scale of interrogative suggestibility. *Personality and Individual Differences, 5,* 303–314.

Gudjonsson, G. H. (1992). *The psychology of interrogations, confessions and testimony.* London: Wiley.

Gudjonsson, G. H. (2003). *The science of interrogations and confessions: A handbook.* Chichester, UK: Wiley.

Guerra, N. G., Tolan, P. H., & Hammond, W. R. (1994). Prevention and treatment of adolescent violence. In L. D. Eron, J. H. Gentry, & P. Schlegel (Eds.), *Reason to hope: A psychosocial perspective on violence and youth.* Washington, DC: American Psychological Association.

Gunnoe, M. L., & Braver, S. L. (2001). The effects of joint legal custody on mothers, fathers, and children: Controlling for factors that predispose a sole maternal versus joint legal award. *Law and Human Behavior, 25,* 25–43.

Guy, L. S., & Edens, J. F. (2003). Juror decision-making in a mock sexually violent predator trial: Gender differences in the impact of divergent types of expert testimony. *Behavioral Sciences and the Law, 21,* 215–237.

Haaga, D. A. F., & Davidson, G. C. (1993). An appraisal of rational-emotive therapy. *Journal of Consulting and Clinical Psychology, 61,* 215–220.

Haapala, D. A., & Kinney, J. M. (1988). Avoiding out-of-home placement of high-risk status offenders through the use of intensive home-based family preservation services. *Criminal Justice and Behavior, 15,* 334–348.

Haber, R. N., & Haber, L. (2000). Experiencing, remembering, and reporting events. *Psychology, Public Policy, and Law, 6,* 1057–1097.

Hall, C. I. (1997). Cultural malpractice: The growing obsolescence of psychology with the changing U.S. population. *American Psychologist, 52,* 642–651.

Hall, N. G. C. (1995). Sexual offender recidivism revisited: A meta-analysis of recent treatment studies. *Journal of Consulting and Clinical Psychology, 63,* 802–809.

Halligan, S. L., Michael, T., Clark, D. M., & Ehlers, A. (2003). Posttraumatic stress disorder following assault: The role of cognitive processing, trauma memory, and appraisals. *Journal of Consulting and Clinical Psychology, 71,* 410–431.

Hamel, M., Gallagher, S., & Soares, C. (2001). The Rorschach: Here we go again. *Journal of Forensic Psychology Practice, 1,* 79–87.

Hanson, R. K. (2001). *Age and sexual recidivism: A comparison of rapists and child molesters.* Ottawa, ON: Department of Solicitor General Canada.

Hanson, R. K. (2005). Twenty years of progress in violence risk assessment. *Journal of Interpersonal Violence, 20,* 212–217.

Hanson, R. K. (2009). The psychological assessment of risk for crime and violence. *Canadian Psychology, 50,* 172–182.

Hanson, R. K., & Bussière, M. T. (1998). Predicting relapse: A meta-analysis of sexual offender recidivism studies. *Journal of Consulting and Clinical Psychology, 66,* 348–362.

Hanson, R. K., & Harris, A. J. R. (1998). *Dynamic predictors of sexual recidivism—1998.* Ottawa, ON, Canada: Public Works and Government Services, Department of the Solicitor General.

Hanson, R. K., & Harris, A. J. R. (2000). Where should we intervene? Dynamic predictors of sexual offense recidivism. *Criminal Justice and Behavior, 27,* 6–35.

Hanson, R. K., Helmus, L., & Thornton, D. (2010). Predicting recidivism amongst sexual offenders: A multi-site study of Static-2002. *Law and Human Behavior, 34,* 198–211.

Hanson, R. K., & Morton-Bourgon, K. E. (2005). The characteristics of persistent sexual offenders: A meta-analysis of recidivism studies. *Journal of Consulting and Clinical Psychology, 73*, 1154–1163.

Hanson, R. K., & Morton-Bourgon, K. E. (2009). The accuracy of recidivism risk assessment for sexual offenders: A meta-analysis of 118 prediction studies. *Psychological Assessment, 21*, 1–21.

Hanson, R. K., & Thornton, D. (2000). Improving risk assessment for sex offenders: A comparison of three actuarial scales. *Law and Human Behavior, 24*, 119–136.

Hanson, R. K., & Thornton, D. (2003). *Notes on the development of Static-2002.* (Corrections Research User Report No. 2003-01). Ottawa, ON: Department of the Solicitor General of Canada.

Hare, R. D. (1980). A research scale for the assessment of psychopathy in criminal populations. *Personality and Individual Differences, 1*, 111–119.

Hare, R. D. (1991). *The Hare Psychopathy Checklist—Revised.* Toronto, ON, Canada: Multi-Health Systems.

Hare, R. D. (1996). Psychopathy: A clinical construct whose time has come. *Criminal Justice and Behavior, 23*, 25–54.

Hare, R. D. (1998). Psychopathy, affect, and behavior. In D. Cooke, A. Forth, & R. Hare (Eds.), *Psychopathy: Theory, research, and implications for society.* Dordecht, The Netherlands: Kluwer.

Hare, R. D., Clark, D., Grann, M., & Thornton, D. (2000). Psychopathy and the predictive validity of the PCL-R: An international perspective. *Behavioral Sciences and the Law, 18*, 623–645.

Hare, R. D., Forth, A. E., & Strachan, K. E. (1992). Psychopathy and crime across the life span. In R. D. Peters, R. J. McMahon, & V. L. Quinsey (Eds.), *Aggression and violence throughout the life span.* Newbury Park, CA: Sage.

Hare, R. D., Hart, S. D., & Harpur, T. J. (1991). Psychopathy and the DSM-IV criteria for antisocial personality disorder. *Journal of Abnormal Psychology, 100*, 391–398.

Harley, K., & Reese, E. (1999). Origins of autobiographical memory. *Developmental Psychology, 35*, 1338–1348.

Harpur, T. J., Hakstian, A., & Hare, R. D. (1988). Factor structure of the Psychopathy Checklist. *Journal of Consulting and Clinical Psychology, 56*, 741–747.

Harris, A. J., Fisher, W., Veysey, B. M., Ragusa, L. M., & Lurigio, A. J. (2010). Sex offending and serious mental illness: Directions for policy and research. *Criminal Justice and Behavior, 37*, 596–612.

Harris, A. J., Lobanov-Rostovsky, C., & Levenson, J. S. (2010). Widening the net: The effects of transitioning to the Adam Walsh Act's federally mandated sex offender classification system. *Criminal Justice and Behavior, 37*, 503–519.

Harris, A. J., & Lurigio, A. J. (2010). Special Issue: Sex offenses and offenders: Toward evidence-based public policy. *Criminal Justice and Behavior, 37*, 477–481.

Harris, G. T., & Rice, M. (2007). Adjusting actuarial violence risk assessments based on aging or the passage of time. *Criminal Justice and Behavior, 34*, 297–313.

Harris, G. T., Rice, M. E., & Quinsey, V. L. (1993). Violent recidivism of mentally disordered offenders: The development of a statistical prediction instrument. *Criminal Justice and Behavior, 20*, 315–325.

Harris, G. T., Rice, M. E., & Quinsey, V. L. (1994). Psychopathy as a taxon: Evidence that psychopaths are a discrete class. *Journal of Consulting and Clinical Psychology, 62*, 387–397.

Hart, S. D., Cox, D. N., & Hare, R. D. (1995). *The Hare Psychopathy Checklist: Screening Version.* Toronto, ON, Canada: Multi-Health Systems.

Hart, S. D., & Dempster, R. J. (1997). Impulsivity and psychopathy. In C. D. Webster & M. A. Jackson (Eds.), *Impulsivity: Theory, assessment, and treatment.* New York: Guilford Press.

Hart, S. D., Hare, R. D., & Forth, A. E. (1993). Psychopathy as a risk marker for violence: Development and validation of a screening version of the Revised Psychopathy Checklist. In J. Monahan & H. Steadman (Eds.), *Violence and mental disorder: Developments in risk assessment.* Chicago: University of Chicago Press.

Hart, S. D., Watt, K. A., & Vincent, G. M. (2002). Commentary on Seagrave and Grisso: Impressions of the state of the art. *Law and Human Behavior, 26*, 241–245.

Hartup, W. W. (2005). The development of aggression: Where do you stand? In R. E. Tremblay, W. W. Hartup, & J. Archer (Eds.), *Developmental origins of aggression.* New York: Guilford Press.

Hasselbrack, A. M. (2001). Opting in to mental health courts (Sample issue). *Corrections Compendium*, pp. 4–5.

Hatcher, C., Mohandie, K., Turner, J., & Gelles, M. G. (1998). The role of the psychologist in crisis/hostage negotiations. *Behavioral Sciences and the Law, 16*, 455–472.

Haugaard, J. J., & Reppucci, N. D. (1988). *The sexual abuse of children.* San Francisco: Jossey-Bass.

Hawkins, D. F. (2003). Editor's introduction. In D. F. Hawkins (Ed.), *Violent crime: Assessing race and ethnic differences.* Cambridge, UK: Cambridge University Press.

Hays-Thomas, R. L. (2000). The silent conversation: Talking about the master's degree. *Professional Psychology: Research and Practice, 31*, 339–345.

Hazelwood, R., & Burgess, A. (1987). Practical aspects of rape investigation: A multidisciplinary approach. New York: Elsevier.

Hazelwood, R., & Burgess, A. (1995). *Practical aspects of rape investigation: A multidisciplinary approach* (2nd ed.). Boca Raton, FL: CRC Press.

Hecker, T., & Steinberg, L. (2002). Psychological evaluation at juvenile court disposition. *Professional Psychology: Research and Practice, 33*, 300–306.

Heilbrun, K. (1987). The assessment of competency for execution: An overview. *Behavioral Sciences & the Law, 5*, 383–396.

Heilbrun, K. (2001). *Principles of forensic mental health assessment.* New York: Kluwer Academic/Plenum.

Heilbrun, K., & Brooks, S. (2010). Forensic psychology and forensic sciences: A proposed agenda for the next decade. *Psychology, Public Policy, and Law, 16*, 219–253.

Heilbrun, K., & Griffin, P. (1999). Forensic treatment: A review of programs and research. In R. Roesch, S. D. Hart, & J. R. P. Ogloff (Eds.), *Psychology and law: The state of the discipline.* New York: Kluwer Academic/Plenum.

Heilbrun, K., Grisso, T., & Goldstein, A. M. (2008). *Foundations of forensic mental health assessment.* New York: Oxford University Press.

Heilbrun, K., Marczyk, G. R., & DeMatteo, D. (2002). *Forensic mental health assessment: A casebook*. New York: Oxford University Press.

Heilbrun, K., O'Neill, M. L., Strohman, L. K., Bowman, Q., & Philipson, J. (2000). Expert approaches to communicating violence risk. *Law and Human Behavior, 24*, 137–148.

Heilbrun, K., Philipson, J., Berman, L., & Warren, J. (1999). Risk communication: Clinicians' reported approaches and perceived values. *Journal of the American Academy of Psychiatry and the Law, 27*, 397–406.

Hellkamp, D. T., & Lewis, J. E. (1995). The consulting psychologist as an expert witness in sexual harassment and retaliation cases. *Consulting Psychology Journal: Practice and Research, 47*, 150–159.

Helms, J. L. (2003). Analysis of Miranda reading levels across jurisdictions: Implications for evaluating waiver competency. *Journal of Forensic Psychology Practice, 3*, 25–37.

Heltzel, T. (2007). Compatibility of therapeutic and forensic roles. Professional Psychology: *Research and Practice, 38*, 122–128.

Hem, E, Berg, A. M., & Ekeberg, Ø. (2001). Suicide in police—A critical review. *Suicide and Life-Threatening Behavior, 31*, 224–233.

Henderson, N. D. (1979). Criterion-related validity of personality and aptitude scales. In C. D. Spielberger (Ed.), *Police selection and evaluation: Issues and techniques*. Washington, DC: Hemisphere.

Henggeler, S. W. (1996). Treatment of violent juvenile offenders—we have the knowledge. *Journal of Family Psychology, 10*, 137–141.

Henggeler, S. W. (2001). Multisystemic therapy. *Residential Treatment for Children and Youth, 18*, 75–85.

Henggeler, S. W., & Borduin, C. M. (1990). Family therapy and beyond: A multisystemic approach to treating the behavior problems of children and adolescents. Pacific Grove, CA: Brooks/Cole.

Henker, B., & Whalen, C. K. (1989). Hyperactivity and attention deficits. *American Psychologist, 44*, 216–244.

Henry, M., & Greenfield, B. J. (2009). Therapeutic effects of psychological autopsies: The impact of investigating suicides on interviewees. *Crisis, 30*, 20–24.

Herek, G. M., Gillis, J. R., & Cogan, J. C. (1999). Psychological sequelae of hate-crime victimization among lesbian, gay, and bisexual adults. *Journal of Consulting and Clinical Psychology, 67*, 945–951.

Herndon, J. S. (2001). Law enforcement suicide: Psychological autopsies and psychometric traces. In D. C. Sheehan & J. I. Warren (Eds.), *Suicide and law enforcement*. Washington, DC: FBI Academy.

Hess, A. K. (1999). Serving as an expert witness. In A. K. Hess & I. B. Weiner (Eds.), *Handbook of forensic psychology* (2nd ed.). New York: Wiley.

Hess, A. K. (2006). Serving as an expert witness. In I. B. Weiner & A. K. Hess (Eds.), *The handbook of forensic psychology* (3rd ed.). Hoboken, NJ: Wiley.

Hess, K. D. (2006). Understanding child domestic law issues: Custody, adoption, and abuse. In I. B. Weinter & A. K. Hess (Eds.), *The handbook of forensic psychology* (3rd ed.). Hoboken, NJ: Wiley.

Heuven, E., & Bakker, A. B. (2003). Emotional dissonance and burnout among cabin attendants. *European Journal of Work and Organizational Psychology, 12*, 81–100.

Hickey, E. W. (1997). *Serial murderers and their victims*. Belmont, CA: Wadsworth.

Hickman, M. J. (2004, September). *50 largest crime labs, 2002*. Washington, DC: U.S. Department of Justice, Bureau of Justice Statistics.

Hiday, V. A. (2003). Outpatient commitment: The state of empirical research on its outcomes. *Psychology, Public Policy, and Law, 9*, 8–32.

Hilgard, E. R. (1986). *Divided consciousness: Multiple controls in human thought and action* (Expanded ed.). New York: Wiley.

Hill, J. (2000). The effects of sexual orientation in the courtroom: A double standard. *Journal of Homosexuality, 39*, 93–111.

Hill, M. S., & Fischer, A. R. (2001). Does entitlement mediate the link between masculinity and rape-related variables? *Journal of Counseling Psychology, 48*, 39–50.

Hillbrand, M. (2001). Homicide-suicide and other forms of co-occurring aggression against self and against others. *Professional Psychology: Research and Practice, 32*, 626–635.

Hiller, M., Belenko, S., Taxman, F., Young, D., Perdoni, M., & Saum, C. (2010). Measuring drug court structure and operations: Key components and beyond. *Criminal Justice and Behavior, 37*, 933–950.

Hilton, N. Z., Harris, G. T., & Rice, M. E. (Eds.) (2010). *Risk assessment for domestically violent men: Tools for criminal justice, offender intervention, and victim services*. Washington, DC: American Psychological Association.

Hoge, S. K., Bonnie, R. G., Poythress, N., Monahan, J., Eisenberg, M., & Feucht-Haviar, T. (1997). The MacArthur Adjudicative Competence Study: Development and validation of a research instrument. *Law and Human Behavior, 21*, 141–179.

Hollin, C. R., Palmer, E. J., & Clark, D. (2003). Level of Service Inventory—Revised profile of English prisoners: A needs analysis. *Criminal Justice and Behavior, 30*, 422–440.

Holmes, R. M., & DeBurger, J. (1985). Profiles in terror: The serial murderer. *Federal Probation, 39*, 29–34.

Holmes, R. M., & DeBurger, J. (1988). *Serial murder*. Newbury Park, CA: Sage.

Holmes, S. T., Hickey, E., & Holmes, R. M. (1991). Female serial murderesses: Constructing differentiating typologies. *Contemporary Journal of Criminal Justice, 7*, 245–256.

Holmes, R. M., & Holmes, S. T. (1998). *Serial murder* (2nd ed.). Thousand Oaks, CA: Sage.

Holmes, S. T., & Holmes, R. M. (2002). *Sex crimes: Patterns and behavior* (2nd ed.). Thousand Oaks, CA: Sage.

Holmes, S. T., Hickey, E., & Holmes, R. M. (1991). Female serial murderesses: Constructing differentiating typologies. *Contemporary Journal of Criminal Justice, 7*, 245–256.

Holtzworth-Munroe, A., & Stuart, G. L. (1994). Typologies of male batterers: Three subtypes and the differences among them. *Psychological Bulletin, 116*, 476–497.

Homant, R. J., & Kennedy, D. B. (1998). Psychological aspects of crime scene profiling. *Criminal Justice and Behavior, 25*, 319–343.

Honig, A. L. (2007, September/October). Facts refute long-standing myths about law enforcement officers. *The National Psychologist, 16*(5), 23.

Honts, C. R. (1987). Interpreting research on polygraph countermeasures. *Journal of Police Science and Administration, 15,* 204–209.

Honts, C. R., & Amato, S. L. (2002). Countermeasures. In M. Kleiner (Ed.), *Handbook of polygraph testing.* San Diego, CA: Academic Press.

Honts, C. R., Devitt, M. K., Winbush, M., & Kircher, J. C. (1996). Mental and physical countermeasures reduce the accuracy of the concealed knowledge test. *Psychophysiology, 33,* 84–92.

Honts, C. R., Hodes, R. L., & Raskin, D. C. (1985). Effects of physical countermeasures on the physiological detection of deception. *Journal of Applied Psychology, 70,* 177–187.

Honts, C. R., & Perry, M. V. (1992). Polygraph admissability: Changes and challenges. *Law and Human Behavior, 16,* 357–379.

Honts, C. R., Raskin, D. C., & Kircher, J. C. (1987). Effects of physical countermeasures and their electromyographic detection during polygraph tests for deception. *Journal of Psychophysiology, 1,* 241–247.

Hornung, C. A., McCullough, B. C., & Sugimoto, T. (1981). Status relationships in marriage: Risk factors in spouse abuse. *Journal of Marriage and the Family, 43,* 675–692.

Horowitz, M., Wilner, N., & Alvarez, W. (1979). Impact of Event Scale: A measure of subjective stress. *Psychometric Medicine, 41,* 209–218.

Horvath, F. S. (1977). The effect of selected variables on interpretation of polygraph records. *Journal of Applied Psychology, 62,* 127–136.

Horvath, L. S., Logan, T. K., & Walker, R. (2002). Child custody cases: A content analysis of evaluations in practice. *Professional Psychology: Research and Practice, 33,* 557–565.

Howarth, J., & Lawson, B. (Eds.). (1995). *Trust betrayed: Munchausen syndrome by proxy, inter-agency child protection and partnership with families.* London: National Children's Bureau Enterprises.

Howe, M. L., & Courage, M. L. (1997). The emergence and early development of autobiographical memory. *Psychological Review, 104,* 499–523.

Howell, J. C. (1998). A new approach to juvenile crime. *Corrections Compendium, 23,* 1–4, 24–25.

Hubbard, D. J., & Pratt, T. C. (2002). A meta-analysis of the predictors of delinquency among girls. *Journal of Offender Rehabilitation, 34,* 1–13.

Huckabee, R. G. (1992). Stress in corrections: An overview of the issues. *Journal of Criminal Justice, 20,* 479–486.

Hucker, S. J. (2008). Sexual masochism: Psychopathology and theory. In D. R. Laws & William T. O'Donohue (Eds.), *Sexual deviance: Theory, assessment, and treatment* (2nd ed.). New York: Guilford.

Hucker, S. J., & Blanchard, R. (1992). Death scene characteristics in 118 fatal cases of autoerotic asphyxia compared with suicidal asphyxia. *Behavioral Sciences & the Law, 10,* 509–523.

Huddleston, C. W., Marlowe, D. B., & Casebolt, R. (2008). Painting the current picture: A national report on drug courts and other problem-solving court programs in the United States. Alexandria, VA: National Drug Court Institute.

Huesmann, L. R., Moise-Titus, J., Podolski, C. L., & Eron, L. D. (2003). Longitudinal relations between children's exposure to TV violence and their aggressive and violent behavior in young adulthood: 1977–1992. *Developmental Psychology, 39,* 201–221.

Hunter, J. A., & Becker, J. V. (1999). Motivators of adolescent sex offenders and treatment perspectives. In J. Shaw (Ed.), *Sexual aggression.* Washington, DC: American Psychiatric Press.

Iacono, W. G. (2007). The detection of deception. In J. Cacioppo, L. Tassinary, & G. Berentson (Eds.), *Handbook of psychophysiology* (3rd ed.). New York: Cambridge University Press.

Iacono, W. G. (2008). Effective policing: Understanding how polygraph tests work and are used. *Criminal Justice and Behavior, 35,* 1295–1308.

Iacono, W. G., & Lykken, D. T. (1997). The validity of the lie detector: Two surveys of scientific opinion. *Journal of Applied Psychology, 82,* 426–433.

Iacono, W. G., & Patrick, C. J. (1999). Polygraph ("lie detector") testing: The state of the art. In A. K. Hess & I. B. Weiner (Eds.), *The handbook of forensic psychology* (2nd ed.). New York: Wiley.

Iacono, W. G., & Patrick, C. J. (2006). Polygraph ("lie detector") testing: Current status and emerging trends. In I. B. Weiner & A. K. Hess (Eds.), *The handbook of forensic psychology* (3rd ed.) New York: Wiley.

Icove, D. J., & Estepp, M. H. (1987, April). Motive-based offender profiles of arson and fire-related crime. *FBI Law Enforcement Bulletin,* 17–23.

Inbau, F. E., & Reid, J. E. (1967). *Criminal interrogation and confessions.* Baltimore: Williams & Wilkins.

Inbau, F. E., Reid, J. E., Buckley, J. P., & Jayne, B. C. (2004). *Criminal interrogation and confessions* (4th ed.). Boston: Jones and Bartlett.

Innocence Project (2010). *Fact Sheet: Eyewitness identification reform.* Retrieved December 14, 2010, from http://www.nacdl.org/public.nsf/defenseupdates/IPResources/$FILE/Eyewitness IdentificationReformFactSheet.pdf.

International Association of Chiefs of Police (IACP). (2002). *Fitness for duty evaluation guidelines.* Alexandria, VA: Author.

Inwald, R. E. (1992). *Inwald Personality Inventory technical manual* (Rev. ed.). Kew Gardens, NY: Hilson Research.

Inwald, R.E., Knatz, H., & Shusman, E. (1982). *The Inwald Personality Inventory manual.* New York: Hilton Research.

Iowa Injury Prevention Research Center. (2002, February). *Workplace violence: A report to the nation.* Iowa City: University of Iowa Press.

Jackson, H. F., Glass, C., & Hope, S. (1987). A functional analysis of recidivistic arson. *British Journal of Clinical Psychology, 26,* 175–185.

Jackson, J. L., van Koppen, P. J., & Herbrink, J. C. M. (1993). *Does the service meet the needs? An evaluation of consumer satisfaction profile analysis and investigative advice offered by the Scientific Research Advisory Unit of the National Criminal Intelligence Division (CRI)—The Netherlands.* Leiden: Netherlands Institute for the Study of Criminality and Law Enforcement.

Jackson, M. S., & Springer, D. W. (1997). Social work practice with African-American juvenile gangs: Professional challenge. In C. A. McNeece & A. R. Roberts (Eds.), *Policy and practice in the justice system.* Chicago: Nelson-Hall.

Jackson, T. L., Petretic-Jackson, P. A., & Witte, T. H. (2002). Mental health assessment tools and techniques for working with battered women. In A. R. Roberts (Ed.), *Handbook of domestic violence intervention strategies.* New York: Oxford University Press.

Janssen, W., Koops, E., Anders, S., Kuhn, S., & Püschel, K. (2005). Forensic aspects of 40 accidental autoerotic deaths in northern Germany. *Forensic Science International, 147S,* S61–S64.

Janus, E. S. (2000). Sexual predator commitment laws: Lessons for law and the behavioral sciences. *Behavioral Sciences and the Law, 18,* 5–21.

Janus, E. S., & Walbek, N. H. (2000). Sex offender commitments in Minnesota: A descriptive study of second-generation commitments. *Behavioral Sciences and the Law, 18,* 343–374.

Jenkins, P. (1988). Serial murder in England, 1940–1985. *Journal of Criminal Justice, 16,* 1–15.

Jenkins, P. (1993). Chance or choice: The selection of serial murder victims. In A. V. Wilson (Ed.), *Homicide: The victim/offender connection.* Cincinnati, OH: Anderson.

Johnson, C. C., & Chanhatasilpa, C. (2003). The race/ethnicity and poverty nexus of violent crime: Reconciling differences in Chicago's community area homicide rates. In D. F. Hawkins (Ed.), *Violent crime: Assessing race and ethnic differences.* Cambridge, UK: Cambridge University Press.

Johnson, L. B. (1991). Job strain among police officers: Gender comparisons. *Police Studies, 14,* 12–16.

Johnson, L. B., Todd, M., & Subramanian, G. (2005). Violence in police families: Work-family spillover. *Journal of Family Violence, 20,* 3–12.

Johnson, M. P. (2006). Conflict and control: Gender symmetry and asymmetry in domestic violence. *Violence Against Women, 12,* 1003–1018.

Johnson, R. (1996). *Hard time: Understanding and reforming the prison* (2nd ed.). Belmont, CA: Wadsworth.

Johnston, J. R. (1995). Research update: Children's adjustment in sole custody compared to joint custody families and principles for custody decision making. *Family and Conciliation Courts Review, 33,* 415–425.

Johnston, J. R., & Girdner, L. K. (2001, January). Family abductors: Descriptive profiles and prevention interventions. *Juvenile Justice Bulletin,* pp. 3–9. Washington, DC: Office of Juvenile Justice and Delinquency.

Johnston, J. R., Girdner, L. K., & Sagatun-Edwards, I. (1999). Developing profiles of risk for parental abduction of childre from comparison families victimized by abduction with families litigating custody. *Behavioral Sciences & the Law, 17,* 305–322.

Jouriles, E. N., McDonald, R., Norwood, W. D., Ware, H. S., Spiller, L. C., & Swank, P. R. (1998). Knives, guns, and interparent violence: Relations with child behavior problems. *Journal of Family Psychology, 12,* 178–194.

Kafrey, D. (1980). Playing with matches: Children and fire. In D. Canter (Ed.), *Fires and human behaviour.* Chichester, UK: Wiley.

Kalmbach, K. C., & Lyons, P. M. (2003). Ethical and legal standards for research in prisons. *Behavioral Sciences and the Law, 21,* 671–686.

Kaplan, M. S., & Green, A. (1995). Incarcerated female sexual offenders: A comparison of sexual histories with eleven female nonsexual offenders. *Sexual Abuse: A Journal of Research and Treatment, 7,* 287–300.

Kapp, M. B., & Mossman, D. (1996). Measuring decisional capacity: Cautions on the construction of a "Capacimeter." *Psychology, Public Policy, and Law, 2,* 45–95.

Karmen, A. (2001). *Crime victims: An introduction to victimology* (4th ed.). Belmont, CA: Wadsworth.

Karmen, A. (2009). *Crime victims: An introduction to victimology* (7th ed.). Florence, KY: Cengage Learning.

Karon, B. P., & Widener, A. J. (1999). Repressed memories: Just the facts. *Professional Psychology: Research and Practice, 30,* 625–626.

Kassin, S. M. (1997). The psychology of confession evidence. *American Psychologist, 52,* 221–233.

Kassin, S. M. (2008). Confession evidence: Commonsense myths and misconceptions. *Criminal Justice and Behavior, 35,* 1309–1322.

Kassin, S. M., Drizin, S. A., Grisso, T., Gudjonsson, G. H., Leo, R. A., & Redlich, A. D. (2010). Police induced confessions: Risk factors and recommendations. *Law & Human Behavior, 34,* 3–38.

Kassin, S. M., Goldstein, C. G., & Savitsky, K. (2003). Behavior confirmation in the interrogation room: On the dangers of presuming guilt. *Law and Human Behavior, 27,* 187–203.

Kassin, S. M., & Gudjonsson, G. H. (2004). The psychology of confessions: A review of the literature and issues. *Psychological Science in the Public Interest, 5,* 33–67.

Kassin, S. M., & Kiechel, K. L. (1996). The social psychology of false confessions: Compliance, internalization, and confabulation. *Psychological Science, 7,* 125–128.

Kassin, S. M., Leo, R. A., Meissner, C. A., Richman, K. D., Colwell, L. H., Leach, A-M., et al. (2007). Police interviewing and interrogation: A self-report survey of police practices and beliefs. *Law and Human Behavior, 31,* 381–400.

Kassin, S. M., & Wrightsman, L. S. (1985). Confession evidence. In S. M. Kassin & L. S. Wrightsman (Eds.), *The psychology of evidence and trial procedure.* Beverly Hills, CA: Sage.

Kaufer, S., & Mattman, J. W. (2002). *Workplace violence: An employer's guide.* Palm Springs, CA: Workplace Violence Research Institute.

Kebbell, M. R., & Wagstaff, G. G. (1998). Hypnotic interviewing: The best way to interview eyewitnesses. *Behavioral Sciences and the Law, 16,* 115–129.

Keeler, E. (1984). *Lie detector man.* Boston: Telshare.

Keenan, K., & Shaw, D. (2003). Starting at the beginning: Exploring the etiology of antisocial behavior in the first years of life. In B. B. Lahey, T. E. Moffitt, & A. Caspi (Eds.), *Causes of conduct disorder and juvenile delinquence.* New York: Guilford Press.

Keilin, W. G., & Bloom, L. J. (1986). Child custody evaluation practices: A survey of experienced professionals. *Professional Psychology: Research and Practice, 17,* 338–346.

Kelly, D. H. (1980). The educational experience and evolving delinquent careers: A neglected institutional link. In D. Schichor & D. H. Kelly (Eds.), *Critical issues in juvenile delinquency.* Lexington, MA: Lexington Books.

Kelly, F., & Baer, D. (1978). *Outward Bound: An alternative to institutionalization for adolescent delinquent boys.* New York: Fandel.

Kelman, H. (1958). Compliance, identification, and internalization. *Journal of Conflict Resolution, 2,* 51–60.

Kendall, P. C., & Hammen, C. (1995). *Abnormal psychology.* Boston: Houghton Mifflin.

Kenrick, D. T., & Springfield, D. O. (1980). Personality traits and the eye of the beholder: Crossing some traditional philosophical boundaries in the search for consistency in all the people. *Psychological Review, 87,* 88–104.

Kessler, R. C., Berglund, P., Demler, O., Jin, R., Merikangas, K. R., & Walter, E. E. (2005). Lifetime prevalence and age-of-onset distributions of DSM-IV disorders in the National Comorbidity Survey Replication. *Archives of General Psychiatry, 62,* 593–602.

Kessler, R. C., Sonnega, A., Bromet, E., Hughes, M., & Nelson, C. B. (1995). Posttraumatic stress disorder in the National Comorbidity Survey. *Archives of General Psychiatry, 52,* 1048–1060.

Kihlstrom, J. F. (2001). Martin T. Orne (1927–2000). *American Psychologist, 56,* 754–755.

Kilmann, P. R., Sabalis, R. F., Gearing, M. L., Bukstel, L. H., & Scovern, A. W. (1982). The treatment of sexual paraphilias: A review of the outcome research. *Journal of Sex Research, 18,* 193–252.

Kilpatrick, D. G., Best, C. L., Saunders, B. E., & Veronen, L. J. (1988). Rape in marriage and in dating relationships: How bad is it for mental health? In R. A. Prentky & V. L. Quinsey (Eds.), *Human sexual aggression: Current perspectives.* New York: New York Academy of Sciences.

Kilpatrick, D. G., Best, C. L., Veronen, L. J., Amick, A. E., Villepontreaux, L. A., & Ruff, G. A. (1985). Mental health correlates of criminal victimization: A random community survey. *Journal of Consulting and Clinical Psychology, 53,* 866–873.

Kilpatrick, D. G., Edmunds, C., & Seymour, A. (1992). *Rape in America: A report to the nation.* Arlington, VA: National Center for Victims of Crime.

Kilpatrick, D. G., & Saunders, B. E. (1997, November). *Prevalence and consequences of child victimization: Results from the National Survey of Adolescents: Final report.* Washington, DC: U.S. Department of Justice, Office of Justice Programs, National Institute of Justice.

Kilpatrick, D. G., Saunders, B. E., Veronen, L. J., Best, C. L., & Von, J. M. (1987). Criminal victimization: Lifetime prevalence, reporting to police, and psychological impact. *Crime and Delinquency, 33,* 479–489.

Kilpatrick, D. G., Seymour, A., & Boyle, J. (1991). *America speaks out: Citizens' attitudes about victims' rights and violence.* Arlington, VA: National Center for Victims of Crime.

Kilpatrick, D. G., Whalley, A., & Edmunds, C. (2002). Sexual assault. In A. Seymour, M. Murray, J. Sigmon, M. Hook, C. Edwards, M. Gaboury, & et al. (Eds.), *National Victim Assistance Academy textbook.* Washington, DC: U.S. Department of Justice, Office for Victims of Crime.

King, L., & Snook, B. (2009). Peering inside a Canadian interrogation room: An examination of the Reid model of interrogation, influence tactics, and coercive strategies. *Criminal Justice and Behavior, 36,* 674–694.

King, R., & Norgard, K. (1999). What about families? Using the impact on death row defendants' family members as a mitigating factor in death penalty sentencing hearing. *Florida State University Law Review, 26,* 1119–1176.

King, W. R., Holmes, S. T., Henderson, M. L., & Latessa, E. J. (2001). The community corrections partnership: Examining the long-term effects of youth participation in an Afrocentric diversion program. *Crime & Delinquency, 47,* 558–572.

Kinports, K. (2002). Sex offenses. In K. L. Hall (Ed.), *The Oxford companion to American law.* New York: Oxford University Press.

Kircher, J. C., & Raskin, D. C. (2002). Computer methods for the psychophysiological detection of deception. In M. Kleiner (Ed.), *Handbook of polygraph testing.* San Diego, CA: Academic Press.

Kirk, T., & Bersoff, D. N. (1996). How many procedural safeguards does it take to get a psychiatrist to leave the light bulb unchanged? A due process analysis of the MacArthur Treatment Competence Study. *Psychology, Public Policy, and Law, 2,* 45–72.

Kirkland, K., & Kirkland, K. (2001). Frequency of child custody evaluation complaints and related disciplinary action: A survey of the association of state and provincial psychology boards. *Professional Psychology: Research and Practice, 32,* 171–174.

Kirschman, E. (2007). *I love a cop: What police families need to know* (Rev. ed.). New York: Guilford.

Kliewer, W., Lepore, S. J., Oskin, D., & Johnson, P. D. (1998). The role of social and cognitive processes in children's adjustment to community violence. *Journal of Consulting and Clinical Psychology, 66,* 199–209.

Klintschar, M., Grasbuschnigg, P., & Beham, A. (1998). Death from electrocution during autoerotic practice: Case report and review of the literature. *American Journal of Forensic Medicine and Pathology, 19,* 190–193.

Knapp, S., & VandeCreek, L. (2000). Recovered memories of child abuse: Is there an underlying professional consensus? *Professional Psychology: Research and Practice, 31,* 365–371.

Knight, K., & Simpson, D. D. (2007, September). Special issue: Offender needs and functioning assessments from a national cooperative research program. *Criminal Justice and Behavior, 34.*

Knight, R. A. (1989). An assessment of the concurrent validity of a child molester typology. *Journal of Interpersonal Violence, 4,* 131–150.

Knight, R. A., Carter, D. L., & Prentky, R. A. (1989). A system for the classification of child molesters: Reliability and application. *Journal of Interpersonal Violence, 4,* 3–23.

Knight, R. A., & Cerce, D. D. (1999). Validation and revision of the Multidimensional Assessment of Sex and Aggression. *Psychologica Belgica, 39,* 135–161.

Knight, R. A., & Prentky, R. A. (1987). The developmental antecedents and adult adaptations of rapist subtypes. *Criminal Justice and Behavior, 14,* 403–426.

Knight, R. A., & Prentky, R. A. (1990). Classifying sexual offenders: The development and corroboration of taxonomic models. In W. L. Marshall, D. R. Laws, & H. E. Barbaree (Eds.), *The handbook of sexual assault: Issues, theories, and treatment of the offender.* New York: Plenum.

Knight, R. A., & Prentky, R. A. (1993). Exploring characteristics for classifying juvenile offenders. In H. E. Barbaree, W. L. Marshall, & S. M. Hudson (Eds.), *The juvenile sex offender.* New York: Guilford Press.

Knight, R. A., Prentky, R. A., & Cerce, D. D. (1994). The development, reliability, and validity of the multidimensional assessment of sex and aggression. *Criminal Justice and Behavior, 21,* 72–94.

Knight, R. A., Rosenberg, R., & Schneider, B. A. (1985). Classification of sexual offenders: Perspectives, methods, and validation. In A. W. Burgess (Ed.), *Rape and sexual assault*. New York: Garland.

Knight, R. A., Warren, J. I., Reboussin, R., & Soley, B. J. (1998). Predicting rapist type from crime-scene variables. *Criminal Justice and Behavior, 25,* 46–80.

Knoll, C., & Sickmund, M. (2010, June). *Cases in juvenile court, 2007.* Washington, DC: U.S. Department of Justice, Office of Juvenile Justice and Delinquency Prevention.

Knoll, J. L. (2008). The psychological autopsy, Part I: Applications and methods. *Journal of Psychiatric Practice, 14,* 393–397.

Knoll, J. L. (2009). The psychological autopsy, Part II: Toward a standardized protocol. *Journal of Psychiatric Practice, 15,* 52–59.

Knutson, J. F., Lawrence, E., Taber, S. M., Bank, L., & DeGarmo, D. S. (2009). Assessing children's exposure to intimate partner violence. *Clinical Child and Family Psychology Review, 12,* 157–173.

Kochanska, G., Murray, K., & Coy, K. (1997). Inhibitory control as a contributor to conscience in childhood: From toddler to early school age. *Child Development, 68,* 263–277.

Kocsis, R. N., Cooksey, R. W., & Irwin, H. J. (2002). Psychological profiling of offender characteristics from crime behaviors in serial rape offenses. *International Journal of Offender Therapy and Comparative Criminology, 46,* 144–169.

Koehn, C. E., & Fisher, R. P. (1997). Constructing facial composites with the Mac-a-Mug Pro system. *Psychology, Crime & Law, 3,* 209–218.

Kolko, D. (Ed). (2002). *Handbook on firesetting in children and youth.* Boston: Academic Press.

Kolko, D. J., & Kazdin, A. E. (1989). The children's firesetting interview with psychiatrically referred and nonreferred children. *Journal of Abnormal Child Psychology, 17,* 609–624.

Koocher, G. P., Goodman, G. S., White, C. S., Friedrich, W. N., Sivan, A. B., & Reynolds, C. R. (1995). Psychological science and the use of anatomically detailed dolls in child-sexual assessments. *Psychological Bulletin, 118,* 199–222.

Koss, M. P. (1985). The hidden rape victim: Personality, attitudinal, and situational characteristics. *Psychology of Women Quarterly, 9,* 192–212.

Koss, M. P., & Dinero, T. E. (1988). Predictors of sexual aggression among a national sample of male college students. In R. A. Prentky & V. L. Quinsey (Eds.), *Human sexual aggression: Current perspectives.* New York: New York Academy of Sciences.

Kosson, D. S., Cyterski, T. D., Steuerwald, B. L., Neuman, C. S., & Walker-Matthes, S. (2002). The reliability and validity of the Psychopathy Checklist Youth Version (PCL:YV) in nonincarcerated adolescent males. *Psychological Assessment, 14,* 97–109.

Kosson, D. S., Smith, S. S., & Newman, J. P. (1990). Evaluating the construct validity of psychopathy in Black and White male inmates: Three preliminary studies. *Journal of Abnormal Psychology, 99,* 250–259.

Kovera, M. B., & Cass, S. A. (2002). Compelled mental health examinations, liability decisions, and damage awards in sexual harassment cases: Issues for jury research. *Psychology, Public Policy, and Law, 8,* 96–114.

Kovera, M. B., & McAuliff, B. D. (2000). The effects of peer review and evidence quality on judge evaluations of psychological science:

Are judges effective gatekeepers? *Journal of Applied Psychology, 85,* 574–586.

Kovera, M. B., Penrod, S. D., Pappas, C., & Thill, D. L. (1997). Identification of computer-generated facial composites. *Journal of Applied Psychology, 82,* 235–246.

Kovera, M. B., Russano, M. B., & McAuliff, B. D. (2002). Assessment of the commonsense psychology underlying Daubert: Legal decision makers' abilities to evaluate expert evidence in hostile work environment cases. *Psychology, Public Policy, and Law, 8,* 180–200.

Kozel, F. A., Johnson, K. A., Mu, A., Grenesko, E. L., Laken, S. J., & George, M. S. (2005). Detecting deception using functional magnetic resonance imaging. *Biological Psychiatry, 58,* 605–613.

Kozu, J. (1999). Domestic violence in Japan. *American Psychologist, 54,* 50–54.

Krafka, C., Dunn, M. A., Johnson, M. T., Cecil, J. S., & Miletich, D. (2002). Judge and attorney experiences, practices, and concerns regarding expert testimony in federal civil trials. *Psychology, Public Policy, and Law, 8,* 309–332.

Krapohl, D. J. (2002). The polygraph in personnel selection. In M. Kleiner (Ed.), *Handbook of polygraph testing.* San Diego, CA: Academic Press.

Kratcoski, P. C. (1994). *Correctional counseling and treatment* (3rd ed.). Prospect Heights, IL: Waveland.

Krauss, D. A., & Sales, B. D. (2000). Legal standards, expertise, and experts in the resolution of contested child custody cases. *Psychology, Public Policy, and Law, 6,* 843–879.

Krauss, D. A., & Sales, B. D. (2001). The effects of clinical and scientific expert testimony on juror decision making in capital sentencing. *Psychology, Public Police, and Law, 7,* 267–310.

Kropp, P. R., & Hart, S. D. (2000). The Spousal Assault Risk Assessment (SARA) guide: Reliability and validity in adult male offenders. *Law and Human Behavior, 24,* 101–118.

Kropp, P. R., Hart, S. D., Webster, C. E., & Eaves, D. (1998). *Spousal Assault Risk Assessment: User's guide.* Toronto, ON, Canada: Multi-Health Systems.

Kruh, I., & Grisso, T. (2009). *Evaluation of juveniles' competence to stand trial.* New York: Oxford University Press.

Kubany, E. S., Haynes, S. N., Leisen, M. B., Ownes, J. A., Kaplan, A. S., Watson, S. B., et al. (2000). Development and preliminary validation of a brief broad-spectrum measure of trauma exposure: The Traumatic Life Events Questionnaire. *Psychological Assessment, 12,* 200–224.

Kubany, E. S., Leisen, M. B., Kaplan, A. S., & Kelly, M. P. (2000). Validation of a brief measure of posttraumatic stress disorder: The Distressing Event Questionnaire (DEQ). *Psychological Assessment, 12,* 197–209.

Kurlychek, M. C., & Kempinen, C. A. (2006). Beyond boot camp: The impact of aftercare on offender re-entry. *Criminology & Public Policy, 5,* 363–388.

Kurt, J. L. (1995). Stalking as a variant of domestic violence. *Bulletin of the American Academy of Psychiatry and Law, 23,* 219–230.

Laboratory of Community Psychology. (1974). *Competency to stand trial and mental illness* (DHEW Pub.No. ADM 74–103). Rockville, MD: U.S. Department of Health, Education, & Welfare.

La Fon, D. S. (2008). The psychological autopsy. In B. E. Turvey (Ed.), Criminal profiling: An introduction to behavioral evidence analysis. Amsterdam: Elsevier/Academic Press.

La Fond, J. Q. (2000). The future of involuntary civil commitment in the U.S.A. after Kansas v. Hendricks. *Behavioral Sciences and the Law, 18,* 153–167.

La Fond, J. Q. (2002). Criminal law principles. In K. L. Hall (Ed.), The Oxford companion to American law. New York: Oxford University Press.

La Fond, J. Q. (2003). Outpatient commitment's next frontier: Sexual predators. *Psychology, Public Policy, and Law, 9,* 159–182.

Laboratory of Community Psychology. (1974). *Competency to stand trial and mental illness* (DHEW Pub. No. ADM 74–103). Rockville, MD: U.S. Department of Health, Education, & Welfare.

LaFortune, K. A., & Carpenter, B. N. (1998). Custody evaluations: A survey of mental health professionals. *Behavioral Sciences & the Law, 16,* 207–224.

Lahey, B. B., Loeber, R., Hart, E. L., Frick, P. J., Applegate, B., Zhang, Q., et al. (1995). Four-year longitudinal study of conduct disorder in boys: Patterns and predictors of persistence. *Journal of Abnormal Psychology, 104,* 83–93.

Lahey, B. B., & Waldman, I. D. (2003). A developmental propensity model of the origins of conduct problems during childhood and adolescence. In B. B. Lahey, T. E. Moffitt, & A. Caspi (Eds.), *Causes of conduct disorder and juvenile delinquence.* New York: Guilford Press.

Laird, R. D., Jordan, K., Dodge, K. A., Pettit, G. S., & Bates, J. E. (2001). Peer rejection in childhood, involvement with antisocial peers in early adolescence, and the development of externalizing problems. *Development and Psychopathology, 13,* 337–354.

Lamb, H. R., Weinberger, I. E., & Gross, B. H. (2004). Mentally ill persons in the criminal justice system: Some perspectives. *Psychiatric Quarterly, 75,* 107–126.

Lambert, E. G., Edwards, C., Camp, S. D., & Saylor, W. G. (2005). Here today, gone tomorrow, back again the next day: Antecedents of correctional absenteeism. *Journal of Criminal Justice, 33,* 165–175.

Lambie, I., McCardle, S., & Coleman, R. (2002). Where there's smoke there's fire: Firesetting behaviour in children and adolescents. *New Zealand Journal of Psychology, 31,* 73–79.

Langan, P. A., & Levin, D. J. (2002, June). *Recidivism of prisoners released in 1994.* Washington, DC: U.S. Department of Justice, Bureau of Justice Statistics.

Langevin, R. (1983). *Sexual strands.* Hillsdale, NJ: Erlbaum.

Langhinrichsen-Rohling, J. (2005). Top 10 greatest "hits": Important findings and future directions for intimate violence research. *Journal of Interpersonal Violence, 20,* 108–118.

Langleben, D. D. (2008). Detection of deception with fMRI: Are we there yet? *Legal and Criminological Psychology, 13,* 1–9.

Langton, L. (2010). *Women in law enforcement, 1987–2008.* U.S. Department of Justice, Office of Justice Programs, Bureau of Justice Statistics. Washington, DC: U.S. Department of Justice.

Lanyon, R. I. (1986). Theory and treatment in child molestation. *Journal of Consulting and Clinical Psychology, 54,* 176–182.

Lara, C., Fayyad, J., de Graaf, R., Kessler, R. C., Aguilar-Gaxiola, S., Angermeyer, M., et al. (2009). Childhood predictors of adult attention-deficit/hyperactivity disorder: Results from the World Health Organization World Mental Health Survey initiative. *Biological Psychiatry, 65,* 46–54.

Larson, J. A. (1932). *Lying and its detection: A study of deception and deception tests.* Chicago: University of Chicago Press.

Laws, D. R. (1995). Central elements in relapse prevention procedures with sex offenders. *Psychology, Crime, and Law, 2,* 41–53.

Le, D., & Macnab, A. J. (2001). Self-strangulation by hanging from cloth towel dispensers in Canadian schools. *Injury Prevention, 7,* 231–233.

LeBlanc, M. M., & Kelloway, K. E. (2002). Predictors and outcomes of workplace violence and aggression. *Journal of Applied Psychology, 87,* 444–453.

LeCroy, C. W., Stevenson, P., & MacNeil, G. (2001). Systems considerations in treating juvenile offenders with mental disorders. In J. B. Ashford, B. D. Sales, & W. H. Reid (Eds.), *Treating adult and juvenile offenders with special needs.* Washington, DC: American Psychological Association.

Lee, M. (2002). Asian battered women: Assessment and treatment. In A. R. Roberts (Ed.), *Handbook of domestic violence: Intervention strategies.* New York: Oxford University Press.

Lee, T. M., Liu, H. L., Tan, L. H., Chan, C. C., Mahankali, S., Feng, C. M., et al. (2002). Lie detection by functional magnetic resonance imaging. *Human Brain Mapping, 15,* 157–164.

Leech, S. L., Day, N. L., Richardson, G. A., & Goldschmidt, L. (2003). Predictors of self-reported delinquent behavior in a sample of young adolescents. *Journal of Early Adolescence, 23,* 78–106.

Lefkowitz, J. (1975). Psychological attributes of policemen: A review of research and opinion. *Journal of Social Issues, 31,* 3–26.

Leiber, M. J. (2002). Disproportionate minority confinement (DMC) of youth: An analysis of state and federal efforts to address the issue. *Crime & Delinquency, 48,* 3–45.

Leistico, A., Salekin, R., DeCoster, J., & Rogers, R. (2008). A large-scale meta-analysis relating the Hare measures of psychopathy to antisocial conduct. *Law and Human Behaviior, 32,* 28–45.

Leitenberg, H., & Henning, K. (1995). Sexual fantasy. *Psychological Bulletin, 117,* 469–496.

Lemley, E. C. (2001). Designing restorative justice policy: An analytical perspective. *Criminal Justice Policy Review, 12,* 43–65.

Leo, R. A. (1996). Miranda's revenge: Police interrogation as a confidence game. *Law & Society Review, 30,* 259–288.

Leo, R. A., & Ofshe, R. J. (1998). The consequences of false confessions: Deprivations of liberty and miscarriages of justice in the age of psychological interrogation. *Journal of Criminal Law & Criminology, 88,* 429–440.

Lesch, K. P., & Merschdorf, U. (2000). Impulsivity, aggression, and serotonin: A molecular psychobiological perspective. *Behavioral Sciences & the Law, 18,* 581–604.

Lester, D., Braswell, M., & Van Voorhis, P. (1992). *Correctional counseling* (2nd ed.). Cincinnati, OH: Anderson.

Levant, R. F., Barbanel, L., & DeLeon, P. H. (2004). Psychology's response to terrorism. In F. M. Moghaddam & A. J. Marsella (Eds.), *Understanding terrorism: Psychosocial roots, consequences, and interventions.* Washington, DC: American Psychological Association.

Levensky, E. R., & Fruzzetti, A. E. (2004). Partner violence: Assessment, prediction, and intervention. In W. T. O'Donohue &

E. R. Levensky (Eds.), *Handbook of forensic psychology: Resource for mental health and legal professionals.* Amsterdam, NL: Elsevier.

Levesque, R. J. R. (2001). *Culture and family violence: Fostering change through human rights law.* Washington, DC: American Psychological Association.

Lewinsohn, P. M., & Rosenbaum, M. (1987). Recall of parental behavior by acute depressives, remitted depressives, and nondepressives. *Journal of Personality and Social Psychology, 52,* 611–619.

Lewis, J. A., Dana, R. Q., & Blevins, G. A. (1994). *Substance abuse counseling: An individualized approach* (2nd ed.). Pacific Grove, CA: Brooks/Cole.

Lidz, C. W., Mulvey, E. P., & Gardner, W. (1993). The accuracy of prediction of violence to others. *Journal of the American Medical Association, 269,* 1007–1011.

Lilienfeld, S. O., & Landfield, K. (2008). Science and pseudoscience in law enforcement: A user-friendly primer. *Criminal Justice and Behavior, 35,* 1215–1230.

Lilienfeld, S. O., & Loftus, E. F. (1998). Repressed memories and World War II: Some cautionary notes. *Professional Psychology: Research and Practice, 29,* 471–475.

Lipsey, M. W. (2009). The primary factors that characterize effective interventions with juvenile offenders: A meta-analytic overview. *Victims and Offenders, 4,* 124–147.

Lipton, D. N., McDonel, E. C., & McFall, R. M. (1987). Heterosocial perception in rapists. *Journal of Consulting and Clinical Psychology, 55,* 17–21.

Litwack, T. R. (2003). The competency of criminal defendants to refuse, for delusional reasons, a viable insanity defense recommended by counsel. *Behavioral Sciences and the Law, 21,* 135–156.

Loeber, R. (1990). Development and risk factors of juvenile antisocial behavior and delinquency. *Clinical Psychological Review, 10,* 1–41.

Loeber, R., Burke, J., & Lahey, B. (2002). What are adolescent antecedents to an antisocial personality disorder? *Criminal Behaviour and Mental Health, 12,* 24–36.

Loeber, R., & Stouthamer-Loeber, M. (1998). Development of juvenile aggression and violence: Some common misconceptions and controversies. *American Psychologist, 53,* 242–259.

Loftus, E. F. (1979). *Eyewitness testimony.* Cambridge, MA: Harvard University Press.

Loftus, E. F. (2004). The devil in confessions. *Psychological Science in the Public Interest, 5,* i–ii.

Lonsway, K. A., & Fitzgerald, L. F. (1994). Rape myths: In review. *Psychology of Women Quarterly, 18,* 133–164.

Lonsway, K. A., & Fitzgerald, L. F. (1995). Attitudinal antecedents of rape myth acceptance: A theoretical and empirical reexamination. *Journal of Personality and Social Psychology, 68,* 704–711.

Loo, R. (2003). A meta-analysis of police suicide: Rates, findings, and issues. *Suicide and Life-Threatening Behavior, 33,* 313–325.

Lord, J. (1997). *Death notification: Breaking the bad news with concern for the professional and compassion for the survivor.* Washington, DC: U.S. Department of Justice, Office for Victims of Crime.

Lord, J. (2001). Death notification training of trainers seminars. *OVC Bulletin.* Washington, DC: U.S. Department of Justice, Office for Victims of Crime.

Louden, J. E., & Skeem, J. (2007). Constructing insanity: Jurors' prototypes, attitudes, and legal decision-making. *Behavioral Sciences and the Law, 25,* 449–470.

Lundy, M., & Grossman, S. F. (2004). Elder abuse: Spouse/intimate partner abuse and family violence among elders. *Journal of Elder Abuse and Neglect, 16,* 85–102.

Lunt, I., & Poortinga, Y. H. (1996). Internationalizing psychology. *American Psychologist, 51,* 504–508.

Lykken, D. T. (1981). *A tremor in the blood.* New York: McGraw-Hill.

Lynam, D. (1997). Pursuing the psychopath: Capturing the fledgling psychopath in a nomological net. *Journal of Abnormal Psychology, 106,* 425–438.

Maccoby, E., Buchanan, C., Mnookin, R., & Dornsbusch, S. (1993). Postdivorce roles of mother and father in the lives of their children. *Journal of Family Psychology, 1,* 24–38.

MacKain, S. J., Myers, B., Ostapiej, L., & Newman, R. A. (2010). Job satisfaction among psychologists working in state prisons: The relative impact of facets assessing economics, management, relationships, and perceived organizational support. *Criminal Justice and Behavior, 37,* 306–318.

MacKain, S. J., Tedeschi, R. G., Durham, T. W., & Goldman, V. J. (2002). So what are master's level psychology practitioners doing? Surveys of employers and recent graduates in North Carolina. *Professional Psychology: Research and Practice, 33,* 408–412.

MacKenzie, D. L. (2000). Evidence-based corrections: Identifying what works. *Crime & Delinquency, 46,* 457–471.

MacKenzie, D. L., Robinson, J. W., & Campbell, C. S. (1989). Long-term incarceration of female offenders: Prison adjustment and coping. *Criminal Justice and Behavior, 16,* 223–238.

MacLin, O. H., MacLin, M. K., & Malpass, R. S. (2001). Race, arousal, attention, exposure, and delay: An examination of factors moderating face recognition. *Psychology, Public Policy, and Law, 7,* 134–152.

MacLin, O. H., & Malpass, R. S. (2001). Racial categorization of faces: The ambiguous race face effect. *Psychology, Public Policy, and Law, 7,* 98–118.

MacLin, O. H., MacLin, M. K., & Malpass, R. S. (2001). Race, arousal, attention, exposure, and delay: An examination of factors moderating face recognition. *Psychology, Public Policy, and Law, 7,* 134–152.

Macnab, A. J., Deevska, M., Gagnon, F., Cannon, W. G., & Andrew, T. (2009). Asphyxial games or "the choking game": A potentially fatal risk behavior. *Injury Prevention, 15,* 45–49.

Magaletta, P. R., Diamond, P. M., Faust, E., Daggett, D., & Camp, S. D. (2009). Estimating the mental illness component of service need in corrections: Results from the Mental Health Prevalence Project. *Criminal Justice and Behavior, 36,* 229–244.

Magaletta, P. R., Patry, M. W., Dietz, E. F., & Ax, R. F. (2007). What is correctional about clinical practice in corrections? *Criminal Justice and Behavior, 34,* 7–21.

Malamuth, N. M. (1981). Rape proclivity among males. *Journal of Social Issues, 37,* 138–157.

Malamuth, N. M., & Brown, L. M. (1994). Sexually aggressive men's perceptions of women's communications: Testing three explanations. *Journal of Personality and Social Psychology, 67,* 699–712.

Malamuth, N. M., Heavey, C. L., & Linz, D. (1993). Predicting men's antisocial behavior against women: The "interaction model" of sexual aggression. In N. G. Hall & R. Hirschman (Eds.), *Sexual aggression: Issues in etiology and assessment treatment and policy.* New York: Hemisphere.

Malamuth, N. M., Linz, D., Heavey, C. L., Barnes, G., & Acker, M. (1995). Using the confluence model of sexual aggression to predict men's conflict with women: A 10-year follow-up study. *Journal of Personality and Social Psychology, 69,* 353–369.

Malamuth, N. M., Sockloskie, R., Koss, M., & Tanaka, J. (1991). The characteristics of aggressors against women: Testing a model using a national sample of college students. *Journal of Consulting and Clinical Psychology, 59,* 670–681.

Malesky, L. A., Jr. (2007). Predatory online behavior: Modus operandi of convicted sex offenders in identifying potential victims and contacting minors over the Internet. *Journal of Child Sexual Abuse: Research, Treatment & Program Innovations for Victims, Survivors, & Offenders, 16,* 23–32.

Mandler, J. M. (1988). How to build a baby: On the development of an accessible representational system. *Cognitive Development, 3,* 113–136.

Mandler, J. M. (1990). Recall of events by preverbal children. In A. Diamond (Ed.), *The development and neural bases of higher cognitive functions.* New York: New York Academy of Science.

Mandracchia, J. T., Morgan, R. D., Gross, S., & Garland, J. T. (2007). Inmate thinking patterns: An empirical investigation. *Criminal Justice and Behavior, 34,* 1029–1043.

Manning, P. K. (1995). The police occupational culture in Anglo-American societies. In W. Bailey (Ed.), *The encyclopedia of police science.* New York: Garland Publishing.

Mannuzza, S., Klein, R. G., Bessler, A., Malloy, P., & LaPadula, M. (1998). Adult psychiatric status of hyperactive boys grown up. *American Journal of Psychiatry, 155,* 493–498.

Maremont, M. (2003, July 1). In corporate crime, paper trail leads to ink analyst's door. *Wall Street Journal,* pp. 1, A4.

Margolin, G., Vickerman, K. A., Ramos, M. C., Serrano, S. D., Gordis, E. B., Iturralde, M. C., et al. (2009). Youth exposed to violence: Stability, co-occurrence, and context. *Clinical Child and Family Psychology Review, 12,* 39–54.

Markesteyn, T. (1992). *The psychological impact of nonsexual criminal offenses on victims.* Ottawa, ON: Ministry of the Solicitor General of Canada, Corrections Branch.

Marshall, C. E., Benton, D., & Brazier, J. M. (2000). Elder abuse: Using clinical tools to identify clues of mistreatment. *Geriatrics, 55,* 42–53.

Marshall, G. N., & Schell, T. L. (2002). Reappraising the link between peritraumatic dissociation and PTSD symptom severity: Evidence from a longitudinal study of community violence survivors. *Journal of Abnormal Psychology, 111,* 626–636.

Marshall, W. B. (1996). Assessment, treatment, and theorizing about sex offenders. *Criminal Justice and Behavior, 23,* 162–199.

Marshall, W. L., & Barbaree, H. (1990). Outcome of comprehensive cognitive-behavioral treatment programs. In W. L. Marshall & H. E. Barbaree (Eds.), *Handbook of sexual assault: Issues, theories, and treatment of offenders.* New York: Plenum.

Marshall, W. L., Barbaree, H. E., & Fernandez, M. (1995). Some aspects of social competence in sexual offenders. *Sexual Abuse: A Journal of Research and Treatment, 7,* 113–127.

Marshall, W. L., & Mazzucco, A. (1995). Self-esteem and parental attachments in child molesters. *Sexual Abuse: A Journal of Research and Treatment, 7,* 229–285.

Mart, E. G. (2007). *Issue-focused forensic child custody assessment.* Sarasota, FL: Professional Resource Press.

Martin, S. E. (1989). Women on the move? A report on the status of women in policing. *Women and Criminal Justice, 1,* 21–40.

Martin, S. E. (1992). The effectiveness of affirmative action: The case of women in policing. *Justice Quarterly, 8,* 489–504.

Martinez, R., Jr. (2002). *Latino homicide: Immigration, violence, and community.* New York: Routledge.

Martinez, R., Jr. (2003). Moving beyond Black and White violence: African American, Haitian, and Latino homicides in Miami. In D. F. Hawkins (Ed.), *Violent crime: Assessing race and ethnic differences.* Cambridge, UK: Cambridge University Press.

Mason, M. A., & Quirk, A. (1997). Are mothers losing custody? Read my lips: Trends in judicial decision-making in custody disputes—1920, 1960, 1990, and 1995. *Family Law Quarterly, 31,* 215–236.

Matarazzo, J. D., Allen, B, V., Saslow, G., & Wiens, A. (1964). Characteristics of successful policemen and firemen applicants. *Journal of Applied Psychology, 48,* 123–133.

Mathews, J. K., Hunter, J. A., & Vuz, J. (1997). Juvenile female sexual offenders: Clinical characteristics and treatment issues. *Sexual Abuse: A Journal of Research and Treatment, 9,* 187–199.

Matsumoto, D. (Ed.). (2010). *APA Handbook of interpersonal communication.* Washington, DC: American Psychological Association.

Mayfield, M. G., & Widom, C. S. (1996). The cycle of violence. *Archives of Pediatric and Adolescent Medicine, 150,* 390–395.

McCann, J. T. (1998). A conceptual framework for identifying various types of confessions. *Behavioral Sciences and the Law, 16,* 441–453.

McCann, L., & Pearlman, L. A. (1990). Constructivist self-development theory as a framework for assessing and treating victims of family violence. In S. M. Stith & M. B. Williams (Eds.), *Violence hits home: Comprehensive treatment approaches to domestic violence.* New York: Springer.

McClave, J. L., Russell, P. J., Lyren, A., O'Riordan, M. A., & Bass, N. E. (2010). The choking game: Physician perspectives. *Pediatrics, 125,* 82–87.

McCormick, E. J. (1979). *Job analysis: Methods and applications.* New York: Amacom.

McDonald, R., Jouriles, E. N., Ramisetty-Mikler, S., Caetano, R., & Green, C. E. (2006). Estimating the number of American children living in partner-violence families. *Journal of Family Psychology, 20,* 137–142.

McEwan, T. E., Mullen, P. E., MacKenzie, R. D., & Ogloff, J. R. P. (2009). Violence in stalking situations. *Psychological Medicine, 39,* 1469–1478.

McEwan, T. E., Mullen, P. E., & Purcell, R. (2007). Identifying risk factors in stalking: A review of current research. *International Journal of Law and Psychiatry, 30,* 1–9.

McFarland, B., Faulkner, L., Bloom, J., Hallaux, R., & Bray, J. (1989). Chronic mental illness and the criminal justice system. *Hospital and Community Psychiatry, 40,* 718–723.

McGee, C. (2000). *Childhood experiences of domestic violence.* London: Jessica Kingsley Publishers.

McGrath, R. J., Cumming, G. F., & Burchard, B. L. (2003). *Current practices and trends in sexual abuser management: The Safer Society 2002 Nationwide Survey.* Brandon, VT: Safe Society Press.

McMahon, M. (1999). Battered women and bad science: The limited validity and utility of battered women syndrome. *Psychiatry, Psychology, and Law, 6,* 23–49.

McNally, R. J. (1991). Assessment of posttraumatic stress disorder in children. *Psychological Assessment, 3,* 531–537.

McNally, R. J., Perlman, C. A., Ristuccia, C. S., & Clancy, S. A. (2008). Clinical characteristics of adults reporting repressed, recovered, or continuous memories of childhood sexual abuse. *Journal of Consulting and Clinical Psychology, 74,* 237–242.

McNeece, C. A., Springer, D. W., & Arnold, E. M. (2001). Treating substance abuse disorders. In J. B. Ashford, B. D. Sales, & W. H. Reid (Eds.), *Treating adult and juvenile offenders with special needs.* Washington, DC: American Psychological Association.

McNeece, C. A., Springer, D. W., Shader, M. A., Malone, R., Smith, M. A., Touchton-Cashwell, S., & et al. (1997). *An evaluation of juvenile assessment centers in Florida.* Tallahassee: Florida State University, Institute for Health and Human Services Research.

McQuiston-Surrett, D., & Saks, M. J. (2009). The testimony of forensic identification science: What expert witnesses say and what factfinders hear. *Law and Human Behavior, 33,* 436–453.

McWhirter, P. T. (1999). La violencia privada: Domestic violence in Chile. *American Psychologist, 54,* 37–40.

Meadow, R. (1977). Munchausen syndrome by proxy: The hinterland of child abuse. *The Lancet, 2,* 343–345.

Mears, D. P., & Bales, W. D. (2009). Supermax incarceration and recidivism. *Criminology, 47,* 1131–1166.

Mears, D. P., & Kelly, W. R. (2002). Linking process and outcomes in evaluating a statewide drug treatment program for youthful offenders. *Crime & Delinquency, 48,* 99–115.

Meehl, P. E. (1954). *Clinical versus statistical prediction: A theoretical analysis and a review of the evidence.* Minneapolis: University of Minnesota Press.

Meehl, P. E. (1989). Law and the fireside inductions (with Postscript): Some reflections of a clinical psychologist. *Behavioral Sciences and the Law, 7,* 521–550.

Meesig, R., & Horvath, F. (1995). A national survey of practices, policies and evaluative comments on the use of pre-employment polygraph screening in police agencies in the United States. *Polygraph, 24,* 57–136.

Megargee, E. I. (1974). Applied psychological research in a correctional setting. *Criminal Justice and Behavior, 1,* 43–50.

Meissner, C. A., & Brigham, J. C. (2001). Thirty years of investigating the own-race bias in memory for faces: A meta-analytic review. *Psychology, Public Policy, and Law, 7,* 3–35.

Meissner, C. A., Hartwig, M., & Russano, M. B. (2010). The need for a positive psychological approach and collaborative effort for improving practice in the interrogation room. *Law & Human Behavior, 34,* 43–45.

Meissner, C. A., & Lassiter, G. D. (2010). Conclusion: What have we learned? Implications for practice, policy, and future research. In G. D. Lassiter & C. A. Meissner (Eds.), *Police interrogations and false confessions: Current research, practice, and policy recommendations.* Washington, DC: American Psychological Association.

Meissner, C. A., Russano, M. B., & Narchet, F. M. (2010). The importance of a laboratory science for improving the diagnostic value of confession evidence. In G. D. Lassiter & C. A. Meissner (Eds.), *Police interrogations and false confessions: Current research, practice, and policy recommendations.* Washington, DC: American Psychological Association.

Meloy, J. R., & Gothard, S. (1995). Demographic and clinical comparisons of obsessional followers and offenders with mental disorders. *American Journal of Psychiatry, 152,* 258–263.

Meloy, M. (2000). Police organizations. In N. H. Rafter (Ed.), *Encyclopedia of women and crime.* Phoenix, AZ: Oryx.

Meloy, M., & Mohandie, K. (2008). Two cases studies of corporate-celebrity male victims: The stalking of Steven Spielberg and Stephen Wynn. In J. R. Meloy, L. Sheridan, & J. Hoffman (Eds.), *Stalking, threatening, and attacking public figures: A psychological and behavioral analysis.* New York: Oxford University Press.

Meloy, M., Mohandie, K., & Green McGowan, M. (2008). A forensic investigation of those who stalk celebrities. In J. R. Meloy, L. Sheridan, & J. Hoffman (Eds.), *Stalking, threatening, and attacking public figures: A psychological and behavioral analysis.* New York: Oxford University Press.

Melton, G. B., Petrila, J., Poythress, N. G., & Slobogin, C. (1997). *Psychological evaluations for the courts: A handbook for mental health professionals and lawyers* (2nd ed.). New York: Guilford Press.

Melton, G. B., Petrila, J., Poythress, N. G., & Slobogin, C. (Eds.) (2007). *Psychological evaluations for the courts: A handbook for mental health professionals and lawyers* (3rd ed.). New York: Guilford Press.

Ménard, K. S., Anderson, A. L., & Godboldt, S. M. (2009). Gender differences in intimate partner recidivism: A 5-year follow-up. *Criminal Justice and Behavior, 36,* 61–76.

Mendell, D. (2003). And the walls keep tumbling down: A demonstration project has come and gone, but detention reform continues to gather steam. *AdvoCasey, 5*(1), 18–27.

Merrill, G. S., & Wolfe, V. A. (2000). Battered gay men: An exploration of abuse, help-seeking, and why they stay. *Journal of Homosexuality, 39,* 1–30.

Merrill, M. A. (1927). Intelligence of policemen. *Journal of Personnel Research, 5,* 511–515.

Merry, S., & Harsent, L. (2000). Intruders, pilferers, raiders, and invaders: The interpersonal dimension of burglary. In D. Canter & L. Alison (Eds.), *Profiling property crimes.* Dartmouth, UK: Ashgate.

Merz-Perez, L., Heide, K. M., & Silverman, I. J. (2001). Childhood cruelty to animals and subsequent violence against humans. *International Journal of Offender Therapy and Comparative Criminology, 45,* 556–573.

Messina, N., Grella, C., Burdon, W., & Prendergast, M. (2007). Childhood adverse events and current traumatic distress: A comparison of men and women drug-dependent prisoners. *Criminal Justice and Behavior, 34,* 1385–1401.

Meuer, T., Seymour, A., & Wallace, H. (2002, June). Domestic violence. In A. Seymour, M. Murray, J. Sigmon, M. Hook, C. Edwards, M. Gaboury, & et al. (Eds.), *National Victim Assistance Academy textbook*. Washington, DC: U.S. Department of Justice, Office for Victims of Crime.

Meyers, L. (2007). Cooperation, not coercion. *Monitor on Psychology, 38*(9), 17–18.

Miccio-Fonseca, L. C. (2006). *Multiplex Empirically Guarded Inventory of Ecological Aggrevates for assessing ssexually abusive youth (ages 19 and under) (MEGA)*. San Diego, CA: Author.

Milan, M. A., Chin, C. E., & Nguyen, Q. X. (1999). Practicing psychology in correctional settings: Assessment, treatment, and substance abuse programs. In A. K. Hess & I. B. Weiner (Eds.), *Handbook of forensic psychology* (2nd ed.). New York: Wiley.

Milgram, S. (1974). *Obedience to authority: An experimental view*. New York: Harper & Row.

Miller, L. (1995). Tough guys: Psychotherapeutic strategies with law enforcement and emergency services personnel. *Psychotherapy, 32*, 592–600.

Miller, L. (2008). Death notification for families of homicide victims: Healing dimensions of a complex process. *Omega: Journal of Death and Dying, 57*, 367–380.

Miller, M., & Hinshaw, S. F. (2010). Does childhood executive function predict adolescent functional outcomes in girls with ADHD? *Journal of Abnormal Child Psychology, 38*, 315–326.

Miller, R. D. (2003). Hospitalization of criminal defendants for evaluation of competence to stand trial or for restoration of competence: Clinical and legal issues. *Behavioral Sciences & the Law, 21*, 369–391.

Millon, T. (1994). *MCMI-III: Manual*. Minneapolis, MN: National Computer Systems.

Mills, R. B. (1969). Use of diagnostic small groups in police recruit selection and training. *Journal of Criminal Law, Criminology, and Police Science, 60*, 238–241.

Mills, R. B. (1976). Simulated stress in police recruit selection. *Journal of Police Science and Administration, 4*, 179–186.

Mills, R. B., McDevitt, R. J., & Tonkin, S. (1966). Situational tests in metropolitan police recruit selection. *Journal of Criminal Law, Criminology, and Police Science, 57*, 99–104.

Miner, M. H., Day, D. M., & Nafpaktitis, M. K. (1989). Assessment of coping skills: Development of situational competency test. In D. R. Laws (Eds.), *Relapse prevention with sex offenders*. New York: Guilford Press.

Mischel, W. (1968). *Personality and assessment*. New York: Wiley.

Mischel, W., & Peake, P. K. (1982). Beyond déjà vu in the search for cross-situational consistency. *Psychological Review, 89*, 730–755.

Mitchell, K., Finkelhor, D., & Wolak, J. (2007). Youth Internet users at risk for the most serious online sexual solicitations. *American Journal of Preventive Medicine, 32*, 532–537.

Mitchell, K. J., Wolak, J., & Finkelhor, D. (2005). Police posing as juveniles online to catch sex offenders: Is it working? *Sexual Abuse: A Journal of Research and Treatment, 17*, 241–267.

Moffitt, T. E. (1990). The neuropsychology of juvenile delinquency: A critical review. In M. Tonry & N. Morris (Eds.), *Crime and justice: A review of research*. Chicago: University of Chicago Press.

Moffitt, T. E. (1993a). Adolescent-limited and the life-course persistent antisocial behavior: A developmental taxonomy. *Psychological Review, 100*, 674–701.

Moffitt, T. E. (1993b). The neuropsychology of conduct disorder. *Development and Psychopathology, 5*, 135–151.

Moffitt, T. E., Arseneault, L., Jaffee, S. R., Kim-Cohen, J., Koenen, K. C., Odgers, C. L., et al. (2008). Research review: DSM-V conduct disorder: Research needs for an evidence base. *Journal of Child Psychology and Psychiatry, 49*, 3–33.

Moffitt, T. E., & Caspi, A. (2001). Childhood predictors differentiate life-course persistent and adolescence limited antisocial pathways among males and females. *Development and Psychopathology, 13*, 355–375.

Moffitt, T. E., Caspi, A., Dickson, N., Silva, P., & Stanton, W. (1996). Childhood-onset versus adolescent-onset antisocial conduct problems in males: Natural history from ages 3 to 18. *Development and Psychopathology, 8*, 399–424.

Moffitt, T. E., & Silva, P. A. (1988). Self-reported delinquency, neuropsychological deficit, and history of attention deficit disorder. *Journal of Abnormal Child Psychology, 16*, 553–569.

Mohandie, K., Meloy, J. R., Green McGowan, M., & Williams, J. (2006). The RECON typology of stalking: Reliability and validity based upon a large sample of North American stalkers. *Journal of Forensic Sciences, 51*, 147–155.

Molina, B. S. G., Bukstein, O. G., & Lynch, K. G. (2002). Attention-deficit/hyperactivity disorder and conduct disorder symptomatology in adolescents with alcohol use disorder. *Psychology of Addictive Behaviors, 16*, 161–164.

Monahan, J. (1996). Violence prediction: The past twenty years and the next twenty years. *Criminal Justice and Behavior, 23*, 107–120.

Monahan, J., & Steadman, H. (1996). Violent storms and violent people: How meteorology can inform risk communication in mental health law. *American Psychologist, 51*, 931–938.

Monahan, J., Steadman, H. J., Silver, E., Appelbaum, P. S., Robbins, P. C., Mulvey, E. P., et al. (2001). *Rethinking risk assessment: The MacArthur Study of Mental Disorder and Violence*. New York: Oxford University Press.

Monahan, K. C., Steinberg, L., & Cauffman, E. (2009). Affiliation with antisocial peers, susceptibility to peer influence, and antisocial behavior during the transition to adulthood. *Developmental Psychology, 45*, 1520–1530.

Money, J., & Werleas, J. (1976). Folie à deux in the parents of psychosocial dwarfs: Two cases. *Bulletin of the American Academy of Psychiatry and the Law, 4*, 351–362.

Morawetz, T. H. (2002). Homicide. In K. L. Hall (Ed.), *The Oxford companion to American law*. New York: Oxford University Press.

Morey, L. C. (1991). *The Personality Assessment Inventory: Professional manual*. Odessa, FL: Psychological Assessment Resources.

Morgan, A. B., & Lilienfeld, S. O. (2000). A meta-analytic review of the relation between antisocial behavior and neuropsychological measures of executive functions. *Clinical Psychology Review, 20*, 113–136.

Morgan, R. D., Winterowd, C. L., & Ferrell, S. W. (1999). A national survey of group psychotherapy services in correctional facilities. *Professional Psychology: Research and Practice, 30*, 600–606.

Morris, A. (1996). Gender and ethnic differences in social constraints among a sample of New York City police officers. *Journal of Occupational Health Psychology, 1,* 224–235.

Morris, E. F. (2001). Clinical practices with African Americans: Juxtaposition of standard clinical practices and Africentricism. *Professional Psychology: Research and Practice, 32,* 563–572.

Morris, R. (2000). *Forensic handwriting identification: Fundamental concepts and principles.* San Diego: Academic Press.

Morris, S. M., Steadman, H. J., & Veysey, B. M. (1997). Mental health services in United States jails: A survey of innovative practices. *Criminal Justice and Behavior, 24,* 3–19.

Morry, M. M., & Winkler, E. (2001). Student acceptance and expectation of sexual assault. *Canadian Journal of Behavioural Science, 33,* 188–192.

Morse, S. J. (2003). Involuntary competence. *Behavioral Sciences and the Law, 21,* 311–328.

Mosher, D. L., & Anderson, R. D. (1986). Macho personality, sexual aggression, and reactions to guided imagery of realistic rape. *Journal of Research in Personality, 20,* 77–94.

Mossman, D. (1987). Assessing and restoring competency to be executed: Should psychologists participate? *Behavioral Sciences & the Law, 5,* 397–409.

Mossman, D. (2003). Daubert, cognitive malingering, and test accuracy. *Law and Human Behavior, 27,* 229–249.

Mulder, R. T., Wells, J. E., Joyce, P. R., & Bushnell, J. A. (1994). Antisocial women. *Journal of Personality Disorders, 8,* 279–287.

Mullen, P. E., Pathé, M., & Purcell, R. (2001). Stalking: New constructions of human behaviour. *Australian and New Zealand Journal of Psychiatry, 35,* 9–16.

Mullen, P. E., Pathe, P. E., Purcell, R., & Stuart, G. W. (1999). Study of stalkers. *American Journal of Psychiatry, 156,* 1244–1249.

Mullen, P. E., Pathe, P. G., & Purcell, R. (2000). Stalkers and their victims. New York: Cambridge University Press.

Mulvey, E. P., Arthur, M. W., & Reppucci, N. D. (1993). The prevention and treatment of juvenile delinquency: A review of the research. *Clinical Psychology Review, 13,* 133–167.

Mumcuoglu, K. Y., Gallili, N., Reshef, A., Brauner, P., & Grant, H. (2004). Use of human lice in forensic entomology. *Journal of Medical Entomology, 41,* 803–806.

Mumley, D. L., Tillbrook, C. E., & Grisso, T. (2003). Five-year research update (1996–2000): Evaluations for competence to stand trial (adjudicative competence). *Behavioral Sciences and the Law, 21,* 329–350.

Muñoz, L. C., Frick, P. J., Kimonis, E. R., & Aucoin, K. J. (2008). Verbal ability and delinquency: Testing the moderating role of psychopathic traits. *Journal of Child Psychology and Psychiatry, 49,* 414–421.

Munsey, C. (2007). Stay involved or get out? *Monitor on Psychology, 38*(9), 16–18.

Murphy, J. J. (1972). Current practices in the use of psychological testing by police agencies. *Journal of Criminal Law, Criminology, and Police Science, 63,* 570–576.

Murphy, K. R., & Davidshofer, C. O. (1998). *Psychological testing: Principles and applications* (4th ed.). Upper Saddle River, NJ: Prentice Hall.

Murphy, S. A., Braun, T., Tillery, L., Cain, K. C., Johnson, L. C., & Beaton, R. D. (1999). PTSD among bereaved parents following the violent deaths of their 12- to 28-year-old children: A longitudinal prospective analysis. *Journal of Traumatic Stress, 12,* 273–291.

Murphy, S. A., Johnson, L. C., & Lohan, J. (2002). The aftermath of the violent death of a child: An integration of the assessments of parents' mental distress and PTSD during first 5 years of bereavement. *Journal of Loss and Trauma, 7,* 202–222.

Murphy, W. D., Coleman, E. M., & Haynes, M. R. (1986). Factors related to coercive sexual behavior in a nonclinical sample of males. *Violence and Victims, 1,* 255–278.

Murray, J. B. (1997). Munchausen syndrome/Munchausen syndrome by proxy. *Journal of Psychology, 131,* 343–350.

Murray, M., & O'Ran, S. (2002). Restitution. In A. Seymour, M. Murray, J. Sigmon, M. Hook, C. Edwards, M. Gaboury, & et al. (Eds.), *National Victim Assistance Academy textbook.* Washington, DC: U.S. Department of Justice, Office of Victims of Crime.

Murrie, D. C., & Cornell, D. G. (2002). Psychopathy screening of incarcerated juveniles: A comparison of measures. *Psychological Assessment, 14,* 390–396.

Myers, B., & Arena, M. P. (2001). Trial consultation: A new direction in applied psychology. *Professional Psychology: Research and Practice, 32,* 386–391.

Myers, J. E. B. (1991). Psychologists' involvement in cases of child maltreatment: Limits of role and expertise. *American Psychologist, 46,* 81–82.

Nagayama-Hall, G. (1992, November/December). Inside the mind of the rapist. *Psychology Today, 25,* 12.

Nagin, D. S., Farrington, D. P., & Moffitt, T. (1995). Life-course trajectories of different types of offenders. *Criminology, 33,* 111–139.

Nagin, D. S., & Land, K. C. (1993). Age, criminal careers, and population heterogeneity: Specification and estimation of a nonparametric mixed Poisson model. *Criminology, 31,* 163–189.

Narag, R. E., Pizarro, J., & Gibbs, C. (2009). Lead exposure and its implications for criminological theory. *Criminal Justice and Behavior, 36,* 954–973.

National Center for the Analysis of Violent Crime (2005, August). *Serial murder: Multi-disciplinary perspectives for investigators.* Washington, DC: U.S. Department of Justice, Federal Bureau of Investigation.

National Center for Victims of Crime. (1999). The NCVC does not support the current language of the proposed crime victims' rights constitutional amendment. Arlington, VA: Author.

National Center for Women & Policing. (2002). *Equality denied: The status of women in policing: 2001.* Los Angeles: Author.

National Center on Elder Abuse. (1999). *Types of elder abuse in domestic settings.* Washington, DC: Author.

National Center on Elder Abuse. (2005). *NCEA Fact Sheet: Elder abuse prevalence and incidence.* Newark, DE: Author.

National Commission on Correctional Health Care. (2008). *Standards for Health Services in Prisons.* Chicago: Author.

National Council of Juvenile and Family Court Judges. (1993). The revised report from the National Task Force on Juvenile Sexual Offending. *Juvenile and Family Court Journal, 44,* 1–120.

National Institute of Mental Health. (1982). *Television and behavior: Ten years of scientific progress and implications for the eighties. Summary report.* Washington, DC: U.S. Government Printing Office.

National Organization for Victim Assistance. (1998). *Community crisis response team training manual* (2nd ed.). Washington, DC: Author.

National Resource Center on Child Sexual Abuse. (1996, March/April). *NRCCSA News.* Huntsville, AL: Author.

National Research Council. (2003). *The polygraph and lie detection.* Washington, DC: The National Academies Press.

Neal, T. M. S., & Clements, C. B. (2010). Prison rape and psychological sequelae: A call for research. *Psychology, Public Policy, and Law, 16,* 284–299.

Neimeyer, R. A. (2000). Searching the meaning of meaning: Grief therapy and the process of reconstruction. *Death Studies, 24,* 541–558.

Neimeyer, R. A., Prigerson, H. G., & Davies, B. (2002). Mourning and meaning. *American Behavioral Scientist, 46,* 235–251.

Nelson, D. W. (2003, Spring). On adolescent crime: Trend to end fad justice. *AdvoCasey 5*(1), 2.

Neubauer, D. W. (1997). *Judicial process* (2nd ed.). Fort Worth, TX: Harcourt Brace.

Neubauer, D. W. (2002). *America's courts and the criminal justice system* (7th ed.). Belmont, CA: Wadsworth.

Newman, G. (1979). *Understanding violence.* New York: J. B. Lippincott.

Newman, J. P., Curtin, J. J., Bertsch, J. D., & Baskin-Sommers, A. R. (2010). Attention moderates the fearlessness of psychopathic offenders. *Biological Psychiatry, 67,* 66–70.

Newman, R. (2010). Diversifying consulting psychology for the future. *Consulting Psychology Journal: Practice and Research, 62,* 73–76.

Nicholson, R. (1999). Forensic assessment. In R. Roesch, S. D. Hart, & J. R. P. (Eds.), *Psychology and law: The state of the discipline.* New York: Kluwer Academic/Plenum.

Nicholson, R., & Norwood, S. (2000). The quality of forensic psychological assessments, reports, and testimony: Acknowledging the gap between promise and practice. *Law and Human Behavior, 24,* 9–44.

Nietzel, M. T., McCarthy, D. M., & Kerr, M. J. (1999). Juries: The current state of the empirical literature. In R. Roesch, S. D. Hart, & J. R. P. Ogloff (Eds.), *Psychology and law: The state of the discipline.* New York: Kluwer Academic.

Nigg, J. T. (2000). On inhibition/disinhibition in developmental psychopathology: Views from cognitive and personality psychology and a working inhibition taxonomy. *Psychological Bulletin, 126,* 220–246.

Nigg, J. T., Butler, K. M., Huang-Pollock, C. L., & Henderson, J. M. (2002). Inhibitory processes in adults with persistent childhood onset ADHD. Journal of Consulting and *Clinical Psychology, 70,* 153–157.

Nigg, J. T., & Huang-Pollock, C. L. (2003). An early-onset model of the role of executive functions and intelligence in conduct disorder/delinquency. In B. B. Lahey, T. E. Moffitt, & A. Caspi (Eds.), *Causes of conduct disorder and juvenile delinquency.* New York: Guilford Press.

Nigg, J. T., John, O. P., Blaskey, L. G., Huang-Pollock, C., Willcutt, E. G., Hinshaw, S. P., et al. (2002). Big Five dimensions and ADHD symptoms: Links between personality traits and clinical symptoms. *Journal of Personality and Social Psychology, 83,* 451–469.

Nigg, J. T., Quamma, J. P., Greenberg, M. T., & Kusche, C. A. (1999). A two-year longitudinal study of neuropsychological and cognitive performance in relation to behavioral problems and competencies in elementary school children. *Journal of Abnormal Child Psychology, 27,* 51–63.

Norris, F. H., & Kaniasty, K. (1994). Psychological distress following criminal victimization in the general population: Cross-sectional, longitudinal, and prospective analysis. *Journal of Consulting and Clinical Psychology, 62,* 111–123.

Norris, F. H., Kaniasty, K., & Scheer, D. A. (1990). Use of mental health services among victims of crime: Frequency, correlates, and subsequent recovery. Journal of *Consulting and Clinical Psychology, 58,* 538–547.

Norris, R. J., & Redlich. A. (2010, Summer). Actual innocence research: Researching compensation policies and other reforms. *American Psychology-Law Society News, 30*(2), 6–7.

Northpointe Institute for Public Management. (1996). *COMPAS* (Computer software). Traverse City, MI: Author.

Oberlander, L. B., Goldstein, N. E., & Ho, C. N. (2001). Pre-adolescent adjudicative competence: Methodological considerations and recommendations for standard practice standards. *Behavioral Sciences & the Law, 19,* 545–563.

Occupational Safety and Health Administration. (2001). *Workplace violence.* Washington, DC: U.S. Department of Labor.

Office for Victims of Crime. (2009). *Victims with disabilities: Collaborative, multidisciplinary first response.* Washington, DC: U.S. Department of Justice, Author.

Office of Juvenile Justice and Delinquency Prevention. (1996). *Juvenile boot camps: Lessons learned.* Washington, DC: U.S. Department of Justice.

Offord, D. R., Boyle, M. C., & Racine, Y. A. (1991). The epidemiology of antisocial behavior in childhood and adolescence. In D. J. Pepler & H. Rubin (Eds.), *The development and treatment of childhood aggression.* Hillsdale, NJ: Erlbaum.

Ogawa, B., & Belle, A. S. (2002). Respecting diversity: Responding to underserved victims of crime. In A. Seymour, M. Murray, J. Sigmon, M. Hook, C. Edwards, M. Gaboury, & et al. (Eds.), *National Victim Assistance Academy textbook.* Washington, DC: U.S. Department of Justice, Office of Victims of Crime.

Ogle, R. S. (2000). Battered women and self-defense, USA. In N. H. Rafter (Ed.), *Encyclopedia of women and crime.* Phoenix, AZ: Oryx.

Ogloff, J. R. P. (1999). Ethical and legal contours of forensic psychology. In R. Roesch, S. D. Hart, & J. R. P. Ogloff (Eds.), *Psychology and law: The state of the discipline.* New York: Kluwer Academic.

Olaya, B., Ezpeleta, L., de la Osa, N., Granero, R., & Doménech, J. M. (2010). Mental health needs of children exposed to intimate partner violence seeking help from mental health services. *Children and Youth Services Review, 32,* 1004–1011.

Olkin, R. (2002). Could you hold the door for me? Including disability in diversity. *Cultural Diversity and Ethnic Minority Psychology, 8,* 130–137.

Olkin, R., & Pledger, C. (2003). Can disability studies and psychology join hands? *American Psychologist, 58,* 296–304.

O'Neill, M. L., Lidz, V., & Heilbrun, K. (2003). Adolescents with psychopathic characteristics in a substance abusing cohort: Treatment process and outcomes. *Law and Human Behavior, 27,* 299–313.

Orne, M. T. (1970). Hypnosis, motivation and the ecological validity of the psychological experiment. In W. J. Arnold & M. M. Page (Eds.), *Nebraska Symposium on Motivation.* Lincoln: University of Nebraska Press.

Orne, M. T., Dinges, D. F., & Orne, E. C. (1984). On the differential diagnosis of multiple personality in the forensic context. *International Journal of Clinical and Experimental Hypnosis, 32,* 118–169.

Orne, M. T., Whitehouse, W. G., Dinges, D. F., & Orne, E. C. (1988). Reconstructing memory through hypnosis: Forensic and clinical implications. In H. M. Pettinati (Ed.), *Hypnosis and memory.* New York: Guilford Press.

Ornstein, P. A., Ceci, S. J., & Loftus, E. F. (1998a). Adult recollections of childhood abuse: Cognitive and developmental perspectives. *Psychology, Public Policy, and Law, 4,* 1025–1051.

Ornstein, P. A., Ceci, S. J., & Loftus, E. F. (1998b). Comment on Alpert, Brown, and Courtois (1998): The science of memory and the practice of psychotherapy. *Psychology, Public Policy, and Law, 4,* 996–1010.

O'Tool, M. E. (2000). *The school shooter: A threat assessment perspective.* Quantico, VA: National Center for the Analysis of Violent Crime, Criminal Incident Response Group.

Otto, R. K., & Heilbrun, K. (2002). The practice of forensic psychology: A look toward the future in light of the past. *American Psychologist, 57,* 5–18.

Otto, R. K., Poythress, N. G., Nicholson, R. A., Edens, J. F., Monahan, J., Bonnie, R. I., et al. (1998). Psychometric properties of the MacArthur Competence Assessment Tool—Criminal Adjudication. *Psychological Assessment, 10,* 435–443.

Owen, B. (2000). Prison security. In N. H. Rafter (Ed.), *Encyclopedia of women and crime.* Phoenix, AZ: Oryx.

Ozer, E. J., Best, S. R., Lipsey, T. L., & Weiss, D. S. (2003). Predictors of posttraumatic stress disorder and symptoms in adults: A meta-analysis. *Psychological Bulletin, 129,* 52–73.

Padela, A. I., & Heisler, M. (2010). The association of perceived abuse and discrimination after September 11, 2001, with psychological distress, level of happiness, and health status among Arab Americans. *American Journal of Public Health, 100,* 284–291.

Palerea, R., Zona, M. A., Lane, J. C., & Langhinrichsen-Rohling, J. (1999). The dangerous nature of intimate relationship stalking: Threats, violence, and associated risk factors. *Behavioral Sciences and the Law, 17,* 269–283.

Palmer, E. J., & Hollin, C. R. (2007). The Level of Service Inventory—Revised with English women prisoners: A needs and reconviction analysis. *Criminal Justice and Behavior, 34,* 91–98.

Palmer, J. W., & Palmer, S. E. (1999). *Constitutional rights of prisoners* (6th ed.). Cincinnati, OH: Anderson.

Palmer, T. (1991). The effectiveness of intervention: Recent trends and current issues. *Crime and Delinquency, 37,* 330–346.

Paoline, E. A., III. (2003). Taking stock: Toward a richer understanding of police culture. *Journal of Criminal Justice, 31,* 199–214.

Parent, D. G., Leiter, V., Kennedy, S., Livens, L., Wentworth, D., & Wilcox, S. (1994). *Conditions of confinement: Juvenile detention and corrections facilities.* Washington, DC: U.S. Department of Justice, Office of Justice Programs, Office of Juvenile Justice and Delinquency Prevention.

Parry, J., & Drogan, E. Y. (2000). *Criminal law handbook on psychiatric and psychological evidence and testimony.* Washington, DC: American Bar Association.

Partlett, D. F., & Nurcombe, B. (1998). Recovered memories of child sexual abuse and liability: Society, science, and the law in a comparative setting. *Psychology, Public Policy, and Law, 4,* 1253–1306.

Paton, D. (2006). Critical incident stress risk in police offices: Managing resilience and vulnerability. *Traumatology, 12,* 198–206.

Patrick, C. J., & Iacono, W. G. (1989). Psychopathy, threat, and polygraph test accuracy. *Journal of Applied Psychology, 74,* 347–355.

Patterson, G. R., (1982). Coercive family processes. Eugene, OR: Castalia Press.

Patterson, G. R., & Yoerger, K. (2002). A developmental model for early- and late-onset delinquency. In J. B. Reid, G. R. Patterson & J. J. Snyder (Eds.), *Antisocial behavior in children and adults: A developmental analysis and the Oregon model for intervention.* Washington, DC: American Psychological Association.

Pearl, P. T. (1995). Identifying and responding to Munchausen syndrome by proxy. *Early Child Development and Care, 106,* 177–185.

Pearson, F. S., Lipton, D. S., Cleland, C. M., & Yee, D. S. (2002). The effects of behavior/cognitive-behavioral programs on recidivism. *Crime & Delinquency, 48,* 476–496.

Pease, T., & Frantz, B. (1994). *Your safety . . . your rights & personal safety and abuse prevention education program to empower adults with disabilities and train service providers.* Doylestown, PA: Network of Victim Assistance.

Penrod, S., & Cutler, B. L. (1995). Witness confidence and witness accuracy: Assessing their forensic relation. *Psychology, Public Policy, and Law, 1,* 817–845.

Pepler, D. J., Byrd, W., & King, G. (1991). A social-cognitively based social skills training program for aggressive children. In D. J. Pepler & K. H. Rubin (Eds.), *The development and treatment of childhood aggression.* Hillsdale, NJ: Lawrence Erlbaum.

Perlin, M. L. (1991). Power imbalances in therapeutic and forensic relationships. *Behavioral Sciences & the Law, 9,* 111–128.

Perlin, M. L. (1994). *The jurisprudence of the insanity defense.* Durham, NC: Carolina Academic Press.

Perlin, M. L. (1996). "Dignity was the first to leave": Godinez v. Moran, Colin Ferguson, and the trial of mentally disabled criminal defendants. *Behavioral Sciences and the Law, 14,* 61–81.

Perlin, M. L. (2003). Beyond Dusky and Godinez: Competency before and after trial. *Behavioral Sciences and the Law, 21,* 297–310.

Perlin, M. L., & Dorfman, D. A. (1996). Is it more than "dodging lions and wastin' time"? Adequacy of counsel, questions of competence, and the judicial process in individual right to refuse treatment cases. *Psychology, Public Policy, and Law, 2,* 114–136.

PERSEREC (The Defense Personnel Security Research Center). (1992). *Police integrity: Use of personality measures to identify corruption-prone officers.* Monterey, CA: Author.

Pérusse, D., & Gendreau, P. (2005). Genetics and the development of aggression. In R. E. Tremblay, W. W. Hartup, & J. Archer (Eds.), *Developmental origins of aggression.* New York: Guilford Press.

Peters, S. D., Wyatt, G. E., & Finkelhor, D. (1986). Prevalence. In D. Finkelhor (Ed.), *Sourcebook on child sexual abuse.* Beverly Hills, CA: Sage.

Peterson, D. R. (1968). The doctor of psychology program at the University of Illinois. *American Psychologist, 23,* 511–516.

Petretic-Jackson, P. A., Witte, T. H., & Jackson, T. L. (2002). Battered women: Treatment goals and treatment planning. In A. R. Roberts (Ed.), *Handbook of domestic violence intervention strategies: Policies, programs, and legal remedies.* New York: Oxford University Press.

Petrila, J. (2005). Introduction to this issue: Diversion from the criminal justice system. *Behavioral Sciences & the Law, 23,* 161–162.

Pfiffner, L. J., McBurnett, K., Lahey, B. B., Loeber, R., Green, S., Frick, P. J., et al. (1999). Association of parental psychopathology to the comorbid disorders of boys with attention deficit–hyperactivity disorder. *Journal of Consulting and Clinical Psychology, 67,* 881–893.

Pierce, C. S., & Brodsky, S. L. (2002). Trust and understanding in the attorney–juvenile relationship. *Behavioral Sciences and the Law, 20,* 89–107.

Pihl, R. O., & Benkelfat, C. (2005). Neuromodulators in the development and expression of inhibition and aggression. In R. E. Tremblay, W. W. Hartup, & J. Archer (Eds.), *Developmental origins of aggression.* New York: Guilford Press.

Pillemer, K., & Finkelhor, D. (1988). The prevalence of elder abuse: A random sample survey. *Gerontologist, 28,* 51–57.

Pinizzotto, A. J. (1984). Forensic psychology: Criminal personality profiling. *Journal of Police Science and Administration, 12,* 32–40.

Pinizzotto, A. J., & Davis, E. F. (1992). *Killed in the line of duty: A study of selected felonious killings of law enforcement officers.* Washington, DC: U. S. Department of Justice.

Pinizzotto, A. J., Davis, E., & Miller, C. (1997). *In the line of fire: Violence against law enforcement.* Washington, DC: U. S. Department of Justice.

Pinizzotto, A. J., Davis, E. F., & Miller, C. E. (2006). *Violent encounters: A study of felonious assaults on our nation's law enforcement officers.* Washington, DC: U. S. Department of Justice.

Pinizzotto, A. J., & Finkel, N. J. (1990). Criminal personality profiling: An outcome and process study. *Law and Human Behavior, 14,* 215–234.

Platt, A. (1969). *The child savers: The invention of delinquency.* Chicago: University of Chicago Press.

Platt, J. J., Bux, D. A., Lamb, R. J., Lidz, V., & Husband, S. D. (1996). *Twenty-four session cognitive-behavioral treatment manual for adolescent substance abusers.* Philadelphia: MCP Hahnemann University.

Podkopacz, M. R., & Feld, B. C. (1996). The end of the line: An empirical study of judicial waiver. *Journal of Criminal Law and Criminology, 86,* 449–492.

Polizzi, D. M., MacKenzie, D. L., & Hickman, L. J. (1999). What works in adult sex offender treatment: A review of prison- and non-prison-based treatment programs. *International Journal of Offender Therapy and Comparative Criminology, 43,* 357–374.

Polusny, M., & Follette, V. (1996). Remembering childhood sexual abuse: A national survey of psychologists' clinical practices, beliefs, and personal experiences. *Professional Psychology: Research and Practice, 27,* 41–52.

Pornari, C. D., & Wood, J. (2010). Peer and cyber aggression in secondary school students: The role of moral disengagement, hostile attribution bias, and outcome expectancies. *Aggressive Behavior, 36,* 81–94.

Porter, S., Fairweather, D., Drugge, J., Hervé, H., Birt, A., & Boer, D. P. (2000). Profiles of psychopathy in incarcerated sexual offenders. *Criminal Justice and Behavior, 27,* 216–233.

Portzky, G., Audenaert, K., & van Heeringen, K. (2009). Psychological and psychiatric factors associated with adolescent suicide: A case-control psychological autopsy study. *Journal of Adolescence, 32,* 849–862.

Potoczniak, M. J., Mourot, J. E., Crosbie-Burnett, M., & Potoczniak, D. J. (2003). Legal and psychological perspectives on same-sex domestic violence: A multisystematic approach. *Journal of Family Violence, 17,* 252–259.

Poythress, N. G. (1979). A proposal for training in forensic psychology. *American Psychologist, 34,* 612–621.

Poythress, N. G., Otto, R. K., Darnes, J., & Starr, L. (1993). APA's expert panel in congressional review of the USS Iowa incident. *American Psychologist, 48,* 8–15.

Prendergast, M. L., Farabee, D., Cartier, J., & Henkin, S. (2002). Involuntary treatment within a prison setting. *Criminal Justice and Behavior, 29,* 5–26.

Prentky, R. A., Burgess, A. W., & Carter, D. L. (1986). Victim responses by rapist type: An empirical and clinical analysis. *Journal of Interpersonal Violence, 1,* 73–98.

Prentky, R. A., Burgess, A. W., Rokous, F., Lee, A., Hartman, C., Ressler, R., et al. (1989). The presumptive role of fantasy in serial sexual homicide. *American Journal of Psychiatry, 146,* 887–891.

Prentky, R. A., Harris, B., Frizzell, K., & Righthand, S. (2000). An actuarial procedure of assessing risk in juvenile sex offenders. *Sexual Abuse: A Journal of Research and Treatment, 12,* 71–93.

Prentky, R. A., & Knight, R. A. (1986). Impulsivity in the lifestyle and criminal behavior of sexual offenders. *Criminal Justice and Behavior, 13,* 141–164.

Prentky, R. A., & Knight, R. A. (1991). Identifying critical dimensions for discriminating among rapists. *Journal of Consulting and Clinical Psychology, 59,* 643–661.

Prentky, R. A., Knight, R. A., & Lee, A. F. S. (1997, June). *Child sexual molestation: Research issues.* Washington, DC: U.S. Department of Justice, Office of Justice Programs.

Prentky, R., & Righthand, S. (2003). *Juvenile Sex Offender Assessment Protocol-II (J-SOAP-II).* Washington, DC: Office of Juvenile Justice and Delinquency Prevention.

Presser, L. & Van Voorhis, P. (2002). Values and evaluation: Assessing processes and outcomes of restorative justice programs. *Crime & Delinquency, 48,* 162–188.

Purcell, R., Moller, B., Flower, T., & Mullen, P. E. (2009). Stalking among juveniles. *British Journal of Psychiatry, 194,* 451–455.

Puritz, P., & Scali, M. A. (1998). *Beyond the walls: Improving conditions of confinement for youth in custody.* Washington, DC: Office of Juvenile Justice and Delinquency Prevention.

Putnam, C. T., & Kirkpatrick, J. T. (2005, May). Juvenile firesetting: A research overview. *Juvenile Justice Bulletin* (NCJ 207606). Washington, DC: U.S. Department of Justice, Office of Juvenile Justice and Delinquency Prevention.

Puzzanchera, C. M. (2009, April). *Juvenile arrests 2007.* Washington, DC: U.S. Department of Justice, Office of Juvenile Justice and Delinquency Prevention.

Puzzanchera, C. M., Adams, B., & Sickmund, M. (2010, March). *Juvenile court statistics, 2006–2007.* Pittsburgh, PA: National Center for Juvenile Justice. Retrieved December 14, 2010, from http://www.OJJDP.NCJRS.GOV/ojstatbb/njcda.

Puzzanchera, C., Stahl, A. L., Finnegan, T. A., Tierney, N. J., & Snyder, H. N. (2003, June). *Juvenile court statistics 1998.* Washington, DC: National Center for Juvenile Justice, Office of Juvenile Justice and Delinquency Prevention.

Puzzanchera, C. M., Stahl, A. L., Finnegan, T. A., Tierney, N., & Snyder, H. N. (2004, December). *Juvenile court statistics 2000.* Washington, DC: Office of Juvenile Justice and Delinquency Prevention, National Center for Juvenile Justice.

Qualls, S. H., Segal, D. L., Norman, S., Niederehe, G., & Gallagher-Thompson, D. (2002). Psychologists in practice with older adults: Current patterns, sources of training, and need for continuing education. *Professional Psychology: Research and Practice, 33,* 435–442.

Quinsey, V. L. (1986). Men who have sex with children. In D. N. Weisstub (Ed.), *Law and mental health: International perspectives* (Vol. 2). New York: Pergamon.

Quinsey, V. L., Harris, G. T., Rice, M. E., & Cormier, C. A. (1998). *Violent offenders: Appraising and managing risk.* Washington, DC: American Psychological Association.

Quinsey, V. L., Harris, G. T., Rice, M. E., & Cormier, C. A. (2006). *Violent offenders: Appraising and managing risk* (2nd ed.). Washington, DC: American Psychological Association.

Quinsey, V. L., Rice, & Harris (1995). Actuarial prediction of sexual recidivism. *Journal of Interpersonal Violence, 10,* 85–105.

Rabe-Hemp, C. E., & Schuck, A. M. (2007). Violence against police officers: Are female officers at greater risk? *Police Quarterly, 10,* 411–428.

Radelet, M. L., & Barnard, G. W. (1986). Ethics and the psychiatric determination of competency to be executed. *Bulletin of the American Academy of Psychiatry and Law, 14,* 37–53.

Raine, A. (1993). The psychopathology of crime: Criminal behavior as a clinical disorder. San Diego, CA: Academic Press.

Raine, A. (2002). Biosocial studies of antisocial and violent behavior in children and adults: A review. *Journal of Abnormal Child Psychology, 30,* 311–326.

Ramchand, R., Schell, T. L., Karney, B. R., Osilla, K. C., Burns, R. M., & Caldarone, L. B. (2010). Disparate prevalence estimates of PTSD among service members who served in Iraq and Afghanistan: Possible explanations. *Journal of Traumatic Stress, 23,* 59–68.

Ramirez, D., McDevitt, J., & Farrell, A. (2000, November). *A resource guide on racial profiling data collection systems: Promising practices and lessons learned.* Boston: Northeastern University Press.

Rand, M. R. (2009, September). *Criminal victimization, 2008.* Washington, DC: U. S. Department of Justice, Office of Justice Programs.

Rand, M. R., & Harrell, E. (2009, October). *Crime against people with disabilities, 2007.* Washington, DC: U. S. Departmet of Justice, Office of Justice Programs.

Raspe, R. E. (1944). *The surprising adventures of Baron Munchausen.* New York: Peter Pauper.

Ravich, T. M. (2007). Is airline passenger profiling necessary? *University of Miami Law Review, 62,* 1–52.

Redding, R. E. (2010, June). Juvenile transfer laws: An effective deterrent to delinquency? *Juvenile Justice Bulletin.* Washington, DC: U.S. Department of Justice, Office of Justice Programs, Office of Juvenile Justice and Delinquency Prevention.

Redding, R. E., Floyd, M. Y., & Hawk, G. L. (2001). What judges and lawyers think about the testimony of mental health experts: A survey of the courts and bar. *Behavioral Sciences & the Law, 19,* 583–594.

Redlich, A. D., & Goodman, G. S. (2003). Taking responsibility for an act not committed: The influence of age and suggestibility. *Law and Human Behavior, 27,* 141–156.

Redlich, A. D., Silverman, M., & Steiner, H. (2003). Pre-adjudicative and adjudicative competence in juveniles and young adults. *Behavioral Sciences and the Law, 21,* 393–410.

Reed, G. M., Levant, R. F., Stout, C. E., Murphy, M. J., & Phelps, R. (2001). Psychology in the current mental health marketplace. *Professional Psychology: Research and Practice, 32,* 65–70

Reichert, J., Adams, S., & Bostwick, L. (2010, April). *Victimization and help-seeking behaviors among female prisoners in Illinois.* Chicago: Illinois Criminal Justice Information Authority.

Reid, J. B. (1993). Prevention of conduct disorders before and after school entry: Relating interventions to developmental findings. *Development and Psychopathology, 5,* 243–262.

Reid, J. E., & Inbau, F. E. (1977). *Truth and deception: The polygraph ("lie detector") technique* (2nd ed.). Baltimore: Williams & Wilkins.

Reidel, M. (2003). Homicide in Los Angeles County: A study of Latino victimization. In D. F. Hawkins (Ed.), *Violent crime: Assessing race and ethnic differences.* Cambridge, UK: Cambridge University Press.

Reiser, M. (1972). *The police psychologist.* Springfield, IL: Charles C Thomas.

Reiser, M. (1982). *Police psychology: Collected papers.* Los Angeles: LEHI.

Reisner, R., Slobogin, C., & Rai, A. (2004). *Law and the mental health system: Civil and criminal aspects* (4th ed.). St. Paul, MN: West Publishing.

Reitzel, L. R. (2003, January). Sexual offender update: Juvenile sexual offender recidivism and treatment effectiveness. *Correctional Psychologist, 35*(1), 3–4.

Rennison, C. (2001, March). *Violent victimization and race, 1993–1998.* Washington, DC: U.S. Department of Justice, Bureau of Justice Statistics.

Rennison, C. (2002a, April). *Hispanic victims of violent crime, 1993–2000.* Washington, DC: U.S. Department of Justice, Bureau of Justice Statistics.

Rennison, C. M. (2002b, August). *Rape and sexual assault: Reporting to police and medical attention, 1992–2000.* Washington, DC: U.S. Department of Justice, Bureau of Justice Statistics.

Reno, J. (1999). Message From the Attorney General. In Technical Working Group for Eyewitness Evidence (Ed.), *Eyewitness evidence: A guide for law enforcement.* Washington, DC: National Institute of Justice.

Renzetti, C. M. (1992). *Violent betrayal: Partner abuse in lesbian relationships.* Newbury Park, CA: Sage.

Reppucci, N. D., & Saunders, J. T. (1974). Social psychology of behavior modification: Problems of implementation in natural settings. *American Psychologist, 29,* 649–660.

Resnick, H. S., Kilpatrick, D. G., Dansky, B. S., Saunders, B. E., & Best, C. L. (1993). Prevalence of civilian trauma in posttraumatic stress disorder in a representative national sample of women. *Journal of Consulting and Clinical Psychology, 61,* 984–991.

Resnick, P. J. (1970). Murder of the newborn: A psychiatric review of neonaticide. *American Journal of Psychiatry, 120,* 1414–1420.

Ressler, R. K., Burgess, A., & Douglas, J. E. (1988). *Sexual homicide: Patterns and motives.* Lexington, MA: Lexington Books.

Rhee, S. H., & Waldman, I. D. (2002). Genetic and environmental influences on antisocial behavior: A meta-analysis of twin and adoption studies. *Psychological Bulletin, 128,* 490–529.

Rice, M. E., & Harris, G. T. (2002). Men who molest their sexually immature daughters: Is a special explanation required? *Journal of Abnormal Psychology, 111,* 329–339.

Rice, M. E., Harris, G. T., & Cormier, C. A. (1992). An evaluation of a maximum security therapeutic community for psychopaths and other mentally disordered offenders. *Lawanda Human Behavior, 16,* 399–412.

Richardson, G., Gudjonsson, G. H., & Kelly, T. P. (1995). Interrogative suggestibility in an adolescent forensic population. *Journal of Adolescence, 18,* 211–216.

Richardson, L. (2003). *Opportunities in correctional psychology.* Washington, DC: American Psychological Association.

Righthand, S., & Welch, C. (2001, March). *Juveniles who have sexually offended: A review of the professional literature.* Washington, DC: U.S. Department of Justice, Office of Juvenile Justice and Delinquency Prevention.

Risinger, D. M., & Loop, J. L. (2002). Three card monted, Monty Hall, modus operandi, and "offender profiling": Some lessons of modern cognitive science for the law of evidence. *Cardozo Law Review, 24,* 193–285.

Ritvo, E., Shanok, S. S., & Lewis, D. O. (1983). Firesetting and nonfiresetting delinquents. *Child Psychiatry and Human Development, 13,* 259–267.

Robbins, E., & Robbins, L. (1964). Arson with special reference to pyromania. *New York State Journal of Medicine, 2,* 795–798.

Robins, P. M., & Sesan, R. (1991). Munchausen syndrome by proxy: Another women's disorder. *Professional Psychology: Research and Practice, 22,* 285–290.

Rodriguez, N. (2007). Restorative justice at work: Examining the impact of restorative justice resolutions on juvenile recidivism. *Crime & Delinquency, 33,* 355–379.

Roediger, H. L., & Bergman, E. T. (1998). The controversy over recovered memories. *Psychology, Public Policy, and Law, 4,* 1091–1109.

Roesch, R., Zapf, P. A., Golding, S. L., & Skeem, J. L. (1999). Defining and assessing competency to stand trial. In A. K. Hess & I. B. Weiner (Eds.), *The handbook of forensic psychology* (2nd ed.). New York: John Wiley.

Rogers, R. (1984). Rogers Criminal Responsibility Assessment Scales (R-CRAS) and test manual. Odessa, FL: Psychological Assessment Resources.

Rogers, R. (1992). *Structured interview of reported symptoms.* Odessa, FL: Psychological Assessment Resources.

Rogers, R. (1997). *Clinical assessment of malingering and deception* (2nd ed.). New York: Guilford Press.

Rogers, R., & Ewing, C. P. (1989). Ultimate issue proscriptions: A cosmetic fix and plea for empiricism. *Law and Human Behavior, 13,* 357–374.

Rogers, R., Hazelwood, L. L., Sewell, K. W., Blackwood, H. L., Rogstad, J. E., & Harrison, K. S. (2009). Development and initial validation of the Miranda Vocabulary Scale. *Law and Human Behavior, 33,* 381–392.

Rogers, R., Rogstad, J. E., Gillard, N. D., Drogin, E. Y., Blackwood, H. L., & Shuman, D. W. (2010). "Everyone knows their Miranda rights"; Implicit assumptions and countervailing evidence. *Psychology, Public Policy, and Law, 16,* 300–318.

Rogers, R., & Sewell, K. W. (1999). The R-CRAS and insanity evaluations: A re-examination of construct validity. *Behavioral Sciences & the Law, 17,* 181–194.

Rogers, R., & Shuman, D. W. (1999). *Conducting insanity evaluations* (2nd ed.). New York: Guilford Press.

Rohde, L. A., Barbosa, G., Polanczyk, G., Eizirik, M., Rasmussen, R. R., Neuman, R. J., et al. (2001). Factor and latent class analysis of DSM-IV ADHD symptoms in a school sample of Brazilian adolescents. *Journal of the American Academy of Child and Adolescent Psychiatry, 40,* 711–718.

Romans, J. S. C., Hays, J. R., & White, T. K. (1996). Stalking and related behaviors experienced by counseling center staff members from current and former clients. *Professional Psychology: Research and Practice, 27,* 595–599.

Root, C., MacKay, S., Henderson, J., Del Bove, G., & Warling, D. (2008). The link between maltreatment and juvenile firesetting: Correlates and underlying mechanisms. *Child Abuse & Neglect, 32,* 161–176.

Root, R. W., & Resnick, R. J. (2003). An update on the diagnosis and treatment of attention deficit/hyperactivity disorder in children. *Professional Psychology: Research and Practice, 34,* 34–41.

Rosenfeld, B., & Harmon, R. (2002). Factors associated with violence in stalking and obsessional harassment cases. *Criminal Justice and Behavior, 29,* 671–691.

Rossmo, D. K. (1997). Geographical profiling. In J. T. Jackson & D. A. Bekerain (Eds.), *Offender profiling: Theory, research and practice.* Chichester, UK: Wiley.

Rostow, C. D., & Davis, R. D. (2004). *A handbook for psychological fitness-for-duty evaluations in law enforcement.* Binghamton, NY: Haworth Press.

Rothman, D. (1980). *Conscience and convenience.* Boston: Little, Brown.

Rubin, K. H., Bukowski, W., & Parker, J. G. (1998). Peer interactions, relationships, and groups. In N. Eisenberg (Ed.), *Handbook of child psychology: Vol. 3. Social, emotional, and personality development* (5th ed.). New York: Wiley.

Rubin, K. H., Burgess, K. B., Dwyer, K. M., & Hastings, P. D. (2003). Predicting preschoolers' externalizing behaviors from toddler temperament, conflict, and maternal negativity. *Developmental Psychology, 39,* 164–176.

Rubinstein, M., Yeager, C. A., Goodstein, C., & Lewis, D. O. (1993). Sexually assaultive male juveniles: A follow-up. *American Journal of Psychiatry, 150,* 262–265.

Russell, B. S. (2010). Revisiting the measurement of shaken baby syndrome awareness. *Child Abuse & Neglect, 34*(9), 671–676.

Sabol, W. J., Hinton, T. D., & Harrison, P. M. (2007, June). *Prison and jail inmates at midyear 2006.* Washington, DC: U.S. Department of Justice, Bureau of Justice Statistics.

Sabol, W. J., West, H. C., & Cooper, M. (2009, December). *Prisoners in 2008.* Washington, DC: U. S. Department of Justice, Bureau of Justice Statistics.

Saks, M. J. (1993). Improving APA science translation amicus briefs. *Law and Human Behavior, 17,* 235–247.

Sale, P. L. (1992). Ego and self-concept development among juvenile delinquent participants in adventure-based programs. *Dissertation Abstracts International, 53,* 2253A.

Salekin, R. T. (2002). Psychopathy and therapeutic pessimism: Clinical lore or clinical reality? *Clinical Psychology Review, 22,* 79–112.

Salekin, R. T., Leistico, A-M. R., Trobst, K. K., Schrum, C. L., & Lochman, J. E. (2005). Adolescent psychopathy and personality theory—the interpersonal circumplex: Expanding evidence of a nomological net. *Journal of Abnormal Child Psychology, 33,* 445–460.

Salekin, R. T., & Lochman, J. (Eds.). (2008). Child and adolescent psychopathy: The search for protective factors [Special issue]. *Criminal Justice and Behavior, 35,* 159–172.

Salekin, R. T., Rogers, R., & Sewell, K. W. (1997). Construct validity of psychopathy in a female offender sample: A multitrait-multimethod evaluation. *Journal of Abnormal Psychology, 106,* 576–585.

Salekin, R. T., Rogers, R., Ustad, K. L., & Sewell, K. W. (1998). Psychopathy and recidivism among female inmates. *Law and Human Behavior, 22,* 109–128.

Salekin, R. T., Rosenbaum, J., & Lee, Z. (2008). Child and adolescent psychopathy: Stability and change. *Psychiatry, Psychology, and Law, 15,* 224–236.

Salisbury, E. J., & Van Voorhis, P. (2009). Gendered pathways: An empirical investigation of women in probationers' path to incarceration. *Criminal Justice and Behavior, 35,* 541–566.

Salter, D., McMillan, D., Richards, M., Talbot, T., Hodges, J., Arnon, B., et al. (2003). Development of sexually abusive behaviour in sexually victimised males: A longitudinal study. *The Lancet, 361,* 108–115.

Sammons, M. T., Gorny, S. W., Zinner, E. S., & Allen, R. P. (2000). Prescriptive authority of psychologists: A consensus of support. *Professional Psychology: Research and Practice, 31,* 604–609.

Sampson, R. J., & Laub, J. H. (1993). Structural variations in juvenile court processing: Inequality, the underclass, and social control. *Law & Society Review, 27,* 285–311.

Sanders, M. J., & Bursch, B. (2002). Forensic assessment of illness falsification, Munchausen by proxy, and factitious disorder, NOS. *Child Maltreatment, 7,* 112–124.

Sandler, J. C., & Freeman, N. J. (2007). Typology of female sex offenders: A test of Vandiver and Kercher. *Sexual Abuse: Journal of Research and Treatment, 19,* 73–89.

Satterfield, J. H., Swanson, J., Schell, A., & Lee, F. (1994). Prediction of antisocial behavior in attention-deficit hyperactivity disorder boys from aggression/defiance scores. *Journal of the American Academy of Child and Adolescent Psychiatry, 33,* 185–191.

Saunders, B. E., Arata, C., & Kilpatrick, D. (1990). Development of a crime-related posttraumatic stress disorder scale for women within the Symptom Checklist-90—Revised. *Journal of Traumatic Stress, 3,* 439–448.

Sauvageau, A. (2008). Autoerotic deaths: A seven-year retrospective epidemiological study. *The Open Forensic Sciences Journal, 1,* 1–5.

Sauvageau, A., & Racette, S. (2006). Autoerotic deaths in the literature from 1954 to 2004: A review. *Journal of Forensic Science, 51,* 140–146.

Savage, J., & Yancey, C. (2008). The effects of media violence exposure on criminal aggression: A meta-analysis. *Criminal Justice and Behavior, 35,* 772–791.

Schaeffer, C. M., & Borduin, C. M. (2005). Long-term follow-up to a randomized clinical trial of multisystemic therapy with serious and violent juvenile offenders. *Journal of Consulting and Clinical Psychology, 73,* 445–453.

Schafer, J. A., Huebner, B. M., & Bynum, T. S. (2006). Fear of crime and criminal victimization: Gender-based contrasts. *Journal of Criminal Justice, 34,* 285–301.

Scheflin, A. W., Spiegel, H., & Spiegel, D. (1999). Forensic uses of hypnosis. In A. K. Hess & I. B. Weiner (Eds.), *The handbook of forensic psychology* (2nd ed.). New York: Wiley.

Schields, L. B. E., Hunsaker, D. M., Hunsacker, J. C. (2005). Autoerotic asphyxia. *American Journal of Forensic Medicine and Pathology, 26,* 45–52.

Schmidt, M. G., Reppucci, N. D., & Woolard, J. L. (2003). Effectiveness of participation as a defendant: The attorney–juvenile client relationship. *Behavioral Sciences and the Law, 21,* 175–198.

Schmucker, M., & Losel, F. (2008). Does sexual offender treatment work? A systematic review of outcome evaluations. *Psychotherma, 20,* 10–19.

Schott, J. C., Davis, G. J., & Hunsaker, J. C., III. (2003). Accidental electrocution during autoeroticism: A shocking case. *American Journal of Forensic Medicine and Pathology, 24,* 92–95.

Schramke, C. J., & Bauer, R. M. (1977). State-dependent learning in older and younger adults. *Psychology and Aging, 12,* 255–262.

Schwartz, B. K. (1995). Characteristics and typologies of sex offenders. In B. K. Schwartz & H. R. Cellini (Eds.), *The sex offender: Corrections, treatment and legal practice.* Kingston, NJ: Civic Research Institute.

Schwartz, I. M. (1989). (In)Justice for juveniles: Rethinking the best interests of the child. Lexington, MA: Lexington Books.

Scott, E. S., Reppucci, N. D., & Woolard, J. L. (1995). Evaluating adolescent decision-making in legal contexts. *Law and Human Behavior, 19,* 221–244.

Scott, E. S., & Steinberg, L. (2008). Adolescent development and regulation of youth crime. *The Future of Children, 18,* 15–33.

Scrivner, E. M. (1994, April). *The role of police psychology in controlling excessive force.* Washington, DC: National Institute of Justice.

Seagrave, D., & Grisso, T. (2002). Adolescent development and measurement of juvenile psychopathy. *Law and Human Behavior, 26,* 219–239.

Sedlak, A. J., & McPherson, K. S. (2010a, May). *Conditions of confinement: Findings from the survey of youth in residential placement.* Washington, DC: U.S. Department of Justice, Office of Juvenile Justice and Delinquency Prevention.

Sedlak, A. J., & McPherson, K. S. (2010b, April). *Youth's needs and services: Findings from the survey of youth in residential placement.* Washington, DC: U.S. Department of Justice, Office of Juvenile Justice and Delinquency Prevention.

Séguin, J. R., & Zelazo, P. D. (2005). Executive function in early physical aggression. In R. E. Tremblay, W. W. Hartup, & J. Archer (Eds.), *Developmental origins of aggression.* New York: Guilford Press.

Seklecki, R., & Paynich, R. (2007). A national survey of female police officers: An overview of findings. *Police Practice and Research, 8,* 17–30.

Seligman, M. E. (1975). *Helplessness: On depression, development, and death.* San Francisco: W. H. Freeman.

Selkin, J. (1975). Rape. *Psychology Today, 8*(8), 70–73.

Selkin, J. (1987). *Psychological autopsy in the courtroom.* Denver: Author.

Selkin, J. (1994). Psychological autopsy: Scientific psychohistory or clinical intuition? *American Psychologist, 49,* 74–75.

Sellbom, M., Fischler, G. L., & Ben-Porath, Y. S. (2007). Identifying MMPI-2 predictors of police officer integrity and misconduct. *Criminal Justice and Behavior, 34,* 985–1004.

Senter, A., Morgan, R. D., Serna-McDonald, C., & Bewley, M. (2010). Correctional psychologist burnout, job satisfaction, and life satisfaction. *Psychological Services, 7,* 190–201.

Serin, R. C., & Amos, N. L. (1995). The role of psychopathy in the assessment of dangerousness. *International Journal of Law & Psychiatry, 18,* 231–238.

Serin, R. C., Peters, R. D., & Barbaree, H. E. (1990). Predictors of psychopathy and release outcome in a criminal population. *Psychological Assessment, 2,* 419–422.

Serin, R. C., & Preston, D. L. (2001). Managing and treating violent offenders. In J. B. Ashford, B. D. Sales, & W. H. Reid (Eds.), *Treating adult and juvenile offenders with special needs.* Washington, DC: American Psychological Association.

Seto, M. C., & Barbaree, H. E. (1999). Psychopathy, treatment behavior, and sex offender recidivism. *Journal of Interpersonal Violence, 14,* 1235–1248.

Sevecke, K., Kosson, D. S., & Krisher, M. K. (2009). The relationship between attention deficit hyperactivity disorder, conduct disorder, and psychopathy in adolescent male and female detainees. *Behavioral Sciences & the Law, 27,* 577–598.

Sexton, T., & Turner, C. W. (2010). The effectiveness of functional family therapy for youth with behavior problems in a community practice setting. *Journal of Family Psychology, 24,* 339–348.

Shahinfar, A., Kupersmidt, J. B., & Matza, L. S. (2001). The relation between exposure to violence and social information processing among incarcerated adolescents. *Journal of Abnormal Psychology, 110,* 136–141.

Shapiro, B. L., & Schwarz, J. C. (1997). Date rape: Its relationship to trauma symptoms and sexual self-esteem. *Journal of Interpersonal Violence, 12,* 407–419.

Shapiro, D. L. (1999). *Criminal responsibility evaluations: A manual for practice.* Sarasota, FL: Professional Resource Press.

Shaw, D. S., Owens, E. B., Giovannelli, J., & Winslow, E. B. (2001). Infant and toddler pathways leading to early externalizing disorders. *Journal of the American Academy of Child and Adolescent Psychiatry, 40,* 36–43.

Shepherd, J. W., & Ellis, H. D. (1973). The effect of attractiveness on recognition memory for faces. *American Journal of Psychology, 86,* 627–633.

Sheridan, L., & Davies, G. M. (2001). Stalking: The elusive crime. *Legal and Criminological Psychology, 6,* 133–147.

Sheridan, M. S. (2003). The deceit continues: An updated literature review of Munchausen syndrome by proxy. *Child Abuse & Neglect, 27,* 431–451.

Shihadeh, E. S., & Barranco, R. E. (2010). Latino immigration, economic deprivation, and violence: Regional differences in the effect of linguistic isolation. *Homicide Studies, 14,* 336–355.

Shirtcliff, E. A., Vitacco, M. J., Gostisha, A. J., Merz, J. L., & Zahn-Waxler, C. (2009). Neurobiology of empathy amd callousness: Implications for the development of antisocial behavior. *Behavioral Sciences & the Law, 27,* 137–171.

Shneidman, E. S. (1981). The psychological autopsy. *Suicide and Life Threatening Behavior, 11,* 325–340.

Shneidman, E. S. (1994a). The psychological autopsy. *American Psychologist, 49,* 75–76.

Shneidman, E. S. (1994b). The psychological autopsy. *Suicide & Life-Threatening Behavior, 11,* 325–340.

Showers, J. (1997). *Executive summary: The National Conference on Shaken Baby Syndrome.* Alexandria, VA: National Association of Children's Hospitals and Related Institutions.

Showers, J. (1999). *Never never never shake a baby: The challenges of shaken baby syndrome.* Alexandria, VA: National Association of Children's Hospitals and Related Institutions.

Shuman, D. W., & Sales, B. D. (2001). Daubert's wager. *Journal of Forensic Psychology Practice, 1,* 69–77.

Shusman, E., Inwald, R., & Landa, B. (1984). A validation and cross-validation study of correction officer job performance as predicted by the IPI and MMPI. *Criminal Justice and Behavior, 11,* 309–329.

Sickmund, M. (2003, June). *Juveniles in court* (Juvenile Offenders and Victims National Report Series). Washington, DC: U.S. Department of Justice, Office of Juvenile Justice and Delinquency Prevention.

Sickmund, M. (2004, June). *Juveniles in corrections.* (NCJ 202885). Washington, DC: U.S. Department of Justice, Office of Juvenile Justice and Delinquency Prevention.

Sickmund, M. (2006, June). *Juvenile residential facility census, 2002: Selected findings.* Washington, DC: U.S. Department of Justice, Office of Juvenile Justice and Delinquency Prevention.

Sickmund, M. (2010, February). *Juveniles in residential placement, 1997–2008.* Washington, DC: U.S. Department of Justice, Office of Juvenile Justice and Delinquency Prevention.

Siegel, A. M., & Elwork, A. (1990). Treating incompetence to stand trial. *Law and Human Behavior, 14,* 57–65.

Siegel, L., & Lane, I. M. (1987). Personnel and organizational psychology (2nd ed.), Homewood, IL: Irwin.

Simon, L. M. J. (2000). An examination of the assumptions of specialization, mental disorder, and dangerousness in sex offenders. *Behavioral Sciences and the Law, 18,* 275–308.

Simon, T., Mercy, J., & Perkins, C. (2001, June). *Injuries from violent crime, 1992–1998.* Washington, DC: U.S. Department of Justice, Bureau of Justice Statistics.

Simourd, D. J., & Hoge, R. D. (2000). Criminal psychopathy: A risk-and-need perspective. *Criminal Justice and Behavior, 27,* 256–272.

Simourd, D. J., & Malcolm, P. B. (1998). Reliability and validity of the Level of Service Inventory—Revised among federally incarcerated offenders. *Journal of Interpersonal Violence, 13,* 261–274.

Simpson, D. W., & Knight, K. (Eds.). (2007). Offender needs and functioning assessments from a national cooperative research program. *Criminal Justice and Behavior, 34,* 1105–1112.

Sinclair, J. J., Pettit, G. S., Harrist, A. W., & Bates, J. E. (1994). Encounters with aggressive peers in early childhood: Frequency, age differences, and correlates of risk for behaviour problems. *International Journal of Behavioural Development, 17,* 675–696.

Singer, M. T., & Nievod, A. (1987). Consulting and testifying in court. In I. B. Weiner & A. K. Hess (Eds.), *Handbook of forensic psychology.* New York: Wiley.

Sipe, R., Jensen, E. L., & Everett, R. S. (1998). Adolescent sexual offenders grown up: Recidivism in young adulthood. *Criminal Justice and Behavior, 25,* 109–124.

Skeem, J. L., Edens, J. F., & Colwell, L. H. (2003, April). *Are there racial differences in levels of psychopathy? A meta-analysis.* Paper presented at the Third Annual Conference of the International Association of Forensic Mental Health Services, Miami, FL.

Skeem, J. L., Edens, J. F., Sanford, G. M., & Colwell, L. H. (2003). Psychopathic personality and racial/ethnic differences reconsidered: A reply to Lynn (2002). *Personality and Individual Differences, 34,* 1–24.

Skeem, J. L., Golding, S. L., Berge, G., & Cohn, N. B. (1998). Logic and reliability of evaluations of competence to stand trial. *Law and Human Behavior, 22,* 519–547.

Skeem, J. L., Monahan, J., & Mulvey, E. P. (2002). Psychopathy, treatment involvement, and subsequent violence among civil psychiatric patients. *Law and Human Behavior, 26,* 577–603.

Skeem, J. L., Poythress, N., Edens, J., Lilienfeld, S., & Cale, E. (in press). Psychopathic personality or personalities? Exploring potential variants of psychopathy and their implications for risk assessment. *Aggression and Violent Behavior.*

Skilling, T. A., Quinsey, V. L., & Craig, W. M. (2001). Evidence of a taxon underlying serious antisocial behavior in boys. *Criminal Justice and Behavior, 28,* 450–470.

Skrapec, C. A. (1996). The sexual component of serial murder. In T. O'Reilly-Fleming (Ed.), *Serial and mass murder: Theory, research and policy.* Toronto, ON: Canadian Scholars' Press.

Skrapec, C. A. (2001). Phenomenology and serial murder: Asking different questions. *Homicide Studies, 5,* 46–63.

Slavkin, M. L. (2001). Enuresis, firesetting, and cruelty to animals: Does the ego triad show predictive validity? *Adolescence, 36,* 461–467.

Slobogin, C. (1999). The admissibility of behavioral science information in criminal trials: From primitivism to Daubert to voice. *Psychology, Public Policy, and Law, 5,* 100–119.

Slobogin, C., & Mashburn, A. (2000). The criminal defense lawyer's fiduciary duty to clients with mental disability. *Fordham Law Review, 68,* 1581–1642.

Slobogin, C., Melton, G. B., & Showalter, C. C. (1984). The feasibility of a brief evaluation of mental state at the the time of the offense. *Law and Human Behavior, 8,* 305–320.

Slot, L. A. B., & Colpaert, F. C. (1999). Recall rendered dependent on an opiate state. *Behavioral Neuroscience, 113,* 337–344.

Slovenko, R. (1999). Civil competency. In A. K. Hess & I. B. Weiner (Eds.), *Handbook of forensic psychology* (2nd ed.). New York: Wiley.

Small, M. H., & Otto, R. K. (1991). Evaluations of competency to be executed: Legal contours and implication for assessment. *Criminal Justice and Behavior, 18,* 146–158.

Smith, B. C., Penrod, S. D., Otto, A. L., & Park, R. C. (1996). Jurors' use of probabilistic evidence. *Law and Human Behavior, 20,* 49–82.

Smith, B. M. (1967). The polygraph. *Scientific American, 216,* 25–31.

Smith, D. (2002a, June). Helping mentally ill offenders. *Monitor on Psychology, 33,* 64.

Smith, D. (2002b, June). On call, 24–7. *Monitor on Psychology, 33,* 65.

Smith, D. (2002c, June). Where are recent grads getting jobs? *Monitor on Psychology, 33,* 28–29.

Smithey, M. (1998). Infant homicide: Victim–offender relationship and causes of death. *Journal of Family Violence, 13,* 285–287.

Snider, J. F., Hane, S., & Berman, A. L. (2006). Standardizing the psychological autopsy: Addressing the Daubert standard. *Suicide and Life-Threatening Behavior, 36,* 511–518.

Snook, B., Cullen, R. M., Bennell, C., Taylor, P. J., & Gendreau, P. (2008). The criminal profiling illusion: What's behind the smoke and mirrors? *Criminal Justice and Behavior, 35,* 1257–1276.

Snyder, H. N. (2000, June). Sexual assault of young children as reported to law enforcement: Victim, incident, and offender characteristics. Washington, DC: U.S. Department of Justice, Bureau of Justice Statistics.

Snyder, H. N. (2008, August). *Juvenile arrests 2005.* Washington, DC: U. S. Department of Justice, Office of Juvenile Justice and Delinquency Prevention.

Snyder, H. N., & Sickmund, M. (1995). *Juvenile offenders and victims: A national report.* Washington, DC: Office of Juvenile Justice and Delinquency Prevention.

Snyder, H. N., & Sickmund, M. (1999). *Juvenile offenders and victims: 1999 national report.* Washington, DC: Office of Juvenile Justice and Delinquency Prevention.

Snyder, H. N., & Sickmund, M. (2006, March). *Juvenile offenders and victims: 2006 national report.* Pittsburgh, PA: National Center for Juvenile Justice.

Solomon, R. M., & Horn, J. M. (1986). Post-shooting traumatic reactions: A pilot study. In J. T. Reese & H. A. Goldstein (Eds.), *Psychological services for law enforcement.* Washington, DC: Government Printing Office.

Sorensen, S. B., & Bowie, P. (1994). Girls and young women. In L. D. Eron, J. H. Gentry, & P. Schlegel (Eds.), *Reason to hope: A psychosocial perspective on violence and youth.* Washington, DC: American Psychological Association.

Spaccarelli, S., Bowden, B., Coatsworth, J. D., & Kim, S. (1997). Psychosocial correlates of male sexual aggression in a chronic delinquent sample. *Criminal Justice and Behavior, 24,* 71–95.

Spiegel, D., & Spiegel, H. (1987). Forensic uses of hypnosis. In I. B. Weiner & A. K. Hess (Eds.), *Handbook of forensic psychology.* New York: Wiley.

Spielberger, C. D. (Ed.). (1979). *Police selection and evaluation.* Washington, DC: Hemisphere.

Spielberger, C. D., Ward, J. C., & Spaulding, H. C. (1979). A model for the selection of law enforcement officers. In C. D. Spielberger (Ed.), *Police selection and evaluation: Issues and techniques.* Washington, DC: Hemisphere.

Sporer, S. L. (2001). The cross-race effect: Beyond recognition of faces in the laboratory. *Psychology, Public Policy, and Law, 7,* 170–200.

Sprang, M. V., McNeil, J. S., & Wright, R. (1989). Psychological changes after the murder of a significant other. *Social Casework: The Journal of Contemporary Social Work, 70,* 159–164.

Stack, S., & Kelley, T. (1999). Police suicide. In D. J. Kenney & R. P. McNamara (Eds.), *Police and policing: Contemporary issues* (2nd ed.). Westport, CT: Praeger.

Stadolnik, R. F. (2000). Drawn to the flame: Assessment and treatment of juvenile firesetting behavior. Sarasota, FL: Professional Resources Press.

Stahl, A. L. (2006, November). *Delinquency cases in juvenile court, 2002.* Washington, DC: Office of Justice Programs, U.S. Department of Justice.

Stark, E. (2002). Preparing for expert testimony in domestic violence cases. In A. R. Roberts (Ed.), *Handbook of domestic violence intervention strategies: Policies, programs, and legal remedies.* New York: Oxford University Press.

Stattin, H., & Klackenberg-Larsson, I. (1993). Early language and intelligence development and their relationship to future criminal behavior. *Journal of Abnormal Psychology, 102,* 369–378.

Stavis, P. F. (1999). The nexus: A modest proposal of self-guardianship by contract: A system of advance directives and surrogate committees-at-large for the intermittently mentally ill. *Journal of Contemporary Health Law & Policy, 1,* 21–22.

Steadman, H. J., Davidson, S., & Brown, C. (2001). Mental health courts: Their promise and unanswered questions. *Psychiatric Services, 54,* 457–458.

Steadman, H. J., Gounis, K., & Dennis, D. (2001). Assessing the New York City involuntary outpatient commitment pilot program. *Psychiatric Services, 52,* 330–336.

Steadman, H. J., McCarty, D. W., & Morrissey, J. P. (1989). *The mentally ill in jail: Planning for essential services.* New York: Guilford Press.

Steadman, H. J., Osher, F. C., Robbins, P. C., Case, B., & Samuels, S. (2009). Prevalence of serious mental illness among jail inmates. *Psychiatric Services, 60,* 761–765.

Steadman, H. J., & Veysey, B. M. (1997). *Providing services for jail inmates with mental disorders.* Washington, DC: U.S. Department of Justice, National Institute of Justice.

Stefan, S. (1996). Race, competence testing, and disability law: A review of the MacArthur competence research. *Psychology, Public Policy, and Law, 2,* 31–44.

Stehlin, I. B. (1995, July/August). FDA's forensic center: Speedy, sophisticated sleuthing. *FDA Consumer Magazine,* pp. 17–28.

Steinberg, L. (2007). Risk taking in adolescence: New perspectives from brain and behavioral science. *Current Directions in Psychological Science, 16,* 55–59.

Steinberg, L. (2008). A social neuroscience perspective on adolescent risk taking. *Developmental Review, 28,* 78–106.

Steinberg, L. (2010). A dual systems model of adolescent risk-taking. *Developmental Psychobiology,* 216–224.

Steinberg, L., Albert, D., Cauffman, E., Banich, M., Graham, S., & Woolard, J. (2008). Age differences in sensation seeking and impulsivity as indexed by behaviour and self-report: Evidence for a dual systems model. *Developmental Psychology, 44,* 1764–1778.

Steinberg, L., Cauffman, E., Woolard, J., Graham, S., & Banich, M. (2009). Are adolescents less mature than adults? Minors' access to abortion, the juvenile death penalty, and the alleged APA "flip-flop." *American Psychologist, 64,* 583–594.

Steinberg, L., Graham, S., O'Brien, L., Woolard, J., Cauffman, E., & Banich, M. (2009). Age differences in future orientation and delay discounting. *Child Develolpment, 80,* 28–44.

Steinberg, L., & Monahan, K. (2007). Age differences in resistance to peer influence. *Developmental Psychology, 43,* 1531–1543.

Steinbock, D. J. (2003). *National identity cards: Fourth and Fifth Amendment issues.* bepress Legal Series, Paper 90. Berkeley, CA: Berkeley Electronic Press.

Stewart, A. E., Lord, J. H., & Mercer, D. L. (2001). Death notification education: A needs assessment study. *Journal of Traumatic Stress, 14,* 221–227.

Stickle, T., & Blechman, E. (2002). Aggression and fire: Antisocial behavior in firesetting and nonfiresetting juvenile offenders. *Journal of Psychopathology and Behavioral Assessment, 24,* 177–193.

Stockdale, M. S., Logan, T. K., & Weston, R. (2009). Sexual harassment and posttraumatic stress disorder: Damages beyond prior abuse. *Law and Human Behavior, 33,* 405–418.

Stockdale, M. S., O'Connor, M., Gutek, B. A., & Geer, T. (2002). The relationship between prior sexual abuse and reactions to sexual harassment: Literature review and empirical study. *Psychology, Public Policy, and Law, 8,* 64–95.

Stone, A. V. (1995). Law enforcement psychological fitness for duty: Clinical issues. In M. Kurke & E. Scrivner (Eds.), *Police psychology into the 21st century.* Hillsdale, NJ: Erlbaum.

Stone, M. H. (1998). Sadistic personality in murders. In T. Millon, E. Simonsen, M. Burket-Smith, & R. Davis (Eds.), *Psychopathy: Antisocial, criminal, and violent behavior.* New York: Guilford Press.

Stowe, R. M., Arnold, D. H., & Ortiz, C. (2000). Gender differences in the relationship of language development to disruptive behavior and peer relationships in preschoolers. *Journal of Applied Developmental Psychology, 20,* 521–536.

Stratton, J. G., Parker, D., & Snabbe, J. (1984). Post-traumatic stress: Study of police officers involved in shooting. *Psychological Reports, 55,* 127–131.

Straus, M. A. (1979). Measuring intrafamily conflict and violence: The Conflict Tactics Scale. *Journal of Marriage and the Family, 41,* 75–88.

Strier, F. (1999). Whither trial consulting? Issues and projections. *Law and Human Behavior, 23,* 93–115.

Straus, M., & Gelles, R. J. (1990). *Physical violence in American families.* New Brunswick, NJ: Transaction Publishers.

Strom, K. J. (2001, September). *Hate crimes reported in NIBRS, 1997–1999.* Washington, DC: U.S. Department of Justice, Bureau of Justice Statistics.

Studebaker, C. L., & Goodman-Delahunty, J. (Eds.). (2002). Expert testimony in the courts: The influence of the Daubert, Joiner, and Kumho decisions, part 3 [Special issue]. *Psychology, Public Policy, and Law, 8.*

Sue, D. W., Arredondo, P., & McDavis, R. J. (1992). Multicultural counseling competencies and standards: A call to the profession. *Journal of Counseling and Development, 70,* 477–486.

Sue, D. W., Bingham, R. P., Porché-Burke, L., & Vasquez, M. (1999). The diversification of psychology: A multicultural revolution. *American Psychologist, 54,* 1061–1069.

Summit, R. C. (1983). The child sexual abuse accommodation syndrome. *Child Abuse & Neglect, 7,* 177–193.

Summit, R. C. (1992). Abuse of the child sexual abuse accommodation syndrome. *Journal of Child Sexual Abuse, 1*(4), 153–163.

Super, J. T. (1999). Forensic psychology and law enforcement. In A. K. Hess & I. B. Weiner (Eds.), *The handbook of forensic psychology* (2nd ed.). New York: Wiley.

Swartz, M. S., Swanson, J. W., & Hiday, V. A. (2001). Randomized controlled trial of outpatient commitment in North Carolina. *Psychiatric Services, 52,* 325–329.

Tappan, P. W. (1947). Who is criminal? *American Sociological Review, 12,* 100–110.

Tappan, P. W. (1949). *Juvenile delinquency.* New York: McGraw-Hill.

Tate, D. C., Reppucci, N. D., & Mulvey, E. P. (1995). Violent juvenile delinquents: Treatment effectiveness and implications for future directions. *American Psychologist, 50,* 777–781.

Teaching-Family Association. (1993). Standards of ethical conduct of the Teaching-Family Association. Asheville, NC: Author.

Teaching-Family Association. (1994). *Elements of the teaching-family model.* Asheville, NC: Author.

Technical Working Group for Eyewitness Evidence. (Ed.). (1999). *Eyewitness evidence: A guide for law enforcement.* Washington, DC: National Institute of Justice.

Teplin, L. A. (1986, April). *Keeping the peace: The parameters of police discretion in relation to the mentally disordered.* Washington, DC: U.S. Department of Justice, National Institute of Justice.

Teplin, L. A. (2000, July). Police discretion and mentally ill persons. *National Institute of Justice Journal,* pp. 8–15.

Teplin, L. A., Abram, K. M., McLelland, G. M., Dulcan, M. K., & Mericle, A. A. (2002). Psychiatric disorders in youth in juvenile detention. *Archives of General Psychiatry, 59,* 1133–1143.

Terr, L. (1979). Children of Chowchilla: A study of psychic trauma. *Psychoanalytic Study of the Child, 34,* 547–623.

Terr, L. (1982). Psychic trauma in children: Observations following the Chowchilla school bus kidnapping. *Annals of Progress in Child Psychiatry and Child Development, 2,* 384–396.

Terr, L. (1983). Chowchilla revisited: The effects of psychic trauma four years after a school-bus kidnapping. *American Journal of Psychiatry, 140,* 1543–1550.

Terr, L. (1991). Childhood traumas: An outline and overview. *American Journal of Psychiatry, 148,* 10–20.

Terr, L. (1994). *Unchained memories.* New York: Basic Books.

Terr, L. C. (2003, Summer). Childhood traumas: An outline and overview. *Focus: The Journal of Lifelong Learning in Psychiatry, 1,* 322–333.

Thompson-Cannino, J., & Cotton, R. (2009). *Picking Cotton: Our memoir of injustice and redemption.* New York: St. Martin's Press.

Till, F. (1980). *Sexual harassment: A report on the sexual harassment of students.* Washington, DC: National Advisory Council on Women's Educational Programs.

Tingle, D., Barnard, G. W., Robbins, L., Newman, G., & Hutchinson, D. (1986). Childhood and adolescent characteristics of pedophiles and rapists. *International Journal of Law and Psychiatry, 9,* 103–116.

Tjaden, P. (1997, November). The crime of stalking: How big is the problem? *NIJ Research Preview.* Washington, DC: U.S. Department of Justice.

Tjaden, P., & Thoennes, N. (1998a, November). *Prevalence, incidence, and consequences of violence against women: Findings from the National Violence Against Women Survey* (Research in brief). Washington, DC: U.S. Department of Justice, National Institute of Justice.

Tjaden, P., & Thoennes, M. (1998b). *Stalking in America: Findings from the National Violence Against Women Survey* (NCJ 169592). Washington, DC: U.S. Department of Justice.

Tobey, A., Grisso, T., & Schwartz, R. (2000). Youths' trial participation as seen by youths and their attorneys: An exploration of competence-based issues. In T. Grisso & R. G. Schwartz (Eds.), *Youth on trial: A developmental perspective on juvenile justice.* Chicago: University of Chicago Press.

Toch, H. (Ed.). (1980). *Therapeutic communities in corrections.* New York: Praeger.

Toch, H. (Ed.). (1992). *Mosaic of despair: Human breakdown in prisons.* Washington, DC: American Psychological Association.

Toch, H., & Adams, K. (2002). *Acting out: Maladaptive behavior in confinement.* Washington, DC: American Psychological Association.

Tombaugh, T. N. (1997). *TOMM: Test of Memory Malingering manual.* Toronto, ON, Canada: Multi-Health Systems.

Tonry, M. (1990). Stated and latent functions of ISP. *Crime & Delinquency, 36,* 174–190.

Topp, B. W., & Kardash, C. A. (1986). Personality, achievement, and attrition: Validation in a multiple-jurisdiction police academy. *Journal of Police Science and Administration, 14,* 234–241.

Torres, A. N., Boccaccini, M. T., & Miller, H. A. (2006). Perceptions of the validity and utility of criminal profiling among forensic psychologists and psychiatrists. *Professional Psychology: Research and Practice, 37,* 51–58.

Tremblay, R. E. (2003). Why socialization fails: The case of chronic physical aggression. In B. B. Lahey, T. E. Moffitt, & A. Caspi (Eds.), *Causes of conduct disorder and juvenile delinquency.* New York: Guilford Press.

Tremblay, R. E., & Côté, S. (2005). The developmental origins of aggression: Where are we going? In R. E. Tremblay, W. W. Hartup, & J. Archer (Eds.), *Developmental origins of aggression.* New York: Guilford Press.

Tremblay, R. E., Hartup, W. W., & Archer, J. (Eds.) (2005). *Developmental origins of aggression.* New York: Guilford Press.

Tremblay, R. E., & Nagin, D. S. (2005). The developmental origins of physical aggression in humans. In R. E. Tremblay, W. W. Hartup, & J. Archer (Eds.), *Developmental origins of aggression.* New York: Guilford Press.

Troup-Leasure, K., & Snyder, H. N. (2005, August). *Statutory rape known to law enforcement.* Washington, DC: U.S. Department of Justice, Office of Juvenile Justice and Delinquency Prevention.

Trovillo, P. V. (1939). A history in lie detection. *Journal of Criminal Law and Criminology, 29,* 848–881.

Truman, D. M., Tokar, D. M., & Fischer, A. R. (1996). Dimensions of masculinity: Relations to date rape–supportive attitudes and sexual aggression in dating situations. *Journal of Counseling and Development, 74,* 555–562.

Tucillo, J. A., DeFilippis, N. A., Denny, R. L., & Dsurney, J. (2002). Licensure requirements for interjurisdictional forensic evaluations. *Professional Psychology: Research and Practice, 33,* 377–383.

Tucker, H. S. (2002). Some seek attention by making pets sick. *Archives of Disease in Childhood, 87,* 263.

Turrell, S. C. (2000). A descriptive analysis of same-sex relationship violence for a diverse sample. *Journal of Family Violence, 15,* 281–293.

Turtle, J., & Want, S. C. (2008). Logic and research versus intuition and past practice as guides to gathering and evaluating eyewitness evidence. *Criminal Justice and Behavior, 35,* 1241–1256.

Turvey, B. (2002). Criminal profiling: An introduction to behavioral evidence analysis (2nd ed.). San Diego: Academic Press.

Tversky, A., & Kahneman, O. (1973). Availability: A heuristic for judging frequency and probability. *Cognitive Psychology, 5,* 207–232.

Tyiska, C. G. (1998). *Working with victims of crime with disabilities.* Washington, DC: U.S. Department of Justice, Office of Victims of Crime.

Ullman, S. E. (2007). A 10-year update of "Review and critique of empirical studies of rape avoidance." *Criminal Justice and Behavior, 34,* 411–429.

Ullman, S. E., Karabatsos, G., & Koss, M. P. (1999). Risk recognition and trauma-related symptoms among sexually revictimized women. *Journal of Consulting and Clinical Psychology, 67,* 705–710.

U.S. Advisory Board on Child Abuse and Neglect. (1995). *A national shame: Fatal child abuse and neglect in the U.S.* (5th report). Washington, DC: Government Printing Office.

U.S. Census Bureau. (2009). *Statistical Abstract of the United States, 2010* (129th ed.) Washington, DC: Author.

U. S. Department of Health and Human Services. (2010). *Child maltreatment 2008.* Washington, DC: Author, Aministration for Children and Family, Childrens' Bureau. Retrieved December 14, 2010, from http://www.acf.hhs.gov/programs/cb/stats_research/index.htm#can.

U.S. Department of Justice. (1988). *Report to the nation on crime and justice: The data* (2nd ed.). Washington, DC: Government Printing Office.

U.S. Department of Justice. (2010, May). The crime of family abduction: A child's and Parent's perspective. Washington, DC: Author.

U.S. Equal Employment Opportunity Commission. (2009, March 11). *Sexual harassment.* Washington, DC: Author.

U.S. Fire Administration. (2009, November). *Intentionally set fires.* Emmitsburg, MD: U.S. Department of Homeland Security, Author.

U.S. Secret Service. (2000). *Safe School Initiative: An interim report on the prevention of targeted violence in schools.* Washington, DC: National Threat Assessment Center.

U.S. Secret Service (2003). National Threat Assessment Center. Washington, DC: Author.

Vaillancourt, T. (2005). Indirect aggression among humans: Social construct or evolutionary adaptation? In R. E. Tremblay, W. W. Hartup, & J. Archer (Eds.), *Developmental origins of aggression.* New York: Guilford Press.

VandenBos, G. R. (2007). *APA dictionary of psychology.* Washington, DC: American Psychological Association.

Van der Kolk, B. A., & Fisler, R. E. (1994). Childhood abuse and neglect and loss of self-regulation. *Bulletin of the Menninger Clinic, 58,* 145–158.

Van der Kolk, B. A., & Fisler, R. E. (1995). Dissociation and the fragmentary nature of traumatic memories: Overview and exploratory study. *Journal of Traumatic Stress, 8,* 505–525.

Vandiver, D. M., & Kercher, G. (2004). Offender and victim characteristics of registered female sexual offenders in Texas: A proposed typology of female sexual offenders. *Sexual Abuse: Journal of Research and Treatment, 16,* 121–137.

Van Goozen, S. H. M. (2005). Hormones and the developmental origins of aggression. In R. E. Tremblay, W. W. Hartup, & J. Archer (Eds.), *Developmental origins of aggression.* New York: Guilford Press.

Van Hasselt, V. B., Flood, J. J., Romano, S. J., Vecchi, G.M., de Fabrique, N., & Dalfonzo, V. A. (2005). Hostage-taking in the context of domestic violence: Some case examples. *Journal of Family Violence, 20,* 21–27.

Van Maanen, J. (1975). Police socialization: A longitudinal examination of job attitudes in an urban police department. *Administrative Science Quarterly, 20,* 207–228.

Van Voorhis, P., Wright, E. M., Salisbury, E., & Bauman, A. (2010). Women's risk factors and their contributions to existing risk/needs assessment: The current status of a gender-responsive supplement. *Criminal Justice and Behavior, 37,* 261–288.

Varela, J. G., Boccaccini, M. T., Scogin, F., Stump, J., & Caputo, A. (2004). Personality testing in law enforcement settings: A meta-analytic review. *Criminal Justice and Behavior, 31,* 649–675.

Vermeiren, R. (2003). Psychopathology and delinquency in adolescents: A descriptive and developmental perspective. *Clinical Psychology Review, 23,* 277–318.

Vermeiren, R., De Clippele, A., Schwab-Stone, M., Ruchkin, V., & Deboutte, D. (2002). Neuropsychological characteristics of three subgroups of Flemish delinquent adolescents. *Neuropsychology, 16,* 49–55.

Vermette, H. S., Pinals, D. A., & Appelbaum, P. S. (2005). Mental health training for law enforcement professionals. *Journal of the American Academy of Psychiatry and Law, 33,* 42–46.

Verona, E., Joiner, T. E., Johnson, F., & Bender, T. W. (2006). Gender specific gene-environment interactions on laboratory-assessed aggression. *Biological Psychology, 71,* 33–41.

Viding, E., & Larsson, H. (2010). Genetics of child and adolescent psychopathy. In R. T. Salekin & D. R. Lynam (Eds.), *Handbook of child and adolescent psychopathy.* New York: Guilford Press.

Vila, B., & Kenney, D. J. (2002). Tired cops: The prevalence and potential consequences of police fatigue. *National Institute of Justice Journal, 248,* 16–21.

Viljoen, J. L., Elkovitch, N., Scalora, M. J., & Ullman, D. (2009). Assessment of reoffense risk in adolescents who have committed sexual offenses: Predictive validity of the ERASOR, PCL:YV, YLS/CMI, and Static-99. *Criminal Justice and Behavior, 36,* 981–1000.

Viljoen, J. L., MacDougall, E. A. M., Gagnon, N. C., & Douglas, K. S. (2010). Psychopathy evidence in legal proceedings involving adolescent offenders. *Psychology, Public Policy, and Law, 16,* 254–283.

Vincent, G. M., Chapman, J., & Cook, N. E. (2010). Risk/needs assessment in juvenile justice: Predictive validity of the SAVRY and racial differences in a detention sample. *Criminal Justice and Behavior, 38,* 42–62.

Violanti, J. M. (1996). *Police suicide: Epidemic in blue.* Springfield, IL: Charles C Thomas.

Violanti, J. M., Fekedulegn, D., Charles, L. E., Andrew, M. E., Hartley, T. A., Mnatsakanova, A., et al. (2009). Suicide in police work: Exploring potential contributing influences. *American Journal of Criminal Justice, 34,* 41–53.

Vitale, J. E., Smith, S. S., Brinkley, C. A., & Newman, J. P. (2002). The reliability and validity of the Psychopathy Checklist—Revised in a sample of female offenders. *Criminal Justice and Behavior, 29,* 202–231.

Viteles, M. S. (1929). Psychological methods in the selection of patrolmen in Europe. *Annals of the American Academy, 146,* 160–165.

Voltz, A. G. (1995). Nursing interventions in Munchausen syndrome by proxy. *Journal of Psychosocial Nursing, 10,* 93–97.

Vossekuil, B., Fein, R. A., Reddy, M., Borum, R., & Mozeleski, W. (2002, May). *The final report and findings of the Safe School Initiative.* Washington, DC: U.S. Secret Service and the U.S. Department of Education.

Wagstaff, G. F. (2008). Hypnosis and the law: Examining the stereotypes. *Criminal Justice and Behavior, 35,* 1277–1294.

Waldron, H. B., & Turner, C. W. (2008). Evidence-based psychosocial treatments for adolescent substance abuse. *Journal of Clinical Child & Adolescent Psychology, 37,* 238–261.

Walker, L. E. (1979). *The battered woman.* New York: Harper Colophone Books.

Walker, L. E. (1984). *The battered woman syndrome.* New York: Springer.

Walker, L. E. (1989). Terrifying love: Why battered women kill and how society responds. New York: HarperCollins.

Walker, L. E. (1999). Psychology and domestic violence around the world. *American Psychologist, 54,* 21–29.

Walker, L. E. (2006). Battered women syndrome empirical findings. In F. L. Enmark, H. H. Krauss, E. Halpern, & J. A. Sechzer (Eds.), Violence and exploitation against women and girls. *Annals of the New York Academy of Sciences.* Malden, MA: Blackwell Publishing.

Walker, L. E. (2009). *The battered woman syndrome* (3rd ed.). New York: Springer.

Walker, S., Alpert, G. P., & Kenney, D. J. (2001, July). *Early warning systems: Responding to the problem police officer.* Washington, DC: U.S. Department of Justice, National Institute of Justice.

Walker, S. D., & Kilpatrick, D. G. (2002). Scope of crime/historical review of the victims' rights discipline. In A. Seymour, M. Murray, J. Sigmon, M. Hook, C. Edwards, M. Gaboury, et al. (Eds.), *National Victim Assistance Academy textbook.* Washington, DC: U.S. Department of Justice, Office of Victims of Crime.

Wallerstein, J. S. (1989, January 23). Children after divorce: Wounds that don't heal. *New York Times Magazine,* pp. 19–21, 41–44.

Walters, G. D. (1996). The Psychological Inventory of Criminal Thinking Styles. Part III. Predictive validity. *International Journal of Offender Therapy and Comparative Criminology, 40,* 105–122.

Walters, G. D. (2006). *The Psychological Inventory of Criminal Thinking Styles (PICTS) professional manual.* Allentown, PA: Center for Lifestyles Studies.

Waltz, J., Babcock, J. C., Jacobson, N. S., & Gottman, J. M. (2000). Testing a typology of batterers. *Journal of Consulting and Clinical Psychology, 68,* 658–669.

Wardwell, J., & Smith, G. S. (2008, September). Recovering erased digital evidence from CD-RW discs in a child exploitation investigation. *Digital Investigation, 5*(1–2), 6–9.

Warr, M. (2002). *Companions in crime: The social aspects of criminal conduct.* New York: Cambridge University Press.

Warren, J. I., Fitch, W. L., Dietz, P. E., & Rosenfeld, B. D. (1991). Criminal offense, psychiatric diagnosis, and psycholegal opinion: An analysis of 894 pretrial referrals. *Bulletin of the American Academy of Psychiatry and Law, 19,* 63–69.

Warren, J. I., Hazelwood, R. R., & Reboussin, R. (1991). Serial rape: The offender and his rape career. In A. Burgess (Ed.), *Rape and sexual assault III.* New York: Garland.

Warren, J. I., Reboussin, R., Hazelwood, R. R., & Wright, J. A. (1989). Serial rape: Correlates of increased aggression and relationship of offender pleasure to victim resistance. *Journal of Interpersonal Violence, 4,* 65–78.

Waschbusch, D. A. (2002). A meta-analytic examination of comorbid hyperactive-impulsive-attention problems and conduct problems. *Psychological Bulletin, 128,* 118–150.

Wasserman, G. A., McReynolds, L. S., Schwalbe, C. S., Keating, J. M., & Jones, S. A. (2010, December). Psychiatric disorder, comorbidity, and suicidal behavior in juvenile justice youth. *Criminal Justice and Behavior, 37*(12), 1361–1376.

Webster, C. D., Harris, G. T., Rice, M. E., Cormier, C., & Quinsey, V. L. (1994). *The violence prediction scheme: Assessing dangerousness in high-risk men.* Toronto, ON, Canada: University of Toronto Press.

Weekes, J. R., Moser, A. E., & Langevin, C. M. (1999). Assessing substance-abusing offenders for treatment. In E. J. Latessa (Ed.), *Strategic solutions.* Lanham, MD: American Correctional Association.

Weiner, I. B., & Hess, A. K. (2006). *The handbook of forensic psychology* (3rd ed.). Hoboken, NJ: Wiley.

Weingartner, H. J., Putnam, F., George, D. T., & Ragan, P. (1995). Drug state-dependent autobiographical knowledge. *Experimental and Clinical Psychopharmacology, 3,* 304–307.

Weisheit, R., & Mahan, S. (1988). *Women, crime, and criminal justice.* Cincinnati, OH: Anderson.

Weiss, D. S., Marmar, C. R., Schlenger, W. E., Fairbank, J. A., Jordan, B. K., Hough, R. L., et al. (1992). The prevalence of lifetime and partial post-traumatic stress disorder in Vietnam theater veterans. *Journal of Traumatic Stress, 5,* 365–376.

Wells, G. L. (2001). Police lineups: Data, theory, and policy. *Psychology, Public Policy, and Law, 1,* 791–801.

Wells, G. L., Small, M., Penrod, S., Malpass, R. S., Fulero, S. M., & Brimacombe, C. A. E. (1998). Eyewitness identification procedures: Recommendations for lineups and photospreads. *Law and Human Behavior, 22,* 603–647.

Welsh, W. (2007). A multisite evaluation of prison-based therapeutic community drug treatment. *Criminal Justice and Behavior, 34,* 1481–1498.

Werth, J. L., Benjamin, G. A. H., & Farrenkopf, T. (2000). Requests for physician-assisted death: Guidelines for assessing mental capacity and impaired judgment. *Psychology, Public Policy, and Law, 6,* 348–372.

Wessler, S., & Moss, M. (2001, October). *Hate crimes on campus: The problem and efforts to confront it.* Washington, DC: U.S. Department of Justice, Office of Justice Programs.

West, C. M. (1998). Leaving a second closet: Outing partner violence in same-sex couples. In J. L. Jasinski & L. M. Williams (Eds.), *Partner violence: A comprehensive review of 20 years of research.* Thousand Oaks, CA: Sage.

West, H. (2010, June). *Prisoners at yearend 2009—Advance count.* Washington, DC: U.S. Department of Justice, Bureau of Justice Statistics.

Whitcomb, D., Hook, M., & Alexander, E. (2002). Child victimization. In A. Seymour, M. Murray, J. Sigmon, M. Hook, C. Edwards, M. Gaboury, & et al. (Eds.), *National Victim Assistance Academy textbook.* Washington, DC: U.S. Department of Justice, Office for Victims of Crime.

White, H. R., Bates, M. E., & Buyske, S. (2001). Adolescence-limited versus persistent delinquency: Extending Moffitt's hypothesis into adulthood. *Journal of Abnormal Psychology, 110,* 600–609.

White, M. D., Goldkamp, J. S., & Campbell, S. P. (2006). Co-occurring mental illness and substance abuse in the criminal justice system. *The Prison Journal, 86,* 301–326.

Whitehead, J. T., & Lab, S. P. (1989). A meta-analysis of juvenile correctional treatment. *Journal of Research in Crime & Delinquency, 26,* 276–295.

Whittaker, J. K., Kinney, J., Tracy, E. N., & Booth, C. (1990). *Reaching high-risk families: Intensive family preservation in human services.* New York: Aldine de Gruyter.

Williamson, S., Hare, R. D., & Wong, S. (1987). Violence: Criminal psychopaths and their victims. *Canadian Journal of Behavioral Science, 19,* 454–462.

Wills, T. A., & Stoolmiller, M. (2002). The role of self-control in early escalation of substance abuse: A time-varying analysis. *Journal of Consulting and Clinical Psychology, 70,* 986–997.

Wills, T. A., Walker, C., Mendoza, D., & Ainette, M. G. (2006). Behavioral and emotional self-control: Relations to substance use in samples of middle and high school students. *Psychology of Addictive Behaviors, 20,* 265–278.

Wilper, A. P., Woolhandler, S., Boyd, J. W., Lasser, K. E., McCormick, D., Bor, D. H., et al. (2009). The health and health care of U.S. prisoners: Results of a nationwide survey. *American Journal of Public Health, 99,* 666–672.

Wilson, J. J. (2001, January). From the administrator. In J. R. Johnson & L. K. Girdner (Eds.), *Family abductors: Descriptive profiles and preventive interventions.* Washington, DC: U.S. Department of Justice, Office of Juvenile Justice and Delinquency.

Wilson, M., & Daly, M. (1993). Spousal homicide risk and estrangement. *Violence and Victims, 8,* 3–16.

Winick, B. J. (1996). The MacArthur Treatment Competence Study: Legal and therapeutic implications. *Psychology, Public Policy, and Law, 2,* 137–166.

Winick, B. J. (2003). Outpatient commitment: A therapeutic jurisprudence analysis. *Psychology, Public Policy, and Law, 9,* 107–144.

Winick, B. J., & Kress, K. (2003a). Foreword: A symposium on outpatient commitment dedicated to Bruce Ennis, Alexander Brooks, and Stanley Herr. *Psychology, Public Policy, and Law, 9,* 3–7.

Winick, B. J., & Kress, K. (Eds.). (2003b). Preventive outpatient commitment for persons with serious mental illness [Special issue]. *Psychology, Public Policy, and Law, 9.*

Witt, A. (2001, June 5). False confessions—Day 3—Police bend, suspend rules. *The Washington Post,* p. A01.

Wolak, J., Finkelhor, D., & Mitchell, K. J. (2004). Internet-initiated sex crimes against minors: Implications for prevention based on findings from a national sample. *Journal of Adolescent Health, 35,* 424.e11–424.e20.

Wolak, J., Finkelhor, D., Mitchell, K. J., & Ybarra, M. L. (2008). Online "predators" and their victims. *American Psychologist, 63,* 111–128.

Wolak, J., Mitchell, K. J., & Finkelhor, D. (2003). *Internet sex crimes against minors: The response of law enforcement* (NCMEC 10–03–022). Alexandria, AV: National Center for Missing & Exploitated Children.

Wolf, M. M., Kirigin, K. A., Fixsen, D. L., Blasé, K. A., & Braukmann, C. J. (1995). The teaching-family model: A case study in data-based program development and refinement (and dragon wrestling). *Journal of Organizational Behavior Management, 15,* 11–68.

Wong, S. (2000). Psychopathic offenders. In S. Hodgins & R. Muller-Isberner (Eds.), Violence, crime and mentally disordered offenders: Concepts and methods for effective treatment and prevention. New York: Wiley.

Wood, R. M., Grossman, L. S., & Fichtner, C. G. (2000). Psychological assessment, treatment, and outcome with sex offenders. *Behavioral Sciences and the Law, 18,* 23–41.

Woodworth, M., & Porter, S. (2002). In cold blood: Characteristics of criminal homicides as a function of psychopathy. *Journal of Abnormal Psychology, 111,* 436–445.

Woody, R. H. (2005). The police culture: Research implications for psychological services. *Professional Psychology: Research and Practice, 36,* 525–529.

Worden, A. P. (1993). The attitudes of women and men in policing: Testing conventional and contemporary wisdom. *Criminology, 31,* 203–242.

Worling, I. R., & Curwen, T. (2001). Estimate of Risk of Adolescent Sexual Offense Recidivism (ERASOR, Version 2.0). In M. C. Calder (Ed.), *Juveniles and children who sexually abuse: Frameworks for assessment*. Lyme Regis, Dorset, UK: Russell House Publishing.

Wormith, J. S., Althouse, R., Simpson, M., Reitzel, L. R., Fagan, T. J., & Morgan, R. D. (2007). The rehabilitation and reintegration of offenders: The current landscape and some future directions for correctional psychology. *Criminal Justice and Behavior, 34*, 879–892.

Wormith, J. S., & Luong, D. (2007). Legal and psychological contributions to the development of corrections in Canada. In R. K. Ax & T. J. Fagan (Eds.), *Corrections, mental health, and social policy: International perspectives*. Springfield, IL: Charles C Thomas.

Yarmey, A. D. (1979). *The psychology of eyewitness testimony*. New York: Free Press.

Yeater, E. A., Treat, T. A., Viken, R. J., & McFall, R. M. (2010). Cognitive processes underlying women's risk judgments: Associations with sexual victimization history and rape myth acceptance. *Journal of Consulting and Clinical Psychology, 78*, 375–386.

Ybarra, M. L. E., & Mitchell, K. J. (2007). Prevalence and frequency of Internet harassment instigation: Implications for adolescent health. *Journal of Adolescent Health, 41*, 189–195.

Yochelson, S., & Samenow, S. E. (1976). *The criminal personality* (Vol. 1). New York: Jason Aronson.

Young, A. T., Fuller, J., & Riley, B. (2008). On-scene mental health counseling provided through police departments. *Journal of Mental Health Counseling, 30*, 345–361.

Young, S., Gudjonsson, G., Misch, P., Collins, P., Carter, P., Redfern, J., et al. (2010). Prevalence of ADHD symptoms among youth in a secure facility: The consistency and accuracy of self- and informant-report ratings. *Journal of Forensic Psychiatry & Psychology, 21*, 238–246.

Young, T. J. (1992). Procedures and problems in conducting a psychological autopsy. *International Journal of Offender Therapy and Comparative Criminology, 36*, 43–52.

Zapf, P. A., Golding, S. L., & Roesch, R. (2006). Criminal responsibility and the insanity defense. In I. B. Weiner & A. K. Hess (Eds.), *The handbook of forensic psychology* (3rd ed.). Hoboken, NJ: Wiley.

Zapf, P. A., Hubbard, K. L., Galloway, V. A., Cox, M., & Ronan, K. A. (2002). *An investigation of discrepancies between forensic examiners and the courts in decisions about competency*. Manuscript submitted for publication.

Zapf, P. A., & Roesch, R. (2006). Competency to stand trial: A guide for evaluators. In I. B. Weiner & A. K. Hess (Eds.), *The handbook of forensic psychology* (3rd ed.). Hoboken, NJ: Wiley.

Zapf, P. A., & Viljoen, J. L. (2003). Issues and considerations regarding the use of assessment instruments in the evaluation of competency to stand trial. *Behavioral Sciences and the Law, 21*, 351–367.

Zelazo, P. D., Carter, A., Reznick, J. S., Frye, D. (1997). Early development of executive functions: A problem-solving framework. *Review of General Psychology, 1*, 198–226.

Zeling, M. (1986). Research needs in the study of post-shooting trauma. In J. T. Reese & H. A. Goldstein (Eds.), *Psychological services for law enforcement*. Washington, DC: Government Printing Office.

Zimring, F. (1998). *American youth violence*. New York: Oxford University Press.

Ziskin, J., & Faust, D. (1994). *Coping with psychiatric and psychological testimony* (5th ed.). Marina Del Rey, CA: Law and Psychology Press.

Zoccolillo, M. (1993). Gender and the development of conduct disorder. *Development and Psychopathology, 5*, 65–78.

Zoccolillo, M., Romano, E., Joubert, D., Mazzarello, T., Côté, S., Boivin, M., et al. (2005). The intergenerational transmission of aggression and antisocial behavior. In R. E. Tremblay, W. W. Hartup, & J. Archer (Eds.), *Developmental origins of aggression*. New York: Guilford Press.

Zona, M. A., Sharma, K. K., & Lane, J. A. (1993). A comparative study of erotomanic and obsessional subjects in a forensic sample. *Journal of Forensic Sciences, 38*, 894–903.

Photo Credits

Photo 2.1. Justin Sullivan/Getty Images News/Getty Images.

Photo 2.2. Washington Post/Getty Images.

Photo 3.1. Robert E Daemmrich/Stone/Getty Images.

Photo 3.2. Stephen Marks/The Image Bank/Getty Images.

Photo 4.1. David McNew/AFP/Getty Images.

Photo 4.2. Ben Gray/AFP/Getty Images.

Photo 5.1. Art Lien/AFP/Getty Images.

Photo 5.2. Alex Wong/ Getty Images News/Getty Images.

Photo 5.3. Joe Raedle/Getty Images News/Getty Images.

Photo 6.1. George Eastman House/Archive Photos/ Getty Images.

Photo 6.2. Scott Olson/ Getty Images News/ Getty Images.

Photo 7.1. Kevin Moloney/Getty Images News/Getty Images.

Photo 7.2. Mark Leffingwell/AFP/Getty Images.

Photo 8.1. Estelle Rancurel/Taxi/ Getty Images.

Photo 8.2. Bride Lane/Popperfoto/Getty Images.

Photo 8.3. RNPS Picture of the Year 2007/HO/Reuters// Corbis.

Photo 9.1. Bob Mahoney/Time & Life Images/Getty Images.

Photo 10.1. Chris Hondros/Getty Images News/Getty Images.

Photo 10.2. Amanda Edwards/Getty Images Entertainment/Getty Images.

Photo 11.1. Larry Dale Gordon/ Stone/Getty Images.

Photo 12.1. Bob Daemmrich/AFP/Getty Images.

Photo 12.2. Cybergabi/Flickr/Getty Images.

Photo 13.1. The Washington Post/Getty Images.

Photo 13.2. Bruce Ayres/ Stone/Getty Images.

Photo 13.3. Ed Eckstein/Corbis.

Name Index

Subject Index

About the Authors

Curt R. Bartol was a college professor for more than 30 years, teaching a wide variety of both undergraduate and graduate courses, including Biopsychology, Criminal Behavior, Juvenile Delinquency, Introduction to Forensic Psychology, Social Psychology, and Psychology and Law. He earned his PhD in personality/social psychology from Northern Illinois University in 1972. He was instrumental in creating and launching Castleton State College's graduate program in forensic psychology and served as its director for 6 years. As a licensed clinical psychologist, he has been a consulting police psychologist to local, municipal, state, and federal law enforcement agencies for over 25 years. In addition to this book, he has written *Criminal Behavior: A Psychosocial Approach* (now in its 9th ed.). He also has coauthored *Juvenile Delinquency: A Systems Approach, Delinquency and Justice: A Psychosocial Approach* (2nd ed.) and *Psychology and Law: Theory, Research, and Application* (3rd ed.). He is also the long-standing editor of SAGE's *Criminal Justice and Behavior*.

Anne M. Bartol earned an MA and a PhD in criminal justice from State University of New York at Albany. She also holds an MA in journalism from the University of Wisconsin–Madison. She taught criminal justice, sociology, and journalism courses over a 20-year college teaching career, primarily at Castleton State College, and has worked as a journalist and a social worker in child and adolescent protective services. In addition to this book, she has coauthored *Juvenile Delinquency: A Systems Approach*; *Delinquency and Justice: A Psychosocial Approach* (2nd ed.); *Psychology and Law: Theory, Research, and Application* (3rd ed.); and *Criminal Behavior* (8th and 9th eds.). She has served as book review editor and managing editor of *Criminal Justice and Behavior* and has published articles on women and criminal justice, rural courts, and the history of forensic psychology.

SAGE Research Methods Online
The essential tool for researchers

Sign up now at
www.sagepub.com/srmo
for more information.

An expert research tool

- An **expertly designed taxonomy** with more than 1,400 unique terms for social and behavioral science research methods
- **Visual and hierarchical search tools** to help you discover material and link to related methods

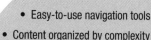

- Easy-to-use navigation tools
- Content organized by complexity
- Tools for citing, printing, and downloading content with ease
- Regularly updated content and features

A wealth of essential content

- The most comprehensive picture of quantitative, qualitative, and mixed methods available today
- More than **100,000 pages of SAGE book and reference material** on research methods as well as editorially selected material from SAGE journals
- More than **600 books** available in their entirety online

Launching 2011!

⑤SAGE research methods online